THE BUTTERFLIES OF
NORTH AMERICA

JAMES A. SCOTT

THE *Butterflies*
OF NORTH AMERICA

A NATURAL HISTORY AND FIELD GUIDE

STANFORD UNIVERSITY PRESS

Stanford, California

Stanford University Press, Stanford, California
© 1986 by the Board of Trustees of the Leland Stanford Junior University
Printed in the United States of America
Original printing 1986
Last figure below indicates year of this printing:
01 00 99 98 97
CIP data appear at the end of the book

PREFACE

In the last century William Henry Edwards and Samuel H. Scudder actively studied the natural history of many eastern U.S. butterflies, but since that time very little information on butterfly natural history has found its way into books, and some of what has appeared is incorrect. When I first became interested in butterflies some 25 years ago, I was ignorant of their behavior and habits, but their fascinating ways became more and more interesting as I learned more about them. Eventually I found that there are many good studies of butterfly habits in the scientific journals, and that much is known though not published by many people who study them, but that this information is scattered and difficult to get to. It became obvious that there was a need for a book like this one, a book that would give all the important natural history information for all the species of North American butterflies in scientifically accurate form, but would present it in such fashion that it would be accessible to everyone.

Thus although this book is more an original work on natural history than an ordinary field guide, everything expected of a field guide is included. Besides all the important information on natural history, I have included information from ecology, behavior, evolution, physiology, genetics, biogeography, and other fields that is directly related to how butterflies live and how they came to exist. Whether for general biological and ecological information (Part I) or for help in identification (Part II) or for data on individual species (Part III), the material offered is as complete and correct as possible, and for all of these purposes the book should be a useful reference source. As a field guide, the book includes maps and color photos for all species, as well as the frequently asked information on where, when, and how to find each species. And because the butterflies on the main color plates are arranged (from top to bottom, left to right, and plate to plate) *according to overall appearance*, rather than by actual genetic relatedness, identifying an unknown butterfly will be found to be much easier and faster than it is likely to be with any other book or method. The provision of maps for all native species is also a unique feature; the maps themselves have never been published before. Finally, I have tried to minimize the use of technical terms: one need not be familiar with a lot of jargon to use this book. A handy glossary is included for those few words the reader might not know.

The book summarizes the findings of many years of study and thousands of published scientific articles. The data on how butterflies overwinter, for example, is based on about 700 sources. Certainly the number of records (mine and others') used for deriving the maps must be several hundred thousand or more. My fieldwork over the years has taken me across much of North America, studying butterflies, especially the western part of the United States and Canada; but I have collected and studied butterflies in the East and Southeast as well, and I have also studied them in Mexico, Hawaii, Colombia, and Africa. My own collection, one of the largest in North America, contains all of the native species and nearly all of the subspecies and strays; it supplied all but about 20 of the specimens used for the color plates. My card file, the most complete now in existence, contains the literature sources for all the larval hostplants given in this book, as well as the references to other biological studies on particular species.

Many people have helped me with the book, and some have greatly improved its content. John F. Emmel, Paul R. Ehrlich, Dennis Murphy, Arthur M. Shapiro, Roy F. Kendall, and J. Richard Heitzman reviewed the book, offering numerous suggestions. Dr. Emmel aided me with many of the western species, Roy Kendall with those of Texas, and Richard Heitzman with eastern U.S. species. Jim Troubridge and David K. Parshall were especially helpful on Canadian and arctic species, Parshall provided hostplant records for arctic species, and H. David Baggett helped out on Florida species. Timothy L. Friedlander provided aid on butterflies that eat hackberry trees. F. Martin Brown advised concerning some taxonomic problems and history. Ray E. Stanford helped with records for the maps and with proofreading. E. N. Woodbury, J. Troubridge, R. Stanford, J. Emmel, R. Humbert, P. Menzel, and D. M. Wright provided numerous valuable photographs. The published works of hundreds of people were consulted, most notably those of William Henry Edwards, Samuel H. Scudder, John A. Comstock, and Charles Dammers.

I am deeply grateful also to the following people for contributing to various aspects of the project: Gary G. Anweiler, George T. Austin, Richard A. Bailowitz, Charles D. Bird, Richard W. Boscoe, Keith S. Brown Jr., John M. Burns, John Calhoun, Frances S. Chew, Ian Common, Charles V. Covell, Charles R. Crowe, Robert P. Dana, Thomas Dimock, Julian P. Donahue, Ernst J. Dornfeld, Malcolm G. Douglas, Christopher J. Durden, Peter L. Eades, Ginter Ekis, John N. Eliot, Marc Epstein, Frank D. Fee, Michael S. Fisher, Gregory S. Forbes, Mecky Furr, Ronald R. Gatrelle, Lawrence E. Gilbert, Carll Goodpasture, Glenn A. Gorelick, L. Paul Grey, John Hafernik, Warren Hamilton, Paul Hammond, Kenneth C. Hansen, Gloria J. Harjes, Jack L. Harry, John B. Heppner, Quimby F. Hess, Lionel G. Higgins, John Hinchliff, Ronald R. Hooper, Maurice L. Howard, I. W. Hughes, Bernard S. Jackson, Kurt Johnson, John Johnstone, Craig Jordan, John Justice, Philip J. Kean, Helmut P. Kimmich, Asao Kitagawa, Paul Klassen, Alexander B. Klots, Steven J. Kohler, Norbert G. Kondla, Tom W. Kral, J. Donald Lafontaine, John Lane, Torben W. Langer, Robert L. Langston, Ross A. Layberry, Zdravko Lorkovic, C. Don MacNeill, William W. McGuire, Lee D. Miller, Molly Monica, James Mori, Douglas Mullins, Erval J. Newcomer, Mogens C. Nielsen, Jim Oberfoell, Charles G. Oliver, Paul A. Opler, Kenelm W. Philip, Edward M. Pike, Austin P. Platt, John Polusny, Jerry A. Powell, Robert Price, Robert M. Pyle, George W. Rawson, Frederick H. Rindge, J. C. Riotte, A. Grant Robinson, Kilian Roever, Ronald Rutowski, Jon H. Shepard, Oakley Shields, Robert W. Sites, Michael J. Smith, Felix A. Sperling, Richard B. Taylor, Fred Thorne, Kenneth J. Thorne, Kenneth Tidwell, J. W. Tilden, Michael Toliver, Fred A. Urquhart, R. Vane-Wright, William A. Weber, Ralph E. Wells, Nathan A. White, Raymond R. White, Walter G. Whitford, E. N. Woodbury, David M. Wright, Allen M. Young, Chen W. Young, Michael E. Young, Joseph Zeligs.

William W. Carver, Editor of Stanford University Press, and Jean D. McIntosh, associate editor of the Press, greatly improved the organization and writing of the book; Paul Psoinos assisted in the final stages. Anita Walker Scott, production manager of the Press, designed the book and saw to its production. Finally, my mother, Juanita M. Scott, helped proofread; and my father, Glenn R. Scott, helped out in numerous ways and stimulated my early interest in nature—this book is dedicated to him.

J.A.S.

CONTENTS

TABLES AND FIGURES

Sixty-four pages of color photographs follow page 272.

ABBREVIATIONS

upf	upperside of forewing	C	central
unf	underside of forewing	N	northern
uph	upperside of hindwing	S	southern
unh	underside of hindwing	E	eastern
		W	western
ups	upperside	NE	northeastern
uns	underside	NW	northwestern
		SE	southeastern
fw	forewing	SW	southwestern
hw	hindwing		
		I.; Is.	Island; Islands
♂	male	mts.; Mts.	mountains; Mountains
♀	female		
		mm	millimeter (= .04 inch)
sp.	species	cm	centimeter (= .39 inch)
ssp.	subspecies	m	meter (= 39.37 inches)
f.	form	km	kilometer (= .62 mile)
assoc.	associated		
esp.	especially	E	early (days 1-10 of month)
vs.	versus	M	mid- (days 11-20 of month)
		L	late (days 21-31 of month)

t   superscript designating hostplants (for example, *Asimina angustifolia*[t]) listed by H. Tietz in his *Index to Life Histories* (a compilation: see "Butterfly References"): plant names so designated are probably valid hostplants, but they have not been verified for the present volume from the original references that Tietz consulted; hostplants listed by Tietz in error have been ignored in this book

THE BUTTERFLIES OF
NORTH AMERICA

INTRODUCTION

Butterflies, creatures of tantalizing beauty, have held a treasured place in human lives for many thousands of years. Ancient peoples carved images of butterflies into stone, and reckoned them messengers from the gods. In the mythologies of diverse cultures today, they continue to be accorded a special status. And people around the world, scientists and nonscientists alike, are drawn to their flashing color patterns and elusive flight, their astonishing life histories and seemingly endless variety, and their fleeting appearance on nature's stage.

We are all struck by the beauty of butterflies. The iridescent blue *Morpho* butterflies of the American tropics, more dazzling than hummingbirds, flap out of the jungle on 13-cm (5-inch) wings, then disappear as quickly again into its recesses. The birdwing butterflies of Indonesia and Malaysia—iridescent blue, yellow, red, and green, reaching 18 cm (7 inches) in wingspan—are among the most beautiful animals in the world. The New Guinea natives use them in headdresses and farm them for sale.

Our temperate-zone butterflies, though seldom as large, are often as beautiful. Each fall, thousands of migrating Monarchs settle briefly along coastal California, spreading their scarlets and blacks across entire groves of trees. A painting of a butterfly, the magnificent Tiger Swallowtail, was done on one of the earliest voyages to the New World by John White, the commander of Sir Walter Raleigh's third expedition to America, in 1587. And even the Pygmy Blue, the world's smallest butterfly, is a pretty sight for those alert enough to spot it—its wings span only a centimeter (less than half an inch).

The origin of the word "butterfly" is obscure. To Chaucer, the word was *boterflye*; in Old English, the word is *buter-flēoge*; in Dutch, *botervlieg*; in German, *butterfliege*. But there the trail ends. The *Oxford English Dictionary* offers the possibility that "the insect was so called from the appearance of its excrement." A happier explanation is that the emergence of butterflies in spring coincided with butter-producing time, a thought that is independent of the color of the butterflies themselves. A third hypothesis, one that *is* related to color, is that the clouds of yellow sulfur butterflies (of the genus *Colias*) feeding at mud puddles reminded someone of "flies" the color of butter. Elsewhere, the word is altogether different: *mariposa* in Spanish, *papilio* in Latin (today, *Papilio* is the scientific name of most swallowtails), *papillon* in French, *schmetterling* or *tagfalter* in German, *borboleta* in Portuguese, *babochka* in Russian, *petaloudha* in modern Greek, *fjaril* in Swedish, *farāsha* in Arabic, *farfalla* in Italian, *parpar* in Hebrew, *chōchō* in Japanese, *hu-tieh* in Chinese, *kipepeo* in Swahili. The ancient Greeks' word for the soul, *psychē*, was also their word for the butterfly, which was seen as an emblem of the immortal soul by reason of its passing through a kind of death in the pupa stage, and a resurrection in the adult.

But in human lives today the place of butterflies is chiefly enjoyment, for the mysteries of metamorphosis have been largely revealed. And butterflies are—for us—harmless: even the farmer or the forester can welcome their annual appearance, for there are very few species that cause enough damage to human crops to be looked upon as pests. What is more, studying butterflies opens up most of nature to the inquiring mind: adult butterflies visit the flowers of many kinds of plants to sip their nectar; female adults search—very selectively—for many other kinds of plants to lay their eggs on; the larvae and pupae are often to be looked for in unlikely places (some bore into roots, and there is even a North American butterfly whose larvae eat aphids—a carnivore!). And of course many different habitats must be sampled, across a vast geography, to find the various butterfly species—almost 700 of them—that occur in the United States and Canada. It took me many years of field observation and laboratory and library research to acquire a knowledge of the variation and natural history of butterflies; what I have tried to offer in this book is a quick and certain means of identifying any species found in North America, as well as immediate access to the interesting details of its life cycle.

Butterflies do not occur in Antarctica, but they are found throughout the rest of the world; even in Greenland there are six species, along the edges of its immense glaciers. Worldwide, there are perhaps 14,500 species of butterflies and skippers, most of them in the tropics. More species are to be found in the American tropics, about 6,000, than anywhere else in the world, and their variety there was important in the development of the concept of mimicry. Henry Walter Bates was in the Amazon from 1848 to 1859, part of the time with his friend Alfred Russel Wallace. Bates was amazed at the pattern of variation in *Heliconius* butterflies: different *Heliconius* species in one region often resemble each other, and others in another region also resemble each other, but the butterflies in the first region do not look like those in the second. Bates's studies were the foundation of the study of mimicry, and one type of mimicry is now named for him. Wallace, who also explored the East Indies, was himself a student of butterflies and a co-founder of the theory of evolution, with Charles Darwin.

Important studies of butterfly mimicry have continued to the present day. In North America, these studies have concentrated on the Monarch (*Danaus plexippus*) and the Viceroy (*Limenitis archippus*), which mimics it; on the Pipevine Swallowtail (*Battus philenor*) and the many butterflies that mimic it (*Papilio glaucus* form *nigra*, *P. polyxenes*, *P. troilus*, etc.); and on a few others. The mimics in these cases, called Batesian mimics, are actually edible to vertebrate predators, but are seldom eaten because their models, the Monarch and the Pipevine Swallowtail, are usually inedible—after vomiting Monarchs a few times, a predator avoids Monarchs and Viceroys alike. Ironically, the *Heliconius* butterflies that Bates himself studied have come to be called Müllerian mimics, in honor of Fritz Müller, another Amazon naturalist; in an association of Müllerian mimics, all species are inedible to birds and lizards and the commonest species in the association tends to be the model for the others.

In recent times, biologists have used butterflies for research into many other phenomena: ecologists have studied the pheromones—the chemicals that help butterflies signal to others of their species their readiness and suitability for mating—as well as the plant chemicals that repel or stimulate butterflies to feed or lay eggs; population biologists have studied the dispersal and migration of butterfly species, and the dispersal within different populations of a single species; and geneticists have studied the remarkable variability within some butterfly species.

For the beauty of butterflies, we have mainly two things to thank: the pigmented scales that cover their wings and their predilection for flying only on bright, sunny days. Butterflies and moths are collectively the Lepidoptera, an order of insects having scale-covered wings. Other insects have scaleless, transparent, usually colorless wings (in many cases, the wings are of the same dull-reddish-brown color as the insect outer skeleton). The scales of butterflies, however, can be filled with pigments, and the scales themselves have evolved into complex shapes that scatter or diffract light into all the colors seen by humans, and even some colors (ultraviolet) that humans cannot see. Most moths, though as thoroughly scaled, fly at night and are rather dull in appearance. Thus moths do not depend on visual stimuli to find each other; the female generally produces a pheromone that attracts males from up to hundreds of meters or even a kilometer (more than half a mile), and when a male finds the female he gives off his own distinct chemical to convince her of his suitability. Because butterflies are day fliers, they have come to use color and pattern in their daily lives. Like many of the day-flying moths, they have evolved bright wing colors and striking wing-color patterns, chiefly for the purpose of mating. Very few butterflies (*Heliconius* are exceptions) locate their mates by sensing long-distance chemicals the way moths do, and instead males or females fly about a particular habitat and locate mates by responding to the colors, patterns, and movements of their wings.

A secondary purpose for the bright colors seems to be as an advertisement to birds and other predators that the butterfly is mostly just fluff, a set of large wings with a small body that is hard to catch and scarcely worth the effort compared to, say, a large immobile worm. I have seen many birds trying to catch butterflies in midair, and they rarely succeed. Too, the impression of a bird's beak often found on the wings of otherwise healthy butterflies (where the scales have come off in a beak-shaped pattern) shows that even when captured, butterflies often escape when the bird tries to swallow. Most butterflies that fail to escape seem in fact to have been attacked when they were too cold to fly, and even then some butterflies scare the attacker away by spreading their wings and revealing prominent eyespots.

Perhaps the most remarkable feature of butterflies is their complete metamorphosis. Most animals, such as alligators and grasshoppers, hatch from an egg as a miniature adult, which then undergoes little change while growing to maturity. The more advanced insects like beetles, wasps, flies, and the Lepidoptera undergo complete metamorphosis, in which the egg hatches into a larva, the larva increases in size and ultimately pupates, and the pupa emerges as an adult when it has matured and the conditions of the environment are right. The advantage of metamorphosis is that it allows the larva and adult to live in completely different environments, the former as a plodding, insatiable eater, the latter as a short-lived, wide-ranging parent. An adult butterfly, equipped as it is with only a slender proboscis, much like a drinking straw, with which it can feed only on fluids, could not possibly draw up enough nutrients—without the larval stage—to reach full size before dying of predation or starvation. Caterpillars (called larvae in this book) are thus feeding machines, with large jaws and small, simple eyes, a huge gut, six true legs, and ten false legs, or prolegs, each proleg equipped with tiny hooks. As it crawls, the larva spins silk threads on the larval hostplant and hooks its prolegs into the silk threads. This attachment procedure is important because the plant is the total habitat for the larva; if it falls off, especially when young, it will probably starve to death before it finds its way back to a suitable plant.

Where the female chooses to lay her eggs is also important; she not only places them on the right plant species for the larva, among hundreds of plants in the habitat (a larva on the wrong plant either will not eat or will die of food poisoning), but she also places them on the right *part* of the plant, and only on plants that are at the right stage of growth (beginning to produce young leaves or flower buds, for example). The larva, finding itself suitably ensconced, then feeds and grows and pupates.

The pupa is a transition stage made necessary by the structural differences between larva and adult and by the need (in many species) to endure long hibernation. The wings of butterflies originate from just a few cells inside the larva; the wings—and likewise the antennae, the proboscis, and other organs—grow enormously inside the older larva and the pupa. The wings of the emerging adult are still small and limp, but body fluids pump them up to full size within half an hour, and their veins and surfaces then quickly stiffen to provide needed structural support.

The diurnal activity and conspicuousness of adult butterflies are characteristic also of many larvae, which are often gaudily colored and employ horns, spines, eyespots, or poisons for defense. Many other larvae take refuge in disguise, in the form of cryptic color patterns. In contrast, many moth larvae and a few skipper larvae are borers, living inside roots or stems or fruits, unseen until they emerge as adults. But in general, moth and butterfly larvae are similar in form and structure and not easily distinguished in overall appearance, unless the characters of particular species are known.

The tiny world of the larva, a single plant or even a single leaf, contrasts with the world of the adult, which may be several hectares (or acres) to several square kilometers (or square miles) in extent, or even larger. With so vast a range per individual butterfly, why are there so many different species of butterflies in the world? There are so many that an accurate count is not possible: about 50,000 different names have been given to genera, species, subspecies, forms, and other categories of butterflies, and more species are discovered and named all the time, particularly in the tropics. There are so many chiefly because there are several hundred thousand plant species in the world for the larvae to feed on, and the world of a larva is so small that some butterfly species subsist quite well on a single plant species. The North American *Euphilotes* butterflies, for instance, feed only on *Eriogonum* plants; the larvae eat the flowers and fruits and the adults sip the nectar. Moreover, the larvae of butterflies often subsist on only one or two parts of the plant. One species may eat the flowers and fruits of the plant, another the leaves, and a few giant-skipper larvae eat only the roots or sap.

If we assume there are 200,000 suitable plant species and seven places per plant for grazers (leaf eaters, flower-and-fruit eaters, flower-nectar sippers, stem borers, root borers, leaf- or stem-sap feeders, root-sap feeders), then there should be ample homes for even 1,400,000 species of herbivorous insects in the world. Since butterfly larvae are mostly leaf eaters or flower-and-fruit eaters—as are most moths, grasshoppers, sawflies, many beetles, some flies, and others—there could be, theoretically, up to 400,000 possible species of these insects. The butterflies' slice of this pie is their roughly 14,500 known species. Some plant species are more popular than others, fed on by many insects; others are eaten by only one or two insect species. A few species (the Ginkgo tree?) seem to have no insect grazers at all, although careful study usually turns up an insect grazer in these cases too.

Why are there so many plant species? Botanists suggest that there are so many because of the numerous climates, terrains, and soil types in the world, entomologists because there are many thousands of species—of bees, and sometimes flies, beetles, butterflies, moths, hummingbirds, and even bats—that pollinate plants, often a single insect species pollinating a single plant species. It is clear in any case that the flowering plants and their pollinators evolved together and increased their numbers and varieties together.

But basically it is efficiency that explains the great number of plant and animal species in the world. In most cases, two species of insects can eat two species of plants more efficiently than one of them could eat both, because each insect can adapt its temperature tolerance, egg-laying and feeding habits, time of appearance during the year, toxin tolerance, mouthparts and other traits to the particular characteristics of one plant species. But for most animals and plants, if too many species occur in an area, the distance between individuals of any one species may be too far for enough individuals to find each other to mate, and it will become extinct. In the Amazon, for instance, there are so many plants and plant species that the distance between individual plants of the same species may be many hundred meters. Insects and other pollinators bridge that distance for most plants; similarly, butterflies and moths have evolved specialized mate-locating behaviors to bring *their* sexes together. These adaptations enable hundreds of species of both plants and animals to occur together, each species at low density.

Another notable feature of butterflies is their generally short lives. The entire cycle from egg to adult may be only a month or two, and adults may live only a week (some live longer, and many arctic/alpine species have two-year life cycles). The short life cycle means that many species that produce only one generation per year fly only a few months out of the year, at a time that depends (1) on when the plants that the larvae eat are at the edible stage and (2) on which particular stage—egg, larva, pupa, or adult—spends the winter in hibernation. Other species produce many generations per year; the numbers of generations and hibernation stages vary greatly from one species or family to the next.

Finally, because butterflies are cold-blooded, they are affected by climate to a considerable degree. Many butterflies are limited in altitudinal distribution, and their ranges generally correlate closely with climatic features—mainly temperature, secondarily precipitation. What is more, adults generally fly only during warm, sunny periods, becoming inactive when clouds obscure the sun or when cold conditions prevail.

One effect of the combination of complete metamorphosis, restricted diet, short life, and critical temperature and sunlight tolerances is that observing and studying butterflies often takes more knowledge (and is thus more interesting) than observing most vertebrates, which have a simple pattern of growth, a broad, unspecialized diet, long lives, and less change of behavior during the year and during the day. To be sure of observing adults of a particular butterfly species, for example, you must know not only the range of the species and the coloration of the adults (the sexes and even the generations may differ), but also the preferred habitat, the time of year when the adults emerge and fly, the sort of place favored by mate-searching males, the plants favored by females for their eggs, and the kinds of food preferred by male and female adults. To find eggs and larvae, you must know the larval hostplants, where the eggs are laid on the plant, the part of the plant eaten, and—in order to estimate when the eggs and larvae will occur on the plants—the timing and duration of the overwintering stage and the adult flight period.

This book provides that sort of specialized information. The material that follows in Part I offers extensive discussion of life cycles, behavior, hostplants, variation, and other topics. Part II provides keys and other tools for the identification of the major butterfly groups, in all life stages. Part III provides detailed data on every recognized species (and the distinctive subspecies) of butterfly (and skipper) that is native to or strays into North America north of Mexico, including Canada, Alaska, Greenland, Iceland, Bermuda, and Hawaii. The appendixes provide information on studying, collecting, and raising butterflies, and about 50 useful references on butterflies and their hostplants.

PART I

Biology and Ecology

The pages that follow offer general information on butterflies—on structure and physiology, life cycle and behavior, habitats and foods, enemies and defenses, variation and adaptations, distribution and migration, and many other topics. This material gives the reader a better understanding of the detailed information presented in Parts II and III.

Scientific and Common Names

Ever since the Swedish naturalist Carl von Linné (Carolus Linnaeus) gave a two-word name to each species that he knew, scientific names have been used to name animals and plants. Although many of the names he adopted had been in general use since the time of the ancients, his *Systema Naturae* (tenth edition, 1758) is generally considered the starting point for scientific names in animals, and his *Species Plantarum* (1753) the starting point for scientific names in plants. Both works have their origin in the first edition of *Systema Naturae*, published in 1735. Many animal and plant species—for example, *Papilio glaucus*, the Tiger Swallowtail, and *Zea mays*, Maize—still carry the names Linnaeus gave them.

A species name, then, consists of two parts, each part usually constructed from one or more Latin or Greek roots. The first part, the genus, is capitalized; the second part, the species, is not. Both are printed in italics (*Papilio glaucus*); the genus name is sometimes abbreviated to its first letter (*P. glaucus*). A subspecies name may follow a species name to represent a particular geographic race of that species: *P. glaucus canadensis* (sometimes given as ssp. *canadensis*), the northern race. The name of a form may also be appended: *P. g. canadensis* f. *arcticus*. With occasional exceptions, zoological and botanical names *mean* something: they describe the organism (in Latin, *papilio* means "butterfly," and *brevicauda* means "with a short tail"; hence our *P. brevicauda* is aptly named), or refer to its locality, or honor its discoverer.

Other scientific names—for families, orders, etc.—are not italicized, but all are capitalized. Family names for butterflies and other animals end in -idae (for instance, Papilionidae, the swallowtails), and plant family names generally end in -aceae (Rosaceae, the rose family). Zoological subfamily names end in -inae (Papilioninae); tribes (intermediate between subfamilies and genera) end in -ini (Papilionini). The names of superfamilies (groups of families) of animals end in -oidea (Papilionoidea).

The basic categories in the taxonomic hierarchy, used by every scientist and for all biological classifications, are phylum (Arthropoda), class (Insecta), order (Lepidoptera), family, genus, and species. Intermediate taxa (including subclass, suborder, section, superfamily, subfamily, tribe, subgenus, subspecies) need not be established, but they are often useful in making sense of relationships in very large groups like the Lepidoptera.

The virtue of scientific names is that they are more precise than common names; the same creatures have the same name in all countries—even in Japan and Russia, which use different alphabets (and quite different common names!), the names are the same, and given in the Roman alphabet, which is used for this purpose throughout the world.

For many decades, zoologists have been developing a system of rules, the International Code of Zoological Nomenclature, for scientific names, and there is even a "Commission" to settle disputes over names. (Botanists have a similar code and commission.) But research and discovery never cease, and in practice, scientists may disagree on which genus a species belongs to, or on whether an isolated subspecies is really a species or vice versa. Under these rules, the oldest scientific name for a given species (or subspecies or genus) is the one that is valid. If two species are combined into one, the older name is used for the union. If someone subsequently gives a different name to a species that proves still later to belong to a species already named, the second name is abandoned and called a synonym (placed in parentheses and preceded by = in this book). The species texts in Part III give only those synonyms that have been widely and recently used, to prevent confusion that might arise in consulting other books.

A species can be thought of as all the individuals, everywhere in the world, that can successfully court and mate with each other and produce fertile offspring (see "Species and Subspecies," below). But for categories above species (genus, family, etc.) there are no such definitions; though it is *hoped* that these categories represent actual branches of the evolutionary tree, they are arbitrary, and from time to time they provoke further disagreements and name changes.

Unlike scientific names, common names are not subject to rules, and anyone can coin them. Most of the common names given in this book are those that have been employed for many years and have become popular. Other common names I have had to invent, either because no name existed or because the existing name was misleading; all such names describe the butterfly's coloration, habitat, behavior, or hostplant.

To simplify cross-references from text or illustrations to particular species texts in Part III, each species has been assigned a number. Thus you might find in Part I, for example, "(see *Ascia monuste*, 83)"; and the color illustrations, which group species by overall similarity rather than by Part III text sequence, give species numbers for every adult illustrated, to allow quick reference to the corresponding text.

Form, Structure, and Movement

Butterflies are fairly typical insects, and as such are enormously different from humans in form, structure, and means of locomotion. The eggs, laid by the female, resemble tiny bird eggs except that they are flattened on the top and bottom and are generally ribbed. The larva develops within the egg, and chews its way out after about a week. Still tiny, it then feeds voraciously, and grows by shedding its skin and its head capsule periodically, as many as four or more times. The larval body is soft; in some species, it may bear various hard spines or plates, and in all stages and all species it bears many short or long hairs (Figs. 1, 46, 47). The hard larval head has tiny eyes, huge chewing mandibles, and tiny antennae (Fig. 2). A spinneret beneath the head produces silk, which the larva uses to spin a mat to walk on or to make a nest (Fig. 3).

Larvae move in a strange manner, using six conventional jointed legs and ten fleshy false legs. At the end of each of the six true legs on the thorax is a

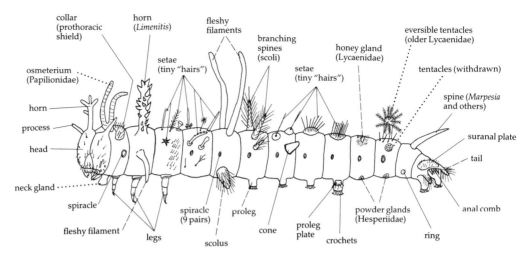

Fig. 1. A composite drawing of all the parts that occur on various butterfly larvae. The type of line from each part's name shows whether that part is hardened (solid line), fleshy and fixed in position (dashed), or fleshy and usually withdrawn into the body (dotted). Scoli (branching spines) are hardened in older larvae, but in young larvae (of Nymphalidae and Papilioninae) they tend to be more fleshy. The six thoracic legs have the same segments as adult legs (Fig. 14), except that in the larva the tarsus has only two segments (the second a claw) and the trochanter and femur are fused. Ten prolegs occur in pairs on abdominal segments 3-6 and 10. Spiracles (breathing holes) occur on the sides of the prothorax and abdominal segments 1-8 (they are larger on the prothorax and on abdominal segment 8). A ring has a hardened rim, as does a spiracle, but is probably a gland. The anal comb, when present, flips away the pellets.

MATURE LARVA   FIRST-STAGE LARVA

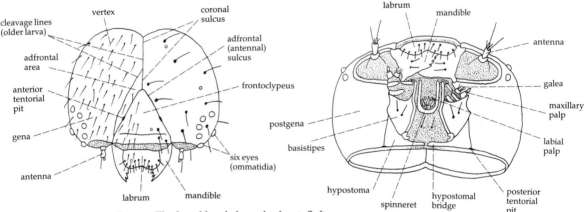

Fig. 2. The larval head, from the front. Soft (membranous) areas are stippled. The mature larva (left side) has many hairs. The cleavage lines usually appear in the third- or fourth-stage larva but do not split until pupation. Two internal ridges (each adfrontal sulcus) join an internal inverted-Y-shaped ridge (the coronal sulcus) to strengthen the head (see Figs. 19, 23). The two cleavage lines run from near the mandibles to the back of the head, and at the coronal sulcus they dive beneath the surface and run beside each other along the base of the Y. The first-stage larva (right side) has few tactile hairs; like the mature larva it has olfactory pits (small circles; the pit on the frontoclypeus is in all butterflies). True ocelli are absent in butterflies; the larval eyes (ommatidia) are often wrongly called ocelli.

Fig. 3. The larval head, from below. Soft (membranous) areas are stippled. During pupation, the head generally bends at the gap in the hypostomal bridge; but in *Celaenor-rhinus* and some other skippers the bridge is broad, and there are three cleavage lines, one at the gap and one lateral to each hypostoma. The maxillary palpi may help direct food to the jaws.

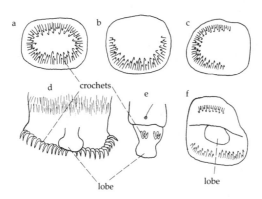

Fig. 4.   Larval prolegs, showing the hooks (crochets) and the fleshy lobe (*d-f*) of Lycaenidae. The crochets may be of three lengths (*a-c* and at the bottom of view *f*), of two lengths (at the top of view *f*), or of one length (*d, e*). Crochets are arranged in various ways: *a*, a circle in skipper prolegs; *b, d, e*, an inner semicircle on the inside of the proleg; *c*, a forward semicircle on the front of all anal prolegs; *f*, an inner semicircle and an outer row on the outside of the proleg. The crochets also vary according to butterfly group: *a*, skippers; *b*, most butterflies; *c*, the anal prolegs of all species; *d*, mature larvae of Lycaenidae; *e*, first-stage larvae of Lycaenidae; *f*, some mature hairstreak larvae (some *Papilio* and *Libytheana* are similar to view *f* but lack a lobe).

claw that can grasp objects. Behind the true legs, on the abdomen, are five pairs of the additional "legs" called prolegs, which are not found on adults and do not have claws. At the tip of each of the ten prolegs are many tiny fishhooks called crochets, arranged in a circle with their bases toward the outside of the tip and their hooks directed toward the center, such that the hook of each crochet points outward and down (Fig. 4). When the proleg lowers (because of the relaxation of a muscle, in conjunction with normal blood pressure), the hooks of the crochets swing down and out and hook into the silk mat or onto the leaf. The proleg is

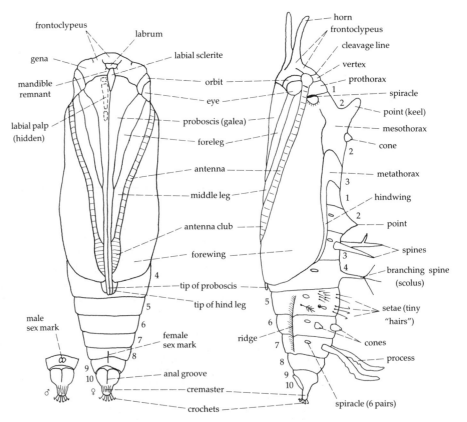

Fig. 5.   Pupal structures, from below.

Fig. 6.   A composite drawing of all the parts that occur on various butterfly pupae, from the left side.

lifted up by a muscle attached to the middle of the circle of crochets. The muscle swings the crochets up and in (and out of the silk mat) and lifts the proleg, all in one motion. Thus the larva moves along in a wavelike motion, lowering and raising its prolegs in turn. An ingenious adaptation, the prolegs prevent the larva from falling to its death; even at night, when the larva rests, the normal blood pressure keeps the crochets attached. The end of the proleg is flexible, and on smooth surfaces, at least in the Lycaenidae, works somewhat like an octopus sucker.

When the larva grows large enough, it starts to wander (skipper larvae stay put) to find a suitable pupation site, and it secures itself to the site by one or another combination of hooks and silk girdles. There the larval skin is shed for the last time, revealing the pupa beneath. The pupa resembles a mummy, although the outlines of wings, antennae, legs, proboscis, and eyes are more or less visible (Figs. 5, 6). Except for its abdomen, which bends at the three joints between segments 4 and 7 (some pupae are fused even at these joints), the pupa is motionless. On the rear of the pupa in most species is a point usually covered with various hooks (crochets). This point, the cremaster, attaches the pupa to a silk pad spun onto a twig or other surface. After a week or so—unless the species is one that hibernates in the pupal stage—the butterfly emerges (Fig. 7), crawls

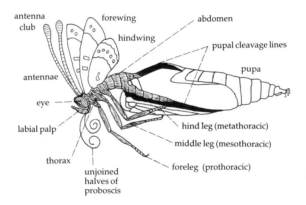

antenna
club
forewing
abdomen
hindwing
pupal cleavage lines
pupa
antennae
eye
labial palp
hind leg (metathoracic)
middle leg (mesothoracic)
thorax
unjoined
halves of
proboscis
foreleg (prothoracic)

Fig. 7. An adult emerging from the pupa, its wings not yet expanded.

to a point where it can hang, and then pumps up its wings to full size; when the wings have hardened it flies away. (Just how the pupating larva and the emerging adult accomplish these transformations is discussed below, under "Molting and Metamorphosis.")

The adult has a head, a narrow neck, a thorax, and a long abdomen. The eyes are enormous, occupying most of the head (Figs. 8-10). Two clubbed antennae and two short scaly palpi adorn the front of the head and detect odors for mating and feeding (Fig. 11). Instead of mandibles, the adult has an extensible strawlike proboscis that allows it to take in only liquids, typically flower nectar. Like those of other insects, the thorax is always divided into three segments, the abdomen into 11 segments, a structure that reflects insects' descent from segmented worms. (In butterflies, the last segments of the abdomen are in fact fused, making ten visible in males, nine in females, and ten in larvae.) The wings and legs of the butterfly are attached to the segments of the thorax (Figs. 12, 13): the prothorax bears a pair of legs, the mesothorax the forewings and the middle pair of legs, and the metathorax the hindwings and the hind pair of legs.

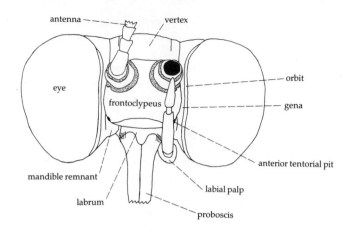

Fig. 8.   Adult head,
from the front.

antenna — vertex — orbit — gena — anterior tentorial pit — labial palp — proboscis — labrum — mandible remnant — frontoclypeus — eye

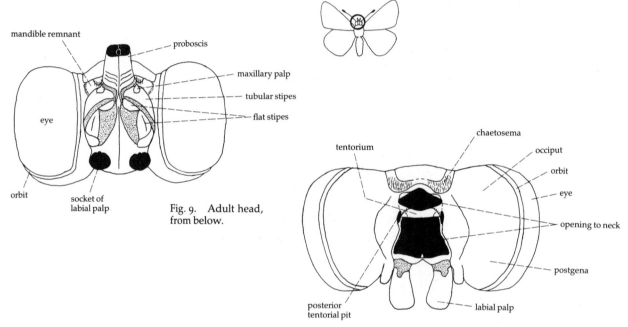

mandible remnant — proboscis — maxillary palp — tubular stipes — flat stipes — eye — orbit — socket of labial palp

Fig. 9.   Adult head,
from below.

chaetosema — occiput — orbit — eye — opening to neck — postgena — labial palp — tentorium — posterior tentorial pit

Fig. 10.   Adult head, from the rear.

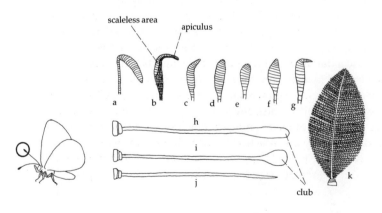

scaleless area — apiculus — club

Fig. 11.   Antennae of adults: *a-g*, skippers; *h*, *i*, other butterflies; *j*, rarely *k* or *h*, moths. *a*, Pyrrhopyginae; *b*, *Epargyreus* (most Pyrginae are similar); *c*, *Pholisora*; *d*, *Pyrgus* and *Heliopetes*; *e*, *Piruna* (*Carterocephalus*, *Copaeodes*, *Ancyloxypha*, *Oarisma*, *Pseudocopaeodes*, *Yvretta* are similar); *f*, *Megathymus*; *g*, *Poanes* (most Hesperiinae are similar); *h*, most butterflies and a few moths; *i*, some Nymphalidae, some Pieridae, Libytheidae; *j*, most moths; *k*, some moths (Cecropia Moth, etc.).

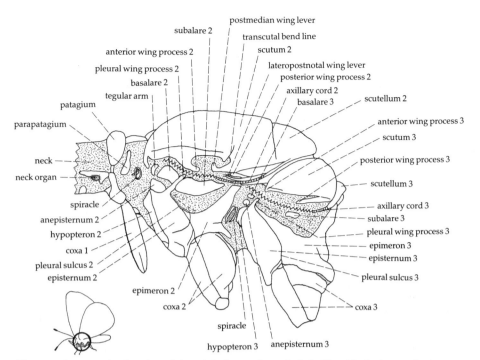

Fig. 12.   A composite drawing of the adult thorax, from the left side with the legs and wings removed, showing all the parts that may occur there in butterflies. Soft (membranous) areas are stippled. The numbers indicate the thoracic segment: *1*, prothorax; *2*, mesothorax; *3*, metathorax. The wings attach at the zigzags, and the wing bases pivot on the pleural wing processes like oars on a rowboat. The muscles from the furcae (see Fig. 22) attach just below the pleural wing processes to keep the bottom of the thorax taut during flight.

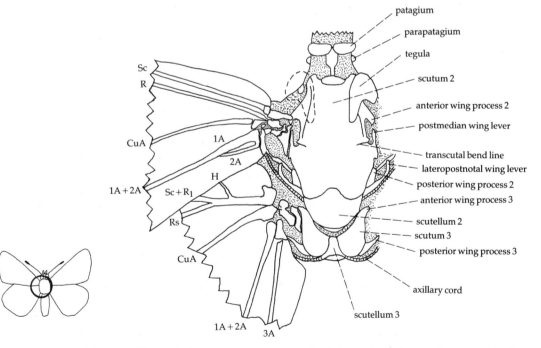

Fig. 13.   The adult thorax, from the top with the right wings and left tegula removed. Soft (membranous) areas are stippled. The numbers beside the names of the structures refer to the thoracic segments on which they occur: *1*, prothorax; *2*, mesothorax; *3*, metathorax. Small hardened parts (axillary sclerites; see Fig. 61) flexibly connect the top of the thorax to the wing; the central one pivots on the pleural wing process (Fig. 12). The tegulae streamline the body during flight and insulate the wing bases.

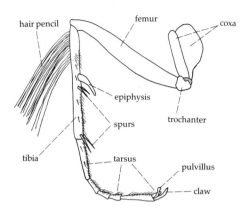

Fig. 14. The usual parts of adult legs. The hair pencil and upper spurs occur only in some skippers, the epiphysis only in the forelegs of skippers and Papilionidae. The coxa is joined to the thorax and moves very little.

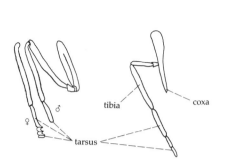

Fig. 15. The miniature forelegs of female and male Nymphalidae.

Fig. 16. The appendix of the coxa of the forelegs in Riodininae.

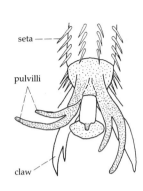

Fig. 17. Parts that may occur on the tip of the tarsus; the parts differ from family to family.

Fig. 18. The adult female abdomen, from the left side. Soft (membranous) areas are stippled.

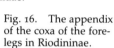
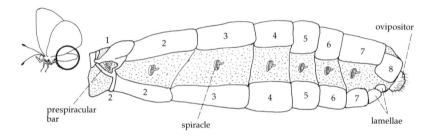

On the tips of the legs are usually claws (Figs. 14, 17), which are used to hang from flowers and vegetation as well as in walking. The scales that cover the wings and body lend the animal its coloration, help to insulate it from the cold, and improve the aerodynamic efficiency of its wings. Just as internal spars are used to strengthen an airplane wing, a network of tubular veins strengthens the butterfly's wing. The abdomen (Fig. 18), which trails behind the thorax and between the hindwings, is made up of several movable segments that telescope into each other somewhat, and on segments 8-10 are the visible reproductive structures: two "claspers," or valvae, on the male, an "egg-layer," or ovipositor, on the female. Thus male adults can be distinguished from females (to distinguish the sexes of pupae and larvae, a far more difficult task, see Part II).

The bodies of butterflies derive structural support not from an internal skeleton, as do human bodies, but from an external skeleton, or exoskeleton. True, an internal "skeleton" of sorts, provided by infoldings of the exoskeleton, lies in the head of larvae and adults (Figs. 19, 20) and in the thorax of adults (Figs. 21, 22), both to strengthen them and to provide extra sites for the attachment of muscles; but the visible exoskeleton provides the main structural support. A second major function of the exoskeleton, shared by all insects, is to provide protection against falls and attacks by predators—allowing beetles, for instance, to become miniature "armored tanks." The exoskeleton also reduces water loss due to evaporation; because small creatures such as insects have more body surface in comparison to their weight than do large animals, drying out poses a greater threat to them. The exoskeleton is ideal for small insects, allowing ants, for example, to carry much more than their own weight. Muscles can be attached to the exoskeleton almost anywhere, not just to a few bones, and the exoskeleton can evolve into odd-shaped parts that can serve as levers, hooks, lenses, fur, spines, etc. Most of the exoskeleton consists of hardened plates called sclerites, and movement occurs at thin flexible membranes between them. A rubberlike protein called resilin occurs in joints that must often bend, such as the wing bases and the proboscis. All these features—a complex system of muscles, levers, and springs mounted in a firm exoskeleton—enable butterflies to fly (see the next section), and allow fleas to jump a hundred times their own length.

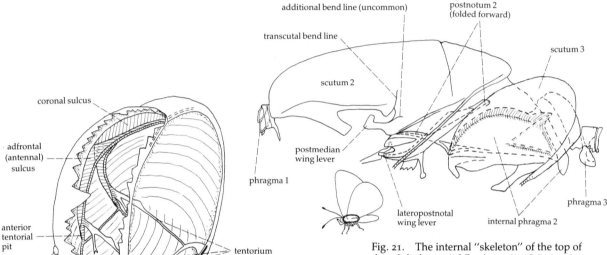

Fig. 19 (*above*).   The internal head "skeleton" of the larva; part of the left side is cut away for viewing.

Fig. 20 (*below*).   The internal head "skeleton" of the adult.

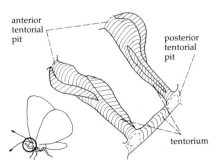

Fig. 21.   The internal "skeleton" of the top of the adult thorax (of *Precis coenia*, 180), consisting of several internal ridges (phragmata). Phragma 2 is a scoop extending back into the metathorax; it allows the large front-to-back forewing muscles to attach there and on the front of the thorax, on scutum 2. These muscles bow the thorax upward like a spring, bending it at the transcutal bend line (and at an additional bend line, also shown, in *Pieris*, *Polyommatus*, and others; J. Sharplin) while the postmedian wing lever raises the base of the wing like the handle of an oar, flapping the wing down. Postnotum 2 is folded forward to the lever, like the laminations in plywood, to strengthen the thorax and allow the front-to-back muscles to act directly on the lever. (See also Fig. 22.)

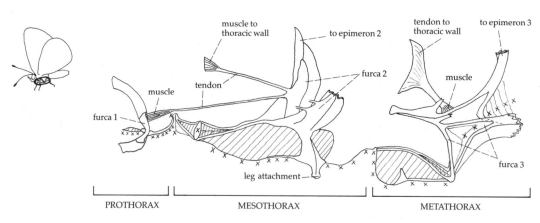

Fig. 22. The internal "skeleton" of the bottom of the adult thorax (of *Precis coenia*, 180). The row of X's marks the midline of the thorax. The three furcae, Y-shaped chairlike structures attached to the bottom and rear of the thoracic segments, are used for attaching muscles. Muscles and tendons from the furcae attach to the side of the thorax and make the wings snap swiftly down in flight (see the text).

Flight and the Mechanism of Flight

For us, the odd flight style of butterflies is part of their appeal. Watching them, one is amazed to see creatures that flap and flutter so erratically able to land precisely on a flower. Yet so confident are they of landing squarely on the flower that the proboscis is uncoiled and ready to drink before they land (see *Pieris rapae*, 76). In equally coordinated maneuvers, *Hamadryas* adults (161-168) land upside down on tree bark, and tropical metalmarks land upside down beneath leaves.

Some butterfly species (most satyrs, in particular) hop up and down erratically in flight, and some swallowtails and whites seem to bob slowly up and down. Other butterflies flutter along quite evenly, without hops. Some hairstreaks, nymphalids, and a few blues zigzag erratically about, but many others travel steadily along in a straight line. Some nymphalids (such as *Heliconius, Precis, Limenitis, Asterocampa*), papilionids, and others have the ability to glide for short distances (even the Cabbage Butterfly can glide for a meter). *Limenitis bredowii* (149) glides lazily along, and the Monarch and some swallowtails appear to soar at times in strong winds, high above the ground.

Insects differ greatly in how fast they flap their wings. Some flies beat their wings as fast as 1,000 times per second, but butterflies flap them rather slowly (5-12 times per second in the Monarch, 20 in some skippers). Most species flap slowly enough that each wingbeat is visible, but others (especially the Hesperiinae skippers and some giant skippers) flap them so fast that the wings are a blur.

Not surprisingly, the butterflies that flap their wings rapidly are often the faster fliers. The fastest butterflies I have seen—*Hesperia miriamae, Ochlodes snowi*, and *Megathymus ursus*—are skippers. Even keeping an eye on these species in flight is difficult. I have seen several dozen *M. ursus* adults in flight, but have yet to catch one. Some satyrs are the slowest species, although their hops and frequent jogs around bushes and trees may make them difficult to follow. The fastest butterflies may travel up to 80 km per hour in brief spurts, the slowest just a few kilometers per hour.

Butterflies also vary in the height at which they typically fly. Most fly about a half to one meter above ground. But many swallowtails fly several meters above ground, and some hairstreaks and *Neophasia* stay mostly in the canopy of tall trees. Yet *Pholisora catullus*, the Common Sooty Wing, and *Philotiella* blues seldom fly more than 5 cm above ground. Even during migrations, butterflies seldom travel more than a few meters above the ground or vegetation. But sometimes when two males who are seeking mates meet, they will fly almost straight up, slowly, until they are nearly out of sight.

The destinations of flying butterflies differ greatly, too. Some fly straight across the habitat, not to be seen again. Most migrants follow this pattern, of course, and some migrants fly enormous distances. The Monarch regularly flies thousands of kilometers, from southeastern Canada to southern Mexico, or from British Columbia to southern California. At the other extreme are *Hypaurotis*, *Philotes*, and other species that generally stay within 100 meters of where they were born. Some species make frequent stops, or may even return repeatedly to one spot; males engaged in locating mates typically show these flight patterns (see "Mate-Finding and Flight Patterns," below).

Probably all butterflies can hover—males often hover near their females—but they do it in different ways. Some skippers move the wings with long strokes, whereas others such as the Zebra Long Wing and courting male buckeyes (*Precis*) hold the wings nearly straight out to the side and flutter them very little.

The actual mechanics of flight are interesting. The main flight muscles of insects are not attached directly to the wings as they are in birds and bats. To understand how a butterfly flies, imagine that the bottom of the thorax is a rowboat, with the wings attached high on its sides like oars, the oar handles inside the rowboat; the top of the thorax is another, upside-down rowboat whose sides are hinged to the handles of the oars. For the downstroke, muscles running along the top of the thorax from the front to the rear (inside the body) contract, bowing the springy top of the thorax upward in the middle where the oars (wing bases) are attached, pulling the oar handles upward and driving the wings downward. For the upstroke, the downstroke muscles relax, and muscles from the top to the bottom of the thorax pull the oar handles down and the oar blades (wings) up. This ingenious system accounts for the basic flapping of the wings.

Some sophisticated refinements have evolved to improve this basic flight system. A split in the side of the thorax along the top (the transcutal bend line in Figs. 12, 13, 21) is full of rubberlike resilin, which allows the top of the thorax to bow upward during the downstroke and spring back downward during the upstroke. A lever on top of the thorax (the postmedian wing lever in Figs. 12, 13, 21) connects the top of the thorax to the forewing base; this lever and several wing processes (Figs. 12, 13, 61) grip the wing base to convert the muscle contractions into wing movements.

Another refinement gives an extra snap to the upstroke and downstroke. The top of the thorax keeps the bases of the wings about the same distance apart; when the wings extend to the side, the bottom of the thorax bows outward like another spring (muscles from the front arms of the furca, Fig. 22, to the thorax wall keep the bottom of the thorax tensed), and this tension helps the muscles snap the wings downward or upward. This snapping mechanism explains why butterflies seldom glide with their wings out to the side (for that, the muscles must be relaxed; most species seldom glide), and explains why in dead butterflies the wings generally lie together above or below the thorax, but not to the side.

Even the inside of the thorax is modified to increase the efficiency of flight. Because butterfly forewings overlap the hindwings, on the downstroke they force the hindwings down too (the downstroke provides most of the lift and forward thrust). The forewing downstroke muscles are in fact much larger than the hindwing downstroke muscles—an internal flange attached to the rear of the second thorax segment, called phragma 2, is enlarged backward (Fig. 21) to allow room for large front-to-back wing muscles for the downstroke. The hindwing and forewing muscles controlling the upstroke are about the same size.

Motion-picture studies show that the forewings incline forward greatly during the downstroke, and incline rearward greatly during the upstroke, both actions tending to move the butterfly forward. This inclination, or twisting, of the forewings is effected partly by muscles attached below the forewings (Fig. 12), some attached to the large basalare (for forward inclination) and some to the subalare and rear part of the wing base (for rearward inclination), and partly by the fact that the front of the forewing—where the wing veins are concentrated—is more rigidly connected to the wing base than is the more flexible remainder of the forewings and hindwings. (The lateropostnotal wing lever may also aid the inclining of the forewing.)

Motion-picture studies also show that in *Pieris* the wings clap nearly together above the back, then nearly together below the body. In both positions, when the front edges of the two clapped-together forewings suddenly move apart, air is sucked between them (because the rear edge of the forewings and the hindwings are still together), driving the butterfly forward. (This mechanism allows some tiny wasps to hover.) In the Monarch and the Mourning Cloak, during gliding the wings are held slightly above the horizontal, and during leisurely flight the wings flap through an angle as little as 45°; but during fast flight the wings are nearly clapped together, through an angle of about 150°. So the clapping mechanism may occur in these species as well, during fast flight; but it occurs only in slow flight in some moths.

The muscles to the basalare below the front of the forewing (Fig. 12) are important to flight control. If the butterfly starts to pitch forward (or rearward), the muscles give less (or more) of a forward inclination to the forewings, so that the airflow returns the butterfly to level flight. They also contribute to turns: for a right turn, the basalare muscles on the left side give more of a forward inclination to the left forewing than those on the right give to the right forewing, which provides more lift and thrust on the left side, causing the butterfly to make a nicely banked right turn. Apparently, the basalare muscles cause these changes not by contracting any more or less, but by contracting earlier (for more wing inclination) or later (for less) during the wingstroke. The butterfly can also use the abdomen for balance and turns, by moving it up or down or right or left, much as a hang-glider shifts his weight to direct his glide. During normal flight, and even in the hovering flight of male buckeyes, the body slants slightly rearward; but in the hovering of skippers (as in most hovering insects) the body is held nearly vertical, and the forward thrust of the wings becomes vertical thrust.

To take off, *Pieris* raise their wings together above the body, then quickly flap them nearly together beneath the body, without inclining the forewings, which shoots them upward. To land, too, they flap their wings without inclining them, and extend their legs.

Unfortunately, the details of insect flight are known well only in the grasshopper and the fly. Thus, a muscle running from the front and top of the butterfly thorax to the tegular arm (Fig. 12) is unexplained (the tegular arm is an internal rod unique to the Lepidoptera, attached to the pleural wing process, on the side of the thorax below the wings). This muscle may aid the inclination of the forewing by pivoting it forward or back on the pleural wing process, or it may move the forewing tip forward (or back), which would make the forewing overlap the hindwing less (or more) to increase (or decrease) the wing area on that side, which would help in turning, or in compensating for wing damage on the other side.

Molting and Metamorphosis

One problem with an exoskeleton is that growth can occur only in jumps, called molts. In a molt, the old exoskeleton is shed and the soft new one beneath is first expanded with blood pressure and then hardened chemically. During a molt, then, the animal is immobilized and must cease feeding; it is also more vulnerable to predators. Some insects, including butterflies, turn this problem to advantage, by using the molt to greatly alter the body and the appendages, thereby preparing themselves for a different way of living. This process, an evolutionary elaboration of the molting phenomenon, is called metamorphosis. Butterflies have what is called complete metamorphosis: a larva, or caterpillar, becomes a pupa, and the pupa becomes an adult butterfly. Hatching from the egg is not a molt; the larva simply grows inside the egg and chews its way out. Larvae molt (typically three to five times) to bigger larvae; the mature larva molts to a pupa; the pupa molts just once, to an adult; and the adult, which might live only a week, neither grows nor molts.

A result of molting is that larvae occur only in certain sizes (called stages in this book, often called instars in other books). A given species passes through a characteristic number of larval stages: although most have five, most Lycaenidae have only four, *Speyeria* six, and many metalmarks six or more (up to nine). The ornamentation and color pattern usually vary from stage to stage, and one can measure the width of the head to determine quite accurately the particular stage a larva is in (in most species, the head dimensions increase about 60 percent at each molt). The pattern of hairs (setae) on the larva is also diagnostic. The first-stage larva of most butterflies has a few setae on the body and head in characteristic positions (Figs. 2, 46-50), the pattern consistent from one individual to the next. Later-stage larvae have more setae, and vary more in shape between species, than do early-stage larvae (Figs. 2, 51).

Molting occurs when the larva has grown sufficiently that the joints between body segments become distended. After a new exoskeleton is formed inside the old one, the old exoskeleton is partially dissolved by enzymes and absorbed. At this point, the larva swallows air and increases in size. The remains of the old exoskeleton then split, starting at the head or neck, and the larva worms its way forward out of the old skin. The pupa and adult escape in a similar manner. Following each molt, the new, larger exoskeleton is hardened chemically.

Generally, the larval head (and the pupa) have well-developed lines of weakness where splitting occurs during molting (Figs. 2, 3, 23). When one larval

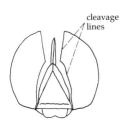

cleavage lines

Fig. 23.   The larval head, from the front, showing where it splits when the pupa emerges. The point is the internal inverted-Y-shaped strengthening ridge shown in Fig. 19.

stage molts to another, the soft new head merely pulls out of the old one through the rear. But when the mature larva pupates, the head surface splits along two special lines (cleavage lines) on the front and top of the head (except in some Lycaenidae, the head of which never splits). The bottom of the head, mostly soft, bends at a gap during pupation; but in species where the bottom of the head is more rigid (including *Celaenorrhinus* and some other skippers), three cleavage lines are to be found there, as well. A middorsal cleavage line on the larval thorax (and sometimes on the front of the abdomen, especially if the animal is pupating) also splits during molting and pupating. Finally, the pupa splits along a middorsal line on the top of the thorax, along lines between the head and thorax, between the antennae and the thorax and wings, and sometimes alongside the legs (Figs. 5, 6; in some Lycaeninae, also between the wings and the abdomen, and in skippers, also along a transverse dorsal line on the head).

Inside the adult are massive internal braces, inward growths of the exoskeleton: an H-shaped brace inside the head, called the tentorium (Figs. 10, 20), and two Y-shaped forks inside the thorax, each called a furca (Fig. 22). Because these structures would be a problem during molting, in larvae the furcae are absent and the tentorium is small (Fig. 19).

In preparation for forming a pupa, the larva stops feeding and voids undigested food from its body. Skipper larvae often then pupate inside their larval leaf nest, attaching themselves to the nest by the cremaster (that pointed projection on the rear) and in many species suspending themselves by a silk girdle as well, about the middle. Larvae of other butterflies start to wander, crawling rapidly about for hours. Finally, a pupation site is selected, and the larvae (in most species) then spin some kind of silk structure (Fig. 52). *Parnassius*, some satyrs, and some Lycaenidae may spin only a few loose threads of silk to connect leaves or litter together (*Parnassius* may spin a loose cocoon). Pieridae, Nymphalidae, Libytheidae, some Lycaenidae, and the other Papilionidae larvae spin a silk mat onto the surface, and a pad of silk onto the mat. They then hook the rearmost pair of prolegs into the pad. Lycaenids may spin a silk girdle that connects the body to a surface, and Papilionidae and Pieridae use the girdle to connect themselves upright to a twig or other surface. Most Nymphalidae and Libytheidae spin a silk pad, then hang upside down attached to the pad by the cremaster (see Fig. 5).

When the larva pupates, its exoskeleton splits, front first, and the pupa worms the larval skin gradually backward for a few minutes. When the larval skin has moved rearward of the wing cases, the cremaster breaks through the larval skin on the dorsal side above the point where the prolegs are attached to the silk pad; the abdomen tip then moves around for 10 seconds or more until the cremaster hooks securely into the silk pad, and the pupa gyrates for about a minute until the larval skin works rearward beyond the cremaster and falls off.

A ligament connects the anal region of the larva with the anal groove of the pupa (J. Osborne). This ligament connects the pupa to the larval skin after the skin is nearly shed and before the pupal cremaster hooks into the silk pad. Without this ligament the pupae that are attached upside down only by the cremaster (Nymphalidae and Libytheidae) might fall and be killed. The gyrations of the pupa after the cremaster is hooked into the silk pad then break the ligament and the skin falls away.

The process of metamorphosis thus looks like four distinct stages (egg, larva, pupa, adult), but in fact, continual changes occur inside the larva (Y. Eassa). The wings develop from tiny clusters of cells already present inside the larva (Fig. 25). Other adult organs grow enormously inside the larva: the tiny galea of the larval head (Fig. 3) becomes the proboscis; the labial palpi greatly expand and grow a third segment; the antennae develop from cells beneath the adfrontal (antennal) sulcus of the larva (Fig. 2), each antenna folding back on itself inside the larval head; the adult compound eye grows from cells beside the larval eyes, which disappear in the pupa; the internal and external male and female reproductive organs start to develop; and the larval legs lengthen to become the adult legs, in the process developing five extra segments. (The larva's prolegs retain no vestige in the adult, nor does the pupa's cremaster.)

Growth of the adult organs accelerates in the mature larva during the day or two before pupation. After the mature larva (except most skippers) wanders to find a pupation site, it becomes a sedentary "prepupa." Its color may change (*Papilio* larvae, for example, become brownish in many cases). Inside the exoskeleton, the antennae, proboscis, wings, and legs pop to the surface of the forming pupa and extend backward over the body in the characteristic pupa fashion (Figs. 5, 6). By the time the larva pupates, the major changes to adult form have already been made.

Inside the pupa, the muscles are reorganized for flight, and when the adult emerges it is perfectly developed, except for the wings themselves. The sperm and many of the eggs mature in the pupa as well; thus in many species, the female is ready to mate almost immediately, in a few cases with a male that has discovered her by scent and has been waiting for her to emerge!

The adult generally emerges shortly after dawn. To emerge, it must swallow air to split the pupal shell. The proboscis of the pupa is not open to the outside, but the adult inside can swallow air through pupal spiracles that open to the outside along the body. The air travels through the tracheal system to spiracles that lie next to the metathorax, then out these spiracles to the space between the pupal shell and the adult inside, and finally through the mouth and into the digestive system to cause the expansion. The pupal shell then splits, and the adult crawls out (Fig. 7). Most butterflies have only the legs to help them emerge, but *Parnassius* adults have hooks on the forewing base (Fig. 61) that can tear open the pupa and any silk covering it, and perhaps even help the adult dig through soil. The adult then crawls to a place where it can hang by the legs if possible, pumps up its wings to full size, and joins the two proboscis halves together (Fig. 7), all within 15-30 minutes of emergence. To pump up its wings, it swallows air into its crop to increase its blood pressure by 15 times. It voids wastes pent up from the pupal stage as a brown, red, or green fluid called meconium. After a few hours spent hardening the wings, it takes flight.

Curiously, the wings can expand without help from the body, even when a wing is cut off and the wound plugged with paraffin; the top and bottom halves of the wing are drawn together by the strands connecting them, increasing the blood pressure within the wing and increasing the area of the wing, much like a balloon pressed flat.

It has long been known that metamorphosis is controlled by hormones, but it took dozens of scientists (starting with C. Williams's work on the Cecropia Moth) 30 years to discover the mechanisms involved (Figs. 32, 33). As a larva grows, stretch detectors in the body joints send nerve signals to the ganglia and brain, which in turn start the production of a protein eclosion hormone. That hormone then circulates through the blood and triggers the prothorax gland, which produces the steroid hormone ecdysone (in insects, 20-hydroxyecdysone). Ecdysone circulates in the blood and causes molting by turning on parts of the DNA in the chromosomes. Eclosion hormone is produced in moths by the ventral ganglia of the nervous system for the later molts of larva to larva and larva to pupa, but by the brain for the molt of pupa to adult (J. Truman and others); in first-stage larvae, both sources produce eclosion hormone. For the molt to the adult, the eclosion hormone travels from the brain to glands called corpora cardiaca, where it is released to the blood.

One other hormone is of particular importance to metamorphosis. The juvenile hormone, a terpenoid, is produced in the corpora allata, in the head. When present, it causes the larva to molt into another larva. When the larva becomes large enough, juvenile-hormone production stops, the adult structures develop rapidly inside the mature larva, and the larva molts into a pupa. Juvenile hormone is produced again in the adult, this time causing the growth of the male and female reproductive organs and eggs. This was proved (by W. Herman and others) in hibernating adults of *Danaus plexippus*, *Nymphalis antiopa*, *Polygonia*, and *Vanessa cardui*, in which long photoperiod in spring causes production of the juvenile hormone; however, in nonhibernating species, such as *Euphydryas*, the juvenile hormone may be produced in the older pupae, as well, when most eggs are formed. (Sperm are produced in the mature larval and pupal stages, generally regardless of the presence of hormones.)

Life Cycle, Life Span, and Time of Flight

All butterflies develop from egg to larva to pupa, and finally to adult, in the sequence of changes called metamorphosis. The species differ, however, in the number of generations per year; in the duration of the egg, larval, pupal, and adult stages; and in the life stage that overwinters (see the next section). The life cycle is largely fixed in each species, although the timing of the flight periods during the year and the number of generations per year may differ between parts of a species' range. The species texts in Part III give the number of generations produced annually and the months when the adults of these generations fly, plus the life stage that endures hibernation.

Each generation in a butterfly is one complete life cycle, from egg to larva to pupa and finally to the adult and its egg-laying. The length of a single generation varies from only a month, for the summer generations of species having many per year, to one year in species with only one generation per year. A few species in cold regions even have a 2-year life cycle. Of course, when there is more than one generation per year, the overwintering generation lasts much longer (commonly 4-8 months longer) than the generations that do not overwinter.

The length of the life cycle depends partly on the nutritional quality of the available food: the aphid eater *Feniseca* (295) develops from the laying of the egg to the emergence of the adult in only 3 weeks. Most flower and fruit feeders like Lycaenidae and Pierinae take only a month to develop from the newly laid egg to the adult, since flowers and fruits tend to be more nutritious and to contain fewer plant poisons than leaves. Most leaf feeders take 6 weeks to 2 months, the grass feeders take 2-3 months or longer, and root feeders may take 6 months. Grasses are less nutritious than most flowering plants, and roots are especially difficult to digest.

The number of generations per year depends partly on climate. Most arctic/alpine species have one generation every 2 years, boreal forest species usually have one per year, many southeastern U.S. species have three, and tropical species have many per year. This variation arises from two factors: the growing season for plants is longer in warmer regions, and butterflies grow and develop faster in warmer temperatures. Of course the species that grow faster as larvae can have more generations per year.

An adult flight is that period of time when the adults of a given generation are active. The time of year when a butterfly species flies depends on which stage hibernates; on how long it takes for the eggs, larvae, and pupae to develop; and on how many generations there are per year. For instance, if it is the half-grown larva that hibernates in a particular species, that larva may resume feeding in late March and take 3 weeks to pupate, in mid-April; the pupal stage may last 2 weeks, to early May, when the first flight of the year takes place; the adults may then take a week to lay more eggs, and the next flight might occur 7 weeks later, in early July, followed by a third in late August. In areas with a cold winter, the species that fly first in the spring are those in which the adult stage overwinters, followed in sequence by species hibernating as pupae, larvae, and eggs. Adult hibernators may spend the fall merely feeding (or, in the Monarch, migrating) before they seek a protected cranny and become torpid.

Climate, latitude, and altitude, too, affect the season of flight. Springlike weather comes earlier in the south and at lower altitude, bringing the butterflies out of winter earlier (too, the larvae grow faster there). In the Arctic the sun shines 24 hours a day in late June, which triggers a tremendous burst of activity; most butterflies there fly in June and July, peaking about late June, and some may fly 24 hours a day. Farther south the number of hours of sun per day varies less, and has less effect. Alpine species fly in July and August in the United States and southern Canada, when temperatures are warmest, usually peaking at the end of July, but about August 10 in the Alpine Zone of the Wyoming Rockies.

The life span of adult butterflies can be guessed from the length of the adult flight period and from the life span of fed adults kept indoors. In nature, of course, many adults are eaten by predators or killed by a storm or some other accident. The mathematical methods mentioned below (see "Population Size and Population Regulation"), when applied to the marking and recapturing of adults, can help us estimate the average life span in nature.

To judge from the several dozen mark-and-recapture studies undertaken in nature so far, most butterfly species live for only about a week as adults, averaging about 7 days for males and about 9 days for females. But some species are exceptions. Adults that overwinter, such as *Nymphalis*, *Polygonia*, and *Danaus*, normally live 7 months to a year, although in areas where there are several generations the summer-flight adults may live only a few weeks. The dry-season adults of some tropical species live several months, and tropical *Heliconius* can live 6 months even in the wet season. Many *Speyeria* live 2-3 months in the summer, and the females delay egg-laying until late summer. *Coenonympha* adults may live a month or more in the dry summer of lowland California. The hibernating eggs, larvae, or pupae of many species live 6 months or more, to survive the fall and winter. The time required for eggs, larvae, and pupae to grow or develop also varies, as just noted.

The structure of a single adult flight is complicated. Most adults emerge by about the middle of the flight, with the rate of emergence peaking a little before the middle of the flight. The maximum adult population occurs later than the time of peak emergence; the longer the average adult life span, the later the time of peak population. Young adults predominate at the start of the flight; old ones predominate at the end. A flight generally lasts from 3 weeks to 2 months, whereas the average life span of an adult is only about a week; thus, some early emergers die before the last individuals emerge, and the composition of the population changes from day to day.

In most species the male and female populations are partially separate and asynchronous, for natural selection has led the females to emerge from their pupae later, when the males are most numerous, so that they can mate quickly. (Since female larvae feed longer than males, the adult females are in fact larger than the males.) Because the males are already flying about the habitat when most females are emerging, their life span can nicely surround the time when most females emerge, and their chances of mating are maximized. This lag between the times of male and female emergence is usually only 1-2 days, but natural selection adjusts the time for each species, to make its mating the most efficient; if the adult life span is long, the lag is also long (a week or 2 in long-lived species like *Speyeria*). Because mating is thus made more efficient, the whole population produces more eggs than it would without the proper lag. If females mated often during their lives and if later matings produced as many eggs as earlier matings, there would be no lag. But since in most species the females are more likely to mate young, and usually only once, most species have evolved the lag. Because the females generally live slightly longer than the males do, and because males emerge earlier than females, males are more common at the start of the flight, both sexes are common in the middle of the flight, and females are much more common at the end.

In Colorado I found (with M. Epstein) that spring flights last longer than summer flights. There are several reasons for the difference: warm and cold fronts interrupt the flights in spring more often than in summer; the microclimate differences between cool north-facing slopes and warm south-facing slopes are greater in spring than in summer (the sun shines at a lower angle in spring, more vertically in summer); the life span of adult butterflies seems to be longer in the cooler temperatures of spring (a phenomenon studied in very few species); and finally, the cooler temperatures of spring retard the rate of development, creating a greater difference in the times of emergence of the slower-growing and faster-growing larvae and pupae than in summer.

In species that have many generations each year, the midsummer-to-fall flights frequently overlap into a continuous flight that makes distinct flights difficult or impossible to discern.

Diapause (Hibernation and Aestivation)

Temperate-zone butterflies survive freezing winters in a stage technically called winter diapause, but more often called hibernation or overwintering. Diapause, which can also occur in the summer (in regions where there is an annual dry season), is a period of hibernation (winter) or aestivation (summer), a quiescent state in which annual periods of unfavorable climate are passed. All hibernations in a given species, regardless of latitude or climate, are passed in the same life stage; in some species that stage is the egg; in some, a particular larval stage; in others, a different larval stage; in many, the pupa; and in a few, the adult. The only exceptions are species with a 2-year life cycle, in which one particular stage passes the first winter, and another stage the second. (A few species pass 2-5 or more years in hibernation, but always in the same life stage.)

During diapause, whether in winter or summer, no feeding, growth, or development occurs; diapausing eggs and pupae do not develop into larvae and adults; diapausing larvae do not molt or pupate; and the metabolism and breathing rate are low. Diapausing adults may fly and feed to build up their body fat, but they do not produce eggs or mate. In diapause, at least in winter, the blood thickens with glycerol (or sorbitol or alcohol in some insects), the water content decreases (from 80 percent to 55 percent in *Limenitis* larvae), and free water is converted to a colloid (like gelatin); these changes, undergone by all hibernating life stages, prevent damage from freezing, in the same way that antifreeze prevents the freezing of car radiators.

The need for diapause can add a molt stage to the normal larval life cycle. Many butterflies (such as *Chlosyne nycteis*, 219; *Phyciodes tharos*, 228; and *Asterocampa*, 140-142) have six larval stages in individuals that overwinter but just five in summer individuals that do not overwinter (W. Edwards); for these species the extra larval stage is specifically adapted to winter. The overwintering larvae differ somewhat in color, too, from those of the summer generations: in *Chlosyne gorgone* (218) and *C. nycteis* (219) the winter larvae are more reddish-brown; in *Plebejus icarioides* (408) they are brown rather than green; in *Problema byssus* (503) they are also darker. And in *Euphydryas editha* (201) the exoskeleton of the diapausing larvae is thicker than that of spring larvae, the better to withstand summer drying.

The overwintering stage is so well adapted in most butterflies that it seldom changes during evolution. All the members of some entire subfamilies hibernate in the same stage. For instance, *Parnassius* hibernate as eggs, except for an arctic species that has a 2-year life cycle. All our Papilioninae hibernate as pupae. The Coliadinae generally hibernate as larvae, the Pierinae as pupae. Among hairstreaks (Theclini), one large section hibernates as eggs, the other as pupae. Most coppers (Lycaenini) hibernate as eggs, but two species of Eurasian origin overwinter as larvae. The blues (Polyommatini) hibernate as larvae or pupae (rarely as eggs), the metalmarks (Riodininae) as larvae. *Danaus, Anaea, Nymphalis, Polygonia,* and *Vanessa* all hibernate as adults. All the other genera of Nymphalinae, all Satyrinae and Apaturinae, and nearly all species of skippers (Hesperiidae) hibernate as larvae.

In the Arctic/Alpine Zone only 1-2 months during each year are suitable for larval growth, and thus most species have a 2-year life cycle. In most arctic/alpine species (for example, *Colias, Neominois, Oeneis,* and *Boloria*), young larvae spend the first winter, and the same larvae spend the second winter nearly mature. Japanese *Parnassius eversmanni* (30) overwinters as eggs during the first winter, then as pupae during the second, and Alaskan *Hesperia comma* (472) spends the first winter as eggs, the second as larvae or pupae.

The alpine *Chlosyne gabbii damoetas* (223) and some lowland *Euphydryas* have a different strategy: half-grown larvae diapause, but every year only a few larvae find a hostplant and become adults; the others hibernate for several successive winters and summers.

Some desert species, which typically have a life cycle of a year or less, are nonetheless able to diapause for several years, until a heavy rain causes the desert plants to resume growth and the diapausing larvae or pupae to become adults. *Papilio polyxenes* (7), which diapauses as pupae, and *Chlosyne gabbii neumoegeni* (223), which diapauses as larvae, produce particularly large adult flights after good rains. Nearly all the Papilionidae and Pieridae that diapause as pupae can persist in that state up to 5-7 years, and *Euphydryas chalcedona* larvae (200) can live up to 5 years. Even when the pupae or larvae are watered, many still fail to hatch or feed; in this fashion these species—and *Chlosyne gabbii damoetas*, in its own fashion (see above)—genetically spread over several years the risk of enduring a bad season.

For species having several generations per year, the number of hours of daylight each day (the photoperiod), and to a lesser extent temperature, controls a butterfly's entry into diapause. The longest day of the year is June 21; the shortest, December 21. When the summer or fall days shorten to a particular length (see the next paragraph) the individual becomes programmed to begin diapause at a certain point later on, either in its current stage or in a later stage. But in many species, including *Pieris rapae* and *Lycaena phlaeas*, high temperatures will prevent the butterflies from entering diapause, regardless of photoperiod.

Because on any given day of spring or summer there are more hours of sunlight in northern latitudes than in more southerly latitudes, butterflies go into hibernation at a longer photoperiod in the north than they do in the south, to be sure of diapausing before winter. For instance, *Papilio machaon* and relatives go into pupal diapause after the larva receives less than 13.0 hours of daylight at 33°N latitude in southern California, less than 13.5 hours at 38°N in northern California, less than 14.0 hours at 42°N in Massachusetts, and less than 16.5 hours at 52°N in Germany. And *Pieris rapae* goes into pupal diapause after larval stages 4 or 5 receive less than about 11 hours daylight at 43°N, about 12 hours at 50°N, and 15 hours at 60°N. But *P. napi* goes into pupal diapause at less than 15 hours daylight at 50°N, less than 17 hours at 60°N. Again, *Limenitis archippus* larvae hibernate in the third stage after the second or early third stage receives less than 13.0 hours daylight at 39°N in Maryland, less than 13.5 hours at 43°N in Vermont, and perhaps less than 15 hours at 50°N. So, although different species have different day-length thresholds, all the species with wide latitudinal ranges go into diapause at longer day length in the north.

Once in diapause, an insect will remain in diapause and eventually die; thus, some stimulus to break diapause is needed. A long period of winter cold, and to a lesser extent long photoperiod, helps end diapause. After months of winter cold, the individual is ready to resume development when the weather warms in spring. The period of winter cold necessary to break diapause must be months long, because if it were shorter the animals would start to develop during a warm spell in fall or winter, and then starve or freeze to death. In adult hibernators the long days of spring cause juvenile hormone to be produced, which triggers reproduction. In other species, such as *Papilio polyxenes*, long days as well as the long period of winter cold help end diapause. Recent data show that a few insects may end diapause automatically after a long passage of time, but these findings may not be widely applicable.

The situation is different for species that have only one generation per year. They always diapause when they reach a particular stage, regardless of time of year, temperature, or the normal photoperiod (though unnaturally long photoperiod or constant light in the lab may trick a few of these into developing).

Examples are the eggs of *Satyrium* and *Lycaena*, the larvae of *Euphydryas* and *Boloria*, and the pupae of *Anthocharis* and *Callophrys*. In these one-generation species, too, the distinction between hibernation and aestivation becomes blurred; for instance, the diapause stage may be reached in late spring or early summer, and the animal then aestivates through the summer and fall and hibernates through the winter, coming out of diapause in the spring. But these one-generation species resemble the multi-generation species in one respect: the long period of winter cold helps end their diapause also.

For overwintering eggs, two strategies predominate. In the method used by most hairstreaks, hibernating eggs are laid on the twigs of hostplant shrubs or trees, where they remain until the new growth of leaves appears the next spring when the larvae emerge to feed. In the other method, used by *Parnassius*, *Satyrium fuliginosum*, *Lycaena*, *Plebejus melissa*, and sometimes *Harkenclenus*, the eggs are laid on litter at the base of the predominantly herbaceous hostplants, where they remain until the next spring's new growth appears. (Because *Speyeria* and arctic/alpine *Boloria* lay their eggs haphazardly near the larval hostplants, they fit into the second group, even though they hibernate as young larvae.) The difference between the two groups is mainly that the first group feeds on shrubs or trees, and the tiny larvae could not climb the trunk in the spring to find the new growth if the eggs were placed near the ground, whereas the second group generally eats herbs, and the newly hatched larvae can locate the new spring growth at ground level. Haphazard egg-laying on loose ground litter in the second group is not as risky as it may seem, for even eggs laid directly on the leaves or stems of the hostplant might be blown away when the plants die in the winter.

In many species that have only one generation per year, aestival (summer) diapause is a prelude to winter diapause, as we have seen. But strictly aestival diapause (which is not continued through the winter) is uncommon among North American butterflies. The adults of some *Speyeria* (251-264) and *Coenonympha* (106) and the larvae of *Agathymus* (422-429) and one *Ochlodes* (506) undergo strictly aestival diapause. Some *Speyeria* emerge in late June or early July and mate, but then diapause through July and early August and emerge from diapause to lay eggs in late August and September (during diapause, they may nonetheless fly and feed). Tropical species often have an aestival diapause during dry seasons, but because they lack the adaptations for winter diapause, they die when a chance freeze occurs, as can happen in southern Texas and Florida. The cause of strictly aestival diapause is poorly studied in butterflies; in moths it is caused by long photoperiod and high temperatures, the opposite of the factors initiating winter diapause.

Diapause in most cases is controlled by the same hormones that control metamorphosis. Adult diapause is caused by a lack of the juvenile hormone that matures the reproductive glands and eggs. Larval (and sometimes pupal) diapause are generally initiated by a failure of the brain to produce eclosion hormone, which in turn means that the prothorax gland cannot produce ecdysone for molting. Pupal diapause in *Papilio machaon* and perhaps many others is caused by the lack of juvenile hormone at pupation (K. Shimada). In eggs, the mechanism is different: a special diapause hormone from the subesophageal ganglion (Fig. 32) generally causes egg diapause.

Physiology and Reproduction

Like humans, butterflies are furnished with respiratory, circulatory, digestive, excretory, and reproductive systems, but how these systems function in butterflies is quite different. And butterflies also make silk and fly.

In humans, air entering the body is drawn only into the lungs, through tubes, and blood vessels and hemoglobin then carry oxygen from the lungs to all parts of the body. By contrast, butterflies are small enough that tiny air tubes (tracheae, each constructed like a vacuum-cleaner hose) can carry air from the outside directly to the body tissues, without the need for lungs or hemoglobin (Figs. 24, 25). Even the wing veins (Figs. 53, 55), which support the butterfly's wings in flight, contain tracheae.

Air enters and leaves the network of tracheae through holes (spiracles) that can be seen as small lateral ovals on the thorax and abdomen. There are spiracles on the sides of the thorax segments (on segment 1 in larvae, between segments 1 and 2 in pupae, and between segments 1 and 2 and between 2 and 3 in adults) and many more spiracles on the sides of the abdomen (on segments 1-8 or larvae, segments 2-7 of pupae, and segments 1-7 of adults). In adults, a lever and a muscle on one side of most spiracles close the spiracles when air is not needed (Figs. 12, 18), in order to prevent water loss.

The tracheae from the spiracles are connected to each other just inside the body (Figs. 24, 25), and in adults at least, slight movements of the body coordi-

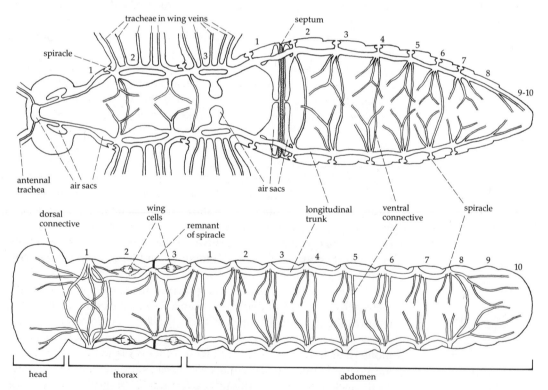

Fig. 24 (*upper drawing*).   Adult breathing tubes (tracheae), from above (after R. Snodgrass, J. Hessel, L. Wasserthal). In adults the air sacs alternately shrink and greatly expand during breathing (see the text).
Fig. 25 (*lower drawing*).   Larval breathing tubes, from above (after R. Snodgrass, A. Petersen).

nated with the opening and closing of the spiracles cause air to be drawn into some spiracles and out others, which in effect constitutes breathing. The internal connections also prevent parts of the body from dying if a nearby spiracle becomes plugged.

In adults, there are two large air sacs in the base of the abdomen and others in the thorax and head (Fig. 24). During the adult breathing cycle, the abdomen expands, air is thereby drawn into the thorax and abdomen, and the air sacs expand like lungs; the abdomen then contracts and the spiracles close, in a wavelike motion starting at the rear, forcing air out of the spiracles ahead of the contraction, and contracting the air sacs as well. The ensuing surge of blood into the thorax that accompanies abdominal contraction forces the air out of the thorax too. And as blood surges out of and into the wing veins, air moves into and out of the wing-vein tracheae.

Eggs breathe in a completely different way. Because they lack spiracles, they exchange air instead through tiny water-repellent pores through the shell (as many as 14,000, occupying as much as 12 percent of the egg's surface area). The pores are so efficient that eggs can survive under raindrops, or even if flooded. The eggs of the Cranberry Bog Copper, *Lycaena epixanthe* (378; see Fig. 31), for example, may be submerged in the winter in cranberry bogs. (Hibernating butterflies, even larvae and pupae, can survive flooding in part because their metabolic rate is low.)

In contrast to their well-developed system of tracheae, the circulatory system of butterflies is incomplete (Figs. 26, 27), and the blood lies freely around the body organs. In larvae a simple dorsally placed heart (seen as a pulsating tube on the middorsal line of the larva) simply pumps blood from the abdomen, via a number of ports, through an aorta in the thorax, and finally to the head and back into the abdomen, via the body cavity. But adult circulation is much more complex. In the adult the heart meanders to the top of the thorax, and the aorta branches to the brain and antennae. Small pumps at the top of the mesothorax and metathorax help suck blood out of the wings. Just after the adult emerges from the pupa, blood is forced into the wings to expand them, but they soon harden and thereafter require little circulation. What little is supplied serves mainly to feed the sense organs on the wing base (in all butterfly species) and the scent-producing glands (in many species). Other small pumps at the base of the legs and proboscis of adults keep the blood in these extremities from stagnating; partitions divide the interiors of these appendages into inflowing and outflowing halves. By undulating, a ventral diaphragm muscle (Fig. 26) just above the nerve cord on the bottom of the body causes blood beneath it to flow rearward; forward flow is prevented by a valve, the muscle septum across the front of the abdomen between the air sacs.

Adult circulation, as well as breathing, is caused mainly by the expansion and contraction of the abdomen (L. Wasserthal). When the abdomen contracts, blood pressure forces the muscle-septum valve against the ventral diaphragm, shutting off rearward circulation beneath the diaphragm, and the heart pumps blood forward to the head. Blood pressure thus rises in the thorax, and blood flows out into the wings. When the abdomen expands, the valve opens, and blood flows back into the abdomen beneath the ventral diaphragm and through the heart, which now beats backward, and blood flows into the thorax from the wings (sucked out in part by the small wing pumps). When the blood is pumped out of the wing veins, the tracheae expand; when the pumps stop, the tracheae shrink and help draw blood back into the wing veins.

Adults feed only on fluids, and for this they use a strawlike proboscis. In the pupa, the two halves of the proboscis are separate (Figs. 5, 7), and after emerging the adult must fit them together, by joining them along grooves like the zippers on some plastic bags. Each proboscis half is concave on the inside, the two thus forming a food channel between them when the front and back edges are zipped together (Figs. 8, 9). The rubbery protein resilin, which is important in the flight structures of the thorax, also causes the proboscis to coil like a clock spring. To uncoil the proboscis, a muscle in each side of the head forces the flat part of the stipes against a flexible flange inside the tubular part of the stipes, forming a closed hydraulic cylinder of blood and forcing the blood

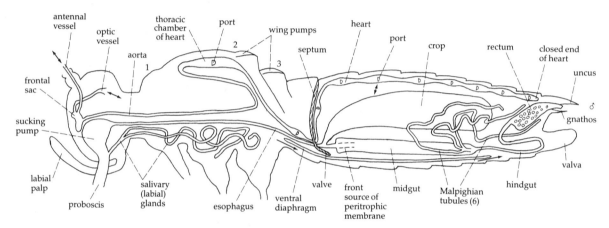

Fig. 26.   Adult structures for digestion and blood circulation. Arrows show the direction of blood flow (see the text). When the abdomen contracts, blood pressure forces the valve and ventral diaphragm against the bottom of the abdomen, and the septum prevents any blood from escaping from the abdomen except through the heart. (After P. Ehrlich, J. Hessel, L. Wasserthal.)

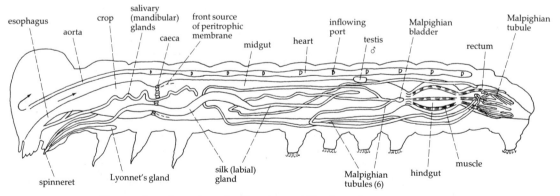

Fig. 27.   Larval structures for digestion and blood circulation. Arrows show the direction of blood flow. The caeca are part of the midgut and occur in at least some moths. Lyonnet's gland, which occurs in at least some moths, lubricates the spinneret. (After S. Scudder, A. Petersen.)

into each proboscis half to uncoil it. When the adult moves from one flower to the next, muscles inside the head can lift the whole proboscis like a crane, raising and lowering it into the adjacent flower, the tip being held vertical all the while. The basal third of the proboscis stays relatively straight after it is uncoiled, but beyond the straightened base the proboscis is very flexible: many tiny muscles (plus a trachea and a nerve) are contained in each proboscis half, and the movements of all but the base of the proboscis while feeding are due to the muscles inside it.

Butterflies have salivary glands, although larvae and adults employ different glands to produce the saliva (Figs. 26, 27). The saliva gland in the adult opens into the base of the proboscis, but unlike mosquitoes and some other insects, butterflies have no saliva tube within the proboscis itself. Thus, only dilute liquid foods can be eaten. Adults also seem to be able to eject saliva in a drop (see "Adult Foods," below) to dissolve solid food. A large sucking pump inside the head (Fig. 26) then sucks up the food.

Larvae have two powerful jaws, which move from side to side for biting and chewing (Figs. 2, 3). But in the larva, the glands that will in the adult produce saliva produce silk instead, and other glands produce saliva (Fig. 27). The silk consists of two protein substances: a thick liquid produced by the narrower tip of the internal silk gland, which rapidly hardens into the tough interior of the silk thread; and a softer gluey substance on the outside of the thread, which is made by the thicker base of the silk gland. The spinneret (just behind the jaws) shapes the silk into a thread. Initially too thick to flow, the silk is daubed onto the plant, and the head then draws silk threads out of the spinneret by moving from side to side, whether to weave a mat for the larva to crawl on or to build a nest. The silk crystallizes and hardens when stretched, and it is because it also shrinks after it is laid down that skippers and others are able to build their leaf nests. Thus the silk threads placed on a leaf cause the leaf to curl very slightly; more threads cause it to curl more; with enough silk the leaf rolls into a half-cylinder; and silk threads placed between the top edges of the cylinder then bring them together to form a tube.

Digestion in butterflies is surprisingly similar to that in humans (Figs. 26, 27). A crop stores the incoming food, a midgut digests it (with help from the saliva) and absorbs its nutrients, and a hindgut and rectum absorb water. In adults, which ingest only nectar and other fluids, the crop is larger than the midgut, whereas in larvae, which ingest large quantities of solid plant material, the midgut is larger. For the most part, adults secrete a single enzyme that digests sugar, whereas larvae produce many kinds of enzymes. To enhance digestion, the midgut encases food in a thin, porous, transparent peritrophic membrane, like a sausage skin; in larvae, once the digested food is absorbed through the membrane, and water is absorbed in the hindgut, only pellets are left. The membrane is usually produced by the front of the midgut, but in some cases (adult skippers and nymphalids, except Danainae) the whole inside of the midgut secretes it.

Some of the nutrition absorbed from the food is used directly, for growth or energy, but fat deposits in the abdomen store energy for future use.

Insects have no kidneys. Rather, six threadlike Malpighian tubules in the abdomen empty into the intestine at the rear of the midgut, three on each side (Figs. 26, 27). Insects produce uric acid, a solid, rather than the fluid urea that

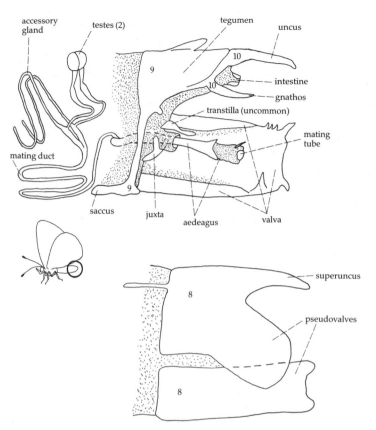

Fig. 28.   A composite drawing of the male reproductive structures, which are useful for identifying some species. Illustrated are the structures on the last abdominal segments and the internal organs, as well as some uncommon structures. During mating, the uncus and gnathos fit beneath the female's ovipositor, the valvae grasp her abdomen from beneath, and the aedeagus—its membranous and sometimes spiny tip everting— extends out of its membranous sheath into her mating tube as far as her bursa copulatrix. The projection above the tegumen is rare (present in *Colias*, some *Anteos*, and some other Coliadinae). The uncus is usually single but may be forked. The gnathos usually has left and right parts, but they may join into one. Hardened parts may be above the intestine (in some *Speyeria*, etc.) or below it (in some Pieridae, *Lycaena*, etc.). The transtilla is uncommon (present in some metalmarks, for example).

Fig. 29.   Rare modifications of male abdominal segment 8. A superuncus (in Libytheidae and in most Papilioninae) performs the function of the uncus when the uncus is missing. The rare pseudovalves (from the top of the abdomen in *Parnassius*, from the bottom in Danainae and *Biblis*) generally serve as a cover for sex glands.

humans produce; the tubules introduce the solid into the rear of the midgut, and it is simply eliminated with the pellets. Like the sealed exterior provided the butterfly by its exoskeleton, the production of solid uric acid helps it avoid water loss. Some wing pigments of Pieridae are related to uric acid, and it may be that storage of it in the wings helps eliminate wastes. The Malpighian tubules of larvae run along the rear of the intestine, where they also help conserve water.

The reproductive system of butterflies is complicated (Figs. 28-30). The two testes are generally joined into a single large sphere and are usually red (yellowish in Lycaenidae). The testes, situated in the top of the abdomen (at about segment 5; see Fig. 27), produce sperm; and two accessory glands in the abdomen produce the other materials transferred to the female in mating.

During mating, the male's uncus fits into a pocket beneath the female's ovipositor to form the main attachment holding the two together, his aedeagus fits into her mating tube, and his valvae clasp her abdomen (in some hairstreaks the valvae also fit into her mating tube).

Using his tubelike aedeagus, the male injects the sperm and other fluids into the mating tube of the female. The first fluids injected form a granular substance; other fluids produce a large, tough, white sac called a spermatophore; and the mating duct produces a polypeptide substance that causes the previously motionless sperm to start swimming. The sperm are supposedly then injected into the spermatophore (but may actually be routed into a gland in the female called

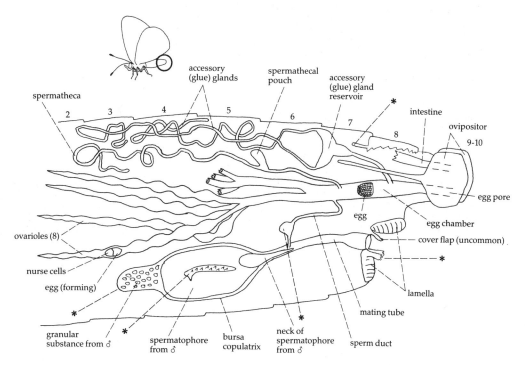

Fig. 30. Female reproductive structures (all except those with an asterisk are typical of most butterflies). The lamellae are variable and may be absent. The cover flap occurs only in all Papilioninae, Coliadinae, and Pierinae. Projections from the lamella may occur above the mating tube in Lycaeninae or below it in *Papilio*.

the spermatheca), and finally the last fluids harden into a clear "neck" that fills the mating tube (counting the remains of these parts inside the female indicates how often she has mated). A hardened structure on the wall of the female's bursa copulatrix is said to rupture the spermatophore, but this seems doubtful since in most butterflies it is absent or lacks a prong. The sperm, released by this or some other means, then travel to the spermatheca, where they are nourished and stored for minutes or even months, until eggs move past the spermatheca to be fertilized. After the sperm have left the spermatophore, the female digests it with enzymes, then uses the protein and fat in it for her own metabolism and for the growth of her eggs. (The granular substance that the male initially transfers to the female may serve to neutralize the digestive enzymes that the female used to digest the last male's spermatophore.) The clear neck that the male transfers to the female behind the spermatophore serves to plug her mating tube, perhaps to prevent the sperm from escaping, perhaps also to prevent her from mating again, at least temporarily. Stretch detectors in the bursa copulatrix tell the brain, via a nerve, when the spermatophore has been mostly digested, typically in about a week; then the female may mate again.

The eggs are produced in eight long tubes called ovarioles, which look like strings of pearls, the small eggs at the tip of each ovariole growing to full size by the time they reach the exit. Nurse cells beside each egg help nourish it. Egg-laying is triggered when an egg becomes large enough to be laid. The mature

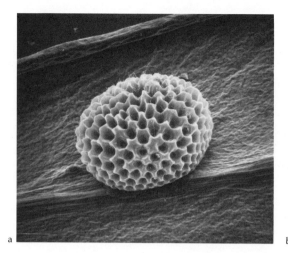

Fig. 31. Egg of *Lycaena epixanthe* (378): *a*, the whole egg (× 110); *b*, close-up of the top of the egg (× 220). The pit at the center contains the micropyles, where the sperm enter. The other pits have many air-breathing pores, too small to see. (David M. Wright)

egg then passes from the ovariole to the egg chamber, where it is fertilized from sperm stored earlier in the adjacent spermatheca. Pores at the top of the egg (the micropyles, Fig. 31) allow the sperm to enter. An accessory gland in the female may provide a fluid medium the sperm can swim through to reach the egg, and the fluid does serve as a glue to fasten the egg to a leaf or other suitable location; the egg is deposited using the two lobes of the ovipositor.

A special gland in male *Parnassius* (28-30) at the base of his pseudovalves (Fig. 29) produces a white fluid substance that is shaped by the pseudovalves into a sphragis, a large structure that hardens onto the female's abdomen tip during mating. The sphragis, useful for distinguishing species (Fig. 62), remains attached to the female *Parnassius* for life and prevents her from ever mating again.

Senses and Responses

Although the nervous system of butterflies includes a brain, many of the detailed functions of leg and wing movement are controlled by ganglia along the ventral nerve cord (Figs. 32, 33). The several ventral ganglia of the larva tend to cluster into fewer ganglia in the adult, to coordinate the movements necessary to flight.

The eyes of adults are enormous, filling most of the head (Figs. 8-10). They are called compound eyes because they are actually composed of hundreds of tiny eyes (ommatidia) grouped together. Each ommatidium consists of a transparent, lenslike cornea, a crystalline cone (the cornea and cone together act as a lens), the cells that produce these parts, and a rodlike structure produced by fingerlike projections of two to six surrounding sensory cells, each cell sensitive to a certain color of light (butterflies see all the colors from red to violet, plus ultraviolet, which humans cannot see). The lens directs the light into the end of the rod, and the light traveling down the rod is detected by the sense cells.

Although the butterfly's compound eyes are very sensitive to movement and color, and each ommatidium is focused on a small angle of incoming light, they cannot adjust for distance, nor can they see detailed patterns or shapes well. A butterfly watching a motion picture would see only a few dozen spots of color on the screen, and each frame of the film would be seen as a different picture rather than blended continuously with the frames before and after. However, the butterfly can see simultaneously up, forward, down, to the sides, and partly to the rear; in detecting movement around a broad periphery, butterfly eyes are far superior to human eyes. And before we insult the compound eye further, we should note that astronomers have copied it, by finding that a cluster of little telescopes, suitably interconnected by computer as in the butterfly eye, is superior to one large telescope, in both performance and cost.

The compound eye of skippers may even be superior to the eye of other butterflies (scudders), because it focuses light on the retina as in the human eye (G. Horridge): behind the corneas and cones and in front of the sense-cell rods (retina) of the skipper eye is a clear zone, through which light can pass from one ommatidium to another (scudders lack a clear zone because their rods and pig-

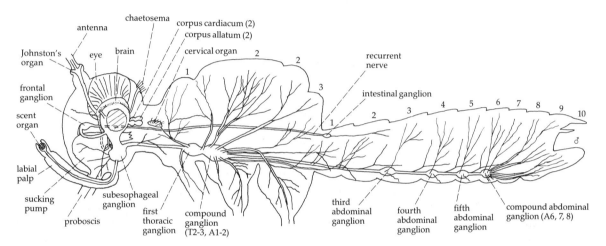

Fig. 32.   The adult nervous system and hormone glands. The ventral ganglia tend to cluster together. The two ganglia in abdominal (*A*) segments 1 and 2 of larvae move to the thorax (*T*) in adults; there is not much need for them in the adult abdomen because the first three abdominal segments are often fused and cannot move separately. (After P. Ehrlich.)

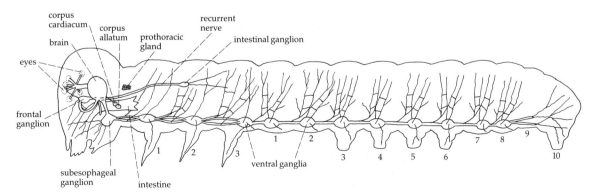

Fig. 33.   The larval nervous system and hormone glands (after A. Peterson).

ment reach the cones), and each ommatidium rod receives light focused by the lenses of dozens of surrounding ommatidia as well as its own. This focused eye allows the accurate fast flight of skippers.

The eyes of larvae are much smaller, each consisting of only six ommatidia arranged in an oval on the lower side of the head (Fig. 2). The structure of each eye is nearly identical to that of a single ommatidium of the adult eye, although larval ommatidia are larger and less densely packed than those of adults. (Ocelli, which occur in many adult insects but not in butterflies in any life stage, have a different structure.) Larvae, too, can distinguish colors, including ultraviolet, in order to find their hostplants.

Like honeybees, butterflies can undoubtedly see polarized light. Light has wavelike properties; thus any given bit of light "vibrates" in only one direction. Polaroid sunglasses let through only the light that vibrates in the same direction as the stretched parallel fibers in the glass. Because each ommatidium rod in the eyes of bees and butterflies is made up of fibers produced by the adjacent light-detecting nerve cells, the insects are able to see polarized light. Bees can use the polarization to find their way to and from their hive, even under partly overcast sky. Whether butterflies make use of polarized light is not known; possibly they use it during migrations, or in traveling about their habitat.

The senses of smell and taste in butterflies are quite unlike those of humans, for the sense organs are numerous, and scattered over the body. The organs of smell are all nerve cells that open to the surface through tiny pores in the exoskeleton. These pores often open all over the surface of tiny, thin-walled olfactory pegs, or at the tip of thick-walled olfactory hairs, or on structures similar to the pegs or hairs but sunken into narrow-mouthed hollows in the exoskeleton (olfactory pits). These organs vary in many minor ways. On the antenna of the Monarch, *Danaus plexippus* (89), J. Myers found about 13,700 leaflike olfactory pegs covering the whole structure except the side facing the wing, about 2,500 longer olfactory pegs on the sides beyond segment 7, about 65 hollow olfactory-pit organs everywhere on the sides except at the base, some olfactory hairs, and a few other types of olfactory pits and pegs. She found, in the female, that the pegs of the most numerous type detect both the particular chemical (pheromone) produced by the male to stimulate mating and the honey odor essential to feeding. (It may be that the other olfactory structures on the antenna and other organs also detect both odors; in moths, the olfactory hairs detect pheromones.)

In adults the antennae are the main sites of smell, and most of the sense organs reside in an area on the antenna club lacking scales (called the nudum; the Monarch antenna is entirely unscaled). However, sense organs occur elsewhere also, especially on the palpi and on the wing bases. At the tip of each labial palp is a hollow odor organ full of sensory hairs (Fig. 32), and on the wing bases many sense cells open through sensory pores to the surface of the veins. D. Minnich cut off the antennae of the Cabbage Butterfly, *Pieris rapae* (76), and found that adults still responded to apple-juice odor (by lowering the proboscis) 42 percent as often as when the antennae were present. S. Nakazema found that male silkworm moths lacking antennae respond to pheromones from the female 24 percent as often as those with antennae do. That they still respond somewhat is because of the odor organs on the palpi, wing bases, and elsewhere. (The palpi may also serve to clean off the proboscis, which rests between them.) Some olfactory pits occur at the top of the legs. At least in moths, odor detectors occur on the proboscis as well, and some, which look like scales, occur even on the wings.

The roughly 70 odor detectors of larvae are scattered about the animal: on the antennae (on olfactory pegs and simple pores), on all the mouthparts, on the surface of the head itself, on the legs, on the last prolegs, and sparsely on the body. The olfactory pits that appear as microscopic light spots on the larval head are so constant in position that taxonomists have assigned names to each of them (Fig. 49).

Undoubtedly, some of the olfactory hairs that serve as odor detectors in butterflies can detect chemicals present in fluids as well. Taste organs are present in the larval mouth and mouthparts and on the proboscis, legs, and antennae of the adult. In many butterflies, at the outside of the proboscis near the tip, are thick, tubular olfactory taste organs; several others are inside the food canal and mouth. *Heliconius* use the proboscis organs to gather pollen for food, as well (see "Adult Foods," below).

Taste organs (olfactory hairs) are also scattered on the ends of all the legs (on the tarsus and the end of the tibia). When the legs come in contact with dissolved sugar, the butterfly usually lowers its proboscis in anticipation of feeding on flower nectar. Experiments (by H. and M. Frings) suggest that in butterflies with normal-size forelegs (Pieridae, and probably Papilionidae and Hesperiidae) the front four legs but not the hind legs taste sugar; by contrast, in the butterflies with small forelegs (Nymphalidae, and probably Libytheidae and Lycaenidae) the hind four legs but not the forelegs detect sugar.

Females use their leg taste receptors to detect appropriate hostplants, as well, often drumming their forelegs against the hostplant to test it before laying an egg. (J. Myers found that *all* six legs of *Danaus* taste the hostplant prior to oviposition.) R. Fox found that the forelegs of females (but not of males) of all butterflies are specially adapted for tasting the hostplant by means of spines on the lower side; beneath each spine lies a cluster of olfactory hairs, whose tips are next to the spine tip (in *Danaus* and *Chlosyne* they are even wrapped around the spine). The female drums the plant with her forelegs, the spines puncture the plant, and the juices or odors flow to the tips of the olfactory hairs, where they are tasted. The ovipositor at the end of the female abdomen probably also has hostplant detectors.

Touch in insects is detected by hairs (tactile setae) that lie in flexible sockets; attached to each seta is a nerve cell that lies beneath the exoskeleton. Most of the visible hairs are of this type, although many of what seem to be setae on adults are really hairlike scales. Tactile setae are present on almost all parts of the adult body, including the legs, proboscis, palpi, antennae, head, thorax, abdomen, and wings. On the lepidopteran wing there are also special scales associated with nerves that detect touch and wing movement. The olfactory setae on *Danaus* antennae may detect both odor and touch.

Tactile setae occur nearly everywhere on the larval antennae, mouth, head, and body. On the first-stage larva the setae are scattered quite evenly over the body, thus maximizing their detecting ability while minimizing their number (Fig. 48). These setae too—again constant in position—have been named according to their location. On the mature larva the setae are much more numerous, but their density is about the same as on the first-stage larva.

Detecting the position of various body parts is important to the control of movement, for both larvae and adults. Microscopic tactile setae on the front of the body segments of larvae detect overlapping folds of the previous segment. On a plate on the side of the adult neck is a neck organ of tactile setae that registers the relative position of the head and body—important information for the control of flight (Fig. 32).

Special internal sense organs called scolopidia, each containing nerve cells sensitive to stretch, detect the positions of the body parts. Scolopidia are found in all adult insects in the mouthparts, intestine, palpi, legs (femur, tibia, and tarsus), antennae, and wing base. The Johnston's organ, in the second antenna segment of adults, contains many scolopidia that detect the position of the antenna, as affected by wind and gravity, for aid in controlling flight and other movements.

Special stretch receptors between the segments in the body of larvae perform similar functions. Each is a long ligament stretching between segments; nerves are attached to each ligament and to a nearby muscle. Nerves attached to tendons, in both larvae and adults, also detect stretching.

Vibrations can be detected by some tactile setae on the body of larvae and adults, and by a special organ called the subgenual organ inside the top of the tibia of each adult leg. Associated with this organ and attached to the leg wall are many scolopidia. The vibrations sensed may signal the approach of a predator and trigger an escape response.

Butterflies can hear, but not well. The tactile setae of *Nymphalis* larvae can pick up noises (D. Minnich); the larva responds by rearing up on its prolegs. In the enlarged veins in the forewing base of some adult Nymphalidae are scolopidia that seem to be able to detect sounds. R. Vogel suggested that a European satyr (*Maniola*) hears with them. The forewing veins are very wide at the base in Satyrinae (and in *Mestra*); because adult satyrs are edible (as larvae they ate grass), they are in greater need of warning, and hearing may help them escape birds or other noisy predators. But perhaps all butterfly adults can hear with their forewing veins, some species better than others. S. Swihart discovered that *Heliconius* and *Hamadryas* butterflies can hear with air sacs covered by a thin translucent exoskeleton on the base of the wings: in *Heliconius*, one on the base of the hindwing where veins $Sc + R_1$ and Cu join, and a second smaller one on the forewing base that is less important in hearing; in *Hamadryas*, two large air sacs on the forewing base (Fig. 64).

In all adult butterflies, on the rear of the head above the neck, are patches of hairs called chaetosemata (Figs. 10, 32), each hair with its own nerve (an extra patch of chaetosema is on the front of the head of skippers). They are poorly studied, but Swihart found that in *Heliconius* they can detect sound (they are inferior to the wing-base ears though). Chaetosemata may also detect touch (they may rub against the prothorax), vibrations, or wind.

Hamadryas males (161-168) and *Megathymus* (417-420) produce clicking sounds (using their abdomen, Fig. 63, or the wings, respectively), perhaps in order to communicate with each other, and a few other butterflies actively make sounds. Males of some tropical American satyrs (*Pharneuptychia*) click while flying near other males, and *Neptis* (Nymphalinae) adults in Vietnam click their forelegs together. When adults of the European *Nymphalis io* are disturbed, they open their wings to display the eyespots and at the same time make a hissing sound by rubbing the veins of the forewings and hindwings together (A. Blest,

J. Swynton). Birds are startled by the eyes and hissing and fly away, which Blest and Swynton ascribed to birds' innate fear of snakes. Although the American *Precis* adults (180-182) have conspicuous eyespots that may startle predators, I have not heard them make this sound, which is undoubtedly faint at best.

Larvae are not known to make sounds, but some pupae can. The transverse ridges on the front edges of the abdomen segments of some Papilionidae and Hesperiidae pupae sometimes rub against fine projections on the rear edges of the preceding segments to make rasping sounds (H. Hinton). The pupa of an Oriental skipper (*Gangara*) has a long striated proboscis that makes a hiss when the ridges on the bottom of abdomen segment 5 rub against it. Pupae of most Lycaenidae (both subfamilies) produce sounds from tiny file-and-peg structures at the joints where abdomen segments 4 and 5, 5 and 6, and 6 and 7 overlap. These faint sounds are random in nature (that is, without any fixed notes) and may protect the pupae from such predators as ants (J. Downey, A. Allyn). *Heliconius erato* pupae produce faint squeaks.

Temperature Regulation, Resting, and Roosting

Although butterflies are "cold-blooded," they can regulate their own body temperature to some extent (by behavioral means) if the air temperature is not too hot or too cold, just as reptiles often do. They can fly when the air is roughly between 16 and 42°C (60-108°F), but they display aberrant behavior at these two extremes, because the optimum temperature inside the body is 28-38°C (82-100°F).

To warm up, butterflies bask in the sun. In dorsal basking, the tactic used by most species, the wings are spread and the upperside of the body is exposed to the sun. Lateral basking, in which the wings are closed and the body is turned sideways to the sun, is used by *Colias*, most satyrs (though *Neominois* bask dorsally, and *Oeneis* sometimes do), most hairstreaks (except *Hypaurotis* and *Strymon*), and occasionally *Euchloe* and *Lycaena* and other butterflies that usually bask dorsally. The Hesperiinae bask dorsally but spread the hindwings more than the forewings. The wings help the warming process by absorbing sunlight and radiating heat into the air around the body (the blood circulation from wings to body is slight). For example, the underside of the hindwings of many species (especially Pieridae) is darker in the spring, which helps heat the air around the body and therefore the body itself. The upper part of the body of *Parnassius* (28-30) is scaleless and black, and the sun thus warms the body directly; the part of the hindwings next to the abdomen is also black, and thus contributes heat. To warm the thorax before flying, some *Danaus, Nymphalis, Polygonia, Vanessa, Atrytone,* and others "shiver" by vibrating the wings slightly. Butterflies may also get warm by resting on warm objects, such as soil or rock.

When the air gets too hot, adults may cool themselves by closing their wings and moving them parallel to the sun's rays, or they may fly to shade, avoid the hot ground, or seek areas that are moist and therefore cooler. J. Rawlins found that when *Papilio polyxenes* adults are cool, they rest with their wings spread and the abdomen not lowered; conversely, when they are hot, they rest with the abdomen lowered into the shade of the spread wings, and blood is pumped between the thorax and the cooler abdomen.

Some species have peculiar resting positions that may have no bearing on temperature regulation. For instance, many Pyrginae skippers keep the wings spread when resting (see "Subfamily Pyrginae," in Part III). Many metalmarks also keep their wings spread when resting, and some tropical forest metalmarks may even rest upside down under leaves. *Parnassius* tend to keep their wings spread when feeding; *Poladryas* spread their wings most of the time; and Papilioninae adults flutter their wings while feeding on flowers, probably because their weight might otherwise cause the flower to sag.

Larvae voluntarily vary their body temperature less than adults do. In cool weather they may move to the top of the plant and bask sideways to the sun. In very hot weather they may move to the base of the plant, where it is cooler. *Colias* larvae prefer cooler temperatures—about 20-29°C (68-84°F)—than adults do. A. Shapiro found that *Pieris* pupae develop to adults even at 3°C (37°F); but the adults emerge only when it is warmer.

In late afternoon, adults seek places to spend the night. The roosting sites may be the same places chosen by basking individuals during the day for temperature regulation, but some species choose special roosting sites that may protect them from predators such as mice. Butterflies usually spend the night on the tops of small trees, shrubs, or other plants. I have often found roosting butterflies of many species on the leaves of small oak trees, and yellow Pieridae often roost on the yellow leaves of shrubs or tall weeds for camouflage. In vacant city lots, also, butterflies often roost on tall weeds, evidently choosing such sites to avoid mice and early-morning birds.

Adults also roost during the day when clouds obscure the sun (they generally fly only when the sun shines). During rains, adults may roost under leaves or crawl into clumps of vegetation. At midday in cloudy weather, *Speyeria* often rest on pine boughs about 3 m off the ground.

Most butterflies roost alone. *Erynnis* skippers roost alone with their wings wrapped around a twig in the manner of a moth. *Pieris rapae* and *P. napi* are known to roost sometimes in small groups, and *Nymphalis milberti* and *N. vau-album* sometimes overwinter in small groups at favorable sites, probably owing to chance findings of the same protected hollow. Some tropical species such as *Heliconius* (271-273), *Smyrna* (169), and *Eumaeus deborah* roost gregariously in true social behavior. *Heliconius*, in fact, gather at the same learned roost every night; each generally returns to the same leaf, night after night, by learning where the site is (*Heliconius* have home ranges). *Heliconius* are distasteful to vertebrates, and they may roost together for defense. For if a bird finds that one tastes bad, he will leave the others alone; and if one adult is startled and flies, the entire flock can take flight.

Dispersal and Migration

Some butterflies are sedentary, a few are great migrants, and the dispersal habits of other species can be anywhere between these extremes. Localized butterflies such as *Hypaurotis crysalus* (297) and *Philotes sonorensis* (397) seldom move more than a few meters from their larval hostplants; adults of most species are fairly local, flying no more than a few hundred meters from where they emerged from pupae; but *Danaus plexippus* (89) and *Vanessa cardui* (186) regularly travel thousands of kilometers.

The dispersal of a species is an adaptation to the stability of its hostplants. By and large, the larvae of sedentary butterflies feed on hostplants (typically perennials such as trees) that have been stable in their distribution for hundreds of years. By contrast, the larvae of migrants often feed on temporary weeds that dry up at certain times of the year; as adult migrants, they then disperse to populate new patches of weeds.

The degree of dispersal in butterflies is largely hereditary, but individual adults, whether migratory or not, modify their flights somewhat to find mates, flowers (thus nectar), mud (thus water), roosting sites, and so forth. Individuals may need to fly some distance from the hostplants to locate plants in flower (sometimes they lay more eggs near their favorite flowers); they may also fly to distant hilltops or other mating sites. And because females generally seem to be more widespread than males and usually fly a little farther than males during their search for hostplants (on which to lay their eggs), females are seen less often than males (though the sex ratio of butterflies is one male to one female).

In nonmigrants, habitat size and population density also affect flight distances. Butterflies in a large habitat fly farther than those in a small one. Species that typically have low-density populations tend to have longer flights than species with high-density populations, both because low-density populations making short flights would become extinct (longer flights are needed to find their scattered mates) and because long flights would decrease the density of a high-density population.

Many species are migrants, and the hatched lines on some of the maps in Part III show the areas where adults migrate beyond their winter range (see "Using the Range Maps" in the opening pages of Part III). The text of Part III details the migratory habits of each species. The aggregations of migrating *Danaus plexippus* are spectacular every year; *Vanessa cardui* also migrates in huge numbers some years; but except for producing occasional hordes, others migrate in less-spectacular fashion.

Migration in North American butterflies certainly increased after the warming following the Ice Age, which opened up a large area to basically tropical butterflies that cannot survive freezes. Migration evidently evolves when the adults moving out of a wintering area produce greater numbers of descendants that manage to fly back into the wintering area than do adults that never leave the area. For such traffic to evolve, two conditions must hold: first, the species is unable to overwinter in freezing temperatures; and second, during the warm months there are hostplants for their larvae in the north, where these freezes occur. (For a discussion of the physiological mechanisms allowing some species to overwinter where freezes occur, see "Diapause," above.)

All migratory species have several generations per year, and because freezes would kill them, they overwinter only in the south, in all but the warmest northern winters. Because most migratory species lack a true diapause, in the southern overwintering range any of the life stages—adults, eggs, larvae, or pupae—may occur at any time of the winter. The Monarch (*Danaus plexippus*) and some others are exceptional in overwintering only as adults, which allows them a quick getaway in spring. Among Monarchs, therefore, there is one generation of individuals—the overwinterers—that migrates twice, once in each direction. Monarchs in fact live for months, from fall to spring (and marked Monarchs lived from February to July, others from July to October). But with the exception of species that hibernate as adults, such as Monarchs, the life span of the individual adult of a migratory species is just about a week, the life span of most other butterflies. In migratory species nearly every individual (of whatever generation) mates at the emergence site (but overwintering Monarchs emerge from their winter roosts and mate), and migration generally starts about 1-2 days after emergence from the pupa (usually after mating). Migration usually ceases when egg-laying begins, in another day or more, although Monarchs often lay eggs en route during the spring flights north.

Migratory species differ in the purposefulness of their flight. The weakest migrants fly north not much more often than south in spring. (Even a species with large flights but no directional preference would spread northward every year as a simple range extension, and then die back if it could not withstand freezing.) Their spread north is accordingly slow, and they do not reach their northern limits until September. Most of these then freeze in the fall and few make it south to the winter haven. Such species qualify only marginally as migrants. The first step toward more truly migratory behavior (achieved, for example, by the eight species mentioned below) is to evolve a stronger fall flight south (to avoid freezing), though the spring migrations may be fairly relaxed. The next step, represented by *Precis coenia* and *Vanessa cardui*, seems to be the evolution of a strong spring flight north as well as the strong fall flight south. The final step, the evolution of truly purposeful northward and southward flights, is represented admirably by *Danaus plexippus*: nearly every Monarch in the entire population flies in a northerly direction in spring; nearly every one heads south in the fall; and very few adults remain in the overwintering area during the summer. In this species the larval feeding grounds and the overwintering grounds are almost totally separate, hundreds or thousands of kilometers apart, but in the other migrant species some adults and larvae remain in the overwintering grounds all summer and a few are to be found all along the migration route, spring and fall.

In many species the fall flights south—a race to stay ahead of the advancing frost—are much more obvious than the unhurried spring and summer flights north. T. Walker placed malaise traps (tentlike nets in which insects bump against a vertical net, fly upward into a net awning, and then enter a killing jar at the apex) in various directions in northern Florida for a whole year to catch migrants; he found that eight species (*Phoebis sennae*, 50; *Eurema lisa*, 63; *Precis coenia*, 180; *Dione vanillae*, 268; *Lerema accius*, 448; *Panoquina ocola*, 561; *Urbanus proteus*, 589; *U. dorantes*, 591) flew south in numbers in the fall (mostly early September to mid-November), but only two (*P. coenia* and to a slight extent *D. vanillae*) flew north in numbers in the spring (April to mid-May). In *Vanessa cardui*, spring flights are more obvious than fall flights, but various observers have seen fall flights.

How many generations fly north, and how many south? In weak migrants, two or three generations have a net movement north, and in the fall one or two generations have predominantly southward flight (the numbers of generations differ because certain death from freezing in the north is a more powerful selective force than the chance of finding food by flying north). Indeed, in the weakest migrants, which have long adult flights but no preferred direction, each generation flies north *and* south, all season long. In the strongest migrants (the Monarch and *Vanessa cardui*) the first generation can migrate far northward, and midsummer generations are sedentary; but even in these two species, some second-generation adults emerging in May in southern states (from eggs laid by the first-generation females on their way north) also fly north, and occasionally more than one generation of *V. cardui* flies south as well.

One hypothesis for the triggering of migration is that the increasing photoperiod (day length) of spring causes adults of migratory species to fly north, and that the shrinking photoperiod of fall triggers (in a later generation) the southward flight. A brief experiment with *Pieris rapae* in Britain suggested that adults exposed to long photoperiod for several days tend to fly north, and those exposed to short photoperiod tend to fly south. It may be that adults head south when the photoperiod falls below a certain critical threshold in late summer and fall. However, photoperiod cannot explain spring migration, because the Monarch flies north about mid-February to late March, and flies south mainly in October and November, when the photoperiod is the same (March 21 and September 21 have identical photoperiod; exceptional adults fly south as early as late July, in Ontario, and others as late as December). And I have seen *Vanessa cardui* migrating south as early as late July at high altitude in Colorado, in mid-August at high altitude in Wyoming. The direction of flight seems related to the hormonal changes during hibernation (see "Diapause," above): the long period of winter cold ends diapause and triggers the northward flight, and short photoperiod causes southward flight and the initiation of diapause. Between these times, say May to September, photoperiod could control the flight direction.

Nymphalis californica (196) is an exceptional migrant, for unlike other migrants it can survive freezing temperatures, and it makes regular altitudinal migrations in California by moving up and down the mountains to where its hostplants are in prime condition (*N. milberti* may do likewise in Colorado). In warmer areas of the world where freezing is no hazard, animals may nonetheless migrate in search of food (the locusts of North Africa and India, for example, and the Wildebeest of East Africa). *Ascia monuste* (83) may be similarly exceptional: E. Nielsen thought that its direction of migration is determined mainly by the direction young adults took from their pupae to their flower-feeding grounds. *Nymphalis vau-album* is another oddity, for it has one generation per year but occasionally spreads out of its normal range, then retreats.

The strong migrants have evolved flight patterns making for efficient travel. Migrating butterflies usually maintain a constant direction at about 20 km per hour all day, within a few meters of the ground (though *Danaus plexippus* is occasionally observed several hundred meters above ground), often flying over houses and trees rather than going around them. In contrast, nonmigrants often backtrack and follow a more haphazard course. Although one theory has migrants flying at a constant angle to the sun, most species studied (including *A. monuste, Kricogonia, Phoebis sennae, Dione vanillae, Vanessa atalanta, V. cardui, V. virginiensis, Precis coenia, Eunica monima, Libytheana, Lampides,* and *Urbanus proteus*) fly in about the same direction at all times of day when migrating. The fall flights of *P. sennae, D. vanillae, P. coenia,* and *U. proteus* are to the south-southeast from September to October in Florida, regardless of wind direction, time of day, or obstacles (T. Walker and others). Two observers of *Phoebis statira* did see migrants reverse direction in the afternoon. Fall-migrant *Danaus* released by F. Urquhart flew southeast in the morning but southwest in the afternoon. And J. Kanz found that in the laboratory, fall-migrating Monarchs often turn toward the sun but nonmigrants do not; released adults of both groups, however, flew with the wind. (Several observers report that the direction of migrating Monarchs does not change during the day.)

In late April and May 1983 I watched migrating Painted Ladies (*Vanessa cardui*) near Denver, Colorado, to check firsthand any change of direction during the day. I recorded directions of 291 adults and the time of day, and found no significant change from early morning to late afternoon in their northeast flight. In 2-hour periods from 8:00 A.M. to 6:00 P.M. (standard time), adults flew 51°, 45°, 59°, 54°, and 42°, averaging 51° over the whole day (east being 0°, north 90°). Northeast flight at Denver implies that the adults must have flown over the Rocky Mountains; and in fact northward migration was observed over Vail Pass, near timberline. Indeed, *V. cardui* was present everywhere in Colorado and adjacent states then (the migration was observed in southern California starting in late March, and in southern New Mexico migrants from Mexico flew northeast in early April). Interestingly, though the overall direction near Denver did not change during the day, some individuals flew at odd directions, and the efficiency of migration gradually increased during the day as fewer took these odd courses. It may be that the butterflies do more feeding in the cool mornings, and make more headway in their travels in the warm afternoons.

The species that overwinter in Mexico or southwestern United States generally fly northeast in spring and southwest in fall, whereas the eastern populations that overwinter in Florida fly northwest (probably north-northwest) in spring, south-southeast in fall.

It is not known, then, how most migrating butterflies maintain a constant direction during the day. Like bees, they may orient by the sun and somehow compensate for its movement across the sky. Like bees, they see polarized light (see "Senses and Responses," above), and polarized light is known to help bees navigate. Almost certainly, butterflies use the position of the sun or the differences in the polarization of light across the sky to navigate. They are also known to use landmarks to navigate (see *Ascia monuste*; see also "Butterfly Intelligence," below), and biologists suspect that they use the stars or moon to navigate, as well, since Monarchs and *Vanessa atalanta* (184) are sometimes observed migrating at night. Birds can use magnetic fields for orientation, but butterflies are not known to. Butterflies do not migrate on cold, cloudy, rainy, or very windy days, but moderate wind, which greatly affects the course of aphids and many other tiny insects, affects migrating butterflies very little.

To study the movements of migrants and nonmigrants, one can mark the adults (see Appendix B). Records of migrations, whether of marked individuals or not, should include the time of day and the flight direction, and are best if continued all day to note any change in direction. Care is essential: glare from looking in the direction of the sun may introduce a bias into this kind of observation.

Mate-Finding and Flight Patterns

Adult butterflies spend most of their time in some aspect of reproduction: males seeking females; females laying eggs. Mate-finding behavior has three components: the flight patterns adults use to locate each other, the locations where they search for mates, and the time of day they devote to the effort.

Butterflies use two basic flight patterns to find mates. In *perching behavior*, males go to certain places at certain times and rest on some handy projection or the ground. From these vantage points they dart out at passing animals and objects to see if they are females of their own species; if not, they return to the vantage points. Females also fly to these places and flutter about until meeting a male, at which time the two mate and the female flies away. These perching places are genetically fixed in each species, and both sexes are instinctively drawn to them.

In *patrolling behavior*, males search for females by flying almost constantly. A few species may use both methods, at different times. Usually pheromones (mating perfumes or scents) are used only in actual courtship, but patrolling males in at least some species occasionally find females by tracking their scent. Patrolling *Heliconius* males follow the scent of female pupae, then land on them and await their emergence.

In general, male butterflies use movement, overall wing color, and sometimes odor in finding females. Their compound eyes see all the colors from red to violet (and even ultraviolet, which humans cannot see), and their eyes are better than ours for detecting rapid movement. Perching males are usually first attracted to moving or fluttering objects, whereas patrolling males are often attracted by motionless objects of the same color as their females.

Many studies have shown that the predominant color of the female is more attractive to a male of that species than are other colors. For instance, male *Neophasia terlootii* (87), seeking the red females, may be lured by any objects that are red. The compound eyes of an insect are poor for detecting shape and pattern, however. Only pronounced differences of wing pattern between large areas of the wings, such as the broad black and white stripes of some *Limenitis*, or the many black and yellow bands of *Papilio xuthus*, are used in searching for a mate of the right species. The details of how butterflies identify their mates are given in "Courtship and Mating," below.

Because butterfly eyes are better at detecting fluttering than detecting detailed shape and pattern, male butterflies looking for females approach birds, wasps, flies, small animals, even blowing leaves. People who see males, especially perching males (which approach fluttering objects to seek mates), approach and investigate other males or other animals often believe that the males are pugnacious or even territorial. But the male actually approaches the passing object simply to smell it and see it, in order to learn if it is a female of his species. If it is not, the male usually flies elsewhere, though males of perching species that mate at special sites such as hilltops may return to rest at or near the same spot as before. They do this not because they are territorial but because that spot is the instinctive mating site for that species. Territoriality is the active defense of an area by an animal; but because adult butterflies lack jaws or antlers with which to fight, they cannot actively defend a territory. A passing butterfly approached by a flying object, including another male of its own species, is indeed likely to fly away, but that is no more than a useful strategy to avoid lurking robber flies, flycatchers, or other predators. Too, a male may fly away simply because he concludes that he is wasting his time investigating another male. Some individuals of some species such as *Papilio zelicaon* and *Philotes sonorensis* have a home range; O. Shields found that *P. zelicaon* males often return to their hilltop when caught and released away from it. But in this case, as in other butterflies, it is doubtful that the males are defending a territory. Some observers have considered all perching species to be territorial, but my mark-and-recapture studies of 11 species demonstrated that males of perching species move about the habitat just as far as males of patrolling species do, even though they spend periods of time at one spot. Further corroboration: of our two most spectacular migrants, the Painted Lady, *Vanessa cardui* (186), is a perching species, and the Monarch, *Danaus plexippus* (89), is a patrolling species.

When a male searching for a mate encounters another male, the two may fly near each other briefly, either flying vertically (most frequent in perching species), flying horizontally (most frequent in patrolling species), or hovering, before going their separate ways.

Many species, especially perching species, mate only in special spots such as hilltops, gulch bottoms, forest nooks, or other sites. Perching behavior seems ideal for mating at restricted sites in the habitat, since perching males usually return to or near the previous spot after an investigative flight. Mating in special sites thus represents a rendezvous strategy in which both sexes know where to fly to find a mate. This strategy, which increases the mating efficiency of a species, is especially useful for the rarer species that could not find enough mates through random searching. The area available at a hilltop site is less than that at gulch bottoms or hillsides, and only a few males can maneuver on a hilltop. I have found, in fact, that hilltop butterflies tend to be rarer than those that mate elsewhere; at one Colorado locality, the populations of the hilltop species averaged only one-fifth the abundance of the others, at least in the spring. In some of the species that mate at special sites such as hilltops, when the population density of the butterflies becomes too great many males search for females away from the hilltop, often around the larval hostplant. Butterfly populations do fluctuate greatly in size, commonly because of weather (heavy snowfall, droughts, wet springs, freezes, etc.), and the use of hilltops for mating rendezvous points helps prevent extinction when the population dwindles in a bad year, by enabling the sexes to find each other readily.

In many cases, closely related butterfly species in the same genus mate at sites of different topography but in the same habitats. For example, *Euchloe olympia*, *Satyrium californica*, *Hesperia pahaska*, and *Erynnis persius* mate on hilltops, but their relatives *Euchloe ausonia*, *Satyrium acadica*, *Hesperia viridis*, and *Erynnis afranius* mate in valley or gulch bottoms. In some of these cases, the two species (or one ancestor species) may have originally mated at sites of the same type until one evolved the new mating-site type. When two species mate at one site, their males waste time and energy investigating males and females of the other species. Especially in the rarer species, such waste cannot be tolerated, because for a given individual most others will be the wrong species. If a genetic change in adults of one of the two species then causes them to mate at a site of different topography, mating will be more efficient there; and in each succeeding generation more of the species will mate at the second site, until finally all members of a distinct population mate there. Although this type of evolutionary change is slow to start, once the process has been set in motion it proceeds rapidly, because those few individuals that continue to try to mate at the original site encounter mostly the wrong species.

Some butterfly species mate primarily on or near the larval hostplant. For instance, *Hypaurotis* males patrol only about the host trees, and *Satyrium acadica* males perch only at or very near the hostplants.

Most species search for mates and mate at any time of day, but some species (including *Nymphalis*, *Polygonia*, most *Vanessa*, some *Asterocampa*, and many hair-streaks) mate only in the afternoon, and other species (including *Neominois*, *Lycaena arota*, Megathyminae, *Amblyscirtes simius*, and *Epargyreus clarus*) mate only in the morning. Nearly all of these examples are perching species, which more often than patrollers mate at restricted times of day as well as at restricted sites in the habitat.

Mate-locating behavior causes some evolutionary changes in wing shape, for males whose wings are shaped best for their mate-finding habits can find more females. Size may be the most important influence on wing shape: very large butterflies like *Danaus* and *Papilio* tend to have long pointed forewings, whereas small butterflies often have rounded forewings. But whether males perch or patrol also correlates with wing shape: males of perching species tend to have more-pointed forewings and thicker, more-muscular thoraxes for quick takeoffs from rest, whereas the patrolling species of related genera tend to have broader forewings and smaller thoraxes for long-range cruising. Compare *Phyciodes orseis* (224) with *P. campestris* (230), *Strymon melinus* (358) with *Phaeostrymon alcestis* (302), *Copaeodes* (461, 462) with *Ancyloxypha* (456, 457), and *Poanes zabulon* (511) with *P. massasoit* (509), for example. Females tend to have more-rounded forewings because they fly for long periods searching for hostplants. Perching species must often beat their wings rapidly, whereas patrolling species more often flutter slowly.

Knowledge of mate-locating behavior is useful in observing butterflies. Males can be found at the mating sites during the mating period, whereas females tend to be spread more widely, near the hostplants. Mate-seeking and flower-feeding flights are the most common flight patterns of males, and flower-feeding and oviposition flights are most common in females. Both males and females may fly purposefully throughout the habitat to find flowers or other feeding sites.

To determine the purpose of a flying butterfly, one must watch to see what it does: a male that pursues passing adults is seeking females; ovipositing females flutter slowly, and often stop to investigate plants; migrating adults appear to fly purposefully in a straight line, often going over trees or buildings rather than around them. Flight patterns often differ with temperature also, and in cold or cloudy weather adults seldom fly.

Courtship and Mating

If a male nears a female who is ready to mate, she lands and they quickly mate, often without any courtship ritual. Or, they may fly in a characteristic pattern such as a zigzag dance, or both may hover beside each other. They may transfer pheromones (perfumes used in mating), or flutter the wings, or tap antennae. If the male is of a species that carries pheromones, he commonly flutters above the female to transfer the scent. The male in some European relatives of *Speyeria* zooms upward in front of the female to transfer pheromones; male Pieridae buffet the female with the wings to transfer them; male Danainae expose their abdominal hair pencils next to the female's antennae to transfer pheromones; and male skippers and others flutter next to the female to transfer pheromones from the wings or legs. Courting satyrs and *Speyeria* are known to position their scent-producing wing glands next to the female's antennae after landing, before mating occurs. To mate, the male curves his abdomen 180° to the side (left or right) while he is alongside the female, his valvae grasp her ab-

domen, and he then turns to face away from her while he injects a spermatophore into her mating tube.

As in humans, unreceptive females tend to have a more complicated courtship than do receptive females; the female may perform a variety of maneuvers
to discourage the male, who then tries other means to make her receptive. For
example, females may perform "rejection dances." In one such dance, she flies
vertically into the air and then quickly downward, so that the male gives up or
cannot follow her. A *Poladryas* male can follow the female upward in this dance,
but when she zooms downward and away he finds it difficult to follow because
of her speed and the visual confusion with the ground. The vertical flights of
females also mimic the encounters between males that employ perching behavior for mate location, and the male may thus become convinced he is following
another male and give up the chase. In another common rejection dance, the
female may flap her wings vigorously; again, this display may serve to convince
the male he is courting another male, since males often flutter their wings during
courtship. Beyond these rituals for discouraging males, an unreceptive female
may simply crawl or fly away, or move her abdomen up between her wings so
that the male cannot join. And as noted below, some females seem to discourage
males chemically.

In some cases these female rejection behaviors may serve to select vigorous,
persistent males for mating, since sometimes a female will mate after prolonged
courtship. Usually, however, if a female does not mate quickly she will not mate
at all, generally because she has recently mated. Most courtships observed in
nature are of this unsuccessful kind.

Mating (see "Physiology and Reproduction," above) lasts from 15 minutes to
3 hours, depending on the species (most often 30-40 minutes). Small butterflies
mate a short time, large butterflies a much longer time. Mating lasts longer
when the weather is cool; and when the male has mated earlier the same day,
mating can last 8 hours or more, for the male needs time to synthesize the
chemicals for another spermatophore. If the mated pair is startled, one individual flies off carrying the other dangling beneath: males fly in Pieridae, *Danaus*,
Heliconius, and blues; females fly in Papilionidae, satyrs, checkerspots, hairstreaks, and skippers; either sex may fly in Argynnini and *Lycaena*. But in
Parnassius, neither sex flies when disturbed; the two remain where they are—
unusual behavior for butterflies. In *Danaus*, the male always flies away carrying
the female shortly after joining, in a "postnuptial flight."

Males can mate many times, but in most cases they must mature for a day
or so after emerging from their pupae. Females on the other hand can usually
mate immediately, and females of some species such as *Parnassius* mate only

Fig. 34 (*facing page; see p. 52*).   Ultraviolet patterns of various butterflies (× 0.67). The white
areas reflect ultraviolet; the black areas absorb it. All are uppersides unless labeled "uns"
(underside).   6, *Papilio zelicaon*.   18, *P. glaucus canadensis*.   19, *P. eurymedon*.   25, *Battus philenor*.   26, *B. polydamas*.   35, *Colias alexandra*: a, ssp. *christina*, Kananaskis, Alta.; b, ssp. *alexandra*, Jefferson Co., Colo.   37, *C. eurytheme*.   38, *C. philodice philodice*.   44, *C. cesonia*.   45,
C. eurydice.   46, *Anteos clorinde*.   48, *Phoebis statira jada*.   51, *P. agarithe*: a, typical form; b, form
alba.   52, *P. argante*.   53, *P. philea*.   56, *Eurema mexicana*.   57, *E. boisduvaliana*.   58, *E. salome*.   59, *E. daira daira* form *jucunda*.   60, *E. dina*.   62, *E. nise*.   63a, b, *E. lisa*.   65, *E. proterpia*.   66, *Kricogonia lyside* form *terissa*.   68, *Anthocharis sara sara*.   79, *Pieris chloridice
beckerii*.   83, *Ascia monuste*.   85, *Appias drusilla*.   86, *Neophasia menapia menapia*.   87a, b,
N. terlootii.   390, *Everes comyntas*.   392, *Celastrina argiolus ladon*: a, typical form; b, form *neglectamajor*, Pendleton Co., W. Va.   393a, b, *C. nigra*.   397, *Philotes sonorensis*.   398, *Philotiella speciosa speciosa*.   405, *Plebejus melissa samuelis*.   671, *Heliopetes laviana*.   (See also Fig. 35.)

Fig. 35 (*facing page*).   Ultraviolet patterns of various butterflies (× 0.85). The white areas reflect ultraviolet; the black areas absorb it. All are uppersides unless labeled "uns" (underside). *143*, *Doxocopa pavon*. *144a, b, D. laure*. *149*, *Limenitis bredowii*. *150, L. fessonia*. *155*, *Eunica monima*. *156, E. tatila*. *157*, *Myscelia ethusa*. *198*, *Nymphalis antiopa*. *251*, *Speyeria diana*. *252, S. aphrodite aphrodite*. *268*, *Dione vanillae*. *293*, *Lasaia sula*. *297*, *Hypaurotis crysalus crysalus*. *298*, *Eumaeus atala*. *306*, *Satyrium sylvinus sylvinus*. *317*, *Ocaria ocrisia*. *318*, *Ministrymon leda*. *320*, *Oenomaus ortygnus*. *322*, *Thereus palegon*. *324*, *Calycopis cecrops*. *325*, *C. isobeon*. *327*, *Tmolus echion*. *342*, *Callophrys spinetorum*. *346, C. goodsoni*. *347, C. miserabilis*. *349*, *Atlides halesus*. *353*, *Hypostrymon critola*. *354*, *Parrhasius m-album*. *367*, *Strymon bazochii*. *368, Erora laeta laeta*. *372*, *Lycaena cupreus snowi*. *373a, b, L. hyllus*. *374, L. mariposa*. *375, L. nivalis nivalis*. *376, L. helloides helloides*. *377, L. dorcas dorcas*, s Ont. *378, L. epixanthe epixanthe*. *379, L. gorgon*. *380a, b, L. heteronea gravenotata*. *381, L. rubidus rubidus*. *384, L. arota virginiensis*. *388*, *Zizula cyna*. (See also Fig. 34.)

once in their lifetime. In most species, just-mated females may be temporarily prevented from remating by the neck of the spermatophore deposited by the male (see "Physiology and Reproduction"). Females of some butterflies may mate many times, and in these species the female tends to remate as soon as the spermatophore she retains is largely digested and absorbed (typically in about a week). As the spermatophore shrinks, she becomes more receptive to mating, and a persistent male may succeed in mating after a time.

At least in *Pieris protodice*, females may prefer larger males to smaller males in courtship, because they deposit larger spermatophores inside the female. A large spermatophore works to the advantage of both sexes: for the female, because she digests it and uses it for energy and making eggs; for the male, because it takes longer to digest, forcing the female to remate later, and increasing the number of offspring that he fathers. (The last male to mate with a female generally fathers her offspring.)

The main purpose of courtship is to make certain that the other butterfly is a healthy member of the right species. To do this, an adult may use color pattern or odor to reject the wrong species. Many species identify visible colors or even the ultraviolet pattern (Figs. 34, 35). Some species such as *Colias* and *Eurema* use both odors (pheromones) and pattern (ultraviolet) to choose the right species.

Visible colors are commonly used to choose a proper mate. In general, males prefer to approach objects that look like females of their species, whether the similarity is in gross pattern or in color or both. For instance, males of *Hypaurotis* (297) approach only those objects showing the violet-to-ultraviolet color of their wing uppersides; *Heliconius erato* (273) and *Neophasia terlootii* (87) males investigate objects that are red like their females; the males of *Papilio glaucus* (18) prefer objects the color of their own females (which are yellow or black, but all absorb ultraviolet; see Fig. 34) rather than the white (ultraviolet-reflecting) of the females of *P. eurymedon* (19); males of *Anthocharis sara* (68) prefer objects that are whitish with red wingtips like their females; and *Limenitis* (146-150) males prefer striped objects like their females.

Ultraviolet light has a wavelength slightly less than that of violet (for it to be seen by humans, a special filter must be fitted over the lens of a camera and a picture taken). Many *Colias*, *Eurema*, other Pieridae, many male *Lycaena*, most male blues, and many subtropical Nymphalidae, *Anaea*, Riodininae, hairstreaks, and Pyrginae reflect ultraviolet. Males of *Phoebis agarithe* (51) and *P. argante* (52) both look orange, but *P. agarithe* reflects ultraviolet from only the forewing, whereas *P. argante* reflects from both the forewing and the hindwing (Fig. 34). White, blue, and a metallic sheen over other colors usually reflect ultraviolet, and yellow, orange, and other colors sometimes reflect ultraviolet. The number of species

in which males reflect ultraviolet is much greater than the number in which females do.

Many butterflies use this ultraviolet pattern of the wings for mating. Females of *Colias eurytheme* (37) require an ultraviolet-reflecting male for mating. Males of *Pieris protodice* (80) pursue butterflies whose wings reflect ultraviolet only modestly (like their females), and females pursue butterflies that reflect not at all (like their males). Since only the males of *Eurema lisa* (63) reflect ultraviolet, they pursue only non-reflecting butterflies. Scientists are only beginning to study how ultraviolet is used by insects, although it has been known for many years that the center of many flowers absorbs ultraviolet and the petal tips reflect it, a combination that guides bees to the nectar (see Fig. 40).

Butterflies often use pheromones during courtship, which may be useful to males in distinguishing other males, useful to males or females in determining whether another butterfly is of the right species, or useful to unreceptive females in repelling males. Both sexes of many species, especially the males, produce noticeable odors (varying from pleasant to unpleasant to our sense of smell), but some known pheromones are undetectable to us. The pheromones are produced by and wafted from glands on many structures of both sexes.

Special wing scales (called androconial scales) commonly waft the pheromone from one sex to the other. Tiny gland cells at the base of the scales produce the pheromone. Sometimes the scales are gathered into a cluster called a stigma. In Pierinae, Nymphalinae, and Satyrinae the scales often have brushlike tips for wafting it into the air (Figs. 36, 37).

The scent-wafting scales in other butterflies look like ordinary wing scales, though they lack scalloped tips and may be longer or shorter or of a different color than normal wing scales. R. Vetter and R. Rutowski noticed that each of these scales in Coliadinae is associated with a scent gland in the wing membrane, the gland causing a characteristic bulge at the base of the scale socket. The scent-wafting wing scales (Fig. 39) may appear as dustlike scale fragments, or as simple hairlike scales, or as long hairlike scales that split at the base and fan out into a miniature broom (Fig. 36). The presence of the scent-gland cells is all that matters: in some *Colias* the scales are at twice the usual scale density, but in young male *Nathalis* they are often missing entirely and the scent diffuses from the glands over the adjacent wing surface and scales.

Fig. 36 (*facing page*). Pheromone-producing parts of Papilionidae and Pieridae. *1, Eurytides marcellus: a,* scent patch ("anal fold") on the hindwing upperside of some Papilionidae; *b,* one of the long tubular scent scales that waft the scent (these scales split and spread out at the base). *5, Papilio machaon,* tip of the female abdomen, with a weakly developed hair pencil of long scales that reportedly wafts a scent. *7, P. polyxenes: a, b,* patches on the forewing underside (*a*), and hindwing upperside (*b*) of both sexes (those in males may be the source of their perfumelike scent); *c,* one of the cross-ridged transparent scales from the patch; *d,* ordinary wing scales. *34, Colias meadii: a,* scent patch on the male hindwing upperside of some Coliadinae; *b,* one of the creamy scent scales; *c,* ordinary wing scales. *50, Phoebis sennae: a,* tip of the female abdomen of some Coliadinae (eleven tentacles—five pairs above, one below—are on the lobelike scent glands, each tentacle covered with hairy protuberances; the male valva may fit into the pocket during mating); *b,* the tip of one tentacle. *63, Eurema lisa: a,* scent patch on the male forewing underside of many Coliadinae (after R. Rutowski; the scent is from a gland in the wing at the base of each scale); *b,* one of the scales that waft the scent (these scales are pale and lack wavy tips). *73, Euchloe ausonia: a,* tip of the female abdomen of some Pierinae, which has eight lobelike scent glands between the abdominal flaps and around the mating tube (the lobes are like hair pencils in shape but fleshy); *b,* fleshy tentacles covering the lobes. *76, Pieris rapae,* one of the brush-tipped scent scales ("androconia") scattered over the forewing upperside of many male Pierinae. *85, Appias drusilla,* a similar scent scale in the same position.

The wings have a good deal of surface area for wafting the mating pheromones, but evaporation may waste most of the chemical. For this reason the
glands often occupy a patch where the forewing and hindwing overlap (in Coliadinae, on the forewing underside of *Eurema*, on the hindwing upperside of
Colias and *Nathalis*). In other groups the glands lie in a flap on the forewing (the
costal fold of Fig. 39) or on the hindwing (the fold of Fig. 36).

Many species solve the evaporation problem by withdrawing the glands
into a pocket inside the body or between the abdomen segments (Figs. 36-39).
The glands may be internal, opening to the surface without scales in males or
females, or they may be associated with scales. Male Pyrginae skippers slide the
tuft of scent hairs on their hind legs into a pouch between the thorax and the
abdomen. The pouch is usually made by a flap (very long in *Celotes*) that grows
back from the rear of the thorax, but in *Celaenorrhinus* a large tuft of long scales
takes the place of the flap, and two diagonal pouches on the underside of the
abdomen probably produce the scent. The hind leg must of course be kept close
to the body to keep the hairs in the pouch.

But having internal glands presents the problem of lacking sufficient sur-

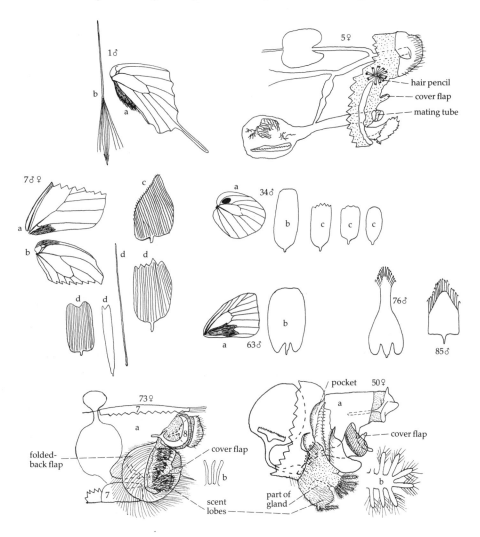

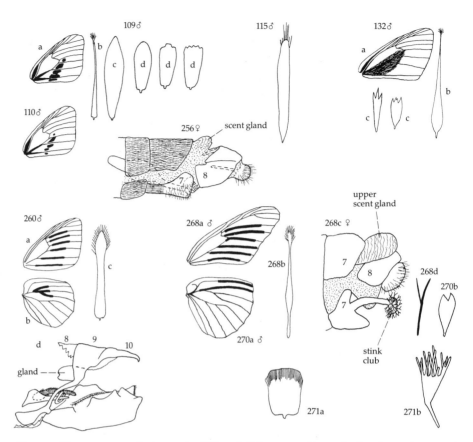

Fig. 37.   Pheromone-producing parts of Nymphalidae.   *109, Cercyonis sthenele*: *a*, stigma on the male forewing upperside; *b*, one of the scent scales scattered among cover scales; *c*, cover scales; *d*, ordinary scales.   *110, Cercyonis meadii*, with a similar stigma.   *115, Erebia magdalena*, one of the scent scales scattered over the male forewing (after B. Warren).   *132, Oeneis jutta*: *a*, stigma on the male forewing upperside; *b*, one of the brown androconial scent scales scattered among brown ordinary scales; *c*, ordinary scales.   *256, Speyeria mormonia*, tip of the female abdomen of Argynnini, with a single scent gland like that of Heliconiini but narrowed in the middle to form two lobes (*Nymphalis* females have similar glands); the hairs on the bottom of segment 7 help waft the scent.   *260, Speyeria atlantis*: *a, b*, male wing upperside of Argynnini; *c*, one of the dark scent scales that lie along the wing veins (positions shown in view *a*); *d*, tip of the male abdomen of Argynnini, with a paired gland normally hidden in abdominal segment 8.   *268, Dione vanillae*: *a*, androconial scent scales on the male forewing upperside veins as usual in Heliconiini; *b*, detail of scent scale; *c*, tip of the female abdomen of Heliconiini, with the upper scent gland everted between segments 7 and 8 (normally withdrawn) and the stink club attached to the plate of sternum 7, which normally swings up and rests in the upper gland but swings down into a male gland at the base of his valva during mating; *d*, detail of a stink-club scent-wafting scale.   *270, Dryas iulia*: *a*, scent scales along the male hindwing upperside veins typical of Heliconiini; *b*, stink-club scale.   *271, Heliconius isabella*: *a*, male wing-vein scent scale; *b*, stink-club scale. (Drawings 268-271 after M. Emsley.)

face area to waft the scent when it is needed. Accordingly, when the glands pop out, a tuft of hairs called a hair pencil commonly wafts the scent. Hair pencils (Figs. 38, 39) are borne on the hind legs of male Pyrginae, but on the abdomen of female Pyrginae, male Danainae, male and female *Biblis*, male *Eumaeus* and some tropical metalmarks, some tropical Pieridae (male *Melete*) and Nymphalidae (male *Morpho*), and questionably even female *Papilio* (Fig. 36). *Typhedanus* males have a tuft of long hairlike scales on top of the hindwing that, like similar structures in some tropical Ithomiinae, may waft pheromones. The stink club of female Heliconiini is a hair pencil of sorts, although the wafting scales in this case are fantastically complicated (even cone-shaped; see Fig. 37). The scent scales (Fig. 39) above the hair pencil in some female Pyrginae are rolled almost into a tube, and these scales are normally telescoped beneath the preceding abdomen segment. In some species the scent scales are actually retracted into a pouch. The glands of female Pieridae (Fig. 36) are shaped like hair pencils but use flexible lobes or hairy tentacles to waft the scent.

Most of these scent structures seem to be used to waft pheromones during

Fig. 38.   Pheromone-producing parts of Nymphalidae and Lycaenidae.   *90, Danaus gilippus*: *a*, male Danainae (left hindwing broken off), showing how his partly extruded abdominal hair pencil fits into his wing pocket when both wings are raised and both hair pencils are inserted at the same time; *b*, during courtship the hair pencils pop out completely, and the long hairlike scales waft the scent to the female and then retract, guided by the pseudovalves (his pseudo-valves work during mating, too, and the true valvae are small like those of *Biblis*, 160*a*).   *160, Biblis hyperia*: *a*, hair pencils on the male abdomen (two on each side; four in all); *b*, details of the dark-brown scales of the front hair pencil; *c*, brown-tipped white scales of the rear hair pencil; *d*, the female abdomen, with only the front pair of hair pencils; *e*, tan scent scales of the female hair pencil (the scent glands at the end of the female abdomen may have something to do with the male's single pseudovalve, which fits beneath her abdomen during mating; the male possibly has glands above his pseudovalve; during mating his weak valvae seem to fit in a pocket inside her flanges).   *310, Satyrium calanus*: *a*, stigma on the forewing upperside of most male Theclini; *b*, scent scale; *c*, ordinary wing scale; *d*, scale on the fringe of the wing.   *382, Lycaena xanthoides*: *a*, one of the scent scales scattered over the wing of male Lycaenini and Polyommatini; *b*, ordinary wing scales.

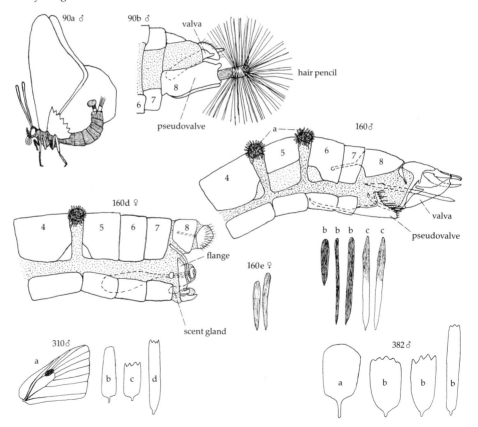

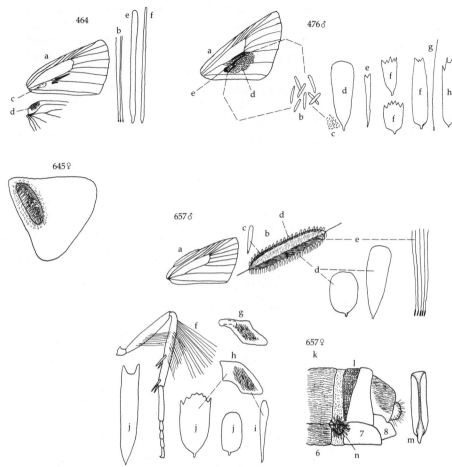

Fig. 39.   Pheromone-producing parts of Hesperiidae.   *464, Thymelicus lineola*: *a*, black stigma on the forewing upperside typical of most male Hesperiinae; *b*, long black stigma scales; *c*, basal patch of light scales on the forewing underside of both sexes; *d*, similar patch on the hindwing upperside base of both sexes; *e*, long wide scale of the forewing patch of both sexes and the hindwing patch of females, which perhaps wafts a scent; *f*, narrower scale of the male hindwing patch.   *476, Hesperia pahaska*: *a*, stigma on the forewing upperside of male Hesperiinae; *b*, *c*, tiny yellow dustlike scale fragments (between the black streaks) that waft the scent; *d*, gray or yellow cover scales that cover the scale fragments (shown in *c* at the correct relative size) between the black streaks (the cover scales also occur in a large patch beyond the stigma); *e*, one of the "jail bar" scales that make up the black streaks and keep the dust from leaving sideways; *f*, ordinary orange or brown wing scales; *g*, one of the hairlike scales covering the wings; *h*, white scale on the forewing underside. (In addition, both sexes have forewing and hindwing patches like those of *Thymelicus*, 464*c*, *d*.)   *645, Ephyriades brunnea*, female scent patch on the abdomen (left-side view of the top of segment 7), the scent scales sunken into a slightly leftward pocket.   *657, Erynnis persius*: *a*, opened-up costal fold on the forewing upperside of many male Pyrginae (the costal fold seems to pop open when the wing is drawn forward in courtship); *b*, close-up of the yellow costal fold opened up; *c*, one of the small scales on the outer part of the flap; *d*, guard scales; *e*, scent-wafting hairlike scales; *f*, hair pencil on the hind leg of many male Pyrginae, which fits between the bottom of the abdomen and a flap on the rear (epimeron) of the thorax (when the hair pencil is to be used, the leg pulls it out; the hair pencil then spreads out to waft the scent); *g*, inside view of the right flap; *h*, top view of the right flap; *i*, yellow flap scales; *j*, ordinary brown flap scales; *k*, tip of the female abdomen of many Pyrginae; *l*, oval scent patch on top of abdominal segment 7, normally retracted beneath segment 6; *m*, detail of the folded scent scales from the patch; *n*, hair pencil covered with ordinary long scales.

courtship, to seduce the partner. The glands of males all seem to produce aphrodisiac perfumes, and the glands of female *Erynnis* (Fig. 39) and probably *Papilio* also seem to produce aphrodisiacs. Male Danainae must fly to plants containing certain chemicals and suck up those chemicals, which are then converted to pheromones and secreted by the male's wing gland. The male then dips his abdominal hair pencils into the wing glands (Fig. 38) to transfer the pheromone to them, in order to be ready for courtship. The female *Danaus gilippus* (90) must be stimulated by the hair-pencil pheromone in order to mate. The pheromone of female Argynnini (Fig. 37) attracts males even when placed on paper. Female pupae of many Heliconiini attract males for subsequent mating, apparently by using a scent from the upper scent gland (Fig. 37).

Some female glands, however, produce pheromones that repel males. During the mating of Heliconiini, the female's stink clubs (Fig. 37) fit into a pocketlike gland at the base of the male's valvae, where they take on another chemical. After mating, when her abdomen is telescoped, the stink clubs swing up into her upper scent gland, where the male chemical may turn off the female's attractant pheromone, or it may allow the production of a third chemical. Whatever the case, after mating, the stink clubs thereafter waft a foul-smelling chemical that repels males. Male Argynnini also have such a gland at the base of the valvae (Fig. 37), but their females lack stink clubs. D. Magnus found that Argynnini males turn away from mated females after antennal contact, suggesting that during the prior mating the male's glands turned off her glands or transferred a pheromone. Female Pieridae repel males by exposing abdominal glands much like hair pencils (Fig. 36) during their abdomen-raised, wings-spread refusal posture.

Mate selection and courtship is discussed in greater detail in the texts for *Papilio xuthus* (4), *P. glaucus* (18), *Colias eurytheme* (37), *C. philodice* (38), *Eurema lisa* (63), *Pieris napi* (77), *Danaus* (89, 90), *Hypolimnas misippus* (175), *Precis coenia* (180), *Heliconius* (272, 273), *Hypaurotis* (297), *Amblyscirtes simius* (535), and others.

Egg-Laying and Larval Nests

The adult female butterfly chooses the larval food. After she emerges from the pupa and mates, she may be able to lay eggs immediately (*Euphydryas* is an example), or she may wait for a few days (*Pieris*, *Precis*, and many others). Most butterflies are probably similar to *Colias* in starting to lay when they are 1-2 days old and continuing a high production until they are several weeks old (if they live that long), when production declines. In some species one female can lay 1,000 eggs in the lab (*Colias* females average 700), but a more common total is a few hundred, and in nature one female may lay less than a hundred.

To oviposit, the female begins a slow fluttering search of the habitat, stopping often to investigate plants. Because these fluttering flights are characteristic and noticeable, the female can be followed to discover the hostplant. She lands on many plants, and upon landing on one she will drum the plant with her forelegs to identify it. To help in this identification, the female foreleg tips bear special clumps of hairlike taste organs (see "Senses and Responses," above). When the right plant is found, she curves her abdomen downward and forward to lay an egg with the ovipositor, which bears hairs sensitive to touch and probably has taste organs as well. Females of species that lay clusters of eggs take a long time, up to an hour or more, and repeatedly return to the same plant and leaf before finally ovipositing.

The eggs are generally laid singly and glued to the substrate. Eggs of *Aga-thymus* females appear to be the only ones that are not glued on; but they fall to the base and usually land on the plant anyway because the leaves of their *Agave* hostplants curve upward.

If eggs are placed on leaves, they are usually laid on the underside, but some species such as *Pholisora* generally oviposit on the top, and *Limenitis* lay the egg on the upperside near the tip.

In some species whose hostplants produce only small amounts of edible parts, a female will not lay eggs on a plant if she sees an egg already there. For if she did lay an egg next to a prior egg, the first larva to hatch might eat most of the available food and the second larva (or both) might starve. *Battus philenor* and some Pierinae that eat Cruciferae plants search the plant for eggs and seldom lay a second egg on any one plant. Females of *Pieris* are apparently even able to smell the eggs. The eggs of some Pieridae turn orange, and A. Shapiro suggested that this signal makes it easier for the female to spot the egg and avoid laying a second egg nearby.

The female usually lays eggs only on plants edible to the larvae, but females of some species lay eggs haphazardly, and mistakes sometimes occur. *Parnassius, Speyeria, Boloria*, the satyrs, and *Hesperia comma* and other Hesperiinae seem to lay eggs rather haphazardly near the hostplants, and many *Lycaena* lay eggs on litter at or near the base of their hostplant rather than on the plant itself. The hostplants of the satyrs and Hesperiinae are generally common nearby, and *Boloria* larvae seem to be able to eat many plants. Because these species (except some *Boloria*) hibernate as eggs or unfed larvae, haphazard oviposition is not the risk it might seem, since the larvae must locate their hostplants again in the spring anyway.

Within a given species, different females and different populations may prefer different hosts. B. Tabashnik and others found an apparently genetic pre-disposition for some females to lay on certain plants, but for others in the same population to lay eggs on different plants. C. Wiklund found that some females of a given species are content with many plants, whereas others prefer only a few plants. This genetic variation in nature is fertile ground for natural selection, which in colonies of *Euphydryas editha* (201) has produced oviposition preference on different plants at different localities. Of course in some species the host-plants change during the season as some plants go to seed and others bloom.

Larvae find food poorly; they see weakly and travel slowly. S. Grant tried to train larvae to turn in a particular direction to find food; his *Vanessa* larvae learned slowly, but *Danaus* larvae never learned. As a result, if the hostplant is eaten or dies, or the female lays an egg on the wrong plant, or the larva falls off, the larva, especially a young one, may starve before it finds proper food, or it may be poisoned by eating the wrong plant. For this reason, females rarely lay eggs on plants that are unsuitable for their larvae; that happens sometimes in Pierinae, which may lay eggs on unsuitable Cruciferae plants introduced from Europe (for instance, *Pieris napi* eggs on *Barbarea vulgaris*), but as time goes on this waste of eggs will probably be selected out.

Luckily, larvae will generally eat many more kinds of plants than are known to be oviposited on in nature, which facilitates raising them in the lab (the texts in Part III, however, give only the plants used in nature, except where a separate notation specifies plants that are eaten only in the lab). The broader choice of plants by larvae than by ovipositing females results from natural selection; survival is much more likely if larvae can eat the plant on which the eggs were laid, and if, when larvae fall off that plant, they are able to eat nearby plants of other species. However, the alternatives larvae are able to eat are generally closely related to the oviposition plants, and larvae refuse to eat or are poisoned by the vast majority of plants.

Generally butterflies lay only one egg at a time, then move on to a new site (another leaf, usually another plant) before laying the next egg, but social egg clustering has evolved in a few species. In the checkerspots, where this pattern is the most highly developed, the eggs are laid in clusters of a few eggs to several hundred, and the young larvae generally feed together and may even make a silk nest and live inside together. Large clusters and communal feeding in *Asterocampa clyton* may facilitate feeding on mature hackberry leaves (*Celtis*). *Nymphalis* and *Hamadryas amphinome* lay large clusters, and a few *Nymphalis* species make nests. Many more species lay eggs in small clusters of several to a dozen; these include *Battus*, *Papilio anchisiades*, *Pieris rapae* in England but not in America, *Ascia monuste*, *Appias drusilla*, *Neophasia menapia*, some *Boloria*, *Polygonia*, some *Hamadryas*, *Asterocampa celtis*, some *Satyrium*, *Eumaeus*, *Thymelicus*, *Calpodes*, and *Urbanus proteus*. *Neophasia* and *Thymelicus*, and sometimes *Battus* and *Nymphalis*, place their eggs single file. *Polygonia* and *Hamadryas* sometimes place them in columns, one on top of another.

The major use of silk is in forming the mat the larval crochets hook into, to prevent a fall. However, some species of butterflies and moths use silk to make nests. The silk webs made by some larvae that feed together, such as *Euphydryas* and some *Nymphalis*, are one type of larval nest. Solitary *Vanessa* may also live in silk nests. *Polygonia* and some *Asterocampa* and *Papilio* may curl a leaf slightly into a type of nest, using silk threads that shrink after they are laid across the surface of the leaf (for the nature of silk and its crucial shrinking property, see "Physiology and Reproduction," above). The best leaf nests are made by the skippers, the *Anaea*, overwintering *Limenitis*, *Vanessa atalanta*, *Hypanartia*, and some metalmarks (*Apodemia*), which silk two adjacent leaves together or roll a large leaf into a tube-shaped nest. Of course the most secure nests are made by the giant skippers (Megathyminae), which burrow out a home within their hostplant roots or in fleshy leaves. When skippers are about to pupate, they produce a waxy white powder (from the bottom of abdomen segments 7 and 8) that sheds water and smooths over rough places. This powder, which waterproofs the nest, is produced by all skippers except *Hesperia ottoe*.

Butterfly Intelligence

Intelligence, as commonly understood, has two components. The first is the inherited ability of an animal to pursue complex behavior that helps it survive in its environment. The second is the animal's ability to learn from experience, to modify its behavior.

In the first sense of the word, butterflies are extremely intelligent, for they demonstrate incredibly complicated behavior that is for the most part genetically programmed into their brains. For instance, the female utilizes a chemical sense equal to any laboratory machine in seeking out one species of plant among hundreds; sizes it up to see whether it is the right size and age; finds the proper place on the plant to lay the egg; determines whether other eggs are already present (and tries elsewhere if they are); places the proper number of eggs on the leaf (even on the proper *side* of the leaf, top or bottom); and glues them on in proper fashion (even single file in some species). The larva, in turn, constructs a complex nest with only strands of silk. Later it wanders a considerable distance in search of a suitable pupation site, and sees to its own seatbelt fastening. And of course the nervous system of the larva directs the incredible transformations of metamorphosis that allow it to lead two separate lives during its brief lifetime. Adults see polarized and ultraviolet light, neither of which we can see, and they can fly (quite deftly) as well as walk; some routinely migrate thousands of miles, navigating to precise destinations by means unknown. They discover mates by flying to certain sites at certain times of day; they use special pheromone "perfumes" and colors to establish identity and induce or refuse mating; they regulate body temperature by modifying their own behavior; and although equipped with only a strawlike proboscis, they have ways to feed even on dry substances.

In their ability to carry out complex instinctive tasks, butterflies are probably superior to humans. Psychologists prefer to deny that any behavior of man, save perhaps suckling, is due to instinct, but biologists appear to have found—partly from studies of identical twins reared apart—that much of peoples' behavior and ability to learn is in part genetic.

In their ability to learn, the second component of intelligence, butterflies do not fare so well. Larvae learn with difficulty. In one experiment, S. Grant tried to train larvae to turn in only one direction, by giving them a food reward: her *Vanessa* larvae learned to do so slowly, but her *Danaus* larvae never did.

Adults are better at learning. N. Tinbergen managed to train European satyrs (*Hipparchia*) to come to certain sap-producing trees to feed, and European *Nymphalis* have been trained to prefer certain colors of flowers for feeding. Males of the *Papilio machaon* group (5-9) that favor hilltops learn the physical features of a selected hill: O. Shields found that marked transplanted males of *P. zelicaon* prefer to return to their own hill. Adults of tropical *Marpesia* (*M. berania*) and *Smyrna* learn the locations of their roosting colonies, and return to them regularly. A *Colias philodice* female (38) can learn the characteristics of one hostplant species and lay eggs mostly on it, while another female at the same site learns to lay eggs on other hostplant species (M. Stanton, R. Cook).

The "smartest" butterflies in their ability to learn, so far as studies to date have demonstrated, are *Heliconius*. Other species tend to wander randomly about a small area or region, finding their needs as they can. But *Heliconius* are able not only to learn landmarks in order to find their way to their communal roosts, and to find their way about their home ranges, but also to learn the locations of hostplants and nectar sites within their home ranges (see "Tribe Heliconiini," in Part III). Most butterflies, when placed in a room with only fluorescent lighting, beat their wings incessantly against the lights; but *Heliconius* quickly adapt and flutter about the room normally (it may be that forest-floor butterflies have adapted to comparable lighting conditions). Much more will surely be discovered about learning in butterflies.

Social and Antisocial Behavior

Most people wrongly think that the only insects to exhibit social behavior are ants, bees, and termites. In fact, the eggs, larvae, and adults of some butterflies are social, too.

The most obviously social behavior is that established when eggs are laid in clusters of up to several hundred by one female (by several cooperating females in *Euphydryas phaeton* and some tropical *Heliconius*). The hatching larvae live together until at least half-grown; they attack and eat one spot of a leaf in unison; they crawl on a communal silk web; and if forcibly scattered, they soon regroup. In nest-building species like *Euphydryas*, several larvae join in making a web, which they all then inhabit. Larvae of the Mexican pierid *Eucheira* live in a communal nest as strong as a paper bag. Larvae of *Papilio anchisiades* (17) and of some tropical *Morpho* feed together at night, then march down the trunk to rest together on the trunk by day. Clustered larvae (and even pupae) of *Nymphalis*, *Euphydryas*, and *Asterocampa* actually twitch in unison to repel predators.

Adults also are social in some species. The communal roosting of *Heliconius* adults keeps local populations of these poisonous butterflies together, so that fewer predators must be taught to avoid them. *Smyrna* and *Eumaeus deborah* roost gregariously in the dry season. *Phoebis* adults sometimes roost where others are, perhaps because they know no predators are likely to be lurking there. Monarchs, during migrations and in winter roosts, gather by the hundreds or thousands on single trees; it has been found that the greater the numbers in the roost, the lower the death rate from predation. Many male butterflies congregate at mud. Males land next to others, and even a dead butterfly placed on the mud will attract them, in the manner of a duck decoy. For by landing next to another, a butterfly can be more certain that no predators such as tiger beetles, toad bugs, frogs, etc., lurk there.

Mate-locating behavior forms a complicated social system in some species that mate at special sites in the habitat, such as on hilltops or in gulch bottoms. Males fly to these sites and perch or patrol in search of females, who fly there, mate, and then fly away. In many species, both males and females conduct these activities only during a fixed period of the day; they essentially agree to meet at a certain place and time for the mating ritual.

Antisocial behavior, however, is nearly nonexistent in adults. Even adults of species that do not roost or sip mud together are content to feed side by side at flowers. Adults in any case lack jaws or other offensive weapons with which to attack or ward off intruders. And although some adults appear to have a temporary (sometimes permanent) home range, and in the process of finding mates may investigate each other, these sallies about a fixed turf are basically mate-seeking behavior rather than aggressive behavior (see "Mate-Finding and Flight Patterns," above). True territoriality, in which an individual chooses one spot and actively defends it from intruders, is rare or absent in butterflies.

But the larvae of butterflies *are* sometimes territorial. Larvae of *Epiphile* (151) and *Diaethria* (152, 153) have long antlers on the head but few spines on the body, an array more useful against their fellows than against predators. A. Muyshondt observed a larva of *Epiphile* on a leaf puncturing another's body with its antlers, and others locking antlers until death. Larvae of European *Iphiclides podalirius* (Papilionidae) are territorial: the silk threads that they lay for walking on twigs have a slight odor (a characteristic perhaps common to most butterfly larvae), and each larva prefers its own silk trail—and will spin silk over another larva's trail (R. Weyh, U. Maschwitz). If two *Iphiclides* larvae meet, the larger may silk the smaller to the branch or they may fight, presumably by biting. The larvae of European *Papilio alexanor* may also be territorial (D. Kahlheber).

Other larvae are sometimes cannibalistic: Lycaenidae larvae must be provided with fresh food frequently or they eat each other; and in crowded conditions the larvae of some species eat newly formed pupae.

Larval Foods

The larva is the main feeding stage of butterflies; the pupa eats nothing at all, and the adult simply sips fluids for energy and moisture. Figure 42 shows how I believe the butterflies evolved, and lists the plants most often eaten by each of the major butterfly groups. Luckily, the food preferences of butterflies—in many cases just one plant species or a handful of related plants—are the best known of any insect food preferences, and two conclusions are evident.

First, the butterflies clearly evolved along with the flowering plants, and the few species that eat nonflowering plants today have evidently switched to them from flowering plants. The nonflowering plants selected today are lichens and fungi (eaten by some tropical Lycaenidae), plants related to ferns (eaten by some tropical Satyrinae, including *Euptychia*), conifers (eaten by *Neophasia*), and cycads (eaten by *Eumaeus*). Some lycaenids have even switched to feeding on aphids and ants.

Second, the ancestor of butterflies and skippers clearly ate dicotyledons, probably the pea family, Leguminosae. The most primitive subfamilies of Hesperiidae (Pyrginae), Papilionidae (Baroniinae), and Pieridae (Dismorphiinae, Coliadinae), and numerous Lycaenidae and Nymphalidae, all eat Leguminosae, which were abundant and diverse even 120 million years ago, before the butterflies evolved. However, several groups, including the Satyrinae and Morphinae, have since switched to monocotyledons. The upper branch of skippers in the figure also switched to monocotyledons; most of them now eat grasses, but some eat sedges or both plants, and a few species eat other monocotyledons (palms, banana, Agavaceae, or plants of the two closely related families Cannaceae and Marantaceae).

Even the dicotyledon feeders have switched hostplant families many times. Some Papilionidae switched from Leguminosae to Aristolochiaceae, and others in turn switched to Magnoliaceae, Annonaceae, and many other dicotyledons. The Charaxinae, Nymphalinae, Acraeinae, Riodininae, hairstreaks, and Pyrginae have switched hostplants so many times that it is difficult to know who ate what when. In fact, about 120 plant families, a bewildering diversity, are now eaten by North American butterflies. Compounding the difficulty in tracing the coevolution of butterflies with flowering plants is the fact that the botanists who devise evolutionary trees for flowering plants cannot agree on where many plant families should be placed on the tree.

Most butterflies feed on the plants of a single family, but there are some exceptions. *Strymon melinus, Celastrina argiolus, Vanessa cardui, V. virginiensis, Hypolimnas misippus, Euptoieta claudia*, and *Boloria* feed on numerous families, but the first two feed only on the flowers and fruits, *V. cardui* prefers thistles, and *V. virginiensis* prefers the plants of one tribe of Compositae; the other three feed on fewer plants than the first four.

The shrub and tree feeders also tend to feed on many families: some species of *Nymphalis, Polygonia, Limenitis, Satyrium, Callophrys, Vaga*, and *Papilio* eat Rosaceae, Salicaceae, Fagaceae, Betulaceae, Oleaceae, and plants of other families scattered all over the plant family tree. These butterflies may choose their hostplants by shrub or tree shape rather than by smell or taste, and may be specialized for eating the tough, dry, nitrogen-poor leaves of trees and shrubs. Most trees also contain tannins, chemicals that prevent leaf protein from being digested; but M. Berenbaum found that tree-eating larvae employ an alkaline intestinal fluid to neutralize the tannins. Still, butterfly larvae that eat herbs grow much faster than those that eat shrubs or trees (J. Scriber, P. Feeny). And even on the same tree, some leaves are far more indigestible than others (J. Schultz); a larva may have to sample many such leaves before finding one that is edible.

Most of the butterfly larvae that eat plants of several families choose closely related plants. Good examples of these plant groups are Urticaceae, Moraceae, and Ulmaceae; Amaranthaceae, Chenopodiaceae, Bataceae, and even Aizoaceae; Passifloraceae, Turneraceae, and Violaceae; Ericaceae and Empetraceae; Lauraceae and Magnoliaceae; Capparidaceae, Cruciferae, and Resedaceae; Asclepiadaceae, Apocynaceae, and Loganiaceae; Cannaceae and Marantaceae; and Gramineae and Cyperaceae. In addition, the checkerspots, *Precis, Anartia, Siproeta, Strymon bazochii,* and *Tmolus echion* treat the plant families Scrophulariaceae, Plantaginaceae, Orobanchaceae, Acanthaceae, and Verbenaceae, and even the Caprifoliaceae, Valerianaceae, Labiatae, and Boraginaceae, as if these plants formed a single natural group; in fact, most botanists believe they are closely related. The plants within each of these ten groups probably contain similar chemical compounds (for example, M. Bowers suggested iridoid glycosides in the last group), which ovipositing females can detect by tapping the plants with their forelegs or by detecting odors from a short distance away.

Some butterflies, however, choose plants that are less closely related botanically. *Pieris rapae* and *Ascia monuste* choose three closely related plant families, the Cruciferae, Capparidaceae, and Resedaceae, and one unrelated family, the Tropaeolaceae, because all four families contain mustard oils or their glucosides that attract the females and stimulate the larvae to feed. *Appias drusilla* eats Capparidaceae and Euphorbiaceae, some of which also contain mustard oils. The *Papilio machaon* group (5-9) feeds on Umbelliferae, Rutaceae, and some Compositae; all contain similar oils, and V. Dethier found them to be oils that stimulate larval feeding. *Callophrys spinetorum* may have evolved feeding on Viscaceae because the plants (mistletoe parasites on conifer trees) look like cedars (cedars are the hostplants of *C. gryneus,* which is closely related to *C. spinetorum*), and conifers and cedars are closely related.

Still other hostplant choices are mysteries. The strangest butterfly diet includes both dicotyledons and monocotyledons (*Tmolus, Caria,* and *Urbanus*). Others that eat plants of several distantly related families include some *Papilio, Colias, Phyciodes frisia, Anartia, Apodemia, Calephelis, Callophrys affinis, Strymon, Calycopis, Chlorostrymon, Leptotes, Plebejus, Hemiargus,* and *Erynnis.*

But why do most butterfly larvae eat the plants of only a few genera or families? The best model for the answer is a perpetual "war" between insects and plants. Ancient insects ate ancient plants; in response, the plants evolved thick, tough, tooth-edged leaves that carry spines or hairs, hooked hairs, gums, resins, high levels of silica, and even raphides (long crystals of calcium oxalate), all of which physically deter animals from eating the leaves. The hooked hairs on one tropical plant, *Passiflora adenopoda,* sometimes hook into the larvae of *Heliconius* and hold them fast until they die (young larvae, however, crawl between the hairs, and older larvae may spin silk over them). The sawtooth leaf edges of some grasses might saw some larvae in half as the wind whips the leaves back and forth (a reason for the silked-leaf nests of skippers). The very woolly leaves of some plants might also deter some larvae. Some *Passiflora* plants produce false stipules (fingerlike projections from the base of a leaf stem) that induce egg-laying by Heliconiini females; these parts, themselves offering minimal nourishment, then drop off, carrying the eggs with them. In some *Aristo-lochia*, a leaf will die around an egg of *Parides* laid on it, and the dead tissue then drops, carrying the egg with it. Plants have also evolved chemical defenses against attack: alkaloids, rotenoids, steroids, glycosides, tannins, terpenoids, and organic cyanides repel or poison animals that try to eat them. Conifers and ferns evolved chemicals that mimic the insect molting hormone ecdysone, and thereby disrupt the metamorphosis of insects that try to eat them. Tomato plants produce chemicals that inhibit most insects' protein-digesting enzymes. Other plants simply do not contain enough nutrients for insect growth.

Along the way, then, plants that were edible to many animals were eaten and extirpated, and only the plants with defenses remained. By evolving one or more of these repellents, a plant could survive all but the few insects able to withstand its defenses and poisons. The few remaining insects then often evolved the ability to use the plant's own poison to find it, for the poison is generally a reliable indicator of plant identity. For instance, the poisons of mustard-family plants deter most insects (actually the plants contain mustard-oil glucosides in some cells and the enzyme myrosinase in other cells, and when the plants are crushed by the jaws these chemicals mix—and the poison, mustard oil, is produced). *Pieris* butterflies, however, can detoxify these chemicals, and have turned the table on the plants by using the mustard-oil glucosides to find them and the mustard oils as a stimulant to feeding. The linear furanocoumarins in plants of the carrot family (Umbelliferae) poison most insects, but *Papilio polyxenes* grows faster when these chemicals are present. A naphthoquinone in *Plumbago* plants prevents some Lepidoptera from molting, but *Leptotes* butterflies eat the plants. Rotenone is a commercial insecticide and fish poison from *Derris* plants, but *Polygonus leo* larvae eat these plants. Sapindaceae plants are used to poison fish, but *Epiphile* butterflies eat the plants. Thus one man's poison is another man's meat.

Why do butterfly species eat only a few plants? Few insect species can detoxify or tolerate the numerous plant poisons residing in a great array of plants; and because most insects can detoxify only a few poisons, most eat only a few plants—generally plants that are closely related. R. Krieger, P. Feeny, and C. Wilkinson studied the level of microsomal oxidase enzymes in the intestines of moths and butterflies. They found that these enzymes, which neutralize and digest plant poisons, were more abundant in species whose larvae feed on many plant species than in those feeding on few plant species.

Some butterfly species do not detoxify the plant poisons. Rather, they somehow evolve other chemical systems to tolerate them. The plant poisons accumulate harmlessly in their bodies, and when one is attacked by a bird or other animal that cannot tolerate the poison, the predator either releases the butterfly or vomits and learns not to hunt that species again. These butterflies, such as *Danaus* and *Battus*, then become the models for mimicry (see "Mimicry and Other Defenses," below).

But there remains the problem that a plant could still be eaten to the ground by those few species that can survive its poisons and defenses. The equalizing factor in this equation is the predators and parasites that attack the butterflies—and that increased in numbers of species along with the species of plants and butterflies. Thus, except in rare instances, the few insects that can eat a given plant and might explode in numbers and eradicate it are held in check by other predatory and parasitic insects.

Adult Foods

Adult butterflies can obtain food only via their tubular proboscis (see "Physiology and Reproduction," above). They usually feed on the nectar of flowers, but sometimes they suck fluids from sap, fruit, aphid honeydew, mud, dung, carrion, or even blood, and can even feed on dry substances like soil, wood, or pollen by dissolving them with a drop of saliva first.

The main food of most adults is flower nectar, which is about 20 percent sugar. In general, neither individuals nor species are choosy, and most butterfly species visit dozens or hundreds of kinds of flowers throughout their range. But in some cases, preferences are exhibited: the western *Hesperia leonardus* (475) feeds almost exclusively on *Liatris punctata* flowers. W. Watt, P. Hoch, and S. Mills found that butterflies generally prefer flowers with relatively dilute nectar containing nitrogen-rich amino acids and sugars of low molecular weight, whereas bees prefer flowers with thicker nectar and high-molecular-weight sugars. Thin nectar may prevent water loss and keep the proboscis from getting clogged. But some butterflies, for example, *Thymelicus lineola* (464), feed on alfalfa and clover nectars with up to 65 percent sugar. D. Murphy and others found that the sugar in nectar allows the adults to live about 50 percent longer and to produce many more eggs after the first few days; but with short-lived butterflies the amino acids in nectar have very little effect.

Butterflies see all colors from red to violet and ultraviolet, and some butterflies seeking nectar (*Parnassius*, Pierinae, *Nathalis*, checkerspots, many Lycaenidae, and some skippers) seem to prefer yellow or white flowers; some prefer blue flowers; but most species show little color preference. Since some flowers reflect ultraviolet around the outer edge of the petals but absorb it in the middle, the ultraviolet appears in ring patterns attractive to bees and probably butterflies (Fig. 40). The ultraviolet also forms a good visual contrast between the flowers and the surrounding leaves or dirt.

Large butterflies like *Papilio* and *Speyeria* prefer tall flowers like thistles, and small butterflies that fly near the ground, such as *Pholisora*, visit small low flowers.

The length of the proboscis is related to the choice of food. Long tubular flowers (like *Penstemon*) are visited only by butterflies such as skippers and *Papilio*, which have a long proboscis. Some butterflies with a short proboscis, like *Oeneis*, *Anaea*, *Feniseca*, and *Hypaurotis*, rarely or never visit flowers. The sap feeders in general tend to have a short proboscis.

Some species (some Compositae-feeding checkerspots, *Apodemia*, *Callophrys polios*, *Euphilotes*, and *Plebejus saepiolus*) often feed on flowers of the larval hostplant (especially *Eriogonum* plants), and may help pollinate these plants. *Danaus plexippus* often pollinates its milkweed hostplants; the claws on the legs pick up the pollen bundles while the adult is feeding. Other butterflies like *Poladryas* never visit the hostplant flowers (*Penstemon*), and *Euphydryas* never visit theirs, apparently because the proboscis is too short.

Phlox and some other flowers (*Lantana*, *Asclepias curassavica*, *Hymenoxys*, *Caesalpinia*, *Zinnia*, *Dyssodia*, *Stachytarpheta*) are pollinated primarily by butterflies; D. Levin and D. Berube found that the proboscis transfers the pollen of *Phlox*, but the head and body scales often transfer the pollen of Compositae flowers, and the legs transfer milkweed pollen. Butterfly-pollinated plants tend either to have many flowers in a flat-topped cluster, like *Senecio*, or to have a landing platform of large petals; each flower tends to have a narrow entrance.

In dry regions, adult hairstreaks are known to seek nourishment by flying downslope to a valley bottom, following the valley down until mud or flowers are found, and then flying up the slope again after feeding. Other species such as *Oeneis* may also do this, in moister regions.

Some groups of butterflies prefer other foods to flower nectar. *Lethe, Cercyonis pegala, Megisto cymela, Anaea, Nymphalis, Polygonia, Vanessa atalanta, Hamadryas, Limenitis, Asterocampa, Feniseca*, and *Hypaurotis* often feed on sap or rotten fruit; D. Wright found that the chemical esters in the sap attract them. Many of these species and others feed also on carrion. Some *Limenitis* feed on flowers, dung, carrion, aphid honeydew, or wood fluids. Many satyrs such as *Oeneis* feed on mud but rarely visit flowers. Male giant skippers (Megathyminae) feed only on mud, and their females do not feed at all.

Males of many species like *Papilio, Colias, Erynnis*, and the blues congregate at wet earth. Their purpose is in part to draw sodium ions from the water (K. Arms, P. Adler, and others). After one male discovers the sodium, others land nearby. Perhaps just the presence of the first adults brings the newcomers, for even a dead adult placed on a moist spot often attracts others, at least briefly. In males, the sodium level is initially about double that in females, and decreases during the male's lifetime, but sodium in the female stays at a fairly constant level, evidently because the male's spermatophore (which is transferred during mating) contains a great deal of sodium, which compensates the female for the loss of sodium due to egg-laying. The observation that urine (which contains sodium) placed on damp earth may attract butterflies has sparked a bizarre collecting technique in the tropics.

Generally it is the males, seldom the females, that feed on mud, carrion, dung, and related substances, but in some tropical Ithomiinae it is the females that feed on bird droppings. The males may be obtaining chemical precursors of male pheromones (a known factor in the choice of certain plants by some male *Danaus*), but this does not seem likely. They may be obtaining nitrogen and amino acids to fuel their metabolism or to make spermatophores, or they may need to replace fluids lost to the exertion of mate-finding efforts. By contrast, females might avoid these substances because the bacteria or other microbes present in them could contaminate their eggs; or, since the females carry more fat than males, they might derive enough water for their needs by metabolizing the fat.

Some butterflies have unusual mechanisms for feeding on dry substances. Generally they eject a drop of fluid from the proboscis onto the substrate, and the fluid dissolves salts, minerals, or organic compounds that are then sucked up. But some skippers are known to eject a drop from the abdomen onto the ground or rock, and then suck up the fluid—after it dissolves various surface substances.

On the sides of the tip of the *Heliconius* proboscis, there are tiny comblike projections. These taste organs (olfactory hairs) are present in some Nymphalidae (including *Heliconius*), Libytheidae, and Lycaenidae, but are generally lacking in Papilionidae, Pieridae, and probably Hesperiidae. *Heliconius* adults use the combs to gather up small bundles of pollen. They then coil the proboscis, and eject from its tip a drop of fluid that fills in the coil and dissolves amino acids from the pollen on the combs. The drop is then sucked up and the amino acids absorbed.

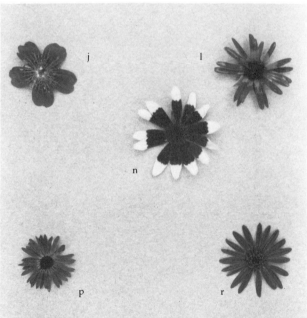

Fig. 40.   Ultraviolet reflection of flowers: *left*, appearance to humans; *right*, ultraviolet reflection (light areas reflect ultraviolet; black areas absorb it)—*a, b, Aster laevis* (blue petals); *c, d, Rudbeckia hirta* (yellow); *e, f, Rudbeckia laciniata* (yellow, a favorite flower of *Speyeria atlantis* butterflies, 260); *g, h, Helianthus petiolaris* (yellow); *i, j, Geranium caespitosum* (pink); *k, l, Heterotheca fulcrata* (yellow); *m, n, Viguiera multiflora* (yellow); *o, p, Aster porteri* (white); *q, r, Heterotheca horrida* (yellow). *Aster, Viguiera,* and *Heterotheca* are visited by *Hesperia, Phyciodes,* and other butterflies, but *R. hirta, Helianthus,* and *Geranium* are seldom visited by butterflies.

To some extent an adult is capable of learning the best food sources in its habitat. *Nymphalis* adults have been trained to prefer certain colors of flowers, and a satyr has been trained to come to some sap-producing trees. *Heliconius* adults can learn where their preferred flowers are in their habitat.

Parasites, Predators, and Other Enemies

The diseases, parasites, and predators that butterflies fall prey to are one reason that their populations seldom explode in large numbers and eat all their hostplants (larvae from migratory flights of *Vanessa cardui*, 186, sometimes do). Other factors that prevent butterfly populations from overeating their hostplants are weather (droughts, freezes, hail, rain, etc.) and accidents (being stepped on by an animal, burned in a fire, crushed by a falling pine cone or branch, etc.).

The microscopic enemies of butterflies include viruses, bacteria, and fungi, all of them common afflictions, and rarely microsporidians, nematodes, and protozoans. Larger nematodes and horsehair worms are occasional parasites. These enemies may attack any stage, but the larvae are the most susceptible because they live longer and because they eat foreign matter, which may contain the microbes or parasite eggs.

Insect parasitoids attack eggs, larvae, and pupae. These wasps or flies feed on body fluids at first, but finally eat the internal organs and kill the butterfly. Wasps (Ichneumonidae, Braconidae, Pteromalidae, Chalcidoidea, Encyrtidae, Eulophidae, Scelionidae, Trichogrammatidae, and others) usually lay eggs inside the host body. Trichogrammatidae, smaller than the size of a pinhead, live inside the butterfly eggs. Some wasps lay only one egg inside the host, and the egg divides to produce many wasps. Some flies (Tachinidae, some Sarcophagidae, etc.) that produce large eggs glue them onto the outside of the host, and the hatching fly larvae then burrow into the interior of the butterfly larva. Other fly species lay many tiny eggs on larval hostplants, some of which then hatch and grow inside the larva that inadvertently eats them, provided that they are not squashed by the mandibles or digested first.

Tiny flies (Ceratopogonidae) or mites are rarely found attached to the wing veins of adults, where they suck blood. Mosquitoes sometimes feed on the blood of larvae.

Most predators of butterflies are other arthropods. Immatures are eaten by praying mantises, lacewings, ladybird beetles, assassin bugs, carabid beetles, spiders, ants, and wasps (Vespidae, Pompilidae, and others). Adults are eaten by robber flies (which catch them in midair), ambush bugs and crab spiders (which ambush them on flowers), dragonflies, ants, wasps (Vespidae and Sphecidae), tiger beetles, and web-spinning spiders. Praying mantises and ambush bugs both have long forelegs that lash out to catch the prey; the last two long segments of their forelegs are toothed where they meet to secure the prey firmly. Ambush bugs are yellow and brown, perfectly camouflaged in late summer on the yellow flowers of Compositae plants, where they lie in wait for butterflies, bees, and other insect prey. Crab spiders, too, are often superbly camouflaged. The sundew plant (*Drosera*) is known to catch some butterflies.

Vertebrate predators including lizards, frogs, toads, mice and other rodents, and birds occasionally eat larvae, pupae, or adults. Sometimes an attacking vertebrate catches only wing fragments. Or an adult that has been caught by the wings flies away when the vertebrate tries to swallow it, escaping with a "beak mark" of missing scales (see the Introduction). A. Shapiro found that 5-7 percent of his butterflies had beak marks; the percentage was largest in the cool seasons when butterflies were too cold to fly. P. Ehrlich saw some tropical lizards jump into the air to snatch passing butterflies.

Other individuals are killed by hail, freezes, or starvation, or by being accidentally eaten or stepped on by grazing animals, by falling from the hostplant, or by being washed off by rain. Averaged over many years, only two eggs from each female survive to become adults, even though the female may lay hundreds of eggs. If any more than two, the population would explode; if any less, it would become extinct.

Mimicry and Other Defenses

Some butterflies are poisonous to vertebrates, and are thus somewhat protected from being eaten—after a few unpleasant experiences, the predator learns to avoid them. In general, if the larva is poisonous, the pupa and adult of that species will be too; but the predator must learn the lesson anew in each case. Poisonous butterflies generally obtain their poisons from their hostplants, as larvae, but the pyrrolizidine alkaloids that adult Danainae and Ithomiinae obtain by feeding on certain plants are also poisons. *Danaus* and *Euphydryas phaeton* larvae, pupae, and adults are poisonous if as larvae they ate poisonous plants, but edible if as larvae they ate nonpoisonous plants. *Battus* and Cruciferae-eating larvae (*Pieris*, *Ascia*, perhaps *Anthocharis*, and others) also derive their poisons from their hostplants.

Some poisonous species, however, make their own poisons. Papilionidae larvae, for example, pop ill-smelling tentacles (osmeteria) out of the thorax to repel threatening intruders; the two acids given off by the osmeteria (isobutyric and 2-methyl-butyric in *Papilio*, *Eurytides*, and Baroniinae; two sesquiterpenes in *Battus*; and numerous other acids, esters, and terpenes in all of these) seem to be manufactured by the larva, and T. and Y. Meinwald found that the acids can even repel ants that have already begun to bite the larva. In *Speyeria*, *Historis*, *Smyrna*, and *Anartia* larvae there is a ventral gland just behind the head that in at least the first three is used for defense. This neck gland (Fig. 1) occurs in some Pieridae, Danainae, Nymphalinae, Libytheidae, skippers, and probably others. The sticky blobs on the spines of larvae of *Dynamine dyonis* (154) presumably have a defensive function. A tropical lycaenid larva (*Teratoneura*) has hairs bearing noxious chemicals (H. Eltringham).

The chemicals of other species may or may not be manufactured by the larva. In adults of *Parides* and *Battus*, scent glands associated with red or yellow abdominal spots emit an acrid odor if the butterfly is pinched (H. Tyler). *Appias drusilla* (85) larvae spit an acrid green fluid when disturbed. Larvae of *Hamadryas amphinome* (168), which are gregarious, exude a foul odor. The spines of *Siproeta stelenes* (176) and *Dryas iulia* (270) larvae supposedly cause a rash when rubbed on the skin, owing in the latter species apparently to a chemical exuded from the spine tips.

Poisonous species often share another feature: because in many cases the bodies of the adults are too tough to crush by pinching, they can recover fully after being tasted and let go. *Parnassius*, *Battus*, and *Danaus* have such bodies.

Poisonous species are often models for other species, which have come to mimic them in general appearance. Models are poisonous; mimics are either edible (Batesian mimics) or poisonous (Müllerian mimics). In each case the mimic evolved to resemble the poisonous model when mutant butterflies that looked a little like the poisonous model were eaten less often and therefore produced more offspring. Mimics gain some protection against being eaten from the behavioral responses of the predators: a predator that has learned to avoid the poisonous model tends to reject other species that resemble it. In this system some models die (though rather fewer of the tough-bodied species) so that many others (and their mimics) may live. Some die because each new predator in the area must learn that the models are poisonous, and of course a predator who has eaten only mimics may try a model, thinking it is edible.

Because in Müllerian mimicry the model and the mimics are *all* poisonous, the evolutionary benefit to the mimics may seem slight. The advantage lies in the fact that the predators must be educated to avoid butterflies of only one color pattern—whereas if the species all looked different, the predators would have to sample each one. Müllerian mimics probably evolve from a convergence toward the color pattern of the most common model, and in some mimicry complexes it is impossible to know which species was the original model. (The Introduction comments on Bates and Müller, the naturalists who are honored by these terms.)

Several mimicry complexes are known in North America:

1. *Battus philenor* (25) is the model for several Batesian mimics: *Papilio troilus* (22), *P. polyxenes* females (7), black *P. glaucus* females (18), *Limenitis arthemis astyanax* (146), and perhaps even *Speyeria diana* females (251). All are basically black on the upperside and bluish on the outer half of the hindwing upperside, and all except *S. diana* have red spots along the margin of the hindwing underside. J. Brower, A. Platt, R. Coppinger, and L. Brower found that inexperienced caged birds eat the mimics, but when then presented with *B. philenor* they refuse it (because of the aristolochic acids derived from its hostplants); but after trying *B. philenor*, most jays refused the mimics. As one would expect, the ranges of *B. philenor*, *P. troilus*, black *P. glaucus*, and *L. a. astyanax* correspond very well in the eastern United States, where this mimicry complex developed.

2. *Danaus* species are models for *Limenitis archippus* (145, a Batesian-Müllerian mimic): (a) *D. plexippus* (89) and *L. a. archippus* are both orange-brown with black veins; (b) *D. gilippus berenice* (90) and *D. eresimus* (91) models and the *L. archippus floridensis* mimic (Florida only) are dark reddish-brown with blackish veins; (c) the *D. gilippus strigosus* model and the *L. archippus obsoleta* mimic (Arizona to west Texas) are mostly brownish, and because the black transverse line on the hindwing of *L. a. obsoleta* is nearly obsolete, it even more closely mimics *Danaus*. J. Brower, L. Brower, A. Platt, and R. Coppinger found that *D. plexippus* and *D. gilippus* are usually unpalatable to birds; they also found that *L. archippus* is relatively palatable but not as palatable as other butterflies (thus intermediate between a Batesian and a Müllerian mimic). Their jays rejected both *Danaus* and *L. archippus* after trying *Danaus*, and they remembered not to eat them for 2 weeks or more. The poisons in *Danaus* are cardiac glycosides (heart poisons, mainly calactin, calotropin, and calotoxin) received from the hostplants. G. Vaughan and A. Jungreis found that glycosides are toxic to animals because they bind to an enzyme in the nervous system, but the high level of potassium in *Danaus* blood prevents them from binding and poisoning *Danaus*. L. Brower found that some milkweed species (*Asclepias*, the larval hostplant) are poisonous and some are not, and that the adult is poisonous only if as a larva it ate a poisonous plant.

3. Some Heliconiini (including *Heliconius erato*, 273, a rare stray into the

United States) are Müllerian mimics in the tropics. Occurring together in southern Florida and southern Texas are three Müllerian mimics of Heliconiini, *Dione vanillae* (268), *Dryas iulia* (270), and *Dryadula phaetusa* (267), all of them orange with blackish stripes. L. Brower, J. Brower, and C. Collins found that *H. erato*, *Dione vanillae*, and *Dryas iulia* are unpalatable to tanagers. *D. iulia* exudes noxious chemicals from the larvae. *Heliconius charitonia* (272) may be unpalatable also, and some Mexican Pieridae (*Itaballia viardi* females) mimic it, but it is not involved in a mimicry complex in the United States. *Heliconius* adults contain cyanogenic glycosides, precursors of cyanide (their *Passiflora* hostplants also contain these chemicals).

4. Most white butterflies seem to belong to a Müllerian mimicry complex, though they have not been well studied and the Pieridae may not be very poisonous. N. Marsh and M. Rothschild found that all three British whites (including *Pieris rapae*, 76, and *P. napi*, 77, which also occur in North America) are noxious; they contain allyl isothiocyanate, mustard oils, and mustard glycosides acquired from the hostplants. *Ascia monuste* (83) is also somewhat distasteful, and T. Eisner found that white *Parnassius phoebus* (28) adults and larvae are noxious. Perhaps the white females of *Colias* benefit from Batesian mimicry of these.

5. Larvae of all *Danaus* (89-91) and the *Papilio machaon* group (5-8) seem to be Müllerian mimics. All have filaments on the thorax and are pale with yellow and black transverse stripes. The *Danaus* larvae are poisonous, and their thoracic filaments somewhat resemble the *Papilio* osmeteria, the smelly tentacles that pop out of the thorax in response to attack. T. Jarvi and others found that the skin of *P. machaon* is distasteful to birds, who released the larvae unharmed after picking them up. Larvae of *Pieris sisymbrii* (82) and *Anthocharis cethura* (69) also look like *Danaus*; rich in mustard oils, they are probably somewhat poisonous also.

6. Certain millipedes and the larvae of *Battus* (25, 26) and *Parnassius* (28-30) are said to be Müllerian models; and the larvae of *Papilio indra* (9) and some *Speyeria* (251-264) may be their Batesian mimics. Though these all have the same shape and the same color pattern (mostly black with paler yellowish or orangish bands or spots), this mimicry complex is nonetheless speculative.

7. *Doxocopa* females (143, 144) resemble *Limenitis bredowii* (149) and *L. lorquini* (148). If they are indeed mimics, it is not known who is mimicking whom. *Limenitis* are somewhat edible, but *Doxocopa* have not been tested for edibility.

8. *Euphydryas chalcedona* (200) may be a model, and *Chlosyne palla palla* females (222), *C. leanira leanira* (209), *Phyciodes campestris campestris* (230), and *P. orseis orseis* (224) may be Batesian mimics. M. Bowers found that *E. chalcedona* is somewhat inedible, but the others have not been tested. In the California lowlands all are mostly black with many yellow spots on the upperside, and somewhat reddish on the underside. But in the higher Sierra Nevada, *E. chalcedona sierra* is reddish on the upperside, and the mimics *C. palla calydon*, *P. campestris montana*, and *P. orseis herlani* become reddish also.

Euphydryas phaeton (199), of the northeastern United States, is blackish above and has red spots on the hindwing underside. Because it thus slightly resembles *Battus philenor* in appearance, it may be a weak Müllerian mimic. M. Bowers found that it is unpalatable to jays when it has fed on *Chelone glabra* (plants of this family, Scrophulariaceae, are known to contain iridoid glycosides, the heart stimulant in digitalis), but not when the larvae eat *Plantago lanceolata*. S. Scudder noted that adults fly very slowly, as if protected. But more likely, *E. phaeton* is the model for the palatable Batesian mimic *Chlosyne harrisii* (220), which has a similar underside and larval pattern, and often flies with *E. phaeton*.

Batesian mimicry is most effective when the palatable mimics are less common and conspicuous than the poisonous models. In accordance with this principle, Batesian mimicry is often limited to females, which halves the abundance of the mimics (our examples are *Papilio glaucus*, *P. polyxenes*, *Speyeria diana*, *Chlosyne palla palla*). Evolution singles out the females for mimicry because the predation death of a female diminishes the number of eggs laid by a population far more than predation on a male would (since there are generally plenty of males available for mating). Batesian mimics also tend to be smaller (examples are our *Limenitis*, *Chlosyne*, and *Phyciodes*), making them less conspicuous and less appealing to predators.

Models, on the other hand, show different trends. Because a predator can more easily remember which species was poisonous if it is conspicuous, the models tend to be brightly colored (blue, orange, white, or black-and-yellow in ours); moreover, they often fly slowly (as in *Danaus*, *Dryas*, *Heliconius*, and *Parnassius*). Models are often tough-bodied, as well, to survive being tasted.

It is important to note that mimicry provides a measure of protection only from vertebrate predators like birds; parasitoids and other invertebrates are not deterred. A. Muyshondt proposed, in fact, that parasitoids actively prefer larvae that are poisonous to vertebrates, for the parasitoids inside a poisonous larva benefit from the diminished predation on the larva itself.

Besides being potentially poisonous, adult butterflies often are not worth the bother to predators large enough to capture them. Many brightly colored butterflies are not eaten by birds simply because they do not look like food to them (R. Coppinger). Since butterflies have very little body compared to their large inedible wings, and since they are hard to catch when in flight, birds may learn that they are not worth the trouble when compared to fat grasshoppers or worms.

Defenses more obvious than mimicry include long spines or hairs on the head or body of larvae. The clubs on the thorax of *Limenitis* larvae (Fig. 51) are used to knock off ants and other predators. Many Hesperiinae pupae have a long horn on the head, and the cremaster on the end of the abdomen is also long and pointed; since the pupa inhabits a rolled-leaf nest, any enemy that crawls into either end of the tube is met by a spear.

The leaf or silk nests of larvae also give a certain amount of protection. The larvae and pupae that live in clusters (*Euphydryas*, *Nymphalis*, *Asterocampa*, etc.) twitch when disturbed, and the sight of many twitching bodies may discourage some predators. Some adult butterflies (*Poladryas* and *Nymphalis*, for example) feign death when handled, which may cause a bird or other predator to ignore them. I noticed that *Ochlodes snowi* adults that I had marked, to study their dispersal, often flew to a tree and remained there for a time; this response might help to protect them until the predator that scared them departs.

The hindwing rubbing of Lycaeninae adults might be useful against the attacks of predators. The resting adults move their hindwings forward and back, the two wings going in opposite directions. The lower corner of the hindwing underside often carries an eyespot (a red spot with a black center) next to a tail, the area thus resembling a head and antennae; the rubbing of the hindwings draws the predator's attention to that part of the wing, causing the predator to peck at the wing rather than at the real head. T. Larsen found that an African hairstreak (*Oxylides*) even turns 180° before landing, in order to place the eyespot and tails where the predator thinks the head should be; curiously, it turns left two-thirds of the landings, right one-third. Species of hairstreaks having well-developed eyespots and tails suffer more hindwing damage owing to predators' attacks that failed to kill them (R. Robbins). Presumably this diversion spares some butterflies, although had they not had such a conspicuous pattern on the wings they might have been spared the attack in the first place. Moreover, a bird's attack on the eyespot might mash the abdomen as well, and in fact the lower corner of the hindwing is elongated in many hairstreaks, perhaps to protect the abdomen from just such damage. Adults of many *Papilio* have an eyespot and a tail, which may also serve for defense.

Some eyespots, larger ones, may in fact repel predators. A. Blest found that the eyespots of adult *Precis* startle birds, which may mistake them for snakes or rodents. The larvae of some *Papilio* (spp. *glaucus*, *troilus*, *palamedes*, etc.) resemble snakes in having large eyespots on an enlarged headlike thorax, and orange osmeteria that look like a snake's tongue.

Some species avoid being eaten by resembling an inedible object. Adult *Anaea*, *Nymphalis*, *Polygonia*, and *Libytheana* (274) look like dead leaves on the underside, and their habit of resting on twigs accentuates their leaflike appearance. Even if a bird discovers them, their bright upperside may startle the bird when the wings are opened for flight. Pupae (Fig. 52) of some *Eurema* and *Phoebis* have enormous wing cases, perhaps to resemble leaves, and the pupae of *Polygonia* and *Limenitis* look like hanging, dead, curled leaves (the larvae of *Limenitis* even hibernate in hanging curled leaves). Yellow *Phoebis* adults may fool predators by roosting on yellow leaves. The overwintering eggs of many hairstreaks and *Lycaena* resemble bark, and many pupae resemble dirt or bark. *Euchloe* pupae resemble dead twigs. The silver spots on some Nymphalidae pupae, when seen against the light, supposedly make them resemble an empty pupal shell. The larvae of *Limenitis* and many *Papilio* resemble bird droppings.

Some larvae mimic their food. *Callophrys spinetorum* larvae (342) take on the color of their food, and many Lycaenidae larvae look like the flowers on which they feed. Many other lycaenid larvae and the larvae and pupae of many other butterflies are of a green shade that matches the leaves or stems of their hostplants. *Cyllopsis pertepida* larvae and pupae (100) are tan with fine brown lines, perfectly resembling dried grass blades.

Many species hide to avoid being eaten. Some tropical Riodininae land under leaves with the wings flat. *Epargyreus* males rest under leaves when not seeking mates. Many larvae, including *Speyeria*, take refuge under leaves, and *Papilio indra* larvae hide at the base of the plant. Many checkerspot larvae, *Plebejus shasta* larvae and pupae, and many other larvae hibernate under rocks. *Euphydryas chalcedona* larvae may hide in hollow stems of their hostplant *Penstemon antirrhinoides*. Young larvae of *Speyeria* sometimes hibernate inside grass stems; *Apodemia mormo* larvae (275) may hibernate inside the inflated stems of *Eriogonum inflatum* plants; and many Lycaeninae larvae live inside fruits or pods. *Atlides halesus* (349) often pupates under loose bark. Adults of *Nymphalis* and *Polygonia* hibernate in cracks or under piles of wood or rocks or in other crannies.

The larvae of Lycaenidae use their remarkable set of defenses to protect themselves against ants, and some lycaenid larvae may actually recruit ants to protect themselves from other predators. Many ant species tend and milk the larvae, and will even move a larva from one spot to another sometimes with their jaws. The ants that tend the lycaenids are of the species that also gather honeydew from aphids. From the lycaenids, too, the ants get honeydew, which is produced by the Newcomer's gland, near the rear on top of abdomen segment 7. (In the Riodininae, the glands are on the side of segment 8; a few Lycaeninae have additional honeydew glands on top of segments 5-8.) The honeydew gland, generally found only in older larvae, also occurs in the pupae of some species. Because the Lycaeninae larvae have thick skin, as well as a small head that can be retracted into the thorax (making them look sluglike), ant bites damage them less. And because movement can cause the ants to attack, the larvae do not move when touched (they feed when the ants are absent, or at night). H. Malicky suggested that tiny glands called ring glands produce a pheromone causing the ants to touch the larva, and the larva then responds by producing honeydew to "bribe" the ants not to attack. N. Pierce and P. Mead found that the ants in turn defend the larva by repelling various parasitoid wasps that try to lay eggs inside it.

Some Lycaenidae have two tentacles that they extrude (on top of abdomen segment 8 just behind the honey glands in Lycaeninae; on the metathorax and sometimes near the rear in Riodininae). G. Clark and C. Dickson think that the tentacles pop out to repel ants or other insects, and that they often pop out when the larva moves. In most species they are hair pencils like those of *Danaus* male adults, and the hairs have many short branches and pop out into a plume (Fig. 1). Generally only older larvae have tentacles, but in some species the first-stage larvae do also. Riodininae also have "vibratory papillae" on the prothorax that pop quickly in and out, for reasons unknown. Nearly all lycaenids associated with ants bear the ring glands, most species have honeydew glands, but only about half the species bear the tentacles. Thus, the ring glands seem to be the most important structures, and larvae with ring glands but without honeydew glands may chemically mimic the species that do have the glands, to fool the ants.

In other parts of the world the larvae of some Lycaeninae species are taken by ants into the ants' nests, where the larvae then feed and grow on the ant larvae. The emerging adult of one Australian species (*Liphyra brassolis*) is covered with hairs, and as it crawls out of the ant nest the ants grab only hair. So far as is known, no North American species lives in ant nests, although ants are known to move some larvae of *Plebejus icarioides* (408) and some Mexican Riodininae from one plant to another or to a different hollow at the base of a plant. Tropical lycaenid larvae in other parts of the world are known to stroke aphids and related insects to feed on the resulting honeydew.

Young Pieridae larvae (of all three subfamilies) have a similar system for protection against ants: forked hairs on the body (D1 and D2; see Fig. 50) dispense honeydew from their tips to bribe the ants. E. Ford noted that ants have been observed attending the young larvae in Britain.

Variation, Genetics, and Convergence

Variation within a single species is especially puzzling to people trying to identify butterflies. The study of this variation is essential to the proper identification of such species and may provide clues both to their evolution and to the nature of evolution itself. The origins of the variation are genetic (inherited), environmental, or both. Genetic variation is especially interesting for its role in natural selection; a genetic trait becomes common if animals (or plants) having that trait manage to produce more offspring than those lacking the trait. For instance, most scientists think that giraffes are tall today because in the past the taller ones survived better and produced more offspring than the shorter ones; the taller ones could reach and eat more leaves of the trees that giraffes feed upon. When Charles Darwin and Alfred Russel Wallace proposed the theory of evolution, genes and heredity were unknown, and some people thought that giraffes became taller by stretching their necks and passing on longer necks to their offspring. Scientists now believe that two things must happen for natural selection to occur: (1) individuals within a population or species must exhibit variation that is genetic and therefore inherited; and (2) some inherited variation or combination of variations must confer greater survival or reproductive capability than others. Geneticists study the nature of this variation and the methods of its inheritance.

A hundred years ago it was not known how traits are inherited. We now know that the chemical DNA (deoxyribonucleic acid) in the chromosomes contains the genes. The DNA shows the cell what kind of proteins to make, and each gene directs the making of one protein; the process can be imagined as the translation of a Greek sentence (the DNA) into an English sentence (the protein). Mutations, which are changes in the sequence of the components of DNA, are caused by "mistakes" in the duplication of the DNA when the eggs or sperm are made; these mutations are rare in nature, but radiation and certain chemicals increase their occurrence. Over many years mutations that increase (or at least do not decrease) the animals' survival can accumulate in a population. Using the technique of electrophoresis, scientists can detect slight differences in the size or electric charge of proteins produced by mutations in the DNA. Many such protein variations occur in most butterflies and other animals, and in fact almost every individual is genetically distinct from every other—in butterflies, even identical twins are impossible, since the egg cannot split. In a given population of animals, about 20 percent of the places for genes on the chromosomes carry two or more different types of genes—but scientists argue whether these minor variations are of any use (or harm) to the animals, beyond providing the potential for change so important to evolution.

Most inherited traits that control the form and behavior of the individuals within a species vary rather continuously along a spectrum, producing many intermediates; these quantitatively inherited traits, or polygenic traits, are assumed to be under the control of many different genes. Good examples are height in humans and the width of the median yellow bands on the wings of the black forms of *Papilio polyxenes* (7), *P. machaon bairdii* (5), and relatives. The orange vs. yellow wing color and black border width of *Colias eurytheme* (37) are similar examples, both due to one or two pairs of genes, without dominance. Quantitatively inherited traits are not much studied because the experiments do not produce simple results.

Other traits are inherited in a dominant-recessive, or Mendelian, fashion, in which one gene dominates the other gene in its effect on the animal's appearance. Because each individual has an even number of chromosomes, grouped into pairs, there are always two genes (sometimes several pairs) regulating a trait, although all of them may be identical. An egg and a sperm each have half the number of chromosomes (and genes) of the resulting individual; when the sperm enters the egg the number doubles, forming the pairs found in larvae, pupae, and adults. The black color of adults in the *Papilio machaon* group (5-9) is said to be dominant to the recessive, yellow color because if an individual has one black (*B*) gene and one yellow (*y*) gene, then as an adult it will be black (*By*) (of course *BB* adults are black also). Only if both are yellow genes (*yy*) will the adult have yellow wings. One can thus predict the coloration of the several offspring when two parents mate. Because half the sperm or eggs of a *By* parent carry *B*, and the other half *y*, two *By* parents produce three black offspring (one *BB*, one *By*, one *yB*) to every yellow offspring (*yy*); the cross *By* × *yy* produces one black offspring (*By*) to every yellow (*yy*); two *BB* parents produce only black (*BB*) offspring; two *yy* parents produce only yellow (*yy*) offspring; and the cross *BB* × *By* produces only black offspring (one *BB* to every *By*). Conversely, a check of the traits of all the offspring of a given pair, especially if carried out over several generations, can yield a good estimate of that pair's genes.

If a trait is beneficial, other genes elsewhere on the chromosome will tend to evolve to make the beneficial trait dominant, whereas if a trait is detrimental, other genes will tend to evolve to make it recessive. Possible examples are the black wings of *Limenitis arthemis astyanax*, *Papilio polyxenes asterias* and *P. glaucus* females, and probably *Speyeria* females; these black forms are dominant, probably because they benefit from mimicry.

Other variations in butterflies known to be inherited in a dominant-recessive fashion are the absence or presence of white bands on *Limenitis arthemis* adults (146); some wing-pattern traits of adult *Pieris napi* (77); red spots or ground color of the larvae of *Papilio machaon*–group species (5-9) and *Chlosyne lacinia* (216); the green color of the larvae of *Pieris napi* and *Colias philodice*; the orange vs. yellow spot on the center of the hindwing upperside of *C. philodice*; and extremely rare white male and female *Colias* (these females usually are confused with form *alba*, which is due to recessive genes).

Traits under the control of genes on the X or Y chromosomes are called sex-linked, because the X and Y chromosomes determine the sex of the animal (they are named for the approximate shapes they take in most animals). Male butterflies have two X sex chromosomes, females one X and one Y (human females have two X chromosomes, males one X and one Y). For example, because the gene for solid-black wings in some *Papilio glaucus* females (18) is on the Y chromosome, daughters are the color of their mother. The ultraviolet reflection of male *Colias eurytheme* (37) is due to a gene on the X chromosome (but just why the reflection occurs only in males is not known, since females have one X). Two other cases might be sex-linked: the white form *alba* of *Colias* females, and some wing traits of *Pieris napi* females. No doubt many other such cases, so far unknown to science, occur in nature.

The great genetic variation within some populations has several causes, the first being mutations, the origin of the variants. Immigration too may introduce new genes. A major cause of variation is hybrid vigor, the increased hardiness of hybrids so familiar among cultivated plants and domestic animals. My hybrids of two *Poladryas* subspecies seemed to thrive on a greater variety of *Penstemon* hostplants, for instance. An individual with different types of genes on the two chromosomes of a pair, say *A* and *a* (written *Aa*)—such as is likely in a hybrid—may have greater survival or reproductive success if each type has a slightly different chemical task in the body, so that a greater range of tasks can be performed than in *AA* or *aa* individuals. R. Fisher proved that in cases in which *Aa* individuals do enjoy greater survival or reproduction, natural selection keeps both genes in the population, perpetuating the variation. Such a state of perpetual genetic variation is called polymorphism. (Natural selection may decrease variation as well, by eliminating harmful genes.)

Some traits remain in a population because the survival or reproduction of individuals having the trait is greater when it is rare. For example, Batesian mimics such as black females of *Papilio glaucus* (18) benefit from mimicry when rare, but if they become common, then predators learn to eat them. Similarly, perching on or patrolling around hilltops is of value at low population density to bring together scattered mates, but is unnecessary at high density.

Sometimes a form can occur across species and subspecies, usually because species and subspecies tend to evolve from populations rather than from individuals; so if a population that gives rise to another species or subspecies contains two or more forms, these same forms can be transferred to the new species or subspecies. That is no doubt why all the *Colias* and related butterflies have a white female form *alba*. Other ways of transferring forms between species are rare hybridization between closely related species, as in the *Papilio machaon* group (5-9), or even the transmission of genes between species by viruses, which has recently been shown to occur.

Environmental variation is caused by differences in a particular habitat over time or by differences between habitats: for example, number of hours of daylight (photoperiod), temperature, and the color or texture of the plant environment in which a larva or pupa lives. The most common environmental variation is seasonal variation: individuals of the spring or fall flights do not look like those of the summer flights. Many cases are noted in the text in all families, especially Pieridae. Often the spring form is darker than the summer form, especially on the underside of the hindwing, which allows more warming sunlight to be absorbed when the days are shorter and the sun is lower in the sky. Photoperiod change is the main physiological cause of seasonal differences because it varies the same way every year (the shortest day of the year is always December 21, the longest June 21). Photoperiod is responsible for the spring forms of *Pieris*, *Ascia*, *Colias*, *Nathalis*, *Anaea*, *Phyciodes*, *Polygonia*, Japanese *Lycaena phlaeas*, and surely many more. In most cases, the ability to produce seasonal forms in response to photoperiod is probably genetically controlled.

Temperature is also influential, affecting, for example, the seasonal forms of *Pieris* (76-82) and *Polygonia* (189-193), but doubtfully the color of *Phyciodes campestris* (230), and possibly the variant forms of *Precis coenia* (180) and *Plebejus icarioides* (408). Adults of many species are smaller in the spring flight than in the summer flight, probably owing to lower temperature. Some altitudinal forms, like those in *Plebejus acmon* (410), might be due to temperature differences, though most seem to be genetic. (In some species, the altitudinal subspecies—for example, in *Parnassius phoebus*, 28; *Euphydryas chalcedona*, 200; *Hesperia comma*, 472; and *Polites sabuleti*, 488—are known to be genetically different.) Temperature also produces many aberrations; these freaks, typically with abnormally blurred or fused wing pattern, can be produced by refrigerating very young pupae for a few days. But some aberrations are mutants, controlled directly by the genes.

Some of the observed variation in larvae and pupae is a response to the local environment. The larvae and pupae of some species are known to change color to match their background. Most Papilionidae and some Pieridae pupae are brown or green depending in part on where they pupate (although in a short photoperiod, all *Papilio* pupae are brown). The lowermost eyes of pupating *Pieris* larvae detect the darkness and color of the background; the resulting pupa is brown on dark (or blue) backgrounds, green on light (or green, yellow, or red) backgrounds (D. Angersbach). Some *Callophrys* and perhaps *Phoebis* larvae approximate the color of their food after eating it for a few days.

Geographic variation, by which most individuals of a species at one locality differ from most at another locality, is sometimes environmental but more frequently genetic in origin: many quantitatively inherited characters change in mix and frequency from place to place. Thus populations often look different because they have different proportions of particular genes; the gradual change of *Papilio machaon* populations (5) from mostly black in the south to yellow in the north is a good example.

Many geographic variants (subspecies) appear to owe their origin to predators, for butterflies that match their background are less easily noticed. Thus California *Oeneis chryxus* adults (128) and *Papilio indra* pupae (9) match the background rocks on the regions where they occur. W. Hovanitz noticed that subspecies or populations that occur in dry, sunny, hot regions are lighter than populations in wetter, cloudier, cooler regions, evidently for better camouflage (darker coloration also absorbs more sunlight during basking). Thus the grassland subspecies of *Coenonympha tullia, Chlosyne harrisii, Hesperia leonardus, H. comma, H. attalus,* and *Atrytone logan* are much lighter than the forest subspecies of these species (*Lethe eurydice,* however, is darker on prairie). Similarly, the desert subspecies of *Pieris napi, Cercyonis pegala,* many *Speyeria, Euphydryas, Chlosyne, Phyciodes picta, Apodemia, Phaeostrymon, Satyrium sylvinus, S. calanus, Hylephila phyleus, Polites sabuleti, Ochlodes sylvanoides,* and *Thorybes mexicana* are paler than the non-desert subspecies. The same phenomenon applies to arctic/alpine habitats, which are wetter, cloudier, and cooler. Thus the subspecies of *Parnassius phoebus, Euphydryas, Chlosyne gabbii,* three *Lycaena, Plebejus shasta, Hesperia comma,* and *Polites sabuleti* are paler at low altitude than at high altitude; and *Pieris napi,* many *Boloria, Plebejus glandon,* and *Hesperia comma* are paler in southern habitats below treeline than in the Arctic. *Oeneis nevadensis* and *Pyrgus ruralis* are also lighter in their southern, drier habitats.

Convergence, a particularly interesting type of geographic variation, occurs when several species in the same locality, species that are elsewhere distinct, resemble each other (mimicry is of course the best example). Convergence can be maddening to people who try to identify such creatures as western *Speyeria,* for instance. Western *Euphydryas* and *Chlosyne* are often convergent as well. Some of this variation results from the need for camouflage, as just noted.

Different species feeding on the same hostplant often converge genetically in a number of ways. For example, the pupae of species whose larvae eat only hackberry trees and shrubs (*Celtis*) look similar: thus the pupae of both *Asterocampa* (140-142) and *Libytheana* (274) are flattened along the sides and bear oblique yellowish lines, perhaps to resemble the hostplant leaves. The larvae of leaf-rolling species and of species that bore into roots or fleshy leaves (Charaxinae and Hesperiidae) generally lose their long hairs and spines, in order to fit into tight quarters; those in large silk nests generally keep them.

Pupation method is also subject to genetic convergence. Pupae of genera that occur frequently where there are no shrubs or trees to pupate on (as is the case in dry grassland and arctic/alpine habitats) sometimes lose the cremaster hooks and pupate in a loose silk cocoon or among debris, sometimes partly underground (*Parnassius*, *Erebia*, *Neominois*, and *Oeneis*); there are few twigs to attach a cremaster to there, and these pupation sites give them some protection from blowing dust and snow (see also *Boloria improba*, 245).

Although these examples can be explained at least in part by natural selection, many examples of convergence remain unexplained: the white hindwing underside bands in several Alaskan and Siberian *Erebia* (113, 114, 116); the orange Florida *Phyciodes frisia* (236) and *P. texana* (234); the wide black hindwing dorsal margin (form *umbrosa*) of three *Polygonia* (189, 190, 193) and *Asterocampa* (142); the tawny hindwing upperside submargin of *Polygonia gracilis* and *P. progne* in the southern Rockies; the obscure hindwing underside of five species of *Callophrys* elfins (331-336) in the west; the large white hindwing underside patches in extinct San Francisco *Glaucopsyche lygdamus xerces* (395) and *Plebejus icarioides pheres* (408); the orange upperside of southern California *P. icarioides*, *P. saepiolus* (407), and *Glaucopsyche piasus* (396); the similarity of *Satyrium fuliginosum* (316) to female *P. icarioides*; the square underside spots on several *Euphilotes* (399, 401) in or near the Sierra Nevada; the spotless white undersides of Oregon *Plebejus idas* (404) and *Everes amyntula* (391); the white hindwing fringes of many southwestern *Erynnis* (646-660); and the large orange unh spots of Fla. *Satyrium liparops* (307), *S. calanus* (310), and *Fixsenia favonius* (351).

To be fair, mention should be made of cases in which related butterflies show divergence rather than convergence. For instance, *Papilio polyxenes* (7) is yellow in the southwest and black elsewhere, but the opposite is true of *P. machaon* (5); *Anthocharis cethura* (69) is yellow in the southwest, but *A. sara* (68) is yellow in the north; *Colias palaeno* (40) is darkest on Baffin Island, where *C. pelidne* (41) is light; and *Hesperia metea* (480) is darkest in Texas, where *H. attalus* (479) is lightest.

Microbiologists may have supplied a clue to the mechanism of convergence by finding that viruses can transfer genes between animals. Closely related species occurring in the same habitats and localities would be the most likely to share viruses, and so would be most likely to exchange genes. Virus-exchanged genes could explain the cases of convergence just noted (including some *Speyeria*) that do not seem (at least with our current knowledge) due to natural selection. Then, too, some cases of convergence could be merely coincidental.

Chromosomes and Chromosome Counts

Chromosomes, which contain the genes of animals, consist of strings of DNA wrapped around special proteins. Although the chromosomes in most animals appear as X-shaped structures, butterfly chromosomes appear as dots, and have been seen as long filaments only a few times. The workings of butterfly chromosomes are poorly known.

Butterflies commonly have about 30 chromosomes in sperm and unfertilized eggs, thus about 60 in other stages. The chromosomes of about one-fourth of the North American butterfly species have been counted (usually from the sperm of adult or pupal testes). The texts in Part III give the counts from the sperm of closely related species that differ in chromosome number, but not of those that do not differ. In most animals, mating between individuals of different chromosome numbers produces few offspring, but in butterflies this seems not to be a problem. Variation in chromosome number is known for more than 30 species of butterflies; in *Philotes sonorensis* it varies from 17 to 44 in one population, and in *Heliconius* from 19 to 32 in one population. (We do know that in many grasshoppers, some gophers, and some other animals, subspecies may have different chromosome numbers.)

In most animals, during the formation of sperm and eggs in the adults, the two strands of a pair of chromosomes are pulled to opposite ends of the dividing cell by fibers attached to a spot on the chromosome called the centromere. If a piece of chromosome breaks off, it is then genetically lost, and the offspring is weak and perhaps unable to survive. But in butterflies and a few other animals and plants, the whole chromosome acts as a diffuse centromere; when a chromosome breaks, both parts function normally and move to the proper end, and a normal offspring therefore results. This means that butterflies with extra chromosome pieces (broken off another chromosome) can function normally.

Butterfly chromosomes are strange in another way also. In most animals, before the chromosomes separate in the production of sperm and eggs, each pair may exchange arms; this happens in the production of Lepidoptera sperm, but not in eggs.

Incredibly, a butterfly can be part male, part female. The sex of each insect cell is determined by the number of X and Y chromosomes: a cell with two X's is male; with one X, female (the Y chromosome has no sex-determining genes, and few genes of any kind). Thus, if a cell starts out XX, therefore male, and then divides, and if in the process one of the two cells loses an X, that cell is left with only one X, and becomes female—through all succeeding cell divisions. Some of the adult will be male, the rest female, such as the *Hesperia columbia* on Color Plate 50. I caught this adult on the side of a boulder on a hilltop, where it had gone to mate, as is the habit of its species; but with which sex it hoped to mate can only be guessed. Other mixed-sex butterflies can happen when a male cell divides and one cell receives 3 X's and dies, and the other receives one X and becomes female; or when a female cell divides and one cell receives only a Y and dies, and the other receives two X's and a Y and becomes male. (Such a rare mixed-sex "gynandromorph" is not possible in humans because the X and Y affect only the gonads, which produce the hormones that produce the sex differences.) One of the most beautiful butterflies ever found was a *Speyeria diana* in which one half was orange and male, the other half blue and female.

Species and Subspecies

Until about 50 years ago, most scientists handled variation by naming each distinguishable group a separate species (the "postage stamp" species concept). When genetics became better known and the theory of evolution gained acceptance, the "biological" species concept became generally accepted. A biological species includes all the individuals and populations that can actually (or potentially, if the populations were brought together) interbreed and still produce normal fertile offspring. This concept takes into account individual and genetic variation, and emphasizes behavioral and physiological barriers to mating and reproduction. Not every pair of a species must be fertile (even in humans about one of five couples is not), but most pairs are, even between subspecies. Using the biological species concept, zoologists revised old classifications, combining "species" that simply look different, splitting others when it was discovered that two similar animals (like *Erynnis persius*, 657, and *E. afranius*, 659) do not interbreed.

Besides being convenient for filing the variation found in nature into descriptive categories, this concept of species is important for an evolutionary reason; for during evolution, biological species have separate fates (since they never or seldom interbreed with other species), whereas subspecies within a species may merge and change, mixing their genes, when glaciers come and go and habitats change. Arguments about particular species still abound because some people incline more toward the postage-stamp species concept, and because at the point when one species evolves into two species the precise assignment of the group as one species or two is impossible.

Scientists apply the biological species concept by looking for localities where two populations fly together (are sympatric) without interbreeding, and by hybridizing populations in the lab. Some distinct species can produce hybrids in the lab by hand-pairing (see "Raising and Breeding" in Appendix B), even though in nature the parents refuse to mate. To circumvent this problem, virgin females raised from the larvae of one population can be released in front of males of a second population, in the field, to study courtship and mating, and the mated females can be brought into the lab and their eggs raised to obtain hybrid females, which can then be mated again with wild males (backcrossed) in nature (of course one should not release any offspring that might become a pest). In a few cases, two not-quite-separate species hybridize in one region but do not in another (for example, *Chlosyne palla*, 222, and *C. gabbii*, 223; *Plebejus acmon*, 410, and *P. lupini*, 411).

Because in the course of evolution each population tends to become adapted to local conditions, and because of chance, the separate populations of a species may look quite different from each other. Each of the subspecies given in the texts in Part III and in the color plates is a geographically distinct part of a species that exhibits easily seen differences in wing pattern. Hundreds of subspecies have been named over the years, but I mention only those that are readily recognizable. It is neither possible nor desirable to name every variation found in nature, but some non-subspecies variations, such as the seasonal forms that help butterflies regulate their temperature, are named and treated as forms in this book.

To evolve into separate species, two populations of a species usually must be isolated for thousands or even millions of years. The gradual adaptation to their local environments and the chance drift away from the ancestral type both progress until, when they do come in contact later, they are no longer able to interbreed. If mating can occur but produces sterile offspring, courtship barriers to mating will also evolve, to prevent useless matings with the wrong species. Natural selection, after all, is driven by numbers of offspring, and the significance of survival is simply that dead organisms cannot reproduce.

In butterflies, several situations might lead to the evolution of two species at one locality. In biennial species, for example, one group of individuals might fly in even-numbered years, and another across the same range in odd-numbered years; reproductive contact between the groups might be sufficiently rare to allow them to evolve separately. Hostplant specificity might also lead to genetic divergence: some species of butterflies are restricted to particular larval hostplants, and the adults fly only when these plants are in bloom. Thus in several cases of *Euphilotes* butterflies (399, 400), one subspecies flies earlier in the summer, when one species of *Eriogonum* blooms, and a second subspecies later in the summer, with the flowering of a second species of *Eriogonum*. The prolonged separation of the two populations could allow them ultimately to evolve into separate species. (They are treated as the same species because they are linked by populations intermediate in appearance and flight period, elsewhere in the overall range of the species.)

Evolution and the Fossil Record

The origin of butterflies is a fascinating subject, one that involves studying butterfly fossils and the rocks and time periods they came from. Studying the behavior and anatomy of living butterflies is just as important, because knowing what their habits and bodies have become allows one to make deductions about the butterfly family tree. Even the study of the earth itself is important, because the idea first put forth by Alfred Wegener in 1912—that the continents split apart eons ago and have since been drifting across the face of the earth—finally has been confirmed by geologists. Because the ancestral butterflies, like everything else, were carried about by the moving continents, the collisions and separations of the continents affected the course of their evolution and distribution.

Geologists now think that the heat produced inside the earth by radioactivity, together with the rotation of the earth, causes the molten rock beneath the continents and ocean crust to move like thick soup in slow currents, only a few centimeters per year. This internal stirring causes the earth's surface to crack into plates that move about like ice floes. New crust is created where the hot rock comes to the surface, at chains of volcanoes along the mid-ocean ridges on the seafloor, and the slow rock currents in the earth then carry the new crust away from the ridge, in both directions. Where one of these spreading seafloor plates collides with a continental plate, the edge of the seafloor plate is forced beneath the edge of the continent, in turn forcing up great mountain ranges. As the Pacific Ocean crust was drawn beneath South America, for example, the Andes were created; and about 260 million years ago (mya) the Ural Mountains were created by the collision of Europe and Asia. Until the earth cools, there will always be continents, and they will evidently continue to drift—for consisting as they do of lighter rock, they float like corks on the heavier deep rock.

The as many as four continents that made up the earth's surface about 600 mya joined into one (called Pangaea by geologists) about 200 mya, when Florida was on the equator. Since then, in sequence, North America and Eurasia have rotated clockwise with respect to northern Africa, moving North America away from the fused South America–western Africa and moving Asia toward eastern Africa (Spain was always adjacent to northern Africa); Antarctica and Australia moved southeastward away from Africa; India moved north from southern Africa and Antarctica and eventually (10 mya or later) smashed into Asia, buckling up the Himalayas; Madagascar split south away from the horn of Africa between 165 and 121 mya; South America moved west away from Africa (they last touched about 80 mya); Australia later moved north to its present position (as late as 60 mya Australia and Antarctica were connected); North America finally separated from Eurasia (as late as 40 mya it was fully or nearly connected to Scandinavia via Greenland, before moving westward), only to collide with Siberia 60 mya (they have been connected that long, but separated by very shallow water except in the Ice Age, when lowered sea level produced the Bering Land Bridge, with important consequences for the spread of plants, animals, *and* man as recently as 10,000 years ago).

These very-large-scale shifts necessarily produced myriad small-scale changes in the lands between major plates. The Yucatán Peninsula and Nicaragua were once squeezed solidly between North and South America where the Gulf of Mexico now lies, and the Greater Antilles lay south of Florida between the two continents, but Yucatán and Nicaragua moved southeastward and the islands moved south to their present positions. The same process of continental drift is now carrying Baja California and much of the California coast (to just north of San Francisco) northwestward toward the Aleutian Islands (movement along the crack here, the San Andreas Fault, caused the 1906 San Francisco earthquake).

Butterflies first arose probably in the tropical areas of Africa, America, and Eurasia about 100-80 mya, when South America still touched Africa, Africa barely touched Eurasia (along Spain), and Europe was still attached to northern North America. They were thus able to spread throughout these areas. India and Madagascar were 400 km or more from Africa and few if any butterflies reached them. Australia was very far from any source of butterflies (they could not have survived the South Pole crossing of Antarctica, to reach Australia from South America), and was not extensively populated by butterflies until recently. Judging from their current distributions, it would seem that all the butterfly families spread throughout the Americas, Africa, and Eurasia before Africa separated completely from South America. But the subfamilies Dismorphiinae, Pseudopontiinae, Trapezitinae, Megathyminae, Coeliadinae, Pyrrhopyginae, and perhaps Riodininae, Curetinae, and Lycaeninae apparently evolved after this split. One skipper genus, *Celaenorrhinus*, is abundant in the tropics of both the Americas and Africa, and may have been present before the split—though perhaps a female was simply blown across the growing Atlantic.

This drift of continents was of course slow: by contrast, a glacier is an avalanche. But all the while, climates were changing, mountains were rising or eroding, and—via the process of evolution—animal and plant life kept pace, adapting endlessly to change in the environment. What drives this process? Any successful undertaking—such as life—has two driving forces: first, the creation of ideas or things; and second, the selection of the best among these. The creative force in evolution is left largely to chance, which on a small scale creates mutations, and on a larger scale produces strange species (and odd structures) that proliferate or dwindle to extinction in later eons. The major changes produced by evolution may require the absence of competitors in a lenient environment, or sufficient isolation of a small colony that chance can allow mutants to spread, so that complex structures, such as a thoracic flap that can become a wing, or the precursor of the eye of a squid or mammal, can develop. Fluctuating populations can also help odd mutations to spread, for during the increases in population the mutants can multiply, and perhaps be spared in the subsequent population crash.

The second driving force in evolution is natural selection, which chooses which of the new creations is to survive. Usually selection merely eliminates harmful mutants that crop up in populations, a janitorial task. But vigorous traits can spread by reproducing more often than others, or, on a larger scale, entire species can become extinct. Both are outcomes of natural selection; the world would be a vastly different place today if some of the extinct species such as dinosaurs were still with us.

In Darwin's day it was thought that evolution proceeds too slowly for changes in a species' form or inherited behavior to be detectable, but that view was pessimistic. We know, for example, that the British Cabbage Butterfly often lays eggs in small clusters, but when introduced to America it relinquished this habit, perhaps because the offspring of those females that laid eggs only singly spread faster across the continent. *Phyciodes picta* (231) has switched from *Aster* as its main hostplant to *Convolvulus* just since the latter weed was introduced from Eurasia. And *Papilio zelicaon* (6) has begun eating *Citrus* trees in some areas. The number of eyespots of the British butterfly *Maniola* changes from year to year and between localities, because the larvae that produce the adults with greater numbers of spots suffer more deaths from parasitoid wasps. Around London (and even around Boston), where pollution has eliminated the pale lichens formerly prevalent on dark tree trunks, the moths resting on the lichens by day used to be pale-colored and thus well camouflaged, but since about 1850 many species have darkened toward a dark brown, simply because of the greater survival of dark mutants that birds could not so readily spot on the dark trunks. And a certain orchard fly has split, within the last 200 years and in the same orchards, into two almost-separate species, each eating a different fruit and flying at a different time of year. In East Africa a pale-colored indoor ecotype of the Yellow Fever Mosquito has evolved in the buried water-storage jars of native villagers just since this storage practice developed (perhaps a few thousand years ago), despite the presence of wild darker mosquitoes that hybridize with the indoor ones in the wet season. The developing resistance of insects to pesticides, and of microorganisms to antibiotics, is proof of astonishing adaptability, and may yet be the downfall of our civilization.

Generally, however, insects—butterflies, pests, or otherwise—take thousands or millions of years to evolve new species (see "Species and Subspecies," above), and our view of each species is like a single snapshot of the growth of a child. But by examining many species, we can deduce most aspects of the evolution of a species, just as the photos of many children and adults can elucidate human growth. Many butterflies are now *in the process* of forming species, and it is difficult, in these cases, to decide whether to give variations one name or two; some authors treat them as subspecies of one species, other authors as different species. Species of the *Papilio machaon* group (5-8) are good examples: very difficult to classify, and known to interbreed somewhat in nature. But the details of a single case, regarding its rates of evolution and whether subspecies will merge or become different species, we cannot tell.

Evolutionary changes have been going on for billions of years. All living things on earth today are thought to be descended from one bacterium-like creature that evolved in some primordial goo, rich in organic compounds, about 3.5-3.0 billion years ago. The first living thing may have been just one molecule like RNA that accidentally developed the ability to duplicate itself. Just one creature probably produced all our earthly life, because all animals and plants use the chemical DNA (or its relative RNA) for their genes, and they all contain left-handed amino acids (the building blocks of proteins). In some other solar system, there may be a planet with only right-handed amino acids.

The probable line of ancestry ultimately producing the butterflies (Fig. 41) can be traced from there on down to the present, through the thicket of branchings and rebranchings of other invertebrate groups, with some confidence

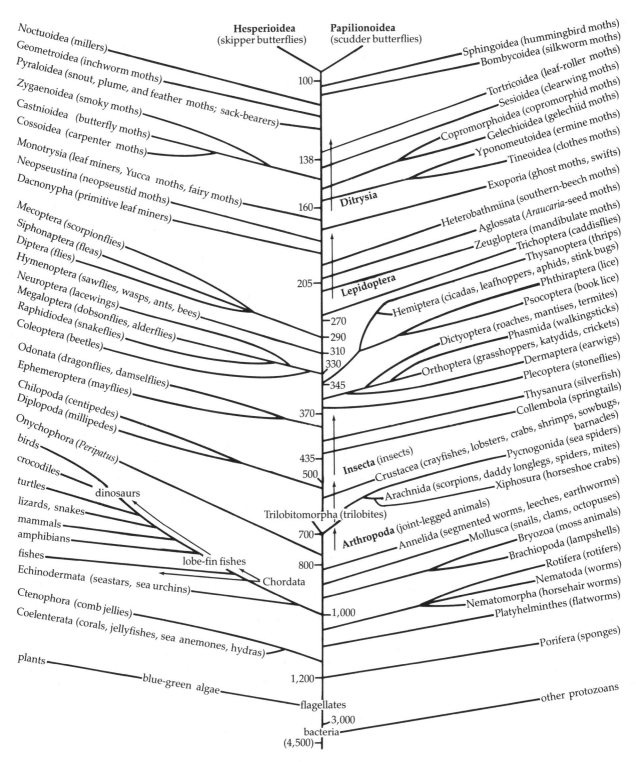

Fig. 41. The evolutionary tree of the animals, especially those along the line that evolved into butterflies. The numbers refer to millions of years ago.

(though of course we cannot be certain of the details). The first advance from the bacterium-like ancestor was the flagellate, still a single cell, but incorporating most of the features of the cells of larger animals, and differing not greatly from a human sperm cell. The next great advance, about 1.2 billion years ago, was the clustering of several different varieties of cell into one animal, represented by the sponges. The coelenterates later developed a primitive type of digestive cavity. Still later, the flatworms added a primitive brain and nerve cord, and the true worms evolved separate intestinal openings for feeding and elimination.

The invertebrate line branched at this point: one branch produced the echinoderms, the vertebrates (including dinosaurs and their living descendants, the crocodiles and birds), and eventually man, while the other produced lamp shells, bryozoans, mollusks, segmented worms, and eventually butterflies. External and internal body segments, like those of insects and other arthropods, were the most important advance made by the segmented worms, or Annelida. They also have brains and ventral nerve cords similar to those of insects, and some even have paddlelike lateral appendages. The next great advance, perhaps 800-600 mya, is represented by the Onychophora, which developed clawed, unsegmented legs on each body segment, as well as eyes and antennae. The living members of Onychophora, *Peripatus*, are soft-bodied creatures about the size of caterpillars, with insectlike tracheae; they prowl the forest floors of the American tropics catching insects by spitting a sticky substance at them. At some point, a creature of the general character of *Peripatus* finally developed a hard exoskeleton and segmented legs, and in the process initiated the Arthropoda. (Some zoologists, in fact, consider the segmented worms and the arthropods to constitute a single phylum.)

The front legs of the early arthropods, which they used for feeding, gradually shrank (and later became the fangs, mandibles, or other mouthparts). This early stage is represented by the trilobites, which flourished about 570-240 mya, then became extinct. Most were about 10 cm long (a few reached two-thirds of a meter) and scurried about the bottom of ancient seas looking for food and mates, each of their numerous legs carrying a gill for the intake of oxygen. Many varieties of primitive arthropods roughly similar to trilobites coexisted with them in the early seas.

One of these varieties produced the arachnids (spiders, scorpions, mites, etc.) and horseshoe crabs. These animals lost their antennae, and combined the head, two pairs of feeding appendages, and four pairs of legs into one "cephalothorax"; the gills (and later, lungs) retracted into the abdomen, and the first pair of legs became pincers in horseshoe crabs, fangs in spiders. The first arachnids were aquatic (a sea scorpion related to arachnids was nearly 2 m long), but land was the destiny of many groups—among the scorpions, for example, there were both aquatic and terrestrial forms. The sea spiders and the horseshoe crabs never left the sea; the latter, which first appear as fossils about 560 mya, have the distinction of being nearly unchanged during the last 200 million years.

Another of the trilobite variations, which later led to insects, developed mandibles from a pair of legs. The crustaceans, which developed from this mandibulate creature more than 500 mya, are a varied assortment of mostly aquatic creatures with gills, a head and thorax (commonly joined into a cephalothorax), an abdomen, and two pairs of antennae. One Japanese crab measures 3.5 m between leg tips.

Finally, at least 435 mya, some arthropods moved onto land. Among them were arachnids (scorpions much like those of today) and the insect ancestor, a mandibulate creature with about 15 or more pairs of legs. The next advance in this many-legger was the incorporation of the first three pairs of legs into the head (these legs in butterfly adults now form the mandible remnants, proboscis, and palpi). The modern centipedes and millipedes have multiplied the numerous body legs of trilobites and some crustaceans, but in the insect ancestor, about 435 mya, the body became divided into a head, a thorax with only six legs, and a legless abdomen.

The various insect orders, then, evolved in the period roughly 435-220 mya. Wings developed just before the ancestor of mayflies and dragonflies branched off the butterfly line (about 330 mya the largest insect that ever lived, a primitive dragonfly with a wingspan of nearly a meter, ruled the air over the swamps). Wings evolved, perhaps 410 mya, from flaplike outgrowths from the thorax segments, outgrowths that may have served as gills in the aquatic young of some early swamp insect (some modern mayfly young have flaplike gills on the abdomen, as well as wing pads on the thorax, and fossil Paleodictyoptera from 320 mya have prothoracic flaps, abdominal gill flaps, *and* wings). The leg muscles of insects attach to the top and sides of the inner walls of the thorax, and one aquatic nymph evidently discovered that these muscles cause the gill flaps to move a little, and thus aid in both swimming and obtaining oxygen in the stagnant swamp water.

Another theory has the flaps used originally to protect the legs and head of a forest-floor insect from falling seeds or other debris, or from the rough ceilings of crannies where the insects scurried; some modern roaches have such flaps on the prothorax as well as broad tough wings. But primitive winged insects have aquatic young, and strong proof of the gill origin of wings may be found in the extensive network of tracheae and veins in the wings of primitive insects, far in excess of any need of the wing itself for oxygen; advanced flying insects have lost most of these veins.

At any rate, because of some chance the flaps on one form were larger, enabling adults, which emerged from the water as do mayflies and dragonflies today, to glide between trees (like flying squirrels), perhaps to find another pool of water or more food or mates, or to escape a predator. Thus the individuals that could flap and glide farther left more offspring, and flight was gradually perfected. The wings had to develop on the thorax because only there were the muscles large enough; four wings were necessary to provide sufficient wing area for gliding (by using rapid wingbeats, flies have since made do with just two); and the wings had to be on the rear of the thorax because that location is closest to the center of weight along the body.

Wing-folding, to roof the wings over the abdomen, developed just before the stoneflies split off (butterflies later lost this ability). This development protected the wings from damage and allowed the insects to prowl through vegetation for food, and to hide in crannies again (the beetles still later turned their forewings into hard covers over the hindwings, making them perfectly adapted for crannies).

Larval and pupal stages, the basis of complete metamorphosis, then evolved just before the beetle and lacewing ancestors branched off. This important step permitted a sedentary larval stage to feed in a small but well-stocked larder, and

a flying adult stage to locate food and mates efficiently. The wasp and fly ancestors evolved next, and at last we come to the orders Trichoptera (caddisflies)
and Lepidoptera (moths and butterflies).

Though there is controversy regarding the origin of some insect groups, it is
universally agreed that the Trichoptera and Lepidoptera are closely related. They
share many traits, such as the production of silk by the larvae for nests and
cocoons, six Malpighian tubules (Figs. 26, 27), and the X and Y chromosomes of
the females (males have two X's). The ancestor of these two orders probably fed
on mosses and liverworts, as some scorpionflies (order Mecoptera) and mandibulate moths (suborder Zeugloptera) still do today. Sometime between 290 and
220 mya the Trichoptera split away from the moth line, and dropped from the
moss into streams and lakes. Today, the larvae in most species have gills and
construct silk cases with sand or debris; they pupate in a silk cocoon like moths,
and the adults chew their way out with the mandibles.

The remaining line (Fig. 41) became the Lepidoptera, the most recently
evolved of all the insect orders, excepting perhaps the fleas. Some Trichoptera
do have wing scales, but they are few and simple in structure, whereas the
Lepidoptera developed a solid covering of broad scales, each having many
ridges. The wing scales may initially have been used for camouflage, or for
decoration in attracting mates; the adults of the primitive Zeugloptera are in fact
day fliers and have metallic spots. The other proven functions of scales are as
"fur" for warmth; improving the airflow during flight (the hairs of Trichoptera
hinder the airflow); and as an escape device when the animals are snared in
spider webs.

The two labial palpi of Lepidoptera each developed a scent organ inside the
tip (Fig. 32); the third (middle) of the three tiny eyes (ocelli) that occur between
the two compound eyes of most adult insects was lost; a special rod developed
from the base of the tegula (Fig. 13) to the side of the thorax; and an epiphysis
(Fig. 14; used to clean the antennae) developed on the forelegs. Although ocelli
are absent in all butterflies (the twelve eyes of larvae are ommatidia) and the
epiphysis is absent in some, the other three traits are present in all Lepidoptera
(along with other more technical traits) and are found in no other insects.

The Lepidoptera then gradually split into eight suborders, one new one at a
time, a process probably completed between about 260 and 160 mya. The oldest
known lepidopteran fossils are several moths from Lebanon that lived about
120 mya (*Parasabatinca* of the suborder Zeugloptera, and others of suborder
Monotrysia). The most advanced of the eight suborders, Ditrysia, is represented
75 mya by a fossil egg that could be a noctuid moth or a skipper. Some wings
that fossilized about 280 mya (*Microptysma, Microptysmodes*), 260 mya, and 220
mya could be Lepidoptera or Trichoptera. Unfortunately, the wings of primitive
Lepidoptera and Trichoptera (and even some scorpionflies, Mecoptera) cannot
be distinguished (though Lepidoptera very rarely have four M veins, which is
usual in the others), so there is no way of knowing what these fossils represent.

The most primitive suborder of Lepidoptera, the Zeugloptera (mandibulate moths) still feed on wet mosses and liverworts, as did the ancestor of the
Lepidoptera. Although they look like so many tiny moths, they are primitive in
structure: adults, pupae, and larvae have grasshopper-like chewing mouthparts
(adults use their mandibles to feed on pollen, and pupae use them to chew out
of a tough silk cocoon); and adults have a cloaca (a combined mating, egg-

laying, and waste-elimination tube) on the abdomen tip. Larvae have rather long, primitive antennae, a small compound eye of clustered ommatidia, eight pairs of pointed abdominal prolegs like those of scorpionflies (order Mecoptera), peculiar suckers on abdomen segments 9 and 10, and four to eight rows of odd scalelike hairs (which reportedly camouflage them on the moss).

The next advance in the Lepidoptera was in the larva, whose antennae and mouthparts were modified, in the process coming to resemble those of butter-flies. The arrangement of larval hairs is primitive, being similar to that of scorpionflies and first-stage butterflies (Fig. 50; species 274). Pupae developed bizarre trumpet-shaped mandibles, each one as long as the width of the head. The Aglossata (represented today by one small Australia-Fiji family, the Aga-thiphagidae) then branched off. Their legless, nearly eyeless larvae bore into seeds, and the pupae use their enormous mandibles to break out of the seed. The adults are small and have grasshopper-like chewing mouthparts like those of the Zeugloptera, with which they probably eat pollen.

In time, the wings of the Lepidoptera lost a crossvein (between the Sc and R veins of the Zeugloptera and Aglossata forewings). The larval head developed adfrontal sulci and the cleavage lines that split during molting (Fig. 2), and the hypostomal bridge developed the narrow gap present today in butterflies (Fig. 3). The Heterobathmiina, represented today by the single family Heterobath-miidae of southern South America, originated at this point. The tiny adults of these moths still have mandibles; the pupae also have enormous mandibles; and the larvae have seven ommatidia in a circle and rather primitive legs but no prolegs. The larvae eat blotch-shaped mines inside the leaves of southern beech (*Nothofagus*—forests of these trees were widespread over the Southern Hemi-sphere as early as 130 mya).

The Lepidoptera line then produced an important innovation: the adult mandibles shrank to stumps, and a strawlike proboscis evolved to replace them (by butterfly standards, the proboscis was primitive: the two halves fit together only during feeding). The larval head also developed a spinneret for the applica-tion of silk. After these changes, the Dacnonypha branched off: their larvae are also leaf miners, mining the middle layer of a leaf (commonly of oak), and like Aglossata (and other leaf miners, even in suborder Ditrysia) they lack legs and prolegs and have only a vestigial eye; the pupae, as before, use enormous mandibles to break out of their silk cocoon; and the adults, which fly in the Northern Hemisphere and Australia, are tiny.

The proboscis of Lepidoptera improved with the addition of internal muscles to help it move, and the wing scales became hollow, as they are in butterflies (perhaps to reduce their weight?). The Neopseustina represent this stage of evolution. The single family Neopseustidae, so far known just from Asia and Chile, are small moths resembling Dacnonypha in most traits, though the odd proboscis has a separate feeding tube in each half, rather than the single com-bined feeding tube of other Lepidoptera; the larvae and pupae are still nearly unknown.

At about this point, the Lepidoptera larva at last developed true prolegs, with crochets and internal muscles, which as in butterfly larvae help to grasp objects (odd eversible lobes on the thorax and abdomen of Heterobathmiina and Dacnonypha larvae, some situated even dorsally, must have been the starting point for these prolegs); and on the true legs the trochanter and femur fused.

The cleavage lines on the larval head became positioned more centrally, like those of butterflies (Figs. 2, 23). The pupa lost the enormous trumpet-shaped mandibles entirely and became mummylike, with only the abdomen movable (the legs, antennae, and wings were previously not glued down). To enable the adult to emerge, a "cocoon-cutter" prong generally developed on the pupal head, together with backward-directed spines on the pupal abdomen that allow the pupa to wriggle partway out of the cocoon. (Some higher Lepidoptera use special thoracic hooks to rip the cocoon open, or dissolve the silk with an enzyme, or depart through an exit constructed like the entrance of a lobster trap; and butterflies have no cocoon at all.) Armed with these changes, the Exoporia branched off. Larvae of the main family Hepialidae (ghost moths, swifts) bore into the roots and stems of plants, and many of their larval hairs are in different positions than in the rest of the Lepidoptera. Ghost moths are small to large in size, usually lack a proboscis and do not feed (other exoporians do feed), and are fast fliers, the females commonly zooming about for a short time at dusk to find the pheromone-producing males. Females scatter up to a thousand tiny eggs during flight, and have three abdominal openings on the fused segments 9-10—for mating, egg-laying (an external groove or a short internal tube connects these two), and waste elimination.

The next advances in the Lepidoptera line mostly improved their flight. The hindwing shrank a little when veins Sc and R_1 combined into one vein and the other four R veins combined into another, Rs (Fig. 53). The coupling of this smaller hindwing to the forewing improved: the hindwings each developed one or more long bristles (the frenulum) that hook into a catch on the forewing (the retinaculum) to couple the wings together, replacing the jugum (a flap on the forewing base of the predecessor moths and caddisflies), which greatly diminished. In addition, the forewing Sc vein became single instead of forked. The proboscis improved with a zipperlike permanent coupling mechanism of the two halves, and the first abdomen segment became membranous beneath, improving oviposition. These changes preceded the split of the remaining Lepidoptera line into the suborders Monotrysia and Ditrysia. The Monotrysia larvae are leaf miners, case makers, or gall makers, or bore into seeds. The best-known monotrysian is the Yucca Moth; the small white female gathers the pollen of yucca flowers and jams it onto the stigma of another flower before laying eggs in the ovary, where the larvae later eat some of the seeds. The Monotrysia are so named because females have a cloaca (a single opening on the fused abdomen segments 9-10 for mating, oviposition, and elimination), as in all previous suborders except Exoporia.

The Ditrysia, the higher moths and butterflies, are so named because they have two openings on the abdomen for reproduction (Fig. 30), one for mating on segment 8 and a second for egg-laying on fused segments 9-10 (an internal sperm duct connects these two), as well as a third, intestinal, opening. These structures are similar to those of the Exoporia, but the two suborders are thought to have developed them independently. The Ditrysia also lost the short hairs so common on the wings of other Lepidoptera and Trichoptera. Adults are tiny to large in size, and the habits of adults and larvae vary greatly. It has been suggested that the ancestor of Ditrysia originally fed on detritus such as animal or plant remains, as some primitive Ditrysia (such as clothes moths) still do, and it was only later that some switched to feeding on living plants. But in the

Cretaceous period (138-63 mya), the flowering plants exploded in numbers of species, and the more advanced Ditrysia ate them and certainly evolved and exploded along with them, as did the bees, which pollinated them.

For some animals, such as fleas, there are no living or fossil intermediates to other, quite different animals, and their evolutionary origin is accordingly uncertain. Quite the reverse is true of the Lepidoptera: collectively, they show an obvious evolutionary progression leading finally to the suborder Ditrysia, to which the butterflies belong. The evolutionary progression itself is unquestioned, but precisely because the progression is almost unbroken, it has led to controversy regarding the names of the suborders (where along the continuum should boundaries be assigned?), and hardly any two authors agree on the same set of divisions or names. Thus the Zeugloptera have at times been named an order, and other suborders have only recently been separated. Most textbooks still lump all the suborders before Monotrysia together under one suborder name, the Homoneura (or Jugatae), and the Monotrysia and Ditrysia are often placed in Heteroneura (or Frenatae) even today, but each of the major branches of the Lepidoptera family tree should be treated equally.

Up to this point in the evolution of the Lepidoptera, we can be somewhat confident of the sequence of branches, owing to the work of N. Kristensen, H. Hinton, and I. Common. Numerous other technical traits (internal organs, etc.) support the sequence. But the Ditrysia—the rest of the Lepidoptera tree, moths and butterflies alike—are exploding in numbers of species, and morphologists have not been able to give them sufficient study (196,000 species, or 98 percent of all known Lepidoptera, are ditrysians; only beetles, with half a million species worldwide, exceed them in the entire animal kingdom). Thus some of the superfamilies that have been named, namely Zygaenoidea, Sesioidea, Yponomeutoidea, Gelechioidea, and Copromorphoidea, are rather doubtful in position, and taxonomists still routinely transfer whole families between some of these. Luckily the overall ditrysian tree can be constructed even though the positions of these side branches remain doubtful. And to alter some side roads, we need not reroute the highway.

The first two branches of ditrysians (Tineoidea-Yponomeutoidea and Gelechioidea-Copromorphoidea; see Fig. 41) have unique long ventral rods on the abdomen to join it to the thorax. In most traits, the Tineoidea (clothes moths, etc.) and Yponomeutoidea compete for the position as the most primitive ditrysian, and they are alone among the primitive ditrysians in usually having the larval hairs L1 and L2 far apart on each abdomen segment, as in Exoporia and Monotrysia. One family of Tineoidea, the Psychidae (bagworm moths) is curious: the female of many species never leaves her larval cocoon, a silked nest of twigs; the male finds the cocoon and mates with the imprisoned female; then she lays her eggs inside the cocoon, the eggs hatch, and the larvae disperse. Epipyropidae (Tineoidea) larvae are external parasites on cicadas and leafhoppers. The Gelechioidea and Copromorphoidea are nearly the only primitive ditrysians whose pupae do not wriggle out of the cocoon; the former has a scaly proboscis like that of the later-evolving Pyralidae.

In the ditrysian trunk, the two long ventral rods on the abdomen joint shrank to two short internal rods, and then the Cossoidea branched off. Their larvae include some wood borers and some leaf eaters; the adults do not feed and their mouthparts are vestigial. Though still primitive in most respects, they are char-

acterized by a unique softened cleft in the epimeron (Fig. 12), discovered by
J. Brock. The most peculiar family of Cossoidea is the Limacodidae: the larva is
saddle-shaped, with stinging hairs, and the prolegs are replaced by about 14
suckers; nearly all the abdomen segments and appendages of the pupa are
movable, and the pupa rests in a cocoon with a silken flanged lid like that on a
sugar bowl. The Zygaenoidea resemble Cossoidea in some ways, though probably branching from the stem of Cossoidea and Castnioidea; many are poisonous
and some are red in color to warn predators.

The Castnioidea (butterfly moths) have often been claimed to be the ancestors of butterflies because (1) they are day fliers with large, colorful wings like
those of butterflies, (2) the antenna club is shaped like that of some skippers,
and (3) the larvae bore through soil or stems, feeding on monocotyledons, in the
fashion of giant skippers. But these similarities are due to convergence. In fact,
at least 16 families of moths have some day-flying species with colorful wings
like those of butterflies (for example, Zygaenidae, Thyrididae, Uraniidae, some
Geometridae and Noctuidae, some Saturniidae and Sphingidae, and even some
Monotrysia, Yponomeutoidea, Gelechioidea, and Tortricoidea). The Uraniidae
resemble *Papilio* butterflies, and several of the butterfly-like moths (Thyrididae
and some Agaristinae noctuids) even have thickened antennae, as do other
moths (Sesiidae and Sphingidae)—although to find a really clubbed antenna we
have to look to the owlflies, in another insect order altogether, the Neuroptera.
The antenna of Castniidae (also of Uraniidae, Apoprogonidae, and Sematuridae)
is clubbed like that of some skippers, but J. Miller found that the microscopic
details of these antennae are totally different (the castniid antenna tip carries
a hairy plume, for instance). True, the larvae of giant skippers also bore into
monocotyledons, but they make a leaf nest when young, as other skippers do,
and there is reason to believe that the ancestral skipper fed on dicotyledons.
I. Common and E. Edwards recently studied the egg, all larval stages, and the
pupa of Castniidae, and their work proved conclusively that castniids are primitive ditrysians, similar to Cossoidea in nearly every respect; indeed the peculiar
positions of three olfactory pits on the larval head suggest that the Castniidae
split off from the base of the Cossoidea branch. The Cossoidea have also been
considered to be the butterfly ancestor, because in some species the heart, like
that of butterflies, has a chamber at the top of the thorax; but in other Cossoidea
the heart merely pulses along the esophagus as it does in most primitive ditrysians. Thus convergence explains even this trait. In fact about 40 major changes
would have to be made in the form of the eggs, larvae, pupae, and adults of
either of these groups, including all those mentioned below leading to the
butterfly line, if one were to transform them into butterflies.

Certainly butterfly moths and many other moths do resemble butterflies.
But why do they, and why don't all moths resemble butterflies? Most nocturnal
moths, and some diurnal ones as well, are dull in appearance because they rest
on bark or under stones by day and must be camouflaged to escape predation;
they find their mates by using pheromones. The female (rarely the male) rests,
and wafts a pheromone during that period of the night (or day) that is typical of
the species; the pheromone is carried downwind, where the male detects it; and
the male flies upwind to the female, where he may waft his own pheromone
to convince her that he is of the right species, at which point they mate. (The
pheromones of hundreds of moth species have now been chemically identified,

and in some cases pheromones synthesized in the laboratory are used in traps to catch wild moths of pest species.) The Sesiidae and some other day-flying moths still use pheromones to find their females, but more of the day-flying Lepidoptera have learned to navigate and locate their mates visually. Since sunlight encourages the development of color vision and colorful wings, for use in both mating and defense, many day fliers have developed butterfly-like wings.

The most important change in the ditrysian line after the Cossoidea and Castnioidea diverged was in the flight mechanism: the basalare of the metathorax (Fig. 12) lost its previous welded connections with the rest of the exoskeleton. Perhaps the first branch following this change was the Sesioidea; these moths mimic wasps, and their larvae bore into stems. After Sesioidea evolved, the main moth line certainly possessed a true pupal cremaster complete with hooks, as in many Tortricoidea, a large group consisting of leaf-rolling species and some fruit borers.

After Tortricoidea, the ditrysian larvae and pupae changed some. The larva lost the third L hair on the prothorax, a hair found on all but the first-stage larvae of earlier ditrysians (a postnatal hair; in butterflies this loss is sometimes obscured by an opposite trend, namely a forest of "secondary" hairs), leaving just two hairs; and the extra L hairs disappeared on abdomen segment 9, leaving only one (Fig. 50). The pupa fused even more, allowing only the three joints between segments 4 and 7 to move (in prior ditrysians, all the joints between segments 2 and 8 in males, and 2 and 7 in females, or even more, can move), and the pupa lost its abdominal spines and no longer must wriggle out of the cocoon. The adult wing lost the M vein in the discal cell.

The section Pyralidina (superfamily Pyraloidea) branched off here. In the Pyralidae there are ears (tympana), one on each side of the abdomen base, that can detect the ultrasonic cries of bats. Bats emit the ultrasound to echo-locate their prey at night and to avoid obstacles; a moth that hears a bat shifts to erratic, zigzag, or spiral flight to avoid being eaten. Some pyralid larvae (Nymphulinae) feed on underwater plants, taking in oxygen through many filamentous gills. Another pyralid, the Wax Moth, feeds on wax in beehives. And in the Pterophoridae, or plume moths, the wings are usually split into about three plumes each. The feather moths, Alucitidae, carry this trend to its bizarre extreme: each wing is split into six or seven "feathers," each formed of one narrow vein and a fringe of long overlapping scales. They truly reinvented the feather, about 50 million years after *Archaeopteryx* displayed the first known bird feathers. In another pyraloid family, the Mimallonidae, or sack-bearers, the larvae travel about with a silked-leaf case that conceals the body, much like the caddisflies (the Mimallonidae have been mistakenly placed in the Bombycoidea).

The prior ditrysians and the seven other suborders are popularly termed microlepidoptera, because of their usually small size. But some are large, and because they are also a diverse lot, the term is useless scientifically.

The remaining ditrysians are jointly called the section Macrolepidoptera, in reference to their usually large size (the six other ditrysian sections are the Pyralidina and the five main branches off the base of the ditrysian trunk of Fig. 41). But unlike the so-called microlepidoptera, they are a distinctive group, and they share many advanced features. The maxillary palpi (Fig. 9) are tiny on adults, absent on pupae (earlier moths have two pairs of palpi). On adults, a fold at the base of the forewing—the last vestige of the jugum of primitive

Lepidoptera—has finally disappeared, the CuP vein (Fig. 53) has become rudimentary, the postmedian wing lever (Fig. 12) has lengthened for more-efficient flight, the internal keel in front of the furca of Figure 22 has increased in size, and the heart always loops to the top of the thorax (this loop does occur in a few other moths). On the larva, hairs L1 and L2 have moved far apart on each abdomen segment (Fig. 50). Some of these traits may appear trivial, a splitting of hairs, but it is just such details that provide the clues to reconstructing the true ancestor of a living organism, because the ancestors themselves have fled the scene. The Macrolepidoptera are the most distinctive group of ditrysians, and attempts to derive their several groups independently from two or three groups of microlepidoptera are misguided and ignore the above traits.

The Geometroidea and Noctuoidea are the earliest lineages of Macrolepidoptera; their larvae usually have only the few primary hairs, and in many of them the crochets are of just one length, as in most microlepidopterans. Adults of several species of Noctuidae (*Calype*) from Laos to Malaysia use their proboscis to suck the blood of live animals; they rock their head left and right to force proboscis halves alternately into the victim. The inchworm moths, Geometridae, their larval prolegs usually only on abdomen segments 6 and 10, travel by looping the middle of the body upward like a ferret, then pushing the body forward, inching forward with each loop. One Hawaiian inchworm is predaceous, mimicking a twig while awaiting a passing insect. Geometroidea have ears (tympana) on the base of the abdomen that probably indicate descent from the ancestor of Pyralidae; the Noctuoidea ears moved to the rear of the thorax, though a hood commonly remains on the abdomen. Half of the North American Lepidoptera species, and the three largest families (Noctuidae, Geometridae, and Pyralidae), have ears, a testimonial to the voracious appetite of bats. The Noctuoidea lay their eggs upright (with the sperm pores on the top), as in butterflies (almost all other Lepidoptera lay their eggs flat, the sperm pores to the side).

The ancestor of Bombycoidea, Sphingoidea (Sphingidae), and butterflies apparently was a day flier, because these groups lack ears, and many of them today are day fliers and beautifully colored. The crochets are always in two lengths in this group (in butterflies, often three), and there are always at least a few extra ("secondary") hairs on older larvae. There are no ocelli on the heads of adults, and a particular ridge on the side of the thorax is missing. The Bombycoidea include the largest moths, among them the Atlas Moth and others up to 25 cm in wingspan, which do not feed as adults. The superfamily also includes the silkworm, whose cocoon, when scalded and unraveled, is the source of silk; each silkworm cocoon can produce a kilometer of silk for use in making thread. Most Bombycoidea retain the featherlike antennae of the Noctuoidea, but the antenna of most Sphingidae, which is shaped like a baseball bat and is even hooked at the tip, may be the true forerunner of the antenna of butterflies. The Sphingidae and butterflies are the only Macrolepidoptera lacking a strong cocoon (Sphingidae pupate in the soil, sometimes in a flimsy cocoon). Sphingidae, variously called hawkmoths, sphinx moths, and hummingbird moths, resemble hummingbirds in flight, and some species have an enormous proboscis, 10 cm long or longer, which they use to feed on tubular flowers while hovering. Most Sphingidae are night fliers or dusk fliers; others are day fliers and mimic bumblebees.

At last we come to the butterflies, subsection Rhopalocera (of section Macrolepidoptera). It consists of two superfamilies, Hesperioidea (skippers) and Papilionoidea (scudders). But whether the name Rhopalocera should be applied to butterflies is open to question, for Brock lumps skippers into the Papilionoidea with scudders, and others feel that names like Rhopalocera should not be used until the Macrolepidoptera classification is more confidently resolved. In the meantime, and regardless of the name one chooses to use, scientists agree that butterflies form a compact group, distinctly separate from moths. But it is also clear that butterflies constitute just one subsection of ditrysian moths, and not a suborder as once classified. Butterflies of course are day fliers, with large vision lobes on the brain, and their antennae are clubbed. Their nonfoldable wings lack the frenulum and retinaculum that hook most moth wings together (except in the skipper *Euschemon*, where they represent, I suspect, a reactivation of dormant genes). But beyond these obvious traits, butterflies are distinguished from the microlepidoptera by all the traits characterizing the Macrolepidoptera, as listed above. And they *differ* from various Macrolepidoptera in many other traits. Adults lack ocelli, but do have chaetosema (Fig. 10; the only other Macrolepidoptera that have chaetosema are Geometroidea); the areole—a small cell enclosed by R veins above the discal cell, present in all other superfamilies—is absent; two membranous clefts on the side of the thorax of these others are absent; the heart has a unique enlarged chamber in the top of the thorax (present in a few Cossoidea moths); and the two ventral rods on the abdomen (that help connect it to the thorax) are tiny. With only the Noctuoidea they share upright eggs and a ventral neck gland on the older larvae, used for defense. The crochets form a circle in most young larvae and in young and old skipper larvae (they form a crescent in most other Macrolepidoptera, and in most older larvae of scudders), and they occur in three lengths (sometimes two, rarely one); older larvae have a forest of hairs, at least on the underside. And the pupae lack a cocoon (the only other Macrolepidoptera to lack a cocoon are the Sphingoidea).

The earliest fossil butterflies known are several species of Papilionidae (one close to modern *Baronia* of the Baroniinae), one species of Nymphalidae (Satyrinae), and one species of Lycaenidae (Riodininae), all from the Eocene period about 48 mya. Many more fossil butterflies, including various Papilionidae, Pieridae, Nymphalidae (Nymphalinae and Satyrinae), Libytheidae, Lycaenidae, and Hesperiidae, are known from the Lower Oligocene period 38 mya. All of the modern butterfly families are thus known to have evolved fully by this time, probably by much earlier (perhaps 100-80 mya), and three of the younger fossils are very similar to species of *Libytheana*, *Doxocopa*, and *Hypanartia* that are found in North America today.

Figure 42 shows how I believe the families and subfamilies of the world's butterflies evolved. Clearly, they evolved along with the flowering plants (see "Larval Foods," above); the original butterfly larva, I believe, ate the leaves of the peas (Leguminosae). This ancestral tree is based on hundreds of external and internal traits of adults, pupae, and larvae, as well as their behavior and habits. It draws heavily, of course, on the findings and theories of others, and the taxonomic names used are time-honored, all more than 30 years old. Another study of the similarity of numerous adult structures, by P. Ehrlich, produced results consonant with the tree in Figure 42. The lines in the figure represent the genealogy of butterflies, and the arrangement of the groups from top to bottom reflects Ehrlich's computer-generated tree of overall similarity. The arguments for the tree's branchings are detailed in the *Journal of Research on the Lepidoptera* (1984), and only the more interesting nontechnical traits can be mentioned here (some traits are used in the keys in Part II, others in the family and subfamily texts in Part III). The tree is controversial chiefly in not raising the subfamilies of Nymphalidae and Lycaenidae to family level. Actually these subfamilies are not as distinctive as those of Papilionidae, Pieridae, and some Hesperiidae. Moreover, the most recent revision of the families of scudders, by Ehrlich, accepts only my five families.

Because all the subfamilies that contain many species are worldwide in distribution, it can be assumed that butterflies diversified into families and most subfamilies *before* Africa, America, and Eurasia split apart and went their separate ways in the process of continental drift, but *after* Australia and Madagascar had split away, because these areas have depauperate butterfly faunas derived from adjacent continents. But because butterflies are strong fliers, migrations

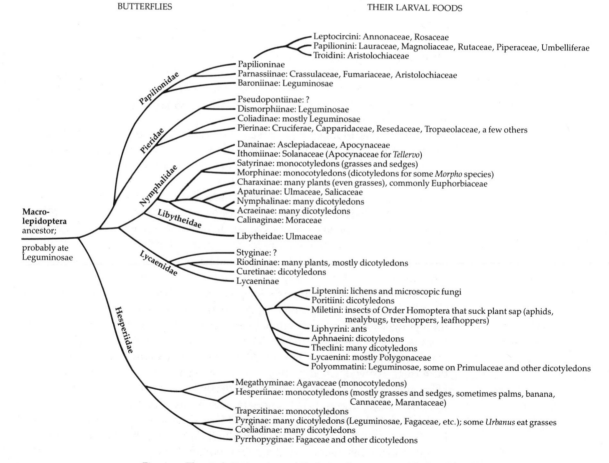

Fig. 42.   The evolutionary tree of the butterfly groups, with their larval hostplants.

and winds have also undoubtedly helped distribute them over most of the world.

Skippers (superfamily Hesperioidea) were the first group to split off from the butterfly line, in the Cretaceous period. Their most distinctive features are their bent antenna club and silked-leaf larval nests. Because outer crochets are needed to grip these nests, each proleg carries a full circle of crochets. The narrow larval neck helps the animal flex about while silking the nest into a tube. Skippers pupate in the nest, and mature larvae use glands beneath abdomen segments 7 and 8 to produce a water-repellent powder that keeps the pupa dry.

Early in their evolution, the skippers split into two groups. The more primitive group, leading to our Pyrginae and Pyrrhopyginae, continues to eat dicotyledons (some *Urbanus* later switched to monocotyledons). Except that it is angled, the antenna club is like that of the scudders (Fig. 11). W. Evans suggests that the widening Atlantic Ocean caused the Pyrrhopyginae and Coeliadinae to diverge. The second group of skippers, producing our Hesperiinae and Megathyminae, switched to monocotyledons (grasses, sedges, etc.) for food. Their antenna tip shrank to an angled point of the club (Fig. 11), a unique basking posture developed (the hindwings are spread more than the forewings), and some of the hairs on first-stage larvae were lost.

The antenna club of scudders (Papilionoidea) remained (or became) straight, but the forewing R veins began to merge with each other. The first branch of scudders, that leading to the Papilionidae and Pieridae, differs from other scudders in the shape of the cells of the retina, in the top of the tarsi of the legs, which took on a covering of spines, and in the metathorax, which is somewhat different in shape. Most males of these two families patrol to seek females, and the primitive members of both families still feed on Leguminosae.

The Papilionidae and Pieridae then diverged. The Papilionidae have a separate little vein 2A on the forewing, not joined to 1A, and except for the primitive Baroniinae, they lack vein 3A on the hindwing, probably because of the scent fold that developed there (a fold like that of *Eurytides*, Fig. 36). Larvae extrude a unique forked organ, the osmeterium, for defense, and pupae have two bumps on the head. The primitive Baroniinae eat Leguminosae, but the remaining Papilionidae evidently switched to Aristolochiaceae before diversifying to their current set of hosts.

The Pieridae are mostly yellow and orange, the color deriving from the many pterine pigments in their scales. Their pupae have only a single cone on the head, and the pupal wings are generally oddly expanded (Fig. 52). The claws on the adult legs are peculiarly forked. One branch of Pieridae, leading to Dismorphiinae and Pseudopontiinae, has strange wing veins (Fig. 55) and equally weird male mating structures. The two subfamilies diverged when the Atlantic Ocean developed (though one genus of Dismorphiinae later spread to Eurasia across the Bering Strait). Females of the other branch of Pieridae, producing Coliadinae and Pierinae, are distinguished by the unique, complex scent lobes on the abdomen (Fig. 36); mated females display these lobes to repel other males.

The branch of scudders leading to Lycaenidae, Libytheidae, and Nymphalidae has relatively small wings and a slightly different shape to the metathorax, and many of their males perch to await females. Strangely, the ancestor of this branch must have had very small forelegs (at least in males), because these families all clean their antennae with the middle legs, using special brushes on the femur and tibia; other Lepidoptera use the forelegs, and the epiphysis on the foreleg of these others (Fig. 14) is designed for cleaning. U. Jander found that the middle leg cleans the antenna even in those Lycaenidae whose forelegs are now large enough to do it.

Lycaenidae larvae evolved many novel features. On their prolegs is a strange extra lobe for crawling, and their bodies are slug-shaped and sport various glands (including honeydew glands) that they use for defense against ants (see "Mimicry and Other Defenses," above). The original lycaenid probably fed on small fruits and flowers that ants visited for nectar, a circumstance that would explain both the small size of lycaenids and their ant defenses. The most primitive subfamily of Lycaenidae is the Styginae. The next two subfamilies, Curetinae and Riodininae, are distinguished by a long extension of the coxa past the trochanter of the male foreleg (Fig. 16). Riodininae developed some odd veins on the hindwing base (Fig. 55), a feather-duster male foreleg, and a unique hairy larval mandible; and the positions of their ant glands changed. The most recently emerging subfamily, Lycaeninae, lost some structures on the mesothorax and on the male abdomen that the other subfamilies retain today. The Riodininae (and Styginae) evolved mainly in the Americas, the Lycaeninae (and Curetinae) largely in the Old World.

The ancestor of Libytheidae and Nymphalidae lost the silken girdle around their pupae, which now hang upside down from the cremaster. The Libytheidae, the first branch from this lineage, have a primitive larva that has even *lost* a few hairs. The Nymphalidae, the remaining scudders, continued the shrinking trend on the foreleg, which in this group is small even in the females. The larvae of Nymphalidae have pursued a trend opposite that of the Libytheidae: they tend to *add* hairs, as well as filaments and spines; the first larval type (in Danainae and Ithomiinae) produced extra hairs on the first stage and fleshy filaments on older larvae, the second type (in Calinaginae, Satyrinae, Morphinae, Charaxinae, Apaturinae) developed head horns and two tails but lacks filaments, and the last type (in Nymphalinae and Acraeinae) developed a fearsome armor of branching spines and lost the tails. Strangely, males of Danainae and Ithomiinae seek certain plants containing the chemical lycopsamine, which they suck up and use to produce their mating pheromones. Satyrinae and Morphinae generally eat monocotyledons, though some *Morpho* have switched to dicotyledons. Morphinae are distinguished chiefly by having an extremely hairy larval head, with hair tufts on the body as well; Satyrinae are notable for their larger third larval eye. The remaining nymphalids generally lack a vein closing the end of the discal cell, and their young larvae pursue the odd practice of silking a ball of dung to a leaf vein after eating away the surrounding leaf. The Charaxinae are an early representative. The Apaturinae larva resembles that of Charaxinae, but adults resemble the Nymphalinae in lacking the anepisternum (Fig. 12). The Acraeinae share with the Nymphalinae the spiny larva, but exhibit some unusual features as well (see "Family Nymphalidae," in Part III).

Much more remains to be learned about the evolution of butterflies. Older fossils would be a boon, and morphological and behavioral studies on living moths and butterflies will help determine who is related to whom. Good studies of the tribes of Hesperiidae, Pieridae, and Nymphalidae have still not been undertaken.

"The Butterfly Census" (below) lists the numbers of species and genera of the butterfly subfamilies and families, as well as of the other suborders of Lepidoptera; the causes of the great diversity of the Lepidoptera are discussed there and in the Introduction.

Habitats and Life Zones

Butterflies can be found in most habitats in North America. Some species (*Colias philodice* and *Vanessa cardui*, for example) are widespread, occurring in numerous habitats, but most species are quite restricted in their habitats, as well as in their hostplants and flight periods. Even areas of mostly bare rock support butterflies if there is vegetation among the rocks (arctic/alpine species like *Erebia magdalena*, *E. occulta*, *Oeneis melissa*, *Chlosyne gabbii damoetas*, and *Lycaena cupreus* occur in very rocky places). Grassy alpine tundra is home for many characteristic species of *Parnassius*, *Colias*, *Erebia*, *Oeneis*, and *Boloria*. Dense forests are not hospitable; almost no butterflies fly there. But bogs within the forest support a few characteristic species such as *Colias scudderi*, *Oeneis jutta*, bog fritillaries (*Boloria*), *Lycaena dorcas*, *L. epixanthe*, and *Plebejus optilete*. Woodland openings may host *Anthocharis sara*, *Pieris napi*, and other species.

Marshes are suitable for a few more species. Characteristic species of these habitats are most of those with sedge-eating larvae, such as *Lethe eurydice*, *Neonympha areolata*, *Problema bulenta*, *Poanes viator*, *P. massasoit*, most *Euphyes*, and others. Wet meadows support many species, including *Speyeria idalia*, *S. nokomis*, *Boloria*, and many *Polites* skippers. *Callophrys hesseli* occurs in white-cedar swamps. *Ochlodes yuma* is found at seeps and along rivers.

Urban areas provide varied habitats for many butterflies, bringing together species usually found in woodlands (such as *Papilio glaucus*, *P. polyxenes*, *Nymphalis antiopa*, *Limenitis*, *Asterocampa*, and *Epargyreus*), moist meadows (*Polites*, *Hylephila*, and *Atalopedes*), and weedy habitats (*Pieris rapae*, *Colias eurytheme*, *Pyrgus communis*, *Pholisora catullus*, and others).

Dry habitats are also home to many characteristic species. Grasslands support many grass-feeding species (such as *Neominois*, *Oarisma*, *Yvretta*, *Hesperia*, *Atrytone*, *Problema byssus*, *Atrytonopsis*, and *Amblyscirtes*), and other butterflies are frequently found in grasslands (*Euchloe olympia*, *Euptoieta*, *Chlosyne gorgone*, and *Megathymus*).

The characteristic species of chaparral habitats (mostly dry hilly areas with many non-thorny shrubs) include *Papilio eurymedon*, *Nymphalis californica*, *Satyrium* hairstreaks, *Oarisma edwardsii*, and some *Erynnis* skippers.

Dunes look inhospitable and dry, but because the rain seeps freely down into the sand, plants like *Eriogonum* with long roots may survive well. *Chlosyne gabbii gabbii*, *Callophrys dumetorum*, some *Euphilotes*, and others fly there.

Deserts, too, have their own characteristic species, such as *Papilio polyxenes coloro*, *Anthocharis cethura*, *Euchloe hyantis*, *Dymasia dymas*, *Texola elada*, *Asterocampa leilia*, *Libytheana carinenta larvata*, *Callophrys xami*, *C. fotis*, *C. mcfarlandi*, *Systasea*, and *Celotes*.

The American tropics support more butterfly species than any other region in the world, and because many range or stray into south Texas, Texas counts more species than any other state or province. Arizona is next, followed by the southern Rocky Mountain states (New Mexico, Colorado, Utah) and California.

Several factors combine to allow greater numbers of species in mountainous regions than in flat regions. Perhaps most important is the greater number of habitats: windy ridges, stream bottoms, hot south-facing slopes, and cool, wooded, north-facing slopes bring different habitats into close proximity, and alpine tundra and desert may occur within a short distance of each other. Hilltops and gulches allow the species that mate in these separate sites to coexist comfortably. Compounding the advantage of mountainous regions is the unfortunate fact that except for some deserts and the Canadian taiga, it is the flat areas that are largely plowed or "developed" by people, thus eliminating many butterfly habitats.

The habitat of each butterfly species may be described by the conspicuous plants present there or by the general shape of the plants, and by the terrain. Since butterflies seem limited in distribution mostly by the distribution of their larval hostplants and by temperature, so-called life zones, based on temperature and predominant plant cover, are often used to characterize butterfly habitats (Fig. 43). These life zones also take into account the change of plants and butter-

Ice

Arctic / Alpine

Hudsonian

Canadian

Transition

Upper Austral / Upper Sonoran

Lower Austral / Lower Sonoran

Subtropical

Fig. 43.   The life zones of North America. The arctic part of the Arctic/Alpine Zone lies along the northern rim of Canada and northern and western Alaska; the alpine part of this zone is in the mountains southward, surrounded by other zones.

flies with altitude and latitude; an increase of 1 m in altitude is equivalent to an increase of about 950 m in latitude in the species of plants and butterflies that occur there.

The Arctic/Alpine Life Zone embraces the treeless area in northern Canada and Alaska (the Arctic) and the cold, treeless tops of forested mountains (the Alpine). The Hudsonian Zone, south of the Arctic and lower than the Alpine, sustains small trees of spruce, fir, willow, and, in Canada, Jack Pine and Tamarack. The Canadian Zone, occupying most of southeastern Canada and moderate altitudes in the mountains to northwestern Georgia and New Mexico, also exhibits fir, spruce, Tamarack, and some pines, but it supports greater stands of aspen, maple, birch, alder, and some hemlock. The Hudsonian and Canadian Zones sustain acid bogs with sphagnum moss, as well. The Transition Zone usually contains Ponderosa Pine in the West, a grassland-forest mixture in the Midwest, and numerous deciduous trees, White Pine, hemlock, etc., in the East. The Austral Zone in the East is divided: the Upper Austral supports relatively pure deciduous woodland, turning to grassland in the West; the Lower Austral, in the Southeast and the coastal plain, is characterized by hard-pine forests, Live Oak, magnolias, palmettos, and swamps. The Sonoran Zone, the western analogue of the Austral Zone, is also divided: the Upper Sonoran grows pinyon-juniper woodland, chaparral, arid sagebrush, and dry prairie; and the Lower Sonoran is the dry thorny desert of southeastern California, southern Nevada, southern Arizona, and west and central Texas. The Subtropical Zone in southern Florida and southern Texas supports many tropical plants and animals.

Species Distributions and Remnant Species

Why does a species occur only in certain places and not in others? Its range may be small, just a few states or a part of a state, and within the range it may occur only at scattered sites. The answer is that butterflies do not survive equally well in all microhabitats and climates; each species has adapted to survive best in places with a particular combination of hostplants, weather, and other necessities. In many cases a species could persist in another area if introduced there, but unsuitable intervening habitats contain it within its present range. For instance, *Boloria alberta* (246) would probably persist in the Alpine Zone of Colorado if it were introduced from the Alpine Zone of Alberta, where it does occur.

Knowing the edges of a species' range can help us understand why it occurs only in certain places. Figure 44a plots the edges of the ranges of all the North American butterflies (ignoring the isolated records of migratory species). Such a "spaghetti diagram" is often used to study the barriers to the distribution of animals and plants. The lines are most dense where many species begin or end their range. From this map, it is obvious that a major boundary to the distribution of many butterfly species is presented by the climatic changes in mountain ranges, such as the Rocky Mountains, the Sierra Nevada, the Mogollon Rim in Arizona, and even the more modest California Coast Ranges and the Appalachian Mountains. Many Rocky Mountain species also occur in separate populations in the hills of western Nebraska and the Black Hills of South Dakota and North Dakota. The arctic treeline and the northern coniferous forest are barriers to many species, and the edge of the eastern deciduous forest, running roughly from eastern Texas to Minnesota, stops many species. The desert edge in Arizona, California, Nevada, and southwestern Oregon is the edge of the range of many species. Freezing temperatures mark the northward limits of many tropical species in Texas and Florida.

Because all these barriers correspond with known temperature or precipitation differences, it is likely that temperature and precipitation are the major factors determining the distribution of butterflies. Corroboration is evidently to be seen in a number of lines running across Canada—the temperature line marking a June average daily maximum of 12.5°C (54.5°F), the line marking a July average daily maximum of 16°C (60°F), the treeline, and the northern range limits of many butterflies—all of which reach almost to the Arctic Ocean along the Mackenzie River Delta (near Alaska), but farther east dip southward around the bottom of Hudson Bay, thence again northward. Summer (and spring) temperatures are more important than winter ones in determining the range of temperate-zone butterflies because the winter diapause stages are capable of withstanding a wide variation of freezing temperatures.

Figures 44c-k, based on the spaghetti diagram (Fig. 44a), show the major butterfly faunas that exist in North America. A "fauna" is all the species that share the same distribution, more or less. (The corresponding term for plant cover is "flora.") The Arctic/Alpine Fauna consists of a few dozen species, many with a biennial life cycle. This fauna occupies the same areas as the Arctic/Alpine Life Zone (Fig. 44c), except that most of the isolated alpine areas, which support alpine plants, have no strictly alpine butterflies, apparently because these areas are too small to support the butterflies, which became extinct there. In the Ice Age most of North America was covered with ice, except for parts of Alaska, the Yukon, Banks Island, and a few other areas (Fig. 44b). The Alpine Zone was widespread in the United States then, even occurring on the southern Wyoming continental divide, which is only 2,150 m high, but by 10,000 years ago the ice melted nearly everywhere except Greenland and a few small localities. The period from about 9,000 to 4,500 years ago was even warmer than today, and the alpine areas shrank to such an extent that only the largest alpine areas of the Rockies retained their alpine species (the Sierra and the White Mountains of California retain very few). Alpine species sometimes disappeared even in major parts of their alpine habitats (for instance, *Erebia callias*, which now occurs only in southwestern Asia and the southernmost Rockies, *E. magdalena*, *Oeneis polixenes*, *O. bore*, *Boloria napaea*, *B. improba*, *B. astarte*, and *B. alberta*). A few arctic species (*Parnassius eversmanni*, *Erebia occulta* and relatives, *Oeneis alpina*, *Boloria natazhati*, and *B. astarte distincta*) survived the Ice Age in the Alaska–northwestern Canada refuge (Fig. 44b) rather than south of the ice.

The Boreal Forest Fauna (Fig. 44d) supports many species in its cold, mostly coniferous forests. It combines the Hudsonian and Canadian Life Zones, because butterflies seldom distinguish these zones (Fig. 44a; many plants are shared by these zones too). The Arctic/Alpine and Boreal Forest Faunas overlap other faunas where they extend southward in the mountains.

The Eastern Deciduous Forest Fauna (Fig. 44e) counts numerous species whose distributions stop at the edge of the northern coniferous forest and Great Plains. It includes the Transition and Upper and Lower Austral Life Zones, because few butterflies stop at the boundaries between these zones, though some species' distributions correspond somewhat with the Lower Austral Zone. A few species of this fauna are limited to the Atlantic and Gulf Coast, often in swamps.

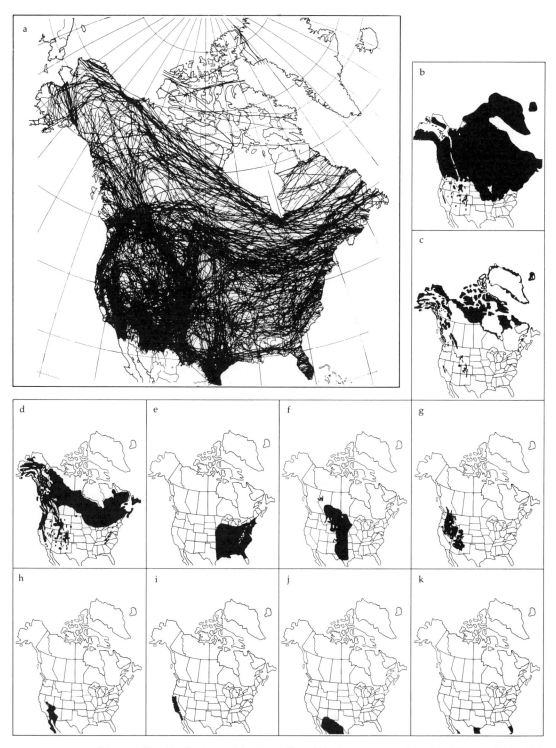

Fig. 44.   The distributions of the butterflies of North America: *a*, "spaghetti diagram," in which each line represents the edge of the range of a species (the lines are densest where mountain ranges or major differences in temperature or rainfall prevent butterflies from spreading); *b*, area of ice in the Ice Age; *c*, Arctic/Alpine Fauna of butterflies; *d*, Boreal Forest Fauna; *e*, Eastern Deciduous Forest Fauna; *f*, Great Plains Fauna; *g*, Great Basin Fauna; *h*, Mojave Desert Fauna; *i*, Californian Fauna; *j*, Mexican Plateau Fauna; *k*, Subtropical Fauna.

The Great Plains Fauna (Fig. 44*f*) consists of a few dozen species, many having grass hostplants. This fauna occupies the Lower Austral/Lower Sonoran, Upper Austral/Upper Sonoran, and Transition Zones from Texas to Canada. A remnant of this fauna even occurs in west-central Alberta in grassland along the Peace River.

The Great Basin Fauna (Fig. 44*g*) occurs in sagebrush and grassland flatlands in the Upper Sonoran Zone, and in the adjacent mountain foothills. Many species of this fauna are paler, thus better camouflaged—*Speyeria callippe* (259) is even gray-green on the underside, to match the sage.

The Mojave Desert Fauna (Fig. 44*h*) occupies the shrubby Lower Sonoran Zone and lower mountains. Butterflies of this fauna fly most abundantly in early spring.

The Californian Fauna (Fig. 44*i*) has many characteristic species in the lowlands of California and Baja California. This area has a "mediterranean" climate, with cool, rainy winters and hot dry summers. Adults fly mostly in spring, except along watercourses. In the Ice Age this fauna was largely southward in Baja California.

The Mexican Plateau Fauna (Fig. 44*j*) includes many characteristic species of the mountains of southeastern Arizona to west Texas, mostly in the Upper Sonoran and Transition Zones. Most of these species extend as far south as Mexico City. Summer rains produce good flights of butterflies here.

The Subtropical Fauna (Fig. 44*k*) is a very large set of species that barely enter southern Texas and Florida, many only as strays. Most of them cannot survive freezing temperatures.

By and large, the distribution of a given species is relatively continuous; the distance between suitable habitats within that distribution is fairly small. However, when the lepidopterist has established all the habitats that should be "suitable" for that species (that have the right climate and hostplants), he or she may find that the species nonetheless occurs in only some of them and is unaccountably absent in some seemingly good habitats. The species may have died out in these spots, or it may never have dispersed there; it may have subtle requirements for overwintering places, or occasional floods, drought, or other factors might make certain localities unsuitable. Some species occur only in the mountains, not in the intervening lowlands. Other species have disjunct ranges of several parts, separated by as much as several hundred kilometers, even though suitable habitats occur between the populated areas. Most likely the intervening areas were once inhabited also, under earlier suitable conditions, but when those earlier conditions changed from suitable to unsuitable (before changing back later to suitable), those populations died out. Many butterflies with this type of distribution are alpine species, as noted above. Some occur in lower mountains, (*Colias pelidne, Erebia theano, Oeneis alberta*, western *Lycaena phlaeas*, and *Plebejus idas* in the southern Rockies).

Other species occur as lower-altitude remnants, and their distributions are mysteries. For examples, look at the maps for *Neonympha areolata mitchellii, Cercyonis meadii*, and *Chlosyne gorgone* colonies; *Apodemia mormo* in Montana; *Habrodais grunus* in Arizona; *Fixsenia favonius* and *Callophrys sheridanii* in New Mexico and Arizona; *Erora laeta, Hesperia attalus, Polites peckius*, and *P. themistocles* in the West; and *Atrytone arogos, Poanes viator*, western *P. hobomok, Euphyes bimacula, E. dukesi, Atrytonopsis hianna, Autochton cellus*, and *Pyrgus ruralis*. These remnant distributions seem to be natural, rather than the result of human destruction of more widespread habitats.

Though the distributions of most species follow the life zones or other vegetational features, there are some odd cases in which one species replaces a second species geographically in the same life zone, even though both have the same hostplant. In rare cases the second species also replaces a third. These species divide up what seems to us to be one habitat. In nearly all cases of geographical replacement the participants are closely related species within the same genus. Thus the maps of Part III show the replacement phenomenon within these groups: *Parnassius clodius* and *eversmanni*; *Papilio zelicaon, polyxenes*, and *brevicauda*; *Pieris napi* and *virginiensis*; *Colias interior, palaeno*, and *pelidne*; *C. alexandra* and *occidentalis*; *Cercyonis sthenele* and *meadii*; *Oeneis nevadensis* and *macounii*; *O. bore* and *polixenes* in the United States (except central Wyoming); *Speyeria aphrodite* and *zerene*; *S. hydaspe* and *adiaste*; *Boloria kriemhild, epithore*, and *bellona*; *Phyciodes morpheus* and *tharos*; *P. batesii* and *campestris*; *Polygonia comma* and *satyrus*; *Limenitis arthemis, weidemeyerii*, and *lorquini*; *Satyrium acadica* and *sylvinus*; *Callophrys eryphon* and *niphon*; *Everes comyntas* and *amyntula*; *Hesperia comma* and *?metea*; *Polites peckius* and *sonora*; *Erynnis martialis* and *pacuvius*; *E. juvenalis* and *telemachus*; *E. tristis* and *horatius*; *Pyrgus ruralis* and *xanthus*.

In two other cases, one species replaces another altitudinally. Thus in the Sierra Nevada, *Plebejus melissa* occupies the high mountains, *P. idas* the boreal forest, whereas in southwestern Colorado *idas* occupies the high mountains, *melissa* the lowlands. And in the higher Sierra and western Wyoming, *Lycaena phlaeas* occupies the Alpine Zone, *L. cupreus* the boreal forest, whereas in Colorado, where *phlaeas* is absent, *cupreus* occupies the Alpine Zone.

At least one case of replacement involves species in different genera: larvae of both *Plebejus optilete* and *Lycaena epixanthe* eat cranberry plants, but *optilete* occupies the northwestern boreal forest, *epixanthe* the southeastern.

Because in each of these cases the species have the same hosts, it is tempting to assume that competition for food drives each species to extinction in the other's territory. But actually there is no shortage of food for any of these species, and competition for food has yet to be proved for any insect that eats live plants. Too, many species do have the same hosts and coexist in the same localities (at least seven species eat *Ceanothus fendleri* and fly together in central Colorado, for instance; see also the Hostplant Catalogue). The most likely explanation for most of these cases is that the two (or three) species have recently evolved from one species, and so are still adapted to the regions where they once were merely subspecies. Thus *Limenitis weidemeyerii* and *L. lorquini* still hybridize (and perhaps are still just subspecies). But this explanation does not suffice for some cases such as the cranberry feeders, which are in different genera. It is known that some wasp parasitoids attack a variety of Lepidoptera larvae, and it could be that these wasps, or just fluctuations of weather, occasionally reduce the total population of larvae so much that the resulting low density of adults causes difficulty in finding mates. At such times one species could exist, but two species, each with half the numbers, would not, and one would become extinct there. All else being equal, the species with better mate-locating behavior would survive. The males of both cranberry feeders, *Lycaena epixanthe* and *Plebejus optilete*, reflect ultraviolet (Fig. 35) for identification in the search for mates, but the former may perch and the latter may patrol, to seek females, perhaps lend-ing the former the advantage in small southern bogs, the latter the advantage in larger northern bogs. *Lycaena mariposa* eats *Vaccinium* and occurs sw of both.

Knowledge of U.S. and Canadian butterfly distributions has progressed sufficiently that extensions of the ranges indicated on the maps in Part III will seldom be reported, though the reader who is persistent in searching out-of-the-way areas or habitats just may discover a range extension. The least known area of North America is the vast wooded center of Quebec; fogbound southwestern Alaska and the northwestern arctic islands of Canada are also poorly known. Latin America, in contrast, offers many opportunities for the discovery of range extensions and even new species.

Population Size and Population Regulation

A "population" is defined as all of the animals (or plants) that occur more or less at the same place and time and might meet or mate with each other. The edge of a population generally is where the hostplants disappear or the habitat changes. Thus all the Cabbage Butterflies in the Denver area qualify as a population, even though some adults may die before others emerge, and even though an adult from a western Denver suburb is not as likely to meet an adult from an eastern suburb as are other eastern adults. All the Monarchs in eastern North America seem to qualify as one vast population when they fly to the over-wintering area in central Mexico, but in spring they fly north to establish many mostly separate populations. The word "population" is often loosely used for subspecies, or for all the animals of a state or the like. A local, isolated population is called a colony. A colony may extend across only 2 hectares (a hectare is 100 by 100 meters, about 2.5 acres), whereas a large population may occupy, say, all of the Denver area (600 km², or 200 sq. mi.) or even—the spring Monarchs—all of eastern North America. Individual butterfly populations vary from many thousands or even millions to as few as 50 or so (do not collect from these). Population density can vary from as high as 1,000 or more per hectare to as low as 3 per hectare in typical butterfly populations, or even less than 1 per hectare in others.

Entomologists studying insect pests, such as the Boll Weevil, Corn Earworm, Spruce Budworm, and Gypsy Moth, devote much of their time to determining the causes of fluctuations in population size. But because few butterflies are pests, there has been little pressure to study them in this regard, and little is known about their population regulation. Besides starvation and mortality owing to natural enemies and accidents (see "Parasites, Predators, and Other Enemies," above), one other factor is important in regulating butterfly populations: success in mating and ovipositing. The number of sons and daughters produced by a butterfly female is the number of eggs she lays minus those that are killed by enemies or accidents before becoming adults. Thus anything that influences mate-finding or ovipositing can affect population size. Cold or cloudy weather can prevent butterfly flight and delay mating; or it can delay or reduce oviposition. British workers sometimes relate small populations of butterflies to bad weather during the life span of the preceding generation. Very hot weather during the adult flight can also reduce life span and the number of eggs laid. S. Courtney found that the key influence on the population size of British *Antho-charis cardamines* is the number of eggs laid during the preceding generation, as affected by the weather.

Most butterfly populations occur in roughly the same numbers from year to year, though nearly every population experiences the occasional boom or bust, and desert species seem particularly prone to dramatic fluctuations in numbers. Density dependence helps keep populations from exploding or dying out. For example, if there are too many larvae in one area or one season, they may eat their hostplants to the ground and starve, and parasitoid insects may multiply and kill most of them; but if the density is low each larva can eat all it wants. Too, if adults are very dense the males tend to interfere with each other in finding and courting females, and the females are courted so persistently by males that they have difficulty laying eggs. In such circumstances, some of both sexes may emigrate, as is known to occur in *Pieris protodice* (80), *Ascia monuste* (83), and *Chlosyne harrisii* (220).

Spatial variations of the habitat are probably the main reason populations seldom die out: typically there are certain core areas within a population's distribution where the hostplants and flowers are lush and the overwintering sites are good, year after year, and where, therefore, adults are successfully raised every year, whereas other habitat areas are marginal, varying in suitability from year to year and producing fewer adults in poor years. Thus in these and other cases an ace in the hole for preventing extinction is dispersal; very often a local population that does disappear is soon recolonized from an adjacent population.

Some butterflies have adopted special tactics to prevent their own extinction. The mate-finding habits of some species tend to prevent extinction: at low density, for example, mating proceeds efficiently at a small rendezvous site such as a hilltop, whereas at high density there are too many males to operate from the same small hilltop, and some of the mating accordingly occurs elsewhere, at lesser efficiency. Staggered emergence of adults is another tactic: in most species that hibernate as pupae, only part of each batch of pupae produces adults in a given year; the others, which wait another year or more before emerging, avoid whatever drought or other disasters might have decimated or eliminated the first group. Similarly, only a small part of a given batch of *Chlosyne gabbii damoetas* larvae (223) grows to adults in a given year, the others hibernating until the following year or longer and perhaps finding more suitable alpine weather when they do emerge.

Studying the population size of a colony is usually done by marking a sampling of adults (see Appendix B), because there are usually far too many individuals in a population to count all of them directly. After marking, releasing, and recapturing adults of a given species during the flight period, you can estimate the size of the local population and even the average life span of its members. To visualize the procedure better, take a jar of rice containing too many grains to count, draw out a spoonful, count them, dye them black, put them back, mix thoroughly, and then draw out another spoonful. If you dyed 230 grains, and the second spoonful held 280 grains of which 9 were black, then there must be about 7,156 grains in the jar (the number marked, 230, divided by the proportion marked, 9/280).

Average life span in nature can also be studied in this fashion. Marking and recapturing (hopefully on at least 3 days) allows one to use modern statistical techniques to estimate the staying rate from one sampling to the next. Staying rate is the proportion of those adults in the population at one sampling time that is still there on second sampling (some individuals may have died or emigrated). If the study area is an isolated, well-bounded colony, or emigration is known to be very small, then the staying-rate estimates represent survival rates (the proportion living rather than dying). The average life span can then be calculated from the survival rate.

Conservation and Extinctions

The conservation of butterflies and other insects, by contrast with that of vertebrates, proceeds from different premises. Because of the large size of the populations of most insects, together with the frequency of new generations and the large number of eggs that each female lays, their populations can rebound quickly from a temporary decrease in numbers. But some insects are rather localized, and cannot readily reach a new, similar habitat if theirs is destroyed. Habitat preservation is therefore the key to butterfly conservation: preserving their habitats is effective, but trying to "manage" their numbers, as is done with fish and deer populations, is not. Organizations like the Nature Conservancy that purchase and preserve natural habitats should therefore be supported.

Laymen often think of vertebrates when they think of conservation of nature, but butterflies and other insects are much more common than vertebrates. A few uninformed governments in countries around the globe, in trying to apply the principles of conservation to a great range of animals, from vertebrates to insects, have banned all collecting of butterflies, while at the same time allowing the destruction of millions of square kilometers of forests and other habitats, thereby destroying trillions of butterflies. Insects in particular depend on their habitats' remaining in the natural state. Construction, plowing, reservoir installation, water diversion, and deforestation are harmful or fatal to butterfly populations. Even the exclusion of fires, pursued so diligently in the name of preservation, has allowed the overgrowth of trees to choke out butterfly habitats in some areas of the national and provincial parks and forests in North America. Many butterfly hostplants prefer habitats that are recovering from recent disturbance, particularly fire.

Collecting butterflies almost never harms a population's chance for survival because there are so many more butterflies than birds or mammals, many thousands per square kilometer in good habitats. K. Coolidge wrote that he once caught "half a million *Brephidium exilis* from several acres of saltbush in several weeks time, without affecting the population noticeably." The only butterfly extinctions we know of resulted from the destruction of the butterflies' habitats. The growth of San Francisco alone extirpated four subspecies or populations, and three others nearby became extinct. Construction of a U.S. Air Force radar station destroyed the only *Speyeria nokomis coerulescens* colony (254) in the United States; an Army Corps of Engineers dam drowned a *Parnassius clodius* population (29) in Washington; and drought, overgrazing, and perhaps introduced European grasses eliminated several subspecies in the Tehachapi Mountains in California. All collectors know of local populations now buried by construction.

Because their numbers on commercial crops are so great, a few butterflies have become pests: for example, *Pieris rapae* (76) on cabbages, etc., sometimes *Neophasia menapia* (86) on pines, *Colias eurytheme* (37) and *C. philodice* (38) on alfalfa and clover, *Vanessa cardui* (186) on soybeans, *Strymon melinus* (358) on hops and beans, *Thymelicus lineola* (464) in Timothy Grass hayfields, *Atalopedes campestris* (500) rarely on golf courses. *P. rapae* and *T. lineola* were inadvertently introduced from Europe; millions of these species could be collected without noticeable effect.

A few butterfly species, however, are limited in distribution and occur only in small isolated habitats or in small localized colonies that should be preserved. For instance, *Hesperia dacotae* (482) and *Eumaeus atala* (298) used to be widespread but now occur only in isolated spots. Examples of colonial species are *Neonympha areolata mitchellii, Erebia theano, Speyeria idalia, S. nokomis, Boloria improba acrocnema* and other bog *Boloria, Calephelis muticum, Callophrys hesseli, Lycaena heteronea clara, Plebejus idas lotis,* and *Ochlodes yuma.* To be on the safe side, one should not disclose the locations of tiny isolated colonies of species having a small distribution, unless their habitats are about to be developed, in which case contact the conservation authorities and obtain a purchase or land-use agreement. Small colonies should be harvested only if abundant. As a rule for collecting colonial butterflies, one should release females and wing-damaged adults unless it becomes obvious that there are hundreds in the population. When first entering a very small colony you can place adults alive in envelopes, to be released later if desired; and you can mark the released adults in order to guess how many are present, which has the virtue of discouraging other persons from collecting the marked ones. You might also try to raise adults in the lab (see Appendix B), for from one female you might be able to raise several hundred adults. But in my experience you will sooner or later find almost every butterfly species in abundance in at least some localities; there, collecting is harmless.

Luckily, no butterfly species that I know of has become extinct, although some subspecies have, for example, *Glaucopsyche lygdamus xerces* (395), which was exterminated by the growth of San Francisco. No butterfly species in the rest of the world has become extinct either, as far as is known, although several British colonies of European species have been exterminated by development, and some species may have been exterminated by destruction of their habitat, unknown to science.

The Butterfly Census

Table 1 shows the place of butterflies in the arthropod world, and gives the estimated numbers of species of the several butterfly families and subfamilies in North America and the world. Out of perhaps 200,000 species of Lepidoptera worldwide, about 14,750 are butterflies and the rest are moths (see "Evolution and the Fossil Record," above). Where there are many plant species, there are many butterfly species. Therefore, most butterfly species are in the tropics, mainly because most plant species occur there; and mountain ranges generally support two to three times the number of species present in flat areas, because of their greater number of habitats and greater number of plant species.

The American tropics, a vast and varied region, have by far the richest butterfly fauna; the second richest is tropical Southeast Asia and the East Indies. More than a third of all the world's species, about 6,000, occur in the American tropics and temperate South America. Elsewhere, there are about 3,500 in the southern Orient (India and Sri Lanka to southern China and Taiwan, through southeast Asia to the East Indies, New Guinea, and the Philippines); 2,450 in sub-Saharan Africa and southern Arabia; 301 in Madagascar; 1,500 in the temperate-climate areas of Eurasia and northern Africa (only 380 of these occur west of the USSR and central Turkey); 360 in Australia; 12 in New Zealand; very few (perhaps a dozen) in Polynesia and other islands of the South Pacific; and nearly 700 in North America.

That there are so many butterfly species in the American tropics is because of the vast areas of rain forest and the mountain ranges there. Tropical Southeast Asia and the East Indies are more limited in area, with smaller mountain ranges. Much of Africa is dry, and the mountains there are few. Too, human disturbance has been greater in the Old World (part of the Sahara Desert was created by overgrazing). Humans first came to the Americas across the Bering Strait about 15,000 years ago, and they multiplied and evidently hunted most of the larger animals to extinction. (It is perhaps no coincidence that the last Woolly Mammoths, mastodons, saber-toothed tigers, giant sloths, and North American camels and horses were fossilized 10,000 years ago, often interred with the spear points of early man.) But American habitats stayed relatively natural until quite recently, and the American butterflies have probably been affected very little by man. In the Old World the desertification of Africa, the Near East, and Central Asia, and the deforestation of Europe, China, India, and Indonesia, by huge numbers of people, may have eliminated entire habitats—and the butterflies that lived there.

Even in North America, which is preponderantly temperate and arctic, the subtropics support the most species, and the southern mountainous regions of the West are second in abundance. Not surprisingly, the arctic regions and the fogbound Aleutian Islands support the fewest.

All of the butterfly families and most of the subfamilies are represented throughout the world, but most of the species of nearly all the subfamilies are confined to the tropics. Some of the smaller subfamilies are more restricted in distribution: Parnassiinae (Northern Hemisphere only), Baroniinae (southern Mexico only), Pseudopontiinae (West Africa), Calinaginae (Asia), Styginae (South America), Curetinae (Orient and East Indies), Megathyminae (North and Central America), Trapezitinae (Australia), Coeliadinae (Old World), and Pyrrhopyginae (New World). The subfamilies not represented in North America are discussed briefly in the family discussions in Part III.

How many individual butterflies are there? If we assume that the average range of each of the nearly 700 species in North America occupies about 300,000 square kilometers (the size of Arizona), and assume on the average about one adult butterfly per hectare (2.5 acres) of its range each generation, or 100 per square kilometer, and assume an average of two generations per year, then there must be about $700 \times 300{,}000 \times 100 \times 2$, or 42 billion adult butterflies in North America. But half are females, and if each female lays an average of 100 eggs, then there must be more than 2 trillion eggs laid per year. A crude estimate, but the numbers are certainly immense. In the whole world there may be a trillion adult butterflies, because far more fly in the tropics than in North America, in many species just as abundantly as in temperate regions, and of course they often fly year-round in the tropics. A species with a small range, such as *Lycaena hermes*, occupies perhaps 50 known localities, with as a guess an average of 500 adults at each; thus as few as 25,000 adults may represent this species. But a widespread common species such as *Strymon melinus* occupies 10 million square kilometers north of Mexico, and a similar number southward, and has an average of perhaps four generations per year. At the rate of one adult per hectare there are 8 billion new adults per year of just this one species. (The number of adults in single populations is discussed above, under "Population Size and Population Regulation.")

TABLE 1 *The Butterfly Census*

Taxonomic Group and Common Name	Genera North America	Genera World	Species North America	Species World	Subspecies North America	Forms North America
Phylum Arthropoda (Joint-Legged Animals)			130,000	2,000,000		
Class Insecta (Insects)			100,000	1,500,000		
Order Lepidoptera (Moths and Butterflies)	1,600	10,000	15,000	200,000		
Suborder Zeugloptera (Mandibulate Moths)	1	7	3	200		
Suborder Aglossata (*Araucaria*-Seed Moths)	0	1	0	2		
Suborder Heterobathmiina (Southern-Beech Moths)	0	1	0	5		
Suborder Dacnonypha (Primitive Leaf Miners)	5	9	20	200		
Suborder Neopseustina (Neopseustid Moths)	0	4	0	9		
Suborder Exoporia (Ghost Moths, Swifts)	2	30	25	500		
Suborder Monotrysia (Leaf Miners, Yucca Moths)	20	150	250	3,000		
Suborder Ditrysia (Higher Moths and Butterflies)	1,500	9,500	14,500	196,000		
Section Macrolepidoptera						
Subsection Rhopalocera (Butterflies)	208	1,500	679	14,750	430	145
Superfamily Papilionoidea (Scudders)	116	950	416	11,100	360	138
Family Papilionidae (Swallowtails)	5	24	30	534	22	18
Subfamily Parnassiinae (Parnassians)	1	8	3	50	8	0
Subfamily Papilioninae (Swallowtails)	4	15	27	483	14	18
Subfamily Baroniinae	0	1	0	1	0	0
Family Pieridae (Whites and Sulfurs)	14	59	58	1,100	25	59
Subfamily Pseudopontiinae	0	1	0	1	0	0
Subfamily Dismorphiinae (Mimic Sulfurs)	1	4	1	100	0	0
Subfamily Coliadinae (Sulfurs)	6	11	36	300	15	40
Subfamily Pierinae (Whites)	7	43	21	700	10	19
Family Nymphalidae (Brush-Footed Butterflies)	52	450	185	4,500	183	39
Subfamily Danainae (Milkweed Butterflies)	2	8	4	157	1	1
Subfamily Ithomiinae (Clear-Wing Butterflies)	0	47	0	400	0	0
Subfamily Satyrinae (Satyrs)	12	200	43	2,000	42	9
Subfamily Morphinae (Morphos, Brassolids)	0	10	0	200	0	0
Subfamily Charaxinae (Goatweed Butterflies)	1	15	4	400	1	2
Subfamily Apaturinae (Emperors)	2	5	5	50	2	2
Subfamily Nymphalinae (Spiny Brush-Footed Butterflies)	35	150	129	1,100	137	25
Subfamily Acraeinae	0	5	0	150	0	0
Subfamily Calinaginae	0	1	0	12	0	0
Family Libytheidae (Snout Butterflies)	1	2	1	8	3	1
Family Lycaenidae (Little Butterflies)	44	425	142	4,700	127	21
Subfamily Styginae	0	1	0	1	0	0
Subfamily Riodininae (Metalmarks)	6	100	20	1,500	11	0
Subfamily Curetinae	0	1	0	10	0	0
Subfamily Lycaeninae (Harvesters, Hair-streaks, Coppers, and Blues)	38	325	122	3,200	116	21
Superfamily Hesperioidea } Family Hesperiidae } (Skippers)	92	530	263	3,650	70	7
Subfamily Megathyminae (Giant Skippers)	3	5	13	20	11	0
Subfamily Hesperiinae (Grass Skippers)	47	315	137	2,150	44	6
Subfamily Trapezitinae	0	16	0	65	0	0
Subfamily Pyrginae (Herb, Shrub, and Tree Skippers)	41	167	112	1,150	15	1
Subfamily Coeliadinae	0	7	0	90	0	0
Subfamily Pyrrhopyginae (Mimic Skippers)	1	20	1	170	0	0

NOTE: Many of the worldwide figures are estimates, especially for moths. The figures for arthropods also include spiders, mites, crusta- ceans, centipedes, etc. The numbers of subspecies and forms are those beyond one per species.

The History and Future of Butterfly Study

The study of butterflies certainly began with prehistoric peoples, but they left no records. In ancient Greece, Aristotle classified numerous animals and studied their habits and structures; his names for beetles (Coleoptera) and flies (Diptera) are used today. But not until the end of the Middle Ages is there an extensive record of butterfly study. Voyagers on the early sailing ships brought back to western Europe many specimens from around the world to naturalists eager to build up their collections. The first museum for these biological treasures was built in Switzerland by the great botanist and zoologist Conrad Gesner, who published an encyclopedia of animals in 1551-58. The first European treatise on insects, a book in Latin describing a few butterflies and other insects, was published in 1634. The oldest butterflies in a museum today may be those of James Petiver, a London silversmith. Given to the British Museum in 1700, his collection includes two skippers from the Carolinas. Petiver had some 75 to 80 associates collecting for him in North America, and his writings provided the basis for many of the names later adopted by the Swedish naturalist Carolus Linnaeus. By 1710, the date of John Ray's *Historia Insectorum*, study of British butterflies was complete enough that all but half a dozen of those now known were recorded.

The first phase in the knowledge of American butterflies was the discovery and naming of most of the species. The first American butterfly known to European naturalists, the Tiger Swallowtail (*Papilio glaucus*), was painted in 1587 by John White, who commanded Sir Walter Raleigh's third expedition to colonize Virginia, but the naming of species began in earnest in 1758 when Linnaeus named 18 U.S. species (among them *P. glaucus*). Half a dozen travelers and adventurers supplied Linnaeus with the specimens for these species, notably Mark Catesby, a Londoner who spent ten years in Virginia, South Carolina, and the Bahamas, and Peter Kalm, Linnaeus's student, who collected in Pennsylvania and New York and was the first to describe Niagara Falls.

This was the golden age of taxonomy; it is said that trumpets heralded the return of Linnaeus from each botanical expedition. Trained in medicine but later a professor of botany, he consistently applied the binomial system of scientific names (genus and species) and initiated a system of plant classification based on characteristics of the flowering parts. He offered genus and species names and Latin descriptions for most of the plants and animals known at that time, including many of those described by earlier workers.

Later in the eighteenth century, Johann Fabricius and Pierre Cramer named many more American butterfly species, and in the nineteenth century the task was continued by Jean Boisduval, William Hewitson, and Jacob Hübner, all Europeans who named species from throughout the world, and by several Americans, Tryon Reakirt, Herman Strecker, Samuel Scudder, and William Edwards. Pierre Lorquin, after failing to find gold in the California Sierra, collected many specimens later named by Boisduval, a French lawyer. Lorquin and other travelers, including James Ridings, a Philadelphia house builder, supplied western U.S. species named by Reakirt. Theodore Mead discovered many Rocky Mountain species that were named by Edwards, a lawyer and businessman. Mead wrote the section on Lepidoptera for the 1871-74 Wheeler Survey, which explored the West; he later married Edwards's daughter. David Bruce, a painter of frescoes and houses in Brockport, New York, conceived and developed the "habitat group" method of museum exhibits. He traveled in the West almost every year from 1883 to 1897, and collected many Rocky Mountain (especially alpine) species. He and Edwards worked together at Glenwood Springs, Colorado, in 1893, raising *Papilio machaon bairdii* and *P. m. brucei*, each from eggs laid by females of the other type, thus proving that these remarkably different creatures are but forms of the same species. Hans Behr, a physician who settled in San Francisco, and William Wright, a southern California storekeeper, part-time bootlegger, and author of *The Butterflies of the West Coast of the United States*, both named some western species. Their collections were stored in the California Academy of Sciences, where most were destroyed in the 1906 San Francisco earthquake and fire. (Ironically, just a year before the fire the Academy curators convinced Wright to remove his collection from his barn because his whiskey-still created a fire hazard.)

The difficult conditions in these early times created numerous taxonomic problems. Apart from Linnaeus, the early collectors did not understand the importance of exact localities, so their specimens often lacked data, or carried erroneous data, and the collectors of the specimens were often unknown. The original specimen of *Speyeria nokomis*, for example, arrived at the Smithsonian Institution in Washington, D.C., in a jar on cotton, with no indication of its locality or collector, creating confusion that persists today. Procuring specimens of butterflies at all in the late eighteenth and early nineteenth century was difficult enough. Thomas Say of the Long Expedition was collecting insects in Colorado and preserving some of them in alcohol, as entomologists still do, when two wranglers hired to handle the pack train ran off with his supplies, threw away the specimens, and drank the alcohol! (Even late in the last century, William Couper's collecting trip to Labrador ended when Indians stole all his specimens and supplies.) In the middle of this century F. Martin Brown published many historical papers deducing the localities and dates for these early specimens and collectors, a task aided greatly by thousands of letters from various naturalists to William Edwards and Herman Strecker (who also named several species).

The life histories and habits of butterflies, however, were generally neglected until late in the nineteenth century. One exception was John Abbot, of Georgia, who painted dozens of butterflies together with their hostplants, larvae, and pupae, and sent his paintings to London. There, the paintings were purchased and published, and the butterflies were named by Boisduval and John LeConte. Abbot also sent specimens to Hübner. One skipper (*Problema bulenta*) in fact was known only from one of Abbot's paintings, published about 1830, until it was rediscovered in 1925.

After about 1860, many people, including Henry Edwards (a San Francisco actor), William Saunders, of Ontario, and especially William Edwards and Samuel Scudder, began publishing valuable basic information on the life histories and habits of various species, and in the process initiated the second phase of North American butterfly study. William Edwards and Scudder published books that remain classics today, Edwards's *Butterflies of North America* and Scudder's *Butterflies of the Eastern United States and Canada, with Special Reference to New England*. They sometimes disagreed in print—about the yearly life cycle of *Boloria*, for instance. Scudder was a renowned scientist at Harvard, with a good grasp of morphology, and an expert on grasshoppers and insect fossils as well. Edwards was not as well organized as Scudder, and clearly his junior in scientific training, but his enthusiasm was unbounded, and for nearly 40 years, from his home in

Coalburgh, West Virginia, he named several hundred new species and sub-species and published a hundred or more descriptions of the early stages and habits of various species from throughout North America.

Although Edwards was not a wealthy man, he financed his own book, with its numerous color plates and extravagant format. To make ends meet, he sold his collection to William Holland, who moved it to his cellar—where many spec-imens molded—and later deposited it in the Carnegie Museum. The whole ex-perience with the book and its finances so discouraged Edwards that at about the turn of the century he gave up butterflies completely, and spent (some say wasted) the next decade working out some of the finer points of the works of Shakespeare. The problem of finance has continued to the present day. One can almost count on one hand the number of people in the world who make their living entirely by studying butterflies. One must hope for a career in teaching or arranging museum exhibits, both fields poorly paying and short in opportuni-ties, or something even farther afield, and study butterflies only in spare mo-ments. Eugene Aaron learned something of this sad state when *Papilio*, a journal he and Henry Edwards edited, and the only journal in the nineteenth century devoted solely to Lepidoptera (running for four years from 1881 to 1884), folded owing to the delinquency of miserly subscribers.

But the late nineteenth century was nonetheless an exciting time for butter-fly enthusiasts, not only because of Edwards and Scudder, but also because of workers such as John Lembert, a hermit who discovered the Sierra Green Sulfur but kept its location hidden for many years; George French and Charles May-nard, who published popular books on butterflies; Herman Strecker, an architect and sculptor, and Henry Skinner, who each named several new species. This was also a time of controversy about evolution. Charles Darwin, like Linnaeus, had a father who wanted him to be a minister, but instead he got an appoint-ment as naturalist on a ship exploring South America and the Galápagos, where he began to ask whether species do change with time, through the greater survi-val or reproduction of some of the varieties existing in the same populations with other varieties. The idea of evolution propounded by Darwin and Wallace encouraged searches for "missing links" between the known creatures.

Perhaps the books by Scudder and Edwards, as well as the very popular *The Butterfly Book* by William Holland, were by their erudition intimidating to their readers. In any case, the start of the twentieth century was an inactive period in the study of butterflies. This was the time, too, when the process of naming new species got out of hand. Darwin's *Origin of Species*, published in 1859, had formed the basis of the concept of species as populations of differing but poten-tially interfertile individuals sharing many common traits, as opposed to a con-cept making all members of a species identically cloned creatures of a single, unvarying type. True, William Edwards himself helped to discredit the clone concept of species by raising many "species" from eggs laid by females of a sec-ond "species," thus proving the two to be merely variants.

But in the early years of the twentieth century the sophisticated species concept we sport today had not crystallized, and most variants, however mod-est, were named as new species. In fact, a fad began, in which aberrations were sought out and named. The fad resulted in some 200 names for the European *Parnassius apollo*, for instance. These excesses were formally reined in by the In-ternational Commission on Zoological Nomenclature, which decreed that names for aberrations would no longer have formal status after 1960. In the field of butterfly study, the work of Cyril dos Passos and L. Paul Grey also helped turn back the trend: in a single paper published in 1947 they reduced 100 or more "species" of *Speyeria* to the dozen or so species we know today. Some new North American species have been named in this century, by such specialists as James McDunnough, Ernest Bell, and especially William Evans (a retired British Army Brigadier, who worked on skippers for several decades in the British Museum), but most of the species we know today had been named earlier.

In the 1920's to 1940's, there was a rebirth of life-history studies in California, where Charles Dammers, a retired British naval officer, and John Comstock published studies on many species. Many other workers—including Karl Coolidge, J. Richard Heitzman, Arthur Shapiro, Vincent Dethier, Roy Kendall, Alexander Klots, Paul Ehrlich, John and Thomas Emmel, and C. Don MacNeill—continued natural-history studies of butterflies into and beyond the middle of this century.

This period saw the introduction of many advanced biological techniques to the study of genetics, physiology, behavior, and ecology. These more sophisticated efforts we can perhaps call the third phase of butterfly study. A prime example is the work of Fred Urquhart, who undertook a study of the migrations and habits of the Monarch Butterfly, *Danaus plexippus*, utilizing hundreds of volunteers in a massive tagging program that culminated after two decades in the discovery that the eastern North American Monarchs all hibernate at a few sites in the mountains of southern Mexico, a discovery now popularized worldwide in films and magazines. Other workers including Lincoln Brower and Miriam Rothschild also unraveled the origins and use of the chemical poisons that Monarchs use to discourage predators from eating them, thus fleshing out the hypotheses on mimicry developed by the English naturalists Henry Bates and Alfred Russel Wallace, in the mid-nineteenth century in the Amazon (see the Introduction and "Mimicry and Other Defenses," above). E. B. Ford in Britain helped pioneer field studies of polymorphism to determine the significance of genetic variations—such as the variable number of eyespots on certain satyrs—in the lives of the butterflies. And Ford's collaboration with the mathematician R. A. Fisher led Fisher to develop numerous mathematical and statistical techniques of great use today. Paul Ehrlich and Peter Raven deciphered how the butterfly families and subfamilies evolved along with the plants, explaining why some major butterfly groups eat only a few related plants. Cyril Clarke and Philip Sheppard in England, through laboratory hybridization and rearing, worked out the modes of inheritance of the numerous forms among the *Papilio machaon* group (species 5-9), a task that Bruce and Edwards had begun some 80 years before. In a second classic study, Clarke and Sheppard worked out the inheritance of the various mimetic forms of African *Papilio*, considerably advancing our knowledge of the evolution of mimicry—a task that Austin Platt is continuing now on our American *Limenitis*, which are mimics both of *Battus* swallowtails and of the Monarch.

In the laboratories of mid-century, physiologists discovered the hormones that trigger successive stages of metamorphosis. Various workers also discovered that photoperiod (day length) affects the diapause of butterflies, and causes most of the seasonal variations that occur. Advances in chemistry permitted the discovery of the exact composition of certain mating pheromones in the Queen

(*Danaus gilippus*) and others (a century earlier, William Wittfeld, a Florida physician, had discovered a female pheromone that leads male Zebra Long Wings, *Heliconius charitonia*, to female pupae). Other studies identified the pheromones that swallowtail larvae use to repel ants, and some of the plant chemicals that females and larvae use to locate their hostplants. Researchers in Japan and elsewhere discovered that some butterflies use ultraviolet reflection to select mates (in the 1920's Frank Lutz had found that insects use ultraviolet to help locate flowers for nectar).

Across all of these areas, the work proceeds, and we can look forward to continued progress in the study of butterflies. The life histories of most of the remaining unstudied North American species should be known in the next few decades, and comparative studies of behavior and ecology will produce new and stronger conclusions than those we now possess. Hostplant-seeking behavior will be studied more systematically, so that we will know, for more species, not only what they eat, but why they select only certain plants and certain parts of plants. Advances in chemistry will result in the identification of many more of the pheromones used for mating and for repelling mates and predators, and many more of the plant chemicals that serve to attract or repel butterfly females and larvae. Knowledge of the genetics and evolution of butterflies can be expected to advance dramatically, and we will come to know more about the adaptational purposes of the forms and genetic variants in the life of the species. The mysterious Lepidoptera chromosome will eventually reveal its peculiarities, and some of the techniques for determining the makeup of DNA in the chromosomes—already developed in fruit flies, bacteria, and mammals—will eventually be applied to the evolution of butterflies. Family trees now based on a few weakly exhibited traits will be improved and fleshed out by the sequences of many biochemicals. And perhaps, before too many years pass, molecular biologists will be able to resurrect some of the chemical DNA from a dried wing of the extinct *Glaucopsyche lygdamus xerces* blue, recombine it in eggs of living *lygdamus*, and "recreate" this extinct creature (or recreate the mastodon and saber-toothed tiger by using DNA from ten-thousand-year-old frozen tissue in some arctic permafrost or glacier).

Or, perhaps, like Mary Shelley's Frankenstein fantasy, the recreation of extinct creatures will remain just a dream, and it will be difficult enough to prevent the extinction of species that now exist. Still, many wonders await. Microscopes will grow more powerful, entomology more sophisticated; the testing machines of science will grow more elaborate and expensive; and some enterprising soul will even begin flying a computerized mechanical butterfly. But when all these findings are set to paper (or computer storage) a hundred years from now, there will still be moments for merely admiring the butterflies flying past, and wondering about their strange habits and life cycles, as people have done for thousands of years.

Identification of Eggs, Larvae, Pupae, and Adults

This part of the book shows how to identify butterflies—eggs, larvae, pupae, and adults. The material that follows discusses each of these life stages, and identifying keys are given for first-stage larvae, mature larvae, pupae, and adults. The keys are generally only to family, subfamily, and tribe, rarely to genus or species. Thus to identify a butterfly to species you must also consult Part III. For eggs, larvae, and pupae, first go through Part II, then turn to Part III. But for adults the color plates, maps, and text of Part III should be consulted first; Part II gives background information on wing veins and mating structures that are sometimes needed for identification; but the key to adults should be consulted only for worn, aberrant, or foreign species. The key to adults works throughout the world; the other keys are intended to apply only to North American butterflies, but they will work for most foreign immatures also.

Using the Keys

Each paragraph of a key begins with a number followed by a second number (or as many as two to four numbers) in parentheses—such as 3 followed by (9), or 4 followed by (8,12). In the Key to First-Stage North American Larvae, for example, begin by comparing the first numbered paragraph, 1(4), with the paragraph numbered in parentheses, 4(1); choose one; then continue on to the numbered paragraphs, following that choice, perhaps 5(12) and 12(5), that best fits your individual. For instance, if 4 fits better than 1, continue on to 5 and 12 rather than to 2 and 3. Continue the comparisons and choices, and stop when you reach a name at the end of a series of dots, perhaps Subfam. Hesperiinae at 7(8). Then turn to the page number indicated. If you find at some point that you have clearly taken a wrong turn in the key, return to the first pair of key numbers where you were uncertain of your choice, and try again. Be patient: butterflies are very small animals, covered liberally with scales and "hairs"; comparing their anatomical details requires care—and often a hand lens or microscope.

Identifying Eggs

Although a butterfly egg is much harder to identify than an adult, its shape can be used to identify it usually to subfamily and sometimes to genus or even species (Fig. 45). Some moth eggs are very similar to butterfly eggs, but nearly all moths glue each egg on its side ("flat") such that the sperm pores face sideways, whereas butterflies (and moths of the superfamily Noctuoidea, Fig. 41) glue each on its bottom ("upright") such that pores face away from the glued bottom (Fig. 31). In addition to egg shape, the plant the eggs are laid on and where they are placed on the plant are good clues to species (identify the plant; the Hostplant Catalogue lists which butterflies eat it). Most females glue their eggs onto the larval hostplant, but in *Agathymus* the unglued eggs fall to the base of the plant. Most species place their eggs carefully, one per plant, but some

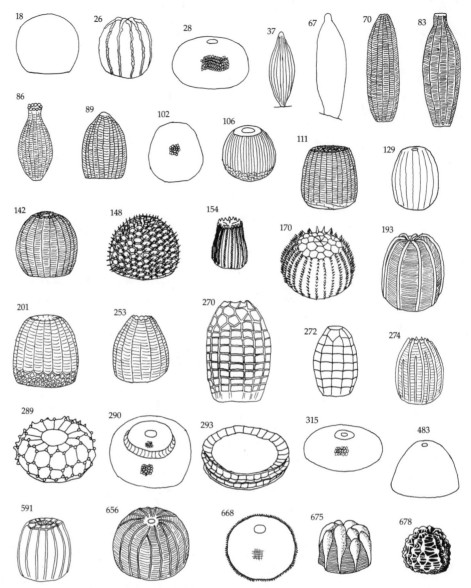

Fig. 45. The major shapes of butterfly eggs. *18, Papilio glaucus* (similar: all *Papilio, Eurytides,* and *Battus*). *26, Battus polydamas*. *28, Parnassius phoebus*. *37, Colias eurytheme* (similar: other *Colias*, 32-45; *Eurema*, 55-65). *67, Nathalis iole*. *70, Anthocharis lanceolata* (similar: *A. midea*, 71; *Euchloe*, 72-75; *Pieris*, 76-82; most Pieridae). *83, Ascia monuste* (similar: *Phoebis*, 48-54, but with rounder top). *86, Neophasia menapia*. *89, Danaus plexippus* (similar: *D. gilippus*, 90). *102, Megisto cymela* (similar: *M. rubricata*, 103; *Neonympha*, 104). *106, Coenonympha tullia*. *111, Cercyonis oetus* (similar: *C. pegala*, 108; *Neominois*, 125, but with rounder top). *129, Oeneis alberta* (similar: other *Oeneis*, 126-135; *Erebia*, 112-123). *142, Asterocampa clyton*. *148, Limenitis lorquini* (similar: *L. archippus*, 145; *L. weidemeyerii*, 147; some tropical *Limenitis*, but others like species 142). *154, Dynamine dyonis*. *170, Historis odius* (similar, with vertical ribs reaching near the top and many thin spikes: *Mestra*, 159; *Biblis*, 160). *193, Polygonia progne* (similar: other *Polygonia, Nymphalis, Vanessa, Precis, Anartia*, 177-198). *201, Euphydryas editha* (similar: all Melitaeini). *253, Speyeria cybele* (similar: other *Speyeria*, 251-264; *Boloria*, 237-250; *Euptoieta claudia*, 265). *270, Dryas iulia* (similar: *Dione vanillae*, 268, slightly longer). *272, Heliconius charitonia* (similar: *H. erato*, 273; *Dryadula*, 267, slightly shorter; *H. isabella*, 271, even shorter). *274, Libytheana carinenta*. *289, Caria ino* (similar: *Calephelis*, 282-288). *290, Emesis emesia*. *293, Lasaia sula* (shaped like two stacked pies). *315, Satyrium behrii* (similar: *Apodemia*, 275-278; *Emesis zela*, 291; all Lycaeninae, though the surface sculpturing varies). *483, Hesperia sassacus* (similar: all Hesperiinae and Megathyminae). *591, Urbanus dorantes*. *656, Erynnis zarucco* (similar: most Pyrginae). *668, Heliopetes ericetorum*. *675, Pholisora catullus*. *678, Hesperopsis alpheus gracielae*. (See also Color Plate 1.)

species lay their eggs haphazardly, and others lay them in clusters (for lists of these species, see "Egg-Laying and Larval Nests," in Part I). When you have narrowed down the possibilities, you can remove eggs from a fresh adult female of the likely species (or a dead female after soaking her abdomen in 0.5 percent trisodium phosphate solution for a day) and, using a microscope, compare them with the eggs you have collected. You can also identify eggs by raising them to adults.

Identifying Larvae

The larva is the growth stage of butterflies—in fact, all of their weight gain occurs in this stage (various appendages, such as wings and antennae, grow enormously during the pupal stage, drawing their substance from nutrients accumulated during the larval stage). The basic body structures of larvae are discussed in Part I, particularly under "Form, Structure, and Movement" and "Physiology and Reproduction."

The hostplant, the position of the larva on the plant, the larva's shape and color, and the presence or absence of nests are all good clues for identification. If the eggs have been laid in clusters—most are not—the young larvae usually feed together. Some species live in special larval nests (see "Egg-Laying and Larval Nests," in Part I, for a list of these). Most species eat leaves, but *Anthocharis*, *Euchloe*, and many Lycaenidae feed on fruits and flowers, and the *Papilio machaon* group (5-9), *Pieris*, *Chlosyne leanira*, *Euphydryas*, *Euptoieta*, and many Lycaenidae eat fruits, flowers, *and* leaves.

Figures 1-4 show the structures of larvae that are important in identifying them. Most common, but ordinarily too small to be useful in identification without a microscope, are "hairs," properly called setae (sing., seta). Setae occur in infinite variety, ranging from hairlike to feathery, clubbed or hooked or forked, branched at the base, bladelike or saw-toothed, etc. A branching spine (scolus) has many setae on a fully or partly hardened cone or spine. Many other hardened structures occur: "antlers" or horns on the head, or spines almost anywhere on the body. Eversible glands, evidently used for chemical defense, pop out behind the head in some species: the dorsal osmeteria of the Papilionidae, a gland beneath the neck in Hesperiidae, Pieridae, Libytheidae, Nymphalinae, Morphinae, Danainae, and probably others.

All larvae have crochets (hooks) on the prolegs that help them grasp the surface (Fig. 4). They are arranged in a circle with the bases of the hooks toward the outside of the circle, the points toward the inside, curving down and outward at their tips. As the larva crawls, the crochets swing down and outward and hook into silk or the surface, and a muscle above the proleg then pulls them up and in again for the next step. In all butterfly larvae of all ages, the crochets on the last pair of prolegs form a curve on the front and sides of the proleg; the other crochets usually form a complete circle in first-stage larvae (except in most Lycaenidae), as well as in the mature larvae of all skippers, some Papilionidae (the *Papilio troilus* and *P. glaucus* groups, 18-24), and some Lycaenidae. In almost all scudders (Papilionoidea), however, the crochets of the eight front prolegs gradually decrease in number on the outside of the proleg until only the crochets on the inside remain in the mature larva. This inner crescent remains because the mature larvae grasp fine twigs, stems, and leaf edges between opposing prolegs, using the crochets on the inside of each proleg; for such acrobatics, the outer crochets would be useless. By contrast, the skippers and the *Papilio troilus* and

P. glaucus groups rest in a concave silked nest or leaf; thus they retain the full circle of crochets because to them the outside ones are useful too. Although the crochets are usually of two or three different lengths (Fig. 4), they may be of only one length in some young larvae (and in older larvae of Satyrinae and others). In Lycaeninae, the crochets of young larvae are usually all of one length; in half-grown larvae, of two lengths; and in mature larvae, generally of three lengths.

In most species, determining the sex of a larva is all but impossible even for specialists, but the sex of some older larvae can be determined. On the abdomen of *Limenitis* at least, midway between segments 7 and 9 on the midventral line, are two microscopic opaque bumps (each with a short hair) on the male, but in place of these on the female are two transparent patches of the exoskeleton.

Unfortunately for butterfly watchers, the larvae of many moths resemble those of the butterflies. Thus you might successfully "identify" an unknown larva with the keys, only to see it emerge later as a moth. The text preceding each of the two larval keys shows how nearly all moths can be separated from butterflies.

Identifying First-Stage Larvae

Newly hatched larvae (Figs. 46-48) are small, only 2-5 mm in length, so they are noticed less often than older larvae. They also differ from older larvae: most have large rounded heads and comparatively few long or short hairs (setae) on a cylindrical body. They may have horns, a hardened "collar" (prothoracic shield), a plate on the rear (suranal plate), other plates on the outsides of the prolegs, and an anal comb.

The setae of a first-stage larva are important for identification. They are generally simple and hairlike, but may be forked or clubbed, and they may be on branching spines, or alone or clustered on hardened plates. The longer setae are generally touch detectors, like cat whiskers (although in certain pyralid and noctuid moths SD1 is a swinging gravity detector). The vulnerable, soft-bodied, weak-eyed larvae use them to feel their way through the vegetation.

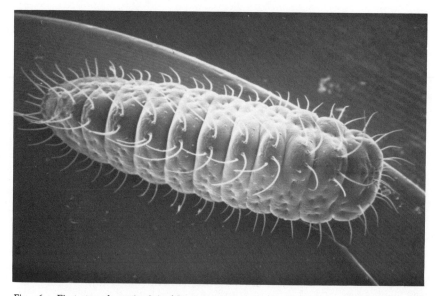

Fig. 46.   First-stage larva (× 80) of *Lycaena epixanthe* (378), from above. (David M. Wright)

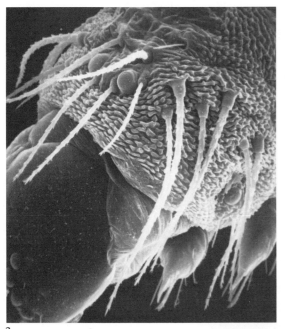

a

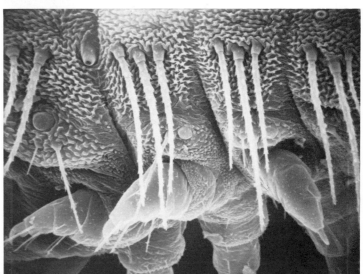

b

c

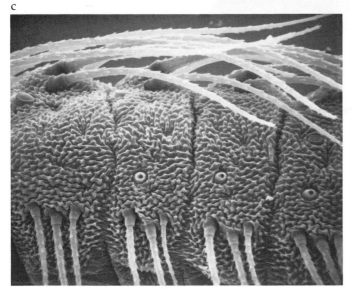

Fig. 47.   First-stage larva (× 260) of *Lycaena
epixanthe* (378), from the left side: *a*, the head,
with the eyes in the lower left-hand corner,
the first thoracic segment, and the first two
thoracic legs; *b*, *c*, the left side of the body.
The skin is wrinkled because this larva was
dissected from the egg; soon after hatching,
the larva fills out, stretching the skin as in Fig.
46. The spiracles are sharply defined lateral
domes with black central breathing holes; the
rounded bumps are glandular rings; the numerous dorsal and lateral short or sawtooth
"hairs" are setae. (David M. Wright)

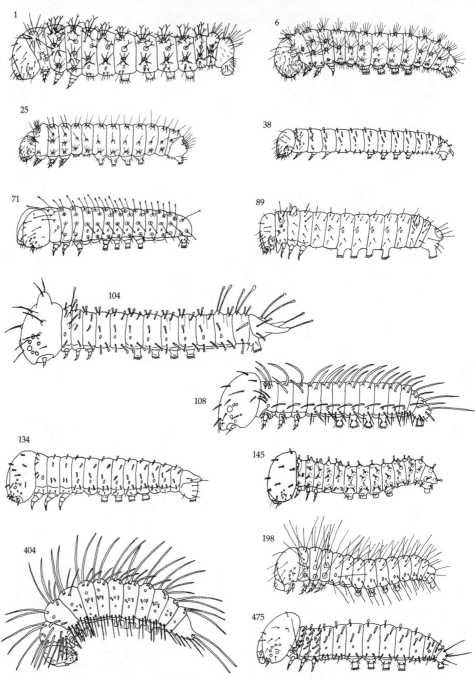

Fig. 48.   The overall appearance of representative first-stage larvae (some of the hairs may not be so accurately positioned as they are in Figs. 49 and 50).   *1, Eurytides marcellus,* many extra forked hairs are on hills (scoli).   *6, Papilio zelicaon* form *nitra,* many unforked extra hairs are on scoli.   *25, Battus philenor,* the extra hairs are on lateral scoli.   *38, Colias philodice* (similar: *Libytheana,* 274, with even shorter straight hairs).   *71, Anthocharis midea.*   *89, Danaus plexippus,* several fleshy cones occur.   *104, Neonympha areolata* (many Satyrinae have horns and tails, and their third eye is bigger; *Asterocampa celtis,* 140, has short tails also but about ten small bumps on the head; see Fig. 49).   *108, Cercyonis pegala,* with scythelike hairs.   *134, Oeneis melissa,* with tails but no horns.   *145, Limenitis archippus,* with many fleshy bumps on top.   *198, Nymphalis antiopa* (similar: most Nymphalinae; but *Speyeria,* 251-264, and *Boloria,* 237-250, have extra hairs at least on the side).   *404, Plebejus idas* (similar: all Lycaenidae, but abdominal segment 9 appears fused with segment 10, and there are many extra secondary hairs at least on the side and usually rings; the subdorsal hairs are shorter and clubbed like this in blues).   *475, Hesperia leonardus* (similar: most skippers, which have rings, and often long hairs on the rear).   (Most drawings after S. Scudder.)

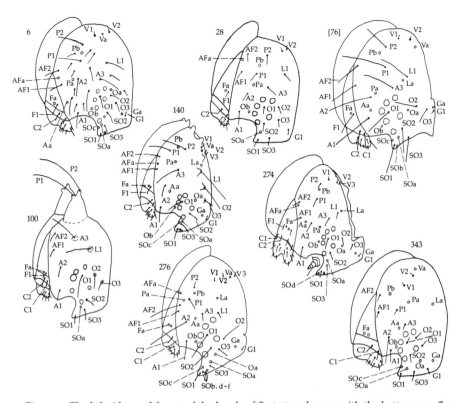

Fig. 49.   The left sides and fronts of the heads of first-stage larvae, with the bottom rear flange bent out so that the O and SO hairs are visible. The hairs are tactile organs (tactile setae). The six large circles are eyes; the tiny circles are olfactory pits. All have special names and are useful in butterfly classification. The "primary" hairs typical of all butterflies are shown for species [76]; the tiny V and G hairs, however, and all the olfactory pits except Fa may be small or absent, so they are not drawn for some species. *6, Papilio zelicaon* form *nitra* (at least some extra hairs occur in all Papilioninae). *28, Parnassius phoebus,* with only primary hairs. *[76], Pieris brassicae* (a European species, but *P. rapae, 76,* is similar; after H. Hinton). *100, Cyllopsis pertepida* (many Satyrinae have horns, and all have the third eye bigger). *140, Asterocampa celtis,* with ten small bumps on the rim. *274, Libytheana carinenta bachmanii,* with an antenna shown. *276, Apodemia nais* (most Lycaenidae lack F1, and L1 is missing in many). *343, Callophrys affinis homoperplexa* (the upper and rear hairs are very short in Lycaeninae and some Riodininae because the head is retracted into the thorax, and the number and positions of hairs may differ).

The setae are sufficiently constant in number and position in Lepidoptera larvae to have been assigned names. Primary setae are those present in primitive moth larvae and most first-stage butterfly larvae (see *Pieris* in Fig. 49 and *Libytheana* in Fig. 50; note that these two genera have fewer than the usual complement of two primary L setae on the prothorax and two primary SD setae each on the mesothorax and metathorax—most Nymphalidae and dicotyledon-eating skippers have the full set). Postnatal ("subprimary") setae are a few additional setae appearing on second-stage to mature larvae that are constant in position (some L setae on the thorax of butterflies and moths and some SV and P on the abdomen). Secondary setae are the numerous extra setae that occur in all older butterfly larvae (and some moth larvae), as well as in the first-stage larvae of some butterfly groups. In the Nymphalinae the branching spines (scoli) of older larvae mostly occur where the primary setae were in the first stage (although the middorsal spines represent fusion of both the two D1 setae). (By contrast, most

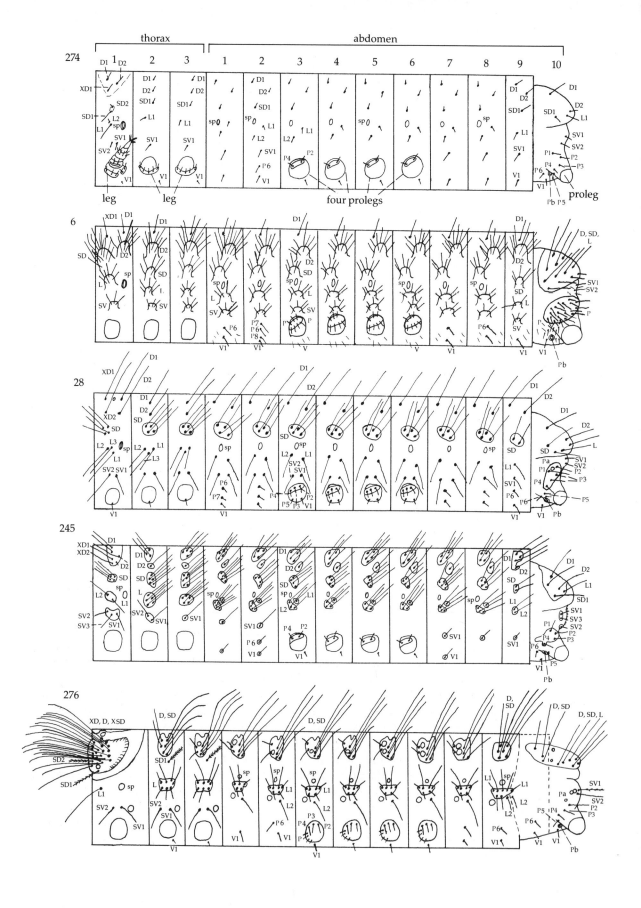

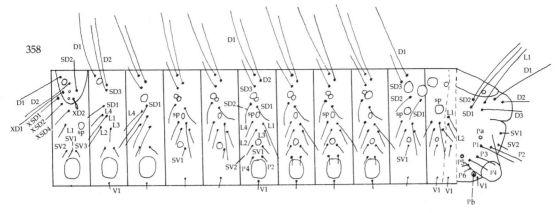

Fig. 50 (*facing page and above*).   The ornamentation on the body of the first-stage larva. The larva is shown as if it had been sliced exactly down the middle and the left half had been placed on the page and rolled flat, like a hot-dog bun. These drawings are called "setal maps." *sp*, spiracles; the other small round circles are rings; the three large circles at the bottom of the thoracic segments are legs; and the large round circles at the bottom of the abdominal segments are prolegs. The names for the hairs are those of H. Hinton, modified as suggested by A. Mutuura and M. Mackay. There are very microscopic hairs on the the top front and bottom front of the segments, too, but they are difficult to study and are not shown; they are tactile organs that detect when the segment in front overlaps them.   *274, Libytheana carinenta bachmanii*, "primary setae," the hairs that are present on nearly all butterfly and moth larvae (except that SD2 is also a primary seta on thoracic segments 2 and 3, present in nearly all Lepidoptera even though missing in *Libytheana*). Pieridae are very similar to species 274 but have longer and usually clubbed hairs, lack L2 on the prothorax, have SD2 on the mesothorax, and may or may not have P6 on abdominal segments 1 and 2. Nymphalidae (except *Boloria improba*, 245, and *Speyeria nokomis*, 254) are also similar to species 274, but they have much longer and mostly unclubbed hairs, often an XD2 below XD1 on the prothorax, and usually SD2 on the mesothorax and metathorax. Hesperiidae are similar, but they have rings and often clubbed or forked hairs; some hairs on the rear are usually very long, and XD2 often occurs below XD1 on the prothorax. In Pyrginae and Pyrrhopyginae skippers, SD2 occurs on the mesothorax and metathorax.   *6, Papilio zelicaon* form *nitra*, with many extra hairs on fleshy bumps except at XD1 and D1.   *28, Parnassius phoebus*, with extra hairs at SD and L on the thorax and at SV above the prolegs.   *245, Boloria improba acrocnema*, with extra hairs at D1, SD, and L (other *Boloria* and *Speyeria* have extra hairs at least at L, but usually not so many).   *276, Apodemia nais*, with numerous XD, D, SD, and L hairs, plus rings on the top plates.   *358, Strymon melinus*, with extra D, SD, and L hairs, many rings, and SV hairs above the prolegs.

moth larvae lack secondary setae and have the same setae, except for the few postnatal ones, in the first stage as when mature.)

Figures 49 and 50 show positions and names of the primary setae of first-stage larvae. The setal map diagrams these setae by showing them from the mid-dorsal line to the midventral line as if the body were sliced down the middle and the left side pressed onto the page. Figures 2 and 3 illustrate other setae on the mouthparts. Each true leg usually has 17 unnamed setae (five, two, six, and four on the first four segments). Some microscopic setae occur on the front of each segment, to inform the larva whether the body segment in front is touching them; these setae, useful in motion control, are too small to show here.

There are amazing differences between the major groups of butterflies in numbers of larval setae and other ornaments, such as horns, tails, hardened plates, combs, and rings—constituting, in fact, most of the variation mentioned in the key. Within the Pieridae, Nymphalidae, and Lycaenidae, for instance, some groups have hardened plates at the base of most setae, and others do not.

The Lycaenidae exhibit the most variation in ornamentation. Tropical *Menander* (Riodininae) even have the dorsal setae in the middle of the body minute or absent, and the lateral setae are scalelike. Among the Lycaeninae, the prothorax tends to be wider in harvesters (Miletini) and coppers (Lycaenini); in both, the two D1 setae are long (one-third to one-half as long as the body) and lie close together on the midline of the top of the body. Miletini are identified by having one row of subdorsal hardened rings, with a long seta behind each ring on the abdomen, and two setae between each ring and the adjacent spiracle (one tiny, posterior; one large, above the spiracle). The head tends to be small compared to the body in hairstreaks (Theclini). Blues (Polyommatini) usually have some short and clubbed SD setae on the abdomen (in *Plebejus glandon* they are long and clubbed, and in *P. melissa* they are small). These SD setae are long and hairlike in most hairstreaks, coppers, and harvesters, though they are absent in some hairstreaks (short in *Erora*) and nearly all coppers (except *Lycaena heteronea*). There are usually two long D setae on the abdomen, but *Euphilotes* have only one, and some hairstreaks have three. The suranal plate on the rear is missing in *Lycaena heteronea*, where it is replaced by rings.

The first-stage larvae are important for classifying butterflies, but because they have been inadequately studied, many differences remain to be discovered and incorporated into the scheme of classification.

A larva known to be in the first stage (hatched from an egg found in nature, for instance) can be identified as a butterfly or moth in most cases. Of course to be a butterfly it must have six thoracic legs and ten prolegs (on abdomen segments 3-6 and 10), each proleg having one row of crochets (usually arranged in a circle). And except for Papilionidae, Lycaenidae, and some Nymphalidae that have secondary setae, all butterflies have only one SV seta on the mesothorax and on the metathorax, only one L seta on abdomen segment 9, and setae L1 and L2 are far apart on each abdomen segment. All moth larvae differ from this pattern, except for perhaps a few Macrolepidoptera. And the peculiar proleg lobes distinguish Lycaenidae from all moths but a few Geometridae, which otherwise lack prolegs on abdomen segments 3-5.

The key that follows is the first of its kind for butterflies.

Key to First-Stage North American Larvae (See Figs. 48-50)

1(4) Prolegs have a fleshy lobe at the tip, the crochets interrupted next to the lobe (Fig. 4) and only a few crochets present (usually four or five), often not in a complete circle; hypostomal bridge (Fig. 3) has a gap as wide as the mandibles; hardened rings usually present on body; secondary setae present on body, often including SV setae above the prolegs; long setae on prothorax often overhang head; head seta F1 missing or extremely small in most species; head setae C1 and C2 far apart; abdomen segments 9 and 10 generally appear fused; Fam. Lycaenidae, go to 2 and 3

2(3) Prothorax covers less than half of the normal-size head; crochets on front prolegs usually arranged in a circle, the circle interrupted in front and back and near the lobe; body often has hardened subdorsal and sublateral setae-bearing plates on every segment (tropical *Anatole* and *Menander* lack the plates); rings when present only subdorsal; often more than two setae on mandible; head setae usually same length on top and front (but short on top in the Mexican *Anatole*) . . . .
. . . . Subfam. Riodininae, p. 348

3(2) Prothorax extends forward to cover half of the often-small head; crochets on front prolegs arranged in an inner semicircle (Fig. 4); hardened body plates only on prothorax and rear; rings present in two to four rows, at least subdorsally and laterally; only two mandible setae; head setae much shorter on top than on front (see text to identify the tribes) .... Subfam. Lycaeninae, p. 355

4(1) Prolegs lack a fleshy lobe, the crochets continuous at least on inner margin and usually in a complete circle; hypostomal bridge (Fig. 3) has only a hairline gap; rings present only in skippers; setae vary; go to 5 and 12

5(12) Hardened rings present on body, subdorsally and sublaterally; head and body have only primary setae (including two L setae on prothorax); setae generally short and clubbed or forked at tip, but sometimes longer and hairlike on the rear and on the body of Megathyminae; head usually much wider than thorax; Fam. Hesperiidae, go to 6 and 9

6(9) Only one SD seta on mesothorax, one on metathorax; rings paired (like a figure 8) on side of thorax segments 2 and 3; rings on abdomen segments 8 and 9 below spiracles; go to 7 and 8

7(8) Setae on middle of body all short and broadened at tip .... Subfam. Hesperiinae, p. 424

8(7) Setae on middle of body long and hairlike .... Subfam. Megathyminae, p. 416

9(6) Two SD setae on side of mesothorax, two on metathorax; no paired rings; rings absent on thorax segments 2 and 3; rings on abdomen segments 8 and/or 9 above spiracles; go to 10 and 11

10(11) Setae clubbed or forked at tip; setae short (less than or equal to the front-to-back length of the segment), the D2 setae not longer; head neither flattened nor bumpy .... Subfam. Pyrginae, p. 469

11(10) Setae hairlike; setae long, the D2 setae much longer than the others (about three times the length of the segment on abdomen segments 7-9); head flattened (ringed with a conspicuous ridge on top and sides), slightly bumpy, with a network of dark "veins" .... *Pyrrhopyge araxes* (Subfam. Pyrrhopyginae), p. 500

12(5) Rings absent; secondary setae present in some species; setae various in shape; head usually about as wide as thorax; go to 13 and 24

13(24) Secondary setae present on body or head; SV setae present above first eight prolegs (except in *Speyeria* and *Boloria*); go to 14 and 21

14(21) Body has some scoli; head has at least one secondary seta, and secondary setae common on body; SV setae above prolegs; clusters of setae do not arise from plates; Subfam. Papilioninae, go to 15 and 18

15(18) Setae, but not scoli, present slightly above abdominal spiracles 2-8 (scoli may occur above this row on *top* of abdomen); *Battus* (Tribe Troidini), go to 16 and 17

16(17) Scoli present on top of abdomen .... *Battus polydamas*, p. 186

17(16) Setae, but no scoli, on top of abdomen .... *Battus philenor*, p. 185

18(15) A row of scoli slightly above abdominal spiracles 2-8; go to 19 and 20

19(20) Some setae on scoli forked at tip .... *Parides* (Tribe Troidini) and *Eurytides* (Tribe Leptocircini), pp. 186 and 162

20(19) No forked setae .... *Papilio* (Tribe Papilionini), p. 164

21(14) No body scoli; head has only primary setae; SV setae present or absent above prolegs; clusters of setae usually arise from plates; go to 22 and 23

22(23) Secondary L setae only on thorax; no secondary D1 setae; secondary SD setae on thorax and abdomen; SV setae present above prolegs; setae hairlike .... Subfam. Parnassiinae, p. 187

23(22) Secondary L setae on thorax and abdomen; secondary D1 setae present in most species; secondary SD setae (three or more on thorax segments, two or more on abdomen segments) present only in some species; SV setae absent above prolegs; setae usually slightly clubbed at tip .... *Boloria* and *Speyeria* (Tribe Argynnini), pp. 317 and 324

24(13) Only primary setae present on body (except a D3 on each abdomen segment in Danainae) and head; SV setae absent above first eight prolegs; Fams. Nymphalidae, Libytheidae, Pieridae, go to 25, 26, and 27

25(26,27) Body has fleshy subdorsal tubercles on thorax segment 2 and sometimes on abdomen segments 2 and/or 8 (in tropics perhaps also on metathorax); setae hairlike; a D3 seta present on each abdomen segment .... Subfam. Danainae, p. 228

26(25,27) Body has about ten fleshy cones on top (on thorax segments 2 and 3 and abdomen segments 2, 7, and 8); setae clubbed; no D3 setae on abdomen ....
.... *Limenitis* (and perhaps a few other Subfam. Nymphalinae), p. 259

27(25,26) No fleshy tubercles or cones on body; setae hairlike or clubbed; no D3 setae on abdomen; go to 28, 29, and 30

28(29,30) Head has several (up to ten) small "horns" along dorsal and lateral rim (Fig. 49); eyes all same size; setae all hairlike; two short tails on rear ....
Asterocampa celtis and some *Doxocopa* (Subfam. Apaturinae), pp. 255 and 257

29(28,30) Head has two conelike bumps or "horns" on top (Fig. 49); third eye (Figs. 2, 48, 49) 50 percent larger than others; body setae clubbed (short or long); usually two short to long tails on rear (except for *Megisto* and others) .... some
Subfam. Satyrinae (*Lethe, Cyllopsis, Megisto, Neonympha,* and others), p. 233

30(28,29) Head has neither bumps nor horns (some *Anaea* have two very small rounded bumps on top of head); eyes all same size or third eye larger; setae vary; tails present or absent; go to 31 and 32

31(32) Third eye (Fig. 2) 50 percent larger than other five; often two fleshy tails on the rear (none in *Cercyonis* and others); body and often head setae clubbed (short or long) or bladelike (like a scythe in *Cercyonis*); head much taller than thorax ....
some Subfam. Satyrinae (*Cercyonis, Erebia, Oeneis,* probably others), p. 240

32(31) All eyes roughly same size; no tails on rear (some Apaturinae have two short tails); body setae clubbed or hairlike, but not bladelike; head about as tall as thorax; go to 33, 34, and 37

33(34,37) Two L setae on prothorax; one SD seta each on mesothorax and metathorax; very wide flange on rear of head behind eyes; setae around rim of labrum (Fig. 2) minute, and all body setae very short, most of them slightly widened at tip; prothorax as large as mesothorax, with slight shoulders . . . . Fam. Libytheidae, p. 344

34(33,37) One L seta on prothorax; two SD setae on mesothorax, one on metathorax; head flange behind eyes not conspicuous; body setae vary; prothorax a bit smaller than mesothorax; Fam. Pieridae, go to 35 and 36

35(36) Body setae clubbed and often glandular (the forked tips of D1 and D2 dispense honeydew attractive to ants), varying from very short (except on the rear in *Colias*) to long (as long as a body segment in Pierinae and *Eurema*) . . . . most Fam. Pieridae (all Pierinae, most Coliadinae), p. 191

36(35) Body setae hairlike (perhaps very slightly enlarged at the tapered tip, perhaps not glandular) and almost as long as a body segment . . . . some Fam. Pieridae (*Nathalis*, perhaps others), p. 210

37(33,34) Two L setae on prothorax; two SD setae each on mesothorax and metathorax; head flange not conspicuous, though an L-shaped plate may occur just behind the head on the neck; body setae hairlike, varying from short to very long; prothorax a bit smaller than mesothorax; Fam. Nymphalidae, go to 38 and 39

38(39) Body setae long, visible to the naked eye . . . . most species of Fam. Nymphalidae, including some species of Subfam. Apaturinae (*Asterocampa clyton* and some *Doxocopa*, both of which may have two short tails) and some species of Tribe Argynnini (*Euptoieta*, but not including *Speyeria* or *Boloria*), p. 227

39(38) Body and head setae very short and clubbed, not visible to the naked eye; head and body mottled with pale dots (the head of *Anaea andria* is smooth, but *A. pithyusa* may have two low bumps on top of head—some tropical species have two to six head horns and two tails) . . . . Subfam. Charaxinae, p. 253

Identifying Mature Larvae

The second larval stage is usually a major transitional stage, in which the structures of the first stage change somewhat and already begin to resemble those of the mature larva. The third and later stages usually closely resemble the mature larva, although the colors and some structures may continue to change somewhat. In general, the transition from first stage to mature larva is marked by an enormous multiplication of small hairs (setae) on the body and an increase in the relative length of the horns, filaments, tails, branching spines (scoli), and other ornaments. Additional glands may appear, such as the ant-related glands of Lycaenidae (Fig. 1; see "Mimicry and Other Defenses," in Part I), the powder glands of Hesperiidae, the osmeteria of Papilionidae, and the ventral neck gland.

Mature larvae can be identified by shape to family, usually to subfamily, and often even to species (Fig. 51). Colors, too, which are given in Part III, are characteristic in many species. The key that follows uses shapes and structures to identify the major groups.

Older larvae of moths and butterflies can usually be separated. All butterfly larvae have six thoracic legs, ten prolegs (on abdomen segments 3-6 and 10), and hundreds of secondary setae all over the head and body; moreover, the crochets are in one row and are of three (sometimes two) lengths (some Satyrinae butterflies have crochets of only one length, but their third larval eye is larger than the other eyes; some Lycaenidae have crochets of only one length, but all lycaenids have their unique proleg lobe on all the prolegs). All Papilioni-

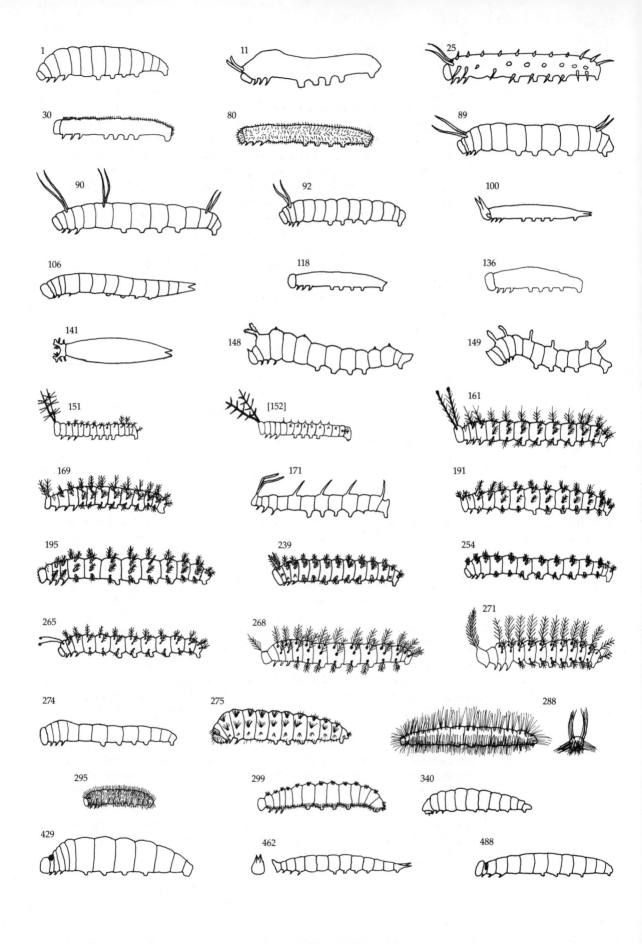

Fig. 51 (*facing page*).   The major shapes of mature larvae, mostly from the left side.   *1, Eurytides marcellus*, with the osmeteria withdrawn.   *11, Papilio cresphontes* (similar: other *Papilio*, 4-24): the two protruded structures behind the head are osmeteria; normally withdrawn into the thorax, they occur in all Papilionidae.   *25, Battus philenor*, with 22 fleshy tubercles on each side and six orange spots on the abdomen; the two osmeteria are withdrawn.   *30, Parnassius eversmanni*.   *80, Pieris protodice* (similar: all Pieridae).   *89, Danaus plexippus*.   *90, Danaus gilippus*.   *92, Lycorea cleobaea*, the tentacles of *Danaus* and *Lycorea* cannot be withdrawn.   *100, Cyllopsis pertepida*, with two head horns and two tails (similar: *Lethe*, 93-97).   *106, Coenonympha tullia*, with two tails (similar: *Megisto*, 102, 103; *Neonympha*, 104; *Cercyonis*, 108-111; most other Satyrinae).   *118, Erebia theano*, with two short tails (similar: *Neominois*, 125; *Oeneis*, 126-135).   *136, Anaea andria*.   *141, Asterocampa leilia*, top view; the plumelike structures in species 141-268 are hard branching spines or antlers (*Doxocopa laure*, 144, has smaller side branches on the horns).   *148, Limenitis lorquini*.   *149, Limenitis bredowii*.   *151, Epiphile adrasta*.   *[152], Diaethria astala* (a tropical species, but *D. asteria*, 152, is probably similar).   *161, Hamadryas februa* (similar: *H. amphinome*, 168, but without middorsal spines on abdominal segments 1-6 and with one middorsal spine on segments 7 and 8; *Eunica monima*, 155; *Myscelia ethusa*, 157; *Biblis*, 160; *Siproeta*, 176; *Anartia*, 177-179).   *169, Smyrna karwinskii*.   *171, Marpesia petreus*.   *191, Polygonia satyrus* (similar: *Historis odius*, 170; *Marpesia chiron*, 173; *Hypolimnas*, 175; also *Precis*, 180-182, but with shorter head antlers).   *195, Nymphalis milberti* (similar: *Hypanartia*, 183; *Vanessa*, 184-187; Melitaeini; also *Phyciodes*, 224-236, but with short spines).   *239, Boloria selene*.   *254, Speyeria nokomis* (similar: most *Boloria*, 238-249).   *265, Euptoieta claudia*.   *268, Dione vanillae* (similar: *D. moneta*, 269; *Dryas*, 270; *Heliconius*, 272, 273).   *271, Heliconius isabella*.   *274, Libytheana carinenta*, sometimes with two small tubercles on the humped thorax.   *275, Apodemia mormo*.   *288, Calephelis wrighti*, side and rear views.   *295, Feniseca tarquinius*.   *299, Eumaeus minijas*.   *340, Callophrys gryneus* (all Lycaeninae are slug-shaped with a carpet of very short hair).   *429, Agathymus stephensi* (similar: all Megathyminae).   *462, Copaeodes aurantiaca*, front and side views, showing the two horns and two tails.   *488, Polites sabuleti* (similar: almost all skippers). (See also Color Plates 2-4.)

dae are distinguished by their unique osmeteria. Some moths (Saturniidae and Sphingidae) have branching spines or body prongs like those of Nymphalinae, but these moths lack head spines and their middorsal body spines occur only on abdomen segments 8 or 9. These indicators should separate nearly all moth and butterfly larvae.

Key to Mature North American Larvae (See Fig. 51)

This key should work for all larvae that are half-grown or older, but not for first- and some second-stage larvae; to identify second-stage larvae, the key to first-stage larvae and the key to mature larvae should both be tried. The key is based partly on the work of S. Scudder, S. Fracker, A. Petersen, and others.

1(12) Abdomen or head armed with hard branching spines or spiny cones (scoli) or branching antlers; many Fam. Nymphalidae, go to 2 and 3

2(3) Body lacks branching spines, is covered merely with tiny hairs (though the head has two thick branching antlers and a few other processes, and rear of body is forked into two "tails"); no larval nests . . . . Subfam. Apaturinae, p. 255

3(2) Body has branching spines or horns; some species have larval nests; Subfam. Nymphalinae, go to 4 and 9

4(9) Spines and horns absent on middorsal line of body; nests only for some hibernating larvae; go to 5 and 6

5(6) Body has 2-12 prickly horns or tubercles, paired on top of body, those on middle of thorax the longest; thorax enlarged; leaf nests only for hibernating larvae; head with very small bumplike horns . . . . *Limenitis* (Tribe Nymphalini), p. 259

6(5) Body has many branching spines; thorax not enlarged; no larval nests; go to 7 and 8

7(8) Head has neither branching spines nor antlers . . . . . Tribe Argynnini, p. 316

8(7) Head has branching spines . . . . Tribe Heliconiini, p. 336

9(4) Spines or horns present on middorsal line of body (only on the rear in *Hamadryas*, tiny in *Diaethria*; both species rare strays to s Tex.); larval nests frequent; go to 10 and 11

10(11) Branching spines horny, fairly narrow, with a distinct single thorn at the tip; usually only one small branching spine at base of first proleg (except two in *Precis* and perhaps others) . . . . Tribe Nymphalini (except *Limenitis*), p. 259

11(10) Branching spines less horny, more conical, with many crowded needles but no single independent needle at the tip; two small branching spines at base of first proleg . . . . Tribe Melitaeini, p. 291

12(1) Abdomen and head have neither hard antlers nor branching spines (though the head in Satyrinae and Hesperiinae sometimes has two conelike horns); go to 13 and 16

13(16) Body has several to many nonretractable fleshy filaments; body nearly hairless; no larval nests; go to 14 and 15

14(15) Body has ten or more long or short filaments on top and sides, plus two orange smelly filaments (osmeteria) that pop out from a dorsal groove behind the head when the larva is disturbed . . . . Tribe Troidini, p. 184

15(14) Body has two long filaments on top of mesothorax, and sometimes filaments on abdomen (two each on top of segments 2 and 8; some foreign tropical species have filaments even on metathorax) . . . . Subfam. Danainae, p. 228

16(13) Body lacks fleshy nonretractable filaments; body hairless or hairy; larval nests in some species; go to 17 and 18

17(18) Prothorax has two orange smelly filaments (osmeteria) that pop out from a dorsal groove behind the head when the larva is disturbed; body nearly hairless; no larval nests . . . . Tribes Leptocircini and Papilionini, pp. 162 and 163

18(17) Body lacks retractable or fixed filaments, horns, antlers, or branching spines (*Parnassius* have osmeteria, though they are never used); hair and nests present or absent; go to 19 and 24

19(24) Crochets on first eight prolegs arranged in a circle (the circle rarely briefly interrupted); body hairs few and small, mostly on underside; ventral glands on abdomen segments 7 and 8 produce waterproofing powder before pupation; Fam. Hesperiidae, go to 20 and 21

20(21) Larvae bore into roots or fleshy leaves of Agavaceae plants; head smaller than prothorax, the body thick throughout . . . . Subfam. Megathyminae, p. 416

21(20) Larvae are external feeders, but live in silked-leaf nests; head much larger than the narrow prothorax; go to 22 and 23

22(23) Monocotyledon eaters; head widest about at middle, sometimes with conical horns (*Copaeodes*); rear of abdomen sometimes has two short tails . . . . Subfam. Hesperiinae, p. 424

23(22) Dicotyledon eaters (except some subtropical *Urbanus* that eat grass); head wider on top than in middle, without horns; abdomen has no tails . . . . Subfams. Pyrginae and Pyrrhopyginae, pp. 469 and 500

24(19) Crochets on first eight prolegs mostly in a semicircle on inside half of proleg, any crochets present on outer half rudimentary; go to 25 and 28

25(28) Semicircle of crochets (on inside of each of the first eight prolegs) interrupted or reduced near the center, and a spatula-like lobe near the interruption (Fig. 4); head often small, always with a wide gap in the hypostomal bridge (Fig. 3); larva usually sluglike; hair sometimes long; often associated with ants; Fam. Lycaenidae, go to 26 and 27

26(27) Head about half the width of body; body usually has tufts of fairly long hairs (very long in *Calephelis*, shorter in *Apodemia*); more than two hairs (often a dozen) on each mandible; body often less sluglike than most Lycaeninae; larva sometimes in a silked-leaf nest; a few crochets on outside of proleg .... Subfam. Riodininae, p. 348

27(26) Head small (rarely more than one-third the diameter of body), retractable into thorax or extensible forward; hairs tiny, coating the body like a carpet; only two hairs on each mandible; body usually sluglike, with heavy skin folds and a lateral ridge (less sluglike and head about one-half width of body in *Feniseca* and *Eumaeus*; the hairs longer in *Feniseca*, slightly longer and in tufts in *Eumaeus*); larva not in a silked nest but sometimes inside fruits or pods; no crochets on outside of proleg .... Subfam. Lycaeninae, p. 355

28(25) Semicircle of crochets lacks both the interruption and the fleshy lobe near the center of the semicircle; head normal in size, with a narrow gap in hypostomal bridge (as in Fig. 3); larva not sluglike; hairs very short; not associated with ants; go to 29 and 30

29(30) Rear of larva forked into two short to medium-length tails (very short in *Erebia magdalena* and perhaps others); third eye (Fig. 2) usually much larger than others; hairs not arising from conelike bumps on body; crochets sometimes of only one length (or of two or three lengths as in other butterflies); head often has two conelike horns; monocotyledon eaters; no larval nests, though some species construct earthen cells for pupation .... Subfam. Satyrinae, p. 233

30(29) Rear of larva rounded, not forked; eyes all the same size; cones occasionally present; crochets of two or three lengths; head horns only in Charaxinae; dicotyledon eaters; larval nests only in Charaxinae; go to 31, 32, 33, and 34

31(32,33,34) Body thickest in middle, tapered at both ends, the head small (only half as wide as body); larvae have osmeteria, like other Papilionidae (though they are never used); body covered all over with a carpet of thousands of short black hairs, the larva black with lateral rows of yellow or orange dots; no neck gland; crochets arranged in two-thirds of a circle (missing on the outside lateral third); no nest, though larvae worm themselves into pebbly soil; hostplants Crassulaceae and Fumariaceae .... Subfam. Parnassiinae, p. 187

32(31,33,34) Body thicker at thorax than at abdomen, the head about as wide as abdomen; no osmeteria; hairs few and tiny except on legs (one on a tiny cone on front of each segment, some coarse bristles on top of head and body); a ventral neck gland; crochets in a semicircle on inside of proleg, a rudimentary row on outside; no nest; hostplants *Celtis* .... Fam. Libytheidae, p. 344

33(31,32,34) Body thickest from middle of thorax to near end of abdomen, the head somewhat narrower than body; no osmeteria; head has many bumps, including several bumplike "horns" on top (foreign species may have four to six horns); body covered with tiny white cones, but tiny hairs mostly lacking except on underside; no neck gland; crochets only in a semicircle on inside of proleg; larva in a rolled-leaf nest; hostplants Euphorbiaceae .... *Anaea* (Subfam. Charaxinae), p. 253

34(31,32,33) Body cylindrical, tapered only at the rear, the head about as wide as body; no osmeteria; body has many tiny hairs, in some cases on tiny cones or plates, and in most Pierinae (except species 76-78 at least) the dorsal primary setae are long bristles; neck gland often present; crochets only in a semicircle on inside of proleg; no nest; hostplants mostly Leguminosae and Cruciferae .... Fam. Pieridae, p. 191

Identifying Pupae

The function of the pupa is to provide a period of time for perfecting the changes needed to turn a caterpillar (larva) into an adult (see "Molting and Metamorphosis," in Part I). Some pupae are cryptically colored, but others are quite beautiful. The name "chrysalis," in fact, often used for butterfly pupae, derives from the gold-colored spots on some Nymphalidae pupae (*chrysos* is the ancient

Fig. 52 (*facing page*).   The major shapes of pupae, mostly from the left side, all in the natural position.   *1, Eurytides marcellus.   9, Papilio indra.   19, Papilio eurymedon* (similar: most *Papilio*, 4-24).   *25, Battus philenor*, side and dorsal views (similar: *Parides*, 27, but without the pointed keel on top of the thorax).   *30, Parnassius eversmanni.   [31, Dismorphia amphione* (a tropical species, but probably similar to *Enantia albania*, 31).   *37, Colias eurytheme* (similar: *Colias cesonia*, 44; *Anteos clorinde*, 46; *Kricogonia*, 66).   *50, Phoebis sennae* (similar: *P. philea*, 53, but with somewhat less protruding wings).   *55, Eurema nicippe* (similar: *E. lisa*, 63, but with less protruding wings).   *67, Nathalis iole.   73, Euchloe ausonia* (similar: *Anthocharis*, 68-71).   *78, Pieris virginiensis* (similar: *P. napi*, 77, but the head cone is shorter and the abdomen flares more subdorsally).   *80, Pieris protodice* (similar: most *Pieris*, 79-82; see the text).   *83, Ascia monuste.   84, Ascia josephina*, with two spines on each side.   *89, Danaus plexippus*, the head lacks a ridge but has two bumps, and the ridge on the abdomen has bumps.   *100, Cyllopsis pertepida*, with two head horns.   *106, Coenonympha tullia* (similar: most Satyrinae).   *134, Oeneis melissa* in a loose silk nest, in loose soil, or under rocks or debris, without cremaster hooks (similar, with similar pupation sites: other *Oeneis; Erebia*, 112-123; *Neominois*, 125).   *136, Anaea andria*, with the cremaster angled backward and a transverse ridge on the head.   *141, Asterocampa leilia*, with two short head horns, the body flattened sideways with a ridge on top of the abdomen (similar: *Doxocopa pavon*, 143; *A. celtis*, 140, and *A. clyton*, 142, also similar, but attached flat to leaf underside).   *144, Doxocopa laure.   145, Limenitis archippus*, with two short head horns.   *149, Limenitis bredowii.   151, Epiphile adrasta* (similar: *Diaethria asteria*, 152, lying flat on leaf or twig).   *154, Dynamine dyonis.   160, Biblis hyperia*, dorsal view.   *161, Hamadryas februa*, with the two horns close together.   *168, Hamadryas amphinome.   170, Historis odius.   171, Marpesia petreus.   176, Siproeta stelenes.   180, Precis coenia* (similar: *Smyrna karwinskii*, 169; *Anartia*, 177-179).   *183, Hypanartia lethe.   186, Vanessa cardui.   196, Nymphalis californica*, with two short head horns (similar: *Polygonia*, 189-193).   *214, Chlosyne janais* (similar: *Euptoieta claudia*, 265; Argynnini; Melitaeini).   *268, Dione vanillae* (similar: *D. moneta*, 269).   *270, Dryas iulia.   271, Heliconius isabella.   272, Heliconius charitonia.   274, Libytheana carinenta.   275, Apodemia mormo.   288, Calephelis wrighti.   295, Feniseca tarquinius*, side and top views.   *298, Eumaeus atala.   340, Callophrys gryneus siva* (similar: most Lycaeninae); Lycaenidae (275-416) sometimes pupate under loose bark or under leaves or rocks.   *417, Megathymus yuccae*, with a broad flat cremaster (similar: *Megathymus*, 417-420; *Stallingsia*, 421).   *429, Agathymus stephensi.   465, Hylephila phyleus*, with the proboscis extending beyond the wings (many other Hesperiinae similar: *Polites*, 489-496; *Atalopedes*, 500; *Ochlodes*, 505, 506; *Paratrytone*, 515; *Amblyscirtes aenus*, 538; some *Hesperia*, 470); skippers (430-679) may be attached by both the cremaster and a silk girdle in a rolled-leaf nest.   *471, Hesperia juba*, with no horn and with the proboscis no longer than the wings (similar: many Hesperiinae).   *560, Panoquina panoquinoides*, with a head horn (some other Hesperiinae similar: *Carterocephalus*, 430; *Cymaenes tripunctus*, 446; *Lerema accius*, 448; *Perichares*, 451; *Copaeodes*, 461, 462; *Thymelicus*, 464; *Lerodea eufala*, 555; *Calpodes*, 558).   *571, Epargyreus clarus* (similar: Pyrginae, but often not so stout).   (See also Color Plates 4, 5.)

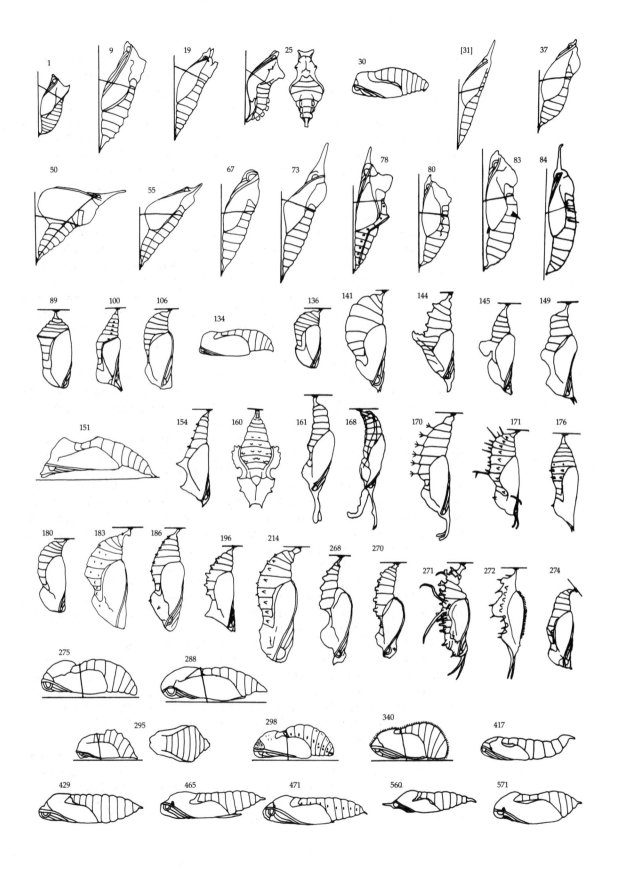

Greek word for gold). Pupae are generally hard to find in nature, because they are nearly motionless and often camouflaged, and because the larva—of all but skippers—wanders far from where it grew up to pupate.

Pupae are capable of very little movement. The legs and antennae do not move at all, and the only possible movement is between the middle segments of the abdomen (between segments 4 and 5, 5 and 6, and 6 and 7). Even at these joints, however, only a few groups of butterflies can move both up-and-down and side-to-side (skippers such as *Megathymus* are the most nimble); many butterflies can move only from side to side, and some Lycaenidae can barely move at all.

Figures 5 and 6 show the structures of pupae. They may have horns, cones, spines, scoli, and setae like those on larvae, and the honeydew glands of larval Lycaenidae may appear also on the pupa. Structures found only in pupae are long ridges, keels, large body points, and irregular body projections. The two anal prolegs and crochets of the larva become the single cremaster with its crochets, which the pupating larva uses to attach itself to a surface (in some species a silk-cable belt provides extra attachment, like that used by a logger climbing a tree). The cremaster is pointed, but in some Lycaenidae it is a mere bump. A slit near the cremaster is very useful for determining the sex of the pupa: on the bottom of abdomen segment 9 of males is a short groove between hemispherical bumps; on segments 8 and 9 of females there is a long slit. On the bottom of segment 10 near the cremaster is another slit, the anal groove, which represents the opening of the larval intestine. It does not function in pupae; rather, the wastes are stored until the adult emerges and voids them.

The two proboscis halves of the pupa taper from the head rearward, midventrally. In some skippers the proboscis case may extend beyond the wings, unattached to the body. The antennae run beside the wings, their clubs and segments clearly visible. Only four legs are visible, beside the proboscis; the last two legs are beneath the antennae, their tips rarely visible. The labial palpi are beneath the proboscis, and only a narrow midventral strip (the labial sclerite, absent in most species) is visible, between the two mandible rudiments. The eyes consist of a smooth, crescent-shaped "orbit" and a rougher "eye." The wings are small compared to those of the adult, and always wrap around the body; the wing bases are on the sides of the thorax, and the wingtips lie next to each other covering the underside of the first four segments of the abdomen. The hindwings are generally visible only as a small sliver (just above the forewings) that tapers backward from the third thorax segment.

Spiracles occur on the sides of abdomen segments 2-7, and there is a vestigial or nonfunctional spiracle on segment 8. A spiracle on segment 1 is always covered by the wing and is useless (in some Nymphalidae the spiracles on abdomen segments 2 and 3 are partly covered as well). There is a lateral spiracle between the prothorax and mesothorax in all pupae; it is generally a slit (in nearly all skippers but Megathyminae it is a plateau), usually about twice as long as the abdominal spiracles, and usually incorporates a feltlike structure.

A day or two before the adult emerges, the colors of the adult wings become visible through the pupal shell. The pupa splits in a peculiar fashion when the adult emerges (Fig. 7; see "Molting and Metamorphosis," in Part I, for details). On the underside of the empty shell is a flap representing the covers of the proboscis, legs, head, and usually the antennae.

Butterfly pupae can be identified at least to family or subfamily (Fig. 52). The species texts in Part III describe the colors and sometimes the shape of the pupae of each species, all of which help in identification. The key that follows uses mainly body structures and attachment habits to identify the major groups. It is based partly on the work of E. Mosher and others.

Key to North American Pupae (See Fig. 52)

1(2) Antennae usually not clubbed; pupa usually in a tough silk cocoon; mandibles present and functional, or if nonfunctional (almost always) then the mandible remnants usually widely separated by the labrum; maxillary palpi often present (as a narrow transverse strip between eye and legs); movement often possible at abdomen joints 2-3, 3-4, and 7-8, rarely at 1-2; backward-directed spines, used to wriggle out of cocoon, often present on abdomen; cremaster present or absent (often absent even on elongate pupae); legs sometimes movable; femur of first leg sometimes visible (as a strip between first leg and proboscis) .... moths

2(1) Antennae clubbed; pupa never in a strong cocoon (some Satyrinae and *Parnassius* may be in a weak silk cocoon, and skippers and others are in a leaf nest); mandibles not functional, the mandible remnants close together (separated usually by a groove, sometimes by a narrow labial sclerite, Fig. 5); maxillary palpi absent; movement possible only at abdomen joints 4-5, 5-6, and 6-7, and often not even at these; no backward-directed spines on abdomen; cremaster present (except in some deer-pellet-shaped Lycaenidae); legs not movable; femur of first leg not visible; butterflies, go to 3 and 10

3(10) Base of proboscis touches orbit of the eye (as in Fig. 5); thoracic spiracle has a large posterior plateau (except in Megathyminae); a prominent transverse cleavage line lies between the antenna bases (the vertex behind the line adheres to the prothorax after adult emergence; Fig. 6); pupa generally plain reddish-brown to green, usually covered with a waxy white powder; pupa in a silked-leaf nest or root; Superfam. Hesperioidea, Fam. Hesperiidae (skippers), go to 4 and 7

4(7) Head only about half as wide as thorax; pupa in a burrow in roots or fleshy leaves of Agavaceae plants; thoracic spiracle a crevice; proboscis does not extend as far as wingtips (actually often nearly to wingtips but almost always covered by wingtips, which are adjacent on the midventral line); Subfam. Megathyminae, go to 5 and 6

5(6) Cremaster broad and flat like a duck bill, with long dense bristles; abdomen segments telescope and move in any direction; pupa moves up and down in the long (a meter or more) root burrow, using the cremaster and abdomen for locomotion; opening of burrow a silk tube covered with dung pellets .... Tribe Megathymini, p. 416

6(5) Cremaster pointed, with small bristles or none; abdomen segments not as movable; pupa rather immobile in short burrow in fleshy leaves; opening of burrow a circular trapdoor .... Tribe Aegialini, p. 420

7(4) Head more than half as wide or as wide as thorax; pupa in a silked nest, usually of leaves, sometimes suspended by a silk girdle; a large plateau behind the thoracic spiracle; proboscis extends to or beyond tips of wing cases; go to 8 and 9

8(9) A unicornlike horn on head, or the proboscis extending far beyond wingtips .... many in Subfam. Hesperiinae, p. 424

9(8) No horn on head, the proboscis extending about as far as wingtips . . . .
. . . . others in Subfam. Hesperiinae, plus Subfams. Pyrginae and Pyrrhopyginae, pp. 424, 469, and 500

10(3) Base of proboscis not touching eye orbit; thoracic spiracle has a small
slanted plateau or is inconspicuous; no cleavage line between antenna
bases; pupa often colorful, lacks waxy powder; pupa sometimes between leaves, in a pod, or under bark or litter, but rarely if ever in a
silked-leaf nest, never in a root; Superfam. Papilionoidea (scudders), go
to 11 and 40

11(40) First and second legs touch the eye or its orbit (the second wedges
between the eye and the antenna a short distance); first leg generally
short; proboscis and antennae usually extend to wingtips; pupa hangs
from a silk button (but some Satyrinae do not hang, and Apaturinae,
Diaethria, and *Epiphile* lie flat on a twig or leaf); Fams. Nymphalidae
and Libytheidae, go to 12 and 23

12(23) Noticeable bumps or cones on top of body (at least on abdomen) in
rows, or a prominent sharp point on top of thorax or abdomen; Subfam. Nymphalinae, go to 13, 16, 17, 18, and 19

13(16,17,18,19) Middorsal cones absent (though there are small middorsal
bumps on the anterior margins of abdomen segments 5-7 and sometimes traces of them on 2-4 and 8); go to 14 and 15

14(15) Head with short to long horns, or at least square-ended; body has a
saddle behind thorax or has very long processes; subdorsal keels on
each abdomen segment . . . . Tribe Heliconiini, p. 336

15(14) Head rounded, lacking horns; body saddle slight; no keels on ab-
domen . . . . Tribe Argynnini, p. 316

16(13,17,18,19) Middorsal cones (including one on top of thorax) very small,
but subdorsal cones present on abdomen, especially above wings, and
the head has two short points . . . . *Siproeta* (Tribe Nymphalini), p. 274

17(13,16,18,19) Middorsal cones absent (or very small, in one tropical species), but abdomen has subdorsal cones and two lateral rows of cones,
and the top of thorax has a small keel . . . *Smyrna* (Tribe Nymphalini), p. 271

18(13,16,17,19) Middorsal spines on abdomen small, but a very prominent
point on top of abdomen segment 2 and a second on top of thorax . . . .
. . . . *Dynamine* (Tribe Nymphalini), p. 264

19(13,16,17,18) Middorsal cones present, at least on abdomen segments 3-8;
go to 20, 21, and 22

20(21,22) Middorsal spines much longer than any others; top of thorax lacks
a prominent point; head has two long processes . . . .
. . . . *Historis* and *Marpesia* (Tribe Nymphalini), pp. 271 and 272

21(20,22) Middorsal cones as large as subdorsal cones; lateral projections on
cremaster base; top of thorax lacks a prominent point; head generally
lacks points or processes . . . . Tribe Melitaeini, p. 291

22(20,21) Middorsal cones smaller than subdorsal cones; no lateral projections on cremaster base; top of thorax often has a prominent point;
head sometimes has two short points . . . .
. . . . Tribe Nymphalini (most genera), p. 259

23(12) Top of body lacks prominent cones or spines or sharp points; go to
24, 25, and 29

24(25,29) No saddle horn or keel on abdomen; a bluntly pointed middorsal ridge on top of thorax; two short horns on head; pupa flat on a leaf or twig ....
..... some of Tribe Nymphalini (*Epiphile*, *Diaethria*, probably others), p. 259

25(24,29) Prominent large saddle horn or large keel on top of abdomen; no ridge on thorax; two short horns on head; go to 26, 27, and 28

26(27,28) Prominent saddle horn on top of abdomen segment 2; body not flattened sideways .... most *Limenitis* (Tribe Nymphalini), p. 259

27(26,28) Small middorsal keel on top of abdomen segment 2; body not flattened sideways .... *Limenitis bredowii* (Tribe Nymphalini), p. 263

28(26,27) Large backward-pointing middorsal keel on top of abdomen segment 3; body appears somewhat flattened sideways ....
.... *Doxocopa laure* (Subfam. Apaturinae), p. 258

29(24,25) No saddle horn or keel on abdomen, though there may be a blunt point or rim or ridge on abdomen; no point or ridge on thorax; head varies; go to 30, 31, 32, and 33

30(31,32,33) Two very long processes on head; no middorsal ridges (though some species have one middorsal point each on abdomen segments 2 and 3); pupa hangs upside down .... *Hamadryas* (Tribe Nymphalini), p. 266

31(30,32,33) Two short horns on head; body flattened sideways, with a slight middorsal ridge on thorax and abdomen, the ridge evenly rounded on top of abdomen in side view; pupa often rests flat on leaf; a white stripe on head horns terminates on top of thorax ....
.... *Asterocampa* and *Doxocopa pavon* (Subfam. Apaturinae), pp. 255 and 257

32(30,31,33) Two short lateral horns on head; body flattened sideways and angled to a blunt point on top of abdomen segment 2 (a yellowish line extends from this point across the wing bases to front of head); pupa hangs upside down; thorax hunched upward; peculiar folds above spiracle on abdomen segment 2 .... Fam. Libytheidae, p. 344

33(30,31,32) Head lacks short horns (but has protruding lateral corners in many Satyrinae); no middorsal ridge; resting position varies; go to 34 and 37

34(37) Abdomen wide on segment 4, where there is a dorsal rim (the rim sometimes weak), the abdomen segments rapidly tapering from rim to cremaster; body short and stout; go to 35 and 36

35(36) Cremaster aimed as much ventrally as posteriorly; rim is on abdomen segment 4 (though segment 4 is rounded and not rimmed in *Anaea pithyusa*); head has a prominent transverse ridge, which extends along eyes and laterally along body; abdomen segments 2, 3, and 4 about same length; proboscis as long as wings .... Subfam. Charaxinae, p. 253

36(35) Cremaster aimed posteriorly; rim is on abdomen segment 3 and has many bumps; head lacks the ridge but has a lateral bump; abdomen segment 2 longer than segments 3 or 4; proboscis shorter than wings
.... Subfam. Danainae, p. 228

37(34) Abdomen evenly decreasing in width toward cremaster, lacking the rim; body usually not short and stout; Subfam. Satyrinae, go to 38 and 39

38(39) Cremaster present, with hooks; pupa hangs upside down from a silk pad; thorax humped on top; body not notably short; head has a transverse ridge and slightly protruding lateral corners; abdomen segments movable . . . . most of Subfam. Satyrinae, p. 233

39(38) Cremaster tiny or absent, lacking hooks (in *Erebia* it is long but has only a few short straight bristles on dorsal side, and no hooks); pupa among silked debris (*Erebia*) or partly underground (completely underground in a British relative, *Hipparchia*); thorax usually not conspicuously humped; body short and stout; head rounded, without ridge; abdomen segments mostly unmovable (except in *Erebia*) . . . .
. . . . *Erebia*, *Neominois*, and *Oeneis* (Subfam. Satyrinae), pp. 243 and 247

40(11) First leg, but never the second, touches the eye or its orbit; first leg short or long; proboscis and antennae vary in length; pupa never hangs from a silk button, and usually has a silk girdle; go to 41 and 49

41(49) Head has no projections; proboscis varies; pupa seldom (only in *Nathalis*) attached with a silk girdle, the cremaster hooking into a silk pad; go to 42, 43, and 44

42(43,44) Pupa long and thin; pupa attached upright with a silk girdle and cremaster; proboscis extending to wingtips; first legs normal length . . . .
. . . . *Nathalis* (Subfam. Coliadinae), p. 210

43(42,44) Pupa large and rounded, even at rear; pupa lacking cremaster, hooks, or silk girdle, in a loose cocoon of a few silk threads or underground; proboscis extending to wingtips; first legs normal length . . . . . .
. . . . Subfam. Parnassiinae, p. 187

44(42,43) Pupa generally small, short, stout, and rounded, like a deer pellet; pupa often has a silk girdle, but is seldom attached upright with the girdle and cremaster (cremaster usually absent, though hooks are usually present); proboscis not extending to wingtips; first legs often shortened; abdomen segments only slightly movable; Fam. Lycaenidae, go to 45 and 46

45(46) Abdomen rounded, not at all pointed at tip (cremaster absent, though hooks may occur); no projections or bumps; antennae not visible from above because prothorax extends forward, making the head ventral . . . .
. . . . Tribes Theclini, Lycaenini, and Polyommatini (most of Subfam. Lycaeninae), pp. 357, 386, and 393

46(45) Abdomen somewhat pointed toward tip (a slight cremaster present, with hooks); other traits vary as noted below; go to 47 and 48

47(48) Abdomen almost twice as wide as thorax, its tip flattened; from top the pupa resembles a monkey's head; antennae not visible from above, because head positioned on bottom of pupa; small rounded dorsal bumps present . . . . *Feniseca* (Tribe Miletini), p. 356

48(47) Abdomen a little wider than thorax; no suggestion of monkey's head; antennae arise anteriorly and may be visible from above, because prothorax shorter . . . . Subfam. Riodininae, p. 348

49(41) Head has one or two prominent projections, or is at least not rounded; proboscis as long as wings; pupa of all species attached with a silk girdle, the cremaster hooking into a silk pad; go to 50 and 57

50(57) Head has two hornlike extensions on front (these extensions very small in a few species, the head merely squared off); hindwings slightly visible on underside; thorax pointed on top; proboscis as long as wings; Subfam. Papilioninae, go to 51 and 52

51(52) Abdomen flaring to the side, to almost twice the width of thorax, and
        has subdorsal keels; two short horns on head and a keel on top of
        thorax; no small bumps on abdomen . . . . Tribe Troidini, p. 184
52(51) Abdomen not flaring, has no keels; horns present or absent; small
        bumps on abdomen present or absent; go to 53 and 54
53(54) Abdomen has small bumps; head has two short horns (nearly absent
        in *Papilio indra*) . . . . most of Tribe Papilionini, p. 163
54(53) Abdomen lacks small bumps; horns short or very small; go to 55
        and 56
55(56) Head has two short horns; a small bump on top of thorax; abdomen
        has a low lateral ridge but no subdorsal ridge . . . . *Papi-
        lio troilus* and *P. palamedes* group, species 22-24 (Tribe Papilionini), p. 183
56(55) Head has two very small horns; a distinct point on top of thorax;
        abdomen has a low subdorsal ridge and a lateral ridge . . . .
        . . . . *Eurytides* (Tribe Leptocircini), p. 162
57(50) Head has only one short to long hornlike projection on front; hind-
        wings not visible on underside; thorax sometimes pointed on top; pro-
        boscis sometimes shorter than wings; Fam. Pieridae, go to 58 and 59
58(59) Wings bulging downward strongly . . . . Subfam. Dismor-
        phiinae and *Phoebis* and *Eurema* (Subfam. Coliadinae), pp. 192, 203, and 206
59(58) Wings projecting downward slightly or not at all; go to 60 and 61
60(61) Projection on head a long cone about as long as thorax; ventrally
        bulging wings form an obtuse angle in side view (Fig. 52) . . . .
        . . . . *Anthocharis* and *Euchloe* (Subfam. Pierinae), pp. 212 and 214
61(60) Projection on head shorter than thorax; wings not bulging, or the
        slight ventral bulge is rounded in side view; go to 62 and 63
62(63) Subdorsal spine on base of abdomen; no ridge on side of abdomen . .
        . . . . *Ascia* and *Appias* (Subfam. Pierinae), pp. 223 and 225
63(62) No spine on abdomen; usually a ridge on side of abdomen; go to 64
        and 65
64(65) Middorsal keel-like ridge on thorax . . . . . *Pieris* (Subfam. Pierinae), p. 216
65(64) No middorsal ridge on thorax . . . .
        . . . . *Colias*, *Anteos*, and *Kricogonia* (Subfam. Coliadinae), pp. 193, 202, and 210

Identifying Adult Butterflies

To identify an adult butterfly, first turn to the color plates; you will find that species comparable in appearance are placed together. In most cases you will be able to match your butterfly with a single species on one of the plates. Next, turn to the maps of that species in text (species having two or more very distinct North American subspecies often require more than one map). If the locality where you found the butterfly is outside the established range of the species, the butterfly is most likely another species, or (very unlikely but possibly) in a new locality. Next, turn to the text to see if the identification hints, time of year of flight, habitat, hostplant, and other data fit what you know of your butterfly. Some species are very similar to each other, and the color or position of certain spots on the wings may be crucial in distinguishing them (study Fig. 54 to learn the wing positions used to describe wing bands and spots).

Wing Veins
(See Figs. 53, 55)

The wing veins are often used for identifying butterflies to family and species. "Veins," best seen on the underside, are in fact tubular struts that

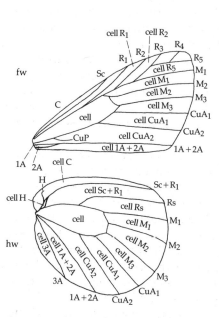

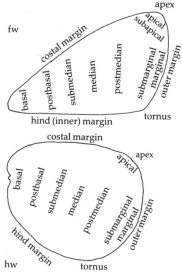

Fig. 53. Names of the wing veins and cells. The area between veins at the wing base is the "cell" or "discal cell," whereas the other cells take their names from the vein in front of them; for instance, cell M_1 is behind vein M_1. (Cells too small to label are named from the vein in front of them, as are the other cells.)

Fig. 54. Names of positions on the wings.

strengthen the wing for flight. The spaces between veins are called cells. Note that there is one cell at the base of each wing that is called merely "the cell" or "the discal cell"; each of the other cells is named from the vein in front of it. The wing-vein pattern is usually like that in Figure 53; the usual variations are shown in Figure 55. The leading edge of the forewing or hindwing (the costa, C) is rarely thickened.

On the forewing there is one Sc (subcostal) vein extending from the base. The R (radial) veins on the forewing all branch from the vein in front of the discal cell. Some R veins (especially R_3, R_4, R_5) generally branch from other R veins, except in skippers and most hairstreaks. The R veins may be reduced in number on the forewing: in Pierinae and Coliadinae there may be only three or four R veins (R_3, R_4, and R_5 may be fused into one vein and may branch from vein M_1); in Charaxinae only two R veins may reach the margin; in Parnassiinae R_2 is missing; and in Lycaenidae (except most hairstreaks) there are only four R veins (R_3 and R_5 may branch from other R veins, and F. Zeuner found that R_4 is often absent).

In the hindwing of all butterflies, veins Sc and R_1 are joined, forming one vein $Sc+R_1$, and the rest of the R veins (R_2 to R_5) are joined into one vein Rs (radial sector). There is also a tiny H (humeral) vein at the hindwing base.

Three M (medial) veins on the forewings and hindwings branch from the end of the discal cell, although most skippers lack vein M_2 on the hindwing. The two CuA (anterior cubitus) veins on the forewing and hindwing branch from the vein behind the discal cell. A vein in primitive moths, the CuP (posterior cubitus), between the Cu and A veins (branching from the Cu base), is represented in adult butterflies only by a crease between the two veins CuA_2 and $1A+2A$ (it is present as a trachea in the pupa but disappears in the adult). Papilioninae show a small remnant of CuP (Fig. 53) arising from the Cu vein behind the discal cell (between CuA and $1A+2A$), and others (Heliconiini, etc.) retain a vestige of it. One or two A (anal) veins, the last veins on each wing, start at the wing base.

Fig. 55.   The major variations of wing veins (fw, forewing; hw, hindwing).   *22, Papilio troilus* (similar: all Papilioninae).   *28, Parnassius phoebus* fw, without vein R₂ (similar: all Parnassiinae).   *31, Enantia albania* male fw (similar: female, but the fw less pointed; all Dismorphiinae).   *38, Colias philodice* fw (similar: *Colias*, 32-45).   *55, Eurema nicippe* fw (similar: most Pieridae, including *Colias* species 44 and 45 sometimes; most *Pieris*).   *72, Euchloe hyantis* fw tip, with short R₄ and R₅.   *73, Euchloe ausonia* fw (similar: most *Euchloe*, 74, 75).   *77, Pieris napi* fw (similar: *Nathalis*, 67).   *95, Lethe anthedon*: fw (similar: most Satyrinae, Nymphalinae, and Libytheidae; only Satyrinae and some Nymphalinae such as *Mestra*, 159, have the enlarged veins on the forewing base); hw (similar: most Nymphalidae; all Libytheidae, 274; also *Heliconius*, 271-273, but the humeral vein is recurved as in *Dione vanillae*, 268).   *136, Anaea andria* fw (similar: all U.S. Charaxinae, with R₁, R₂, R₃ tiny).   *204, Microtia elva*.   *219, Chlosyne nycteis* fw (similar: usually Nymphalinae tribes Melitaeini, Argynnini, and Heliconiini; most Danainae; occasionally other Nymphalidae).   *265, Euptoieta claudia* hw, with the discal cell open at the end (similar: all Nymphalinae except Heliconiini).   *268, Dione vanillae*: fw (similar: *Euptoieta claudia*, 265; *Phyciodes frisia*, 236); hw, with the humeral vein pointed to the body (similar: all Heliconiini, but *Heliconius*, 271-273, have the discal cell closed).   *282, Calephelis borealis* hw base, with a thick costa, C (similar: all Riodininae; in contrast, Lycaeninae lack the costa and humeral vein; the thick costa is absent in other butterflies except skippers).   *295, Feniseca tarquinius* fw (similar: some Pieridae).   *298, Eumaeus atala* fw.   *329, Callophrys niphon* fw (similar: all hairstreaks except *Hypaurotis*, 297, and *Habrodais*, 296).   *395, Glaucopsyche lygdamus* fw (similar: all Riodininae; most Lycaeninae, including the hairstreaks *Habrodais* and *Hypaurotis*).   *510, Poanes viator*: fw, with M₂ starting near M₃ (similar: Hesperiinae; Megathyminae); hw, with M₂ missing or weak, the costa thickened, and the humeral vein pointed to the base (similar: all Hesperiidae).   *604, Achalarus lyciades* fw, with M₂ starting midway between M₁ and M₃ (similar: Pyrginae; Pyrrhopyginae).   (Most drawings after S. Scudder.)

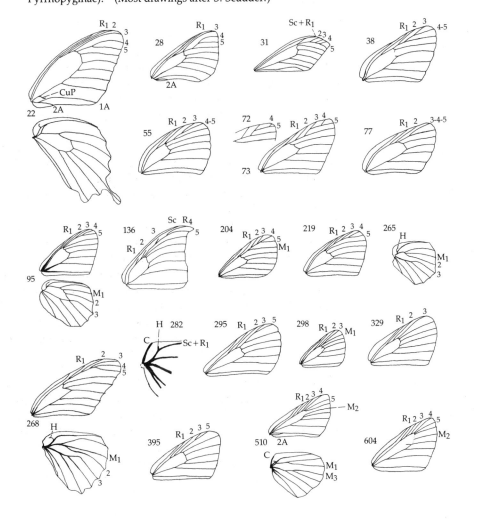

The veins 1A and 2A, both present in the pupa, combine in the adult to form one vein 1A+2A on forewing and hindwing (but in Papilionidae 2A is a separate vein branching to the hind margin), and in many skippers, Danainae, and others a fork can be seen at the adult wing base where 1A and 2A join. A second anal vein 3A occurs on the hindwing but not the forewing, but most Papilionidae lack vein 3A on both wings.

At the end of the discal cell on each wing are connecting veins called discocellular veins: the lower one connects veins M_2 and M_3; the middle one connects M_1 and M_2; and in a few species a short upper one connects R_5 and M_1. The discocellular veins are often faint or missing, especially on the hindwing of skippers and on both wings of Nymphalinae, Apaturinae, and Charaxinae.

The names of these veins (Fig. 53) were developed by J. Comstock, R. Tillyard, F. Zeuner, and others, by studying the veins of other insects and moths and by studying the tracheae in the growing wings of pupae (veins derive from tracheae). The M veins, for example, branch from a trachea in the pupa, but the base becomes lost in the adult, though traces of it can be seen running through the discal cell of some species. Generally only the wings of fossil insects are preserved, so the veins must serve as the keys to the identity of fossils as well as living forms.

Separating Males from Females

Gender and sexual structures are clues to identification as well. In many species, color alone is sufficient to distinguish the sexes; in these cases, the color plates illustrate both. In some species minor wing differences occur: males of many species have more strongly pointed forewings than females, or a round or oblong dark patch of scent scales, called a stigma, on their forewings or hindwings (Figs. 36-39); this type of information is more often supplied in the species texts in Part III.

The adult male and female genitalia, often useful in species identification, are often easily used for distinguishing the sexes, as well. The end of the abdomen of males (Fig. 28) has several hooks (the uncus and gnathos) on top and two claspers (the valvae) on the bottom, all of which grasp the female's abdomen during mating. The aedeagus, which often protrudes from the end of the abdomen, identifies males of hairstreaks and others. Females have two pillowlike structures, jointly forming the ovipositor, on the top of the end of the abdomen and a plate on the bottom (Fig. 30). Looking at these parts may be necessary for identification. Before dissecting the abdomen to examine these parts (see Appendix B), brush away the scales at the abdomen's end (using a camel's-hair brush, clipped short) to see if the identifying structures are visible. Clearing away the scales (and sometimes carefully breaking away the shell around the male genitalia with fine-pointed dissecting tweezers and a stereoscopic microscope) usually makes actual dissection unnecessary.

Key to Adult Butterflies Worldwide

The color plates will usually be the best place to begin in identifying a North American butterfly, but the following key to adults is useful for identifying an individual that is badly worn or aberrant, or a stray from abroad. So as to be useful for adults found in foreign countries, the key includes all the families and subfamilies of the entire world. The asterisks indicate those groups not found in North America. The key is based in part on the work of P. Ehrlich, J. Eliot, W. Evans, E. Munroe, and others.

1(2) Antenna usually hairlike or featherlike (Fig. 11), not clubbed; *or*, if antenna clubbed, a spine (frenulum) on the base of the hindwing fits into a hooklike apparatus (retinaculum) on the base of the forewing underside; most species night fliers; two small ocelli sometimes present on top of head between eyes .... moths

2(1) Antenna clubbed; no frenulum or retinaculum (except in males of Australian *Euschemon*, Pyrginae); day fliers; ocelli absent in all species; butterflies, go to 3 and 13

3(13) Antenna club asymmetrical (bent near tip, middle, or base of club; see Fig. 11); forewing has five unbranched R veins (Fig. 55); hindwing vein M_2 generally missing or weak; thick-bodied, powerful fliers; epiphysis (Fig. 14) present on foreleg tibia; Superfam. Hesperioidea, Fam. Hesperiidae (skippers), go to 4 and 5

4(5) Antenna club bent back at base of club, the antenna thus suggesting a putter-type golf club (Fig. 11); base of forewing vein M_2 about equally distant between veins M_1 and M_3 (Fig. 55); forewing discal cell of both sexes very long, more than two-thirds as long as leading edge of wing; all species large, the wingspan about 4 cm; American tropics (and southwest U.S.) only .... Subfam. Pyrrhopyginae, p. 500

5(4) Antenna club bent back in middle or at tip; position of vein M_2 varies; forewing discal cell less than two-thirds as long as wing; species large to small; go to 6, 7, and 10

6(7,10) Base of forewing vein M_2 varies in position; end of hindwing discal cell sloping toward body; antenna variable; palpi variable; wings often yellowish or orangish; hair pencil and costal fold absent; a male stigma often present on wing; Australia and New Guinea only ....
.... Subfam. Trapezitinae*, p. 416

7(6,10) Base of forewing vein M_2 about equally distant between veins M_1 and M_3; end of hindwing discal cell vertical or sloping outward; antenna bent in middle or merely asymmetrical at tip; palpi often projecting forward; wings seldom yellowish or orangish in ground color; a hair pencil often present on hind leg of male; a male stigma and costal fold sometimes present on wing (Fig. 39); go to 8 and 9

8(9) Palpi erect, but last segment long and projecting forward; a stigma often present on male forewing, but costal fold absent; Africa and Australasia only .... Subfam. Coeliadinae*, p. 415

9(8) Palpi erect and last segment small, or all segments projecting forward; male stigma absent, but costal fold often present on male forewing (Fig. 39); worldwide .... Subfam. Pyrginae, p. 469

10(6,7) Base of forewing vein M_2 closer to vein M_3 than to M_1; end of hindwing discal cell vertical or sloping outward; antenna bent in middle or at tip (in North America usually bent at tip, except in *Carterocephalus* and *Piruna*); palpi rarely projecting forward (only in *Carterocephalus* and *Piruna* in North America); wings often yellowish or orangish; hair pencil and costal fold absent; a male stigma often present on wing; worldwide; go to 11 and 12

11(12) Head about as wide as thorax; antennae far apart (usually more than half width of head); wingspan 1.5-5 cm; worldwide ....
.... Subfam. Hesperiinae, p. 424

12(11) Head only about half the width of thorax; antennae closer together (about half width of head); wingspan 3.5-7 cm; North and Central America only . . . . Subfam. Megathyminae, p. 416

13(3) Antenna club symmetrical (not bent, though often flattened on one or both sides; see Fig. 11); forewing has some posterior R veins branched, or if unbranched (in Theclini) only three R veins occur (Fig. 55); hindwing vein M_2 present; most species fairly thin-bodied, often weak fliers; epiphysis present only in Papilionidae; Superfam. Papilionoidea (scudders), go to 14 and 15

14(15) Palpi on front of head pointed forward and very long, about as long as thorax; species medium-sized (wingspan 3-4 cm), brown and orange (blue in foreign males) with small white spots on forewings; male forelegs much less than half, female forelegs half, the length of hind legs; male has a superuncus (Fig. 29); worldwide . . . . . . Fam. Libytheidae, p. 344

15(14) Palpi usually shorter than thorax, angled upward; other traits variable; go to 16 and 31

16(31) Eyes usually indented at least slightly next to antennae; face much taller than wide between the eyes; wingspan 4 cm or less, usually less than 2 cm; Fam. Lycaenidae, go to 17 and 20

17(20) First segment of male foreleg (the coxa, attached to the body) extends like a spine below the joint with the rest of the leg (Fig. 16); hindwing has H and often C veins, or the antenna base has ventral bristles; go to 18 and 19

18(19) Male foreleg less than half the length of the other legs, and covered with long scales like a feather duster; base of antenna shaft lacks bristles; hindwing has a tiny H vein at base (concealed by forewing on upperside) and often a unique C vein along base of front margin of hindwing (Figs. 53, 55); most species rest with wings spread; worldwide in warmer regions, but most species in tropical America . . . . Subfam. Riodininae, p. 348

19(18) Male foreleg more than half the length of the other legs, and lacks long scales; base of antenna shaft has unique ventral bristles; hindwing has no H or C veins; a dozen species in the Orient and East Indies . . . . Subfam. Curetinae*, p. 348

20(17) First segment of male foreleg (coxa) does not extend below the joint with the rest of leg; hindwing lacks C and often H veins; antenna base lacks ventral bristles; go to 21 and 22

21(22) Male foreleg less than half the length of other legs, but tarsus has movable segments and claws; palpi only as long as head; traces of two M veins within forewing discal cell at its end; eye not notched beside antenna (technically, the anepisternum of Fig. 12 is large on the mesothorax, and the male has the transtilla of Fig. 28; both traits occur in Riodininae and Curetinae but are absent or rudimentary in Lycaeninae); a single Andean species . . . . Subfam. Styginae*, p. 348

22(21) Male foreleg more than half the length of other legs, but tarsus segments are fused and rarely clawed; palpi usually longer than head; rarely a trace of just one vein within forewing discal cell, or none; eye usually slightly notched beside antenna; worldwide; Subfam. Lycaeninae, go to 23 and 24

23(24) Ten forewing veins (three R veins, none branched); male forewing often has a small oval stigma (Fig. 38) . . . .
. . . . Tribe Theclini (all genera except *Habrodais* and *Hypaurotis*), p. 357

24(23) Eleven forewing veins (the forewing has four R veins, R_3 and R_5 branched from one vein); male forewing lacks a stigma; go to 25 and 28

25(28) Antenna club cylindrical, not flattened beneath; tibiae on four hind legs spurred or unspurred; go to 26 and 27

26(27) None of the four hind legs has spurs on end of tibia; hindwing untailed . . . . Tribe Miletini, p. 356

27(26) Each of the four hind legs has a pair of spurs on end of tibia; hind-wing often tailed . . . . *Habrodais* and *Hypaurotis* (Tribe Theclini), p. 357

28(25) Antenna club flattened beneath; four hind legs have tibia spurs; go to 29 and 30

29(30) Bases of last forewing R vein and vein M_1 close together at discal cell; uncus lobes of male genitalia (Fig. 28) long and finger-shaped; thorax thicker in relation to wings; males blue only in *Lycaena heteronea* . . . .
. . . . Tribe Lycaenini, p. 386

30(29) Bases of last forewing R vein and vein M_1 separate, sometimes widely so, at discal cell; uncus lobes shorter; thorax narrower and flight weaker; males in most species blue on upperside . . . . Tribe Polyommatini, p. 393

31(16) Eyes not indented next to antennae; face as wide as tall between the eyes; wingspan 2-10 cm; go to 32 and 48

32(48) Front two legs small, much less than half the size of hind four legs; Fam. Nymphalidae, go to 33 and 42

33(42) Anepisternum (Fig. 12) absent on side of mesothorax (brush away the scales to see this; if this is difficult, go to all four choices 34, 37, 43, and 44); go to 34 and 37

34(37) Forewing vein 2A visible (as a fork at the base of 1A+2A; Fig. 53); coxa of middle leg (Fig. 12) has a prominent bulge on the rear (unique except for some Acraeinae); end of discal cell on forewing and hindwing closed by a tubular vein; go to 35 and 36

35(36) Antennae lack scales (scaled in all other Nymphalidae, except some Acraeinae, Satyrinae, and Morphinae); two hair pencils on male ab-domen tip, these popping out into a plume during courting (Fig. 38), but none on wings; female foreleg tip strongly clubbed, the tarsus with only four segments; worldwide . . . . Subfam. Danainae, p. 228

36(35) Antennae scaled; hair pencils on male wings but not on abdomen; female foreleg tip not clubbed, the tarsus with four or five segments; American tropics and New Guinea only . . . . . . Subfam. Ithomiinae*, p. 228

37(34) Forewing vein 2A not visible; coxa of middle leg only rarely has the bulge (in some Acraeinae); discal cells vary; go to 38 and 39

38(39) End of hindwing (and forewing) discal cell closed by a tubular vein; each of the two claws on each leg tip forked, or one of the pair larger than the other (claws rarely unforked and the same size, as in other Nymphalidae); tropical America, Africa, and Australasia . . . .
. . . . Subfam. Acraeinae*, p. 238

39(38) End of hindwing (and usually forewing) discal cell open to margin (except in *Heliconius* and *Eueides*) (Fig. 55); claws not forked, each claw of a pair the same size; go to 40 and 41

40(41) Forewing of both sexes pointed, the margin indented; hindwing scalloped (extending outward at each vein) and slightly lobed at vein CuA_2, the margin indented in males (some foreign Nymphalinae may key here); warm areas worldwide . . . . Subfam. Apaturinae, p. 255

41(40) Forewing and hindwing shapes various, but not presenting the combination of traits of most Apaturinae; worldwide . . . .
. . . . Subfams. Apaturinae and Nymphalinae, pp. 255 and 258

42(33) Anepisternum (Fig. 12) present on side of thorax (small in Satyrinae); go to 43 and 44

43(44) Some forewing veins swollen at the base in nearly all species (Fig. 55), a unique trait except for a few Nymphalinae; end of hindwing discal cell usually closed by a tubular vein; anepisternum much smaller than in Figure 12; forewing vein 2A rarely visible; worldwide . . . .
. . . . Subfam. Satyrinae, p. 233

44(43) Forewing veins not swollen at the base; hindwing discal cell varies; anepisternum as large as in Figure 12; forewing vein 2A varies; go to 45, 46, and 47

45(46,47) End of forewing discal cell closed by a tubular vein (Fig. 55), that of hindwing closed or open to margin; forewing vein 2A rarely visible (as a fork at the base of 1A+2A); female foreleg lacks claws; tropical America, southeast Asia, East Indies . . . . Subfam. Morphinae*, p. 228

46(45,47) End of forewing and hindwing discal cells open to margin (Fig. 55); forewing vein 2A not visible; female foreleg lacks claws (in our North American species, forewing veins R_1 to R_3 are vestigial, but they are normal in some foreign species; the parapatagia, Fig. 12, are hardened on the prothorax, unlike all other Nymphalidae); worldwide, mostly tropical . . . . Subfam. Charaxinae, p. 253

47(45,46) End of forewing and hindwing discal cells closed by a tubular vein; forewing vein 2A visible; female foreleg has tiny claws (other Nymphalidae lack foreleg claws except for some female Ithomiinae; male Nymphalidae always lack claws); Oriental . . . .
. . . . Subfam. Calinaginae*, p. 228

48(32) Front two legs almost same size as hind four legs; go to 49 and 57

49(57) Foreleg has a projection (epiphysis, Fig. 14) on upper part of tibia; hindwing has only one A vein (except in Baroniinae in southern Mexico; Fig. 53); forewing vein 2A runs to hind margin; two claws on leg tips not forked; butterflies large, the color variable; Fam. Papilionidae, go to 50 and 51

50(51) Hindwing has two A veins (1A+2A and 3A); one orange-and-black species with 3-cm wingspan; s Mexico . . . . Subfam. Baroniinae*, p. 161

51(50) Hindwing has only one A vein (1A+2A); vein 3A missing; go to 52 and 53

52(53) Forewing vein CuP absent (if rudimentary, legs unscaled); antennae 11 mm or shorter; two hooks on forewing base in at least *Parnassius* (Fig. 61); wingspan 5-7 cm; forewing vein R_2 often absent (Fig. 55); western North America and Eurasia only . . . . . Subfam. Parnassiinae, p. 187

53(52) Forewing vein CuP present (Fig. 53; if weak, legs scaled); antennae 11 mm or longer; no hooks on forewing base; wingspan 6-15 cm; forewing vein R_2 present; worldwide; Subfam. Papilioninae, go to 54, 55, and 56

54(55,56) Tibiae and tarsi of legs unscaled, the sides spined but not indented; a fold containing scent scales on hind margin of male hindwing in most species (Fig. 36); male superuncus present . . . . . . Tribe Troidini, p. 184

55(54,56) Tibiae and tarsi scaled, the sides spineless and indented; a fold containing scent scales on hind margin of male hindwing in many species; male superuncus present or absent . . . . Tribe Leptocircini, p. 162

56(54,55) Tibiae and tarsi unscaled, the sides spineless and indented; no hindwing scent fold, the wing folded down there ("fluted"); male superuncus present . . . . Tribe Papilionini, p. 163

57(49) Foreleg epiphysis absent; hindwing always has two A veins; forewing veins 1A+2A joined; two claws on each leg tip each forked in two; butterflies small to large, generally white, yellow, or orange; Fam. Pieridae, go to 58 and 59

58(59) Each wing nearly round; vein M_2 arises from vein R_{345} on forewing, and from vein M_1 on hindwing, but not from discal cell; hindwing veins $Sc+R_1$ and Rs fused together beyond discal cell; one white west African species . . . . Subfam. Pseudopontiinae*, p. 192

59(58) Wings not especially rounded; vein M_2 arises from end of discal cell; hindwing veins $Sc+R_1$ and Rs not fused together; go to 60 and 61

60(61) Forewing has five R veins, all branching from one vein extending from the discal cell, and R_1 is connected to Sc (Fig. 55); base of forewing vein M_2 closer to vein M_3 than to M_1; male forewing much narrower than hindwing in most species; uncus forked and the two valvae partly fused together, as in Pseudopontiinae; American tropics, and one Eurasian genus having normal-size male forewing . . . .
. . . . Subfam. Dismorphiinae, p. 192

61(60) Forewing has three to five R veins branching from at least two veins extending from the discal cell; base of forewing vein M_2 closer to M_1 than to M_3; male forewing about as wide as hindwing; uncus not forked, the valvae not fused together; worldwide; go to 62 and 63

62(63) Prothorax has two hardened lobelike subdorsal bumps (patagia; see Fig. 12); H vein on hindwing base usually minute or absent; tegumen on male abdomen usually much shorter than uncus; wings mostly yellow or orange, sometimes white or green or other colors . . . .
. . . . Subfam. Coliadinae, p. 192

63(62) Prothorax lacks the two hardened lobelike subdorsal bumps; H vein on hindwing base usually long (Fig. 53); tegumen longer than uncus (Fig. 28); wings mostly white, sometimes yellow or orange-tipped or other colors . . . . Subfam. Pierinae, p. 211

PART III

The Butterflies

This part of the book provides detailed information on identification, distribution, ecology, and behavior for every species of butterfly recorded from the United States and Canada, including the native species and those that have been known to stray into the area. The book also offers complete coverage of the adjacent islands (Greenland, Hawaii, Iceland, and Bermuda; see Appendix A) and of Mexico's westernmost extremity, Baja California, except for two species (*Ascia sevata*, Pierinae; and *Opsiphanes boisduvalii*, Morphinae) that do not range north of southern Baja.

Using the Text

The discussions are arranged in taxonomic order, to reflect modern classifications of the world of butterflies, from superfamily through family, subfamily, tribe, and genus. The opening texts for these groups offer useful generalizations (in fact, if all the members of a family exhibit a certain trait, that trait is not repeated in the subfamily and tribe texts).

For each species, the following information is given in sequence, wherever known. The heading line contains the species number (a number assigned to facilitate cross-referencing in this book); the scientific name (with commonly used synonyms occasionally given in parentheses after an = sign; a name in quotes is a valid name but has been commonly misapplied to this species and properly names another species); and the common name. Designation of the color plate(s) and (if any) drawing(s) illustrating that species is given in the margin, as is the range map for that species also.

The text for a species usually consists of four paragraphs, each offering the same material in all species texts (if little is known about a species, it is all in a single paragraph). The first paragraph gives identification hints for adults, if needed, and such subspecies or other distinct variations or forms that occur, and their inheritance if known. Each subspecies or form is given in boldface type where it first occurs. A form is given the same name in all the species in which it occurs if the form seems to have the same genetic and environmental cause (for instance, white females of all the species of Coliadinae are called form *alba*). (The Catalogue/Checklist listed in "Butterfly References" gives the persons who named each scientific name, the year and library reference for each, and type localities.) Information on mimicry is also given in the first paragraph.

The second paragraph gives the preferred habitat of the species (often with reference to the life zones shown in Fig. 43); the range beyond North America (for example, Siberia, Europe, or south to Argentina) if this range has not been presented already in connection with the subspecies in the first paragraph; and the larval hostplants in nature, their plant family, and their life form (herbs, shrubs, trees, grasses, etc.; the "Hostplant Catalogue" indexes these hosts by genus and gives their common names).

The third paragraph gives information on the early stages, including where on the plant the eggs are laid (leaves, flower buds, etc.) and whether they are clustered; the part of the hostplant eaten by the larvae; whether the larvae make nests and, if so, the type of nest made; other unusual larval habits; brief descriptions of the egg, the mature larva, and the pupa; and the life stage that hibernates. If larvae or pupae vary, the word "*or*" appears between descriptions of the most extreme variants, and the reader should know that intermediates also occur in most species (except *Papilio* species whose pupae are generally green or brown with few intermediates).

The fourth paragraph gives information on the adults, beginning with the number of generations (flights) and when these fly during the season (E, M, and L refer to the early, middle, and late thirds of a month, specifically, days 1-10, 11-20, and 21-31). Usually the times of flight are given only for the extremes of the species' range, such as north and south; thus if you are in the middle of the range, you will have to estimate an intermediate time of flight (in general, butterflies fly later, and have fewer flights, northward and at higher altitude). The fourth paragraph also discusses the dispersal tendencies, migration patterns, and flying distances of the adults; the adult foods; and mate-locating and mating behavior. Because nearly all butterfly adults sip flower nectar, their food preference is not mentioned unless they also take moisture from mud, sap, etc., or feed on other foods, or unless related species (such as satyrs and Nymphalini) do not feed from flowers. The times of day (such as 8:30 A.M.) are standard times; to obtain daylight saving time, add one hour (8:30 + 1 = 9:30 A.M. daylight saving time).

To identify an adult butterfly, first compare the butterfly you have found with the butterflies illustrated on the color plates, and settle on its probable identity. Next, use the species number beside that plate specimen to turn to the map and text below: check the map to see that the range accords with the locality where you found the butterfly, and confirm the identification with the identification hints given in the species text. Then read the natural history of the species and the other information offered there.

If you want to find a certain species in nature, first consult the map to find the proper region to visit, and then read about the habitat, larval hostplants, and time of flight during the year, so that you can plan a productive trip. A plant book (see "Plant References") may illustrate the hostplants and give habitats for them. To find eggs or larvae, also look up the overwintering stage along with the adult flight time during the season in order to estimate when eggs or larvae will be present on the hostplants.

For keys to the larvae, pupae, and adults of all major butterfly groups (families, subfamilies, and tribes), see Part II. For general information on all aspects of the lives of butterflies, see Part I.

Using the Range Maps

Range maps are provided in Part III for all North American species except for several Hawaiian species and those rare strays that occur only in southern Texas or southern Florida. (Throughout this book, "Hawaii" means the entire state, not just the single island.) For some species with two or more very distinct subspecies, there are two or more maps.

The solid-black areas on the maps indicate year-round range, the records so dense as to blanket a region. Adjacent areas crossed by parallel lines on some maps are regions occupied only by regular or (usually) rare migrants (the species texts that follow give more information on migratory habits). Truly isolated localities are indicated with a black dot or patch—which in some cases has been enlarged beyond actual distribution limits just enough to be visible. Similarly isolated records of migrants are shown by two short parallel lines. Arrows on the maps point to small areas of distribution that the reader might otherwise overlook. Where the natural range of a species extends beyond North America, that information is given in the species texts.

The maps are based on more-detailed maps that I have prepared from data gathered over many years. These larger maps (see, for example, Fig. 56) indicate the location of each known occurrence by a dot; they are based on hundreds of thousands of records, both published and unpublished, by hundreds of lepidopterists and butterfly enthusiasts throughout North America, and include records in the season's summaries of the *News of the Lepidopterists' Society*.

Fig. 56.   The distribution of *Oeneis jutta* (132), an example of the dot maps from which the range maps of Part III were drawn.

SUPERFAMILY PAPILIONOIDEA: SCUDDERS

The Papilionoidea, which comprise all the butterflies except the skippers, number about 11,100 species worldwide, and occur on all continents except Antarctica. Two characters distinguish them dependably from skippers: the antenna club is straight (in the skippers it is bent), and the forewing R veins are either branched from each other or fewer than five.

Because they are generally less-powerful fliers than are the skippers, I venture to call them scudders; the old name, "true butterflies," is a poor description of them, and insults the skippers. The name "scudder" not only reflects their scudding flight, but also honors Samuel H. Scudder, one of the world's foremost authorities on butterflies in the last century.

Although scudders tend to be more beautiful and thinner-bodied than are most skippers, they are so varied in habits and appearance that few other generalizations can be made about them.

The five families of the Papilionoidea are all represented in North America.

FAMILY PAPILIONIDAE: SWALLOWTAILS

The Papilionidae, about 534 species, are generally very large, and the family includes the largest butterflies in the world. They occur worldwide, mostly in the tropics. Although some extend into the Arctic, the 30 species in North America are mostly in the southern U.S.

In the adults, all six legs are about the same size, there is only one hindwing A vein (Mexican *Baronia* have two), the forewing vein 2A is separate from 1A, and (except in *Parnassius*) the forewing vein M_2 starts from what looks like the CuA vein (Fig. 55). The larvae, which eat several families of dicotyledons, lack spines or horns, but have an osmeterium, a forked, foul-smelling, fleshy "snake-tongue" gland that pops out behind the head to repel ants and other predators. In many cases the skin of the larva is distasteful to birds (see *Papilio machaon*, 5). The pupae vary in shape, and in most cases the pupae hibernate.

Mimicry is common; the *Aristolochia*-feeding species are models for other swallowtails and for some Nymphalidae, and the white *Parnassius* seem to be Müllerian mimics with some Pieridae.

Most Papilionidae flap along with just a few wingbeats per second. They usually fly several meters above ground, and can travel rather fast because of their size. Few species migrate, although adults of some species travel long distances. They spread their wings when resting or basking, but the Papilioninae are unique in continuing to flutter while feeding on flower nectar, presumably lest their weight tilt the flowers. All Papilionidae species visit flowers. Males generally patrol to seek females, although some species often perch also. Females generally fly when a mated pair is startled.

Two subfamilies, the Parnassiinae and Papilioninae, occur in North America. The third subfamily, the Baroniinae, consists of a single southern Mexican species whose larvae eat *Cassia* (Leguminosae). The Baroniinae are like the Parnassiinae in forewing shape and in lacking the vestige of vein CuP (present in the Papilioninae) on the base of the forewing. *Baronia*, unlike other Papilionidae, have two hindwing A veins; but the larvae, like others in the family, have osmeteria. The larva of *Baronia* (even the first stage) has numerous forked hairs on the body and on the bumpy head; it is cylindrical, as in Pieridae, and striped, as in *Oeneis* (Nymphalidae). The pupa, in an earthen cell, is shaped like that of *Parnassius*.

Subfamily Papilioninae: Swallowtails

The Papilioninae occur worldwide, but most of the 483 species are found in the tropics. The birdwing butterflies, large species ranging from southeastern Asia to northern Australia, are among the largest and most beautiful butterflies in the world. The 27 North American species are found mostly in the southern U.S., but one species (*Papilio machaon*) ranges north to treeline.

Adults are distinguished by the small CuP vein at the forewing base (only a remnant occurs in Heliconiini and others). A small cell at the base of the hindwing between the humeral vein and $Sc+R_1$ also occurs in some Nymphalidae and skippers. The antennae are longer than in other Papilionidae.

Larvae eat dicotyledons: often Rosaceae and Umbelliferae, and often primitive plants such as Aristolochiaceae, Magnoliaceae, Lauraceae, and Annonaceae. The first-stage larvae have extra hairs on the body and sometimes on the head, and some SV hairs above the first eight prolegs (Fig. 50); they also bear fleshy cones with stiff hairs (scoli). Some larvae also produce permanent fleshy filaments. The older larvae have inconspicuous tiny hairs, and a forked organ (osmeterium) that pops out of the thorax when the larva is disturbed; the smells of two acids given off by this organ repel predators like ants (see *Papilio machaon*, 5; the two acids are isobutyric and 2-methyl-butyric, but *Battus* osmeteria contain two sesquiterpene chemicals instead).

Pupae, which generally have two head horns and a prong on the thorax, are upright, attached to a surface both by a silk girdle around the middle and by the cremaster. They often take on different colors, from green to brown, depending on photoperiod and background color and texture. Pupae generally hibernate.

The adults of the *Aristolochia* feeders have tough bodies, and are models for other Papilionidae and Nymphalidae that mimic them.

Although the adults are generally large enough and strong enough to migrate, few species migrate readily. They flap their wings slowly, but because of their size they can move quite fast. The tiger-striped species (such as *Eurytides* and *Papilio eurymedon*) seem to bob up and down a bit more than the others. Adults generally rest and bask with the wings spread. While feeding at flowers, they continue to flutter their wings—perhaps a useful behavior, because these heavy butterflies might cause the flowers to tilt. Males usually patrol to seek females. If a mating pair is disturbed, the female flies carrying the male.

The three tribes are the Leptocircini, Papilionini, and Troidini.

Tribe Leptocircini: Kite Swallowtails

The Leptocircini (=Graphiini) comprise 144 species worldwide, most of them tropical. Only one species, of the eastern U.S., is native to North America; two others are rare strays to Texas and Florida.

Males, like those of the Troidini, have a fold of scent scales on the hind margin of the hindwing. Adults usually have very long tails, and the wings are often zebra-striped and sometimes transparent. Older larvae lack filaments, and often feed on pawpaw (Annonaceae) and Rosaceae. Pupae have smaller horns than do other Papilioninae. Pupae hibernate.

Our species are not distasteful or involved in mimicry.

Adults do not migrate. They flap about a meter above ground with an interesting bobbing flight.

1. Eurytides marcellus   Zebra Swallowtail

Easily identified. Spring individuals are small, light, with shorter tails. Summer forms are larger, with broader dark areas and longer tails (form **lecontei**).

Color Plates 4 (pupa), 7
Figs. 36 (scent fold), 48,
51, 52

Habitat mostly Austral to lower Transition Zone semi-wooded areas, often in low moist spots. Hostplants shrub Annonaceae: *Asimina triloba, parviflora, speciosa, pygmaea, obovata, reticulata, "longifolia," angustifolia*[t], *incana*[t], *(palustris?)*.

Eggs pale green, laid singly on the hostplant. Larvae live under leaves (without nests) and eat leaves. Larva (Figs. 48, 51) green, with transverse rows of black dots, yellow bands between segments, many narrow black transverse lines, and a velvety-black dorsal stripe (edged behind with yellow) between the thorax and abdomen, the head green; *or* larva mostly black, with orangish transverse bands between the segments and many white transverse lines, the head black. Pupa (Fig. 52) brown to green, reddish, or yellowish, more compact than *Papilio* pupa; abdomen with a small cream subdorsal ridge (with cream oblique dashes beneath it) and cream ridges on each side that meet at a peak on top of the thorax; two short horns on head. Pupae usually beneath leaves. Photoperiod does not affect pupal color, but diapausing pupae are most often brown. Pupae hibernate.

Two flights, mostly May-Aug., northward; many flights, Mar.-Dec., in Fla. Some pupae of each flight hibernate until the next year. Adults sip flower nectar and mud. Males seem to patrol near the hosts to seek females, displaying an interesting batlike flight.

2. Eurytides celadon   Cuban Kite Swallowtail

Stray only
Color Plate 58

Like small spring *E. marcellus*, but the red unh line lacks the white inner edge of *marcellus*, and the black unf postbasal band is narrow and separate from the small black spot just beyond it (the band is broad with a light band through it in *marcellus*). A very rare stray into s Fla. from Cuba, where it flies most of the year (or an error: one caught 1945, and other records doubtful). Eggs light green.

3. Eurytides philolaus   Dark Kite Swallowtail

Stray only
Color Plate 58

Much blacker than *E. marcellus*. Females similar to males or almost solid black. Hostplants shrubby Annonaceae: *Annona*. A very rare stray into s Tex. (July) from Mex., where it flies most of the year. Ranges south to Honduras. Adults sip mud.

Tribe Papilionini: Fluted Swallowtails

The Papilionini comprise 203 species worldwide, many in the temperate zones. The 21 North American species occur from southern Canada southward, though *Papilio machaon* and *P. glaucus* range into the Arctic.

The hind margin of the hindwing of males is bent downward ("fluted"), unlike that in other Papilioninae. Older larvae, which lack tubercles, feed on several plant families, especially Umbelliferae and Rutaceae. The young larvae of many species (4-17) and older larvae of some (10-17) curiously resemble bird droppings. Other larvae (18-24) resemble miniature snakes, with eyes and an orange tongue-like osmeterium that pops out. Pupae, which have two head horns and a prong on the thorax, are yellow-green or brown, depending on background color and photoperiod. Pupae hibernate.

Adults are edible to birds, so are not models, but some species mimic Troidini species. The females of *Papilio polyxenes asterias* and *P. machaon bairdii* have lost the median yellow bands on the upper hindwing, in imitation of the swallowtail *Battus philenor*.

In the *Papilio machaon* group (5-9), most species have two very different forms, one mostly yellow and one mostly black. Just why this dimorphism occurs has not been explained. Probably the black form developed in *P. polyxenes* or *P. machaon* in order to mimic *Battus*, the adults of which are poisonous to birds; the other species may then have picked up the black form by occasional hybridization (the "species" are not really distinct in this group). The existence of yellow and black forms cannot have been caused by climatic adaptation, since the yellow form of *P. machaon* occurs in cold regions, the yellow form of *P. polyxenes* in hot regions.

Adults flap swiftly about, and those of some species occasionally migrate. Species in the *P. machaon* group commonly fly only a meter above ground, but the others, whose larvae eat trees, commonly fly several meters or more above ground. Although males usually patrol to seek females, those of the *P. machaon* group perch and patrol.

4. Papilio xuthus   Asian Swallowtail

Hawaii only
Color Plate 63

The only *Papilio* in Hawaii, identified by having many yellow streaks in the fw cell. Introduced in 1971 by military planes from Guam or by Japanese tourists, now on at least six islands.

Habitat tropical woodlands and cities. Hostplants tree Rutaceae: *Citrus* in Hawaii, many genera in Japan.

Larva green, with a black lateral band edged below with white, a black transverse band edged behind with white spots (with an eyespot at each end of the band) on the rear of the thorax, four U-shaped black oblique stripes (each edged above with white) crossing over the body and connecting to the lateral band, and two orange subdorsal bumps in the second U-shaped band. Pupa green, brown, or orange, with two large head horns and a horn on top of the thorax. A short photoperiod acting on the larva produces diapausing pupae that are green or orange; non-diapause pupae are green or brown (T. Hidaka and others). Brown and orange pupae are produced when the brain stimulates a ganglion behind the neck to release a hormone that controls the making of pteridine and melanic pigments producing the color.

Many flights all year in Hawaii. Flight is strong and swift; adults probably colonized most islands by flying between them. Males patrol about trees to seek females. The striped pattern (not the color) of yellowish-greenish and black attracts the male to the female (Hidaka and Y. Yamashita). When a male finds a resting female with wings spread, he contacts her wings with his forelegs, he lands, and they mate.

5. Papilio machaon   Artemisia Swallowtail

Color Plates 1 (egg), 2 (larva), 7
Figs. 36 (hair pencil?), 57-59

As in *P. zelicaon* (6) and *P. polyxenes* (7), some adults are mostly yellow and others mostly black, but most *machaon* can be identified by the uph eyespot, in which the black dot usually touches the abdominal wing margin (Fig. 57). The unh has few orange spots (placed at the end of the discal cell usually), in contrast to *P. polyxenes*. Yellow-winged *machaon* forms differ from *P. zelicaon* on the abdomen, which is mostly yellow (one broad and one narrow yellow stripe on each side, and a yellow midventral line; Fig. 58). Black-winged *machaon* forms differ from *P. polyxenes* and black *P. zelicaon* form *nitra* by having strongly yellow

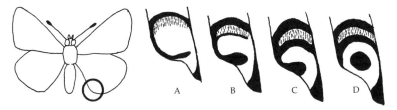

Fig. 57. The eyespot (right uph) of the *Papilio machaon* group (species 5-9). A blue crescent (hatched area) rests atop orange (white area). Letters *A* to *D* correspond to eyespot shapes in Table 2.

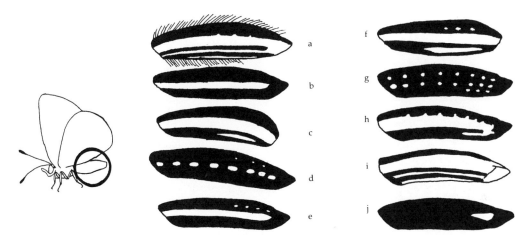

Fig. 58. The color patterns on the sides of the abdomens of the *Papilio machaon* group (species 5-9). *a, Papilio machaon aliaska* male (similar: female; *P. m. hudsonianus*); the hairs are long in ssp. *aliaska*, shorter in other species and subspecies; traces of yellow dots are present on top of the uppermost yellow band only in some *P. m. hudsonianus*; the yellow midventral stripe may be absent. *b, P. zelicaon* male. *c, P. zelicaon* female. *d, P. zelicaon* form *nitra* male (female the same); the upper yellow dots vary in number to six or more but are usually small or absent; *P. machaon bairdii* females are often similar but have more upper dots. *e, P. polyxenes coloro* male. *f, P. polyxenes coloro* female (some males look like this also, and extreme adults of both sexes may resemble view *i*). *g, P. polyxenes asterias* male (similar: female; *P. p. kahli* male and female; *P. p. coloro* form *clarki* male and female; *P. brevicauda* male and female; *P. machaon bairdii* male); the size of the spots varies somewhat; the uppermost and lowermost rows may be reduced in size, the lowermost often absent. *h, P. machaon bairdii* form *hollandii*; the region between the upper and middle rows of yellow dots is washed with yellow; *hollandii* varies completely to form *bairdii* with the region black. *i, P. machaon brucei* male (similar: female, but the tip is darker; some *P. polyxenes coloro*; most *P. p. asterias* form *pseudoamericus*; *P. machaon oregonius*, but yellower and with the two black side bands reduced to narrow lines). *j, P. indra* male (female the same); the pale yellow dash may be absent or half as long as the abdomen, but the front half of the abdomen is always black.

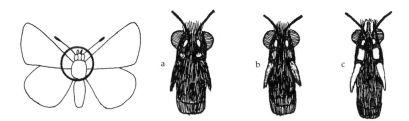

Fig. 59. The top of the thorax and head of the *Papilio machaon* group (species 5-9), showing the color variation of the tegulae: *a*, sometimes black (*Papilio polyxenes*); *b*, slightly yellow (*P. zelicaon* form *nitra*); *c*, yellow (*P. machaon bairdii*). For the color of the tegulae of other forms, see Table 2.

TABLE 2 *Traits Useful for Identifying the Species and Varieties of the* Papilio machaon *Group*

Name	Postbasal and basal unh color	Abdominal pattern (Fig. 58)	Tegular color (Fig. 59)	Typical eyespot (Fig. 57)	Width of yellow uph median band	Number of red unh spots	Unf discal-cell base color	Other
P. machaon aliaska	yellow	a	mostly yellow	A	≅ 12 mm	few	yellow	tail often short
P. machaon hudsonianus	yellow	a	mostly yellow	B	≅ 12 mm	few	yellow	fw less pointed
P. m. hudsonianus form comstocki[a]	yellow	a	mostly yellow	B	≅ 8 mm	few	yellow	
P. machaon oregonius	yellow	i (black lines narrower)	yellow	C	≅ 12 mm	few	yellow	
P. machaon form and ssp. brucei	yellow	i	yellow	C	≅ 12 mm	few	black	
P. machaon brucei form comstocki	yellow	i	yellow	C	≅ 8 mm	few	black	
P. machaon form hollandii[a] (♀[b])	black	h	yellow	C	♂ 2–7 mm ♀ 0–2 mm	few	black	
P. machaon form and ssp. bairdii	black	g (♀ fewer spots)	yellow	C	♂ 2–6 mm ♀ 0–2 mm	few	black	
P. machaon form ampliata[a] (♂ only)	black		yellow	C	♂ 0–2 mm	few	black	
P. zelicaon	yellow	b (♂), c (♀)	mostly yellow	D (rarely A in Alta.)	≅ 12 mm	few	black	
P. zelicaon form comstocki[a]	yellow		mostly yellow	D	≅ 7–10 mm	few	black	
P. zelicaon form nitra[a]	black	d	black to slightly yellow	D	♂ 2–7 mm ♀ 1–5 mm	few	black	
P. zelicaon form ampliatanitra[b]	black	d	mostly black	D	♂ 0–2 mm ♀ 0–1 mm	few	black	
P. polyxenes asterias	black	g	mostly black	D	♂ 2–7 mm ♀ 0–2 mm	many, large	black	
P. p. asterias form ampliata (♂ only)[a]	black	g	mostly black	D	♂ 0–2 mm	many, large	black	
P. p. asterias form pseudoamericus[b]	yellow	i (sometimes h or g)	yellow	D	≅ 8–10 mm	many	black	
P. polyxenes kahli	black	g	mostly black	C (sometimes B, D)	♂ 3–7 mm ♀ 1–5 mm		black	
P. p. kahli form comstocki[b]	yellow	a (slightly darker)	yellow		≅ 8 mm		slightly yellow	
P. polyxenes coloro	yellow	e, f (♂), f (♀), rarely i	somewhat yellow	D	≅ 10 mm	few to (usually) many	black	uph black postmedian band broad, fw submarginal spots more rounded
P. p. coloro form comstocki	yellow		somewhat yellow	D	≅ 7 mm		black	
P. p. coloro form clarki	black	g	mostly black	D	♂ 2–6 mm ♀ 1–3 mm		black	
P. brevicauda	black	g	slightly yellow	D	2–6 mm	many, large	black	tail very short, ups bands often orange, fw less pointed
P. indra	black	j (or solid black)	slightly yellow	D	0–6 mm	few	black	tail often very short

NOTE: Traits are listed in the order of decreasing utility.
[a] Uncommon.
[b] Quite rare.

northern ssp.

tegulae (Fig. 59), from *nitra* in having two rows (plus a partial third row) of yellow dots on each side of the abdomen (Fig. 58), and from most *polyxenes* in having only a few orange unh spots (in the middle of the median band) as in *nitra*. *P. machaon, zelicaon, polyxenes, brevicauda,* and *indra* belong to the *machaon*-group; all except *indra* hybridize and exchange genes so much that some individuals are hard to identify, but *indra* never hybridizes with the others (forced *P. indra* × *polyxenes* lab hybrids die as eggs or young larvae; T. and J. Emmel). Table 2 lists the features useful in identifying the members of this group. Ssp. **aliaska** (Alaska to N B.C.) resembles European, N African, and Asian populations (ssp. *machaon* and others) in having the uph eyespot containing a large orange disk capped by a blue crescent, these nearly surrounded by a black line (Fig. 57), the yellow unf submarginal band is wider than in any other ssp. or spp., and the abdomen is covered with long yellowish hair. The eyespot of *P. zelicaon, polyxenes, brevicauda,* and *indra* nearly always has a black crescent separating the orange disk from the blue crescent, a black line caps the blue crescent, and the black line of *aliaska* below the orange disk has moved inward to form a black spot usually isolated in the middle of the orange disk (Fig. 57). Ssp. **hudsonianus** (N Alta to Que.) has eyespots intermediate between those of *aliaska* and these other spp.; most have a black dot or bar at the bottom of the orange disk, usually joined to the margin, and the black line separating the orange and blue is reduced. In addition the unf submarginal band is fairly wide, the unf discal-cell base is yellow, and the abdomen is sometimes somewhat hairy but less so than in *aliaska* (other ssp. and spp. lack the long hairs). In c and s Man. the yellow ups median band is sometimes narrow (ssp. *hudsonianus* form **comstocki**), owing to past transfer of genes from *P. polyxenes*. Ssp. *aliaska* and *hudsonianus* have a somewhat stubby fw and slightly less-yellow tegulae compared to other *machaon* ssp., though populations along the Peace River of E B.C.-w Alta., referable to ssp. *oregonius* by hostplant, also have rather stubby fw and less-yellow tegulae. Ssp. **oregonius** (s B.C.-Ore., w Mont., Ida.) resembles *hudsonianus* in unf submarginal band width and unf discal-cell color, and the eyespot is similar (the black dot usually is connected to the margin, and a black crescent usually separates the orange and blue; *aliaska*-type eyespots occur rarely), but the fw is more pointed, the tegulae strongly yellow, and the abdomen never hairy. Ssp. *oregonius* intergrades to ssp. *brucei* in at least Uintah Co., Utah, and Moffat Co., Colo. Ssp. **brucei** (= *dodi*) (SE Alta.-Sask. south to Neb.-N Colo., west to N Utah-N Nev.) has yellow wings as in the previous ssp., but the yellow is a little less widespread, the unf discal-cell base is black, and the unf submarginal band is narrower (sometimes almost broken into spots). Ssp. *brucei* differs from *P. polyxenes coloro* by having the black hw postmedian band narrower, the yellow upf submarginal spots more rectangular, and the red unh spots usually few. The width of the yellow ups median band varies in yellow-wing *brucei* (the narrow-band form is **comstocki**) as in *P. zelicaon* and *P. p. coloro* (*comstocki* is most frequent southward in the range of ssp. *bairdii*; see below). From c Nev. east to NW Colo., ssp. *brucei* contains form **brucei**, because black-winged adults (form **bairdii**) also occur. The polymorphism of forms *brucei* and *bairdii* forms a cline between 34° and 41° latitude (the map shows the northern limit of *bairdii* as a white line). North of Nev.-Utah-Colo. all are yellow (except one *bairdii* known from SE Alta.), in N Nev.-N Utah-N Colo. most are yellow, from s Utah-s Colo. about 20 percent are yellow, and from s Calif. to c N.M. only about 1-5 percent are yellow. W. Edwards and D. Bruce proved that forms *brucei* and *bairdii* are the same

southern ssp.

species by raising each from eggs laid by the other. Ssp. **bairdii** is applied to the mostly black-form populations from s Nev.-s Utah-s Colo.-w Kans. southward, with the understanding that all or nearly all *bairdii* populations contain a percentage of form *brucei*. In black-winged adults also, the yellow postmedian bands of males are highly variable in width (sometimes absent, form **ampliata**, which resembles females), and in females they are usually absent (but sometimes several millimeters wide). In black-winged forms the abdomen also occasionally has a yellow flush between the yellow dots on the side, varying rarely to mostly yellow on each side (form **hollandii**; Fig. 58); the abdomen varies independently of the wings. Ssp. *oregonius*, *brucei*, and *bairdii* were considered a distinct species (*P. bairdii*), and *oregonius* has been raised to species rank, but they share the *Artemisia* hostplant and many adult traits (eyespots, unf-cell color, unf submarginal band width, abdominal color, etc.) with ssp. *aliaska* and *hudsonianus*. The ssp. form an obvious progression of traits from *aliaska* to *hudsonianus* to Peace River populations to *oregonius* to *brucei* to *bairdii*, as each ssp. is intermediate in adult traits to the traits of the adjacent ssp. The body enzymes of ssp. *aliaska* and *hudsonianus* are more similar to those of *oregonius* than to those of *P. zelicaon* (F. Sperling). C. Clarke, P. Sheppard, S. Ae, and C. Remington studied the genetics of *machaon*-group species (5-8). Black adult forms (which have the unh basal and postbasal area black and one, rarely no, yellow fw-cell bar) are dominant to yellow forms (which have the unh base yellow and two fw-cell bars). Orange or red larval spots (in notches of the black transverse bands) are dominant to yellow spots (other genes control red vs. orange). The following traits seem to be quantitatively inherited: eyespot pattern, amount of orange or yellow in the unh submarginal spots, amount of yellow or black on the legs, amount of yellow on the unf-cell base, and amount of yellow between the apical unf spots. Long tails may be dominant to short tails. Modifier genes affect the width of the yellow ups median bands, affect the sexual difference in the median-band width of black forms (this sexual difference is great in *P. machaon bairdii* and *P. polyxenes asterias*, absent in *P. brevicauda* and *P. indra*, and intermediate in the others in the table, so the genes show no dominance or are quantitative), and affect the number of flights (*brevicauda* has only one flight, genetically determined). Modifier genes also vary the abdominal pattern. Yellow dots on the side of the abdomen (Fig. 58) seem dominant to yellow stripes, and the abdomen genes seem to be closely linked to the black- and yellow-wing genes because yellow forms usually have striped abdomens and black forms have spotted abdomens. Clarke and Sheppard made lab crosses and backcrosses (crosses between a hybrid and a parent species) between most of the *machaon*-group species; hybrids are usually produced, and backcrosses are generally fertile, though brother and sister hybrid matings seldom produce offspring. *P. machaon* ssp. seem to hybridize occasionally with *P. zelicaon* and *P. polyxenes* wherever they contact them. NE B.C. *machaon* sometimes have *zelicaon* eyespots, and s Alta. *zelicaon* sometimes have *P. m. aliaska* eyespots and wide yellow abdominal bands. (S. Sims produced *aliaska*-like eyespots in a few *zelicaon* adults by chilling the pupae, but under natural conditions the eyespot traits are inherited.) In c and s Alta., ssp. *hudsonianus* and *P. zelicaon* hybridize extensively in some areas, very little in others (Sperling). Occasional hybridization between ssp. *brucei* and *P. zelicaon* seems to occur from c Nev. to w Colo., and hybridization between ssp. *bairdii* and *P. polyxenes* is known occasionally in c Colo.

Habitat Canadian to Hudsonian Zone woods and barely onto the arctic tundra from Alaska to Que., Transition Zone prairie-aspen along the Peace River, mostly Upper Sonoran to Transition (rarely Canadian) Zone arid canyons, hills, and prairie southward. Hostplants herb Compositae: *Artemisia norvegica* ssp. *arctica* in Alaska, Yukon, and B.C., *A. dracunculus* along the Peace River and for ssp. *oregonius, brucei,* and *bairdii, Petasites frigidus* in N.W. Terr. (var. *palmatus* in Sask.); Umbelliferae: *Heracleum lanatum* in Yukon and N Alta., *Zizia aptera* in N Alta. and Man., many genera in Europe; Rutaceae: *Ruta* sp. in Europe. Some Compositae and Umbelliferae are very similar biochemically. *A. dracunculus* contains an oil also found in plants of the Umbelliferae, anisic aldehyde, which stimulates larvae to eat. Lab larvae of U.S. ssp. grow well eating Umbelliferae (*Foeniculum vulgare, Daucus carota, Pastinaca sativa*), and European *machaon* larvae almost always eat umbels, but Compositae seem to be preferred in nature in N. Amer. even in arctic populations; Yukon females in the lab prefer to oviposit on *Artemisia norvegica* rather than on Umbelliferae by 20 to 1 (H. Kimmich).

Eggs cream or greenish-yellow, developing a reddish ring and top, laid singly on the host. Some females in Sweden lay eggs on many Umbelliferae, even those not eaten by larvae, whereas other females lay only on the preferred host species as long as it is available (C. Wiklund). This variation between females seems useful for adaptation to different localities with different Umbelliferae species. Young larvae eat leaves, but after the second stage, larvae feeding on umbels prefer the inflorescence; no nests. Young larva (stages 1-3) of the *machaon*-group black with a white saddle, like a bird dropping. Mature larva (Yukon) pale bluish-green, with colored (see below) spots in notches of the front edge of the black transverse bands, with black lines between segments, the rear facelike (with black eyes, mustache, and sideburns, as in the next four *Papilio* species); head bluish-green, with a black spot in front and black bands beside the spot and on each side, the eyes in a black patch. One Sask. larva similar, but yellowish-green. Larva (U.S.) green to pale grayish-green or bluish-green, with the black marks similar but enlarged in some larvae, which appear mostly black; head like that of *P. zelicaon.* Mainly-black larvae occur sometimes in England. Spots in notches of the black bands orange in Calif., orange or red at least in Colo., Ariz., Japan, and Europe, mostly orange in SE Alta., yellow (rarely orange) Ore.-B.C., yellow in Yukon and Sask. Birds reject larvae after tasting their skin (all the larvae were let go and survived); other chemicals on the osmeteria also repel ants and other arthropod predators (T. Jarvi, B. Sillen-Tullberg, and Wiklund). These researchers think that older larvae are both cryptic, blending among vegetation, and warningly colored, resembling *Danaus* (89-91) larvae. Pupa grayish-brown to lighter brown or brown with a tan pattern and lateral abdominal and middorsal bands like those of *P. polyxenes* (the wing margins, head, and antennae often blackish at least in the Yukon); *or* pupa yellowish-green or green, unbanded. Pupa shaped as in the next three species, with two short horns on the head, a point on top of the thorax, and bumps at the base of the wings. Wiklund, who studied the mortality of brown and green pupae in nature, found that predators ate 50 percent more of the pupae he placed on contrasting color backgrounds than of those he placed on backgrounds matching the pupa color. Pupae hibernate.

One flight, mostly June-E July, in Alaska-N B.C.-Que. and N Europe; two or three flights, usually May-Sep., southward and in S Europe. Somewhat migratory in Europe, occasionally flying from France to England. Adults sip flower nectar and mud. Males can fly several kilometers to reach hilltops and ridgetops, where they perch and patrol all day to await females.

6. Papilio zelicaon (=*gothica*)   Western Swallowtail

Color Plates 7, 63
Figs. 34 (ultraviolet), 48-50, 57-59

The usual yellow form of *zelicaon* resembles *P. machaon* (5) and *P. polyxenes coloro* (7), but the eyespot differs from that in most *machaon*, and the abdomen (Fig. 58) usually has one narrow yellow stripe on each side in males, and one or two stripes in females, thus differing from *machaon* and most *coloro*. The unh usually has orange spots only at the apex and in the center of the median band, fewer than most *coloro* (for other differences from *coloro*, see *P. polyxenes*). The tegulae are mostly yellow, or black in many black adults (Fig. 59). The yellow ups median bands of yellow adults are sometimes narrower (form **comstocki**). *P. "gothica"* is a synonym, indistinguishable from spring Calif. *zelicaon*, which differ in several minor details from summer adults (A. Shapiro). Some s Alta. adults slightly resemble *machaon*, and in N Alta. *machaon* and *zelicaon* hybridize extensively in some areas, very little in others (F. Sperling). An uncommon black form **nitra** (5-20 percent of adults) occurs from s Alta. south to c Colo. and w Dakotas generally east of the continental divide. Form *nitra* is identified by the single row of yellow dots on each side of the abdomen (Fig. 58; occasionally one complete row of dots and a partial second row above it), by the few orange unh spots, and by the mostly black tegulae. M. Fisher, J. Oberfoell, R. Hooper, and I proved that *nitra* is a form of *zelicaon*; both forms were raised from eggs laid by a single form. Form *nitra* occurs rarely in N N.M., N Utah, and Ida. Very rare black adults are known from near San Francisco and San Diego; three females from near Los Angeles are black but have a yellow abdominal stripe. The width of the yellow postmedian bands of *nitra* varies from wide to narrow like the bands of *P. polyxenes* in Colo., Alta., and elsewhere. These bands are rarely nearly absent (form **ampliatanitra**), and they are usually narrower in females than in males. Form *nitra* derived from occasional hybridization with *polyxenes*, and occurs where *zelicaon* meets *polyxenes* in Colo., but mostly farther west than *polyxenes* in Mont. and Alta.; I observed one natural mating of a *zelicaon* male with a *polyxenes* female. Form *nitra* apparently remains in the population because the male perching sites are slightly more restricted to the topmost point of a series of hills than those of yellow males; this habit may allow them to mate more often because females fly to hilltops to mate. In addition, *nitra* may have a larval or pupal survival advantage at low altitude, whereas the yellow form may survive better at higher altitude.

Habitat mostly Transition to Hudsonian Zone mountains, ranging from sea level to rarely above timberline. Hostplants (n, known hosts of form *nitra*; all the plants are eaten by the usual form) herb Umbelliferae: *Anethum graveolens*[n], *Angelica*[n] *ampla, arguta, hendersonii, kingii, lineariloba, tomentosa, lucida, Apium graveolens, Cicuta maculata, Conioselinum scopulorum, Daucus carota* (and var. *sativus*), *pusillus, Conium maculatum, Carum carvi, Foeniculum vulgare, Harbouria trachypleura*[n], *Heracleum lanatum*[n], *sphondylium* (and ssp. *montanum*), *Ligusticum porteri, grayi, Lomatium nuttallii*[n], *californicum, dasycarpum, utriculatum, parryi, grayi, triternatum, marginatum, martindalei?, dissectum* var. *multifidum, Oenanthe sarmentosa, Zizia aptera*[n], *Pseudocymopterus montanus, Pimpinella, Petroselinum crispum, Pter-*

yxia hendersoni, petraea, terebinthina var. *californica, Pastinaca sativa, Perideridia bolanderi, gairdneri, kelloggii, Sphenosciadium capitellatum, Tauschia arguta, parishii;* Rutaceae trees and herbs: *Citrus sinensis, limon, Ruta graveolens. P. zelicaon* invaded lowland Calif. after *Foeniculum* was introduced, and now larvae eat *Citrus* there, and are pests within orange groves. *Citrus* and plants of the Umbelliferae contain similar oils: methyl chavicol in *Citrus*; anethole and anisic aldehyde in Umbelliferae. These oils stimulate some *Papilio* larvae to eat (V. Dethier). Larvae refuse *Artemisia dracunculus*, a *P. machaon* host (J. Hopfinger).

Eggs cream, developing a reddish-brown ring and top, laid singly on leaves and inflorescences. Larvae (Figs. 48-50) eat leaves, but older larvae prefer the inflorescence; no nests. Larva usually green or bluish-green (rarely mostly black— S. Sims produced mostly black larvae by raising them at high temperature), with notched black transverse bands, black lines between segments, and as in other *machaon*-group species two black spots above the legs; spots in the notches of the black bands yellow (sometimes orange or red) in Calif., yellow or orange in Alta., usually yellow in Colo. (sometimes orange w of Denver); head greenish, with a black spot in front and another among the eyes, the black vertical bands in front of the eyes and on each side joined or nearly joined at the top. Pupa yellowish-gray, or light brown to blackish-brown, with a brown lateral band and a brown middorsal band; or pupa yellowish-green, unbanded. Pupae hibernate.

One flight, mostly May-E June (mostly L May-E July in Alta. and higher mountains); several flights, mostly May-Aug. in Wash.-Ore., Mar.-Sep. in lowland Calif., nearly all year in s Calif. Males patrol and perch all day on hilltops to await females. O. Shields recaptured males after up to 29 days on the same hilltop, and found that transferred males returned to the hilltop from up to 5 km away, showing a preference for the hill they were caught on. L. Gilbert also found that some hilltopping males remain at the same learned spot for many days. When Shields released virgin and mated reared females, only the virgins flew to hilltops, where they slowly flew about until spotted by a male. Females are pursued by males for long distances, but other males are not pursued far (Gilbert); tethered males are ignored when they stop fluttering upon landing, but males try to mate with females when they have stopped fluttering. This shows that males can tell the sexes apart, probably by sensing the perfumelike odor of all *machaon*- and *glaucus*-group males (see also Fig. 36). In courtship, the male flies around the female with a bobbing flight, the female lands, the male lands, and mating begins; sometimes mating is initiated rapidly, without preliminaries. After mating, the female flies rapidly downhill.

eastern ssp.

Color Plates 2 (larva), 4 (pupa), 6-8, 63
Figs. 36 (scent patch), 57-59

7. Papilio polyxenes (= *joanae*)   American Swallowtail (Black Swallowtail)

The wings are mostly black in E N. Amer., mostly yellow in Calif. and vicinity, but most adults everywhere have orange in most of the unh median and submarginal spots. Ssp. **asterias** (most of the range except w Ariz. westward and Sask.-Man.) is black, with most unh (and often unf) spots strongly orange, rather than mostly yellow as in *P. machaon* (5) and *zelicaon* (6). The tegulae (Fig. 59) are mostly or completely black (yellow in *machaon*), and the abdomen (Fig. 58) is black with two rows (plus a partial row) of yellow dots on each side. The yellow uph postmedian bands of males are highly variable, from absent (form **ampliata**, which resembles a female) to 1 cm wide. Females usually have narrow postmedian bands (or none) in N. Amer. in order to mimic *Battus philenor* (25); the bands are wide in Cuba (ssp. *polyxenes*), where *B. philenor* is absent and the *Battus* species also have light bands. The median bands are narrower when the larvae are raised under low light intensity (J. Heitzman). A yellow form (ssp. *asterias* form **pseudoamericus**) appears very rarely (Ill., Colo., N.M., w Tex., SE Ariz., but commoner in E Mex.); its abdomen (Fig. 58) is suffused with yellow on each side between the yellow dots (or rarely blacker with rows of dots). *P.* "*joanae*," slightly darker, from C Mo. (possibly ranging east to the Appalachians), I treat as a synonym of *asterias*; Heitzman treats it as a distinct species because it is said to occur only in woods, to lack orange larval spots and melanic larvae, and to normally have the black segmental larval bands broken into spots. The status of *joanae* should be studied further. Ssp. **kahli** (SE Sask. in aspen parkland, s Man. east to Winnipeg and north to C Man., and Turtle Mts., N.D.) resembles ssp. *asterias*, but the black eyespot dot or bar is usually below the center and often connected to the margin, the black line between the blue and red in the eyespot is often narrow or absent, the unh usually has less orange (from none to completely orange in each spot), the female ups median bands are sometimes as wide as those of males, and the tegulae often have a trace of yellow. In form **comstocki** of ssp. *kahli* (rare: 0.003 of the larvae found on *Zizia* plants and raised to adults by J. Troubridge) the yellow covers most of the unh, but the uph median band of females is only 1 cm wide (probably about 1.5 cm in males), and the abdomen has yellow stripes on each side. *P. machaon hudsonianus* form *comstocki* may have a slightly hairier abdomen than *kahli* form *comstocki*, and more yellow in the unf cell, though the distinction is unclear because *P. polyxenes* and *machaon* probably hybridize occasionally in Man. and Sask. C. Remington raised both typical *kahli* and *kahli* form *comstocki* from a cross of two wild black *kahli* adults with fairly wide yellow median bands. Ssp. *kahli* evolved through a transfer of genes from *P. machaon* to *polyxenes* in past hybridization. Ssp. **coloro** (= *rudkini*; in deserts from C Ariz. and sw Utah west to s Calif. east of the South Coast Range) has yellow (**coloro**) and black (**clarki**) forms; the frequency of yellow forms increases westward but never reaches 100 percent (10 percent of adults are the yellow form NE of Phoenix, 50 percent at Yuma, Ariz., about 80 percent in the Providence Mts., Calif., 86 percent in Clark Co., Nev., about 98 percent in the Ivanpah Mts. and in San Diego Co., Calif.). Both forms almost always have orange in most of the yellow unh median and submarginal spots and the unf median band. Yellow-wing ssp. *coloro* adults always have the unh base yellow, but rarely have narrow uph median bands (1 cm, form **comstocki** of ssp. *coloro*). The *coloro* tegulae are slightly yellow. The abdomen of yellow forms (Fig. 58) in males usually has a fairly narrow yellow stripe and above it often a row of yellow dots, and in females one (plus a partial stripe) or two yellow stripes and often dots. Ssp. *coloro* meets *P. zelicaon* at the w edge of the s Calif. deserts, where yellow *coloro* forms are distinguished by having the male abdomen and red unh spots usually differing from those in *zelicaon*, the unf submarginal spots usually more rounded (rarely in a band as in most *zelicaon*), the yellow uph streak in cell CuA_2 usually longer than the one in CuA_1 (usually shorter in *zelicaon*), and the black uph postmedian band wider. Black form *clarki* is like ssp. *asterias* (on the abdomen also), but the unh spots usually have less red, and females have a narrow yellow fw median band. F. Thorne hybridized *coloro* and *asterias* and their offspring for many generations in the lab,

ssp. *coloro*

and he and D. Bauer both raised both black and yellow forms from eggs laid by either yellow or black females, proving that they belong to one species. Other ssp. of *polyxenes* occur south to Colombia-Peru, where black and yellow forms also fly together. *P. polyxenes* seems to hybridize occasionally with *P. machaon*, *zelicaon*, and *brevicauda*.

Habitat Subtropical to lower Canadian Zone woods, mountains, and suburbs; mostly Lower Sonoran Zone desert for ssp. *coloro*. Hostplants (a or no letter, ssp. *asterias*; c, ssp. *coloro*; k, ssp. *kahli*; j, "*joanae*") herb Umbelliferae: *Angelica ampla, atropurpurea, venenosa, Anethum graveolens, Apium graveolens, Conium maculatum, Daucus pusillus, carota*[ack] (and var. *sativus*[a]), *Cryptotaenia canadensis, Foeniculum vulgare*[ac], *Harbouria trachypleura, Heracleum lanatum,* sp.[k] (rarely used), *Levisticum officinale, Ligusticum scothicum, Berula erecta, Osmorhiza longistylis, Oxypolis canbyi, Pastinaca sativa*[ak], *Petroselinum crispum*[ack], *Ptilimnium capillaceum, Carum carvi, Cicuta maculata, bulbifera, douglasii, Sium suave, Spermolepis divaricata, Taenidia integerrima*[aj], *Thaspium barbinode*[aj], *Zizia aurea*[kj], *aptera*[k] (main host of *kahli* and its form *comstocki*), *Cymopterus panamintensis* var. *acutifolius*[c] (occasionally), *Tauschia parishii*[c], *arguta*[c] (*Hydrocotyle* is doubtful because lab larvae refused *H. umbellata* and *americana*); herb and shrub Rutaceae: *Thamnosma texana*[a], *montana*[c] (usual host), *Ruta graveolens*[ac] (Penn., Ill., Ga., Mo., Tex., Mass., Calif.), *Dictamnus albus.* Larvae are attracted to the Umbelliferae oils methyl chavicol, anethole, anisic aldehyde, anisic acid, carvone, coriandrol, and sedanolid, and to the Rutaceae oil methyl-nonyl-ketone (V. Dethier); lab larvae will eat even *Cosmos* and *Solidago* (Compositae), which have similar oils. Umbelliferae plants produce certain chemicals, linear furanocoumarins (psoralins), to repel insects that try to eat them. Larvae are resistant to psoralins that kill other insects because the intestine and body rapidly detoxify and eliminate them, but angular furanocoumarins reduce larval growth (M. Berenbaum, P. Feeny, G. Ivie, and others); the psoralins discourage other insects, and some Umbelliferae species now produce the angular ones to discourage *polyxenes*. The psoralins actually increase the growth rate and decrease the mortality of *polyxenes* eating them (Berenbaum). J. Erickson and J. Scriber raised *polyxenes* on many other lab Umbelliferae; larvae grew 25 percent faster on cultivated than on wild Umbelliferae, probably because some insect-repelling chemicals, such as the angular ones, have been bred out of the cultivated species to make them more edible for people. *P. polyxenes* can survive on *Magnolia* leaves in the lab. Ssp. *coloro* larvae refuse *Citrus*, which *P. zelicaon* larvae eat.

Eggs cream, developing a reddish-brown ring and top, laid singly on leaves and inflorescences of the host (ssp. *kahli* prefers to lay on the inflorescence). Females lay an average of 206-435 eggs in the lab, about 36-53 per day, starting when about 2-4 days old (W. Blau and R. Lederhouse). Larvae eat leaves and the inflorescence; older larvae often prefer the inflorescence; no nests. Ssp. *asterias* larva green, yellow-green, bluish-green, or whitish-green, with black lines between segments and yellow spots (sometimes orange or red; mostly orange on Cape Breton I., N.S.) in the notches of the black transverse bands, the black lines and bands variable in thickness (sometimes the larva mostly black); head like that of *zelicaon*. Ssp. *kahli* larva similar, light green to pale bluish-green, with yellow spots in the notches (or interruptions) of the black bands. Ssp. *coloro* larva similar, green or white to almost totally black (usually black with narrow white bands in Utah), the spots in the notches orange in Calif., orange or yellow in Utah (orange also in Costa Rica). The "*joanae*" larva similar, light green, some-times with wide black stripes (the black bands usually broken by pale spots) or bluish-green in color, as in some ssp. *asterias* larvae; spots in the notches pale yellow-orange or yellow (to whitish in the bluish-green larvae). Pupa light brown, with a brown-to-black lateral band and a light-brown-to-black middorsal band, the wing-case margins brown; *or* pupa green (often with yellow on top), or (some "*joanae*") bluish-green, unbanded. The "*joanae*" larvae that are light green produce green or brown pupae, whereas blue-green larvae produce blue-green or brown pupae (Heitzman). Pupae are brown in short-day photoperiods, but green or brown in long-day photoperiods (D. West, W. Snellings, and W. Hazel). In long-day photoperiods, pupae are brown when they pupate on rough sur-faces, but green on smooth surfaces; on artificial (mostly smooth) lab back-grounds, they tend to be green on green (and especially yellow) backgrounds, and brown on blue and red backgrounds. These factors affecting pupal color tend to ensure that overwintering pupae will be brown, and that summer pupae will match the background color, providing camouflage to reduce the chance of being eaten (see *P. machaon*, 5). Pupae are found on thick stems, rocks, etc., within a meter above the ground. Pupae hibernate (some pupae of each flight hibernate in "*joanae*" and in other populations as well). C. Oliver found that pupal diapause is triggered by short photoperiod (except in Costa Rica); long photoperiod or cold help end diapause.

One flight, L May-L June in Man.-Sask., L June-M Aug. in Colo. moun-tains; several flights L Apr.-Sep. in lowland Colo. and N U.S., L May-M June and M July-L Sep. at Ottawa, Feb.-Oct. in s Calif.; many flights all year in Fla. In the Mojave Desert, rains initiate a large adult emergence. Adults feed on flower nectar and mud. Blau found that adults can live as long as a month in Costa Rica, and that females there disperse more than males. To seek females, males perch and patrol all day, mostly on hilltops or ridgetops (patrolling is more common in flat areas). Lederhouse found that males typically choose an area about 70 m^2, where they perch about 67 percent of the time, patrol 25 percent, feed 6 percent, and interact with others 2 percent. He found that males often change sites; at the most preferred site for seeking mates he studied, only 52 per-cent of males new to the site remained the next day, but if they did remain their likelihood of staying increased (92 percent of males remaining for four days were there a fifth day). Females fly to hilltops to mate, and males chase butterflies that resemble *P. polyxenes* longer than they chase other butterflies. Lederhouse and Heitzman studied mating. The male and female flutter near each other briefly, landing an average of about 20 m from where courtship started, then mate shortly after landing. Successful courtship lasts an average of 42 sec; unsuc-cessful courtship lasts 100 sec. Mating itself lasts an average of 31 min (Mo. "*joanae*") to 45 min (N.Y.). Females fly high in the air (like the encounters be-tween two males), then rapidly downward to reject and evade courting males. Those females surviving a week or more often mate a second time (rarely a third) to maximize the fertilization success of their eggs.

8. Papilio brevicauda   Short-Tailed Swallowtail

Resembles *P. polyxenes asterias* (7) and has the same abdominal pattern (Fig. 58) and unh spots (which in most individuals are completely orange), but the tails are short (as in some *P. machaon*, 5), females have median bands as wide

Color Plate 7
Figs. 57, 58

as those of males, the tegulae (Fig. 59) are slightly yellow, the fw is shorter (as in *machaon*), and the wing bands are frequently orange on the ups as well as the uns. The ups bands are usually orange in Nfld. (ssp. **brevicauda**), becoming more yellow westward (ssp. **gaspeensis**), in a cline. Once was considered a ssp. of *polyxenes*, but J. McDunnough found that *brevicauda* flies with *polyxenes* on Cape Breton I., N.S., where it has one flight between the full flight and the partial second flight of *polyxenes*, and its larval forms occur at different frequencies there (most are light green, very few blackish, whereas *polyxenes* has mostly blackish larvae there). C. Clarke and P. Sheppard found that *brevicauda* is as distinct from *polyxenes* as is *machaon*, based on their hybridization studies. D. Ferguson found a few apparent hybrid *brevicauda* × *polyxenes* in nature.

Habitat Canadian Zone taiga to lower Alpine Zone, often near the sea. Hostplants herb Umbelliferae: *Ligusticum scothicum* (a favorite), *Coelopleurum lucidum*, *Heracleum lanatum*, *Angelica atropurpurea*, *Pastinaca sativa*, *Conioselinum chinense*, *Daucus carota* var. *sativus*, *Petroselinum crispum*, *Apium graveolens*. The last three plants are used in town gardens. A female oviposited on *Dictamnus albus* (Rutaceae), a possible host, and on *Matricaria chamomilla* (Compositae), on which the larvae died (a mistake by the female). B. Jackson, J. McDunnough, and Ferguson discovered most of these hostplants. Unlike *P. polyxenes*, larvae evidently tolerate eating angular furanocoumarins, which four of these hosts possess.

Eggs cream, developing a reddish-brown ring and top, laid singly on host inflorescences or on top of leaves. Larvae eat leaves and the inflorescence; no nests. Larva pale green to creamy-greenish-white, with black lines between segments, the width of these lines and of the black transverse bands variable (larva rarely mainly black); notches or interruptions in black bands yellow (mostly orange on Cape Breton I.); head like that of *P. zelicaon* (6). Pupa green, with a yellowish subdorsal band and a dark-green lateral band; *or* pupa blackish-brown, or intermediate in color. Pupae hibernate, sometimes under stones.

One flight, M June-July. Males await females on hilltops.

9. Papilio indra   Cliff Swallowtail

Color Plates 2 (larva),
7, 8
Figs. 52, 57, 58

Identified by the abdomen (Fig. 58), which is black with one short pale-yellow dash on the side near the rear, or completely black. The wings are mostly black with pale-yellow bands and spots, and the tails are very short except in the southern Great Basin and s Calif. The tegulae (Fig. 59) are slightly yellow. Ssp. **indra** (the Rockies and Cascades south to c Calif.) has the tails very short (2 mm) and the uph postmedian band about 5 mm wide. Ssp. **pergamus** (coastal s Calif.) has similar 5 mm bands, but the tails are longer (5-7 mm) as in the remaining ssp. Ssp. **fordi** (Mojave Desert, Calif.) has wider wing bands (6-7 mm), which decrease in width northward and eastward in its range; in c Nev. highly variable intergrade populations occur. Ssp. **kaibabensis** (Grand Can., Ariz.) is large, with postmedian bands nearly obsolete and blue areas much larger; the bands become slightly wider northeastward to sw Colo. (ssp. **minori**).

Habitat mostly Upper Sonoran to Transition Zone desert mountains or canyons to Ponderosa Pine forest. Hostplants bushy odorous herb Umbelliferae growing among rocks: *Cymopterus purpurea*, *panamintensis* var. *acutifolius*, *Aletes acaulis*, *Harbouria trachypleura* (the only host not bushy and not preferring rocks), *Lomatium lucidum*, *parryi*, *nuttallii*, *eastwoodi*, *marginatum*, *scabrum*, *latilobum*, *junceum, grayi, triternatum, dissectum* var. *multifidum, Pteryxia hendersonii, petraea, terebinthina* var. *californica, Tauschia parishii, arguta.* Larvae eat *Thamnosma montana* (Rutaceae) in nature when the normal hosts are consumed.

Eggs greenish-cream, developing a brownish ring and top within 2 days, laid singly on the underside of host leaves. Young larvae eat notches at the edge of leaves. Larvae eat only leaves, and conceal themselves by resting at the base of the plant; no nests. Young larva like a bird dropping. Mature larva mostly black (the blackest larvae resembling *Parnassius*); in ssp. *pergamus* the black transverse lines between segments absent (these lines typical in the other four ssp. in the *P. machaon* group, 5-8); in the other *indra* ssp. the bands expanded backward to the front of the next segment, the color between the bands whitish (usually in s Calif.), pink (usually in ssp. *minori* and the s Sierra), pinkish-gray, yellowish, salmon, or slightly bluish, depending on locality; spots in the notches of the black bands yellowish (orange in ssp. *minori* and in the s Sierra); lower part of the body black (with light spots above the prolegs and on the lower side); head yellow to orange, marked like that of *P. zelicaon* (6), or mostly black. Pupa (Fig. 52) tan, blackish, grayish, reddish, or greenish-brown, tending to resemble the background rocks at each locality (J. Emmel); pupa shorter, with smaller projections, than other *machaon*-group pupae. Pupae hibernate.

One flight, mostly May-June northward, May southward, M Mar.-Apr. in Mojave Desert; one early flight, L Apr.-May, plus a full or partial flight, July-Aug., from sw Colo. to N Ariz. and c Nev. and rarely the s Sierra and Mojave Desert. Adults sip flower nectar and mud. Males perch all day not on the hilltop, but on rocky places just below the hilltop or mesa top, to await females. Adults in the Grand Canyon can move several kilometers upward from hostplants to the canyon rim to mate. In courtship the male and female flutter close together briefly, then the female lands and flutters slightly, the male lands, and they join.

Color Plate 9

10. **Papilio andraemon**   Bahamas Swallowtail

Resembles *P. aristodemus* (13) but has additional smaller tails, usually lacks yellow upf submarginal spots, and has a yellow spot on the tail and a yellow bar at the end of the upf cell.

Habitat tropical wooded areas. Caribbean migrants (known from the Bahamas, Cuba, and Jamaica) occasionally establish temporary populations on islands south of Miami, and rare strays are known in Miami. Hostplants Rutaceae: *Citrus aurantifolia, aurantium, Zanthoxylum* (all trees), *Ruta graveolens* (herb).

Eggs laid singly on host leaves. Larva olive-green to reddish-brown to black, with white prothorax, a white saddle in the middle of the body, white on top of the rear, and blue dots along the back, the underside lilac; head dark brown. Pupa resembling that of *P. cresphontes* (11), slightly reddish-brown mottled with blackish; abdomen and wing cases somewhat greenish.

Several flights, Apr.-Oct. at least. Adults sometimes fly out over the ocean between islands, and hurricanes may transport them between islands.

11. **Papilio cresphontes**   Giant Swallowtail

Easily recognized in most of its range. In the southwest resembles *P. thoas* (12) except in the fw spots (see *thoas*) and the male abdomen (Fig. 60).

Fig. 60.   Top view of rear half of male abdomen: *left*, *Papilio cresphontes* (11); *right*, *P. thoas* (12).

Color Plates 6, 8
Figs. 51, 60

Habitat tropical to Transition Zone woodland and *Citrus* groves. Ranges south to Colombia, Bimini, and Cuba. Hostplants tree and herb Rutaceae: *Citrus sinensis, limon, aurantium, grandis*[t], *Zanthoxylum fagara, americanum, clava-herculis, hirsutum, Ptelea trifoliata, Ruta graveolens, Casimiroa edulis, Dictamnus albus, Amyris elemifera, Choisya*; Piperaceae: four spp. of *Piper* in Cuba. R. Sim observed eggs laid on (and larvae eating) Staphyleaceae: *Staphylea trifolia*. Records of *Nyssa sylvatica* (Nyssaceae), *Persea borbonia* (Lauraceae), and *Populus* (Salicaceae) seem erroneous. Both *P. cresphontes* and *P. zelicaon* (6) fed on *Citrus* in the San Joaquin Valley, Calif., though *cresphontes* was a stray there and is now eradicated.

Eggs yellowish or light green, sometimes orange, laid singly on host leaves and twigs. Larvae (Orange Dogs) eat new shoots and young and older leaves. Young larvae stay under leaves; no nests. Larva (Fig. 51) resembles bird dung, mottled brown, with a cream band (aimed toward the osmeteria) on the sides of the thorax, a cream saddle in the middle of the body, cream on top of the rear, and a transverse ridge on top of the thorax; head brown. Pupa mottled gray-brown or brown, or green with yellow and brown patches; wing cases projecting slightly ventrally. Pupae hibernate.

Two flights northward, L May-E Sep.; many flights all year in s Tex. and s Fla. Somewhat migratory, straying rarely to Que., N.D., and Bermuda. Adults sip flower nectar, mud, and the juices from manure. Males patrol to seek females.

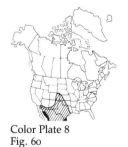

Color Plate 8
Fig. 60

12. **Papilio thoas**   King Swallowtail

P. thoas and *P. cresphontes* (11) both have only two red unh postmedian spots, unlike other similar *Papilio*; but *thoas* is only a southern stray. The yellow upf postmedian spots next to the cell are rectangular and placed in a neat row (the middle two spots in *cresphontes* are round, one smaller than the other). The upf submarginal spots outside the yellow spots usually number four in *thoas*, three in *cresphontes*. The abdomen is longer on top in male *thoas*; when viewed from above, no space is visible between the valvae (*cresphontes* has a space; Fig. 60). *P. thoas* is mostly in Tex. (ssp. **autocles**) and Mex.; ssp. *thoas* and other ssp. extend to Argentina, Cuba, and Jamaica. *P. thoas* has 27 chromosomes; *P. cresphontes* and *P. ornythion* have 30.

Habitat open subtropical areas. Hostplants in Latin Amer. herb and tree Rutaceae: *Zanthoxylum, Citrus limon, Ptelea, Ruta graveolens*; Piperaceae: six spp. of *Piper. Monnieria trifolia* (Scrophulariaceae) is doubtful.

Larvae rest exposed, usually on the upperside of a leaf. Larva olive-green mottled with brown (the rear white on top), with a dirty-white irregular lateral band, above which (and on top of the body) is a wide olive-green dorsal band (narrowest in the middle of the body), which contains blue points (and yellow rings on the thorax); head brownish or olive-green. Larva like that of *P. an-*

draemon (10), but lacking white above the third and fourth prolegs. Species 10-16 are in the *P. thoas* group, whose larvae resemble bird droppings even when mature (other *Papilio* larvae may resemble dung only when young). Pupa like that of *P. cresphontes*, gray-brown, or dark brown with gray or greenish shading, with four rows of tiny dorsal bumps.

Many flights all year in Mex.; an occasional stray into s Tex. (July-Sep.) and a rare migrant in Kans. and Colo. Adults sip flower nectar and mud.

13. **Papilio aristodemus**   Island Swallowtail

Color Plate 8

Somewhat similar to *P. cresphontes* (11), but the pale ups bands are narrow, a long wide rust band is next to the blue unh spots, and the tail lacks a yellow spot.

Habitat subtropical wooded areas in the Bahamas, Greater Antilles, and s Fla. islands, rarely north to Miami. Hostplants tree Rutaceae: *Amyris elemifera*, *Zanthoxylum fagara*.

Eggs pale greenish-cream, laid singly on top of host leaves. Larvae eat new growth, so the preferred habitats are advancing hammocks or cut-over areas rather than mature hammocks protected from disturbance. No nests. Larva maroon-brown, with white or cream blotches along the sides (the blotches bigger in the middle and at the ends of the larva) and blue dots on the back; prolegs whitish; head maroon-brown. Pupa like that of *P. cresphontes*, rusty-brown, varying to gray etched with green. Parasitoid wasps and flies are so common in immatures that only about 3 percent of the eggs laid in nature become adults. Pupae hibernate.

One flight, L Apr.-June (mostly May); rarely, a partial second flight (L July-E Sep.). Adults often fly 1 km or more between adjacent islands. Males patrol all day about the tree canopy to seek females.

14. **Papilio ornythion**   Ornythion Swallowtail

Color Plates 8, 58

Resembles *P. astyalus* (15), but males lack a yellow upf spot in the cell and have about four small yellow dashes between the unf postmedian and submarginal bands, and the yellow male postmedian bands are narrower. Females have tails, and either look like males (though the bands are narrower and whiter) or have the postmedian bands nearly gone and the uph submarginal spots suffused with brown. Habitat subtropical wooded areas. Hostplants tree Rutaceae: *Citrus*. Larva like that of *P. thoas* (12), but more yellow. Many flights probably all year in s Tex.; somewhat migratory, rarely straying to s Ariz. and N.M. Ranges south to Guatemala.

15. **Papilio astyalus**   Astyalus Swallowtail

Color Plates 8, 58

P. astyalus, like *P. ornythion* (14), has the yellow upf submarginal spots next to the margin. Both spp. have wide yellow bands with small submarginal spots on the males and no yellow on the tail. *P. astyalus* males have a yellow spot in the upf cell. Females are very dark like *P. androgeus*, but they have only one tail or none; yellow postmedian bands are absent; the uph has three bands—orangish (or blue with a posterior red spot), blue, and cream or yellow—from the center to the margin (these bands sometimes reduced to two blue rows on the uph); red spots lie near the hind angle (tornus); and the fw is lighter in the middle of the wing than at the base.

Habitat subtropical wooded areas. Ranges south to Argentina. Hostplants tree Rutaceae: *Citrus sinensis, limon*.

Larva like that of *P. thoas* (12), more strongly marbled, the patches yellow. Pupa more slender than that of *P. thoas*, the thoracic point longer.

Many flights all year in s Tex.; somewhat migratory, straying rarely to Ariz. and NE Tex.

16. Papilio androgeus   Queen Swallowtail

Color Plates 8, 9

P. androgeus, P. astyalus (15), and *P. ornython* (14) are similar in having a long row of reddish unh median spots. *P. androgeus* males differ in having very wide yellow bands on the fw without pale submarginal spots, the uph submarginal spots brown, and the tail lacking yellow. Females are markedly different, mostly black, with two narrow (and one wide) green uph bands, one linear tail, and several smaller tails.

Habitat subtropical and tropical woods. Ranges south to Argentina and the Greater Antilles. Common in orange groves in s Fla. since 1976, introduced from Latin Amer. Hostplants tree Rutaceae: in Fla. *Citrus sinensis*, in Latin Amer. *C. reticulata* and *Zanthoxylum elephantiasus*.

Larvae ("Orange Puppies") rest on the upperside of a leaf. Larva dark olive-green, or gray-brown to black, with an orange lateral line on the neck, greenish-white lateral blotches, a greenish-white saddle in the middle of the body, a greenish-white saddle on the rear, and small bumps with blue spots on the back; head olive-brown. Pupa dark brown with creamy lengthwise bands, wing cases with green shading. Pupae hibernate.

Many flights, Mar.-Sep. at least. Adults sip flower nectar and mud. Males patrol to seek females on hilltops in Colombia (J. Scott) and in other countries.

17. Papilio anchisiades   Red-Spotted Swallowtail

Color Plate 8

Easily identified.

Habitat subtropical woodlands and *Citrus* groves. Ranges south to Argentina. Hostplants tree Rutaceae in Mex.: *Citrus limon* and other spp., *Casimiroa edulis*.

Eggs laid in clusters on the host. Larvae feed at night and rest gregariously on the trunk or stems by day. Larva greenish-brown, with small cream spots, a cream patch on each side in the middle of the body, and rows of small bumps; head brown. Pupa light brown, with light-green mottling.

Many flights, Apr.-Nov. at least, in s Tex.; apparently a resident in Tex. and a rare migrant north to Kans.

18. Papilio glaucus   Tiger Swallowtail

Color Plates 2 (larva), 4 (pupa), 6-8
Figs. 34 (ultraviolet), 45, 71

Easily identified by its yellow tiger-striped wings. In ssp. **glaucus** (E U.S. north to Transition Zone, and most of the Great Plains) the unh marginal spots are red, and the unf marginal spots are separate except in spring (the unf spots joined into a yellow band in the spring form **canadensis**). Ssp. **canadensis** (Canadian Zone in NE U.S. to Alaska and B.C.) has red unh marginal spots and a yellow unf marginal band (as in occasional spring ssp. *glaucus*) and a wider black unh stripe on the abdominal margin. Ssp. *canadensis* is genetically smaller than ssp. *glaucus*, and its larval foodplant preference seems to be genetically different

ssp. *glaucus, canadensis*

ssp. *rutulus*

(J. Scriber). Ssp. *canadensis* form **arcticus** (Alaska-Yukon) is like ssp. *glaucus* form *canadensis*, but it has few or no red unh marginal spots (like ssp. *rutulus*). Ssp. **rutulus** (sw B.C. to w Mont., south to Calif., Ariz., and the Rockies, and outlying colonies in the mountains of w Dakotas and w Neb.) has yellow unh marginal spots, a yellow unf marginal band, an unbranched spine on the male valva (the other two ssp. have several branches; Fig. 71), and broader lobes like a cottonwood leaf on the female lamella (the other two ssp. have bladelike lobes; Fig. 71). Ssp. *rutulus* is usually treated as a distinct species because its mating structures are more similar to those of *P. eurymedon* (19) and *P. multicaudata* (20) than to those of ssp. *glaucus*, but the larval foods of *rutulus* are more similar to those of ssp. *canadensis* than to those of ssp. *glaucus*, *P. eurymedon*, or *P. multicaudata*. Also, ssp. *rutulus* is reproductively isolated from *P. eurymedon* and *P. multicaudata*, but not from ssp. *glaucus*. The white line on the first map is the northern boundary of ssp. *glaucus*. Ssp. *rutulus* and *glaucus* intergrade in the Black Hills (L. Brower), and ssp. *rutulus* and *canadensis* intergrade in se B.C., in wing pattern and in male and female genitalia (Brower, J. Scott, J. Shepard). Males of the yellow species do not approach whitish butterflies (the color of *P. eurymedon*) for mating (Brower); males may prefer butterflies that absorb ultraviolet, since both yellow and black *P. glaucus* absorb ultraviolet, whereas *P. eurymedon* reflects it. C. Clarke and P. Sheppard hybridized and backcrossed ssp. *rutulus* and Chicago ssp. *glaucus* in the lab, and the few crosses to date produced adults, indicating that there may be little or no infertility between them, although female pupae from the cross of male *rutulus* × female *glaucus* (but not the reverse) stayed in diapause and never hatched. No one has hybridized ssp. *rutulus* with ssp. *canadensis*, which is more closely related. The unf submarginal stripe (vs. separate spots) and the red unh spots (vs. yellow) are both inherited quantitatively (Clarke and Sheppard); wing-pattern intermediates found in nature where the subspecies meet are thus due to hybridization. The cross of *glaucus* × *eurymedon*, in contrast, had much infertility and no female offspring (Clarke and Sheppard). Some females of ssp. *glaucus* are black, form **nigra** (found from Mass. west to s Minn., e Colo. south to the Gulf Coast, but rare in Fla., rare in Nfld.); black coloration is determined by a gene on the Y chromosome (according to Clarke and Sheppard and to U. Mittwoch), so each female is the color of her mother. Some genes of ssp. *rutulus* (not on the Y chromosome) make the blackish hybrids of *nigra* × *rutulus* less black and more yellow. Form *nigra* is thought to mimic the poisonous *Battus philenor* (25). Black and yellow forms are edible to birds. J. Sternburg, G. Waldbauer, and M. Jeffords painted some Promethea Moths to look like *B. philenor*, some to look like *Danaus plexippus* (89), and others to look like yellow *P. glaucus*; they released them in nature and then tried to recapture them. They recaptured fewer of the yellow *glaucus* type, suggesting that resembling *B. philenor* (and *D. plexippus*) discourages birds from attacking. J. Burns thought that the polymorphism is maintained by two opposing forces: the black form benefits from mimicry, but males prefer the yellow female form. His data showed that yellow females mated more often than black females. S. Makielski, M. Levin, and T. Pliske, however, found no differences in mating frequency, reproduction, or life span between the two forms, and T. Prout and others noted that opposing selective forces within the same generation cannot maintain any polymorphism. Mimicry may favor the black form in localities where *B. philenor* is common, whereas survival differences may favor the yellow form; as a further complication, adults may move between areas where the black form is rare and where it is common. Prout suggested that there may be "frequency-dependent selection," by which mimicry favors the black form when it is rare, but when it is common birds learn to eat it.

Habitat subtropical to tundra-edge deciduous wooded areas. Ranges south (as ssp. *alexiares*) to Veracruz, Mex. Hostplants many trees and shrubs (g, ssp. *glaucus*; c, *canadensis*; r, *rutulus*; ?, dubious): Rosaceae: *Prunus cerasus*[gcr], *domestica*[g] (and var. *galatensis*[r]), *americana*[gr], *serotina*[gc], *pennsylvanica*[gc], *virginiana*[grc], *persica*[gcr] (ssp. *glaucus* larvae refuse it), *emarginata*[r], *ilicifolia*[rt], *armeniaca*[r], *caroliniana*[r], *Amelanchier canadensis*[c], *Crataegus*[gc], *Malus pumila*[gcr], *Sorbus americana*[c], *Cydonia oblonga*[g], *Rubus*?[r]; Salicaceae: *Populus balsamifera*[rc], *tremuloides*[gcr], *grandidentata*[c], *trichocarpa*[r], *angustifolia*[r], *deltoides*[g], *Salix lasiolepis*[r], *lasiandra*[r], *scouleriana*[r], *exigua*[r], *babylonica*[r], *hookeriana*[rt], sp.[c]; Betulaceae: *Betula alba*[c], *lenta*[c], *alleghaniensis*[c], *papyrifera*[c] var. *commutata*[r], *Carpinus caroliniana*[g], *Corylus*[c], *Alnus rugosa*[c], *incana*[g], *tenuifolia*[r], *viridis*[r], *crispa*[rt], *rubra*[r]; Aceraceae: *Acer*[cr]; Juglandaceae: *Carya*[gc]; Ulmaceae: *Ulmus*[cr]; Platanaceae: *Platanus racemosa*[r]; Tiliaceae: *Tilia americana*[gc]; Bignoniaceae: *Catalpa bignonioides*[g]; Magnoliaceae: *Liriodendron tulipifera*[g], *Magnolia*[(r?)] *acuminata*[g], *virginiana*[g]; Lauraceae: *Cinnamomum camphora*[g], *Lindera benzoin*[g], *Sassafras albidum* var. *molle*[g], *Persea americana*[r]; Styracaceae: *Styrax americana*?[g]; Oleaceae: *Fraxinus*[r] *americana*[gc], *nigra*[g], *caroliniana*[g], *pennsylvanica* (vars. *lanceolata*[gc] and *subintegerrima*[c]), "swamp ash"[g], *Syringa vulgaris*[gcr]; Rutaceae: *Ptelea trifoliata*[g], *baldwinii*[r], *Zanthoxylum americanum*[g]; Fagaceae: *Quercus velutina*?[g], *chrysolepis*[rt]. All three ssp. eat *Prunus*, *Malus* (*rutulus* oviposits on this but larvae refuse it), *Alnus*, *Fraxinus*, and *Syringa*, although ssp. *rutulus* and ssp. *canadensis* seem to prefer Salicaceae and Betulaceae as well, whereas ssp. *glaucus* often prefers *Liriodendron*. Ssp. *glaucus* larvae die eating *Populus tremuloides*, and refuse *Salix*; hybrid *glaucus* × *canadensis* larvae survive on *Populus* and *Liriodendron*; ssp. *canadensis* die eating *Liriodendron* and *Lindera benzoin*; and ssp. *rutulus* refuse *Liriodendron* and *Malus* (W. Edwards, J. Scriber).

Eggs (Fig. 45) green, soon becoming greenish-yellow speckled with reddish-brown, laid singly on host leaves. Larvae eat leaves, and rest on a silk mat on top of a leaf, which usually bows the leaf upward somewhat. Larvae of *P. glaucus*, *P. eurymedon*, and *P. multicaudata* very similar, green, with a yellow subdorsal eyespot (with a blue center), on the rear of the thorax (several yellow spots above it), a black transverse dorsal stripe (edged in front with yellow) between abdomen segments 1 and 2, two subdorsal rows and one lateral row of small black-rimmed blue spots (especially on abdomen segments 4-7); head reddish-brown. Larval eyespots of ssp. *rutulus*, *P. eurymedon*, and *P. multicaudata* have two yellow satellite spots above them (the lower one attached to the eyespot); ssp. *glaucus* lacks the upper spot. Larva turns brown before pupating. Pupa light brown, often with green patches and black markings, a brown or black lateral stripe, a light- or dark-brown dorsal band, two short horns on the head, a peak on top of the thorax, and a bump at the base of the wing. Pupa in ground litter, sometimes on fences or tree trunks. Pupae of all three ssp. hibernate.

One flight for ssp. *canadensis* and in higher mountains, June-July; several flights elsewhere, June-Aug. on Colo. plains, M May-Aug. in N.Y., Mar.-Nov. in Fla., Mar.-Sep. in lowland Calif. J. Fales marked adults in his yard and found that a third of them returned; one was recaptured 1.5 km away. Adults sip flower nectar, carrion juices, etc. Males congregate at wet spots to get sodium ions from the water. Males patrol all day in woodland lanes or moist wooded valley bottoms to seek females. Colo. males sometimes patrol in forest lanes on hilltops, but they do not stay there for more than a few minutes. In courtship the male and female flutter about each other before landing and mating. Males of *glaucus* and species 19 and 20 have a perfumelike pheromone used in courtship.

19. Papilio eurymedon   Pallid Tiger Swallowtail

Color Plate 7
Figs. 34 (ultraviolet), 52

Like *P. glaucus* (18) but whitish, with thicker black stripes.

Habitat foothills and mountains, typically Transition and Canadian Zones. Hostplants tree and shrub Rosaceae: *Prunus emarginata, virginiana* (and ssp. *demissa*), *ilicifolia, persica, domestica, Malus pumila, Holodiscus discolor, Amelanchier alnifolia?, Crataegus rivularis, douglasii;* Rhamnaceae: *Ceanothus fendleri, velutinus, prostratus, sanguineus, Rhamnus crocea, californica* (and var. *rubra*); Betulaceae: *Alnus rubra*. Doubtful are *Salix* (Salicaceae) and *Ribes inerme* (Grossulariaceae).

Eggs yellowish-green, with reddish-brown blotches, laid singly on host leaves. Larval and pupal habits like those of *P. glaucus*. Larva like that of *P. glaucus rutulus*, though eyespot slightly narrower. Pupa (Fig. 52) like that of *P. glaucus* in shape, light brown, with a brown lateral band, the front and top half mottled blackish-brown. Pupae hibernate.

One flight, mostly June (May-June in c Calif.); several flights, L Mar.-Aug., in s Calif. Adults sip flower nectar and mud. To seek females, males generally patrol back and forth, but they sometimes perch, all day in forest lanes on hill-tops. However, males usually do not stay more than a few hours at one point on a ridge, and can travel several kilometers (O. Shields and L. Gilbert).

20. Papilio multicaudata   Two-Tailed Tiger Swallowtail

Color Plate 7

Like *P. glaucus* (18), but each hw has two tails, and the black stripes are usually narrower. Spring adults are smaller.

Habitat Upper Sonoran to Transition Zone foothills, mountains, or canyons. Ranges south to Guatemala. Hostplants tree and shrub Rosaceae: *Prunus virginiana* (and ssp. *demissa*), *americana, emarginata, cerasus, capuli, ilicifolia?, Amelanchier, Vauquelina californica;* Oleaceae: *Fraxinus oregonius, latifolia, anomala, viridis, pennsylvanica* var. *lanceolata, Ligustrum lucidum, vulgare;* Rutaceae: *Ptelea trifoliata* (and var. *angustifolia*), *baldwinii, crenulata;* Platanaceae: *Platanus racemosa. Salix* (Salicaceae) and *Umbellularia californica* (Lauraceae) are doubtful.

Eggs greenish-yellow, with reddish patches, laid singly on host leaves. Larval and pupal habits like those of *P. glaucus*. Larva like that of *P. glaucus rutulus*, with tiny white circles around the hairs on the ventral half of the body. Pupa mottled greenish-brown to yellowish-brown, with a brown lateral stripe, a light-brown band on top of the abdomen, light-brown wings, and brown horns and bumps, shaped like that of *glaucus*. Pupae hibernate.

One flight, mostly L May-June in B.C., May-June in c Calif., M June-E Aug. in Colo. mountains; several flights, mostly L Apr.-E Aug., in the Colo. foothills and southward; many flights, Feb.-Nov., in Tex. Adults sip flower nectar and mud. Males patrol all day along canyon bottoms to seek females.

21. Papilio pilumnus   Three-Tailed Tiger Swallowtail

Stray only
Color Plate 58

Like *P. glaucus* (18) but with several tails. The fw has one less black band than in *P. multicaudata* (20).

Habitat tropical woodland. Ranges south to Guatemala. Hostplants tree Lauraceae: *Litsea*.

Larva green, with a yellow transverse ridge on the neck, two brown eye-spots edged with black (with two black spots in each center) at the rear of the thorax, and a yellow lateral line with brown beneath; abdomen with four dorsal rows of blue rings and a row of blue sublateral spots; head tan. Pupa pale green or pink, with lateral ridges, a purple subdorsal line (with purple dots next to it at the front), two purple projections on the head, and one purple projection on the thorax.

Many flights nearly all year in Mex.; a rare stray into s Tex. (Ariz.-N.M. records are errors). Adults sip mud.

22. Papilio troilus   Spicebush Swallowtail

Differs from other *Papilio* in having a broad greenish-blue band in the middle of the uph and the uph submarginal spots usually greenish-blue also. The uph is greener in males, bluer in females. Ssp. **ilioneus** (Fla.) has larger more-yellow uph submarginal spots than ssp. **troilus** elsewhere. A Batesian (palatable) mimic of *Battus philenor* (25).

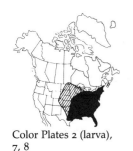

Color Plates 2 (larva), 7, 8
Fig. 55 (veins)

Habitat Subtropical to Transition Zone deciduous woodland. Hostplants shrub and tree Lauraceae: *Sassafras albidum* var. *molle* and *Lindera benzoin* (the two usual hosts), *Cinnamomum camphora*, *Persea borbonia*; Magnoliaceae: *Lirio-dendron tulipifera*, *Magnolia virginiana*. The following are doubtful—Rosaceae: *Prunus persica*, *serotina*, *Pyrus arbutifolia*; Leguminosae: *Cercis canadensis*; Oleaceae: *Syringa vulgaris*. Rutaceae are questionable: *Zanthoxylum americanum*, *fraxineum*, *clava-herculis*.

Eggs greenish-white, laid singly on the underside of leaves. Larvae eat leaves. First- and second-stage larvae live in a silked bent-over flap of a leaf. Older larvae live in a tube made by bringing two sides of a leaf upward and together with silk. Larva green, with a broad yellow lateral band (edged beneath with a fine black line, then grayish-tan beneath the line), two subdorsal rows and one lateral row (below the yellow band) of blue (black-rimmed) spots on the abdomen, a large orange subdorsal (black-rimmed) eyespot (with a blue dot above a black blotch inside) on the rear of the thorax, and a smaller orangish subdorsal (black-rimmed) spot (with a blue center) on abdomen segment 1, the area behind the osmeteria orange and black; head green. Pupa yellowish-green to reddish-yellow or reddish-brown, with some black dorsal dots and a brown or grayish lateral ridge edged beneath with white; wing cases projecting ventrally slightly. Pupae usually near the ground on slender stems. Short photoperiod produces brown diapausing pupae, whereas with long photoperiod green and brown pupae occur. Pupae hibernate.

Several flights, M May-M Sep., northward; many flights, Mar.-Dec., in Fla. A rare stray west to Man. and Colo., and to Cuba. Adults sip flower nectar and mud. Males patrol all day in wooded areas to seek females.

23. Papilio palamedes   Laurel Swallowtail

The long narrow yellow stripe on the unh base is diagnostic, along with the unbroken yellow uph median band.

Habitat wooded areas, esp. swampy woods, on the SE U.S. coastal plain,

Color Plate 8

with a few exceptions that may be strays. Hostplants Lauraceae trees: *Persea borbonia* (and var. *pubescens*), *Sassafras albidum* var. *molle*. J. Brooks found that lab larvae eat these plants, plus *Persea americana* and three other Lauraceae, but would not eat *Magnolia virginiana* (Magnoliaceae) or *Citrus* (Rutaceae).

Eggs pale yellowish-green, laid singly on the host. Larvae eat leaves, and rest on a silk mat in the center of a leaf, which bows the leaf upward, as do larvae of *P. glaucus* (18). Larva green, with many blue spots like those of *P. troilus* (22) and a narrow yellow lateral line (edged beneath by a fine black line, with red-brown beneath it on the underside), the orange eyespot on the front of the abdomen very small, that on the rear of the thorax a black circle containing a ring of orange and a large black center. Pupa green, with a whitish lateral line edged above with brown and two short horns. Pupae probably hibernate.

Several flights, L May-Sep., in Va.; many flights, Mar.-Dec., in Fla. L. Harris saw a small migratory (?) flight to the northwest in Ga., and some records of strays as far as Neb., N.Y., and Cuba seem to indicate long flights. Three or four adults sometimes roost together on a palmetto leaf (S. Scudder). Adults sip flower nectar and mud. Males patrol all day in wooded areas to seek females.

24. Papilio victorinus

Stray only
Color Plate 58

Resembles some *P. astyalus* (15) females, but the yellow upf spots are not on the margin, and females have broader greenish uph postmedian spots.

Habitat tropical woodland. Ranges south to Costa Rica. Hostplant tree Lauraceae: *Persea americana*.

Larva green (gray on the sides), with orange subdorsal eyespots at the rear of the thorax, a gray transverse band between these eyespots enclosing black spots, behind this band green dotted with white, and then a white transverse line interrupted by four pale-blue dots; abdomen with gray triangles (containing green spots inside) near the rear and a white transverse ridge on the rear, the first segment gray with a black transverse band on its rear; head gray. Pupal head and thorax brown, the thorax with a triangular green patch on each side, the abdomen green, with a white-edged brown middorsal band and a similar lateral band, the wings and underside green; *or* pupa uniformly gray. Pupae hibernate.

Many flights, at least Jan.-Nov., in Mex.; a rare stray into s Tex. (Aug.).

Tribe Troidini: *Aristolochia* Swallowtails

The Troidini, which include the birdwing butterflies of the East Indies, comprise 136 species worldwide, mostly tropical. Three species occur in North America, mostly in southern U.S., one of them a rare import.

Males generally have a fold of scent scales on the hind margin of the hindwing (full of white fluff in *Parides*). K. Brown found that in courtship males hover over females, occasionally darting back and forth, appearing to brush this wing fold against the female's antennae and head. Larvae feed on *Aristolochia* plants. They are mostly black with red spots and red filaments. First-stage larvae have fewer secondary hairs than do other Papilioninae; there may be only a few on the head, and the body scoli may be limited to the lower part of the body. Pupae have flaring ridges on the abdomen in addition to the two head horns and the prong on the thorax. Pupae hibernate.

Because *Aristolochia* plants are poisonous to vertebrates, the Troidini are also poisonous and are often mimicked by other butterflies.

Adults flap about fairly swiftly, though the species of the forest genus *Parides* are slower. Most species are nonmigratory, but *Battus* sometimes migrate.

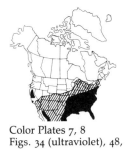

Color Plates 7, 8
Figs. 34 (ultraviolet), 48,
51, 52

25. Battus philenor   Pipevine Swallowtail

Easily recognized, with little variation. Females have less blue and larger pale spots on the uph than males. Adults are poisonous to vertebrates and are mimicked by the edible *Papilio troilus* (22), female *P. polyxenes* (7), black females of *P. glaucus* (18), female *Speyeria diana* (251), and *Limenitis arthemis astyanax* (146) (see "Mimicry and Other Defenses," in Part I). The red spots on the abdomen of *Battus* and *Parides* have glands that emit an acrid odor when pinched (H. Tyler). The ranges of the mimics fit the range of *B. philenor* in the east where the mimicry developed, but not in the west. *L. a. astyanax* and black female *P. glaucus* seem limited to areas where *philenor* is common. *B. philenor* has a tough bite-resistant body, which allows it to survive after being tasted.

Habitat tropical to Upper Austral/Upper Sonoran Zone mostly brushy or wooded areas. Ranges south to Veracruz, Mex. Hostplants vine and herb Aristolochiaceae: *Aristolochia californica* (for c Calif. nonmigratory populations), *serpentaria*, *elegans* (preferred by adults but most larvae die eating it), *durior*, *longiflora*, *macrophylla*, *reticulata*, *tomentosa*, *watsoni*; *Asarum canadense* is doubtful because females and larvae usually refuse it. Other recorded plants not normally used are mostly vines: *Calonyction aculeatum* (Convolvulaceae) and three Polygonaceae, *Polygonum convolvulus*, *cristatum*, and *hydropiper* (not a vine). One larva fed to pupation on *Azalea indica* (Ericaceae). Females use plant shape as well as chemical cues to identify hostplants (M. Rauscher), which may explain the records for Convolvulaceae and Polygonaceae (which are probably not eaten by larvae) because these plants are mostly vines like the hostplants. Females search for eggs on the plant before laying, and fly away if an egg is found. Rauscher found that larvae eating *Aristolochia serpentaria* or *reticulata*, both small herbs, may have to find and eat 25 plants before pupating. In E Tex. the first-flight females prefer to lay on *reticulata*, which is much more common then, and the second-flight females prefer *serpentaria*; larval survival is greater on *serpentaria* for the second flight but not for the first flight. Young and mature leaves of *serpentaria* are eaten, but because mature leaves of *reticulata* are tough and nitrogen-poor, they are not eaten by larvae or used by the second Texas flight. Rauscher and P. Feeny proposed that larvae ate so many *serpentaria* plants that *serpentaria* evolved underground flowers and fruits, most of the plant matter became placed in the roots, and the leaves became tough and nutrient-poor.

Eggs reddish-brown, laid in clusters of 1-20 (average 2.2 in Tex.) under host leaves and petioles, mainly in sunny areas (even though eggs and larvae survive better in the shade). Young larvae gregarious. Larvae eat leaves, stems, and seed capsules; no nests. Larva (Figs. 48, 51) dark purplish-brown, with two long dark filaments on the prothorax below a black collar, a 4-mm filament on each side of the last two thorax segments, a small filament above the spiracle on abdomen segment 1, a 4-mm filament below the spiracle of abdomen segment 2, short filaments above the prolegs, a short sublateral filament on abdomen segments 7 and 8, short subdorsal filaments on every segment behind the prothorax (these orange on the abdomen and longer, 5 mm long on abdomen segment 9), lateral orange spots on the abdomen, and a red-brown plate on the rear; head reddish-brown, black between the eyes. Pupa (Fig. 52) brown to green, often with yellow patches, with a point on top of the thorax, two short horns on the head, and two undulating ridges on top of the abdomen; wing widened into a lateral ridge. Pupae found on tree trunks and other exposed surfaces. Pupae brown on most rough surfaces such as twigs, green on smooth (or yellow) surfaces such as leaves, sometimes green on red or green surfaces (D. West and W. Hazel). Photoperiod affects the pupal color very little, not as in *P. polyxenes*, although diapausing pupae (in winter in Va.; Calif. pupae may enter diapause as early as July) are most often brown. Pupae hibernate.

Many flights from spring to fall (but commonest in spring in Calif.); three flights, mostly May and July-Sep., at Philadelphia; two flights M Mar.-May in E Tex. Except in C Calif., adults fly long distances, migrating rarely even to Maine, Mich., and Colo. Adults often sip the nectar of flowers, esp. pinkish to purplish ones, and mud. Males patrol all day to seek females, usually near the hostplants, but sometimes on hilltops. In courtship, after fluttering near each other the female and then the male land and they mate quickly. Males have scent scales next to the abdomen on the hw as in *Eurytides* (1-3; see Fig. 36), which other papilionids use to induce the female to land for mating. Half a dozen adults often roost communally on a tree.

26. Battus polydamas Gold Rim

Easily recognized. Probably distasteful like *B. philenor* (25).

Habitat Subtropical Zone disturbed areas more than virgin forest, temporarily established northward. Ranges to Argentina and throughout the Antilles and Bahamas. Hostplants Aristolochiaceae, mostly vines: *Aristolochia durior, pentandra, ringens, elegans, serpentaria, sipho, macrophylla*, plus many more spp. in Latin Amer.

Color Plate 8
Figs. 34 (ultraviolet), 45

Eggs (Fig. 45) pale yellow to dark greenish-orange, laid in tight clusters of about 10-14 on young hostplant stems or growing tips of vines, mostly in sunny areas (even though eggs and larvae survive better in the shade). Larvae gregarious when young. Larvae eat leaves; no nests. Larva black (usually), brownish-gray, red-brown, greenish-brown, brownish-yellow, or reddish-yellow, with blackish transverse bands and with many filaments positioned like those in *B. philenor* (all filaments dark yellow or orange, tipped with black); prothorax with a reddish-orange or yellow collar; head brownish-black. Pupa brown mottled with rusty-yellow, sometimes green mottled with yellow (the yellow mostly above the wings and on the head, the ridges and protrusions sometimes tipped with bluish), shaped like that of *philenor*. Pupae hibernate.

Many flights all year in S Tex. and S Fla. (rare in winter). Adults are fairly sedentary in Costa Rica and Brazil around the hostplants and flowers, although they may move several hundred meters or a kilometer (A. Young and K. Brown); U.S. adults rarely migrate north to Ky. and Mo. Adults sip flower nectar and mud. They live about a week on the average (rarely up to 28 days) in Brazil.

27. Parides eurimedes (= *arcas*) Cattle Heart

Stray only
Color Plate 58

In males the abdominal edge of the hw contains a brown patch of scent scales. The sexes differ but both have an orange hw fringe and a red hw patch.

Habitat tropical forest. Ssp. **mylotes** is in U.S. and Mex.; other ssp. range to S. Amer. Hostplants Aristolochiaceae: many *Aristolochia* spp. in Costa Rica.

Eggs deep rusty-brown, laid singly or in loose clusters of two to five, mostly on the upperside of older host leaves. Larvae usually eat young leaves; no nests. Larva purplish-brown (turning grayish-tan), with black blotches, a transverse stripe behind the head, and white tubercles dorsally on abdomen segments 4 and 7 and laterally on segments 7, 8, and 10. Pupa light green (yellow dorsally), shaped like that of *Battus* (25, 26) but without the point on top of the thorax.

Many flights all year in Mex.; a very rare stray into the U.S. (one record from Fort Worth, probably a human import). Males patrol on sunlit forest edges to seek females, mainly in the morning.

Subfamily Parnassiinae: Parnassians

The Parnassiinae include about 50 medium-sized, usually white or yellow species with rounded forewings. Only three species occur in North America, in the western mountains; the rest are found in temperate Eurasia.

Parnassiinae adults lack the forewing vein R_2 (except Eurasian genera; see Fig. 55). The larval osmeteria are rarely or never used. First-stage larvae have extra (secondary) hairs only on the sides of the body. Older larvae have a carpet of short hairs, unlike Papilioninae. Larvae eat Aristolochiaceae, Zygophyllaceae, Crassulaceae, and Fumariaceae plants. Because they can squeeze through small holes, they can rest in soil, and they pupate underground or under rocks. They sometimes make slight silk cocoons (including a silk girdle) when pupating. Pupae are not attached by the cremaster (in Papilioninae they are). Eggs and sometimes pupae hibernate.

Larvae and adults are poisonous to vertebrates. Both stages have tough

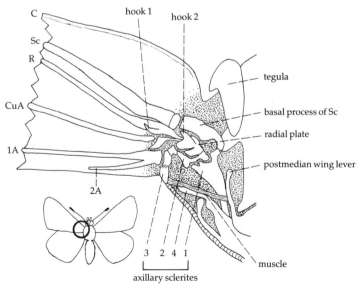

Fig. 61.   The left forewing base of *Parnassius clodius* (29), showing the hooks the adult uses emerging from its pupa.

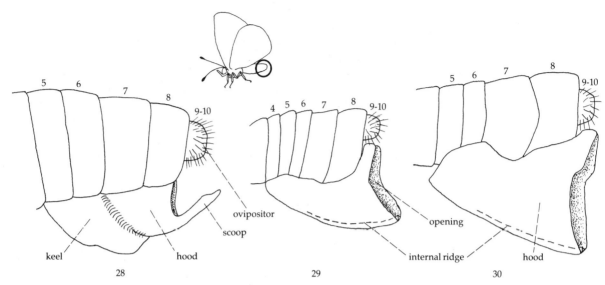

Fig. 62.   The shape of the sphragis on the end of the female abdomen: *28, Parnassius phoebus; 29, P. clodius; 30, P. eversmanni.* The sphragis, a whitish structure preventing the female from remating, is secreted during mating by a gland beneath the male's pseudovalves (see Fig. 29) that pops out during mating. (See also the females of species 28 and 29 in Color Plate 9.)

leathery bodies, and seem to be involved in mimicry. The larvae are supposedly Müllerian mimics with millipedes (but I have never seen these millipedes), and the adults seem to be Müllerian mimics with white Pierinae adults.

The forewing base of *Parnassius* has two hooks (Fig. 61), discovered by M. Hering, that apparently aid the newly emerged adult in escaping from the pupa, the loose cocoon, or the underground pupation site. The first hook is pressed against the top of a vein and is thus useless in the fully hardened adult, but it should be usable when the wing vein is still soft. Both could hook onto pebbles, silk threads, or the pupal case when the unexpanded wings are flapped. Such hooks are unknown in other butterflies, but similar hooks occur on the thorax of Luna Moths.

Adults fly rather slowly, fluttering evenly along, and the wings seem to travel less during each stroke than do those of most other butterflies. Adults, which never migrate, rest and bask with the wings spread. Males patrol to seek females. Adult courtship has disappeared, and the male glues a structure called a sphragis onto the female to prevent her from mating again (Fig. 62). Neither sex seems to fly if a mating pair is disturbed, unique behavior among butterflies. Because adults of at least some species are poisonous to predators, mating pairs are relatively safe.

28. Parnassius phoebus   Small Apollo

Color Plates 2 (larva), 4 (pupa), 9
Figs. 45, 49, 50, 55 (veins), 62

Differs from other *Parnassius* in having the antenna shaft alternately ringed with black and white, and often in having more red and black fw spots. Ssp. **smintheus** is in most of the area, north to interior and sw Alaska. High-altitude populations in the Rockies (ssp. **hermodur**) are small and much darker, esp. in females; they are genetically distinct in wing pattern from low-altitude ssp. *smintheus* in Colo. (my lab-raised adults remained distinct). Ssp. **montanulus**

(lowland w Mont.) has blackish females. Ssp. **sternitzkyi** (N Calif.) has large red spots; ssp. **behrii** (Calif. Sierra near timberline) has orange-yellow spots. Ssp. **pseudorotgeri** (San Juan Mts., Colo.) has a broad gray margin and postmedian band on the fw. Ssp. **apricatus** (Kodiak I. and Seward Pen., Alaska) has four red unh basal spots; males have large red uph spots, and females have wide smoky ups submarginal-marginal borders. Ssp. *phoebus* and other ssp. are in the European Alps and Asia. Adults appear to be Müllerian mimics with other white butterflies (see "Mimicry and Other Defenses," in Part I). Adults have tough leathery bodies that resist bites. Birds refuse to eat adults (T. Eisner) but chipmunks eat them (C. Guppy); body fluids irritate at least humans.

Habitat Transition to Alpine Zone mountain meadows, grassland, and open forest, often on the north side of ridges. Hostplants succulent herb Crassulaceae: *Sedum lanceolatum, stenopetalum, debile, obtusatum* (and ssp. *boreale*), *rhodanthum, rosea* ssp. *integrifolium*. In Europe reported on *Saxifraga aizoides*, but W. Edwards's Colo. larvae would not eat it.

Eggs (Fig. 45) white, laid singly on anything nearby, from soil to plant litter to living plants of many kinds. Larvae (Figs. 49, 50) eat leaves, sometimes flowers and fruits also. They make no nests, but can squeeze into very small holes. Larva black, with many short black hairs, with yellow spots (on each segment one small subdorsal spot and two small and one large supralateral spots), these spots sometimes orange or white; osmeteria short, yellow; head black. Pupa cylindrical, finely granulated, yellow-brown with a green tint, or chocolate or reddish-brown with tan spots (positioned like those of the larva) on the abdomen, the head rounded, the cremaster lacking hooks. Lab pupae sometimes pupate under leaves drawn together with a few silk threads (a loose "cocoon") or under debris (Edwards); larvae in nature worm themselves into pebbly soil, where they probably pupate (J. Scott). Eggs hibernate; possibly biennial in some arctic areas, where older larvae or pupae may spend the second winter.

One flight, mostly June at low altitude, July-M Aug. at high altitude. Movements are usually less than 1 km, but rarely can be many kilometers (J. Scott). Adults often sip the nectar of flowers, esp. yellow Compositae and *Sedum*; they pollinate *Senecio* and other Compositae and become covered with pollen. Males patrol all day with a steady flight just above the ground to seek virgin females. When a male finds a female (by sight, and often by detecting the female's odor when she is hidden in a clump of grass with wings not yet expanded), he drops onto her and crawls over her to grasp her underside. Mating lasts several hours, while the male secretes the sphragis onto her abdomen to prevent her from mating again. The sphragis is flattened ventrally with a scoop and keel (Fig. 62, Color Plate 9), whereas other *Parnassius* have a pointed hoodlike sphragis. Both sexes emit a powerful odor, which is probably used for defense or for mating.

29. Parnassius clodius   American Apollo

P. clodius and *P. eversmanni* have solid-black antennae, unlike *P. phoebus*. The sphragis, formed on the female's abdomen during mating, lacks the scoop and keel of *phoebus* (Fig. 62, Color Plate 9). The red central spot on the hw is not attached to the black corner bar. There is much variation in size and color with altitude and locality. One extreme population with smaller spots (ssp. **strohbeeni**, Santa Cruz Mts., Calif.) is extinct. Alaska adults are darker (ssp. **incredibilis**). Ssp. **clodius** occurs elsewhere.

Color Plate 9
Figs. 61 (fw hooks), 62

Habitat mainly Canadian to Hudsonian Zone open mountain woods. Host-plants herb Fumariaceae: *Dicentra uniflora, formosa, pauciflora*. These plants have poisonous alkaloids; larvae, pupae, and adults may be poisonous too.

Eggs tan, laid singly, scattered haphazardly (even on shrubs) near the host. Larva black, with short black hair and yellow or orange supralateral spots (1-3 per segment); *or* larva (high-altitude) gray-brown or pinkish-gray, with a yellow supralateral band (edged above with black semicircles, 1 per segment) and mid-dorsal black V's aimed forward (each V outwardly edged by yellow, and the point of the V filled with black); osmeteria small, not used; head black. High-altitude larvae are cryptic, whereas low-altitude larvae mimic poisonous millipedes (*Harpaphe haydeniana*: D. McCorkle, J. Emmel). Pupa reddish-black, rounded except for square shoulders at the base of the wings, in a whitish, strong, single-layered silk cocoon above ground, which no doubt requires the wing hooks (Fig. 61) to break. Eggs hibernate; possibly biennial at high altitude, hibernating there perhaps also as older larvae or pupae.

One flight, mostly L June-M July (May in Snake R. Canyon of SE Wash., mostly July at high altitude). Males patrol all day with a peculiar bobbing flight, mainly in meadows and swales, to seek females. Males capture females by grabbing them in midair; both then fall to the ground and mate.

30. Parnassius eversmanni   Yellow Apollo

Differs from *P. clodius* in having yellow males (females are white), longer dark fw bands, and the red central hw spot attached to a black bar that extends to the corner of the hw. The sphragis is like that of *clodius* (Fig. 62).

Habitat lower Arctic to Hudsonian Zone open areas, mostly near forest, in NW N. Amer. and Asia. Hostplants herb Fumariaceae: in Asia *Corydalis gigantea*, in Japan *Dicentra peregrina*.

Color Plates 9, 11
Figs. 51, 52, 62

Eggs white, laid singly (sometimes two together) and haphazardly under stones, on leaves or stalks, etc., near the host. Larvae eat leaves and buds, but prefer flower stalks. Larvae usually rest in the open (as in *P. phoebus*), and are probably distasteful. Larva (Fig. 51) black, with short black hair and a lateral row of white to yellowish dashes separated by dots of the same color; two osmeteria on the prothorax seldom used; head black. Pupa (Fig. 52) dark reddish-brown, in a thin silk cocoon, lacking a silk belt, the cremaster rudimentary. Eggs hibernate the first winter, pupae the second.

One flight, mostly June. Biennial in the alps of Honshu, Japan, but annual in the Disetsu Mts., Japan (Y. Tabuchi).

FAMILY PIERIDAE:
WHITES AND SULFURS

The Pieridae comprise about 1,100 species worldwide. Of the 58 species in North America, most are medium-sized, though a few are small and some are large; most species are common and widespread.

White, yellow, and orange are the predominant colors. The wings generally contain pterine pigments, which are found in some other butterflies also. Many species reflect ultraviolet from the structures of the wing scales, and the wing pigments may also absorb ultraviolet on some areas of the wing, producing an ultraviolet pattern (Fig. 34). Males and females often use ultraviolet to identify the opposite sex.

In Pieridae the six legs are of equal length, and the claws on the leg tips are always strongly forked (in other families, excepting the Libytheidae, the claws are rarely forked), but the pulvilli (Fig. 14) beside the claws are wide and not forked. Larvae eat many dicotyledons, especially Cruciferae and Leguminosae. The larvae are cylindrical and covered with short hair. Only primary hairs occur on the first-stage larvae (Fig. 50); these are usually clubbed or forked, and the upper ones are glandular, emitting honeydew attractive to ants. Pupae are upright, attached (as in the Papilioninae) both by the cremaster and by a silk girdle around the middle. The pupal head usually has one short horn, often prolonged into a cone.

The white species may be Müllerian mimics, because at least in some cases the mustard oils from their larval food render them distasteful.

Flight is generally straight, steady, and fluttering, without any hops or glides. *Pieris napi* and *P. rapae* seem to fly more slowly than others in the family, bobbing up and down somewhat. The flight of *Colias meadii* and many other species is quite fast, and *Eurema nicippe* flies both fast and erratically. *Nathalis iole* flies just above the ground, but the large species such as *Colias cesonia*, *Anteos*, and *Phoebis* commonly fly several meters above the ground. The others fly at intermediate heights. Adult Pieridae generally disperse more than other butterflies, and many migrate. *Phoebis sennae*, for example, has regularly been seen hundreds of kilometers north of its hostplants, flying along at a brisk pace about 2 m above ground. Pieridae usually rest with the wings closed, and they tend to bask by spreading the wings, but *Colias* and occasionally *Euchloe* and other species sometimes bask sideways to the sun with the wings closed. All Pieridae species visit flowers. Except in some tropical species, males always patrol to seek females, and usually produce pheromones to seduce them (Fig. 36). If a mating pair is disturbed, the male nearly always flies, toting the female who dangles beneath. Female Pierinae and Coliadinae employ a special tactic for rejecting males: they spread the wings and raise the abdomen vertically so that the male cannot join, and glands on the end of the abdomen apparently produce a repellent chemical as well (Fig. 36).

The oddest feature of Pieridae is their occurrence in seasonally different adult forms, a phenomenon due to different day lengths. The spring-form underside usually becomes redder or darker, and the *Eurema proterpia* hindwing even grows a tail. Pupae may change color depending on the background, as in Papilionidae.

Three subfamilies of Pieridae occur in North America, the Dismorphiinae, Coliadinae, and Pierinae. The only subfamily that does not occur here is the Pseudopontiinae, of tropical west Africa; its one species is characterized by having peculiarly branched wing veins and round wings. This species is related to the Dismorphiinae and shares that group's peculiar male abdominal structures. The pupa has a cone on the head, and enlarged wings, as in some Coliadinae (*Phoebis* and *Eurema*).

Subfamily Dismorphiinae: Mimic Sulfurs

Except for one Palaearctic genus, the Dismorphiinae occur only in the American tropics. There are about 100 species; only one species, a stray into southern Texas, is found in North America.

Adults are characterized by having five R veins in the forewing (all of which branch from one vein that starts from the discal cell), the base of vein M_2 arising next to vein M_3, and the forewings markedly narrower in males than in females. The male mating structures are distinctive, as noted in the key (see Part II). Larvae usually eat plants of the Leguminosae, and are shaped like those of other Pieridae. Pupae have a long cone on the head and the wings extend downward, in the manner of *Phoebis* of the Coliadinae (Fig. 52).

Adults often mimic *Heliconius* or other butterflies.

Mimic sulfurs flutter fairly slowly. None of the species migrates. Females lack the pheromone glands on the tip of the abdomen that are present among Pierinae and Coliadinae. C. Wiklund found that unreceptive European females (of *Leptidea*) do not show the characteristic rejection behavior found among Pierinae and Coliadinae; instead, they keep the abdomen between the closed wings, thereby preventing the male from joining. They may also fly vertically.

31. Enantia albania (*"melite"*)   Dimorphic Sulfur

Stray only
Color Plate 58
Fig. 55 (veins)

The antennae are long. Males are yellow, with a narrow fw and brown unh patches; females are white, with a wide fw and a long brown unh streak. A tropical Mexican species. Many flights in Mex.; a rare stray into s Tex. (one old record, and one record in Sep. 1972).

Subfamily Coliadinae: Sulfurs

The Coliadinae (about 300 species) occur worldwide, and the 36 North American species range from the subtropics to the Arctic.

The sulfurs are distinguished in several ways: they are mostly yellow or orange in color, the humeral vein on the hindwing is reduced or absent, and other structural traits differ (see the key in Part II). The larvae, similar in shape to those of other Pieridae, generally eat plants of the Leguminosae. Pupae may have a head horn like that in the Pierinae, and some species have enormous wing cases (Fig. 52), which may convince birds or lizards that they are leaves. In the temperate-zone species, the larvae usually hibernate.

Mimicry seems to be absent, although the white females of many species may be mimics of some Pierinae.

Adults have a powerful, steady, flapping flight, carrying them usually in a straight line, though the flight of *Eurema nicippe* is erratic. The smaller species such as *Nathalis* fly near the ground, the medium-sized species usually fly about a half a meter to a meter above ground, and the large species of *Phoebis* and *Anteos* fly higher, commonly several meters or so. Except for the native *Colias*, most Coliadinae are somewhat migratory. *Colias* and perhaps others bask by turning sideways to the sun.

32. Colias nastes   Arctic Green Sulfur

Color Plate 11

Identified by the greenish wings with light spots in the black upf border of both males and females (other *Colias* have light spots in the border only on females). The unh middle spot is smeared outwardly. W. Hovanitz has documented numerous arctic populations in which hybridization with *C. hecla* (33) occurs; some hybrids are greenish-orange, some have intermediate male borders, and some have both traits. From Coppermine east to Coral Harbour in Canada, populations tend to have both parental types and swarms of intermediates of every combination, indicating extensive hybridization. Most hybrids in the populations from the Baker Lake region, N.W. Terr., are orange, but the wing borders vary. A population from Pink Mt., B.C., is orangish-green. Hybrids in scattered populations from Meade River, Alaska, to Payne Bay, Que., are greenish, with all types of border. *C. "boothii"* is a name given to these part-orange hybrids, and is therefore not a species name. Other hybrids reported as *"boothii"* were from Baffin I., Churchill, Man., Mayo in the Yukon, c Alaska (including McKinley Park, where adults are often yellowish with narrow borders). In N Alaska adults are greenish with very narrow black borders (ssp. **thula**) and occur with *C. hecla* and with some broader-bordered individuals resembling ssp. **nastes** (as at Meade R.); ssp. *nastes* has wider black borders and occurs everywhere except N Alaska (ssp. *thula*) and Churchill (ssp. **moina**, the pale upf border spots large). I treat *thula* as a ssp. of *nastes*. The variability of border width may be due to an intermixture of genes from ssp. *nastes* or *C. hecla*, or due to *thula*'s Eurasian origin; *C. nastes werdandi* from Scandinavia somewhat resembles *thula* (most have narrow borders but some have wide *nastes*-type borders), which indicates past movement of Siberian adults into Alaska. K. Philip thinks that *thula* is a distinct species, which intergrades with *"boothii"* in NE Alaska. This complicated mess needs study. *C. nastes* males absorb ultraviolet, but orange hybrid males, like *C. hecla*, reflect ultraviolet. Neither *nastes* nor *hecla* has an uph male stigma that produces a pheromone; in other *Colias*, females use this scent to identify their males. The females may rely on ultraviolet to identify their males, and the often-cloudy arctic weather may confuse the adults and account for the extensive hybridization.

Habitat arctic/alpine tundra (esp. dry ridges and eskers). Hostplants herb Leguminosae: *Astragalus alpinus*, *Hedysarum alpinum* var. *americanum* (in Europe?), *Oxytropis deflexa* (Europe), *campestris* (main host at Churchill), *maydelliana* (Coral Harbour), *Lupinus arcticus* (for *thula*). *Salix arctica* (Salicaceae) seems doubtful.

Larva dark green, with tiny black points, a yellow subdorsal stripe (lined above with red), and a white lateral stripe (lined with reddish below); head lighter, with a pair of yellow and white lateral stripes. Hibernation has been reported for young, third-stage, and full-grown larvae; probably biennial.

One flight, L June-E Aug. northward, M July-M Aug. in Lab., July-Aug. in Alta.

33. **Colias hecla**   Arctic Orange

Color Plate 13

This orange species hybridizes with *C. nastes* (32), and the unh middle spot is also smeared outwardly. Resembles *C. meadii* (34), and males of both reflect ultraviolet, but *hecla* males lack the round scent patch found on the uph base of *meadii* males; their ranges are separate also (*hecla* ranges south to Nordegg, Alta., but occurs in the taiga at elevations as low as 1,000 m, whereas *meadii* is near timberline in s Alta.). Where *hecla* and *C. alexandra christina* (35) fly together, *hecla* has a more rounded fw and the smeared unh spot. Ssp. **hecla** (arctic) is always on tundra, females rarely white (form **alba**). Ssp. **canadensis** (s Alaska-Alta., taiga to lower tundra) often has narrower borders and paler orange color; females usually *alba*; flies with ssp. *hecla* in s Alaska-s Yukon but usually earlier and at lower altitude.* Hybrids with *C. nastes* occur ("*boothii*").

Habitat lush Arctic/Alpine Zone tundra and Hudsonian Zone taiga (Canadian Zone in N Alta.). Ranges to Scandinavia and Siberia. Hostplants herb Leguminosae: *Astragalus alpinus* (in Lapland), *eucosmus*, *Hedysarum mackenziei*, *alpinum* var. *americanum*, *Lupinus arcticus*; Salicaceae: *Salix arctica*.

Larva green, with light lateral stripes and tiny black points. Larvae hibernate; probably biennial, hibernating as young larvae in the first winter, as fully grown larvae in the second.

One flight, mostly L June-July (June-E July for *canadensis*).

34. **Colias meadii**   Alpine Orange

Color Plate 13
Fig. 36

Like *C. eurytheme* (37) in having orange wings, but the unh is greenish without brown submarginal dots. The N Mont.-Alta. ssp. **elis** has narrower borders than the s Mont.-N.M. ssp. **meadii**. White females (form **alba**) are rare. The male has a round stigma on the uph base in cell $Sc+R_1$ (Fig. 36). Also Siberia (ssp. **hyperborea**, duskier, possible in arctic N. Amer.: one male known from Bernard Harbour, N.W. Terr.).

Habitat alpine tundra and subalpine meadows. *C. meadii* can live in the Alpine Zone because the adults can fly at lower air temperatures than other species such as *C. philodice* (38; J. Kingsolver). Hostplants herb Leguminosae: *Trifolium dasyphyllum*, *nanum*, *parryi*, *Astragalus alpinus*, *Oxytropis deflexa*, *Vicia americana*.

Eggs yellow-green, later turning crimson, laid singly on leaves. Larvae eat leaves. Larva dark yellow-green, with black points, a pale-yellow subdorsal stripe with black spots on its lower edge, and a narrow white lateral line; head green, with black points. Pupa yellow-green, with a middorsal dark line and a faint subdorsal line; all but the wings dotted with whitish; head projection yellow. Larvae hibernate in the third or fourth (rarely fifth) stage, and according to T. Bean *C. meadii* is biennial in Alta., where first-stage larvae hibernate the first winter, probably nearly mature larvae the second.

*While this book was in press, new data showed *C. canadensis* to be a distinct species.

One flight, July-Aug. Adults typically move 0.5 km in their lives (one moved 1.7 km), tending to go downslope (W. Watt and others). Males live an average of 6-7 days in nature; females, 4 days. In different populations at altitudes only 350 m apart Watt found several genes for body enzymes present in different frequencies, suggesting that populations adapt locally to even minor differences in altitude. Males patrol all day in open areas to seek females.

35. Colias alexandra   Ultraviolet Sulfur

three ssp.

Color Plates 12, 13
Fig. 34 (ultraviolet)

ssp. *harfordii*

Adults vary in visible color and pattern, but the males always reflect ultraviolet only from the outer part of the wings. Ssp. **christina** (Black Hills of S.D. to Wyo., Man., Alta., NE B.C., and E Alaska) is orange on the outer half of the uph and the outer two-thirds of the upf (yellow on the wing bases), and the unh often has brown submarginal dots and rarely a central satellite spot. In the Black Hills and NE B.C.-Alaska, the upf orange extends nearly to the wing base, as in *C. eurytheme* (37). In NW Wyo., Mont., and Utah, *christina* intergrades to ssp. **alexandra**; in this ssp., which occurs in most of the range, including N.D. and SW Sask., the wings are yellow, the unh is grayish with a silver spot lacking a rim, and the fringes are yellow. Ssp. **columbiensis** (S B.C., N Wash., N Ida., and Lincoln Co., Mont.) has yellow wings without orange, a more rounded fw, a rim on the silver unh spot, and often brown unh submarginal dots. Ssp. **harfordii** (S Calif.) is yellow, the silver unh spot has a rim (rarely a satellite spot), and the unh has brown submarginal dots. Some females of all ssp. are white, esp. in the central Rockies (form **alba**). Ssp. *columbiensis* and a Crook Co., Ore., population seem to have hybridized with *C. occidentalis* (36), and the unh submarginal dots of *christina* and *harfordii* may be due to hybridization with *C. eurytheme*. Males of all populations reflect ultraviolet on the outer part of the uph, and on most, a little, or none of the upf (C. Ferris). The orange populations, and some yellow ones in N and C Nev.-NE Calif., have an orange uph spot, and these populations tend to reflect ultraviolet extensively on the upf also. Most yellow populations reflect ultraviolet on the upf only narrowly inside the black border. Ssp. *harfordii* (thought to be possibly a distinct species because J. Burns found that the enzymes of *harfordii* and *alexandra* differ somewhat) has an orange uph spot, and the uph reflects ultraviolet as usual, but the upf reflects only a trace.

Habitat usually Transition to Canadian Zone openings in coniferous forest, sagebrush, and grassland; also open oak woodland in S Calif. Hostplants (c, *christina*, h, *harfordii*, a or no letter, *alexandra*) herb Leguminosae: *Astragalus miser* (and var. *oblongifolius*), *lentiginosus* (vars. *diphysus*, *araneosus*, *salinus*), *eremiticus*, *canadensis*, *serotinus*, *alpinus*, *douglasii*[h] (and var. *parishii*[h]), *antiselli*[h], *bisulcatus* var. *haydenianus*, (doubtfully *crotalariae*[h]), *Hedysarum boreale* (and var. *mackenzii*[c]), *alpinum* var. *americanum*[c], *Lathyrus leucanthus*, *Lotus scoparius*[h], *Lupinus*[ca], *Medicago sativa*, *Oxytropis lambertii*, *splendens*[c], *Thermopsis divaricarpa*, *pinetorum*, *montana*, *rhombifolia*, *Trifolium pratense*, *Vicia americana*.

Eggs yellow-green or cream, later turning crimson, laid singly on host leaves (all *Colias* lay eggs on the upperside of leaves). While finding that females can lay up to 600 eggs, J. Hayes determined that the number of eggs laid is proportional to the population size of the next generation; adult mortality or bad weather that prevents oviposition may thus affect the population size the following generation. Larvae eat leaves; no nests. Larva (ssp. *alexandra* and ssp. *christina*) yellow-green, with tiny black points and a white lateral band (with orange dashes running through it); head yellow-green, with small black points. Larva (ssp. *harfordii*) green, with black points and a white lateral stripe around a red line. Pupa (ssp. *alexandra* and ssp. *christina*) yellow-green (dorsally darker), with three small reddish spots on the ventral side of the abdomen next to the wing cases and (in ssp. *christina*) a yellowish lateral stripe running around the top of the wing case and edged beneath with red-brown on the abdomen. Pupa (ssp. *harfordii*) yellow-green, the abdomen yellowish with a pale lateral stripe. Larvae hibernate (ssp. *harfordii*; third-stage in ssp. *alexandra*).

One flight, L June-E Aug. in most places, M Apr.-M May in s Nev.; two flights, L May-M June and L July-M Aug., in N.D. (and perhaps in sw Sask.), Neb., and the Colo. plains; several flights, Mar.-May and L June-Aug., for ssp. *harfordii*. Adults move up to 8 km but average only 0.6 km in a lifetime (W. Watt and others). Adults sip flower nectar and mud. Males live up to a month, but average only 6-12 days' life span in nature (females less). Males patrol all day in open areas to seek females.

36. Colias occidentalis   Golden Sulfur

Color Plate 12

Adults large, yellow; males do not reflect ultraviolet. The unh is marked by a few brown submarginal dots and a large sometimes pearly middle spot with a red rim and rarely a satellite spot. This middle spot is less silvery than that of *C. philodice* (38) and is surrounded by only one red ring. Females are usually yellow, rarely white (form **alba**). The Calif. ssp. **chrysomelas** has a darker unh and wider black upf borders; ssp. **occidentalis** occurs in Ore.-B.C. Closely related to *C. alexandra* (35), with which it seems to hybridize from Ore. to B.C.

Habitat Transition to Canadian Zone fairly open pine and Douglas fir forest. Hostplants herb Leguminosae: *Vicia angustifolia*, *Lathyrus lanszwertii*, *Lupinus latifolius*, *Melilotus alba*.

Eggs laid singly on host leaves.

One flight, L May-June. Adults sip flower nectar and mud. Males patrol all day near the hosts or in valley bottoms to seek females.

37. Colias eurytheme   Orange Sulfur (Alfalfa Butterfly)

Color Plates 12, 13
Figs. 34 (ultraviolet), 45, 52

The ups is wholly or mostly orange, except on some white females. The unh has a silver spot, with two red rings and a satellite spot, and brownish submarginal dots. Adults are a little larger than *C. philodice* (38), and in females the black upf border is wider with larger pale spots. The orange vs. yellow color of *eurytheme* vs. *philodice*, and the wide vs. narrow black upf borders are controlled by one or two pairs of genes without dominance. Males reflect ultraviolet all over the ups (but no *Colias* reflects from the black border). (Rare males, probably mutants, are yellow, but still reflect ultraviolet.) The ultraviolet reflection, limited to males, is determined by a recessive gene on the X chromosome. Short photoperiod acting on the third- and fourth-stage larva produces the spring form (**vernalis**), which is smaller than the summer form and has narrower borders, darker unh, and yellow on the outer part of the upf (S. Ae and S. Hoffman). (Cold temperature during the pupal stage can also produce *vernalis*; A. Shapiro.) The darker unh (also found in arctic/alpine *Colias*) helps warm them when they bask laterally in cool spring days (W. Watt). Females are often white (form **alba**), owing to a dominant gene affecting only females. The white females of *Colias* species have the same temperature preference as normal females, but the nitrogen that goes into the orange pigment of normal females is used by white females to produce faster development, more fat, and larger eggs, giving them a reproductive advantage (Watt and associates). But normal females (of *C. alexandra* and *C. scudderii* at least) are preferred by males for mating. White females generally are more prevalent in northern N. Amer. populations of *Colias* than in the south (W. Hovanitz); a faster developmental rate may be more useful in arctic climates.

Habitat open areas everywhere at all altitudes. Ranges to s Mex. After the cutting of forests, it became common in New England, where a century ago it was rare (there are some early SE Canada records). J. Boisduval recorded it from N.Y. before 1840, but it did not become common in New England and D.C. until 1929-33. Hostplants herb Leguminosae: *Astragalus drummondii, flexuosus, racemosus, bisulcatus, crassicarpus* or *plattensis, crotalariae, antiselli, whitneyi, alpinus, Baptisia, Cassia, Coronilla, Glycine max*[t], *Glycyrrhiza lepidota, Lotus scoparius, purshianus*[t], *grandiflorus*[t], *crassifolius, subpinnatus, strigosus, Lathyrus leucanthus, jepsoni* ssp. *californicus, Lespedeza, Lupinus minimus, perennis*[t], *succulentus, bicolor, Medicago sativa, hispida, lupulina, Melilotus officinalis, alba, Phaseolus, Pisum sativum, Psoralea, Sesbania exalata, Thermopsis montana, Trifolium repens, nanum, pratense, reflexum, stoloniferum, tridentatum, longipes, wormskjoldii, Vicia americana, cracca, angustifolia, sativa.*

Eggs (Fig. 45) cream or greenish-white, turning crimson in a few days, laid singly on host leaves. Females start laying eggs when several days old. Lab females lay an average of 700 lifetime eggs, and can live up to 39 days. Young larvae of *C. eurytheme* and *C. philodice* eat holes in the top of leaves, and later eat leaves from the tip; older larvae eat each half of the leaf separately. No larval nests. When the weather is too hot or cold, older larvae move to the plant base (P. Sherman and W. Watt). Larvae of *eurytheme* prefer 23°-29°C (73°-84°F), of *philodice* 20°-26°C (68°-79°F), whereas adults of both species prefer 35°-39°C (95°-102°F), perhaps explaining how *philodice* can live farther north. *C. eurytheme* takes 31 days from egg to adult in the lab, *philodice* only 29-30 days, which also helps *philodice* in the short northern summer. Larva green, with raised points, a faint darker-green dorsal line, sometimes a strong white subdorsal line, and a white lateral band (with a line of yellow, pink, or red through it, and edged beneath with blackish dashes). Short photoperiod produces larvae with prominent black lateral patches. Pupa (Fig. 52) green, with yellowish-white and black mottling and a yellow lateral band. Third- and fourth-stage larvae hibernate, although the diapause may not be properly adapted to the northern photoperiod.

Many flights, spring-fall. Because of its recent spread north, diapause is poorly adapted there, allowing ill-fated emergence of some adults in warm periods in late fall at the latitude of N.Y. and Penn. Movements are probably large, larger than those of *C. alexandra*. Although adults do not seem to be strong migrants, N. Criddle reported a southward flight in Aug. in Man.; *C. eurytheme* rarely occurs in N Alta. and N Man. Adults sip flower nectar and mud. Males patrol all day regardless of topography to seek females. Mating is very simple, and receptive females move little: males approach females, the female lands if she was flying, he buffets her with his wings, he then lands, and they mate. Recently mated males court females with less vigor than other males do, and give up more quickly (R. Rutowski). R. Silberglied, O. Taylor, and J. Grula studied how adults choose their mates. Males recognize females visually; they are attracted to the greenish-yellow female unh and are repelled by ultraviolet. Females do not care about the orange or yellow male color. *C. eurytheme* males reflect ultraviolet from the ups, but *C. philodice* males do not reflect ultraviolet; female *eurytheme* must have an ultraviolet-reflecting male to mate. In addition, *eurytheme* and *philodice* each has its own male pheromone (from an uph basal patch), and females mate only with males having the right pheromone. The *eurytheme* pheromone is 13-methylheptacosane, in addition to several straight-chain hydrocarbons that are also found in females and in *philodice*. The male pheromone causes the female to lower her abdomen so that he can mate. Females less than an hour old, esp. females of *eurytheme*, cannot distinguish between the two species very well; thus, most hybrids result from matings between high-density *philodice* males and young *eurytheme* females. This cross, however, usually produces sterile and inviable female offspring, whereas the cross between *eurytheme* males and *philodice* females produces very fertile and viable offspring. The two species hybridize often but not randomly. The sex ratio of hybrids is usually normal (1:1). The genes controlling female mate choice, male phero-mones, male ultraviolet reflection, orange or yellow color, width of the black fw border, size, and developmental rate are all on the X chromosome, forming a "supergene" (Grula and O. Taylor); *eurytheme* and *philodice* have different X chro-mosomes. Because *eurytheme* × *philodice* female hybrids preferably mate with a male of their father's species, the X chromosomes stay in the proper species and do not end up in the other species in the way other chromosomes may. And because nearly all the differences between *philodice* and *eurytheme* result from genes on the X chromosome, even the hybrids sort into *philodice* or *eurytheme*, according to the source of their X chromosomes. The two species remain dis-tinct, and the *eurytheme/philodice* situation is essentially a case of chromosome polymorphism.

38. Colias philodice   Common Sulfur

As in *C. eurytheme* (37), the unh has brownish submarginal dots and a silver spot in the center with two red rings around it and usually a satellite spot. But in contrast, adults are yellow, males do not reflect ultraviolet, adults are a little smaller than *eurytheme*, in females the black upf border is narrower with smaller light spots, and the range of *philodice* extends farther north. Many yellow-orange hybrids with *eurytheme* occur, and white females of the two species (form **alba**) sometimes cannot be distinguished. Ssp. **vitabunda** (N B.C. to Alaska tundra) has narrower borders and mostly white females; ssp. **philodice** occurs else-where. Rare in SE U.S., and once found briefly on Bermuda. The spring form **vernalis** is small, with a darker underside. An orange uph central spot is domi-nant in inheritance to a yellow spot in males, and dominant to a pale-orange spot in females (the spot is never yellow in females; C. Remington).

Habitat open areas at all altitudes and north to the Arctic. Ranges south to Guatemala. Hostplants mostly herb Leguminosae: *Astragalus miser, adsurgens, decumbens, crassicarpus* or *plattensis, Baptisia tinctoria, Caragana, Cytisus, Hedysarum boreale, Lathyrus leucanthus, Lotus, Lupinus perennis, Medicago sativa, hispida, Me-lilotus alba, Pisum sativum, Robinia pseudoacacia* (a tree), *Thermopsis divaricarpa, Trifolium repens, pratense, agrarium, hybridum, longipes, Vicia cracca, americana*. In the east it may prefer *Trifolium* to *Medicago*, but in Colo., Nev., and NE Calif., *C. philodice* and *C. eurytheme* are common in *Medicago* (alfalfa) fields, and *philodice* is now extending its range westward through Ariz. into SE Calif. in alfalfa fields.

Color Plates 10, 12
Figs. 34 (ultraviolet), 48,
55 (veins)

Eggs cream, turning crimson in a day or two, laid singly on host starting 2-4 days after emergence. Larvae (Fig. 48) eat leaves; no nests. Larva like that of *C. eurytheme*, green, sometimes pale yellow on the side, with raised points, a fainter green middorsal line, and a white lateral band (with a rosy line through it and black dashes beneath it); head green. Rare blue-green or yellow-green larvae are recessive to normal green larvae, and yellow-green is recessive to blue-green (Remington). Pupa like that of *C. eurytheme*. Third-stage (sometimes fourth-) larvae hibernate.

Generally several to many flights, spring-fall; one flight, mainly June-M July, for ssp. *vitabunda*, and probably one flight, June-July, in Nfld. Colo. adults move farther than a kilometer sometimes, averaging about 250 m for the 70 percent of the population that relocates; females moved more than males in the second flight, but less in the first (W. Watt and associates). Pest populations in alfalfa fields, however, averaged less than 100-m movement and had more overlapping flights than native populations, though some dispersal does occur. Colo. adults live an average of only 2-3 days in nature, although the maximum life span is several weeks. Adults sip flower nectar and mud. Mate-locating behavior is like that of *C. eurytheme*, as is mating, although females do not need an ultraviolet-reflecting male. The male buffets the female with his wings, transferring his pheromone from a patch on the uph base (at the base of cell $Sc+R_1$), which causes the female to extend the abdomen out from the hindwings such that the male can join. A. Clark suggested that the male forewings are drawn forward while fluttering, perhaps to uncover the uph patch, and may strike the female at that time. The female must be contacted by his wings during the pheromone transfer before she will lower her abdomen. The pheromone consists of three esters (n-hexyl myristate, n-hexyl palmitate, and n-hexyl stearate), in addition to several straight-chain hydrocarbons also found in females and in *C. eurytheme*. A female that is ready to mate will approach a male if a male has not found her first (R. Rutowski).

39. Colias interior   Pink-Edged Sulfur

Identified by the very conspicuous pink fringes, by the uniformly yellow unh (with very few dark scales), and by the red ring around the white unh central spot (which rarely has a satellite spot); the uph shows a weak orangish central spot. Females are almost always yellow (white form **alba** females rare), with somewhat narrower dark borders. *C. interior*, *C. palaeno* (40), and *C. pelidne* (41) are closely related and perhaps hybridize occasionally. The range to the northwest is odd, and shows evidence of replacement by *palaeno*. Males do not reflect ultraviolet.

Habitat Canadian to Hudsonian Zone shrubby forest openings. Hostplants low Ericaceae: *Vaccinium myrtilloides, cespitosum, angustifolium, ?crassifolium*[t], probably *vacillans*. Lab larvae eat *Vaccinium* but refuse willow and legumes.

Eggs white, tinged with greenish-yellow, soon turning reddish-orange. Larvae eat leaves. Larva dark yellowish-green, with black points, a narrow darker dorsal stripe margined with bluish-green, and the usual white lateral stripe with a red line through it; head dark yellow-green, with dark points. Pupa green, with yellowish-white dorsal mottling, a yellowish-white head projection, a darker-green middorsal line, and a paler lateral band on the abdomen (with a

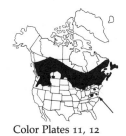

Color Plates 11, 12

reddish-brown stripe beneath it). Third-stage (rarely first- or second-) larvae hibernate.

One flight, mostly M June-M Aug. (M June-M July near Ottawa, M July-M Aug. in Nfld. and Sask.). Adults sip flower nectar and mud. Males patrol slowly to seek females.

40. Colias palaeno   Arctic Sulfur

Color Plate 11

Males are pale yellow with the uph central spot pale yellow (rarely missing) rather than orange. The single white unh central spot lacks a rim, and the black upf central spot is usually missing. The black borders are usually wide, and the unh is darker greenish than on *C. interior* (39). Females are often white (form **alba**). Males do not reflect ultraviolet. Ssp. **baffinensis** (Baffin I.) is darker on the unh; ssp. **chippewa** occurs elsewhere in N. Amer.; ssp. *palaeno* and other ssp. are in the Alps, Scandinavia, and Asia. Habitat upper Canadian to Arctic Zone taiga openings and tundra, often in boggy areas. Overlaps the range of *C. interior* from NE B.C. to N Ont., and extends south to C Alta. and N Man. Hostplants Ericaceae: *Vaccinium uliginosum* and perhaps *cespitosum*. Third-stage larvae hibernate. One flight, L June-E Aug.

41. Colias pelidne   Blueberry Sulfur

Color Plate 11

Males are yellow. The uph central spot is usually missing on males (not orange or pale), often slightly orange on females. The black upf spot is small or absent, as in *C. interior* (39). The unh has greenish suffusion, as in *C. palaeno* (40), but the white unh spot has a definite red rim, and rarely a satellite spot. Differs from *interior* in lacking the orange uph central spot and in having a darker unh and base of uph. The unh is darker than that of *C. alexandra* (35), and lacks the brown submarginal dots of *C. philodice* (38). Females are almost always white (form **alba**), except in Wyo., where almost half the females are yellow. *C. pelidne* flies with *palaeno* on Baffin I., and in N Lab., N Ont., and N Que., and with *interior* in the Rockies without interbreeding; also from Nfld. to Natashquan, Que. Ssp. **pelidne** (arctic) lacks the dark unf flush of ssp. **minisni** (Alta.-Wyo.), and more closely resembles *interior*. Males do not reflect ultraviolet. Habitat upper Canadian to Arctic/Alpine Zone forest clearings and tundra. Hostplants low Ericaceae: *Vaccinium, Gaultheria humifusa*. *Salix* (Salicaceae) seems erroneous. One flight, July-E Aug. in Nfld., M July-Aug. in the Rockies and Lab. To seek females, males patrol all day about 0.3 m above the ground near *Vaccinium* and willow, mostly in valley bottoms or on lower slopes.

42. Colias scudderi   Willow Sulfur

Color Plate 11

The fringes are pinkish like those of *C. interior* (39), but the unh is greener. The white unh spot has a red rim and often a satellite spot, but there are no dark submarginal dots like those of *C. philodice* (38). The unf lacks the dark suffusion of *C. pelidne* (41) from the Rockies. Yellow *C. alexandra* (35) and *C. palaeno* (40) differ in their unh spot. Females are often white (form **alba**), esp. in N Man. and C Colo., where they predominate; females usually lack the black upf border. Males do not reflect ultraviolet. Compared to the northern ssp. **gigantea**, ssp. **scudderi** (s Wyo.-N.M.-Ut.) has wider black borders, a more-green unh, and less often a satellite spot beside the unh central spot (these traits seem to form a north-south cline in the U.S.). Uph spot usually yellow, except in females.

Habitat Canadian to Arctic/Alpine Zone willow bogs. Hostplants (s, *scudderi*; g, *gigantea*) shrubby Salicaceae: *Salix reticulata*ᵍ, *lutea*ᵍ, *planifolia* var. *monica*ˢ; low Ericaceae: *Vaccinium cespitosum*ˢ. *Salix* seems to be the main host based on 11 records and field associations, but there are three valid egg-laying records on *Vaccinium* (one record of many eggs); S. Ae and W. Edwards found that Colo. lab larvae eat *Vaccinium* and *Salix babylonica*, but refuse *Trifolium repens* (a legume).

Eggs laid singly on the leaves of young hostplants (on *Salix*). Larvae eat leaves. Half-grown larvae (in the second, third, and fourth stages) hibernate.

One flight, mostly L June-July (July-Aug. in Colo.). Colo. individuals move an average of 0.8 km between captures; dispersal is greater along creeks than in isolated willow bogs (W. Watt and others). To seek females, males patrol all day near shrub willows in the bogs and along creeks.

43. **Colias behrii**   Sierra Green Sulfur

Color Plate 11

Identified by the green wings and small size, which make it less conspicuous than the brighter *Colias*. Some females are lighter green than others; thus, the two female forms are less distinct than in most *Colias* (pure-white females do not occur). Males do not reflect ultraviolet.

Habitat Hudsonian Zone meadow. Hostplants shrub Salicaceae: *Salix* (oviposition, and an attached pupa); low Ericaceae: *Vaccinium cespitosum*.

Eggs greenish-white, undoubtedly turning crimson later. Larvae probably eat leaves. Larva green, with a narrow pinkish-white middorsal line (narrowly edged with black), a white subdorsal line (pinkish in the center and edged above with black dashes), and a whitish lateral band (pinkish in the center and with a black border extending upward around the spiracles). Pupa like that of other *Colias*, yellowish-green, with a pale lateral line on the abdomen.

One flight, L July-M Aug. Males patrol about 0.5 m above the ground to seek females.

44. **Colias cesonia**   Dog Face

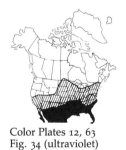

Color Plates 12, 63
Fig. 34 (ultraviolet)

Both sexes have a "dog face" with a black eye on the upf. The outer half of the dog face reflects ultraviolet (the entire dog head reflects in *C. eurydice*, 45). The male has a small red stigma on the uph base. The fall and early-spring form **rosa** has red on the unh. Rare females (form **immaculsecunda**), like *eurydice* females, lack the black dog-face marks.

Habitat mostly Subtropical to Lower Austral/Lower Sonoran Zone open areas, straying north. Ranges south to Argentina, Cuba, and Hispaniola. Hostplants herb Leguminosae: *Amorpha fruticosa*, *californica*, *canescens*, *Glycine*, *Medicago sativa*, *Dalea pogonathera*, *frutescens*, *Petalostemon alba*, *purpurea*, *Trifolium*.

Eggs yellow-green, later turning crimson, laid singly on the underside of terminal host leaves. Larvae eat leaves; no nests. Larva usually light or dark yellow-green, with many black points and a yellowish-white lateral band containing orange dashes; some larvae transversely banded with yellow to orange, or black, or both; or larva striped lengthwise with yellow and black; head yellow-green, with black points. Pupa (similar to 37 in Fig. 52) bluish-green (sometimes yellow-green), with whitish streaks, black subdorsal dots, and a lateral gray line (white on the abdomen), the abdomen yellow-green beneath; wings darker green, with yellow veins. Probably no diapause, though adults may survive mild southern winters.

Many flights all year in s Tex. and s Fla.; fewer northward, where it migrates from the south. Doubtfully overwinters north of 35°N, and seems to be a migrant into Calif., Colo., and as far north as Man. Adults sip flower nectar and mud. Males patrol all day in open areas to seek females. The male buffets the female with his wings to transfer pheromone from his uph base during courtship.

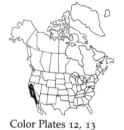

Color Plates 12, 13
Fig. 34 (ultraviolet)

45. **Colias eurydice**   California Dog Face
Males have broader upf borders and narrower hw borders than *C. cesonia* (44), and the "dog face" has a violet sheen. The dark borders are very narrow on females, which lack the dog face. The fw is more pointed than that of any other *Colias*. White females (form **alba**) are rare. *C. eurydice* and *cesonia* have been caught together at a few places; they hybridize somewhat in the San Bernardino and San Jacinto Mts., Calif., where intermediates in color and wing border result. S. Amer. ssp. of *cesonia* are more different than *eurydice* is from *cesonia* in N. Amer., so the two may be the same sp.

Habitat Upper Sonoran to Transition Zone chaparral and oak or coniferous woodland. Hostplants herb Leguminosae: usually *Amorpha californica*, occasionally *Medicago sativa* and *Dalea*.

Eggs pale green or yellow-green, later turning crimson, laid singly on the hostplant. Larvae eat leaves; no nests. Larva dull green, with tiny black points, a white lateral band (edged below with red, with a black dot above the red band on each segment, the black dots largest on the thorax), and a whitish transverse band on each segment (rare larvae have more black spots or have black transverse bands); head dull green, with tiny black points. Pupa pale green, the abdomen with a whitish lateral line.

Many flights, Feb.-Dec. in s Calif. (most common Apr.-May and July-Aug. in N and s Calif.). Adults fly swiftly and probably move many kilometers. Males patrol to seek females.

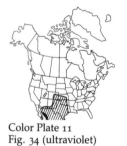

Color Plate 11
Fig. 34 (ultraviolet)

46. **Anteos clorinde**   Ghost Brimstone
Identified by the white color of both sexes, the large size, and the wing shape. The orange upf spot of males reflects ultraviolet; the female sometimes has this spot but it does not reflect.

Habitat subtropical brushy areas, straying northward. Ranges south to Argentina and the Greater Antilles. Hostplants shrub Leguminosae: *Cassia spectabilis* in Cuba and Mex., *Pithecellobium*.

Eggs pale green to pale yellow or white, probably later turning reddish, laid singly, mostly on the edge of a hostplant leaf. Larva light green, with many hairs, a yellow stripe above a whitish-green lateral stripe, and a row of dark lateral bumps, the underside light green; head yellowish-green, with small green bumps. Pupa (similar to 37 in Fig. 52) light green to yellow to cream-white, the abdomen with a red-brown middorsal line and a red-brown lateral line, the lateral one also edging the top of the wing case and continuing to the tip of the head; wing cases bulging ventrally.

Many flights, all year in Mex., recorded May-Dec. in s Tex. Flies high and fast, and rarely migrates as far north as Colo.

47. Anteos maerula   Yellow Brimstone

Both sexes resemble *A. clorinde*, but the wings are solid yellow without the orange upf spot. Males do not reflect ultraviolet.

Habitat subtropical open woods; a stray northward. Ranges south to Peru and the Greater Antilles. Hostplant tree Leguminosae: *Cassia emarginata* (Puerto Rico).

Larvae eat leaves. Larva olive-green, with black points, a subdorsal row of blotches, and a yellowish lateral band.

Many flights, all year in Mex., mainly Aug.-Dec. in s Tex. A strong migrant, straying rarely as far north as Neb. from Mex., and rarely into Fla. (Apr., July) from Cuba. Flies high and fast.

Color Plates 12, 13

48. Phoebis statira   Migrant Sulfur

Males have the ups wing bases yellow, but the outer parts mealy-white. Females resemble *P. sennae* (in lacking upf postmedian spots), but the upf border is a wavy band (not spots), and the unh central circle is usually absent, or single and small (rarely double as in *sennae*). Females are orangish (form **naranja**), yellowish, or white (form **alba**). Males have one stigma on the unf base, and another on the uph base. The upf base reflects ultraviolet moderately in the Tex. ssp. **jada**, but not in the Fla. ssp. **floridensis**. Ssp. *statira* and other ssp. range south to Argentina and the Greater and Lesser Antilles.

Habitat subtropics. Hostplants tree, shrub, and vine Leguminosae: *Calliandra* and *Dalbergia ecastophyllum* in Fla., *Cassia* and *Entada gigas* in the Antilles; supposedly Sapindaceae: *Melicocca bijuga* in the Antilles.

Eggs laid singly on hostplant leaves and seedlings. Larva orange, with a greenish tinge, a blue-black sublateral band (rust-colored posteriorly), the head orange; *or* larva (Jamaica) blue-green, with orange and yellow lateral stripes and many tiny blue dorsal dots, the head green with two black "eyes." Pupa (Jamaica) pale blue-green to gray, with a cream lateral line on the abdomen and a reddish dorsal line.

Many flights all year in s Fla.; migratory from Mex. into s Tex. (Sep.-Oct.), and flying as far north as Mass. and Neb. Adults sip flower nectar and mud.

Color Plate 12
Fig. 34 (ultraviolet)

49. Phoebis orbis   Orbed Sulfur

The male of this rare stray has an orange upf basal orb, mealy-white ups borders, and a pale-yellow uns. Both sexes have one large and one small unh circle. Females are like *P. sennae*, but the ups is orangish-yellow with a brown upf marginal band (not dots). Habitat tropical Antilles (Cuba, Hispaniola). One stray from Cuba was caught on flowers in the Fla. Keys (Apr. 1973). Hostplant shrub Leguminosae: *Caesalpinia pulcherrima* (pollinated by butterflies) in the Antilles. Larva green, tending to orange at the rear, with transverse lines, yellowish tubercles, and a lateral line of dark olive edged beneath by green. Many flights in Cuba.

Stray only
Color Plate 58

Color Plate 12
Figs. 36 (repellent
glands), 52

50. Phoebis sennae   Cloudless Sulfur

Males are yellow. Females are yellow, orangish-yellow, or whitish (form **alba**), differing from other *Phoebis* (except *P. statira*) in having the upf postmedian line faint; the upf border is a series of spots, not a line as in *statira*. The winter form **rosa** has more unh spots. Females are usually orangish-yellow in winter, but whitish (form *alba*) in the summer and fall (J. Brown).

Habitat open or brushy areas in s U.S., straying north. Ranges south to Patagonia, the Bahamas, and the Antilles. Hostplants herb and shrub Leguminosae: *Cassia bicapsularis, nictitans, marilandica, occidentalis, fasciculata*[t], *obtusifolia, corymbosa, covesii, tomentosa, cinerea, Crotalaria agatiflora,* "bean" (*Phaseolus*?).

Eggs cream, later turning reddish, laid singly on young hostplant leaves or flower buds. Larvae eat leaves; no nests. Larva pale yellowish-green or yellow, with black points, a yellowish lateral line often edged beneath with whitish, and bluish-black transverse bands (many containing a white line); larva turning oranger before pupation. Pupa (Fig. 52) green, with white specks, a yellow lateral stripe bordered ventrally with green, and a darker middorsal line; *or* pupa pink, with greenish-yellow lines on each side, the back, and wings, the head pointed, the wings greatly expanded downward.

Many flights, all year in s Tex. and s Fla., sporadic northward from spring to fall. A strong migrant every year (to as far north as Maine and Mont.); a permanent resident in Bermuda. In se U.S., adults migrate northwest in spring, southeast in Aug.-Nov. (N.C. and Conn. autumn flights were to the southwest, though on the se S.C. coast many adults migrate northeast all day long L Aug.-E Oct., a lesser number to the southwest). In Ala. one flight flew southward in every 10-minute period from 11:17 A.M. to 3:36 P.M., without change in direction. In N Fla., adults migrate to the south-southeast Sep.-E Nov., peaking about Oct. 1 (T. Walker, A. Riordan). Adults sip flower nectar and mud. Males patrol all day to seek females. In courtship, the male approaches the female and flutters over her while she lands, he hovers and touches his wings or legs to her wings, she usually opens and closes her wings briefly, and then he lands; after mating, the male usually flies away, with the female dangling beneath (R. Rutowski). Unreceptive females spread the wings and raise the abdomen.

Color Plates 12, 13
Fig. 34 (ultraviolet)

51. Phoebis agarithe   Large Orange Sulfur

Males are solid orange; females are white (form **alba**) or orange. The only *Phoebis* to have the unf postmedian line (and the upf line of females) straight, not jagged. Males reflect ultraviolet only on the upf.

Habitat subtropical brushy areas or open woods. Ranges south to Brazil and throughout the Antilles. Hostplants shrub and tree Leguminosae: in Fla. *Pithecellobium keyense*, in Tex. *P. flexicaule*, in Latin Amer. *P. dulce, Cassia, Inga vera. Cassia bicapsularis* is not used in Fla.

Eggs cream-white, later turning orange-red. Larvae eat only tender young leaves. Larva green, later becoming greenish-yellow with blackish-green specks, with a yellowish-white lateral band edged with dark green (sometimes developing a crimson line above the lateral band, and sometimes black edging beneath it); head yellowish-green. Pupa green mottled with purplish, with a purplish middorsal line, a yellowish lateral line, and three white irregular spots on each side of the abdomen.

Many flights, all year in s Tex., Mar.-Dec. in Fla.; a strong migrant, straying as far north as Wis. and Maine.

52. Phoebis argante   Apricot Sulfur

Color Plate 13
Fig. 34 (ultraviolet)

Orange like *P. agarithe*, but the unf postmedian line is broken and offset. Females of *P. argante* and *agarithe* have upf postmedian spots, unlike female *P. sennae* and *P. statira*. Females may be white (form **alba**). Males reflect ultraviolet from the uph as well as the upf.

Habitat subtropical brushy or wooded areas. Ranges south to Paraguay and the Greater Antilles. Hostplants shrub and tree Leguminosae in Latin Amer.: *Pithecellobium, Inga vera, laurina, Cassia fruticosa, Caesalpinia, Pentaclethra macroloba*; supposedly also Capparidaceae in Brazil (dubious).

Eggs laid singly on leaf buds and young leaves. Larva green or yellow-green, with cream spots, brown bumps, and a white or yellow lateral line. Pupa rosy-purplish, with a yellow-green dorsal stripe edged by white, a yellow-green lateral stripe, yellow-green lines on the wings, and yellow-green transverse lines on the abdomen; *or* pupa yellow-green, with brown spots and grayish dorsal patches, a reddish-brown lateral band on the thorax and head, brown lateral spots with white centers on the abdomen, and a light dorsal stripe, the posterior part of the wing brown or with a broad brown V, the wings like those of *P. philea* (less protruding than those of *P. sennae*).

Many flights all year in Mex.; a strong migrant, rarely as far north as Kans. Adults sip flower nectar and mud.

53. Phoebis philea   Orange-Barred Sulfur

Color Plate 13
Fig. 34 (ultraviolet)

The largest *Phoebis*. Males are yellow, the uph border orange; an orange upf bar reflects ultraviolet. Females are larger than other *Phoebis*, with prominent upf postmedian spots. Females resemble males (form **alamacho**) or are uniformly cream (form **crema**) like females of *P. sennae* and *P. argante* or rarely white (form **alba**). The winter form (form **rosa**) has more unh spots; winter females usually resemble males on the ups.

Habitat subtropical areas. Ranges south to Argentina and the Greater Antilles. Hostplants herb, shrub, and tree Leguminosae: *Cassia corymbosa, marilandica, occidentalis* (Mex. and Puerto Rico), *grandis* (Puerto Rico), *bicapsularis, fistula, Pithecellobium, Caesalpinia pulcherrima* (Puerto Rico).

Eggs laid singly on leaves and inflorescences. Larvae eat flowers in preference to leaves. Larva green, with many black points, orange areas on each segment, and a lighter lateral band, the sides of the abdomen blue-black; *or* larva yellow, with black-tipped green points, a dark-green subdorsal band, and a white band just below it, the head yellow with four black dots across the face; *or* larva yellowish-green, with a yellow lateral band containing whitish-ringed red-black spots and with a reddish-black band above the lateral band. W. Schoenherr stated that larvae become yellow on *Cassia fistula* flowers, green on foliage (the pupae differ in color also); this should be studied. Pupa (similar to 50 in Fig. 52) light grayish-green to bluish-green, with a yellowish lateral line on the abdomen and a dark-green middorsal line, the wing veins lighter green, the head projection tipped with dark brown; *or* pupa light purplish-rose marbled with white and yellow, the wing veins and lateral abdominal band yellow.

Many flights, all year in s Fla., Aug.-Dec. at least in s Tex.; a strong migrant, flying as far north as Wis. and Nova Scotia. Adults sip flower nectar and mud.

Color Plate 58

54. Phoebis intermedia   Tailed Sulfur

Both sexes have tails. The male has an orangish uph border and an orange patch on the middle of the upf. The female is whitish (form **alba**) or yellowish. The C. Amer. *P. intermedia* may be a ssp. of S. Amer. *P. rurina*. A rare migrant from Mex. into Ariz. (Douglas) and s Tex. (Sep.); these records were reported for *P. cypris* form *neocypris*, but must be for *intermedia* because *cypris* does not occur in Mex.

Color Plate 13
Figs. 52, 55 (veins)

55. Eurema nicippe   Rambling Orange

The orange wings and broad black hw borders are distinctive. Winter adults (form **rosa**) have a redder unh than summer adults. Females are very rarely yellow on the ups. Males do not reflect ultraviolet.

Habitat tropical to Lower Austral Zone open areas, straying northward. Ranges southward to Brazil, the Bahamas, and the Greater Antilles. Hostplants herb Leguminosae: *Cassia marilandica, occidentalis, nictitans, lindheimeriana, corymbosa, covesii, obtusifolia, fasciculata, armata, tomentosa, Trifolium.*

Eggs pale greenish-yellow, turning reddish later, laid singly under host leaves or sometimes on flower buds. Larvae eat leaves, the tips first. Larva green to grayish-green, with tiny black points and a yellow lateral band (or the band whitish containing orange spots, or rarely containing an orange line, the band bordered below with dark blue); head yellow-green. Pupa (Fig. 52) green to black (W. Evans raised these extremes from eggs laid by a single female), with white raised corrugations and dark-brownish spots, several white spots on the mesothorax, and a darker middorsal line, the lateral ridges cream, the head pointed, the wings expanded downward. Overwinters as an adult, probably only in the south.

Many flights all year in s Calif., s Tex., and s Fla.; migratory northward (few spring records, most common in late summer), rarely as far as Wyo. and Ont. Adults sip flower nectar and mud. Males patrol all day mainly in gulches and flats to seek females. The male buffets the female with his wings to transfer pheromone from his unf base during courtship. This unf patch is orange (becoming white) at the base of the cell CuA_2.

Color Plate 12
Fig. 34 (ultraviolet)

56. Eurema mexicana   Wolf-Face Sulfur

The fw has a "wolf face" pattern. The orange uph spot reflects ultraviolet in males of *E. mexicana* (also in *E. boisduvaliana*, 57, and *E. salome*, 58). The fall form **rosa** has a reddish unh. Habitat open areas in s U.S., straying northward. Ranges south to Colombia. Hostplants herb and tree Leguminosae: *Cassia, Acacia hirta, Robinia neomexicana*. Many flights, nearly all year in s Tex., Apr.-Nov. in N.M.; a stray northward, where it is most common in late summer. Migratory north as far as Sask., but does not overwinter there. Adults sip flower nectar and mud. Males patrol all day, more slowly than *E. nicippe*.

Color Plate 12
Fig. 34 (ultraviolet)

Color Plate 12
Fig. 34 (ultraviolet)

Color Plate 12
Fig. 34 (ultraviolet)

57. **Eurema boisduvaliana** Poodle-Face Sulfur

The male has a black "poodle face" upf border and a tooth on the black uph border, and the female has a small black uph border. The unh is redder in the winter form **rosa** than in the summer form. Habitat subtropical and desert woodland. Ranges south to Costa Rica and Cuba. Hostplants herb Leguminosae: *Cassia bicapsularis* in Tex., *occidentalis* in Mex. Many flights and a native in Mex., straying northward in the summer (common in SE Ariz. in the summer, and in s Tex. June-Nov.). Not native to the Antilles, thus probably a stray (perhaps a resident) in s Fla. (May-June). Males patrol all day in gulches and flats to seek females.

58. **Eurema salome** Monkey-Face Sulfur

Like *E. boisduvaliana* (57), but the black male fw border is shaped like a monkey face, the male uph border is linear (not toothed), and the female uph border is absent. Tropical; ranges south to Peru. Many flights all year in Mex.; a rare stray into s Tex. (Aug.-Sep.) and s Ariz. (doubtful in N.M.).

59. **Eurema daira** Barred Sulfur

Variable. Males and many females have a black bar on the rear of the upf like that of *Nathalis* (67), but the black border on the front of the uph is absent or weak. Females lacking the fw bar resemble *E. lisa* (63), but the black uph border is shaped like one-fourth of a pie. Females vary from yellow to whitish (form **alba**) throughout the range. The upf of males is always yellow, and their uph is also yellow in most of the range (ssp. **daira**), but in extreme s Fla. and s Tex. southward the uph is whitish (ssp. **palmira**; the male has a narrower upf bar in the winter form). In summer (Apr.-Oct.) the unh is white, and the black upf posterior bar is usually present in females (but often reduced to a trace). In the larger winter form **rosa**, the unh is reddish-brown, the uph borders broader, and the black upf bar usually absent in females. In spring or fall some are intermediate, and J. Haskin raised identical adults from eggs of both forms. Males reflect ultraviolet from the upf.

Habitat subtropical open or brushy areas. Ranges south to Brazil and throughout the Antilles. Hostplants herb Leguminosae: in the U.S. *Stylosanthes biflora, Cassia, Glycine, Trifolium, Medicago lupulina, Aeschynomeme viscidula*, in the Antilles *A. americana, Desmodium, Meibomia*, in Mex. *Mimosa pudica*.

Eggs white, probably turning reddish later, laid singly on the upperside of leaves or leaf buds. Larvae eat leaves. Larva light waxy-green (or bluish-green), with tiny white dots beneath short hairs, a slightly darker middorsal heart line, and a pale lateral stripe edged by blue-green; head green. Pupa pale waxy-green or greenish-yellow, with a few brown markings, sometimes a brown ventral streak, and a dark lateral line turning to dots on the abdomen; some females heavily marked with brown. Form *rosa* adults "hibernate" up to 4-5 months during the dry season in Costa Rica, whereas wet-season adults live only 1-10 days (P. Opler).

Many flights, all year in s Fla., Apr.-Oct. in c Ga. Somewhat migratory, straying rarely into s Tex. (at least Aug.-Oct.) and Neb. Adults sip flower nectar and mud. Males patrol all day in open areas to seek females. In courtship, the male hovers until the female lands, he lands and moves one forewing out from between the hindwings, and then he flaps only that forewing about 20 times in each 5-sec. bout so that its hind margin (beside the unf pheromone patch) rubs her antenna; meanwhile, she flicks her wings, then she lowers her abdomen, and they join. Unreceptive females behave like *E. lisa*, and the male may flap his forewing (R. Rutowski).

Color Plates 12, 13, 63
Fig. 34 (ultraviolet)

60. Eurema dina   Bush Sulfur

The male is orange (very rarely yellow), the female mostly yellow. Both sexes are bigger than *E. lisa* (63) and have a narrow black upf border and three black unh dots (at the base of veins M_1 and M_3 and in the middle of the cell). The female unh has a brown often triangular blotch at the apex and a brown sub-apical unf blotch. Ssp. **westwoodi** (Tex.) is a little bigger, with a less-spotted unh, than ssp. **helios** (Fla.). Ssp. *dina* occurs in the Antilles. Seasonal forms occur. Males reflect ultraviolet all over the ups. Habitat dense subtropical bush-land. Ranges south to Panama, the Bahamas, and the Greater Antilles. Host-plants shrub and tree Simaroubaceae: *Alvaradoa amorphoides* in Fla., *Picramnia pentandra* and *andicola* in Mex. Many flights in Mex., all year in s Fla. (native); a stray from Mex. into s Tex. (Nov.) and s Ariz. (Oct.).

Stray only
Color Plate 58

61. Eurema chamberlaini   Bahamas Sulfur

The ups is pale orange to orangish-yellow in males (more yellow than *E. dina*, 60), yellowish (like *dina*) in females. The uph margin is orangish in both sexes. The wingspan is only 2 cm, the size of *E. lisa* (63; wingspan 3 cm in *dina*). A black dot lies at the end of the unf cell and the unh cell (*dina* has three dots on the unh and usually lacks a dot on the unf), and the unf does not have a brown subapical blotch. The male upf may have a submarginal zone of scales of differ-ent texture inside the narrow black border. The pink unh submarginal patch in females is round as in *E. nise* (62; it is sometimes triangular in *dina*). Habitat sub-tropical Bahamas, where many flights occur all year; a rare stray into s Fla. (Dade Co., one adult recorded in Mar., perhaps a misidentified *E. dina*).

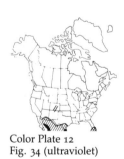

Color Plate 12
Fig. 34 (ultraviolet)

62. Eurema nise   Blacktip Sulfur

Like *E. lisa* (63), but lacks the black upf dash at the end of the cell and the black border on the uph. Seasonal forms occur.

Habitat subtropical brushy areas. Ranges south to Argentina and the Greater Antilles. Hostplants herb Leguminosae: *Mimosa pudica*, *Lysiloma latisili-qua*, in the Antilles *Desmanthus virgatus*.

Larva green, with tiny white hairs and a whitish lateral line, the heart line darker. Pupa yellowish-green, mottled with greenish-white and brownish specks, occasionally much darker.

Many flights all year in s Tex.; a native but rare at least May-Dec. in s Fla. Somewhat migratory (one female recorded in Colo.).

63. Eurema lisa   Little Sulfur

Males and most females are yellow, with a black dash at the end of the upf cell, not as in the other small *Eurema*, and the uph has a black border. Females

Color Plate 12
Figs. 34 (ultraviolet), 36
(stigma)

have a round blotch at the unh apex, and are sometimes white (form **alba**). Male *E. lisa* (and *E. nise*, 62) reflect ultraviolet all over the ups.

Habitat open areas, esp. in the s U.S. Ranges south to Costa Rica, and throughout the Antilles. Hostplants herb Leguminosae: *Cassia fasciculata, marilandica, occidentalis, nictitans, Amphicarpa, Desmanthus*, in Puerto Rico *Glycine*, in the Antilles *Mimosa pudica*.

Eggs light green, probably turning reddish later, laid singly on the upperside of host leaves, usually on a rachis between leaflets or on a midrib. Larvae eat leaves; no nests. Larva grass green, with many white points, a white or light-green lateral line, and a dark-green middorsal line; head green. Pupa green, with black dots, the head pointed, the wings only slightly expanded downward. Overwinters only in the south (possibly no diapause).

Many flights, all year in s Fla. and s Tex., spring-fall northward (M June-Sep. at Ottawa, where it is rare). Migrates northward rarely as far as Que., Man., and Wyo., mostly in M to L summer; in fall, adults fly southward. Occasionally migrates to Bermuda, but not established there. Adults sip flower nectar and mud. Males patrol all day to seek females. The male approaches the female, strikes her with his wings and legs, she may flutter, then she spreads her antennae, and when she detects the male pheromone (from the male unf base; Fig. 36), she lowers her abdomen out from between her closed wings, the male lands on her and crawls onto the side of her thorax, and mating begins (R. Rutowski). Unreceptive females flutter strongly or fly straight up in the air, rarely adopting the Pieridae rejection posture (wings spread, abdomen raised). Because only males reflect ultraviolet, males avoid individuals that reflect. They also avoid butterflies with the wing bar of *E. daira* (59) and *Nathalis iole* (67) and those with the grayish underside of *E. daira*.

64. Eurema messalina

Stray only
Color Plate 58

Adults are white, with the black upf border angled inward. Males show a pink unf bar (a stigma producing a pheromone), which disappears after death. Habitat subtropical shrubby areas; an Antillean species (Bahamas, Cuba, Jamaica), straying once to Fla. (Oct.). Hostplant herb Leguminosae: *Desmodium*. Eggs laid singly on top of leaves. Larva resembles that of *E. daira* (59). Adults fly slowly, and are reportedly not attracted to mud puddles, which males of nearly all other Pieridae visit.

65. Eurema proterpia   Tailed Orange

Color Plate 13
Fig. 34 (ultraviolet)

The only tailed orange *Eurema*. The summer form has rounded tails and black veins. The winter form **gundlachia** has longer tails, different black borders, no black veins, and reddish unh spots. Some females are white (form **alba**). Males reflect ultraviolet all over the ups. Habitat subtropical and desert open areas. Ranges south to Peru and the Greater Antilles. Hostplants herb and tree Leguminosae: *Cassia texana* and *Prosopis reptans* in Tex., *Desmodium* in the Antilles. Many flights all year in Mex.; migrates northward in spring, arriving in Ariz. about July-Oct. (sometimes common), in s Tex. Aug.-Nov., and rarely as far north as Okla. Adults sip flower nectar and mud. Males patrol all day in gulches and flats to seek females.

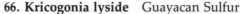

Color Plates 10-12
Fig. 34 (ultraviolet)

66. Kricogonia lyside   Guayacan Sulfur

Extremely variable. The only black markings are those at the wing apices, these often absent. Males are white, with a yellow upf basal patch that reflects ultraviolet; some (form **terissa**, s Tex.) show a black uph apical bar. T. Turner raised both forms from eggs laid by either form. Females often have the yellow upf basal patch (but it reflects less ultraviolet than the males'), but sometimes lack it (form **anorbus**); they may be pure yellow (form **unicolor**) to pure white; and their upf margin may be tipped with black (form **fantasia**). These three female traits vary independently.

Habitat subtropical open areas. Ranges south to Venezuela, the Bahamas, and the Greater Antilles. Hostplants tree and shrub Zygophyllaceae: *Porlieria angustifolia*, in the Antilles *Guaiacum officinale*.

Larva dull green, with a silvery dorsal line bordered broadly and irregularly with brown, the side yellow with a silvery lateral line edged with brown; head green. Larvae feed at night and hide under bark by day. Pupa bluish-gray, with a whitish bloom.

Many flights all year in s Tex.; perhaps a native in s Fla. (at least May-Aug.). Migratory, straying north rarely to Neb.

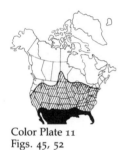

Color Plate 11
Figs. 45, 52

67. Nathalis iole   Dainty Sulfur

Easily recognized by the small size, the black bar on the rear of the upf, and the black bar on the front of the uph. The spring form **viridis** has a greenish unh, owing to short photoperiod; summer adults have a yellow unh, owing to long photoperiod (M. Douglas and J. Grula). In some females the uph is orange. Whitish adults sometimes occur in Fla. (form **pallida**).

Habitat open areas and roadsides (many hostplants are roadside weeds) mostly in s U.S. Ranges south to Colombia, the Bahamas, and the Greater Antilles. Hostplants small herb Compositae: *Dyssodia papposa, Bidens pilosa, Helenium autumnale, bigelovii*[t], *Cosmos, Palafoxia linearis, Tagetes, Thelesperma trifidum, megapotamicum*. Non-Compositae records are unusual and probably represent oviposition errors: *Erodium cicutarium* (Geraniaceae; K. Coolidge), *Stellaria media* (Caryophyllaceae; L. Berry, both oviposition and lab food), *Mollugo verticillata* (Aizoaceae; oviposition), *Galium* (Rubiaceae).

Eggs (Fig. 45) lemon-yellow or orange-yellow, laid singly on leaves (rarely sepals) of hostplant seedlings. Larvae probably eat leaves. Larva whitish-green to dark green, covered with tiny hairs, usually with a broad chocolate or dark-green or red middorsal stripe, and a narrow chocolate dorsal edging to a yellow lateral stripe (or merely a light-green to whitish lateral line); *or* larva solid dark green; prothorax with two reddish dorsal bumps; head light green to yellow; overall appearance resembling a hostplant stem. Pupa (Fig. 52) green or yellow-green, with yellow-white dots, mottled with light and dark green, lacking a projection on the head. Probably no diapause stage.

Many flights, Mar.-Dec., in the south; because adults overwinter only in the south, they do not become common northward until late summer. The tiny adults migrate, gradually spreading northward during the spring and summer. In some years, northern areas are populated by individual migrants from the south; strays are known above timberline and as far as c Man. Migrates into

Calif. mostly in wet years. The range is continuous (not broken into three parts as has been suggested), although Fla. adults do not migrate. Adults sip the nectar of low flowers, esp. yellow Compositae. Males patrol all day several centimeters above the ground in flats and low areas to seek females. The male has a scent patch at the base of uph cell $Sc+R_1$, which is orange but fades to yellow after death (the color and pheromone glands are in the wing itself, not in the scales—in fact some males hatch from pupae without scales on the patch). In courtship, which lasts 5-14 sec, a flying male approaches a flying or resting female, she lands if not resting, the male lands beside her (sometimes after hovering above her briefly), she lowers her abdomen from between the wings, and the male bends his abdomen, usually with his wings closed, to join (R. Rutowski). The female often briefly shows a rejection behavior of mated females (spreading her wings and raising the abdomen, or fluttering her wings), in which case the male, while in front of her and facing away, usually spreads his wings and moves his forewings forward to expose his scent patch, and then he tries again to mate.

Subfamily Pierinae: Whites

Usually white in color, the Pierinae, about 700 species, occur worldwide. The 21 species of North America occur as far north as the limit of trees.

Adults differ from Coliadinae in having a long humeral vein on the hindwing base and in several other traits noted in the key to adults, in Part II. Larvae (except for *Neophasia*, which eat conifers) eat plants of the Cruciferae and the related Capparidaceae, Tropaeolaceae, and Resedaceae; Bataceae and Euphorbiaceae are also eaten by some species. All of these plants (except the conifers) contain mustard oils. Some Cruciferae, such as *Erysimum*, *Thlaspi arvense*, and *Capsella bursa-pastoris*, seem to be poor hostplants (*Erysimum* contain cardenolide heart poisons). *Lesquerella* are never eaten. *Barbarea vulgaris* is unsuitable for *Pieris napi* but fine for *P. rapae* (both *B. vulgaris* and *P. rapae* have been introduced from Europe, and *P. napi* has not yet adapted). *P. rapae* larvae have been found to grow slowly on *Lepidium virginicum* and *Lunaria annua*. F. Slansky, Jr., and P. Feeny suggested that *T. arvense* and *L. virginicum* are less nourishing because organic cyanides are produced from certain chemicals when the plants are crushed by the jaws of an insect, and *Lunaria* is less suitable because the seeds (and likely other parts as well) contain alkaloids. The larvae are much like those of Coliadinae. Pupae generally hibernate, although in *Neophasia* it is the eggs that hibernate.

The whites are conspicuous enough to attract predators. However, most or all of the Cruciferae-eating whites may be poisonous to vertebrates because of the mustard oils they consume, and they seem to be involved in Müllerian mimicry (with *Parnassius*, which is also distasteful). Thus predators may learn to ignore white butterflies.

The flight of the whites is straight, fluttering, and usually fast, although *Pieris napi* and *P. rapae* fly more slowly and bob up and down more. Nonmigratory adults can fly several kilometers, and *Ascia* and *Appias* migrate. Adults usually bask with the wings spread, but *Euchloe* and perhaps others sometimes bask with the wings closed, sideways to the sun. To seek females, *Neophasia* males circle lazily about the treetops, *Pieris sisymbrii* flies low above the ridge-tops, and *P. chloridice* flies swiftly up and down gullies.

One of the more remarkable species of Pierinae is *Eucheira socialis*, a Mexican species related to *Neophasia*; its larvae live gregariously in a silk nest on their hostplant trees, and the nest is said to be strong enough and tight enough to hold water.

Color Plate 11
Fig. 34 (ultraviolet)

68. Anthocharis sara   Western Orange Tip

Identified by the rounded fw with a red apical spot and by the fine unh mottling that is not clumped into bands. Females are all yellow from the high Sierra Nevada (where males are slightly yellow), N Utah, and Wyo. northward (ssp. **stella**), mostly whitish elsewhere (ssp. **sara**). A black line edges the orange fw tip of males near the coast (a very thick black line on Santa Catalina I., Calif.), but it is usually broken into a black cell bar and black marginal dash in the Rockies and to some extent in the high Sierra; this black cell bar is thicker in s Ariz. and s N.M. The unh mottling is blacker in Ariz-N.M., more yellowish northward. The variation accords poorly with the subspecies distinction because the traits vary independently. Second-flight adults in the Calif. Coast Ranges are larger, with the unh more weakly mottled (ssp. *sara* form **pallida**). Males reflect ultraviolet from the orange spot; other *Anthocharis* do not.

Habitat Lower Sonoran Zone desert to mostly wooded areas in Upper Sonoran to Canadian or occasionally Hudsonian Zone. Hostplants herb Cruciferae: *Arabis perennans, duriuscula, glabra, lyalli, platysperma, sparsiflora* (vars. *arcuata, atrorubens*), *Athysanus pusillus, Barbarea vulgaris, verna, orthoceras, Brassica geniculata, nigra, campestris, napus, kaber, hirta*[t], *rapa*[t], *Erysimum asperum*[t], *Capsella bursa-pastoris, Dentaria californica, Descurainia pinnata, Nasturtium, Raphanus sativus, Caulanthus lasiophyllus, Sisymbrium officinale, Streptanthus breweri, glandulosus, tortuosus, Thysanocarpus curvipes.*

Eggs cream, turning orange-red in a few hours, laid singly on the underside of host leaves and on inflorescences, but mainly on stalks and petioles near the top of the plant. Young larvae may eat leaves, but older larvae eat flowers and fruits; no nests. Larva green (darker green beneath), with black points and a cream lateral stripe (edged below by a dark-green line), this stripe extending onto the green head. Pupa light brown, with brown spots, to dark green, with a brown middorsal line, a brown-above-white line above the spiracles, and a brown lateral line, the wings expanded downward to a point. *Anthocharis* and *Euchloe* pupae have a long conelike head. Pupae hibernate.

One flight, from Mar. in the Ariz. desert to June in the north; one primary flight in coastal Calif., Feb.-Apr., and a second partial uncommon flight May-June. Males patrol all day to seek females, mainly in valley bottoms. W. Evans noted that males fly up and down canyons, frequently returning to the same spot. He used dead *A. sara* adults to attract males.

69. Anthocharis cethura   Desert Orange Tip

Like *A. sara*, but the green unh mottling is more fused into bands, the orange spot is usually yellowish and smaller or it extends into the cell, the males may be yellow, the fw is more hooked at the tip, and the black fw apical mark-

Color Plate 11

ings differ. Ssp. **morrisoni** (w Nev. to Inyo Co. and s San Joaquin Valley, Calif.) has very heavy green unh mottling, and females lack orange; ssp. **pima** (Ariz. to Providence Mts., Calif., and west of Yuma) is yellow in both sexes. Elsewhere in s Calif., yellow individuals are polymorphic forms (form **caliente**) of the mostly white ssp. **cethura**. Ssp. *cethura* form **deserti** all but lacks the orange spot and resembles *Euchloe hyantis* (72), but the upf apical markings differ.

Habitat Lower to Upper Sonoran Zone lowland desert; also the more moist Santa Catalina I., Calif. Hostplants herb Cruciferae: *Caulanthus cooperi, coulteri, inflatus, Thelypodium lasiophyllum, Descurainia pinnata* (and var. *menziesii*), *Streptanthella longirostris*.

Eggs bluish-green, soon turning orange, laid singly on the host. Larvae eat blossoms and pods; no nests. Larva has a white lateral stripe (interrupted by orange spots beneath black spots, the latter sometimes joined into a black line edging the white stripe), many alternating orange-yellow and bluish-gray or green transverse bands on the top, and many tiny black bumps on the body; head green tinged with maroon, becoming black with a white lateral patch. Pupa light brown to dark gray or blackish, with a long cone on the head and with brown lateral, subdorsal, and middorsal lines on the abdomen, the wings not much expanded downward. Pupae hibernate.

One flight, Feb.-Apr. southward, May northward. Adults sip flower nectar of the hostplants and other plants. Males patrol on hilltops all day to seek females. Virgin females fly to hilltops to mate, where they approach males (O. Shields). One male was recaptured on a hilltop 14 days after being marked, showing that at least some adults are fairly sedentary.

70. Anthocharis lanceolata   California White Tip

Color Plate 11
Fig. 45

The fw is somewhat pointed, without orange, and the unh is very finely striated with brown.

Habitat Upper Sonoran to Transition Zone open woodland canyons. Hostplants herb Cruciferae: *Arabis glabra, drummondi, perennans, sparsiflora* var. *arcuata, holboelli* var. *refracta, Sisymbrium officinale, Streptanthus tortuosus*.

Eggs (Fig. 45) laid singly on the host inflorescences and leaves. Larvae prefer to eat blossoms and fruits; no nests. Larva green, with a white lateral line and black dots. Pupa dark gray-brown with the head cone curved upward, the wings expanded downward somewhat to a point. Pupae hibernate.

One flight, mainly Mar.-May (May-June at higher altitudes). Males patrol all day in valley bottoms or steep draws to seek females.

71. Anthocharis midea   Falcate Orange Tip

Color Plate 11
Fig. 48

Identified by the range, the hooked fw, and the fine yellow-and-brown unh mottling. Males have orange fw tips, but females lack orange.

Habitat mostly Lower and Upper Austral Zones in or near open woods. Hostplants herb Cruciferae: *Arabidopsis thaliana, Arabis glabra, canadensis, laevigata, lyrata, Barbarea verna, Cardamine bulbosa, parviflora* (and var. *arenicola*), *hirsuta, Sisymbrium, Dentaria laciniata, diphylla*[t], *heterophylla*[t], *Lepidium densiflorum*. Females oviposit on *Barbarea vulgaris, Capsella bursa-pastoris,* and *Draba,* but larvae refuse to eat them (larvae die on *B. vulgaris*).

Eggs (similar to 70 in Fig. 45) yellow-green, soon turning orange, laid singly on a host flower stalk usually on the rachis at the base of the flower, rarely on leaves. Females can detect eggs on the host, and never lay more than one egg per plant (A. Shapiro and H. Schönborn). Larvae (Fig. 48) eat flower buds, flowers, and mainly fruits; no nests. Larva olive-green, with black points, a broad white lateral stripe edged above with pale yellow, and an orange middorsal stripe edged broadly by blue-green; head green with dark-green blotches, white on the side. Pupa yellowish, covered with black dots, with a long cone on the head, the wings expanded slightly downward. Pupae hibernate.

One flight, mostly Apr.-May (Mar. in s Tex.). Males patrol all day on hilltops and flats in search of females.

Color Plate 11
Figs. 55, 71 (juxta)

72. Euchloe hyantis   Western Marble

Like other *Euchloe* spp. in having broad green unh bands but no orange; wing pattern is enough to identify most *Euchloe*. Very similar to *E. ausonia*, but has fewer than eight (usually zero, about five in *E. hyantis andrewsi*) white scales in the black upf bar at the end of the cell whereas *ausonia* has 20-120 (*E. creusa* 1-35; *E. olympia* 0-5). A good identifying feature is the length of the two veins (R_4 and R_5) at the fw tip (Fig. 55): very short in *hyantis* because they usually branch off of the stem vein very close to the tip (some individuals are almost like *ausonia*), but as long as the stem in the other *Euchloe* because they branch much closer to the base. The unh white is more pearly in *hyantis*, and the uncus more tapered, than in the other *Euchloe*. *E. hyantis* may be related to *E. simplonia* of Europe. The desert and pinyon-juniper ssp. **lotta** tends to have a wide black bar at the end of the fw cell; ssp. **hyantis** (mountains of N Calif. from chaparral to Canadian Zone open forest) has a narrower bar. Ssp. **andrewsi** (San Bernardino Mts., Calif., pine forest) looks like *E. ausonia* (which does not occur there), but has four to six white scales in the black upf spot (vs. zero or one in the other ssp.).

Habitat the upper Lower Sonoran Zone to Canadian Zone desert, chaparral, sagebrush, and open woodland. Hostplants herb Cruciferae: *Arabis glabra, holboellii* var. *pinetorum, Caulanthus inflatus, amplexicaulis, crassicaulis, major, Descurainia pinnata* ssp. *menziesii* (and var. *nelsoni*), *richardsonii, Isatis tinctoria, Lepidium fremontii, virginicum, Sisymbrium altissimum, Stanleya pinnata, Streptanthus breweri, glandulosus, tortuosus* (and var. *orbiculatus*), *bernardinus, polygaloides, Streptanthella longirostris, Thelypodium stenopetalum.* Ssp. *hyantis* often prefers *Streptanthus.*

Eggs resemble those of *E. ausonia*, laid singly, usually on hostplant leaves. Larvae prefer to eat flowers and fruits; no nests. Larva green, with many black points, and with a white lateral band (yellow in some w Sierra Nevada colonies) bordered above with a purplish line, the area above this line purplish-gray in Nev., yellowish-green near Los Angeles, green elsewhere; head green. Pupa yellowish to brown, with brown to black middorsal, lateral, and sublateral lines; in all *Euchloe* pupae, the head is lengthened into a cone, and the wings are expanded downward slightly to a blunt point. Pupae hibernate.

One flight, Apr.-May in most areas, M Mar.-E May southward, June in mountains. Males patrol all day on hilltops (or sometimes near hostplants) to seek females.

73. Euchloe ausonia   Dappled Marble

See *E. hyantis* for identification using wing pattern. Also distinguished by the V-shaped male juxta (Y-shaped in other *Euchloe*; Fig. 71). Females are often

Color Plates 2 (larva), 4 (pupa), 11
Figs. 36, 52, 55 (veins), 71

yellowish (form **flavidalis**). Some females reflect ultraviolet and others do not. There is minor geographic variation; **ausonides** is the American ssp., according to L. Higgins and N. Riley (ssp. *ausonia* and other ssp. occur in N Africa and Eurasia).

Habitat Transition to Hudsonian Zone open areas. The range is extending eastward through Canada. Hostplants herb Cruciferae: *Arabis drummondi, glabra, lyalli, duriuscula, hirsuta, fendleri* var. *spatifolia, sparsiflora* var. *atrorubens, Barbarea orthoceras, vulgaris, Brassica campestris, kaber, nigra, napus, geniculata, Descurainia californica, richardsonii, Isatis tinctoria, Lepidium densiflorum* var. *bourgeanum, Raphanus sativus, Sisymbrium altissimum, officinale, Thelypodium lasiophyllum*, rarely *Erysimum capitatum* (the larvae may die on *Erysimum*).

Eggs bluish-green, turning orange the first day, laid singly on host flower buds. Females seldom lay eggs on plants that already have orange eggs (A. Shapiro). Larvae eat flowers and fruit, rarely leaves; no nests. Larva dark bluish-gray, with many black points, a yellow subdorsal band, and a white lateral band edged beneath with yellow, the underside green; head greenish-gray. Pupa (Fig. 52) whitish-gray to tan, with a brown lateral line and a narrow brown dorsal line. Pupae hibernate.

One flight, mostly May-June (June-E July northward); two flights, Mar.-Apr. and L May-June, at low altitude in N Calif. Adults disperse randomly over distances of at least several kilometers, the females slightly farther than males. Adults sip the nectar of flowers, mostly yellow or whitish flowers of the larval hosts. They bask dorsally and laterally to get warm. Males patrol all day, mainly in valley bottoms, to seek females. They usually hover and then land and mate, but if a male finds a resting female, he may land and mate quickly. Unreceptive females reject males by spreading the wings and raising the abdomen, exposing glands (Fig. 36) that probably produce a pheromone to repel the male (who cannot join with her in this position), or the female flies high in the air until the male leaves.

Color Plate 11
Fig. 71 (juxta)

74. Euchloe creusa   Northern Marble

Like *E. ausonia*, with which it flies, but has more-uniform green unh mottling, fewer than 35 white scales in the black bar at the end of the upf cell (*ausonia* usually has 50-100), usually more hair on the body, a more shiny-white unh, and a blacker uph base. The female lamella is more sinuous in *E. creusa* and *E. olympia* than in other *Euchloe. E. creusa* ranges farther north than does *E. hyantis*.

Habitat Canadian to lower Arctic/Alpine Zone, mainly in taiga clearings and on talus slopes. Hostplants herb Cruciferae: *Draba lanceolata, Arabis glabra*.

Eggs laid singly on unopened host flower buds. Larvae undoubtedly eat flowers and fruits. Pupa like that of *E. ausonia*.

One flight, mostly June-M July.

Color Plate 9

75. Euchloe olympia   Rosy Marble

Easily identified by the fewer unh bands, the often rosy unh tint, and the pure-white antennae. *E. olympia* and *E. creusa* are similar structurally and replace each other east to west, although their wing pattern is very different. W. Wagner notes a smaller Mich.-Ont. dune variety.

Habitat mostly Upper Austral (Lower Austral in Tex.) to Transition Zone, usually in fairly dry clearings with few plants in E U.S., also prairie and (in

Colo.) foothill chaparral. Its range is expanding in Ont. Hostplants herb Cruciferae: *Arabis lyrata, serotina, laevigata, missouriensis, drummondii, viridis, glabra, Descurainia pinnata, Sisymbrium officinale*. Lab larvae refused *Barbarea vulgaris* (Cruciferae).

Eggs resemble those of *E. ausonia*, laid singly on unopened host flower buds. Young larvae eat flowers and fruits; older larvae, the leaves and stems also. No larval nests. Larva resembles that of *E. ausonia*, bluish-gray, with many black points, a green (yellow-centered) subdorsal band, and a white lateral band edged beneath with large yellow spots; head bluish-gray. Pupa gray-brown to tan, with a brown lateral band. Pupae hibernate.

One flight, M Apr.-M May in Va., L Apr.-E June in s Ont. and Colo. Males patrol on hilltops all day to seek females.

76. Pieris rapae   Cabbage Butterfly (Small White)

Color Plates 1 (egg), 9
Figs. 36 (androconia), 49

Identified by the yellowish or greenish-gray unmarked unh. The male has one black fw spot beyond the cell, whereas females have two; both fw and hw have black apical spots. Spring adults (form **metra**) are small, with smaller spots than on summer adults.

Habitat mostly Lower Austral/Lower Sonoran to Canadian Zone, usually in towns, but also in some natural habitats, mostly in valley bottoms. This N African and Eurasian agricultural pest was introduced into Que. about 1860 and into Calif. about 1866(?). By 1871 it occupied all of New England, by 1881 all of the eastern U.S., and it now ranges to s Mex. Introduced since then into Hawaii, Bermuda, Australia, and New Zealand, where it is permanently established, and into Iceland. Hostplants herb Cruciferae: *Arabis glabra, Armoracia lapathifolia, aquatica, Barbarea vulgaris, orthoceras, verna?, Brassica oleracea* (vars. *capitata, acephala, botrytis, gemmifera, viridis*[t]*), rapa, caulorapa, napus, juncea, hirta, nigra, napobrassica, kaber* (and var. *pinnatifida*), *geniculata, Caulanthus cooperi, Cakile edentula, Cardaria draba, Capsella bursa-pastoris* (females oviposit but larvae refuse it), *Dentaria diphylla, Descurainia sophia, Eruca sativa, Erysimum perenne, Hesperis matronalis, Lepidium latifolium, virginicum* (retards larval growth), *campestre, densiflorum, Lobularia maritima, Lunaria annua* (retards larval growth), *Matthiola incana, Nasturtium officinale, Raphanus sativus, raphanistrum, Rorippa curvisiliqua, islandica, Sisymbrium irio, altissimum, officinale* (and var. *leiocarpum*), *Streptanthus tortuosus, Thlaspi arvense* (larvae grow slowly or refuse it); Capparidaceae: *Cleome serrulata, Capparis sandwichiana*; Tropaeolaceae: *Tropaeolum majus*; Resedaceae: *Reseda odorata*. A record on Aizoaceae (*Cryophytum crystallinum*) seems dubious. All these plants except *Cryophytum* contain mustard oils; females use these oils to locate the plants, and the larvae need them to feed. Mustard oils inside *P. rapae* and *P. napi* make them distasteful to birds (N. Marsh and M. Rothschild). Larvae adjust their feeding rate to maintain a constant rate of nitrogen uptake (F. Slansky, Jr., and P. Feeny). Larvae eating plants with low nitrogen content (1.5 percent dry weight) eat faster and utilize nitrogen more efficiently (but they utilize other nutrients less efficiently) than larvae on high-nitrogen-content plants (5 percent or more); through this mechanism larval growth rates are the same on the two diets.

Eggs white or pale yellow, laid singly on host leaves (sometimes in small clusters in England). R. Jones found that fewer eggs are laid on plants in clumps than on isolated plants. She found that egg production peaks after about a week in the lab, and that females can live up to 3 weeks. In Japan, M. Yamamoto and T. Ohtani found that ovipositing peaks at 3-6 days of age in the lab, declining until few eggs are laid after several weeks (total production is about 700 lifetime eggs per female). Larvae (similar to 76 in Fig. 49) eat mostly leaves, and bore into the interior of cabbages. Larva bluish-green, with tiny black points, a black ring around the spiracles, a lateral row of yellow dashes, and a yellow middorsal line; head green. Pupa brown to mottled-gray to green (tending to match the brown or green background), shaped like that of *P. napi*, but the head cone longer, the abdomen not flaring as much laterally, the flared subdorsal ridge whitish, and the flared points brown on green pupae. All pupae are brown when mature larvae are raised in darkness (H. Okamoto and J. Kolyer). Pupae hibernate. Short photoperiod (actually, long nights) causes pupal diapause, and high temperature tends to prevent diapause (R. Barker and others).

Generally many flights, from E spring to fall; several flights, M Apr.-Oct., as far north as Ottawa and s Sask.; probably one flight, mostly June, in the far north. Migratory in Europe, but not in N. Amer. Adults can move many kilometers in individual flights (up to 12 km in F. Chew's study), and there are records from as far north as N.W. Terr. T. Shreeve marked adults in British woods; recaptured males had moved an average of 394 m, females an average of 310 m. Each female flies about 0.7 km per day, and typically ends up 0.45 km from where she started; oddly, each butterfly maintains a preferred direction throughout one day, but the direction changes unpredictably from day to day (Jones and others). Adults sip flower nectar, rarely mud. Adults seeking flowers first look for green vegetation, then certain colors (purple, blue, and yellow are preferred to white, red, and green), which they approach; they extend the proboscis before landing, then probe for nectar after landing (M. Miyakawa). N. Ohsaki found that in Japan adults live an average of about 5 days in nature. He and N. McFarland found that *P. rapae* (and *P. napi*) often roost in small groups. Males patrol all day about the hostplants to seek females. In Japan (ssp. *crucivora*) females reflect more ultraviolet than males, and Y. Obara found that males use ultraviolet to identify females. In Europe and America (ssp. **rapae**), however, females and males both absorb ultraviolet. Y. Suzuki and others studied courtship in Japan. The male lands beside a resting female, or if she is flying, he zigzags up-and-down below and in front of her until she lands, and then he lands beside her. After landing, the male flutters, he catches her closed forewings with his legs, and he mates while spreading his wings (which causes her to lean). Then he usually flies a short distance, with her dangling beneath. Unreceptive females may fly vertically, or spread the wings and raise the abdomen in the usual pierid rejection posture.

77. **Pieris napi**   Sharp-Veined White

Variable, but the unh veins are usually sharply defined by dark scales. The fw lacks a black bar, but may have black central spots. The second flight is lighter in many southern populations and in s Ont. and s Que. (form **napaeae**). Some of these summer individuals (frequent in w Colo., for example) are nearly spotless and can be confused with *P. rapae*, but *rapae* nearly always has its characteristic fw pattern, the *napi* male androconial scales are much broader (those of *rapae*

Color Plates 2 (larva), 9
Fig. 55 (veins)

have a narrow neck), the male juxta of *napi* is narrower, and the plate on female bursa is triangular and tailed in *napi* (rounded in *rapae*). Diapausing pupae produce the dark spring form; non-diapausing pupae produce the dark form only when chilled (A. Shapiro). In ssp. **hulda** (Alaska and the N.W. Terr.) the unh veins are dark and the female ups is darker than in other ssp. Calif. lowland populations often have a black fw central spot and dark unh veins (ssp. **venosa**). Ssp. **oleracea** occurs elsewhere; individuals from N N.M. to Mont. and the Great Basin are often lighter. Ssp. *napi* and other ssp. occur in N Africa and Eurasia. Ssp. *hulda* is very similar to *napi bryoniae* of Europe (which was studied by B. Petersen, Z. Lorkovic, and S. Bowden) and has the same forms (and should perhaps have the same name). Ssp. *bryoniae* prefers cooler temperatures than ssp. *napi* for mating and oviposition, occurs at higher altitude, and has fewer flights. *P. n. bryoniae* and *hulda* females may show brownish veins on the upf and uph (form **bryoniae**), owing to a dominant gene B, or a brownish-yellow dorsal ground color (form **flava**), owing to a partially dominant gene Y. Some *bryoniae* and *hulda* have a greenish-yellow unh (form **subflava**), owing to a recessive gene w (the dominant gene W produces form **subtalba** with a white unh in males, a light-yellow unh in females). Some females from Ore., Marin Co. (Calif.), and Europe have a pale-yellow ups (form **sulphurea**), owing to a recessive gene at the same chromosome site as w and W. Ssp. *napi* and *bryoniae* hybridize extensively in the southern Alps, but not in the northern Alps. Males of the two ssp. are not attracted to the upperside of *bryoniae* females as much as they are to *napi* females, but the underside is attractive. In Scandinavia a ssp. like *bryoniae* intergrades with *napi* completely. After studying the genetics of 20 different adult body enzymes of *napi* and *bryoniae* in Europe, H. Geiger found very little difference between them (different samples of ssp. *napi* sometimes had greater differences). This genetic information undoubtedly applies to N. Amer. populations also, esp. to ssp. *hulda*. Ssp. *hulda* produces its dark form even in the lab, but never form *napaeae*, and apparently lacks the genes to do so (A. Shapiro). The distinct narrow unh vein borders of *napi oleracea* and *n. venosa* (form **acuta**) are dominant to the broad vein borders of *P. virginiensis* and European *napi* (and probably ssp. *hulda*). The black upf median spots of European *napi* and ssp. *venosa* (and some w Colo. individuals) are dominant to the lack of spots (form **restricta**) in ssp. *oleracea*. Forms *acuta* and *restricta* are due to genes on the same chromosome. Some females, esp. in the Rockies and in form *flava*, reflect ultraviolet, owing to the structure of the wing scales, but wing pigments in males absorb ultraviolet. The number of chromosomes varies in populations at some European sites (Z. Lorkovic).

Habitat Transition to Hudsonian Zone shaded streamsides (barely onto arctic tundra). *P. napi* is the only butterfly known from the Pribilof Is., Alaska. F. Chew found that *napi* declined in range in the NE U.S. because of forest cutting (a major host, *Dentaria diphylla*, grows only in forests) and the invasion of *Barbarea vulgaris* (which does not support larval growth), rather than from competition with *P. rapae*. Hostplants herb Cruciferae: *Arabis drummondi, glabra, Armoracia lapathifolia, Barbarea verna, orthoceras, Brassica oleracea* (vars. *gemmifera, capitata*), *rapa, hirta*[t], *nigra*[t], *Cardamine cordifolia, pratensis* var. *palustro, Dentaria diphylla, californica, Descurainia richardsonii, sophioides, Draba aurea, Lepidium virginicum* var. *pubescens, Nasturtium officinale, Raphanus sativus, raphanistrum, Rorippa islandica, Sisymbrium officinale, Thlaspi montanum*; females oviposit on *Barba-*

rea vulgaris and *Thlaspi arvense*, but larvae refuse to eat them or die if they do. Native Colo. *D. richardsonii* and introduced *T. arvense* have similar mustard oils, but *D. richardsonii* is unaccountably preferred by the larvae, whereas larvae die on *T. arvense* (Chew). Females and larvae both refused *Erysimum asperum*, which contains cardenolides (heart poisons) and sulfur-bearing mustard oils.

Eggs white or pale yellow, tinged with green, laid singly, mostly on leaves or stems of the host. M. Yamamoto and T. Ohtani found that Japanese females oviposit rather continuously (without a peak) from 4-5 days to several weeks of age (producing only about 300 lifetime eggs per female). Larvae bore into leaves, like larvae of *P. rapae*; no nests. Larva green, with black points, an unmarked green middorsal stripe, and a greenish-yellow or whitish lateral stripe. Pupa (similar to 78 in Fig. 52) light bluish-gray, tan, or green, dotted with black, with light or yellowish dorsal and lateral stripes, darker above the lateral ridge on the abdomen, the thorax expanded upward to a point, the abdomen with a dorsolateral ridge above the end of the wing, the head with a short cone. Pupae hibernate.

One flight, mostly June, from Nfld. to Alaska and in the Rockies south to N N.M. (June-July in the Arctic, M June-E Aug. in Nfld. and Lab.); two or three flights, spring-summer, elsewhere (two flights, M May-M Sep., at Ottawa, for instance). In c coastal Calif. a Feb.-Apr. flight is followed by a second full or partial May-June flight. *P. napi* seems more local than other *Pieris*, although three mass movements have been observed in Europe. Chew found four individuals that moved more than 2 km (maximum 5 km). In English woods males moved an average of 352 m, the females 349 m (T. Shreeve). Males patrol all day to seek females, mainly along shaded streams. Y. Suzuki studied courtship in Japan. A male lands beside a resting female; or, if she is flying, he zigzags up-and-down from just below her to in front of her until she lands, and then he lands beside her. She usually opens her wings quickly, and is often unreceptive for a time, but then she closes them, he flutters his wings, he catches her closed forewings with his legs, and he mates while opening his wings (which causes her to lean somewhat). Usually the male then flies briefly (with her dangling beneath). Unreceptive females spread their wings and raise the abdomen in the usual pierid rejection posture. G. Bergstrom and L. Lundgren found that the male pheromones of *napi* and *rapae* differ, and are different from those of other *Pieris*.

78. Pieris virginiensis   Diffuse-Veined White

This dingy species differs from *P. napi* in lacking the yellow unh tint and in having the unh veins more diffusely outlined, not sharp. Southern populations are lighter. The unh is whitish because the W gene (the same as in *P. napi* form *subtalba*) is fixed (S. Bowden). The usual poor success of lab hybrids proves that *virginiensis* is a distinct species from *napi*, and they fly together in various sites in six states and provinces. *P. virginiensis* has 26 chromosomes, vs. 25 in *napi napi* and *napi bryoniae*. However, several cross-species mating pairs have been found in nature, some lab crosses produce fertile offspring, and W. Hovanitz noted some intergradation between them. Bowden concluded that *virginiensis* evolved recently from eastern *napi oleracea* for several reasons: its pupa is very different in shape from pupae of the *napi* and *bryoniae* from Ore.-Wash. and Europe, but less different from the ssp. *oleracea* pupa; *virginiensis* and *oleracea* have shorter

Color Plate 9
Fig. 52

antennae than the other American and European *napi*; *virginiensis, oleracea*, and Ore.-Wash. *napi* lack yellow rings around the larval spiracles (which European *napi* and *bryoniae* have); and the American *virginiensis* and *napi* ssp. larvae die on *Alliaria*, which all European ssp. eat. A. Shapiro found that continuous lab light produces a second generation of adults, with no gray unh veining, that is nearly indistinguishable from *napi oleracea* (this flight does not occur in nature).

Habitat Transition Zone deciduous woods, in drier areas than *P. napi*. Hostplants herb Cruciferae: *Dentaria diphylla, laciniata* (the usual hosts), *Cardamine pennsylvanica, Brassica*; many others in the lab.

Eggs laid singly on the host. Larvae probably eat leaves. Larva dark yellowish-green, with black points formed by the hairs and their bases, a yellowish-green lateral stripe, and a narrow yellowish-green middorsal stripe. Pupa (Fig. 52) tan with dark dots (with a brown lateral band on the abdominal ridge and extending along the lateral edge of the wing); *or* pupa yellowish-white or light green; shape thinner than in *P. napi*, the cone on the head longer and the abdominal ridge flaring more. Pupae hibernate.

One flight, May northward, Apr.-May southward. Adults are very local, and fly more slowly than *P. napi*. Adults sip flower nectar and mud. Males patrol slowly all day to seek females.

79. **Pieris chloridice**   Great Basin White

The unh is distinctive with its broad green vein edging, the white space beyond the cell, and the middle green patch on the costa, which juts forward away from its vein (Rs). The spring form **vernalis** has much heavier green unh mottling. The American ssp. is **beckerii**, according to L. Higgins and N. Riley; ssp. *chloridice* ranges from the Balkans and Turkey to Mongolia.

Habitat mainly arid Upper Sonoran Zone deserts and foothills. Hostplants herb and bushy Cruciferae: *Isomeris arborea, Stanleya pinnata, elata, Arabis lignifera, Brassica nigra, Sisymbrium altissimum, loeseli, Lepidium perfoliatum, virginicum, Descurainia sophia, richardsonii* var. *viscosa, Thelypodium laciniatum* var. *streptanthoides*.

Eggs lemon-yellow, in a few days turning orange, laid singly on host flower buds, leaves, stems, and pods. Larvae prefer flower buds and fruits; no nests. Larva vivid yellowish-green or greenish-white, with small black bumps, mottled with bright purple esp. dorsally, orangish-yellow or orange at the joints between segments, with a pale-green or pale-yellow middorsal line, the body pale bluish-green beneath; head pale green, with black points. Pupa brownish-green, with a pale middorsal line, the wings cream, the first two abdomen segments gray-white; shape as in *P. sisymbrii*.

Two to four flights, mostly Apr.-Sep. (Mar.-Oct. in s Nev.). Males patrol up and down gulches all day to seek females. The ultraviolet of the unh is very striking (white reflects and green absorbs ultraviolet; see Fig. 34), in contrast to other *Pieris*, and may be used by males to identify mates of their own species.

80. **Pieris protodice**   Checkered White

P. protodice and *P. callidice* are very similar, esp. in spring. The marginal fw marks are much smaller in male *protodice* than in male *callidice*, and the dark fw spots in *protodice* females are brown (black in *callidice*). The unh veins in female

Color Plate 9
Fig. 34

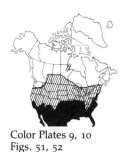

Color Plates 9, 10
Figs. 51, 52

and many male *callidice* are greenish, whereas in *protodice* they are yellowish-brown (white in summer *protodice* males). Both species have spring and high-altitude forms that are smaller with darker unh veins; short photoperiod (long nights) acting on older larvae produces the spring form **vernalis** regardless of temperature, and cold temperature causes pupae raised in long-day conditions to produce *vernalis* (A. Shapiro). V. Chang found that the black spot on the lower unf corner is large in summer *protodice* (about 3 mm wide; smaller, 1-3 mm, in spring), small in *callidice* (about 1.5 mm); the fw vein M_2 is usually the second vein to split off from the vein at the upper edge of the fw discal cell in *protodice*, usually the third vein in *callidice*; technically the male saccus is usually less than 0.7 mm long in *protodice*, usually greater than 0.8 mm in *callidice*; the aedeagus is smaller in *protodice*; and the hardened plate on the female bursa copulatrix is usually shorter than 0.85 mm in *protodice*, usually longer than 0.85 mm in *callidice*. Most individuals can be identified by wing pattern, but these anatomical details are useful to confirm important records. Eastern (Penn. and N.J. at least) males occasionally have black marginal spots at the end of the uph veins, which Shapiro found are due to a recessive gene.

Habitat Subtropical to Canadian Zone (straying to other zones) open areas including desert, plains, and disturbed areas. Ranges to s Mex. and Cuba. Host-plants herb Cruciferae: *Arabis glabra, drummondii, Barbarea vulgaris, Brassica geniculata, campestris, nigra, oleracea* (vars. *capitata, botrytis*), *rapa, kaber*[t], *Caulanthus, Cardaria draba, Cakile edentula*[t], *Capsella bursa-pastoris, Descurainia sophia, pinnata* (and ssp. *glabra* and *halictorum*), *Lepidium densiflorum, fremontii, latifolium, virginicum* (and var. *pubescens*), *lasiocarpum, Lobularia maritima, Malcolmia africana, Physaria, Rorippa curvisiliqua, Raphanus sativus, Selenia aurea, Sisymbrium altissimum, Thelypodium elegans, lasiophyllum, Thlaspi arvense*; Capparidaceae: *Wislizenia refralta, Cleome serrulata, lutea*; Resedaceae: *Reseda*.

Eggs pale yellow, soon turning orange, laid singly on hostplant inflorescences and leaves. Females seldom lay eggs on plants that already have orange eggs (Shapiro). Larvae prefer flower buds, flowers, and fruits, but also eat leaves; no nests. On cabbage the larva eats only the outer leaves (*P. rapae* can bore into the interior). Larva (Fig. 51) pale blue-green to bluish-gray, with black points and yellow subdorsal and lateral stripes; head yellowish, with reddish dots. Pupa (Fig. 52) light bluish-gray (sometimes with yellowish dorsal and lateral stripes), speckled with black, shaped like that of *P. rapae* but the abdomen less expanded sideways. Pupae hibernate.

Many flights, E spring-fall. Native in the south but sporadic in the north; the exact northern limits of year-round residency are poorly known. Adults travel many kilometers to populate new stands of their weedy hostplants. O. Shields found only a 15 percent recapture rate on hilltops, indicating that most adults dispersed. The life span (about a week in nature) is longer in cool weather (Shapiro). Males patrol on hilltops and near hostplants to seek females. At high density the patrolling males courted the females so often that the females dispersed from the area (Shapiro). Both *P. protodice* and *P. callidice* lack the androconial scales of other *Pieris*; they use ultraviolet reflection instead of pheromones to identify their mates. Males absorb ultraviolet, but females reflect ultraviolet somewhat, owing to different wing pigments. Males and females can distinguish the sexes by using ultraviolet reflection (R. Rutowski); the males prefer to chase slightly reflecting adults (rather than non-reflecting or strongly reflecting ones), and females prefer to chase non-reflecting adults. Males preferentially court larger and older females (whose wings reflect more ultraviolet, owing to the loss of scales). He found that females approach males when they want to mate if no male has approached them first. In courtship, the female lands (if she has been flying) when the male approaches her; the male flutters and contacts her with wings and legs for several seconds, then lands on her side and mates. This same courtship pattern occurs in *Colias* and *Eurema* also (Rutowski). Unreceptive females flutter their wings, fly vertically, adopt the pierid rejection posture (wings spread, abdomen raised), or fly away. After mating, the male courts less often, while he replenishes his reproductive glands. The females remate when their spermatophore (transferred by the male during the last mating) has been digested.

81. Pieris callidice   Peak White

Color Plate 9

See *P. protodice* for identification. In addition, *P. callidice* is more heavily marked on the unh than *protodice*, esp. the spring form **vernalis**, which also occurs at high altitude in the summer; *vernalis* is caused by short photoperiod, and many long-photoperiod pupae produce *vernalis* when subjected to more than a week of cold (less than 6°C; A. Shapiro). Ssp. **occidentalis** occurs in most of N. Amer.; ssp. **nelsoni** (Alaska) has slightly smaller spots on males; ssp. *callidice* and other ssp. occur in Eurasia. Ssp. *nelsoni* produces fewer summer-form individuals under long photoperiod than ssp. *occidentalis* (Shapiro). Crosses of European *callidice* males and Alaskan *nelsoni* females produced adults, but the eggs from two female *callidice* mated to *nelsoni* males died; more crosses may show that they are different species, though adults look nearly identical (Shapiro).

Habitat Transition to Alpine Zone (even onto tundra) natural (sometimes disturbed) open areas. Hostplants herb Cruciferae: *Arabis drummondii, glabra, holboellii* (vars. *pinetorum, retrofracta*), *breweri, platysperma, Barbarea vulgaris, Brassica nigra, Chorispora tenella, Caulanthus, Athysanus pusillus, Phoenicaulis cheiranthoides, Descurainia richardsonii* (and ssp. *viscosa*), *sophia, Draba cuneifolia, howellii, crassifolia, Lepidium campestre, virginicum* (and var. *pubescens*), *densiflorum* var. *bourgeanum, Sisymbrium altissimum, Streptanthus tortuosus, barbatus, Thlaspi alpestri, Thelypodium lasiophyllum*; perhaps rarely Capparidaceae: *Cleome*. In Europe also *Reseda* (Resedaceae), *Erysimum* (Cruciferae, undoubtedly rarely), and reportedly *Sempervivum* (Crassulaceae), which is very dubious. Females sometimes lay eggs on plants (*Thlaspi arvense*) that are fatal to the hatching larvae (F. Chew).

Eggs laid singly on the hostplant. Larvae prefer flower buds, flowers, and fruits; no nests. Larva like that of *P. protodice*, bluish-gray, with black points and yellow subdorsal and lateral stripes, or with orange spots anteriorly in a yellow subdorsal stripe; color slightly darker than that of *protodice*, esp. in ssp. *nelsoni*. Pupa usually light gray, with a few black points on the wing veins and body, the prominences red-tinted; shape as in *protodice*. Pupae hibernate.

One flight, mostly July near timberline, June-E July (plus a rare partial second flight in Aug.) in Alaska; usually two flights, about May and July, at lower altitude or latitude; three flights, Apr., June, Aug.-Sep., at one Boulder Co., Colo., upper-plains site. Males patrol on hilltops and around the hostplants all day to seek females.

Color Plate 9

82. Pieris sisymbrii   Spring White

Like *P. callidice* but smaller, with the ventral markings blackish-brown (not greenish or tan) and the fw spot at the end of the cell narrower. Some females are yellowish (form **flava**), esp. northward.

Habitat the upper Lower Sonoran to Transition Zone desert to pine forest; also the Alpine Zone of Olympic Mts. and the Canadian Zone in the N.W. Terr. (probably on dry slopes). Hostplants herb Cruciferae: *Arabis glabra, holboellii* var. *retrofracta, sparsiflora* var. *atrorubens, Caulanthus coulteri, Descurainia richardsonii, Sisymbrium, Streptanthus glandulosus, breweri* (and var. *hesperidis*), *tortuosus, polygaloides, barbatus*; I saw one oviposition on *Erysimum*, but larvae probably refuse it.

Eggs bluish-green, soon turning orange, laid singly anywhere on the hostplant. Females lay fewer eggs on plants that already have orange eggs, and *Streptanthus breweri* plants growing on serpentine have orange growths on the upper leaves that resemble eggs, which trick the females into not laying (A. Shapiro). Larvae usually start eating leaves, but older larvae prefer inflorescences. Larva light yellow (with two broad wavy black transverse stripes on each segment, white between them), with a black lateral line; head black, with white dots and with an inverted white V on the face. Pupa dark brown, with many darker spots, varying to black, the head tan, the prominences very small. Pupae hibernate.

One flight, Feb.-Mar. in the southern desert, Apr.-May in Colo., M May-June in Canada. Males patrol on hilltops (sometimes in canyon bottoms in Calif.) all day to seek females.

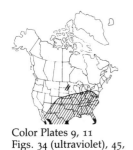

Color Plates 9, 11
Figs. 34 (ultraviolet), 45,
52

83. Ascia monuste   Southern White

The unh is distinctive. The fw lacks a round spot at the end of the cell, except in some blackish females. Females darker than males. The Fla. ssp. **phileta** lacks the tan unh veins of the Tex.-S. Amer. ssp. **monuste**, and has some very dark females. Long photoperiod produces dark-gray females (form **nigra**) that fly M Apr.-July, whereas short photoperiod produces light ones (R. Pease, Jr.). Both forms migrate. Just why form *nigra* occurs is unknown; the white form presumably benefits from Müllerian mimicry with other white butterflies that store mustard oils in the body. Females are less palatable to birds than males, and both sexes are less palatable than other butterflies (H. Pough and L. Brower).

Habitat open subtropical areas, esp. near the coast in SE U.S., straying northward. Ranges to Argentina and throughout the Antilles. Hostplants herb Bataceae: *Batis maritima* (the main host in Fla.); Cruciferae: *Armoracia lapathifolia, Brassica oleracea* (vars. *capitata, botrytis, acephala*), *rapa, Capsella, Cakile maritima, edentula, Lepidium virginicum* (a favorite in Fla.), *Nasturtium, Raphanus sativus*; Tropaeolaceae: *Tropaeolum*; Capparidaceae: *Cleome spinosa, rufidosperma, Pedicellaria pentaphylla, Polanisia*, and in Puerto Rico and Mex. three spp. of *Capparis*. In Puerto Rico *Allium cepa* (Liliaceae) was eaten when the Cruciferae were gone.

Eggs (Fig. 45) pale yellow, often laid in shade. Eggs laid singly (or a few together) on the two favorite Fla. hosts, but in clusters of up to 50 on *Tropaeolum* and *Cleome* (E. Nielsen). In Mex. C. Jordan found that eggs are laid in clusters of 1-38 (average 16) under young expanded leaves (up to 840-1,000 lifetime eggs per female). Eggs can withstand salt water. Larvae apparently eat leaves; no nests. Young larvae are gregarious if the eggs were clustered. Gregarious larvae grow faster, because together they are better able to attack the edge of tough leaves, whereas single larvae eat the tough underside (Jordan). Larva (Mex.) mottled gray, with tiny and larger black spots on the gray areas and with orange bands (a narrow middorsal, a wide subdorsal, a narrow lateral); prolegs yellow; collar orange; head straw, with black spots and with an orange triangle on the face. The orange body bands yellow in Brazil, yellow laterally and yellow or greenish dorsally in Fla.; the gray areas sometimes brownish-green in Fla. Pupa (Fla.; Fig. 52) green, gray, white, or black, depending on background, or (Mex.) white, with olive-black on the head and the top of the thorax, many black dots, and orange-yellow middorsal and lateral bands on the abdomen, the wings with broad dark dorsal margins; a spine on each side. No diapause; in cold winters the population survives only in s Tex. and Miami southward.

Many flights, all year in s Fla. and s Tex., Mar.-Sep. in Ga. Nielsen found that adults can be nonmigratory or migratory. Nonmigratory individuals slowly disperse over an area of a few square kilometers, and movement decreases with age. Initiation of migration is mainly a response to crowding, though the continuation of migration north to Colo., Iowa, and Va. occurs at very low density. Females mate before migrating, and rarely feed during migration. Migration occurs mainly on the day after emergence, and before egg-laying starts at about 1.5 days of age (at 2 days in highly crowded conditions). Adults migrate only above 23°-26°C (73°-79°F). Migrations usually start at 9-10 A.M., and the direction of flight seems determined by the course the first adults travel from the roosting site to morning flower-feeding sites. Small flights last 2 hours, but large flights from very crowded populations can last 10 hours one day and several hours the next (in the same direction on the second day). (But several groups from the same colony often migrate in opposite directions.) Adults apparently navigate by using landmarks and polarized light from patches of blue sky. Each flight travels in a narrow somewhat linear stream about 1-3 m above ground at 10-15 km per hour, following the beach or a road. Flights typically travel 30-60 km, but marked groups flew up to 160 km. In Fla. K. Hodges observed mostly northward flights in summer, mostly southward flights in winter until May or June. K. Hayward observed similar migrations in Argentina. Adults sip flower nectar; females visit flowers earlier in the day than do males. Males live about 5 days in nature on the average; females, about 8-10 (up to 16 in the lab). Males patrol near the hostplants to seek females. Females adopt the same two rejection behaviors as *Euchloe ausonia* (73) to discourage courting males.

84. Ascia josephina   Giant White

Like *A. monuste* but larger, and it has a round spot at the end of the fw cell (rarely absent in females).

Habitat subtropical open woodland. Ranges to C. Amer. and the Greater Antilles. Hostplants tree Capparidaceae: *Capparis frondosa* (Mex.), *ferruginea* (Jamaica), *Forchammeria hintonii* (Mex.).

Eggs laid singly on mature leaves, up to 300 lifetime eggs per female. Young larvae have large heads, enabling them to feed on older leaves (C. Jordan). Larva green, with yellowish and bluish mottling, a yellowish middorsal line, many thick short black hairs on the top half of the body, and a red lateral line just above many long sublateral hairs; last abdomen segment white; head green, with short

Color Plate 11
Fig. 52

black spikes on the top half and longer white hairs on the lower part. Pupa (Fig. 52) bluish-white, with small black subdorsal dots and some fainter dark dorsal dots, two black spines extending laterally from abdomen segments 2 and 3 just above the wings, and a single very long unicorn horn on the head.

Many flights all year in Mex.; at least a temporary resident in s Tex. (Sep.-Dec., often common), migrating rarely as far north as Kans. Adults often fly long distances.

85. Appias drusilla   Tropical White

Adults are unspotted, with pearly fw bases and a distinctive fw shape. Males are white. Females slightly yellowish-white with a narrow dark upf border (this near-white form seems to be a dry-season form in the Antilles), or yellow on the uph with a broader upf border (form **amarilla**); both forms with a yellow unf base.

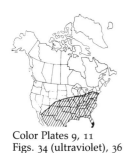

Habitat subtropical woods (in hardwood groves in s Fla.). Ranges to s Brazil and throughout the Antilles. Hostplants tree Capparidaceae: *Capparis* in Brazil, *C. lateriflora* in Fla., *C. frondosa* and *Forchammeria hintonii* in Mex.; Euphorbiaceae: *Drypetes lateriflora* in Fla.

Eggs white, later turning yellow, laid in groups of two or three on young hostplant leaves (laid singly in Mex. on young expanded leaves; up to 1,000 lifetime eggs per female). Larvae eat leaves, mostly under overcast or at night, and are often cannibalistic. They normally rest on petioles, and when disturbed they rear up and may exude an acrid green substance (C. Jordan). Larva green, with short bluish-black spines and minute yellow dots, a lateral line (yellowish in front and whiter toward the rear), and two short tails; underside pale green with whitish hairs; head yellowish-green, with bluish-green points. Pupa pale grayish-green or yellowish-green (sometimes ashy-brown dorsally), with small reddish spots, a white (black on the head) middorsal line (edged by white spots on the abdomen), and sometimes a yellow lateral line, the wings slightly pinkish, and above each wing a dorsolateral spine is red-brown margined with white.

Many flights all year in s Fla.; a stray elsewhere. Adults often fly long distances, migrating rarely as far as N.Y. and Neb. Males patrol erratically to seek females.

86. Neophasia menapia   Pine White

Easily identified by pattern and the mostly white fw cell. Ssp. **melanica** (Outer Coast Range in Mendocino and Sonoma Cos., Calif.) has larger black fw patches; ssp. **menapia** occurs elsewhere.

Habitat Upper Sonoran to Canadian Zone coniferous forest. Hostplants tree Pinaceae: *Pinus ponderosa* (the favorite), *contorta* (and var. *latifolia*), *edulis*, *jeffreyi*, *monticola*, *Pseudotsuga taxifolia*, *Tsuga heterophylla*, *Abies balsamea*, *grandis*, *Picea sitchensis*. Rarely a forest pest in the northwest.

Eggs (Fig. 45) bluish-green with a whitish crown, laid in one row of 3-22, the eggs angled and glued together, on a leaf near the top of the host tree. Young larvae feed gregariously, in clusters circling the needle, perhaps to stop the resin flow; older larvae feed alone. Larvae prefer older needles; no nests. Larva green, with a purplish tinge, a white lateral band, a white subdorsal band, and two short tails on the rear, the heart faintly purplish; head green. Larvae pupate on bark or twigs, or lower themselves by a silk thread to ground vegetation. Pupa yellowish-green (male) or dark-brown (female) with yellowish-white bands (one on wing, one lateral band also running along top of wing, one subdorsal band, one middorsal). R. Stretch found that pupae on green leaves are green, and most on bark are blackish-brown, but W. Cole states that these colors are due to the pupa's sex. Eggs hibernate. S. Kohler found 12 spp. of predators and 12 spp. of parasitoids eating the early stages.

One flight, mainly L July-E Sep. (July for ssp. *melanica*). Adults sip flower nectar. Males patrol lazily around the host trees all day to seek females.

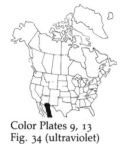

Color Plates 9, 13
Fig. 34 (ultraviolet)

87. Neophasia terlootii   Mexican Pine White

Like *N. menapia*, but the fw cell is all black, and females are orange. Habitat mostly Transition Zone coniferous forest of desert mountains. Ranges to w Mex. Hostplant tree Pinaceae: *Pinus ponderosa*. Larva green, with white lines. Two flights, June-July (uncommon, perhaps a partial first flight) and Sep.-Nov. Males patrol about the host trees to seek females, and are attracted to orange objects (the color of the female).

Color Plate 58

88. Catasticta nimbice

Easily identified. Many adults have been recorded in the Chisos Mts. of w Tex. (Mar.-May at least). Habitat Subtropical to Upper Sonoran Zones in Mex. Hostplant mistletoe parasite (Loranthaceae) on trees in Mex.: *Phoradendron velutinum*. Many flights all year in Mex.

FAMILY NYMPHALIDAE: BRUSH-FOOTED BUTTERFLIES

The Nymphalidae, about 4,500 species, are found throughout the world. They range in size from small to large, but of the 185 species in North America, most are of medium size.

In adult appearance, the Nymphalidae are the most diverse family of butterflies. Many are extremely beautiful, others look like dead leaves, and some have eyespots or other odd markings. Larval and pupal shapes are also the most diverse (the Riodininae of the Lycaenidae are more diverse in egg shape).

Nymphalidae are called "brush-footed" because in both sexes the forelegs are very small and covered with hair, vaguely resembling a brush. In most cases, the forelegs are less than half normal size and lack claws (a few female Ithomiinae and Calinaginae on other continents do have small claws), and in males the tarsal segments are fused together; adults walk on only the hind four legs. It has been thought that the forelegs, with their important hostplant detectors, are small so as to be less susceptible to accidental loss, but J. Myers found that *Danaus* adults can detect the hostplant with the other legs also (and in Libytheidae and Lycaenidae the male forelegs are smaller than those of the females). The hind four legs of nymphalids detect sugar for feeding (in Pieridae, the first four legs detect sugar). Adults are distinct in one other way: at least three of the forewing R veins branch from one stem that arises from the discal cell, and no R veins arise from M_1 (except in *Microtia*).

Larvae vary in shape and eat many different kinds of plants. In certain details, the first-stage larvae are like some skipper larvae and others; for one thing, they lack secondary hairs except in some Argynnini, Morphinae, and Danainae. The older larvae are characterized by having prominent ornaments, such as branching spines or antlers, though these are almost absent in some groups. The pupae never have a silk girdle, but hang upside down from the cremaster (except for some cold-climate Satyrinae that pupate among debris or partly underground or in a loose silk-and-leaf cocoon, and a few tropical Nymphalinae and Apaturinae that lie flat on a leaf). Larvae generally hibernate; a dozen species hibernate as adults.

Some species are involved in mimicry; in the Danainae and Heliconiini most species serve as the models for others. The other Nymphalidae rely mostly on camouflage or deceptive coloring for protection, either resembling leaves or displaying eyespots.

The flight habits of the Nymphalidae are quite variable. Some species migrate, including the most famous migrants of all—*Danaus plexippus* (89) and *Vanessa cardui* (186). The resting positions vary. Most species bask by spreading the wings, although some Satyrinae (*Oeneis* and perhaps others) often bask sideways with the wings closed. Mate-locating habits also vary. When a mating pair is scared, the female generally flies (the male dangling beneath), but in Argynnini either sex may fly, and in Heliconiini only the male flies.

Five subfamilies—the Danainae, Satyrinae, Charaxinae, Apaturinae, and Nymphalinae—are found in North America. Four others—the Ithomiinae, Morphinae, Calinaginae, and Acraeinae—occur elsewhere in the world. The Ithomiinae, of the American tropics (except for the Papuan East Indies *Tellervo*), are medium-sized species with long wings like those of the Heliconiini, often banded with yellow and brown and mimicking *Heliconius*, and sometimes having transparent wings. Their larvae eat plants of the potato family (Solanaceae), though *Tellervo* eat plants of the Apocynaceae and perhaps Aristolochiaceae. The Ithomiinae are very closely related to the Danainae, but the antennae have scales, the males lack their hair pencils on the abdomen (they occur on the wings in some species), and they rarely migrate. Like the Danainae, they visit plants containing pyrrolizidine alkaloids to obtain chemicals that they apparently use for making courtship pheromones. One or more species of Ithomiinae may eventually stray into south Texas from Mexico, or be blown in by a hurricane, but to date none has been recorded.

The Morphinae are large butterflies that occur in the American tropics, Malaya, and the East Indies. This subfamily includes the large, brilliantly iridescent blue *Morpho* butterflies of the American tropics. They are nearly identical to the Satyrinae (the larvae are very similar), but they lack several specialized traits of the Satyrinae (swollen forewing veins, for example). As in the Satyrinae, the larvae eat monocotyledons, though some species of *Morpho* eat dicotyledons. First-stage larvae (of *Morpho* and *Opsiphanes*) have many extra hairs on the body and hundreds of forked hairs on the fuzzy head.

The Calinaginae consist of a dozen Oriental species that seem to resemble the ancestor of all Nymphalidae except the Danainae and Ithomiinae. Larvae eat *Morus* (Moraceae), and have two horns and two tails, as in Satyrinae.

The fourth subfamily not occurring in North America, Acraeinae, comprises many tropical species worldwide. This subfamily is related to the Nymphalinae, but the hindwings lack a flap next to the abdomen, the discal cell is closed by crossveins as in most butterflies, and the middle legs often have forked claws as in the Pieridae. In some species, the male deposits a sphragis on the female to prevent her from mating again, as in *Parnassius*. Larvae bear branching spines on the body like those of the Nymphalinae, and are often gregarious on stems of the hostplants, which include species in many families. Many adults are probably poisonous to vertebrates, and the American tropical species flutter slowly about, in the manner of distasteful species. The Acraeinae are a curious group, as primitive as *Parnassius* in some of their behavior.

Subfamily Danainae: Milkweed Butterflies

The Danainae, about 200 species, are widespread in the tropical regions of the world. Four species occur in the southern U.S. and one, the Monarch, migrates every year to southern Canada.

Adults are large, the antennae lack scales, and the female foreleg has only four tarsal segments. A hair pencil on the male's abdomen wafts a scent to seduce the female. Larvae eat Asclepiadaceae and Apocynaceae plants. Larvae (even the tropical *Anetia*) have pairs of fleshy filaments on top of the body (the first-stage larvae have bumps), but lack branching spines. Pupae are stout in shape.

The hostplants are poisonous to vertebrates (milkweed plants contain milky juice, often an indication that a plant is poisonous). Because the adults and larvae are frequently poisonous as well, these butterflies are mimicked by other butterflies, especially the Viceroy, *Limenitis archippus* (145), and the larvae of some *Papilio*.

Adults are strong fliers, flapping slowly but strongly, and the Monarch often soars or glides between wing flaps. The Monarch is the most strongly migratory butterfly in the world, and most of the adults in the eastern U.S. and Canada hibernate in just a few sites in central Mexico. Adults commonly rest with the wings closed, although they generally bask by spreading the wings. Adults of all species visit flowers. Males patrol to seek females. The Danainae seem to be the only butterflies to have a "postnuptial flight"; the male flies away after joining, the female dangling beneath. In other butterflies the mating pair flies only if disturbed.

The hair pencils on the abdomen of all male Danainae, and the hindwing gland of male *Danaus*, produce pheromones for mating. Male adults are attracted to certain plants (such as *Heliotropium*, *Eupatorium*, *Senecio*, and *Crotalaria*) that contain the alkaloid lycopsamine (chemically 1,2-dihydropyrrolizidine alkaloid). The males feed on the juices of these plants, and the lycopsamine is chemically converted to dihydropyrrolizine, a pheromone secreted by the wing glands. After the hair pencils are inserted into these wing glands (Fig. 38), chemical changes occur and they are ready for use in mating. A ketone called danaidone is the pheromone in most *Danaus* (see *D. gilippus*, 90), a similar aldehyde called hydroxydanaidal is the pheromone in some *Danaus* and relatives, and a third related chemical called danaidal occurs with the other two pheromones in other *Danaus*. The related Ithomiinae males produce, on the hair pencils on the hindwing upperside, a lactone pheromone also derived from lycopsamine. J. Edgar proposed that when this pheromone system evolved, the hostplants produced lycopsamine, but then the plants stopped producing lycopsamine to gain a survival advantage, to force the females to lay their eggs elsewhere, thereby sparing the plants from larval damage.

89. Danaus plexippus   Monarch

Easily identified, though the Viceroy (*Limenitis archippus*, 145) mimics it. After birds ate poisonous Monarchs they vomited, and then refused both Monarchs and Viceroys, an association that protects the edible Viceroy from attack (J. Brower). Some *Asclepias* hostplants have cardiac glycosides (heart poisons, mainly calactin, calotropin, and calotoxin) in large amounts, whereas others do not (L. Brower and M. Rothschild). L. Brower and others found that female Monarchs have more glycosides than do males, more northeastern U.S. adults are poisonous than southern U.S. and Calif. adults (90 percent in Mass., 71 percent in Mex., and 53 percent in Calif.), and the wings and abdomen store more poison than the rest of the body. A Monarch is poisonous only if its larva ate a poisonous plant. Despite this protection, birds do eat some Monarchs (B. Petersen, L. Brower, W. Calvert, and others). Both palatable and unpalatable butterflies

Color Plates 19, 64 (egg, larva, pupa, roosting adults)
Figs. 45, 48, 51, 52

are killed at Calif. overwintering sites, and millions are eaten in Mexican over-wintering sites by Black-Headed Grosbeaks that eat the whole butterfly and are immune to the poison (Monarchs are their main food) and by orioles and jays that have learned to discard the wings and eat only the thoracic muscles and abdominal contents (warblers and chickadees refuse all Monarchs). Overwinter-ing Monarchs become less poisonous with time, which increases predation upon them. L. Fink and L. Brower found that the larvae of most overwintering Mexi-can Monarchs had fed on *Asclepias syriaca* and *A. tuberosa*, and because these plants produce relatively nonpoisonous adults, they suggested that historical increases in the abundance of both plants in ᴇ N. Amer. have increased preda-tion, even in Mex. The Mexican butterflies were found to be safer in large colo-nies than in small ones; a greater percentage of small ones suffered predation because birds concentrated on the edges of each colony. In general, then, al-though birds do eat many Monarchs, many more are protected by some being poisonous, and the Viceroy is also somewhat protected by resembling them. In Hawaii, albinos (form **alba**) constitute 10-20 percent of the population.

Habitat mostly open places, esp. moist valley bottoms; breeding from the subtropics to the lower Canadian Zone. Rarely strays to w Europe, even Greece; nearly all European records are Aug.-Oct., apparently of migrants transported from the U.S. on ships. Ranges south to Argentina and the Bahamas and An-tilles; established in Bermuda, Hawaii, the Solomons, New Caledonia, New Zea-land (1840), Australia (1870), New Guinea, Ceylon, India, the Azores, and the Canary Is. Hostplants herb Asclepiadaceae: *Asclepias amplexicaulis, cordifolia, cu-rassavica, nivea, purpurascens, verticillata, speciosa, syriaca, tuberosa* (and ssp. *rolf-sii), incarnata, subverticillata, fascicularis, eriocarpa, humistrata, curtissii, californica, exaltata, subulata, erosa, asperula, physocarpus, Matelea laevis, reticulata, Sarco-stemma clausa, Calotropis procera, gigantea*; Apocynaceae: ?*Apocynum androsaemi-folium. A. curassavica* is pollinated by butterflies.

Eggs (Fig. 45) greenish-white or cream, laid singly under host leaves, stems, and inflorescences. More eggs laid on large plants, and larval survival is greater there. Larvae eat leaves and flowers; no nests. Larva (Figs. 48, 51) striped trans-versely with black, yellow, and white stripes (some larvae darker, appearing to have equally thick transverse black and yellow rings), with two long black fila-ments on the mesothorax and two short ones on abdomen segment 8; prolegs black; head with black rings. Pupa (Fig. 52) stout, green, with a black gold-edged transverse band behind abdomen segment 3 and with many gold spots esp. on the thorax. Adults hibernate by roosting in trees, but only on the Calif. coast from near San Francisco into Baja Calif., in the mountains of ᴄ Mex. (at least 16 locations in Michoacán and probably elsewhere, mostly on sw-facing wooded slopes at an average altitude of 2,800 m, or 9,300 ft), and to some extent in sw Ariz. and Fla.; some scattered adults hibernate along the Gulf Coast. Trees provide important resting sites for overwintering; treeless clearings in Mex. are subject to colder night temperatures near the ground that kill some adults (a Jan. 1981 freeze killed 2.5 million Mex. adults).

Five or more flights all year in Calif. and s Fla., but absent in winter else-where; several flights, Mar.-Nov., in N.M. and s Nev.; one or two flights, mostly May-Oct., in the northeast, Aug.-Oct. in Nfld. F. Urquhart found, by marking thousands with wing tags, that Monarchs migrate each spring from the wintering sites, from Calif. to the Pacific Northwest and Great Basin, from Mex. and Fla. to the Great Plains, E U.S., and SE Canada. One individual marked near Mexico City was recaptured in N.Y; another in Toronto (Sep.) flew to S Mex. (Jan.). Females lay eggs on the way north. In the fall, adults of subsequent generations fly back to the wintering places, feeding and growing fat along the way. Some fly through Fla. to Cuba and the Yucatán. Strong winds are known to change their course. Adults often sip flower nectar. They pollinate some milkweeds; milkweed pollen bundles are often found hanging from their legs. At the overwintering sites, thousands of adults sip moisture from creek banks. In the summer, males patrol all day near the hostplants to seek females. With many females available in the overwintering colonies, and little chance of mating with the wrong species, courtship has disappeared, and males capture females and mate with them. The male nudges the female, he flies after her, he grabs her, they fall to the ground where he touches her with his antennae, and they mate. Then the male flies away carrying the dangling female. Unreceptive females try to fly away or keep their abdomen away from the male. The Monarch lacks the ketone pheromone in his abdominal hair pencils (used by *D. gilippus* to seduce females), his hair pencils are small, he does not run them through his uph gland as *gilippus* males do, and only rarely does he expose his hair pencils before grappling with a female. Curiously, Monarch antennae respond to the *gilippus* pheromone, and Monarchs are attracted to *Heliotropium* and an *Epidendrum* orchid (sources of male pheromone), apparently a remnant behavior from the past when Monarchs produced pheromones. Hibernating Monarchs mate in late winter.

90. Danaus gilippus   Queen

Identified by the brownish color and the white postmedian spots in cells M_3, CuA_1, and CuA_2. Largely replaces the Monarch (*D. plexippus*) in SE U.S. (ssp. **berenice**) and sw U.S. (ssp. **strigosus**, paler). Ssp. *gilippus* and others range to Argentina, the Bahamas, and the Greater Antilles. Brown ssp. of the Viceroy (*Limenitis archippus*, 145) mimic the Queen rather than the Monarch in s U.S. where the Queen is more common, because the Queen is poisonous also. *D. gilippus* is perhaps a ssp. of the African *D. chrysippus*.

Habitat open woodland, fields, and desert in s U.S. Hostplants herb Asclepiadaceae: *Asclepias curassavica, amplexicaulis, albicans, erosa, fascicularis, mexicana, humistrata, nivea, asperula, subulata, tuberosa* ssp. *rolfsii, Stapelia, Sarcostemma hirtellum, clausa* (Jamaica), *cynanchoides* var. *hartwegii, Matelea hirsuta, carolinensis*[t], *Cynanchum palustre, angustifolium*, in Jamaica *Calotropis procera*; supposedly Apocynaceae: *Nerium*.

Eggs (similar to 89 in Fig. 45) pale green or white, laid singly on leaves, stems, and flower buds of the host. Larvae eat leaves, flowers, and stems; no nests. Larva (Fig. 51) bluish-white, reddish-brown beneath, with narrow to wide transverse stripes of reddish-black (each divided dorsally by a transverse yellow band or row of yellow spots), other narrow black transverse stripes, a lateral row of yellow spots, and six brownish-black dorsal filaments (sometimes with red bases); head whitish with black triangles on the face. Pupa like that of *D. plexippus*, green (rarely pale pink) with gold spots and a black transverse band edged with gold on the abdomen. Overwinters only in the south.

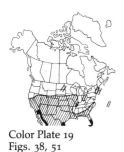

Color Plate 19
Figs. 38, 51

Many flights, all year in s Tex. and s Fla., Apr.-Nov. in s Calif. and s Nev. In N Fla. migrates north in spring, and south from Aug. or Sep. to Oct. A few large migrations are known, and temporary colonies occur as far north as Colo. A rare stray into N.D. and Bermuda. Adults sip flower nectar and mud. Males patrol all day to seek females. Females can mate up to 15 times, a record for butterflies. In courtship, the male pursues and overtakes the female, he exposes his hair pencils (Fig. 38) and brings them near her antennae, she lands, he hovers near her with hair pencils exposed, she closes her wings (or if she flutters he drops repeatedly onto her to induce her to fly, and courtship is repeated), and he lands on her side and palpates her with his antennae while they join. Then he flies away with her dangling beneath. An unreceptive female may spread her wings or try to escape. Each Queen male produces a pheromone, which he transfers to his large hair pencils by running them through his black uph wing-pocket gland (Fig. 38). L. Brower, J. Myers, T. Pliske, and others proved that this hair-pencil pheromone (the ketone danaidone, 2,3-dihydro-7-methyl-1H-pyrrolizin-1-one, identified by J. and Y. Meinwald and P. Mazzocchi), plus a hair-pencil diol that glues the pheromone onto her antennae, are required for the female to land. Myers and others found that the female may also have a pheromone. The thin-walled olfactory pegs on the female antennae detect the male pheromone and also respond to honey odor for feeding; in contrast, the larval foodplant detectors are on the tips (tarsi) of all six legs. Pliske and T. Eisner found that lab-raised males lacked the ketone danaidone and courted poorly; M. Boppre, R. Petty, D. Schneider, and J. Meinwald discovered why, working on the African *Danaus chrysippus*, which has the same courtship and pheromone as *gilippus*. The males must fly to heliotrope (Boraginaceae) or other plants that contain pyrrolizidine alkaloids and suck up these precursor compounds; danaidone is synthesized from these and stored in the wing glands; males must then draw the hair pencils through the uph glands to pick up the danaidone. This explains why Danainae and Ithomiinae (tropical butterflies with similar pheromones) are attracted to rotting plants of heliotrope, crushed and set out as bait. Adults often roost communally.

91. Danaus eresimus   Soldier

Like *D. gilippus*, but the ups is darker in the basal half, the upf lacks the white postmedian spots in cells M_3, CuA_1, and CuA_2, and the unh has an irregular brown median band. Chromosomes 30, vs. 29 in *gilippus*.

Habitat subtropical open areas. Ranges south to Brazil and the Greater Antilles. Hostplants in Latin Amer. herb Asclepiadaceae: *Sarcostemma clausa* (Fla.), *Cynanchum undulatum*, *unifarium*, *Calotropis procera*; Loganiaceae: *Spigelia anthelmia*.

Eggs bright orange. Larva black, with a subdorsal row of tan spots, with ten broad and many narrow white (yellow laterally) spotless transverse bands, and six black filaments like those of *D. gilippus*.

Many flights, Feb.-Oct., in s Fla. (fairly common at times and apparently a resident); common in s Tex. at least from Aug. to Jan. Somewhat migratory, but less so than *D. gilippus*.

Color Plate 19

92. Lycorea cleobaea ("ceres")   Large Tiger

Resembles *Heliconius isabella* (271) but has a black hw loop.
Habitat tropical forest. Ranges south to Argentina and the Greater Antilles.

Color Plate 58
Fig. 51

Hostplants in Latin Amer. herb Asclepiadaceae: *Asclepias curassavica*; Caricaceae: *Carica papaya*, *Jacaratia*; Moraceae: *Ficus mexicana*, *maxima*.

Larvae eat leaves. Larva (Fig. 51) pale green, with ten broad black transverse bands that send dashes to touch the black uns; only two black filaments (on mesothorax); head black. Pupa ellipsoidal, bright yellow with about sixty scattered black spots, cremaster black.

Many flights all year in Mex.; a rare stray from Mex. into w Tex. (Sep.), and from the Antilles into s Fla. (Jan., Apr.). The male has large hair pencils and the same ketone pheromone (danaidone) as does the Queen (*D. gilippus*, 90).

Subfamily Satyrinae: Satyrs

About 2,000 species of satyrs occur throughout the world, in every habitat. The 43 North American species are found from the subtropics to the arctic tundra.

Adults are mostly medium-sized and brown or more or less orange. Characteristic swollen veins on the forewing base contain hearing organs (*Mestra* of the Nymphalinae also have swollen forewing veins).

Larvae eat monocotyledons (mostly grasses or sedges), although a few tropical species are known to eat *Selaginella*, which are mossy fernlike plants. Because eating grass seems to make all stages edible to vertebrates, the larvae and pupae tend to be cryptically colored green or tan, and adults tend to be camouflaged in various shades of brown to yellow to orange, rather than colored brilliantly (they are not involved in mimicry). The hearing organs may allow them to detect predators better. Larvae generally have two "tails" on the rear (they are nearly absent in *Erebia* and some others) that resemble those of the Apaturinae and some Hesperiinae. The head often has two conelike horns, and the third eye is larger than the others; the body lacks spines and has only a few short hairs, which in first-stage larvae are usually clubbed. Pupae usually have a humped thorax and two head horns, except in one group (*Erebia*, *Neominois*, and *Oeneis*) that is adapted to grasslands and arctic climates. These three are also peculiar in lacking hooks on the cremaster (the last two have nearly lost the cremaster itself), and they pupate in silked-leaf nests or under rocks or partly underground; the other Satyrinae hang upside down as usual. Larvae hibernate.

Most Satyrinae "hop" peculiarly in flight, except for *Erebia*, which merely flutters evenly along. The hops seem due to slow wingbeats: each downstroke lifting them up is followed by a downdrift during the upstroke. The flight is not powerful in most species, although the arctic *Oeneis alpina* can fly as fast as the fritillaries. Adults, which never migrate, always rest with the wings closed. They usually bask with the wings spread, but *Coenonympha*, *Oeneis*, and others often bask with the wings closed sideways to the sun. Adults of many species prefer sap to flowers. Most species patrol to seek females, but some (*Neominois*, some *Oeneis*, and *Lethe*) perch. The males often have a dark streak (stigma) of scent scales on the forewing for mating (Fig. 37). If a mated pair is scared, the female flies with the male dangling beneath.

93. Lethe creola   Creole Pearly Eye

Males are easily identified by the pointed fw and dark upf sex scales (along the veins) that other *Lethe* lack. Females look like *L. portlandia* and *L. anthedon*,

Color Plate 16

but *L. creola* has five unf eyespots and its unf postmedian line is offset at vein M$_1$ (vs. four eyespots and a straight line at M$_1$ in the others).

Habitat Lower Austral to southern Upper Austral Zone damp places and streamsides in woodlands. Hostplants grasses (bamboo): *Arundinaria tecta* and undoubtedly *gigantea*.

Larva like that of *L. portlandia* but lighter in color. Larvae hibernate.

Several flights, M June-M Sep. northward, May-Sep. southward. Adults sip moisture from carrion, manure, sap, mud, and rotting fruit, but not flowers. Males perch on tree trunks (often upside down) to await females, late in the day at least, perhaps all day on cloudy days.

94. Lethe portlandia   Southern Pearly Eye

Resembles *L. anthedon* and females of *L. creola*, but the unf eyespots are not in a straight line, the antenna club is orange, the unh usually shows much white marking, and the male uncus is straight like a stork bill. Ssp. **portlandia** (E Ala. eastward) has three large fw eyespots (often even bigger in C Fla.); ssp. **missarkae** (C Ala. westward) has one or two large fw eyespots (tiny or absent in cell M$_3$, and often absent in cell M$_1$), and the female unh eyespots are clouded with yellow-orange.

Habitat mostly Lower Austral Zone damp places in woods and along streamsides. Hostplants grasses (bamboo): *Arundinaria gigantea, tecta*.

Eggs of all *Lethe* are apparently laid singly on or near the hostplant. Larvae eat leaves; no nests. Larva yellowish-green, with two red tails; head with two horns tipped with red. Pupa green. Larvae hibernate.

Many flights, mostly M Apr.-M Nov. Adults feed on carrion, manure, sap, mud, and rotting fruit, but never on flower nectar. On the basis of preliminary reports, males awaiting females seem to perch on tree trunks (often upside down), at least at dusk.

Color Plate 16
Fig. 55 (veins)

95. Lethe anthedon   Northern Pearly Eye

Like *L. portlandia* and females of *L. creola*, but the unf eyespots are nearly in a straight line, the antenna club is orange and ringed with black, the unh is brown without much white, the unh eyespots have white centers, and the uncus droops like a pelican bill (as in *creola*). The eyespot in upf cell M$_3$ is usually large. Once considered a ssp. of *portlandia*, but *anthedon* flies with *portlandia* without interbreeding. M. Angevine and P. Brussard found that some adult body enzymes are very different from those of *L. eurydice*.

Habitat Upper Austral to lower Canadian Zone woods, often in shady areas. Hostplants grasses: *Erianthus, Brachyelytrum erectum, Uniola latifolia, Schizachne purpurascens, Phalaris arundinacea, Hystrix patula, Leersia virginica*.

Eggs greenish-white. Larva (similar to 100 in Fig. 51) yellow-green, with a dark-green middorsal line, a green subdorsal line above a yellow stripe, a green lateral line above a yellow stripe, and a yellow sublateral line; tails red; head yellow-green, with two red horns and white lateral cones. Pupa pale green, sometimes blue-green, lighter ventrally, the dorsal edge of the wings and the top of the head cream-white. Third- and fourth-stage larvae hibernate.

One flight, L June-E Aug. (rarely early Sep.), northward; two flights, L May–E Sep. (peaking M June and M Aug.), southward. Adults feed on sap, dung, fungi, carrion, and mud, but not on flower nectar. Males perch (often upside down) all day on tree trunks or foliage 0.5-3 m above ground at the edge of small clearings to await females, and after investigating a passing butterfly may patrol back and forth briefly before landing.

96. Lethe eurydice   Marsh Eyed Brown

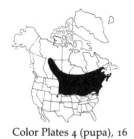

Color Plates 4 (pupa), 16

Like *L. appalachia*, but the unh postmedian line zigzags in cells CuA$_1$ and CuA$_2$. Ssp. **fumosa**, from Neb., S.D., sw Minn., Iowa, w Ill. (wingspan slightly larger in Colo.), is darker than ssp. **eurydice** elsewhere. Adults near N.Y. City show tendencies of hybridizing with *appalachia*.

Habitat northern Upper Austral to Canadian Zone open sedge marsh. Hostplants sedges (Cyperaceae): *Carex bromoides, lacustris, stricta, rostrata, trichocarpa, lupulina, Scirpus rubricosus*. Larvae do poorly on grasses, although one dry-field population near Ithaca, N.Y., ate both grasses and sedges in the lab (A. Shapiro).

Eggs greenish-white, laid singly and haphazardly on many plants. Larvae eat leaves; no nests. Larva green, with a dark-green middorsal band edged by a pale-green band, then a yellow-green stripe, a pale-green line, a dark-green band with faint yellow lines through it, and a yellow stripe above the legs, the rear forked; head green, with a white subdorsal band running to the two red horns and a red stripe from each horn extending to the eyes (with small tubercles lying all along the stripe). Pupa green, with yellowish-white lines (subdorsal, lateral, and two faint dorsal ones, the lateral one extending along the top edge of the wing case); a large point on top of the thorax and two points on the head. Third- and fourth-stage larvae turn straw-yellow and hibernate.

One flight, L June-July, plus a partial second flight of often dark individuals in E Aug. in upstate N.Y. Adults seldom feed but will consume sap and flower nectar infrequently. M. Angevine, P. Brussard, and A. Shapiro found that marked adults stayed within an open marsh. Males patrol, and occasionally perch on low leaves, apparently all day, to seek females.

97. Lethe appalachia   Woods Eyed Brown

Color Plates 14, 16

Like *L. eurydice*, but the unh postmedian line is straight in cells CuA$_1$ and CuA$_2$, males are a smokier color on the ups, the male tegumen is flatter, and adults occur in woods, not in the open.

Habitat Lower Austral to Transition Zone floodplain forest and bush swamp, often within sight of water. Hostplants sedges (Cyperaceae): *Carex lacustris, stricta* (associated with *gracillima, lanuginosa, Scirpus georgianus*), *Rhynchospora inundata*. Larvae refused grasses in the lab.

Larva like that of *L. eurydice*, green, with yellowish subdorsal and sublateral lines (with two faint whitish lines between them), and a yellowish lateral line on the forked tail; head with a yellowish stripe behind each horn (the red stripe on the head horn not extending below the horn base, and the tubercles larger than those of *eurydice* and only at the horn base). Third- and fourth-stage larvae turn straw-yellow and hibernate.

One flight, L June-July (rarely E Sep.), northward; two flights, June-July and L Aug.-E Oct., southward and in coastal Va. A. Shapiro, M. Angevine, and P. Brussard found that adults move freely through woods and are not local. They also found that the enzymes are slightly different from those of *L. eurydice*. Adults sip mud and sap. Males patrol back and forth and occasionally perch on low leaves in small sunlit forest openings to seek females.

98. Paramacera xicaque   Mexican Pine Satyr

Color Plate 13

The unh is unique. Ssp. **allyni** is in Ariz.; ssp. *xicaque* ranges south to Chiapas, Mex. Habitat Transition Zone grassy pine-forest openings. One flight, L June - M Aug. Adults sip mud. Males seem to patrol to seek females.

99. Cyllopsis pyracmon   Mexican Arroyo Satyr

Color Plate 13

Like *C. pertepida*, but the unh postmedian line is straight to the forward margin. In the Aug.-Sep. generation (form **nabokovi**), this line usually extends outward a short distance, making a ray along vein M_1 (the May-June generation lacks this ray), the unh is lighter, the bands redder, and the unf median and submarginal bands farther apart than in the earlier generation. The spring form should produce the late summer one when raised, and both forms have the same abdominal structures; L. Miller treated them as separate species, but this seems doubtful because *C. gemma* shows these seasonal forms also. Ssp. **henshawi** is in the U.S. Ssp. *pyracmon*, which occurs only south of Durango, Mex., shows the same seasonal forms. Habitat mainly Upper Sonoran Zone oak and pinyon woodland. Ranges south to Guatemala. Hostplant unknown, probably grass. Eggs pale green. Two flights, mostly May-June and Aug.-Sep.

100. Cyllopsis pertepida   Arroyo Satyr

Color Plate 13
Figs. 49, 51, 52

Like *C. pyracmon*, but the unh postmedian line curves toward the margin above the black spots, then usually disappears. Females have redder ups than males. Ssp. **dorothea** is in the U.S.; ssp. *pertepida* ranges to s Mex.

Habitat Upper Sonoran to Transition Zone, mainly pinyon-juniper and oak woodland. Hostplant unknown. The grass *Poa pratensis* is eaten in the lab.

Eggs laid singly. Larvae eat leaves; no nests. Larva (Figs. 49, 51) resembles dead grass; straw-colored, with a brown sublateral band, many faint brown lines, and two long tails; head straw, with two long horns with brown stripes like those of *C. gemma* (a stripe on each side extending vertically to the horn tips, plus a stripe on each cheek forming an inverted brown V on the front). Pupa (Fig. 52) straw-colored, with many brown longitudinal striations, and slightly paler subdorsal and lateral stripes on the abdomen; two short horns on the head. Half-grown larvae hibernate.

One flight northward, M June-July in the foothills, July-M Aug. in higher mountains; several flights, May-E Oct., southward and in s Nev. Adults almost never feed (on flower nectar rarely, and once observed at mud). They often fly through oak thickets and in the shade of trees, avoiding clearings. Males patrol all day up and down narrow, dry, shaded gulches to seek females.

101. Cyllopsis gemma   Jeweled Satyr

Color Plate 13

Like *C. pertepida* but lacks red, is smaller, and occurs farther east. The spring form **inductura** is darker on the uns, with the bands less sharp and often closer together.

Habitat subtropical to Transition Zone grassy areas near water. Ranges south to Guatemala. Hostplant unknown. Larvae eat grass in the lab.

Eggs yellow-green. Larva tan in Aug. (light yellow-green in May), with a gray middorsal line (darker in May), a broad tan band beside it (yellow in May), a reddish subdorsal line, next a broad gray band (yellow in May), below it a narrow tan stripe, and a yellow-tan lateral stripe (yellow in May) with blackish dashes beneath; two reddish tails; head tan (greenish-white in May), with a black-brown rim (red-brown in May) on the horns (the black-brown extending between the horns and onto the side of the head) and two brown vertical stripes on the face below the horns. Pupa (Aug.) yellow-tan, the wing cases more yellow, with several brown stripes; *or* pupa (May) bluish-green, with whitish and red streaks; head always forked. *C. gemma* is one of only a few butterflies known to have seasonal forms in both larvae and pupae. Fourth-stage larvae hibernate.

Many flights, L Apr.-E Oct. in Va., Feb.-Nov. southward.

102. **Megisto cymela**   Little Wood Satyr

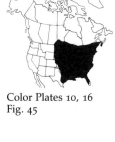

Identified by the two upf eyespots. Form **viola** (SE U.S.) is somewhat larger, with larger eyespots (at least in Fla.), thicker more sinuous brown postmedian lines on the uns, and a slightly less whitish uns. Possibly *viola* is a different species, flying with *M. cymela* from c Fla. to s S.C., west to c Tex., s La., and c Ark.; its larva is said to be paler brown, and adults have only one flight, but species-level distinction has not been proved (its abdominal structures and other wing traits do not differ, and *M. cymela* generally has only one flight).

Habitat grassy wooded places from the Gulf Coast to lower Canadian Zone; prefers shade. Hostplants grasses: *Dactylis glomerata*, *Eremochloa ophiuroides*; larvae eat many grasses in the lab.

Color Plates 10, 16
Fig. 45

Eggs (Fig. 45) pale yellowish-green, laid singly on dead or live grass, the bases of tree trunks, soil, etc. Larvae eat leaves, at night; no nests. Larva (similar to 106 in Fig. 51) pale brown or yellow-brown, often tinged with green, with a dark middorsal stripe (edged by brown patches), a brown wavy subdorsal line (above a yellow wavy subdorsal line), and a brown oblique lateral stripe on each segment, the sublateral area yellowish; two red-tipped tails; head yellow-brown, with only traces of horns. Pupa pale yellow-brown, with fine brown streaks, dark-brown spots on margins of the wing cases, two brown ventral stripes on the abdomen, brown lateral dots, and two low ridges on the abdomen. Fourth-stage larvae hibernate.

One flight, June-E July northward, L Mar.-May on the Gulf Coast (most common in May in Miss., Apr. in Fla.; records along the Gulf as late as Sep. seem to be partial extra flights). Adults feed on sap and aphid honeydew, occasionally on flower nectar. Males patrol all day, mostly in shade, to seek females. Adults have a slow bouncing flight around trees and among bushes.

103. **Megisto rubricata**   Red Satyr

Like *M. cymela*, but the upf has only one eyespot, and the fw has an orangish flush. This orange-red fw patch is the size of the hw patch in Ariz. and w N.M. (ssp. **cheneyorum**), but much larger elsewhere (ssp. **rubricata**).

Habitat Lower Austral and Upper Sonoran Zone grassland hills and open mesquite, pine, or oak woodland. Ranges south to Guatemala. Hostplant unknown. Larvae eat grass in the lab.

Color Plate 16

Eggs (similar to 102 in Fig. 45) cream, after several days mottled with pink, laid singly, scattered haphazardly. Larva light tan (some larvae darker), with a dark middorsal stripe, two light bands beside, next a very dark band containing white dots, and two light lateral bands; two short tails; head light mottled tan, with three dark diagonal bands on each side (and one dark band across the top in some individuals), the horns reduced to low nodules. Pupa yellowish (blackish-brown beyond the wing tips), with brown dots on the abdomen, dark points at the wing edges, a black line above a white stripe on the lateral margin of the wing case, a small middorsal ridge on the thorax; and two traces of head horns. Mature larvae hibernate.

Many flights, Feb.-Dec. in Tex., at least May-Aug. in N.M. Males patrol all day, mainly in semi-shaded gulches and other shady areas, to seek females.

ssp. *areolata*,
septentrionalis

Color Plate 16
Fig. 48

ssp. *mitchellii*,
unnamed

104. Neonympha areolata　Orange-Oval Satyr

Identified by a large orangish oval around the row of unh eyespots. In ssp. **areolata** (s U.S. and the eastern coastal plain north to SE Va., where it intergrades with ssp. *septentrionalis*), these eyespots are elongated, and the uns lines are orange. Ssp. **septentrionalis** (s N.J., south on the western coastal plain to w S.C., and, strangely, in extreme NW Fla. and s Fla.; intergrading with *areolata* in N.C.-Va.) is similar, but the eyespots are not as elongated; the uns lines are orange to orangish-brown, the eyespots are ringed with ochre inside a rim of dark brown, and the unf eyespots are faint or absent. In ssp. **mitchellii** (Mich., Ind., Ohio), the uns lines are orangish-brown, the unh postmedian line is straighter, the unh eyespots are oval with yellow rings but no dark-brown rim, and the unf has four (sometimes three, rarely two) eyespots. Ssp. *mitchellii* is connected to *areolata* by *septentrionalis*, which has intermediate eyespots and line color.* N N.J. populations are close to *mitchellii*, but often have fewer (two to four) unf eyespots; the unh eye-spots are usually like those of *mitchellii*, but sometimes more elongated with a dark-brown rim around the yellow ring. Ssp. **unnamed** (s-c N.C. sphagnum bogs) resembles *mitchellii* but is darker with dark-red uns lines. The ssp. form a patchwork pattern rather than a cline (three ssp. occur in s-c N.C., for instance). The ssp. prefer different habitats: sphagnum bogs for the unnamed ssp. and *mitchellii*, wet or marshy areas for ssp. *septentrionalis*, pine flats for ssp. *areolata*.

Habitat open bogs northward, and moist grassy areas, wet meadows, and pine flats southward. Hostplants probably sedges (Cyperaceae). Mich. larvae ate *Carex alopecoides* and *Scirpus atrovirens* in the lab. Ga. and Fla. larvae were raised on the grasses *Digitaria sanguinalis* (in the lab) and *Sorghastrum nutans* (in the lab?, J. Abbot), but W. Edwards's Ga. larvae refused most grasses, accepting the grass *Dactyloctenium aegyptium* somewhat, but then dying.

Eggs (similar to 102 in Fig. 45) greenish-white to cream, becoming tan before hatching, laid singly on stems, etc. Larvae (Fig. 48; similar to 106 in Fig. 51) eat leaves; no nests. Larva lime-green, with fine green and tiny white bumps, a whitish-green line along the spiracles, and three more longitudinal lines to the top (the middle line broader); tails brownish or reddish; head with two tan bumps. Ssp. *mitchellii* and *areolata* larvae very similar. Pupa light lime-green, more bluish-green on the wing veins and abdomen, minutely mottled with pale greenish on the thorax and abdomen, the wings with a dark ridge at the hind edge, the head with two bumps. Fourth-stage larvae hibernate.

*While this book was in press, *N. mitchellii* (including ssp. unnamed) was proved to be a distinct species, which differs in valva shape and flies near *N. areolata* in N.C. without hybridizing.

One flight, end of June-M July, northward and in w N.C.; two flights, L Apr.-E Sep., in se Va. and w S.C. (E June and E Aug. for N.C. unnamed); many flights southward, M Apr.-E Oct. in La., all year in Fla. Males patrol with a low and slow bobbing flight to seek females.

105. Hermeuptychia hermes   Southern Satyr

Color Plate 16

Like *Megisto cymela* (102), but lacks upf eyespots.

Habitat tropical to Transition Zone grassy places and woods. Ranges to S. Amer. Hostplants grasses: *Axonopus compressus*, *Cynodon dactylon*, *Eremochloa ophiuroides*.

Eggs pale green. Larvae eat leaves; no nests. Larva light green, with dark-green stripes and many hairy yellow points. Pupa green (the abdomen yellow-green, with two small dorsal ridges and three black lateral dots).

Many flights, all year in Fla. and Tex., L Apr.-E Oct. in Va. Adults feed on sap, rotting fruit, and mud, but not on flowers. Males patrol all day to seek females.

106. Coenonympha tullia   Ringlet

Color Plate 13
Figs. 45, 51-52

Very variable geographically, darkest (orange-brown) in the east and palest (cream) in Calif. and Alaska, but easily identified. Eyespots common on wings. Ssp. **inornata** (e U.S. and Canada, expanding southward in New England, west to ne Minn. and c Man.) is dark on the ups (orange-brown in males, ochre in females) and gray on the uns, with few eyespots. A local ssp. in sw Nfld. (**macisaaci**) is the same, but dark sooty-brown on the ups. A local *inornata* variety "heinemani" from Thousand Is. near Clayton, N.Y. has more eyespots (always one on the unf, which only one-half to two-thirds of ssp. *inornata* individuals have, and often one on the upf and unh), and the uph submarginal marks are rarely present; previously treated as a separate species because it flies in Aug.-Sep. and supposedly (an error) does not come from the June flight. F. Brown noted, however, that the early flight there looks like the later flight, and the early stages are similar. Actually, two flights occur all over se Ont. from Mt. Forest to Kitchener, Ottawa, Montreal, n N.Y., N.H., and even s Vt. in ssp. *inornata*, and W. Kiel and W. Eberlie raised the second flight from the first. Many first-flight larvae produce the second flight, but some hibernate in the fourth stage (rarely in the third). The second flight is usually uncommon or rare in Ont. (R. Layberry). Ssp. *inornata* intergrades westward in the Dakotas, Alta., and lowland Mont. (ssp. **benjamini**, lighter) to *ochracea*. Ssp. **ochracea** (mountains in Mont. to Colo.) is ochre in both sexes, with few to many eyespots. Ssp. **brenda** (mountains, Utah and n N.M., e and s Nev.) is the same, but has many unh eyespots. Ssp. **furcae** (Grand Can., Ariz.) is like *brenda* but pale ochre. Ssp. **subfusca** (White Mts., Ariz.) is like *brenda* but each unh eyespot is surrounded by a narrow yellow ring. Ssp. **ampelos**, mostly in lowlands from e Calif., nw Nev. (intergrading to *brenda* in Elko Co.), Ida., north to B.C., is like *ochracea* but usually has no eyespots, and the ground color is light ochre. Ssp. **eunomia** (Ore. west of the Cascades) is similar but dark ochre. Ssp. **mixturata** (ne Alaska-N.W. Terr.) is like *ampelos* but darker (more grayish) ochre. Ssp. **kodiak** (w and s Alaska) is the same but very dark. Ssp. **mackenziei** (near Great Slave Lake, N.W. Terr.) is ochre like *ochracea*, but the fringe is whitish like *mixturata*. Ssp. **california** (lowland Calif.-sw Ore.) is cream-colored, and its spring form **sis-**

kiyouensis is gray below. Some of these ssp. have been considered distinct species, but D. Davenport showed that they form one species. Ssp. *tullia* and many other ssp. are in Eurasia.

Habitat Upper Sonoran to Hudsonian Zone prairie, woodland, salt marsh, and arctic tundra. Hostplants grasses: *Stipa, Poa pratensis*; oviposits near *Melica bulbosa*; in the lab, larvae eat *Festuca* and *Agrostis*. In Europe larvae eat sedges (Cyperaceae), including *Eriophorum angustifolium* and *Rhynchospora alba*.

Eggs (Fig. 45) pale yellow-green, becoming mottled with reddish-brown. Larva (Fig. 51) green, covered with tiny bumps, with a dark-green dorsal line, a strong green lateral stripe, and a fainter green lateral stripe above a whitish-yellow lateral ridge, with two short pink tails, the head green or tan, covered with tiny bumps; *or* larva (Calif.) dark green to brown, with dark and light stripes. Pupa (Fig. 52) green (green to brown in Calif.), with nine black stripes. Larvae hibernate, usually in the third or fourth stage, mostly in the first stage (occasionally second) north of Lake Ontario, and in the first stage in Calif.; in Europe young larvae hibernate (though there is a two-year life cycle in part of Europe). Larvae hibernate in thick mats of dead grass (W. Eberlie).

One flight, June-July northward and in the Rockies, M July-M Aug. in N.B., M May-E June in ssp. *furcae*; two flights, June-E July and M Aug.-M Sep., north of Lake Ontario; several flights, May-E Sep. from Ore., Wash., and s Ida. south to Carson City and lowland Eureka Co., Nev. (only one flight in the mountains of Elko and Lander Cos., Nev.); many flights, Mar.-Oct. in Calif. Adults often sip flower nectar. Adults live an average of only 3-4 days in a localized British colony (J. Turner). Adults aestivate in Calif. summers and live many weeks. To seek females, males patrol all day with a hopping flight.

107. **Coenonympha haydenii**   Yellowstone Ringlet

Color Plate 13

Males are dark brown; females ochre brown. The unh eyespots are distinctive in having orange rings. Habitat Transition to Canadian Zone forest clearings and bogs. Larva (half-grown) yellowish-green, with three white dorsal stripes, and two white lateral stripes each edged by a purple-pink line. One flight, L June-E Aug. Adults often sip flower nectar. Males patrol to seek females.

108. **Cercyonis pegala**   Wood Nymph (Goggle Eye)

Color Plate 16
Fig. 48

The biggest *Cercyonis* (male fw length 26 mm, female 30 mm). The male stigma is only in cells CuA$_1$, CuA$_2$, and 1A+2A. The lower fw eyespot is bigger than the upper (sometimes the same size in males) in the west, where *C. sthenele* occurs. Ssp. **pegala** (c Tex. to Kans., east to Fla., Penn., coastal Maine) has a large yellow fw patch; it intergrades west and north to the patchless ssp. **nephele** (Nova Scotia, c Penn., and Ill. north and west to the Rockies and the Pacific). Ssp. **gabbii** (SE Ore., extreme NE Calif., Nev. to N Utah) has heavy brown unh striations, many unh eyespots, and a yellow unf flush (many adults, esp. females, are yellow around the fw eyespots and whiter on the unh, form **stephensi**, which is commonest in NW Nev. and vicinity).

Habitat moist grassy places from the Gulf Coast and Upper Sonoran Zone to Canadian Zone. Hostplants various grasses: *Andropogon, Tridens flavus, Avena fatua*^{t}, *Stipa spartea*^{t}, ?*Puccinellia*. All *Cercyonis* eat *Poa pratensis* in the lab.

Eggs (similar to 111 in Fig. 45) pale lemon-yellow or white, turning tan in a

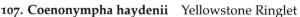

few days, developing orange-brown or pinkish mottling, laid haphazardly on or near grasses. Larvae (Fig. 48; similar to 106 in Fig. 51) eat leaves; no nests. *C. pegala* females lay 200-300 eggs (other *Cercyonis* lay only 100-150; T. Emmel). Larva yellow-green or grass green, frosted with hair, with a dark-green middorsal stripe, sometimes a white (or yellow) subdorsal stripe, and a usually yellow lateral stripe (but white in ssp. *gabbii*); two reddish tails; head green, without horns. Pupa yellow-green, with a whitish line along the dorsal edge of the wing case, a whitish line on top of the mesothorax, a transverse white line on the head, sometimes a yellowish subdorsal band on the thorax and abdomen, and sometimes a yellowish middorsal band all along the body. Pupa (ssp. *gabbii*) green, or white with many black stripes, or intermediate in color and pattern. Unfed first-stage larvae hibernate.

One flight, mostly L June-E Sep. (June-July in coastal Calif.). Adults sip flower nectar and rarely sap and dung. Males patrol all day in grassy areas to seek females. In courtship (of *C. pegala* and *C. oetus*), the male pursues the female, who lands (if flying) and then remains motionless with her wings closed; the male then lands and flutters his wings at full stroke while butting her head with his head (his forewings drawn forward to transfer pheromone from his upf patch); next, he moves to her side and flutters his partly opened wings with smaller strokes, and then bends his abdomen to mate. When an unreceptive airborne female continues to hover or fly slowly, both sexes fly in a series of 10-cm rises, as the male flies beneath her and rises up to place his upf patches near her antennae to induce her to land and she rises 10 cm to escape him. An unreceptive resting female may hold her wings nearly to the side and flutter them with small strokes until the male leaves (he may hover over the fluttering female or dip down to contact her repeatedly before departing), or she may crawl or fly vertically or horizontally to escape.

109. Cercyonis sthenele   Scrub Wood Nymph

Like *C. pegala* but smaller (male fw length 22 mm, female 24 mm), without yellow suffusion (sometimes slightly yellowish on female fw), and with the upper fw eyespot bigger than the lower in males (the same size in females). The male upf sex patch (stigma) extends into cell M_3 in addition to cells CuA_1, CuA_2, and $1A+2A$, where the *pegala* stigma occurs (Fig. 37). In ssp. **sthenele** (San Francisco, extinct about 1880; a similar population still occurs on Santa Cruz I.) the unh has a dark white-edged median band. Ssp. **behrii** in the Calif. Coast Ranges has a slight unh median band; intermediates to *sthenele* still occur in Marin Co., Calif. Ssp. **silvestris** (rest of Calif.-B.C.) lacks the dark unh band. Ssp. **paulus** (SE Ore., east of the Sierra to Colo.) has a dark unh median band, whitish unh mottling, and many unh eyespots; it sometimes hybridizes with *C. pegala* in Delta and Montrose Cos., Colo. (T. Emmel). In the Grand Canyon some (form **damei**) have an orange flush around the fw eyespots (esp. on the unf of females), owing to past hybridization (introgression) with *C. meadii*. Northwest of Grand Canyon Park, *sthenele* and *meadii* fly together with many hybrids of every possible combination; the two are thus not completely distinct species, and may be ssp., though both spp. fly in several counties in SE Utah and vicinity. Populations intermediate between *sthenele* and *meadii* also occur in the Chuska Mts., Ariz.

Color Plates 16, 63
Fig. 37

Habitat mostly Upper Sonoran Zone open woodland, chaparral, sagebrush. Hostplants unknown grasses.

Eggs like those of *C. pegala*, laid singly. Larva light green, with a dark-green middorsal stripe and dark-green-edged subdorsal and lateral stripes (these stripes yellow in ssp. *silvestris*, white in ssp. *paulus*); tails reddish; head light green. Pupa uniformly grass green. Unfed first-stage larvae hibernate.

One flight, mostly L June - E Aug. (M June - M July in the Coast Ranges). Adults sip flower nectar. Males patrol all day, often in valley bottoms, to seek females.

110. Cercyonis meadii   Red Wood Nymph

Color Plate 15
Fig. 37

Like *C. sthenele*, of which it may be a ssp.; identified by the orange unf (*sthenele* form *damei* from the Grand Canyon usually has only a trace of orange) and by the small size of the male stigma, mostly in cell CuA_1 plus an upper and lower part in cell CuA_2 (Fig. 37). The unh median bands are variable. Some adults (ssp. **alamosa**) from the San Luis Valley, Colo., have a whiter unh than ssp. **meadii** elsewhere in the range.

Habitat mostly Transition Zone open woodland. Hostplants unknown grasses, undoubtedly *Bouteloua gracilis* in Colo.

Eggs like those of *C. pegala*, laid singly. Larva yellow-green, covered with fine whitish hair, with a dark-green yellowish-edged middorsal stripe, a yellow-white subdorsal stripe, and a yellow lateral stripe; tails red; head green, with fine white hair. Larva like that of *C. oetus*, but the subdorsal stripe as wide as the lateral stripe. Pupa light yellow-green, the top of the head and the top edges of wing cases cream-white. Unfed first-stage larvae hibernate.

One flight, L July - E Sep. Adults sip flower nectar and mud. Males patrol all day throughout the habitat to seek females.

111. Cercyonis oetus   Small Wood Nymph

Color Plate 15
Fig. 45

C. oetus is the smallest *Cercyonis* (fw length 21 mm). Identified by the absence of a complete unf postmedian line (when rarely present, found only basal to the lower eyespot) and by the inward jut of the unh postmedian line in cell M_2. The prominent male stigma is in upf cells M_3, CuA_1, CuA_2, and 1A+2A. The unh is darkest in the Rockies (ssp. **charon**), lightest in sagebrush areas in the Great Basin (ssp. **oetus**).

Habitat Transition to Canadian (sometimes Hudsonian) Zone grassland, chaparral, sagebrush, and open woodland (very rarely Alpine Zone in Calif.). Hostplants unknown grasses.

Eggs (Fig. 45) lemon-yellow, becoming mottled with orange-brown, laid singly. Females do not oviposit until about 5 days old. Larva yellowish to whitish-green, with fine whitish hair, a dark-green yellowish-edged middorsal line, and yellow or whitish subdorsal and lateral stripes; two reddish tails; head green, without horns. Pupa pale yellow-green, with whitish dots, a whitish middorsal stripe, and a whitish subdorsal stripe, the top of the head lined with white; *or* pupa uniformly whitish-green, or greenish-black with gray stripes, or dark brown with thick blackish and pinkish-white stripes. Unfed first-stage larvae hibernate.

One flight, L June - Aug. Adults sip flower nectar. Males patrol all day throughout the habitat to seek females.

112. Erebia vidleri   Cascades Alpine

Identified by the sharply edged yellow-orange jagged upf band containing two or three eyespots. Habitat Hudsonian to Alpine Zone meadows and flowery rockslides. Larvae may eat grass. One flight, July-M Aug. Adults sip flower nectar.

113. Erebia rossii   Two-Dot Alpine

The fw has two eyespots like those of *E. epipsodea* (119; fw sometimes lacks eyespots, or has two extra small ones) but lacks a reddish upf patch or band. In ssp. **ornata** (Churchill, Man.) the two fw eyespots are joined into one. Ssp. **rossii** elsewhere usually has two eyespots, but may have none (form **brucei**, common on Boothia Pen.). Other ssp. are in Siberia. Habitat arctic tundra (also in Hudsonian Zone forest westward), mainly in wet sedge meadows. Hostplants sedges (Cyperaceae): *Carex atrofusca, rariflora* (oviposits at Churchill, D. Parshall). One flight, M June-July. Adults sip flower nectar and mud.

114. Erebia disa   White-Spot Alpine

Identified by the white spot in the middle of the unh (rarely absent) and usually by another white spot on the front edge of the unh. The upf has four eyespots in a row. Ssp. **mancinus** has a red flush in the middle of the fw, and the unh is dark, with the white spots conspicuous. Ssp. **steckeri** (Alaska-N.W. Terr.) lacks the red flush and has distinct whitish unh bands, in which the white spots are almost lost. Ssp. *disa* and other ssp. are in Scandinavia and Siberia. Habitat Canadian to Hudsonian Zone spruce bogs to lower arctic tundra. One flight, June-M July. Biennial, flying in odd years in Alaska and Sask., even years in part of Sask., every year at Churchill, Man. Adults sip mud at least. They commonly rest on trees.

115. Erebia magdalena   Rockslide Alpine

Identified by the solid-black wings, although some adults carry faint traces of unh bands. The Alaska and Siberia ssp. **erinnyn** (=*mackinleyensis*) has an orange fw flush (esp. in the Brooks Range) that the southern ssp. **magdalena** rarely has. They intergrade in the Yukon.

Habitat Arctic/Alpine Zone rockslides, usually near vegetation. Hostplant unknown. Larvae eat grass in the lab.

Eggs pale yellow-brown, with numerous strong ribs, laid singly on the side of rocks near Juncaceae (*Luzula spicata*), and on Gramineae and Cyperaceae (*Carex atrata*) near rockslides. Larvae eat leaves; no nests. Larva dark green mottled with yellow, with many short hairs, a dark-green middorsal line on the thorax, two paired brown lateral lines, green middorsal crescents (with yellow spots beside them) on the abdomen, and a dark-green transverse line on each segment that ascends and then curves posteriorly beneath each of the yellow dorsal spots; shape sluglike; no tails; head brown, without horns. Pupal head and wing cases blackish-green, the abdomen brown with black dots and a brown middorsal stripe (2 mm wide) edged by tan; cremaster with several or no hooks. Larvae hibernate; possibly biennial.

One flight, mostly July southward, L June-July in the Arctic. Males patrol all day over rockslides, mainly in depressions in the slides, to seek females.

Color Plate 15

Color Plate 15

Color Plate 15

Color Plate 15
Fig. 51

Color Plate 15

116. Erebia fasciata   White-Band Alpine

Like *E. magdalena* (115) on the ups, but the unh has striking whitish bands. Form **avinoffi** has narrower white unh bands. Habitat moist cotton-"grass" swales in arctic/alpine tundra; also in Siberia. Hostplant unknown. Adults assoc. with the sedge *Eriophorum* (cotton grass). One flight, L June-M July.

117. Erebia discoidalis   Red-Disk Alpine

Identified by the reddish fw, the mottled unh, and the lack of eyespots. Habitat open dry grassy areas and moist prairie, often on gravelly knolls, from the Canadian Zone to the edge of arctic tundra (where it may be in boggy areas); also in Asia. Hostplants grasses: *Poa canbyi, glauca, alpina.* Fourth-stage larvae (and supposedly pupae) hibernate; probably biennial. One flight, M May-M June southward, June-M July in the Arctic. Flight is slow and near the ground.

118. Erebia theano   Banded Alpine

Identified by the postmedian bands of red spots and the absence of eye-spots. Ssp. **ethela**, in most of N. Amer., usually has a red spot in the middle of the fw; ssp. **pawloskii** (Yukon to Siberia) lacks this spot and has fewer band spots. Ssp. *theano* and other ssp. are in Asia.

Habitat Hudsonian to lower Arctic/Alpine (occasionally Canadian) Zone grassy areas, sometimes in bogs. Hostplant unknown. Larvae eat grass in the lab.

Eggs cream, with many reddish-brown spots, weakly ribbed, laid singly on dead blades near five different species of grass, sedge, and rush in Colo. Fe-males often lay eggs on *Salix* (Salicaeae) at Churchill, Man. (D. Parshall). Larvae eat leaves; no nests. Larva (Fig. 51) tan, with a dark-brown middorsal stripe and three dark-brown stripes on each side; two short bumps on the rear; body and hornless head, covered with thick club-shaped hairs. Biennial, hibernating as young larva the first winter, probably as nearly mature larva the second, as in both British *Erebia* spp.

One flight, mostly July northward, M July-E Aug. southward, flying mostly in even years in Colo. and Wyo. Adults are very local (a colony may exist in only one hectare); they seldom fly, mainly resting in the grass. They often sip the nec-tar of yellow and white flowers. To seek females, males occasionally patrol slowly above the grass in swales and on hillsides, at any time of day.

119. Erebia epipsodea   Common Alpine

Identified by the two large fw eyespots, sometimes with additional smaller eyespots on the fw and others on the hw. The eyespots are sometimes absent in Alpine Zone individuals (form **brucei**, very rare except up to 15 percent in a few spots in c Colo.). W. Edwards raised normal *epipsodea* from *brucei* eggs.

Habitat moist open grassy areas and meadows, mostly Canadian to Hudso-nian Zone, often Alpine Zone, occasionally Transition Zone southward. Host-plant unknown. Larvae eat grass (Gramineae) and sedge (Cyperaceae) in the lab. Adults fly near the grass *Poa fendleriana*.

Eggs whitish, laid on grasses, dead leaves, etc. Larva yellow-green, with a dark middorsal line and yellowish subdorsal and lateral stripes (both edged below with brown, the latter widely edged); two short tails; head yellow-brown, without horns. Larvae pupate among leaves silked together. Pupa (similar to 134 in Fig. 52) whitish-brown, with brown longitudinal stripes on the wings, a brown transverse stripe on each abdomen segment, and brown dorsal dots; cremaster with only a few straight bristles. Third- and fourth-stage larvae hibernate.

One flight, mostly June at low altitude and in Sask., M July-E Aug. above timberline, L June-July in Alaska. P. Brussard and P. Ehrlich found that adults moved large distances (up to 13 km; more than 10 percent of recaptures had traveled more than 500 m), dispersing from high-density areas. Adults often sip flower nectar and mud. They bask dorsally. Males patrol all day in moist meadows and swales to seek females.

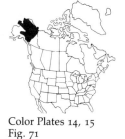

Color Plates 14, 15
Fig. 71

120. Erebia dabanensis   Four-Dot Alpine

E. dabanensis and *E. kozhantshikovi* (121) have four black fw eyespots like those of *E. disa* (114) but lack its white unh spots. The short unh hair of *dabanensis* is always reddish, as in *kozhantshikovi* (whitish in *E. occulta*, 122). The antenna club, on the unscaled side facing the other antenna, has an ochre line between a long thick brown dorsal patch and another brown ventral patch (or series of small brown ventral dots), unlike that of *kozhantshikovi*. The orange patches and black eyespots are usually large, and the orange unf patches are often joined into a broad band, whereas *kozhantshikovi* seldom has an orangish unf band, and *occulta* has small orangish spots. The male valva (Fig. 71) has a shortened tip, and the spined ridge is thus short (36-47 percent of the length of the top of the valva, averaging 43 percent), shorter than that of *kozhantshikovi* and *occulta*. The neck of the valva appears narrow, because the spined ridge rises steeply from the base of the valva. The unh is generally grizzled dark brown (the ground-color scales are usually dark brown or blackish in males, brown in females, with scattered white and red scales), but rare adults are smooth brown, tinted with reddish, like *kozhantshikovi*. The fringes are often checkered (darker brown at the vein tips); they are never checkered in *kozhantshikovi*. The American ssp. **youngi** has usually more-elliptical black pupils in the orange fw spots, usually fewer orange hw spots, and darker unh bands than the Siberian ssp. *dabanensis*; the valva tip is shortened (ssp. *dabanensis* has a longer tip, so the toothed ridge is usually longer than that of ssp. *youngi*, 47-67 percent of the length of the valva). Adults from Mt. McKinley, w Alaska, and coastal Yukon have slightly less unf orange and somewhat smaller hw spots. Habitat Arctic/Alpine Zone dry tundra (esp. short grass and sedge tundra), occasionally rocky scree in some places. One flight, L June-July; possibly biennial. Adults sip mud.

Color Plate 14
Fig. 71

121. Erebia kozhantshikovi   Reddish Four-Dot Alpine

Resembles *E. disa* (114) and *E. dabanensis* (120) but lacks the white unh spots of *disa*. The short unh hair is always reddish, as in *dabanensis* (whitish in *E. occulta*, 122). The antenna club has one large brown patch covering most of the scaleless side that faces the other antenna, without an ochre median line (*dabanensis* and *occulta* have an ochre median line along the club). The toothed part of the male valva (Fig. 71) is about half the length of the top of the valva (50-59 percent, averaging 54 percent), which is longer than the toothed part in *dabanensis youngi*, slightly shorter than that in *occulta*. The valva neck appears wider than in *dabanensis*. The spines on the valva are usually coarser than those of *occulta*. The unh has the same number of red scales and hairs as in *dabanensis*, but fewer white scales than in most *dabanensis*, and the ground-color scales are paler (brown in males, often tan in females), so that the unh looks smooth and slightly redder than in most *dabanensis*. The grayish unh postmedian band often has tiny points into the dark median band in the middle of each cell, as well as along the veins (only along the veins in the other species). The fringes are never checkered (often slightly checkered in *dabanensis*). The amount of fw orange and the width and jaggedness of the unh bands vary, as they do in *dabanensis*, but the unf very seldom has the orange patches joined into a band (as is common in *dabanensis*). In the American ssp. **lafontainei** the eyespots are usually smaller, the unh postmedian band is usually darker, and the valva spines are usually coarser than in ssp. *kozhantshikovi* from Siberia. Habitat Arctic/Alpine Zone shrub tundra, generally in short-sedge patches among low willows and birches, sometimes near forest. One flight, M June-M July; possibly biennial. Adults sip mud.

Color Plate 15
Fig. 71

122. **Erebia occulta** (=*phellea*)   Eskimo Alpine

Resembles *E. dabanensis* (120) and *E. kozhantshikovi* (121) in having four reddish or yellowish fw spots, but easily identified by the tiny white or cream unh hairs (the hairs red in the other species) producing an obscured dark-brown look. The fw patches (yellowish-red in males, reddish-yellow in females, as in the other two species) are small, the black pupils are tiny or absent (the black pupils usually large in the other two species), and the front two fw patches are usually slightly larger than the hind two (usually the same size or smaller in the other species). The toothed part of the male valva (Fig. 71) is about two-thirds the length of the top of the valva (62-72 percent, averaging 67 percent), much longer than that of *dabanensis youngi* and slightly longer than that of *kozhantshikovi*. The valva neck appears wide. The unh median band is rather obscure except in the Alaska Range, the dark unh submarginal band is indistinct or absent, and there are often yellow unh submarginal spots. The unh has dark-brown ground-color scales, fewer red scales than in *dabanensis* and *kozhantshikovi*, and fewer white scales than in most *dabanensis*. The antenna club, on the scaleless side facing the other antenna, is most like that of *dabanensis*, with brown dorsal and ventral patches (separated by a paler ochre line) of about equal size. Adults from the Seward Pen., w Brooks Range, and Siberia, lack the orange unf suffusion often present eastward. The name *inuitica* has been applied to *occulta*, but the type of *inuitica* seems to be a European *E. pharte*, mislabeled Alaska. Habitat Arctic/Alpine Zone dry rocky places, preferably areas with small rocks rather than massive boulder scree. One flight, M June-M July; possibly biennial.

Color Plate 15

123. **Erebia callias**   Relict Gray Alpine

Identified by the lead-gray or gray-brown unh and by the two fw eyespots in a red patch (the eyespots sometimes absent in NW Wyo., form **brucei**). Habitat alpine grassy areas; also in Asia. Hostplant unknown. Eggs laid singly on dead blades near four different species of grasses and sedges in Colo. Adults usually assoc. with the sedge *Kobresia myosuroides*. One flight, mostly M July-M Aug. (E-M Aug. in c Wyo.). Adults often sip flower nectar and mud. Males patrol all day over grassy areas, especially on knolls, to seek females.

Color Plate 15

Color Plate 13

124. **Gyrocheilus patrobas**   Red-Rim Satyr

Habitat Upper Sonoran to Transition Zone open woodland. Ranges to s Mex. One flight, Sep.-Oct. Males patrol all day, throughout the habitat but usually in shady areas, to seek females.

125. **Neominois ridingsii**   Grasshopper Satyr

The gray wings with white patches are unique. Varies geographically some-what, but not in a consistent fashion. Some colonies in Nev. and w Colo. are slightly yellowish (large in w Colo.), and some Calif. and Wyo. colonies are whiter.

Habitat Lower Sonoran to Canadian Zone (occasionally Hudsonian Zone southward) prairie, open woodland, and sagebrush. Hostplant grass: *Bouteloua gracilis*.

Eggs (similar to 111 in Fig. 45) white, laid singly on the host or on other plants and shrubs. Larvae eat leaves; no nests. Larva (similar to 118 in Fig. 51) reddish-tan, with short white hairs, whitish lines between stripes, which are positioned like those of *Oeneis chryxus* (128), stripe #1 pale black, #2 tan, #3 whitish-tan, #4 blackish, #5 brownish-green, #6 greenish-tan; two short tails; head brown-yellow, with six pale-brown vertical stripes, without horns. Pupa (similar to 134 in Fig. 52) red-brown, the wing cases and abdomen joints green; pupa in a soil hole made by the larva. Third- and fourth-stage larvae hibernate (probably annual at lower altitude and in Rocky Mts.). Biennial in Hudsonian Zone of Tuolumne Co., Calif., where it flies only in even-numbered years, probably hibernating as young larvae the first winter, as old larvae the second.

One flight, June-E July at low altitude, M July-E Aug. at high altitude. Marked adults moved an average of 94 m for males, 119 m for females during their lifetime (J. Scott). Adults feed rarely, mostly on the nectar of yellow com-posites. They live an average of 11 days in nature in a cool year, and 5 days in a hot year (Scott). They bask dorsally. In hot weather adults seek shade, or the tops of plants where females lay eggs. Males perch from about 7:50 to 11:00 A.M. on small grassy hilltops, mesas, and saddles to await females. The male pursues a passing female, they land, the male nudges her abdomen with his head, either sex may flick the wings rapidly, and then they join.

Color Plate 15

126. **Oeneis nevadensis**   Pacific Arctic

Along with *O. macounii* (127), the largest *Oeneis*. The hw margin looks wavy, and the unh is covered with white and has less brown striation than *O. chryxus* (128) or *O. uhleri* (131). The valva is like that of *O. bore* (130). In ssp. **gigas** (Vancouver I.) the unh is darker. In ssp. **iduna** (Mendocino-Sonoma Cos., Calif.) the ups is yellow-orange (more orange in other ssp.). Ssp. **nevadensis** occurs elsewhere.

Habitat mainly Canadian Zone forest glades and rocky hills. Hostplant un-known. Larvae eat grass in the lab.

Eggs gray-white. Larvae eat leaves; no nests. Larva like that of *O. macounii*, striped like that of *O. chryxus*; stripe #1 black, #2 whitish (shading outwardly to brown, with black streaks at lower edge), #3 pale tan mottled with brown,

#4 black (brown in front), #5 greenish-tan, #6 yellowish-white; head with six dark stripes. Biennial, hibernating as second- or third-stage larvae the first winter, as fifth-stage (mature) larvae the second winter.

One flight L May-M July; mostly in even-numbered years. To await females, males perch all day on fallen trees, etc., in glades in valley bottoms and on hilltops.

Color Plate 15

127. Oeneis macounii   Canada Arctic

Females identical to *O. nevadensis* (126); males lack the dark upf patch of *nevadensis* containing the androconial scales. *O. macounii* occurs farther east than *nevadensis*. Probably a ssp. of *nevadensis*: their behavior and habitats are similar (J. Masters), and early stages are very similar (W. Edwards). The two species are found within 30 km of each other in B.C. without any intermediates (male *macounii* have no androconia at all there). The androconia of *nevadensis* may produce a pheromone required by the female to mate; if so, the two may be distinct species.

Habitat Canadian to lower Hudsonian Zone open Jack Pine–forest clearings and stony spruce ridges. Hostplant unknown. Larvae eat grasses and sedges in the lab.

Eggs gray-white. Larva striped like that of *O. chryxus* (128); stripe #1 pale black, #2 and #3 brownish-tan, #4 greenish-black, #5 greenish-tan, #6 gray-green; head greenish-yellow. Biennial, hibernating as first- or second-stage larvae the first winter, as mature larvae the second winter.

One flight, M June-M July; in odd years from Alta. to Riding Mts., Man., in even years eastward. Adults occasionally sip flower nectar. Males perch on bushes or trees in small glades to await females.

Color Plate 15

128. Oeneis chryxus   Brown Arctic

This medium-sized brown species is smaller than *O. nevadensis* (126) and usually bigger than *O. uhleri* (131). The unh has heavy brown striations and a darker median band sometimes edged with white. Most adults have an unf postmedian line. The valva is like that of *O. bore* (130; Fig. 71). Ssp. **chryxus** (Rockies) is very variable; from Sonora Pass to Carson Pass in the Calif. Sierra similar populations occur, which intergrade to ssp. **ivallda** (ups color cream) northward and southward in the Sierra. In ssp. **strigulosa** (s Ont.-Mich.) the unh is evenly brown-striated, and the upf is orange except for the stigma. In ssp. **calais** northward (Que.-Man.) the upf base is browner, and the unh is similarly striated but has a stronger median band. In Calif. the wing color tends to match the color of the background rocks (ssp. *ivallda* flies on grayish rock and ssp. *chryxus* on darker metamorphic rock).

Habitat in the west Transition to Alpine Zone bunchgrass, open woodland, and alpine tundra, in the east Canadian to Hudsonian Zone dry, sandy, or rocky areas. Hostplants grasses: *Danthonia spicata* (raised on, in Ont.), *Oryzopsis pungens* and *Phalaris arundinacea* (both oviposition, in Ont.); larvae eat other grasses in the lab. Assoc. with the sedge *Carex spectabilis* in Calif., and a larva (probably *chryxus*) was found on it.

Eggs white, laid singly on grasses and sedges, etc., in Colo. Larva (similar to 118 in Fig. 51) greenish-tan to tan, with reddish hairs, a tan middorsal stripe

(#1) that is black at the joints, a brownish or whitish-tan stripe (#2), a reddish-tan or whitish stripe (#3), a broad (#4) then a narrower (#5) mottled tan stripe along the spiracles, and a tan stripe (#6) above the legs; whitish lines separating all six stripes (the widest line on the lateral ridge between stripes #5 and #6); head yellow-brown, with six brown vertical stripes on the top half, without horns. The six dark body stripes and the six on the head occur in all *Oeneis* (studied by W. Edwards): stripes #1, #4, and #6 darker than the others, #3 lightest, and #1, #5, and #6 narrower than the others. Pupa brown, the thorax yellow-brown, the abdomen light yellow-brown, with black dots. Biennial; larvae hibernate in the first or second stage the first winter, in the third, fourth, or fifth (mature) stage the second winter.

One flight, M May-M June in Mich. and c Sask., L May-M July in low-altitude Colo., L June-E Aug. in the Arctic/Alpine Zone (M July-M Aug. in alpine Calif.); mostly in even years in Colo., odd years in NW Wyo. and Calif., every year in Mich. and Man. Adults sip mud. Males mainly perch all day, usually on hilltops or ridgetops (but in gulches near timberline in some places in the San Juan Mts., Colo.), to await females.

Color Plate 15
Fig. 45

129. Oeneis alberta   Prairie Arctic

Most like *O. uhleri* (131), but *O. alberta* has a pointed unf postmedian line, is a little smaller (the smallest *Oeneis*), and tends to be grayish in color with a strong dark unh band. Very variable; brownish-gray adults occur, and the number of eyespots varies from few to many. The valva is like that of *O. bore* (130), not *uhleri*. Ssp. **daura** (Ariz.) is a little larger, the unh more striated. Ssp. **alberta** elsewhere has a more distinct unh median band with white edges.

Habitat mainly Canadian Zone dry bunchgrass hills. Hostplant bunchgrass; reported on *Festuca* grass, and larvae eat grass in the lab.

Eggs (Fig. 45) pale-green, rapidly changing to gray-white, laid singly and haphazardly in the lab. Larvae eat leaves; no nests. Larva striped like that of *O. chryxus* (128), dark brown; stripe #1 black, #4 greenish-black, #5 green speckled with black, #6 bluish-green, the lateral ridge between #5 and #6 brown; head brownish-green, the six dark stripes broad. Larva (Ariz.) white, with the usual bands; head white, with grayish-black pits. Pupa greenish-gray, the abdomen yellow-brown with black dots, the wing cases olive-green. Probably hibernates as older larva; possibly biennial.

One flight, M May-M June. Adults sip mud. Males perch and often patrol all day, usually in sloping swales among bunchgrasses, to await females.

Color Plates 1 (egg), 2
(larva), 15
Fig. 71

130. Oeneis bore   Arctic Grayling

This arctic/alpine species resembles *O. melissa* (134) and *O. polixenes* (135); best identified by the valva (Fig. 71), which has a lobe near the base, and by the long narrow uncus protruding from the end of the male abdomen about 1 mm. The unf has a brown postmedian line (sometimes faint) lacking in the other two spp. The ups is grayish or orangish-brown (males grayer, females more brownish). The unh usually lacks eyespots and has a dark median band bordered by heavy white bands; the unh veins are variable, mostly white but often dark esp. in the Arctic. White-veined adults were treated as a separate species, but most populations vary in this trait. Some *O. chryxus* (128), *alberta* (129), *alpina* (133), and arctic *polixenes* have white veins also. Ssp. **taygete** is in N. Amer.; ssp. *bore* and other ssp. are in Scandinavia and Asia.

Habitat Arctic/Alpine Zone tundra, esp. moist hummocky areas. Hostplants: hummock sedge *Carex misandra* at Churchill, Man. (many ovipositions in nature and larvae raised, D. Parshall); grasses, esp. *Festuca ovina* in Europe, oviposits on *F. mibra*, *brachyphylla*, *vivipara* at Churchill, and larvae eat grass in the lab.

Eggs white, laid on dead blades. Larval head and body (fourth stage at Churchill; J. Troubridge) striped like those of *O. chryxus*; stripe #1 brown (black at joints), #2 mottled whitish-brown, #3 mottled reddish-white, #4 dark brown, #5 mottled light reddish-brown, #6 brown, the lines between stripes white, the body joints paler. Biennial; fourth- and fifth-stage (mature) larvae hibernate in the second winter, probably young larvae in the first winter.

One flight, mostly L June - E Aug. (M June - July in western Arctic); in even years in Lab. and at Churchill, every year in Colo.-Wyo. (but the odd-year cohort looks a little different from the even-year cohort in N Wyo.) and Baker Lake, N.W. Terr. Adults occasionally sip flower nectar. Males perch and patrol all day, mostly in sloping swales and on grassy hillsides, to seek females.

Color Plate 15
Fig. 71

131. **Oeneis uhleri**   Rocky Mountain Arctic

Small and brownish. The unh is striated esp. in the inner half and usually lacks a dark median band; a brown unf postmedian line is nearly absent. There are few to many eyespots. The ups veins are dark. The valva is unique (triangular, without lobes or teeth; Fig. 71). Ssp. **nahanni** (Yukon and N.W. Terr.) is often dark brown, with a strong black unh median band, though some adults may be ochre in color. Ssp. **uhleri** elsewhere is brown and variable.

Habitat Transition to Hudsonian Zone dry bunchgrass. Hostplant unknown, probably grass; larvae eat grass in the lab.

Eggs white, laid singly on grasses and sedges, etc., in Colo. Larva (Colo.) striped like that of *O. chryxus* (128), greenish-tan; stripe #1 black, #2 gray-black, #3 greenish-tan, #4 black, #5 greenish-tan, #6 blackish; head brown, with six dark-brown stripes. Larva (s Canada) variable, often green; stripe #1 (and area between stripes #2 and #3) solid black or having black dashes; head greenish-yellow. Pupa (Colo.) yellow-brown, the abdomen darker, the wing cases greenish-tinted; pupa (Canada) greenish-yellow-brown, the abdomen greenish-yellow. Pupates just under the soil like *Neominois*. Larvae hibernate in the second, third, fourth, or fifth (mature) stage; probably biennial, at least in Alta.

One flight, L May - E July; mostly odd years in the Yukon, perhaps more common in odd years in Colo. Adults sip mud. Males perch and occasionally patrol all day in bunchgrass to await females, usually in slight hollows at the base of slopes, on hills in Neb.

132. **Oeneis jutta**   Forest Arctic

The only *Oeneis* with orange rings or bands around the ups eyespots that contrast with the dark-brown color. As large as *O. chryxus* (128) or larger, it has a mottled grayish unh, often with a darker median band. The unf of females usually has a postmedian line. The valva is like that of *O. melissa* (134). The orange ups bands vary somewhat in width. Ssp. **reducta** (Mont.-Colo.) has the outer third of the ups more orange, and similar populations occur in Riding

Color Plate 15
Figs. 37 (stigma), 56 (dot range map)

Mts., Man. (ssp. **ridingiana**). Ssp. **jutta** elsewhere in N. Amer. (plus Scandinavia and Asia) is darker.

Habitat Canadian to Hudsonian Zone, in spruce bogs in the east and north to the edge of tundra, and in mature grassy Lodgepole Pine forest from Alta. to Colo. Hostplants sedges (Cyperaceae): *Eriophorum spissum* in four areas, *Carex geyeri*, *concinna* (and *oligosperma*, in lab only?); Juncaceae: *Juncus* sp. In the lab, larvae eat grasses and *Juncus articulatus*, but T. Fyles's larvae preferred sedge to grass.

Eggs yellow-white, laid haphazardly near the host. Larvae eat leaves; no nests. Larva striped like that of *O. chryxus*, pale green with reddish hairs; stripes #1, #5, and #6 green (sometimes dark brown; #1 black at body joints), #2 and #4 pale green, #3 mottled white; head reddish-brown, or greenish with six rows of brownish dots. Pupa yellow-green, the abdomen with a darker middorsal line and many rows of brown to black dots, the wing cases light green, the head reddish. Biennial, hibernating as young larvae (first to third stage) the first winter, as older larvae (fourth to sixth stage) the second winter.

One flight, mostly M June-M July; M June-E July southeastward, L May-M June at Ottawa, M June-E Aug. from Nfld. to Lab.; in odd years in Alaska, Mich., Wis., Minn., Sask., Lab., and NW Wyo., and in even years in Colo., Man. (both years at Churchill), Ont., and eastward to Nfld. Adults occasionally sip flower nectar. Males perch (and occasionally patrol) on logs or low plants in small forest clearings, esp. in gentle swales, to await females. The female may have a pheromone; Fyles and J. Masters note that males come to females that are tethered or newly emerged.

Color Plates 14, 15, 63
Fig. 71

133. Oeneis alpina   Eskimo Arctic

Like *O. chryxus* (128), but males and females almost always have two hw eyespots (in cells M_3 and CuA_1), unlike almost all *chryxus*. In males the basal two-thirds of the uph is brown (orange in *chryxus*), the outer third orange, and the orange upf band usually narrower, formed of orange spots. The male valva (Fig. 71), like that of *O. melissa* (134) and *O. jutta* (132), lacks the tooth present in *chryxus*. The female ups is mostly orange, usually with a broad brown median (and basal uph) band at least on the uph. Eyespots are in fw cell M_1 (and usually cells M_3 and CuA_1 of females) and in the two hw cells. Ssp. **excubitor** occurs in N. Amer.; ssp. *alpina*, from E Siberia, has very similar male genitalia but often more eyespots than most *excubitor*. Habitat S Arctic/Alpine Zone scree and rocky tundra hills. One flight, mostly L June-M July; apparently biennial, mostly in odd years westward, mostly in even years in Mackenzie Delta and eastward. Adults fly rather fast for *Oeneis*. Males perch on hilltops to await females.

Color Plate 13
Figs. 48, 52, 71

134. Oeneis melissa   Mottled Arctic

This arctic/alpine species is best identified by the male valva (Fig. 71), which is broad without a basal lobe and has many teeth on the wide end. The wings are grayish-brown, the unh heavily mottled with a darker mottled median band. Eyespots when present (infrequently, in some females) are usually small. In ssp. **beanii** (C Wyo.-S Alta.-B.C.) the wings are dark smoky-gray even for females, whereas ssp. **melissa** elsewhere has gray-brown males and brownish females with variable unh markings.

Habitat Arctic/Alpine Zone dry tundra, esp. ridgetops and rocky places; also in Siberia. Hostplants sedges (Cyperaceae): *Carex bigelowii* (N.H.), *rupestris* (Man., N.W. Terr.; D. Parshall); larvae eat sedges and grasses in the lab.

Eggs gray-white, laid on or near host. Larvae (Fig. 48) eat leaves. Larva (N.H.) striped like that of *O. chryxus* (128), varying from dusky-green to red-brown, or red-brown with green sides in different individuals; stripes #1 and #2 with black interruptions, #3 gray-green, #4 blackish, #5 gray-green, #6 dusky-green; head dark brown or reddish-brown, with six blackish stripes. Larva (Colo.) with stripe #1 whitish (black at joints), #2 and #3 whitish with a series of triangles with black tips, #4 yellow-green with black edges, #5 whitish, #6 a black line. Pupa (N.H.) dark brown, the abdomen lighter yellowish with black spots; pupa (Colo.; Fig. 52) with the top of the thorax greenish-yellow, the abdomen banded with yellow and brown-gray. Pupates under moss and stones or partly in the soil. Biennial, hibernating as young larvae (commonly in the second or third stage) the first winter, as fifth-stage (mature) larvae the second.

One flight, mostly July, M July-M Aug. in Alta., M June-July in the Arctic, E-M Aug. in c Wyo.; every year in most places, but mostly in odd years at Churchill, Man. Adults rarely sip flower nectar. Males perch and often patrol all day on rocky ridgetops (and sometimes at other rocky places) to await females.

Color Plate 13
Fig. 71

135. Oeneis polixenes   Banded Arctic

This arctic/alpine species is best identified by the male valva (Fig. 71), which lacks a basal lobe and is narrowed and curved upward to a point bearing fine teeth. The ups is gray to brown, and the unh has a dark band edged with white bands like those of *O. bore* (130) and some *O. chryxus* (128). Eyespots are rare (except in some females), though ssp. **katahdin** (Maine) usually has one or two on the fw. Ssp. **brucei** (s Mont.-N.M.) has more-transparent gray-brown wings (esp. females). Ssp. **polixenes** occurs elsewhere.

Habitat Arctic/Alpine Zone tundra, esp. in moist or wet hummocky places. *O. polixenes* and *O. bore* almost never occur together in the Rockies from N.M. to Alta. (except in the Wind River Mts.), probably because they occur in the same moist habitat and interfere with each other while locating mates. In the Yukon, J. Troubridge found *polixenes* on fairly dry tundra hillsides, *bore* in wet hummock tundra. Hostplants sedge (Cyperaceae): *Carex misandra* (many ovipositions at Churchill, Man.; D. Parshall); grass: *Festuca mibra* (few ovipositions there). Larvae eat sedge and grass in the lab.

Eggs dull white. Larva striped like that of *O. chryxus*: stripe #1 gray-green (black at joints), #2 gray-tan with blackish streaks, #3 tan with brown streaks, #4 black, #5 dark gray, #6 gray; head greenish-yellow, the middle stripes on each side broken. Biennial, the larvae hibernating in the first and perhaps the second or third stage the first winter, in the fourth or fifth (mature) stage the second winter.

One flight, mostly L June-E Aug.; M June-July in the Arctic, July-M Aug. in Lab. (similar in Alta.); in odd years in Alaska, at Baker Lake (N.W. Terr.), Lab., Churchill, mainly in even years in Maine, every year in Colo. Adults occasionally sip flower nectar. Males patrol and sometimes perch all day in grassy swales (located on slopes, or on flatter hummocky areas), to await females.

Subfamily Charaxinae: Goatweed Butterflies

The Charaxinae are widespread in tropical regions of the world, just a few of their 400 species ranging into the southern temperate zone. The four species that occur in the southern U.S. include one (*Anaea andria*) that ranges north to Canada.

Adults are medium-sized. They resemble the Nymphalinae in having the discal cells open to the margin, but in our species the forewing veins R_1, R_2, and R_3 are rudimentary, and an Sc vein takes their place, nearly reaching the outer margin. On the prothorax the parapatagium (Fig. 12) has become partly hardened (it is membranous in nearly all species of Nymphalinae). Larvae eat plants of the Euphorbiaceae in North America, but elsewhere they eat plants of many kinds, and some species even eat grasses. The larvae live in rolled-leaf nests. Young larvae make a resting perch on a leaf vein by eating away all of the leaf but the vein. First-stage larvae resemble those of the Nymphalinae, although some foreign species have horns and tails and many extra hairs on the head and body. Older larvae lack the branching spines characteristic of the Nymphalinae, although on top of the head are rudimentary horns (some African and Australian species have up to six protuberances on the head, and these and neotropical species may have two tails on the rear). Pupae, like those of the Danainae, are stout. In our northernmost species, the adults hibernate.

The Charaxinae have a strong flight, with powerful wing beats. Some species are somewhat migratory, rarely flying as far as several hundred kilometers. Adults often feed on sap or rotting fruit, but not on flowers. They rest with the wings closed, but seem to bask with them open. Males generally perch to await females, generally on twigs 2-4 m above ground.

136. Anaea andria   Goatweed Butterfly

Resembles *A. troglodyta*, but the hw margin is smooth. The fall overwintering form **morrisonii** has a more pointed fw, and heavier ups lines on females, than the July flight; T. Riley found that the hibernating form results from short photoperiod acting on the mature larva. Males have fewer ups lines than females.

Habitat Subtropical to Upper Austral/Upper Sonoran Zone wooded areas, roadsides, recently cleared fields, railroad tracks, and prairie cottonwood groves. Ranges south to Veracruz, Mex. Hostplants herb Euphorbiaceae: *Croton texensis, capitatus, monanthogynus*.

Eggs greenish-cream, becoming mottled with red on the top, laid singly under host leaves. Larvae eat leaves; first- and second-stage larvae eat the leaf tip except for the midrib, and rest on the midrib, and silk dung pellets to the midrib perhaps to repel ants. Third-stage larvae live in a folded-leaf tent; large ones live in rolled leaves, the leaf edges joined together above the larva. Larva (Fig. 51) gray-green with many pale points, odd-shaped (thickest at the rear of the thorax); abdomen often with subdorsal black patches; head gray-green, with many paler points, the four dorsal bumps (plus smaller bumps on top and side) orange (or whitish with brown bases, or the inner bumps white, the outer ones black), the eyes black. Pupa (Fig. 52) stout, light green, speckled with white and sometimes speckled with brown, the edges of the wing cases and top of head whitish. Adults hibernate, in bark crannies, etc.

Color Plate 17
Figs. 51, 52, 55 (veins)

Two flights northward (July-M Aug. and Sep. overwintering to Apr. in Colo.); probably three or four flights all year on the Gulf Coast. Somewhat migratory, straying to N Wyo. and Mich. Adults feed on sap, dung, fruit, and rotting wood; the proboscis is too short for many flowers. Adults of *A. andria* and *A. troglodyta* often land with wings closed on the underside of twigs and branches, where they resemble dead leaves, but seldom land on leaves. Adults often pretend to be dead when handled, which may help them survive predation. Males perch all day in clearings, on branches up to 3 m high, to await females; in the east, males also concentrate along ridgetops (P. Opler). Overwintering adults mate in the spring.

137. Anaea troglodyta   Leaf Wing

Color Plate 17

Resembles *A. andria*, but the hw margin protrudes at the end of each vein. Ssp. **floridalis** (Fla.) is red; ssp. **aidea** (Ariz.-Tex. southward) is orange-brown. The fw is more hooked in the fall and winter form **morrisonii**.

Habitat subtropical pine-palmetto scrub and desert wooded areas. Ranges south to Honduras and the Greater and Lesser Antilles. Hostplants herb Euphorbiaceae: *Croton linearis* (Fla.), *humilis* (Puerto Rico), *soliman* (Mex.).

Larvae eat leaves; older larvae live in a nest of leaves silked together. Larva yellow-green, with many tiny white points, a yellow lateral stripe, a large black crescent on top of abdomen segment 2, and an oval black patch on segments 8-10; head light green with two very small black horns and seven tiny orange bumps. Pupa pale green.

Many flights, all year in s Fla., Apr.-Nov. at least in s Tex. Migrates north rarely to Kans. and Ill. Adults feed on sap.

138. Anaea glycerium   Angled Leaf Wing

Color Plate 59

Identified by the fw, which is pointed at vein CuA$_2$. Habitat subtropical woods and scrub. Ranges south to Argentina, Jamaica, and Hispaniola. Many flights all year in Mex.; a rare stray to Ariz. and s Tex. (July at least).

139. Anaea pithyusa   Blue Leaf Wing

s Tex. only
Color Plate 16

Black and blue, unlike other N. Amer. *Anaea*.

Habitat subtropical open woods. Ranges south to Bolivia. Hostplant tree Euphorbiaceae: *Croton reflexifolius* and *niveus* in El Salvador.

Eggs transparent pale green, laid singly under host leaves. Larvae eat mature leaves. Young larvae rest on the eaten-away midrib with dung pellets silked to the midrib; older larvae rest in a rolled leaf. Larva green to brownish-green, with many light points, a thick black stripe above the spiracles (darkest on the thorax and near the end of the abdomen where the black stripe is edged beneath by white), a black transverse bar edged behind and below by white on top of abdomen segment 2; top of rear black; head black, with yellow tubercles, two very short forked horns, two yellow inverted V-shaped marks on the face, and two yellow vertical lines on each side. Pupa purplish-brown, with a black band dorsally on abdomen segment 5, a pale band outlining the wing cases (except ventrally), and a dark middorsal stripe on the thorax.

Many flights all year in Mex.; apparently a native in s Tex. (Mar.-Dec.). Adults feed on fruit and dung. Males perch on trees to await females.

Subfamily Apaturinae: Emperors

The 50 species of the Apaturinae occur worldwide in temperate and tropical regions, mostly in the tropics. Five species occur in North America, none farther north than southern Canada.

Adults are medium-sized, and not well distinguished from the Nymphalinae, although their wing shape is characteristic. Larvae eat *Celtis* in North America, but European species also eat plants of the Salicaceae (*Salix*, *Populus*). The larvae are distinguished by lacking branching spines on the body, by having two short tails on the rear, and by having thick antlers and other processes on the head (first-stage larvae have tails, and some species, but not others, have small bumps on the head). Pupae are flattened sideways, and have two head horns. Pupae resemble leaves, and two of ours (*Asterocampa celtis*, *A. clyton*) rest flat on a leaf, unlike most other Nymphalidae (our others hang; British *Apatura* hang upside down from a leaf after silking the stem to the twig). Larvae hibernate.

The females of *Doxocopa* resemble both sexes of *Limenitis*; this may be a case of mimicry, but it is not known whether either is distasteful.

Adults are swift and powerful fliers, but they can glide readily, and the flights between stops are generally less than 10 meters; they do not migrate. Adults seem to prefer sap and rotting fruit to flower nectar. They commonly rest and bask with the wings spread. Males generally perch to await females. Mating often takes place late in the day.

Color Plates 1 (egg), 19, 22
Fig. 49

140. Asterocampa celtis   Hackberry Butterfly

The upf cell has one bar and two spots (unlike *A. leilia*), and the fw has eyespots in cells CuA_1 and often in cell M_3. Ssp. **celtis** (E Kans. to N.Y.) is darker. In ssp. **alicia** (SE U.S.) the outer half of the fw is dark, and the ground color is orangish. Ssp. **antonia** is in SW U.S. The submarginal spot in fw cell M_3 is usually white in E U.S., black (or black with a white center) in SW U.S. The spot below it in cell CuA_1 is usually black, occasionally a black ring in SW U.S. Most *Asterocampa* ssp. have been recently treated as separate species, but the morphology, wing pattern, and ecology show that there are only three species north of Mex. (T. Friedlander).

Habitat subtropical to Transition Zone wooded areas. Ranges to S Mex. Hostplants tree Ulmaceae: *Celtis occidentalis, reticulata, laevigata, tenuifolia, lindheimeri, pallida*.

Eggs pale green or cream, usually laid singly (sometimes in groups of several to 20, and rarely in larger clusters) on young hostplants or on new growth, under host leaves, sometimes on twigs and bark. Larvae (similar to 104 in Fig. 48; Fig. 49) eat leaves (esp. new leaves), are not gregarious, and rest on the underside of leaves; no nests. Larva green with blue-green sides, speckled with light dots below the hairs, with yellow middorsal dashes and yellow subdorsal and lateral lines (with a zigzag yellow line between these lines); head green with four vertical cream stripes, or brown, with two long forked horns, a yellow line behind each horn. Larvae develop faster than those of *A. clyton*. Pupa yellow to blue-green, with a yellow middorsal line, light dots on the abdomen, many white subdorsal oblique lines (a thick line starts from the tornus of the wing, and the other thick line runs from the top of each of the two head horns and extends backward onto the middle of the thorax nearly to the dorsal line), and a

white wavy line on the side of the abdomen that extends around the top of the wings. Third-stage larvae hibernate, turning brown before winter.

Many flights, Mar.-Nov., in s Tex. and Fla.; three flights in Mo.; about two flights, June-Sep., northward. Adults feed on sap and fruit, and sometimes on flower nectar, mud, carrion, and dung. Males perch all day to await females, but most often from early afternoon to dusk, on small trees, sunlit tree trunks, or other elevated objects (commonly a human head) in sunny patches near the host trees (in gulches in mountainous regions).

141. **Asterocampa leilia**   Desert Hackberry Butterfly

Color Plate 19
Figs. 51, 52

Resembles *A. celtis*, but the fw cell has two bars, and the eyespots in fw cells M₃ and CuA₁ are both usually black.

Habitat mostly Lower Sonoran/Lower Austral Zone desert and subtropical thorn forest. Ranges to s Mex. Hostplant tree Ulmaceae: *Celtis pallida*.

Eggs pale yellow, turning white later, laid in clusters of 10-15 (rarely 89) usually on the upperside of leaves. Larva (Fig. 51) green, with tiny yellow dots and a yellow subdorsal stripe; head green, with a yellowish line around each cheek and two brown antlers like thick television antennae. Pupa (Fig. 52) yellow-green (a more even grayish-green than in *A. celtis*), with tiny yellow dots, a white dorsal ridge, and two points on the head. Third-stage larvae hibernate (all *Asterocampa* sometimes begin diapause in late summer).

Many flights, Feb.-Nov. in s Tex., Apr.-Nov. in Ariz. Adults feed on sap and dung, occasionally on flower nectar. G. Austin found that males perch most of the day to await females, often on the ground, in washes near the hostplant. Adults live as long as 17 days in nature. Adult *Asterocampa* bask dorsally (with the wings spread).

142. **Asterocampa clyton**   Tawny Emperor

Color Plates 2 (larva), 4 (pupa), 19
Fig. 45

Identified by the lack of upf eyespots and by having fewer unh basal marks than other *Asterocampa*. *Euptoieta* (265, 266) are similar in overall appearance, but the pattern details differ. The unh varies from uniformly grayish, form **apunctus**, to marked with white bands and spots. In e U.S. north of the Gulf Coast, the outer part of the uph is often black (form **geneumbrosa**; as in form *umbrosa* of *Polygonia*, 189, 190, 193); because this form flies with the normal form, it is probably genetic in origin. Ariz.-w Tex. ("*subpallida*") and s Tex. ("*louisa*") populations have somewhat different larvae, but in adult appearance are ordinary *clyton*.

Habitat subtropical to Transition Zone woods. Ranges to s Mex. Females seem to prefer mature trees in groves lining streams and rivers (T. Friedlander). Hostplants tree Ulmaceae: *Celtis occidentalis, tenuifolia, laevigata, lindheimeri, reticulata*.

Eggs (Fig. 45) greenish-cream, laid in large clusters of almost 200 to 500 eggs, in several layers, usually on the underside of mature host leaves, occasionally on bark. Larvae gregarious under leaves for the first three stages; older larvae solitary. Larvae eat leaves, often mature leaves (very young larvae skeletonize them). Young larvae make no nests, but hibernating larvae may tie leaves together and live inside, and mature larvae may live on the underside of a leaf curled downward with silk. The E U.S. larva light green, with white dots below hairs, a broad yellow dorsal band (divided by a bluish-green middorsal line and edged by a whitish subdorsal band), two yellow bands (not zigzags) on each side, and two tails; head pale green (rarely brown), with four vertical white stripes and two branched antlers, the antlers generally shorter than those of *A. celtis* and *A. leilia*. All *A. clyton* larvae have a brown spot on the front of each antler (rarely absent in E U.S. larvae), a variable amount of brown extending down from each antler, and other lateral protuberances on the head; the antlers and protuberances sometimes brown-tipped. The bands on the body are all white in Ont. The *clyton* larva from C to S Tex. to Ariz. green or yellow-green (the middorsal line bluish-green), with white or yellowish subdorsal and lateral bands (and a white or yellowish zigzag line of dashes between them); head mostly brown (often green ventrally, rarely green with a brown spot on the two horns), with four white vertical stripes on the front. S Tex. (and Fla. population) larva also has yellowish transverse dorsal crescents. C Tex. larva sometimes with brownish-black head. The head horns are longer in S Tex. and esp. in Ariz. than in NE U.S. The Fla. larva yellow-green, with a dark-bluish-green middorsal line, a whiter subdorsal band, a whitish zigzag line of dashes beneath it, and a dull-green lateral stripe; head green, with black patches and a black triangle on the front, a white H on the front, and a white vertical stripe on the side (head rarely mostly white, nearly unmarked). Pupa pale green (darker ventrally), with two horns on the head, the horns blunter than those of *celtis* and *leilia*, the yellowish dorsal stripe and whitish pattern the same as in *celtis*. Third-stage larvae turn pinkish-brown in the fall and hibernate; groups averaging 9 or 10 larvae move to a leaf at the end of a branch, silk the leaf to the branch, and hibernate in the resulting dead-curled-leaf hibernaculum.

Many flights, all year in S Tex., Mar.-Nov. in Fla., at least June-Sep. in Ariz.; two flights in Mo.; one flight, L June-M Aug., in the north. Adults feed on sap, fruit, carrion, and occasionally flower nectar and mud. Friedlander found that males perch on tree foliage in full sun to await females, from late morning to late afternoon, earlier than *A. celtis*. This difference, plus the difference in the age of the foliage chosen for oviposition, allows *clyton* and *celtis* to occupy the same habitats without much competition.

143. Doxocopa pavon   Purple Emperor

Stray only
Color Plate 17
Fig. 35 (ultraviolet)

The uns is not silver, and the male has a purple ups, unlike *D. laure*. Females of *Doxocopa* strangely resemble *Limenitis bredowii* (149).

Habitat subtropical woods. Ranges at least to S Mex. Hostplants tree and shrub Ulmaceae: *Celtis pallida*, in Mex. *iguanaea*.

Larva green, with a lateral line of paler dots and a pointed tail; head greenish, with black eyes, black mandibles, and black bars on the front extending onto two long horns that have forked black tips. Pupa (similar to 141 in Fig. 52) green, strongly arched and keeled ventrally on the abdomen, with short horns on the head.

Many flights in Mex.; a regular stray north into S Tex. (May and Aug.-Dec. at least). Male *Doxocopa* perch on trees in full sun to await females, esp. about midday (T. Friedlander).

Stray only
Color Plate 17
Figs. 35 (ultraviolet), 52

144. Doxocopa laure   Silver Emperor

The female resembles *D. pavon*, but the unh is silver. The male resembles the female but has an orange upf median band.

Habitat subtropical wooded areas. Ranges south to Venezuela, Cuba, and Jamaica. Hostplants tree and shrub Ulmaceae: *Celtis pallida*, in Mex. *iguanaea*. *Casearia* (Flacourtiaceae) is an error.

Eggs greenish, laid singly (sometimes 2 or 3 together) mostly on new growth. Young larvae make a resting perch (usually without dung pellets) on top of a leaf. Larva (similar to 141 in Fig. 51) green, with tiny yellow dots esp. on sides, yellowish oblique lines from the spiracles back up to near a pale middorsal line, four triangular yellow plates behind abdomen segment 2 (W. Müller noted forward-sloping white middorsal bumps on the front of abdomen segments 2, 4, and 7, and whitish spots in place of these on segments 5 and 6 and on the mesothorax), and a pointed tail; head bluish, with yellowish-white sides, many small spines, and two very long green horns (with a black bar at the horn base and black forked tips). Pupa (Fig. 52) clear green powdered with white, with many white (sometimes darker green, or brown on the line from horn to keel) diagonal lines on each side, a large pointed keel on top of abdomen segment 3, several smaller middorsal points on segments 6 and 7, sometimes colored brown on the keel and posterior wing edge, with two head horns.

Many flights in Mex., regularly moving north to s Tex. (July-Dec.).

Subfamily Nymphalinae: Spiny Brush-Footed Butterflies

The Nymphalinae occur throughout the world, from the tropics to the tundra. Of almost 1,100 species worldwide, 129 range across North America.

Adults, larvae, and pupae vary greatly in shape. Adults have the forewing and hindwing discal cells open to the margin (except in *Heliconius*, which have crossveins closing the hindwing cell as in other Nymphalidae). The antennae are scaled, just a few species (*Mestra*, for example) have swollen forewing veins, and the side of the prothorax lacks the hardened structure found in Charaxinae. Larvae eat many kinds of dicotyledonous plants. First-stage larvae usually have very long hairs; those of *Limenitis* have fleshy tubercles, and those of *Speyeria* and *Boloria* have some extra hairs. Older larvae are easily identified because the body or head is armed with hardened branching spines or spiny tubercles (scoli) and branching antlers (hence the common name). These branching spines are present only in Nymphalinae and Acraeinae, young larvae of Papilioninae, and some moths like Saturniidae (io moths). Pupae sometimes have long processes or branching spines or bumps, and frequently some gold or silver spots. Larvae usually hibernate, but in some Nymphalini the adults hibernate.

Mimicry is common in the group.

The flight habits, resting habits, and mate-locating habits vary. Some species are very local; others are great migrants. Adults of many species feed on sap rather than flowers. Most species bask by spreading the wings. In most species, the female of a mating pair flies if the pair is startled.

The four tribes are the Nymphalini, Melitaeini, Argynnini, and Heliconiini.

Tribe Nymphalini: Varied Brush-Footed Butterflies (Leaf Butterflies)

The Nymphalini occur worldwide. Some 54 species occur throughout North America, except in the Arctic.

Adults are often brilliantly colored, with many different colors (white, red, orange, green, blue, brown), patterns, and shapes (leaflike, tailed, etc.). The H vein (Fig. 53) is aimed toward the wing tip. The Nymphalini are in fact a hodgepodge of species, and some authors divide the group into additional tribes, but I find no clear justifications for them. Larvae and pupae have also evolved in different directions (those of *Limenitis* are the most different), and as much variety in shapes occurs among the Nymphalini as in all other butterflies and skippers combined (Figs. 51, 52). Larvae eat many dicotyledons (commonly Moraceae, or the related Urticaceae or Ulmaceae), and many tropical genera eat Euphorbiaceae. Young larvae commonly make a resting perch of a leaf vein to which dung pellets are silked. Larvae are characterized by having horns or spines on the head or middorsal spines on the body. Larvae usually hibernate, although in *Nymphalis*, *Polygonia*, and *Vanessa* the adults hibernate.

The Nymphalini are masters of deceit. One species of *Limenitis* mimics the Monarch, and females of *Hypolimnas* mimic another Danainae species. Many species resemble dead leaves on the underside (*Nymphalis*, *Polygonia*, some *Vanessa*, *Hypanartia*, *Marpesia*, *Smyrna*, *Historis*, *Myscelia*, *Epiphile*). *Hamadryas* resemble tree bark. *Precis* use eyespots to scare predators. The larvae of *Limenitis* resemble bird droppings. Many species are brilliant orange, blue, or green on the upperside, which is normally hidden when not in flight.

Adults generally have a powerful, fluttering flight. The *Anartia* fly more slowly than most other species do, seemingly hopping about and often dipping into crannies in the vegetation. *Limenitis bredowii*, *Hamadryas*, and to a lesser extent *Precis* often glide with the wings spread. *Biblis* and *Mestra* seem to flutter more slowly and weakly than most. *Marpesia* fly in a fast, flapping manner like that of some *Papilio*. Many species migrate. Adults of many species feed on sap and seldom visit flowers. Most species usually close their wings when resting, but they generally bask with the wings spread. *Precis* adults usually rest and bask with the wings spread, displaying the eyespots. *Hamadryas* adults rest upside down on tree trunks with their wings spread flat to look like bark; they can make cracking sounds during flight. (European *Nymphalis* can make a hissing sound.) *Eunica* adults commonly rest on branches inside thorny shrubs or trees, and *Polygonia* and *Nymphalis* often land on twigs also. Males usually perch to await females, although some patrol. The female usually flies if a mating pair is startled.

145. **Limenitis archippus**   Viceroy

Mimics the Monarch and Queen (*Danaus*, 89, 90) but is smaller, with a black line across the hw. Ssp. **archippus** (most of range) is orangish and mimics *D. plexippus*. In the south where *D. gilippus* occurs, *L. archippus* becomes darker: ssp. **floridensis** (Fla. to S.C. coast, similar on the Gulf Coast west to Ark. and E Tex.) is reddish-brown and mimics *D. g. berenice*; ssp. **obsoleta** (w Tex.-Ariz.) is brown mimicking *D. g. strigosus*, and the uph line is nearly absent. Rare hybrids occur between *archippus* and *Limenitis* species 146-148.

Habitat subtropical to Canadian Zone watercourses, and deciduous woodlands in E U.S. Ranges to s Mex. Hostplants tree Salicaceae: *Salix exigua, sericea,*

Color Plates 19, 64
(larva, adult)
Figs. 48, 52

nigra, interior, cordata, discolor, caroliniana, Populus gileadensis, fremontii[t], heterophylla[t], trichocarpa, grandidentata, tremuloides, alba, deltoides, balsamifera, nigra (and
var. italica); Betulaceae: Betula papyrifera; Rosaceae: Prunus domestica, serotina,
Malus pumila, Pyrus communis[t], Crataegus[t], Amelanchier, Chrysobalanus oblongifolius; reportedly but somewhat doubtfully Fagaceae: Quercus ilicifolia, rubra. Salicaceae are preferred everywhere.

Eggs (similar to 148 in Fig. 45) pale green or pale yellow, turning grayish
later, laid singly, preferably on the upperside of the tips of young host leaves.
Larvae feed (often at night), on catkins in spring, later on leaves. First-stage (Fig.
48) and second-stage Limenitis larvae eat the tips of leaves, except the midrib on
which they rest, and they silk together a ball of leaf bits and dung that hangs
near the feeding area; the ball blows in the wind, and S. Scudder suggested that
it diverts predators' attention from the larva. Larval nests only during hibernation (see below). The mature larva resembles a bird dropping. Ssp. archippus
larva brownish-yellow or olive-green (the thorax tan), with a pinkish-white or
creamy ragged-edged saddlelike patch in the middle of the abdomen, a lateral
line of cream blotches on the abdomen, and five pairs of small dorsal spines;
thorax enlarged, with two plumelike black horns on top, the horns shorter than
those of other Limenitis; head reddish-brown, with two small toothed bumplike
"horns" and two smaller horns behind them. Scudder and A. Clark noted that
the larva is greenish on willow but brownish on poplar, but A. Platt found that
the difference in color is probably genetic, because most larvae are brownish,
and a few green, on both plants. Ssp. obsoleta larva similar, but yellowish-brown,
brown at the rear (the thorax blotched with grayish-white), with the usual whitish saddle and lateral line of whitish spots on the abdomen. Ssp. floridensis larva
more reddish, the ground color olive-green, the thorax pale red-brown, the
saddle either reddish-brown or pinkish-white, the lateral abdominal band greenish-white, the thorax horns longer; head pale red. The unusual-looking pupa of
ssp. archippus (Fig. 52) resembles a finless dolphin with a western saddle, mottled with blackish-green, tan, pinkish, and gray, palest on the abdomen, the
saddle horn angled more toward the head than in other Limenitis. Ssp. obsoleta
pupa brownish, the middle of the abdomen whitish. Ssp. floridensis pupa brown,
with silver marks on the head and above the wings, the wing cases, saddle horn,
and end of the abdomen dark brown, the base of the saddle horn black, the
abdomen yellowish with green mottling. The third-stage larva hibernates in a
rolled leaf (hibernaculum); the larva eats the tip of the leaf except the midrib,
silks the remainder into a tube, silks the leaf petiole to the twig, and then enters
it in such a way that the head is next to the petiole. Platt, S. Clark, and J. Hong
found that short photoperiod acting on the second- and early third-stage larva
causes diapause.

One flight, probably June-July, in the far north; two flights, mostly June
and Aug., in N U.S. and Ottawa; four or more flights from spring to fall in the
south. Adults sip flower nectar, aphid honeydew, moisture from rotting wood,
fungi, dung, mud, sap, etc. Males perch 1-2 m above ground on vegetation and
patrol all day near the hosts to seek females.

146. Limenitis arthemis   White Admiral (northern ssp.), Red-Spotted
Purple (southern ssp.)
Ssp. **arthemis** (E Canada and NE U.S.) and ssp. **rubrofasciata** (W Man. to

Color Plates 8, 16, 17, 22

Alaska, the unh redder) have black and white bands and are not mimics. The fw tip is black (unlike that of *L. lorquini*), and the unh base lacks white (unlike that of *L. weidemeyerii*). Ssp. **astyanax** (E U.S.) and ssp. **arizonensis** (w Tex.-Ariz., the uph submarginal spots white) are bluish without white bands, and are Batesian mimics of the poisonous *Battus philenor* (25). W. Nakahara, A. Platt, L. Brower, and others proved without doubt that ssp. *arthemis* and *astyanax* are the same species. Hybrids between them are healthy and fertile. They found that the white band is due to a recessive gene, but the blue hw (vs. black) and the red uph spots (vs. none) are due to several genes. There are no structural differences between the ssp., and they intergrade in a band about 40°-46° latitude from Minn. to Penn. and Maine (the white lines on the map bound the intergradation zone), where all combinations of traits occur. Southward, all adults have a blue uph, without red spots or a white band; northward, the white band is always present, but the bluish uph and the red uph spots remain variable. J. Maudsley found adults with white bands as far south as the Great Smoky Mts.; one adult resembling *astyanax* has been caught in Que.

Habitat Lower Austral (Upper Sonoran westward) to Hudsonian Zone deciduous wooded areas. Hostplants (n, ssp. *arthemis* and *rubrofasciata*; s, *astyanax* and *arizonensis*) tree Salicaceae: *Salix*[ns], *Populus balsamifera*[n(st)], *alba*[s], *tremuloides*[sn], *deltoides*[ns], *grandidentata*[ns], *heterophylla*[st], *nigra* var. *italica*[st]; Betulaceae: *Betula lenta*[n], *lutea*[n], *Alnus rugosa*[n], *Carpinus caroliniana*[ns], *?Ostrya virginiana*[s]; Rosaceae: *Prunus pennsylvanica*[nt], *serotina*[ns], *virginiana*[ns], *cerasus*[s], *domestica*[s], *Malus pumila*[ns], *Pyrus communis*[s(nt)], *Crataegus*[ns], *Amelanchier*[n], *Cydonia oblonga*[s], *?Rosa*[s]; Fagaceae: *Fagus grandifolia*[n], *Quercus phellos*[s], *ilicifolia*[s], *palustris*[s], *velutina*[n]; Ulmaceae: *Ulmus americana*[n], *Celtis?*[s]; Tiliaceae: *Tilia americana*[ns]; questionable are Grossulariaceae: *Ribes*[s] *lacustre*[st], *sativum*[st].

Eggs grayish-green, laid singly on the upperside of host leaf tips, preferably of young plants. Larvae eat leaves; no nests. Larva brown (sometimes green around the saddle), or green, or even whitish-green; all with a white to reddish-cream saddle, a whitish to pink lateral line on the abdomen, and white patches on the thorax; head brownish-red, with two small toothed horns. In ssp. *arthemis* larva, the long blackish thoracic horns are clubbed (with short thicker warts), whereas in ssp. *astyanax* the horns are not clubbed (and have slender warts) and the body tends to have more warts. Pupa like that of *L. archippus*, but the saddle horn less angled. Pupa (ssp. *arthemis*) whitish-gray, yellowish-white on top of the abdomen, with various darker streaks and silver marks above the wings, the saddle horn and the end of the abdomen brown, the wings margined with greenish-brown, the bump at the base of the wing appearing as a backward-directed point. Pupa (ssp. *astyanax*) similar in shape, yellow-brown and pinkish, mottled with dark green and dark gray. Third-stage larvae hibernate in a hibernaculum.

One flight in the north, M July-M Aug. in Lab., M June-M Aug. in s Sask.; one flight, M June-M July and a partial second flight in Aug., at Ottawa; two flights, June-Sep., in N.Y.; many flights in the south (Mar.-Nov. in Fla., Apr.-Nov. in Ariz.). Adults feed on sap, fruit, flower nectar, carrion, dung, honeydew, decaying wood, etc. Ssp. *astyanax* males perch on trees and tall bushes, and rarely patrol, to await females. Ssp. *arizonensis* males patrol all day near the hosts (rarely on hilltops) to seek females.

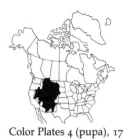

Color Plates 4 (pupa), 17

147. Limenitis weidemeyerii   Western Admiral

Like *L. arthemis rubrofasciata* (whose range is mostly separate), but the unh ground color is mostly white instead of red, and on the unh the inner row of blue marginal crescents is thicker than the outer row. The white median bands are wider in the Great Basin. From Mono Co., Calif., to N and C Nev. and w Mont., adults with the fw tip slightly orange and with a red line between the rows of blue unh marginal crescents (form **fridayi**) may be recent hybrids with *L. lorquini*, but most are probably due to introgression (transfer of genes owing to past hybridization) because *lorquini* is rare or absent there (except Mont.). *L. lorquini* and *weidemeyerii* are closely related and may be ssp., although their male valvae differ slightly. They hybridize in E Ida. and w Mont. also.

Habitat Upper Sonoran to Canadian Zone wooded mountain canyons, streamsides, and suburbs. Hostplants tree and shrub Salicaceae: *Salix subcoerulea, exigua, Populus tremuloides, angustifolia*; Rosaceae: *Prunus virginiana, Amelanchier alnifolia, utahensis, Holodiscus boursieri, microphyllus, discolor, dumosus*.

Eggs (similar to 148 in Fig. 45) grayish-green, laid singly on the upperside of host leaf tips, often on young plants. Larvae eat leaves. Larva olive-green, the thorax mostly yellowish-tan; *or* larva grayish, mottled with gray and white patches; shape like that of other *Limenitis*; abdomen with a whitish or yellowish-tan saddle on the middle and a whitish lateral band; head red-brown, with small tubercles on top. Pupa blackish-brown (including the end of the abdomen and the saddle horn), with a black streak extending obliquely back from the saddle horn, the basal two-thirds of the wings whitish, the top of the head and thorax tan, the abdomen whitish with a pink tint and some tan and slight greenish mottling on top, the saddle horn slightly more circular in outline than in *L. archippus*. Third-stage (rarely fourth?) larvae hibernate in a hibernaculum.

One flight, mainly June-July, in the Canadian Zone; two flights, June-Aug., at lower altitude and southward. Adults feed on tree sap, flower nectar, carrion, mud, etc. Males perch on shrubs and trees all day to await females, and rarely patrol, preferably in gulches.

Color Plate 17
Figs. 45, 51

148. Limenitis lorquini   Orange-Tip Admiral

Resembles *L. weidemeyerii*; identified by the orange fw tip and by the diffuse red line between the marginal rows of blue unh crescents (this line is black in *weidemeyerii*). The unh has much white, as in *weidemeyerii*, but in a population at Tweedsmuir Park, B.C., the unh is redder, probably from hybridizing with *L. arthemis* (*lorquini* hybridizes sometimes with *arthemis* in NW Mont. as well as sw B.C.). By hybridizing *lorquini* with *L. arthemis arthemis* in the lab, A. Platt found that the reddish fw tip is genetically dominant to the black tip of *arthemis*, the creamy median bands of *lorquini* (and of *L. bredowii* and some *L. arthemis rubrofasciata*) are dominant to the white *arthemis* bands (these creamy bands absorb ultraviolet; compare *L. bredowii* and *L. fessonia* in Fig. 35), and the whitish unh base of *lorquini* is dominant to the reddish unh base of *arthemis*.

Habitat mainly Upper Sonoran to Canadian Zone mountain canyons and deciduous woods. Hostplants tree and shrub Salicaceae: *Salix lasiandra, lutea, lasiolepis, Populus tremuloides, trichocarpa*; Rosaceae: *Prunus domestica* (and var. *galatensis*), *virginiana* (and var. *demissa*), *emarginata, Cotoneaster, Holodiscus discolor, Spiraea douglasii, Malus pumila*; Rhamnaceae: *Ceanothus*; Fagaceae: ?*Quercus*.

Eggs (Fig. 45) silvery pale green, laid singly on dorsal leaf tips of the host, often on young plants. Larvae eat leaves; no nests. Larva and pupa shaped like those of other *Limenitis*. Larva (Fig. 51) olive-brown, with pale-pinkish mottling on the thorax, a pale-olive-yellow hump on abdomen segment 2, a whitish saddle on the middle of the abdomen, a white lateral line on the abdomen, some bluish dorsal bumps, and two blackish-brown plumelike horns on the thorax; head dull olive-brown, with two tiny horns. Pupa light gray, mottled with dull purplish on the thorax, with dark-olive-gray wing cases, a blackish saddle horn, and a black bar angling back from the saddle horn, the end of the abdomen black. Half-grown larvae hibernate, in the rolled-leaf hibernaculum usual for the genus.

Several flights, Apr.-Oct., in Calif.; perhaps just one flight, June-M Aug., in Wash. and Mont. Males perch all day on shrubs and trees in valley bottoms to await females, and sometimes patrol.

149. Limenitis bredowii   Sister

Color Plate 17
Figs. 35 (ultraviolet), 51, 52

Identified by the orange fw apical spot and by the broken white fw band. Ssp. **bredowii** (Nev.-Tex.-Mex.) has one orange unh cell bar and two wavy blue unh submarginal lines; ssp. **californica** (Calif.-Ore.) usually has two orange bars and one straighter blue line.

Habitat mostly Upper Sonoran to Transition Zone lower mountains near oaks. Ranges south to Honduras. Hostplants tree Fagaceae: *Quercus chrysolepis, vaccinifolia, agrifolia, douglasii, wizlizenii, kelloggii, gambelii, turbinella, Castanopsis chrysophylla.*

Eggs green, laid singly on the leaf edge at the base of a spine. Larvae eat mature leaves. Young larvae make a long resting perch by extending the vein of a leaf with silk and silking dung pellets to it (J. Harry). Larva (Fig. 51) dark green on top and sides, brown on the abdomen, with a pale lateral line on the abdomen, the middle of the body paler, the collar pale brown; *or* larva yellow-orange, with a brown lateral line bordering the tan lower half; both forms with four to six pairs of yellow dorsal tubercles (those on the thorax longest) and small spines just above the paler lateral band; head tan, with brown vertical bands, yellow-brown (often black-tipped) points, and two black-tipped points on top. Pupa (Fig. 52) straw, with fine brown marks, brown streaks above the wings, the lower wing edges and several dorsal areas shot with gold, the saddle horn a mere ridge, the head with two horns. Larvae hibernate.

Several flights, June-Aug. in Ore., Apr.-Oct. southward; somewhat migratory, straying into Wash., s Colo., and Kans. Adults feed on fruit, mud, aphid honeydew, and sometimes flower nectar. Males perch and patrol all day, usually in gulches, to seek females.

150. Limenitis fessonia   Mexican Sister

Stray only
Color Plate 17
Fig. 35 (ultraviolet)

Resembles *L. bredowii*, but the white fw band runs solidly from front margin to rear. Tropical, a regular stray into s Tex. (all year) from Mex. Ranges south to Costa Rica. Hostplants tree and shrub Ulmaceae: *Celtis lindheimeri* in Tex.; Rubiaceae: *Randia* in El Salvador.

151. Epiphile adrasta   Dimorphic Bark Wing

Stray only
Color Plate 59
Figs. 51, 52

Males and females of this stray differ enormously on the ups, but the uns is always mottled brown like bark.

Habitat tropical forested areas. Ranges to S. Amer. Hostplants vine Sapindaceae: in El Salvador *Paullinia fuscescens*, *Serjania*, *Urvillea*, and *Cardiospermum*, in Mex. *P. tomentosa*, *Serjania racemosa*, and *S. brachycarpa*. Since these plants are used to poison fish in the tropics, the butterflies may be somewhat toxic also.

Eggs white, turning gray before hatching, laid singly under mature leaves. Young larvae rest on a bared leaf vein to which dung pellets have been silked. When disturbed, the larva strikes with its horns, and may puncture another larva. Larva (Fig. 51) green, with a yellow lateral stripe on the thorax, thin yellow longitudinal lines on top, oblique lateral areas of whitish-green, yellow irregular lines and tubercles on each side, subdorsal branching spines (yellowish-orange at the bases with black tips), and two middorsal spines on abdomen segments 7 and 8, the latter longer; head brown, reddish tinted, with thin whitish spines surrounding the head, a light triangular spot on the front, and two very long (1 cm) branched horns like television antennae. Pupa (Fig. 52) dark green, light green on the abdomen beyond the wings, with brown edging on the lateral edges of the wings and between the dark-green and light-green dorsal areas, a pointed brown-tipped middorsal keel on the thorax, a silver oval on the side of the thorax, and silver streaks on the side of the head; pupa dorsally flattened somewhat, with two short bumps on the head. Pupa somewhat resembling dung, attached (by the cremaster) to the top of a leaf or twig, unlike that of other Nymphalidae. Pupae may make creaking sounds by moving the abdomen when disturbed.

Many flights all year in Mex., once straying to s Tex. (Oct.). Adults fly swiftly. They feed on rotten fruit, sap, and dung, but not on flower nectar.

152. Diaethria asteria   Mexican 88 Butterfly

Stray only
Color Plate 59

The ups is violet, with a white upf apical spot; the unh has two figure eights within two black circles. Larva and pupa unknown, probably similar to Mex. species (Figs. 51, 52). Tropical, ranging to s Mex.; a rare stray from Mex. into s Tex. (July).

153. Diaethria clymena   88 Butterfly

Stray only
Color Plate 59

Named for the 88 or 89 unh pattern. The ups is black, with bluish stripes on the margins. Tropical; three records from Fla. (Feb., Mar., July), but these seem to be airplane imports from S. Amer., not natives (absent in the Antilles). Hostplant Ulmaceae: *Trema micrantha* in Brazil. Young larvae make resting perches with dung pellets. Larval and pupal shape and habits of *D. astala* (not in the U.S.; Figs. 51, 52) are like those of *Epiphile* (151; pupa also dorsally flattened), except that the larval spines are very small (the lateral spines on abdomen segment 9 are long); the head horns of the larva and the pupation site are also like those of *Epiphile*.

154. Dynamine dyonis   Blue-Eyed Green Wing

The unh is unique, slightly resembling a pair of fried eggs. Males are green on the ups; females are black and white.

Habitat tropics, south to Honduras. Hostplant herb Euphorbiaceae: *Tragia ramosa*.

Eggs (Fig. 45) silvery-white, laid singly on hostplant leaves and stems. Young larvae eat young leaves; older larvae eat mature leaves. Larvae rest under leaves; no nests. Larva green, with a darker-green middorsal line, a faint white subdorsal stripe, and many branching spines (including middorsal spines on the abdomen), each tipped with a sticky blob (J. Doyle); shape somewhat sluglike; head green, with short white hair, without horns. Pupa (Fig. 52) green, with brown or silver marks on the large middorsal point on the thorax and on a large point on abdomen segment 2, the top of the abdomen with an arrow-shaped mark and short middorsal spines, the head with two short lateral points on the end.

Many flights in Mex.; a stray into s Tex. (June-Nov., rarely common).

Color Plate 16
Figs. 45, 52

155. **Eunica monima**   Dingy Purple Wing

Resembles a small satyr, but males have a faint violet sheen on the ups.

Habitat subtropical wooded areas and hammocks. Ranges south to Venezuela, the Bahamas, and the Greater Antilles. Hostplant tree Rutaceae: *Zanthoxylum pentamon*.

Larva (similar to 161 in Fig. 51) dull orange to reddish-green, with a black or white lateral band, a few black spines on the side of the thorax and near the end of the body, and small black spines scattered elsewhere; head black or pale orange, with long black or yellow branching horns. Pupa green, shaped like pupa of *Myscelia* (157, 158).

Many flights in Mex.; a stray into Tex. (June-Sep., sometimes common), usually rare but native in s Fla. (May-Dec.). Several mass migrations are known. Adults feed on fruit, dung, sap, and mud, seldom flower nectar. Adults often rest on tree trunks, sometimes within thorny trees where they are impossible to catch.

Color Plate 16
Fig. 35 (ultraviolet)

156. **Eunica tatila**   Large Purple Wing

Larger than *E. monima*, the fw more angled, the ups more violet esp. in males, with more white fw spots. Habitat subtropical woodlands and hammocks. Ranges south to Argentina, the Bahamas, and the Greater Antilles. Many flights all year in s Fla. (where it is a resident); migratory in Argentina and Mex., straying from Mex. to s Tex. (Aug.-Sep.) and rarely north to Kans.

Color Plate 16
Fig. 35 (ultraviolet)

157. **Myscelia ethusa**   Blue Wave

Males have two blue upf cell stripes and three blue uph bands; females have one cell stripe, but have four blue uph bands and more white upf spots. Habitat subtropical wooded areas. Ranges to C. Amer. Young larvae make a resting perch by silking dung pellets to a leaf vein from which the leaf has been eaten away. Tropical *Myscelia* (*M. orsis*) larvae (hostplant *Dalechampia*, Euphorbiaceae) have many branching body spines and two very long spined horns on the head, aimed forward at rest (similar to 161 in Fig. 51); pupa flattened dorsally, with two short conelike points on the head. Many flights all year in s Tex. Adults sip mud and rotting fruit. They often rest on tree trunks with wings closed, the dark uns resembling bark.

s Tex. only
Color Plates 16, 22
Fig. 35 (ultraviolet)

Color Plate 59

Color Plate 9

Color Plate 17
Figs. 38 (scent glands),
52

Stray only
Color Plate 59
Figs. 51, 52, 63, 64

158. Myscelia cyananthe (=*skinneri*)   Dark Blue Wave

Blue like *M. ethusa*, but the middle of the fw is black. Many flights in subtropical Mex. (ranges to s Mex.); a rare stray into s Tex. (Oct.) and N.M. Adults feed on rotten fruit and mud.

159. Mestra amymone   Noseburn Wanderer (Texas Bagvein)

The whitish color and unh pattern are unique. Wet-season adults are reportedly darker.

Habitat subtropical open fields and woods edges, straying northward. Ranges south to C. Amer. Hostplants vine Euphorbiaceae: in Costa Rica *Dalechampia scandens*, *Tragia volubilis*, in U.S. undoubtedly *T. neptifolia* (which ranges north to Neb.).

Larva has two long head spines.

Many flights all year in s Tex. (common), migrating northward (sometimes in numbers) as far as Minn.

160. Biblis hyperia   Red Rim

Identified by the black wings and red hw band.

Habitat subtropical open woods. Ranges south to Paraguay and throughout the Antilles (except Jamaica and Cuba). Hostplant vine Euphorbiaceae: *Tragia volubilis*.

Eggs (similar to 170 in Fig. 45) whitish, laid singly or two or three together, on young hostplant shoots. The young larva makes a resting perch with dung pellets; larvae rest with only the prolegs attached. Larva (similar to 161 in Fig. 51) gray-brown (tiny greenish bumps give the body a greenish tinge), with reddish oblique lines extending rearward up to those spines just above the spiracles, a wedge-shaped reddish-yellow spot on abdomen segment 4 (with two bright bands angling down from its rear), and many yellow spines; head black, with two very long kinked and spined horns (a bright band below the tip of the horn). Pupa (Fig. 52) faint green mixed with pink, the wings yellow with reddish veins, a dark spot on the upper wing edge, and another at the wingtip; *or* pupa mostly brown-black mixed with pink; both forms with the abdomen light beneath and with a bright spot on the hw, many dorsal bumps on the abdomen, a wide lateral flange on the margin of the fw and another smaller flange at the wing base, and two small conelike head horns.

Many flights all year in s Tex. (sometimes common); a rare stray into c Tex. Adults fly slowly. They feed on fruit.

161. Hamadryas februa   Gray Cracker

Like *H. glauconome* (162) in that the white unh has submarginal eyespots, each consisting of a brown ring containing a black crescent (some crescents are part of a faint black circle), and the uph eyespots generally have orange scales before the black crescent (all other *Hamadryas* species but these two lack orange eyespot scales). Differs from *glauconome* in having at least some red in a bar in the fw discal cell; the male upf is not greatly whitened in the outer part, and the unf has a black submarginal patch in cell CuA$_1$, never a black ring.

Habitat open subtropical woods or cultivated areas with trees. Ranges south to Argentina. Hostplants in Latin Amer. vine and herb Euphorbiaceae: *Dale-champia scandens, heteromorpha, triphylla, pruriens, tiliafolia, Tragia volubilis*.

Eggs dull white, turning dirty-brown two days before hatching, laid singly (or two or three on top of each other) under mature leaves or sepals. The very young larva makes a resting perch of dung pellets, as in some *Limenitis, Anaea*, and other Nymphalidae. Larva (Fig. 51) solitary, black (the sides more white), with green spines, six yellow longitudinal lines on each half of the body (next to the spines), transverse bands of black dashes between segments, orange spots on either side of the abdominal middorsal spines (and often orange around the base of the subdorsal spines); *or* larva more orange or tan, with black lateral

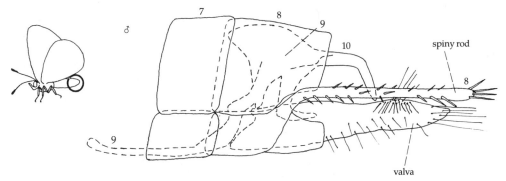

Fig. 63.   The sound-producing organs of *Hamadryas februa* (161; other *Hamadryas* are similar). The cracking sound of males no doubt is made by twanging the two immovable spiny rods on the tip of the male abdomen with the two spiny valvae just below them.

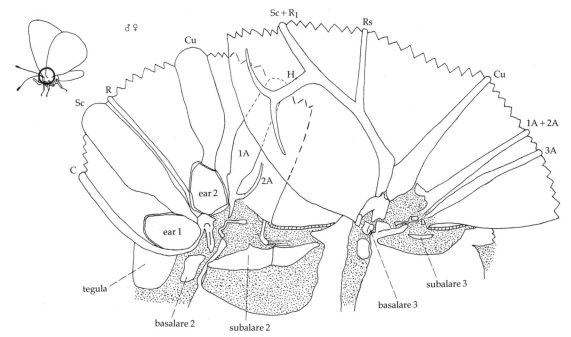

Fig. 64.   The hearing organs of *Hamadryas februa* (161; other *Hamadryas* are similar). The fore-wing underside of both sexes has two ears, white translucent membranes connected to nerves; S. Swihart proved the membranes can detect sound but cannot produce it.

bands; *or* larva more tan, with the back green, the many spines (including the middorsal spines on abdomen segments 1-8) mostly yellow but some longer and black; head red, turning black, with very long clubbed horns. Pupa (Fig. 52) light brown to reddish-brown; *or* pupa green with a mixture of yellow spots and slightly darker subddorsal and lateral bands; all forms with a black midventral line, a pair of white ventral dots on the wings, and two long projections on the head that are joined in their centers but flare apart at the tip.

Many flights all year in Mex.; a rare stray into s Tex. (Aug.-Oct.). Adults feed on rotting fruit, sap, and mud, but not on flowers. *Hamadryas* adults land upside down with the barklike wings flattened against tree trunks for camouflage. To await females, males perch on trees and dart out at passing butterflies, insects, even people, often making a "cracking" sound with the abdomen. Males of all *Hamadryas* species—except perhaps *H. atlantis* (163) and *H. iphthime* (166), which are poorly studied—share this behavior, which males evidently use to discriminate males from females (males may pursue only non-cracking adults), and which accounts for their common name. *Hamadryas* males have two long lateral spiny rods extending backward from abdomen segment 8 (Fig. 63), which probably produce the cracking sound when the valvae twang the rods (using a spiny dorsal part of the valva; the spiny parts and rods are longer in species that often crack). The sounds are produced only in flight, for unknown reasons. Both sexes have two tympana on the unf base (Fig. 64), which S. Swihart proved detect sound but cannot produce it. Adults do not always perch on the same trees, so they are not strictly territorial (G. Ross).

162. Hamadryas glauconome (=*ferox*, =*amphichloe*)   Pale Cracker

Stray only
Color Plate 56

Like *H. februa* (161) in that the white unh has submarginal eyespots consisting of a brown ring containing a black crescent (some crescents are part of a faint black circle), and the uph eyespots generally have orange scales before the black crescent (these are the only two *Hamadryas* spp. having orange eyespot scales). Differs from *februa* in having no reddish bar in the fw discal cell, the outer half or third of the upf usually whitish in males, and often a black submarginal ring in unf cell CuA_1 (always a ring in ssp. *glauconome* of E Mex., which may eventually be found in s Tex., and in ssp. *grisea* of NW Mex.; a black patch or a small ring in the Greater Antilles and rarely Fla. ssp. **diasia**). The only U.S. species that have this ring are some *glauconome* and all *H. feronia* (164) and *H. guatemalena* (165). Other ssp. range south to Peru. Habitat tropical moist or semidesert open areas with trees. Hostplant vine Euphorbiaceae: *Dalechampia scandens* in Guatemala. Many flights all year in Latin Amer.; a rare stray into s Fla. (July). Adults feed on fruit, carrion, and mud, but not on flowers. Males make a cracking noise in flight.

163. Hamadryas atlantis   Dusky Cracker

Color Plate 59

Easily identified by the five black lines in the unf discal cell; the outer half of the unf is black in males (but not in females, which have a white subapical band), and the ups is dark bluish (often greenish). The fw cell lacks a red bar. The uph submarginal eyespots are like those of *H. iphthime* (166). The unh is white, as in *H. februa* (161), but the eyespots are narrow black circles surrounding a blue-centered black spot. Tropical, in valley bottoms in fairly dry open areas with trees. Ranges south to Honduras. Many flights, at least May-Nov., in Mex.; a rare stray into SE Ariz. (Aug.). Adults feed on rotten fruit and mud, but not on flowers. Thus far, adults have not been heard to make a cracking noise in flight.

164. Hamadryas feronia   Blue Cracker

Stray only
Color Plates 56, 59

The unh is white or tan-white, with black submarginal rings like those of *H. guatemalena* (165) and *H. iphthime* (166). The fw has a red bar in the discal cell, and the unf has a black submarginal ring in cell CuA$_1$, as in *guatemalena*, but not as in *iphthime*. Each uph submarginal eyespot of *H. feronia* has a blue ring, then a black spot containing a white center; the *guatemalena* eyespots are more complex. The white unf subapical spot in cell R$_3$ is usually small or absent in *feronia*, large in *guatemalena*.

Habitat tropical open areas with trees. Ranges south to Paraguay (a rare stray to Hispaniola). Hostplant vine Euphorbiaceae: *Dalechampia triphylla* (and ssp. *stenosepala*) in S. Amer.

Larva black (blue-black above), with brownish-white dots, reddish lateral spots, and some yellow spines; *or* larva dirty-gray-green, with a pale interrupted lateral line; shape like that of *H. februa*; middorsal spines on thorax segments 2 and 3 and on abdomen segments 7 and 8 (some spines on the thorax and rear segments resembling a bottle brush). Pupa has two long head processes.

Many flights all year in Mex., esp. June-Sep.; a rare stray into s Tex. (Aug.-Nov.). Adults feed on rotting fruit, not on flowers. Males perch on tree trunks to await females. Males make a cracking sound in flight.

165. Hamadryas guatemalena   Central American Cracker

Stray only
Color Plate 56

The unh is tan-white with black submarginal rings like those of *H. feronia* (164) and *H. iphthime* (166). The fw has a red bar in the discal cell, and the unf has a black submarginal ring in cell CuA$_1$, as in *feronia*, but not as in *iphthime*. Each uph submarginal eyespot of *H. guatemalena* consists of a blue ring, a wide black ring, a blue ring, then a mottled brown-and-white center; these eyespots are simpler in *feronia*. The white unf subapical spot in cell R$_3$ is large in *guatemalena*, small or absent in *feronia*.

Habitat tropical open areas with trees. Ranges south to Costa Rica. Hostplant vine Euphorbiaceae: *Dalechampia scandens* in C. Amer.

Eggs white, laid singly (or two or three in a stack) under mature leaves. Larvae solitary. Larva black, with a wide yellow patch on top of each segment, two yellow spots above each abdominal spiracle just beside each dorsal patch, and many dull-yellow branching spines (the middorsal abdominal spines only on segments 7 and 8; some subdorsal and both middorsal spines shaped like a bottle brush); head black, with dull-yellow spiny horns. Pupa light green, with a wide dark-green subdorsal band (which edges the wings also), two white bumps on each leg, and two processes on the head shaped like Bighorn Sheep horns.

Many flights all year in Mex.; a rare stray into s Tex. Adults feed on rotten fruit, manure, sap, and very rarely on flowers. Males perch on tree trunks, and make a cracking sound in flight.

166. Hamadryas iphthime   Ringless Blue Cracker

Stray only
Color Plate 56

The unh is white, with black submarginal rings like those of *H. feronia* (164) and *H. guatemalena* (165), but the fw lacks a red bar in the discal cell, and the unf has a black submarginal patch in cell CuA_1 instead of a black ring. Each uph submarginal eyespot consists of a blue ring, a narrow brown ring, a light-blue ring, then a black center containing a white oval or crescent. One stray known from c Tex. (Burnet Co., perhaps mislabeled) of ssp. **joannae** (Tex.-Costa Rica); ssp. *iphthime* (Panama-Paraguay) has a red fw-cell bar.

Habitat openings in tropical forest. Hostplants vine Euphorbiaceae: in Panama *Dalechampia cissifolia*, in Brazil *D. triphylla*, *ficifolia*, *stipulacea*.

Eggs laid singly beneath leaves. Larvae solitary; rest with head horns pointed forward and only the prolegs touching the surface. Larva black (reddish-flecked below the spiracles), with distinct or indistinct yellow lines (one middorsal, one subdorsal, one above the spiracles); spines mostly pale (but dark on abdomen segments 1, 3, 7, and 8), including middorsals on abdomen segments 1-8. Pupa bright green, with a wide white middorsal band behind the mesothorax (divided by a green middorsal line on the abdomen) and with a lateral white band reaching the midventral line near the abdomen tip and then running along the wing margin (where it is silvery) onto the top of the head, the wings yellow-green with darker veins, the head with two long "rabbit ears," each green with a white seam, arranged in a V like those of *H. fornax* (167) and *H. amphinome* (168).

Many flights nearly all year in Mex., esp. July-Aug.; a rare stray into c Tex. (Aug.). Adults feed on rotten fruit.

167. Hamadryas fornax   Yellow Cracker

Stray only
Color Plate 59

Easily identified by the orangish-yellow unh with a few black-capped white submarginal spots and by the red bar in the fw cell. Ssp. **fornacalia** is in the U.S. to Colombia; ssp. *fornax* ranges south to Argentina.

Habitat tropical open areas with trees. Hostplants vine Euphorbiaceae: in El Salvador *Dalechampia scandens*, in Brazil *D. triphylla*, *ficifolia*, *stipulacea*.

Eggs white, laid in strings of five to ten on top of each other under leaves. Larvae gregarious. Larva black (the top yellow), mostly reddish in the area below the spiracles, with many bright spots above the spiracles, and many bottlebrush spines (the middorsal spines only on abdomen segments 7 and 8), each supraspiracular spine with a yellow crescent extending down and forward in front of it, and another down behind it and then up to the subdorsal spine; *or* larva greenish; head black, with two long horns. Pupa blackish-brown, with a white pattern like that of *H. iphthime* (166) including a white middorsal stripe (in the light form the white pattern includes a sublateral abdominal stripe, white wings and legs, and a white spot on the thorax, in the dark form only a narrow lateral white spot on the wing edge), the head with two long "rabbit ear" projections.

Many flights all year in Mex., esp. summer; one stray known from s Tex. (Aug.). Males make a cracking sound in flight.

168. Hamadryas amphinome   Red Cracker

Stray only
Color Plate 59
Fig. 52

Easily identified by the brick-red unh (yellow-orange in NW Mex.), with most eyespots absorbed by the white margin, and by the broad white fw band. The fw cell lacks a red bar. Ssp. **mexicana** ranges from Texas to Colombia and

Cuba; ssp. *mazai* occurs in NW Mex. and may eventually stray to Ariz. Other ssp. range south to Argentina.

Habitat tropical forest clearings. Hostplants vine Euphorbiaceae: in Costa Rica *Dalechampia scandens*, in Brazil *D. triphylla*, *ficifolia*, and *stipulacea*.

Eggs yellowish-white, turning gray when about to hatch, laid in strings of five to ten on top of each other, 30-100 eggs in a cluster, under hostplant leaves. The gregarious young larvae of *H. amphinome* and *H. fornax* (167) do not make resting perches of dung, as the solitary larvae of other *Hamadryas* do. Larva (similar to 161 in Fig. 51) foul-smelling, black, with white OTO-shaped marks on top of each segment in the middle of the body (these segments with orangish spines and sublateral spots), many usually black branching spines (midddorsal abdominal spines only on segments 7 and 8); head black (white between the horns), with two white-clubbed horns. Pupa (Fig. 52) light brown (the thorax and underside green), with paired brown dorsal and ventral lines; *or* pupa brown, darker dorsally; head with two very long "rabbit ear" projections.

Many flights all year in Mex., esp. July-Oct.; a rare stray into s Tex. (June and Sep.). Adults feed on rotten fruit and mud, but not on flowers. Adults may wave their wings up and down while on a tree trunk, like *H. fornax*, and may move in short hops around the tree trunk to avoid a predator.

169. Smyrna karwinskii   Nettle Bark Wing

Stray only
Color Plate 59
Fig. 51

The ups of this stray is orange except for the black fw tip; the uns is mottled with lines and eyespots for camouflage. (Another Mex. species, *Smyrna blomfildia*, may also occur in s Tex. It resembles *S. karwinskii*, but *both* lobes on the hind corner of the unh contain large black spots; only one is spotted in *karwinskii*. Its hosts and habits are the same as those of *karwinskii*, except that adults roost singly and never leave the lowlands. The egg, larva, and pupa are similar to those of *karwinskii*, but the larvae vary in being tan, or greenish-white with black stripes, and in having many middorsal spines; the pupae lack abdominal cones.)

Habitat tropical woodlands. Ranges to C. Amer. Hostplants tree (El Salvador; A. Muyshondt) Urticaceae: *Urticastrum mexicanum*, *Urera caracasana*, *baccifera*.

Eggs light green, laid singly on the underside of leaves. Larvae eat leaves, and rest on the underside; no nests. Larva (Fig. 51) tan, with about nine black sinuous longitudinal lines, many short tan spines (only one middorsal spine, on abdomen segment 8); head black with tan front and two spiny horns. Pupa (similar to 180 in Fig. 52) mottled tan, with dark-brown spots at the base of wing cases, stubby in shape, with six rows of subdorsal and lateral bumps on the abdomen and a tiny keel on top of the thorax.

Many flights all year in the tropics; a rare or doubtful stray from Mex. to near Brownsville, Tex. Adults feed on sap, fruit, and mud. In the dry season, El Salvador adults move to the high mountains, where they roost gregariously, aestivating for a month or more. Males perch head down on tree trunks to await females.

170. Historis odius   Stinky Leaf Wing

Stray only
Color Plate 59
Figs. 45, 52

The uns of this rare stray is very leaflike. (*H. acheronta*, which may also occur in s Tex., resembles *H. odius*, but it has a sharp hw tail and many white subapical upf spots. Its host is also *Cecropia mexicana*, but the larva is black with yellow patches on top of abdomen segments 2, 4, and 6, the head is red with black horns, and the pupal horns are short and far apart.)

Habitat tropical wooded areas. Ranges south to Argentina and the Greater Antilles. Hostplants (Latin Amer.) tree and shrub Moraceae: *Cecropia mexicana, peltata*; reportedly also *Tabebuia* (Bignoniaceae) and *Inga vera* (Leguminosae).

Eggs (Fig. 45) tan, laid singly on top of mature host leaves. Larvae eat leaves, and when young rest on a vein with silked-together dung pellets. Larva (Jamaica) light green, with brown transverse stripes, the dorsal spines black, the other spines white; head whitish, with a black cross and two black horns. Larva (El Salvador; similar to 191 in Fig. 51) white with red spines, or light yellow with yellow spines (both forms with red transverse stripes and a red underside), with middorsal spines on the abdomen; the spines treelike; head dark brown (some larvae have a light cheek spot), with many spines and two short spiny orange horns. Larva (as in *Smyrna*, 169), with a ventral neck gland used for defense. Pupa (Jamaica) pale yellow changing to red-brown, with darker marks, a lateral black band, and some processes (including two on the head). Pupa (El Salvador; Fig. 52) pinkish-brown, with reddish (black-tipped) treelike dorsal spines on the abdomen and red rings around two long head horns, the horns joined into a hook.

Many flights all year in the tropics; a rare stray into s Fla. (June) or an error. Adults feed on fruit, sap, dung, and mud, but rarely on flowers. Adults are powerful and fast fliers, with a muscular thorax, and they rest on tree trunks. Males perch on tree trunks, usually on hilltops, to await females.

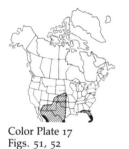

Color Plate 17
Figs. 51, 52

171. **Marpesia petreus**   Red Dagger Wing

The tails are reminiscent of *Papilio*, whereas the red ups resembles most *Anaea* (136-139). Narrow lines cross the wings, and the fw lines are straight.

Habitat subtropical wooded areas. Ranges south to Brazil, Puerto Rico, and the Lesser Antilles. Hostplants tree Moraceae: in Fla. *Ficus populina* var. *brevifolia, aurea, carica*, in Latin Amer. *F. citrifolia, padifolia*. Doubtful is *Anacardium occidentale* (Anacardiaceae).

Eggs pale yellow. Larva (Fig. 51) brick red or purplish or yellowish-white, with black diagonal lateral dashes (edged beneath with white), a dark-orange lateral band, black sublateral spots, and pinkish or yellow saddles between spines; abdomen segments 2, 4, 6, and 8 with a long red spine on top, the spines tipped with black, with black patches below them, the last spine edged with white; head pinkish (or yellowish-white or orange), with two long filaments, these black with white or yellow tips. Pupa (Fig. 52) light green, with a black spot on top of the thorax and black subdorsal spots on the abdomen; *or* pupa shiny gray-white, with black patches on the thorax and upper edges of wing cases, and a black subdorsal band on the abdomen; pupa armed with a long black spine and a few smaller ones on top of the abdomen, a black spine at wing base, and a curved black-and-green spine in front of each eye.

Many flights, all year in s Fla. (native); migratory from Mex. into s Tex. (regularly recorded) and rarely Neb. Adults sip flower nectar and mud. Males perch 5-10 m above ground on sunlit trees to await females.

Using the Color Plates

Each of the 64 pages that follow is a color plate, whether it presents several photos (like this page, Plate 1) or a single full-page photo (like Plate 7). A reference beside the text for each species in Part III lists the color plate or plates illustrating that species. In the plates, the numbers beside the butterflies and in the legends are the numbers assigned to species in Part III; they are not page numbers. The species are listed in numerical order in the legends, but not on the plates. Many species are illustrated more than once on the same plate; such multiple illustrations are distinguished by the letters ("a," "b," etc.) that appear beside the number of the species. A few Mexican species not yet known from the U.S. that resemble numbered U.S. species are shown on Plates 59, 61, 62, and 63 with the number of the species they resemble in brackets.

To simplify identification, the butterflies are arranged on the full-page plates by overall appearance, not by text order or genetic relationship: white butterflies are shown together in one group, small green butterflies are in another group, and so on. Thus, taxonomically unrelated mimics and their models (the Viceroy and the Monarch, for instance, species 145 and 89) are placed together on the same plate rather than with their genetic relatives; males and females of a single species that differ greatly in appearance are shown on different plates (for example, those of *Speyeria diana*, species 251); and if the subspecies or forms of a species look notably different (for example, the variants of *Limenitis arthemis*, species 146), they too appear on different plates, along with the species they most resemble.

All the butterflies on the full-page plates are shown from the underside (except those labeled "ups," upperside), because most butterflies are easier to identify from the underside. A place name in the legend for any butterfly simply identifies where the butterfly shown was photographed or collected; to determine the range of the butterfly, turn to the map for that species in Part III.

Plates 1 through 5 illustrate eggs, larvae, and pupae; Plates 6 through 57, 60, and 64 illustrate butterflies native to the continental United States and Canada; Plates 58, 59, and 61 through 63 show strays from Latin America; Plate 63 also includes Hawaiian species that do not occur in North America.

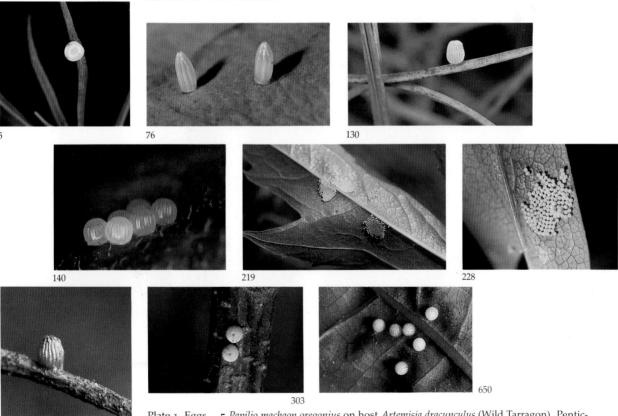

Plate 1. Eggs. **5** *Papilio machaon oregonius* on host *Artemisia dracunculus* (Wild Tarragon), Penticton, B.C. (J. Troubridge). **76** *Pieris rapae* (Cabbage Butterfly), normally solitary in nature, Marion, Ind. (R. Humbert). **130** *Oeneis bore taygete* on dead grass, Churchill, Man. (J. Troubridge). **140** *Asterocampa celtis celtis*, Brandywine Creek, Del. (E. Woodbury). **219** *Chlosyne nycteis drusius* on host *Rudbeckia laciniata* (Tall Cone-Flower), four females have laid four egg masses, Jefferson Co., Colo. **228** *Phyciodes tharos* (Pearl Crescent), eggs laid by a single female on host *Aster*, Elbert Co., Colo. **240** *Boloria titania boisduvalii* on twig, Marathon, Ont. (J. Troubridge). **303** *Harkenclenus titus titus* on twig, normally solitary in nature, Caledonia, Ont. (J. Troubridge). **650** *Erynnis juvenalis juvenalis*, normally solitary in nature, St. Williams, Ont. (J. Troubridge).

Plate 2. Mature larvae.   **5** *Papilio machaon brucei* on host *Artemisia dracunculus* (Wild Tarragon), Red Deer R., Alta. (J. Troubridge).   **7** *Papilio polyxenes asterias* on host *Daucus carota* (Carrot), Faulkland, Del. (E. Woodbury).   **9** *Papilio indra indra* on host *Harbouria trachypleura* (Whisk-Broom Parsley), Jefferson Co., Colo.   **18** *Papilio glaucus glaucus* (Tiger Swallowtail) in curled-leaf nest, Newcastle Co., Del. (E. Woodbury).   **22** *Papilio troilus troilus*, a green larva that turned yellow before pupating, Faulkland, Del. (E. Woodbury).   **28** *Parnassius phoebus hermodur*, normally solitary, on host *Sedum rosea* ssp. *integrifolium* (King's Crown), Mt. Evans, Colo.   **73** *Euchloe ausonia ausonides* on pods of host *Arabis glabra* (Tower Mustard), Red Rocks, Colo.   **77** *Pieris napi oleracea*, Howdenvale, Ont. (J. Troubridge).   **130** *Oeneis bore taygete* (fourth stage) on sedge, Churchill, Man. (J. Troubridge).   **142** *Asterocampa clyton* on host *Celtis* (hackberry), Eastern Neck I., Md. (E. Woodbury).   **180** *Precis coenia* (Buckeye) on host *Antirrhinum majus* (Snapdragon), Little Creek, Del. (E. Woodbury).   **184** *Vanessa atalanta* (Red Admiral) wandering to pupate, Jefferson Co., Colo.   **187** *Vanessa virginiensis* on host *Gnaphalium* (cudweed), N.J. (E. Woodbury).   **191** *Polygonia satyrus* (fourth stage) on host *Urtica dioica* ssp. *gracilis* (Nettle), Jefferson Co., Colo.   **192** *Polygonia gracilis zephyrus* on host *Ribes cereum* (Wax Currant), Tinytown, Colo.

Plate 3. Mature larvae.   **193** *Polygonia progne nigrozephyrus* on host *Ribes inerme* (Gooseberry), showing how prolegs grasp small stems, Cedaredge, Colo.   **196** *Nymphalis californica* on host *Ceanothus fendleri* (Buckbrush), Jefferson Co., Colo.   **198** *Nymphalis antiopa* (Mourning Cloak) on host *Salix* (willow), Snow Hill, Md. (E. Woodbury).   **218** *Chlosyne gorgone*: **a**, form *bicolor* on host *Helianthus annuus* (Sunflower); **b**, form *rufa* on host *H. annuus*; both at Vineland, Colo.   **219** *Chlosyne nycteis drusius* (third stage) on underside of host *Rudbeckia laciniata* (Tall Cone-Flower) leaf, Golden Gate Canyon, Colo.   **224** *Phyciodes orseis orseis*, Siskiyou Co., Calif. **231** *Phyciodes picta*, Arapahoe Co., Colo.   **239** *Boloria selene myrina* on host *Viola nephrophylla* (Blue Violet), Elbert Co., Colo.   **254** *Speyeria nokomis nokomis*, normally solitary, on host *Viola nephrophylla* (Blue Violet), Chuska Mts., N.M.   **260** *Speyeria atlantis atlantis* (last stage and third stage), normally solitary, on host *Viola canadensis* (Violet), Tinytown, Colo.   **265** *Euptoieta claudia* (Variegated Fritillary) on host *Linum australe* (Flax), Arroyo del Agua, N.M.   **268** *Dione vanillae* (Gulf Fritillary) on host *Passiflora* (passion vine), Dade Co., Fla. (E. Woodbury).   **295** *Feniseca tarquinius* (Harvester) on twig beside carcasses of aphids it has eaten, St. Williams, Ont. (J. Troubridge).   **303** *Harkenclenus titus titus*, State College, Pa. (E. Woodbury).   **329** *Callophrys niphon clarki* on host pine needles, St. Williams, Ont. (J. Troubridge).   **334** *Callophrys augustus augustus*, Pinery, Ont. (J. Troubridge).

193

196

219

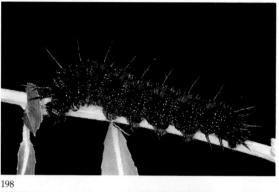

198

218a

218b

224

231

239

254

260

303

265

268

295

329

334

Plate 4. Mature larvae and pupae. Larvae: **335** *Callophrys mossii doudoroffi* on flower buds of host *Dudleya cymosa* (Live-Forever), El Dorado Co., Calif. **343** *Callophrys affinis homoperplexa*, Golden Gate Canyon, Colo. **345** *Callophrys sheridanii paradoxa* eating leaf of host *Eriogonum corymbosum* (Wild Buckwheat), Mesa Co., Colo. (J. Emmel). **372** *Lycaena cupreus snowi* on leaf of host *Oxyria digyna* (Alpine Sorrel), Loveland Pass, Colo. **378** *Lycaena epixanthe phaedra*, Ont. (J. Troubridge). **395** *Glaucopsyche lygdamus couperi*, Britt, Ont.(J. Troubridge). **407** *Plebejus saepiolus amica*, Ont. (J. Troubridge). **424** *Agathymus alliae alliae* removed from its leaf burrow in *Agave utahensis* (Century Plant), Grand Canyon, Ariz. **511** *Poanes zabulon taxiles* removed from silked-leaf nest, Jefferson Co., Colo. **647** *Erynnis brizo brizo* on host *Quercus* (oak), the leaf nest broken open, St. Williams, Ont. (J. Troubridge).

Pupae: **1** *Eurytides marcellus* (Zebra Swallowtail) on bark (J. Troubridge). **7** *Papilio polyxenes asterias*, Newcastle Co., Del. (E. Woodbury). **18** *Papilio glaucus glaucus* (Tiger Swallowtail), Faulkland, Del. (E. Woodbury). **28** *Parnassius phoebus hermodur* and one cast larval skin (normally underground or under rocks), Mt. Evans, Colo. **73** *Euchloe ausonia ausonides*, with silk girdle, Sandilands, Man. (J. Troubridge). **96** *Lethe eurydice*, camouflaged pupa and cast skin and head, Ont. (J. Troubridge). **142** *Asterocampa clyton* on host *Celtis* (hackberry); normally rests flat on the silk mat on leaf underside, rather than off to the side as here; Eastern Neck, Md. (E. Woodbury). **147** *Limenitis weidemeyerii* on twig of host *Salix exigua* (Sandbar Willow), Cherry Creek, Colo. (R. Stanford).

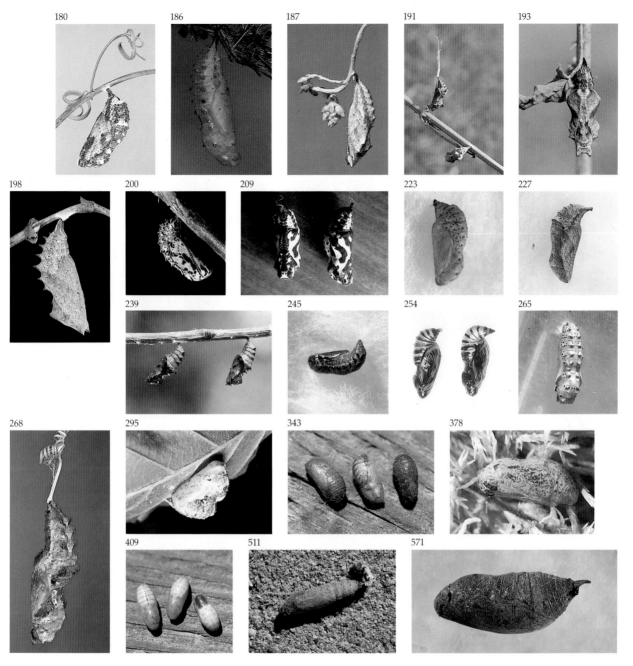

Plate 5. Pupae. **180** *Precis coenia* (Buckeye), Little Creek, Del. (E. Woodbury). **186** *Vanessa cardui* (Painted Lady), Faulkland, Del. (E. Woodbury). **187** *Vanessa virginiensis*, Faulkland, Del. (E. Woodbury). **191** *Polygonia satyrus*, Mt. Vernon Historic Site, Colo. **193** *Polygonia progne nigrozephyrus* on host *Ribes inerme* (Gooseberry), Cedaredge, Colo. **198** *Nymphalis antiopa* (Mourning Cloak), Snow Hill, Md. (E. Woodbury). **200** *Euphydryas chalcedona chalcedona*, Jasper Ridge, Calif. (R. Humbert). **209** *Chlosyne leanira alma*, Uravan, Colo. **223** *Chlosyne gabbii damoetas*, Loveland Pass, Colo. **227** *Phyciodes morpheus*, Golden Gate Canyon, Colo. **239** *Boloria selene myrina* (normally solitary), Elbert Co., Colo. **245** *Boloria improba acrocnema* (normally horizontal among leaves, etc., silked together), San Juan Mts., Colo. **254** *Speyeria nokomis nokomis*, Chuska Mts., N.M. **265** *Euptoieta claudia* (Variegated Fritillary), Arroyo del Agua, N.M. **268** *Dione vanillae* (Gulf Fritillary), Dade Co., Fla. (E. Woodbury). **295** *Feniseca tarquinius* (Harvester), attached by cremaster and silk girdle to underside of leaf, Ont. (J. Troubridge). **343** *Callophrys affinis homoperplexa*, Golden Gate Canyon, Colo. **378** *Lycaena epixanthe phaedra*, Ont. (J. Troubridge). **409** *Plebejus shasta pitkinensis* (normally solitary beneath rocks, attached by cremaster and silk girdle; the darker pupa at right is about to hatch), Uncompahgre Peak, Colo. **511** *Poanes zabulon taxiles*, with cast skin; removed from silked-leaf nest, Jefferson Co., Colo. **571** *Epargyreus clarus* (Silver-Spotted Skipper), removed from leaf nest, Lakewood, Colo.

7♀

18♂

11♂

Plate 6. **7** *Papilio polyxenes kahli* form *comstocki* (*P. machaon hudsonianus* form *comstocki*, species 5, is very similar; see text), Riding Mt., Man. (J. Troubridge). **11** *Papilio cresphontes* (Giant Swallowtail) on *Cornus florida* (Flowering Dogwood), Del. (E. Woodbury). **18** *Papilio glaucus glaucus* (Tiger Swallowtail), Berkeley Heights, N.J. (E. Woodbury).

Plate 7 (× 0.7). **1** *Eurytides marcellus* (Zebra Swallowtail). **5** *Papilio machaon:* **a**, ssp. *aliaska;* **b, c,** ssp. *brucei,* Chaffee Co., Colo.; **d**, ssp. *bairdii* form *hollandii;* **e**, ssp. *bairdii.* **6** *Papilio zelicaon:* **a, b,** typical form; **c**, form *nitra.* **7** *Papilio polyxenes:* **a, b,** ssp. *coloro;* **c**, ssp. *asterias.* **8** *Papilio brevicauda brevicauda,* Anticosti I., Que. **9** *Papilio indra:* **a**, ssp. *indra;* **b**, ssp. *fordi,* Granite Mts., San Bernardino Co., Calif. **18** *Papilio glaucus* (Tiger Swallowtail): **a**, ssp. *glaucus;* **b**, ssp. *rutulus.* **19** *Papilio eurymedon.* **20** *Papilio multicaudata.* **22** *Papilio troilus troilus.* **25** *Battus philenor* (Pipevine Swallowtail).

Plate 8 (× 0.7). **7** *Papilio polyxenes asterias.* **9** *Papilio indra kaibabensis.* **11** *Papilio cresphontes* (Giant Swallowtail). **12 a, b,** *Papilio thoas autocles.* **13** *Papilio aristodemus.* **14 a, b,** *Papilio ornythion.* **15 a, b,** *Papilio astyalus.* **16** *Papilio androgeus.* **17** *Papilio anchisiades.* **18** *Papilio glaucus glaucus* form *nigra* (black form of Tiger Swallowtail). **22** *Papilio troilus troilus.* **23** *Papilio palamedes.* **25** *Battus philenor* (Pipevine Swallowtail). **26** *Battus polydamas.* **146** *Limenitis arthemis astyanax* (Red-Spotted Purple). **251** *Speyeria diana.* **254** *Speyeria nokomis coerulescens.*

Plate 9 (× 0.9). **10** *Papilio andraemon.* **16** *Papilio androgeus.* **28** *Parnassius phoebus:* **a**, ssp. *smintheus,* Kananaskis, Alta.; **b**, ssp. *smintheus,* Moffat Co., Colo.; **c**, ssp. *pseudorotgeri.* **29 a, b,** *Parnassius clodius clodius.* **30** *Parnassius eversmanni.* **75** *Euchloe olympia.* **76 a, b,** *Pieris rapae* (Cabbage Butterfly). **77** *Pieris napi:* **a**, ssp. *hulda,* Aklavik, N.W. Terr.; **b**, ssp. *hulda,* Route 9, Yukon; **c**, ssp. *oleracea* form *napaeae,* Teton Co., Wyo.; **d**, ssp. *oleracea,* San Juan Co., Colo.; **e**, ssp. *oleracea,* Gunnison Co., Colo.; **f**, ssp. *venosa,* Marin Co., Calif. **78** *Pieris virginiensis.* **79** *Pieris chloridice beckerii.* **80** *Pieris protodice:* **a**, form *vernalis;* **b, c,** typical form. **81** *Pieris callidice occidentalis:* **a, b,** typical form; **c**, form *vernalis.* **82** *Pieris sisymbrii.* **83** *Ascia monuste monuste.* **85 a, b,** *Appias drusilla.* **86** *Neophasia menapia:* **a**, ssp. *melanica;* **b**, ssp. *menapia.* **87** *Neophasia terlootii.* **159** *Mestra amymone.* **179** *Anartia jatrophae.*

1♂

19♂

18a ♂

18b ♂

20♂

7a ♀

6a ♀

5b ♂

5a ♂

7b ♂

6b ♂

5c ♀ ups

5e ♂ ups

9a ♂

7c ♂

5d ♂

9b ♀

8♂

6c ♂

22♂

25♂

Color Plate 7

23♂

18♀

15a ♀

26♂

25♂ ups

22♂ ups

146♂ ups

7♀ ups

9♂ ups

17♂

254♀ ups

251♀ ups

16♀ ups

14a ♀

12a ♂ ups

11♂ ups

15b ♂ ups

12b ♂

14b ♂ ups

13♂

Color Plate 8

10♂

16♂ ups

179♂ ups

159♂ ups

30♀

28a ♂

28b ♀

28c ♀

29a ♀

29b ♂

86a ♂

87 ♂

86b ♀

77a ♂

77b ♀ ups

76a ♂

77c ♂

77d ♂ ups

77f ♂ ups

78♂

77e ♂

82♂

81a ♀

81b ♂

80a ♂

80b ♀

76b ♀

79♂

81c ♂

85a ♀ ups

85b ♀ ups

83♂ ups

75♂

80c ♂

Color Plate 9

38♀

80♀

66♀

Plate 10. **38** *Colias philodice* (Common Sulfur) caught by ambush bug on flower of *Liatris punctata* (Blazing Star), Green Mt., Colo. **66** *Kricogonia lyside*, Santa Ana Refuge, Rio Grande Valley, Tex. (E. Woodbury). **80** *Pieris protodice* on *Tagetes* (marigold), Denver, Colo. (R. Stanford). **102** *Megisto cymela*, Nottingham Co. Park, Pa. (E. Woodbury).

102

Plate 11 (× 0.9). **30** *Parnassius eversmanni*. **32** *Colias nastes*: **a**, ssp. *nastes*, Snow Creek Pass, Alta.; **b**, ssp. *moina*; **c**, ssp. *thula*. **39 a, b**, *Colias interior*. **40 a-c** *Colias palaeno chippewa*. **41** *Colias pelidne*: **a**, ssp. *pelidne*; **b-d**, ssp. *minisni*. **42** *Colias scudderi*: **a, b**, ssp. *scudderi*, Colo.; **c**, ssp. *gigantea*, Wyo.; **d**, ssp. *gigantea*, Man. **43** *Colias behrii*. **46 a, b**, *Anteos clorinde*. **66** *Kricogonia lyside*: **a**, typical form; **b**, form *terissa*. **67** *Nathalis iole*: **a, b**, typical form; **c**, form *viridis*. **68** *Anthocharis sara*: **a**, ssp. *sara*, Saguache Co., Colo.; **b**, ssp. *stella*, Benton Co., Ore.; **c**, ssp. *stella*, El Dorado Co., Calif. **69** *Anthocharis cethura*: **a**, ssp. *pima*; **b, c**, ssp. *cethura*. **70** *Anthocharis lanceolata*. **71 a-c** *Anthocharis midea*. **72** *Euchloe hyantis*: **a**, ssp. *hyantis*; **b**, ssp. *lotta*. **73** *Euchloe ausonia ausonides*: **a**, Colo.; **b, c**, Calif. **74** *Euchloe creusa*. **83** *Ascia monuste phileta*. **84** *Ascia josephina*. **85** *Appias drusilla*.

Plate 12 (× 0.9). **35** *Colias alexandra*: **a**, ssp. *alexandra*, Jefferson Co., Colo.; **b**, ssp. *alexandra*, Clear Creek Co., Colo.; **c**, ssp. *alexandra* × *christina*, Bighorn Co., Wyo.; **d**, ssp. *christina* form *alba*, Kananaskis, Alta.; **e**, ssp. *harfordii*. **36 a, b**, *Colias occidentalis chrysomelas*. **37** *Colias eurytheme* form *vernalis*. **38** *Colias philodice* (Common Sulfur): **a-c**, ssp. *philodice*; **d**, ssp. *vitabunda* form *alba*; **e**, ssp. *vitabunda*. **39** *Colias interior*. **44** *Colias cesonia* (Dog Face). **45** *Colias eurydice*. **47** *Anteos maerula*. **48** *Phoebis statira*: **a**, ssp. *floridensis*; **b**, ssp. *jada*. **50** *Phoebis sennae*: **a, b**, typical form; **c**, form *alba*. **51** *Phoebis agarithe*. **56 a, b**, *Eurema mexicana*. **57 a, b**, *Eurema boisduvaliana*. **58 a, b**, *Eurema salome*. **59** *Eurema daira*: **a**, ssp. *daira*; **b, c**, ssp. *daira* form *rosa*; **d**, ssp. *palmira*. **60** *Eurema dina*: **a**, ssp. *westwoodi*; **b**, ssp. *helios*. **62 a, b**, *Eurema nise*. **63 a, b**, *Eurema lisa*. **66** *Kricogonia lyside* form *unicolor*.

Plate 13 (× 0.8). **33** *Colias hecla*: **a**, ssp. *canadensis*, Nordegg, Alta.; **b**, ssp. *hecla*, Baker Lake, N.W. Terr.; **c**, hybrid *hecla hecla* × *nastes* ("*boothii*"), Eskimo Point, N.W. Terr. **34** *Colias meadii*: **a**, ssp. *meadii*; **b**, ssp. *elis*. **35** *Colias alexandra christina*: **a**, Jasper, Alta.; **b**, Pennington Co., S.D. **37** *Colias eurytheme*: **a**, form *alba*; **b-d**, typical form. **45** *Colias eurydice*. **47** *Anteos maerula*. **51** *Phoebis agarithe*. **52** *Phoebis argante*. **53** *Phoebis philea*: **a, b**, typical form; **c**, form *alamacho*; **d**, form *crema*. **55 a, b**, *Eurema nicippe*. **60** *Eurema dina helios*. **65** *Eurema proterpia*: **a**, form *gundlachia*; **b, c**, typical form. **87** *Neophasia terlootii*. **98** *Paramacera xicaque*. **99** *Cyllopsis pyracmon henshawi*: **a**, typical form; **b**, form *nabokovi*. **100** *Cyllopsis pertepida dorothea*. **101** *Cyllopsis gemma*. **106** *Coenonympha tullia*: **a**, ssp. *california*; **b**, ssp. *inornata*, Carleton Co., Ont.; **c**, ssp. *furcae*; **d**, ssp. *kodiak*, Seward Pen., Alaska; **e**, ssp. *brenda*, Kane Co., Utah. **107** *Coenonympha haydenii*. **125** *Neominois ridingsii*. **134** *Oeneis melissa*: **a**, ssp. *melissa*; **b**, ssp. *beanii*. **135** *Oeneis polixenes*: **a**, ssp. *brucei*; **b**, ssp. *polixenes*.

Color Plate 11

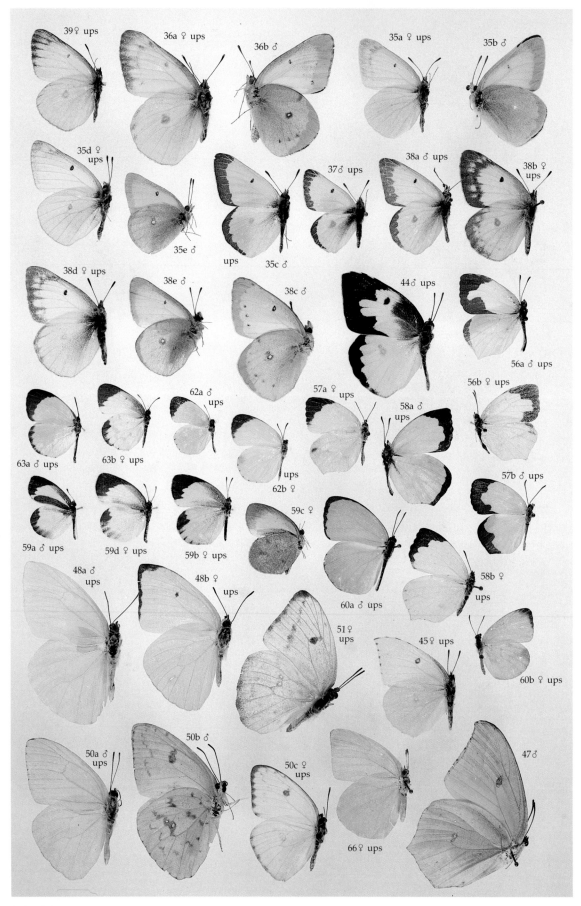

Color Plate 12

47♂ ups

53a ♂

53b ♂ ups

53c ♀ ups

53d ♀ ups

52♂

51♂

60♂ ups

45♂ ups

ups

65a ♂

33a ♀ ups

33c ♂ ups

33b ♂

55a ♀ ups

55b ♂ ups

ups 65b ♂

65c ♀ ups

37a ♀ ups

37b ♂

34a ♂

34b ♀

37c ♂ ups

37d ♀ ups

87 ♀

ups 35a ♂

35b ♀ ups

106a ♂

98♂

100♂

99a ♂

99b ♂

101♂

106b ♂

135a ♂

134a ♀

125♂

106d ♂

135b ♂

106c ♂

134b ♂

107♂

106e ♂

97

Plate 14.   **97** *Lethe appalachia*, Brandywine Creek State Park, Del. (E. Woodbury). **120** *Erebia dabanensis youngi*, Alaska. **121** *Erebia kozhantshikovi lafontainei*, Alaska. **133** *Oeneis alpina excubitor*, Mt. Chambers, Yukon (J. Troubridge).

120♂   121♂ 133♀

Plate 15 (× 0.8).   **110** *Cercyonis meadii meadii*. **111** *Cercyonis oetus*: **a**, ssp. *charon*; **b**, ssp. *oetus*, Austin Summit, Lander Co., Nev. **112** *Erebia vidleri*. **113** *Erebia rossii*: **a**, ssp. *rossii*; **b**, ssp. *ornata*. **114** *Erebia disa*: **a**, ssp. *mancinus*; **b**, ssp. *steckeri*. **115** *Erebia magdalena*: **a**, ssp. *erinnyn*; **b**, ssp. *magdalena*. **116** *Erebia fasciata*. **117** *Erebia discoidalis*. **118** *Erebia theano*: **a**, ssp. *pawloskii*, Haines Jct., Yukon; **b**, ssp. *ethela*, Sublette Co., Wyo. **119 a, b,** *Erebia epipsodea*. **120** *Erebia dabanensis youngi*. **122 a, b,** *Erebia occulta*. **123** *Erebia callias*. **124** *Gyrocheilus patrobas*. **126** *Oeneis nevadensis*: **a**, ssp. *iduna*; **b**, ssp. *nevadensis*. **127 a, b,** *Oeneis macounii*. **128** *Oeneis chryxus*: **a**, ssp. *chryxus*, Haines Road, Yukon; **b**, ssp. *chryxus*, Wilmore, Alta.; **c**, ssp. *chryxus*, Sweetgrass Co., Mont.; **d**, ssp. *chryxus*, Lemhi Co., Ida.; **e**, ssp. *strigulosa*; **f**, ssp. *ivallda*. **129** *Oeneis alberta*: **a**, ssp. *daura*; **b**, ssp. *alberta*, Union Co., N.M.; **c**, ssp. *alberta*, Park Co., Colo. **130** *Oeneis bore taygete*: **a, b,** Chaffee Co., Colo.; **c**, Churchill, Man. **131** *Oeneis uhleri*: **a**, ssp. *nahanni*; **b, c,** ssp. *uhleri*. **132** *Oeneis jutta*: **a**, ssp. *jutta*, Hwy. 11, Yukon; **b**, ssp. *jutta*, Ottawa, Ont.; **c**, ssp. *reducta*, Grand Co., Colo. **133** *Oeneis alpina excubitor*.

Plate 16 (× 0.8).   **93 a-c** *Lethe creola*. **94** *Lethe portlandia*; **a, b,** ssp. *missarkae*; **c, d,** ssp. *portlandia*. **95 a, b,** *Lethe anthedon*. **96** *Lethe eurydice eurydice*. **97** *Lethe appalachia*. **102** *Megisto cymela*. **103** *Megisto rubricata cheneyorum*. **104** *Neonympha areolata*: **a**, ssp. *mitchellii*; **b**, ssp. *areolata*; **c**, ssp. *septentrionalis*. **105** *Hermeuptychia hermes*. **108** *Cercyonis pegala* (Wood Nymph): **a, b,** ssp. *nephele*; **c**, ssp. *pegala*; **d**, ssp. *gabbii* form *stephensi*; **e**, ssp. *gabbii*, typical male. **109** *Cercyonis sthenele*: **a**, ssp. *paulus* form *damei*; **b**, ssp. *paulus*, Mesa Co., Colo.; **c**, ssp. *behrii*, Marin Co., Calif.; **d**, ssp. *behrii*, Humboldt Co., Calif.; **e**, ssp. *silvestris*, Kern Co., Calif. **139** *Anaea pithyusa*. **146** *Limenitis arthemis astyanax* (Red-Spotted Purple). **154 a-c** *Dynamine dyonis*. **155 a, b,** *Eunica monima*. **156** *Eunica tatila*. **157** *Myscelia ethusa*. **176** *Siproeta stelenes*. **177** *Anartia fatima*.

Plate 17 (× 0.7).   **136 a-c** *Anaea andria*. **137** *Anaea troglodyta*: **a, b,** ssp. *aidea*; **c**, ssp. *floridalis*. **143 a-c** *Doxocopa pavon*. **144 a, b,** *Doxocopa laure*. **146** *Limenitis arthemis* (White Admiral): **a**, ssp. *rubrofasciata*; **b**, ssp. *arthemis*. **147** *Limenitis weidemeyerii*. **148** *Limenitis lorquini*. **149** *Limenitis bredowii californica*. **150** *Limenitis fessonia*. **160** *Biblis hyperia*. **171** *Marpesia petreus*. **173 a, b,** *Marpesia chiron*. **184** *Vanessa atalanta* (Red Admiral). **192** *Polygonia gracilis*: **a, b,** ssp. *zephyrus*; **c**, ssp. *gracilis*. **193** *Polygonia progne*: **a, b,** ssp. *progne*; **c**, ssp. *progne* form *umbrosa*; **d**, ssp. *oreas*, Contra Costa Co., Calif.; **e**, ssp. *oreas*, Cascade Co., Mont.; **f**, ssp. near *oreas*, Nez Perce Co., Ida. **194** *Polygonia faunus*: **a, b,** ssp. *hylas*; **c**, ssp. *hylas* form *silvius*; **d**, ssp. *faunus*. **195 a, b,** *Nymphalis milberti*. **196 a, b,** *Nymphalis californica*. **197 a, b,** *Nymphalis vau-album*. **198** *Nymphalis antiopa* (Mourning Cloak). **272** *Heliconius charitonia*.

Color Plate 15

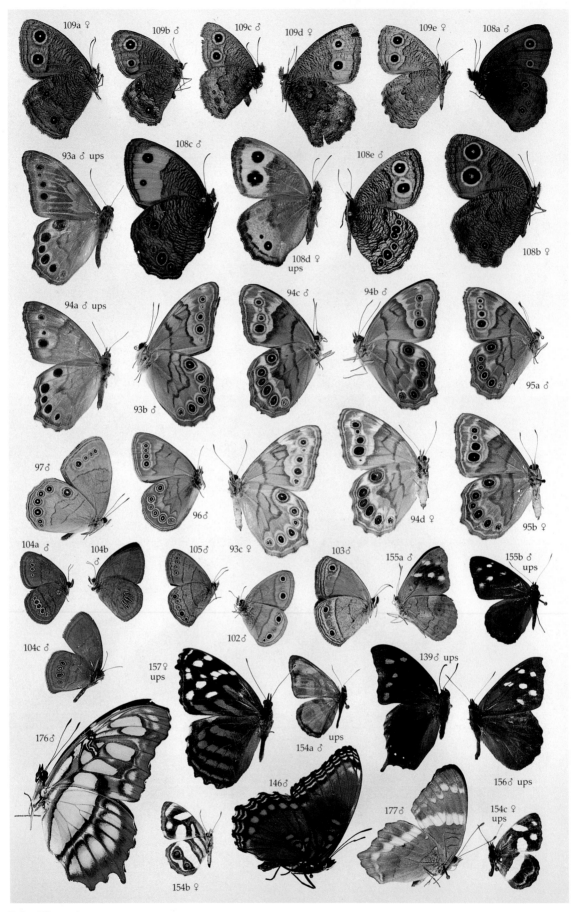

Color Plate 16

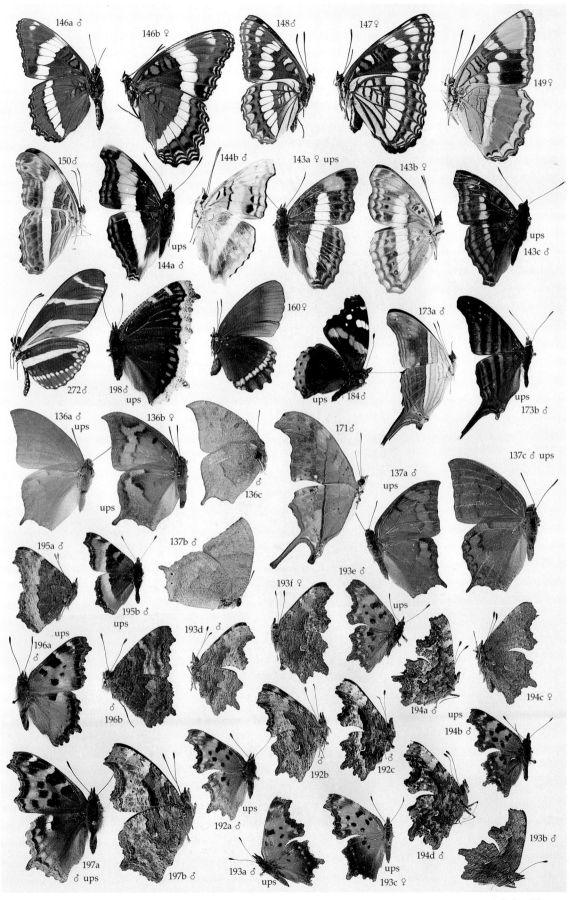

146a ♂
146b ♀
148♂
147♀
149♀
150♂
144b ♂
143a ♀ ups
143b ♀
ups
143c ♂
ups
144a ♂
272♂
198 ups
160♀
173a ♂
ups
184♂
ups
173b ♂
136a ♂ ups
136b ♀
171♂
137c ♂ ups
137a ♂ ups
ups
♂
136c
195a ♂
137b ♂
193f ♀
193e ♂
ups
195b ♂
ups
196a ♂
193d ♂
194a ♂ ups
194c ♀
♂
196b
194b ♂
197a ♂ ups
192a ♂
192b
♂
192c
♂
194d ♂
197b ♂
193a ♂ ups
193c ♀ ups
193b ♂

Color Plate 17

181a ♂ ups   181c ♀ ups

181b ♂   181d ♀

182a ♂ ups   182c ♀ ups

182b ♂   182d ♀

♀ 371 ♂

Plate 18. **181** *Precis evarete zonalis*: **a**, **b**, Key Largo, Fla.; **c**, **d**, Homestead, Fla. **182 a-d** *Precis genoveva*, New Smyrna Beach, Fla. **371** *Lycaena phlaeas*, mating pair, Lakehurst, N.J. (E. Woodbury).

Plate 19 (× 0.7). **89** *Danaus plexippus* (Monarch). **90** *Danaus gilippus* (Queen): **a**, ssp. *strigosus*; **b**, ssp. *berenice*. **91** *Danaus eresimus*. **140** *Asterocampa celtis*: **a-c**, ssp. *antonia*; **d**, ssp. *alicia*. **141 a**, **b**, *Asterocampa leilia*. **142** *Asterocampa clyton*: **a**, **c**, Tarrant Co., Tex.; **b**, Pima Co., Ariz.; **d**, form *geneumbrosa*, Montgomery Co., Ala. **145** *Limenitis archippus* (Viceroy): **a**, ssp. *archippus*; **b**, ssp. *obsoleta*; **c**, ssp. *floridensis*. **180** *Precis coenia* (Buckeye; hybrid Tex. × Calif.). **181** *Precis evarete*: **a**, ssp. *nigrosuffusa*, Aransas Co., Tex.; **b**, ssp. *nigrosuffusa*, Cameron Co., Tex.; **c**, ssp. *zonalis*. **186 a**, **b**, *Vanessa cardui* (Painted Lady). **187** *Vanessa virginiensis*. **188 a**, **b**, *Vanessa carye annabella*. **189** *Polygonia interrogationis* (Question Mark): **a**, form *umbrosa* (probably a hybrid with *P. comma*, because unh silver mark a comma); **b**, **c**, typical form. **190 a-c** *Polygonia comma*. **191 a-e** *Polygonia satyrus*. **194** *Polygonia faunus smythi*. **270** *Dryas iulia*. **274** *Libytheana carinenta* (Snout Butterfly): **a**, ssp. *larvata*; **b**, ssp. *bachmanii*; **c**, ssp. *bachmanii* form *kirtlandi*; **d**, ssp. *mexicana*.

Plate 20 (× 0.8). **251** *Speyeria diana*. **252** *Speyeria aphrodite*: **a**, ssp. *aphrodite* form *alcestis*, Ill.; **b**, **c**, ssp. *aphrodite*, Mont.; **d**, ssp. *aphrodite*, Jaffray, B.C.; **e**, ssp. *aphrodite*, Ont.; **f**, ssp. *byblis*. **253** *Speyeria cybele*: **a-c**, ssp. *leto*; **d**, ssp. *charlotti*; **e**, ssp. *cybele*, Archuleta Co., Colo.; **f**, ssp. *cybele*, Johnson Co., Kans.; **g**, ssp. *cybele*, Cuyahoga Co., Ohio. **254** *Speyeria nokomis*: **a-c**, ssp. *nokomis*; **d**, ssp. *apacheana*. **255** *Speyeria idalia*. **260** *Speyeria atlantis*: **a**, ssp. *nausicaa*; **b**, ssp. *chitone*; **c**, ssp. *schellbachi*; **d**, **e**, ssp. *dorothea*; **f**, ssp. *atlantis* × *hesperis*, Saguache Co., Colo.; **g**, **h**, ssp. *atlantis*, Ont.; **i**, ssp. *atlantis*, Eagle Co., Colo.; **j**, ssp. *dennisi*. **265 a**, **b**, *Euptoieta claudia* (Variegated Fritillary). **266 a**, **b**, *Euptoieta hegesia*. **268** *Dione vanillae* (Gulf Fritillary). **269** *Dione moneta*.

Plate 21 (× 0.7). **258** *Speyeria hydaspe*: **a**, ssp. *purpurascens*; **b**, ssp. *rhodope*; **c**, **d**, ssp. *hydaspe*; **e**, ssp. *viridicornis*. **259** *Speyeria callippe*: **a**, **b**, ssp. *liliana*, Lake Co., Calif.; **c**, ssp. *liliana*, Jackson Co., Ore.; **d**, ssp. *juba*; **e**, **f**, ssp. *macaria*; **g**, **h**, ssp. *callippe*; **i**, ssp. *juba* × *nevadensis*, El Dorado Co., Calif. **260** *Speyeria atlantis*: **a**, **b**, ssp. *irene*; **c**, ssp. *hesperis*, Jefferson Co., Colo.; **d**, ssp. *wasatchia*. **261** *Speyeria egleis*: **a**, **b**, ssp. *oweni*; **c**, ssp. *secreta*; **d**, ssp. *oweni* × *linda*, Crook Co., Ore.; **e**, ssp. *utahensis*; **f**, ssp. *tehachapina*. **262** *Speyeria zerene*: **a**, **b**, ssp. *bremnerii*, Thurston Co., Wash.; **c**, ssp. *bremnerii*, Clatsop Co., Ore.; **d**, ssp. *myrtleae*; **e**, ssp. *behrensii*; **f**, ssp. *gloriosa*; **g-j**, ssp. *zerene*; **k**, ssp. *picta*; **l**, ssp. *sinope*. **263** *Speyeria coronis*: **a-c**, ssp. *halcyone*; **d**, **e**, ssp. *coronis*.

194♂

190a ♂

ups

190b ♂

189a ♂ ups

190c ♀

191a ♀

ups

189b ♂

189c

191b ♀

♂

191c

191d ♀ ups

191e ♂ ups

ups

181c ♀

ups

181a ♂

ups

181b ♂

ups

180 ♀

ups

187 ♀

186a ♀

274a ♂

274b

274c

188a ♂

188b ♂ ups

186b ♂ ups

274d ♂ ups

90a ♀

145b ♂

91♂

145a

♂

89 ♀

145c ♀

90b ♀

270 ♀

ups

140a ♂

ups

140b ♀

142b ♀ ups

140d ♂ ups

ups

141a ♂

ups

142a ♂

141b ♂

140c ♂

142d ♂

142c ♀

Color Plate 19

251♂
266a ♂ ups
266b ♂
265a ♂
265b ♂ ups
269♂
254a ♀ ups
254b ♀
253a ♀
255♂
253d ♀ ups
253e ♀
268♂
253g ♂ ups
ups 253b ♀
253f ♀
253c ♂
254c ♂
254d ♂ ups
252d ♂
252a ♂
252c ♀ ups
260a ♀
252b ♀
ups 260e ♂
260b ♀
ups
260c ♀
260d ♂
ups 252e ♂
252f ♂
260f ♀
ups 260g ♀
260h ♂
ups 260j ♀
ups 260i ♂

Color Plate 20

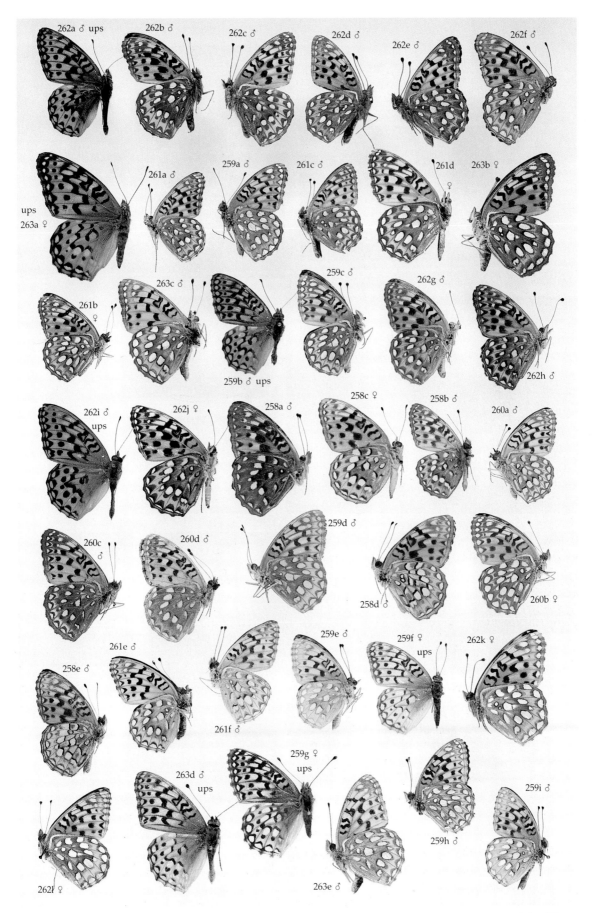

262a ♂ ups
262b ♂
262c ♂
262d ♂
262e ♂
262f ♂

ups
263a ♀
261a ♂
259a ♂
261c ♂
261d ♀
263b ♀

261b ♀
263c ♂
259c ♂
262g ♂
259b ♂ ups
262h ♂

262i ♂ ups
262j ♀
258a ♂
258c ♀
258b ♂
260a ♂

260c ♂
260d ♂
259d ♂
258d ♂
260b ♀

258e ♂
261e ♂
259e ♂
259f ♀ ups
262k ♀
261f ♂

263d ♂ ups
259g ♀ ups
259h ♂
259i ♂
262l ♀
263e ♂

Color Plate 21

Plate 22. **140** *Asterocampa celtis celtis* basking, Brandywine Creek, Del. (E. Woodbury). **146** *Limenitis arthemis astyanax* (Red-Spotted Purple) basking, Redden Forest, Del. (E. Woodbury). **157** *Myscelia ethusa* basking, Tex. (E. Woodbury). **180** *Precis coenia* (Buckeye) in normal resting position, sipping nectar from *Solidago* (goldenrod), Cambridge, Md. (E. Woodbury). **189** *Polygonia interrogationis* (Question Mark) form *umbrosa* basking, Chatham, Pa. (E. Woodbury). **190** *Polygonia comma* sipping organic fluids (note camouflaged uns), Blacksburg, Va. (E. Woodbury). **194** *Polygonia faunus faunus* basking, Mt. Washington, N.H. (E. Woodbury). **198** *Nymphalis antiopa* (Mourning Cloak) basking, Brandywine Creek, Del. (E. Woodbury). **274** *Libytheana carinenta larvata* (Snout Butterfly) basking, Alamo, Tex. (E. Woodbury).

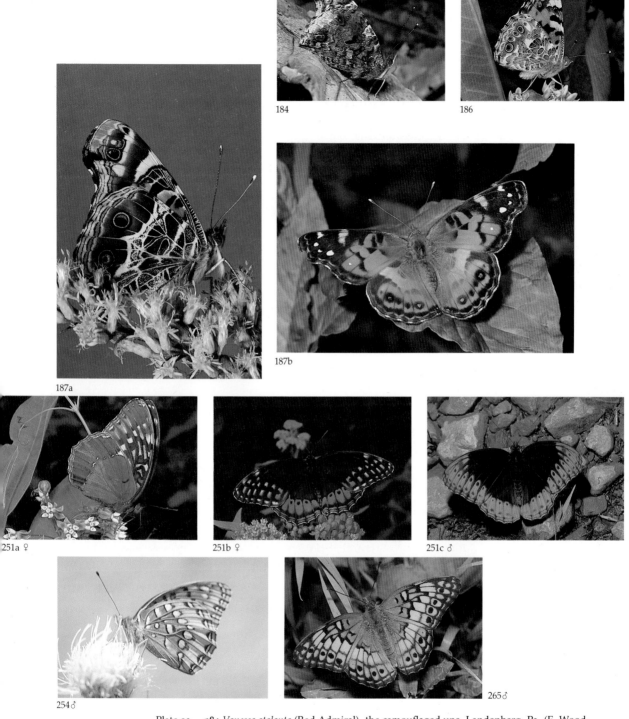

184

186

187b

187a

251a ♀

251b ♀

251c ♂

254♂

265♂

Plate 23. **184** *Vanessa atalanta* (Red Admiral), the camouflaged uns, Landenberg, Pa. (E. Woodbury). **186** *Vanessa cardui* (Painted Lady) sipping nectar from *Asclepias* (milkweed), Oceanville, N.J. (E. Woodbury). **187** *Vanessa virginiensis*: **a**, sipping nectar from *Solidago* (goldenrod), Faulkland, Del.; **b**, basking, Newcastle Co., Del. (both photos E. Woodbury). **251** *Speyeria diana*: **a**, female (mimics *Battus philenor*, species 25), basking and sipping nectar from *Asclepias* (milkweed), Blacksburg, Va.; **b**, female sipping nectar from *Asclepias* (milkweed), Poverty Hollow, Va.; **c**, male (not a mimic) basking, Blacksburg, Va. (all photos E. Woodbury). **254** *Speyeria nokomis nokomis* sipping nectar from *Cirsium* (thistle), La Plata Co., Colo. (R. Stanford). **265** *Euptoieta claudia* (Variegated Fritillary) basking, Landenberg, Pa. (E. Woodbury).

Color Plate 23

Plate 24.   **239** *Boloria selene myrina* basking (the enlarged black upf spots are aberrant), Arendtsville, Pa. (E. Woodbury).   **250** *Boloria natazhati*: **a**, feeding on wet soil; **b**, basking; both at Victoria I., N.W. Terr.

239♂

250a ♂

250b ♀

Plate 25 (×0.8).   **252** *Speyeria aphrodite manitoba*.   **254** *Speyeria nokomis*: **a**, ssp. *apacheana*; **b**, ssp. near *apacheana*, Duchesne Co., Utah; **c**, **d**, ssp. *coerulescens*.   **256** *Speyeria mormonia*: **a**, ssp. *mormonia*; **b**, ssp. *eurynome*, Wasatch Co., Utah; **c**, ssp. *eurynome*, Fremont Co., Wyo.; **d**, **e**, ssp. *eurynome*, Granite Co., Mont.; **f**, ssp. *artonis*; **g**, ssp. *luski*.   **257** *Speyeria adiaste*: **a**, ssp. *clemencei*; **b**, ssp. *adiaste*.   **259** *Speyeria callippe*: **a**, ssp. *macaria*; **b**, ssp. *nevadensis*, Storey Co., Nev.; **c**, ssp. *semivirida*; **d**, ssp. *meadii*.   **260** *Speyeria atlantis*: **a**, ssp. *dennisi*; **b**, **c**, ssp. *ratonensis*; **d**, ssp. *greyi*.   **261** *Speyeria egleis*: **a**, **b**, ssp. *egleis*; **c**, **d**, ssp. near *utahensis*; **e-g**, ssp. *albrighti*; **h**, ssp. *linda*.   **262** *Speyeria zerene*: **a**, **b**, ssp. *malcolmi*; **c**, ssp. *carolae*; **d**, **e**, ssp. *platina*; **f**, ssp. *gunderi*.   **263** *Speyeria coronis*: **a**, **b**, ssp. *semiramis*; **c**, **d**, ssp. *snyderi*.   **264** *Speyeria edwardsii*.

Plate 26 (× 1.0).   **224 a-c** *Phyciodes orseis orseis*.   **225 a**, **b**, *Phyciodes mylitta mylitta*.   **226 a-d** *Phyciodes pallida*.   **230 a**, **b**, *Phyciodes campestris campestris*.   **237** *Boloria napaea*: **a**, **b**, ssp. *alaskensis*; **c**, **d**, ssp. *halli*.   **238** *Boloria eunomia*: **a**, ssp. *triclaris*, Churchill, Man.; **b**, ssp. *triclaris*, Nigel Pass, Alta.; **c**, ssp. *caelestis*, Summit Co., Colo.; **d**, ssp. *caelestis*, Clear Creek Co., Colo.   **239** *Boloria selene*: **a**, ssp. *nebraskensis*; **b**, ssp. *atrocostalis*; **c**, ssp. *myrina*.   **240** *Boloria titania*: **a**, ssp. *boisduvalii*, Canmore, Alta.; **b**, ssp. *boisduvalii*, Coos Co., N.H.; **c**, ssp. *boisduvalii*, Banff, Alta.; **d**, ssp. *chariclea*; **e**, ssp. *helena*.   **241** *Boloria kriemhild*.   **242** *Boloria epithore chermocki*.   **243** *Boloria bellona bellona*.   **244** *Boloria frigga*: **a**, ssp. *sagata*; **b**, ssp. *gibsoni*.   **245** *Boloria improba*: **a-c**, ssp. *improba*; **d**, **e**, ssp. *acrocnema*.   **246 a-c** *Boloria alberta*.   **247** *Boloria astarte*: **a**, ssp. *distincta*, Richardson Mts., N.W. Terr.; **b**, ssp. *astarte*; **c**, ssp. *tschukotkensis*.   **248** *Boloria polaris*.   **249** *Boloria freija browni*.   **256** *Speyeria mormonia eurynome*.

Plate 27 (× 0.9).   **203** *Poladryas minuta*: **a**, ssp. *monache*; **b**, ssp. *minuta*.   **205 a**, **b**, *Dymasia dymas chara*.   **206** *Texola elada*.   **207 a**, **b**, *Chlosyne chinatiensis*.   **208** *Chlosyne theona*: **a**, ssp. *bolli*; **b**, ssp. *thekla*.   **209** *Chlosyne leanira*: **a-c**, ssp. *fulvia*; **d**, ssp. *alma*; **e**, ssp. *leanira* × *alma*, Little Rock, Los Angeles Co., Calif.; **f**, **g**, ssp. *leanira*.   **210 a**, **b**, *Chlosyne cyneas*.   **211** *Chlosyne definita definita*.   **212** *Chlosyne endeis pardelina*.   **214 a**, **b**, *Chlosyne janais*.   **215 a**, **b**, *Chlosyne rosita browni*.   **216** *Chlosyne lacinia*: **a**, ssp. *crocale*; **b**, **c**, ssp. *adjutrix*.   **217** *Chlosyne californica*.   **224 a**, **b**, *Phyciodes orseis herlani*.   **225** *Phyciodes mylitta*: **a**, **b**, ssp. *mylitta*; **c**, ssp. *callina*.   **227 a-c** *Phyciodes morpheus*, Colo. (most females resemble 228b).   **228** *Phyciodes tharos* (Pearl Crescent): **a**, Grand Co., Utah; **b**, Abbeville Co., S.C.   **229 a-c** *Phyciodes batesii*, Mich.   **230** *Phyciodes campestris*: **a**, **b**, ssp. *montana*; **c**, **d**, ssp. *campestris*.   **231 a**, **b**, *Phyciodes picta*.   **232** *Phyciodes phaon*: **a**, form *marcia*; **b**, typical form.   **233** *Phyciodes vesta*.   **234** *Phyciodes texana*: **a**, ssp. *texana*; **b**, ssp. *seminole*.   **235** *Phyciodes ptolyca*.   **236** *Phyciodes frisia*: **a**, **b**, ssp. *tulcis*; **c**, ssp. *frisia*.   **277** *Apodemia phyciodoides*.   **294** *Melanis pixe*.

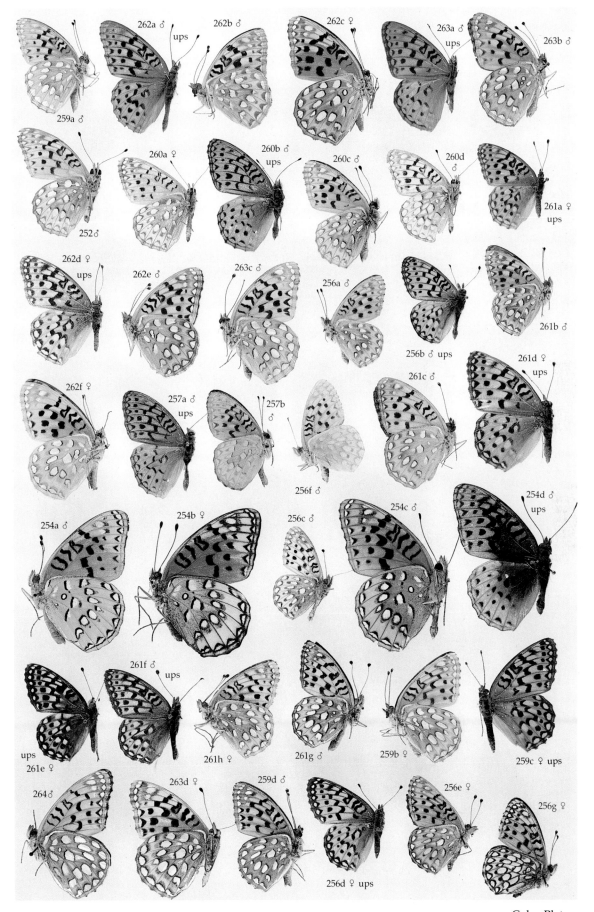

259a ♂
262a ♂ ups
262b ♂
262c ♀
263a ♂ ups
263b ♂

260a ♀
260b ♂ ups
260c ♂
260d ♂
252♂
261a ♀ ups

262d ♀ ups
262e ♂
263c ♂
256a ♂
256b ♂ ups
261b ♂

262f ♀
257a ♂ ups
257b ♂
256f ♂
261c ♂
261d ♀ ups

254a ♂
254b ♀
256c ♂
254c ♂
254d ♂ ups

ups
261e ♀
261f ♂ ups
261h ♀
261g ♂
259b ♀
259c ♀ ups

264♂
263d ♀
259d ♂
256d ♀ ups
256e ♀
256g ♀

Color Plate 25

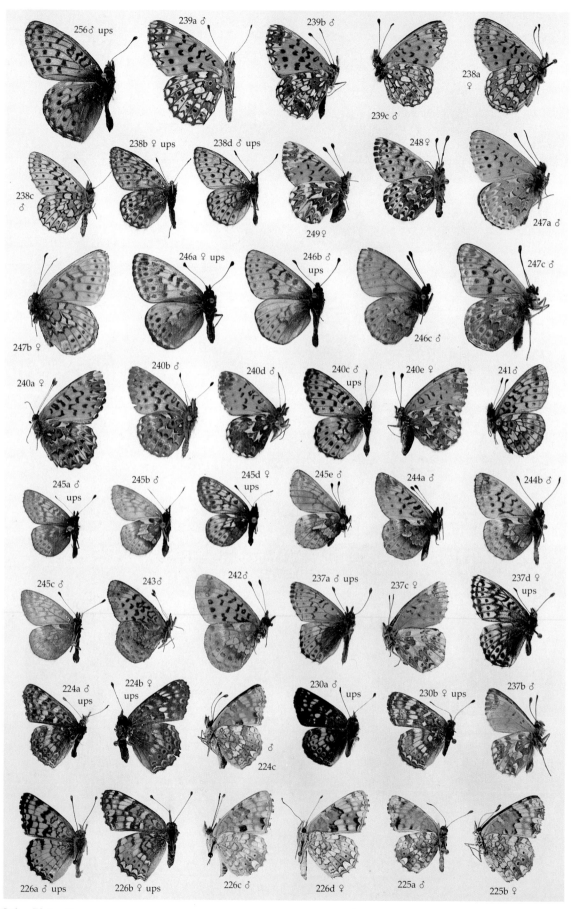

256♂ ups

239a ♂

239b ♂

239c ♂

238a ♀

238b ♀ ups

238d ♂ ups

238c ♂

248♀

247a ♂

249♀

247b ♀

246a ♀ ups

246b ♂ ups

246c ♂

247c ♂

240a ♀

240b ♂

240d ♂

240c ♂ ups

240e ♀

241♂

245a ♂ ups

245b ♂

245d ♀ ups

245e ♂

244a ♂

244b ♂

245c ♂

243♂

242♂

237a ♂ ups

237c ♀

237d ♀ ups

224a ♂ ups

224b ♀ ups

224c ♂

230a ♂ ups

230b ♀ ups

237b ♂

226a ♂ ups

226b ♀ ups

226c ♂

226d ♀

225a ♂

225b ♀

Color Plate 26

225a ♂ ups
225c ♀ ups
225b ♂
230a ♂
224a ♂
ups
224b ♀

232a ♂
232b ♀
231a ♀
231b ♂
230c ♂
230d ♀
230b ♂ ups

227a ♂ ups
228a ♀ ups
228b ♀ ups
ups
227b ♀
♂
227c
229a ♂

229b ♂ ups
229c ♀ ups
233 ♀
235 ♂
236a
236b ♀ ups
236c ♂ ups

214a ♂ ups
214b ♂
215b ♀
215a ♀ ups
234a ♂
ups
234b ♂

216a ♂ ups
216b ♀
216c ♂ ups
217 ♂
211 ♂
294 ♂

210a ♂ ups
209a ♂ ups
207a ♀ ups
207b ♂
208a ♀
208b ♂
212 ♀

210b ♂
209b ♂
209d ♂ ups
209c ♀ ups
209e ♀ ups
209f ♂ ups

ups
205a ♂
205b ♀
206 ♀
203a ♂
203b ♀
277 ♂
209g ♂

Color Plate 27

199♀

373♀

♂ 377 ♀

Plate 28.   **199** *Euphydryas phaeton phaeton* feeding and basking, Great Meadow, N.J. (E. Woodbury).   **373** *Lycaena hyllus* sipping nectar from *Asclepias* (milkweed), N.J. (E. Woodbury).   **377** *Lycaena dorcas dorcas*, mating pair, Howdenvale, Ont. (J. Troubridge).

Plate 29 (× 0.9).   **199** *Euphydryas phaeton phaeton*.   **200** *Euphydryas chalcedona*: **a**, ssp. *chalcedona*; **b**, ssp. *wallacensis*; **c**, ssp. *dwinellei*; **d**, ssp. *sierra*; **e**, ssp. *kingstonensis*; **f**, ssp. *bernadetta*, Washoe Co., Nev.; **g**, ssp. *bernadetta*, Harney Co., Ore.; **h**, ssp. *anicia*, Snow Creek Pass, Alta.; **i**, ssp. *anicia*, Custer Co., Colo.; **j**, ssp. *magdalena*; **k**, ssp. *wheeleri*; **l**, ssp. *chuskae*; **m**, ssp. *capella*; **n**, ssp. *morandi*.   **201** *Euphydryas editha*: **a**, ssp. *editha*, Santa Clara Co., Calif.; **b**, ssp. *editha*, Benton Co., Ore.; **c**, ssp. *beani*, Snow Creek Pass, Alta.; **d**, ssp. *beani*, Iron Co., Utah; **e**, ssp. *beani*, Piute Co., Utah; **f**, ssp. *nubigena*, Mariposa Co., Calif.; **g**, ssp. *nubigena*, Tuolumne Co., Calif.   **202** *Euphydryas gillettii*.   **218** *Chlosyne gorgone*.   **219** *Chlosyne nycteis*: **a**, ssp. *drusius*; **b**, ssp. *nycteis*; **c**, ssp. *reversa*.   **220** *Chlosyne harrisii*: **a**, **b**, ssp. *harrisii*; **c**, ssp. *hanhami*.   **221** *Chlosyne hoffmanni*: **a**, **b**, ssp. *hoffmanni*; **c**, ssp. near *segregata*, Siskiyou Co., Calif.   **222** *Chlosyne palla*: **a-c**, ssp. *palla*; **d**, ssp. *calydon*, Alpine Co., Calif.; **e**, ssp. *flavula*.   **223** *Chlosyne gabbii*: **a**, ssp. *gabbii*; **b**, ssp. *neumoegeni*: **c**, **d**, ssp. *sabina*; **e**, **f**, ssp. *acastus*; **g**, ssp. *dorothyi*; **h**, **i**, ssp. *damoetas*; **j**, ssp. *whitneyi*.

Plate 30 (× 1.0).   **295 a-c** *Feniseca tarquinius* (Harvester).   **371** *Lycaena phlaeas*: **a**, ssp. *arethusa*; **b**, ssp. *polaris*, Sweetgrass Co., Mont.; **c**, **d**, ssp. *americana*.   **372** *Lycaena cupreus*: **a**, **b**, ssp. *cupreus*; **c**, **d**, ssp. *snowi*.   **373 a-c** *Lycaena hyllus*.   **374 a-c** *Lycaena mariposa*.   **375** *Lycaena nivalis*: **a-c**, ssp. *nivalis*; **d**, **e**, ssp. *browni*.   **376** *Lycaena helloides*: **a**, **b**, ssp. *helloides*; **c**, ssp. *florus* (variant resembling ssp. *helloides*); **d**, **e**, ssp. *florus*; **f**, ssp. *megaloceras*.   **377** *Lycaena dorcas*: **a**, ssp. *dorcas*, Clinton Co., Mich.; **b**, **c**, ssp. *dorcas*, Livingston Co., Mich.; **d**, ssp. *dospassosi*.   **378** *Lycaena epixanthe*: **a**, ssp. *epixanthe*; **b**, ssp. *phaedra*.   **379 a-c** *Lycaena gorgon*.   **381** *Lycaena rubidus*: **a**, ssp. *rubidus*, Denver Co., Colo.; **b**, ssp. *rubidus*, Fremont Co., Colo.; **c**, ssp. *rubidus* form *sirius*, Gunnison Co., Colo.; **d**, ssp. *ferrisi*.   **382** *Lycaena xanthoides*: **a**, **b**, ssp. *dione*; **c**, ssp. *xanthoides*; **d**, **e**, ssp. *editha*.   **383 a**, **b**, *Lycaena hermes*.   **384 a**, **b**, *Lycaena arota virginiensis*.

Plate 31 (× 1.1).   **275** *Apodemia mormo*: **a**, ssp. *duryi*; **b**, ssp. *mormo*; **c**, ssp. *mejicanus*, Saguache Co., Colo.; **d**, ssp. *deserti*; **e**, ssp. *langei*; **f**, ssp. *virgulti*.   **276** *Apodemia nais*: **a**, **b**, ssp. *nais*; **c**, ssp. *chisosensis*.   **278 a**, **b**, *Apodemia palmerii*.   **279** *Apodemia hepburni*.   **280 a**, **b**, *Apodemia walkeri*.   **282 a**, **b**, *Calephelis borealis*.   **283 a**, **b**, *Calephelis muticum*.   **284 a**, **b**, *Calephelis virginiensis*.   **285 a**, **b**, *Calephelis nilus perditalis*.   **286 a-c** *Calephelis nemesis*.   **287** *Calephelis rawsoni*: **a**, **b**, ssp. *arizonensis*; **c**, ssp. *rawsoni*.   **288 a**, **b**, *Calephelis wrighti*.   **289 a**, **b**, *Caria ino melicerta*.   **290** *Emesis emesia*.   **291 a-c** *Emesis zela cleis*.   **292 a**, **b**, *Emesis ares*.   **296** *Habrodais grunus*: **a**, **b**, ssp. *grunus*; **c**, ssp. *herri*.   **315** *Satyrium behrii*: **a**, **b**, ssp. *behrii*; **c**, ssp. *crossi*.   **328** *Callophrys eryphon*: **a**, **b**, ssp. *eryphon*; **c**, ssp. *sheltonensis*.   **329** *Callophrys niphon*: **a**, **b**, ssp. *clarki*; **c**, ssp. *niphon*.   **330 a**, **b**, *Callophrys lanoraieensis*.   **334** *Callophrys augustus*: **a**, ssp. *augustus*; **b**, ssp. *iroides*, Marin Co., Calif.; **c**, ssp. *iroides*, Boulder Co., Colo.   **335** *Callophrys mossii*: **a**, ssp. *mossii*, Jefferson Co., Colo.; **b**, ssp. *mossii*, Boulder Co., Colo.; **c**, ssp. *doudoroffi*, Nevada Co., Calif.; **d**, ssp. *doudoroffi*, San Luis Obispo Co., Calif.; **e**, ssp. *doudoroffi*, San Mateo Co., Calif.

221a
♂ ups

221c ♂ ups

221b ♀

222d ♀ ups

222a ♂
ups

222b ♂

♀
223a

223b ♂
ups

223d ♂
ups

223c
♂

223e ♂

222e ♀

223f ♀ ups

222c ♀ ups

223g ♀
ups

223h ♂

223i ♀ ups

223j ♀ ups

219a ♂ ups

220a ♂
ups

219b ♀

219c ♀
ups

220c ♀
ups

220b ♀

218♂

202 ♀

199♂

200a ♂
ups

200f ♂ ups

200b ♂
ups

201a ♂

200h ♂ ups

200j ♂ ups

201c ♂ ups

201b ♀
ups

200c ♀
ups

200d ♂
ups

201f ♂ ups

201d ♀

200g ♂ ups

201e ♂ ups

200k ♀ ups

201g ♀
ups

200l ♀

200i ♂

200m ♂
ups

200n ♂ ups

200e ♀ ups

381a ♂ ups

ups
381d ♀

381c ♀ ups

381b ♂

372a ♂ ups

372b ♂

ups
371a ♂

ups
371b ♂

ups
371c ♂

371d ♂

372c ♂

372d ♀ ups

382b ♀

382a ♂ ups

382c ♂

382d ♂

382e ♀ ups

374a ♀ ups

373a ♂ ups

373b ♀ ups

373c ♂

384a ♂

374b ♂

ups
374c ♂

383b ♂

379a ♂ ups

379b ♀ ups

379c ♂

384b ♀ ups

383a ♂ ups

378a ♂

375a ♂ ups

375b ♀ ups

375d ♀ ups

375e ♀

375c ♂

378b ♂

376a ♂ ups

376c ♀ ups

376d ♀ ups

376f ♀ ups

376b ♀

376e ♂

377a ♂ ups

377b ♀ ups

377c ♂

377d ♀ ups

295a ♀

295b ♂ ups

295c ♀ ups

Color Plate 30

276a ♂ ups
276b ♂
276c ♂
275a ♀ ups
275b ♂ ups
275c ♂

280a ♀ ups
279♂ ups
278a ♂ ups
278b ♀
275d ♀ ups
275e ♂ ups
275f ♂

280b ♂
288a ♂ ups
288b ♂
287a ♂ ups
287b ♀ ups
286a ♂ ups
286b ♀ ups

286c ♂
287c ♂
285a ♂ ups
285b ♂
282a ♀ ups
282b ♂
283a ♂ ups

291a ♀
290♂
289a ♂
289b ♀
284a ♂
284b ♂ ups
283b ♂

291b ♂ ups
291c ♀ ups
292a ♂ ups
292b ♀ ups
296a ♂ ups
296c ♂ ups

329a ♀ ups
329c ♂ ups
315a ♀ ups
315b ♀
315c ♂
296b ♀

328a ♀ ups
328c ♂
328b ♂
329b ♀
330a ♀
330b ♀ ups
335a ♂ ups

335b ♂
335e ♀ ups

334a ♂ ups
334b ♀ ups
334c ♂
335c ♂
335d ♂

Color Plate 31

Plate 32.   **297** *Hypaurotis crysalus crysalus* basking on host *Quercus gambelii* (Gambel Oak), Tiny-town, Colo.   **303** *Harkenclenus titus titus*, Lakehurst, N.J. (E. Woodbury).   **310** *Satyrium calanus falacer* sipping nectar from *Asclepias* (milkweed), N.J. (E. Woodbury).   **332** *Callophrys henrici henrici*, Lakehurst, N.J. (E. Woodbury).

297 ♀

303 ♀

310 ♀

332

Plate 33 (× 1.0).   **302 a**, **b**, *Phaeostrymon alcestis alcestis*.   **307 a-c** *Satyrium liparops strigosum*. **308** *Satyrium kingi*.   **309** *Satyrium caryaevorus*.   **310** *Satyrium calanus*: **a**, ssp. *calanus*; **b**, **c**, ssp. *falacer*.   **311** *Satyrium edwardsii*.   **312 a-c** *Satyrium auretorum*.   **313 a**, **b**, *Satyrium saepium*. **314 a-c** *Satyrium tetra*.   **331** *Callophrys irus*: **a**, **b**, ssp. *hadros*; **c**, ssp. *irus*.   **332** *Callophrys henrici*: **a**, **b**, ssp. *henrici*; **c**, ssp. *solatus*.   **333 a**, **b**, *Callophrys polios*.   **336 a**, **b**, *Callophrys fotis*.   **340** *Callophrys gryneus*: **a**, ssp. *nelsoni*, El Dorado Co., Calif.; **b**, ssp. *nelsoni*, Robson, B.C.; **c**, ssp. *muiri*; **d**, ssp. *thornei*; **e**, ssp. *chalcosiva*, Lassen Co., Calif.; **f**, ssp. *chalcosiva*, Douglas Co., Nev. **341 a-c** *Callophrys johnsoni*.   **351** *Fixsenia favonius*: **a**, **b**, ssp. *favonius*; **c**, ssp. near *ontario*, Cum-berland Co., N.C.; **d**, ssp. *autolycus*; **e**, ssp. *ilavia*.   **352 a**, **b**, *Fixsenia polingi*.   **369 a**, **b**, *Electro-strymon endymion*.   **370 a**, **b**, *Electrostrymon angelia*.

Plate 34 (× 1.0).   **303** *Harkenclenus titus*: **a-c**, ssp. *titus*; **d**, ssp. *immaculosus*.   **304 a**, **b**, *Satyrium acadica*.   **305 a-c** *Satyrium californica*.   **306** *Satyrium sylvinus*: **a**, ssp. unnamed; **b**, ssp. *dryope*; **c-e**, ssp. *sylvinus*.   **318** *Ministrymon leda*: **a**, **b**, typical form; **c**, form *ines*.   **319 a**, **b**, *Ministrymon clytie*.   **324 a**, **b**, *Calycopis cecrops*.   **325** *Calycopis isobeon*.   **326 a-c** *Tmolus azia*.   **327 a-c** *Tmolus echion*.   **349 a**, **b**, *Atlides halesus*.   **353** *Hypostrymon critola*: **a**, Baja California Sur, Mex.; **b**, Santa Cruz Co., Ariz.   **354 a**, **b**, *Parrhasius m-album*.   **355 a**, **b**, *Strymon acis*.   **356 a**, **b**, *Strymon mar-tialis*.   **357 a**, **b**, *Strymon avalona*.   **358 a**, **b**, *Strymon melinus* (Gray Hairstreak).   **359 a**, **b**, *Strymon bebrycia*.   **360** *Strymon alea*.   **361** *Strymon rufofusca*.   **362 a**, **b**, *Strymon albata*.   **363 a**, **b**, *Strymon yojoa*.   **364 a**, **b**, *Strymon columella*.   **366 a**, **b**, *Strymon cestri*.   **367 a**, **b**, *Strymon bazochii*.

Plate 35 (× 1.0).   **293 a-c** *Lasaia sula*.   **297** *Hypaurotis crysalus*: **a**, **b**, ssp. *crysalus*; **c**, ssp. *citima*. **298 a**, **b**, *Eumaeus atala*.   **342 a**, **b**, *Callophrys spinetorum spinetorum*.   **380** *Lycaena heteronea*: **a**, ssp. *gravenotata*; **b**, ssp. *clara*.   **385 a**, **b**, *Lampides boeticus* (Hawaii only).   **386 a-c** *Leptotes ma-rina*.   **387 a-c** *Leptotes cassius*.   **390 a-c** *Everes comyntas*.   **391** *Everes amyntula*: **a**, **b**, typical form; **c**, form *immaculata*, Klamath Co., Ore.   **395** *Glaucopsyche lygdamus*: **a**, ssp. *lygdamus*; **b**, **c**, ssp. *couperi*; **d**, ssp. *columbia*; **e**, ssp. *australis*; **f**, ssp. *xerces* (intermediate toward ssp. *incognitus*); **g**, ssp. *xerces*; **h**, ssp. *incognitus*; **i**, ssp. *oro*.   **396** *Glaucopsyche piasus*: **a**, **b**, ssp. *daunia*; **c**, ssp. *piasus*. **397 a-c** *Philotes sonorensis*.   **403** *Plebejus glandon*: **a**, ssp. *aquilo*; **b**, **c**, ssp. *rustica*; **d**, ssp. *podarce*. **414 a-c** *Hemiargus isola*.   **415** *Hemiargus ceraunus*: **a**, **b**, ssp. *antibubastus*; **c**, **d**, ssp. *zachaeina*; **e**, ssp. *gyas*.   **416 a**, **b**, *Hemiargus thomasi*.

ups
331a ♀ ups
332a ♂
332b ♂
332c ♂
331c ♀
331b ♂

340a ♀
340c ♀
ups
336a ♀
336b ♂
333a ♀
ups
333b ♀

340b ♀ ups
340d ♂
340e ♀
ups
340f ♂
341a ♀
ups
341b ♂

ups
370b ♂
370a ♂
369b ♂
369a ♂ ups
313a ♀
ups
313b ♂
ups
341c ♀

312a ♀ ups
312b ♀
312c ♂
314a ♀
ups
314b ♀
314c ♂

351d ♂
351e ♂
351b ♂ ups
351c ♀
ups
351a ♂
352a ♂

310a ♂
310b ♂
310c ♀
302a ♂ ups
302b ♂
352b ♂ ups

311 ♂
309 ♂
308 ♀
307a ♂
307b ♂ ups
307c ♀ ups

Color Plate 34

297a ♂ ups

297c ♂ ups

297b ♀

298a ♂ ups

298b ♂

342b ♂

342a ♀ ups

390a ♂ ups

390b ♀ ups

391a ♀ ups

390c ♂

391b ♂

386b ♀ ups

386a ♂ ups

386c ♂

387a ♂ ups

387b ♀ ups

387c ♀

391c ♂

385a ♂

385b ♂ ups

293a ♂ ups

293b ♀ ups

293c ♀

397a ♀ ups

395a ♂

395b ♂

395d ♂

395e ♂

397b ♂

397c ♂ ups

395f ♀

395g ♀

395c ♂ ups

395h ♂ ups

395i ♀ ups

396a ♂

403a ♂ ups

403b ♀ ups

403c ♂

403d ♀

396b ♂ ups

396c ♂

416a ♂ ups

416b ♀

415a ♂

415c ♂

415d ♀ ups

380a ♂ ups

380b ♀ ups

414a ♂

414b ♀ ups

ups

414c ♂

415e ♂

415b ♂ ups

Color Plate 35

♂ 405 ♀

Plate 36. **339** *Callophrys hesseli hesseli* on flowers of *Arctostaphylos uva-ursi* (Bearberry), Burlington Co., N.J. (E. Woodbury). **405** *Plebejus melissa samuelis*, mating pair, N.Y. (E. Woodbury). **406** *Plebejus optilete*, Churchill, Man. (J. Troubridge). **408** *Plebejus icarioides pembina* basking on *Artemisia tridentata* (Big Sagebrush), Aspen, Colo. (R. Stanford).

339   406♂   408♂

Plate 37 (× 1.1). **316 a, b**, *Satyrium fuliginosum*. **380** *Lycaena heteronea*: **a**, ssp. *heteronea*; **b**, ssp. *gravenotata*. **399** *Euphilotes battoides*: **a, b**, ssp. *glaucon*; **c, d**, ssp. *centralis*; **e**, ssp. *ellisii*, Mesa Co., Colo.; **f**, ssp. unnamed, San Juan Co., N.M.; **g**, ssp. *comstocki*, Tulare Co., Calif.; **h**, ssp. *intermedia*; **i**, ssp. *battoides*; **j**, ssp. *bernardino*. **400** *Euphilotes enoptes*: **a**, ssp. *columbiae*; **b, c**, ssp. unnamed; **d**, ssp. *dammersi*; **e, f**, ssp. *ancilla*; **g**, ssp. *smithi*; **h, i**, ssp. *mojave*; **j**, ssp. *enoptes*; **k**, ssp. *bayensis*. **401** *Euphilotes rita*: **a, b**, ssp. *coloradensis*; **c**, ssp. *emmeli*; **d**, ssp. *rita*; **e, f**, ssp. *elvirae*; **g**, ssp. *pallescens*. **406 a, b**, *Plebejus optilete*. **407** *Plebejus saepiolus*: **a**, ssp. *amica*; **b**, ssp. *gertschi*; **c**, ssp. *hilda*; **d**, ssp. *insulanus*, Teton Co., Wyo. **408** *Plebejus icarioides*: **a**, ssp. *pembina*, Lander Co., Nev.; **b**, ssp. *pembina*, Clark Co., Ida.; **c**, ssp. *pembina*, Arapahoe Co., Colo.; **d, e**, ssp. *icarioides* form *evius*; **f**, ssp. *icarioides*; **g**, ssp. *pardalis*; **h**, ssp. *pheres*. **409** *Plebejus shasta*: **a, b**, ssp. *shasta*; **c**, ssp. *minnehaha*; **d, e**, ssp. *pitkinensis*. **410** *Plebejus acmon*: **a**, ssp. *acmon*; **b**, ssp. *lutzi*; **c, d**, ssp. *lutzi* form *spangelatus*, Clallam Co., Wash.; **e**, ssp. *lutzi* × *texanus*, Boulder Co., Colo.; **f**, ssp. *texanus*.

Plate 38 (× 1.1). **301 a, b**, *Chlorostrymon maesites telea*. **346 a-c** *Callophrys goodsoni*. **347 a-c** *Callophrys miserabilis*. **368** *Erora laeta*: **a, b**, ssp. *quaderna*; **c, d**, ssp. *laeta*. **388 a, b**, *Zizula cyna*. **389** *Brephidium exilis*: **a**, ssp. *pseudofea*; **b, c**, ssp. *exilis*. **392** *Celastrina argiolus*: **a**, ssp. *ladon* form *marginata*; **b, c**, ssp. *ladon* form *violacea*; **d, e**, ssp. *ladon* form *neglectamajor*, Jefferson Co., Colo.; **f**, ssp. *ladon* form *neglectamajor*, Pendleton Co., W.Va.; **g**, ssp. *ladon* form *lucimargina*; **h**, ssp. *lucia*; **i**, ssp. *echo*; **j**, ssp. near *gozora*, Pima Co., Ariz. **393 a-c** *Celastrina nigra*. **398 a-c** *Philotiella speciosa speciosa*. **402 a-c** *Euphilotes spaldingi pinjuna*. **404** *Plebejus idas*: **a**, ssp. *scudderi*, Mayo Lake Road, Yukon; **b**, ssp. *scudderi*, Sandilands, Man.; **c**, ssp. *scudderi*, Nigel Pass, Alta.; **d**, ssp. *atrapraetextus*, Hinsdale Co., Colo.; **e**, ssp. *anna*; **f**, ssp. *lotis*, Mendocino Co., Calif. **405** *Plebejus melissa*: **a, b**, ssp. *melissa*; **c**, ssp. *melissa* form *annetta*, Tuolumne Co., Calif.; **d, e**, ssp. *samuelis*. **410** *Plebejus acmon acmon* form *cottlei*. **411** *Plebejus lupini*: **a, b**, ssp. *monticola*; **c-e**, ssp. *lupini*. **412 a, b**, *Plebejus neurona*. **413 a, b**, *Plebejus emigdionis*.

Plate 39 (× 1.1). **300 a-c** *Chlorostrymon simaethis*. **337 a, b**, *Callophrys mcfarlandi*. **338 a, b**, *Callophrys xami*. **339 a, b**, *Callophrys hesseli hesseli*. **340** *Callophrys gryneus*: **a**, ssp. *gryneus*, Travis Co., Tex.; **b**, ssp. *gryneus*, Benton Co., Mo.; **c**, ssp. *gryneus* form *smilacis*, Benton Co., Mo.; **d**, ssp. *sweadneri*; **e**, ssp. *loki*; **f**, ssp. *siva*, Ventura Co., Calif.; **g**, ssp. *siva*, Sierra Co., N.M. **343** *Callophrys affinis*: **a-c**, ssp. *homoperplexa*; **d**, ssp. *apama*; **e, f**, ssp. *affinis*; **g**, ssp. *perplexa*, Mason Co., Wash.; **h**, ssp. *perplexa*, Marin Co., Calif. **344** *Callophrys dumetorum*: **a, b**, ssp. unnamed; **c, d**, ssp. *dumetorum*. **345** *Callophrys sheridanii*: **a**, ssp. *sheridanii*; **b**, ssp. *newcomeri*; **c-e**, ssp. *lemberti*; **f**, ssp. *lemberti* × *comstocki*, Churchill Co., Nev.; **g**, ssp. *paradoxa*; **h**, ssp. *comstocki*. **576** *Chioides zilpa*. **577** *Chioides catillus*. **589 a, b**, *Urbanus proteus*. **591 a, b**, *Urbanus dorantes*. **592** *Urbanus teleus*. **595** *Urbanus procne*.

380a ♂ 380b ♀ 408a ♂ ups 408d ♂ ups 408b ♀ ups

408e ♀ 408g ♂ 408c ♂ 408f ♂ 408h ♂

316a ♂ ups 316b ♂ 407a ♂ ups 407b ♀ ups 407c ♀ ups 407d ♂

406a ♀ ups 406b ♂ 399a ♂ ups 399c ♀ ups 399d ♀ 399b ♂ 399e ♂

400a ♂ 399f ♂ 400b ♂ ups 400c ♂ 401a ♂ 400d ♂ 400e ♀

400g ♂ 400h ♂ 400i ♀ ups 399g ♂ 399h ♂ 400j ♂ 401c ♀

401e ♂ ups 401b ♂ ups 401d ♀ ups 399i ♂ 401f ♂ 399j ♂ 401g ♂

400k ♂ ups 400f ♀ ups 409a ♂ ups 409b ♀ ups 409d ♀ ups 409c ♀ 409e ♂

410a ♂ ups 410b ♂ ups 410f ♀ ups 410c ♂ ups 410d ♂ 410e ♂

Color Plate 37

410 ♀ ups

411a ♂ ups

411c ♂ ups

411b ♀ ups

411d ♀ ups

411e ♂

412a ♂ ups

412b ♂

413a ♂ ups

413b ♀

402a ♂ ups

402b ♀ ups

402c ♂

404a ♂ ups

405a ♀ ups

405d ♀ ups

405e ♂

405c ♂

405b ♂

404d ♀ ups

404e ♂

404f ♂

404b ♂

404c ♂

392a ♂

393a ♂ ups

393b ♀ ups

393c ♂

392i ♂ ups

392b ♀ ups

392c ♂

392h ♂ ups

392d ♀ ups

392e ♂

392f ♂

392g ♂

ups
392j ♂

398a ♂ ups

398b ♀ ups

398c ♂

388a ♀

388b ♂ ups

389a ♂

389b ♂ ups

389c ♀

368d ♀

368b ♀

368a ♂ ups

368c ♀ ups

347a ♂ ups

347b ♀ ups

ups
346a ♂

346b ♀ ups

346c ♂

347c ♀

301a ♀ ups

301b ♂

Color Plate 38

300a ♂ ups

300b ♀ ups

300c ♂

337a ♀ ups

337b ♀

338a ♀ ups

338b ♀

339a ♂

340a ♀

340c ♂

340d ♂

340e ♀

340f ♀

340g ♂

ups 339b ♀

ups

340b ♂ ups

345d ♀ ups

345a ♂

345b ♂

345c ♂

343a ♂

343b ♀

343d ♀

345g ♂

345h ♂

345f ♂

345e ♂

343e ♂

343g ♂

343h ♂

344a ♂

344c ♀

344d ♂

344b ♂ ups

343f ♀ ups

343c ♀ ups

589a ♂ ups

591a ♂ ups

595 ♂

577 ♀

576 ♂

589b ♀

591b ♂

592 ♀

Color Plate 39

589♂

591♂

651♀

663♂

Plate 40.   **589** *Urbanus proteus* basking, Tamaulipas, Mex.   **591** *Urbanus dorantes* basking, Santa Cruz Co., Ariz.   **651** *Erynnis telemachus* basking, Fremont Co., Colo.   **663** *Pyrgus xanthus* basking and sipping mud, Otero Co., N.M.

Plate 41 (× 0.9).   **558** *Calpodes ethlius*.   **567** *Phocides pigmalion okeechobee*.   **569** *Phocides polybius lilea*.   **571** *Epargyreus clarus* (Silver-Spotted Skipper).   **572** *Epargyreus zestos*.   **574 a, b,** *Polygonus leo*.   **575** *Polygonus manueli*.   **584** *Zestusa dorus*.   **585** *Codatractus arizonensis* (similar: *C. melon*, Color Plate 61).   **597 a, b,** *Astraptes fulgerator*.   **601** *Autochton cellus*.   **603** *Autochton cincta*.   **609** *Thorybes pylades*: **a,** ssp. *albosuffusa*; **b, c,** ssp. *pylades*.   **610 a-c** *Thorybes bathyllus*.   **611** *Thorybes mexicana*: **a, b,** ssp. *mexicana*; **c,** ssp. *blanca*.   **612 a-c** *Thorybes confusis*.   **613 a-c** *Thorybes diversus*.   **615 a, b,** *Thorybes valeriana*.   **616** *Cabares potrillo*.   **619** *Spathilepia clonius*.   **620 a, b,** *Cogia hippalus*.   **621 a, b,** *Cogia outis*.   **623 a, b,** *Cogia calchas*.   **679** *Pyrrhopyge araxes*.

Plate 42 (× 0.9).   **604** *Achalarus lyciades*.   **605 a, b,** *Achalarus casica*.   **607 a, b,** *Achalarus toxeus*.   **614 a, b,** *Thorybes drusius*.   **622 a, b,** *Cogia caicus*.   **640** *Achlyodes mithridates tamenund*.   **642** *Timochares ruptifasciatus*.   **644** *Gesta gesta*.   **646 a-c** *Erynnis icelus*.   **647 a-c** *Erynnis brizo brizo*.   **648 a, b,** *Erynnis martialis*.   **649** *Erynnis pacuvius*: **a,** ssp. *callidus*, Marin Co., Calif.; **b,** ssp. *callidus*, Siskiyou Co., Calif.; **c, d,** ssp. *pacuvius*.   **650** *Erynnis juvenalis*: **a-c,** ssp. *juvenalis*; **d,** ssp. *clitus*.   **651 a-c** *Erynnis telemachus*.   **652** *Erynnis propertius*: **a-c,** ssp. *propertius*; **d-f,** ssp. *meridianus*.   **653** *Erynnis scudderi*.   **654 a-c** *Erynnis horatius*.   **655** *Erynnis tristis*: **a-c,** ssp. *tatius*; **d, e,** ssp. *tristis*.

Plate 43 (× 1.0).   **630 a, b,** *Staphylus hayhurstii*.   **631 a, b,** *Staphylus mazans*.   **633 a, b,** *Staphylus ceos*.   **637** *Xenophanes trixus*.   **638 a, b,** *Systasea pulverulenta*.   **639** *Systasea zampa*.   **643 a, b,** *Chiomara asychis*.   **645 a-c** *Ephyriades brunnea*.   **656** *Erynnis zarucco*: **a, b,** ssp. *zarucco*; **c, d,** ssp. *funeralis*.   **657 a-c** *Erynnis persius*.   **658 a, b,** *Erynnis lucilius*.   **659 a-c** *Erynnis afranius*.   **660 a-c** *Erynnis baptisiae*.   **661** *Pyrgus centaureae*: **a,** ssp. *wyandot*; **b, c,** ssp. *loki*.   **673 a, b,** *Celotes nessus*.   **674 a, b,** *Celotes limpia*.   **675** *Pholisora catullus* (Common Sooty Wing).   **676** *Pholisora mejicanus*.   **677** *Hesperopsis libya*: **a, b,** ssp. *libya*; **c,** ssp. *lena*.   **678** *Hesperopsis alpheus*: **a, b,** ssp. *gracielae*; **c,** ssp. *texana*; **d, e,** ssp. *alpheus*.

569♂

567♂

584♂

558♂

ups
574a♀

679♂

597a ♂

597b ♂
ups

575♀

574b ♀

585♂

619♂

603♂

601♂

571♂

572♂

616♀

620a ♂
ups

620b ♂

621a ♂

621b ♀ ups

610a ♀ ups

613a ♂

ups
612a ♂

612b ♀
ups

612c ♂

610b ♂

610c ♂ ups

613b ♂ ups

613c ♀ ups

609a ♂ ups

609b ♀
ups

609c ♂

611a ♂ ups

623a ♂

623b ♂ ups

615a ♂ ups

615b ♂

611c ♂

611b ♀

Color Plate 41

614a ♀
614b ♀ ups
622a ♂ ups
622b ♂
605a ♂
605b ♂ ups

644♂ ups
640♂ ups
642♂
604♂
607a ♀
607b ♂

646a ♂ ups
646b ♀ ups
646c ♂
647a ♂ ups

647b ♀ ups
647c ♀
648a ♂ ups
648b ♂
649a ♂ ups
649b ♂ ups

650a ♂ ups
650b ♀ ups
650c ♂
650d ♂ ups
649c ♀
649d ♀ ups

651a ♂ ups
651b ♀ ups
651c ♂
652a ♂ ups
652b ♀ ups
652c ♂

652d ♂ ups
652e ♀ ups
652f ♂
653♂ ups
654a ♂ ups
654b ♀ ups

655a ♂ ups
655b ♀ ups
655c ♂
655d ♂
655e ♂ ups
654c ♂

Color Plate 42

656d ♀ ups
657a ♂
656a ♂
ups
656b ♂
ups
656c ♂

660a ♂ ups
660b ♀ ups
660c ♂
657b ♂ ups
657c ♀ ups

658a ♂ ups
658b ♂
659a ♀
659b ♂ ups
659c ♀ ups

645a ♂ ups
645b ♀ ups
645c ♂
630a ♂ ups
631a ♂ ups
633a ♂ ups

678a ♂ ups
678b ♂
676♂
675♂
630b ♀ ups
631b ♀ ups
633b ♀ ups

677a ♀ ups
678c ♂ ups
678d ♀ ups
678e ♀
677c ♂
677b ♂

639 ♀ ups
638a ♂ ups
638b ♂
637♂ ups
643a ♂ ups
643b ♂

674a ♂ ups
674b ♂
673a ♂ ups
673b ♂
661a ♂ ups
661b ♀ ups
661c ♂

Color Plate 43

465♂

472♀

Plate 44. **465** *Hylephila phyleus muertovalle* (Fiery Skipper) sipping nectar, Palo Alto, Calif. (R. Humbert). **472** *Hesperia comma assiniboia* feeding on nectar from flower of *Machaeranthera pattersoni* (Aster) and basking in the characteristic fashion of Hesperiinae and Megathyminae (fw spread partway, hw fully), Platte Canyon, Colo. (R. Stanford). **475** *Hesperia leonardus pawnee* sipping nectar from *Liatris punctata* (Blazing Star), Jefferson Co., Colo. **640** *Achlyodes mithridates tamenund* resting, Hidalgo Co., Tex.

475♂

640♂

Plate 45 (× 1.0). **446 a-c** *Cymaenes tripunctus*. **447 a, b,** *Cymaenes odilia*. **448 a-c** *Lerema accius*. **526** *Asbolis capucinus*. **559 a, b,** *Panoquina panoquin*. **560** *Panoquina panoquinoides*: **a-c,** ssp. *panoquinoides*; **d,** ssp. *errans*. **561 a, b,** *Panoquina ocola*. **562 a, b,** *Panoquina hecebolus*. **563 a, b,** *Panoquina sylvicola*. **565** *Nyctelius nyctelius*. **662** *Pyrgus ruralis*: **a, b,** ssp. *ruralis*; **c,** ssp. *lagunae*. **663 a, b,** *Pyrgus xanthus*. **664** *Pyrgus scriptura*: **a, b,** typical form; **c,** form *pseudoxanthus*. **665** *Pyrgus communis* (Checkered Skipper): **a-c,** ssp. *communis*; **d,** ssp. *albescens*. **666 a-c** *Pyrgus oileus*. **667 a-c** *Pyrgus philetas*. **668 a-c** *Heliopetes ericetorum*. **669 a, b,** *Heliopetes domicella*. **670** *Heliopetes macaira*. **671** *Heliopetes laviana*.

Plate 46 (× 1.0). **436 a, b,** *Synapte malitiosa*. **441 a, b,** *Vidius perigenes*. **442** *Monca telata tyrtaeus*. **443 a-d** *Nastra lherminier*. **444 a-d** *Nastra neamathla*. **445 a-c** *Nastra julia*. **538** *Amblyscirtes aenus linda*. **540 a-c** *Amblyscirtes texanae*. **541 a, b,** *Amblyscirtes hegon*. **542 a, b,** *Amblyscirtes nereus*. **543** *Amblyscirtes celia*: **a-c,** ssp. *celia*; **d-f,** ssp. *belli*. **544 a, b,** *Amblyscirtes eos*. **545** *Amblyscirtes* unnamed. **546** *Amblyscirtes tolteca*: **a-c,** ssp. *tolteca*; **d,** ssp. *prenda*. **547 a, b,** *Amblyscirtes nysa*. **548 a-c** *Amblyscirtes alternata*. **549 a, b,** *Amblyscirtes vialis*. **551 a-c** *Amblyscirtes reversa*. **552 a, b,** *Amblyscirtes carolina*. **555 a, b,** *Lerodea eufala*. **556** *Lerodea arabus*: **a,** ssp. *arabus*; **b, c,** ssp. *dysaules*.

Plate 47 (× 1.1). **454 a-c** *Decinea percosius*. **524** *Euphyes vestris*. **527** *Atrytonopsis hianna*: **a,** ssp. *loammi*; **b,** ssp. *hianna*, Armstrong Co., Tex.; **c,** ssp. *hianna*, Cumberland Co., N.C.; **d,** ssp. *hianna*, Custer Co., Colo. **528 a-c** *Atrytonopsis deva*. **529 a-c** *Atrytonopsis vierecki*. **530** *Atrytonopsis lunus*. **531 a, b,** *Atrytonopsis pittacus*. **532 a, b,** *Atrytonopsis cestus*. **533 a, b,** *Atrytonopsis python python*. **534 a, b,** *Atrytonopsis ovinia zaovinia*. **535** *Amblyscirtes simius*: **a,** form *nigra*; **b,** form *rufa*; **c, d,** typical form. **536 a-c** *Amblyscirtes oslari*. **537 a, b,** *Amblyscirtes cassus*. **538** *Amblyscirtes aenus*: **a,** ssp. *aenus* form *erna*, Baca Co., Colo.; **b,** ssp. *aenus*, Boulder Co., Colo.; **c,** ssp. *aenus*, Armstrong Co., Tex.; **d,** ssp. *aenus*, Pueblo Co., Colo.; **e,** ssp. unnamed, Santa Cruz Co., Ariz. **539 a, b,** *Amblyscirtes exoteria*. **553 a, b,** *Amblyscirtes phylace*. **554 a, b,** *Amblyscirtes fimbriata*. **557** *Oligoria maculata*.

664a ♂ ups 664c ♂ ups 664b ♂ 663a ♀ ups 663b ♂ 662a ♂ ups 662b ♂

665a ♀ ups 665b ♂ ups 665c ♂ 666a ♂ 667a ♂ 662c ♂ ups

665d ♀ ups 666b ♂ ups 666c ♀ ups 667b ♂ ups 667c ♀ ups 669a ♂ ups

671 ♀ 668a ♂ ups 668b ♀ ups 668c ♂ 669b ♂

670 ♂ 561a ♀ 562a ♂ 563a ♀ 526 ♂

560a ♂ ups 560b ♀ ups 560c ♀ 561b ♂ ups 562b ♂ ups 563b ♂ ups

560d ♀ 559a ♂ ups 559b ♀ 565 ♂ 447a ♂ 447b ♀

448a ♂ ups 448b ♀ ups 448c ♂ 446a ♂ ups 446b ♀ ups 446c ♀

442♂

436a ♂ ups

436b ♂

441a ♀ ups

441b ♀

445a ♂ ups

444a ♂ ups

ups
444b ♀

444c ♂

444d ♀

445b ♂

♀ ups
445c

443a ♂ ups

443b ♀ ups

443c ♂

443d ♀

555a ♂ ups

555b ♂

548a ♂

547a ♀ ups

547b ♂

556a ♂

556b ♀

556c ♀ ups

548b ♂ ups

548c ♀ ups

549a ♂ ups

549b ♀

541a ♂ ups

541b ♂

542a ♂ ups

542b ♂

551a ♂ ups

551b ♀ ups

551c ♂

552a ♂

546a ♂ ups

546b ♀ ups

546c ♂

546d ♂

545♂

552b ♂ ups

543a ♂ ups

543b ♀ ups

543c ♂

540a ♂

544a ♀

544b ♂ ups

543d ♂ ups

543e ♀ ups

543f ♂

540b ♂ ups

540c ♀ ups

538♂

Color Plate 46

538a ♀
538b ♂
538e ♂
538c ♂ ups
538d ♀ ups
ups
539a ♂

536a ♂
ups
536b ♀ ups
536c ♂
537a ♂ ups
537b ♂
539b ♂

535a ♂ ups
535b ♂ ups
535c ♀ ups
535d ♂
534a ♂
ups
534b ♂

530 ♀
532a ♂ ups
532b ♂
531a ♀ ups
531b ♂

529a ♂ ups
529b ♀ ups
529c ♂
533a ♂
ups
533b ♂

528a ♂ ups
528b ♀ ups
528c ♀
527b ♂
527a ♀

527c ♂
ups
527d ♀ ups
557 ♀
454a ♂ ups
ups
454b ♀

553a ♂ ups
553b ♂
554a ♂
554b ♀ ups
524 ♂ ups
454c ♂

489♂

Plate 48. **489** *Polites peckius* being sucked dry by the female of a mating pair of ambush bugs, on flowers of *Liatris punctata* (Blazing Star), Jefferson Co., Colo. **500** *Atalopedes campestris* (Sachem) basking, Davis Mts., Tex. **511** *Poanes zabulon taxiles*, Red Rocks, Colo. **515** *Paratrytone melane melane* basking (see legend for *Hesperia comma*, species 472, in Color Plate 44), Palo Alto, Calif. (R. Humbert).

511♂   515

Plate 49 (× 1.0). **466 a-c** *Yvretta rhesus*. **467** *Yvretta carus*: **a**, **b**, ssp. *carus*; **c**, ssp. *sub-reticulata*. **470 a-c** *Hesperia uncas uncas*. **480** *Hesperia metea*: **a**, **b**, ssp. *licinius*; **c**, **d**, ssp. *metea*. **496** *Polites vibex*: **a**, ssp. *praeceps*; **b**, ssp. *vibex*. **497 a-c** *Wallengrenia egeremet*. **498** *Wallengrenia otho*: **a-c**, ssp. *curassavica*; **d**, ssp. *otho*. **499 a-c** *Pompeius verna*. **500 a**, **b**, *Atalopedes campestris* (Sachem). **508 a-c** *Ochlodes snowi*. **509 a-c** *Poanes massasoit massasoit*. **511 a**, **b**, *Poanes zabulon zabulon*. **512** *Poanes hobomok hobomok* form *pocahontas*. **515** *Paratrytone melane*: **a**, ssp. *vitellina*; **b**, **c**, ssp. *melane*. **524 a**, **b**, *Euphyes vestris*. **525 a-c** *Euphyes dukesi*. **550 a-c** *Amblyscirtes aesculapius*.

Plate 50 (× 1.0). **469 a-c** *Stinga morrisoni*. **470** *Hesperia uncas macswaini*: **a**, Lander Co., Nev.; **b**, Mono Co., Calif. **471 a-c** *Hesperia juba*. **472** *Hesperia comma*: **a**, ssp. *harpalus*, Tooele Co., Utah; **b**, ssp. *harpalus*, Sweetgrass Co., Mont.; **c**, ssp. *oroplata*; **d**, ssp. *laurentina*; **e**, ssp. *manitoba*, Gilpin Co., Colo.; **f**, ssp. *manitoba*, Churchill, Man.; **g**, ssp. *dodgei*; **h**, ssp. *assiniboia*; **i**, ssp. *yosemite*, Santa Clara Co., Calif.; **j**, ssp. *yosemite*, San Diego Co., Calif. **473 a-c** *Hesperia wood-gatei*. **475** *Hesperia leonardus*: **a-c**, ssp. *leonardus*; **d**, ssp. *pawnee* × *leonardus*, Sherburne Co., Minn.; **e**, **f**, ssp. *montana*. **476 a-c** *Hesperia pahaska pahaska*. **477** *Hesperia columbia*: **a**, gynandro-morph (left side female, right side male); **b**, normal male. **478 a-c** *Hesperia viridis*. **484 a-c** *Hesperia lindseyi*, Napa Co., Calif. **485 a**, **b**, *Hesperia miriamae*. **486 a-c** *Hesperia nevada*. **491 a-c** *Polites mystic*. **506** *Ochlodes sylvanoides santacruza*.

Plate 51 (× 1.0). **465** *Hylephila phyleus* (Fiery Skipper): **a-c**, ssp. *phyleus*; **d**, **e**, ssp. *muer-tovalle*. **487 a-c** *Polites draco*. **488** *Polites sabuleti*: **a**, ssp. *tecumseh*; **b**, **c**, ssp. *ministigma*; **d**, **e**, ssp. *chusca*; **f**, ssp. *sabuleti*. **489 a-c** *Polites peckius*. **490 a-c** *Polites mardon*. **491** *Polites mystic*. **492** *Polites sonora*: **a**, **b**, ssp. *sonora*; **c-e**, ssp. *utahensis*. **496** *Polites vibex*: **a**, ssp. *praeceps*; **b**, ssp. *vibex*. **500 a**, **b**, *Atalopedes campestris* (Sachem). **506** *Ochlodes sylvanoides*: **a**, ssp. *sylvanoides*, El Paso Co., Colo.; **b**, ssp. *sylvanoides*, Davis, Yolo Co., Calif.; **c**, ssp. *sylvanoides*, King Co., Wash.; **d**, ssp. *orecoasta*; **e**, **f**, ssp. *bonnevilla*. **510 a**, **b**, *Poanes viator*. **511** *Poanes zabulon*: **a**, **b**, ssp. *zabulon*; **c-f**, ssp. *taxiles*. **512** *Poanes hobomok*: **a**, ssp. *wetona*; **b**, **c**, ssp. *hobomok*.

524a ♀ ups

524b ♂

497a ♂ ups

497b ♀ ups

497c ♀

499a ♂

515a ♂ ups

508a ♂ ups

508b ♀ ups

508c ♂

499b ♂ ups

499c ♀ ups

515b ♂ ups

515c ♂

498a ♂ ups

498b ♀ ups

498c ♂

498d ♂

496a ♀ ups

496b ♀

512 ♀

511a ♀

511b ♀ ups

500a ♀ ups

509a ♂ ups

525a ♂ ups

525b ♀ ups

525c ♂

500b ♀

509b ♀ ups

509c ♂

550a ♂ ups

550b ♀ ups

550c ♂

466a ♂ ups

480a ♂ ups

467a ♂ ups

467c ♀ ups

467b ♀

466b ♀

466c ♀ ups

480c ♀ ups

480b ♂

480d ♂

470a ♂ ups

470b ♀ ups

470c ♂

Color Plate 49

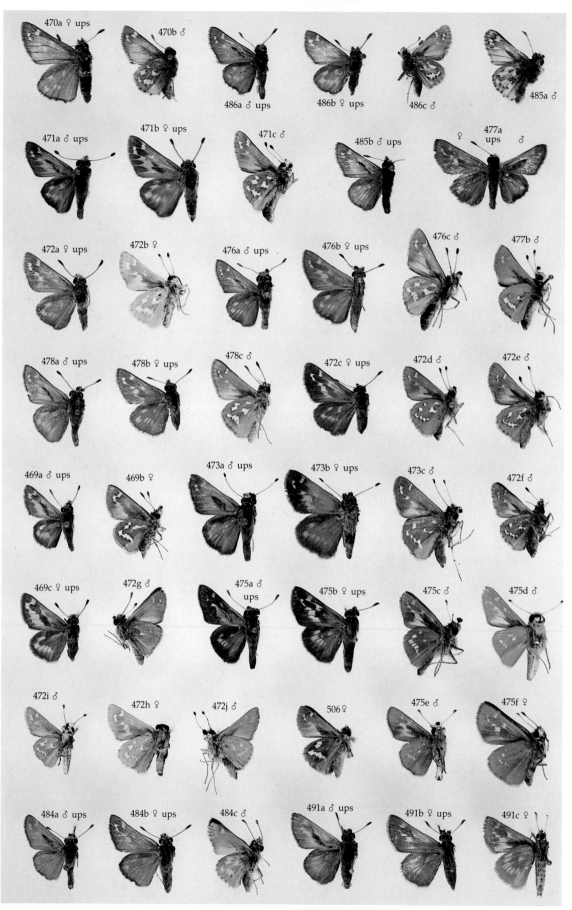

Color Plate 50

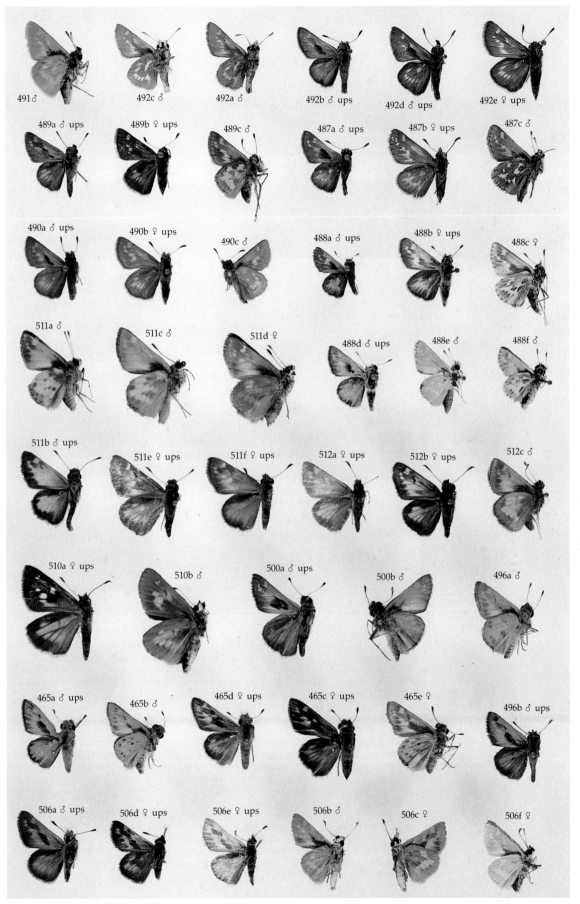

491♂ 492c ♂ 492a ♂ 492b ♂ ups 492d ♂ ups 492e ♀ ups

489a ♂ ups 489b ♀ ups 489c ♂ 487a ♂ ups 487b ♀ ups 487c ♂

490a ♂ ups 490b ♀ ups 490c ♂ 488a ♂ ups 488b ♀ ups 488c ♀

511a ♂ 511c ♂ 511d ♀ 488d ♂ ups 488e ♂ 488f ♂

511b ♂ ups 511e ♀ ups 511f ♀ ups 512a ♀ ups 512b ♀ ups 512c ♂

510a ♀ ups 510b ♂ 500a ♂ ups 500b ♂ 496a ♂

465a ♂ ups 465b ♂ 465d ♀ ups 465c ♀ ups 465e ♀ 496b ♂ ups

506a ♂ ups 506d ♀ ups 506e ♀ ups 506b ♂ 506c ♀ 506f ♀

Color Plate 51

418♀

Plate 52.　**418** *Megathymus ursus ursus*, Cochise Co., Ariz.　**506** *Ochlodes sylvanoides sylvanoides* sipping nectar from *Cirsium vulgare* (Bull Thistle), Golden Gate Canyon, Colo.　**571** *Epargyreus clarus* (Silver-Spotted Skipper) sipping mud, Idledale, Colo.　**574** *Polygonus leo* basking and perhaps feeding, Key Largo, Fla.

506♂　　　　　　　　　　571♂　　　　　　　　　　574♂

Plate 53 (× 1.0).　**474 a-c** *Hesperia ottoe*.　**475 a-c** *Hesperia leonardus pawnee*.　**479** *Hesperia attalus*: **a-c**, ssp. *slossonae*; **d**, **e**, ssp. *attalus*.　**481 a-c** *Hesperia meskei*.　**482 a-d** *Hesperia dacotae*. **483 a-c** *Hesperia sassacus*.　**502** *Atrytone logan*: **a**, ssp. *lagus*; **b**, **c**, ssp. *logan*.　**503 a-c** *Problema byssus*.　**504 a-c** *Problema bulenta*.　**505 a-c** *Ochlodes yuma*.　**507 a-c** *Ochlodes agricola*.　**513 a-c** *Poanes aaroni*.　**514 a-c** *Poanes yehl*.　**518 a-c** *Euphyes pilatka*.

Plate 54 (× 1.1).　**430 a-c** *Carterocephalus palaemon*.　**431 a**, **b**, *Piruna pirus*.　**432** *Piruna haferniki*.　**433 a**, **b**, *Piruna polingii*.　**434 a-c** *Piruna cingo*.　**435 a**, **b**, *Piruna microsticta*.　**456 a**, **b**, *Ancyloxypha numitor*.　**457 a-c** *Ancyloxypha arene*.　**463 a-c** *Adopaeoides prittwitzi*.　**493 a-c** *Polites themistocles*.　**494 a-c** *Polites baracoa*.　**495** *Polites origenes*: **a**, **b**, ssp. *rhena*; **c**, ssp. *origenes*. **501 a-c** *Atrytone arogos*.　**519 a-c** *Euphyes conspicua*.　**520** *Euphyes dion*: **a**, Tarrant Co., Tex.; **b**, Va.; **c**, Mo.　**521 a-c** *Euphyes berryi*.　**522** *Euphyes bimacula*: **a**, **b**, Colo.; **c**, Me.　**523 a-c** *Euphyes arpa*.

Plate 55 (× 1.1).　**421 a**, **b**, *Stallingsia smithi maculosus*.　**424** *Agathymus alliae*: **a**, ssp. unnamed, Ivanpah Mts., Calif.; **b**, ssp. *alliae*.　**427 a-c** *Agathymus remingtoni valverdiensis*.　**428** *Agathymus mariae*: **a-c**, Culberson Co., Tex.; **d**, Val Verde Co., Tex. (darker variant).　**429 a-c** *Agathymus stephensi stephensi*.　**458 a-c** *Oarisma powesheik*.　**459 a-c** *Oarisma garita*.　**460 a-c** *Oarisma edwardsii*.　**461 a-c** *Copaeodes minima*.　**462 a-c** *Copaeodes aurantiaca*.　**464 a-c** *Thymelicus lineola*. **468** *Pseudocopaeodes eunus*: **a-c**, ssp. *eunus*; **d**, ssp. *alinea*.

507a ♂ ups
507b ♀
507c ♂
ups 483a ♂
ups 483b ♀
483c ♂

505a ♂ ups
505b ♀ ups
482a ♂ ups
482b ♂
482c ♀ ups
482d ♀

505c ♂
475a ♂
474a ♂
474b ♂ ups
474c ♀ ups

475b ♂ ups
475c ♀ ups
479a ♂ ups
479b ♀ ups
479d ♂
479c ♀

514a ♂ ups
514b ♂
481a ♂ ups
481b ♀ ups
481c ♂
479e ♀ ups

514c ♀ ups
ups 518a ♂
518b ♀ ups
518c ♂
513a ♂

504a ♂ ups
ups 504b ♀
504c ♂
513b ♂ ups
513c ♀ ups

503a ♂ ups
503b ♀ ups
503c ♂
502a ♂ ups
502b ♀ ups
502c ♀

501a ♂ ups
501b ♀ ups
501c ♂
ups 523a ♂
523b ♀ ups
521a ♂ ups
521b ♀ ups
521c ♂
522a ♂
523c ♂
522b ♂ ups
522c ♀ ups
520a ♂ ups
520b ♀ ups
520c ♂
519a ♂ ups
519b ♀ ups
519c ♂
494a ♂ ups
494b ♀ ups
494c ♂
495a ♂ ups
495c ♀ ups
495b ♂
493a ♂ ups
493b ♀ ups
493c ♂
430a ♂ ups
430b ♀ ups
430c ♂
434a ♂ ups
434b ♀ ups
434c ♂
435a ♀
456a ♂ ups
431a ♀ ups
431b ♂
432♂
433a ♂ ups
433b ♂
435b ♀ ups
456b ♂
457a ♂ ups
457b ♀ ups
457c ♂
463a ♂ ups
463b ♀ ups
463c ♂

Color Plate 54

464a ♂ ups

464b ♀ ups

464c ♂

468a ♂ ups

468b ♀ ups

468c ♂

462a ♂ ups

462b ♀ ups

462c ♂

461a ♂ ups

461b ♀ ups

461c ♂

468d ♂

460a ♂ ups

460b ♀ ups

460c ♂

459a ♂ ups

459b ♀ ups

459c ♂

421a ♂ ups

421b ♀

458a ♂ ups

458b ♀ ups

458c ♂

427a ♂ ups

427b ♀ ups

427c ♀

428a ♂ ups

428d ♂ ups

428b ♀ ups

428c ♂

429a ♂ ups

429b ♀ ups

429c ♂

424a ♂ ups

424b ♂ ups

162b ♀   165b ♂   166b ♀

162a ♂   164♂   165a ♀   166a ♂

Plate 56. **162 a**, **b**, *Hamadryas glauconome diasia*, Haiti. **164** *Hamadryas feronia*, Mex. **165 a**, **b**, *Hamadryas guatemalena*, Mex. **166 a**, **b**, *Hamadryas iphthime joannae*, Guatemala. **403** *Plebejus glandon rustica* (many, mostly males) and **407** *Plebejus saepiolus whitmeri* (several, males and females), all sipping mud, Jones Pass, Colo.

403 and 407

Plate 57 (× 0.8). **417** *Megathymus yuccae*: **a**, ssp. *coloradensis*, Bexar Co., Tex.; **b**, **c**, ssp. *coloradensis*, Washington Co., Utah; **d**, ssp. *yuccae*, Charleston Co., S.C. **418 a**, **b**, *Megathymus ursus violae*. **419** *Megathymus streckeri*: **a-c**, ssp. *texanus*; **d**, **e**, ssp. *streckeri*. **420** *Megathymus cofaqui cofaqui*. **422** *Agathymus neumoegeni*: **a-c**, ssp. *neumoegeni*; **d**, ssp. *chisosensis*. **423** *Agathymus aryxna*: **a-c**, ssp. *aryxna*; **d**, **e**, ssp. *freemani*; **f**, ssp. *baueri*. **424 a**, **b**, *Agathymus alliae alliae*. **425 a-c** *Agathymus evansi*. **426** *Agathymus polingi*: **a**, **b**, Pima Co., Ariz.; **c**, Gila Co., Ariz.

Plate 58 (× 0.7). Strays from Latin America. **2 a**, **b**, *Eurytides celadon*. **3** *Eurytides philolaus*. **14** *Papilio ornythion*. **15 a**, **b**, *Papilio astyalus*. **21** *Papilio pilumnus*. **24** *Papilio victorinus*. **27 a**, **b**, *Parides eurimides mylotes* (× 0.5). **31 a**, **b**, *Enantia albania*. **49 a**, **b**, *Phoebis orbis*. **54** *Phoebis intermedia*. **61 a-c** *Eurema chamberlaini*. **64 a**, **b**, *Eurema messalina*. **88** *Catasticta nimbice*. **92** *Lycorea cleobaea*. **204** *Microtia elva*. **213** *Chlosyne marina eumeda* (× 0.8). **267** *Dryadula phaetusa*. **271** *Heliconius isabella eva*. **273** *Heliconius erato petiverana*.

Plate 59 (× 0.7). Strays from Latin America. **138** *Anaea glycerium*. **151 a-c** *Epiphile adrasta*. **152** *Diaethria asteria*. **153** *Diaethria clymena*. **158** *Myscelia cyananthe*. **161 a**, **b**, *Hamadryas februa*. **163 a**, **b**, *Hamadryas atlantis*. **164** *Hamadryas feronia*. **167** *Hamadryas fornax*. **168** *Hamadryas amphinome*. **169** *Smyrna karwinskii*. **170** *Historis odius*. **172 a**, **b**, *Marpesia eleuchea*, Cuba. **174** *Marpesia coresia*. **175 a**, **b**, *Hypolimnas misippus*. **178** *Anartia lytrea chrysopelea*. **183** *Hypanartia lethe*. **213 a** *Chlosyne marina melitaeoides*. **[213] b**, **c**, *Chlosyne erodyle* (similar to species 213). **274** *Libytheana carinenta motya* (Snout Butterfly): **a**, Cameron Co., Tex.; **b**, **c**, Cuba.

424a ♀ ups   424b ♂   423a ♂ ups   423b ♀ ups   423c ♂

ups   423d ♀   423e ♂   423f ♂ ups   425a ♂ ups

426a ♂ ups   426b ♀ ups   426c ♀   425b ♀ ups   425c ♂

ups   422a ♂   ups   422b ♀   422c ♂   ups   422d ♀

418a ♀ ups   418b ♂   420 ♀   419a ♀

419d ♂ ups   419e ♀ ups   419b ♀ ups   419c ♂

417a ♂ ups   417b ♀ ups   417d ♀ ups   417c ♂

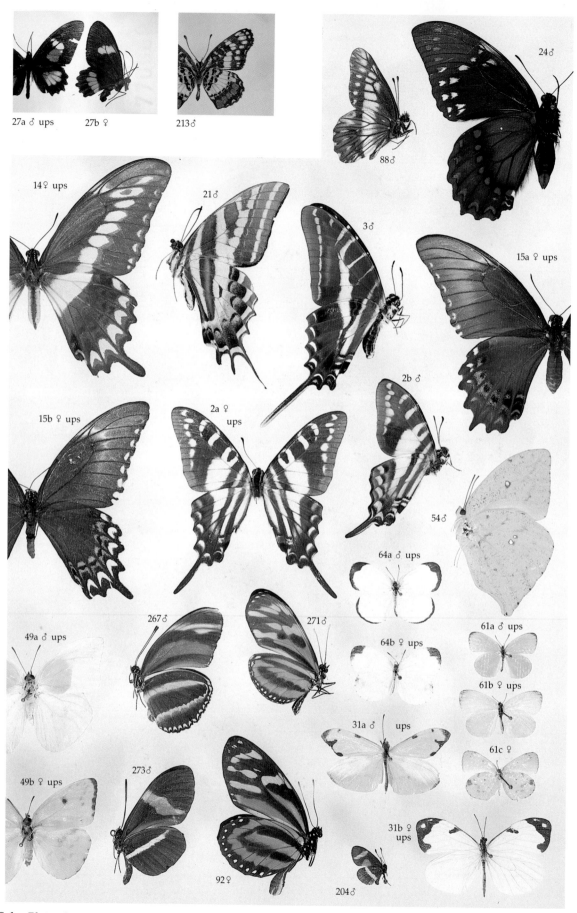

27a ♂ ups 27b ♀ 213♂

88♂ 24♂

14♀ ups 21♂ 3♂ 15a ♀ ups

2b ♂

15b ♀ ups 2a ♀ ups 54♂

64a ♂ ups

267♂ 271♂ 61a ♂ ups

49a ♂ ups 64b ♀ ups 61b ♀ ups

31a ♂ ups 61c ♀

49b ♀ ups 273♂ 31b ♀ ups

92♀ 204♂

Color Plate 58

163a ♀ ups
163b ♂
164♂
161a ♂
161b ♂ ups
167♂
168♂
169♂
170♂ ups
151a ♂ ups
151b ♀ ups
151c ♀
183♂
158♂ ups
175a ♀ ups
172a ♂
172b ♀ ups
152♂
178♀ ups
175b ♂ ups
174♂
138♂ ups
153♂
213a ♀
[213]b ♀
[213]c ♀ ups
274a ♀ ups
274b ♀ ups
274c ♂

Color Plate 59

216♀

245♀

Plate 60. **216** *Chlosyne lacinia adjutrix* basking, Alamo, Tex. (E. Woodbury). **220** *Chlosyne harrisii harrisii* basking, Great Meadows, N.J. (E. Woodbury). **245** *Boloria improba acrocnema* basking and about to oviposit on host *Salix reticulata* ssp. *nivalis* (Snow Willow), Uncompahgre Peak, Colo. **282** *Calephelis borealis* resting, Springdale, N.J. (E. Woodbury).

282♂

220♂

Plate 61 (× 1.0). Strays from Latin America. **277** *Apodemia phyciodoides*. **281 a**, **b**, *Apodemia multiplaga*. **299 a**, **b**, *Eumaeus minijas*. **317 a**, **b**, *Ocaria ocrisia*. **320 a**, **b**, *Oenomaus ortygnus*. **321 a-c** *Thereus zebina*. **322 a**, **b**, *Thereus palegon*. **323 a**, **b**, *Allosmaitia pion*. **348 a-c** *Callophrys herodotus*. **350 a**, **b**, *Arawacus jada*. **365 a**, **b**, *Strymon limenia*. **450 a**, **b**, *Vettius fantasos*. **451** *Perichares philetes*. **453 a**, **b**, *Rhinthon cubana osca*. **564** *Panoquina fusina evansi*. **566** *Thespieus macareus*. **[585]** *Codatractus melon* (similar to *C. arizonensis*, species 585, shown in Color Plate 41). **602** *Autochton pseudocellus*. **617** *Celaenorrhinus fritzgaertneri*. **618** *Celaenorrhinus stallingsi*. **624 a**, **b**, *Arteurotia tractipennis*. **636 a-c** *Carrhenes canescens*. **641** *Grais stigmaticus*. **672** *Heliopetes arsalte*.

Plate 62 (× 0.9). Strays from Latin America. **568** *Phocides urania*. **570** *Proteides mercurius*. **573** *Epargyreus exadeus*. **578 a**, **b**, *Aguna asander*. **579 a**, **b**, *Aguna claxon*. **580** *Aguna metophis*. **581** *Typhedanus undulatus*. **582** *Polythrix octomaculata*. **583** *Polythrix asine*. **586 a** *Codatractus alcaeus*. **[586] b** *Codatractus carlos* (similar to species 586). **587** *Urbanus doryssus*. **588 a**, **b**, *Urbanus esmeraldus*. **590** *Urbanus pronus*, Hidalgo Co., Tex. **593** *Urbanus tanna*. **594** *Urbanus simplicius*. **596 a**, **b**, *Astraptes egregius*. **598 a**, **b**, *Astraptes alector hopfferi*. **599 a**, **b**, *Astraptes alardus*. **600 a**, **b**, *Astraptes anaphus*. **606** *Achalarus albociliatus*. **608** *Achalarus jalapus*. **628 a**, **b**, *Bolla brennus*. **629 a**, **b**, *Bolla clytius*. **632 a**, **b**, *Staphylus azteca*.

Plate 63 (× 0.8). Strays from Latin America; Hawaiian species; miscellaneous species. **4** *Papilio xuthus*. **6** *Papilio zelicaon* form *ampliatanitra*. **7** *Papilio polyxenes asterias*: **a**, **b**, Benton Co., Mo. (both originally named *joanae*, a synonym of *asterias*); **c**, form *pseudoamericus*, Denver, Colo. **44** *Colias cesonia* (Dog Face). **60** *Eurema dina helios*. **109** *Cercyonis sthenele*, individual near ssp. *sthenele*, Santa Cruz I., Calif. **133 a**, **b**, *Oeneis alpina excubitor*. **185** *Vanessa tameamea*. **213** *Chlosyne marina melitaeoides*. **301 a**, **b**, *Chlorostrymon maesites maesites*. **385 a-c** *Lampides boeticus*. **394 a-c** *Vaga blackburni*. **437 a**, **b**, *Synapte salenus*. **438 a**, **b**, *Synapte syraces*. **439 a**, **b**, *Corticea corticea*. **440 a**, **b**, *Callimormus saturnus*. **449** *Lerema ancillaris*. **452** *Erionota thrax*. **455 a-c** *Conga chydaea*. **516 a** *Choranthus haitensis*. **[516] b**, **c**, *Choranthus radians* (similar to species 516). **517** *Mellana eulogius*: **a-c**, light; **d**, dark; **e**, normal coloring. **625 a**, **b**, *Nisoniades rubescens*. **626** *Pellicia dimidiata*. **627 a-c** *Pellicia costimacula arina*. **634 a-d** *Gorgythion begga* (most females resemble 634c). **635 a-c** *Sostrata bifasciata nordica*.

277♂ ups

281a ♂ ups

281b ♂

299a ♀

299b ♂ ups

348a ♂ ups

348b ♂

348c ♀ ups

317a ♀

320a ♂

320b ♂ ups

322a ♀ ups

322b ♀

317b ♂ ups

365a ♀ ups

323a ♀

323b ♂ ups

321a ♀ ups

321b ♂ ups

321c ♂

365b ♂

350a ♂

350b ♂ ups

624a ♂ ups

624b ♂

602♂

672♀

450a ♂ ups

453a ♂ ups

453b ♂

618♂

617♂

450b ♀

566♂

564♂

636a ♂

641♂

636b ♂ ups

636c ♀ ups

[585]♀

451♂

Color Plate 61

598a ♂ ups
598b ♀
568♂
600a ♂ ups
600b ♂
599a ♀ ups
573♀
570♂
596a ♂ ups
599b ♂
579a ♂ ups
608♂
578a ♂
578b ♂ ups
596b ♂
606♂
579b ♂
582♀
583♀
580♂
581♂
587♂
ups
590♂
[586]b ♀
586a ♀
588a ♂
588b ♂ ups
593♀
594♀
629a ♂ ups
632a ♂ ups
628a ♂ ups
629b ♀ ups
632b ♀ ups
628b ♀ ups

Color Plate 62

634a ups 634b ♂ ups 634c ♂ ups 634d ♂ 635a ♀ ups 635b ♂ 635c ♂ ups

625a ♂ ups 625b ♀ ups 626♂ ups 627a ♂ ups 627c ♂ 449♂

627b ♀ ups

455a ♀ 455b ♂ ups 455c ♀ ups 439a ♂ ups 440a ♂ ups 440b ♂

439b ♂

438a ♂ ups 437a ♂ 437b ♀ ups 517a ♀ ups 517b ♀

438b ♂

516a ♂ [516]b ♂ ups 517c ♂ ups 517d ♂ ups 517e ♂

[516]c ♀

213 ♀ ups 60 ♀ 452♂ 44 ♀ ups

394a ♂

301a ♂ 4 ♀ 185♂ 394b ♂ ups

301b ♀ ups 6♂ ups

109♂ 394c ♀ ups

385b ♂ 385c ♀ ups

7a ♂ ups 385a ♂ ups 7b ♀ ups 133a ♂ 7c ♂ ups

133b ♀ ups

89a 89b 89c 89d

89e 89f

145a

89g 145b ♂

Plate 64. Monarchs and their Viceroy mimics. **89** *Danaus plexippus* (Monarch): **a**, egg, Faulkland, Del. (E. Woodbury); **b**, larva, Marion, Ind. (R. Humbert); **c**, larva, Morrison, Colo.; **d**, pupae, Morrison, Colo.; **e-g**, Monarchs roosting in winter, covering the trees in Michoacán, Mex. (all P. Menzel). **145** *Limenitis archippus* (Viceroy): **a**, ssp. *archippus* larva (mimics bird dropping), Faulkland, Del. (E. Woodbury); **b**, ssp. *floridensis* basking (mimics *Danaus*; see Part I), Levy Co., Fla. (R. Stanford).

Stray only
Color Plate 59

172. Marpesia eleuchea   Antillean Dagger Wing

The wings are more rounded than those of *M. petreus*, and the middle dark upf line is angled outward. Possibly a ssp. of *petreus*. Tropical, normally found only in the Bahamas and Greater Antilles, where it replaces *petreus*. Many flights all year in the Caribbean; a rare stray into s Fla. (Jan., Oct., Dec.). Hostplant tree Moraceae: *Ficus*.

Color Plate 17

173. Marpesia chiron   Banded Dagger Wing

Identified by the long tail, the white fw subapical spots, and the many wing bands.

Habitat tropical woodland openings. Ranges south to Argentina and the Greater Antilles. Hostplants in the tropics tree and shrub Moraceae: *Artocarpus heterophyllus*, *Chlorophora tinctoria*, *Ficus*, *Morus*. *Zanthoxylum* (Rutaceae) is dubious.

Eggs pale greenish, laid on buds. Young larvae make a resting perch with dung pellets. Larva (similar to 191 in Fig. 51) orangish-yellow, with reddish-brown transverse streaks, two black dorsal stripes, and many black spines, the side greenish-yellow with dark-red lateral lines; head greenish-yellow, with black lines leading to two black horns (with yellow bases) that are ringed with white. Pupa grayish-white on the thorax and head, with two orange spots on the head and several short black dorsal spines, the wing cases yellowish-white with black spots, the abdomen red-brown.

Many flights in Mex.; migrating occasionally from Mex. to s Tex. (Feb., July-Oct.) and rarely to Kans., rarely from the Antilles to s Fla. (June-July). Adults sip flower nectar and mud.

Color Plate 59

174. Marpesia coresia   Waiter

The basal half of unf and unh are contrasting white; the ups is uniformly dark brown. A rare stray to w and s Tex. (July, Oct.) from tropical Mex., where it has many flights. Ranges south to Brazil.

Color Plate 59

175. Hypolimnas misippus   Mimic

Males and females look very different. Males are black, with unique white and blue ups spots; the orange females mimic the African *Danaus chrysippus*, and do not greatly resemble any American butterfly. This African and Indian sp. may have come to America on slave-trade ships, or possibly by natural migration; now found in the Guianas and throughout the Antilles.

Habitat the tropics. Common in the s Antilles, but very rare in Cuba, the Bahamas, and Fla. (Apr., May, Sep., Nov., Dec.) and probably not native, though one adult was raised from a larva recorded in Fla. Sighted in Miss. (Aug.), and one stray caught in N.C. (Nov.). Hostplants in other countries mostly herb Portulacaceae: *Portulaca*, *Talinum*; Acanthaceae: *Asystasia*, *Ruellia*, *Justicia*, *Blepharis*, *Pseuderanthemum*; Crassulaceae: *Sedum*; Malvaceae: *Abutilon*, *Abelmoschus*, *Hibiscus*; Amaranthaceae: *Amaranthus*; Convolvulaceae: *Ipomoea*; tree Moraceae: *Ficus*.

Larvae gregarious. Larva blackish, with a black middorsal line, transverse bands of tan points, a black middorsal line, and many gray or white branching spines; dark brown beneath; prolegs red; head reddish, with two long black branched spines on top. Pupa tan, variegated and streaked with yellowish-tan, short and thick, with small bumps.

Many flights, all year, southward; migratory, found 322 km (200 miles) out in the ocean. Males perch on or near the ground to await females. The male rises to follow a passing female, he quivers his wings while in a vertical position, the female quivers and lands with her wings partly open, the male lands and pushes under her wings, and they mate. Unreceptive females close their wings, drop into herbage, or fly vertically (often quivering). Males are attracted by fluttering, and are attracted to female (but not male) wings (esp. to the uph and its orange color). American forms are unstudied, but in Africa females are orange, with the fw tips black (form **misippus**) or orange (form **inaria**), the black tips genetically dominant to orange. The uph is white in form **alcippoides**. The white forms better mimic *Danaus chrysippus*. White is not attractive to males, leading G. Stride to suggest that white forms are uncommon because males prefer orange females, but M. Edmunds found little difference in the courtship of orange and white females. Edmunds found that white females fly more slowly, as in *D. chrysippus*, and that marked white-form adults survived longer when *chrysippus* was common (but shorter when *chrysippus* was rare), proving the value of the mimicry in Africa. Unaccountably, form *inaria* survived longer than the *misippus* form; the *misippus* form may have better survival of larvae or pupae.

176. Siproeta stelenes   Malachite

The green patches on adults vary (in C. Amer. at least) from proportionately large (form **claro**), to small (form **oscuro**). Form *claro* may be a dry-season form, and *oscuro* a wet-season one. In Costa Rica, young adults move to higher elevations for the duration of the dry season (P. Opler).

Habitat subtropical wooded areas. Ranges south to Brazil and the Greater Antilles. Hostplants (in Latin Amer. unless stated) semi-woody herb Acanthaceae: *Blechum brownei* (Fla.), *blechum, pyramidatum, Justicia candalerianae, carthaginensis, Ruellia* sp. (Tex.), *coccinea, metallica*; Plantaginaceae: *Plantago*.

Color Plate 16
Fig. 52

Eggs dark green, laid singly (or two or three eggs in a loose cluster) under host leaves, mainly on unfolding leaf buds or seedlings. Larvae eat leaves, and rest on the underside. Larva (similar to 161 in Fig. 51) black, colored purplish or dark red between segments, with many branching spines, the lower spines black, the subdorsal ones pink, orange, or red with black tips and arising from round orange spots (middorsal spines absent except on abdomen segments 7 and 8); prolegs dull purple or pink; head black, with two long red or black horns. A. Young and A. Muyshondt note that the larva "spits" a green fluid when disturbed, and the spines of older larvae can cause a rash when rubbed on human skin. Pupa (Fig. 52) pale green with a whitish bloom, with rows of tiny black dots, a small black point on top of the thorax, four rows of short pinkish (yellow and red) spikes on top of the abdomen (the subdorsal spikes on abdomen segments 4 and 5 several mm long, the others tiny and mostly black), and two head horns (each black dorsally); cremaster black.

Many flights, all year in s Fla. (native) and s Tex. (at times common); a rare stray into Kans. Adults sip flower nectar, rotting fruit, mud, dung, and moist leaf litter, and roost in loose groups on low shrubs. Males perch on shrubby vegetation, and sometimes patrol slowly back and forth, to await females.

Color Plate 16

177. **Anartia fatima** Brown Peacock

Identified by the brown wings with whitish and red bands.

Habitat subtropical open areas and disturbed places. Ranges south to Panama, and a related sp. or ssp. (*A. amathea*) continues on in S. Amer. Hostplants herb Acanthaceae: in Tex. *Ruellia*, in Latin Amer. *Blechum brownei, pyramidatum, costaricense, Justicia candalerianae, Dicliptera unguiculata*.

Eggs green, laid singly and haphazardly on or near the host, esp. on the sepals and bracts of flower clusters, preferring fresh tall plants; up to 200-400 eggs per female. Larva (similar to 161 in Fig. 51) black, with longitudinal stripes (including a lateral stripe) of light dots; spines reddish-brown or blackish-brown; head purplish-black, with two long clubbed horns. A ventral gland on the neck is everted during pupation for unknown reasons. Pupa translucent green, with dots where the lateral spines were in the larva, the cremaster dull pink dorsally and black ventrally; *or* pupa all black; head forked very slightly.

Many flights, sometimes common all year in s Tex. but absent some years; one stray known in Kans. Adults can fly several hundred meters routinely, and occasionally much farther. Adults sip flower nectar. O. Taylor found that adults live up to 38 days in nature in Costa Rica, where adults may diapause in the dry season. Adults sometimes roost in aggregations. Male *A. fatima* patrol with an erratic flight, and sometimes perch on vegetation, to seek females. The courtship of *fatima* and *A. jatrophae* is peculiar. When a patrolling male approaches a female, she closes her wings and leans to one side, the male hovers over that side, then she leans to the other side and he hovers over that side, etc. This seems to be a rejection dance by the female. In successful courtship the male flies behind her with a bobbing flight, she lands, he lands and bends his abdomen to mate. Adults with yellow ups postmedian bands in Costa Rica seem to be genetically different from cream-banded adults upon emergence from pupae, although both fade in sunlight to white-banded. T. Emmel and Taylor found that males approach white-banded adults more often, perhaps because females tend to have whiter bands even when young than males. A. Aiello and R. Silberglied found that the red uph median band is genetically dominant to orange and that males prefer females having a red band.

Stray only
Color Plate 59

178. **Anartia lytrea** Caribbean Peacock

Tropical, found Feb. and Apr. 1972 and 1973 in s Fla., a temporary stray of ssp. **chrysopelea** from Cuba. Ssp. *lytrea* is on Hispaniola. Hostplant herb Verbenaceae: *Lippia* in Cuba. Eggs bluish-yellow, laid singly on host. Larva yellowish-green, with fine maroon mottling and many spines; head bluish-yellow.

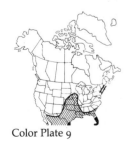

Color Plate 9

179. **Anartia jatrophae** White Peacock

The wings are whitish, with a characteristic pattern. Summer adults are darker. Ssp. **guantanamo** (Fla.) is a little darker than ssp. **luteipicta** (Tex.). Ssp. *jatrophae* and other ssp. range to Argentina and throughout the Bahamas and Antilles.

Habitat subtropical open areas, disturbed and swampy places, often with *Precis coenia* (180). Hostplants (mostly Latin Amer.) herb Verbenaceae: *Lippia* (Fla.), *citriodora, Phyla* (Tex.); Acanthaceae: *Blechum brownei, pyramidatum, Ruellia occidentalis* (Tex.), *tuberosa*; Scrophulariaceae: *Bacopa monnieri* (Fla.), *Lindernia dif-*

fusa; Labiatae: *Mentha piperita, pulegium, Melissa officinalis. Jatropha* (Euphorbiaceae) is an error.

Eggs pale yellow, laid singly and haphazardly near the host or on the underside of host leaves. Larva like that of *A. fatima*, dark brown to black, with transverse rows of silver or white spots (esp. on top but including whitish lateral spots below the spiracles), the lateral fold dark orangish, and a neck gland like that of *fatima*; spines many, black, orangish, or black with orange bases; head black, with two long clubbed horns. Pupa like that of *fatima*, light green, with brown below the cremaster, yellow eyes, many rows of small black dots on the abdomen and top of the thorax, and sometimes a black dorsal line; *or* pupa occasionally greenish-black or all black.

Many flights, all year in s Fla. and s Tex., where it is native and common; migratory northward rarely to Iowa and Mass. Adults sip flower nectar. To seek females, males patrol as in *A. fatima* (but glide frequently), and may perch also.

180. Precis coenia   Buckeye

Color Plates 2 (larva), 5 (pupa), 19, 22
Figs. 21 and 22 (skeleton), 52

Identified by the white on the body side of the large upf eyespot (which is ringed with whitish, then brown) and by the front uph eyespot, which contains a red crescent and is generally larger than the other eyespots. The unh varies from tan to red (form **rosa**); red may be due to cold or to short photoperiod because f. *rosa* flies mainly in late fall in E U.S.

Habitat mostly subtropical to Upper Sonoran/Upper Austral Zone, in open areas and weedy places. Ranges to s Mex., Cuba, the Bahamas, and Bermuda. Hostplants herb Plantaginaceae: *Plantago lanceolata, virginica, coronopus, major, rugelii, helleri, hookeriana* ssp. *californica*; Scrophulariaceae: *Linaria vulgaris, maroccana, canadensis, Kickxia spuria, Digitalis*[t], *Orthocarpus purpurascens, lacerus, Penstemon azureus, Mimulus* (prob. *M. guttatus*), *Antirrhinum majus, Maurandya antirrhiniflora, Gerardia grandiflora, harperi, tenuifolia, stictifolia, purpurea, fasciculata, homalantha, maritima, Seymeria cassioides, Buchnera floridana, Castilleja purpurea, Russelia equisetiformis* (a shrub), *Cymbalaria muralis, Veronica comosa, anagalis-aquatica, americana*; Verbenaceae: *Lippia lanceolata, nodiflora* (vars. *canescens* and *rosea*), ?*Verbena prostrata*; Acanthaceae: *Dyschoriste linearis, Ruellia nudiflora* (oviposition rare), *runyonii*; Cornaceae: *Aucuba* (once at a nursery). "Iridoid glycoside" chemicals in these plants may stimulate females to oviposit; *Euphydryas* (199-202) also choose this chemical (M. D. Bowers) and have nearly the same hosts.

Eggs dark green, laid singly on host leaves (mostly on the upperside) or leaf buds. Larvae eat leaves, buds, and fruits; no nests. Larva (similar to 191 in Fig. 51) usually nearly black, with two middorsal rows of orangish-cream spots (sometimes in Fla. streaking downward into the dark subdorsal area), two lateral rows of cream spots (extensively whitish between lateral rows in E U.S.), and many black branching spines (the spine bases bluish on top of the larva, orange on the side); prolegs orange; head black, with cream points, an orange spot on the front, and two short black spines on top, the top and sides orange. Larva rarely blacker with smaller pale areas, or paler. Pupa (Fig. 52) very light cream with reddish-brown blotches, varying in other individuals to nearly black. Larvae and perhaps adults overwinter, but only in the south and in Calif. lowlands (perhaps no diapause).

Many flights all year in Fla., Tex., and s Calif.; migratory northward mostly

June-Oct., sometimes becoming common in late summer. Several mass migrations are known, and past migrants created a permanent population on Bermuda. T. Walker and associates found (by using malaise traps in N Fla.) that adults fly northward in the spring, to the south-southeast in the fall (E Sep.-E Nov.); P. Opler noted a spring flight to the northwest in Ga. In a sedentary Calif. colony, marked adult males move an average of about 160 m, and females 190 m (maximum 1,100 m), between their farthest capture points (J. Scott). Adults in warmer Tex. temperatures averaged 172 m for males and 286 m for females (J. Hafernik). Tan unh adults, and adults emerging from light-colored pupae, move longer distances than do red-unh adults (form *rosa*) and adults emerging from dark pupae (Scott). A. Clark also thought that form *rosa* is more sedentary than the tan-unh form. Adult *Precis* often glide between wing flaps. Adults sip flower nectar and mud. They live about 10 days on the average in nature and up to a month in the lab. They bask and often rest on the ground with their wings spread and eyespots displayed (in hot weather the wings are closed). A. Blest, working on European *Nymphalis io*, found that such eyespots scare away inexperienced predators such as young birds. Males perch all day on bare ground or low plants on flat areas and gulch bottoms to await females. Although the male behavior of chasing passing objects looks pugnacious, males are not truly territorial but merely looking for females. Courtship is variable. In some cases a passing female is pursued by the male, she lands and closes her wings, the male lands similarly, and they mate. Other times (in the most complex cases), when the female lands she flaps her wings, the male hovers over her and then flutters after landing behind her, and he nudges her from behind before they join. An unreceptive female rejects a male by flapping the wings vigorously, by raising the abdomen or spreading the wings so he cannot join, or by flying away.

181. Precis evarete   Smoky Buckeye

Color Plates 18, 19

Resembles *P. coenia*, but the large upf eyespot has brown toward the body (the *coenia* eyespot is in a white patch except at the rear), the white upf postmedian band is suffused with brown, orangish, or orangish-white (pure white in *coenia*), and the ups ground color is blacker. Except in some Tex. adults, the front uph eyespot lacks orange and is usually the same size as or smaller than the hind upf eyespot. Occurs only in the extreme south. Differs from *P. genoveva* in having most of the antenna club ochre, the ups smoky-brown, and the upf postmedian band seldom orange. In ssp. **zonalis** (first found in s Fla. in 1978, widespread by 1981, and throughout the Antilles, Panama, and Colombia; tropical E Mex. to Costa Rica "*zonalis*" are an unnamed ssp. with an orange upf postmedian band) the upf postmedian band is orangish-white and much broader than in *genoveva* (because the brown ground color does not extend as far into the band in cells M$_2$ and M$_3$), and the unh median line is straighter; as in *genoveva*, the hind upf eyespot is ringed with orange but lacks a complete brown ring, and the front uph eyespot is small and usually lacks orange. Ssp. **nigrosuffusa** (Ariz.-Tex. south to upland C Mex. and s Baja Calif.) is the same, but the upf postmedian band is usually brown (sometimes orange); because of past hybridization with *P. coenia* the hind upf eyespot is ringed with reddish or whitish, which in turn is usually within a complete brown ring, and the front uph eyespot is the same size as or a little bigger than the hind upf eyespot and occasionally has red in it. Ssp. *evarete* and other ssp. are in S. Amer. to Argentina. The cold-winter form **rosa** has a redder unh. J. Hafernik's females of ssp. *zonalis* (from Puerto Rico), when released in front of *P. coenia* males, mated and produced vigorous hybrids, but the hybrids were mostly sterile. He also hybridized Tex. ssp. *nigrosuffusa* with the unnamed Guatemalan ssp. and with *coenia*; these hybrids and backcrosses were completely normal and fertile. Nevertheless, *P. coenia* is treated as a separate species from *P. evarete* on the basis of his statistical analysis of wing pattern variation and his studies of courtship in nature. Ssp. *nigrosuffusa* males refuse to court *coenia* females because of their white upf postmedian band and lighter color, and male *coenia* usually refuse to court *evarete* females because of their orange or brown upf band and dark ground color (male *coenia* also refuse *coenia* females that are painted black—however, A. Shapiro found that aberrant *coenia* females without the white band are courted in 49 percent of their encounters with normal wild males [vs. 74 percent for normal females], so a pheromone may prevent this much hybridization between species in nature). Occasional hybridization occurs between *nigrosuffusa* and *coenia* in Tex. (and sometimes in c Ariz. and sw N.M.), mainly male *coenia* × female *nigrosuffusa*, resulting in the larger front uph eyespot (occasionally containing orange) of *nigrosuffusa*. Hafernik thought that *nigrosuffusa* evolved its dark wings to prevent hybridization with *coenia*. Pheromones may allow *P. evarete* and *P. genoveva* to identify themselves; A. Clark noted that *coenia* males possess a "sweet sugary" odor, perhaps a pheromone.

Habitat dry Upper Sonoran Zone open woodland, and subtropical open fields, often in disturbed areas. Hostplants herb Scrophulariaceae: *Stemodia tomentosa* (the main host in Tex.), *Gerardia maritima* (Tex.), *purpurea* (Tex.), *stictifolia* (rarely eaten by Tex. *nigrosuffusa* × *coenia* hybrids), *Mimulus* (Ariz.); Verbenaceae: *Stachytarpheta jamaicensis* (main host in Fla. and the Antilles), *indica* (Puerto Rico); Acanthaceae: *Blechum pyramidatum* (Jamaica, Costa Rica, El Salvador), *Ruellia tuberosa* (Jamaica), *nudiflora* (oviposition rare, and only in Tex.); Convolvulaceae: supposedly *Ipomoea* in Brazil. Texas lab larvae also eat *Plantago lanceolata* (Plantaginaceae). Tex. larvae prefer *Stemodia*, which Guatemala and U.S. *P. coenia* larvae refuse because of its hairy leaves (young *nigrosuffusa* larvae burrow through the hairs). Conversely, a major host of *coenia* in Tex. (*Gerardia stictifolia*) is not used by *evarete*; each species thus has a major food of its own, preventing competition.

Eggs laid singly on the host. Larvae eat leaves at least; no nests. Larva (ssp. *nigrosuffusa*) black (usually darker than that of *P. coenia*, but some are identical), with cream points, two middorsal rows of orangish-cream spots, and two lateral rows of cream blotches, the dorsal three rows of spines black with bluish bases, the lateral three rows of spines orange at the base; legs and prolegs orange; head black, with cream points, an orange spot on the front, and two short black spines on top, sometimes orangish on the top and side. Larva (Fla. ssp. *zonalis*, R. Boscoe; similar in C. Amer.) black, usually darker than that of *nigrosuffusa*, with two faint middorsal rows of cream dots and some faint cream lateral dots, the spines black with bluish bases, the lateral and sublateral spines sometimes slightly orangish at the base; legs and prolegs paler tan; head black (the top rear somewhat orangish), with cream points, an orangish spot on the front, and two short black spines on top. Older larvae are darker than those of *coenia*; young larvae are black in ssp. *zonalis*, cream in *coenia*. J. Swainson notes that the black *zonalis* larva is camouflaged on the purplish-black stems of *Stachytarpheta*. Pupa like that of *coenia*, light to dark brown (usually tan) mottled with cream, with dorsal cones (edged behind with white).

Many flights, all year in s Fla. and s Tex., at least Apr.-Oct. in Ariz. Northward migrations occur in Argentina in Mar. and Apr., but are rare in N. Amer. (one migration invaded s N.M. in Apr. 1983, and strays occasionally fly from s to c Tex.). Various observers state that ssp. *zonalis* flies less strongly and less readily than does *P. genoveva*; nevertheless, *zonalis* has invaded Fla. from Cuba and spread through s Fla. Males in a Tex. island colony ranged an average of 189 m (females 286 m) between the farthest capture points (maximum 1,400 m, J. Hafernik). Adults sip flower nectar; they pollinate the hostplant *Stachytarpheta* in Jamaica (M. Percival). Males perch all day to await females, mostly on flat areas on the top of vegetation such as sedges, but sometimes on bare ground. When two perching *nigrosuffusa* males interact, they do not fly vertically as *P. coenia* males do. Mating is like that of *coenia*; the male pursues the female, who lands, and the male may nudge her from the rear before they join. Unreceptive females flutter the wings, move the abdomen away from the male, or try to fly away.

Color Plate 18

182. Precis genoveva   Black-Mangrove Buckeye

Differs from *P. coenia* in having the upf postmedian band orangish or orangish-white, the upf eyespot ringed only with orange (not with brown), no white on the body side of this eyespot, the front uph eyespot lacking orange and usually the same size as or smaller than the hind upf eyespot, and the range only in s Fla. and s Tex. Differs from the Fla. *P. evarete zonalis* in having a narrower orangish upf postmedian band (the brown color extending farther out into the band in cells M$_2$ and M$_3$) and in having the unh median line more jagged. Differs from the Tex. *P. evarete nigrosuffusa* in having the upf postmedian band never brown, the hind upf eyespot never completely ringed with brown, and the front uph eyespot without orange and seldom larger than the hind upf eyespot. In addition, differs from both *P. evarete* ssp. in having most of the antenna club brown, the ups ground color lighter (brown), and an orange uph submarginal band in males (seldom present in male *evarete*; present in females of both species); less noticeably, the wingspan is usually slightly larger, the fw tip protrudes very slightly more, and the unh is seldom banded and often lacks eyespots (often with reddish-brown bands and eyespots in *P. evarete zonalis*). The unh is usually tan, though in cold winters it is redder (form **rosa**). Occasional hybrids with *coenia* occur in Fla., though they are probably sterile; Pacific-Coast Mexican populations may represent hybridization with *coenia*. E. Munroe treated *P. genoveva* as a dry-season form of *P. evarete*, but W. Comstock and T. Turner considered it a species. African *Precis octavia* has temperature-induced adult and larval forms (adults blue-black at low temperature, pale red at high; L. McLeod), giving rise to the theory that *genoveva* is a form of *evarete*. But most traits of our *Precis* except form *rosa* seem not to vary seasonally, and *genoveva* has always been present in s Fla., whereas *zonalis* is very recent.

Habitat subtropical coastal Black Mangrove swamps and tidal flats. Ranges south to the Bahamas, Greater Antilles, St. Croix, and the Atlantic coast of Mex. (Yucatán and Veracruz north rarely to Tex.). Hostplants herb Verbenaceae: *Avicennia germinans* (Fla., R. Boscoe; Jamaica), *Lippia* (Cuba) *nodiflora* and *reptans* (both Puerto Rico). The Puerto Rico hosts possibly refer to *P. e. zonalis*, but they probably refer to *P. genoveva* because R. Boscoe found that Fla. *P. e. zonalis* females refused to oviposit on *Lippia*.

Eggs laid singly on the host, most often on the upperside. Larvae eat leaves; no nests. Larva (Fla., R. Boscoe) black, darker than that of *P. evarete nigrosuffusa* but slightly more orange than that of *P. e. zonalis*, with cream points, two faint middorsal rows of cream dots, and a faint lateral row of cream dots; spines black, with bluish bases (but the lateral and sublateral spines orangish at the base); legs and prolegs orange; head black (the top rear orange), with cream dots, an orange spot on the front, and two short black spines on top. Pupa similar to that of *P. evarete*.

Many flights, all year in s Fla.; a rare stray from Mex. to s Tex. and from s to c Fla. Adults sip flower nectar.

183. Hypanartia lethe   Orange Map Wing

Stray only
Color Plate 59
Fig. 52

Mostly orange, the uns camouflaged, resembling bark or a map. Tropical; doubtfully recorded in s Tex., a stray from Mex. Ranges to S. Amer. Hostplants in Brazil herb and tree Urticaceae: *Boehmeria caudata*; Ulmaceae: *Celtis* probably *braziliensis*, *Trema*. Larvae live in rolled-leaf nests. Larva (similar to 195 in Fig. 51) nearly white, turning ochre, then turning greenish at pupation, with many black spines, but apparently no head horns. Pupa (Fig. 52) whitish-green, with pure-green oblique lines slanting forward on the top and each side of the abdomen, a dark spot at the wing base, many dorsal cones (those in the saddle silver), and two short horns on the head. Many flights in Mex. Males perch on small trees in gulches and along roadsides in Colombia to await females; their flight is swift.

184. Vanessa atalanta   Red Admiral

The wing pattern is unique.

Color Plates 2 (larva),
17, 23

Habitat almost everywhere from the subtropics to the edge of arctic tundra south to Guatemala and the Greater Antilles. Also native to N. Africa and Eurasia, and established on the Canary Is., the Azores, New Zealand, Hawaii, and Bermuda; a stray to Iceland. Hostplants herb Urticaceae: *Urtica dioica* (and ssp. *gracilis*, *holosericea*), *urens*, *Soleirolia soleirolii*, *Parietaria pennsylvanica*, *floridana*, *Boehmeria cylindrica*, *Pipturus albidus*, *Laportea canadensis*; Moraceae: *Humulus lupulus*.

Eggs pale green, laid singly on the upperside of host leaves, which larvae eat. Young larvae live and eat inside a nest made by silking young leaves (or parts of one leaf) together; an older larva bites through the petiole making the leaf droop, then silks the leaf edges together above it and lives inside the tube, eating the end of the leaf. Larva (similar to 195 in Fig. 51) yellowish, yellow-green, grayish, reddish, or mostly black in different individuals (some have greenish-yellow lateral patches), with white dots, and with many branching spines (including one on top of abdomen segment 1), the spines usually black but sometimes pale yellow-white with reddish bases; head black (brown in the paler larvae). Pupa reddish-gray or gray-brown, densely reticulated with black (*or* pupa greenish-gray with a bronze dorsal sheen, if the larva was light), with yellowish dorsal cones, dorsal gold spots, and a darker lateral abdominal band. British pupae are said to be yellow-golden when attached to their host, but blackish when attached to tree trunks. Adults (and doubtfully pupae) hibernate.

Two flights northward (L June-E Aug., and L Aug. overwintering to May, in Colo.); about four or more flights nearly all year in s Fla., s Tex., and lowland Calif. Migratory; several mass movements are known in the U.S. and Canada, many in Europe. A stray into Iceland; the Alaska-N Canada records may all be strays. A permanent resident in Bermuda and Hawaii. O. Shields marked adults of all four Calif. *Vanessa* species on hilltops. Fewer than 7 percent were recaptured after a day, and the maximum time of stay was only 3 days for *V. atalanta* and 2 for *V. carye*, illustrating the great movements of *Vanessa*. Adults feed on sap, fruit, dung, and flower nectar. Males perch on hilltops (on shrubs or the ground), porch roofs on flat land, etc., mainly in the afternoon to evening, to await females. Males arrive on hilltops later at higher temperatures—12:30 P.M. at 15°C (59°F), 3 P.M. at 30°C (86°F)—and slightly later at high humidity (Shields). In Iowa flatlands, males perch mostly near linear features (sidewalks, walls, lanes of trees), esp. from 5 to 7:30 P.M., and usually move to a different spot every day (R. Bitzer and K. Shaw).

185. Vanessa tameamea   Kamehameha Butterfly

Hawaii only
Color Plate 63

Like *V. atalanta*, but the fw has more orange, and *V. tameamea* occurs only in Hawaii (all the main islands).

Habitat montane tropical woods. Hostplants herb Urticaceae: *Pipturus albidus, Boehmeria nivea, Neraudia, Touchardia, Urera.*

Eggs laid singly on host. Larvae eat leaves, and live in rolled-leaf nests until mature. Larva usually green, with a cream lateral stripe (below a darker line), *or* larva wine-brown or purplish (either with a yellowish lateral line) or multicolored; branching spines many, red, black-tipped, the two on the end of the abdomen very large; head the color of the body, black around the eyes, with a maroon spot on the front and many large white-tipped tubercles.

Many flights all year. Adults feed on sap.

186. Vanessa cardui   Painted Lady

Color Plates 5 (pupa), 19, 23
Fig. 52

Orange-patterned on the ups like *V. carye* and *V. virginiensis*, but the upf subapical spot is white unlike that of *carye*, and the unh has four or five eyespots (only two in *virginiensis*). The most widely distributed butterfly in the world, ssp. **cardui** occurs in N. Amer. (straying to Bermuda and Iceland) south to Venezuela and throughout the Bahamas and Antilles; also throughout Eurasia, Africa, Madagascar, the Azores and Canary Is., India, and Ceylon. Ssp. **kershawi** (Australia and New Zealand, straying into Fiji) has only four uph submarginal dots, these with bluer centers. Hawaii adults are intermediate between *cardui* and *kershawi* (E. Zimmerman), and both forms develop from the eggs of a single female (R. Perkins).

Habitat everywhere, mostly in open or disturbed areas. Hostplants herb (rarely shrub or tree) Compositae: *Cirsium arvense, texanum, discolor, vulgare, occidentale, muticum, altissimum, undulatum, breweri, neomexicanum, centaureae, solstitialis, hydrophilum, scopulorum, hesperium, Cynara scolymus, Onopordum acanthium, Silybum marianum, Carduus nutans, acanthoides, crispus, Arctium lappa, minus, Lappa officinalis, Cnicus benedictus, Artemisia frigida, stelleriana, vulgaris, ludoviciana* var. *gnaphalodes, Calendula officinalis, Centaurea solstitialis, nigra, Achillea millefolium, Anaphalis margaritacea, Helianthus annuus, argophyllus, Helianthella, Filago arvensis* (Europe), *Helichrysum, Lactuca sativa, Chrysanthemum, Parthenium argentatum, Senecio maritima*[t]*, cineraria*[t]*, Serratula*[t]*, Wyethia glabra, Tanacetum, Xanthium pennsylvanicum* var. *canadense*; Boraginaceae: *Amsinckia douglasiana, Borago officinalis, Cryptantha angustifolia, Echium vulgare, Nonea, Anchusa officinalis, Symphytum officinale, Lycopsis*; Malvaceae: *Althaea rosea, officinalis, Malva parviflora, sylvestris, neglecta, nicaeensis, moschata, Sida hederacea, Sphaeralcea ambigua, Gossypium*; Chenopodiaceae: *Beta vulgaris, Chenopodium album*[t]; Hydrophyllaceae: *Eriodictyon californicum, Phacelia campanularia*; Leguminosae: *Glycine max, Lupinus bicolor, albifrons, formosus, perennis, arboreus, argenteus, succulentus, arcticus* var. *subalpinus, Medicago sativa, Phaseolus vulgaris, Pisum sativum, Trifolium*; Urticaceae: *Soleirolia* (*Helxine*), *Parietaria, Urtica urens, dioica* ssp. *gracilis*[t]; Labiatae: *Mentha, Salvia, Stachys sieboldii*; Verbenaceae: *Lantana*; Solanaceae: *Nicotiana glauca, Petunia, Solanum tuberosum*; Rosaceae: *Fragaria, Prunus* (a tree); Convolvulaceae: *Ipomoea batatas*; Plantaginaceae: *Plantago lanceolata*; Cruciferae: *Raphanus sativus*; Polygonaceae: *Rumex*; Umbelliferae: *Eryngium*; vine Cucurbitaceae: *Cucumis melo*; shrub Rhamnaceae: *Rhamnus*; tree Ulmaceae: *Ulmus americana*; tree Rutaceae: *Citrus sinensis*; the grass *Zea mays* (in Europe). Obviously prefers Compositae, esp. *Cirsium*. Sometimes a pest on Iowa soybeans (*Glycine*). One larva eats about 234 cm^2 of soybean leaves in its lifetime, all but 7 cm^2 in the last two larval stages (F. Poston).

Eggs pale green, laid singly on the upperside of host leaves. Larvae eat leaves, and live in silk nests on top of leaves. Larva grayish-brown (the front and rear of the body blacker, the underside often red-brown), with many yellowish transverse lines on the front and back of each segment; or larva mostly black; all larvae with a dark middorsal line (in a yellowish band) and a yellowish lateral stripe; spines many, yellowish, orangish, or brownish-white tipped with black, bluish-gray around their bases, the base of the lateral abdominal spines usually orange; head black or reddish-brown, wider than that of *V. carye*, with many short white hairs, the long dorsal hairs on the cones black, not white as in *V. atalanta*. Pupa (Fig. 52) metallic-greenish, bluish-white, whitish-gold, or brown, with brown patches and gold points. Adults hibernate (doubtfully also pupae), but only in mild winters or in the south. The male and female reproductive systems stop functioning (no eggs are produced) in Sep.-Oct., in preparation for hibernating, owing to short photoperiod (W. Herman and S. Dallmann).

Many flights all year in s Tex. (very rare in summer), s Fla., and s Calif. Migratory and irregular northward, from spring to fall; flying thousands of kilometers to Iceland, Bermuda (not a resident there), the Arctic, N Greenland, and Hawaii. In cold winters overwinters only in sw U.S. and Mex. deserts and in s Fla. Records accumulated by C. Williams show that adults fly north (often in large flights) from spring through July, returning south in less-spectacular fashion from L July-Aug. (at high altitude) through fall. In California, migration is to the northwest in L Mar.-Apr., to the south (southeast?) in L Oct.-E Dec. In sw U.S., migration is to the northeast in spring, to the southwest in late summer and fall (starting as early as L July at high altitude; see "Dispersal and Migration," in Part I). The main puzzle regarding *V. cardui* is the weak return flight in late summer and fall. The only return flights I have seen were to the southwest in L July and M Aug. above timberline. In the Canadian Zone of Colo., T. Emmel and R. Wobus noted no movement M July-M Aug., but most adults suddenly moved south and south-southwest in L Aug., a few stragglers continuing southward through M Sep. Plains adults in Sep.-Oct. mostly just feed, though a large southward flight was noted in Ont. in L Sep. by W. Henson, a flight to the southwest in s N.M. in M Oct. by S. Cary. Adults sip flower nectar, and sometimes aphid honeydew. Mate location is like that of *V. atalanta*. In courtship, the male and female fly in a fast figure-eight pattern.

Color Plates 2 (larva), 5 (pupa), 19, 23

187. Vanessa virginiensis   American Painted Lady

Identified by the two large unh eyespots beyond the cobweb pattern.

Habitat nearly everywhere in open areas from subtropics to lower Canadian Zone, a stray northward. Ranges to Venezuela and the Greater Antilles, and rarely strays to Hawaii, the Azores, Britain, and sw Europe; apparently established on the Canary Is. Hostplants herb Compositae: *Gnaphalium palustre, obtusifolium, bicolor, purpureum, Antennaria parvifolia, plantaginifolia, neodioica, Anaphalis margaritacea, Artemisia douglasiana, absinthium*[t], *stelleriana*[t], *ludoviciana, Arctium lappa, Cirsium arvense, Carduus, Onopordum acanthium, Silybum marianum, Helianthus, Vernonia, Senecio maritima*[t], *cineraria*; Boraginaceae: *Echium vulgare, Myosotis*; Leguminosae: *Lupinus*; Malvaceae: *Althaea rosea, Malva*; Urticaceae: *Urtica*; Balsaminaceae: *Impatiens capensis*[t]; Scrophulariaceae: *Antirrhinum*. Prefers the Compositae tribe Inuleae (the first three genera).

Eggs pale yellowish-green, laid singly on the upperside of leaves, which the larvae eat. Larvae live inside silk nests; plant hairs are used in the nest of young larvae, and several leaves are silked together by older larvae. Larva whitish or yellowish, with many black transverse lines, a whitish, yellowish, or orangish lateral band, broad black transverse bands on the top half (these bands contain black branching spines with orange or red at their bases, and white subdorsal spots on the abdomen); head black. Pupa grayish-white, golden-green with purplish areas, yellow, or pale brown; all with dark dots, brown ventral and lateral stripes, and many orange points. Adults (doubtfully also pupae) hibernate.

Many flights all year in s Fla., s Tex., and s Calif.; only two flights in the north, the second flight apparently overwintering (active M May-Sep. at Ottawa). Somewhat migratory, rarely flying to Lab., Iceland, Hawaii, and islands west of Africa. Adults sip flower nectar and mud. Mate-locating behavior is like that of *V. atalanta* (184), occurring as late as 7:45 P.M.

Color Plate 19

188. Vanessa carye   Western Painted Lady

Like *V. cardui* (186), but the fw is angled, and the upf postmedian bar is orange (white in *cardui*). Hybrids with *V. atalanta* (184) sometimes occur in Calif. The valva of the N. Amer. ssp. **annabella** differs somewhat from ssp. *carye* of S. Amer. (south to Argentina, and known in Easter I.), which W. Field treated as a distinct species, but the male gnathos is very variable and the wing pattern is nearly identical.

Habitat mostly Upper Sonoran to Canadian Zone, in open areas and suburbs. Hostplants herb Malvaceae: *Althaea rosea, Malacothamnus fasciculatus, Lavatera assurgentifolia, Malvastrum exile, Malva parviflora, sylvestris, neglecta, nicaeensis, rotundifolia, Sida hederacea, Sidalcea malvaeflora, glaucescens, oregana* ssp. *spicata, Sphaeralcea ambigua*; Urticaceae: *Urtica urens, dioica* ssp. *holosericea*. Doubtful hosts are Leguminosae: *Lupinus succulentus, arboreus*; Oleaceae: *Ligustrum ovalifolium*[t], *vulgare*; Labiatae: *Lavandula latifolia*.

Eggs pale green, laid singly on host leaves (probably on the upperside). Larvae eat leaves, and live inside a silk nest among the leaves. Larva variable, tan to reddish or blackish with orange blotches; head covered with many tiny white hairs and several long black dorsal hairs on cones. G. Okumura found that the head is smaller than that of *V. cardui* (2.5 mm wide vs. 3.3 mm in *cardui*), the head cones are much larger, and the hairs on the body scoli are longer. Pupa light brown, with gold spots. Adults hibernate.

Many flights all year in lowland Calif.; two flights, the first in midsummer, the second from fall apparently overwintering to spring, in the Rockies; perhaps one flight in higher mountains, or a migrant there. Several mass flights seen in Calif. and Argentina; a stray into c B.C. and e N.D. Adults sip flower nectar and manure. Dispersal and mate-seeking are like that of *V. atalanta*.

Color Plates 19, 22

189. Polygonia interrogationis   Question Mark

Named for the unique silver unh mark. The uns is brown; wing margins are smooth, but the fw is quite hooked. The upf cell M_2 has a black postmedian spot, and the uph tail is often violet-tipped. In non-hibernating adults (form **umbrosa**) the outer half of the uph is darker than in hibernating adults; W. Edwards raised each form from the other.

Habitat Subtropical to Transition Zone woodlands and suburbs. Ranges south to c Mex. Hostplants tree Ulmaceae: *Ulmus americana, rubra, pumila, parvifolia, crassifolius, Celtis occidentalis, laevigata*; vine Moraceae: *Humulus lupulus, japonicus*; herb Urticaceae: *Urtica dioica* (and ssp. *gracilis*), *Boehmeria cylindrica*. These three families are very closely related. Doubtful hosts are *Populus tremuloides* (Salicaceae), *Tilia americana* (Tiliaceae), *Bignonia capreolata* (Bignoniaceae).

Eggs pale green, laid singly (or stacked in a pile of up to eight) on the underside of young host leaves. Larvae live alone (or often with a few others) under leaves, which they eat, and seldom make nests with the leaf edges drawn down the way *P. comma* does. Larva black, with many white dots, two orange wavy lateral stripes on each side, several yellowish dorsal lines, and many orange branching spines (the lateral spines yellow); head red-brown (all *Polygonia* have two black spiny clubs on the head and black eyes). Pupa dark brown, orangish, yellow-brown, gray-brown, or greenish, with silver or gold spots in the saddle, sometimes a dark-green lateral abdominal band, a dorsal keel on the thorax, two short horns on the head, and many dorsal cones on the abdomen. Adults hibernate.

Two flights, M June-E Aug., and L Aug. overwintering to May in the north (perhaps migrating to Ottawa and not overwintering); three or four flights (May-June, July, Sep. overwintering to Apr.) in Tex. and Ga. Movements are large, and a few small migrations are known; rarely flies to w Colo., Nfld., and Cuba. Adults feed on sap, fruit, mud, and carrion, rarely flowers. Males perch on tree trunks or leaves in the afternoon to await females.

190. Polygonia comma   Comma Anglewing

The uns is brown, and the silver mark is like a comma, but swollen at both ends, not as in other *Polygonia* (except some *satyrus*). The brown uph border surrounds the pale spots and is wider than the upf border. In non-hibernating

Color Plates 19, 22

adults (form **umbrosa**) the outer half of the uph is blacker than in hibernating adults; W. Edwards raised both forms from each other.

Habitat Lower Austral to Transition Zone woods and suburbs. Hostplants tree Ulmaceae: *Ulmus americana*; vine Moraceae: *Humulus lupulus*; herb Urticaceae: *Urtica dioica* (and ssp. *gracilis*), *Laportea canadensis*, *Boehmeria cylindrica*. Doubtful hosts are *Betula papyrifera* (Betulaceae), *Tilia* (Tiliaceae), *Ribes* (Grossulariaceae). In contrast to *P. interrogationis*, larvae unwillingly eat *Celtis occidentalis* (Ulmaceae).

Eggs pale green, laid singly or stacked like hotcakes (up to nine in a pile) on the underside of young host leaves or stems. Larvae eat leaves at night, usually live alone, and when older live under a leaf with the edges drawn down toward each other with silk. Larva greenish-white or cream-white, almost without markings (with whitish or yellow spines); *or* larva greenish-brown or black (with yellow black-tipped spines, white transverse lines on the rear of each segment, a white V in front of each middorsal spine, an oblique white bar in front of each subdorsal spine, and a yellow lateral stripe below white dashes on each segment); *or* larva red-brown (the uns greenish or amber, with an orangish patch around the spines above the spiracles); head dull pink with two short reddish spines in light-colored larvae, *or* head black with black spines in dark larvae (the front may be greenish), with many tiny white spines. Pupa dark mottled brown (with yellower patches) or brown (with a dark lateral line and greenish streaks) or white (with yellow-brown shading and a bronze luster over the front and the wing cases); all with gold or silver spots in the saddle. Adults hibernate. Japanese workers have found that short photoperiod brings about *Polygonia* diapause and that the ovaries make eggs only in the spring; these processes are due to different hormones. The hormone that causes the eggs to mature in the long days of spring also triggers female pheromone production.

Two flights, L June–E Aug., and L Aug. overwintering to May, in N U.S. and at Ottawa; probably one flight, L July overwintering to June, in Man. and Maine; about three flights in the south. A rare stray into c Colo. Adults feed on sap and fruit, rarely on flower nectar. Males perch on the flat ground or side branches of trees to await females, at least from 3:15 to 6 P.M. (and probably perch in ravines earlier in the afternoon).

Color Plates 2 (larva), 5
(pupa), 19
Fig. 51

191. Polygonia satyrus   Golden Anglewing

The unh is usually more golden-brown than in *P. interrogationis* or *P. comma*, and the females less mottled. The brown uph border is so narrow that the light uph submarginal spots tend to blend into the yellowish middle of the wing. The base of upf cell CuA$_1$ has a dark spot like the one behind it; this spot is rare in *comma*. The median unh line is more straight than in *comma*. The uph nearly always has a black spot in the middle, which is variable in the other species.

Habitat mostly Transition to Canadian Zone, along streams and valley bottoms. Hostplants herb Urticaceae: *Urtica dioica* (ssp. *gracilis*, *holosericea*); vine Moraceae: *Humulus lupulus*; shrub Salicaceae: *Salix* (s Ariz.). Other records probably refer to other *Polygonia*: an oviposition on *Ribes* (Grossulariaceae), and B. McGugan's rearings from *Alnus* and *Betula* (both Betulaceae).

Eggs green, laid singly (or in groups or stacks of three or four) on the underside of host leaves. Larvae eat leaves. Older larvae make nests on the underside of leaves by cutting the leaf base slightly (making it droop), drawing down the leaf edges, and fastening them together, as in *P. comma*. Larva (Fig. 51) black, with greenish-yellow on the top of the body (ochre-yellow anteriorly), faint dark V-shaped dorsal marks except behind the head, orange dashes behind the spiracles, and a pale-yellow lateral band (orange between the segments) containing pale-yellow spines; head black, with an inverted cream V on the front and two short black antlers. Pupa tan (sometimes yellowish dorsally) or light brown, with brown abdominal lines (two dorsal lines and lateral and ventral bands) and gold spots in the saddle. Adults hibernate.

About three flights, active Feb.-Nov. and then overwintering, in Calif.; two flights, L June-E Aug., and Sep. overwintering to May, in Colo., Nev., and Sask.; one flight, mostly L July overwintering to June, in the far north, Nfld., and N.S. Adults feed on flower nectar, sap, and mud. Males perch in valley bottoms from about 12:30 P.M. to late afternoon to await females. Hibernating *Polygonia* spend the fall feeding, and usually mate only in the spring.

192. Polygonia gracilis   Hoary Comma (Hoary Anglewing)

The uns is gray (paler than *P. progne*), much darker on the inner half than the outer. The light uph submarginal spots are in a dark band. In ssp. **zephyrus** (sw Sask.-s Alta.-s B.C. southward) the uns is a little less two-toned, and the yellow uph submarginal spots near the abdomen tend to enlarge and blend into the median color more than in ssp. **gracilis** (Alaska-Nfld.), which has a two-toned uns. The two ssp. were treated as separate species, but they intergrade from Man. to Alaska, even Wash., and most are intermediate from Kananaskis to Jasper, Alta. They have the same narrow down-curved gnathos and broad tegumen (Fig. 71), and their ranges fit together nicely. Where two or more generations occur, summer-flight adults have the uph submargin slightly paler than hibernating adults (it is much darker in *Polygonia* spp. 189, 190, 193).

Habitat Canadian to Hudsonian Zone taiga northward, Transition to Hudsonian Zone valleys southward. Hostplants (g, *gracilis*; z, *zephyrus*) shrub Grossulariaceae: *Ribes* (usually currant, rarely gooseberry) *triste*[g] and *glandulosum*[g], both Alaska, *cereum*[z], *inerme*[z], *montigenum*[z], *lacustre*[z], *sanguineum*[z], and on Anticosti I., Que., "currant"[g]; Ericaceae: *Rhododendron occidentale*[z], *Menziesia glabella*[z]. One larva was found on *Rosa*[z] (Rosaceae) but ate it reluctantly. Doubtful are *Humulus lupulus*[z] (Moraceae) and *Ulmus*[z] (Ulmaceae).

Eggs green, laid on host leaves (usually on the underside and petioles). Larvae eat leaves, and rest on the underside; no nests. Larva black, orange with orange-red spines on top of the thorax and abdomen segments 1 and 2, cream with cream spines on top of segments 3-8 (with sharp dark V-shaped marks on the cream segments, the point of each V obscure at each middorsal spine), with a weak black middorsal line (cream on the thorax), black and cream transverse rings between segments, a wavy slightly red line above the spiracles broken by black spines, and a wavy slightly red lateral line broken by black (sometimes white) spines; head black, sometimes with an orange inverted V, and black spiny horns. Pupa light brown (or creamy gray or tinged with green), with gold or silver spots in the saddle, the abdomen mottled brown, with brown lateral and midventral bands. Adults hibernate.

ssp. *zephyrus*

Color Plates 2 (larva), 17
Fig. 71

ssp. *gracilis*

One flight, Aug. overwintering to June, northward; two flights, L June-E Aug., and end of Aug. overwintering to May, in lower mountains southward (Colo., Nev.); perhaps three flights in lowland Calif. Uncommon in E N. Amer. Adults sip flower nectar, sap, and mud. Summer adults often fly to the higher mountains (even to the Alpine Zone) to feed on flowers, and presumably fly downward in the fall. Males perch on shrubs or other plants in valley bottoms from about 12:30 P.M. to late afternoon to await females.

ssp. *progne*

Color Plates 3 (larva), 5 (pupa), 17
Figs. 45, 71

western ssp.

193. Polygonia progne   Dark-Gray Comma (Dark-Gray Anglewing)

Identified by the blackish-gray uns (sometimes brownish-gray in the east or nearly black in the northwest) with little contrast between inner and outer halves. The uns of *P. gracilis* and *P. faunus* is also gray, but the *gracilis* uns is lighter gray, often with a white postmedian band, western *P. gracilis zephyrus* has the uph submarginal area usually paler (except in the southern Rockies), and *faunus* has more ragged wing margins and usually many green uns spots. Ssp. **progne** (E and N N. Amer., Great Plains, west to SE Alta.-C B.C.) has very small orangish uph submarginal spots enclosed in the black band (this band is very wide in the non-hibernating adult form **umbrosa**, a form absent in the other ssp.), and the black median spot in upf cell CuA_2 is small. Ssp. **oreas** (N Rockies, E Wash.-E Ore.-N Calif.; Outer Coast Range of C Calif., where it is not sympatric with *P. gracilis zephyrus*, which flies in the Inner Coast Range) is blackish-gray on the uns in both sexes as in ssp. *progne*, but the orange or yellowish uph submarginal spots are usually larger (occasionally as large as those of *P. g. zephyrus*), and the upf spot in cell CuA_2 is usually large (but some *oreas* adults are identical to overwintering ssp. *progne*, esp. in C Mont. where adults seem to intergrade with *progne* somewhat). Ssp. **nigrozephyrus** (Colo.-S Wyo.-Utah) resembles *oreas* but the pale uph submarginal spots are usually large as in *P. g. zephyrus*; these adults were formerly considered a dark-uns form of *zephyrus*, but the gnathos and tegumen confirm that *nigrozephyrus* belongs to *P. progne*. Ssp. **silenus** (the Cascades north to SW B.C., intergrading to ssp. *oreas* in NW Mont. and NW Calif. in Mendocino Co.; an adult recorded from Klotassin R., Yukon, is probably mislabeled) is like *oreas* but the uns is nearly black in males, dark blackish-gray in females, narrowly edged with russet, the black spot in upf cell CuA_2 is very large, and the ups is a bit darker. The silver mark of *progne* ssp. tapers at both ends like that of *P. gracilis* and *faunus*, though the lower arm is short in ssp. *progne* more often than in the other ssp. and spp. Ssp. *progne* was considered a separate species from western ssp., but their ranges fit together like a jigsaw puzzle, some adults cannot be distinguished, and all *P. progne* ssp. have the same wide gnathos and long tegumen (the gnathos is narrower and more down-curved and the tegumen shorter in *P. gracilis* ssp.; see Fig. 71).

Habitat coastal Redwood forest and Transition to Hudsonian Zone woodland (also Upper Austral Zone in E U.S.). Hostplants (superscript is first letter of ssp.) shrub Grossulariaceae: *Ribes* (mainly gooseberry, rarely currant) *divaricatum*[o s], *Ribes* sp. with spiny fruits[o], *R. rotundifolium*[p], *missouriense*[p], *inerme*[n], *leptanthum*[n], gooseberry[p], currant[p]; Ericaceae: *Rhododendron nudiflorum*[p]; Betulaceae: occasionally *Betula papyrifera*[p]. *Ulmus americana* (Ulmaceae) is dubious.

Eggs (Fig. 45) green, laid singly (sometimes on the ups) on host leaves. Larvae eat leaves, and rest on the underside or on stems, with the front of the body bent sideways, the rear bent up; no nests. Larva (ssp. *oreas* from Calif.) dark brown, yellowish-orange on top of the thorax and abdomen segments 1 and 2, orangish-yellow on top of 3 and 4, then pale yellowish on top of 5-8, with blackish V-marks around the middorsal spines of segments 3-8 (these broader and much more strongly connected into U's than those of *P. gracilis*), a larger brown middorsal triangle within each V, black and cream transverse rings between segments, a wavy orange line above the spiracles containing orange spines, and a wavy pale-yellow lateral line containing pale-yellow spines, the dorsal thoracic spines black (orange in *gracilis*) with pale bases; head black, with many tiny orange cones, a large orange W on the front, orange surrounding both black eye patches, and an orange notch between two spiny black horns. Larva (ssp. *nigrozephyrus*) the same except orangish-yellow on top of the thorax and abdomen segments 1 and 2, pale yellow on top of segments 3-8, and the wavy orange line above the spiracles thin and cream-colored between segments. Larva (ssp. *progne*, W. Edwards) variable, often yellowish-brown, identical to that of ssp. *oreas* in details, except the top of the abdomen does not change as markedly from orange in front to yellowish behind; some summer-generation larvae blacker, with orangish patches on the sides, the spines more orangish. Pupa mottled brown (ssp. *oreas*) or pinkish-tan or sometimes blackish-gray (ssp. *nigrozephyrus*), reddish-brown on top of abdomen segments 2 and 3, with gold or silver spots in the saddle, the abdomen marked with a brown-edged middorsal line and tan-edged lateral and midventral bands, the dark band on the wing often greenish. Pupa (ssp. *progne*) variable, usually pinkish-brown (often greenish on the head and thorax), with a green band on the pinkish-tan or yellow-brown wing and with stripes and lines on the abdomen (a pinkish-tan dorsal stripe, a dark-green lateral stripe, some pinkish oblique lines); *or* pupa dark brown without bands or stripes; all have metallic spots in the saddle. Adults hibernate.

One flight, L July overwintering to E June, north of s Canada and in Wash., the Rockies, and higher mountains; two flights, L June-E Aug., and Sep. overwintering to May, in s Sask., Ottawa, E U.S. (M June-M July, and L Aug. overwintering to Apr., in Calif.-sw Ore.). Uncommon in w N. Amer. Some peripheral records of ssp. *progne* (such as w Kans.) may be strays; all *Polygonia* seem to have fairly large movements. Adults feed on sap, fruit, and mud, rarely flower nectar. Colo. *progne*, *gracilis*, and *faunus* adults roost on twigs with the forewings moved far forward, hiding the antennae between them for camouflage. Males perch in the afternoon on shrubs and small trees (ssp. *oreas* in valley bottoms, ssp. *progne* at the edge of clearings) to await females.

194. Polygonia faunus   Green Comma (Green Anglewing)

Identified by the very ragged wing margins and by the variegated unh that often has green submarginal spots. The yellow uph submarginal spots are always in a dark band. Ssp. **faunus** in the northeast has a brownish uns; ssp. **smythi** (W. Va. southward) is larger with a dark brownish uns. Ssp. **hylas** (Sask. westward, except Calif.) is smaller, with a gray uns (the green unh spots smaller south of c Wyo.). Ssp. **rusticus** (Calif.) is larger, the uns more brownish-gray esp. in the Coast Ranges. Females are variable in w N. Amer. (uns as in males, or varying to nearly unmarked in the usual form **silvius**, which is rare in N.Y.).

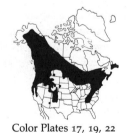

Color Plates 17, 19, 22

Habitat Canadian to Hudsonian Zone, mostly along streams. Hostplants tree and shrub Salicaceae: *Salix humilis*, *Salix* sp. in Colo., *Populus tremuloides*; Betulaceae: *Betula papyrifera*, *lenta*, *allegheniensis*, *Alnus crispa*; Ericaceae: *Rhododendron occidentale* (main Calif. host), *Vaccinium* (sometimes in Mich.); Grossulariaceae: *Ribes* sp., *inerme*. One record of *Ulmus americana* (Ulmaceae) perhaps refers to *P. comma*. The *Ribes* records are from five people, although F. Caulfield notes that *Salix* is preferred. Larvae eat *Urtica* (Urticaceae) in the lab.

Eggs green, laid singly on the bottom and top of host leaves and twigs. Larvae eat leaves, and rest on the underside of leaves; no nests. Larva black, orange on top of the thorax and abdomen segments 1 and 2, white with black oblique dashes on top of abdomen segments 3 to 8, with cream and black transverse lines between segments, a wavy orange line containing dark-orange spines above the spiracles, and a wavy orange lateral line containing white spines; head black, with an orange W on the front and two short black horns. Pupa light brown or dark gray, with gold spots and often an orange flush in the saddle, abdominal bands like those of *P. satyrus*, two long head horns, and many subdorsal bumps; shape more elongate than in other *Polygonia* pupae. Adults hibernate.

One flight, L July overwintering to June northward, Aug. overwintering to May in Colo. and N.S.; two flights, M June - M July, and L Aug. overwintering to Apr., in Calif. - Ariz., apparently L June - M Aug., and Sep. overwintering to May in Va. Adults often sip flower nectar, also mud, carrion, and dung. Males perch in valley bottoms, from about 1 P.M. to late afternoon, to await females.

195. Nymphalis milberti   Fire-Rim Tortoise Shell

The flamelike ups bands are unique.

Color Plate 17
Fig. 51

Habitat mainly Transition to Hudsonian Zone mountains and woods. Hostplants herb Urticaceae: *Urtica dioica* (and ssp. *gracilis* and *holosericea*), *procera*; *Laportea canadensis* in the lab at least. Dubious is *Ulmus* (Ulmaceae).

Eggs pale green, laid in clusters of several hundred (as many as 713) on the underside of host leaves. Larvae gregarious when young, in a silk nest near the top of plant; older larvae, usually solitary, may live in a leaf that is rolled (usually upward) and tied above the larva with silk. Larva (Fig. 51) black above, with orange-and-white dots, a black lateral line (bordered by greenish-yellow), and a black dorsal line (edged with yellow), the uns greenish; many black spines including one on top of abdomen segment 2 (but none on segment 1 or the head); head black. Pupa whitish, golden-brown, golden-green, or nearly black. Adults hibernate, sometimes two or three together.

One flight, mostly L July overwintering to June, in the far north and Colo.; two flights, L June - E Aug., and L Aug. overwintering to May, in N N.Y.; perhaps three flights in Penn. - Ind. Semi-migratory, straying to N.C., etc. A common alpine species in Colo., where adults seem to be migrants from lower altitude (the hosts do not occur in the alpine areas); they feed on alpine flowers in July-Aug., and apparently return to the lower mountains in Sep. to hibernate. Adults sip flower nectar, sometimes sap. Males perch to await females, from about 11 A.M. or 12:30 P.M. to 5 P.M., usually on rocky places just below a hilltop (as in *Papilio indra*, 9), and sometimes on gulch banks on the plains where there are no hilltops.

Color Plates 3 (larva), 17
Fig. 52

196. Nymphalis californica　Western Tortoise Shell

The unh lacks a silver mark, the ups is more orange than that of *N. vau-album*, and the uns is darker.

Habitat Transition to Hudsonian Zone chaparral and woodland. Hostplants shrub Rhamnaceae: *Ceanothus thrysiflorus, integerrimus, velutinus, cordulatus, fendleri, sanguineus, cuneatus.*

Eggs laid in clusters on the host. Larvae gregarious until the third molt. Larvae eat leaves; no nests. Larva black or reddish-black, with tiny white dots, a black middorsal line (edged with yellow), a whitish lateral band, and many orange or black branching spines (the middorsal row yellow); head blackish. Some Calif. larvae are slightly more black with white hairs, and other larvae have larger yellow dorsal patches, with the base of the spines paler. Pupa (Fig. 52) ashy-gray with a bluish tint (the abdomen tan), or orangish or nearly black; all with dorsal bumps on the saddle, the bumps whitish at the base (all the bumps have black, then orange, tips). Adults hibernate.

One flight in Colo., emerging and feeding in July, then overwintering to May; three or more flights in Calif.; perhaps just one flight in B.C. In c Calif. to Wash. there are spectacular migrations. In c Calif., adults overwinter in the Coast Ranges and Sierra foothills through Mar. These produce the first non-overwintering flight in L May-E June, which migrates east across the Central Valley to the higher Sierra. These then produce a second flight in July-Aug., which often produces a third flight in L Sep.-Oct.; in early fall the surviving second- and third-flight adults migrate west to the Sierra foothills and Coast Ranges, where they hibernate and become active the next year in Feb.-E Apr. (A. Shapiro). In N Calif. the flights tend to be toward the north or northeast in the spring, and toward the south or southwest in the fall. Perhaps a native east of Alta., since there are 16 records in a band from Sask. to Penn. (one in Mo. and one in s Vt.); a colony in N.Y. survived at least 20 years. Adults sip nectar and mud. Males usually perch in late afternoon (about 2-5 P.M.), usually on hilltops (but sometimes on foliage on the margins of open areas, on gulch banks, etc.), to await females.

Color Plate 17

197. Nymphalis vau-album　Comma Tortoise Shell

The uns is leaflike, and the unh has a silver J-mark as in some *Polygonia*.

Habitat Canadian to Hudsonian Zone deciduous woodland. Ranges also from E Europe to Japan. Hostplants tree Betulaceae: *Betula populifolia, papyrifera, alba, lenta, allegheniensis*; Salicaceae: *Salix, Populus tremuloides*; Ulmaceae: *Ulmus americana*; Rosaceae: ?*Malus pumila*[t]; Moraceae: ?*Humulus lupulus*[t]; in Europe Fagaceae: *Fagus grandifolia.*

Eggs laid in small clusters on the host. Larvae gregarious. Larvae eat leaves; no nests. Larva green, with white dots, lighter stripes, and many spines; head with black spines on top. Pupa tan or reddish-tan, sometimes supposedly whitish-green, with gold spots in the saddle, a rounded bump on top of the thorax, many dorsal points, and two short head horns. Adults hibernate under bark and in holes, sometimes gregariously.

One flight: adults emerge from pupae M July-E Aug., feed on sap, fruit, mud, occasionally flower nectar, then hibernate, mate, and lay eggs the following spring. This sequence of behavior seems to occur in hibernating adults of all

Nymphalis, *Polygonia*, and *Vanessa*. Native only to the U.S.-Canada border region (and Eurasia) and possibly to the Black Hills and MacKenzie R., but straying thousands of kilometers, rarely to Calif., Fla., and Baker Lake, N.W. Terr. A few mass migrations are known. Varies greatly in abundance.

Color Plates 3 (larva), 5 (pupa), 17, 22
Figs. 35 (ultraviolet), 48

198. Nymphalis antiopa   Mourning Cloak

The yellow borders are unique. The flight is similar to that of some *Papilio*, but more erratic and circling. Ssp. **hyperborea** (Alaska; Mackenzie District, N.W. Terr.) has smaller size, darker borders, and larger blue spots than ssp. **antiopa**, which ranges south to Venezuela and throughout Eurasia (native from Spain to Lapland east to Siberia, and rarely straying to England, where it is called the Camberwell Beauty).

Habitat deciduous woodland and suburbs from the subtropics to the edge of the arctic tundra. Hostplants mostly trees—Salicaceae: *Salix exigua, amygdaloides, bebbiana, discolor, lasiandra, jepsoni, babylonica, nigra, interior, lutea, candida, sericea, Populus gileadensis, trichocarpa, tremuloides, deltoides, alba, eugenei, balsamifera, grandidentata, nigra* var. *italica;* Betulaceae: *Betula papyrifera, alleghaniensis, glandulosa, alba, Alnus, Ostrya virginiana;* Aceraceae: *Acer;* Ulmaceae: *Ulmus pumila, americana, rubra, Celtis reticulata, occidentalis;* Moraceae: *Humulus lupulus* (a vine), *Morus rubra;* Oleaceae: *Fraxinus americana;* Rosaceae: *Pyrus communis, Sorbus, Spiraea latifolia, Rubus* and *Rosa* (both shrubs); Tiliaceae: *Tilia americana;* Polygonaceae: *Rumex acetosella* (a herb). Some wandering mature larvae even eat *Sparganium* (Sparganiaceae).

Eggs whitish, becoming tan when about to hatch, laid in clusters (up to 250), in one layer, in rings circling a host twig near its tip, rarely on leaves. Larvae (Fig. 48) eat leaves, and are gregarious throughout life; no nests. Larva black, with many tiny white dots, orange subdorsal spots, and long black branching spines (but none on top of abdomen segment 2 or the head); prolegs red; head black. Pupa blackish-gray to whitish-tan to light brown, with many pink-tipped, conelike dorsal bumps. Larvae and pupae (if clustered) twitch in unison when disturbed. Adults hibernate.

One flight in the far north and high mountains, probably mostly L July overwintering to June, and perhaps one in the Central Valley of Calif., the adults apparently aestivating in the summer (or migrating?); two flights, L June-M Aug., and L Aug. overwintering to May, in s N.Y., lowland Colo., and coastal Calif.; probably three flights in Va. Migratory, with a few recorded mass movements, rarely straying to s Tex., s Fla., and Bermuda. H. Roer marked and released hundreds in Europe, and found that adults fly up to 70 km after emergence in June-July, go into aestivation until the fall, feed and grow fat, then hibernate and mate in the spring. This pattern may occur also in Canada. Adults sip flower nectar, sap, fruit, and mud; they land on the trunk above the sap, and then crawl down to it. Males perch from about 11:30 A.M. to 5 P.M. on branches in valley bottoms to await females.

Tribe Melitaeini: Checkerspots and Crescents

The Melitaeini occur throughout the Northern Hemisphere. Some species occur in the American tropics, but there is apparently none in the Asian or African tropics. The 38 species occurring in North America include a few that extend almost to the Arctic.

Adults are mostly small, usually some shade of orange, or black and orange. Most species lay eggs in clusters, and the larvae feed together, sometimes inside a silk nest, before hibernating, generally when half grown. The larvae eat many plants, often of Compositae, or of Scrophulariaceae or related plants. Larvae lack branching spines on the head, but have many on the body, including middorsal spines; the spines are generally rather conical, more blunt than those of other Nymphalinae. Pupae have only small dorsal bumps. Larvae generally hibernate.

There are few Melitaeini mimics in North America (see "Mimicry and Other Defenses," in Part I) but some tropical *Phyciodes* mimic some Heliconiini.

Adults flutter in a fairly slow, straight-line flight, but some species are faster than others. Most species fly fairly near the ground and are rather local, but some migrate. All species feed on flowers. Adults usually rest with the wings spread, and also bask by spreading the wings. Even while flower-feeding they commonly spread the wings. *Poladryas* adults keep the wings spread when perching, basking, or feeding, for example, and seem to close them only when roosting or in cold weather. *Phyciodes*, when feeding, may close the wings more often than the others do. Depending on the species, some males perch to await females, and others patrol. The female generally flies when a mating pair is scared, the male dangling beneath her.

199. Euphydryas phaeton   Baltimore

Color Plates 28, 29

Identified by the many cream unh postmedian spots. There is a cline from small adults with red borders in the northeast (ssp. **phaeton**) to larger ones with little red in the southwest (ssp. **ozarkae**).

Habitat upper Lower Austral to lower Canadian Zone; most colonies in the northeast are in wet meadows around *Chelone*, but some (and most of the southwest populations) choose drier ridges and other sites. Hostplants herb and shrub Scrophulariaceae: *Chelone glabra, Gerardia grandiflora, flava, pedicularia, Mimulus ringens, Pedicularis canadensis, Seymeria macrophylla, Penstemon hirsutus, Scrophularia marilandica, Veronica*; Valerianaceae: *Valerianella radiata*; Caprifoliaceae: *Lonicera canadensis, oblongifolia, xylosteum*[t], *Symphoricarpus orbiculatus, Viburnum dentatum, recognitum*; Plantaginaceae: *Plantago lanceolata*; Oleaceae: *Fraxinus americana* (a favorite, six records); rarely Compositae: *Solidago, Actinomeris alternifolia*; in spring rarely shrub Rosaceae. Several ovipositions were also seen on Labiatae: *Galeopsis tetrahit* (introduced). Females and young larvae before hibernation are very choosy, preferring *Chelone* in most places, *G. grandiflora* in Mo., Ark., s Conn., and parts of N.Y., *Plantago lanceolata* in parts of N.Y., *Penstemon* in N.J. and one Ohio site, and *L. canadensis*. After hibernation, larvae are most tolerant, eating all the plants listed, some of which are very different botanically. According to M. D. Bowers, larvae, pupae, and adults that eat *Chelone* are poisonous to Blue Jays, but after feeding on *P. lanceolata* in the lab for several larval stages they become edible. She found that the plant poison is iridoid glycoside, which also stimulates larvae to feed. Ssp. *phaeton*, which usually eats *Chelone*, flies weakly, as if advertising its inedibility. (Western *E. chalcedona* and *E. editha* are also somewhat poisonous.)

Eggs yellow, turning orange in a few days, laid in clusters of 100-600 (average 274) under host leaves, mainly large leaves on the upper half of plant stalks near the perimeter of a cluster of plants. A third of the clusters are laid next to other clusters. Larvae eat leaves. Young larvae move from the lower leaves, where the eggs were laid, to the top of the plant, where they make a silk nest (N. Stamp). Small groups of larvae have more difficulty moving to the plant top because they lay fewer trails of silk for others to follow, and some little larvae fall off the plant; large clusters of many hundred larvae have greater mortality, owing to parasitoids. Young larvae molt inside the webs, but parasitoids can lay eggs through the web into larvae resting just inside the web. Young larvae are gregarious in this silk nest before hibernation; hibernating larvae make a different silk nest near the ground. In spring, the older larvae rarely make nests but are still gregarious when possible; however, because of mortality and their search for food they are mostly solitary. *Euphydryas* larvae snap their heads up when disturbed to knock off parasitoids and predators. Larvae also regurgitate onto predators (Stamp), or may wiggle, crawl away, or flee into the silk nest. Larva black, with orange transverse and lateral stripes and black branching spines. Pupa bluish-white, with velvety-black dots and orange dorsal bumps and with black dashes on the wings; legs orange and black. Third- or fourth-stage larvae hibernate, under ground litter. Diapause is obligatory in nearly all *Euphydryas*, occurring even in continuous light.

One flight, L June-E Aug. in N.S., M June-M July at Ottawa, M May-June in the south. Adults sip the nectar of flowers, but not that of *Chelone*. Colonies seem local but adults become widespread in the Ozarks during population outbreaks. P. Brussard and A. Vawter have proposed that the polymorphism of genes for particular enzymes in tiny colonies is probably maintained by the movement of individuals between colonies. Males perch near the ground to await females.

short-valva-prong ssp.

Color Plates 5 (pupa), 29
Fig. 71

long-valva-prong ssp.

200. Euphydryas chalcedona   Western Checkerspot

Similar to *E. editha* but usually larger, the fw more pointed, the abdomen often with white subdorsal dots, the male uncus with two long hooks, and the upper prong of the antler on the inside of the valva short or curved downward (Fig. 71). This species has been split into two or three species—*chalcedona, colon,* and *anicia*—on the basis of the male valva, but *chalcedona* and *colon* have the same valva shape, with a short upper prong on the male valva antler (J. Scott, $N = 500$), and they intergrade in valva shape with Rocky Mts.-Great Basin *anicia* (in which the valva has a long downcurved upper prong) in certain populations in Ariz., E Calif., Nev., Ida., NE Ore., Wash., Mont., and B.C. The ssp. seem to form a "ring of races," in which *colon* ([n]) races intergrade with *chalcedona* ([c]), and *chalcedona* races with *anicia* ([a]), but *colon* races are usually reproductively isolated from *anicia* races. There is enormous geographic variation, with 38 ssp. named, many of them poorly defined. In ssp. **chalcedona**[c] (lowland Calif. and SW Ore.), the ups is mostly black with cream spots. Ssp. **dwinellei**[c] (local, near Mt. Shasta in N Calif.), also black with cream spots, has a red upf median band. Ssp. **colon**[n] (Ore.-W B.C.) is black with cream spots as in ssp. *chalcedona*, but the cream spots are fewer or smaller. Ssp. **wallacensis**[n] (Ida.-W Mont.-NE Ore.-NE Nev.-extreme NW Utah) resembles ssp. *colon*, but the upper valva prong is longer, intermediate to that of ssp. *anicia*. In ssp. **kingstonensis**[c] (Mojave Desert in Calif., lowland S Nev., W Ariz.), the uph is yellowish-orange, the upf darker. Ssp. **hermosa**[a] (mountains, S Ariz. in scattered sites to SW Utah) resembles *kingstonensis* but has a long upper valva prong. Ssp. **morandi**[a] (higher Spring Mts., S Nev.) resembles *kingstonensis* but the ups wing bases are nearly black, and the upper valva prong is long. In ssp. **sierra**[c] (high-altitude Sierra and Trinity Alps, Calif.), the ups is mostly reddish, with occasional yellowish spots. Ssp. **corralensis**[c] (desert E and NE of San Bernardino Mts., Calif.) is reddish, similar to ssp. *sierra*, but the front part of the uph is more uniformly red. Ssp. **wheeleri**[a] (Nev. and the lowlands of Utah, w Colo., NW N.M.) resembles ssp. *sierra*, but the upper valva prong is long (short to long in *sierra*). In ssp. **anicia**[a] (Rockies in Canadian to Alpine Zone, including Utah), the ups is mostly reddish with thicker dark lines (the ups more black at high altitude). Ssp. **magdalena**[a] (White Mts., Ariz.) is small, the ups mostly reddish-brown, with uniform dark lines. In ssp. **capella**[a] (s N.M. to the foothills of the Colo. Front Range), the ups is brick red without yellow spots. Ssp. **chuskae**[a] (Chuska Mts., Ariz.) resembles *capella* on the ups, but the unh is more yellowish. Ssp. **bernadetta**[a] (lowlands, in sagebrush areas of SE Wash., E Ore., NW Nev., s Mont. to NW Colo., and w Neb. hills) looks whitish because the cream ups spots are large on a blackish background. Ssp. **hennei**[c] (San Diego Co. north to Riverside, Calif.) also looks whitish, but the upper valva prong is mostly short (long in *bernadetta*). Ssp. **olancha**[c] (some s Sierra Nevada colonies) is very similar to ssp. *hennei*, but the ups usually has more red. Mixed-color populations (black to red, whitish to red, etc.) are scattered from B.C. south to Calif. and Nev., even w Colo. Because the alpine Colo. populations (ssp. *anicia*) stay dark when reared in the lab, they are genetically different from the lowland populations (ssp. *capella*) in wing pattern (J. Scott). The variation in the valva antler is largely independent of the variation in wing pattern. Near the coast the upper prong of the antler is usually short (in ssp. *chalcedona, dwinellei, colon*), slightly longer eastward (ssp. *olancha, hennei, sierra, corralensis, kingstonensis*, and esp. *wallacensis*), and long farther east (ssp. *hermosa, morandi, wheeleri, magdalena, anicia, capella, chuskae, bernadetta*). The *colon* races seem to blend completely with the *chalcedona* races, which in turn intergrade completely with the *anicia* races at many sites in E Calif., w Nev., and Ariz., both in wing pattern and in prong length. And D. Murphy hybridized ssp. *chalcedona* and *anicia* and obtained several generations of fertile hybrids (which resemble ssp. *bernadetta*). However, ssp. *wallacensis* flies with the *anicia* races without interbreeding, in NE Nev. (Pequop Mts., though in the Owyhee Valley red adults indicate some hybridization), at some sites in Ida., w Mont., and Kittitas Co., Wash. (though *wallacensis* usually flies a month earlier and at lower altitude in these three areas, and its longer upper prong indicates some past hybridization), and in NE Ore. (in Harney Co. *wallacensis* generally occurs in forest, *bernadetta* in dry sagebrush, but they fly together at a few sites). The biological species concept does not handle a circle of races well, but the circle is treated as one "species" because there is no clear point at which to divide it.

Habitat Upper Sonoran to Alpine Zone desert hills, chaparral, open forest, and alpine tundra. Hostplants (c or no letter, ssp. *chalcedona*; n, *colon*; a, *anicia*) herb and shrub (mostly perennial) Scrophulariaceae: *Besseya alpina*[a], *Castilleja integra*[a], *linariaefolia*[a], *occidentalis*[a], *affinis, chromosa*[ca], *latifolia, foliolosa, martinii, applegatei, Collinsia heterophylla, bicolor, Cymbalaria muralis*[t], *Diplacus aurantiacus, longiflorus, Mimulus nasutus, Orthocarpus*[a], *Penstemon antirrhinoides*[c] (and ssp. *microphyllum*), *cordifolius, ternatus, shastensis, bridgesi*[a], *breviflorus, lemmonii, deustus, procerus, newberryi, subserratus*[n], *barbatus*[t], *whippleanus*[a], *strictus*[a], *barretae*[a], *heterophyllus, gloriosus*[a], *serratulus*[a], *speciosa*[a], *retrorsus*[a], *alpinus*[a], *virgatus* ssp. *asa-*

grayi[a], *eatoni* ssp. *exsetus*[a], *Scrophularia californica*, *Pedicularis densiflorus*, *centranthera*[a], *Veronica anagallis-aquatica*, *Verbascum thapsus*[n]; Valerianaceae: *Plectritis*; Orobanchaceae: *Orobanche fasciculata* var. *franciscana*; Plantaginaceae: *Plantago*[a] *lanceolata*, *major*[cn], *hookeriana*; Caprifoliaceae: *Lonicera*, *Symphoricarpus albus*[cna], *vaccinioides*[n], *mollis*[n]; and occasionally Boraginaceae: *Mertensia ciliata* var. *stomatechoides*[ca]; Labiatae: *Trichostema lanatum*, *Stachys palustris*[t]; Rosaceae: *Rosa minutifolia*, *blanda*[t], *carolina*[t]; Loganiaceae: *Buddleja davidii*. Larvae on *Diplacus* prefer leaves away from the branch tips because they have less sticky resin than the tips (H. Mooney and associates). The resin lowers larval survival and growth because it combines with plant nitrogen, making the tissues less digestible. Larvae, pupae, and adults are probably poisonous to vertebrates, as in *E. phaeton*.

Eggs yellow, turning reddish-brown later, laid in large clusters, mainly on the underside of leaves of sunlit hosts. Young larvae live in a silk nest before winter. Larvae eat leaves and sometimes flowers or bracts. Larva varying from black with middorsal and lateral rows of small yellow dots between the yellowish (not orangish) spines in w Colo., to black speckled with white (with narrow whitish lateral and dorsal bands) in Calif., s Ariz., and Ida. (fewer white bands in coastal Calif.), to longitudinally banded with narrow black and wide white bands in much of the area (northwestern populations including ssp. *colon* and ssp. *sierra* may have the hairs more white, and may have a yellow-orange flush on the thorax), to ivory-white with narrower black stripes in E Ariz. and c Colo.; a dark middorsal line sometimes present; spines above the spiracles and above the legs orangish, the middorsal spines always orange at least at the base (this distinguishes from *Chlosyne leanira*, 209, which may be on the same plant), the other spines black; head black. Geographical variation in larval color is independent of wing color or valva-antler variation. Pupa (Calif. and Colo.) white with brown or black spots and orange dorsal bumps (and orange lateral abdominal bumps). Third- and fourth-stage larvae hibernate in litter or under rocks, rarely in hollow stems. Alpine larvae, and lowland larvae during drought, can hibernate for several years.

One flight, Apr. in the Calif. desert, May-June in most of Calif. and Ore., June-E July in Canadian Zone, mostly July above timberline, to L June-M July in far north; several flights, Apr.-Oct., in w Ariz. (and sometimes more than one flight in the Mojave Desert of Calif. and s Nev.). P. Ehrlich, R. White, and others found that *E. chalcedona* adults generally fly farther than *E. editha*. Flight distance between recaptures averaged 65 m at one site, 146 m at another, for males, but only 18 m for females (several males and females dispersed 3 km, however, demonstrating that female dispersal is probably not less than male dispersal). Average life span for males was 9-10 days in nature. Males seek females all day, by patrolling all over the habitat or by perching (esp. on hilltops, but often on exposed vegetation in clearings), depending on the locality. In courtship, the female lands with the male behind, he may flutter his wings, and then they mate. Unreceptive females flutter their wings.

201. **Euphydryas editha**   Ridge Checkerspot

Very similar to some *E. chalcedona*, but the fw usually more rounded, the size usually smaller, the abdomen without white subdorsal dots, the cream postmedian spot in unf cell CuA_2 usually with more black edging on its inner (basal) side than on the outer side, the red unh postmedian band often extending

Color Plate 29
Figs. 45, 71

slightly onto the median band, the uncus with two short blunt projections, and the upper prong of the valva antler pointed upward (Fig. 71). Geographically variable. Coastal populations (Coast Ranges from s Calif. to lowland w Ore., w Wash., and sw B.C.) tend to be blackish with some red and cream spots and very rounded fw (ssp. **editha**), Pacific-states montane populations (San Bernardino Mts., Sierra Nevada, and higher Cascade Mts. of Ore.-Wash.) tend to be red (ssp. **nubigena**), and Great Basin (including c Ore.) and Rocky Mts. adults tend to be small, mottled with red, black, and cream spots (ssp. **beani**). Dozens of localized races have been named, but they all fit into these three ssp. High-altitude populations are smaller and darker everywhere.

Habitat mountains, typically on ridgetops, from coastal chaparral and Transition Zone open woodland to alpine tundra (alpine sometimes in the Sierra and the N Cascades, always alpine in Alta.). Hostplants herb (often annual, rarely shrub) Scrophulariaceae: *Castilleja nana, pilosa, foliolosa, affinis, linariaefolia, lemmonii, flava, applegatei, lapidicola, chromosa, Collinsia childii, callosa, parviflora, tinctoria, bartsiaefolia, sparsiflora, greenei, heterophylla, bicolor, torreyi, Orthocarpus densiflorus, Pedicularis densiflora, semibarbata, centranthera, Mimulus whitneyi, Penstemon heterodoxus, speciosus*; Valerianaceae: *Plectritis ciliosa, Valerianella*; Plantaginaceae: *Plantago lanceolata, pusilla, erecta, insularis, maritima, hookeriana* var. *californica*; Caprifoliaceae: *Lonicera interrupta*. The same plant families are used by the other *Euphydryas* and by *Precis coenia* (180), but *E. editha* (and to a lesser extent other *Euphydryas*) tends to prefer only one or a few species at each locality, and its egg-laying habits, larval hostplant preference, movements, and mate-locating behavior are also locally adapted (P. Ehrlich, R. White, M. Singer). Larvae, pupae, and adults are somewhat poisonous to vertebrates, as in *E. phaeton*.

Eggs (Fig. 45) greenish-yellow, later turning orangish-brown, laid in clusters of 20-350 (except that females in populations that eat *Collinsia tinctoria* lay about 50 small clusters per female), up to 1,200 per female lifetime, on the underside of host leaves or on the inflorescence, in sunlight or in shade depending on the population. Larvae live in loose silk webs during the first three stages; larvae eat leaves, occasionally flowers, and may eat the whole plant and then starve trying to find another. Different hostplant species are eaten before and after hibernation at many sites. Some coastal Calif. populations occur only on serpentine ridges; *Plantago erecta*, on which the eggs are laid, dies early, and the larvae that manage to crawl to *Orthocarpus* plants, which locally grow only on serpentine, are the only ones that survive to hibernation; the *editha* population size even depends on the abundance of *Orthocarpus* the preceding year. And the abundance of the hostplants depends in turn on the weather; thus, adults are scarce the year after a drought. Larva black, or spotted with white or orange, or striped with white esp. on the side and top; dorsal, subdorsal, and lateral spines often orange at the base; head black. Pupa white or gray (some with extensive black markings), with black blotches and streaks and orange dorsal cones. Third- and fourth-stage larvae hibernate, often under stones; diapausing larvae have thicker and hairier skins.

One flight, Mar.-Apr. on the Calif. coast, June in the Great Basin, L June-E Aug. above timberline. White and Ehrlich found that average movements between recaptures range from less than 25 m up to 193 m, depending on the population (a maximum of 10 km for one adult); if there are no flowers nearby, adults often commute between valley flowers and ridge hostplants. Adults from a population where individuals flew short distances moved much more when transferred to a population where the flowers and hosts were separate. Adults live about a week on the average. Males seek females all day by perching on ridgetops or by patrolling through the habitat, depending on the population and the distribution of its hostplants and flowers. In a patrolling population a flying male spots a resting female (or pursues a flying female who lands), he lands and nudges or pushes under her hindwings, and then they mate (P. Labine). Virgins placed in the habitat were found randomly after an average time of 51 min. by males in the same study (this time depends on the density of males: the higher the density, the shorter the time). Unreceptive females reject males by flapping their wings or by trying to escape; receptive females are passive. Ovipositing females are no longer attractive to males, perhaps because only virgin females have a pheromone; and females generally mate only once, in part because the neck of the male's spermatophore plugs the female's mating tube at least temporarily.

202. Euphydryas gillettii   Yellowstone Checkerspot

Color Plate 29

The broad orange submarginal bands identify it. *E. gillettii* and *Coenonympha haydeni* (107) have similar ranges, and resemble Asian butterflies more than American ones; they apparently resemble ancient butterflies that came from Asia. *E. gillettii* has been introduced into c Colo., but it may not survive there.

Habitat upper Transition to Canadian Zone moist valley openings and meadows near streams and conifers (mostly spruce and pine), sometimes with sagebrush nearby; also Hudsonian Zone meadows in c Wyo. Hostplants shrub and herb Caprifoliaceae: the herb *Veronica wormskjoldii* (for the subalpine ecotype), *Lonicera involucrata* (the usual host), *Symphoricarpus albus* (K. Coolidge); Scrophulariaceae: *Castilleja miniata, linariaefolia, Pedicularis bracteosa*; Valerianaceae: *Valeriana occidentalis* (all occasional spring hosts). Lab larvae also eat *Plantago* (Plantaginaceae).

Eggs yellowish-green, later turning pinkish-red, laid in clusters (averaging 146 eggs) under young host leaves. Eggs are placed mostly under leaves whose upper surfaces face the morning sun (E. Williams); the eggs develop faster there because of the warmth. Larvae eat leaves and leaf buds; young larvae feed communally in a silk nest wrapped around several leaves and the stem until they diapause. Larva (raised by P. Ehrlich) black, with a yellow dorsal stripe and a white lateral stripe; dorsal spines yellow, the other spines black; head black. Pupa white with many black spots, with many orange bumps on the abdomen and top of the thorax. Fourth-stage larvae hibernate (sometimes in the second or third stage) in lowland populations; J. Harry found that the subalpine ecotype hibernates in the second, third, or fourth stage after feeding for 2 weeks, then hibernates the second winter in the unfed fifth stage.

One flight, mostly L June-July (L July-M Aug. for the subalpine ecotype). Adults fly slowly. They sip flower nectar and mud, and usually spread their wings when feeding. They roost singly on conifers. Males seem to patrol to seek females, mainly around treetops, where females evidently fly to mate.

203. Poladryas minuta   Beardtongue Checkerspot

Identified by the two marginal rows of white unh spots before the fringe

ssp. *minuta*

Color Plate 27

ssp. *monache, arachne*

and by the black dashes in the white unh median band. Ssp. **minuta** (Tex., E N.M. plains, south to s Mex.; extinct near Kerrville and Comfort, Tex.) has wider red unh bands and a black line on the unh margin. Ssp. **monache** (s Sierra) has wide white unh bands. Ssp. **arachne** occurs elsewhere, south to w Mex.; populations from Spring Mts., Nev., and Pine Valley Mts., sw Utah, have the *arachne* unh, but the black ups spots are smaller, as in *monache*. Hybridized and backcrossed ssp. *minuta* × *arachne* were obtained by releasing females in nature in front of perching males, resulting in no infertility or inviability of the hybrids (J. Scott).

Habitat (for ssp. *minuta*) limestone ridges in mesquite woodland and plains, (for other ssp.) open mountain hills from Upper Sonoran to Canadian Zone. Hostplants herb (occasionally shrub) Scrophulariaceae: *Penstemon* (beardtongue) *cobaea* and *albidus* (both for ssp. *minuta*), *speciosus* (for ssp. *monache*), and (all for ssp. *arachne*) *dasyphyllus*, *virgatus* (ssp. *arizonicus* and *asagrayi*), *alpinus*, *cyathophorus*, *barbatus* ssp. *torreyi*, all green thin-leaved species. I found that *Penstemon* with thick grayish leaves are not eaten (*P. secundiflorus* is eaten by ssp. *arachne* only when young and green).

Eggs pale yellow, laid in clusters averaging 38 eggs on the underside of the leaves of young hostplants. Larvae gregarious when young. Larvae eat leaves; no nests. Larva (ssp. *arachne*) white, with a black middorsal band and a wide black band above the spiracles, the body below the spiracles dark brown (mottled with gray between the appendages); head orangish-brown, with black around the eyes and a brown bell-shaped spot on the front. Ssp. *monache* larva similar. Larva (ssp. *minuta*) all orange, with a trace of a black middorsal band on the thorax; head like that of *arachne*, but flanges on the "bell" usually smaller or absent. The body spines of all ssp. all black, except that the subdorsal spines have orange bases. Larval (and adult) color-pattern traits are inherited quantitatively; hybrids and backcrosses between the ssp. have a pattern intermediate to that of their parents (Scott). Pupa white, with black patches and dorsal rows of orange bumps. Third-stage larvae hibernate; some Tex. larvae diapause even in spring.

Several flights, at least Jan.-Sep. for the extinct Kerrville population, June-E Sep. in Colo. and Calif., May-Sep. in N.M. and s Nev. The flights overlap. Mark-and-recapture studies showed fairly limited movements of males, averaging about 100 m (Scott); males live an average of about 5 days in nature. Adults sip the nectar of flowers, esp. yellow Compositae, but not *Penstemon*. To seek females, males in Colo., N.M., and Tex. perch on ridgetops and hilltops from about 7:00 A.M. to 12:30 P.M.; then in the afternoon they leave the ridgetops and patrol around flowers. In courtship, the male flies behind the female, she lands, he lands beside her, and they mate. The male may hover above the landed female, may flutter behind her, and may push under her wings to try to mate if she spreads her wings. Females sometimes flutter slightly. Unreceptive females reject males by flying vertically, then rapidly downward, or (on the ground) by flapping the wings in a ritualistic rejection dance, by spreading the wings, by raising the abdomen so he cannot join, or by trying to crawl or fly away.

204. Microtia elva   Little Elf

A rare stray into s Tex. (Aug.), Mo. (one record), and Ariz. from tropical Mex., where it has many flights. Ranges south to Venezuela. Adults sip flower nectar and mud. Males patrol slowly all day to seek females.

Color Plate 58
Fig. 55 (veins)

Color Plate 27

205. Dymasia dymas   Tiny Checkerspot

Like *Texola elada* (206), but smaller, and the unh margin has only a black marginal line and white spots. Males are more black on the ups in ssp. **chara** (Calif., Ariz.), orange like females in ssp. **dymas** (N.M., Tex.).

Habitat Lower Austral/Lower Sonoran Zone desert scrub and woodland, and subtropical thorn forest. Ranges south to c Mex. Hostplants Acanthaceae: *Beloperone californica* (a shrub), *Siphonoglossa pilosella* (a herb).

Eggs pale lemon-yellow, darkening slightly, laid in small clusters on the host. Larvae eat leaves. Larva gray (camouflaged on the grayish *Beloperone* stems), with black and white mottling, a middorsal black line, a narrow white band along the spiracles, and another wider white band below them; spines pale but black-needled, the dorsal spines with orange bases, the lateral spines with a narrow orange basal ring; head black, with whitish points, a whitish spot on the lower face, and whitish bars around the eyes. Pupa whitish-gray, finely mottled with black, with tiny dorsal bumps.

Several flights, Feb.-Nov. in s Tex., Mar.-Oct. in N.M. and Calif. Males patrol slowly, esp. in gulches and flats, to seek females.

Color Plate 27

206. Texola elada   Small Checkerspot

Like *Dymasia dymas* (205), but the unh margin has orange spots at the wing edge beyond the white spots. Habitat mostly Lower Austral/Lower Sonoran Zone and subtropical desert scrub and open thorn forest. Ranges south to Oaxaca, Mex. Hostplants Compositae: a small yellow-flowered sp. in Mex., doubtfully *Baccharis glutinosa* in w Tex.; in the lab, Acanthaceae: *Siphonoglossa pilosella*. Many flights, Apr.-Oct. at least. Males patrol slowly all day, often on flats, to seek females.

Color Plate 27

207. Chlosyne chinatiensis   Lechuguilla Checkerspot

The unh resembles *C. theona* (208), but the unf and ups are spotless orange.

Habitat Lower Sonoran Zone desert hills with *Agave lechuguilla* and other thorny shrubs. Hostplant herb Scrophulariaceae: *Leucophyllum minus*.

Eggs laid in clusters on host. Larvae eat leaves. Larva (half-grown) brown, with many small cream dots, a faint darker dorsal line, a lighter lateral band and many black spines; head orangish-brown. Pupa white, with black dots and five alternating black-and-orange-checked longitudinal stripes (the ventral stripe meeting a black stripe on the proboscis); wing case with three black stripes; head with a black staple-shaped mark. Half-grown larvae hibernate (J. Harry).

Many flights, probably Apr.-Oct. (records are June-July, Sep.-Oct.). Males patrol all day just above the ground, mainly on ridgetops, to seek females.

Color Plate 27

208. Chlosyne theona   Mexican Checkerspot

The unh pattern is simpler than that of the other checkerspots except *C. chinatiensis* (207); *C. theona* has distinct unf and ups spots. Ssp. **bollii** (Tex.) is slightly darker on the ups than ssp. **thekla** (Ariz.-N.M.). Ssp. *theona* and other ssp. range to Venezuela.

Habitat Upper Sonoran Zone desert foothills, open pinyon or oak woodland, and subtropical thorn forest. Hostplants herb Scrophulariaceae: *Castilleja lanata, Leucophyllum texanum, frutescens, Brachiostygma*; Verbenaceae: *Verbena*.

Eggs laid in clusters on the host. Larvae eat leaves at least. Larva velvety brownish-black dorsally, with many small cream dots, a faint darker middorsal line, and a yellowish lateral band; head yellow-brown or orange. Pupa white, with black-and-orange longitudinal stripes and black dots, resembling that of *chinatiensis* but the stripes narrower. Fourth-(third?-)stage larvae hibernate.

Many flights, Apr.-Oct. Adults sip flower nectar and mud. To seek females, males patrol all day in Mex., but in w Tex.-Ariz. they often perch on hilltops.

ssp. *leanira, alma*

Color Plates 5 (pupa), 27

209. Chlosyne leanira   Paintbrush Checkerspot

Easily recognized by the cream unh with black veins and a black postmedian chain. *C. cyneas* (210) in s Ariz. is similar but has the ups more black. In ssp. **leanira** (Calif.-Ore. except the desert), the ups is black, the unh basal marks thick, and the palpi are orange-tipped. Ssp. **alma** (Mojave Desert to Nev., Utah., w-c Colo., intergrading to *leanira* in the w Mojave Desert) has the ups orange in both sexes, with thin black unh basal marks, the palpi orange-tipped. In ssp. **fulvia** (Ariz., s Utah, sw and c Colo., Kans., south to c Mex.), males are partly black on the ups, females orange, both usually lacking black unh basal marks, and the palpi are black and white.

ssp. *fulvia*

Habitat Upper Sonoran to Transition Zone (to Canadian Zone in Colo.) open prairie, foothills, and desert hills, often on gypsum and limestone in Colo., ssp. *alma* often on limestone in Calif. Hostplants herb Scrophulariaceae (l, ssp. *leanira*; a, *alma*; f, *fulvia*): *Castilleja integra*[f], *lanata*[f], *chromosa*[a], *foliolosa*[l], *affinis*[l], *martinii*[l]. Doubtful are *Penstemon*[f], *Cordylanthus pilosus*[l], *tenuis*[l].

Eggs pale lemon-yellow, changing to orange, laid in clusters on the underside of lower host leaves. Young larvae seem to eat leaves and inflorescences; older larvae usually eat the inflorescence. Young larvae gregarious in a loose web. Larva orange (Calif., w Nev.), yellow-orange (w Colo.), ochre-yellow (s Colo.), or yellow (Ariz., s Utah), with black middorsal and lateral lines and a black subdorsal band (this band is very wide in s Calif., and contains white dots in ssp. *leanira* but not in other ssp.); head orange (Ariz., s Utah), reddish-brown (s Colo.), or nearly black (elsewhere). The larval variation does not correspond to the adult variation. Pupa white, with black bars and dots and orange between adjacent black spots. Third-stage larvae hibernate.

One flight for ssp. *leanira* and *alma*, Apr.-June in s Calif. (and a rare fall flight in s Calif. *alma* after heavy summer rains), L Apr.-May in s Nev., May-June northward. Ssp. *fulvia* has one flight (July) in the s Colo. Canadian Zone; three flights, May-E Sep. in lowland Colo., Apr.-Oct. southward. Males mainly perch and occasionally patrol all day on hilltops to seek females.

Color Plate 27

210. Chlosyne cyneas   Black Checkerspot

Like *C. leanira fulvia* (209) in unh pattern and palpi color, but the ups in both sexes black, with cream dots and orange borders. Probably a ssp. of *leanira*, because orangish adults (hybrids with *C. leanira fulvia*?) have been caught in the Huachuca Mts. Also, an intermediate population was found in the lower Chiricahua Mts. in 1985. *C. cyneas* occurs in Ariz. in the Huachuca Mts. (above 1,800 m, or 6,000 ft.) and Chiricahua Mts. (but not since 1916 in the latter, mislabeled?), and *leanira fulvia* occurs on the flats around the Huachuca Mts. (at about 1,200 m, plus one canyon record about 1,800 m) and Chiricahua Mts.

Habitat open woodland (oak, pinyon, and Ponderosa Pine) in mountains. Ranges to s Mex. Hostplants herb Scrophulariaceae: *Seymeria tenuisecta* in Mex., probably *Brachiostygma* in Ariz. Larvae eat *Castilleja* in the lab.

Larva like that of *C. leanira fulvia*, cream-yellow, with a black middorsal line, a wide black subdorsal band (with tiny white dots in it), a black lateral line, and many black branching spines; collar black; head orange, with black at the eyes. Pupa white, with black stripes and spots, orange between adjacent black spots, and rows of dorsal cones. When D. Mullins raised *cyneas* and *leanira fulvia* together, the *fulvia* larvae diapaused whereas the *cyneas* grew to adults.

Several flights, Apr.-Oct.

Color Plate 27

211. Chlosyne definita   Coahuila Checkerspot

The white dot in the orange unh submarginal band is distinctive (*C. endeis*, 212, has it also, but *endeis* is larger and darker). In ssp. **schausi** (s Tex.), the ups is darker than ssp. **definita** westward. Habitat Lower Sonoran Zone shrubby desert hills, and subtropical thorn forest. Ranges south to s Mex. Hostplant herb Acanthaceae: *Stenandrium barbatum*. Many flights, Apr.-Oct., perhaps over a longer span in s Tex. Males patrol all day just above the ground of ridges and gulches to seek females.

Color Plate 27

212. Chlosyne endeis

The unh has white fw spots and resembles that of *C. definita* (211), but *C. endeis* is much larger and darker. The fw is more orange in males, more white-spotted in females. Ssp. **pardelina** is in the U.S.; ssp. *endeis* is in s Mex. Habitat subtropical chaparral and thorn forest. Many flights, at least Mar.-Dec. in s Tex.; a rare stray into c Tex.

Stray only
Color Plates 58, 59, 63

213. Chlosyne marina

One adult was caught in s Tex. and a second in sw Ariz. (Ajo), strays from Mex. The unh submarginal pattern resembles that of *C. definita* (211) and *C. endeis* (212), but the unh is yellow from the base to the red spots. White or yellowish (but not orange) spots are all over the black fw. Ssp. **melitaeoides** (Tex., NE Mex.) lacks a fw band; ssp. *marina* (c and s Mex.) has a broken yellow fw median band; ssp. **eumeda** (Ariz. and Pacific slope of Mex.) has a broad yellow fw median band. Doubtful records of *Chlosyne erodyle* (Color Plate 59) from s Tex. may refer to *C. marina* (*erodyle* is like *marina melitaeoides* but has only one or two red spots at the uph corner, vs. four or five in *marina*, and the yellow on the uph and unh is limited to two basal and postbasal bands). Habitat subtropical and desert thorn forest. Many flights, most of the year, in Mex.

Color Plate 27
Fig. 52

214. Chlosyne janais   Giant Patch

The fw is black with white spots, and the unh base is yellow like that of *C. marina* (213) and *C. erodyle* (see under 213), but the uph has a red patch. Also, between the yellow base and the margin the unh has an orange postmedian band that is not connected to the hind margin (it is connected in species 215-217), white submarginal dots, and yellow marginal spots.

Habitat subtropical woodland. Ranges south to Colombia. Hostplants shrub

Acanthaceae: *Odontonema callistachyum* in Mex. along shaded streams, *Anisacanthus wrightii* in Tex.

Eggs laid in clusters under host leaves. Larvae feed on the underside of leaves. Larva metallic grayish-green (the prothorax light orange), with black transverse bands connecting the black spines, interrupted sublateral rows of black spots, and many narrow black transverse lines; head orange-red, the lower part black. Pupa (Fig. 52) white or grayish-green, with many small black dashes and spots and many black dorsal and subdorsal points.

Many flights, at least July-Nov., in s Tex.; somewhat migratory, straying into N Tex.

215. Chlosyne rosita   Rosy Patch

s Tex. only (stray Ariz.)
Color Plate 27

Resembles *C. janais* (214) and some *C. lacinia* (216), but lacks marginal spots. Ssp. **browni** (Tex., NE Mex.) has the hw patch yellowish at the base, then red; ssp. **mazarum** (Ariz. rarely, w Mex.) has the uph red replaced by black, the unh red replaced by red-brown; ssp. *rosita* is in s Mex.-El Salvador. Habitat subtropical woodland. Hostplants herb Acanthaceae: *Dicliptera vahliana, brachiata* var. *alternata*; in the lab *Siphonoglossa pilosella*. Eggs laid in clusters on the underside of leaves. Many flights, most of the year, in s Tex., and one stray from Mex. known in SE Ariz.

216. Chlosyne lacinia   Sunflower Patch

Color Plates 27, 60

Differs from *C. rosita* (215) and *C. californica* (217) in having marginal spots and a red-orange postmedian spot at the unh hind corner; the unf cell lacks orange, and the orangish uph postmedian-submarginal spot (or band when present) reaches the abdominal margin as in *californica*. The ups bands vary from almost completely black to white, yellow, orange, or red-and-white. Orange ups postmedian bands are usual from SE N.M. to Tex. (ssp. **adjutrix**); white bands, westward (ssp. **crocale**). Ssp. *lacinia* and other ssp. extend to Argentina.

Habitat Subtropical to Upper Sonoran Zone desert hills, pinyon or oak woodland, and thorn forest. Hostplants mostly herb Compositae (*, major hosts found by R. Neck): *Ambrosia artemisiifolia, trifida* var. *texana*, Baltimora, Calyptocarpus vialis, Eupatorium, Gaillardia pulchella, Helianthus annuus** (and ssp. *lenticularis*), *ciliaris, argophyllus, maximiliani, tuberosus, debilis* var. *cucumerifolius, Heterotheca latifolia, Palafoxia* (probably *sphacelata*), *Parthenium hysterophorus, Silphium asperrimum, Simsia calva, Viguiera dentata, deltoidea* var. *parishii, Verbesina encelioides*, virginica, Xanthium pennsylvanicum* (vars. *strumarium, canadense, saccharatum*), *Zexmenia hispida*.

Eggs pale greenish-yellow, turning reddish, laid in clusters averaging 139 eggs on the underside of host leaves. Young larvae eat the underside of leaves and are gregarious; older larvae eat leaves, stems, rarely buds and flowers, and are solitary. Larvae do not make nests. Neck found that there are three basic larval forms, though modifying genes produce nearly continuous variation between them. The orange-red "**rufa**" form is due to a dominant gene R at one chromosome region that prevents the other two forms from appearing. If the recessive gene r is present, a form "**bicolor**" (black with an orange dorsal stripe) is dominant to the recessive form "**nigra**" (mostly black), owing to the alternative genes B and b at a second chromosome region. Pupa nearly black, or white with black marks, or nearly white. Third-stage larvae go into hibernation, triggered by short photoperiod. Third-(also fourth?-)stage larvae may also diapause in summer.

Many flights, Mar.-Oct. in Calif., all year in s Tex. Ssp. *adjutrix* is migratory, straying north to Minn. rarely. Adults sip the nectar of flowers, esp. yellow and white ones, and males feed on dung, carrion, and mud. To seek females, males patrol and sometimes perch on hilltops, or patrol near the hosts, all day.

Color Plate 27

217. **Chlosyne californica**   California Patch

Like *C. lacinia* (216), but the unf has orange in the cell, and the median band and submarginal spots are orange. The red unh spot near the abdomen tends to blend into the median band, whereas it is usually separate in *lacinia*. The two fly together but do not interbreed.

Habitat Lower Sonoran to lower Upper Sonoran Zone desert canyons and washes. Hostplants Compositae: shrub *Viguiera deltoidea* var. *parishii*, occasionally the herb *Helianthus annuus*.

Eggs pale yellowish-green when young, laid in clusters on the underside of host leaves. Larvae eat leaves. Larvae velvety-black with transverse rows of tiny cream dots (*or* larva orange dorsally, or mostly orange, varying as in *C. lacinia*); head black. Pupa usually white with brownish-black bars and spots and with many black-rimmed orange dorsal cones; *or* pupa mostly black, or unmarked white. Third-stage larvae hibernate.

Many flights, Mar.-Nov. Males perch on hilltops from 7:00 A.M. to 2:00 P.M. (usually 8:00-11:00 A.M.) to await females.

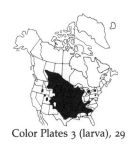
Color Plates 3 (larva), 29

218. **Chlosyne gorgone**   Great Plains Checkerspot

Identified by the unh median band of white arrowheads.

Habitat Lower Austral to lower Canadian Zone open areas. Basically a Great Plains species, offshoots occur in Ponderosa Pine forests in the Rockies (even Ida. and Utah), in old fields, railroad tracks, and woods edges in Mo., hardwood forest in Ga., and the Canadian Zone in an odd N N.Y. colony and an extinct Toronto colony. Hostplants herb and shrublike Compositae: *Helianthus annuus, pumilus, petiolaris, laetiflorus, trachelifolius, Ambrosia trifida, Iva xanthifolia, Viguiera multiflora.*

Eggs pale green when young, laid in clusters under host leaves. Larvae eat leaves (feeding gregariously under the leaf when young); no nests. R. Neck found that the same three larval forms occur as in *C. lacinia* (216), and control of inheritance is the same. Larva (form **bicolor**; Colo.) with wide black subdorsal and sublateral bands, containing many tiny whitish dots, usually with yellow-orange or orange-red between the bands. Larva (form **nigra**; Colo.) with narrow yellow lines (rather than orangish bands), a black middorsal line, and black lateral mottling between the very wide black bands. Larva (form **rufa**; uncommon in s Colo. and Tex., rare in c Colo.) orange (but the spines black). Larval head and branching spines black in all forms. Pupa (from *rufa* larva) cream with fine reddish mottling, or (from *nigra* larva) blackish-brown owing to fine blackish mottling, or intermediate (from *bicolor* larva); all with a row of pale dots across the wings and many small dorsal bumps on the abdomen. Third-stage larvae hibernate, in a special reddish-brown skin.

One flight, M May-E July, in the Colo. mountains, Canada, and N.Y.; two flights, June-Aug., in N.D.-Wis.; several flights, L Apr.-M Sep. southward and on the plains. Adults sip the nectar of flowers, esp. yellow ones. Males perch on hilltops all day, or patrol near the hosts, to seek females. Courting males fly up and down about 15 cm above the female several times between attempts to mate. Unreceptive females flutter to reject males, and may try to escape by flying vertically and then zooming down and away.

Color Plates 1 (egg), 3 (larva), 29
Fig. 55 (veins)

219. Chlosyne nycteis   Streamside Checkerspot

Identified by the large white spot in cell M_3 of the unh margin (with brown in cell M_2 beside it) and by the dark upf tip. The ups is darker in the Rockies (ssp. **drusius**), lightest in s Man. (ssp. **reversa**). Ssp. **nycteis** is elsewhere. "Wet season" Tex. adults resemble ssp. *drusius* (C. Durden).

Habitat Lower Austral to Canadian Zone streamsides, moist meadows, open moist deciduous woods. Hostplants herb Compositae: *Rudbeckia laciniata, Actinomeris alternifolia, Aster puniceus, umbellatus, Helianthus divaricatus, tuberosus, strumosus, annuus, decapetalus, Verbesina helianthoides, virginica, Conyza canadensis*[t], *Solidago*.

Eggs whitish-green when young, laid in clusters averaging 121 eggs on the underside of host leaves. Larvae eat leaves. Young larvae gregarious; no nests. Larva brownish-black speckled with tiny white dots, with an orange lateral stripe (in Colo., two lateral rows of pale-orangish dashes), purplish lateral streaks, and many brown spines; head black. Pupa white with blackish spots and brownish streaks, or greenish-yellow, pinkish-brown, gray-brown, or nearly black; many orange dorsal cones (edged in front with brown). Third-stage larvae hibernate in a special reddish-brown skin, as in *C. gorgone* (218).

One flight June-M July, northward and in the Rockies; two flights, May-Sep., Ill. to Penn.; several flights, Mar.-Sep., in Tex. Adults sip flower nectar, and in the east may congregate at mud. Males patrol all day around the hosts to seek females. Courting males fly in loops about 20 cm in diameter behind and above the female, as in *Phyciodes texana* (234). Unreceptive females flutter the wings to reject courting males.

Color Plates 29, 60

220. Chlosyne harrisii   Eastern Checkerspot

The uns resembles that of *C. palla* (222), but *C. harrisii* has black uph postmedian dots (as do *C. gorgone*, 218, and *C. nycteis*, 219), darker ups wingtips, and a range only in E N. Amer. The ups is lighter in s Man. (ssp. **hanhami**), darkest in the southeast (ssp. **harrisii**). The male valva is like that of *palla*.

Habitat Transition to lower Canadian Zone moist meadows, marsh edges, and forest openings. Hostplants herb Compositae: *Aster umbellatus*, occasionally *Verbesina helianthoides, Solidago,* ? *Actinomeris alternifolia*[t].

Eggs lemon-yellow, laid in clusters averaging 200 eggs on the underside of host leaves. Young larvae live in a silk nest (which often binds a leaf to a stem), which they strengthen in winter; no nests in spring. Larvae eat leaves (young larvae eat the underside), often defoliating small plants, and then often starving to death trying to find another. A. Shapiro found that parasitized larvae crawl to the top of the plant, where predators can more easily carry the doomed larva and its parasitoids away, perhaps saving some fellow *harrisii* from parasitoids.

Larva orange, with black transverse bands (one broad band containing the black branching spines, one narrow band in front, and two narrow bands behind the spines on each segment), a black middorsal line, and the rear nearly black; head black. Pupa white, with variable-size black spots and stripes, many orange dorsal cones (edged in front with black), and orange joints, the end of abdomen black. Third- and fourth-stage larvae hibernate.

One flight, mostly M June-M July (June-E July near Ottawa). After V. Dethier and R. MacArthur stocked 20,000 extra larvae in a field, the resulting adult population was five times larger than normal, but since most adults emigrated, the next year's population was back to normal. Roadsides are often routes of dispersal.

221. Chlosyne hoffmanni   Pacific Checkerspot

Color Plate 29
Fig. 71

The light unh spots are cream-colored as in *C. palla* (222; spots not white or pearly). Ssp. **hoffmanni** (Sierra Nevada) is easily distinguished from *palla* by the broad blended upf postmedian band and by the dark uph base. Ssp. **segregata** (Wash., intergrading to ssp. *hoffmanni* in N Calif.-Ore.) is best distinguished from *palla* by the male valva (which has a shorter posterior process; Fig. 71); other differences are that the upf median band is still blended into the postmedian band more than in *palla*, and the uph median band is a neater row of more rectangular cream spots, this band contrasting more with the background than it does in *palla* (in *palla* this row is slightly more orange, and the spot in cell CuA_1 seems rounder and more offset toward the base).

Habitat Canadian Zone forest openings. Hostplants herb Compositae: *Aster conspicuus* in Wash., *A. ledophyllus* and *Chrysopsis breweri* in Calif.

Eggs light green when young, laid in clusters on the underside of host leaves. Larvae eat leaves, feeding gregariously when young on the underside of leaves in silk nests. Larva black, speckled with white, with a cream lateral line and white circles around the lateral spiracles. Pupa pearly white, tan, or brown, with brown to black patches. Half-grown larvae hibernate.

One flight, July in the Sierra, June-E July in Wash. Adults sip flower nectar and mud. Males patrol all day near the hosts, mainly in valley bottoms, to seek females.

222. Chlosyne palla   Creamy Checkerspot

Color Plate 29
Fig. 71

The unh has yellowish or cream spots as in *C. hoffmanni* (221; note its small range), but the posterior prong of the valva is longer (Fig. 71). In ssp. **palla** (s Calif. to Ore., E Wash., and s Ida.) the female ups is black with white spots (esp. in Ore.-Wash., where males may also be pale whitish-orange). In ssp. **calydon** (higher-altitude Sierra, E slope of Cascade Mts. in Ore., east to the Rockies), females are orange on the ups. In ssp. **flavula** (Utah and w Colo.), both sexes are paler orange. Populations in the s Sierra (Tulare Co.) in June look a bit like *C. gabbii acastus* and *g. neumoegeni* (223), apparently from past hybridizing. Near Frazier Park and Frazier Mt. in Kern and Ventura Cos., Calif., the population tends toward *C. g. gabbii*, and some individuals are closer to *gabbii* than to *palla*, evidently owing to hybridization.

Habitat coastal chaparral and open woodland, and Transition to Canadian Zone moist wooded areas and clearings. Hostplants herb and shrub Compositae: *Aster radulinus, occidentalis, conspicuus, Chrysothamnus nauseosus, vis-cidiflorus, paniculatus, Erigeron speciosus* var. *macranthus, Solidago californica, Senecio triangularis.*

Eggs pale green when young, laid in clusters on the underside of host leaves. Larvae eat leaves (young larvae eat the underside, gregariously); no nests, or sometimes a slight silk nest when young. Larva black, with white dots (conspic-uously including two rows of white dots along the dorsal spines and a lateral line of white dots), and two dorsal and two lateral rows of orange dashes. Pupa pale tan to brown, or gray to mostly black, with mottled spots and shining dor-sal bumps. Half-grown larvae hibernate.

One flight, L Apr.-M June in lowland Calif. and Wash., May-June in Ore. and B.C., M June-M July inland and in mountains. R. Schrier and associates found that adults move fairly large distances (often 1.6 km, averaging 477 m be-tween captures). Adults sip flower nectar and mud. Males patrol all day to seek females, mainly around the larval hostplants, and frequently perch (esp. on small shelflike areas) in valley bottoms.

ssp. *gabbii*

Color Plates 5 (pupa), 29

ssp. *neumoegeni, sabina*

ssp. *acastus, vallis-mortis, dorothyi*

223. Chlosyne gabbii   Pearly Checkerspot

Identified by the white or pearly unh spots. Ssp. **gabbii** (Calif. Coast Ranges) is dark on the ups, with pearly unh spots. Ssp. **neumoegeni** (Mojave Desert, Calif., and w Ariz.) is very light orange on the ups, with pearly unh spots. Ssp. **sabina** (foothills from NW Ariz. to sw N.M., intergrading with *neumoegeni* at low altitude) is darker on the ups, with pearly unh spots. In ssp. **acastus** (lowlands in E-c Calif., c Nev., NW N.M., north to Alta. and Neb.), the ups is slightly less black than in *sabina* (except in s-c Colo.), and the unh spots more dull white than pearly. Ssp. *acastus* replaces *neumoegeni* northward and may intergrade with it in some areas. Ssp. **vallismortis** (Panamint Mts. and near Death Valley, Calif., to the Spring Mts. of s Nev.) most resembles ssp. *acastus*, but probable inter-breeding with *C. palla* (222) and ssp. *neumoegeni* in the past is suggested by the usually slightly yellowish unh spots and by the broadly orange unf like that in *neumoegeni*. Ssp. *vallismortis* has been treated as a ssp. of *palla*, and may derive from *palla* populations that were stranded in the mountains after the Ice Age and subsequently hybridized with *gabbii*. Ssp. **dorothyi** (Snake and Burnt River can-yons in NE Ore.) also resembles ssp. *acastus*, but both sexes have whiter ups spots. Two alpine rockslide ssp. have a dull greasy ups, a slightly less-angled fw, and whitish unh spots: ssp. **whitneyi** (=*malcolmi*), from alpine Sierra Nevada, has an orange (sometimes cream in females) ups pattern like that of *acastus*; ssp. **damoetas** (alpine Rockies; in Alta. and B.C. somewhat similar to *whitneyi*) is darker on the ups, esp. in s Colo. where females are sometimes greatly suffused with black. Lab-raised ssp. *damoetas* resemble wild adults, so the difference between ssp. *damoetas* and *acastus* seems to be genetic. Some ssp. have been treated as distinct species, but the early stages and most adult traits are very similar. In one former treatment, most ssp. (and *C. palla flavula*) were considered one species (*C. gabbii* including individuals from all over w U.S.). *C. palla* is closely related also; its valva is identical to that of *C. gabbii* (see Fig. 71). *C. palla* seems to hybridize with *gabbii* (see *palla*). *C. palla palla* and *gabbii dorothyi* seem to converge in wing pattern somewhat, as do *p. flavula* and *g. acastus*. The latter two

ssp. *whitneyi, damoetas*

butterflies are sympatric at three w Colo. sites with only one hybrid known.*

Habitat coastal dunes, chaparral, and open woodland in s Calif., Lower Sonoran to Transition Zone desert scrub, shrubby prairie hills and badlands, pinyon-juniper woodland, and sagebrush inland, alpine rockslides in the Rockies and Sierra. Hostplants herb and shrub Compositae (superscript=first letter of ssp.): *Corethrogyne filaginifolia* var. *bernardina*[g] (the main host[g]), *Haplopappus squarrosus*[g], *Baccharis plummerae*[g], *Heterotheca grandiflora*[g], *Acamptopappus shockleyi*[n], *sphaerocephalus* var. *hirtellus*[n], *Machaeranthera tortifolia*[n], *canescens*[a], *viscosa*[a], *Asters*[s], *Chrysothamnus viscidiflorus*[a] (also in association[n]), *Erigeron leiomeris*[d], *pygmaeus*[w], *Solidago multiradiata*[w].

Eggs pale green when young, laid in clusters on the underside of host leaves and sometimes on flower buds. Larvae eat leaves, and (in s Nev. at least) often eat flowers. Young larvae are gregarious on leaves or flowers; no nests. Larva (ssp. *damoetas*; ssp. *whitneyi, gabbii,* and *acastus* similar) resembles that of *C. palla,* black with many black spines, covered with cream dots, brown ventrally, with a narrow black middorsal line, the orange crescents on each side of the middorsal spines forming two orange dorsal stripes, and the orange crescentic bars on the ventral base of the spines above the spiracles (plus small orangish bars at the ventral base of the spines below the spiracles) forming two orange lateral stripes with cream dots frequent between them; head black. Larva (ssp. *neumoegeni*) the same, but the orange stripes (always the dorsal ones, occasionally the lateral ones) replaced by gray (the spines are the same length in *neumoegeni* and *acastus,* contrary to one report). Pupa (ssp. *damoetas*) tan, shaded in front with black, with a bluish-white tint on the abdomen, five dorsal rows of orange bumps, a lateral row of orange dots on the abdomen, lateral black dots, and black spiracles. Pupa (ssp. *gabbii*) similar, but tending to have black blotches. Pupa (ssp. *neumoegeni*) gray, extensively mottled with black. Larvae of ssp. *neumoegeni* and *whitneyi* hibernate half grown; ssp. *neumoegeni* can diapause for many months or perhaps years, and heavy summer rains produce a large adult flight. Ssp. *damoetas* larvae diapause about half grown (in the third or fourth stage) under rocks, and each year some of the numerous diapausing larvae seem to find a hostplant and become adults (many diapause for two or more years, allowing them to survive bad-weather years); the lengthy diapause allowed ssp. *damoetas* to adapt easily to the Alpine Zone. Third-stage ssp. *gabbii* larvae also hibernate.

One flight, July-E Aug. above timberline, Apr.-May for ssp. *gabbii* (rarely a partial summer flight), mainly Apr. for ssp. *neumoegeni* (rarely a partial summer flight) and *sabina,* M May-M June for the other ssp.; two flights (the second partial?), June-Aug., in Sask.-N.D.; about three flights (the second and third apparently partial), May-Sep., in Utah-w Colo.-s N.M. Adults sip flower nectar and mud. Males seek females all day, in ssp. *neumoegeni* and *acastus* by perching and sometimes patrolling in gulches, in ssp. *damoetas* and *whitneyi* by patrolling and sometimes perching in the rocky hollows of rockslides and rocky chutes.

*While this book was in press, matings between the subspecies in the lab (J. Emmel) showed that three species exist: *C. gabbii,* the Coast Checkerspot; *C. acastus* (and ssp. *neumoegeni, sabina, vallismortis, dorothyi*), the Sagebrush Checkerspot; and *C. whitneyi* (and ssp. *damoetas*), the Alpine Checkerspot. Hybrids between these three species died as larvae; hybrids within species produced several generations of adults. The larval spines of *C. acastus* and *C. palla* are longer than those of *C. gabbii* and *C. whitneyi.*

M. Howard observed several male *damoetas* attracted to the scent of a newly emerged female, hidden beside her pupal shell under a rock, demonstrating that the female's pheromone attracts the male at short range.

Color Plates 3 (larva), 26, 27

224. Phyciodes orseis   Long-Wing Crescent

Can be confused only with *P. mylitta* (225) and *P. campestris* (230), with which it flies. The fw is angled like that of *mylitta*, but *orseis* is somewhat larger. Antenna club mostly orange (esp. in males) as in *mylitta* (brown in *campestris*). Ssp. **orseis** (s Ore. to Trinity Alps of Calif.; extinct or mislabeled from Napa, Sonoma, and Marin Cos. and San Francisco) is dark like *campestris* on the ups, but the fw is angled, and the unh is mottled as in *mylitta*, not mostly orange as in *campestris*. Ssp. **herlani** (Sierra Nevada) is light yellow-orange on the ups, but the unh is uniformly yellow with fine brown lines all over, not mottled with brown as in *mylitta*, and not orangish with a marginal brown patch as in *campestris*. The two ssp. intergrade in N Calif.

Habitat mainly Canadian Zone mountain valleys. Hostplants herb Compositae: *Cirsium*; assoc. with *C. cymosum* in N Calif.

Eggs pale yellowish-green, laid in large clusters on the underside of host leaves. Larvae eat leaves; no nests. Larva (similar to 195 in Fig. 51) maroon-black all over the dorsal half (two middorsal lines and a wide lateral band are ochre-brown in ssp. *herlani*, orange in ssp. *orseis*), more brown beneath; head black, with a cream subdorsal stripe (with a cream spot below it). Pupa mottled light to dark brown, with small bumps. Third-stage larvae hibernate.

One flight, M May-June (Apr.-May for extinct Calif. populations). Males perch all day in gulches and along creeks to await females.

Color Plates 26, 27

225. Phyciodes mylitta   Thistle Crescent

Small (16-17 mm fw length), having the fw angled, lacking the large black upf spot of *P. pallida* (226), and tending to be darker and more mottled on the unh. Ssp. **callina** (sw Colo.-Ariz.-N.M.-s Mex.) is often larger, with a bigger spot, but *pallida* does not fly with it. Ssp. **mylitta** elsewhere in the U.S.

Habitat mainly Transition Zone mountains, agricultural fields (even in the Central Valley of Calif.), and towns. Ranges south to s Mex. Hostplants herb Compositae (tribe Cynareae): *Cirsium occidentale, proteanum, californicum, vulgare, breweri, hydrophilum, arvense, Silybum marianum, Carduus pycnocephalus, ?Centaurea solstitialis*; Scrophulariaceae: *Mimulus guttatus*.

Eggs pale yellowish-green, laid in large clusters on the underside of host leaves. Larvae eat leaves; young larvae sometimes live in a small silk-web nest. Larva maroon-brown to black with many pale dots, the underside brown, with two cream middorsal lines and on each side two cream lateral lines; many black spines, the lateral spines orangish; head black, with a cream subdorsal stripe (rarely a cream spot below it) and rarely a cream crescent above the eyes. Pupa mottled brown to ashy gray. Half-grown larvae hibernate.

Many flights, Feb.-Nov. southward, Apr.-Sep. northward. In wet years strays (mostly females) occur in the New York and Panamint Mts. and others in the Mojave Desert. Males perch all day in gulches or along creeks, or patrol in agricultural fields, to await or seek females.

Color Plate 26

Color Plates 5 (pupa), 27
Figs. 65, 71

226. Phyciodes pallida   Pale Crescent

Very similar to *P. mylitta* (225), but larger (fw 20-22 mm), with the black markings usually small on the ups, a large black upf median spot next to the hw, and the unh submarginal spots of females silvery white without much brown.

Habitat mainly Upper Sonoran and Transition Zone valleys. Hostplants herb Compositae: *Cirsium*.

Eggs pale yellowish-green, laid in large clusters on the underside of host leaves. Larvae eat leaves; no nests. Larva ochre, with a brown middorsal line and a brown band above the spiracles; head black, with a cream subdorsal stripe on each temple and a cream crescent above the eyes. Pupa light mottled brown.

One flight, mostly L May-June (L Apr.-M June in Ore.). Males perch all day in gulches, and rarely patrol on ridges, to await or seek females.

227. Phyciodes morpheus (*=selenis, =pascoensis*)   Orange Crescent

P. morpheus is most like *P. tharos* (228), with which it was long confused (see Fig. 65). The ups is orange with broad black borders, though adults are larger than *tharos* (fw length 16-18 mm in males, 18-20 mm in females). The orange ups patches are not divided by black postmedian lines as much as in *tharos* (esp. on the uph). Females are usually much blacker than males, esp. on the upf, and the upf median spots are usually much paler (cream) than the spots beyond them (*tharos* females are more uniformly orange). Males sometimes have creamy upf median spots also. The black ups borders seldom have the creamy submarginal spots as well developed as those of *tharos*. The antenna club is almost always orange and black, unlike *P. batesii* (229), which has black-and-white clubs (*tharos* has black-and-white clubs southward, orange-and-black clubs northward). The two hooks on the male uncus are a bit thicker and shorter than in *tharos* (Fig. 71). *P. morpheus* usually occurs farther north than *tharos*, and has fewer flights (generally only one, sometimes a partial second flight). *P. morpheus* was treated as the summer form of *tharos*, but actually the summer form of *tharos* is little different from the spring form on the ups. Form **marcia** (the unh more brown) is rare in *morpheus* and is limited to localities where the late-summer or fall larvae from a partial second flight experience a short photoperiod the preceding year. *P. morpheus* and *P. tharos* fly together in areas of W.Va., Va., Penn., Mich., and probably the Black Hills and elsewhere (C. Oliver and P. Opler). In W.Va. and Va. they differ in size, wing pattern, antenna color, number of flights, time of flight, and the frequency of several body-enzyme genes. The main flight of *morpheus* usually falls more or less between the first two flights of *tharos*. At one W.Va. site, where only a few possible hybrids are known, *morpheus* and *tharos* differ in the frequency of two particular enzymes (A. Vawter). By comparison, enzyme frequencies were very similar among populations of *tharos* in N.Y., Tex., and Ala. (Vawter and P. Brussard). C. Oliver hybridized *morpheus* and *tharos* in lab cages, and found that the viability and the sex ratio of hybrid and backcross individuals are normal. He found that the mother may influence the developmental time of hybrid larvae; some grow faster and others more slowly than normal. Courtship barriers may minimize mating in nature (as do the mostly separate ranges and flight periods), but there may be some hybridization; and some individuals cannot be identified. *P. tharos* may have secondarily invaded the range of *morpheus* in some places, following deforestation. The name *mor-*

Fig. 65. *Phyciodes tharos* and relatives. All are uppersides unless labeled "uns" (underside). *227, P. morpheus: a*, Custer Co., Colo.; *b*, Eagle Co., Colo.; *c*, Jefferson Co., Colo.; *d*, Penobscot Co., Maine. *228, P. tharos: a*, Montgomery Co., Kans.; *b*, San Luis Potosí, Mex.; *c*, Slope Co., N.D.; *d*, Boone Co., Ky.; *e*, form *marcia*, Slope Co., N.D. *229, P. batesii: a*, Pennington Co., S.D.; *b*, Grand Traverse Co., Mich.; *c*, Oakville, Ont.

pheus is used here because it is the oldest name for the species (the original description mentions the orange-and-black antennae and the type locality of "America Boreali," which I restrict to N.S. to avoid confusion with *P. tharos*), and because it has been used for the large summer adults now placed in *P. morpheus*. (But see the end of the text of *P. tharos*.)

Habitat Transition to lower Hudsonian Zone moist meadows, moist fields, valley bottoms, and streamsides. In Penn. and vicinity *P. morpheus* often occupies "barrens" habitats (brushy ledges or gravelly areas), whereas *P. tharos* is in moist fields (Oliver); elsewhere *morpheus* seems to prefer moister areas. Hostplants herb Compositae: *Aster laevis* in Colo., *A. umbellatus* in N.S.; assoc. with *A. simplex*, *prenanthoides* in Pa., Vt., W.Va. T. Mead's record of *A. novae-angliae* in the Catskill Mts., N.Y., may refer to *P. morpheus*.

Eggs pale green, laid in large clusters under hostplant leaves (averaging about 40 per cluster). Larvae eat leaves (young larvae are gregarious and eat only the underside); no nests. Larva chocolate-brown or reddish-brown, covered with tiny white dots, with a blackish middorsal line, a cream subdorsal band edged beneath with black dashes, a cream lateral band edged beneath with blackish (with a sinuous row of white dots above it), and many whitish-tipped brown branching spines, these spines orange-based on the cream bands; head black, with a cream triangle on the front, a cream crescent around the eyes, and a cream streak (orangish in Ont.) extending forward on each side of the top (the lower part of the streak sometimes isolated). Reddish-brown larvae are frequent in *P. morpheus*, but absent in *P. tharos*. Pupa cream (usually whiter than *P. tharos* pupa), with brownish streaks (one streak edges a transverse dorsal ridge across the abdomen); some mostly cream and others mottled cream and brown; all with a faint cream subdorsal band and a faint cream-above-brown lateral band on the abdomen; shape like that of *P. tharos*. Third-stage larvae hibernate. June and July larvae usually diapause, whereas *tharos* larvae do not (Oliver).

One flight, M June-E July in W.Va. and Penn. (a partial second flight in Aug. in Penn.), L May-M July in the Colo. foothills, mostly June in Alta.-Sask., June-M July at Ottawa (a partial second flight in L July-E Sep. in Sask., Ottawa, and Maine), L June-E Aug. in higher mountains, Nfld., and the far north. Adults are rather local, and they sip flower nectar and mud. Males patrol all day near the hostplants, mostly in valley bottoms, to seek females.

Color Plates 1 (egg), 27
Figs. 65, 71

228. Phyciodes tharos　Pearl Crescent

The ups has thick black borders (Fig. 65), but the middle is more broadly orange than in the other *Phyciodes* except *P. morpheus* (227). *P. tharos* usually occurs farther south than *morpheus*, is smaller (fw length 14-16 mm in males, 16-18 mm in females), and has orange ups patches divided by black postmedian lines. Females are somewhat darker than males, but not usually as dark as female *morpheus*. An often well developed creamy submarginal band of spots on the uph and upf seems less well developed or absent in *morpheus*. Because *tharos* has black-and-white antenna clubs southward, in Va. and W.Va. it is easily distinguished from *morpheus*, which generally has orange-and-black antenna clubs. However, from s Maine to N.Y. and in some Penn. colonies, west to the Dakotas, Alta., Neb., and Colo., *tharos* also has orange-and-black antenna clubs, so the other traits must be used. The two hooks on the male uncus are slightly thinner and longer than in *P. morpheus* (Fig. 71). *P. tharos* has many flights, unlike *morpheus*. In early-spring and late-fall form **marcia**, the unh is brown, resulting from a short photoperiod acting on the larva just before diapause (C. Oliver). Form *marcia* sometimes has pearly unh postmedian spots, giving rise to the common name.

Habitat Subtropical to lower Transition Zone moist meadows, moist fields, moist prairie, and streamsides. Ranges south to s Mex. and Bimini. Hostplants herb Compositae: *Aster praealtus* and *texanus* (both Tex.), *laevis*, *pilosus*, *ericoides* (all Staten I., N.Y.), *simplex* (Penn., N.Y.), *puniceus*, *dumosus*, *lateriflorus*, *novae-angliae*, *acuminatus* (all N.Y.; some spp. possibly refer to *P. morpheus*), *solidagineus* (E U.S.). *Verbesina helianthoides* is somewhat doubtful; larvae eat *Erigeron peregrinus* in the lab.

Eggs pale green, laid in clusters of 20-300 (averaging about 63) on the underside of hostplant leaves, up to 700 eggs per female. Larvae eat leaves (young larvae are gregarious and eat only the underside); no nests. Larva chocolate-brown (rarely brown), covered with tiny white dots, with a blackish middorsal line, a cream subdorsal band edged beneath with black dashes, a cream lateral band edged beneath with blackish (with a sinuous row of whitish dots above it), and many often whitish-tipped brown branching spines, these spines orange-based on the cream bands; head black, with a cream triangle on the front, a cream crescent around the eyes, and a cream streak extending forward on each side of the top (the lower part of the streak sometimes isolated into a spot). Pupa creamy-tan (sometimes yellow-brown, and usually oranger than *P. morpheus* pupa), with brownish streaks (a transverse dorsal ridge across abdomen segment 4 edges one streak; lesser ridges top segments 5-7 as in *P. morpheus*), the wings often tinted with yellow-brown, the abdomen with a faint cream subdorsal band and a faint cream-above-brown lateral band; shape like *P. morpheus* pupa, more angular than that of *P. batesii* (229), with many small dorsal bumps present. Third-stage larvae hibernate.

Many flights all year in s Tex. and s Fla.; about three or four flights, L Apr.-Oct., in Va.; several flights, May-Sep., in N.Y. and the Colo. plains; two flights, L May-Aug., in Sask. Adults are fairly local, and they sip flower nectar and mud. Males patrol all day near the hostplants, mostly in valley bottoms, to seek females. (Since the writing of the accounts of *P. morpheus* and *P. tharos*, *morpheus* females from the Colo. mountains were reared and released in front of Colo. plains *tharos* males, and many natural matings and viable adult hybrids resulted [J. Scott]; and in the lab, thousands of hybrids and backcrosses between *morpheus* and *tharos* from many areas were reared [Oliver]. Thus, *P. tharos tharos* and *P. tharos morpheus* are merely subspecies in Colorado, but behave as separate species in W.Va.-Va.-Penn. In courtship [of *tharos*, *morpheus*, and *P. campestris*; Scott], the male pursues the female, who lands [if flying] and keeps her wings mostly spread; next, the male lands behind her [rarely after hovering for a second] and may display his wings [by spreading them nearly to the side, often moving the forewings forward, and often vibrating them imperceptibly; this display frequently done while facing her], and occasionally may flutter his wings as well; with his wings slightly open he then crawls under her hindwings to mate. For highly receptive females, which are usually motionless, the male seldom displays or flutters before mating; but an unreceptive female flutters her spread wings, which may cause him to fly away, or she raises her abdomen [such that he cannot join], turns or crawls away, drops down into the vegetation, or flies horizontally or vertically to escape.)

229. Phyciodes batesii   Dark Crescent

The ups has dark borders like those of *P. tharos* (228) and *P. morpheus* (227), but *P. batesii* is somewhat darker on the upf (Fig. 65), the black unf lower median spot is larger than the black subapical spot, the black unf median spots tend to form a band, the creamy-orange upf postmedian band is paler than the orange submarginal area (*tharos* and *morpheus* are usually more uniformly orange, except for occasional adults and *morpheus* females), and the underside of the antenna club is white and black rather than orange and black. The black-and-white antenna club separates it from most *morpheus* and *tharos*, except from Ga. to W.Va. and Va., where many *batesii* populations are extinct. The brown unh mar-

Color Plate 27
Figs. 65, 71

ginal patch is often smaller than that of *morpheus* and *tharos*, and the unh sub-marginal dots are always dark. The lateral margins of the male uncus just anterior to the two hooks form a more obtuse angle than in *tharos* and *morpheus* (Fig. 71). Appalachian *batesii* are slightly less orange on the upf than Great Lakes *batesii*, and the unh is slightly more yellow, with fewer brown lines and a smaller brown marginal patch; *batesii* from Man. westward often have more brown unh patches than usual. *P. batesii* often flies with *P. morpheus* and sometimes with *P. tharos*; it flies with *P. campestris* (230) from w Neb. north to Canada.

Habitat northern Upper Austral to Canadian Zone, in drier sites such as slopes with little vegetation in the northeast, in moist areas in Mich.-Wis. Host-plants herb Compositae: *Aster undulatus* (main host), possibly *A. simplex*, which was eaten by an introduced population.

Eggs pale green, laid in clusters on the underside of host leaves. Larvae eat leaves. First- and second-stage larvae live under a loose silk web spun on the leaf underside, unlike those of *P. tharos* and *P. morpheus*; older larvae make no nests. Larva dark purple-brown, with a pinkish tinge, a heavier, more even pale-yellowish subdorsal stripe than *tharos* and *morpheus*, a wider pale-yellowish lateral band, and many white-tipped blackish-brown spines (Que.) or tan-tipped light-pinkish-brown spines (N.Y.); head black, with a few variable white patches on the front and sides of the head that are smaller than those of *tharos*. Pupa light mottled brown, much more rounded than that of *tharos*, with the dorsal bumps nearly absent. Third-stage larvae hibernate.

One flight, M May-June southward and at Ottawa (usually flying between the first two flights of *P. tharos* from Penn. southward), M June-July in the north (largely between the flights of *tharos* and *morpheus* in s Sask.); sometimes a partial second flight in Mich.

Color Plates 26, 27

230. Phyciodes campestris (=*pratensis*)   Field Crescent

The ups is blackish, except in the Calif. Sierra. Differs from *P. tharos* (228), *morpheus* (227), and *batesii* (229) on the unf in usually having a yellow bar just beyond the base in the discal cell, and the unf black patches are small. Ssp. **montana** (montane Sierra) is mostly orange on the ups and usually lacks the bar; it differs from sympatric *P. mylitta* (225) and *P. orseis* (224) in having a rounder fw, usually lighter upf median spots, and a usually oranger unh with less-distinct brown lines and a large brown marginal patch. Ssp. **campestris**, elsewhere (and south to s Mex.) is blackish on the ups. J. Emmel raised *montana* at San Francisco and got normal *montana* adults; the difference between ssp. *montana* and *campestris* thus seems to be genetic.

Habitat plains to mountains and taiga. Hostplants herb Compositae: *Aster occidentalis*, *chilensis* (and ssp. *adscendens*), *hesperius*, *ericoides*, *greatai*, *conspicuum*, *integrifolius*, *foliaceus* var. *parryi*, *Machaeranthera pattersonii*.

Eggs pale yellow-green, laid singly in large clusters on the underside of host leaves, esp. on young plants. Larvae eat leaves; young larvae sometimes live under a loose web. Larva patterned like that of *P. picta* (231), but darker, blackish-brown; head black, with weak cream dorsal stripes and a lighter crescent around the eyes. Pupa mottled with brown and cream, with small dorsal bumps. Half-grown larvae hibernate.

Three or four flights, Apr.-Oct. in lowland Calif., May-Sep. in the Colo.

plains; one flight, L June - E Aug., in the far north and in high mountains. Males patrol all day just above the vegetation in meadows and swales to seek females.

231. Phyciodes picta   Painted Crescent

Color Plates 3 (larva), 27

Small, resembling *P. phaon* (232), but the unh and the tip of the unf are almost unmarked (yellow in males, cream in females) (the winter form **marcia** has a few slight marks on the unh).

Habitat mostly Upper Sonoran Zone dry alkaline valley bottoms, roadsides, and fields. Ranges south to N Mex. Hostplants herb Convolvulaceae: *Convolvulus arvensis*. Larvae eat *Aster laevis* (Compositae) and *Siphonoglossa pilosella* (Acanthaceae) in the lab. The original host may have been *Aster*, but I found the introduced European *C. arvensis* to be the main host now in Colo. and N.M. (on the basis of many ovipositions in nature, the supporting of growth from larvae to adults, and field associations).

Eggs pale yellow-green, laid in clusters of about 50-100 on the underside of host leaves. Larvae eat leaves; no nests. Larva yellowish-brown, with three faint brown dorsal lines, a brown subdorsal line (edged above by a cream line), and a brown lateral line (edged above by a cream stripe); head brown, with two cream stripes on the top and a cream crescent around the eyes, the face cream. Pupa smooth, light mottled brown. Second- to fourth-(probably mostly third-)stage larvae hibernate.

Three flights, M May - E Sep. in Colo., Apr. - Sep. in N.M.; a native in Colo., but an E Neb. and a reputed Iowa record may be strays. Males patrol all day on flats near the hosts to seek females.

232. Phyciodes phaon   Mat-Plant Crescent

Color Plate 27

Identified by the fw, which has a thick black median band, a whitish postmedian band, and an orange submarginal band. The unh is yellowish-cream, with narrow brown lines in females. The winter form **marcia** has a darker unh, owing to short photoperiod.

Habitat Lower Austral/Lower Sonoran Zone fairly moist open areas, esp. lakeshores and rocky creek beds, straying northward. Ranges south to Guatemala, Cuba, and the Cayman Is. Hostplants herb Verbenaceae: *Lippia lanceolata*, *nodiflora*.

Eggs laid in clusters on the underside of host leaves. Larvae eat leaves; no nests. Larva dark-brown (brown dorsally), with tiny white dots, a blackish middorsal line, a tan subdorsal band edged beneath by dark dashes, a tan mottled band along the spiracles, and a cream lateral line edged beneath by a blackish line; many cream spines; head blackish-brown, with white patches like those of *P. picta* but enlarged and joined. Pupa tan, mottled with cream and black, with many tiny brown dorsal bumps.

Many flights, all year in S Tex. and S Fla., Feb. - Oct. in Calif., Apr. - Sep. in N.M.; native in N Ark. and extreme S Mo., but somewhat migratory, straying as far as Iowa - Neb. Males patrol all day on flats near the hosts to seek females.

233. Phyciodes vesta   Mesquite Crescent

Color Plate 27

Easily recognized by the chainlike series of black unf postmedian circles. The winter form **marcia** is a little darker on the unh.

Habitat open mesquite and thorn woodland, southern prairie, and desert. Ranges south to Guatemala. Hostplant herb Acanthaceae: *Siphonoglossa pilosella*.

Eggs laid in clusters on host leaves. Larvae eat leaves.

Many flights, Feb.-Dec. in s Tex., Apr.-Sep. northward; native only in c N.M. southward, but somewhat migratory, straying north to Neb. Males patrol all day in low areas to seek females.

Color Plate 27

234. Phyciodes texana   Texas Crescent

In *P. texana*, *P. ptolyca* (235), and *P. frisia* (236) the fw margin is indented, but *texana* has light upf marginal spots that the other two lack. Ssp. **seminole** (New Orleans-Fla.) has orange fw bases; ssp. **texana** (westward) has darker bases.

Habitat southern open areas and desert. Ranges south to Guatemala. Hostplants herb Acanthaceae: *Dicliptera brachiata*, *Jacobinia carnea*, *Ruellia carolinensis*; larvae eat *Beloperone guttata* and *Siphonoglossa* in the lab.

Eggs laid in clusters on the underside of host leaves. Larvae eat leaves.

Many flights, all year in s Tex., Mar.-Nov. in s Fla. and Ariz.; somewhat migratory, a rare stray into Minn., N.D., and s Calif. Males usually perch in gulches all day to await females. Courting males fly in loops above the female (as in *Chlosyne nycteis*, 219).

Stray only
Color Plate 27
Fig. 71

235. Phyciodes ptolyca   False Black Crescent

The light unf marginal spot in cell M_3 separates *P. ptolyca* from *P. frisia* (236): in *ptolyca* the cream cap is thinner than the yellow base, and there are similar but smaller adjacent spots in cells M_2 and CuA_1; in *frisia* the cream cap is thicker than (or as thick as) the yellow base, and there is a slightly smaller similar spot in cell CuA_1, but the spot in cell M_2 is small and obscure, or absent. *P. ptolyca* has more-distinct uns markings, the end of the male uncus is membranous without tiny spines, and the valva has a small spine (between the tip and the large spine) that arises from the underside of the valva (Fig. 71). Habitat subtropics, south to Nicaragua. Many flights in Mex.; a rare stray into s Tex. (Mar., Dec.).

Color Plate 27
Fig. 71

236. Phyciodes frisia   Black Crescent

Consult the similar *P. ptolyca* (235) for identification. In addition, *P. frisia* is more widespread, the uns markings are usually less distinct and less suffused with yellowish, the orange upf basal spots are seldom present, the male uncus has tiny spines on the end, and the tiny spine on the valva (between the tip and the large spine) arises from the top of the valva (Fig. 71). Ssp. **tulcis** (Tex.) is black and white on the ups. Ssp. **frisia** (Fla.) is orange and black.

Habitat subtropical usually open areas, straying northward. Ranges south to Argentina, the Bahamas, and the Greater Antilles. Hostplants herb Acanthaceae: *Beloperone guttata*, *Dicliptera*, *Ruellia*; Euphorbiaceae: *Drypetes lateriflora*.

Eggs pale green, laid in clusters of 25-80 on the underside of young host leaves. Larvae eat the underside of leaves at night; no nests. Larva gray, with tiny yellow dots, a black middorsal line (bordered by yellowish-white, then black), and a whitish or black lateral line, the underside grayish-white, the appendages yellowish; many grayish-yellow spines; head yellowish-tan or gray, with the "temples" and lower face paler. Pupa tan or dark brown, with two rounded projections on the head and conelike dorsal bumps.

Many flights all year in s Fla. and s Tex.; somewhat migratory, rarely straying to s Ariz. (Aug.) and Mo.

Tribe Argynnini: Fritillaries

Argynnini are widespread in the Northern Hemisphere, and a few species occur in Africa, the Asian tropics, and South America, some in the Andes. The 30 species in North America range from the Arctic to Mexico.

Adults are medium-sized, usually more or less orange in color with darker wing veins and spots, often with silver or white hindwing spots on the underside. They are essentially the temperate-zone counterparts of the Heliconiini; like them, the males often have androconial scales on the wing veins; and the females have glands on the abdomen tip that produce a scent attractive to males (Fig. 37). Larvae bear many branching spines, and like the Heliconiini, they lack middorsal spines; but unlike the Heliconiini, they lack head spines. Pupae may bear small dorsal bumps, but lack the long processes of some Heliconiini. In *Speyeria*, the first-stage larvae hibernate; in *Boloria*, it is usually the fourth-stage larvae that hibernate (in the biennial arctic species the young larva also hibernates through its first winter); and *Euptoieta* may not have a true diapause.

Larvae eat various dicotyledons, especially violets. All *Speyeria* eat *Viola* (in the lab, they grow on every American species tested, but the European *V. odorata* kills them). Many *Boloria* seem to be able to eat many plants. Females (except *Euptoieta*) usually oviposit haphazardly near (sometimes on) the larval hostplants, rather than carefully placing them on the plant as most butterflies do. *Speyeria* are known to oviposit on twigs, leaves, stones, cones, even under J. Lembert's shoe, near the green violets. In many of the dry-habitat *Speyeria* (*aphrodite, callippe*, etc.), females seem to delay laying most of their eggs until late August or September. They then usually oviposit in places where the violets have dried up for the year (perhaps the female can smell the violet roots). Adult *Speyeria* live longer (several weeks or months) than most butterflies, and males emerge a week or so before females.

Mimicry is rare, although *Speyeria* look like *Dione*, which is probably distasteful. But because the ranges of the two genera are mostly separate, mimicry in this case would have to be based on a bird's wintering in *Dione*'s range, flying north, and then avoiding summer *Speyeria* for fear of being poisoned.

Adults have a fluttering, straight-line flight that is fairly strong, especially in the larger species. The largest fly about a meter above ground, the small *Boloria* only a fourth to a half meter above ground. *Euptoieta* migrates, and *Speyeria* may fly many kilometers, especially in late summer; but *Boloria* may be quite local. All species feed on flowers. Adults usually rest with the wings closed; but because they bask with them spread, the mountain species, more in need of the sun's heat, are often observed with open wings. Males patrol to seek females. When a mating pair is disturbed, either sex may fly; this is one of the few groups in which such flexibility occurs.

D. Magnus studied the mating behavior of the European *Argynnis paphia*, which is undoubtedly similar in behavior to our *Speyeria*. He found that he could attract patrolling males to artificial butterflies that flutter rapidly and are of the same color and size as the female. The eversible female glands on the end of the abdomen produce a pheromone that is attractive to males even when placed on filter paper. The male pursues the female and zooms up in front of her repeatedly, apparently to place his pheromone (from the scent scales along the veins on his upperside) next to her antennae. She lands, the male flies around her and then lands, he "bows" by spreading his forewings a little and moving them forward near her antennae, he bumps her with his palpi and touches her head with his antennae, and then they mate. This elaborate courtship, involving both male and female pheromones, may be necessary to prevent mating with the wrong species (many *Speyeria* look similar, and the pheromones probably differ between species). The courting males of *Speyeria* (see *S. atlantis*, 260, below) keep the forewings in the forward position and open and close them spasmodically near the resting female, to waft pheromones. Unreceptive *Speyeria* females flutter their wings to reject males.

Some of our female *Speyeria* are black, and others are orange like the males. Both forms occur in European *Argynnis paphia* females (and in our *S. cybele*), in which the black form is dominant to the orange (R. Goldschmidt). Although *A. paphia* males prefer orange females, the black ones manage to mate anyway. Our black *S. diana* females benefit from mimicry.

Some western *Speyeria* have many subspecies, and in certain regions even the species may resemble each other. By studying tens of thousands of adults and charting how the wing pattern changes from region to region, L. Grey and C. dos Passos demonstrated that the hundred or so species of *Speyeria* that had been named belong in fact to only 14 species. Because *Speyeria* species 259-263 (the *callippe* group) are very similar in certain areas of the western U.S., more space is given to identifying them. To identify western *Speyeria* one should first try species 251-258 and 264, and if unsuccessful there, consult the maps to find which other species occur in the area, then read the descriptions for each subspecies in the area. J. Brittnacher, S. Sims, and F. Ayala used electrophoresis to study the body enzymes of ten California *Speyeria* species and found that the five *callippe*-group species could not be distinguished, whereas the other species could be, although the enzymes of *S. hydaspe* and *adiaste* were similar. *S. callippe* and *coronis* each has 30 chromosomes, and *atlantis*, *egleis*, and *zerene* each has 29, although further research may show that the number varies within a species.

Color Plate 26

237. **Boloria napaea**   Mountain Fritillary
Identified by the angled fw and characteristic unh; that part of the unh median band inside the discal cell is white, but the rest of the band is yellow or tan. The ups of males is orange; of females, blackish and cream. Ssp. **alaskensis** (Arctic to Alta.) has silver unh marginal spots; ssp. **halli** (Wind River Mts., Wyo.) lacks the silver, has a yellower unh, and has less black on the uph base. Ssp. *napaea* (which resembles *alaskensis*) and other ssp. range from the Pyrenees to Siberia. Habitat Arctic/Alpine Zone moist tundra (in lower Alpine and Hudsonian Zone meadows in Wyo.). Hostplants herb Polygonaceae: *Polygonum viviparum* (B.C. and Europe), probably *P. bistortoides* in Wyo.; possibly *Viola* (Violaceae) and *Vaccinium* (Ericaceae) in Europe. Eggs laid haphazardly near hosts. First-stage larvae hibernate (J. Harry); older larvae probably hibernate the second winter. One flight, L July-M Aug. in Wyo., L June-July in the Arctic. Males patrol all day, about a third of a meter above ground in moist meadows near *Polygonum*, to seek females.

Color Plate 26

238. Boloria eunomia   Ocellate Bog Fritillary

Identified on the unh by the row of white-centered postmedian circles, the large marginal spots (silvered to clear yellowish like the median band), and the median spot in cell CuA$_2$, which is convex outwardly (concave in the other *Boloria* except *B. epithore*, 242). Ssp. **dawsoni** (s Man.-Maine) is brownish above, with silver unh spots. Ssp. **triclaris** (Lab. to Alaska to Alta.) is oranger above (alpine Alta. populations often browner), with silver unh spots. Ssp. **caelestis** (=*alticola*) (sw Mont.-Colo.) is orangish or cream above, with yellowish unh spots. Ssp. *eunomia* and other ssp. are Eurasian (Pyrenees to Siberia).

Habitat Canadian to Alpine Zone bogs and moist tundra. Hostplants (E. Pike, D. Parshall, J. Harry, J. Scott) shrubby Salicaceae: *Salix* (Alta.); herb Polygonaceae: *Polygonum viviparum* (Man. and Europe); Violaceae: *Viola palustris* (Man. and Europe), *adunca* (and ssp. *bellidifolia*; Wyo., Colo.). Oviposition observed on other plants that are doubtful hosts—in Ont. Ericaceae: *Vaccinium oxycoccos*, *Gaultheria hispidula*; in Colo. Ranunculaceae: *Thalictrum alpinum*, *Caltha leptosepala*; in Colo. Rosaceae: *Pentaphylloides floribunda*. Colo. lab larvae eat *Salix* and *Viola* well, *P. floribunda* a little, *Thalictrum* not at all (Scott). Some Alta. lab larvae prefer *Salix* to *Viola* and *Polygonum* (J. Shepard); others eat the *Polygonum viviparum* inflorescence (Pike).

Eggs cream, becoming tan, laid in clusters of 2-4 (rarely 20) under the leaves of numerous plants. Larvae eat leaves, the somewhat gregarious younger larvae eating holes in them. Larva (Colo.-Wyo.) pale reddish-brown, with many reddish spines. Larva (Europe) silver-gray, finely dotted with white above, with paler lateral and sublateral bands, the underside black-brown; spines white or flesh-colored; head brownish-yellow. Third- and fourth-stage larvae hibernate.

One flight, July-E Aug. southward, M June-July in the north, M July-Aug. in Lab. and c Wyo. Adults of *B. eunomia* and *B. titania* (240) often move a few hundred meters through dry pine woods between wet habitat areas (Shepard). Males patrol all day in bogs to seek females.

Color Plates 3 (larva), 5 (pupa), 24, 26
Fig. 51

239. Boloria selene   Silver Meadow Fritillary

Identified on the unh by the four rows of silver spots (including the postmedian and the large marginal spots) and by the absence of the white-centered circles of *B. eunomia* (238). Ssp. **atrocostalis** (Canada-Alaska), which has black dorsal borders, remains distinct when raised in the lab. Ssp. **nebraskensis** (E Neb.-Ohio) is large and light. Ssp. **myrina** occurs elsewhere. Ssp. *selene* and others are Eurasian (Spain to Korea).

Habitat mostly northern Upper Austral to Hudsonian Zone moist meadows, bogs, and spring-fed meadows (even in shortgrass prairie). Hostplants herb Violaceae: *Viola nephrophylla*, *glabella*, in England *canina*. Larvae eat many other *Viola* spp. in the lab. Possible European hosts are *Fragaria* (Rosaceae) and *Vaccinium uliginosum* (Ericaceae).

Eggs pale-green or yellowish-white, becoming tan, laid singly and haphazardly near but seldom on *Viola*. Oviposition sometimes near *Salix* (Salicaceae), but larvae may not eat it (*Viola* is probably nearby). Larvae eat leaves, the underside when young; no nests. Larva (Fig. 51) dark grayish-black with a bluish tint, with many black dots, black patches around the dorsal spines, and an orange-brown lateral line; spines orangish-ochre with black tips and black hairs, the black dorsal prothoracic spines three times as long as the others; head blackish. Pupa brown (the wing cases more yellow-brown) or yellow-brown, with a row of subdorsal cones (those on the thorax and abdomen segments 1 and 2 metallic reddish-gold or silvery), a point on top of the thorax, and two brown cones on the head. Larvae hibernate in second to fourth stages (mostly third).

Three flights, M May-M Sep., in lowland U.S.; two flights, June and Aug., from N.S. to Sask., L June-E Sep. in Nfld.; one flight, July-E Aug. in high Colo. mountains, L June-E Aug. in c Alta., L June-July in the far north. Males patrol all day about the meadows to seek females. Females have abdominal glands like those of *Speyeria* (251-264) that are probably used in courtship. The male may hover above the female, and may flutter after landing behind her. Unreceptive females seem to flutter while at rest.

Color Plates 1 (egg), 26

240. **Boloria titania**   Purple Bog Fritillary

Identified on the unh by thin white marginal spots (rarely missing) capped by brown crescents or triangles pointed inward. *B. eunomia* (238), *B. freija* (249), and *B. selene* (239) differ on the rest of the wing. Ssp. **chariclea** (mostly Arctic/ Alpine Zone north of 61° latitude and in Scandinavia and Siberia) has about four or more white or silver unh spots, and females are slightly darker than males. It was considered a distinct species, but it intergrades with ssp. *boisduvalii* in many places all across the Arctic; E. Pike found that it is a ssp. of *titania*. Ssp. **boisdu-valii** (Alaska-Alta.-Lab.-Nfld.-N.S.-Minn.-c B.C., extending north of 61°N along the Mackenzie R. and in lowland Alaska and the Yukon) is dark, the unh median band suffused with reddish or brown. Ssp. **helena** (s B.C. and Mont. southward) is lighter, the unh median band yellowish. Females are paler on the ups, with broad upf veins in the Sangre de Cristo Mts., Colo., and the Beartooth Plateau of Wyo.-Mont. (form **sangredecristo**). There is much individual variation and some other minor geographic variation. Ssp. *titania* and other ssp. are in the European Alps and s Asia.

Habitat Canadian Zone moist valley bottoms, to arctic/alpine tundra. Host-plants herb and shrub Salicaceae: *Salix* sp. (Alta.), *reticulata* (s Alaska and Chur-chill, Man.), *arctica* (Churchill); Polygonaceae: *Polygonum* (Europe), *P. bistortoides* (Wash.), ?*viviparum* (N. Amer.); Violaceae: *Viola pallens* (Ont.), *adunca* (Wyo.); Rosaceae: *Dryas integrifolia* (Greenland). Assoc. with *Salix herbacea* in se Can. and with *S. reticulata* ssp. *nivalis* in Colo. Young larvae eat *Viola* in the lab (Colo., J. Scott). Oviposition observed on *Vaccinium angustifolium* (Ericaceae, Ont.), *V.* sp. (N Que.), and *V. scoparium* (Colo.), all possible hosts, and on *Trollius laxus* (Ranunculaceae, Colo.), a doubtful host.

Eggs whitish, laid singly on the underside of the leaves of many plants. Larvae eat leaves; no nests. Larva gray, with black dorsal and lateral stripes and orange spines (the first subdorsal pair longer and yellow); head black. First- and fourth-stage larvae hibernate in Alta. and the Arctic, where the species is bien-nial; larvae are known to hibernate in the first stage in Wash. and N.H. and in the fourth stage in Colo., where it may be biennial also.

One flight, July-Aug. southward, M July-L Aug. in Alta.-Sask., L June-E Aug. in the Arctic, July-E Aug. in Lab. Ssp. *chariclea* (and perhaps all ssp.) biennial, flying in odd years in Alaska and the Yukon. Males patrol all day in valley bottoms and along bog edges to seek females. I observed a male courting a female who was upside down on a grass stem, with wings spread and fluttering. She everted two red glands on the end of her abdomen, probably wafting a pheromone.

Color Plate 26

241. Boloria kriemhild   Relict Meadow Fritillary

Like *B. epithore* (242) and *B. titania* (240), but the unh has a uniformly yellowish median band, a small postbasal spot, and the brown submarginal crescents pointed outward, and it lacks the silver or yellow marginal spots of *B. eunomia* (238).

Habitat Canadian to Hudsonian Zone moist meadows and clearings. Hostplant herb Violaceae: *Viola*.

Fourth-stage larvae hibernate.

One flight, M June-E Aug. Males patrol in moist meadows all day to seek females.

Color Plate 26

242. Boloria epithore   Western Meadow Fritillary

Similar to *B. frigga* (244) and *B. bellona* (243), but the range is mostly separate, the fw more rounded, and the unh slightly more yellow-brown with a more distinct yellow median band. Ssp. **epithore** (Santa Cruz Mts., Calif.) has smaller black ups spots than ssp. **chermocki** elsewhere.

Habitat Transition to Alpine (mostly Canadian) Zone moist forest openings and wet meadows. Hostplants herb Violaceae: *Viola ocellata, glabella, sempervirens,* probably *nephrophylla.*

Larva gray, the top and the lower part of each side dark (the area between streaked with black), with two gray middorsal lines and a reddish-brown sublateral stripe; spines mostly reddish (those on front and rear black); head black. Pupa pale brown, the top of the head and the thorax pale brown mottled with white, the wing cases white at the edge, the abdomen whitish (mottled with pale brown) with dark-brown lateral patches. Fourth-stage larvae hibernate.

One flight, M May-June in Coast Ranges, June-July inland, July-M Aug. at high altitude. Males patrol all day in meadows and moist woods, mainly in valley bottoms, to seek females.

Color Plate 26

243. Boloria bellona   Meadow Fritillary

Similar to *B. frigga* (244) and *B. epithore* (242), but the fw tips are squared off. Darker northward (ssp. **toddi**, Lab.-N Man.-N.W. Terr.); ssp. **bellona** elsewhere.

Habitat upper Transition to Hudsonian Zone moist meadows; range expanding southward in Mo., Ky., and Va. Hostplants herb Violaceae: *Viola sororia, pallens;* several other spp. in the lab.

Eggs whitish, laid haphazardly on twigs, grass stems, other plants, etc., rarely on violets. Larvae eat leaves at night; no nests. Larva purplish-black, sometimes with yellowish mottling, with light dots at the base of the hairs and a white subdorsal (and a fainter lateral) line of dashes; many brown spines about equal in length; head black. Pupa brown, with gold dorsal cones, the abdomen with yellow mottling and yellow subdorsal and lateral lines of dashes. Third- or fourth-stage larvae hibernate.

Three flights southward (and at Ottawa), M May-E Sep.; two flights, L May-

Aug., from Que. to c Alta.; one flight westward, M June-July in Colo., L May-E July in Wash. Males patrol all day in moist meadows to seek females. In courtship the male hovers in front of the female, who may also flutter.

Color Plate 26

244. Boloria frigga   Willow-Bog Fritillary

Identified by the unh, which has a dark-violet-gray outer part and a white patch (containing a dark spot) next to the fw, the patch shorter than that of *B. improba*. The fw is rather pointed. Ssp. **sagata** (Wyo.-Colo.) is lighter on the ups. Ssp. **saga** (most of the range) has darker-brown ups wing bases. Ssp. **gibsoni** (=*alaskensis*; Arctic from NE Alaska to Hudson Bay) is lighter and more yellow, the unh median band sometimes yellow (brown in other ssp.). Ssp. *frigga* and others are in Scandinavia and Siberia.

Habitat Canadian to Arctic/Alpine Zone shrub-willow (half a meter tall) bogs and arctic tundra. Hostplants mostly shrub Salicaceae: *Salix* (Colo., Alta); Betulaceae: dwarf *Betula* (Mich.); Rosaceae: *Rubus chamaemorus* in Europe, and the herb *Dryas integrifolia* (oviposition on, in Alaska).

Nearly mature larvae hibernate.

One flight, mostly June-July (July-E Aug. in Lab.). Males patrol all day, esp. in low spots of willow bogs, to seek females.

Color Plates 5 (pupa), 26, 60
Fig. 50

245. Boloria improba   Dingy Arctic Fritillary

Small and dingy, identified by the large blended blackish upf postmedian spots. The outer half of the unh is usually grayish, as in *B. frigga* (244), but the unh median band is placed farther out than in *frigga*. Ssp. **acrocnema** (San Juan Mts., Colo.) is whiter, the fw very rounded, the fw discal-cell spot a blotch, the unh median band paler, and the spot in unh cell M_2 apparently longer. Ssp. **harryi** (Wind River Mts., Wyo.) resembles *acrocnema*, but the pointier fw and fw discal-cell bar are as in ssp. *improba*, and a few other details are intermediate to *improba*; however, the black upf postmedian line is thicker, the outer third of the unh is a little grayer, and the red unh bands contrast more with the median band than in other ssp. Ssp. **unnamed** (w-c Alta.) is like ssp. *improba*, but the fw is shorter and the unh median band is paler tan; the ups median band is creamier, and the outer third of the ups is oranger than in any other ssp. Ssp. **improba** elsewhere, including Eurasia (Scandinavia, Novaya Zemlya north of mainland Russia, probably Siberia), is suffused with brown; some adults in and near the Yukon are yellowish (form **youngi**). Ssp. *acrocnema* was named a separate species, but its ecology, morphology, and most wing traits are like those of *improba*, and the other two ssp. are intermediate in wing shape and pattern.

Habitat Arctic/Alpine Zone tundra, in moist places with a carpet of dwarf willow. Hostplants tiny prostrate Salicaceae: *Salix reticulata* ssp. *nivalis* in Colo. (eggs rarely laid on *Polygonum viviparum* there), a tiny *Salix* (possibly *reticulata*) in N.W. Terr., *S. arctica* in Wyo., probably *S. herbacea* in Europe; adults assoc. with *Salix* everywhere.

Eggs cream, becoming tan later, laid singly, mostly on host stems. Larvae (Fig. 50; similar to 254 in Fig. 51) eat leaves; no nests. Larva mottled dark brown (tan beneath), with a brown middorsal line and a blackish-edged bright-cream subdorsal line; spines reddish-brown; head black, with a brown subdorsal bar on top of the head and a brown spot above the eyes. Pupa mottled brown, with a tan subdorsal line when young and with many subdorsal bumps, the fifth to seventh abdomen segments each having a small middorsal "saddle horn" in the front at the point of a gray flaring triangle (each triangle between two black semi-circular spots in ssp. *acrocnema*, these areas domes between black triangles in ssp. *harryi*), the intersegmental membrane in the front of segments 5-7 reddish; pupa usually horizontal between leaves, etc., loosely silked together. Biennial; newly hatched larvae hibernate the first winter, unfed fourth-stage larvae the second (J. Scott, J. Harry).

One flight, mostly L June-July (M July-E Aug. in Colo., E-M Aug. in Wyo.); flies in even years in c Alta., every year in Colo. and Wyo. Adults fly slowly unless disturbed, often rest, and are very local esp. in Colo., but they sometimes stray 50 m or more from a colony. Life span is up to a week in nature. Populations may be more than 2,000 in 1 hectare (2.5 acres) during the total flight period of about 3-4 weeks, but in many years and in most Colo. colonies they are much less common to uncommon. Adults sometimes sip flower nectar and often probe soil with the proboscis for moisture. Males patrol all day to seek females, just above the ground near the hostplant.

246. Boloria alberta   Alberta Alpine Fritillary

Color Plate 26

The fw is rounded, and the unh median band is suffused with brownish. Males are dingy orange; females dingy brownish and paler orange.

Habitat alpine rock garden and scree; also in Siberia. Hostplant probably herb Rosaceae: *Dryas octopetala* (on the basis of association and lab oviposition).

Eggs pale yellow when laid. First-stage larvae hibernate (W. Edwards); probably older larvae pass the second winter.

One flight, L July-E Aug.; biennial, flying mostly in even years. Males patrol low to the ground all day near *Dryas* on hillsides (rarely on flats) to seek females (J. Scott); they seldom if ever patrol on hilltops.

247. Boloria astarte   Arctic Ridge Fritillary

Color Plate 26

Identified by the uniform row of white unh postmedian crescents, followed by black dots. The unh base has only three white spots (four in *B. polaris*, 248). Ssp. **astarte** (NE B.C. to Alta. southward) has pearly-white unh median spots and a fairly pointed fw. In ssp. **distincta** (NW B.C. northward) the unh is orangish, the unh median spots are broader and suffused with tan, and the fw is more rounded. Ssp. **unnamed** (Brooks Range, Alaska) resembles *distincta*, but its unh is more dingy-brown. Ssp. **tschukotkensis** (w Alaska and Siberia) resembles *distincta*, but the unh is more grayish.

Habitat alpine/arctic rocky ridges. Hostplant herb Saxifragaceae: *Saxifraga bronchialis* (Alta., Siberia).

Eggs laid on or near the host.

One flight, July-M Aug. in Alta., L June-July in the Arctic; biennial, mostly flying in even years in Wash., every year in Alta., even or odd years in the Arctic. Males in the Yukon, B.C., and Alta. patrol swiftly all day to seek females, near the ground on scree slopes (usually south-facing) near the hostplant, often along the leeward edge of ridgetops and hilltops (J. Troubridge, J. Scott).

Color Plate 26

248. Boloria polaris   Polar Fritillary

Identified on the unh by the white marginal streak extending from each brown submarginal spot to the margin and by the whitish postbasal discal-cell spot (between the basal spot and the median band in this cell). These marginal streaks are much shorter in *B. astarte distincta* (247), which usually lacks the white cell spot and has the unh base orange-brown (red-brown in *B. polaris*). *B. freija* (249) has similar marginal streaks, but the rest of the unh differs.

Habitat arctic tundra; ranges also to Scandinavia and Asia. Hostplants herb Rosaceae: *Dryas integrifolia, octopetala*; Ericaceae: many eggs laid on *Vaccinium uliginosum* (and var. *alpinus*) in nature, and lab larvae eat it (D. Parshall).

Eggs laid singly or in clusters of 2-20. Third- and fourth-stage larvae hibernate (E. Pike). Newly hatched larvae probably hibernate also; larvae of northern Ellesmere I. (N.W. Terr.) *Boloria* (*polaris* and/or *titania chariclea*, 240) hibernate both when newly hatched and when "well grown" (J. Downes).

One flight, mostly L June-July (M July-M Aug. in Lab.); biennial, flying in odd years in c Alaska and at Churchill, Man., mostly in odd years at Baker Lake, N.W. Terr., in even years most other places including Coral Harbour, N.W. Terr. They often bask dorsally in protected hollows to keep warm.

Color Plate 26

249. Boloria freija   Zigzag Fritillary

Identified on the unh by the characteristic sawtooth median band (shared only by *B. natazhati*, 250) with its two white spots, the arrowhead white spot near the base, and the yellow-brown base of the postmedian band in cells Rs and M_1. The unh has reddish areas, unlike *B. natazhati*. Arctic populations (in Eurasia also) are darker on the ups, esp. in N.W. Terr. (ssp. **freija**); s Rockies populations are lighter on the ups (ssp. **browni**).

Habitat Canadian Zone bogs and valley forest openings, to arctic/alpine tundra valleys. Ranges to Scandinavia, Siberia, and Japan. Hostplants shrubs and herbs—Ericaceae: *Vaccinium cespitosum* (Wash., Colo., Man.), *uliginosum* (Man., Europe), *Arctostaphylos uva-ursi* (Alta., Man., and Europe), *Rhododendron aureum* (Japan); Empetraceae: *Empetrum nigrum* (Europe): Rosaceae: *Rubus chamaemorus* (Man., Europe), *Sieversia* (Japan). Oviposition on the herb *Dryas integrifolia* (Rosaceae) in Man. Empetraceae and Rosaceae may not be eaten much by larvae.

Eggs laid singly and haphazardly near or on the hostplant. Larvae eat leaves; no nests. Half-grown larva dark brown, with light areas above and below the many black spines; head black. Fourth-stage larvae hibernate.

One flight, L May-E July in Colo., M May-M June in Alta.-Sask., June-M July in the Arctic (M June-M Aug. in Lab.). Males patrol all day near the hostplants to seek females.

Color Plate 24

250. Boloria natazhati   Pleistocene Fritillary

The unh has the same sawtooth median band as *B. freija* (249), but the unh ground color is ochre, not red. *B. natazhati* is much darker than *freija*, the basal two-thirds of the unh and uph being mostly dark brown (the unh brown extending outward from the median band somewhat, and largely obscuring the arrowhead-shaped white spot that is present in *freija* on the unh base). The body and wing bases of *natazhati* are covered with long hairs, unlike *freija*, the ups has a greasy-bluish sheen reminiscent of *Chlosyne gabbii damoetas* (223), and the fw is more pointed than that of *freija*. The ochre space at the end of the fw cell is slightly larger in *natazhati*. *B. natazhati* has been treated as a ssp. of *freija*, because the wing-pattern elements and male abdominal parts are like those of *freija*. It seems distinct because both *natazhati* and *freija* have been found at Coppermine, N.W. Terr., with no evidence of intergrading. So far *natazhati* has been found only in three widely separated regions (Coppermine and Bernard Harbour, N.W. Terr., and adjacent Victoria I.; north of Mt. Natazhat on the sw Yukon-Alaska border, and the adjacent Mentasta Mts. of se Alaska, both in the Alaska Range; and the Richardson Mts., N.W. Terr.); it probably occurs in e Yukon. No geographic variation. Habitat arctic/alpine tundra, mostly in rather barren areas esp. scree of dark boulders. One flight, M June-July; probably biennial, though recorded in both even and odd years.

251. Speyeria diana   Great Smokies Fritillary

Color Plates 8, 20, 23
Figs. 35 (ultraviolet), 71 (uncus)

The unh is unique. Males are orange; females blue. Females may mimic *Battus philenor* (25).

Habitat mostly Upper Austral to Transition Zone deciduous and pine woodland near streams. Common in the s Appalachians from w Va. and W.Va. to ne Ga., and in the Ark. Ozarks, but apparently uncommon or extinct elsewhere, and some records may be strays. It became extinct in se Va. about 1951, and the records from most other regions except the Appalachians and Ozarks are more than 50 years old. Hostplants herb Violaceae: *Viola papilionacea, cucullata*. Lab larvae eat many *Viola*, and have been partially raised on *Vernonia noveboracensis* (Compositae).

Eggs laid singly and haphazardly near *Viola*, mostly in late summer. Larvae eat leaves and flowers; no nests. Larva black, with many spines and with two white dots between the dorsal pairs of spines (all *Speyeria* have six rows of large spines, none on the dorsal line), the spines orange at the base, longer than those of *S. cybele* (253) and *S. aphrodite* (252); head brown, orangish behind. Pupa light brown mottled with darker brown, with about 18 dark conical subdorsal bumps, the abdomen slightly darker brown, with red mottling on the sides. Unfed first-stage larvae hibernate.

One flight, M June-E Aug., rarely Sep. Adults sip flower nectar and feed on dung. Males patrol to seek females.

252. Speyeria aphrodite   Aphrodite Fritillary

Color Plates 20, 25
Figs. 35 (ultraviolet), 71

Differs from *S. cybele* (253; and from some western *Speyeria*) by having a black spot at the base of fw cell CuA$_2$ (except sometimes in ssp. *manitoba*) and little dark sex scaling on the narrow male upf veins. The basal two-thirds of the unh is brown. The unh always has silver spots (except in some adults in Bear Paw Mts., Mont.). The unh is always streaked with reddish-brown, which tends to diffuse a little onto the pale unh submarginal band; in the Midwest (esp. Iowa-Ind.) the pale unh band is often completely brown (form **alcestis**). The uncus differs from that of the *S. callippe* group (259-263; the uncus of *aphrodite*, *diana*, *cybele*, *nokomis*, and *idalia* in side view is thick with a notch beneath the tip, whereas all other *Speyeria* have a thin uncus without much of a notch; see

Fig. 71). *S. aphrodite* females have a two-chambered bursa copulatrix as in *diana*, *idalia*, and *cybele*; other *Speyeria* have one chamber. Ssp. **manitoba** (N Great Plains) adults are paler. Ssp. **byblis** (Ariz.-w Colo.) adults are smaller. Ssp. **aphrodite** (elsewhere) is very similar to *S. atlantis atlantis* (260) in the west, but usually larger (male fw length 30-33 mm, female 32-38 mm, vs. *atlantis* male fw length 26-29 mm, female 27-32), with narrower male upf veins and a slightly narrower pale unh submarginal band than *atlantis*. In w Colo., ssp. *byblis* is the same size as *atlantis*, but *byblis* males have narrower dark upf veins and a slightly redder ups; *byblis* females have the unh Rs vein bordered above with pale cream (about 1 mm wide) from near the wing base to the submarginal spot (in *atlantis* the brown color covers the vein at least in the middle).

Habitat dry Transition to Canadian Zone brushland or open woods, tall prairie. Hostplants herb Violaceae: *Viola lanceolata*, *fimbriatula*, *nuttallii*, *papiliona-cea*, *nephrophylla*, *primulifolia* var. *acuta*.

Eggs cream, turning violet-tan with a cream lateral ring, laid singly and hap-hazardly near *Viola*, or where *Viola* will appear the next spring (often under shrubs). Larvae eat leaves; no nests. Larva blackish-brown (form *alcestis* black-ish), with many black-tipped spines (the dorsal spines ochre on the thorax and brown on the abdomen, the subdorsal and esp. the lateral spines ochre), a black middorsal line, and a black patch around each spine; head black, orangish be-hind, with two small cones on top. Pupa (ssp. *aphrodite*) mottled yellowish-brown, the head brownish-black, the abdomen grayish, with a blackish trans-verse band on the front of each segment; pupa (form *alcestis*) darker, mottled red-brown, with a black wing patch and black wing veins. Unfed first-stage larvae hibernate.

One flight, L June-M Sep. Females may lay eggs in L June-July, but usually not until M Aug.-Sep. Males patrol all day, mainly in open areas, to seek females.

Color Plate 20
Fig. 45

253. Speyeria cybele   Great Spangled Fritillary

The lack of a black spot near the base of fw cell CuA$_2$ separates *S. cybele* from all other similar species except *S. nokomis* (254; *S. aphrodite*, 252, and *S. atlantis*, 260, from Sask. and Man. rarely lack this spot). The basal two-thirds of the unh of western *cybele leto* is dark brown (darker than in *nokomis*), and there is only one black bar at the end of the uph cell (two in *nokomis* and the *S. callippe* group, 259-263). *S. cybele* is always silvered, and always has heavy sex scaling on the male upf, resulting in wide black upf veins, unlike *aphrodite*. The pale unh sub-marginal band is very wide, and the female has a two-chambered bursa copu-latrix. In ssp. **cybele** (E U.S.), both sexes are brown; darkest in the northeast, it becomes smaller and lighter in sw Colo. and Man.-Alta. In N Mich and adjacent Ont. (rarely elsewhere), paler females are frequent (form **krautwurmi** of ssp. *cybele*). In ssp. **charlotti** (NW Colo., La Sal Mts. of Utah, s Wyo.), most females are cream-colored. In Alta. and Mont. where ssp. *cybele* intergrades with ssp. *leto*, many males are intermediate, but females tend to be whitish or tan (inter-mediates are probably rare because pale females are dominant to tan ones in in-heritance). In ssp. **leto** (w Mont. to sw Wyo. and c Utah westward), males are bright orange, with the fw pointed and the black lines narrow; females are nearly white.

Habitat Transition to Canadian Zone moist deciduous woods and moist meadows. Hostplants herb Violaceae: *Viola rotundifolia, papilionacea, palustris, adunca* var. *bellidifolia;* assoc. with *V. canadensis.*

Eggs (Fig. 45) pale yellow, becoming tan, laid singly and haphazardly near *Viola.* Larvae eat leaves; no nests. Larva velvety-black, with two middorsal lines of gray dots and many black-tipped spines (the base of the spines reddish-yellow, sometimes yellow esp. on the subdorsal thoracic spines and the lateral abdominal spines); head dark brown, reddish-yellow behind. Larva resembles *S. diana* (251), but the dorsal spines are shorter and sometimes darker. Pupa dark mottled brown (the abdomen mostly unmottled), sometimes with reddish-orange mottling, the outer edge of the wing case sometimes lighter, the abdomen with dorsal bumps (black in front, yellow behind). Unfed first-stage larvae hibernate.

One flight, mostly M June-M Sep. (sometimes starting in May in E U.S.), mostly July-Aug. in the west. Females may lay eggs in L June-July but often not until Aug.-Sep. Adults sip flower nectar and occasionally feed on dung. Males patrol all day to seek females. The courting male moves his forewings forward and opens and closes them near the female, apparently transferring pheromones (A. Clark).

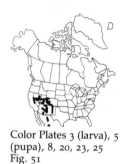

Color Plates 3 (larva), 5 (pupa), 8, 20, 23, 25 Fig. 51

254. Speyeria nokomis   Western Seep Fritillary

Characterized by the large size, by females that are black basally and whitish outwardly (males are orangish), and by the lack of a black spot near the base of fw cell CuA_2. The unh is always silvered. Only *S. cybele leto* (253) from Utah-Calif. can be confused with it, but *leto* has a dark-brown unh, only one black uph bar at the end of the discal cell, narrow upf veins of males, and uph postmedian spots in cells M_3 and CuA_1 shaped like one-third moons. In ssp. **apacheana** (Calif.-Nev.), the unh is yellow in males, green in females. Ssp. *apacheana* intergrades in a cline through sw Utah, NE Utah, w Colo., to sw Colo. and N N.M., where the basal two-thirds of the unh is light brown in males, brown-black in females (ssp. **nokomis**). From C Ariz. to sw N.M., ssp. *nokomis* is a little darker, with the pale unh submarginal band suffused a little with tan in males, and most females have more ups black. In ssp. **coerulescens** (s Ariz., s N.M. to Durango, Mex.) the male wing bases are dark brown, and females are bluish-white on the outer part of the ups; the basal two-thirds of the unh is brown or greenish-brown in males, brown to green in females.

Habitat Upper Sonoran to Canadian Zone moist meadows near streams, permanent spring-fed meadows, and seeps. Hostplant herb Violaceae: *Viola nephrophylla.*

Eggs cream, soon speckled with brown, becoming tan (dirty-white with purplish markings), laid singly and haphazardly near *Viola.* Larvae eat leaves; no nests. Larva (Fig. 51) orangish-ochre, dark beneath, with six rows of long orangish-ochre spines, black patches around dorsal and subdorsal spines, two black transverse stripes on the rear of each segment, and orangish-ochre lateral and dorsal stripes; head black, orangish on top rear. Pupa orangish-ochre, with a black transverse serrate band on the front of each abdomen segment, the thorax and all but the center of the wing black, and the top of the thorax with an orangish triangular spot. Unfed first-stage larvae hibernate (half-grown larvae may aestivate also in the Apr.-June Mexican drought).

One flight, usually L July-M Sep. (M Aug.-M Sep. southward). Adults sip the nectar of flowers, esp. thistles. Males patrol all day about the meadows or seeps to seek females.

255. Speyeria idalia   Regal Fritillary

The outer part of the uph is black with white spots.

Habitat Upper Austral to Transition Zone wet meadows and moist prairie. Many colonies have disappeared recently, owing to habitat destruction. Hostplants herb Violaceae: *Viola pedatifida, papilionacea, lanceolata, pedata*.

Eggs laid singly and haphazardly near *Viola*. Larvae eat leaves; no nests. Larva resembles that of *S. nokomis* (254), ochre-yellow to orangish, yellow on the rear, with a black middorsal line, black blotches in front of the dorsal and subdorsal spines, two black transverse lines on each segment behind the spines, and yellowish middorsal and lateral stripes, the dorsal spines silvery at the base, the subdorsal and lateral spines orange at the base; head black, orangish on top rear. Pupa light mottled brown tinged with pink, with small black spots on the wings and thorax, short dorsal cones, and yellow transverse bands on the abdomen. Unfed first-stage larvae hibernate.

One flight, June-E Sep. Females do not lay many eggs until Aug. Males patrol all day to seek females.

Color Plate 20

256. Speyeria mormonia   Mormon Fritillary

Identified by the small size (male fw length about 24 mm, female 26 mm), the rounded fw, the very narrow (almost undarkened) upf veins of males, and the mostly subalpine habitat. The dark unh crescents capping the silver marginal spots are mostly cone-shaped. The basal two-thirds of the unh usually has many lighter areas among the ground color, which is greenish to brownish (ssp. **eurynome**, in most of the Rockies, with silver spots in the south, very variable and often unsilvered northward), reddish-brown (ssp. **erinna**, the Cascades from NW Calif. to s Wash., usually silvered), light brown (ssp. **mormonia**, Sierra Nevada of Calif. only, usually silvered), ochre (ssp. **artonis**, N Nev. and SE Ore., the entire unh ochre-yellow with only faint traces of spots, unsilvered; the arctic ssp. **bischoffii** is the same but the ups is darker, and a few are silvered), or greenish-yellow (ssp. **luski**, White Mts., Ariz., the whole unh greenish-yellow, with thick black lines around where the silver spots would be, unsilvered). The Sierra ssp. *mormonia* differs from the very similar *S. egleis egleis* (261), which is also small, in several characters: the fw is more rounded, the male upf veins are narrower (less dark scaling), the black upf median spots of males are narrower, the uph marginal crescents touch the black line more, the ups borders of females are darker, and the unf orange tends to be more uniform. Ssp. *erinna* generally has a greenish tinge to the abdominal margin of the unh, separating it from *S. egleis*.

Habitat upper Canadian to lower Alpine Zone meadows. Hostplants herb Violaceae: *Viola nuttallii, nephrophylla, palustris, adunca* var. *bellidifolia*.

Eggs yellowish, becoming purplish-tan, laid singly and haphazardly near *Viola*. Larvae eat leaves; no nests. Larva grayish-brown to tan, patterned like other *Speyeria*, with a light middorsal stripe and short spines having pale bases. Unfed first-stage larvae hibernate.

Color Plates 25, 26
Fig. 37 (scent gland)

One flight, M July - E Sep. southward, July - Aug. northward. Adults (esp. females) can fly far; they occasionally stray to foothills or even the Colo. plains. Adults sip flower nectar and mud. Males patrol all day in open areas near the ground to seek females.

257. Speyeria adiaste   Coast Fritillary

Color Plate 25

Identified by the washed-out ghostlike unsilvered unh, which has a violet tinge, and by the coastal Calif. range. The unh of unsilvered *S. callippe macaria* (259) differs by having reddish outlining the positions of the absent silver spots. Ssp. **atossa** (extinct since 1959; previously Mt. Pinos - Tehachapi Mts. - Tejon Mts., Calif.) was pale yellow-orange; about one out of 500 adults was silvered. Ssp. **clemencei** (Monterey - San Luis Obispo Cos.) is darker (orange). Ssp. **adiaste** (Santa Cruz Mts.) is darkest (reddish).

Habitat Redwood-forest openings northward, higher mountains southward. J. Emmel thinks that *S. adiaste* has become more scarce owing to man's suppression of wildfires and the resulting habitat change. Hostplants herb Violaceae: *Viola quercetorum*, possibly *ocellata*, ?*purpurea*.

Eggs laid singly and haphazardly near *Viola*. Larvae eat leaves; no nests. Larva like that of *S. callippe*, but the sides lighter gray and the top rear of the head yellow. Pupa like that of *callippe*, but the wing cases a little lighter. Unfed first-stage larvae hibernate.

One flight, mostly June - July, rarely as late as E Sep.

258. Speyeria hydaspe   Lavender Fritillary

Color Plate 21

The unh is red-brown with a lavender tint, the pale unh submarginal band is uniformly lightly suffused with this color also, the unh has large round unsilvered spots, and the ups wing bases are dark. B.C. and some Wash. adults (ssp. **rhodope**) are a little smaller, darker on the ups, reddish-brown on the unh, and sometimes silvered on the unh. In Ore. - N Calif., the basal two-thirds of the unh is very dark black-purple to reddish-brown beneath (ssp. **purpurascens**). Sierra Nevada adults are a little lighter on the unh (ssp. **hydaspe**). The basal two-thirds of the unh is much lighter, pinkish-red-brown with yellow scaling, in the Greenhorn Mts., Calif. (ssp. **viridicornis**). Ssp. **sakuntala** occurs elsewhere. *S. atlantis* (260) from Calif., Ore., and east to Ida. is similar, but lacks the lavender tint, and the pale unh submarginal band does not blend into the ground color (when it does blend in Ida., Wyo., and Utah, the band is still pale outwardly and the ups is lighter than in *hydaspe*). *S. zerene zerene* (262) in the Calif. Sierra is extremely similar to *hydaspe* because the *zerene* unh is violet-tinted and unsilvered, but *zerene* differs in several characters: the unh spots are smaller and more elongated, the red-brown streaks extending into the paler unh submarginal band seem longer, and in unh cell Rs the tiny median bar and cream postmedian spot are much farther apart. (Both *hydaspe* and *zerene platina* were recorded from N.M. from the same two sites, a case of mislabeled specimens.)

Habitat Transition to Canadian Zone (to Hudsonian Zone in Wash.) moist dense woodland. Hostplants herb Violaceae: *Viola glabella, orbiculata, nuttallii, purpurea, adunca, V.* sp. similar to *lobata* ssp. *psychodes*, probably *V. sheltonii* in Calif.

Eggs laid singly and haphazardly near violets. Larvae eat leaves; no nests. Larva nearly black, lacking a middorsal stripe; dorsal spines black, the lateral spines yellow-orange to orange-brown at their bases. Unfed first-stage larvae hibernate.

One flight, June-Sep.; adults are most common July-M Aug.

259. Speyeria callippe   Callippe Fritillary

Color Plates 21, 25

Characterized everywhere by the pallid unh marginal spots, which are triangular and capped with a thin triangle of green or brown. The silver spots tend to show through as light areas on the uph. The ups is more yellowish-brown than bright orange (esp. in females), except that the ups is more orange in N Calif.-s Ore. The silver spots tend to be elongated. Ssp. **callippe** (Calif. Coast Ranges from San Francisco to Baja Calif.) has dark ups wing bases, a pale ups median band (the always-silver spots show through as light areas on the uph), and orange ups submarginal areas. The basal two-thirds of the unh is light brown with large elongated silver spots. Ssp. **liliana** (Lake and Mendocino Cos., Calif., very similar in S Cascades, Ore.) is more reddish on the ups, the ups wing bases are not as dark, without a distinct pale ups band, and the basal two-thirds of the unh is darker brown; with silver spots. Ssp. *callippe* once intergraded with ssp. *liliana* north of San Francisco, but this population is now extinct. Ssp. **rupestris** (Tehama Co., Calif., to N Calif.) is similar, with somewhat darker ups wing bases, unsilvered. In N Calif. and even S Ore., some *rupestris* adults resemble ssp. **juba** (w slope of the Sierra Nevada), which is unsilvered with the basal two-thirds of the unh brown, the ups more yellowish-orange. Ssp. *juba* differs from *S. hydaspe* (258), *zerene* (262), and *atlantis irene* (260) in having the basal two-thirds of the unh a more-uniform brown with no lavender flush. Ssp. **macaria** (S Sierra) is paler than *juba*, with narrower black median spots on the ups, and the basal two-thirds of the unh a light brown; mostly unsilvered in the Greenhorn Mts., but becoming mostly silvered north of Los Angeles. In ssp. **semivirida** (Cascades of B.C.-C Ore. to NE Calif.) the basal two-thirds of the unh is brownish-green to brown. Populations intermediate between *semivirida* and *rupestris* (the unh green to brown) occur near Bartle in Lassen Co., Calif. Other brown-to-green populations (mostly intermediate between ssp. *juba* and *nevadensis*) occur in the Piute Mts. and Sierra Co., Calif., and in w Nev. W. Hovanitz and L. Grey proved that the green-unh ssp. belong to *callippe* as well as the brown-unh ssp. Ssp. **nevadensis** (SE B.C., the Great Basin east to Sask. and w Colo.) has the basal two-thirds of the unh light gray-green, and has silver spots. *S. egleis* (261), *coronis* (263), and some *zerene* also have a greenish unh, but *callippe* (*nevadensis* and some *semivirida*) has the basal two-thirds of the unh gray-green on a cream background, the ups ground color is yellowish-orange, the silver unh marginal spots and their caps are triangular, and the silver spots tend to be elongated. Ssp. **meadii** (Front Range of Colo. and SE Wyo.) is darker on the ups and is the only *Speyeria* having the uns completely grass-green (usually on the submargin also) between the silver spots.

Habitat Upper Sonoran to Transition Zone (and Canadian Zone in the Great Basin) chaparral, fairly dry woodland, sagebrush, and prairie hills. Hostplants herb Violaceae: *Viola purpurea, beckwithii, pedunculata, douglasii, nuttallii, ?quercetorum.*

Eggs pale yellow, becoming pinkish-brown, laid singly and haphazardly near dried-up *Viola*, mainly under shrubs where *Viola* will come up the next spring. Larvae eat leaves; no nests. Larva gray, with many black-bristled spines (spines orange in ssp. *callippe*, black in ssp. *macaria*), a black middorsal line, large black patches around the dorsal spines, and black dashes around the subdorsal spines; head black. Pupa whitish, with black markings like those of *S. nokomis* (254). Unfed first-stage larvae hibernate.

One flight, mostly M June-M Aug. (June-July in Calif.). O. Shields recaptured only 13 percent of marked males after one or more days on s Calif. hilltops, indicating some dispersal (but one male was recaptured after 17 days). Males patrol and perch on hilltops until just after noon, then patrol on hillsides near the ground to seek females (ssp. *meadii* and *callippe*); males of some other ssp. patrol in flatter areas.

Color Plates 3 (larva), 20, 21, 25
Fig. 37 (scent patches)

260. Speyeria atlantis   Atlantis Fritillary

The silver unh marginal spots are most similar to those of *S. callippe* (259), roughly triangular, and usually with fairly thin brownish triangular caps. The basal two-thirds of the unh is always brownish (never green) with small silver or white spots; the ups is always orange-brown (lighter in ssp. *greyi* and *wasatchia*) without lighter median areas, and the silver spots do not show through on the uph. More than half of the unf is always orangish. Ssp. **atlantis** (E U.S. and most of the Rockies and Canada) has fairly dark ups wing bases and dark margins, and the basal two-thirds of the unh is dark brown, sometimes reddish (the unh from Alta. to Colo. is usually reddish, about half are reddish in N N.M.), with silver spots. Ssp. *atlantis* is esp. dark from NE U.S. to Alaska; in B.C., NE Wash., and Alta. southeast to N.M. and SE Utah, it is a little lighter on the ups and resembles *S. aphrodite* (252; see it for identification). Ssp. *atlantis* has darker ups wing margins, a darker basal two-thirds of the unh, and more extensive and uniform orange on the unf than does *S. zerene picta* (262). Ssp. **dennisi** (N Great Plains from s Man. to s Alta. and N.D.) is much paler than forest *atlantis*, with narrow black ups lines and a tan silver-spotted unh, in some ways resembling *S. aphrodite manitoba*. Ssp. *dennisi* is claimed to occur at Duck Mt. and the Riding Mts., Man., without interbreeding with ssp. *atlantis*, but the two ssp. occur in different habitats except in a few places where both occur as forms; R. Hooper found them intergrading at Meadow Lake Park, Sask., and they also intergrade in w Alta. Several isolates resemble *dennisi*. Ssp. **ratonensis** (Colfax Co., N.M., and adjacent Colo.) is like *dennisi*, but it has slightly thicker black fw spots, and sometimes the basal two-thirds of its unh is a lighter tan. Ssp. **greyi** (NE Nev.) resembles *atlantis*, but its ups is lighter yellowish-orange, and the basal two-thirds of the unh is a light brown (some even tinged with green); it resembles *ratonensis*, and both ssp. are silvered, but the silver spots of *greyi* are larger. Ssp. **hesperis** (Black Hills of S.D., Bighorn Mts. of Wyo., eastern slope of Colo. Rockies) occurs in a polymorphic population. Most adults are unsilvered with the basal two-thirds of the unh red-brown, but owing to intergradation with ssp. *atlantis*, some are half-silvered, others silvered with brown on the unh; unsilvered *hesperis* forms occur more often at low Transition Zone altitudes and in drier habitats, and silvered brown-unh *atlantis* forms at higher Canadian Zone altitudes and in wet meadow–stream-bank habitats. The genetics of this needs to be studied. Ssp. **wasatchia** (NW Wyo. to N Utah, intergrading with ssp. *hesperis* in

Bighorn Mts., Wyo.) resembles *hesperis* in that the basal two-thirds of the unh is red-brown and mostly unsilvered, but the red-brown very often also covers the pale unh submarginal band and the ups is more yellowish-orange. Ssp. *wasatchia* intergrades westward to ssp. *irene* and in Wash. and B.C. to ssp. *atlantis* somewhat. Ssp. **irene** (c Ida., NW Elko Co. in Nev., Ore., Calif.) has an orange-brown ups as usual (darkest northwestward, lightest in Calif. and in the N Humboldt Mts., Nev.) and is always unsilvered; the basal two-thirds of the unh is redbrown but has pale streaks, and the unh submarginal band is pale yellowish esp. in Calif. Ssp. *irene* differs from *S. hydaspe* (258) in lacking the unh lavender tint and in having a paler unh submarginal band. Ssp. **chitone** (s Utah) has the basal two-thirds of the unh red-brown, like that of *wasatchia*, but the pale unh submarginal band is not suffused, most adults are silvered, the fw is more pointed, and the ups wing bases are darker. Ssp. **schellbachi** (Kaibab Plateau, Ariz.) is more extreme, the fw quite pointed, the ups wing bases very dark, the black ups median spots very thick, and the unh usually silvered. Ssp. **nausicaa** (c Ariz. to w N.M.) retains the pointed fw but is larger and more reddish-brown on the ups, with the black ups spots narrow as usual, the unh always silvered, the basal two-thirds of the unh red-brown with gray over much of it, and the pale unh submarginal band somewhat suffused with tan. Ssp. **dorothea** in c N.M. intergrades between *nausicaa* and N N.M. *atlantis*.

Habitat Canadian to Hudsonian Zone (Transition to Canadian Zone in Calif. and Colo.) forest openings, often in moist meadows and streamsides. Hostplants herb Violaceae: *Viola adunca* (and var. *bellidifolia*), *purpurea*, *canadensis*, *nephrophylla*, *nuttallii* var. *linguaefolia*. Assoc. with *V. septentrionalis*.

Eggs pale greenish-yellow, soon becoming tan, laid singly and haphazardly near *Viola*. Larvae eat leaves; no nests. Larva (ssp. *atlantis*, Vt.) greenish-yellow on the top (with a black middorsal line), greenish-gray subdorsally with gray spines, gray on the side with a rust-red tint and rust-colored spines, with large brown-black patches around the top spines and black dashes along the subdorsal spines, the hairs on the spines about half the length of the spines; head dark brown, yellowish behind. W. Forbes described ssp. *atlantis* as deep purplish. Larva (ssp. *hesperis*, Colo.) velvet-black or brown-black, with yellowish spines; head brown, yellowish behind. In the Black Hills, S.D., larva blackish with orange spines, the middorsal stripes light brown in the *atlantis* form, grayish-white in the *hesperis* form. Pupa mottled dark brown and black, the wing cases graybrown (ssp. *atlantis*, Vt.) to dark brown (ssp. *hesperis*, Colo.), the rear of each abdomen segment paler yellow-brown. Pupa of Black Hills *atlantis* form darker, with less of the light-brown mottling of the *hesperis* form there. Unfed first-stage larvae hibernate.

One flight, L June-Aug. Adults sip flower nectar, sometimes mud and dung. Males patrol all day in open areas, esp. moist valley bottoms, to seek females. In courtship, the male pursues the female (and possibly rises up beneath her as in *Argynnis* to induce her to land), she lands and remains motionless with closed wings, the male lands and faces toward her, draws his forewings forward, and flicks his closed wings slightly open (wingtips 0 to 1 cm apart) in quick bursts, each burst of two to five flicks lasting less than a second, to waft his ups pheromone to her antennae, and then he moves alongside her and they join. An unreceptive female spreads her wings nearly to the side and flutters them with small strokes until he departs, or she crawls away or raises her abdomen between closed wings so that he cannot join. (Courtship in *S. aphrodite*, 252, is similar but the male flicks his wings open wider.)

Color Plates 21, 25

261. Speyeria egleis   Great Basin Fritillary

Normally small, 24-28 mm fw length, little bigger than *S. mormonia* (256) esp. in the Pacific states, though c Nev.-Utah-Ida. adults are the size of *S. zerene* (262; fw to 32 mm). The silver unh marginal spots are similar to those of *S. zerene* (spots lenslike, capped with narrow plateaus of brown or green). The other silver spots are a little smaller in size than those of *S. callippe* (259), *S. zerene*, and *S. coronis* (263). The unf color is dull yellowish with very little (if any) orange at the base, except in Calif.-Ore populations. The ups is orange-brown except in ssp. *albrighti*, *macdunnoughi*, and Ida. *linda*. Ssp. **egleis** (Sierra Nevada) is small like *S. mormonia*, the ups orange-brown, the basal two-thirds of the unh reddish-brown with lighter areas, and the unf with more orange than usual; it resembles *S. mormonia mormonia* (see the *mormonia* discussion for differences), and the two are the only silvered *Speyeria* in much of the Sierra (esp. in s Sierra). Ssp. **tehachapina** (Tehachapi Mts., Calif.) resembles *egleis*, but is completely unsilvered and a little lighter and larger; it resembles unsilvered *S. callippe macaria*, but in *macaria* the basal two-thirds of the unh is more uniformly reddish-brown and the unh marginal spots are triangular with thin triangular caps. All other *S. egleis* ssp. are usually silvered, although about half the ssp. *egleis* adults are unsilvered around Lake Tahoe, and in Plumas Co. and the Siskiyou Mts., Calif., and individuals are often unsilvered in sw Mont., w Wyo., and the Wasatch Mts., Utah. Ssp. **oweni** (Coast Ranges and n Calif. to s Ore.) resembles ssp. *egleis*, but is bigger at most sites and darker, with a slight lavender tint to the red-brown unh, the ground color tending to suffuse somewhat into the pale unh submarginal band. Ssp. *oweni* is smaller than *S. zerene* and *S. hydaspe* (258) where the ranges overlap, and its unh spots are smaller and more heavily silvered. The other ssp. are larger (esp. in Utah and c Nev.) with less unf orange. In ssp. **utahensis** (Wasatch Mts., Utah) the basal two-thirds of the unh is light brown (tan to green in the Oquirrh Mts., Utah; tan in s Utah). Light adults differ from *S. zerene platina* and *zerene gunderi* in having smaller less-round silver unh spots (*utahensis* is sometimes unsilvered) and in having a more dull-yellowish color on the unf (unf has less orange in *utahensis*). Female *utahensis* may have orange on the unf, but the ups is orange-brown, not yellow-brown as in *platina*. Ssp. **linda** (c Ida.-sw Mont. and Stansbury Mts., Utah) has the basal two-thirds of the unh green; it intergrades with ssp. *utahensis* in NE Nev. (unh green, sometimes tan), and with ssp. *oweni* in Wash. and NE Ore. (unh brown to green). In ssp. **albrighti** (c Mont.) the basal two-thirds of the unh is darker brownish-green (some adults brown, some green); the ups (esp. in females) is darker black at the base, and the ups postmedian areas are lighter yellowish (esp. in females). Northwestern *S. egleis* tends to be smaller than *S. zerene picta*, the male fw is less pointed, the silver spots are smaller, and the basal two-thirds of the unh varies from chocolate-brown to green (rather than red-brown in *picta*). Ssp. *linda* and *albrighti* have a greenish unh, so could be confused with *S. callippe nevadensis*, but their silver spots are smaller, the unh marginal spots less triangular, and the green darker (usually brownish-green). *S. egleis* is smaller than *S. coronis snyderi*, with smaller silver spots, much less orange on the unf base, and narrower unh marginal caps to the silver spots. Southward, ssp. **macdunnoughi** (Wyo.) resembles ssp. *albrighti* but has the basal two-thirds of the unh greenish-brown; ssp. *linda*, *utahensis*, and *macdunnoughi* all intergrade in SE Ida. and sw Wyo. Ssp. **secreta** (NW Colo. and s Wyo.) is orangish on the ups like *utahensis*, but the basal two-thirds of the unh is red-brown and diffuses considerably over the pale unh submarginal band; the unh is always silvered. Ssp. *secreta* resembles *S. atlantis*, but the pale unh band is more suffused, the silver unh marginal spots and caps are less triangular, the red unf flush is nearly absent on a dull-yellowish ground color, the ups wing bases are a little less dark, and the silver spots show through on the uph a little more.

Habitat Transition to Canadian Zone (upper Transition to Hudsonian Zone in the Sierra) forest openings, but usually on exposed rocky ridges from Calif. to Wash. Hostplants herb Violaceae: *Viola adunca*, *purpurea* (and vars. *venosa*, *integrifolia*), *nuttallii*, *walteri*.

Eggs pale yellow, becoming tan, laid singly and haphazardly near *Viola*. Larvae eat leaves; no nests. Larva gray-brown, with a dark middorsal line within a yellowish dorsal band, black streaks (edged with white) around the black-tipped dorsal and subdorsal spines (the dorsal spines white at the base, the other spines yellowish at the base); head black, yellowish behind. Pupa dark mottled brown, the wing cases dark, the abdomen yellow-brown with a dark anterior border on each segment as in *S. nokomis* (254). Unfed first-stage larvae hibernate.

One flight, L June - M Aug. To seek females, males patrol all day low to the ground, along shaded forest lanes in Colo., mostly on hilltops in Calif.

262. Speyeria zerene   Zerene Fritillary

Color Plates 21, 25

The pallid unh marginal spots are not as extreme as those of *S. coronis* (263); they are a little more triangular, capped with narrow plateaus of brown or greenish-brown. The silver spots are fairly large. Ssp. **zerene** (Sierra to Ore. Cascades, south to Inner Coast Range in Lake Co., Calif.) is dark reddish-orange on the ups, with heavy black uph median lines, a reddish-brown unh with a lavender tint, a pale unh submarginal band suffused with brown, and small unsilvered unh spots; it resembles *S. hydaspe* (258; see *hydaspe* to distinguish it). Ssp. **malcolmi** (E side of the Sierra, intergrading to *zerene* in some places) is paler, the unh less reddish with less lavender tint; unh usually silvered. Ssp. **carolae** (Spring Mts. of s Nev.) is very large, darker in color, very similar to *malcolmi*, the ups reddish with thick black lines, with a pale-lavender tint to the usually silvered unh. Some *carolae* have unsilvered spots like ssp. *zerene*, and some resemble *S. coronis halcyone* on the uns; the only *Speyeria* in the Spring Mts., *carolae* is a "connecting link" between *zerene* and *coronis*. The other ssp. are all silvered. In ssp. **bremnerii** (coast ranges of extreme NW Calif. to Haines, Alaska), the ups is less reddish with dark wing bases, and the unh is reddish-brown with the pale unh submarginal band little suffused (although reddish dashes extend into the band as in ssp. *zerene*). Ssp. *bremnerii* is smaller on the Ore.-Wash. coast; it intergrades to *zerene zerene* in variable sw Ore. populations (ssp. **gloriosa**), and intergrades to ssp. *behrensii*. Ssp. **behrensii** (Calif. Outer Coast Range from s Humboldt to Mendocino Cos.) resembles *bremnerii* somewhat, but the pale unh submarginal band is mostly obliterated with red-brown.

Ssp. **myrtleae** (San Mateo Co. (extinct) and Marin Co., Calif.) also resembles *bremnerii*, but the basal two-thirds of the unh is slightly lighter and more yellow-tinged (sometimes greenish-tinged). Ssp. *bremnerii* intergrades inland to ssp. *picta*. Ssp. **picta** (NE Ore., E Wash., and B.C. southeastward to Wyo. and Ida.) is yellowish-orange on the ups like *bremnerii*, but the ups wing bases are less darkened, and the basal two-thirds of the unh is light reddish-brown to light brown (sometimes with a greenish tint). Ssp. *picta* becomes lighter southeastward, and in ssp. **sinope** (S Wyo. and NW Colo.) the green unh tint is pronounced. Ssp. **platina** (N Utah) is paler, the basal two-thirds of the unh pale tan, with a wider yellow unh submarginal band. Ssp. **gunderi** (=*cynna*; sw Ida., SE Ore., N Nev.) is the palest of all, the unh tan to yellow, the ups yellow-brown; it intergrades to ssp. *zerene* in the Warner Mts., Calif. Ssp. *sinope* resembles *S. coronis* in NW Colo., but the silver unh marginal spots are narrowly capped with greenish (not broadly capped with brown as in *coronis*), and *sinope* is slightly more heavily marked.

Habitat Transition to Canadian Zone conifer woodland, sagebrush, salt-spray meadows, and moist coastal dunes. Hostplants herb Violaceae: *Viola adunca, cuneata, lobata* (and ssp. *psychodes*), *nuttallii, purpurea*.

Eggs cream, turning pinkish-tan, laid singly and haphazardly near *Viola*. Larvae eat leaves; no nests. Larva resembles that of *S. coronis*, orangish (ssp. *bremneri*) or grayish-straw (on the Ore. coast), with extensive blackish-brown markings (patterned as in *S. callippe*), a black middorsal line, and wide blackish patches near the grayish-based spines (the spine needles hinged and capable of being folded upward); a ventral eversible neck gland produces a musky smell, perhaps for defense against ants (D. McCorkle); head blackish. Pupa like that of *S. nokomis* (254), hanging vertically within silked-together leaves as in most *Speyeria*. Unfed first-stage larvae hibernate on a thin silk mat.

One flight, M June–E Sep. (adults most common during L June–M Aug.). Females diapause (delay egg-laying for a month or so) as in *S. coronis*, at least in Calif. Adults can disperse 2-3 km in Ore. (McCorkle). Males patrol all day to seek females.

Color Plates 21, 25

263. **Speyeria coronis**   Coronis Fritillary

The uns is always silvered, and the silver unh marginal spots tend to be lenslike (not triangular) and capped with thick wide plateaus of green or brown; the other silver spots are large and round, and do not show through on the uph, except in ssp. *coronis*. The ups is orangish. Wingspan large, as in *S. zerene* (262). Males tend to have a pointed fw in the Great Basin and in Colo. In ssp. **halcyone** (Colo. Front Range to s Wyo.), the basal two-thirds of the unh is brown with thick wide brown caps to the silver marginal spots. It intergrades in c Wyo. and w Colo. to the Great Basin ssp. **snyderi**, which tends to be very large (smaller in Wash.), with the basal two-thirds of the unh greenish-brown to green (varying in color northward), with broad marginal caps. Ssp. *snyderi* resembles *S. zerene* in w Colo. (see the *zerene* discussion for identification), and sometimes resembles *S. callippe* (259); the marginal unh caps are wider than those of *callippe*, the green is darker, the ups is oranger, the unf is much more orange than on the green-unh ssp. of *callippe* (*nevadensis*, some *semivirida*), the wingspan is greater, and the silver spots are larger (see also the *callippe* discussion for identification). In ssp. **semiramis** (S Calif.), the ups is redder, the black ups lines are narrower, and the basal two-thirds of the unh is light brown (sometimes the pale submarginal band is slightly tan); it is possibly related to *S. zerene*. In ssp. **coronis** (Calif. Coast Ranges from Santa Barbara Co. north to the Bay Area), the basal two-thirds of the unh is light brown and the unh submarginal band is occasionally suffused with brownish, but the ups is paler yellow-brown, lighter in the middle of the wing where the silver spots show through slightly on the uph (this is reminiscent of *callippe* but much less extreme).

Habitat Transition to sometimes Canadian Zone chaparral, sagebrush, and conifer woodland. Hostplants herb Violaceae: *Viola nuttallii, purpurea, douglasii, beckwithii*.

Eggs laid singly and haphazardly near *Viola*. Larvae eat leaves; no nests. Larva mottled brown and black, patterned as in *S. callippe*, with many black spines, the lateral spines orange. Pupa resembles that of *callippe*. Unfed first-stage larvae hibernate.

One flight, June-E Sep. (most common during L June-July). Females diapause (delaying oviposition) in Calif., appearing in late Aug.-Sep. (sometimes in places where males are rarely seen). West-coast (Ore.) larvae feed in the drier lowlands, then adults fly to higher mountains in midsummer when flowers are abundant, then return to the lowlands in late summer to oviposit (P. Hammond). In contrast, sympatric *S. callippe* remains in the lowlands. Adults sip flower nectar, occasionally mud. Males patrol all day in open areas, often in valley bottoms, to seek females.

264. Speyeria edwardsii   Green Fritillary

Color Plate 25
Fig. 71

The unh is green with silver spots. Similar to *S. callippe* (259), but larger (male fw length 33 mm, female 37 mm), the unf more red, the unh veins brownish, the ups borders dark, and the male fw more pointed. The ups is much lighter than *S. egleis albrighti* (261). The narrow prong on the male valva is only a third to a half as thick as that of all other *Speyeria* (Fig. 71).

Habitat Transition to Canadian Zone chaparral, forest openings, and prairie. Hostplants herb Violaceae: *Viola nuttallii, adunca*.

Eggs greenish-yellow, becoming tan, laid singly and haphazardly near *Viola*, or where *Viola* will appear the next spring, usually not laid until about Aug. Larvae eat leaves; no nests. Larva dark yellow on top, gray subdorsally (the side gray mottled with reddish-yellow), with a black middorsal line, and with black white-edged patches around the dorsal and subdorsal spines, the base of the upper spines gray-green, the base of the lower spines yellow; head brown-black, yellowish behind. Pupa mottled yellow-brown, the front reddish-brown, the abdomen mottled gray, with a serrated dark-brown transverse stripe on the front of each segment. Unfed first-stage larvae hibernate.

One flight, L June-E Sep. Adults sip flower nectar and dung. Males patrol all day in open areas to seek females, and frequently patrol and mate in shrubby areas on the sunny side of a hilltop just below the top.

265. Euptoieta claudia   Variegated Fritillary

The unh pattern is unique.

Habitat open areas such as grassland, fields, scrub, and open woodland, mainly in s U.S., straying northward. Ranges south to Argentina, the Bahamas, and the Greater Antilles. More common at low altitude. Hostplants herb Viola-

Color Plates 3 (larva), 5 (pupa), 20, 23 Figs. 51, 55 (veins)

ceae: *Viola papilionacea, fimbriatula, rafinesquii, tricolor* ssp. *hortensis, Hybanthus verticillatus;* Linaceae: *Linum australe, rigidum, sulcatum*[t]; Nyctaginaceae: *Boerhaavia erecta* var. *intermedia;* Asclepiadaceae: *Metastelma arizonicum;* Passifloraceae: *Passiflora foetida, caerulea, incarnata;* Turneraceae: *Turnera ulmifolia;* Crassulaceae: *Sedum lanceolatum, purpureum*[t]; Menispermaceae: *Menispermum;* Portulacaceae: ?*Portulaca oleracea;* Plantaginaceae: *Plantago.* Somewhat doubtful plants stated by J. Abbot are *Desmodium paniculatum* (Leguminosae), *Cynoglossum* (Boraginaceae), *Podophyllum peltatum* (Berberidaceae).

Eggs pale green or cream, laid singly on leaves and stems of the hostplant. Larvae eat flowers and leaves, feeding by day at least; no nests. Larva (Fig. 51) white, with five red longitudinal bands (the dorsal one with white dashes through it, one per segment) and six rows of black spines in the white areas; head red, with two very long black spines. Pupa pale shining blue-green, with small black dots, a black proboscis, yellow antennae, orange spots on the eyes, and gold dorsal tubercles. The larva and pupa are very beautiful. Probably overwinters only in the south; flies north each spring and summer.

Many flights, all year in s Tex., Mar.-Dec. in Fla.; spreading northward in spring (spring-fall northward but more common in late summer). Migratory, straying to N.W. Terr. and s Canada. Males patrol just above the ground all day, throughout the habitat, to seek females. In courtship, the male pursues the female, who lands and holds her wings mostly closed and her abdomen raised slightly, the male lands behind and flutters his wings slowly, then he draws alongside and flutters his nearly vertical wings rapidly, then they mate. During mating, the female spreads her wings more than the male, and both wave the wings occasionally, the male more often than the female.

266. Euptoieta hegesia   Mexican Fritillary

Resembles *E. claudia,* but lacks black uph median marks.

Habitat open subtropical areas. Ranges south to Argentina, the Bahamas, and the Greater Antilles. Hostplants herb Passifloraceae: *Passiflora foetida;* Turneraceae: *Turnera ulmifolia* (Mex. and the Antilles); Convolvulaceae: *Ipomoea maritima* in Brazil. *Euptoieta* and *Dione* (268) both eat *Passiflora,* and seem to be the connecting links between fritillaries and *Dryas* (270).

Larva shiny red, with a black-edged middorsal line of silver spots, a subdorsal row of white black-edged spots, a silver black-edged lateral line, and six rows of black spines; head red, with two long black clubbed horns. Pupa dark brown or rarely tan, with short gold lateral and subdorsal cones, gold eyes, and a black T on the wing case.

Many flights, all year in Mex., at least July-Dec. in s Tex. Somewhat migratory, straying north to s Calif. rarely.

Color Plate 20

Tribe Heliconiini: Longwings

The Heliconiini are medium-sized tropical butterflies. Some 65 species are found in the Americas, and 11 or more others occur in tropical Asia (*Cethosia* and possibly *Terinos* and *Vindula*). Seven species occur in the southern U.S., most barely entering the U.S.; *Dione vanillae,* the exception, ranges northward.

In all Heliconiini, the hindwing humeral vein is aimed toward the body, a trait unique among the North American scudders. The "stink clubs" on the female abdomen (Fig. 37) are found only in the Heliconiini, though they are absent in *Dryadula*. Larvae bear many branching spines on the body and on the head (small on the head in some tropical species); the Argynnini have only body spines. Pupae often have long processes, unlike the Argynnini. None of the Heliconiini seems to have a true winter diapause, and they are killed by freezes.

Larvae eat passion-flower plants (Passifloraceae) and rarely the closely related Turneraceae. Because these hostplants are poisonous, most Heliconiini are poisonous to vertebrates, and for this reason they are often mimicked by other butterflies or other Heliconiini.

K. Brown, Jr., W. Benson, M. Emsley, L. Gilbert, J. Crane, W. Beebe, H. Fleming, and others have studied the Heliconiini extensively in the last 25 years, and they have discovered amazing variation in habits between species. Adult *Heliconius*, which can learn readily where to find flowers and their communal roosting sites, seem to be the "smartest" butterflies. All species sip flower nectar. Adult *Heliconius* often feed on pollen, a diet unique among butterflies. The knobs on the proboscis gather the pollen, and a drop of saliva from the coiled proboscis dissolves some of the pollen nutrients. Females may search out plants partly by leaf shape, and the leaves of tropical *Passiflora* vary greatly in shape, often mimicking those of other common tropical plants, partly to avoid being eaten. Most species lay the eggs singly, but some lay them in large clusters. Females do not lay eggs on parts of plants that already bear eggs, and some plants have accordingly evolved bulges (on stipules, which are projections from the joints, or on other plant parts) that look like eggs or young larvae, to fool the females into flying away and laying their eggs somewhere else. Some plants produce stipules that look like tendrils (the growing tips of vines), and the stipules are then shed, along with any eggs placed there by females that were lured to them. The plants also produce a nectar from the stems or leaves; the nectar attracts ants, which then kill and eat the Heliconiini eggs and small larvae.

Adults flutter slowly about, often turning and exploring vegetation, except for *Dione*, which flaps faster, in the manner of fritillaries. The adults are generally very local, but many species occasionally migrate hundreds of kilometers, and *Dione* are regular migrants. Adults often rest and bask with the wings spread. The males patrol to seek females. Male *Heliconius* are often attracted to female pupae by their odor, and the male mates with the female just before she emerges from the pupa. The male transfers a chemical onto the female's abdominal stink clubs during mating, which repels other males later. If a mating pair is startled, the male flies and the female hangs beneath, at least in *Heliconius*.

267. Dryadula phaetusa   Banded Orange

This stray is vaguely similar to *Heliconius isabella* (271) and *Lycorea* (92), but the fw is less spotted.

Habitat tropical lowland damp fields and marshes. Ranges south to Paraguay. Hostplants vine (rarely shrub) Passifloraceae in Latin Amer.: many spp. and subgenera of *Passiflora*.

Eggs (similar to 272 in Fig. 45) pale yellow, becoming mottled with brown before hatching, laid singly on leaves and stems. Larvae eat leaves, chewing an oblique slot into the leaf; and rest in a J-shape. Larva velvety dark brownish-black, the rear brown, the true legs orange; many black spines; a black collar;

Color Plate 58

head orange, with two long spines on top. Pupa brown like that of *Dione vanillae* (268), with gold spots on the saddle and above the wing bases; shape like that of *vanillae*, with two fairly long head processes and several small subdorsal keels on the abdomen.

Many flights all year in Mex.; a rare stray from Mex. into s Fla. (Feb. 1932, 1947) and s Tex. (Dec. 1933). Adults are fairly local, but migration sometimes occurs. Adults usually fly within several meters of the ground. They sip the nectar of flowers (esp. whitish ones) and feed on bird droppings, and males sometimes sip mud. Adults roost in small loose groups, mostly under grass blades. Females normally mate only once, just after hatching from the pupa.

268. Dione vanillae   Gulf Fritillary

Resembles *Speyeria* (253), but the fw is longer, and the silver unh spots are lengthened. A "connecting link" between Heliconiini and Argynnini; *Dione* and *Euptoieta* (265, 266) have similar hostplants, and *Speyeria* also have silver unh spots like those of *Dione*.

Color Plates 3 (larva), 5 (pupa), 20

Figs. 35 (ultraviolet), 37 (scent organs), 51, 52, 55 (veins)

Habitat s U.S. forest margins, fields, scrub, and suburbs. Ranges south to Argentina and throughout the Antilles and Bahamas. Hostplants vine (rarely herbs or shrubs in Latin Amer.) Passifloraceae: *Passiflora caerulea, incarnata, lutea, tenuiloba, affinis, laurifolia, umbrosa, manicata, alato-caerulea, suberosa, edulis, mollissima, foetida* var. *gossypifolia*, plus numerous spp. and subgenera of *Passiflora* and *Tetrastylis* in Latin Amer. Females are more particular than larvae; they rarely oviposit on the last two *Passiflora* spp., though larvae can eat them (N. Copp and D. Davenport).

Eggs yellow, becoming mottled with brown before hatching, laid singly on hostplant leaves, stems, tendrils, and buds. Larvae eat these parts at night, and rest in a J-shape. Larva (Fig. 51) grayish-black with cream dots (the underside black with tiny white dots), with two reddish middorsal lines, a reddish subdorsal row of crescents below the spines, and a reddish broken lateral band (with a whitish band beneath it); six rows of long black branching spines; a darker collar; head creamy white (or black), with a reddish-brown patch on top and on each side, a reddish crescent on each side of the face, and two spines on top. Some larvae lighter, with much yellow, more orange, and a lighter head. Pupa (Fig. 52) brown (mottled with gray and brown patches), or greenish-brown, or blacker, with a reddish-tan lateral band on the abdomen (edged beneath with greenish-brown), two pink spots on the head case, a black figure 3 on the wing case, silver spots on top of the saddle, small subdorsal keels on abdomen, subdorsal bumps on the thorax, and two short appendages on the head, the wings bulging downward. Overwinters only in the south.

Many flights, all year in s Fla., s Tex., and s Calif.; migrates northward. Copp and Davenport marked adults in a suburb and found that there was little movement between vines even 300 m apart. Migrations have been seen in Kans., however, rarely as far north as Man., and as far south as Argentina. Now established in Los Angeles, around San Francisco, and in Hawaii (since 1977, spreading to all the large islands by 1980), Bermuda, and the Galápagos Is. In N Fla., T. Walker and others found that adults fly northward about Feb.-June, southward Aug.-Nov. T. Walker and A. Riordan studied the fall flight in N Fla., which flew to the south-southeast about E Sep.-L Oct., peaking about Sep. 22. Adults fly rapidly within several meters of the ground; males patrol to seek females. Adults sip the nectar of flowers (esp. red and white ones), and males sometimes feed on mud; adults do not feed on pollen and live only a few weeks to a month in nature. S. Scudder and others found that adults may roost in groups of 6-16 or alone, mostly near the ground on grass leaves. In courtship (R. Rutowski, J. Schaefer), the female lands, the male lands beside her (often after hovering over her), and he opens his wings halfway, closes and opens them about 30 times in a 5-second burst to waft his upf pheromone to her antenna (which often rests between his wings), and then bends his abdomen to mate (some males do not flap before mating). Receptive females are nearly motionless (the abdominal glands, hidden between the hindwings, are possibly exposed), but unreceptive females flutter their wings or spread them and raise the abdomen, exposing the abdominal glands which, after mating, possibly waft a scent to repel males. Females mate several times.

Color Plate 20

269. Dione moneta   Mexican Silver-Spotted Fritillary

Resembles *D. vanillae*, but the unf has black median rings, and the ups wing bases are brown.

Habitat subtropical and tropical fields and scrub. Ranges south to Brazil. Hostplants vine Passifloraceae: many spp. of *Passiflora* and *Tetrastylis* in Latin Amer.

Eggs lemon-yellow or white, probably becoming mottled with brown before hatching, laid singly (or in clusters of 1-20) under young host leaves or on stems, tendrils, or buds. Larvae sometimes feed gregariously; they eat an oblique slot into the leaf, and rest in a J-shape. Larva (similar to 268 in Fig. 51) dark red, with three parallel yellow dorsal stripes (sometimes edged with grayish-white), a cream to white lateral stripe (sometimes tinged with purple), many black spines, and a dark broad collar; head black and white with two prominent branching spines. Pupa (similar to 268 in Fig. 52) dull rust-brown, with a few dark wing streaks, metallic spots on abdomen segment 2, large flanges on the abdomen, and short head appendages.

Many flights in Mex.; rarely migrates north to Tex. (Apr., July, Oct.-Dec., briefly established in 1968) and s Calif. (July). Adults fly rapidly, usually within several meters of the ground. Adults sip the nectar of flowers (mostly reddish ones), and males sometimes sip mud. Adults may roost in loose groups, mostly near the ground on grass.

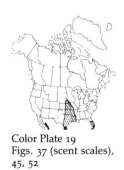

Color Plate 19
Figs. 37 (scent scales), 45, 52

270. Dryas iulia   Orange Long Wing

Identified by the very long orange wings. Females are darker than males. Ssp. **largo** (Fla.) males have two brown upf spots; ssp. **moderata** (Tex.) males have one. Ssp. *iulia* and other ssp. range south to Paraguay and throughout the Antilles and Bahamas.

Habitat subtropical open sunny forest clearings. Hostplants vine Passiflora-ceae (occasionally shrubs in Latin Amer.): *Passiflora lutea* var. *glabriflora*, and in Latin Amer. many other species and subgenera of *Passiflora*.

Eggs (Fig. 45) lemon-yellow, turning orange or mottled brown just before hatching, laid singly on tender leaves or new tendrils, sometimes on old leaves, of the host. Larvae eat leaves (they eat an oblique slot into the leaf) and rest in a J-shape; no nests. They cause a rash on human skin (A. Muyshondt), probably because of a yellow fluid exuded from the spine tips. Larva (similar to 268 in Fig. 51) pinkish-gray (grayish-green beneath) with thin black transverse lines, a broad cream lateral stripe broken with maroon (connected to four oblique cream patches on the abdomen), a pinkish-gray middorsal band on the abdomen, many blackish and cream branching spines, and a dark slender collar; head black or maroon (the sides cream), with an inverted cream Y on the front and two black or brown spines on top. Pupa (Fig. 52) brown, slightly mottled with cream, gray, and tan, with gold or silver spots in the saddle, many subdorsal black spots, and subdorsal cones on the thorax, the wing cases cream, the abdomen segments with small subdorsal keels, the wings extended downward somewhat, the head appendages very small.

Many flights all year in s Fla. and s Tex. (common in the fall); rarely migrates north to Neb. Adults fly mostly in the middle story of tropical forests, slowly to rapidly. They sip the nectar of flowers, esp. red and bluish ones, and males often sip mud. Adults live only a few weeks. Roosting occurs alone or in small groups near the ground on grass leaves, etc. Males patrol all day to seek females. A. and P. Ehrlich found that females can mate up to four times, unlike most *Heliconius*, which generally mate only once; they first mate after emerging from pupae (often when a week or two old). In J. Crane's courtship studies, males approach females from behind, the female flies if she was not already flying, the male flies above and in front of the female, fanning her with his scent scales, the female tries to rise above the male but eventually lands, the male fans her while above and in front of her (facing the same direction), the female spreads her hindwings and partly spreads her forewings, she vibrates them while raising her abdomen and extruding her scent glands, he fans her from behind and then from in front, she closes her wings, lowers her abdomen, and withdraws the scent glands, he lands, and they mate.

Color Plate 58
Figs. 37 (scent scales),
51, 52

271. **Heliconius isabella**   Isabella Tiger

Similar to *Lycorea cleobaea* (92) but smaller, without the black hw loop. Males have a gray patch on the front of the uph containing scent scales. Females have lighter-colored antennae. Ssp. **eva** is in the U.S. and Mex.; ssp. *isabella* and other ssp. range south to Brazil, Cuba, and Hispaniola.

Habitat tropical second-growth forest and woodland margins. Hostplants vine Passifloraceae: many *Passiflora* in Latin Amer., mainly the subgenus *Granadilla*, although one sp. of subgenus *Distephana* is eaten.

Eggs (similar to 272 in Fig. 45) pale greenish to cream, probably turning orangish before hatching, laid singly (rarely in clusters of two or three) mostly under host leaves (often old leaves) and on tendrils. Larvae eat leaves and tendrils; no nests. Larva (Fig. 51) brown-black dorsally, with gray or white transverse streaks (of variable thickness), a wide pale-yellow lateral band, and a gray middorsal band on the abdomen, the end of the abdomen orange (the tip itself yellow to white); larva later turning maroon; branching spines blackish (often pale-tipped, the rear two spines cream); collar black and four-parted; head black or mostly white, gray on the front, with two black or gray dorsal spines (larger than those of *H. erato*, 273, and *Dryas iulia*, 270) and with gray crescents below the spines. Pupa (Fig. 52) cream, with light-grayish-green mottling, three dark spots at the tornus of the wing case (see Fig. 54), no metallic spots, many short subdorsal filaments and four long filaments on the abdomen, and several long curved filaments on the head.

Many flights in Mex.; a rare stray into s Tex. (Apr.-Dec., briefly established at times). Colonies are fairly local, although adults rarely migrate to w Tex. from Mex. Adults fly fairly rapidly, usually in the middle story of the forest. They sip the nectar of flowers, esp. whitish ones. Roosting occurs alone, mostly under leaves. Males seem to patrol to seek females; mating sometimes occurs on hilltops, and courtship is like that of *Dryas iulia*. Females may mate several times.

272. Heliconius charitonia   Zebra Long Wing

Identified by the long wings and zebra pattern.

Habitat subtropical woods edges and scrub. Ranges south to Peru and throughout the Antilles and Bahamas. Hostplants vine Passifloraceae: in Fla. *Passiflora suberosa*, in s Tex. *lutea* and *affinis*, plus in Latin Amer. many other spp. esp. the subgenus *Plectostemma*.

Eggs (Fig. 45) pale yellow, becoming mottled with orange-brown before hatching, laid singly (or occasionally in clusters of two to five) on terminal leaf buds or the leaves of the host. Larvae feed at night on young and old leaves; no nests. Larva (similar to 268 in Fig. 51) bluish-white or pure white, with six rows of long black branching spines, brown lateral spots, many rows of brown-black spots, and a slender dark collar; legs and prolegs brown; head greenish-white, with black spots on the front and around the eyes, and two black spines on top. Pupa (Fig. 52) brownish-orange or tan (mottled with brown and some darker lines), with paler areas on the wing cases, silver or gold spots in the saddle and on the head, dorsolateral flanges on the abdomen (including a large flange in middle of the abdomen), many short spines, and two long flanged horns on the head.

Many flights, all year in s Fla., at least Apr.-Nov. in s Tex.; rarely migrates northward as far as Neb. Adults are generally fairly local, moving up to 500 m but usually less than 200 m. They fly very slowly and look almost ghostlike. Adults sip the nectar of flowers (esp. white or bluish ones) and gather pollen loads with the proboscis as does *H. erato*. L. Cook and A. Young found that adults often live 3 months in nature (a maximum of 130 days). Lab adults can live up to 4.5 months, and females can each lay 1,000 eggs if they eat nectar and pollen, but in the lab without pollen L. Gilbert found that they live only a month. Adults roost in groups of up to 70 or more (usually within 2 m of the ground on twigs, tendrils, or leaves), returning to the same roost every night. Males patrol to seek females, mostly within several meters of the ground. The male is attracted to female but not male pupae (W. Wittfeld). A male lands on the female pupa, turns, and hangs downward. Up to three males are present, and when the female is about to emerge a male breaks through the pupal shell with his abdomen and mates with her before she has emerged. The male deposits a repellent pheromone on the female stink clubs as in *H. erato*.

Color Plate 17
Figs. 45, 52

273. **Heliconius erato**   Red Passion-Flower Butterfly

Stray only
Color Plate 58

This rare stray is easily identified. Ssp. **petiverana** is in the U.S. and Mex.; ssp. *erato* and many other ssp. extend to S. Amer. In the tropics it forms Müllerian mimicry assemblages with other *Heliconius*, notably *H. melpomene*. In one region both species look alike; in another region, both look alike, although the wing pattern differs from that in the first region. Adults are unpalatable to tanagers (L. and J. Brower and C. Collins); some *Heliconius* adults are known to contain the poisons cyanogenic glycosides. With the red patch painted out, adults in nature disappeared more frequently and received more predator damage (W. Benson), probably because predators use the red spot to recognize them as unpalatable.

Habitat tropical forest margins. Ranges south to Paraguay. Hostplants vine (occasionally shrub) Passifloraceae in Latin Amer.: many subgenera and spp. of *Passiflora*, plus a few spp. of *Tetrastylis* and *Dilkea*. Larvae eat the plant species that females oviposit on, plus others that females ignore (J. Smiley). L. Gilbert found that one plant (*Passiflora adenopoda*) kills some larvae feeding on it when its recurved hairs hook into the larvae. He found that most *Passiflora* have nectar glands on stems or other parts to attract insect predators such as ants that eat *Heliconius* immatures.

Oviposition starts 3-7 days after emergence. Females do not lay on plants if they see an egg there, and some plants try to fool females by producing various structures (tendrils, flower buds, glands, spots, and stipules) that look like eggs, to keep the female from ovipositing (K. Williams and L. Gilbert). Eggs (similar to 272 in Fig. 45) yellow, turning orange the day before hatching, laid singly on young shoots and tendrils. Larvae eat these parts; no nests. Larva white, sometimes with a darker lateral band, dull orange beneath, with many black spots, black branching spines, orange rings around the topmost spines, and a slender black collar; head white, with two black rectangles on the front, a black patch above the mouthparts (in Trinidad, black around the eyes and with black patches on top), and two long dark spines. Pupa light brown like that of *H. charitonia*, with gold spots on the saddle, many subdorsal spines, several large flanges on the abdomen, many spines along the antennae, and long flanged head appendages; it makes faint sounds.

Many flights all year in Mex.; a rare stray into s Tex. (Jan., June, Aug., and Dec. records). Adults roost gregariously (usually in small groups 2-10 m above ground on twigs or tendrils) after several days of age, returning to the same leaves for weeks to months. The home ranges, which J. Turner found to be as small as 30 m wide, perhaps benefit *H. erato* because fewer predators need to be taught that they are distasteful. Adults sip the nectar of flowers, esp. red ones, pollinating those of *Anguria* and *Gurania* (the favorites; Cucurbitaceae) in the process. Females gather more pollen than males, and Gilbert found that the pollen sticks to knobs on the proboscis. By exuding a drop of fluid (saliva, etc.) from the proboscis while it is coiled, adults are able to dissolve amino acids from the pollen and use them to make eggs and to live for several months (adults live up to 3 months in nature). Males patrol most of the day to seek females, usually within a few meters of the ground. Males locate female pupae and mate as the female emerges, as in *H. charitonia*. J. Crane studied the courtship of the occasional females that are not mated before emergence. She found that the red fw patch attracts males (females painted black fail to attract males; adults can see all the colors from red to ultraviolet). The male detects a resting female or pursues a flying female, who lands. The male sometimes nudges the female, making her fly; the male or female may try to fly above the other before landing. The male fans the resting female from behind, she elevates her abdomen and extrudes her dorsal abdominal glands (see Fig. 37; these glands probably also produce the pheromone attractant in the pupa), and she closes the anterior margin of the forewings, but the posterior margin and the hindwings are spread and vibrated. The male then fans her from in front, separating his forewings and hindwings, apparently to transfer pheromone from the uph scent scales to the female. The female closes her wings, lowers her abdomen, and withdraws the glands; the male lands, still quivering, and joins. Young females have fewer wing movements in courtship than older females. Gilbert found that while mating, the male transfers a chemical from a gland in his valvae to two "stink clubs" possessed by all *Heliconius* females on the end of the abdomen. These then produce an odor that, in mated females, causes approaching males to depart. Unreceptive females also spread their wings so that the male cannot join. C. Boggs and Gilbert also found that females digest their spermatophores and use them to produce eggs. *Heliconius* adults evidently have complicated behavior and are good at learning. They can learn to live in a room lit with only fluorescent bulbs (most butterflies fly incessantly into the lights); they can also learn the locations of roosting and flower sites, to return there repeatedly, and can use the colors of flowers to locate those in season.

FAMILY LIBYTHEIDAE: SNOUT BUTTERFLIES

The Libytheidae, a family of only about eight species, occur throughout the tropical and subtropical regions of the world. One species extends into the southern and eastern U.S.

The long palpi ("snout," Fig. 7) on the front of the head are aimed forward (in some Hesperiinae the palpi are directed forward but are not as long, and in a few foreign Nymphalidae the palpi are as long as those of some Libytheidae). The forewings are always square-tipped, and the wings are generally brown or orange-brown with white spots, but the males of some Old World species are blue. In the males, the forelegs are much smaller than the hind four legs and their tarsal segments are fused (lacking claws), but the forelegs of the female are nearly normal size (two-thirds the length of the other legs) and clawed. Larvae usually eat *Celtis*, though in some species they eat Rosaceae. Larvae are shaped like those of the Pieridae, although the thorax region is slightly enlarged; they lack the spines and horns of most Nymphalidae. On the pupa, the first and second leg cases touch the eye, and the thoracic spiracle is a slit; both are characters they share with the Nymphalidae. Pupae have a crest on the abdomen and two points on the head (Fig. 52); they lack the dorsal bumps of most Nymphalinae. The pupae of hackberry (*Celtis*) feeders—Libytheidae and Apaturinae (Nymphalidae)—may appear green with a yellow diagonal stripe for camouflage against a leaf. The pupae of Apaturinae rest prone on a leaf, but those of the Libytheidae hang upside down even though the cremaster is aimed ventrally. Adults seem to hibernate in Eurasia and North America.

Adults are not involved in mimicry.

The flight, fluttering but fairly strong, resembles that of fritillaries (*Speyeria*), about a meter above ground, and most species migrate. Adults rest with the wings closed, but bask with the wings spread. While resting, they are leaflike (especially when they rest parallel to a twig with the "leaf stalk" palpi and antennae angled close to the twig). The palpi "snout" evidently evolved to perfect this leaflike camouflage. Males seem to perch to await females.

Color Plates 19, 22, 59
Figs. 45, 49, 50-52

274. Libytheana carinenta Snout Butterfly

The characteristic huge palpi on the adult head (the "snout") seem to be used for camouflage. When an adult is resting on a twig, the palpi resemble a leaf petiole (the palpi and antennae are pressed close together and angled toward the twig) and the closed wings resemble a leaf, presumably as camouflage to fool predators. C. Michener studied American *Libytheana*, and found that ssp. *carinenta* (S. Amer. to Argentina), **mexicana** (lowland Mex. and C. Amer.), **larvata** (Mexican Plateau and sw U.S. east to c Tex.), and **bachmanii** (Kans. and

E Tex. to E U.S.) all form a cline (a gradual gradient) in several traits: increasing area and brilliance of orange markings, increasing area of white spots (those on females larger than those on males), increasing nearness of the white fw spot along the front margin to the white spot beyond the fw cell, decreasing acuity of the hw hind corner, increasing acuity of the angle at the end of vein M_2 of the fw, increasing waviness of the outer margin of the hw, and decreasing size. He treated them as two species, only because the first two ssp. have a more blunt prong on top of abdomen segment 8. However, dissection shows that intermediates occur in this trait also (J. Scott). The narrowest prongs are in E U.S., ssp. *larvata* has thicker prongs, and in a population with *larvata* wing pattern from Acatlán, Puebla, Mex., some individuals have blunt prongs resembling ssp. *mexicana* and some have prongs resembling *larvata*. The white fw spot traits also vary somewhat. Larvae (see below) are alike in ssp. *larvata* and *mexicana*, but not in ssp. *bachmanii*. Migration explains the presence of individuals of one ssp. within the range of another, such as rare *larvata* and *mexicana* in the range of *bachmanii* in Kans., rare *mexicana* (May-Nov.) in the range of *larvata* in s Ariz. and c and s Tex., rare *bachmanii* in the range of *larvata* at Austin, Tex., and rare *larvata* in the range of *mexicana* in lowland Mex. Two s Tex. females caught in June 1968 (Color Plate 59) resemble the Cuban ssp. **motya**; they were probably strays from Cuba but might have been variants within the *larvata* population. Ssp. *motya* has all the orange (except at the fw base in and near the cell) replaced by white, and the spot at the end of the fw cell is very large, white, and oval, without a satellite spot. Two forms occur in all ssp.: the unh is either pale tan with brown dashes and brown median and submarginal bands, or nearly uniform violet-gray (form **kirtlandi**; *kirtlandi* may be a wet-weather form). Two other ssp. occur on Hispaniola and Dominique in the Antilles.

Habitat mostly Subtropical to Lower Austral/Lower Sonoran Zone woodland and thorn forest, migrating northward. Hostplants tree Ulmaceae: *Celtis occidentalis, laevigata, douglasii, pallida, reticulata, tenuifolia*, and in S. Amer. *spinosa* and *boliviensis*. *Symphoricarpus occidentalis* (Caprifoliaceae) is not a normal host, although H. Barber raised adults from a few larvae found on it when *Celtis* was scarce in E Neb.

Eggs (Fig. 45) pale green, laid singly on young terminal leaves of the hostplant, usually on the petiole, occasionally on the leaf underside. Larvae prefer young leaves; no nests. Larva (ssp. *mexicana*; ssp. *larvata* similar) dark green, yellowish-green beneath, with many yellowish points and with a faint yellow lateral line on the abdomen; larva (ssp. *bachmanii*; Figs. 49-51) similar, but with a yellow middorsal line, a small black subdorsal cone ringed with yellow on the hump on top of the mesothorax, and (perhaps in all ssp.) a hair on a cone on the front of each segment; head green, the eyes black or brown over a narrow yellow base. T. Friedlander noted that ssp. *bachmanii* larvae (from College Station, Tex., eastward) have black thorax cones, whereas ssp. *larvata* (from Austin and the Rio Grande valley, Tex., from Ariz., and from Puebla and Oaxaca, Mex.) and ssp. *mexicana* (from Veracruz and Oaxaca, Mex.) both lack the black cones. W. Edwards noted that last-generation larvae in E U.S. are occasionally dark green on top, edged on either side by a gray line, a yellow band, a gray line, and finally a black band, with the metathorax and abdomen segment 2 partly black; another occasional larval variety green, with a black sublateral band and a few other black patches on the metathorax and the rear (owing to bacterial infections?).

Friedlander noted that larvae are grayer when eating more slowly. Pupa (ssp. *mexicana*; Fig. 52) green, yellowish-green on the abdomen; pupa (ssp. *bachmanii*) deep green, to bluish-green, or yellowish-green, the abdomen sprinkled with yellowish dots; both ssp. with a slight whitish or yellowish lateral line on the abdomen and a whitish or yellowish diagonal line from the point on top of the abdomen across the wing bases to the end of the head, the wing veins green edged with white points. Friedlander found no differences between the pupae of the three U.S. ssp. Pupa attached only by the cremaster (as in the Nymphalidae), the pupa hung upside down from twigs, etc., despite the cremaster being aimed ventrally. Overwinters as adults, but only in the south, migrating northward.

Many flights, all year in s Tex. and s Fla., Apr.-Sep. in Va. (common in SE U.S.); rarely migrates north to Calif., Ont., N.D., and Maine, but sometimes common northward in late summer. A strong migrant; huge flights are frequent in ssp. *larvata* (I once saw about 200 adults on one tree during a migration in s Tex.), and one flight coursed from Tex. north-northeast to Kans. in Aug.-Sep. Adults sip flower nectar, mud, and fruit. Friedlander noted that males mainly perch to await females, although they seldom return to a previous resting site; mating seems to occur all day.

FAMILY LYCAENIDAE:
LITTLE BUTTERFLIES

The 4,700 species of the Lycaenidae are distributed throughout the world, especially in the tropics. North American species number 142, and several of these occur even in the Arctic.

The eyes of adults are indented near the antennae and the face is narrow. The forewing R veins are simple (Fig. 55). The forelegs of males are slightly or moderately smaller than the hind four legs and have fused tips without claws, but the forelegs of females are of almost normal size and do bear claws. Older larvae and sometimes pupae of both subfamilies of Lycaenidae are often tended by ants for the honeydew they produce, and in both groups eversible tentacles produce a pheromone that may alarm ants. Larvae eat dicotyledons of many families, some species even eat aphids or ants, and a few tropical species eat lichens or fungi. Larvae are sluglike in most species, though less so in the Riodininae than in the Lycaeninae. Older Lycaeninae larvae are usually covered with a carpet of very short hair, whereas Riodininae larval hairs are longer and tufted. In the larvae of all Lycaenidae, the semicircle of crochets on the prolegs is interrupted, and a spatula-like fleshy lobe occurs in the center of the proleg beside the interruption (Fig. 4); H. Hinton suggested that the lobe may function as an adhesive organ to stick the proleg to a surface. The pupa is usually attached to a surface by a silk girdle, and the cremaster is frequently absent, although the normal hooks are present, usually on an oval-shaped area. The pupae are mostly oval in shape, rounded at both ends. The pupal head tends not to be visible from the dorsal side, especially in the Lycaeninae. The abdomen segments are nearly immovable, but tiny pegs and ribs between the overlapping segments may produce faint squeaks when the segments move. The hibernation stage varies.

Adults, other than those of a few Oriental and New Guinea species, do not seem to be involved in mimicry. Many species have eyespots and a hairlike tail on the hindwing, which somewhat resemble an eye and antenna, perhaps drawing a predator's attention away from the real head.

Most Lycaenidae are local and do not migrate, but some blues (including the smallest butterfly in the world, the Pygmy Blue of southwestern U.S., with a 1-cm wingspan) are migratory. Most Lycaenidae have a large body, relative to the wings, and a strong flight. Most hairstreaks and metalmarks fly swiftly but erratically, usually covering no more than several meters without landing; coppers are not quite as swift or erratic as hairstreaks. Most blues have a small thorax and rounded wings, and most flutter along at a steady pace (*Lampides* and *Leptotes* fly like hairstreaks). Lycaenidae generally rest with the wings closed, but usually bask with the wings open. Some hairstreaks (but not *Hypaurotis*) bask with the wings closed sideways to the sun. Males of most groups usually perch to await females; male blues generally patrol to seek females.

Two subfamilies of Lycaenidae, the Riodininae and Lycaeninae, occur in North America. The two subfamilies not found here are Styginae and Curetinae. The former consists of a single little-known Andean species that may resemble the ancestor of Lycaenidae in most respects. The Australasian Curetinae eat green plants, and occupy an intermediate position between Riodininae and Lycaeninae.

Subfamily Riodininae: Metalmarks

The Riodininae occur worldwide, nearly all of them in the tropics, especially the American tropics, where there are about 1,500 species; only a few occur in the Old World. The 20 North American species occur mainly in the southern U.S., though one ranges slightly into Canada. The wings of the tropical species display nearly every color and shape imaginable.

Adults are identified by the male foreleg, which is less than half the length of the other legs; its first segment (coxa) extends like a spine beyond the joint with the rest of the leg (Fig. 16). The hindwing usually has a humeral vein, and often a noticeable costal vein (Fig. 55). The larvae of some species are, like the Lycaeninae, associated with ants, although the positions of the honey glands and other structures differ in the Riodininae (see "Mimicry and Other Defenses," in Part I). Larvae eat many dicotyledons. They are less sluglike than in the Lycaeninae, and have slightly wider heads (about half the width of the body) and longer hairs on the body. First-stage larvae have normal-size heads, and the prothorax does not cover the head as much as in the Lycaeninae; the upper head hairs are usually as long as the lower ones, but shorter in some species. On the first-stage larvae in some species, unlike those of the Lycaeninae, the body hairs arise from hardened plates on every body segment. Pupae are a little less rounded than those of the Lycaeninae. Eggs vary enormously in shape (Fig. 45). In the temperate-zone species, the larvae hibernate.

Flight is usually rather swift and erratic, weaker in *Calephelis*. The Riodininae are rather local, seldom fly far, and almost never migrate. All species feed on flower nectar. Adults usually rest, bask, and feed with the wings opened nearly flat. Some species rest upside down under leaves with the wings spread. Males commonly perch to await females, though some species may patrol also.

275. Apodemia mormo   Mormon Metalmark

The pattern of white spots on the brown unh and the orange on the basal two-thirds of the unf are characteristic. There is much geographic variation, which fits poorly into subspecies. Ssp. **mormo** (Great Basin, the c Sierra Nevada above 2,500 m, and Ariz.) has red only on the fw. The form or ssp. **dialeuca** (higher altitudes in N Baja Calif., San Bernardino Mts., Calif., and White Mts., Ariz.) nearly lacks ups red. Ssp. **deserti** (Mojave Desert) is similar but has larger white ups spots and a more whitish unh. Ssp. **langei** (near Antioch, c Calif.) has the fw (including the spots in the cell) and the uph base red. In ssp. **cythera** (along the E base of the Sierra) the fw and the uph submarginal band are red-

Color Plate 31
Figs. 51, 52

orange. Ssp. **mejicanus** (s Ariz. to w Tex., then northward, east of the continental divide, to Sask.) resembles *cythera* but often has more orange, including some on the unh. Ssp. **virgulti** (s Calif.) resembles *cythera*, but the unh is blackish. Ssp. **tuolumnensis** (Calif., near Yosemite south to Tejon Mts.) also resembles *cythera* but is slightly more orange, with a brown unh. In ssp. **duryi** (Organ Mts., N.M.) the ups is mostly orange.

Habitat mostly Lower Sonoran to lower Canadian Zone (rarely higher-altitude) grassland, chaparral, open woodland, and dunes. Ranges to Sinaloa, Mex. Hostplants herb and shrublike Polygonaceae: *Eriogonum corymbosum, cinereum, elatum, elongatum, fasciculatum* (vars. *polifolium, foliolosum, fasciculatum*), *inflatum, hastatum, latifolium, deflexum, leptocladon, nudum* (and ssp. *indictum, auriculatum, sulphureum*), *lonchophyllum, microthecum* (and var. *foliosum*), *umbellatum* (and ssp. *behiiforme*), *wrighti* ssp. *subscaposum, jamesi* var. *jamesi, kearneyi* var. *kearneyi, plumatella* var. *plumatella*; in Sask. assoc. with *E. multiceps*; in w Tex. Krameriaceae: *Krameria glandulosa*.

Eggs pale pink, later turning deep violet, laid in small clusters of two to four on drying lower leaves, sometimes singly at stem junctions or under petiole sheaths or on leaves or inflorescences. Young larvae eat the upperside of leaves; older larvae eat leaves and stems, rarely flowers, at night and live in a nest of leaves silked together. Larva (Fig. 51) dark violet (lighter beneath), with six rows of clustered cactuslike spines, the dorsal rows black at their bases, the lateral rows ochre. Pupa (Fig. 52) hairy, mottled brown, with dark spots on the abdomen; in litter. Young larvae hibernate, sometimes inside the inflated stems of *E. inflatum* or inside the dried flower heads of *E. fasciculatum*, usually under litter.

One flight, mainly Aug., in most of area (even into Sep. in high Sierra); several flights, Mar.-E Oct., from s Calif. and s Nev. to w Tex. (rarely Jan.-Dec. in s Calif.). Adults are fairly local, moving an average of 49 m for males and 64 m for females (maximum 617 m) during their life spans, which average about 9 days for males, 11 days for females (R. Arnold, J. Powell). Adults sip flower nectar, mostly of *Eriogonum*. Males perch mostly in hillside depressions to await females, from about 11 A.M. to 2:30 P.M. (mated pairs were seen from 1-4 P.M. in Calif.). In courtship, the male pursues a passing female, both land, she may flutter briefly, and then he flutters next to her and nudges her before they join.

276. Apodemia nais   Coppermark

Identified by the unh, which somewhat resembles that of *Lycaena hyllus* (373); the ups resembles a checkerspot (Melitaeini). First named as a copper (Lycaenini). Ssp. **chisosensis** (Big Bend, Tex.) is slightly paler on the ups, the unh lacks orange central spots, and the black unh postmedian dots are more in a line. Ssp. **nais** is elsewhere.

Habitat Upper Sonoran to Canadian Zone chaparral and open woodland. Hostplants shrub Rhamnaceae: *Ceanothus fendleri* (Colo.); Rosaceae: *Prunus havardii* (Tex.). Both hosts induce oviposition in nature and lab feeding. Ariz. lab larvae also eat wild plum (*Prunus*).

Eggs greenish-white, laid singly on host inflorescences and adjacent leaves (of *Ceanothus*) or under leaves (of *Prunus*). Larvae (Figs. 49, 50) eat leaves of both

Color Plate 31
Figs. 49, 50

plants and probably eat fruits. Larvae live in nests of leaves silked together. Larva light pinkish (greenish ventrally), with a dark dorsal line, red subdorsal marks, and six rows of black clustered spines; head black, lighter above, spiny. Pupa gray-brown (dark greenish on the abdomen, the eye orange) with several gray-brown lines and a silk girdle, covered with white hair except on the wing cases. Larva and pupa somewhat resemble those of *Phyciodes* (224-236) in shape, but are larger in the middle. Half-grown to nearly mature larvae hibernate under fallen leaves, etc.

One flight, L June-July, in Colo.; one May flight in w Tex., plus a partial second flight of rare adults in Aug. Adults sip flower nectar and mud. Males perch in small gulch mouths and in hillside depressions, and perch near and patrol erratically around the hostplant, from about 8:50 A.M. to 2:30 P.M., to seek females.

Color Plates 27, 61

277. **Apodemia phyciodoides**   Crescentmark

Named for its resemblance to *Phyciodes*; in overall appearance resembles *Phyciodes mylitta* (225), but the pattern details differ. The ups resembles *A. nais*, but the unh lacks an orange band and has a strong white band. Only two individuals have been found in the U.S. ("Paradise, Chiricahua Mts., Ariz."); they were undoubtedly mislabeled from Mex. (Chihuahua and Sonora), where the original discoverers also collected. Habitat in Mex. Upper Sonoran Zone near cottonwood/willow woodland. Several flights (Apr.-Sep. at least in Mex.). Adults sip nectar of *Aloysia* (Verbenaceae) and *Eriogonum abertianum* (Polygonaceae) flowers.

Color Plate 31

278. **Apodemia palmerii**   Mesquite Metalmark

Identified by the orange uns with white bands and by the orange ups margins.

Habitat mesquite desert. Ranges to c Mex. Hostplants tree Leguminosae: *Prosopis glandulosa, pubescens*.

Eggs greenish-white, laid singly on young host leaves. Larvae eat leaves, and live in a nest of leaves silked together; larvae venture out to feed, as in *A. nais*. Larva pale bluish-green, with yellow middorsal and subdorsal lines and six rows of clustered spines. Pupa pale bluish-green (the wing cases straw) with a cream subdorsal line. Third-stage larvae hibernate.

Many flights, Apr.-Nov., southward; two flights, May-Sep., in Nev. and Utah.

Color Plate 31

279. **Apodemia hepburni**

Darker than *A. palmerii*, with smaller white spots, lacking the white submarginal spots of *palmerii*, and having the ups margins less orange. Usually treated as a form of *palmerii*, but the valva is a little shorter, and G. Forbes caught both together at several sites. Raising eggs would determine whether *hepburni* is a form of *palmerii*. Habitat desert mountains near Mex. Ranges to c Mex. In U.S. known only from the Chisos Mts., Tex. Many flights, at least Mar.-Nov., in Mex.

280. Apodemia walkeri   White Metalmark

Stray only
Color Plate 31

Like *A. hepburni*, but the uns is mostly white, the ups is brown with smeared white areas instead of distinct white spots. Subtropical. Ranges south to Oaxaca, Mex. Common in Mex. all year, occasionally flying to s Tex. (May-Dec.).

281. Apodemia multiplaga   Pointed Metalmark

Stray only
Color Plate 61

The fw is pointed with a wavy margin, the ups is dark brown with large white spots. The uns is similar, but the unf base is orange and the unh base is mostly white. Many flights all year in subtropical Mex. (ranges south to Puebla); a rare stray into s Tex. (Oct., Nov.).

282. Calephelis borealis   Northern Metalmark

Identified by the range, large size, rounded male fw, and dark ups median band. The male transtilla is shorter than the valva and not pointed (Fig. 71), and the female lamella has a characteristic shape (Fig. 71).

Habitat Upper Austral to Transition Zone woods openings (often on limestone outcrops). Hostplant herb Compositae: *Senecio obovatus*.

Color Plates 31, 60
Figs. 55 (veins), 71

Eggs pale lavender, turning purple, deep red, and finally waxy-white a day or two before hatching, laid singly beneath host leaves. Larvae eat leaves (young larvae eat the underside); no nests. Larva greenish, with long whitish hairs dorsally and laterally, resembling *C. muticum*, but the black dorsal spots prominent. Pupa resembles that of *muticum*, light brown (the abdomen yellow), with rows of black dorsal spots, black lateral spots on the abdomen, and many long white hairs; attached by a silk girdle. Larvae hibernate in the fifth or sixth stage (of eight or nine).

Mostly one flight, L June-July (two flights, L May-June and M Aug., in sw Mo.). Adults bask dorsally, and often rest upside down under leaves. Males perch to await females.

283. Calephelis muticum   Swamp Metalmark

Like *C. borealis* but smaller, and the male fw is pointed; in both sexes the ups is reddish-brown without a dark median band, and the two rows of silver median unh dots extend into cell 1A + 2A (only the outer row does in *borealis*). The male transtilla is pointed and as long as the valva (Fig. 71), and the female lamella has a characteristic shape (Fig. 71). *C. muticum* and *C. virginiensis* have brown fringes; other *Calephelis* have a few faint white fringe spots.

Color Plate 31
Fig. 71

Habitat Upper Austral to Transition Zone swamps, bogs, and wet meadows. Hostplant herb Compositae: *Cirsium muticum, altissimum*.

Eggs reddish, becoming waxy-white just before hatching, laid singly under young host leaves. Larvae eat leaves (young larvae eat the leaf underside); no nests. Larva whitish-green, with a dorsal row (next to a middorsal line) and a lateral row of long (half the length of the larva) whitish hairs (the prothoracic hairs extend over the cream head, those of the rear extend posteriorly), the subdorsal area covered with tiny six-pronged processes and black spots. Pupa pale green (the abdomen yellowish-green), sometimes mottled with darker blotches, with black dorsal spots, covered with many larval hairs and tiny hooked bristles;

usually under leaves attached by a silk girdle. Larvae hibernate in fourth or fifth stage (of eight or nine) under lower leaves.

One flight, M July-Aug., northward; two flights, June and Aug.-Sep., in Mo. and Ark. Adults sip the nectar of yellow flowers. They bask dorsally, and often rest upside down under leaves.

284. Calephelis virginiensis   Little Metalmark

Color Plate 31
Fig. 71

The only *Calephelis* in most of the coastal SE U.S. range. Very small, reddish-brown, without a dark median ups band, the male fw rather rounded. The male transtilla and valva are truncated, and the transtilla is as long as the valva (Fig. 71). The four lateral processes of the transtilla are long in *C. borealis*, *muticum*, and *virginiensis*, short in the other *Calephelis*. The female lamella has a notch in these three species, but not in other *Calephelis* (Fig. 71).

Habitat Lower Austral Zone open pine woods, savannah, salt-marsh meadows, and grassy areas of the coastal plain. Hostplant herb Compositae: *Cirsium horridulum*.

Eggs laid singly on host leaves. Larvae eat leaves, resting beneath them by day. Larva pale green, with dorsal and lateral hair tufts like those of *C. muticum*, and reddish-brown spots beside the dorsal tufts on abdomen segments 5-10. Pupa pale green on the abdomen, the wing cases cream or pale yellow.

Three flights, L Apr.-May, July-Aug., Sep.-E Oct., in Va.; many flights all year in Fla. (most common in Aug.-Oct.), Mar.-Nov. in Tex. A rare stray to Cuba. Males perch on low vegetation to await females.

285. Calephelis nilus   Rounded Metalmark

Color Plate 31
Fig. 71

C. nilus flies only with *C. nemesis* and *C. rawsoni*. The ups has a dark median band, unlike that of *rawsoni*. The male fw is rounded (unlike those of *nemesis* and *rawsoni*). The male transtilla is like that of *nemesis* (Fig. 71). The female lamella has a fairly straight posterior margin as in *rawsoni* (Fig. 71). The U.S. ssp. is **perditalis** (*wellingi*, *clenchi*, and *browni* also seem to be C. Amer. ssp. of the Venezuelan *nilus*).

Habitat subtropical open areas. Hostplant herb Compositae: *Eupatorium odoratum*, probably *serotinum* and *betonicifolium*.

Eggs laid singly, mostly in host leaf axils. Larvae eat leaves. Larva has tufts of white hairs. Pupa light green, becoming darker, found under leaves.

Many flights all year (adults most common Mar.-Nov.).

286. Calephelis nemesis (=*guadeloupe*)   Mexican Metalmark

Color Plate 31
Fig. 71

Often flies with *C. rawsoni*, *C. nilus*, and *C. wrighti*. The ups is brown with a dark median band and a lighter-brown area beyond it, the band darker than that of *wrighti* and *rawsoni*. Males have a pointed fw, unlike that of *nilus*. The male transtilla is very short and pointed, as in *nilus* (Fig. 71), but the posterior margin of the female lamella is convex (Fig. 71). Some individuals and populations are redder or have less-dark ups median bands.

Habitat mostly Lower Sonoran/Lower Austral Zone desert canyons and chaparral, esp. along creeks, and subtropical open areas and fence rows. Ranges south to Oaxaca, Mex. Hostplants shrub and vine Compositae: *Baccharis gluti-*

nosa and *Encelia californica* in Calif.; Ranunculaceae: *Clematis henryi* and *drummondi* in s Tex.

Eggs reddish with white ridges, laid singly on host leaves. Larvae eat leaves; no nests. Larva dark gray, with tiny silvery processes, blackish lateral spots, and arising from chestnut blotches dorsal and lateral rows of long whitish to brownish hairs, the hair shorter than in *C. wrighti*. Pupa pale dirty-yellow (the abdomen sometimes greenish above and below) with a few brown middorsal and lateral spots and a silk girdle.

Many flights, all year in s Tex., Feb.-Oct. in Calif. Both sexes fly weakly about the hostplants. Adults sip flower nectar and mud.

Color Plate 31
Fig. 71

287. Calephelis rawsoni   Southwest Metalmark

Usually occurs with *C. nemesis*, and with *C. nilus* in c and s Tex. The male fw is pointed, unlike that of *nilus*, and a dark ups median band is weak or absent, not as in *nemesis* and *nilus*. Spring adults have more-contrasting ups median bands than do summer adults. The female lamella has a straight posterior margin, like that of *nilus*, in all ssp. (Fig. 71). The male transtilla (Fig. 71) is long, extending beyond the valvae, in c Tex. (ssp. **rawsoni**), extending usually to and sometimes beyond the ends of the valvae in w Tex. (ssp. **freemani**), and sometimes extending to but usually not as far as the ends of the valvae in s Ariz. (ssp. **arizonensis**). The wing pattern, female lamella, hostplants, and behavior are so similar among these groups that I treat them as ssp. of *rawsoni*; there seems to be a cline in the transtilla length. Widespread in Mex. south to Michoacán (ssp. *dreisbachi*, which was recorded for s Ariz. on the basis of one doubtful female, ssp. *sinaloensis*, *nuevoleon*, and probably *matheri*). W. McAlpine states that hybrids of *C. nemesis* × *rawsoni arizonensis* occur.

Habitat semi-shaded limestone outcrops in c Tex., desert foothill canyons in w Tex. and s Ariz. Hostplants Compositae: *Eupatorium havanense* (c and w Tex., a shrub), *greggii* (w Tex., a herb), a riparian yellow-flowered daisy in Ariz.

Eggs laid singly on host leaf axils or dead leaves. Larvae eat leaves; no nests.

Many flights Feb.-Nov. Ariz. and w Tex. males perch all day in narrow dry gulches (or at the side of larger gulches) to await females.

Color Plate 31
Figs. 51, 52, 71

288. Calephelis wrighti   Sweetbush Metalmark

Very distinct, the ups is uniformly reddish-brown with a faint whitish sheen (without the dark median band of *C. nemesis*), the wing fringe has few white spots, and the male fw is pointed. The male transtilla is broadly truncated and as long as the valva (Fig. 71). The female lamella has upturned corners (Fig. 71).

Habitat Lower Sonoran Zone desert washes and canyons. Hostplant bushy herb Compositae: *Bebbia juncea*.

Eggs reddish with white ridges, laid singly at host stem junctions. Larvae eat the greenish covering of stems; no nests. Larva (Fig. 51) grayish-white or lilac-white, with raised tiny white processes, black dots, dorsal and lateral rows of very long thick white hair, and yellow spots (lined above with black) above the spiracles. Pupa (Fig. 52) light grayish-green (the abdomen brownish-tinged), with hair tufts on the body but not on the wing cases.

Many flights Feb.-Dec. (mostly Mar.-Oct.). Adults sip hostplant flower nectar. Males seem to perch on larval hosts or nearby, and may patrol, to seek females.

289. Caria ino   Small Curvy Wing

Color Plate 31
Fig. 45

The front fw edge is oddly curved. Males are darker on the ups and redder on the uns than females. Ssp. **melicerta** is in U.S. and E Mex., ssp. *ino* in w Mex.

Habitat subtropical thorn forest. Ranges south to Yucatán, Mex. Hostplant tree Ulmaceae: *Celtis pallida*; Bromeliaceae: *Tillandsia caput-medusae*.

Eggs (Fig. 45) laid singly at the base of host leaf petioles. Larvae eat leaves, and live in a nest of leaves silked together or in a rolled (often dead) leaf. Mature larvae hibernate, but cannot withstand freezing.

Many flights all year in s Tex. (most common Apr.-Nov.). Adults often rest under leaves.

290. Emesis emesia   Big Curvy Wing

Stray only
Color Plate 31
Fig. 45

The leading edge of the fw is curved. Larger than *Caria ino* (289), *E. emesia* has a white fw dash. Subtropical. Ranges south to Nicaragua. Hostplant herb Leguminosae: *Caesalpinia mexicana*. Eggs (Fig. 45) laid under host leaflets. Larvae eat leaves; they rest under leaves, without nests. Many flights all year in Mex.; a rare stray into s Tex. (Oct.-Nov.; few records, although breeding is occasional).

291. Emesis zela   Arizona Metalmark

Color Plate 31

Resembles *E. ares*, but the fw tip is slightly hooked, the uph has a dark median stripe, the upf lacks black submarginal spots, the uph is more orange, and the female often has a more yellow upf. Somewhat variable, esp. in summer, when adults resemble *ares* a bit more closely. Ssp. **cleis** is in U.S.; ssp. *zela* is in C. and S. Amer. (to Venezuela). Habitat Upper Sonoran to Transition Zone mountains. Eggs (similar to 315 in Fig. 45) white. Several flights, Mar.-Apr. and June-M Aug. (perhaps only one flight, M June-E July, in N Ariz.). Males perch in valley bottom openings to await females.

292. Emesis ares   Chiricahua Metalmark

Color Plate 31

Like *E. zela*, but the fw tip is rounded, the upf of both sexes is uniformly brown with black submarginal and other spots, and the uph is more red-orange. The uncus has a smaller notch than that of *zela*, although *zela* varies. *E. ares* is perhaps an extreme seasonal form of *zela*, which flies with *ares* E-M Aug.; R. Bailowitz noted some adults intermediate between the two in Sycamore Canyon near Nogales, Ariz., in L Aug. Habitat the oak zone of desert mountains. Hostplant tree Fagaceae: a pupa found on *Quercus* leaves. One flight July-Sep. (most common in Aug.).

293. Lasaia sula   Blue Metalmark

s Tex. only
Color Plate 35
Fig. 35 (ultraviolet), 45

A subtropical species, common at times in s Tex. Egg strangely shaped (Fig. 45). Many flights, Apr.-Nov. at least. Ranges south to Honduras.

Stray only
Color Plate 27

294. Melanis pixe   Pixy Metalmark

Easily identified. Subtropical. Ranges south to Panama. Hostplant tree Leguminosae: *Pithecellobium dulce*. Larvae eat leaves. Larva hairy. Pupa light, with dark points, and with small bumps on top of the abdomen. Many flights all year in s Tex., but occurring only after several years without frost, when adults move north from Mex. In Colombia the hairy larvae of *M. pronostriga* eat leaves of the ornamental leguminous tree *Samanea saman*; males patrol around the canopy of this tree and about the roofs of adjacent tall buildings from about 5 P.M. to dusk to seek females (J. Scott).

Subfamily Lycaeninae: Harvesters, Hairstreaks, Coppers, and Blues

The Lycaeninae, about 3,200 species, occur worldwide, even in the Arctic. The 122 North American species are found everywhere.

The forelegs of the male are somewhat smaller than the rear legs but not as small as those of Riodininae; they lack the extended first segment found in the Riodininae. The hindwing, at least in North America, lacks the humeral vein and thickened costal vein of the Riodininae. Larvae are often tended by ants, and produce honeydew for them (see "Mimicry and Other Defenses," in Part I). A few species are even carried by the ants into ant nests, where the larvae eat ant grubs. Larvae feed on many dicotyledons, often eating the flowers and young fruits. In fact, one way to find the larvae of these groups is to pick flowers of plants suspected of being hostplants (but not of rare plants!), place them in a screened box, and wait until the flowers dry; the larvae then leave the plants, crawl up the sides of the box, and become visible. Older larvae, which are covered with a carpet of tiny hairs, are generally sluglike, with small heads that can be retracted within the prothorax or extended to bore out fruits. First-stage larvae have hardened body plates only on the prothorax and rear, and many long hairs on the body; the prothorax covers most of the head, and the upper hairs on the head are much smaller than normal. Pupae are rounded like deer pellets, and are found in leaf litter or under bark or in other crannies. The hibernation stage varies.

Basking, flight habits, and mate-locating behavior also vary. Adults commonly rest with the wings above the body, and move the hindwings forward and back, the left and right wings moving in opposite directions ("hindwing rubbing"; see "Mimicry and Other Defenses," in Part I). This behavior may draw a bird's attention to eyespots and antenna-like tails on the hindwing, leading the bird to peck at the wing instead of the body.

Four tribes occur in North America, the Miletini, Theclini, Lycaenini, and Polyommatini. Four other tribes occur in the rest of the world (the heartland of the Lycaeninae is southeastern Asia). Larvae of the African tribe Liptenini eat lichens and microscopic fungi, whereas larvae of the related southeastern Asian tribe Poritiini are gregarious and eat green plants. Larvae of both tribes have fairly wide heads and long tufts of hair, like larvae of the Riodininae, traits perhaps inherited from the original Lycaenidae ancestor. The Liphyrini are Old World tropical species whose larvae live in ant nests and eat the ants. The sides of these larvae are widened into a leathery skirt that extends down to the nest, to keep the ants from biting the legs. The Old World Aphnaeini eat green plants, and are related to the Theclini.

Tribe Miletini: Harvesters

The Miletini are a small tribe (about 50 species) that occurs in the Asian and African tropics, with a few species extending into Eurasia (several into the Palaearctic) and one into southeastern North America.

Adults are characterized by lacking spurs on the end of the tibias of the rear four legs. The common name derives from the predaceous habit of the larvae: these carnivores eat insects of the order Homoptera (aphids, mealybugs, leafhoppers, and treehoppers). All other North American butterfly larvae eat plants, although a few other tropical tribes related to the Miletini are also carnivorous, and some larvae of other groups of Lycaenidae may eat ant larvae. The larvae are more cylindrical than in other Lycaeninae. Pupae are very wide and in top view look like a monkey's head (Fig. 52).

The flight of harvesters is weaker than that of hairstreaks and somewhat erratic; they seldom fly far and are very local. Adults do not feed on flowers. They usually rest with the wings closed. "Hindwing rubbing" is not done.

Color Plates 3 (larva), 5 (pupa), 30
Figs. 51, 52, 55 (veins)

295. Feniseca tarquinius   Harvester

The wing pattern is unique, somewhat resembling that of a copper (Lycaenini). Darker in spring in the northeast, but in the midwest it is slightly lighter and larger in spring.

Habitat Lower Austral to lower Canadian Zone deciduous woods, often near streams. Larval foods are aphids (insects that suck sap from plants—Order Homoptera, Family Aphididae), usually on trees: *Prociphilus tessellatus* aphids (on *Alnus rugosa* and on *Ilex verticillata* plants), *Meliarhizophagus fraxinifolii* (on *Fraxinus americana*), *Fagiphagus imbricator* (on *Fagus grandifolia*), *Neoprociphilus aceris* (on *Acer saccharinum*, *Smilax herbacea*), unknown aphids (on *Hamamelis virginiana*, *Alnus serrulata*, *incana*, *Smilax hispida*, *Malus pumila*, *Echinocystis lobata*, probably *Ulmus*). Adults were also seen flying around Fulgoridae (also Order Homoptera) (on *Parthenocissus quinquifolia*), which are possibly eaten by larvae.

Eggs pale greenish-white, with weaker ridges than in other Lycaenidae, laid singly among aphids, under leaves or under twigs of the host. They take only 3-4 days to hatch. Larvae eat aphids. To avoid ants, larvae usually live inside a silk web covered with aphid carcasses, occasionally in leaves silked together, but some live exposed. Larva (Fig. 51) light to dark gray, tinged with greenish in front, with contrasting white (yellow on top) subdorsal bumps, and dull-dark-brown to brick-red or pink middorsal and subdorsal streaks, the heart darker and edged with white; or larva unmarked uniform pale pink; all with long hairs in masses on six rows of whitish bumps. The four larval stages complete growth in as little as 8 days. Pupa (Fig. 52) whitish (with brown flecks) on the thorax and wings, cream (mottled with greenish-brown) on the abdomen, with small rounded dorsal bumps (the upper bumps orange), the abdomen tip shaped like a broad spatula; shape in dorsal view resembling a monkey's head. Pupae take only 8-11 days until emergence; the life cycle is thus only 3 weeks. Hibernation stage poorly known, probably older larva.

Two flights northward (L May-E June, July-E Sep. near Ottawa); many flights, Feb.-Dec., in Fla. Adults are very local, but the flight is fast and erratic. Adults sip aphid honeydew, sap, carrion, mud, and dung, but not flower nectar; the proboscis is very short. Males perch on leaves 2-3 m above ground to await females, and when they take off they patrol back and forth and around the area (seldom flying more than 10 m in any direction) for several minutes before landing near the previous spot (J. Heitzman).

Tribe Theclini: Hairstreaks

The Theclini occur worldwide, with about 2,000 species, especially in the American tropics, where about a thousand species occur; 75 species occur in North America.

Most hairstreaks are identified by having only 10 forewing veins (there are only 3 unbranched R veins on the forewing); this group is very common in the American tropics, and a few species occur in the Old World. Two hairstreaks (*Habrodais* and *Hypaurotis*) have 11 forewing veins (four R veins) and form a second group common in Eurasia. Hairstreaks are often very beautiful, commonly show blue on the upperside, and often have a complicated underside pattern. Males often have hairlike tails on the hindwing, plus streaks of white or brown, giving rise to the common name. The larvae, which eat a wide variety of dicotyledons, resemble those of coppers and blues, although the *Eumaeus* larva is less sluglike than the others. Pupae are also similar to those of coppers and blues. In species whose larvae eat shrubs or trees, the eggs usually hibernate; in species whose larvae eat herbs or succulents, the pupae usually hibernate.

Adults generally have fairly muscular thoraxes and are swift, erratic fliers. They seldom fly far, however, and rarely migrate. *Habrodais* and *Hypaurotis* adults feed on mud and sap, but not flowers, whereas all other hairstreaks often visit flowers. Adults usually rest with the wings closed, and usually bask with the wings closed, sideways to the sun. Males usually perch to await females, but in some species they patrol. Mating occurs only in the afternoon or early evening in many species. If a mating pair is startled, the female usually flies carrying the hanging male.

296. Habrodais grunus   Live-Oak Hairstreak

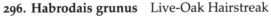

Easily identified by its rounded wings, which are ochre beneath. Ssp. **grunus** (coastal Calif., slightly paler in the Sierra) is mostly brown on the ups. Ssp. **herri** (N Calif.-Ore.) has more orange on the ups. A third ssp. from N Baja Calif. (*poodiae*) is very light, mostly ochre, on the ups. Elsewhere known only from Mt. Graham and the Mogollon Rim in Ariz.

Habitat mostly Upper Sonoran to Transition Zone oak woodland. Host-plants tree Fagaceae: *Quercus chrysolepis, chrysolepis × vaccinifolia, vaccinifolia, Lithocarpus densiflorus, Castanopsis chrysophylla.*

Eggs laid on host twigs. Larvae eat young leaves; no nests. Larva pale bluish-green, with tan dots at the base of numerous hairs, a yellowish subdorsal line, and a bluish-white lateral band. Pupa green or pale bluish-green, covered with brownish dots and minute hairs, with a pale-yellow subdorsal line. Eggs hibernate.

One flight, L June-E Aug. southward, L July-E Sep. in Ore. Adults feed on

Color Plate 31

mud, but apparently not on flowers. Males patrol around the canopy of trees, about 2-7 P.M., to seek females.

Color Plates 32, 35
Fig. 35 (ultraviolet)

297. Hypaurotis crysalus   Colorado Hairstreak

Easily identified and one of our most beautiful butterflies. Ssp. **citima** (c Utah, intergrading to ssp. *crysalus* in w Colo.) lacks the orange ups spots of ssp. **crysalus** elsewhere.

Habitat Upper Sonoran to Canadian Zone oak woodland. Ranges to w Mex. Hostplant tree Fagaceae: *Quercus gambelii.*

Eggs laid singly on host twigs. Eggs hibernate.

One flight, L June-July at low altitude, M July-Aug. at high altitude. Marked adults move throughout small groves of oaks, but rarely between groves (J. Scott). Males live an average of 5 days in nature, females 9 days. Adults feed only on tree sap, mud, and raindrops. The proboscis is very short (too short for most flowers); but by flying in midsummer afternoons, when rains are frequent in the southwest, adults can suck raindrops to dilute the thick oak sap. Males patrol the oak canopy about 2-6:30 P.M., esp. in cloudy weather, to seek females, who bask dorsally then (and in the morning) to keep warm. Using colored paper, newly killed adults, and oven-dried adults pinned to oak leaves, I found that males are attracted to the violet/ultraviolet color (but not to the orange spots). When the male lands, he tries to mate with newly killed females but not with oven-dried females, suggesting that a female pheromone may be involved. After landing and before mating, the male holds his wings vertically, rapidly vibrates them open a little, then stops, then repeats the process a few times for a few seconds. An unreceptive female tries to escape or raises her abdomen so that the male cannot join.

Color Plate 35
Figs. 35 (ultraviolet), 52, 55

298. Eumaeus atala   Coontie Hairstreak

Resembles *E. minijas,* but the wing fringes are black. The hostplant *Zamia* is poisonous, and the larvae, pupae, and adults of *Eumaeus* are brightly colored, probably to warn predators. Adults can be touched without disturbing them. Birds and esp. lizards try to eat some adults, many of which have beak marks on the wings.

Habitat subtropical brushy areas and hammocks, mostly in pinelands; sometimes in open areas in the Bahamas. Ranges to the Bahamas, Cuba, and the Isle of Pines. Hostplant fernlike shrubby Cycadaceae: *Zamia floridana, integrifolia, angustifolia* (all sometimes treated as varieties of *Z. pumila*), in Cuba *Cycas revoluta.* The roots of the hosts were used for food by the Seminole Indians, who may have propagated the plants. Once feared extinct, a few colonies of the butterfly still exist throughout s Fla. (of course every colony deserves protection from development and excess collecting).

Eggs grayish-white, laid in clusters (usually a dozen, but up to 50), mainly on the upperside of the leaf tips of host seedlings, but sometimes in the Bahamas on the conelike inflorescence. Larvae eat young leaves (young larvae eat only the upperside) and must crawl to other hostplants when the seedling is eaten; no nests. Larva bright brownish-red (the neck and rear yellowish-brown), with two dorsal rows of yellow spots (on either side of the midline) and many tubercles covered with dark hair, the body not as slug-shaped as in other lycaenids; prolegs yellow; head yellowish-brown. Pupa (Fig. 52) light reddish-brown, with yellow spots showing through and brown dots.

Many flights, all year in Fla. Males rarely stray from a colony, but females may stray as far away as 50 m (rarely farther) looking for seedlings. Most Fla. colonies are small, but large ones exist in the Bahamas. Adults fly very slowly unless disturbed, and roost in low trees. Adults sip flower nectar, mainly in the early morning and late afternoon. Male *Eumaeus* have hair pencils on the abdomen, used in courtship, when the male hovers in front of the female.

299. Eumaeus minijas   White-Rim Cycad Hairstreak

Stray only
Color Plate 61
Fig. 51

This doubtful U.S. species resembles *E. atala*, but the fringes are white. Adults have acrid body fluids, and are undoubtedly distasteful to birds.

Habitat tropical woodland, mainly pine/oak forest in Mex. Ranges to S. Amer. Hostplant fernlike shrub Cycadaceae: *Zamia loddigesii* in Mex.

Eggs cream, turning pinkish the day before hatching, laid in clusters of three to eight under tender new host fronds. Larvae eat young leaves (in winter, larvae may eat older leaves to the midrib), and young larvae eat the epidermis; no nests. Larva (Fig. 51) hairy, bright red, with pale translucent subdorsal tubercles (having many hairs), yellow figure-eight marks below those tubercles in the middle of the body, and a collar; shape not as sluglike as in other Lycaenidae; head brownish-orange. Pupa glossy brownish-orange with many small black spots, usually fastened to the substrate only by a silk girdle.

Many flights, all year in Mex. One adult from s Fla. probably arrived with an introduced cycad (*E. minijas* is not in the Antilles). s Tex. records are doubtful. Adults fly very slowly, but often stray a kilometer or more beyond areas with the hostplant.

300. Chlorostrymon simaethis   Silver-Banded Hairstreak

Color Plate 39

The ups is violet, and the uns is green with a distinctive silver-white band.

Habitat subtropical woodland and Lower Sonoran Zone desert. Ranges south to Argentina and to the Greater and Lesser Antilles. Hostplants vine Sapindaceae: *Cardiospermum halicacabum* in Fla. and Tex., *corindum* in Tex.; shrub Compositae: *Eupatorium villosum* in the Antilles.

Eggs shiny waxy-green, laid singly on young fruits. Larvae eat young seeds and live inside the developing pods. Early stages similar to those of *C. maesites*. Larva yellowish-green or light green; *or* larva light brown (turning brick-red before pupating); all with a vague blackish wavy subdorsal band and a greenish-black middorsal stripe (edged on each segment by reddish-brown ovals, those on the metathorax very wide); segments prominent; head tan. Pupa tan to dark grayish-brown (lighter beneath) with black and brown specks, with a faint black middorsal line, the eye black; attached by a silk pad and silk girdle.

Many flights; a native in Fla. (at least May-Dec.) and perhaps s Tex. (records June-Dec.), straying from Mex. to s Calif. (Oct.) and s Ariz.

Color Plates 38, 63

301. Chlorostrymon maesites   Verde Azul

Resembles *C. simaethis* with its bluish ups and green uns, but the unh postmedian band is narrow, broken into spots. In ssp. **telea** (Tex. to Bolivia) the white unh band forms a W, and the brownish unh marginal patch is smaller than in ssp. **maesites** (Fla. and most of the Antilles). They may be two distinct species.

Habitat subtropical woods. Adults in Fla. often rest on top of the tree *Swietenia mahagoni* (Meliaceae), growing in sand or coral rock (although poachers have cut most of these trees), sometimes on other trees. R. Boscoe found that lab females oviposit on *Albizzia lebbeck* (Leguminosae) and larvae eat the flower buds.

Eggs bright green. Larvae eat flower buds. Larva yellow-green (with lighter chevrons), a red spot several segments behind the head (on each side of the dorsal midline). Pupa mostly tan, with darker speckles (esp. on wing cases); attached to the substrate by a silk pad and silk girdle.

Many flights, all year in Fla. (native but rare); a stray from Mex. to s Tex. (June).

Color Plate 33

302. Phaeostrymon alcestis   Soapberry Hairstreak

Identified by the white dash in the middle of the unf and unh and by the solid-brown ups. In ssp. **oslari** (w Tex. to Ariz.) the uns is lighter tan than in ssp. **alcestis** elsewhere.

Habitat southern prairie valleys, hedgerows, and desert foothill canyons. Hostplant tree Sapindaceae: *Sapindus saponaria* var. *drummondii*.

Eggs laid singly on host twigs. Larvae eat young leaves; no nests. Eggs hibernate.

One flight, Apr.-June southward, M June-E July northward. Adults sip flower nectar, as in all the remaining hairstreaks. Males patrol around the host canopy about 2-6 P.M. to seek females.

Color Plates 1 (egg), 3 (larva), 32, 34

303. Harkenclenus titus   Coral Hairstreak

Identified by the unh marginal spots, which are the color of Italian coral used in jewelry. Orange upf spots often occur. The black unh spots tend to be smaller in the Great Basin ssp. **immaculosus**; ssp. **titus** is elsewhere. Rare in c Tex.

Habitat N Lower Austral and Upper Sonoran to lower Canadian Zone shrubby and wooded areas. Hostplants tree Rosaceae: *Prunus virginiana, serotina, americana, domestica, angustifolia, cerasus*[t], *ilicifolia*[t].

Eggs pale green, turning white, laid singly on host twigs, sometimes on trash at the base of the plant. Larvae eat leaves and fruits at night, and rest at the plant base during the day. Larvae are associated with ants; no nests. Larva green (or dull yellowish-green), with a dark-green middorsal line, and with three reddish patches bordered with white spots (on the prothorax, top of thorax, and rear). Pupa pale brown with black dots, with a dorsal stripe of dark dots on the abdomen. Eggs hibernate.

One flight, L May-E July southward, M July-Aug. in the north and at high altitude. Males perch on shrubs on hilltops (if available), from about 10 A.M. to late afternoon, to await females.

Color Plate 34

304. Satyrium acadica   Northern Willow Hairstreak

The ups is gray. The unh is brownish-gray, with many orange submarginal spots and an orange crescent capping the blue spot. Differs from *S. californica* (305) and *S. sylvinus* (306) by having only one orange uph spot and many orange unh submarginal spots. Possibly a ssp. of *californica*, *acadica* stops a few kilometers from the mountains in Colo., and *californica* takes over in the foothills, though one apparent *californica* adult was found in a Denver *acadica* colony.

Habitat along streams with willows, mostly Transition Zone and on the c plains. Hostplants tree-shrub Salicaceae: *Salix exigua, discolor, sericea, nigra, petiolaris*.

Eggs whitish, with green and pink tints, laid on host twigs. Larvae eat leaves. They are associated with ants; no nests. Larva grass-green, with a white lateral line, a dark-green middorsal band (edged by white bands blended laterally with the ground color), and narrow white oblique subdorsal dashes (with green between them). Pupa yellowish-brown, with small darker-brown spots, a dark ventral stripe on the abdomen, and dark dorsal and lateral bands. Eggs hibernate.

One flight, L June-E Aug. Adults sip the nectar of flowers, esp. milkweed. Males perch and seldom patrol on low plants near the host, from about 1:50 P.M. to dusk, to await females.

Color Plate 34

305. Satyrium californica   Western Hairstreak

S. californica and *S. sylvinus* (306) have smeared orange spots on the ups (rarely only one), esp. on the uph and on females, unlike *S. acadica* (304). The uns is brownish to brownish-gray, with several to many orange unh crescents and usually with a thin red crescent capping the blue unh spot.

Habitat Upper Sonoran to Transition Zone chaparral and open woodland. Hostplants shrub and tree Rosaceae: *Amelanchier alnifolia, Cercocarpus montanus, betuloides, Prunus virginiana*; Fagaceae: *Quercus*, probably *Q. lobata*; Rhamnaceae: *Ceanothus cuneatus, velutinus*; Salicaceae: *Salix*.

Eggs whitish, laid in clusters of about two to four in crevices of host twigs, cemented with copious clear glue. Larvae eat leaves; no nests. Larva gray-brown, with large gray middorsal spots, white subdorsal chevrons, cream dashes above the spiracles, and a cream lateral ridge; prothorax black on top. Pupa red-brown mottled with black spots, with ivory-green wing cases and underside. Eggs hibernate.

One flight, M June-E Aug. Males perch and sometimes patrol on top of trees, usually on hilltops, from about 2 P.M. to dusk to await females.

Color Plate 34
Fig. 35 (ultraviolet)

306. Satyrium sylvinus   Western Willow Hairstreak

Resembles *S. acadica* (304) and *S. californica* (305), but lacks the orange crescent capping the blue unh spot (rarely with a touch of orange), has just one or a few orange unh spots, and often has small black unh spots; the unh is whiter except in the northwest. Ssp. **sylvinus** (most of the area, including mountains in Nev. and lowlands in w and E Ore.-sw Ida.-c Wash.) has tails and a whitish-gray uns. Ssp. **dryope** (Santa Clara Co., Calif., south to the Tehachapi Mts.; Mono Co., Calif., to lowland c Nev.) lacks tails, and the uns is nearly white. Ssp. **unnamed** (Cascades, Blue Mts., and Rockies from N Calif. to s B.C., and the mountains of Ida., NE Nev., N Utah, and C Wyo.) has tails and a gray uns (it lacks the orange cap and has fewer orange spots than *S. californica*). *S. sylvinus* occurs with *acadica* on the plains of Fremont Co., Colo., without interbreeding.

Habitat Upper Sonoran to Canadian Zone streamsides and ditches with willows. Hostplants tree-shrub Salicaceae: *Salix exigua, hindsiana, lasiolepis*.

Eggs pale greenish-white, laid singly on host stems. Larvae eat leaves; no nests. Larva pale green, with a white subdorsal line and two white oblique dorso-lateral dashes on each segment, the lateral ridge yellow. Pupa pale olive-green mottled with dark green, the abdomen pale greenish-brown with brown dorsal mottling. Eggs hibernate.

One flight, May at low altitude in N Calif., June in the Calif. Coast Ranges, M July-M Aug. in the north and at high altitude. Adults sip the nectar of flowers, esp. milkweed. Males perch on low plants near the hosts to await females, and seldom patrol about the hosts, from about 9:50 A.M. to 3 P.M.

Color Plate 33

307. Satyrium liparops   Striped Hairstreak

The numerous white lines and bands on the dark uns are diagnostic. The blue unh spot of *S. liparops* and *S. kingi* (308) is capped with orange, and males have an extra small scent pad (stigma) on the upf between the bases of veins M_3 and CuA_1. In *liparops* the unf median bands are wider and more tilted than in *kingi*. The orange upf patch is small or absent in most areas (ssp. **strigosum**), very large in s Ga.-Fla. (ssp. **liparops**; marginal orange and blue unh spots larger).

Habitat Gulf Coast to lower Canadian Zone deciduous woods, prairie streamsides, and (westward) foothill canyons. Hostplants tree and shrub (rarely herb) Rosaceae: *Prunus pennsylvanica, nigra, serotina, virginiana, americana, domestica, cerasus*[t], *ilicifolia*[t], hybrid *cistena, Rubus, Malus pumila, Pyrus melanocarpa, Crataegus boyntoni, pruinosa, Amelanchier canadensis, Sorbus*; Juglandaceae: *Carya*; Betulaceae: *Betula papyrifera, Carpinus caroliniana*; Fagaceae: *Castanea dentata, Quercus rubra, laevis*; Oleaceae: *Fraxinus*; Ericaceae: *Rhododendron calendulaceum, Vaccinium arboreum, corymbosum*; Salicaceae: *Populus tremuloides, ?Salix*. Doubtful are *Ilex opaca* (Aquifoliaceae), *Liquidambar styraciflua* (Hamamelidaceae; pupation site), *Podophyllum peltatum*[t] (Berberidaceae).

Eggs reddish-purple, laid singly on host twigs and buds. Larvae eat fruits, buds, and leaves, preferring the fruits of some plants; no nests. Larva green (more white beneath), with a yellowish middorsal and a yellowish lateral line, many yellowish oblique subdorsal lines, and a yellowish lateral patch on the rear. Pupa dull yellowish-brown or dark reddish-brown, with brown markings, a brown dorsal band, and a dark ventral abdominal line. Eggs hibernate.

One flight, M May-June southward, July-E Aug. northward and in mountains. Males perch on bushes, etc., all day, mainly in gulches, to await females.

Color Plate 33

308. Satyrium kingi   Sweetleaf Hairstreak

The unf is similar to that of *S. caryaevorus* (309), but the unh has an orange cap on the blue spot.

Habitat Lower Austral Zone open brushy hardwood forest. Hostplants shrub and tree Symplocaceae: *Symplocos tinctoria* (main host, in Ark., Ga., Fla., S.C., N.C.); Ericaceae: raised on *Rhododendron calendulaceum* (assoc. with *Vaccinium crassifolium*); also assoc. with Hamamelidaceae: *Liquidambar styraciflua*.

Eggs laid singly on host twigs. Larvae eat leaf buds and leaves, refusing flowers and fruits. Larva green, with darker-green oblique lateral stripes. Pupa tan with many black specks. Eggs hibernate.

One flight, M May-M June (rarely Aug.) southward and along the coast, M July-M Aug. in mountains.

Color Plate 33
Fig. 71

309. Satyrium caryaevorus   Hickory Hairstreak

S. caryaevorus lacks the orange cap on the blue unh spot present in *S. kingi* (308) and *S. liparops* (307). The dark unf postmedian band is usually wider than in *S. calanus* (310), with the middle dashes more offset toward the wing base. The white line on the blue unh spot is much closer to the wing base than is the white line on the orange-and-black eyespot, and the black unh spot is usually thicker than its orange cap. A few *caryaevorus* are like *calanus* in these traits. The male stigma is thinner than that of *calanus*. The male genitalia has two spines aimed at each other (Fig. 71; *liparops* has small spines, *calanus* none). The female has two spadelike projections around the ostium bursa (Fig. 71), seen by brushing away the scales at the end of the abdomen (absent in the other spp.).

Habitat Upper Austral to lower Canadian Zone deciduous woods. Hostplants tree Juglandaceae: *Carya ovata, glabra, cordiformis, Juglans cinerea*; Oleaceae: *Fraxinus nigra, americana*; Fagaceae: *Quercus rubra, Castanea dentata*; possibly Rosaceae: *Crataegus*.

Larvae eat the lower surface of leaves; no nests. Larva yellowish-green (sometimes yellowish-brown on the sides), with a dark-green middorsal band (edged by white dashes), dark-green or brownish diagonal subdorsal streaks (edged by whitish or light green), and a white or yellowish lateral line; *or* larva lacking dark dorsal and lateral markings; head green. Pupa light mottled brown. Eggs hibernate.

One flight, June-E July southward, L June-E Aug. northward. Males perch nearly all day high in the trees to await females.

Color Plates 32, 33
Figs. 38 (stigma), 71

310. Satyrium calanus   Banded Hairstreak

Most like *S. caryaevorus* (309) and *S. edwardsii* (311) in lacking an orange cap on the blue spot, and in having the unf postmedian band usually narrow, but somewhat variable. The orange-red cap in cell CuA_1 is usually as thick as or thicker than the black spot. Males lack the two genitalia spines and females lack the two lamella processes found on *caryaevorus* (Fig. 71). Ssp. **calanus** (Fla., SE Ga., and to some extent s La.) is larger and has an orange uph spot on the female and larger unh marginal spots (sometimes the red unh patch is as large as in some *Fixsenia favonius favonius*, 351). In ssp. **albidus** (w Colo.), the uns is tan instead of blackish-brown (a form **heathi**, with a mostly white uns, is frequent in Routt Co., Colo., but rare elsewhere; this character is present but rare in other hairstreaks also). In ssp. **falacer** (=*boreale*; most of the range), the uns is blackish-brown, and the unh has small red spots.

Habitat open deciduous woodland from the Gulf Coast to lower Canadian Zone. Hostplants tree Fagaceae: *Quercus prinus, macrocarpa, alba, rubra, laevis, falcata, incana, gambelii, Castanea dentata*; Juglandaceae: *Carya glabra, ovata, Juglans cinerea, nigra, microcarpa*; Rosaceae: *Malus pumila*[t] (assoc. with *Prunus virginiana*); Aceraceae: *Acer negundo*; Oleaceae: *Fraxinus*.

Eggs pale green, laid on host twigs. Larvae eat catkins and they eat holes in leaves; no nests. Larva grass-green, with lighter-green (or whitish) and darker-green longitudinal lines and a dorsal line of dark triangles; *or* larva pinkish-brown without markings (sometimes with heavy dark markings on the front and rear, with a darker middorsal band); head green or greenish-brown. Pupa light brown to darker brown, mottled with dark brown. Eggs hibernate.

One flight, L Apr.- E June southward, July-M Aug. in the north and in high mountains. Adults sip the nectar of yellow and white flowers. Males perch on shrubs, etc., all day, mainly in gullies or in small clearings, to await females.

311. **Satyrium edwardsii** Scrub-Oak Hairstreak

Color Plate 33

Like *S. calanus* (310), but the unf postmedian spots are edged inwardly with more white and shaped more like a chain than a continuous stripe. The unh spots are orange and number about five, including an orange streak next to the abdomen that is as long as the blue spot (*calanus* usually has two to four). The male and female genitalia resemble those of *calanus*.

Habitat Transition to lower Canadian Zone oak woodland, often on sandy soil or on ridges. Hostplants tree Fagaceae: *Quercus ilicifolia, coccinea, macrocarpa, velutina, alba*. Doubtful are *Crataegus* (Rosaceae), *Carya illinoensis*[t] (Juglandaceae).

Eggs laid singly (rarely up to four in a cluster) in the crevices of twigs of young host trees. Young larvae eat host buds by day; older larvae eat leaves at night, and in the day rest around the trunk base within a chimney of litter built by ants. These ants (*Formica integra*) stay near the larvae and feed on honeydew produced by the fourth-stage larvae and on the honeydew of treehoppers and scale insects (R. Webster, M. Nielsen). Larva dark brown or greenish-brown, with a dark middorsal band (with narrow whitish somewhat oblique dashes beside it) and narrow whitish dashes on the lateral line. Pupa yellowish-brown, with darker-brown marks and a dark lateral band. Eggs hibernate.

One flight, M May-E July southward, L June-E Aug. northward. Males perch all day on oaks or nearby trees to await females.

312. **Satyrium auretorum** Gold-Hunter's Hairstreak

Color Plate 33

Resembles *S. calanus* (310) somewhat, but the range differs, the uns spots are vague, and the ups may have orange patches (esp. in females).

Habitat lowland Calif. chaparral and oak woodland. Hostplants tree Fagaceae: *Quercus wislizenii, douglasii, dumosa*.

Eggs green, turning purple, laid singly on host stems. Larvae eat leaves; no nests. Larva apple-green with white points and a white lateral band (often edged beneath by pink); *or* larva pale orange with a lemon-white lateral band; neck with a reddish shield. Pupa pinkish-tan, with dark-brown dots (the wings sometimes whitish) and brown middorsal dashes and spots. Eggs hibernate.

One flight, L May-M July. Males perch and sometimes patrol on treetops on hilltops to await females, and sometimes court on flowers, from about 2:45 P.M. to dusk.

313. **Satyrium saepium** Buckthorn Hairstreak

The uniformly metallic-reddish-brown ups is diagnostic.

Habitat chaparral and pine woodland, mostly in Upper Sonoran to Transi-

Color Plate 33

tion Zone. Hostplants shrub Rhamnaceae: *Ceanothus fendleri, cuneatus, megacarpus, greggii, velutinus, sanguineus, integerrimus.* Oviposited on *Quercus* (Fagaceae), but larvae refused it. *Cercocarpus betuloides* (Rosaceae) is dubious.

Eggs greenish-white, laid singly on host twigs, leaves, and buds. Larvae eat the upside of leaves (making holes in them) and flower buds; no nests. Larva green, frosted with numerous whitish points, with faint greenish-yellow dorsolateral chevrons and a whitish or yellow lateral stripe. Pupa brown with blackish mottling. Eggs hibernate.

One flight, M July-Aug. in Colo., L May-E Sep. (but mainly July) from Wash to N Calif., L May-July in s Calif., L Apr.-June on Santa Cruz I. Males perch all day on the side of shrubs (or on top of small ones) on hilltops to await females.

Color Plate 33

314. Satyrium tetra (=*adenostomatis*)   Chaparral Hairstreak

The ups is gray, and the unh has white suffusion beyond the white median line.

Habitat Upper Sonoran to Transition Zone chaparral and pine woodland. Hostplants shrub Rosaceae: *Cercocarpus betuloides*, assoc. with *ledifolius*, possibly *minutiflorus*.

Eggs laid singly or in small clusters on the host, probably usually on twigs but sometimes on leaves. Larvae eat leaves. Larva pale green, covered with orange hairs, with four pale bluish-white diagonal bands on each side of each segment and with a white middorsal band, the prothorax with orange dorsal lines, the shield on the neck reddish (with orange in the center). Pupa pale brown mottled with black. Eggs hibernate.

One flight, June-July. Males perch to await females on the side of shrubs, usually on hilltops but sometimes on valley hostplants, mainly from afternoon to dusk.

Color Plate 31
Fig. 45

315. Satyrium behrii   Orange Hairstreak

Easily identified by the orange ups color and by the broad brown borders on the leading edge of the upf. Ssp. **crossi** (east of the continental divide in Colo.-N.M.) is larger, and darker on the unh. Ssp. **behrii** is elsewhere.

Habitat Upper Sonoran to lower Transition Zone chaparral, sagebrush scrub, and pine woodland. Hostplants shrub Rosaceae: *Purshia tridentata* and *glandulosa* for ssp. *behrii*, *Cercocarpus montanus* for ssp. *crossi*.

Eggs (Fig. 45) greenish-white, turning white, laid singly on host twigs or sometimes leaves. Larvae eat leaves; no nests. Larva green (a few brownish), with a whitish middorsal line (bordered with dark green spots), diagonal lines of yellow, white, and green, and two yellow lateral lines edging a dark-green stripe. Pupa light tan with tiny dark-brown blotches. Eggs hibernate.

One flight, June-E July in s Calif. and sw Colo., mostly July elsewhere. Males perch all day on shrubs on hilltops to await females.

316. Satyrium fuliginosum   Sooty Hairstreak

Identified by the rounded fw, the sooty-brown ups, and the dingy-light-brown uns with a few postmedian and postbasal spots. Resembles females of *Plebejus icarioides* (408, a species of blue) in appearance, patrolling behavior, oviposition, and hostplant use, a good example of convergence. Adults are slightly darker in N Calif.-sw Ore.

Habitat Transition to Hudsonian Zone sagebrush, mostly in hilly areas. Hostplants shrub Leguminosae: *Lupinus arbustus, andersonii, meionanthus, croceus, albicaulis.*

Eggs greenish-white, laid singly on the host or on trash at its base. Eggs overwinter.

One flight, mainly July. To seek females, males occasionally patrol erratically (and sometimes perch) near the hostplants (mainly on ridges), at least in the afternoon.

Color Plate 37

Stray only
Color Plate 61
Fig. 35 (ultraviolet)

317. Ocaria ocrisia   Black Hairstreak

Identified by the black uns ground color and by the blue ups. Tropical; one stray from Mex. recorded in s Tex. (Nov.). Ranges to S. Amer.

318. Ministrymon leda   Mesquite Hairstreak

This little species has a sky-blue ups, a grizzled-grayish uns, a dash in the middle of the unf, and several postbasal dashes on the unh. Form **ines** (in the fall, sometimes in spring) has a dark unh median band without red; *ines* intergrades to the summer form in Sep.

Habitat Lower Sonoran Zone desert thorn forest. Hostplant tree Leguminosae: *Prosopis juliflora* var. *torreyana.*

Eggs pale green with whitish ridges, laid singly on host flowers. Larvae probably eat flowers. Larva yellowish-green, with yellowish-white oblique ridges (connected to a yellowish-white lateral ridge), the ridges sometimes edged with reddish; a cream band above the legs; neck shield reddish (with a lighter band). Pupa pale olive-brown (the abdomen light brown), with black blotches and dots.

Many flights, Apr.-Nov.

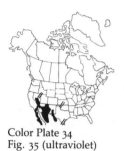

Color Plate 34
Fig. 35 (ultraviolet)

Color Plate 34

319. Ministrymon clytie   Silver-Blue Hairstreak

Silvery-blue on the ups, somewhat resembling *M. leda*, but the unh has large red postbasal spots and a thicker red postmedian band (with white beyond it). The unf has a median dash, unlike most *Strymon* (355-367). Habitat subtropical thorn forest. Ranges to s Mex. Hostplants tree Leguminosae: *Prosopis reptans* and other legumes. Many flights, all year in s Tex.; a stray from Mex. into Ariz. (Sep., sometimes common and temporarily breeding).

Stray only
Color Plate 61
Fig. 35 (ultraviolet)

320. Oenomaus ortygnus   Large Brilliant Hairstreak

The uns is unique. Tropical. Ranges to S. Amer. Hostplant shrub Annonaceae: *Annona globifolia* in Mex. Eggs laid singly on fruits. Larvae bore into fruits; they make no nests, but are sometimes concealed within the fruit. Two strays from Mex. recorded in s Tex. (Dec. 1962).

Stray only
Color Plate 61

321. Thereus zebina   Double-Spotted Slate Hairstreak

Males are blue on the ups, dark gray-brown on the uns; females are whitish-brown on the ups, gray on the uns. Identified by the large size and uns pattern, but in the tropics many other hairstreaks are similar. Tropical. In Colombia, larvae of this species or a close relative feed on a bushy legume with large white oval leaves. Three strays from Mex. (where it flies all year) were recorded in s Tex. (Sep., Nov.).

322. Thereus palegon   Slated Hairstreak

Stray only
Color Plate 61
Fig. 35 (ultraviolet)

The uns is unique. Tropical; one stray from Mex. was recorded in s Tex. (Nov.). Ranges to S. Amer.

323. Allosmaitia pion   Blue-Metal Hairstreak

Stray only
Color Plate 61

Resembles *Thereus zebina* (321), but males have a scent pad on the base of the uph (at the front edge), and on the upf the blue covers only the lower edge. The unh corner has an orange eyespot, then a blue spot capped by a black line (the line broken in *zebina*), then a black spot at the corner (this spot sometimes has a narrow red cap; it is black and orange in *zebina*). The female is more gray-blue than the male. Habitat subtropical woods and scrub. Ranges to C. Amer. One stray from Mex. recorded in s Tex. (Nov.).

324. Calycopis cecrops   Red-Banded Hairstreak

Color Plate 34
Fig. 35 (ultraviolet)

Red uns bands on a brown background identify *Calycopis*. Resembles *C. isobeon* but widespread in se U.S.; the black in the unh eyespot is larger than the red cap, and the red unf band is wide.

Habitat mostly Lower Austral to Upper Austral Zone brush and open dry woods. Hostplants shrub Anacardiaceae: *Rhus copallina, typhina, aromatica;* Myricaceae: *Myrica cerifera;* herb Euphorbiaceae: *Croton linearis.* Doubtful is *Gossypium herbaceum* (Malvaceae). Larvae probably eat mainly detritus on the ground.

Eggs pearly-white, turning tan before hatching, laid singly on the underside of dead leaves, etc., beneath the host. Larvae eat leaves (young larvae eat the underside) and flower buds; no nests. Larva olive-green, with dark-brown hairs and a bluish-green dorsal stripe. Pupa pale brown, with many black dorsal and lateral blotches. Early fourth-stage larvae hibernate.

Several flights, Apr.-Oct. northward, all year in Fla.; a rare stray north into Mich. and Sask. Adults sip flower nectar and mud. Males perch on low trees and shrubs, esp. in the afternoon, to await females.

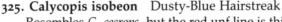

325. Calycopis isobeon   Dusty-Blue Hairstreak

Color Plate 34
Fig. 35 (ultraviolet)

Resembles *C. cecrops,* but the red unf line is thinner and the black unh dot in the eyespot is about as thick as the red cap; *isobeon* is mainly Texan.

Habitat subtropical open areas. Ranges south to Panama. Hostplants primarily dead (even moldy) leaves and fruits or seeds on the ground. Lab larvae can eat fresh and dead leaves, seeds, and berries of dozens of plant families, even poison ivy, bread crumbs, hair follicles, dead insects, and fellow larvae (S. Johnson).

Eggs pale greenish, soon turning white, laid singly on shaded detritus on the ground; the larvae do not climb stems to seek green food. Larva dark brown, with two middorsal blackish bands, with long black hairs; collar a black polygon;

spiracles black, the two on abdomen segment 8 positioned subdorsally resembling two tiny eyes, which possibly startle predators (disturbed larvae even crawl backward briefly). Pupa ochre, with large irregular black blotches on the side of thorax and wings and over the top of abdomen; *or* rarely all ochre; covered with black hair, fastened with 15–30 silk strands over the top.

Many flights, all year in s Tex.; migratory, rarely straying into Kans. and La.

326. Tmolus azia   Tiny Hairstreak

Color Plate 34

Somewhat resembles *Strymon rufofusca* but very small (8-10 mm fw length), the red uns postmedian band wide and fairly continuous. The ups is gray-tan, but may have a whitish hw suffusion (esp. on females).

Habitat subtropics. Ranges south to S. Amer., Jamaica, and Hispaniola. Hostplants herb Leguminosae: *Mimosa malacophylla* in s Tex., *Leucaena latisiliqua* in Fla. Lab females oviposited on flower buds (not leaves) of *Leucaena, Acacia,* and *Lysiloma bahamensis,* and the larvae were raised on the first two (R. Boscoe).

Eggs pale green. Larvae eat flower buds; no nests. Larva whitish, or yellow with orange markings, conspicuously constricted between segments. Pupa tan with darker specks.

Many flights all year in Mex.; an apparent resident in s Tex. (at least Mar.-Oct., occasionally common) and established in s Fla. in 1976 (at least Apr.-Dec.). Two inadvertent imports were recorded in Colo.

327. Tmolus echion   Four-Spotted Hairstreak

Hawaii only (stray Tex.)
Color Plate 34
Fig. 35 (ultraviolet)

Resembles *Ministrymon clytie* (319), but larger (10-13 mm fw length), the ups darker blue, and the unh with large orange postbasal and postmedian spots.

Habitat subtropical scrub and open forest. Ranges to S. Amer. Hostplants (all in Hawaii, except the last five in Latin Amer.) herb Solanaceae: *Capsicum frutescens* (and var. *longum*), "bull-nosed pepper," *Datura arborea, Solanum melongena, nudiflorum, sanitwongsei, tuberosum;* Verbenaceae: *Lantana camara;* Boraginaceae: *Cordia sebestena;* Labiatae: *Hyptis;* Anacardiaceae: *Mangifera indica;* Malpighiaceae: *Stigmaphyllon lindenianum;* Acanthaceae: *Aphelandra deppeana. Ananas* seems to refer to *Strymon basilides,* not to *T. echion.*

Eggs pale green, becoming white, laid singly on host flowers. Larvae eat flowers and fruits, sometimes leaves; no nests. Larva light green, with short white hair. Pupa light brown.

Many flights all year in Hawaii (rare, introduced by entomologists into Hawaii in 1902 to help control *Lantana*) and Mex.; a rare stray into s Tex. (May).

328. Callophrys eryphon   Western Pine Elfin

Color Plate 31

The unh is reddish-brown, patterned as in *C. niphon* (329), but with brown cones beyond the zigzag unh submarginal line. Females are more orange on the ups than are males. "Elfins" lack hairlike tails. They generally appear in early spring. In ssp. **sheltonensis** (Puget Sound, Wash.) the unh is more purplish, with more marginal gray. Ssp. **eryphon** is elsewhere. The eastern N. Amer. records are recent, possibly of introductions from transplanted trees or Christmas trees.

Habitat Transition to Hudsonian Zone (north to Canadian Zone in the east) coniferous forest. Hostplants tree Pinaceae: *Pinus ponderosa, contorta* (and ssp. *latifolia*)*, muricata, monticola, banksiana, flexilis, strobus, Tsuga heterophylla, Pseudotsuga taxifolia*; Cupressaceae: *Thuja plicata*. Assoc. with *P. resinosa, edulis, Abies concolor, Picea mariana* (all Pinaceae).

Eggs pale green, turning white, laid singly at the base of young needles. Larvae bore into the base of young needles and male catkins, and refuse old leaves. Larva dark green, with cream subdorsal and lateral stripes. Pupa brown with dark dorsal spots. Pupae hibernate.

One flight, May-June at low altitude, June-M July at high altitude, mostly May in the north. Males perch all day on the sides of small trees and shrubs in gulch bottoms to await females.

329. **Callophrys niphon**   Eastern Pine Elfin

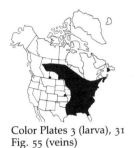

Color Plates 3 (larva), 31
Fig. 55 (veins)

Resembles *C. eryphon* (328), but the unh margin has gray marginal spots with flat brownish caps beyond the black submarginal line, this line jagged but not uniformly zigzag as in *eryphon*. The southeastern ssp. **niphon** has two bars in the middle of the unf (one in *eryphon*), but ssp. **clarki** in Canada has just one bar visible; *clarki* is also smaller, the female ups more orange.

Habitat Gulf Coast to Hudsonian Zone coniferous forest. Hostplants tree Pinaceae: *Pinus banksiana, resinosa, rigida, virginiana, strobus, sylvestris, echinata, taeda, Picea glauca*; probably Cupressaceae: *Juniperus virginiana*. Assoc. with *Pinus clausa, Picea mariana, Larix laricina* (all Pinaceae).

Eggs pale green, turning whiter, laid singly on the new growth of young plants. Young larvae bore through the needle sheath; older larvae eat the leaf tip to the base. Larva green (young larva brown) with a pale-green middorsal line, a narrow white or yellowish lateral line (with a pale-green stripe above it), and white subdorsal stripes (the subdorsals sometimes turning yellowish or orangish in the middle of segments). Pupa dark mottled brown, the abdomen blackish on top. Pupae hibernate.

One flight, Mar.-Apr. southward, May-M June northward. Adults sip flower nectar and mud. Males perch on pines to await females.

330. **Callophrys lanoraieensis**   Spruce-Bog Elfin

Color Plate 31

Resembles *C. niphon* (329) but smaller; the unh is grayer and more obscurely patterned, the white unh spots in cells Sc + R$_1$ and Rs are only 0.6 mm apart (1.5-2 mm in *niphon*), the black unh submarginal crescents are more prominent, and females are brown (not orange) on the ups.

Habitat Canadian Zone spruce bogs, and sometimes *Pinus strobus* barrens in s N.S. Hostplants tree Pinaceae: *Picea mariana* (the main host), occasionally *glauca* and *rubens*.

Young larvae bore into young shoots; older larvae eat whole leaves. Larva green, with a wide white lateral stripe (and perhaps a subdorsal stripe?). Pupae hibernate.

One flight, M May-M June. Adults fly about the tops of the host trees.

Color Plate 33

331. **Callophrys irus**   Frosted Elfin

Identified by the black unh submarginal spot in cell CuA$_1$ (unique to this elfin and rarely absent) and by a stubby tail on hw vein CuA$_2$. The white unf line is more crooked than that of *C. henrici*. The unh is variegated in ssp. **irus**, but more obscure in the sw Ark.-Tex. ssp. **hadros**. (The western ssp. of the next four elfins are also more obscure beneath; no explanation has been proposed.)

Habitat southern to Transition Zone open second-growth woods and scrub. Hostplants herb and shrub Leguminosae: *Baptisia tinctoria, australis, Lupinus perennis, Crotalaria sagittalis*.

Eggs greenish-white or bluish-white, turning yellowish-white, laid singly on host inflorescence. Larvae eat flowers and fruits; no nests. Larva pale bluish-green (the underside whiter), with faint markings, including three whitish dorsal lines, whitish oblique subdorsal dashes, and a whitish lateral line. Pupa brownish-yellow (sometimes with a greenish or reddish tinge) with dark blotches (often on the side of the abdomen); *or* pupa nearly black. Pupae hibernate, in silked-together litter.

One flight, M Mar.-Apr. southward, May northward.

Color Plates 32, 33

332. **Callophrys henrici**   Woodland Elfin

Distinguished from all other elfins by the lack of a male upf stigma; a stubby tail on vein CuA$_2$ of the hw is also characteristic. The white unf line is fairly straight. In most of the range ssp. **henrici** is easily distinguished by the dark-brown edging inside the white unh postmedian line. Ssp. **margaretae** (s Ga. and Fla.) has longer tails and a less-contrasting unh median band. In ssp. **solatus** (c Tex.-N.M.) the unh is more obscurely patterned.

Habitat Gulf Coast to lower Canadian Zone open woods and moist scrub; mesquite woodland in the southwest. Hostplants tree, shrub, and herb Leguminosae: *Cercis canadensis, Sophora secundiflora, Lupinus texensis*; Rosaceae: *Prunus pennsylvanica, susquehanae, americana, serotina*[t]; Ericaceae: *Vaccinium pallidum, corymbosum, vacillans, Leucothoe racemosa* (? J. Abbot), *Gaylussacia baccata*; Aquifoliaceae: *Ilex opaca, vomitoria, cassine*; Ebenaceae: *Diospyros texana*; Caprifoliaceae: *Viburnum acerifolium*; Cyrillaceae: *Cyrilla racemiflora* (possible, J. Abbot).

Eggs pale green with white ridges, turning white, laid singly on the host inflorescence or on a leaf upperside next to leaf buds. Larvae eat flowers, fruits, and young leaves; no nests. Larva green to maroon or red, with pale middorsal and lateral lines and yellowish comma-shaped oblique subdorsal marks. Pupa orange-brown, mottled with brown to blackish, the abdomen broader than that of other species. Pupae hibernate.

One flight, Mar.-Apr. southward, May-E June northward. Adults sip flower nectar and mud. Males perch to await females.

Color Plate 33

333. **Callophrys polios**   Hoary Elfin

The unh is grayish on the outer half, the base darker.

Habitat upper Transition to Hudsonian Zone dry sites or bogs in forest. Hostplants shrubby Ericaceae: *Arctostaphylos uva-ursi, Epigaea repens*.

Eggs greenish-white, laid singly on flower pedicels or on the base of leaf buds. Larva bright green, with a light-green middorsal stripe, pale oblique dashes on the flanks, a light-green lateral line, and a white star-shaped mark on top of the neck. Pupa yellowish-brown to dark brown, with brown middorsal and sub-dorsal spots on the abdomen. Pupae hibernate.

One flight, L Apr.-M June northward and in high mountains, Apr.-M May southward. Males perch all day on vegetation in open low spots (such as gulch bottoms or swales) to await females.

Color Plates 3 (larva), 31

334. Callophrys augustus (=augustinus)   Brown Elfin
Identified by the reddish-brown unh. The unh base is darker, but it varies, and tends to be darkest in the northeast (ssp. **augustus**), lightest in the south-west (ssp. **iroides**, sw Colo.-Calif. southward).

Habitat upper Transition to Hudsonian Zone open woods, scrub, or bogs in most of the range; mostly Upper Sonoran to Transition Zone chaparral or open woods in the southwest and in Calif. Hostplants shrubs, trees, vines, herbs—eastward: Ericaceae: *Arctostaphylos uva-ursi* (Colo. and N.W. Terr. as well as N.J.), *Chamaedaphne calyculata, Vaccinium angustifolium, corymbosum, vacillans, Gaylus-sacia baccata, Ledum groenlandicum, Rhododendron, Kalmia angustifolia* (oviposition, but larvae refuse it); on the west coast: Ericaceae: *Arctostaphylos, Arbutus men-ziesii, Gaultheria shallon*; Rhamnaceae: *Ceanothus velutinus* (Utah), *cuneatus, integer-rimus*; Cuscutaceae: *Cuscuta* (?*gronovii*[t]); Polygonaceae: *Eriogonum*[t]; Hydrophylla-ceae: *Eriodictyon californicum*; Rosaceae: *Malus pumila, Holodiscus discolor*; Liliaceae: *Chlorogalum pomeridianum*.

Eggs pale bluish-green, turning pale yellow-green and finally white, laid singly on host inflorescences. Larvae eat flowers and fruits (older larvae and starving young ones also eat leaves); no nests. Larva (Utah, Calif.) olive-green to light green, with white subdorsal triangles (with a weak reddish-brown spot at the top inside each one, the triangle on abdomen segment 1 mostly replaced by reddish-brown) and a lateral abdominal band of white dashes (each with a weak reddish-brown spot above and below); larva (N.J.) vivid yellow-green, with or without bright yellow markings; larva (Ont.) green with yellow subdorsal bars (and pale crescents beneath them), a yellow lateral line, and a white dorsal line. Pupa light brown with dark blotches. Pupae hibernate.

One flight, May-E June northward and at high altitude (M May-L June in Nfld. and in the Sierra above 2,300 m), L Mar.-M Apr. in Ga., Apr.-May in the southwest. Males perch all day in openings on ridges or on small trees in hillside clearings to await females, and may spend many days at one perching site (males can live up to 16 days in nature). J. Powell found that courtship is most frequent in the afternoon; the male vibrates his wings as in *Hypaurotis* (297) before joining.

Color Plates 4 (larva), 31

335. Callophrys mossii   Stonecrop Elfin
Identified by the red-brown along the unh margin and by the gray edging just beyond the white unh median line. In ssp. **mossii** (most of the range) the white line (and gray edging) is prominent, but it is weaker in the Calif. ssp. **doudoroffi**, which may resemble *C. augustus* (334) somewhat. Ssp. *doudoroffi* dif-fers from Calif. *augustus* in having the unh red-brown only on the outer fourth of the wing (the outer half in *augustus*), the hw fringe more scalloped because of

a brown spot at the end of each vein (evenly curved in *augustus*), the hw fringe with a whiter line midway through the fringe scales, and gray just beyond the white unh median line (esp. toward the rear).

Habitat Transition to lower Canadian Zone wooded canyons; in Calif. Upper Sonoran to Hudsonian Zone rocky areas and cliffs in open woodland. Host-plants succulent Crassulaceae: *Sedum lanceolatum, spathulifolium* (including ssp. *anomalum*), *obtusatum, oregonense, stenopetalum, Dudleya cymosa, Parvisedum pumilum*; assoc. with *S. oreganum*.

Eggs pale bluish-green, turning white just before hatching, laid singly, mainly on the underside of host leaves. Young larvae (in the first and second stages) eat leaves (older larvae prefer flowers and fruits); no nests. Larva usually entirely scarlet (esp. in Calif.); *or* larva pink, reddish with a greenish undertone, yellowish, or (often in Colo.) greenish; all but the reddest usually marked with two red dorsal bands, oblique subdorsal dashes of white above red, and a whitish lateral band below another reddish band. Pupa chocolate-brown with a dark middorsal line, dark dorsal spots, and reddish dorsal lines, Pupae hibernate.

One flight, mostly M Mar.-May (in Calif. Mar. at low altitude to May-June at high altitude). Adults are local, moving an average of only 50 m for males, 52 m for females (maximum 250 m), during their life spans, which average 7 days in males, 8 in females (R. Arnold). To await females, males perch all day in gulches in Colo., on shrubs on slopes (where tall vegetation borders low) or on the top of cliffs in Calif. In courtship, the male pursues the female, they land, flutter, and nudge slightly, and then they join.

Color Plate 33

336. **Callophrys fotis**   Desert Elfin

The only desert elfin except *C. augustus* (334), identified by the whitish-gray outer half of the unh. In sw Colo.-NW N.M. populations, the unh is often yellowish-gray, and the ups is orangish in females.

Habitat Upper Sonoran Zone desert scrub. Hostplant shrub Rosaceae: *Cowania mexicana* ssp. *stansburiana*.

Eggs laid singly on hostplant inflorescences. Larvae eat flower buds, flowers, and young fruits (J. Johnson). Larva dark green (sometimes with subdorsal check-shaped chevrons) or light yellow-green (some larvae with brown shading; about 50 percent of all larvae plain green without markings); larva sometimes developing a red tint before pupating. Pupa brown, sometimes with slight green shading. Pupae hibernate.

One flight, Mar.-Apr. in Calif. (Apr.-June in the higher Panamint Mts.), Apr.-May in Utah. Males perch 1-2 m up on trees and shrubs near the hostplant to await females.

Color Plate 39

337. **Callophrys mcfarlandi**   Beargrass Hairstreak

The green tailless unh with a white oval along the margin is unique.

Habitat Upper Sonoran Zone foothills and high plains. Hostplant shrub Agavaceae: *Nolina erumpens* ssp. *compacta* in U.S., *N. texana* in Mex.

Eggs laid on host flower stalks. Larvae eat flowers and fruits; no nests; assoc. with ants. Larva tan or dark maroon, sometimes pink or light green, with or without whitish middorsal, oblique lateral, and lateral stripes and spots. Pupae hibernate.

Several flights, Feb.-June northward, Feb.-Aug. southward, generally most common early in the season.

338. Callophrys xami   Succulent Hairstreak

Color Plate 39

Resembles *C. gryneus siva* (340) on the uns, but the white unh line is straight from the front margin to vein CuA$_1$, where it projects in a W toward each tail.

Habitat subtropical and Lower Sonoran Zone canyons (including urban gardens in Mexico City). Ranges south to Chiapas, Mex. Hostplants succulent Crassulaceae: in Mex. *Sedum allantoides, texana, Echeveria gibbiflora,* in Ariz. *Graptopetulatum bartrami, rusbii.*

Eggs pale green, turning dull cream, laid singly on host leaves (usually on the underside near the base of the leaf). Larva burrows partly or completely into the thick leaf, usually where the egg is laid; no nests. Larva uniformly yellowish-green, or pale yellow-green with red dashes beside the green heart line and a red lateral stripe, or dull scarlet without marks; all with a darker heart line. Pupa orangish-tan (grayish on top), with fine black mottling and with large middorsal and subdorsal black spots on the abdomen.

Many flights Mar.-Dec.

339. Callophrys hesseli   White-Cedar Hairstreak

Color Plates 36, 39

The first spot in the white unf postmedian band is offset outward, a unique trait. The tailed green unh is patterned like that of *C. gryneus* (340) but grizzled with red-brown patches esp. just beyond the white postmedian line in cells M$_1$, M$_2$, and CuA$_2$. There is often a white dot near the unf base, usually lacking in *gryneus.* Ssp. **unnamed** (Fla.-w S.C.) has two hw tails, and the unh is more boldly marked blue-green to brownish-green. Ssp. **hesseli** northward has one tail.

Habitat coastal-plain stream banks and swamps near the host. The hostplant grows from Maine to La., but *C. hesseli* is not yet known west of Fla. Hostplant tree Cupressaceae: *Chamaecyparis thyoides.* (Lab larvae can also eat *Juniperus virginiana.*)

Eggs light green, turning yellowish-white just before hatching, less prominently reticulate than eggs of *C. gryneus,* laid singly on host foliage. Females can live up to 3 weeks in the lab and lay up to 90 eggs. Larvae eat foliage (young larvae eat new growth); no nests. Larva deep bluish-green or dark green, with a faint light middorsal stripe, white curved subdorsal dashes (oblique in the rear to more transverse in front), white oblique lateral dashes, and four white transverse dashes on top of the thorax. Pupa dark brown with dark distinct marks and a lighter dorsal line. Pupae hibernate.

One flight, M-L May, in Mass.; two flights, L Apr.-May and July-E Aug. in N.J. (the latter flight partial), at least M Mar.-Apr. and May-June southward. Adults can fly as far as a kilometer from the host to obtain nectar, and they sip mud. Males perch on top of the host trees to await females.

340. Callophrys gryneus   Cedar Hairstreak

Color Plates 33, 39
Figs. 51, 52

The unh varies from green to brown, and adults can be confused with *C. hesseli* (339) on the east coast, *C. johnsoni* (341) from Calif. to Wash., and *C. xami* (338) from s Ariz. to s Tex. (For identification, see those species.) In ssp. **gryneus**

ssp. *gryneus, sweadneri*

ssp. *siva*

three brown-unh ssp.

ssp. *thornei, loki*

(Tex. to E Neb. eastward, native as far as E Neb.), the unh is green, with white postbasal bars and a white zigzag postmedian line; summer broods (form **smilacis**) have less orange on the ups, and the orange is sometimes paler esp. westward. Ssp. **sweadneri** (Fla.) is similar but lacks the red unh spot (a larger black spot replaces it), the white unh postbasal bars are smaller, the white unh median line is straighter, and the ups lacks orange (but is sometimes yellow-orange in w Fla.). In ssp. **siva** (Mont. to w Tex., west to Utah and s Calif.), the unh is green as in ssp. *gryneus* (yellowish-green from Ariz. to s Calif.), but there are no postbasal marks, and the white postmedian line is fairly straight. In ssp. **chalcosiva** (Stansbury Mts., Utah, to Nev. and NE Calif., s Ida., and E Ore.), the uns is brown (or green turning brown with age) without postbasal marks, with the unh postmedian line as in ssp. *siva*. In ssp. **nelsoni** (s B.C., extreme NW Mont., south in Ore. and Calif. to the high-altitude San Bernardino Mts. and Laguna Mts. in s Calif., N Baja Calif.), the uns is brown with a violet tint, without white postbasal marks, and the white unh postmedian line is straight but faint. Ssp. **muiri** (c Calif. Coast Ranges, and Guadeloupe I., Mex.) is the same, but the unh is darker violet-brown. In ssp. **thornei** (lowland coastal San Diego Co., Calif.; Cedros I., Mex.), the unh is violet-brown also, occasionally varying to brownish-green, with white unh postbasal marks. In ssp. **loki** (lowland s Calif. south of ssp. *siva*, east and south of Riverside), the unh is green with faint white postbasal marks, and the white unh postmedian line is prominent and angled, suggesting past hybridization with ssp. *gryneus*. Populations of ssp. *siva* tending toward *loki* occur in chaparral habitats in c Ariz. Nearly all the ssp. have been treated as distinct species, but wherever two C. *gryneus* ssp. range near each other they intergrade. Ssp. *gryneus* and *siva* intergrade in the Davis Mts., Tex. (Mt. Locke), and at Sitting Bull Falls in SE N.M., where both *siva* and intergrades between the two occur (the unh postbasal spots are present or absent, and the white unh postmedian band is straight to zigzag); K. Roever and R. Bailowitz found that the abdominal structures of the two ssp. are the same. It was once thought that ssp. *gryneus* is sympatric with ssp. *siva* in s Ariz., but *gryneus* does not occur in Ariz. (in the Baboquivari Mts., ssp. *siva* rarely does have white unh postbasal bars, as in ssp. *gryneus*). Ssp. *nelsoni, muiri*, and *loki* (including populations of ssp. *nelsoni* in the northwest with a hardened spot on the female bursa copulatrix) have also been treated as distinct species; they, too, intergrade, and the abdominal traits by which they were once distinguished are too variable to be the basis for species. In one green-unh population connecting *siva* and *loki*, north of Los Angeles, five different wing traits are intermediate between the two (J. Comstock). Ssp. *thornei* seems to represent a mixture of ssp. *loki* and *muiri* or *nelsoni*, and ssp. *loki* intergrades with ssp. *nelsoni* in the Laguna Mts. of San Diego Co., Calif. Ssp. *siva* and ssp. *nelsoni* intergrade in at least four areas: from w Utah to NE Calif., ssp. *chalcosiva* represents clinal intergrading populations, because the unh green becomes brown (some green adults turn brown with age) and the white unh line varies from strong eastward to weak westward; near Big Bear Lake in the San Bernardino Mts., Calif., the unh is green to brown, with variable white markings; at Kennedy Meadows in Tulare Co., Calif., the unh varies like that at Big Bear Lake; and in E San Luis Obispo Co., Calif., the unh green becomes darker, approaching the brown coastal ssp. *muiri*.

Habitat Lower Austral/Upper Sonoran to Hudsonian Zone dry or rocky open areas wherever juniper-like trees occur. Hostplants (superscript = first letter of ssp. except W=*sweadneri*; capitalized superscripts record oviposition or larvae found in nature, uncapitalized superscripts merely adults found on the plant) tree Cupressaceae: *Juniperus virginiana*[Gs] (plus hybrids with *scopulorum*[gs] and *horizontalis*[gs]), *scopulorum*[Nsc], *asheii*[g], *pinchotii*[gs], *deppeana*[gs], *communis*[g], *silicicola*[Wg], *occidentalis*[nsc], *californica*[Lmst], *osteosperma*[sc], *flaccida*[s], *monosperma*[s], *Thuja plicata*[N], *Calocedrus decurrens*[N], *Cupressus forbesii*[T], *macnabiana*[mn], *sargenti*[m]; Pinaceae: *Tsuga heterophylla*[N]. Local populations may prefer one plant, although in the lab a *C. forbesii*[T] population ate *J. californica*, a *J. californica*[L] population fed on *Cupressus guadaloupensis*, a *C. decurrens*[N] population ate *Thuja*, and a *J. virginiana*[G] population ate *Chamaecyparis thyoides* (the host of *C. hesseli*).

Eggs pale green, the ridges whiter, laid singly on host foliage tips (esp. on new growth) and on blossoming twigs. Larvae eat foliage tips; no nests. Larva (ssp. *gryneus* and *sweadneri*; Fig. 51) dark green, with a faint light middorsal line, white lateral dashes in a line, white subdorsal dashes (these dashes long and nearly parallel near the rear, short and oblique in the middle of the larva, transverse and yellowish on the thorax), and thin white comma-shaped marks that flare down and backward from the subdorsal dashes on the abdomen. Larva of the western ssp. (*siva, nelsoni, thornei, loki*) nearly identical: vivid green, with darker-green bumps, a faint light middorsal line, a light-yellowish lateral line of dashes, and lemon-yellow subdorsal dashes (with smaller crescents flaring down and backward from the centers of these dashes). The lateral and subdorsal pale dashes are thinner in ssp. *siva* and *nelsoni* than in ssp. *gryneus, sweadneri*, and *loki*. All *C. gryneus* ssp. differ from *C. hesseli* in having light commas flaring from the pale subdorsal dashes, the white lateral dashes in a more even band, and the subdorsal thoracic dashes slightly smaller and yellowish. Pupa (ssp. *gryneus*) brown to pale brown mottled with blackish, the abdomen tinged with reddish. Pupa (western ssp.; Fig. 52) dark brown. Pupae hibernate.

Two flights, L Apr.-E June and L June-E Aug. in the northeast and midwest; several flights, L Mar.-E June and M July-Sep. in SE U.S. and Tex., Mar. and sometimes E to M June in w San Diego Co., Mar.-Apr., L June-July, L Aug.-E Oct. (rarely in Nov.) from lowland s Calif. to w Tex.; one flight, mostly M May-June (occasionally as early as Apr. or as late as July) in most of the west, Apr.-May on most of the Pacific coast. Adults can (rarely) stray up to 15 km from hostplants. Males perch all day on the top and sides of the host trees to await females, more often on ridges than in valleys in the west.

Color Plate 33

341. Callophrys johnsoni   Brown Mistletoe Hairstreak

The ups is mostly brown in males, mostly orange in females. Differs from *C. gryneus nelsoni* (340) in being larger and in having the white unh line complete and narrowly white, the unh without a lilac tint, and the orange upf areas diffused without the dark border of *C. g. nelsoni*.

Habitat Transition to Canadian Zone coniferous forest. Hostplants mistletoe (Viscaceae), which are juniper-like parasites on Pinaceae trees: *Arceuthobium campylopodum* (form *tsugensis* parasitic on *Tsuga heterophylla*, and form *campylopodum* on *Pinus sabiniana*). The similar appearance of *Arceuthobium* to *Juniperus*, the host of *C. gryneus*, may have allowed the forerunner of *C. johnsoni* to transfer to *Arceuthobium* as its hostplant.

Larva indistinguishable from that of *C. spinetorum* (342), yellowish-olive, with red, yellow, and white diagonal subdorsal bars. Pupa dark brown. Pupae hibernate.

One flight, L May-M July, northward and at high altitude; two flights, L Feb.-Mar. and July-Aug., in lowland Calif. Adults sip flower nectar and mud, and fly down valleys to seek them. Males perch on treetops on ridges or hilltops to await females.

Color Plate 35
Fig. 35 (ultraviolet)

342. **Callophrys spinetorum**   Blue Mistletoe Hairstreak

Identified by the steel-blue ups (brownish in *C. johnsoni*, 341) and the reddish-brown uns. Occasional adults from the Sacramento Mts., N.M., have a trace of a white unh postbasal band, present in the Mex. ssp. *millerorum* ranging to Durango and Hidalgo.

Habitat Upper Sonoran to lower Hudsonian Zone coniferous forest. Hostplants mistletoe (Viscaceae), which are juniper-like parasites on Pinaceae trees: *Arceuthobium vaginatum* (parasitic on *Pinus ponderosa*), *A. campylopodum* (form *campylopodum* on *P. ponderosa*, *P. sabiniana*, *P. jeffreyi*; f. *divaricatum* on *P. edulis*, *monophylla*; f. *abietum* on *Abies concolor*; f. *blumeri* on *P. reflexa*, *P. lambertiana*; f. *laricis* on *Abies lasiocarpa*, *Larix occidentalis*; f. *cyanocarpum* on *Pinus aristata*), *A. globosum* (on *P. michoacana*), *A. americanum* (on *P. contorta*).

Eggs laid singly on the host. Larvae eat all external parts; no nests. Larva green, with a light-olive middorsal band, an oblique subdorsal ridge on each segment (each ridge orange-red-brown, edged obliquely below by white except on the mesothorax and on abdomen segment 1), and a lateral white stripe (containing orange-red-brown blotches before pupation), the neck shield reddish with an olive bar; *or* larva greener or redder, changing color to match the hostplant color. Pupa dark chestnut-brown (wing cases slightly greenish), mottled with black. Pupae hibernate.

One flight, mostly June, northward; several flights, Mar.-Aug. (mostly May and July), in s Ariz.-N.M.-s Nev. and lowland Calif. Adults sip flower nectar and mud. Males perch all day on top of prominent trees (esp. on hilltops) to await females.

ssp. *perplexa*, *affinis*

Color Plate 4 (larva), 5 (pupa), 39
Fig. 49

343. **Callophrys affinis** ("*dumetorum*")   Green Hairstreak

The unh is green, without tails. Similar to *C. dumetorum* (344) in coastal Calif. (see its discussion for identification in that region). Similar to *C. sheridanii* (345), but *C. affinis* is much larger (usually 12-15 mm fw length, vs. 10-13 in *sheridanii*), the ups and unf often have orange, the white unh line is almost never straight, and adults fly somewhat later in spring. The white unh line is usually reduced to just a few spots except in Ariz.-N.M. In ssp. **perplexa** (lowland Calif. to w Ore., Carson Range, Nev., and Puget Sound, Wash.), the ups is gray in males, mostly orange in females, and the unf is half orange. Ssp. **affinis** (Nev., E Wash., Mont., s Ida. to N Utah and NW Colo.) has the male ups slightly orange-tinted, the female ups very orange, the unh more yellow-green, the unf mostly green in front and gray behind, the unh fringe mostly white (not mostly brown as in all other ssp.). Ssp. *perplexa* and *affinis* intergrade (J. Scott, J. Justice): sw Wash. populations are closest to *perplexa* (one adult has the unh band shape of *apama*); N Wash. populations are closest to *affinis* (some adults are bluish-green on the unh as in *C. dumetorum*); and Blue Mts. (of Ore.-Wash.) popu-

ssp. *homoperplexa, apama*

lations are intermediate between sw Wash. populations and *affinis*. Ssp. *affinis* changes to ssp. *homoperplexa* in a narrow zone in w-c Colo., s-c Wyo., and Utah. Ssp. **homoperplexa** (E and sw Colo., s Utah, intergrading southward to ssp. *apama*) resembles ssp. *perplexa*. (Ssp. *perplexa* and *homoperplexa* are similar also in that their larvae both eat plants of several families.) In ssp. **apama** (Ariz.-N.M.), the unf is mostly orange, and the white unh line is complete and bulges outward strongly. Ssp. *perplexa*, *homoperplexa*, and *apama* have been treated as distinct species but they intergrade. In N Kern Co., Calif., ssp. *perplexa* has more unh spots, a grayish-green unh, little or no orange on the unf, and more white on the unh fringe; it intergrades clinally in w Inyo Co. to *C. sheridanii comstocki* at NW Inyo Co., and they have similar larvae (J. Emmel).

Habitat Upper Sonoran to Canadian Zone woodland, chaparral, scrub, dunes, and sagebrush. Hostplants (p, *perplexa*; a, *affinis*; h, *homoperplexa*; x, *apama*) herb Polygonaceae: *Eriogonum*[x] *umbellatum*[ha] (and var. *majus*[a]), *flavum*[a], *latifolium*[P] (rarely), *nudum*[P], *fasciculatum*[P] (ssp. *fasciculatum, polifolium, foliolosum*), probably *wrighti* ssp. *trachygonum*[P]; Leguminosae (Wash. and Calif.): *Lotus scoparius*[P], *crassifolius*[P], *oblongifolius*[P] (and var. *nevadensis*), *strigosus*[P], *argophyllus* var. *ornithopus*[P]; Rhamnaceae: *Ceanothus fendleri*[h] (a major Colo. host along with *Eriogonum*).

Eggs pale green, laid singly on host flower buds, occasionally on leaves. Larvae (Fig. 49) eat flowers and young fruits, occasionally leaves; no nests. Larva (ssp. *perplexa*) light yellow-green with a whitish subdorsal line and a white lateral line, *or* larva paler without lines; body turning pink just before pupation, the shield on the neck reddish, the body ridges less pronounced than in *C. dumetorum*. Larva (Polk Co., Ore.) similar to ssp. *perplexa*, bluish-green with faint light subdorsal and lateral lines. Larva (ssp. *affinis*) grass-green, *or* larva deep red; all with whitish subdorsal and lateral lines and subdorsal ridges. Larva (ssp. *homoperplexa*) usually red, *or* larva green; all but the reddest with a white lateral line and white dashes on the subdorsal ridges; segmental ridges present. Pupa brown with fine blackish mottling, or (*homoperplexa*) reddish-brown with wings tan to brown or green. Pupae hibernate.

One flight, usually May-June (mostly Mar.-E May in Calif., June-July at higher altitudes in Colo.). Adults seem to be rather local; ssp. *homoperplexa* moves very little (J. Scott). Adults may live at least 19 days in nature. O. Shields recaptured 37 percent of males in s Calif. after a day or more on hilltops, including one male after 18 days. Males perch all day to await females, in gulches for ssp. *homoperplexa*, mostly on hilltops for ssp. *affinis*, near the host or on small hills in Calif. and Wash., often in gulches near the s Calif. desert. In courtship, the male pursues the female and flutters behind her, she lands and may occasionally quiver her partly open wings, he lands behind her and may flutter, and they mate.

344. **Callophrys dumetorum** (=*viridis*)   Coastal Green Hairstreak

Like *C. affinis perplexa* (343) in having the unh green without tails, but *C. dumetorum* occurs only near the Pacific coast, the antenna shaft in most adults is whiter beneath (usually solid white on the last 3-6 mm of the shaft, whereas in *affinis* there are more black and white rings), the unh fringe is mostly white except at the base (mostly brown in Calif. *affinis*), the unh is often bluish-green, the unf usually lacks orange and the green usually covers half or more of the unf,

Color Plate 39

and both sexes are gray on the ups (usually with no orange). The unh has zero to many white spots, averaging slightly more than *affinis* (many more at the southern end of the range). *C. dumetorum* was treated as a ssp. of *C. affinis* because they appear to hybridize wherever their ranges overlap. However, J. Emmel found that both species fly together at one coastal site in Monterey Co., Calif. (*dumetorum* mostly M Mar.-M June, *affinis perplexa* mostly M Feb.-Apr. and rarely M June), where less than 10 percent of the adults are intermediate in appearance; each sp. prefers a hostplant (mostly *Eriogonum* for *dumetorum*, mostly *Lotus* and rarely *Eriogonum* for *affinis*), and adults fly mainly near that host. G. Gorelick also found larval differences between the two species, and A. Douglas found that *dumetorum* pupae are more likely to emerge (rather than diapause as nearly all *affinis* pupae do), producing the longer flight period of *dumetorum*. At one time *affinis* also flew near *dumetorum* in San Francisco, but *affinis* is now absent there. In the Inner Coast Range in Stanislaus and Trinity Cos., Calif., are several populations (ssp. **unnamed**) that in adult and larval appearance are mostly *dumetorum*, but somewhat similar to *affinis perplexa*. Ssp. **dumetorum** is elsewhere.

Habitat coastal dunes and foggy hills from Mendocino to Monterey Cos., and several Inner Coast Range sites in oak woodland from Stanislaus to Trinity Cos. Hostplants herb Polygonaceae: *Eriogonum latifolium* (the main host near the coast), *nudum* (in Trinity Co., and var. *auriculatum* in Stanislaus Co. and occasionally in the San Bruno Mts.); Leguminosae: *Lotus scoparius* (often eaten in San Francisco, rarely elsewhere; Emmel).

Eggs pale green, laid singly on host flower buds and under leaves. Larvae eat flowers, young fruits, sometimes leaves (Gorelick, Emmel); no nests. Larva (ssp. *dumetorum*) light yellow-green with a small amount of pink or red (usually on the subdorsal ridges), *or* larva whitish with extensive red; some with light subdorsal and lateral lines; all with light chevrons on subdorsal ridges, the body with segmental ridges. Larva (unnamed ssp.; these larvae eat leaves) yellowish-green, with a yellowish lateral line, faint pale subdorsal chevrons, and a faint subdorsal band; *or* larva dull red to dull pink or purplish-pink (the lateral line dirty-white except in the reddest larvae); all with reduced subdorsal ridges. Pupa (ssp. *dumetorum*) brown to orangish-brown, with fine blackish mottling; *or* pupa (unnamed ssp.) pale orangish-brown to reddish-brown, with fine black specks. Pupae hibernate.

One flight, mostly M Mar.-M June along the coast, Mar.-Apr. in the San Bruno Mts. and Inner Coast Range. Adults are very local. Males perch all day near the hosts to await females. In courtship, the male pursues the female and flutters behind her, they land, he again flutters behind her, and they mate.

Color Plate 4 (larva), 39

345. **Callophrys sheridanii**   Little Green Hairstreak

Slightly smaller than *C. affinis* (343), about 10-13 mm fw length vs. 12-15 in *affinis*; the ups is always gray, the unh is grass-green to grayish-green, the unf is never orange, and the white unh line is well developed and straight (except in s Ore., the Sierra, and the s Great Basin). Both *sheridanii* and *affinis* show parallel variation in the southwest, where the white unh line bulges outward and the unf has less green. Ssp. **sheridanii** (s Mont. south to E Ariz. and s N.M.) has a thick straight white unh line. Ssp. **newcomeri** (w Mont.-Wash.-NE Ore.) has a thin straight white unh line, and seems to intergrade in Ore. to ssp. **lemberti** (s Ore. to Sierra Nevada, Calif., at high altitude), in which the white unh line is absent to complete, straight to bulging outward. Ssp. *lemberti* intergrades in variable populations in sw Nev.-Inyo Co., Calif., to ssp. *comstocki*. In ssp. **comstocki** (NE Mojave Desert, Calif., s Nev., sw Utah, NW Ariz.), the white unh line is complete (sometimes only a few spots) and bulging outward, the unf has less green and more gray in the middle of the wing, the unh is more grayish-green (dark grass-green in the other ssp.), and a faint white line is inside the black base of the unh fringe. A desert ssp., **paradoxa** (lowland w Colo., and E Utah), completes the circle: it is intermediate between *comstocki* and *sheridanii*, with the white unh band bulging to nearly straight (although the band may be complete to nearly absent), the green grayish-green to usually dark green as in ssp. *sheridanii*, and the unf gray extensive as in ssp. *comstocki*.

Habitat Transition to Canadian Zone (rarely Alpine) woodland, sagebrush, and chaparral in the Rockies and NW U.S.; Hudsonian to Alpine Zone rock garden, open woodland, and scrub from s Ore. to the Sierra (down to Transition Zone in the Carson Range, Nev.), mostly Upper Sonoran Zone desert canyons for ssp. *paradoxa* and *comstocki* and populations intergrading with them. Hostplants (superscript = first letter of ssp.) herb Polygonaceae: *Eriogonum*[nc] *umbellatum*[sl] (and var. *dichrocephalum*[s]), *elatum*[l], *incanum*[l], *heermanni*[c], a vinelike sp.[s], *jamesi* var. *wootonii*[s], *compositum* var. *lieanthum*[n], *nudum* var. *deductum*[l], *corymbosum*[p], *kennedyi*[c]; assoc. with *E. marifolium*[l], *ovalifolium*[lc].

Eggs very pale green, turning white prior to hatching, laid singly on the hostplant, mostly on leaves. Larvae eat the surface of leaves or they eat holes through them (*C. dumetorum*, 344, and *affinis*, 343, prefer flowers and young fruits). Larva (ssp. *sheridanii*) green, with a white subdorsal line and a faint light lateral line; larva (ssp. *paradoxa*) green or pale pinkish-green, with pale-yellow lateral, subdorsal, and narrow middorsal lines; larva (ssp. *newcomeri*) green to pink. Larva (ssp. *lemberti*) green to bluish-green, with a pale yellowish to white lateral line, and with pale whitish subdorsal lines on moderate ridges; *or* larva grayish-green, with whitish (edged with red) lateral and subdorsal lines; *or* larva dull red to dull pink, the subdorsal and lateral lines faint (except the lateral line sometimes dirty-white). Larva (ssp. *comstocki*) green, with a cream lateral line, a cream subdorsal line, and faint whitish chevrons on moderate subdorsal ridges. All five ssp. have moderate subdorsal and segmental ridges somewhat resembling the ridges of *C. dumetorum*. Pupa medium brown (in ssp. *lemberti* and *paradoxa*, pale orange-brown to reddish-brown), with fine dark mottling (less on the wings). Pupae hibernate.

One flight, L Mar.-M May from lowland Colo. to Wash., M June-July at high altitude, Mar.-Apr. (with partial flights in June-July and Aug.-Sep.) in the Calif.-Nev.-sw Utah desert, M Apr.-M May in the E Utah-w Colo. desert. Males perch all day to await females, in hillside swales (or depressions in flat land) in most ssp., in gulch bottoms in ssp. *comstocki* and *paradoxa* (and in c Nev. *lemberti-comstocki* populations).

346. Callophrys goodsoni   Silvery Green Hairstreak

s Tex. only
Color Plate 38
Fig. 35 (ultraviolet)

Identified by the silvery-blue on the uph and the lower part of the upf, by the lack of tails, and by the presence of only one brown spot in the hind corner of the green unh. Habitat subtropical streamside woodland. Ranges south to Costa Rica. Hostplant herb Phytolaccaceae: *Rivina humilis*. Eggs laid singly on host inflorescences. Many flights, at least June–Nov. in s Tex.

347. Callophrys miserabilis   Sad Green Hairstreak

s Tex. only
Color Plate 38
Fig. 35 (ultraviolet)

Resembles *C. goodsoni* (346), but males are steel-blue all over the ups, the hw is tailed, and several brown spots may dot the green unh. Subtropical. Ranges south to Costa Rica. Hostplant tree Leguminosae: *Parkinsonia aculeata*. Many flights, at least May–Dec. in s Tex.

348. Callophrys herodotus   Tropical Green Hairstreak

Stray only
Color Plate 61

Very similar to *C. miserabilis* (347), but the unh usually has just one brown dot on the hind corner. Subtropical; one stray into s Tex. (June). Hostplants (in Latin Amer.) tree and shrub Anacardiaceae: *Lithraea brasiliensis*, *Schinus molle*, *polygamus*, *Mangifera indica*; Compositae: *Mikania*; Verbenaceae: *Clerodendron paniculatum*, *Lantana camara*, *Cornutia grandifolia*. Eggs laid singly on flowers and flower stalks. Larvae eat flowers and leaves. Larva green.

349. Atlides halesus   Great Blue Hairstreak

Color Plate 34
Fig. 35 (ultraviolet)

Identified by the blue ups and by the mostly black uns with red basal spots.

Habitat wooded areas, mostly south of 38° latitude, but north on the coasts to N.Y. and nw Ore. Ranges to s Mex. Hostplants mistletoe parasites (Loranthaceae) on trees: *Phoradendron flavescens* (var. *macrophyllum* on *Populus*, *Platanus racemosa*, *Juglans*, *Fraxinus*; var. *villosum* on *Quercus*), *californicum* (on *Olneya tesota*, *Prosopis glandulosa*), *bolleanum* var. *densum* (on conifers), *juniperinum* (on *Juniperus*).

Larvae eat male flowers and leaves: young larvae eat the epidermis; older larvae eat the whole leaf. Larva green with traces of reddish, with a yellowish lateral stripe, a darker middorsal line, and short orange hair. Pupa brown, heavily mottled with black. Pupae hibernate, at the base of the tree or under loose bark. Parasitoid wasps are very common in pupae (J. Scott).

Many flights, mostly Mar.–Nov. (all year in Fla. and s Tex.). Males can live for up to 24 days, and are fairly local, often returning to the same tree to await females (J. Alcock). Males perch on treetops on hilltops from about noon to 7:30 P.M. (quitting as early as 4:30 on cool days) to await females.

350. Arawacus jada   Nightshade Hairstreak

Color Plate 61

The banded cream uns is diagnostic. Habitat subtropical open areas. Ranges to C. Amer. Hostplant herb Solanaceae: *Solanum umbellatum*. Larvae eat foliage; no nests. Many flights, all year in Mex.; a rare stray into Ariz. (May).

351. Fixsenia favonius   Southern Oak Hairstreak

Color Plate 33

The wing pattern and shape is like that of *Strymon* (355–367), without any unf median spots, but the uns is brown and the male stigma is large and merely grayish. Ssp. **ontario** (e U.S.) has no (or small) red upf spots. Ssp. **favonius** (the coast of se Ga. and south through peninsular Fla., straying to N.J. or a rare variation there) has the white unf postmedian band offset, the red unh spots fused

ssp. *favonius*

three inland ssp.

Color Plate 33

Color Plate 34
Fig. 35 (ultraviolet)

Color Plate 34
Fig. 35 (ultraviolet)

and smeared, their white caps straighter, a small unh postbasal dash in both sexes, and red upf spots. Populations intergrading between these ssp. occur in coastal N.C. (close to *ontario*), S.C. (intermediate but closest to *ontario* at Charleston), and Ga. (at Savannah close to *favonius*); M. Fisher found that sw Ga., s Ala., s Miss., and Fla.-panhandle populations are also somewhat intermediate. Ssp. *ontario* intergrades clinally through Mo. to ssp. **autolycus** (Okla.-Tex.-NE N.M.), which has large orange upf spots, but the red unh spots are like those of ssp. *ontario*. Ssp. **ilavia** (sw N.M. westward) resembles *autolycus* on the ups, but the unh spots are vague.

Habitat Subtropical to Transition Zone oak woodland. Hostplants (super-script = first letter of ssp.) tree Fagaceae: *Quercus virginiana*fa, *falcata*f, *marilan-dica*f, *nigra*f, *laurifolia*ao, *gambelii*a, *alba*o, *stellata*o.

Eggs laid singly on host twigs. Larvae eat male catkins, buds, and leaves; no nests. Larva yellowish-green, with many green stripes and a yellowish sublateral stripe. Pupa pale brown, slightly mottled with black, with a lateral row of black dots. Eggs hibernate.

One flight, M Mar.-E May in Fla., L Apr.-May in Ga. and Tex., May-June in the north.

352. **Fixsenia polingi**   Rounded Oak Hairstreak

Like *F. favonius autolycus* (351) on the uns, but the ups is all brown, the male fw is rounded, and the male stigma is a small upf spot on the leading edge (large in *favonius*).

Habitat oak woodland of Davis and Chisos Mts., Tex., and Organ Mts., N.M. Closely related to *F. favonius*, which does not occur there. Hostplants tree Fagaceae: *Quercus* (assoc. with *grisea* and *emoryi*).

Eggs laid on twigs in the lab. Eggs hibernate.

Two flights, M May-June and M Aug.-E Sep., the latter perhaps partial. Adults rest on oaks and fly about them.

353. **Hypostrymon critola**   Grizzled Hairstreak

Identified by the gray uns with numerous darker streaks, the blue ups, and the very large male upf stigma. In the summer form the unh is less striated, and the unh postmedian line is orange, compared to the spring form **ines**. Habitat streamside woodland among desert scrub in s Ariz. Ranges to sw Mex. On Baja Calif. beaches assoc. with the shrub *Maytenus phyllanthoides* (Celastraceae). Several flights, May and Sep. in Ariz., all year in Mex.

354. **Parrhasius m-album**   White-M Hairstreak

Similar to *Strymon* (355-367) on the uns, but mostly blue on the ups. The common name comes from the white M on the unh.

Habitat Subtropical to lower Transition Zone woods, generally near oak. Ranges south from Mex. to Venezuela. Hostplants tree Fagaceae: *Quercus virgini-ana*, *marilandica*; Tiliaceae: larvae were taken from *Tilia americana* and raised by G. Pilate. Assoc. with *Q. alba*; larvae eat *Q. virginiana* and *alba* in the lab, as well as other *Quercus* spp. with willow-shaped and lobed leaves. Other reported hosts seem doubtful.

Eggs white. Larva brownish-olive-green or light yellowish-green (the heart darker green), with duller darker-green subdorsal diagonal marks. Pupa brown, with brown dorsal blotches on the abdomen and a black dorsal ridge between abdomen segments 5 and 6 that squeaks.

Three flights, mostly May, July, and Sep., northward; many flights, Mar.-Dec., in Fla.

Color Plate 34

355. Strymon acis   Antillean Hairstreak

In *S. acis* and *S. martialis* (356) the unh postmedian line touches the large red spot; *acis* lacks blue and has two unh postbasal spots.

Habitat subtropical wooded areas. Ranges throughout the Bahamas and Antilles. Hostplants shrub Euphorbiaceae: *Croton linearis* in Fla. pinelands, *discolor* in Jamaica.

Eggs pearly-gray, laid singly on host flower stalks. Young larvae eat flowers, fruits, and the upperside of leaves; older larvae prefer leaves; no nests. Larva whitish-green, yellowish-green, or yellowish-tan, with pale subdorsal and lateral bumps, a pale lateral line, and a dark-green or tan middorsal band (edged with white), the body covered with short tan hair. Pupa pale gray-green or whitish-tan, with small reddish dots, small subdorsal bumps, a dark band on top of the abdomen, and a black dot on front of the thorax.

Many flights all year in s Fla.

Color Plate 34

356. Strymon martialis   Blue-and-Gray Hairstreak

Resembles *S. acis* (355), but the ups is blue and the unh lacks postbasal spots. Habitat subtropical Fla. Ranges throughout the Bahamas and Greater Antilles. Hostplants shrub and tree Ulmaceae: *Trema micrantha* in woods and hammocks; Simaroubaceae: *Suriana maritima* on beaches. Young larvae eat flowers, fruits, and young leaves; older larvae prefer leaves. Larva green, with a faint yellow lateral line, faint yellow oblique subdorsal lines, and dense short white hair. Many flights all year in s Fla.

Color Plate 34

357. Strymon avalona   Catalina Hairstreak

The unh spots are smaller than those of *S. melinus* (358), and *melinus* is rare on Santa Catalina I., Calif., where *S. avalona* lives. Possibly a ssp. of *melinus*. Though *S. avalona* has a different chromosome number than *melinus*, *melinus* has been introduced to Santa Catalina I., and G. Gorelick found intermediates there; the introduced *melinus* may be absorbed by the *avalona* population. The two species share identical male abdominal structures.

Habitat grassy areas and chaparral, common all over the island. Hostplants herb Leguminosae: *Lotus argophyllus* var. *ornithopus*; Polygonaceae: *Eriogonum grande, giganteum*.

Eggs pale gray-green with a bluish cast, laid on blossoms and terminal buds. Larva pale green or pale pink. Pupa pale pinkish-brown or brown (the abdomen ochre, the thorax and head pinkish-white), with olive mottling and several rows of dark-olive spots.

Many flights, Feb.-Dec.

Color Plate 34
Fig. 50

358. Strymon melinus   Gray Hairstreak

The ups is blackish with a conspicuous orange hw spot; the orange spot is larger than in other *Strymon*. The uns is gray, darker gray in early spring than in summer adults, and darker in males than females. The male abdomen is orange.

Habitat tropical to Transition Zone open areas. Ranges south to Venezuela, and an odd ssp. flies on Clarion I. west of mainland Mex. Hostplants herb (occasionally shrub or tree) Leguminosae: *Amorpha, Amphicarpa bracteata*[t], *comosa*[t], *Astragalus bisulcatus, mexicanus, crotalariae*[t], *mollissimus*[t], *Cassia puberula, alata, Desmodium canadense*[t], *nudiflorum*[t], *Glycyrrhiza lepidota, Indigofera texana, Lespedeza hirta, capitata, Lupinus argenteus, texensis, diffusus, Medicago sativa, Melilotus alba, Phaseolus limensis, vulgaris, lunatus* var. *macrocarpus, Pisum sativum, Sesbania drummondi, Trifolium oliganthum, tridentatum, repens, arvense, incarnatum, Vicia, Vigna sinensis;* Malvaceae: *Hibiscus esculentus, syriacus, tubiflorus, Gossypium herbaceum* (cotton; the larva is called the Cotton Square Borer in Tex.), *Callirhoe leiocarpa, Malva parviflora, nicaeensis, neglecta, rotundifolia, Sida hederacea, Sphaeralcea ambigua;* Boraginaceae: *Cynoglossum officinale;* Rhamnaceae: *Rhamnus californica;* Polygonaceae: *Eriogonum effusum, alatum, parvifolium* var. *parvifolium, Polygonum lapathifolium, phytolaccaefolium, Rumex salicifolius* ssp. *triangulivalvis;* Myricaceae: *Comptonia peregrina* var. *asplenifolia;* Zygophyllaceae: *Porlieria angustifolia;* Ericaceae: *Rhododendron calendulaceum;* Loasaceae: *Mentzelia;* Verbenaceae: *Lantana macropoda;* Moraceae: *Humulus lupulus;* Scrophulariaceae: *Verbascum thapsus;* Labiatae: *Hyptis emoryi, Lamium amplexicaule, Salvia mellifera;* Hypericaceae: *Hypericum aureum;* Rutaceae: *Citrus limon;* Euphorbiaceae: *Croton monanthogynus, capitatus, Eremocarpus setigerus;* Rosaceae: *Crataegus marshalii*[t], *pedicellata*[t], *apiifolia* or *coccinea, Eriobotrya japonica, Malus pumila, Rosa californica*[t], *Rubus idaeus* var. *strigosus, Fragaria;* Juglandaceae: *Carya illinoensis*[t]; Ebenaceae: *Diospyros texana;* Apocynaceae: *Echites;* Asclepiadaceae: *Asclepias tuberosa;* Bignoniaceae: *Tecoma stans;* Fagaceae: *Quercus virginiana;* Crassulaceae: *Sedum;* Cactaceae: *Neolloydia intertexta* var. *dasyacantha;* Gramineae: *Zea mays;* Agavaceae: *Nolina microcarpa;* Pinaceae: *Pinus;* Palmae: *Sabal megacarpa.*

Eggs pale green, laid singly on host inflorescences. Larvae (Fig. 50) eat flowers and fruits, rarely young leaves; no nests. Larva straw, purplish-white, pink, reddish-brown, or green, with various other paler marks; head yellowish-brown. Pupa brownish. Pupae hibernate.

Many flights, from spring to fall. Adults bask dorsally. Males perch on small trees and shrubs from about 1 P.M. (rarely as early as 11:15) to dusk, preferably on hilltops, to await females.

Color Plate 34

359. Strymon bebrycia (=*buchholzi*)   Balloon-Vine Hairstreak

Resembles *S. melinus* (358), but the unh postmedian line is red and white (with very little black), there are white unh submarginal dashes like those of *S. alea* (360), the red hw spot is small, and the male stigma is large (black and oval). In *S. rufofusca* (361) and *Tmolus azia* (326), the unh is similar but the postmedian band is shaped differently. Habitat subtropical thorn forest, also desert scrub in Big Bend, Tex. Ranges to c Mex. Hostplant vine Sapindaceae: *Cardiospermum halicacabum;* adults assoc. with *Prunus havardii* in Big Bend. Many flights, all year in Mex., all year in s Tex. (rare), Mar.-Sep. at least in w Tex. Males perch on hilltop bushes to await females in w Tex. (C. Durden).

Color Plate 34

360. Strymon alea (=*laceyi*)   Tarugo Hairstreak

Resembles *S. columella* (364), *bebrycia* (359), and *yojoa* (363), but identified on the unh by having the postmedian spots joined to form a band and the several postbasal spots separate from each other. The uns is darker in winter than in summer adults. Habitat subtropical thorn forest and along creeks. Ranges to s Mex. Hostplant shrub Euphorbiaceae: *Bernardia myricaefolia*. Larvae eat blossoms and buds. Many flights all year in s Tex.

s Tex. only
Color Plate 34

361. Strymon rufofusca   Red-Crescent Hairstreak

Resembles *S. bebrycia* (359) and *S. alea* (360), but the unh postmedian line is red and broken into spots. Habitat subtropical thorn forest. Ranges south to Paraguay and the Lesser Antilles. Hostplant herb Malvaceae: *Malvastrum coromandelianum* in Mex. Eggs laid singly on host flower buds. Many flights, at least Mar.-Dec. in s Tex.

Stray only
Color Plate 34

362. Strymon albata   White Hairstreak

Resembles *S. alea* (360) but identified by the white ups areas. Subtropical. Ranges south to Guatemala. Hostplant bushy herb Malvaceae: *Abutilon incanum*. Eggs laid singly on flower buds and on young leaves of host. Larvae eat flower buds and young fruits. Many flights all year in Mex.; an occasional stray into s Tex. (July, Nov.-Dec.), briefly multiplying at times.

s Tex. only
Color Plate 34

363. Strymon yojoa   White-Stripe Hairstreak

Identified by the white unh postbasal stripe and the two black spots on the uph corner. Habitat subtropical thorn forest. Ranges to C. Amer. Hostplants (Latin Amer.) herb Malvaceae: *Hibiscus* sp. and *tubiflorus*; Leguminosae: *Desmodium axillare*; Gesneriaceae: *Kohleria tubiflora*. Eggs green, laid singly on host flowers. Larvae eat flowers and fruits; no nests. Many flights all year in s Tex.

Color Plate 34

364. Strymon columella   Dotted Hairstreak

Identified by the black unh postbasal dots, by the unh postmedian line, this line broken into dots, and by the two black uph corner spots.

Habitat subtropical open areas and Lower Sonoran Zone desert; two adults near Buffalo, N.Y., were apparently temporary imports. Ranges south to Brazil and through most of the Bahamas and Antilles. Hostplants herb Malvaceae: *Sida hederacea*, *Abutilon permolle*, *Hibiscus denudatus*.

Eggs pale green. Larvae eat stems and young leaves; no nests. Larva dark green, with a darker middorsal line, a paler lateral ridge, and a light diamond-shaped spot just behind the head. Pupa pinkish-tan (the wings pale greenish), the abdomen with black dots and a greenish dorsal band, the side of the thorax blotched with brown.

Many flights, all year in Tex. and Fla., Mar.-Oct. in s Calif.

Stray only
Color Plate 61

365. Strymon limenia   Disguised Hairstreak

Resembles *S. columella* (364), but the uph corner lobe is narrowly orange, the orange unh spot is a little longer, and the unh postmedian line angles toward the corner. Subtropical, temporarily established 1971-76 on the Fla. Keys (from the Greater Antilles) but no longer present. Many flights, at least Mar.-Dec.

366. **Strymon cestri**   Spotted Hairstreak

s Tex. only
Color Plate 34

S. cestri and *S. bazochii* (367) lack tails and orange spots. *S. cestri*, however, has many black unh spots, including one on the margin, and males have very little blue on the ups (females have much blue). Subtropical. Also in s Baja Calif.; ranges to C. Amer. Many flights in s Tex. (Mar.-Oct.); rare.

367. **Strymon bazochii**   Mottled Hairstreak

Color Plate 34
Fig. 35 (ultraviolet)

Resembles *S. cestri* (366), but males are blue on the ups (almost as blue as females), and the unh is vaguely mottled. Habitat subtropical open areas. Ranges south to Brazil and the Greater Antilles, and to Hawaii. Hostplants herb Verbenaceae: *Lippia alba* and *graveolens* (both Tex.), *Lantana camara*; Labiatae: *Hyptis pectinata*, *Ocimum basilicum* (all Hawaii). Introduced into Hawaii to control *Lantana*, which is still common (and *Lantana* is pollinated by butterflies!). Eggs laid singly on host inflorescences. Larvae eat flowers and fruits; no nests. Larva dull green, covered with white and dark bristles. Pupa light brown, with dark spots. Many flights all year.

368. **Erora laeta**   Turquoise Hairstreak

Color Plate 38
Fig. 35 (ultraviolet)

Identified by the untailed turquoise unh with orange spots. The Ariz.-Tex.-Mex.-Guatemala ssp. **quaderna** has a little less blue on the male ups and a little more orange on the female fringe, but these traits are variable. Common in sw U.S., but the eastern ssp. **laeta** is seldom seen.

Habitat upper Transition to Canadian Zone oak, hazelnut, or beech forest in the east, mostly Upper Sonoran Zone mountain oak/pine/juniper woods in the west. Hostplants (l, *laeta*; q, *quaderna*) tree Betulaceae: *Corylus cornuta*[l]; Fagaceae: *Fagus grandifolia*[l], almost surely *Quercus* in nature[l], *Q. emoryi*[q]; supposedly also Rhamnaceae: *Ceanothus*[q]. H. Mousley observed oviposition on *F. grandifolia*, and R. Whittaker found a larva on it. F. Rindge raised larvae on *Corylus cornuta*. W. Wright, Jr., raised lab *laeta* larvae successfully on *C. cornuta*, *Quercus alba*, and *Salix* (Salicaceae), but was not successful with *Fagus* or *Betula* (Betulaceae); his young larvae were greener in color on *Salix*, rustier on *Corylus*. *Salix* is a possible host in nature. M. Douglas raised lab *laeta* larvae on leaves of a white-oak species (*Quercus*) with small leaf lobes, and ssp. *quaderna* larvae on an Arizona white oak with willow-shaped leaves and on another oak species. A. Klots found a *quaderna* larva on *Q. emoryi*.

Eggs pale green, turning gray-white, laid singly, on at least the underside of leaves. Larvae eat leaves (young larvae skeletonize them), and older larvae also eat fruits; no nests. Larva (ssp. *laeta*) pale-green (often yellowish-green) or rusty-brown, with a carpet of short pale hair, two reddish spots on top of the mesothorax, dark green on abdomen segment 1 above the side (with two reddish dorsal spots), a large rusty or brown patch on top of abdomen segment 6 (extending but decreasing in width to segment 8), and a green lateral patch above the first four pairs of prolegs; head tan. Larva (ssp. *quaderna*) pale green, with a carpet of short tan hair, a pair of yellowish-brown spots on the mesothorax, some slightly darker subdorsal patches, and darker patches on top of abdomen segments 6 and 7. Pupa (both ssp.) rust-colored with dark-brown specks, turning a more uniform brown after a day or two. Pupae possibly hibernate.

Two flights, May-M June and July-E Aug. in the northeast, M Apr.-M May and L June-July (rarely a partial third flight L Aug.-E Sep.) in the Appalachians, L Mar.-Apr. and L June-July in the southwest. Adults sip flower nectar and mud, and often fly down valleys to find them. Males perch on top of trees on hilltops (probably on the tallest trees in level E U.S. woods) at least in the afternoon, to await females. Scared adults fly to the top of the nearest tall tree.

369. Electrostrymon endymion   Ruddy Hairstreak

Stray only
Color Plate 33

Identified by the orange ups (with a broad brown margin on the front of the upf), the tan uns, and the red unh line. Subtropical, occurring in s Tex.; one record from s Fla. (Feb.) in 1982. Ranges to s Brazil. Many flights, at least Apr.-Dec. in s Tex. Males perch on shrubs on hilltops (in Colombia) to await females.

370. Electrostrymon angelia   Fulvous Hairstreak

Color Plate 33

Resembles *E. endymion* (369), but the ups is coppery-brown, the unh postmedian line consists of a few white dots, and the blue and orange unh spots are smeared toward the wing base.

Habitat subtropical shrubby areas. Ranges to the Bahamas, Greater Antilles, and Virgin Is. Hostplant shrub Anacardiaceae: *Schinus terebinthifolius*.

Eggs pale green, laid singly on leaves and stems. Larvae eat leaves, esp. young leaves. Larva dark reddish-brown with a bluish tinge. Pupa reddish-brown on the abdomen, the thorax and wing cases tan with darker markings.

Many flights all year. An Antillean native recently established in s Fla.

Tribe Lycaenini: Coppers

The Lycaenini (about 50 species) occur mainly in Eurasia and North America, but a few species occur in New Zealand, New Guinea, the Asian tropics, Africa, and tropical America. The 14 North American species occur from the central U.S. north to the Arctic.

Adults are often "coppery" in color, hence the common name, but they may be yellow, gray, blue, or brown above, often white beneath. Larvae usually eat Polygonaceae plants. Larvae and pupae are like those of hairstreaks and blues. Eggs usually hibernate in North America, but in many Palaearctic species and in two American species recently arrived from Asia the larvae hibernate.

The thorax is rather thick, and flight is strong but fluttery, not as erratic as that of the hairstreaks. Adults do not migrate and are fairly local. All species feed on flower nectar as adults. Males of most species perch to await females, but some patrol. *Lycaena heteronea* (380) patrols like the blues, and like them is blue. It was first named as a blue, and in appearance, behavior, and larval hostplant it is a blue, but its body structures resemble those of coppers. It flies more swiftly than the blues, and makes longer flights than most coppers. If a mating pair of coppers is startled, either the male or the female flies, toting the other below.

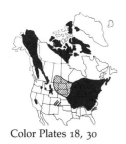

Color Plates 18, 30

371. Lycaena phlaeas Small Copper

Identified by having the unh mostly gray with an orange marginal band, the uph mostly gray-brown, and the upf mostly shiny red or orange. Ssp. **americana** (Ont.-Kans., eastward; a rare introduction in the Great Plains) is bright orange, the spring flight lighter. Form **fasciata**, with larger black upf spots, is usually rare, but it makes up half the adults at one Penn. site. Ssp. **arethusa** (Alta., but doubtful in c Alaska; the upf suffused with brown) and ssp. **polaris** (the rest of the west, the Arctic, and Scandinavia; the upf shining yellow-orange) sometimes have blue uph submarginal spots (form **caeruleopunctata**). Ssp. *phlaeas* is in Europe. Also occurs in Asia and N Africa (I found it at the base of Mt. Kenya).

Habitat Transition to Canadian Zone waste places for ssp. *americana*, Canadian to (usually) Alpine Zone rocky places in the Rockies, alpine fell-fields in the Sierra, and arctic tundra. Hostplants herb Polygonaceae: *Rumex acetosella, crispus, acetosa, Oxyria digyna*, in Europe occasionally *Polygonum*; assoc. with *R. alpestris*.

Eggs greenish-white, soon turning white, laid singly on host leaves or stems. Larvae eat leaves (young larvae eat the underside); no nests. Larva red (with yellowish laterally), light-green (with a dusky middorsal line, sometimes with red dorsal dashes, sometimes with a red lateral stripe), or yellowish-green. Pupa light brown or reddish, tinged with yellowish-green, with many dark dots. Half-grown larvae hibernate. T. Sakai and S. Masaki found that diapause is triggered by short photoperiod and low temperature (the pale-adult Japanese spring form is also triggered by short photoperiod).

Several flights in ssp. *americana* (June-Sep. northward, M Apr.-M Oct. southward); one flight in the other ssp. (July in the Arctic, July-Aug. southward). Adults move short distances (averaging only 43 m in Britain; T. Shreeve). Japanese adults live up to 14 days in nature. Adults bask dorsally, and roost in low vegetation. Males perch (and sometimes patrol) all day to await females, mainly in low spots on the leaves and flowers of low weeds (alpine males perch in nooks at the base of rocky slopes). They investigate fluttering objects, and can distinguish resting females from males by the uns wing pattern (males do not court resting males). A receptive female lands, the male lands beside her with his wings spread halfway, and he bends his abdomen to mate. An unreceptive female may flutter her wings, crawl away, or fly vertically (Y. Suzuki).

Color Plates 4 (larva), 30
Fig. 35 (ultraviolet)

372. Lycaena cupreus Lustrous Copper

The uns is like that of *L. phlaeas* (371), but the ups is mostly shiny red or orange. Although the female uph may be suffused with brown, it is more orange than in *phlaeas*. Ssp. **cupreus** (Calif.) is shiny red on the ups, and the unh is cream with a long red marginal band. In ssp. **artemisia** (NE Nev., Utah, Wyo. to c Mont.), the ups is usually shiny reddish-orange (the female uph is sometimes brownish), the unh is usually creamy-gray, and the black spots are larger. Ssp. **snowi** (alpine Rockies in Colo. and s Wyo., N Utah, Alta.-B.C.) is shiny brassy-orange on the ups, dark gray on the unh.

Habitat Alpine Zone, esp. in glacial cirques (ssp. *snowi*), Canadian (rarely Transition) to Alpine Zone open areas in Calif., and Transition to Hudsonian Zone sagebrush and meadows elsewhere. Hostplants herb Polygonaceae: *Rumex paucifolius, acetosella, acetosa, Oxyria digyna*.

Eggs laid singly on or next to the host. Larvae eat leaves; no nests. Larva light green (sometimes reddish, or with a red lateral stripe and red dorsal dashes). Half-grown larvae hibernate.

One flight, L June - M Aug. Males perch and often patrol all day in hollows and the rocky depressions of open areas to await females.

373. **Lycaena hyllus**   Bronze Copper

Color Plates 28, 30
Fig. 35 (ultraviolet)

The unh is mostly white, the unf mostly orange, and the uph mostly brown with an orange border. The upf is reddish-brown in males, mostly orange in females.

Habitat Upper Austral to lower Canadian Zone moist meadows, marshes, and lakeshores. Hostplants herb Polygonaceae: *Rumex crispus, verticillatus, obtusifolius, "longifolius," patientia*[t], *Polygonum coccineum*.

Eggs white or greenish-white, laid singly on leaves, petioles, or seeds (or on dead leaves if the plant grows in water). Larvae eat leaves; no nests. Larva velvety yellowish-green, with a dark-green dorsal stripe (edged with yellow). Pupa light yellowish-brown, with brown dots. Eggs hibernate.

Two flights, M June - M July, M Aug. - M Sep., in most of the range; one flight, M July - M Aug., in Alta., Sask., and the s Colo. mountains. Males perch all day on low vegetation to await females.

374. **Lycaena mariposa**   Forest Copper

Color Plate 30
Fig. 35 (ultraviolet)

The mottled gray unh is distinctive. Habitat Canadian to Hudsonian Zone forest bogs and clearings. Hostplant Ericaceae: *Vaccinium arbuscula* in Calif. Eggs hibernate. One flight, M July - Aug. Males perch all day in depressions to await females.

375. **Lycaena nivalis**   Lilac-Edged Copper

Color Plate 30
Fig. 35 (ultraviolet)

The unh is yellow or cream, usually with a pinkish flush on the outer third. Males are tan above, females brown to mostly orange. Geographically variable. In ssp. **nivalis** (Sierra Nevada) the unh is light yellow at the base with a pinkish tint outwardly, and females have yellow patches on the upf. Similar adults from the Warner Mts., Calif., have larger black unh spots, and the females are brown on the upf. In ssp. **browni** (elsewhere), the unh is yellow (pinkish outwardly) and females are yellow to brown on the upf (upf yellow in the Cascade Mts. of Ore. and NW Calif.).

Habitat Canadian to Hudsonian (sometimes Alpine) Zone rocky valley bottoms, open woodland, or sagebrush terraces near streams. Hostplants herb Polygonaceae: *Polygonum douglasii*; larvae eat *Rumex* in the lab.

Eggs pale bluish-white, turning white, laid singly at or near the base of the host. Larvae eat leaves; no nests. Larva pale green, with a red dorsal line (edged with white), brownish dorsal and lateral hairs, and small dorsal tubercles. Pupa pale straw-yellow, with brown spots and tiny trumpet-shaped hairs. Eggs hibernate.

One flight, L June - E Aug. Males perch all day in bare shallow depressions in open areas to await females.

Color Plate 30
Fig. 35 (ultraviolet)

376. Lycaena helloides   Purplish Copper

Identified by the orangish unh tint. Resembles *L. dorcas* (377), but is larger (male fw length 14-15 mm, females 15-16 mm); the male fw is pointed, the black fw postmedian spots are farther from the wing base, and the unh is uniformly orangish-ochre. In ssp. **helloides** (most of the range, mostly in lowlands), females are occasionally dark brown but usually quite orange on the ups, and males are brown on the ups, usually with about four orange uph lunules. Ssp. **florus** (high-altitude Rocky Mts. from N.M. to Alta., northwest to Alaska) usually has less ups orange on females and few uph lunules on males; it has been placed in *L. dorcas* (377), but most traits and hostplants are as in *L. helloides*. Ssp. **megaloceras** (mountains in s Mont. and N Wyo.) resembles *florus* but the female upf is cream instead of orange, and the red unh band is reduced.

Habitat coastal and Upper Sonoran to Hudsonian Zone streamsides and valley bottoms. Hostplants herb Polygonaceae: *Polygonum aviculare, lapathifolium, hydropiperoides, persicaria, punctatum, amphibium* (and var. *stipulaceum*), *douglasii*, sp. (probably *hartwrightii* or *careyi*), *Rumex persicarioides, conglomeratus, crispus, hymenosepalus, acetosella, densiflorus, salicifolius* ssp. *triangulivalvis, maritimus* var. *fueginus*; Rosaceae: *Potentilla egedei* var. *grandis* in a Calif. coastal marsh. Yukon adults sip the nectar of and oviposit on *Solidago decumbens* (Compositae, D. Parshall), which is probably not a hostplant.

Eggs pale greenish-white, turning white, laid singly and haphazardly at the base of the host. Larvae eat leaves; no nests. Larva grass-green, with a weak yellowish lateral stripe, two faint yellow middorsal lines, and faint yellow oblique lateral dashes. Pupa yellow-green on the abdomen and grass-green on the thorax, with a fine black middorsal line and dark dots, the wing cases cream. Eggs hibernate.

Several flights, M May-M Oct., in most of the range (June-M Oct. in Sask., Apr.-Oct. in Calif.); one flight M July-Aug. at high altitude, M July-M Aug. in the far north. Adults sip the nectar of flowers, including *Pentaphylloides floribunda* (the *L. dorcas* host), but females do not oviposit on it. Males perch and sometimes patrol all day in depressions to await females.

377. Lycaena dorcas   Cinquefoil Copper

Resembles *L. helloides* (376) but is smaller (male fw length 12-13 mm, females 13-14 mm); the male fw is rounded like that of females, the black fw postmedian spots are a little closer to the wing base than in *helloides*, the unh is purplish-brownish-ochre (with marginal red spots edged by brown, and the ground color is darker inside the black postmedian spots), males have only one or two red uph lunules, and females have very few orange upf spots. Ssp. **dorcas** (most of the range) is small and dark. Ssp. **dospassosi** (N.B.) is larger, with larger black spots, and lighter, tending toward *helloides*.

Habitat Canadian to Hudsonian Zone, in bogs, drier sites in Maine, salt marsh in N.B. Hostplant shrub Rosaceae: *Pentaphylloides floribunda* (= "*Potentilla fruticosa*") for ssp. *dorcas*, probably *Potentilla egedei* var. *groenlandica* for ssp. *dospassosi*. Oviposits on *Vaccinium oxycoccos* (Ericaceae).

Eggs white, laid singly, usually under host leaves near the top of small plants. Larvae eat leaves; no nests. Larva pale green, with short hair, four faint white lines from the top to the side of each segment, and a middorsal dark-green line,

Color Plates 28, 30
Fig. 35 (ultraviolet)

the lateral fold whitish, the prothorax with a diamond-shaped shield; head tan. Pupa green, black, brown, or even purplish, sometimes with faint pale bands on the side of the abdomen. Eggs hibernate.

One flight, mostly July-E Aug. (L July-Aug. in Maine, Nfld., and Lab.). Males seem to patrol and perch near the host to seek females.

Color Plates 4 (larva), 5 (pupa), 30
Figs. 31, 35 (ultraviolet), 46, 47

378. Lycaena epixanthe   Cranberry-Bog Copper

Small, the unh yellowish to cream with small red marginal spots. The ups is brownish, with broad brown uph borders. Resembles *L. dorcas* (377), but has a paler unh. The unh is grayish-cream in ssp. **phaedra** (northeast and west), usually pale yellowish in ssp. **epixanthe** (N.Y., Mass., N.J.).

Habitat cranberry bogs, mostly in Transition to Canadian Zones. Adult density can be more than 1,000 per hectare. Hostplants shrubby Ericaceae: *Vaccinium macrocarpon, oxycoccos*.

Eggs (Fig. 31) white, laid singly beneath leaves and stems near the base of the host. Larvae (Fig. 47) eat shoots and leaves. Larva bluish-green, with white hairs, a dark-green middorsal band (edged with whitish dashes, the band red in young larvae), slightly darker-green oblique dashes on the flanks, and a lighter-green lateral line. Pupa pale yellowish-green to green, with brown blotches and with white dots on the back; *or* pupa rarely solid dark purple. Eggs hibernate (the larva fully developed inside), often under water.

One flight, mostly L June-E Aug. (M June-M July near Ottawa, M July-M Aug. in Nfld.). Adults visit cranberry flowers and sip raindrops. Males perch all day (mostly 10 A.M. to 6 P.M.) on low plants (usually cranberry) to await females. In courtship, the perched male pursues a passing female, she lands, he lands behind and vibrates his wings, and then they mate. A mated unreceptive female flutters her wings, and the male departs.

Color Plate 30
Fig. 35 (ultraviolet)

379. Lycaena gorgon   Buckwheat Copper

Identified by the grayish-white uns (with black spots and red margin), the uniformly reddish-brown male ups, and the creamy-yellow female ups spots.

Habitat foothill woodland and chaparral. Hostplants herb Polygonaceae: *Eriogonum nudum* (vars. *nudum, auriculatum*), *elongatum*.

Eggs pale greenish, turning creamy-white, laid singly on forks of host flower stalks. Larvae eat leaves; no nests. Larva pale turquoise-green, with short white hair, the lateral ridge cream. Pupa pale blue-green, with longitudinal rows of slightly darker dots except on wings, the abdomen with a slightly yellowish shade. Eggs hibernate.

One flight, M May-June. Males patrol and perch all day near the hostplants to seek females.

Color Plates 35, 37
Fig. 35 (ultraviolet)

380. Lycaena heteronea   Blue Copper

The uns is white with black spots, separating it from all other coppers except *L. rubidus* (381). *L. heteronea* males have a blue ups, and females are brown (occasionally with some blue) without any orange, not as in *rubidus*. The unf has more black spots than the blues (Polyommatini), including at least two spots in the discal cell and a black median spot in cell CuA_2. Some females have blue on the ups, esp. in s Calif. (ssp. **clara**). In ssp. **gravenotata** (east of the continental divide in Colo. and s Wyo.; the Cascade Mts. of Ore. and NW Calif.), the unh spots are large and black. Ssp. **heteronea** (elsewhere) has small or no unh spots.

Habitat Upper Sonoran to Hudsonian Zone open woods, brushy areas, sagebrush, and prairie. Hostplants herb Polygonaceae: *Eriogonum umbellatum* (vars. *umbellatum, majus, munzi*), *jamesi* (vars. *jamesi, flavescens*), *microthecum, latifolium, nudum, heermannii, fasciculatum* ssp. *polifolium, compositum* var. *lieanthum*; assoc. with *E. wrighti*.

Eggs white, laid singly on bracts under the host umbels in Colo., under leaves for ssp. *clara*. Larvae eat young leaves (the young larvae eat the underside); no nests. Larva gray or grayish-green, frosted with white dots, with two pale middorsal lines, pale oblique subdorsal lines, and a whitish lateral line. Pupa light green (greenish-gray on the wing cases), with grayish-white mottling, a darker middorsal line, a pale lateral stripe, and greenish subdorsal spots. Eggs hibernate.

One flight, mostly M July-Aug. (earlier near the coast, and L June-E Aug. in s Calif.). Adults sip the nectar of flowers, including *Eriogonum*. Colo. males patrol all day near the hosts to seek females, but N Calif. males and ssp. *clara* males mainly perch. *L. heteronea* is remarkably similar to (convergent with) the *Euphilotes* blues (399-401) that use the same hostplants: both are blue in males and brown in females, and both patrol, though adult *heteronea* fly more swiftly than most blues.

Color Plate 30
Fig. 35 (ultraviolet)

381. Lycaena rubidus   Ruddy Copper

The uns is mostly white as in *L. heteronea* (380), but the male ups is orange and the female ups is brown to orange, always with an orange uph border lacking in *heteronea*. Females tend to be darker (brown instead of orange on the upf, form **sirius**) at high altitude. In ssp. **ferrisi** (White Mts., Ariz.), the unf is usually more orange, and black unh dots are larger than in ssp. **rubidus** elsewhere.

Habitat Upper Sonoran to Hudsonian Zone streamsides and valley bottoms in woodland, prairie, and sagebrush. Hostplants herb Polygonaceae: *Rumex occidentalis, densiflorus, hymenosepalus, venosus, transitorius, crispus, salicifolius* ssp. *triangulivalvis, Oxyria digyna*.

Eggs white, laid singly at or near the base of the host. Larva brown, with a dark-reddish middorsal band (edged by yellow). Eggs hibernate.

One flight, M June-July at low altitude, M July-Aug. at high altitude. Males perch all day along streams and in open gulches and meadows to await females.

ssp. *dione*

Color Plate 30
Fig. 38 (scent scales)

382. Lycaena xanthoides   Gray Copper

Similar to some hairstreaks (Theclini) in the gray ups ground color, but *L. xanthoides* lacks tails and has many spots at the unh base. Males are uniformly gray on the ups; females are also gray but usually have cream to orange upf spots. The unh red forms a marginal band in the Great Plains ssp. **dione**, which may be a distinct species. In the other ssp., there are only a few red unh marginal spots and the middle brown unh spots have light centers: the mountain ssp. **editha** (Calif. to Colo. and s Alta.) is smaller with larger unh spots than the lowland Calif.-w Ore. ssp. **xanthoides**. Ssp. **nevadensis** (N Elko and Humboldt Cos., Nev.) resembles *editha* but is paler on the ups, and the unh is more whitish

ssp. *editha, nevadensis*

ssp. *xanthoides*

with indistinct spots. Ssp. *editha* was considered a separate species but it intergrades to ssp. *xanthoides* at middle altitudes in N Calif. and the Sierra (J. Scott).

Habitat mostly Upper Sonoran to Transition Zone prairie streamsides, moist meadows, or fields (ssp. *xanthoides* and *dione*), Canadian to Hudsonian Zone mountain valley bottoms (ssp. *editha* and *nevadensis*). Hostplants (superscript = first letter of ssp.) herb Polygonaceae: *Rumex hymenosepalus*x, *pulcher*x, *californicus*x, *conglomeratus*x, *crispus*xd, *occidentalis*d, *obtusifolius*d, "*longifolius*"d, *acetosella*e, *paucifolius*e, *salicifolius* ssp. *triangulivalvis*d, *Polygonum phytolaccaefolium*e. Ssp. *editha* uses smaller hostplants than ssp. *xanthoides* and *dione*.

Eggs pale green, becoming white, laid singly at or near the base of the host. Larvae eat leaves (the young larvae eat the underside); no nests. Larva green with a darker middorsal band; *or* larva yellowish-green (with a reddish middorsal band, sometimes yellow-edged, sometimes with reddish lateral lines); *or* larva dark orange with a reddish middorsal band, and with three green-edged red bars on the side of each segment; neck shield green with a bluish bar. Pupa pinkish-tan, with numerous black blotches, in a loose silk cocoon with dirt particles. Eggs hibernate.

One flight, L May-E July for ssp. *xanthoides*, M June-July for ssp. *dione*, July for ssp. *nevadensis*, July-Aug. for ssp. *editha*. Adults are rather local (P. Opler). Marked adults of ssp. *xanthoides* lived an average of 9 days for males and 14 days for females in nature. Males perch all day in low spots to await females. Males hover over the female or flutter behind her before joining. Unreceptive females flutter as in *L. arota* (384) to discourage males.

Color Plate 30

383. Lycaena hermes   Yellow Copper

The yellow unh and tails are unique.

Habitat chaparral, only in San Diego Co., Calif., and Baja Calif. Hostplant shrub Rhamnaceae: *Rhamnus crocea*.

Eggs white, laid singly on host twigs. Larvae eat young leaves; no nests. Larva apple-green, with a yellowish-edged dark-green middorsal line, paired yellowish lateral lines, paler oblique dashes, and a shield on the neck shaped like a double-barbed spear point. Pupa grass-green, with tiny brown dots, three yellow middorsal lines, and yellow oblique abdominal bars. Eggs hibernate.

One flight, June-E July. Males perch to await females.

Color Plate 30
Fig. 35 (ultraviolet)

384. Lycaena arota   Tailed Copper

The unh pattern, which is more complex than that of hairstreaks (Theclini), and the tails are unique. In ssp. **virginiensis** (east of the Sierra to Colo.), the unh is more brown and the male unf has an orange flush. In ssp. **arota** (Calif.), the unh is more whitish. In ssp. **nubila** (Los Angeles vicinity), the female upf is less orange.

Habitat Upper Sonoran to Canadian Zone open woodland. Hostplants shrub Grossulariaceae: *Ribes roezlii, velutinum, leptanthum, cereum, californicum* ssp. *hesperium, aureum* var. *gracillimum*.

Eggs white, laid singly on twigs, dead leaves, etc., on or under the host. Larvae eat leaves; no nests. Larva green, with minute white bumps below short hairs, a pair of white middorsal lines, and a yellowish lateral line. Pupa blackish-brown or mottled tan or yellow-brown, the larval lines faint. Eggs hibernate.

One flight, mostly July-Aug. (L May-July in s Calif.). Adults are sedentary; marked individuals moved as far as 214 m but averaged only 15 m for males and 29 m for females around attractive flowers, and they lived an average of only 4 days because of hot weather and predation by robberflies and ambush bugs (J. Scott). Adults sip the nectar of flowers (esp. yellow or white ones), mud, and berry juices. Adults pollinated *Hymenoxys richardsonii* (Compositae) flowers in Colo. Adults bask dorsally. Males perch on shrubs, etc., in small clearings, from as early as 7 A.M. to noon, to await females. The male pursues a passing female, she lands, he lands and opens his wings a little and vibrates them narrowly, and they mate. Unreceptive females flap their wings to reject males.

Tribe Polyommatini: Blues

The Polyommatini occur worldwide, with many species in North America and Eurasia, and a few in the American tropics. The 32 North American species are found from treeline to the tropics.

Males are usually blue, females usually brown. The amount of blue on the females varies greatly in some species. The role of the blue color of males has not been explained, but it is undoubtedly a signaling system to allow the males to ignore each other while searching for females; females, except species 393 and 412, may require a blue male to mate (and see species 404). Larvae often eat plants of the Leguminosae, but also many others. Larvae and pupae are like those of hairstreaks and coppers. Larvae or pupae usually hibernate; in two species, the eggs hibernate.

Adults generally have small thoraxes, rounded forewings, and weak fluttering flight. They fly about the tops of their hostplants and between them. The Pygmy Blue is so small as it flutters around its host bushes that it is difficult to see, yet it is known to migrate. The larger species have stronger flights. Two exceptional blues (*Leptotes*, especially *L. marina*, and *Lampides*) fly swiftly and erratically about a third to a half meter above ground. Several blues migrate, which suggests that it is genetic coding rather than powerful flight that makes a migrant. Adults of all species sip flower nectar. They rest with the wings closed, and often perform the "hindwing rubbing" characteristic of other Lycaeninae. They generally bask with the wings spread. In all cases, males patrol to seek females (*Everes amyntula* occasionally perches as well). The males usually fly with the females hanging passively when mating pairs are scared.

385. Lampides boeticus   Long-Tailed Blue

Hawaii only
Color Plates 35, 63

The striped uns of this Hawaiian sp. resembles that of *Leptotes* (386, 387) but *Lampides* has tails and orange unh spots.

Habitat tropical open fields and woodland in the main Hawaiian Is. Ranges from Africa to s Europe, east to Japan, India, Ceylon, the Philippines, Australia, and Samoa. Hostplants herb Leguminosae: *Crotalaria longirostra, saltiana, Vicia faba, Phaseolus vulgaris, limensis, Pisum sativum, Gliricidia sepium, Dolichos lablab, Cajanus cajan, Sesbania tomentosa, Sophora chrysophylla, Ulex europaeus.*

Eggs laid singly on host flower stalks. Larvae eat flowers, pods, and seeds; no nests. Larva green, with darker dark-green lines along the body and a paler lateral stripe.

Many flights all year. Migratory in Eurasia and Africa; Asian migrants have colonized the main Hawaiian Is. Adults have a fast erratic flight like that of *Leptotes marina*. Males patrol to seek females, about a fourth of a meter above ground.

386. Leptotes marina   Striped Blue

Color Plate 35

The uns is characteristically "zebra-striped" with tan and white.

Habitat subtropical and southwestern open areas, alfalfa fields, and desert, migrating northward. Ranges south to C. Amer. (a rare stray in Puerto Rico) Hostplants herb Leguminosae: *Astragalus, Amorpha californica, Acacia greggii, Dalea purpurea, Dolichos lablab, Galactia, Glycyrrhiza lepidota, Prosopis glandulosa, Lysiloma thornberi, Lathyrus odoratus,* "*larvatus,*" *Medicago sativa, Lotus scoparius* ssp. *dendroides, Phaseolus, Wisteria sinensis*; Plumbaginaceae: *Plumbago.*

Eggs pale green, turning white, laid singly on host flower buds. Larvae eat flowers and fruits; no nests. Larva light green or brown, with dark bands and diagonal stripes. Pupa pale ochre-brown, with gray wing cases and brown spots.

Many flights, all year in s Calif. (mostly Mar.-Oct.) and s Tex., May-Oct. northward. Migratory, straying to Minn., Ind., Miss., and Ky.; sometimes common as far north as Utah and Colo. Adults sip flower nectar and mud. Males patrol erratically all day to seek females.

387. Leptotes cassius   Tropical Striped Blue

Color Plate 35

The uns is striped with tan and white bands as in *L. marina* (386), but the unf hind margin is not striped.

Habitat subtropical open areas and woods edges. Ranges south to Argentina and throughout the Antilles. Hostplants (mostly Latin Amer.) herb Leguminosae: *Galactia volubilis* (Fla.), *Macroptilium lathyroides* (Fla.), *Phaseolus limensis* (Mo.), *vulgaris* (Tex.), *lunatus* var. *lunonanus* (Mo.), *Pithecellobium* (a shrub or tree), *Crotalaria incana, vitellina, Desmodium, Indigofera anil*; Malpighiaceae: *Malpighia glabra* (Tex.); Plumbaginaceae: *Plumbago scandens* (Tex.), *auriculata* (Fla.), *capensis* (Fla., Brazil).

Eggs pale green, turning white, laid singly among host flowers. Larvae eat flowers and fruits; no nests; associated with ants. Larva green, with a russet-red or pink tinge, sometimes a pink dorsal stripe, a green or pink lateral stripe, a white lateral ridge, and two dorsal rows of white specks. Pupa tan, with a brown middorsal line, dark-gray specks, and a dark lateral line, the wings sometimes greenish. The pupa makes faint squeaks.

Many flights, all year in s Tex. and s Fla.; migrates very rarely as far north as Iowa and Utah (perhaps misidentified *L. marina?*).

388. Zizula cyna   Tiny Blue

Color Plate 38
Fig. 35 (ultraviolet)

A tiny species resembling *Philotiella* (398), identified by the long narrow wings, the uns submarginal cones, and the rounded black uns spots. Habitat subtropical and desert open areas. Ranges south to Colombia. Many flights, all year in Mex., Mar.-Sep. in Tex. Somewhat migratory; apparently native in s and w Tex., but straying to N Tex. and s Ariz.

389. Brephidium exilis   Pygmy Blue

Identified by the row of large black and blue unh marginal spots, without a red submarginal band. In ssp. **pseudofea** (New Orleans eastward), the uns and

ssp. *pseudofea*

Color Plate 38

ssp. *exilis*

wing fringe are browner. In ssp. **exilis** (sw La. and Ark. westward, introduced into Hawaii about 1979), the uns and wing fringes are whiter, and ups wing bases sometimes have blue. Ssp. *pseudofea* was considered a separate species, but it has the same abdominal structures as does ssp. *exilis*; these ssp. are connected by the intermediate Antillean ssp. *isopthalma*, and intermediates between *exilis* and *pseudofea* are reported from La. populations (a *pseudofea* reported as a "stray" from Galveston, Tex., and another reported as "*pseudofea*" from s Tex. are no doubt just extremes of ssp. *exilis* populations there).

Habitat mostly lower-altitude alkaline areas, including salt marsh, desert, prairie, and wasteland, mostly along the coast in se U.S., inland in sw U.S. Ranges south to Venezuela, the Bahamas, and the Greater Antilles. Hostplants (for ssp. *exilis* unless noted) shrub and herb Chenopodiaceae: *Atriplex canescens, coulteri, serenana, leucophylla, patula* (and var. *hastata*), *semibaccata, rosea, cordulata, hymenelytra, coronata, lentiformis* var. *breweri, Suaeda fruticosa, californica, torreyana, Salicornia bigelovii* (for ssp. *pseudofea*), *virginica* (for both U.S. ssp.), *Chenopodium album, leptophyllum, Salsola iberica, kali* var. *tenuifolia, Halogeton glomeratus*; Aizoaceae: *Trianthema portulacastrum, Sesuvium verrucosum*; probably Bataceae: *Batis maritima* (both ssp. assoc. with it, and *pseudofea* larvae eat it in the lab). *Petunia parviflora* (Solanaceae) is a dubious host.

Eggs pale bluish-green, turning white, laid singly everywhere on the host, most often on the upperside of leaves. Larvae eat flowers, fruits, leaves, and stems; no nests. Larva (ssp. *exilis*) yellowish-green with a yellow lateral band and a yellowish-white (pinkish-tinged) middorsal line; *or* larva green with a rosy or dark-green middorsal line and sometimes a rosy lateral band; *or* larva solid dark green; head dull brown. Larva (ssp. *pseudofea*) green with whitish tubercles; head blackish. Pupa (ssp. *exilis*) variable, usually light yellowish-brown (with yellowish wing cases), with a weak brown middorsal line, brown spots on the wings, and brown subdorsal dots on the abdomen; *or* pupa brownish-yellow, or solid pale green, or yellow-white with a reddish head. Pupa (ssp. *pseudofea*) green. Pupae hibernate.

Many flights, all year in s Calif., Tex., and Fla., Mar.-E Dec. in s Nev. Ssp. *exilis* migrates northward as far as Neb., Ark., and Ore., and northward is most common in late summer. Variable in abundance in Ga. and Fla. (absent for several years, then abundant), suggesting migration (one proven stray known in N Ga.). Males patrol all day over the host canopy to seek females.

Color Plate 35
Figs. 34 (ultraviolet), 71

390. Everes comyntas   Tailed Blue

Resembles *E. amyntula* (391), but in *E. comyntas* the unh has two orange spots, the black unh spots are distinct, and the uph often has an orange spot in males (two in females). Spring females are bluer on the ups (form **meinersi**), summer females mostly brown. The end of the male uncus, when viewed from above, is concave with a point in the middle (Fig. 71).

Habitat Upper Sonoran Zone (Lower Austral Zone in E U.S.) to lower Canadian Zone desert foothills, moist meadows, streamsides, and forest clearings (to the tropics of E Mex., south to Costa Rica). *E. comyntas* and *E. amyntula* are largely allopatric; *comyntas* is the sole occupant of the lower Canadian Zone in the east, *amyntula* in the west. Hostplants herb (sometimes shrub) Leguminosae: *Astragalus, Baptisia tinctoria, Desmodium canescens, marilandicum, rigidum, Galactia, Lotus purshianus, scoparius, strigosus, Lathyrus ochroleucus, jepsonii* ssp. *californicus, Les-*

pedeza stipulacea, hirta, capitata, texana, intermedia, Lupinus perennis, bicolor, nanus ssp. latifolius, Phaseolus polystachios, Medicago lupulina, Melilotus indicus, officinalis, Trifolium hybridum, repens, pratense, tridentatum, Vicia angustifolia, sativa, americana, villosa, cracca.

Eggs pale green with white ridges, laid singly on host flowers, sometimes on young leaves. Larvae eat flowers, fruits, and sometimes young leaves; no nests. Larva usually dark green, with many pale dots, a dark green or brownish middorsal stripe, obscure brownish oblique subdorsal marks, and a whitish lateral line (edged by reddish) in the middle of the body; or larva red-brown (sometimes with green stripes), violet-brown, or yellow-brown. Pupa pale or dark green (the abdomen yellowish-green or brownish-yellow), with a middorsal stripe of dark green (edged with black spots) or blackish, and with black oblique dashes on the side of the abdomen; or pupa whitish dorsally and whitish on the abdomen. Nearly mature larvae hibernate, sometimes within the host pods.

Several flights, May-Oct. northward, Feb.-Nov. on the Gulf Coast, M May-M Sep. in Colo., Mar.-Sep. in Calif. Adults sip flower nectar and mud. Males patrol all day near the host to seek females.

Color Plate 35
Fig. 71

391. Everes amyntula   Western Tailed Blue

Resembles E. comyntas (390), which flies with it (at least in Ont., Man., Minn., Colo., and N Calif.), but E. amyntula has only one orange unh spot (a second spot sometimes present but faint), and its black unh spots are usually less distinct. Mostly at higher altitude and latitude than comyntas. Form **immaculata**, with few or no unh spots, is frequent westward, esp. in Ore.-Wash., where it may predominate. The male uncus is convex with a point (Fig. 71), as in Eurasian E. argiades, but the valva differs.

Habitat mostly Transition to lower Hudsonian Zone (rarely Upper Sonoran Zone, and rarely Alpine Zone in N Calif.) woodland openings, sometimes even chaparral. Isolated populations in N N.B. and Gaspé, Que. Hostplants herb Leguminosae: Astragalus flexuosus, miser, whitneyi (and ssp. siskiyouensis), douglasii, nuttallii (doubtfully crotalariae), Lathyrus ochroleucus, polyphyllus, venosus, leucanthus, jepsoni ssp. californicus, Oxytropis lambertii, Vicia americana, californica, gigantea.

Eggs pale green with white ridges, laid singly on host flowers and young pods (sometimes on stems). Larvae eat flowers and fruits; no nests, but larvae inside pods seal up the entrance hole with silk. Larva greenish-straw (with a red middorsal line, pink or red oblique dashes, and a pink lateral ridge); or larva solid green with a darker middorsal line. Pupa pale tan, sometimes greenish-gray or olive-white, with a dark-brown middorsal band and subdorsal blackish spots. Nearly mature larvae hibernate.

Several flights, Mar.-Apr. in s Calif., L Apr.-M Aug. in most of the west (later flights are often partial); one flight, L May-M July northward (M June-July in the Arctic). Adults sip flower nectar and mud. Males patrol (and perch in small depressions in valley bottoms) all day to seek females.

392. Celastrina argiolus   Spring Azure

Identified by the white unh, which has many dark dashes and submarginal zigzags, the rounded fw, and the ups, which is blue in males and blue or white

Color Plate 38
Fig. 34 (ultraviolet)

in females. Ssp. **lucia** (the Arctic, south to c Alta.) is pale silvery-blue on the ups of males and females; the unh always has dark marginal marks, and often a dark central patch (see the forms of ssp. *ladon*). In ssp. **gozora** (Panama north to c Tex., and intergrading with ssp. *echo* in s Ariz. and w Tex.), the uph of males is white, and females have a white ups. Ssp. **echo** (B.C. to Calif., east to w Tex.) has the ups of females blue, small unh spots, and no seasonal forms. Ssp. **ladon** in the rest of N. Amer. has several seasonal forms: in the early-spring flight the ups of females is blue; the unh usually has only small black dots (form **violacea**), but it may have a dark central blotch (form **lucia**) or a dark margin (form **marginata**) or both the blotch and dark margin (form **lucimargina**). A few weeks later (mostly L May) the late-spring flight appears, in which the unh is white with only small dark spots, the ups of females is mostly white, and the size is often larger (form **neglectamajor**). A few more weeks later a full second flight appears, which is similar to *neglectamajor* or even whiter (form **neglecta**). Both *neglecta* and *neglectamajor* produce other flights like *neglecta* later in the summer. The range of form *violacea* is the same as the range of ssp. *ladon*. Form *lucia* occurs south to Va. and Ark., but is frequent only in n N.Y. and the n Great Lakes northward, and from nw N.M. to Mont. in the wetter mountain ranges, rarely Ore., northward to the Arctic. Forms *marginata* and *lucimargina* have similar ranges. Form *neglectamajor* occurs from Ga. to Penn., N.Y., N.S., Ont., and the Black Hills of S.D., and a smaller version of it is found west of Denver. The summer form *neglecta* is rare in the north and the Rockies (Colo.) but common southward. The uns of ssp. *gozora* and *echo* resembles *neglecta*. Genetic and temperature/photoperiod studies are needed on these forms; some ssp. may even be environmental forms. C. Oliver found that long photoperiod causes the offspring of form *violacea* to resemble form *neglecta* (and sometimes to resemble f. *neglectamajor*). Long photoperiod does not eliminate the unh blotch of form *lucia*, which is apparently genetically controlled. W. Edwards found that *violacea* produces *neglecta* (and some pupae from both forms hibernate until the next spring). He thought that *neglectamajor* comes from hibernating pupae and produces hibernating pupae and form *neglecta*; however, *neglectamajor* probably comes from eggs laid by early-spring *violacea*. Ssp. *argiolus* and other ssp. occur in n Africa, Europe, and Asia.

Habitat wooded areas from the Gulf Coast and desert foothills to the edge of the tundra. Hostplants (*, frequent hosts; n, form *neglectamajor*) tree and shrub (occasionally herb and vine) Rosaceae: *Adenostoma fasciculatum, Chamaebatiaria millefolium, Holodiscus dumosus, discolor, Malus pumila*[t], *Physocarpus monogynus, Petrophytum caespitosum, Peraphyllum ramosissimum, Prunus serotina, virginiana, americana**, *Rubus cuneifolius*[t], *idaeus* var. *aculeatissimus, Spiraea salicifolia*; Aceraceae: *Acer spicatum*; Hippocastanaceae: *Aesculus californica**; Araliaceae: *Aralia elata, hispida*[n]; Ericaceae: *Arctostaphylos, Ledum palustre, Vaccinium corymbosum*; Ranunculaceae: *Cimicifuga racemosa*[n], ?*Aquilegia canadensis*; Rhamnaceae: *Ceanothus americanus** (and var. *pitcheri), integerrimus*; Cornaceae: *Cornus florida**, *acerifolium**, *stolonifera**, *racemosa**, *alternifolia**; Moraceae: *Humulus lupulus*[n] (Colo.); Fagaceae: *Quercus*; Hamamelidaceae: *Hamamelis virginiana*?; Aquifoliaceae: *Ilex*; Oleaceae: *Ligustrum*; Caprifoliaceae: *Lonicera sempervirens, Viburnum cassinoides**, *acerifolium*[n], *lentago*; Leguminosae: *Lupinus densiflorus, chamissonis, Apios americana, Amphicarpa, Lespedeza, Melilotus officinalis, Crotalaria sagittalis*[t], *Erythrina herbacea, tuberosa, Lotus scoparius* ssp. *dendroideus*; Saxifragaceae: *Jamesia* *americana**; Anacardiaceae: *Rhus typhina*; Labiatae: *Collinsonia canadensis*; Compositae: *Verbesina helianthoides, virginica, Actinomeris alternifolia**, *Chrysanthemum leucanthemum, Helianthus*ᵗ. Females lay eggs on *Sambucus canadensis*, but the larvae die because the plants contain hydrocyanic acid (Oliver).

Eggs pale green with white ridges, laid singly on host flower buds. Larvae eat flowers and fruits; no nests. Larvae are tended by ants. Larva (all at one Colo. site; similar in W.Va.) pale green, olive-green, yellowish, greenish-white, pinkish, or reddish-brown, usually with a dark-green or brown middorsal line (edged with cream triangles). Pupa light brown or light brownish-yellow, often with brown blotches. Pupae hibernate.

One flight, mostly M June-E Aug. in Nfld.-Lab., M May-M June in the Arctic, May-M June (a partial second flight is rare in July) in Sask., mostly May in the Rockies; several flights, Mar.-July in Ore.-Calif., Apr.-Sep. in most of E N. Amer. (M Apr.-E June, L June-M Aug. at Ottawa), where the first flight is usually more common than the later flights, and the later flights are sometimes missing (summer flights are supposedly more common at London, Ont.); several flights (about equally common), M Mar.-Oct. in s Nev., Feb.-Nov. in N.M. Adults move rather large distances in England, even between separate patches of forest, averaging 1.7 km for males and 2 km for females (T. Shreeve). In N. Amer., adults are often local, the form *neglectamajor*, for instance, being found only near its hostplants, although adults may move farther in continuous woods. Adults sip flower nectar, mud, dung, etc. Males usually patrol all day near the hosts to seek females, but in s Calif. and w Tex., males often perch and patrol about shrubs on hilltops.

393. **Celastrina nigra** (=*ebenina*)   Spring Sooty

Color Plate 38
Fig. 34 (ultraviolet)

Males are brown, not blue, and females are white with a touch of blue at the ups wing bases. The uns most resembles that of *C. argiolus* (392), but both sexes can be identified by the many conspicuous black unh marginal dots. Considered a form of *argiolus* until recently; more rearings should be done where *nigra* occurs with *argiolus*. The type specimen of form *nigra* Edwards 1884 was also the type specimen of *C. ebenina* Clench 1972. The code of zoological nomenclature states that "A name is or remains available even though before 1961, it was proposed as a 'variety' or 'form.'" *Nigra* was named as a form, so *ebenina* is a synonym of *nigra*.

Habitat Upper Austral to Transition Zone north-facing deciduous woods slopes and vicinity. Hostplant herb Rosaceae: *Aruncus dioicus*.

Eggs bluish-gray, laid singly under young host leaflets or on flower stalks. Larvae eat leaves, occasionally young flower stalks (mature larvae prefer flowers); no nests. Larvae tended by ants. Larva resembles one larval form of *C. argiolus*: pale whitish-blue-green, with two yellowish-white lateral stripes, whitish subdorsal dashes (corresponding to the subdorsal triangles of *argiolus*), and yellow-white dots on the side. Pupa light brown, like that of *argiolus*. Pupae hibernate.

One flight, Apr.-M May. Adults seem to be local, but have been caught 0.5 km from hostplants. Adults sip the nectar of flowers (they feed on geraniums by resting under the petals) and mud. Males patrol to seek females.

394. **Vaga blackburni**   Green Hawaiian Blue

Hawaii only
Color Plate 63

The green uns, the violet ups, the lack of tails, and the Hawaiian range make it unmistakable. Found only on the larger Hawaiian Is.

Habitat tropical woods. Hostplants shrub and tree Leguminosae: *Acacia koa* (the main host), *A.* sp., *Pithecellobium*, *Samanea saman*, *Perottetia sandwicensis*; Sapindaceae: *Dodonaea viscosa*; Urticaceae: *Pipturus albidus*; Rubiaceae: *Kadua*.

Larvae eat flowers, fruits, and rarely leaves; no nests. Larvae lack honey glands, apparently because there are no ants native to Hawaii. Larva yellow-green (occasionally orange-brown with a darker middorsal stripe), with paler oblique stripes on the side.

Many flights all year. Males seem to patrol the canopy of trees on hilltops to seek females.

395. **Glaucopsyche lygdamus**   Silvery Blue

Color Plates 4 (larva), 35
Fig. 55 (veins)

Identified by the round black postmedian spots on the grayish-tan uns and by the absence of uns submarginal or marginal marks. The blue of males and many females is silvery in most ssp. In ssp. **lygdamus** (Mo., Ill., Ala.-N.Y.), the uns is brownish, and the large black postmedian spots are nearer the margin than in other ssp. Ssp. **couperi** (Nfld.-Minn.-Alaska) is very pale silvery-blue, and its unh has small spots. Ssp. **mildredae** (Cape Breton I.) is a local form with deeper blue and larger uns spots. Ssp. **oro** (Rocky Mts. and Great Basin) has a gray unh with large spots. Ssp. **jacki** (Kans.-Okla.) is intermediate between *oro* and *lygdamus*. Ssp. **arizonensis** (SE Ariz.-SW N.M.) resembles *oro* but the male upf has a broader border. In ssp. **columbia** (Wash. to the Sierra of Calif.), the unh spots are small. Ssp. **australis** (S Calif.) has large spots on the unf, small spots on the unh. In ssp. **incognitus** (N and C Calif. coast), the unh and unf spots are large and the ups is deep blue. In ssp. **xerces** (San Francisco, extinct), the uns was pale tan, and the black unh spots were totally replaced by white in many adults. Ssp. *xerces* has been treated as a distinct species by a few people, but it was connected to *incognitus* by numerous intergrading forms having small black dots in the white spots and by a form having a grayer uns and large black unh spots as in *incognitus*; the early stages of *xerces* and *incognitus* were identical, and its hosts and hibernating stage were the same. Adults of *xerces* in museums are now slightly less silvery-blue than *incognitus* adults (although *incognitus* is very similar), owing to fading of the blue (the blue of old *Plebejus icarioides* from extinct San Francisco populations fades in the same way). Ssp. *xerces* was found on Lone Mt. and its cemetery, Parkside, Lake Merced, Fort Funston, Presidio, Sunset District, the W slope of Twin Peaks, North Beach, and west of Marine Hospital; it was last caught Mar. 23, 1943, on the beach side of Sloat Blvd. A conservation society is named for it.

Habitat coastal dunes, moist prairie, open woodland, etc., from the N Lower Austral Zone (in the west from lower Transition Zone) to the edge of the arctic/alpine tundra. Hostplants herb and shrub Leguminosae: *Astragalus miser*, *adsurgens*, *trichopodus* ssp. *leucopsis*, *A.* sp. (ssp. *incognitus*), *Hedysarum boreale*, *Lathyrus venosus*, *japonicus*, "couperi," *ochroleucus*, "carolina," *jepsonii* var. *californicus*, *Lotus scoparius* (the main host for ssp. *xerces*, and also eaten by *incognitus*), *purshianus*, *Lupinus ammophilus*, *argenteus*, *polycarpus* (=*micranthus*, for *incognitus* and *xerces*), *arboreus* (*incognitus* and *xerces*), *succulentus*, *bakeri* (and ssp. *amplus*), *caudatus, floribundus, parviflorus, sericeus, variicolor, arcticus* var. *subalpinus, polyphyllus* ssp. *superbus, Medicago sativa, Melilotus alba, Oxytropis lambertii, Thermopsis montana, divaricarpa, Vicia villosa, caroliniana, sativa, cracca, gigantea, americana.* Ssp. *xerces* larvae ate *Astragalus nuttallii* var. *virgatus* in the lab.

Eggs pale bluish-green with white ridges, turning white, laid singly on host flower buds and sometimes on young leaves. Larvae eat flowers, fruits, and young leaves, and are tended by ants; no nests. D. Breedlove and P. Ehrlich found that larvae destroy up to 50 percent of *Lupinus* flowers. Some plants bloom very early in spring to avoid much larval damage, some so early that at one site a spring freeze destroyed the flowers and *G. lygdamus* became temporarily extinct. The *Lupinus* species eaten most by *lygdamus* have more alkaloid chemicals than other species. Larva gray-green with purple on the rear, or pale green, green, pale brown, or purplish, often with a darker green to red to reddish-brown dorsal band (edged with whitish or yellow), often with lighter oblique subdorsal lines, and often with a whitish or yellowish lateral line (edged by red). Pupa wood-brown (the thorax and wing cases often paler, the wing cases often greenish-brown), with a dark middorsal line and various light-brown patches and black dots; *or* pupa blackish with no marks. One pupa was found in an ant nest. Pupae hibernate (in ssp. *xerces* also).

One flight, Feb.-Apr. in s Calif., M Mar.-M May near San Francisco, L Mar.- Apr. in Ga., M May-M July at high altitude and in the north (M June-M July in Nfld.). Males patrol all day near the host to seek females.

Color Plate 35

396. **Glaucopsyche piasus**   Arrowhead Blue

Named for the white arrowhead-shaped unh submarginal spots. The unh has a distinctive white postbasal dash, the fw is somewhat pointed, and the fringes are checkered, not as in other large blues. Ssp. **piasus** (sw Ore. to s Calif.) is paler (esp. on the uns) than other ssp. In ssp. **sagittigera** (Los Angeles) the female ups has yellowish margins. Ssp. **daunia** occurs elsewhere.

Habitat mostly Transition to Canadian Zone woods (also coastal dunes and Upper Sonoran Zone woods in Calif.). Hostplants shrub and herb Leguminosae: *Lupinus argenteus, hirsutissimus, albifrons, caudatus, excubitus* ssp. *halli, Astragalus.*

Eggs pale green with white ridges, becoming white, laid singly on host flower buds, sometimes on leaves or stems. Larvae eat flowers and fruits, sometimes leaves; no nests. Larva yellow-brown, with a gray-brown middorsal line, oblique subdorsal dashes (whitish dashes above reddish-brown ones), and a whitish lateral stripe (edged above by gray-green and below by red-brown); *or* larva bluish-green, with faint paler lines and pinkish sides; *or* larva greenish-white, with whitish and red specks, red dorsal and subdorsal dashes, and a pale-blue area (mottled with red) on the prothorax. Pupa yellowish-tan (the abdomen reddish-brown beneath), with a yellowish middorsal line (edged by brownish), the wing cases bluish-green to greenish-yellow. Pupae hibernate.

One flight, L May-E July in most of the range (L Mar.-May in s Calif.). Males patrol all day near the host to seek females.

397. **Philotes sonorensis**   Stonecrop Blue

The red unf spots are unique.

Habitat desert to Canadian Zone canyons, mainly at rocky places and small

Color Plate 35
Fig. 34 (ultraviolet)

cliffs. Hostplants succulent Crassulaceae: *Dudleya cymosa* (ssp. *cymosa, minor*), *lanceolata, saxosa*; assoc. with other spp.

Eggs pale green, turning white, laid singly on upper- or underside of leaves, rarely on flower stalks. Larvae bore into leaves, and are tended by ants. Larva usually mostly red (esp. on thorax) with whitish oblique dorsolateral stripes and a green uns; *or* larva pale yellow-white or greenish-gray, with a red middorsal band and red lateral dashes; *or* larva greenish-yellow, with blue-white oblique lateral dashes and a bluish middorsal line; *or* larva solidly pale yellow. Pupa olive-green (wood-brown on the abdomen). Pupae undoubtedly hibernate.

One flight, mostly Feb.-Mar. Adults rarely visit flowers and mud. Males patrol weakly all day near the host, often at the base of south-facing cliffs, to seek females.

Color Plate 38
Fig. 34 (ultraviolet)

398. Philotiella speciosa   Small Blue

Identified by the small size, the absence of any uns marginal spots, and the elongated wing shape (as in *Zizula cyna*, 388). This wing shape is useful for crawling into tubular flowers (P. Ehrlich); and because, aerodynamically, tiny insects "swim" through the air, oar-shaped wings are more efficient. Ssp. **bohartorum** (Mariposa Co., Calif.) is darker blue and has wider dark male ups borders than does ssp. **speciosa** elsewhere.

Habitat Lower to Upper Sonoran Zone shrubby desert (Upper Sonoran Zone in the Sierra). Hostplants annual herb Polygonaceae: *Oxytheca perfoliata, trilobata, Eriogonum reniforme,* ?*pusillum*; ssp. *bohartorum* is assoc. with *Chorizanthe membranacea,* and ssp. *speciosa* larvae ate *C. californica* in the lab.

Eggs creamy-white, laid singly on the leafy structures below flowers. Larvae eat the saucer-like fleshy flanges at the joints of *Oxytheca* (larvae rest in the saucers when young), and the flowers of *Eriogonum.* Larva apple-green, with short white hair, a lateral rose-edged yellow band, and usually a dark-red wavy dorsal line, the rear tinged with reddish. Pupa chestnut-brown, the front darkening. Pupae hibernate.

One flight, usually Apr.-E May (L May-E June northward). Males patrol all day about 10 cm above ground, mainly in swales or gulches, to seek females.

Color Plate 37
Fig. 71

399. Euphilotes battoides   Buckwheat Blue

Euphilotes have a spotted whitish uns, with a red unh submarginal band, and they lack any shiny metallic tint beside the black unh marginal dots; they resemble *Plebejus acmon* (410), but *acmon* and other similar *Plebejus* spp. have metallic (blue, green, or yellow) around the black unh marginal spots, and less-checkered fringes. *E. battoides, enoptes,* and *rita* are very similar in some regions, but there is much geographic variation. The male valva is the safest way to identify *battoides*; it has a forked prong at the end (Fig. 71), which can be seen by brushing the scales away from the abdomen tip or by squeezing the abdomen of a fresh male with forceps. By consulting the maps and reading the description, flight times, and hosts for each ssp. one can identify most adults without dissection. When observing *Euphilotes,* it is helpful to identify the sp. of host *Eriogonum.* After each ssp. the range, adult flight time, and hosts are listed. Ssp. **battoides** (high-altitude s Sierra Nevada, Calif.; July-Aug.; hostplants *Eriogonum lobbii* var. *lobbii, E. incanum, polypodum*) has very large square black uns spots.

Ssp. **bernardino** (Coast Ranges south of San Francisco to Baja Calif., northeast to Inyo Co., Calif.; mostly May-June, but Apr.-June in the desert; *E. fasciculatum* [ssp. *fasciculatum, polifolium, foliolosum, flavoviride*], *E. heermannii* [vars. *humilis, floccosum, sulcatum*]) is small, with smaller but still fairly large square black uns spots. Ssp. **allyni** (near Los Angeles and southward to San Diego Co., often on dunes; mostly July; *E. parvifolium* var. *parvifolium, E. cinereum, fasciculatum* var. *fasciculatum*) resembles ssp. *bernardino*, but the spots are large on the unh as well as the unf. Ssp. **baueri** (Inyo Co., Calif., and most of Nev., and similar near Fredonia, Ariz.; mostly May; *E. ovalifolium* [vars. *ovalifolium, multiscapum*], *E. shockleyi* ssp. *longilobum*) resembles *bernardino*, but the dark male upf border is narrow, and the female is bluish on the ups. Ssp. **martini** (s Nye Co., Nev., Inyo Co., Calif., southeast to s Ariz.; mostly Apr.-E May; *E. fasciculatum* ssp. *polifolium*) resembles *bernardino*, but the uns is lighter, the ups is lighter blue, and the orange unh band is very thick. Ssp. **glaucon** (B.C. to NE Calif., the E side of the Sierra Nevada, s Ida.; June usually, July in Ore.; *E. umbellatum* [vars. *umbellatum, chlorothamnus, stellatum, subaridum, nevadense*], *E. ovalifolium* var. *nivale, E. heracleoides* [vars. *heracleoides, angustifolium*], *E. sphaerocephalum* var. *halimioides, E. flavum* var. *piperi*) has the unf spots rounder, and often has a smoky unf suffusion, as in *E. enoptes columbiae*. In ssp. **oregonensis** (a local form in s Ore.; mostly July; *E. marifolium*), the uns spots are a little larger than in ssp. *glaucon*, and the male upf border is very wide and dark. In ssp. **intermedia** (N Calif. to the Sierra Nevada near Lake Tahoe; mostly July; *E. incanum, marifolium*), the uns spots are very small, the orange unh band is narrow, the unf is smoky-gray, and the male upf border is wide. Ssp. **comstocki** (middle-altitude s Sierra, extinct in the Tehachapi Mts. or mislabeled there; July; *E. umbellatum*) resembles *intermedia* but has no dark unf suffusion on the whitish uns, and the male upf border is narrower. Ssp. **ellisii** (N Ariz., s and E Utah, Mesa Co., Colo.; M Aug.-E Sep.; *E. corymbosum* [vars. *corymbosum, velutinum, glutinosum, orbiculatum*], *E. batemanii*) resembles *glaucon* but has a wide orange unh band. Ssp. **unnamed** (E San Bernardino Co., Calif., and Spring Mts. in s Nev., Aug.-Sep., *E. microthecum*; and similar adults in NW N.M., Aug.-Sep., *E. corymbosum* var. *velutinum*) has no smoky unf suffusion and the orange unh band is narrow. Ssp. **centralis** (s Colo., N-c N.M.; mostly July-E Aug.; *E. jamesi* var. *jamesi*) resembles ssp. *intermedia*, and usually has a smoky postmedian suffusion between the unf spots and a narrower orange unh band than does ssp. *ellisii*. *E. battoides* exhibits complex geographic variation in appearance, flight period, and hostplants, and seems to illustrate the concept of "hostplant subspecies," in which local groups of populations are adapted to one or several hostplant species (O. Shields). Adults feed mainly on the flowers of the host, larvae eat only the flowers and fruits, and most mating pairs are found on the host; each population flies at the time that most hostplants are starting to bloom. Several pairs of subspecies even occur together at one locality, flying at different times around different spp. of *Eriogonum* and thus never meeting: ssp. *ellisii* and ssp. similar to *baueri* near Fredonia, Ariz.; ssp. *martini* and the unnamed ssp. in the Providence and Clark Mts., Calif.; ssp. *baueri* and a ssp. similar to *glaucon* at Westgard Pass, Inyo Co., Calif. Other cases of two ssp. supposedly flying at the same locality at the same time are errors: ssp. *comstocki* and *bernardino* in the Tehachapi Mts., Calif. (doubtful because based on only two adults of *bernardino*, because *comstocki* probably occurred at higher altitude, and because *comstocki* is extinct there now or was mislabeled, so that *bernardino* may have moved in later); ssp. *battoides* and *intermedia* at Gold Lake, Sierra Co., Calif. (the ssp. *battoides* individuals from there were mislabeled). Ssp. *bernardino* and *glaucon* both occur west of Independence, Inyo Co. (both ssp. at the edges of their ranges). Perhaps *bernardino*, *allyni*, *baueri*, and *martini*, which are all closely related, should be treated as a separate sp. from *battoides* (and all other ssp.). Some ssp. are known to intergrade somewhat, including *glaucon*, *oregonensis*, and *intermedia*, plus *ellisii* and *centralis*, *martini* and *bernardino*, *allyni* and *bernardino*, *battoides* and *glaucon*, supposedly *bernardino* and *ellisii*, and supposedly *baueri* and *glaucon*. Also, ssp. *comstocki* and esp. ssp. *centralis* are very similar to ssp. *intermedia*. These similarities make dividing the species difficult. Because both sexes are restricted to the hostplant, apparently even if two ssp. were to occur together and were completely fertile with each other (belonging to one species), little hybridization would take place if each prefers a different *Eriogonum* sp. The only possibility for hybrids would occur when adults fly between plants, but it is known that in patrolling species females often mate before they are old enough to fly; thus, in high-density populations when females mate young, almost no hybrids would occur.

Habitat mostly Lower Sonoran to Transition Zone prairie, desert, open woodland, chaparral, and dunes, plus alpine rock garden in the Sierra Nevada. Hostplants herb and shrublike Polygonaceae: *Eriogonum* (the species are detailed above, generally perennials).

Eggs pale bluish-white, turning white, laid singly on host flowers. Larvae eat flowers and young fruits, and are tended by ants; no nests. Larva pale blue-green, green with chocolate marks, lemon-yellow with chocolate marks, pale soiled-yellow, pale reddish-brown, or uniform pink; the body often with chocolate middorsal, subdorsal, and paired lateral stripes. Pupa pale brown (with a green tinge on the wing cases) or orange-brown. Pupae hibernate in litter or sand, rarely at a leaf base.

One flight, as detailed above. Adults at a tiny remnant colony in Los Angeles are extremely local, flying an average of only 6 m for males, 11 m for females, during their life spans, which average 4 days for males, 5 for females (R. Arnold). Adults sip the nectar of flowers (esp. host flowers) and (esp. males) mud. Males patrol all day about the host to seek females.

400. Euphilotes enoptes   Dotted Blue

Resembles *E. battoides* in some regions, esp. the Pacific Northwest and Great Basin. The male valva is very different, rectangular with one downward-pointing toothed prong at the end (Fig. 71). The unh lacks the metallic marginal spots of *Plebejus acmon* (410). Geographically variable: after each ssp. the range, adult flight time, and hosts are listed. Ssp. **dammersi** (s Nev., E Mojave Desert and w Colorado Desert of Calif., eastward to c Ariz.; mostly Sep.; hostplants *Eriogonum nudum* var. *pauciflorum*, *E. elongatum* var. *elongatum*, *E. wrightii* [vars. *wrightii*, *trachygonum*, *membranaceum*]) has large unf spots, a smoky unf postmedian suffusion, and a whitish unh. Populations on the w edge of the Mojave Desert in Inyo, Kern (including E edge of the Sierra), and Los Angeles Cos., Calif. (L Aug.-M Sep.; *E. wrightii* var. *subscaposum*) are similar. Ssp. **unnamed** (Spring Mts. of s Nev.; M June-July; *E. umbellatum* var. *subaridum*) is similar to *dammersi*, but the male upf border is very wide, and the unh is bluish-white.

Color Plate 37
Fig. 71

Ssp. **smithi** (coastal Monterey to Ventura Cos., Calif.; mostly July-Aug.; *E. latifolium, parvifolium* [vars. *parvifolium, paynei*]) has no smoky unf suffusion, the uns is whitish, and the unh spots are not large. Ssp. **tildeni** (Inner Coast Range from Stanislaus to Kern Cos., and mountains of Ventura Co., Calif.; Aug.-Sep. southward, but two flights, May-E June and July-Sep., in Stanislaus Co., or possibly two different one-generation populations there; *E. nudum* [vars. *nudum, auriculatum, indictum, saxicola*] for the July-Sep. flight, *E. parvifolium* var. *paynei* for a June flight, *E. covilleanum* for a May flight at a separate locality) resembles *smithi* but is grayer on the unh. Ssp. **bayensis** (coastal Santa Cruz to Humboldt Cos., Calif.; mostly June; *E. nudum* [vars. *nudum, auriculatum*]) resembles *tildeni* and *enoptes* but has a narrow male upf border and small unh spots. Ssp. **enoptes** (sw Ore. south to Mendocino Co., Calif., and the Sierra Nevada to the mountains near Los Angeles; mostly July, sometimes earlier; *E. nudum* [vars. *nudum, saxicola, pauciflorum, deductum, pubiflorum, scapigerum, sulphureum*], *E. wrightii* var. *subscaposum, E. roseum, saxatile, davidsonii*) has the orange unh band very narrow, the dark male upf border very wide, the unh spots small, and the unh grayish-white. In ssp. **columbiae** (Wash., N Ore.; mostly May-June; *E. compositum* var. *compositum*, and assoc. with *E. heracleoides* var. *angustifolium*) the male uph marginal border has a prominent row of black dots and the unh has a strong black marginal line, unlike other ssp. Ssp. **ancilla** (SE Ore., Nev. eastward to Mont., Colo., NW N.M.; mostly June-July; *E. umbellatum* [vars. *umbellatum, majus, aureum, nevadense*], *E. flavum* var. *crassifolium, E. ovalifolium* var. *ovalifolium, E. heracleoides* var. *heracleoides, E. lobbii* var. *robustius, E. strictum* var. *proliferum*) has the uns bluish-gray-white, the black male upf border is a little wider than in *columbiae*, and the unf sometimes has a smoky postmedian suffusion. In ssp. **mojave** (Mojave Desert, Calif., and edge of the s end of the Sierra, the Virgin Mts. of s Nev.; mostly Apr., but M Apr.-May in the Sierra, May in s Nev. and Inyo Co., June at Doble in the San Bernardino Mts.; *E. nudum* [var. *pubiflorum*, and a yellow-flowered var.], *E. pusillum* [an annual], *kennedyi* [vars. *purpusii, kennedyi*], *?reniforme*), the female ups is mostly blue unlike other ssp., and the bluish-white unh has small spots and a narrow orange band. The most distinct ssp. (*dammersi*) occurs with ssp. *mojave* in the Mojave Desert, but flies five months later. The smoky unf suffusion of *dammersi* lessens westward; the Sep.-flying *dammersi* is connected to the spring-flying ssp. by ssp. *smithi* and ssp. *tildeni*, which can have late-summer or spring flights. Ssp. *mojave* was treated as a distinct species, but it resembles other ssp., and may be connected to ssp. *ancilla* by small w Colo. populations. Most ssp. intergrade with each other.

Habitat usually Transition to Canadian Zone open woodland, sagebrush, and chaparral; also Lower Sonoran Zone desert in sw U.S. Hostplants herb and shrubby Polygonaceae: *Eriogonum* (the species detailed above, most of them perennials).

Eggs pale bluish-green, turning white, laid singly on host flowers or flower buds. Larvae eat flowers and young fruits, and are tended by ants; no nests. Larva (ssp. *dammersi*) ivory-white, with tinges of pink, a pinkish-brown dorsal stripe, brown oblique subdorsal dashes, and a pinkish sublateral line (with pink blotches above it); *or* larva more lightly or darkly marked; the body covered with whitish hairs; pupa uniformly pale brown. Larva (ssp. *mojave*) yellow, with many dark-red lateral and red subdorsal and dorsal bands and marks, the body covered with whitish hairs; pupa brown with a yellow tinge on the abdomen. Larva (ssp. *bayensis*) uniformly rose-yellow, with a few rose depressions, the body covered with yellowish hairs; pupa translucent yellow. Larva (ssp. *smithi*) yellowish or pinkish-brown. Pupae hibernate, mostly in litter.

One flight, as detailed above; possibly two for ssp. *tildeni*. Adults are local, flying an average of 26 m for males, 35 m for females (maximum distance 226 m), during their life spans, which average 4 days for males, 5 for females (R. Arnold). Adults sip the nectar of flowers (esp. host flowers) and mud. Males patrol all day about the host to seek females. In courtship, the male lands after the female, and both sexes may flutter and nudge each other before joining.

Color Plate 37
Fig. 71

401. Euphilotes rita   Desert Buckwheat Blue

Resembles *Plebejus acmon* (410) but lacks metallic unh spots. Similar to *E. battoides* and *E. enoptes* but usually flies in Aug. and differs enough to be identified usually without looking at the male valva, which is boot-shaped, with one toothed prong projecting downward from the toe (Fig. 71). The range, adult flight time, and hostplants are listed for each ssp. Ssp. **rita** (c Ariz. to w Tex.; intergrading to ssp. *coloradensis* in c N.M.; L. Aug.-E Sep.; hostplants *Eriogonum wrightii* var. *wrightii*, *E. polycladon*, *rotundifolium*, *corymbosum* var. *velutinum*) has round uns spots and a very wide orange unh band. Ssp. **coloradensis** (Colo.-Wyo.; mostly Aug.; *E. effusum* var. *effusum*, *E. flavum* var. *flavum*) resembles ssp. *rita*, but the unf has a smoky postmedian suffusion, and the orange unh band is normal width. Ssp. **emmeli** (N Ariz., s Utah, sw Colo.; L Aug.-E Sep.; *E. leptocladon* [vars. *leptocladon*, *ramosissimum*, *papiliunculi*], *E. smithii*) resembles *coloradensis* but has less-smoky unf suffusion. Ssp. **pallescens** (NW Utah, Nev., Mono Co., Calif.; mostly Aug.; *E. microthecum* [vars. *foliolosum*, *laxiflorum*], *E. kearneyi* var. *kearneyi*, *E. baileyi* [vars. *baileyi*, *divaricatum*], *E. heermanni* var. *humilis*) has the male upf border narrow, the unh pale cream, the orange unh band narrow, the unf spots normal-size (smaller and rounder than those of ssp. *elvirae*). Ssp. **elvirae** (s Mono Co. to s Calif.; mostly Aug.; *E. microthecum* var. *ambiguum*, *E. kearneyi* [vars. *monoense*, *kearneyi*], *E. plumatella* [vars. *plumatella*, *jaegeri*], assoc. with *E. wrightii*) resembles *pallescens*, but the uns spots are large (square on the unf). The ssp. all seem to intergrade (*pallescens* with *emmeli* in Washington Co., Utah, and ssp. *emmeli* is intermediate between the w and E ssp. in the number of teeth on the male valva, for example; O. Shields).

Habitat mostly Lower and Upper Sonoran Zone desert, prairie, and sand dunes (the hostplants grow on pure sawdust at one site); Transition Zone prairies in E Colo.-Wyo. Hostplants shrublike (sometimes herb) Polygonaceae: *Eriogonum* (the species detailed above, all perennials).

Eggs greenish-white, turning white, laid singly inside host flowers. Larvae eat flowers and young fruits, and are tended by ants; no nests. Larva (ssp. *elvirae*) ivory-white with a slightly green tinge, pinkish-brown middorsal dashes, and brownish-pink oblique subdorsal dashes. Larva (ssp. *coloradensis*) more reddish. Pupa orange-yellow. Pupae hibernate.

One flight, as detailed above. Adults feed on host flowers and mud. Males patrol all day about the host to seek females.

402. Euphilotes spaldingi   Colorado-Plateau Blue

Identified by the orange unf marginal band (in addition to the orange unh band) and by the lack of metallic unh marginal spots (present in the similar *Plebejus melissa*, 405, and *P. idas*, 404). The male valva resembles that of *E. rita* (Fig.

Color Plate 38
Fig. 71

71), but the female lamella is much broader (Fig. 71). In ssp. **spaldingi** (Utah-Ariz.), the orange band is broad on the unf, narrow on the unh. In ssp. **pinjuna** (Colo.-N.M.), the band is wide on both the unf and unh, and the uns is darker. Habitat Upper Sonoran Zone pinyon-juniper woodland. Hostplant herb Polygonaceae: *Eriogonum racemosum*. One flight, mainly July. Adults sip the nectar of flowers (esp. *Eriogonum jamesi* in s-c Colo., but not *E. racemosum* flowers, which are on a single tall stalk) and (males) mud. Males patrol all day near the host to seek females, flying more erratically and higher above ground (0.5 m) than other *Euphilotes*.

Color Plates 35, 56

403. Plebejus glandon   Primrose Blue

Identified by both the white arrowhead-shaped unh submarginal spots and the large white unh postbasal and median spots. In ssp. **aquilo** (from the Arctic of Scandinavia, Siberia, and N. Amer., south to Alta. and Wash., intermediate to *rustica* in alpine Wind River Mts., Wyo.), the unh ground color is pale brown, males often have a whitish upf submarginal band, and females often have white upf dots. Ssp. **franklinii** (N Man., N Sask., NE Alta., east to Lab.) is similar, but the black unf and unh spots are larger, with white rings. In ssp. **rustica** (the Alta. plains east to s Man. and southward), the uns is whitish (very similar to ssp. *glandon* from Spain, the Alps, Balkans, and Turkey). In ssp. **podarce** (Calif.-Ore.), the unh is tan with prominent black spots, and females are orangish-brown on the ups.

Habitat usually Canadian to Arctic/Alpine Zone (as low as Upper Sonoran Zone in s Colo.) prairie, open woodland, and tundra. Hostplants (superscript= first letter of ssp.; g, European *glandon*) herb Primulaceae: *Androsace septentrionalis*[gr] (vars. *puberulenta*, *subumbellata*), *chamaejasme* ssp. *carinata*[r], *Soldanella alpina*[g], *Gregoria*[g], *Dodecatheon jeffreyi*[p], possibly *alpinum*[p]; Leguminosae: *Astragalus alpinus*[a] (Europe); Diapensiaceae: *Diapensia lapponica*[a]; Saxifragaceae: *Saxifraga oppositifolia*[a], *tricuspidata*[a]. *Vaccinium nivictum*[p] (Ericaceae, based on assoc.) is probably an error.

Eggs greenish-white, laid singly under host leaves, sometimes on bracts or sepals. Larvae eat blossoms in Europe. Larva green with reddish marks. Larvae or pupae hibernate.

One flight, July-Aug. in most of the range, M June-M July at low altitude in Colo., June-M July in SE Alta.-Sask., L June-July in the Arctic and Nfld., L July-M Aug. in Lab. Adults fly as late as midnight on Ellesmere I. under the arctic sun. Males patrol all day near the host to seek females.

Color Plate 38
Figs. 48, 71

404. Plebejus idas ("argyrognomon")   Northern Blue

The uns is whitish (usually with an orange marginal band) and the unh has metallic marginal spots as in *P. melissa* (405). The orange bands may be small or absent in some areas, however, and they are generally broken into spots (a continuous band in *P. melissa melissa*). The unh margin is edged with a very thin black line, and black spots lie at the end of the veins. From Colo. to B.C. east to Wis., the male abdomen is the best character for identification; the gnathos is shorter and thicker near the tip (in ventral view; the valvae must be spread or removed) than that of *melissa* (Fig. 71). Ssp. **anna** (Sierra Nevada, Calif., to sw B.C.) is easily identified; the uns is whitish, the orange uns spots are absent or very small, and the black uns spots are small. In ssp. **lotis** (Mendocino Co., Calif., and the Warner Mts., Calif.), the uns is whitish with small black spots, and the orange spots are always present and small. Ssp. **atrapraetextus** (Mont. to s Alta., southeastward to Colo.) resembles *P. melissa*, but the orange spots are a little smaller, and the uns is bluish-white. The gnathos is a little longer than usual in NW Wyo.-Colo., perhaps because of past hybridization with *P. melissa*. Ssp. **scudderi** (c and SE B.C. northward to Alaska, and east to Nfld.) has the black spots normal-size but the orange spots small; Alaska females tend to have more blue on the ups. Ssp. **empetri** (N.S. and Prince Edward I.) resembles *scudderi*, but the uns spots are large and black. Ssp. *idas* and other ssp. are in Eurasia. Since V. Nabokov studied the taxonomy of *P. idas* (which he called *argyrognomon*), *P. melissa*, and their relatives using a detailed examination of wing pattern and male abdominal structures, name changes in Europe arising from a study of type specimens mean that Nabokov's "*argyrognomon*" is *idas*, and his "*ismenias*" is *argyrognomon*, which occurs only in Eurasia.

Habitat Canadian to Arctic/Alpine Zone forest clearings, meadows, and tundra. Hostplants herb and shrub Leguminosae westward: *Astragalus alpinus*, *whitneyi* (and ssp. *siskiyouensis*), *Lathyrus torreyi*, *polyphyllus*, *Lupinus parviflorus*, *Lotus oblongifolius* var. *nevadensis*, *Vicia exigua*; Empetraceae: *Empetrum nigrum* from N.S. to Nfld.; Ericaceae from Minn. to N.S.: *Ledum palustre* ssp. *decumbens*, *Kalmia polifolia*, *Vaccinium cespitosum*.

Eggs greenish-white, laid singly on stems and on trash below the host. Larvae associated with ants, and often pupate in ant nests in Europe. Larva (Fig. 48) in Europe green, with dark-red and brown dorsal stripes and red-brown lateral marks, with oblique white marks between them; *or* larva tan. Eggs hibernate.

One flight, mostly L June-M Aug. (L July-M Aug. in Nfld.-Lab.). Adults sip flower nectar and (males) mud. Males patrol all day near the host to seek females. Males are attracted to blue butterflies, but in seeking mates they look mainly for adults with the wings closed and head downward, showing the orange-margined white uns (the normal resting position; males are much less attracted to adults with head upward), and males flutter over these, transferring male pheromone. If the resting adult has the proper female pheromone, the male buffets the passive female with his wings, he lands beside her and vibrates his wings very rapidly, and they join (O. Pellmyr). Unreceptive (mated) females vibrate their wings rapidly, bend the abdomen up so that the male cannot join, or try to escape. (The blue color of male blues seems useful to allow males to recognize other males, and in most species females may require a blue adult for mating.)

405. Plebejus melissa   Orange-Margined Blue

Resembles *P. idas* (404), but the orange uns band is usually fused (not separate spots), and the unh margin has a wider black line on the edge (thicker at the veins). The red band is on both the unh and unf (only the unh in *P. acmon*, 410), and the unh has metallic marginal spots, lacking in *Euphilotes spaldingi* (402). The male gnathos (in ventral view) is longer and thinner at the tip than that of *idas* (Fig. 71). Ssp. **melissa** (most of the range) has a thick orange uns band and larger black spots. Form **annetta** of ssp. *melissa* (the higher Wasatch Mts., Utah, where *idas* does not occur, the alpine Sierra Nevada, and rarely

Color Plates 36, 38
Figs. 34 (ultraviolet), 71

higher-altitude c Colo.) has smaller orange spots and smaller black dots. Ssp. **samuelis** (SE Minn. eastward) has smaller orange and black spots (but the orange spots are still larger than those of *idas* there), and the dark male upf border is narrower than in *idas*.

Habitat Upper Sonoran to Canadian (sometimes Alpine) Zone clearings, shrubland, and prairie, mostly on sandy-soil prairie for ssp. *samuelis*. Hostplants herb and shrub Leguminosae: *Astragalus drummondi, mollissimus, miser, caryocarpus, whitneyi, flexuosus*, sp. similar to *bisulcatus, Glycyrrhiza lepidota, Hedysarum boreale, Lotus purshianus, Lupinus perennis, caudatus, parviflorus, argenteus* (and var. *alpestris*), *barbiger, Medicago sativa, Oxytropis sericea, Vicia*; assoc. with *Psoralea tenuiflora*. One oviposition (seen by G. Scott) on *Eriogonum umbellatum* var. *majus* (Polygonaceae), which is probably not a host, demonstrates the ease of the *Eriogonum*-legume host crossover (*P. acmon* and *Callophrys affinis*, 343, eat plants of both groups).

Eggs pale green with white ridges, turning white. The female lands on the plant and walks down a stem, laying eggs singly on stems or trash near the plant base (as in most *Lycaena*, 371-384, *Harkenclenus*, 303, or *Satyrium fuliginosum*, 316), sometimes laying on leaves, pods, etc. Larvae eat leaves and flowers. Larva green or whitish-green, covered with white hairs, with a cream lateral stripe; honey glands and tentacles are used when ants are near. Pupa yellow-green, the wings sometimes straw, the abdomen sometimes whitish. Eggs hibernate in ssp. *samuelis* and ssp. *melissa* (R. Dana; records of larval hibernation seem to be errors).

Several flights, L May-E Sep. in Canadian Zone, Apr.-Oct. southward; one flight, L June-July in c Alta., M July-M Aug. for the high-altitude form *annetta*. Adults sip flower nectar and mud. Males patrol all day about the hosts to seek females.

Color Plates 36, 37

406. Plebejus optilete   Cranberry Blue

Most like *P. saepiolus* (407), but identified by the violet-blue color of males, the orange unh spot, and the straight row of black unf postmedian spots like those of *P. melissa* (405; not curved as in *P. saepiolus* and *P. icarioides*, 408), and the black unh postmedian spots are large. The uns is grayish. Habitat Canadian to lower Arctic Zone cranberry swamps, forest clearings, and tundra. Ranges also from N Europe to Japan. Hostplants shrublike Ericaceae: *Vaccinium myrtillus, oxycoccos*; assoc. with *V. vitis-idaea*. Larvae lack tentacles and honey glands. Larvae hibernate. One flight, mostly E-M July.

Color Plates 4 (larva), 37, 56

407. Plebejus saepiolus   Greenish Clover Blue

The uns is whitish to tan, with many black spots and very little or no unh orange. Resembles *P. icarioides* (408) but is slightly smaller, and the male upf is shiny light blue (usually greenish-tinged) with a black central dash. The unh cell CuA$_1$ usually has a black marginal dot and a black submarginal crescent (sometimes capping an orange spot). The unf submarginal spots are usually as well developed as the postmedian ones (in *icarioides* the marginal and submarginal spots are usually weak). Females are brown to blue on the ups, usually with some uph marginal orange, and browner than males on the uns. In ssp. **saepio-**

lus (Calif. Sierra), the uns has large spots, the ups of females is orangish-brown, and the dark upf male border is wide. Ssp. **insulanus** (NW Calif. north to SW B.C., east to Mont., W Colo., Nev., N Utah) is the same, but males have narrow dark upf borders. The remaining ssp. have narrow male borders (except *hilda*), but otherwise resemble ssp. *saepiolus* except that ssp. **hilda** (s Calif.) females usually have orange ups margins (seldom orange in other ssp.), ssp. **gertschi** (s Utah-N Ariz.) females are mostly blue on the ups, ssp. **whitmeri** (east of continental divide in s Wyo. and Colo., N N.M.) females are partly blue on the ups, and ssp. **amica** (Alaska, Canada, E U.S.) has small uns spots.

Habitat moist meadows and streamsides from the high Transition Zone prairie to the Alpine Zone and edge of the tundra. Some investigators think that *P. saepiolus* invaded the E parts of its range recently, but it was in N.S. in 1908, and is more likely expanding its range along roadsides and in clearings. Hostplants herb Leguminosae: *Trifolium hybridum, repens, longipes* (and var. *atrorubens*), *thompsonii, monanthum, wormskjoldii, productum, breweri, parryi, variegatum, cyathiferum*. Females oviposit on *Lotus* when *Trifolium* dries up.

Eggs greenish-white, laid singly among host flowers. Larvae eat flowers and fruits; no nests. Larva greenish, greenish-white (with purplish front and rear), or red. Pupa sometimes gray mottled with black. Half-grown (and perhaps young) larvae hibernate.

One flight, L May-July at low altitude, L June-M Aug. in high mountains and northward. Adults are very local near the host. They sip the nectar of flowers (esp. *Trifolium*) and mud. Males patrol all day about the hosts to seek females.

408. Plebejus icarioides   Lupine Blue

Color Plates 36, 37

The largest blue. Males differ from *P. saepiolus* (407) in usually lacking the black upf dash and in having a bluer ups; both sexes differ in having the unf postmedian spots more prominent than the submarginal-marginal ones, and in unh-cell CuA_1 the black marginal dot of *saepiolus* is absent or weak (the black submarginal crescent is often present, and almost never with any orange). The black unh postmedian spots are usually ringed with white, and usually smaller than those of the unf. In ssp. **icarioides** (most of Calif. and w Ore.), the black unh postmedian spots are encircled by narrow white rings, and most females have orange on the uph margin. Female form **evius** of this ssp. (s Calif., and Spring Mts., s Nev.) is orange on the ups; it has been raised from normal Sierra Nevada females with less orange, and so may be a temperature form. In ssp. **pardalis** (Santa Clara to Contra Costa Cos., Calif., intergrading to ssp. *icarioides* nearby), the white rings around the black unh spots are almost absent, and the unh is gray in males and tan in females. In ssp. **pheres** (Point Reyes; extinct nearby in San Francisco), the unh postmedian spots are white (without a black dot), and females have a white spot in the upf center. Populations intermediate between *pheres* and *pardalis* still occur on Twin Peaks and San Bruno Mt. south of San Francisco. Males of ssp. **buchholzi** (White Mts., Ariz.) have wide dark ups borders, and females often have an orange uph spot. Males of ssp. **blackmorei** (Vancouver I., B.C.) are silvery-blue with a wide dark ups border, and the black spots are small on the unf and absent on the unh. Ssp. **pembina** (rest of the range, including the Rockies and Great Basin) has thick white rings around the unh spots.

Habitat Transition to Hudsonian Zone woods clearings, prairie, and sagebrush. Hostplants shrub Leguminosae: *Lupinus argenteus* (and vars. *alpestris, stenophyllus, rubricaulis, tenellus), plattensis, caudatus* (and ssp. *argophyllus), elatus, chamissonis, albifrons* (and var. *collinus), andersonii, arbustus* (and vars. *neolaxiflorus, calcaratus, silvicola, pseudoparviflorus), fulcratus, latifolius* (and var. *columbianus), sitgreavesii, spathulatus, succulentus, wyethii, meionanthus, micranthus, variicolor, glacialis, holosericeus, floribundus, hillii, palmeri, parviflorus, sericeus* (and ssp. *egglestonianus), leptostachyus, ammophilus, formosus, albicaulis, leucophyllus, densiflorus* var. *gloreosus, bakeri* ssp. *amplus.* Wherever two or more lupine species occur at a locality, females oviposit mostly on the hairiest one (esp. on *L. caudatus* and *sericeus*; J. Downey).

Eggs greenish-white, laid singly on leaves (more often on the underside than the upper), stems, flowers, and pods, esp. on new growth. Larvae eat leaves, then transfer to flowers and fruits; in spring they eat young shoots. Larvae are tended by ants, and sometimes rest by day in holes dug by ants below the plant; no other nests. Larva green, with short white hair, a red-purple mid-dorsal line, three rows of faint white oblique bars on each side, and a purplish-edged whitish lateral ridge; *or* larva mostly red-purple. Pupa green, the abdomen green or reddish-brown with green blotches, the head brownish-green. Second-stage larvae turn brown and hibernate, usually in litter.

One flight, M June-M Aug. in most of the range, June-July in Ore., Apr.-June in s Calif.; apparently two flights, L May-June and Aug.-E Sep., around the Black Forest on the Colo. plains. Adults are fairly local, flying an average of 27 m for males, 32 m for females, in a small colony (maximum distance 162 m), during their life spans, which average 8 days for both sexes (R. Arnold). Adults feed on mud, occasionally on flower nectar. Males patrol all day near the hosts to seek females.

Color Plates 5 (pupa), 37

409. Plebejus shasta   Cushion-Plant Blue

The wing pattern is like that of *P. acmon* (410), but the unh postmedian spots are brown (not black like those of the unf), and black dashes usually occur in the middle of the upf and uph. In ssp. **shasta** (Calif. to Wash., Canadian to Alpine Zone), males have wide dark upf borders, and the unf usually has a black post-basal spot. In ssp. **minnehaha** (most of the range, on prairie, mostly Transition to Canadian Zone, plus Alpine Zone in Teton Mts., Wyo.), the male upf border is narrower, and the unf spot is usually absent. Ssp. **charlestonensis** (Spring Mts., Nev.) is similar, but the unh postmedian spots are sharper and blacker. In ssp. **pitkinensis** (Alpine and Hudsonian Zone in Colo.-s Wyo.), the unh is darker gray, and the ups dashes are less distinct. Lab-raised ssp. *pitkinensis* remain distinct from ssp. *minnehaha*, so they are genetically different. Between local populations in Colo., the ups color varies from blue to blue-gray, and the male upf border width also varies.

Habitat mostly open cushion-plant communities on ridges (sometimes in forest openings for ssp. *shasta*), from high plains and sagebrush hills to Alpine Zone. Hostplants herb Leguminosae: *Trifolium dasyphyllum, nanum, gymnocarpon, monoense, Astragalus calycosus* (and var. *mancus), newberryi, purshii, whitneyi, platytropis, kentrophyta* (vars. *implexus, elatus), chamaeleuce, Lupinus lyallii, arbustus, breweri* var. *bryoides, Oxytropis parryi;* assoc. with *A. spatulatus.*

Eggs laid singly, mainly on host leaves, sometimes on stems or seed pods. Larvae eat leaves and flowers; no nests. Larva (Calif.) brown (with a blackish middorsal band edged with tan, a blackish lateral band, and blackish oblique subdorsal bars), white (with a brown middorsal band, a faint brown lateral band, and brown oblique subdorsal bars), or green. Larva (Colo.) solid grass-green. Pupa (Calif.) light tan to pale greenish-tan with green wing cases; pupa (Colo.) green, the head and end of the abdomen tan, the outer part of the wings sometimes tan; usually attached to underside of a rock by a silk girdle. Biennial, hibernating as eggs first winter, nearly mature larvae second winter.

One flight, mostly L June-July (M July-M Aug. near or above timberline). Males patrol all day just above the ground near the host to seek females.

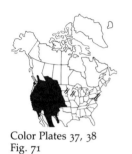

Color Plates 37, 38
Fig. 71

410. **Plebejus acmon**   Silver-Studded Blue

This common species is identified by the whitish uns, the orange hw submarginal band, and the pale uncheckered fringes. Differs from *Euphilotes* (399-402) in having metallic unh marginal spots. Calif. *acmon* adults can be confused with *P. lupini* (411), but they are usually smaller, the male dark upf border is narrower (about 0.5 mm vs. 1 mm), the uph marginal band is pink without dark inside edging, the male uncus has a deep cleft (Fig. 71), and the female lamella is narrow with just a few irregular hardened spots (Fig. 71). *P. acmon* sometimes hybridizes with *lupini* in Ore.-Wash. and c Nev. (C. Goodpasture). In ssp. **acmon** (Calif., w Nev., sw Ore.), the male upf border is narrow, and the pink male uph border lacks dark inner edging. Spring females (form **cottlei**, in Calif. at least) are bluer on the ups. Ssp. *acmon* intergrades in E Ore., sw Ida., and SE Wash. to *lutzi*. Ssp. **lutzi** (NW Ore. to B.C., southeast to N Utah and N Colo.) has the wing pattern of *P. lupini* (the male upf border is wide, and the orange male uph band has dark inner edging), but the genitalia resemble those of ssp. *acmon*. The alpine form **spangelatus** of ssp. *lutzi* (Wash., Alta., Colo.) is darker gray on the uns, and the orange uph spots are small. Ssp. **texanus** (Neb. to s Colo., southwestward to s Nev. and Ariz., south to c Mex., intergrading to ssp. *lutzi* in c and s Colo., and intergrading to ssp. *acmon* in the E Mojave Desert, Calif.) has the wing pattern of ssp. *lutzi* and *P. lupini*, but males usually have dark scales in the middle of the upf (*P. lupini* from Mono Pass, Calif., resembles *texanus* in this trait), and the genitalia are intermediate between those of ssp. *lutzi* and *P. lupini* or are even closer to those of *lupini* (Fig. 71). Ssp. *texanus* is therefore closely related to *P. lupini*. *P. acmon* and *P. lupini* seem to be a case of circular overlap, in which the characters gradually change from ssp. *acmon* to ssp. *lutzi* to ssp. *texanus* to *P. lupini*; the ends of the circle thus overlap (ssp. *acmon* and *P. lupini*) but nonetheless do not interbreed.

Habitat Lower Sonoran to Canadian (rarely Alpine) Zone open woodland, fields, desert, and prairie. Hostplants herb and shrubby Polygonaceae: *Eriogonum effusum, flavum* (and var. *xanthum*), *racemosum, umbellatum* (and var. *majus*), *latifolium, nudum* (ssp. *nudum, sulphureum*), *strictum, sphaerocephalum, elatum, gracillimum, elongatum, wrightii* (vars. *wrightii, membranaceum, subscaposum, trachygonum*), *parvifolium, plumatella, albertianum, compositum* (vars. *compositum, lieanthum*), *corymbosum* var. *velutinum, Polygonum aviculare*; Leguminosae: *Lotus scoparius, procumbens, denticulatus, humistratus, purshianus, micranthus, "parviflora," oblongifolius* var. *nevadensis, Astragalus lentiginosus, wootoni, Lupinus, Melilotus alba*; assoc. with *E. annuum, heracleoides, cernuum, lobbii* var. *robustius, marifolium, pyrolaefolium*. Ssp. *lutzi* eats mostly shrubby *Eriogonum*, ssp. *texanus* eats shrubby *Eriogonum* and *Lupinus*, and ssp. *acmon* eats herbs and shrubs of both families.

Eggs greenish-white, laid singly on host leaves or flowers. Larvae eat flowers, pods, and leaves, and are tended by ants; no nests, though sometimes larvae are inside pods. Larva dirty-yellow, with a greenish middorsal stripe, a few black spots, variable lateral markings, and short hairs. Pupa brown or tan, the abdomen greenish, the top of the thorax sometimes greenish. Second-stage (and third-stage?) larvae hibernate.

Many flights, Mar.-Oct. on the coast and from Ariz. to Tex., M May-M Sep. elsewhere; one flight, M June-E July in Alta.-Sask., July-E Aug. above timberline. Strays are known from se Minn. and ne N.D., demonstrating that some dispersal occurs; introduced to N.J. in 1969 but not persisting. Adults sip flower nectar and mud. Males patrol all day near the hosts to seek females.

Color Plate 38
Fig. 71

411. Plebejus lupini   Large Silver-Studded Blue

Like *P. acmon* (410) but usually larger; the male dark upf border is wider (1 mm), the male orange uph band is edged inside with a dark line, the male uncus is cleft only a short distance (Fig. 71), and the female lamella has a knobby plate at the end (Fig. 71). Some *acmon* ssp. resemble *lupini*, but only outside of Calif. Ssp. **lupini** from the Sierra Nevada northward has deep-blue males; it hybridizes with *acmon lutzi* in c Nev. and the Ore.-Wash. Cascades. Ssp. **monticola** (Pinnacles Nat. Mon. and Tulare Co., Calif., southward) is lighter sky-blue (except in San Diego Co.). In the Tehachapi and Tejon mts., s Calif., some males are greenish-blue on the ups (form **chlorina**), and some females have the fw border orange as in *P. neurona* (412; perhaps indicating past hybridization with *neurona*) but differ in the lamella. Rare males from the Tehachapi Mts. (form **transvestitus**) are brown like females.

Habitat Coast Ranges chaparral to Hudsonian Zone, often in sandy or gravelly areas. Hostplants mostly shrublike Polygonaceae: *Eriogonum ovalifolium, kearneyi, palmerianum, marifolium, fasciculatum* (and var. *polifolium*), *umbellatum* (var. *covillei*), *wrightii* var. *membranaceum*.

Eggs laid singly, mainly on host flowers, which larvae presumably eat. Larva reddish or greenish, indistinguishable from that of *P. acmon*. Pupa resembles *acmon* pupa. Second-stage larvae hibernate.

One flight, L June-M Aug., in the Sierra; several flights elsewhere, Mar.-M June in Coast Ranges, Mar.-July in s Calif. Males patrol all day near the host to seek females.

Color Plate 38

412. Plebejus neurona   Transvestite Blue

Like *P. acmon* (410) on the uns and in genitalia, but both sexes are brown on the ups and have an orange upf band extending inward along the veins. Differs from *P. melissa* (405) in having only a few orange spots on the lower corner of the unf.

Habitat Transition to Canadian Zone open wooded areas. Hostplants prostrate shrublike Polygonaceae: *Eriogonum wrightii* (vars. *subscaposum, trachygonum*), *kennedyi*.

Eggs greenish-white with white ridges, laid singly on host leaves, which larvae presumably eat. Larva apple-green (with a gray overcast due to tiny hairs), with a white lateral band, a faint dark middorsal line edged with cream, and two rows of broad white diagonal streaks on each side. Pupa vivid green, the rear yellowish-green, the wing cases bluish-gray. Second-stage larvae hibernate.

One or two flights, mostly L May-M July, but records from as late as Aug.- E Sep. indicate at least a partial second flight.

413. **Plebejus emigdionis**   Saltbush Blue

Color Plate 38

Resembles *P. acmon* (410), but the orange unh spots are small, the uph orange blends into the brown, and two black spots are elongated in the zigzag unf postmedian band. Males are mostly blue on the ups with an orange uph band; females are brown with bluish bases on the ups and with orange ups margins.

Habitat Lower Sonoran Zone desert canyons and along riverbeds. Hostplant shrub Chenopodiaceae: *Atriplex canescens*. *Lotus purshianus* (Leguminosae; W. Wright) is doubtful.

Eggs greenish-gray, laid singly on host leaves. Larvae eat leaves; no nests. Larva greenish, blue-green, gray, or brown, with a dark middorsal line and many tiny black spots, the dorsal bumps and lateral ridge purplish; abdominal tentacles protruded when the larva touched, as part of the relationship of larvae with ants. Pupa green or yellowish, with a middorsal green line on the abdomen. Older larvae hibernate.

Three flights, L Apr.-May, L June-E July, Aug.-E Sep.

414. **Hemiargus isola**   Mexican Blue

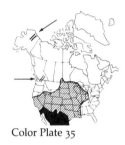

Color Plate 35

Identified by the chain of large round black unf spots and by the black unh spots at the hind corner.

Habitat Subtropical to Alpine Zone woodland, prairie, desert, moist meadows, creeksides, and fields. Ranges south to Costa Rica. Hostplants herb and shrub Leguminosae: *Acacia roemeriana, angustissima* var. *hirta, Albizzia julibrissin, Astragalus, Dalea candida, scoparia, purpurea, pogonanthera* var. *walkerae, Desmanthus, Glycyrrhiza lepidota, Indigofera lindheimeriana, miniata* var. *leptosepala, Lotus, Medicago sativa, Melilotus officinalis, indicus, alba, Mimosa, Prosopis juliflora, Trifolium repens, longipes, fragiferum,* "pin clover."

Eggs laid singly on host flower buds. Larvae eat flowers, fruits, sometimes young leaves, and are attended by ants; no nests.

Many flights, all year in s Tex., Apr.-Oct. in Calif., M May-Oct. in Colo., Apr.-Sep. in Ill.; migratory, straying to Sask. rarely, probably not native north of Tex., Ariz., and s Calif. Adults sip flower nectar and mud. Males patrol all day near the hosts to seek females.

415. **Hemiargus ceraunus** ("*hanno*")   Southern Blue

Color Plate 35

The uns has tan dashes rather than black dots, as in *Everes* (390, 391), but the hw lacks tails, and the orange caps on the black dots at the unh hind corner are small or absent. The unh lacks the black spot in the corner that *H. thomasi* has. In ssp. **antibubastus** (Fla.-Ala.), the uns is tan, and the unh has one black dot (in cell CuA$_1$). Ssp. **zachaeina** (Tex.) has a whitish-tan uns, and two black unh dots (in cells M$_3$ and CuA$_1$). Ssp. **gyas** (N.M.-Calif.) has a whitish uns and one black unh dot (in cell CuA$_1$). A Jamaica ssp. *ceraunus* and other ssp. range south to Costa Rica and throughout the Bahamas and Antilles.

Habitat Subtropical to Upper Sonoran Zone open woodland and desert. Hostplants herb and shrub Leguminosae: *Abrus precatorius, Acacia angustissima* var. *hirta, Astragalus crotalariae, Cassia brachiata, aspera, Macroptilium lathyroides, Medicago sativa, Prosopis juliflora, pubescens, Psorothamnus fremontii, Rhynchosia minima,* and in Latin Amer. *Crotalaria verrucosa, Mimosa pudica, Phaseolus.*

Eggs pale bluish-white or greenish-white, laid singly on host flower buds or young leaves. Larvae eat flowers and fruits, sometimes young leaves; no nests. Larva green, often with a yellow (purplish-edged) lateral ridge, sometimes also with a purplish (yellow-edged) middorsal band and with two dark-green oblique bands on each segment; *or* larva reddish with a green tinge; *or* larva light yellow to dark yellow; *or* larva solid pale green. Pupa pale green to bright green, often slightly purplish, with a dark middorsal line.

Many flights, all year in Fla. and Tex., L Mar.-Nov. in s Calif. Males patrol all day to seek females.

416. Hemiargus thomasi   Caribbean Blue

Like *H. ceraunus*, but only in s Fla. Identified by the two black unh dots, the one in cell CuA$_1$ usually having a red cap (this spot is also red on the ups in females), the other at the corner in cell CuA$_2$. The unh has a strong white postmedian band. Females are bluer on the ups in winter than in summer.

Habitat Subtropical Zone open areas. Ranges throughout most of the Bahamas and Antilles. Hostplants herb Leguminosae: *Caesalpinia crista, Pithecellobium keyense*; Sapindaceae: *Cardiospermum halicacabum. Chiococca alba* (Rubiaceae) is doubtful (one oviposition).

Eggs bluish-white with white ridges, laid singly on host flower buds. Larvae eat flowers and fruits, and often live inside the growing pods, eating the seeds. M. Douglas found many *Chlorostrymon simaethis* (300) larvae in the same pods. Larva green, with a dark brownish-red dorsal line and a white lateral line (edged with reddish).

Many flights all year.

Color Plate 35

SUPERFAMILY HESPERIOIDEA, FAMILY HESPERIIDAE: SKIPPERS

Worldwide in distribution, skippers are most numerous in the tropics. Hesperiidae is the only family. Of the 3,650 species in the world, about 2,300 are found in the Americas, 850 in Eurasia and Australia (especially in tropical Asia), and 500 in Africa south of the Sahara. Several hundred more species will surely be discovered in the future. Some 263 species occur in North America, mostly in southern U.S., and a few species range to tree line.

Skippers are distinct in having the antenna club bent (Fig. 11); in the few species in which the antennae have the same shape as in other butterflies, they are asymmetrical at the tip. The forewing radial veins are all unbranched. Larvae eat plants of many families, although the subfamilies have distinct preferences. The larvae look simple, and in most cases they are adorned only with tiny hairs, although some have horns and tails. The neck is narrower than the head (except in Giant Skippers) to enable the animal to turn and silk together a leaf tube, which is where most larvae live and pupate. The pupa may rest in a Y-shaped silk girdle inside the leaf nest made by the larva. Pupae are simple in shape; some have a head horn and others a long proboscis. Most skippers hibernate as larvae.

Some tropical skippers, perhaps owing to mimicry, are highly convergent in appearance.

Hesperiidae are called skippers because of their powerful flight. The thorax is generally thick and well muscled, giving them a faster flight than most butterflies. The wings seem shorter because of the thick body. Skippers, however, seldom fly far, and few species migrate. The Hesperiinae and Megathyminae have a characteristic and readily recognized basking posture in which the forewings are spread partly, the hindwings fully. The other skippers generally bask with all wings spread. When merely resting, most skippers hold their wings above the back, but some Pyrginae species such as *Staphylus*, *Systasea*, *Celotes*, *Pholisora*, and *Hesperopsis* keep the wings spread. The mate-locating habits of skippers vary, but most species perch to await females, and their powerful thoraxes suit the practice well. However, some skippers (such as *Oarisma*) have narrow bodies, and the males patrol to seek females. Some of the scent-producing structures used for mating (Fig. 39) are unique to skippers. When a mated pair is frightened, generally the female flies away, the male hanging beneath.

Four subfamilies, the Megathyminae, Hesperiinae, Pyrginae, and Pyrrhopyginae, are found in North America. Two subfamilies of skippers do not occur in North America. The Coeliadinae (about 90 species in the African and Australasian tropics) are characterized by adult palpi having the second segment stout and erect and the third segment long and projecting forward; this group is related to the Pyrginae and Pyrrhopyginae. The Trapezitinae (about 65 species in Australia and a few in New Guinea) are characterized by having the end of the hindwing discal cell sloping toward the body; this group is very closely related to the Hesperiinae and may not be a distinct subfamily.

The Hesperiidae and Papilionidae are the only butterfly families that have been given systematic worldwide treatment. When he retired from his post as a British Army officer in India, William Henry Evans turned to working full-time in the British Museum of Natural History, which has by far the best butterfly collection in the world. From 1937 to 1955, Evans published revisions of the Hesperiidae of the entire world, naming many new species.

Subfamily Megathyminae: Giant Skippers

These are the only butterflies whose larvae always bore into fleshy leaves or roots. About 20 species are found from the southern U.S. (13 species) to Central America.

The Megathyminae are closely related to the Hesperiinae, but the head is smaller than the prothorax. Traits common to these two subfamilies (but not to the other two subfamilies) are the shape of the antenna club (bent slightly toward the tip), the location of the base of forewing vein M_2 (closer to M_3 than to M_1), the spot pattern of the wings, the basking posture (the forewings spread partway, the hindwings fully), the larval hairs, and the larval hostplants (monocotyledons). Megathyminae are in fact essentially Hesperiinae that have switched to boring into *Yucca*-like plants (Agavaceae). The ancestor of giant skippers undoubtedly ate the leaves, and the larva rested in a silk nest among the leaves, as the young larvae of *Megathymus* do today. The thick bodies and small heads of older giant-skipper larvae are adaptations to the larval burrows that enable the larva to turn around in a burrow little wider than the width of the body (the narrow neck of other skippers, useful in constructing a leaf tube, is an adaptation not needed here). The hairs of first-stage larvae are longer than those of other first-stage skippers. Pupae are like those of other skippers, except that the plateau behind the thoracic spiracle is missing, perhaps because it would have scraped against the burrow wall. Larvae hibernate, and in some species also aestivate.

Mimicry does not seem to occur.

Adults have thick muscular bodies and can fly very fast, although they may return to the same spot repeatedly. There is little hope of catching most of them, although males can sometimes be caught while feeding at mud or perching, and females while they are ovipositing. Adults do not migrate, and they never feed on flowers. They rest with the wings closed, but bask with the peculiar posture noted above. The males perch to await females, commonly resting on the hostplant or on other bushes or rocks.

The two tribes are the Megathymini and Aegialini.

Tribe
Megathymini:
Tent-Making
Giant Skippers

There are six species of Megathymini, all in Mexico and the U.S., and five of these are found in the southern U.S.

Megathymini larvae feed on soapweed (*Yucca*) and aloe (*Polianthes*). Eggs are glued onto the leaves, and the young larvae eat leaves while reposing in a silk

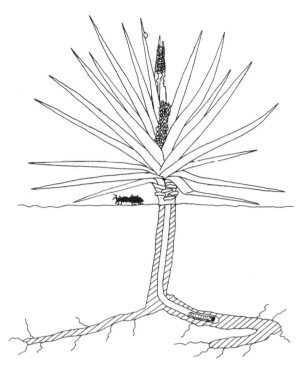

Fig. 66.   Habits of the early stages of *Megathymus*: egg on leaf tip; silk nest among *Yucca* leaf tips, where young larva resides and feeds; and root tunnel, where older larva lives and feeds, occasionally coming up to a dung-covered silk tube (usually sealed) to deposit another pellet.

nest; older larvae eat roots and the enlarged stem at the base of the plant (their burrows are long) and make a cigar-shaped, dung-covered exit tent (Fig. 66). Pupae have a broad cremaster, which they use to move up and down in the burrow; it is covered with short, unhooked bristles.

The adults usually fly in spring or early summer, but may have a flight in the spring and another in the fall.

Color Plate 57
Fig. 52

417. Megathymus yuccae   Yucca Skipper

Identified by the large white triangular postbasal spot in unh cell Sc+R$_1$ (there are few other unh spots), by the separation of the fw-cell spot from the postmedian band, and by the usually uniformly unscalloped uph marginal band. The upf postmedian band is fairly thick behind vein M$_3$; females have this band thicker and may have uph postmedian spots. Ssp. **yuccae** (La. eastward) has orangish-yellow ups spots. Ssp. **coloradensis** (westward) has yellowish spots. Ssp. **reubeni** (Hueco Mts., w Tex., and northward along the Rio Grande) has large yellowish spots. Ssp. **wilsonorum** (extreme s Tex.) has small yellowish spots. K. Roever found that the E and W ssp. are the same species, despite a reported difference in the number of chromosomes; chromosome numbers vary somewhat within populations of *M. yuccae*.

Habitat Subtropical to Lower Austral/Lower Sonoran Zone (up to Transition Zone in s Rockies) desert, open woodland, and grassland. Ranges south to c Mex. Hostplants shrub and tree Agavaceae: *Yucca flaccida, gloriosa, aloifolia, glauca, schidigera, baileyi, harrimaniae, arkansana, pallida, louisianensis, freemanii,*

brevifolia, thornberi, campestris, treculeana, carnerosana, thompsoniana, torreyi, re-verchoni, constricta, rupicola, necopina, schottii, "intermedia" var. ramosa, baccata (and var. vespertina), elata, verdiensis, baccata × arizonica (=confinis), smalliana, filamentosa, angustifolia, tenuistyla, navajoa; the only U.S. species definitely not eaten is Y. whipplei. One larva developed abnormally in a transplanted Agave sp.

Eggs pale bluish-green, becoming pinkish-white and finally yellowish-brown, laid singly, glued mostly to host leaves. First- and second-stage larvae eat leaves, webbing together several leaves into a nest if the leaves are small. Larvae then (or sometimes after hatching) burrow into the root, making a cigar-shaped "tent" of silk and dung that usually sticks out among the topmost leaves. Larva whitish, with tiny reddish hairs, the collar a little darker than the body, the suranal plate is black or brown; head black. Pupa (Fig. 52) brown-black, paler on the abdomen, covered with powder in the burrow. Pupae can move up and down in the burrow using the broad bristly cremaster on the abdomen tip that is characteristic of all Megathymus. Mature larvae hibernate.

One flight, mostly Mar.-Apr. (Apr.-May or even June in the Colo. Transition Zone). Adults have a very fast flight. Males sip mud, but females never feed. Males perch near the host in the morning to await females.

Color Plates 52, 57

418. **Megathymus ursus**   Desert Yucca Skipper

Identified by the all-white antenna club and by the thick upf postmedian band, the band barely touching (male) or connected to (female) a small discal-cell spot. The unh resembles that of M. yuccae. In Ssp. **violae** (east of the Rio Grande), the fw spots (except the subapical ones) are orange. Ssp. **ursus** (westward) has the fw spots yellow in males, orange-yellow in females. Ssp. **deserti** (c Ariz.) has yellow fw spots in both sexes and may have white unh postmedian spots.

Habitat mostly Upper Sonoran Zone (sometimes Lower Sonoran or Transition Zone) open desert woodland and grassy shrubland. Ranges south to c Mex. Hostplants shrub Agavaceae: Yucca arizonica, baccata × arizonica (=confinis), baccata, thornberi, schottii (main host in s Ariz.), faxoniana, treculeana, torreyi (main host in N.M.).

Eggs greenish-white, becoming creamy-white with brown blotches, laid singly on host leaves. Like M. yuccae, young larvae sometimes feed on leaves, then burrow into the root and make a tent, but the tent is smaller than that of yuccae until just before pupation (R. and D. Wielgus). Larva creamy-yellowish-white, with fine black setae, the collar and suranal plate black; head black. Pupa dark reddish-brown, living in the powdered burrow. Third-, fourth-, and fifth-stage larvae hibernate.

One flight, mostly July-Aug. in Ariz., L June-Aug. in SE N.M., L Apr.-June in Chisos Mts., Tex.

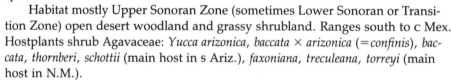

Color Plate 57

419. **Megathymus streckeri**   Plains Yucca Skipper

Resembles M. yuccae, but the wings are broader, the unh median spot at the front edge is not smaller than the postbasal spot, the unh has postmedian spots, the yellow uph margin is usually more scalloped, the upf postmedian band has the spots shrinking rearward from vein M_3 in males, and females often have very large spots. M. streckeri may be a ssp. of M. cofaqui. In ssp. **texanus** (east of the Rio Grande), females tend to have large spots including an uph postmedian band; *texanus* intergrades in the San Luis Valley, Colo., and just east of the Rio Grande, to *streckeri*. In ssp. **streckeri** (west of Rio Grande), females more closely resemble males (the uph postmedian spots are small or absent).

Habitat shortgrass to mixed-grass prairie on the Great Plains, in the southwest mostly Upper Sonoran Zone shrubland and open woodland. Hostplants shrub Agavaceae: *Yucca baileyi, angustissima, glauca, constricta, navajoa*.

Eggs creamy-white, laid singly, glued to host leaves. Larvae do not eat leaves (although R. Leussler's young lab larvae ate the tender parts of a leaf in a silk case before burrowing into the cork). Larvae burrow into the stem to the rhizome root, packing dung behind them, without making a tent; when about to pupate they come to the surface through the stem or soil, construct a tent with silk and bits of soil or plants, powder the burrow, and then pupate. Larva yellowish-white, with brownish hairs, the collar and suranal plate yellowish-white; head dark reddish-brown. Pupa pinkish-yellow on the abdomen, the wing cases pinkish-brown, the head gray, the collar dark brown; cremaster short, broad, bristly. Larvae hibernate.

One flight, May-June in most areas, Apr.-May southward, M June-E July in N.D. and the Colo. mountains. Females make clicking sounds as they fly. Males perch and sometimes patrol all day near the host to await females. Adults often bask on old *Yucca* stalks, where the pattern on the spread uph makes the adult camouflaged to resemble old split pods.

Color Plate 57

420. Megathymus cofaqui   Southern Yucca Skipper

Resembles *M. yuccae*, but the fw is shorter and less pointed, and the fw postmedian band is broadly connected to the one in the discal cell (as in some females of *M. streckeri*, which occurs farther west). The ups has long hairs like those of *streckeri*, and the unh is like that of *streckeri* but with smaller spots. Ssp. **cofaqui** (Fla., SE Ga.) has small unh spots. Ssp. **harrisi** (C Ga. westward) is slightly darker, with the unh spots nearly absent and the uph band more broken into spots. Possibly in Tenn. (on the basis only of larval tents).

Habitat Subtropical to Lower Austral Zone open woodland and shrubland. Hostplants shrub Agavaceae: *Yucca filamentosa, smalliana, aloifolia*, perhaps *gloriosa*.

Eggs creamy-white, laid singly on host leaves. Larvae do not eat leaves. They burrow into the stem and root as in *M. streckeri*, packing dung behind them. When ready to pupate, larvae construct a camouflaged tent at the surface of the soil (or sometimes above ground on the stem of the *Yucca* in Fla.); then they powder the burrow and pupate. Larva creamy-white, the collar and suranal plate whitish; head brownish-black. Pupa like that of *streckeri*. Larvae hibernate, about half-grown.

One flight, mostly M July-M Aug., in Ga.; two flights, Mar.-M Apr. and Aug.-Sep. in N Fla., Mar.-Apr. and M Oct.-Nov. in S Fla. Adults often rest on shady tree trunks in the afternoon (K. Karalus); the males probably perch to await females in the morning.

421. Stallingsia smithi   Aloe Skipper

Identified by the small fw postmedian spots like those of *Agathymus remingtoni* males (427), but *S. smithi* males lack uph spots, the unh is less gray, the unf is brown (not black with a gray tip), and the female unf spot in cell CuA_2 is

Color Plate 55

blended with the wing. Ssp. **maculosus** is in U.S. and NE Mex.; ssp. *smithi* is in s Mex.

Habitat Subtropical Zone thorn forest. Hostplant succulent Agavaceae: *Polianthes maculosa*, a small *Agave*-like plant with red flowers and rubbery leaves.

Eggs yellow-green, turning white, laid singly, glued to host leaves and inflorescences. Young larvae usually bore down through the inflorescence to the root, but they may bore first into leaves and then into the root, or they may bore directly into the root. The larva makes a small tent of silk and dung in the center of the plant as does *Megathymus yuccae* (417); the tent is enlarged before pupation, when the larva powders the burrow. Larva white, with tan hairs, the collar brown, the suranal plate whitish; head pale tan. Pupa (similar to 417 in Fig. 52) yellow; cremaster spade-shaped with bristles, as in *Megathymus* (pupae use the cremaster to move up and down the burrow as do *Megathymus*). Larvae hibernate.

Two flights, L Apr.-May and Sep.-Oct. Adults are not known to feed.

Tribe Aegialini: Trapdoor Giant Skippers

About 14 species of trapdoor giant skippers occur south to Central America, and 8 of these are found in the southwestern U.S.

Aegialini larvae feed only on century plants (*Agave*). Some of these plants may grow for a decade or two, then flower and die. The eggs are not glued onto the plant, but since the base of the plant has concave leaves in a rosette, fallen eggs usually land lower down on the plant anyway. The young larva crawls to the leaf tip and bores into a tunnel there; the older larva leaves that tunnel and makes a short tunnel in the fleshy leaf base (or through several leaves at the base), where it feeds on sap. The larva makes a plate-shaped trapdoor out of thick sticky silk before pupating (Fig. 67). The pupal cremaster is narrow, and the pupa does not move much in its short burrow.

Fig. 67.   Burrows of *Agathymus* larvae: burrow of a young larva in an *Agave* leaf tip; burrow of an older larva in leaf base, with the pupa inside and a silk trapdoor.

Adults usually fly in late summer (Aug.-Nov.).

Mescal is distilled from the sap of *Agave americana*, the Century Plant, one hostplant of this tribe; the larvae found in bottles of mescal are a Mexican species of the tribe (*Aegiale hesperiaris*) that eats *A. americana*.

422. Agathymus neumoegeni   Tawny Giant Skipper

Color Plate 57

Identified by the orange upf spots, by the orange suffusion of males (the upf postmedian band is straight from fw cells M_3 to CuA_2), and by the orange upf suffusion of females over nearly the whole wing. *A. aryxna* (423), *A. evansi* (425), and *A. polingi* (426) may have the spots orangish-yellow as in *neumoegeni*, but the ranges differ: *neumoegeni* does not fly with *evansi*, and it flies with *aryxna* only in sw N.M., with *polingi* only north of Phoenix. Ssp. **chisosensis** (Chisos Mts., Tex.) has slightly less fw orange in females than ssp. **neumoegeni** elsewhere.

ssp. *chisosensis*

ssp. *neumoegeni*

Ssp. *chisosensis* may be a distinct species because the first-stage larva differs somewhat and it reportedly has 18 chromosomes vs. 10 in ssp. *neumoegeni* (but see "Chromosomes and Chromosome Counts," in Part I).

Habitat mostly Upper Sonoran (sometimes lower Transition Zone) open woodland or shrub-grassland. Hostplants shrub Agavaceae: *Agave parryi* (and var. *gracilipes, cousii*), *parryi* × *lechuguilla*. Larvae are usually found in small plants in Ariz. One larva ate *A. lechuguilla*, but reports of *A. scabra* and *chisosensis* are errors.

Eggs pale yellowish, later turning dark red and orange, laid singly on or near the host but (as in all *Agathymus*) the eggs are not glued on, so they fall to the base. Female *Agathymus* lay about 80-150 eggs, and live less than a week (K. Roever). Young larvae bore into leaf tips where they eat pulp, then hibernate. Third-stage larvae bore into the upperside of a leaf base, depositing dung outside the hole, and silking over the entrance when molting; these and older larvae eat sap inside an oval burrow at the leaf base. When mature larvae stop feeding about midsummer, they silk over the tunnel opening, making a silk plug just within the entrance. After several weeks or months of quiescence they powder the burrow using glands on the uns of abdomen segments 7 and 8 (present in nearly all Hesperiidae—the powder keeps the nest dry). They then remove the silk plug, enlarge the narrow entrance, and use a thick viscid silk to make a round tan trapdoor like a dinner plate, which is usually placed on the upperside of the leaf with silk surrounding it on the leaf. Then they pupate. Larva whitish, slightly bluish, or greenish; head and collar dark. Pupa light brown; all *Agathymus* have a pointed cremaster on the end of the abdomen that lacks conspicuous bristles. Larvae hibernate, mostly in the first stage.

One flight, mostly M Sep.-M Oct. Males feed only on mud or manure. *Agathymus* never visit flowers, and females never feed. Males perch near the host from about 7:30 A.M. to noon to await females.

ssp. *aryxna*

Color Plate 57

ssp. *baueri, freemani*

423. Agathymus aryxna   Arizona Giant Skipper

A. aryxna flies with *A. evansi* (425) and *A. polingi* (426), and it is found with or near *A. neumoegeni* and *A. alliae* (see those species for identification). The male fw has a row of orangish-yellow spots; the postmedian spots form a band on the male upf and on the uph of both sexes. Ssp. **aryxna** (s Ariz.-N.M.-NW Mex.) intergrades in E Pinal, sw Gila, and E Maricopa Cos., Ariz., to ssp. **baueri** (NE Maricopa, w Gila, E Yavapai Cos., Ariz., and sw Ariz.), which has smaller fw spots. Ssp. *baueri* intergrades in s-c Yavapai Co. to ssp. **freemani** (NW Maricopa and w Mohave Cos., Ariz., and E Mojave Desert, Calif.), which has larger yellowish-orange spots and large white unh postbasal and postmedian bands. Ssp. *aryxna* reportedly has 5 chromosomes, vs. 15 in the other two ssp., and has been treated as a separate species, but they all reportedly intergrade.

Habitat mostly Upper Sonoran Zone open grassy woodland. Hostplants shrub Agavaceae: *Agave palmeri, palmeri* × *parryi, chrysantha, chrysantha* × *parryi* (*parryi* is not eaten), *deserti*.

Eggs pale green, developing pinkish marbling, becoming gray-green, laid singly on or near the host, without glue. Egg, larval, and pupal habits like those of *A. neumoegeni*. Young larvae live and hibernate in leaf tips; older larvae live in leaf bases. Mature larvae stop feeding mostly in May. Trapdoor smooth, usually dark brown, usually on the underside of the leaf. Young larvae hibernate.

One flight, mostly E Sep.-Oct. Males feed on mud, but not flower nectar; females never feed. Males perch near the host from about 7:30 A.M. to noon to await females. Mating behavior similar to that of *A. polingi*.

Color Plates 4 (larva), 55, 57

424. Agathymus alliae   Canyonlands Giant Skipper

Found only near *A. aryxna* (423), but never in the same localities. Usually has smaller ups spots and much smaller unh spots than does *aryxna freemani*, whose range is near. The orangish-yellow ups spots usually form separate spots on the male upf, but form a band on the uph; they form a wide band on the female fw as in *A. a. freemani* and *A. evansi* (425). The ups base has an orange-yellow flush. The spot in fw cell CuA$_1$ is longer than the others, except in Calif. Ssp. **unnamed** (E Mojave Desert) has smaller spots. Ssp. **alliae** is elsewhere.

Habitat mostly upper Sonoran Zone open pine-woodland canyons and desert. Hostplant shrub Agavaceae: *Agave utahensis* (and vars. *eborispina, kaibabensis, nevadensis*).

Eggs pale olive-green, developing a dull ochre band across the top, turning dull brownish-red after a day or two, becoming light bluish-gray before hatching, laid singly on or near the host, not glued on. Egg, larval, and pupal habits as in *A. neumoegeni* (422). Young larvae live and hibernate in the leaf tip; older larvae live in a burrow in the bases of several leaves. Mature larvae stop feeding in Aug. Trapdoor thin, white, usually on the underside of the leaf. Larva greenish-white to bluish-white. Pupa light brown. Young larvae hibernate.

One flight, mostly L Aug.-E Oct. Males sip mud. Males perch near the larval host from about 7:30 A.M. to noon to await females.

Color Plate 57

425. Agathymus evansi   Huachuca Giant Skipper

Only in the Huachuca Mts., Ariz. (and NW Mex.), *A. evansi* resembles *A. aryxna* (423; the only other *Agathymus* there), but both sexes have broader fw, the fw spots are larger, the upf spot in cell CuA$_1$ is wider than the spots in cells M$_3$ and CuA$_2$, the upf spots in cells M$_2$ and M$_3$ touch, and females usually have wider postmedian bands (6-8 mm in upf cell CuA$_1$ vs. 4-6 mm in *aryxna*) that are usually broadly connected to the cell spot.

Habitat Upper Sonoran Zone open woodland. Hostplant shrub Agavaceae: *Agave parryi* var. *huachucensis*. *A. palmeri* is dubious.

Eggs laid singly on hostplant, without glue. Egg, larval, and pupal habits as in *A. neumoegeni* (422). Young larvae bore a gallery usually about halfway from the leaf base to the tip, where they hibernate. Older larvae live in the leaf base, and stop feeding in L June-E July. Trapdoor black, rough, with a flange, usually on the underside of the leaf. Larva pale reddish-green or bluish-green (before pupating covered with white powder), the last segment blackish-brown, the heart line green, the divided collar black; head reddish-brown. Pupa light brown. Young larvae hibernate.

One flight, mostly L Aug.-M Sep. Males feed on mud, etc., but not on flower nectar; females never feed. Males perch near the host from about 7:30 A.M. to noon to await females.

426. Agathymus polingi   Little Giant Skipper

A. polingi flies only with *A. aryxna* (423) and *A. evansi* (425), and ranges near *A. neumoegeni* (422). Small (male fw length 19-20 mm, female 20-23 mm), the fw-

Color Plate 57

cell spot is large (and broadly connected to the postmedian band in females), the uph band at the end of the cell is pointed toward the body slightly more than the band of other species, the male upf spots are in a postmedian band, and the wing bases are mostly orangish-yellow.

Habitat mostly Upper Sonoran Zone open woodland. Ranges to NW Mex. Hostplants shrub Agavaceae: *Agave schottii* in S Ariz., *toumeyana* in C Ariz.

Eggs resemble those of *A. neumoegeni*, laid singly on or near the host. Egg, larval, and pupal habits as in *neumoegeni*. Young larvae live and hibernate in a leaf-tip burrow; older larvae burrow into the bases of several leaves, and partly into the stem. Mature larvae stop feeding in July. Trapdoor silky whitish, on the underside of the leaf base. Pupa light brown. Young larvae hibernate.

One flight, L Sep.-Oct. Adults never feed. Males perch near the host from about 7:30 A.M. to noon to await females. When a virgin female comes near a male, he pursues, she lands, the male lands behind, she flutters her wings briefly, and when she lowers her abdomen from between her wings they join. Virgin females may release a pheromone, because males do not approach very close to mated females.

Color Plate 55

427. Agathymus remingtoni   Coahuila Giant Skipper

Flies only with *A. mariae* (428) and near *A. neumoegeni* (422). Identifiable by the small uph postmedian spots, which shrink from front to rear, whereas in *mariae* the spots are larger in a band that is widest near the abdomen. The wings are black with small cream spots in males, blackish-brown with larger orangish-yellow spots in females. Ssp. **valverdiensis** is in the U.S.; ssp. *remingtoni* and others range to C Mex.

Habitat Lower Sonoran Zone desert hills and thorn forest. Hostplant shrub Agavaceae: *Agave lechuguilla*.

Egg, larval, and pupal habits like those of *A. neumoegeni*. Young larvae live and hibernate in the leaf tip; older larvae live in a tunnel through the bases of several leaves and the stem. Trapdoor tan, usually on the upperside of the leaf base. Larva light tan (just before pupation covered with white powder), the collar black, the suranal plate and head reddish-brown. Pupa light brown. Young larvae hibernate.

One flight, mostly M Sep.-E Oct., earlier than for *A. mariae*. Males perch in the morning near the larval host to await females.

Color Plate 55

428. Agathymus mariae   Lechuguilla Giant Skipper

Flies only with *A. remingtoni* (427) and *A. neumoegeni* (422). The spots are larger than those of *remingtoni*, the uph postmedian band is widest near the abdomen, and the uns is grayer (the unf apical spots are immersed in gray, not just touching the gray as in *remingtoni*). Several worthless ssp. names have been given to *mariae* populations, including a narrow-banded variant that is sympatric with another and supposedly has 21 chromosomes (vs. 22 for the others); this difference expresses individual variation, and because pupae are used for chromosome counts and adults provide the basis for identification, the chromosome count was not validly associated with adult identification for this variant. All *mariae* populations have some slightly darker individuals, and I found a solid-brown male with no spots at all. Several *mariae* × *neumoegeni* hybrids are known.

Habitat mostly Lower Sonoran Zone desert hills and thorn forest. Ranges to

NE Mex. Hostplant shrub Agavaceae: *Agave lechuguilla*, occasionally *A. l.* × *parryi* var. *gracilipes*.

Egg, larval, and pupal habits like those of *A. neumoegeni*. Young larvae live and hibernate in the leaf tip; older larvae live in a tunnel through the bases of several leaves and the stem. Trapdoor tan, usually on the upperside of the leaf base. Larva pale bluish, the collar black; head black. Pupa light brown. Young larvae hibernate.

One flight, mostly Oct. Males perch in the morning near the host to await females.

Color Plate 55
Figs. 51, 52

429. Agathymus stephensi   California Giant Skipper

The only *Agathymus* in extreme s Calif. (*A. alliae*, 424, and *A. aryxna*, 423, are only in the E Mojave Desert). Most closely resembles *A. remingtoni* (427), but the unh has large cream postmedian and postbasal spots (not just the straight postmedian row of *remingtoni*). Ssp. **stephensi** occurs in Calif.; other ssp. (*dawsoni, comstocki*) occur in N Baja Calif.

Habitat Lower to Upper Sonoran Zone desert. Hostplant shrub Agavaceae: *Agave deserti*.

Eggs pale blue-green, after several days blotched with red, laid singly on or near the host, without glue. Egg, larval, and pupal habits as in *A. neumoegeni*. Young larvae live and hibernate in the leaf tip; older larvae live in a bulbous tunnel in the leaf base. Trapdoor tan, usually on the upperside of the leaf base, with some silk around the door. Larva (Fig. 51) whitish, tinged with blue-green, the collar brown, the suranal plate dark; head brown. Pupa (Fig. 52) light brown, the abdomen greenish-yellow with a green middorsal line. Young larvae hibernate.

One flight, M Sep.-E Oct. Males feed on mud, esp. in the late afternoon; females do not feed. Adults roost on bushes, the males mainly in canyon bottoms. Males perch near the host to await females, probably only in the morning.

Subfamily Hesperiinae: Grass Skippers

The Hesperiinae, about 2,150 species, occur throughout the world. Several of the 137 species occurring in North America range north to treeline.

Adults are mostly orange or brown, and the antenna club is oval, usually with a small point called an apiculus angling from the tip (Fig. 11). Sometimes the antenna is oval and lacks the apiculus, but the club is bent slightly toward the tip. *Carterocephalus* and *Piruna* are unusual for the subfamily, since, like some Pyrginae, they lack the apiculus and have the antenna club bent in the middle, and the palpi extend forward in front of the head like those of many Pyrginae. In all adults, the base of forewing vein M_2 is closer to vein M_3 than to M_1 (Fig. 55); the subfamily shares this and other characters with the Megathyminae. Larvae eat monocotyledons. Most seem able to eat many plant species (grass feeders usually feed on many grasses, sedge feeders on many sedges), but some species are more restricted. The larvae live in silked-leaf nests, and some species make their nests partly underground (which protects them from cows and lawn-mowers!). Larvae are usually green or tan with a dark head and black collar. Some have two conelike horns and even short tails. Pupae generally rest in the larval nest; they may have a horn on the head, and often a long proboscis, sometimes extending beyond the cremaster. Larvae generally hibernate.

Mimicry is rare (see Pyrrhopyginae).

Adult flight is generally strong and fast, straight and not erratic. However, a few small species, including *Piruna, Ancyloxypha, Oarisma, Adopaeoides,* and several larger *Poanes* (*viator* and *massasoit*), flutter along more slowly; they patrol to seek females rather than perching as most Hesperiinae do. The flight of *Hesperia miriamae, Ochlodes snowi,* and some others is so fast that they are often difficult to see. Most species are fairly local, but a few species (including *Calpodes,* which has an extremely fast flight) migrate. Adults of all species seem to visit flowers, and sap-feeding is absent or rare. Adults rest with the wings closed. They bask by spreading the hindwings to the side, but the forewings only to about 45°, a posture unique to Hesperiinae and Megathyminae. Males usually perch to await females, with the exceptions noted above. Males commonly have a black streak (stigma) of scent scales on the forewing (Fig. 39) for seducing females. Females fly when mating pairs are startled, the male dangling beneath.

Color Plate 54

430. **Carterocephalus palaemon**   Arctic Skipperling

The unh pattern is unique.

Habitat Upper Transition to Hudsonian Zone grassy forest glades in moist valley bottoms. Also Eurasia (Britain to Japan). Hostplants grasses: *Calamagrostis purpurascens* in Calif., *Bromus* and *Brachypodium sylvaticum* in Europe. Larvae eat many grasses, esp. wide-leaved species, in the lab.

Eggs pale greenish-white. Larvae eat leaves, and live in nests of leaves silked together. Larva cream to whitish-green, with a darker-green middorsal line and a pale whitish or yellowish lateral stripe above a line of blackish spots; head green. Pupa with a conical horn on the head (similar to 560 in Fig. 52). Larvae hibernate.

One flight, mostly L May-June (June-E July in the far north, L June-M July in Nfld.). Females rarely fly up to 3 km in Europe. Males perch on low objects and often patrol in grassy swales in valley bottoms, all day, to await females.

Color Plate 54

431. **Piruna pirus**   Russet Skipperling

Identified by the small size and the spotless red-brown unh. Habitat Upper Sonoran to Transition Zone moist valley bottoms. Hostplants probably grasses such as *Poa.* One flight, June-E July in foothills, mostly July at higher altitude. Adults sip the nectar of flowers, esp. *Geranium,* and sip mud. Males patrol all day just above low vegetation, mostly in valley bottoms, to seek females.

Color Plate 54

432. **Piruna haferniki**   Chisos Skipperling

Identified by the gray base of the unspotted unh. So far known only from the Chisos Mts., Tex., the Carmen Mts., Mex., and Hidalgo, Mex. Habitat Upper Sonoran Zone open oak/pine woodland. Many flights, at least Mar.-Aug. in Tex.

433. **Piruna polingii**   Spotted Skipperling

Like *P. pirus* (431), but the unh has white postbasal and median spots (but not submarginal spots). Habitat Transition Zone open woodland grassy areas. One flight, L June-E Aug.

Color Plate 54

Color Plate 54

Stray only
Color Plate 54

s Tex. only
Color Plate 46
Fig. 71

Stray only
Color Plate 63

434. Piruna cingo (= *mexicana*)   Mexican Skipperling

P. cingo and *P. microsticta* (435) have white submarginal and median spots on the unh. In *cingo* the unh spot in cell Sc+R$_1$ lies farther out from the wing base than the spot at the end of the discal cell, and the fringes are not checked. Habitat Upper Sonoran Zone desert grassland and open woodland. Ranges south to Guatemala. Common around Nogales, Ariz. One flight, Aug.-E Sep.

435. Piruna microsticta   Tamaulipas Skipperling

Resembles *P. cingo* (434), but the unh spot in cell Sc+R$_1$ is placed above the spot at the end of the discal cell, there are three spots in a row in the middle of the unf (including one on the leading edge that *cingo* lacks), and the male uns fringe is slightly checkered. Habitat subtropical arid chaparral and Upper Sonoran Zone open woodland. Ranges south to Guerrero, Mex. Many flights, probably most of the year in Mex. (Aug. at least), rare in s Tex. (Oct.).

436. Synapte malitiosa   Shady Skipper

Identified by the rounded wings, the uniform yellowish-brown unh (with many brown striations), and the dark-brown ups with a yellow-brown upf band from cell M$_3$ to cell CuA$_2$, where the band extends inward to the base. The uph is mostly dark brown (yellowish-brown from the discal cell to the hind corner); the ups may be plain brown in females. The gnathos arms are very narrow (Fig. 71). Habitat subtropical shaded woods areas. Ranges south to Argentina, Cuba, and Jamaica. Hostplants grasses: *Paspalum* in Tex., *Panicum maximum* in Mex. Many flights all year in s Tex. (regular, occasionally common). Adults fly more often in the afternoon.

437. Synapte salenus

Like *S. malitiosa* (436) but dark brown (the yellowish-brown dorsal bands are fainter in males, absent in females). The unh is brown (some adults are grayish near the base and reddish-brown near the margin) striated with dark brown, leaving a large dark-brown triangular area on the unh front margin (absent in *malitiosa*) and a smaller dark-brown central area (sometimes present in *malitiosa*). The unf front margin is reddish-brown. The gnathos arms are much thicker than those of *malitiosa* at the base, as in *S. syraces* (438), and the spine on the valva tip is nearly as long as the spine on the arm (similar to 438 in Fig. 71). Subtropical; a rare stray into s Tex. (Aug.) from Mex. Ranges south to Bolivia.

Color Plate 63
Fig. 71

438. Synapte syraces

Brighter than *S. malitiosa* (436), the orange upf median band and orange apical spots are joined, and the uph has a tawny patch. The unh has white scaling and brown striations, a large dark triangular area on the front margin, and a dark bar beyond the discal cell. The gnathos is like that of *S. salenus* (437), and the valva has a long spine on the arm (in *malitiosa* it is a broader lobe) and a tiny spine on the tip (Fig. 71). Subtropical; one stray from Mex. known in s Ariz. (Aug.). Ranges south to El Salvador.

439. Corticea corticea   Redundant Swarthy Skipper

Stray only
Color Plate 63
Fig. 71

Somewhat similar to *Nastra julia* (445) and *Synapte malitiosa* (436). *C. corticea* differs from *julia* in lacking spurs on the middle-leg tibia and in having the unh more orangish-brown than yellowish-brown and the fringes more yellow than whitish-tan. Resembles *S. malitiosa* on the ups (which is brown, often with yellowish-brown spots in fw cells M_3 and CuA_2), but the uns is yellowish-brown without striations. The male valva is distinctive (Fig. 71). Subtropical; a rare stray from Mex. into s Tex. (Sep.-Dec.). Ranges south to Paraguay.

440. Callimormus saturnus

Stray only
Color Plate 63

Small like *Lerodea* (555, 556) or *Nastra* (443-445). The unh is distinctive for its tan postmedian area bordered by brown dots (tan inside this area to the base) and its darker margin. The fw and ups are dark brown, with several yellowish fw postmedian spots. Subtropical; common in woodland areas in Mex. most of the year, a rare stray into s Tex. (an error?). Ranges south to Argentina.

441. Vidius perigenes

s Tex. only
Color Plate 46

Brown on the ups and yellow-brown on the uns like *Nastra neamathla* (444), but the unh has a whitish streak. Habitat subtropical grassy areas in thorn forest. Ranges south to Colombia. Hostplants grasses. Many flights, Mar.-Oct. at least, in s Tex.; sometimes common.

442. Monca telata

Easily identified by the whitish unh patches and by the unf, which is reddish then gray at the tip and has a white spot in the middle of the leading edge. Ssp. **tyrtaeus**, from U.S.-C. Amer., has been considered a distinct species (E. Bell). Ssp. *telata* is in S. Amer. south to Brazil. Habitat subtropical shady woods. Hostplant grass: *Paspalum*. Many flights all year in s Tex.; regular, occasionally common in wet years. Adults fly more at dawn and at dusk (W. McGuire).

Color Plate 46

443. Nastra lherminier   Swarthy Skipper

Color Plate 46
Fig. 71

Nastra species are all very similar. Males lack a stigma, and the antenna shaft is brown above, white beneath, and checkered in front, unlike that of most skippers. The fringes are light. *N. lherminier* is smaller than *N. julia*, the brown wings have no fw light spots (or have traces of two), the unh and tip of the unf are dark yellow-brown, most of the unf is black, and the unh often has lighter veins. The male valva (Fig. 71) narrows to a point with a flange on the end. *N. neamathla* is similar, but in *lherminier* the black unf area is larger and blends with the yellow-brown tip less, and the unh is darker with lighter veins.

Habitat the Gulf Coast to the lower edge of the Transition Zone, in grassy often moist places. South to Tampa, Fla., and west to near Dallas, Freestone, and Harris Cos., Tex.; one record in N Minn. Hostplants grasses: *Andropogon scoparius*; larvae eat *Sorghum halepense* in the lab.

Eggs shiny white.

Two flights M June-L July and M Aug.-E Sep., northward; several flights, L May-Sep. in Va., Mar.-Oct. in Fla.

Color Plate 46
Fig. 71

444. Nastra neamathla   Southern Swarthy Skipper

Like *N. lherminier*, but the range is SE U.S. south of 32° latitude, the unh is more yellow-brown without light veins, and the unf black occupies not much more than half the wing and is blended into the yellow-brown tip. The valva is notched at the end between two knobs (Fig. 71). Habitat southern grassy places, preferably open grassy pine forest in Fla. West to Limestone, Harris, and Galveston Cos., Tex. (a male close to *neamathla* is known from Comal Co., Tex.); probable in s Ga. Hostplant grass: *Eragrostis* (at least in the lab); lab larvae also eat *Sorghum halepense*. Many flights, Feb.-Oct. in Fla., Mar.-Oct. in Tex.

Color Plate 46
Fig. 71

445. Nastra julia   Western Swarthy Skipper

Like *N. neamathla*, but ranges farther west (except in E Tex.), is slightly larger, and has two to five distinct yellow fw spots (absent or a trace of two in *N. lherminier* and *neamathla*). The unh and unf tips are yellowish-brown (or orangish-brown) without light unh veins. The male valva lacks the notch and has one knob (Fig. 71). *Corticea corticea* (439) is similar in s Tex. (see it for identification). *N. julia* ranges south to Costa Rica, and east to Dallas, Limestone, Freestone, Harris, and Galveston Cos., Tex., flying with *neamathla* and *lherminier* in most of these counties. Hybridization with *neamathla* may occur in Galveston, Limestone, and Comal Cos., Tex., although completely intermediate adults are not seen (J. Scott). Habitat Subtropical to Lower Sonoran Zone moist grassy places, stream banks, and grassy ditches. Hostplants grasses: *Cynodon dactylon*; larvae eat *Sorghum halepense* and *Stenotaphrum secundatum* in the lab. Many flights, all year in s Tex., Apr.-Oct. elsewhere. Males perch all day in grassy swales to await females.

Color Plate 45

446. Cymaenes tripunctus   Dingy Dotted Skipper

Both sexes are dark brown, the fw with small white spots, the unh slightly yellowish-brown with faint light postmedian spots. Males lack the stigma of *Lerema* (448, 449). Females resemble *Pompeius verna* (499; see it for identification), but the spots are smaller (with only a trace of one in unf cell CuA$_2$), the unh has a slightly different tint, and the two species meet only in c Fla. *Lerodea eufala* (555) is grayer beneath and has shorter antennae.

Habitat subtropical grassy areas. Ranges south to Argentina, the Bahamas (Andros I.), the Greater Antilles, and the Virgin Is. Hostplants grasses in the Antilles: *Saccharum officinarum*, *Panicum maximum*.

Eggs pale green to white, laid on the upperside of hostplant leaves. Larvae eat leaves; larvae and pupae live in rolled-leaf nests. Larva bluish-green, with many greenish and grayish-green bands; head white, with dark-brown marginal stripes, varying to brown, with a white stripe on each side of the face forming a white V on the front. Pupa (similar to 560 in Fig. 52) light green, with a narrow yellow subdorsal line on the abdomen, the proboscis pinkish where it extends to the end of the abdomen; head with a long horn.

Many flights, Feb.-Nov., in s Fla.

447. Cymaenes odilia   Fawn-Spotted Skipper

s Tex. only
Color Plate 45

Like *C. tripunctus*, but identified by the two faint light unh bands (the inner one touching the leading edge of the wing, not as in *Lerema accius*, 448). The unf lacks the white spot of *Monca telata* (442) in the middle of the leading edge. The male lacks the stigma of *Lerema*. The female looks like *accius* but is a little smaller, and the unh pattern is a little different. Ssp. **trebius** is in U.S. and C. Amer.; ssp. *odilia* and other ssp. are in S. Amer., south to Argentina. Habitat subtropical shaded trails and grassy woods. Hostplant grasses: *Paspalum* in Tex., *Panicum maximum* in Mex. Many flights, Apr.-Dec., in s Tex.; common in some wet years. Often found in shade, it also flies at dusk.

448. Lerema accius   Clouded Skipper

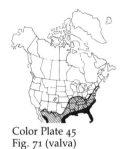

Color Plate 45
Fig. 71 (valva)

Identified by the dark-brown ups with distinct white spots on the fw and by a brown unh central patch edged by large faint postmedian spots. The unh is gray-brown, the margins slightly gray. The uns differs from that of the other "witches" (see *Pompeius*, 499) and of *Lerodea arabus* (556), which is smaller.

Habitat Subtropical to s Lower Austral Zone grassy fields and open woods. Ranges south to Venezuela. Hostplants grasses: *Stenotaphrum secundatum*, *Zea mays*, *Erianthus alopecuroides*, *Paspalum ciliatifolium*, *Pennisetum ciliare*, *Oryzopsis*[t], *Panicum capillare*[t], *Sorghum halepense*[t], *Andropogon*, in Latin Amer. *Echinochloa poiretiana*.

Larva whitish, mottled with dark lines and points on the front of each segment, the collar black; head white, with a black band around the sides and top and three black vertical streaks on the face. Pupa (similar to 560 in Fig. 52) greenish-white, the proboscis extending to the abdomen tip; head with a long horn.

Many flights, all year in s Tex. and s Fla., Feb.-Nov. on the Gulf Coast; migrates northward, reaching Va. mostly July-E Oct., reaching N.Y. by Sep.-Oct., rarely reaching Ind. and Mass. In the fall, T. Walker caught many adults in N Fla. malaise traps migrating south, but very few going north; few were caught in the spring.

449. Lerema ancillaris

Stray only
Color Plate 63
Fig. 71

Like *L. accius* (448) in having a stigma on the male, but the unh is uniformly slightly yellowish-brown without a dark patch inside the tiny whitish median spots. The valva has a spine on the bottom, unlike that of *accius* (Fig. 71). Ssp. **liris** is in the U.S. and C. Amer.; ssp. *ancillaris* is in S. Amer., south to Brazil. Subtropical. Hostplants grasses (larvae eat many grasses including bamboo and sugarcane in the lab). Many flights all year in Mex.; a rare stray into s Tex. (Aug.-Oct.).

450. Vettius fantasos   Fantastic Skipper

Stray only
Color Plate 61

The unh is unique. Habitat subtropical thorn forest. Ranges south to Paraguay. Hostplants grasses: *Lasiacis* sp. (*divaricata*?) and *Panicum ramosum* in Latin Amer. Larva green. Many flights in Mex.; a rare stray into s Tex. (Oct.).

451. Perichares philetes   Gaudy Skipper

Stray only
Color Plate 61

Easily recognized by the unh pattern and fw spots. The male has a stigma.

Habitat subtropical open areas and open woodland. Ranges south to Argentina and the Greater Antilles. Hostplants in Latin Amer. grasses: *Saccharum offici-*

narum, Zea mays, Panicum maximum, Bambusa vulgaris (a bamboo); Palmae: *Desmonicus, Hyospathe elegans.*

Eggs laid singly on the upperside or underside of host leaves. Larvae eat leaves. Larva shiny green (pale bluish-green on the underside, with a chalky-white blotch on the underside behind the true legs), with a greenish-yellow dorsal stripe, the sides greenish-yellow; head light yellow to green. Pupa green (the wing cases whitish), with two yellow dorsal lines, the proboscis extending about 7 mm beyond the abdomen, the head with a projection (similar to 560 in Fig. 52).

Many flights in Mex.; a rare stray into s Tex. (Nov.-Dec.). Adults are supposedly crepuscular.

452. Erionota thrax   Banana Skipper

Hawaii only
Color Plate 63

Easily recognized. Native to SE Asia and the East Indies, introduced to Oahu, Hawaii, from Guam in Aug. 1973, since spreading to the island of Hawaii. Habitat tropical woodlands and banana plantations. Hostplant tree Musaceae: *Musa paradisiaca* var. *sapientum.* Larvae eat leaves. Many flights all year.

453. Rhinthon cubana

Stray only
Color Plate 61

The head and thorax are greenish. The ups spots are like those of *Polygonus leo* (574), including one in the discal cell (the spot is divided in males), but the unh is uniformly brown with several small white dots showing through on the uph. The size and wing shape are similar to those of *Thespieus* (566) and *Calpodes* (558), but *Rhinthon* lacks large white spots on the uph and in upf cell CuA_2. Ssp. **osca** occurs from the U.S. to Ecuador; ssp. *cubana* is in the Antilles (Cuba, Jamaica). Habitat subtropical wooded areas. A rare stray into s Tex. (Oct.) from Mex.

454. Decinea percosius

s Tex. only
Color Plate 47

Identified by the angled white spot in fw cell CuA_1, the tiny white spot in the middle of the hw, and the slightly yellowish-brown unh (often with dark-brown postmedian dots). There is no stigma. Subtropical. Ranges south to British Guiana. Hostplants grasses; larvae eat several grasses in the lab. Larvae eat leaves, mostly at night, and live in rolled- or tied-leaf nests. Many flights, Apr.-Nov., in s Tex.; apparently a resident because frequently caught in some years.

455. Conga chydaea

Stray only
Color Plate 63

Identified by the white streak in unf cell CuA_2. Similar to *Decinea percosius* (454, which also lacks a stigma); the ups is brown, the fw apical spots are tiny or absent, a small spot is in fw cell M_3, an hourglass-shaped spot is in fw cell CuA_1 (the spots are smaller or absent in females), the unh is brown to yellowish-brown with more or less dull-gray scaling (with suffused pale postmedian spots and spots at the end of the cell). The antenna hook (apiculus) is much shorter than the width of the club (greater than the width in *Decinea*). Subtropical; a rare stray into s Tex. (July-Oct.) from Mex. Ranges south to Argentina.

Color Plate 54

456. Ancyloxypha numitor　Least Skipperling

Easily recognized by the broad borders and orange hw.

Habitat Subtropical to lower Canadian Zone moist grassy places and stream-sides. Hostplants grasses: *Zizaniopsis miliacea*, *Oryza sativa*, *Poa*, *Leersia oryzoides*, *Spartina*, *Setaria*, *Panicum*, *Zea mays*[t].

Eggs pale yellow, soon developing an orange-red ring, laid singly, prefera-bly on broadleaf grasses. Larvae eat leaves, and live in rolled- or tied-leaf nests. Larva light green; head dark brown, with white spots or bands on the face and a white patch behind the eyes. Pupa cream, with brown marks. Third- and fourth-stage larvae hibernate.

Several flights northward, M June-E July and Aug.-E Sep. near Ottawa and in Colo.; many flights, Feb.-Dec., in Fla. Males patrol weakly all day over grasses in meadows and along streams to seek females.

Color Plate 54

457. Ancyloxypha arene　Orange Least Skipperling

The wings are orange with a narrow dark border, unlike those of *A. numitor*. The fw borders are broader than those of *Copaeodes* (462) and *Oarisma* (459, 460). Habitat Subtropical to Upper Sonoran Zone moist grassy places, in-cluding desert lakes and springs. Ranges south to Costa Rica. Several flights, Apr.-Sep. Males patrol weakly over valley-bottom grasses, all day, to seek females.

Color Plate 55

458. Oarisma powesheik　Eastern Skipperling

Like *O. garita*, but the unh hind margin is all black (rarely with a narrow streak of orange), the unh veins are whiter, and the unf is mostly black. Possibly a ssp. of *garita*, since the male abdominal structures are alike, though T. McCabe notes that *garita* flies a little earlier than *powesheik* in N.D. (perhaps because of its drier habitat) and no intermediate adults were seen (though the ranges are mostly separate, both species are recorded for Ransom and Cass Cos., N.D., so some contact is possible).

Habitat Transition Zone grassy lake margins, moist meadows, and tallgrass prairie. Hostplants sedges (Cyperaceae): oviposition on *Eleocharis elliptica* and another sedge. Larvae eat sedge readily in the lab and refuse several grasses (they reluctantly eat *Poa pratensis*).

Eggs pale yellow-green, laid singly on host leaves. Larvae eat leaves. Larva green, with a wide dark-green middorsal band (edged with white) and six other white lines on each side; head pale green. Pupa light colored, the thorax and head darker. Fifth-stage larvae hibernate (the larvae go through about seven stages).

One flight, M June-July. Males patrol just above the sedges to seek females.

Color Plate 55

459. Oarisma garita　Western Skipperling

The wings are stubby, and the ups is mostly brown. Like *O. powesheik*, but the unh hind margin is orange.

Habitat Transition to Canadian Zone grassy places, prairie, and open wood-land. Recent records from La Cloche area of Lake Huron may be an introduction in hay. Ranges to s Mex. Hostplants grasses: *Sitanion hystrix*, *Blepharoneuron tri-*

cholepis, *Stipa columbiana*, *Poa pratensis*, *agassizensis*, *Bouteloua gracilis*. One egg was laid on *Arenaria* (a grasslike Caryophyllaceae), which is not a host.

Eggs creamy-white, laid singly, mostly on host leaves or stems. Larva green, with a white dorsal line and seven white lines on each side; head pale green. Fourth-stage larvae hibernate.

One flight, mostly M June-July (June-M July at low altitude in Colo.). Males patrol all day in grassy places to seek females. When a female flies near a male, he pursues, she lands on a grass stem, and then he lands and flutters vigorously while jerking his thorax toward the female occasionally.

Color Plate 55

460. Oarisma edwardsii   Orange Skipperling

Like *O. garita* but more orange, the hind margin of the unh orange (occasionally with a black streak), the unh veins not whitened, the hw more triangular, and the antenna shaft more checkered on the underside. *O. garita* is intermediate between *edwardsii* and *powesheik* in several traits. The unh of *edwardsii* is darker than that of *Copaeodes* (462). Habitat dry Upper Sonoran to Transition Zone chaparral and open woodland. Ranges to Puebla, Mex. One flight, L June-July, in Colo.; several flights, Apr.-Sep., southward. Males patrol rapidly all day throughout the habitat but more often in valley bottoms to seek females.

Color Plate 55

461. Copaeodes minima   Tiny Skipper

Identified by the tiny orange wings and the white unh streak. Females may have black ups veins near the margin. Ranges south to Panama. Habitat subtropical to southern non-arid grassy places. Hostplant grass: *Cynodon dactylon*. Two flights, M May-M June and M Aug.-M Sep., northward; many flights all year in s Fla. and s Tex. Possibly migrates northward to some extent. Flight is slower than that of *C. aurantiaca*, but is still fairly fast. Adults sip flower nectar and mud.

Color Plate 55
Fig. 51

462. Copaeodes aurantiaca   Western Tiny Skipper

Like *C. minima*, but without a white unh stripe. Females may have a dark ups border and veins.

Habitat arid southwestern grassland and open woodland. Ranges south to Panama. Hostplants grasses: *Cynodon dactylon*, ?*Distichlis spicata*; larvae eat grasses in the lab.

Eggs cream. Larva (Fig. 51) green, with a pale middorsal line edged by wide purple bands that become red on each of the two pointed tails, and with two wide dark-green bands on each side; head with four vertical pink bands, a purplish area on each side, and two horns. Pupa (similar to 560 in Fig. 52) pale yellow, with brown middorsal and lateral lines, two white subdorsal lines on each side (the lower line edged with pink), and a long horn on the head.

Many flights, Apr.-Oct. northward, Mar.-Dec. in s Calif., all year in s Tex. Probably migratory, straying to c Kans. and Colo. (apparently not native there). Adults have very fast flight, amazing considering the tiny size. Males perch all day in gulches to await females.

Color Plate 54

463. **Adopaeoides prittwitzi**   Black-Veined Skipperling

The sexes are similar (females a little darker than males), orange, with heavy dark ups veins like those of *Thymelicus* (464). The unh has a white stripe as in *Copaeodes minima* (461), but adults are larger and have much darker ups veins than any *minima*. Habitat mostly Upper Sonoran Zone springs in desert grassland and open woodland. Ranges south to Guerrero, Mex. Several flights, at least May-June and Sep. Adults sip the nectar of watercress and other flowers. Males patrol somewhat weakly over flowers and grasses at springs, at least in the morning, to seek females.

Color Plate 55
Fig. 39 (scent patches)

464. **Thymelicus lineola**   European Skipperling

Identified by the orange-brown color, the dark veins near the ups margins, the short male stigma, and the northern range. A light form **pallida** is very rare in most areas. Found in Colo. mts. in 1985.

Habitat upper Transition to Canadian Zone meadows and hayfields. Eurasian, from N Africa to Britain east to Asia. Hostplants grasses: *Phleum pratense* (the favorite), *Agrostis alba*. An economic pest on *Phleum*. Some 22 parasitoid species have been raised from immatures, and a nucleopolyhedrosis virus also attacks immatures.

Eggs whitish, laid in strings around the lower hostplant stem. Larvae eat leaves, and live in tied-leaf nests. Larva green, with a dark dorsal stripe and two yellow lateral lines; head light brown with two yellowish stripes down the face. Pupa green, the abdomen more yellowish (with stripes), the head with a hooked horn (similar to 560 in Fig. 52). Eggs hibernate.

One flight, mostly June-M July (M June-M July at Ottawa, L July-E Aug. in Nfld.). Introduced from Europe to London, Ont., about 1910, it has since spread an average of 25 km per year (faster after 1960) to occupy nearly all suitable habitats in the east. Another introduction to Terrace, W B.C., in 1960 has spread to SE B.C. At this rate *T. lineola* will occupy Alaska and the N Rockies in less than 50 years. The rate of spread is rapid; many movements may result from eggs in transported hay and in transported waste from cleaning *Phleum* seed. T. Shreeve found that during their lifetimes adults moved fairly large distances in England, averaging 545 m for males and 415 m for females. Oddly, nectar-seeking adults enter the slipper of orchid flowers (*Cypripedium*) and become trapped and die, as many as 24 bodies having been found in one flower; the native skippers are immune to this fate. Males patrol all day through the grass to seek females.

Color Plates 44, 51
Fig. 52

465. **Hylephila phyleus**   Fiery Skipper

Identified by the short antennae and the yellow unh (brownish-yellow in some females) with dark spots like those of male *Polites vibex* (496). Male *H. phyleus* have yellow ups marginal veins (unlike *vibex*) and narrow jagged uph borders. Females from Fla. to Tex. and Argentina (ssp. **phyleus**) are usually dark brownish on the ups with orange bands. Females are much lighter orange-yellow in Calif.-Ariz. (and esp. in the desert at Las Vegas and Death Valley, where even males are lighter; ssp. **muertovalle**).

Habitat southern urban lawns and grassy places, straying northward. Ranges south to Argentina and throughout the Antilles. Hostplants grasses: *Cynodon dactylon* (sometimes a lawn pest on this grass), *Stenotaphrum secundatum*, *Agros-*

tis, Eragrostis hypnoides, Poa pratensis, and in the Antilles *Digitaria sanguinalis, Saccharum officinarum, Paspalum conjugatum, Axonopus compressus.*

Eggs pale bluish-white or greenish-white, laid singly, mostly on the underside of hostplant leaves, but also on many other plants and objects. Larvae eat leaves. They roll and tie leaves to make nests, which are horizontal in mowed lawns. Larva dark yellow-brown, gray, greenish-brown, or dull green, usually with brown dorsal and lateral stripes, the collar dark brown or black; head dark brown or black with red-brown vertical stripes. Pupa (Fig. 52) yellowish-brown (sometimes reddish or pale green), with brown dorsal mottling, a blackish dorsal line, and a black subdorsal stripe on the thorax, the abdomen with black lateral spots.

Many flights all year in s Fla. and s Tex.; a native on the Gulf Coast (mostly Mar.-Nov.) and in lowland Calif. (Apr.-Dec.) and Hawaii (introduced in 1970, spreading to five Hawaiian Is. by 1980, flying all year); a rare stray or failed introduction to Bermuda. Migrates north as far as Ont. and Prince Edward I. (mostly Sep.-Oct. in the north, rare before July-Aug.). Adults move an average of about 100 m between captures in Davis, Calif., but considerable dispersal out of the area apparently occurs (I. Shapiro). Males perch all day in grassy swales and lawns to await females. A passing female is pursued by the male, she lands, he lands and thrusts his head and antennae onto her abdomen and wings, then he flutters and crawls beside her, and they mate (Shapiro). Unreceptive females flutter the wings, raise the abdomen, or fly away.

Color Plate 49

466. Yvretta rhesus   Prairie Cobweb Skipper

The unh has white veins on dark areas as in *Hesperia uncas* (470), but *Y. rhesus* lacks orange-brown on the ups, and the male stigma is absent. Males have fewer white fw spots than females.

Habitat Upper Sonoran to lower Canadian Zone shortgrass and mixed-grass prairie. Hostplant grass: *Bouteloua gracilis.*

Eggs laid singly on the host.

One flight, mostly May (L May-M June at high altitude). Adults sip the nectar of flowers, esp. white-flowered *Astragalus drummondii*. Males perch all day on small prairie mesa tops (2 m high), or on flats where no hills exist, to await females.

Color Plate 49

467. Yvretta carus   Mexican Cobweb Skipper

Both sexes lack the ups orange of *Hesperia* (470-486). The male has a narrow upf stigma. The unh is grayish-yellow, without the black patches of *Y. rhesus* (466). Ssp. **carus** (Ariz.-Calif.) has pale unh veins and white upf spots. In ssp. **subreticulata** (w Tex. south to Panama), the unh veins are scarcely lighter than the ground color, and the upf has yellowish spots. Habitat mostly Upper Sonoran Zone desert grassland and oak/pinyon woodland. Several flights, Apr.-Sep. Adults sip flower nectar and mud. Males perch on flat bare ground next to the presumed shortgrass host, at least in the afternoon, to await females.

468. Pseudocopaeodes eunus   Alkali Skipperling

In both sexes of this Calif.-Nev. species, the ups wing veins are typically dark at the margins (females darker than males). Males have a narrow black upf

Color Plate 55

Color Plate 50

Color Plates 49, 50
Fig. 71

stigma. Both sexes have two whitish unh streaks, one in the discal cell and the other in cell CuA$_2$, edged with brown. Ssp. **alinea** (c Mohave Desert-s Nev.) is almost unmarked orange (the dark veins and white unh streaks are very faint), but the stigma, female border, and size differ from those of *Copaeodes* (461, 462). Ssp. **eunus** elsewhere (and w Nev.) has darker veins and prominent white unh streaks. Habitat Lower to Upper Sonoran Zone grassy places on alkali flats. Ranges south to Colima, Mex. Hostplant grass: *Distichlis spicata* var. *stricta*. Eggs cream. Several flights, June-Aug. northward, Apr.-Sep. southward.

469. Stinga morrisoni   Arrowhead Skipper

Identified by the silver unh streak from the base to the middle (forming an arrowhead with the postmedian band), not as in *Hesperia* (470-486), which it otherwise resembles. Habitat Upper Sonoran to Transition Zone open pinyon and Ponderosa Pine forest. One flight, May-M June in the Colo. foothills, L May-E July at higher altitude; several flights, M Apr.-M May and Sep. in w Tex. Males perch all day on hilltops, usually next to shrubs or trees, to await females. Adults sip nectar and mud.

470. Hesperia uncas   White-Vein Skipper

Except in Calif.-w Nev., easily identified by the white unh veins. The ups is usually quite orange except in some females of ssp. *uncas*. In ssp. **macswaini** (high-altitude mountains in w Nev.-Calif.-s Ore.), the unh veins are very little whitened; it resembles *H. nevada* (486), except that the white spot in unh cell CuA$_2$ is broadly connected to the postmedian band; it differs from *H. miriamae* (485) in unh ground color. Ssp. **lasus** (Utah-Ariz.-E Nev.) is lighter than ssp. **uncas** elsewhere; both ssp. have white unh veins. The male uncus is blunt and the valva may have small teeth on the end (Fig. 71). The female lamella also helps in identification (Fig. 71).

Habitat prairie, open woodland, and sagebrush in the Upper Sonoran to lower Canadian Zone (the Alpine Zone occasionally in Colo. and Calif., and mostly Canadian to Hudsonian Zone for ssp. *macswaini*). Ranges to s Mex. Hostplants grasses: *Bouteloua gracilis* in most of the range, *B. uniflora* in Mex., *Erioneuron pilosum* in Kans., *Stipa nevadensis* and *pinetorum* for ssp. *macswaini*.

Eggs pale greenish-white, laid singly on or near the host. Larvae eat leaves, and live in tied-leaf nests. Larva resembles that of *H. pahaska* (476); head sometimes pale laterally. Pupa similar to that of *pahaska*, the setae longer, the proboscis extending 1.3 mm beyond the legs, the cremaster very wide.

One flight, M June-July for ssp. *macswaini* and at high altitude in Colo.; usually two flights, mainly June and Aug., on the plains; several flights, L Apr.-M Sep., southward. Males perch all day on small prairie mesa tops or small hilltops to await females, and sometimes court at flowers elsewhere. Mate-locating behavior and adult appearance are similar to those of *Yvretta rhesus* (466), another grassland species, in an example of convergent evolution.

471. Hesperia juba   Jagged-Border Skipper

Identified by the contrasting indented upf borders, by the slightly greenish unh with a jagged white postmedian band (which has the rear spot in cell CuA$_2$ offset toward the base), by the two brown spots below the fw cell of females,

Color Plate 50
Figs. 52, 71

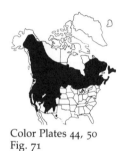

Color Plates 44, 50
Fig. 71

and by the short antennal club. The male uncus and valva are like those of *H. comma* (472; Fig. 71), but the female lamella is broader (Fig. 71).

Habitat Upper Sonoran to Transition Zone sagebrush, chaparral, and open woodland. Hostplants grasses: *Deschampsia elongata*, *Stipa* sp. similar to *nevadensis*, *Bromus rubens*, *Poa pratensis*, *agassizensis*.

Eggs creamy-white, soon becoming pinkish, then dull grayish-white, laid singly on or near the host. Larvae eat leaves, and live in tied-leaf nests. Larva like like that of *H. pahaska* (476). Pupa (Fig. 52) like that of *pahaska*, the proboscis not extending beyond the legs, the setae hooked. Larvae probably hibernate.

Two flights, mainly May-M June and Sep. Adults sip flower nectar and mud. Males perch all day in gulches to await females.

472. Hesperia comma   Holarctic Grass Skipper

Hard to identify because of individual and geographic variation. Western and northern, *H. comma* flies late in the summer (except in w Nev.-s Calif.); the upf border does not blend much with the orange, and the unh spots are nearly always well developed (except on the n Calif. coast). The male uncus is blunt (as in *H. juba*, 471, *uncas*, 470, *woodgatei*, 473, and *ottoe*, 474; Fig. 71), whereas it is triangular in the *leonardus* group (475-477) and highly pointed in other *Hesperia*; the valva teeth are close together (Fig. 71). The female lamella may also aid in identification (Fig. 71). In ssp. **laurentina** (SE Man.-NE Minn. east to N.B.-Maine), the unh is brownish-ochre with small spots. Ssp. **manitoba** (Alaska east to N Man. and Lab., south in the Cascades to N Calif., south in the Rockies to sw Colo.) is dark on the ups and greenish-brown on the unh; the postmedian spot in unh cell CuA$_2$ sometimes is placed closer to the thorax as in *H. nevada* (486), but the upf border is darker and the unh is not as greenish. Ssp. **assiniboia** (prairie, sw Man. to E-C B.C. south to Mont. and S.D.) is orangish, the unh yellow to yellow-gray with the postmedian spots yellowish. Ssp. *assiniboia* intergrades in the Front Range of Colo. to ssp. *oroplata*. In ssp. **oroplata** (s-c Colo. and NE N.M., intergrading at higher altitude to ssp. *manitoba*), the unh is yellow with a silver V-shaped postmedian band. High-altitude *manitoba* differs genetically from *oroplata* in Colo.; lab-raised *manitoba* are darker, and require a shorter time from egg-laying to adult (2.5 vs. 4 months; J. Scott). In ssp. **susanae** (N.M.-Ariz.), the unh is ochre-brown with normal-size white spots. In ssp. **harpalus** (Great Basin), the unh is gray-green with silver spots. Ssp. **yosemite** (w slope of the Sierra Nevada, s Calif., and the Inner Coast Range of Calif.) is orangish, and the unh is yellowish-brown with yellow (sometimes absent) postmedian spots. In ssp. **dodgei** (a local ssp. in the Outer Coast Range near San Francisco), the unh is chocolate with white spots, the usual spots toward the hind corner missing. In ssp. **unnamed** (near the NW Calif. and sw Ore. coast), the unh is chocolate but lacks spots. Ssp. *comma* and other ssp. are in N Africa, Europe, and Asia.

Habitat Upper Sonoran to Hudsonian Zone (and tundra edge) open woodland and grassland. Hostplants grasses: *Festuca ovina* (Europe), *rubra*, *Poa scabrella*, *glauca*, *arctica*, *Muhlenbergia*, *Stipa thurberiana*, *Andropogon saccharoides*, *Lolium*, *Bromus*, *Bouteloua gracilis*; sedges (Cyperaceae): *Carex* in Japan, and sometimes oviposition site in Colo. Larvae eat grasses in the lab.

Eggs creamy-white, turning salmon-pink, then grayish-white, laid somewhat haphazardly on or near the host (or on *Eriogonum* or dead twigs in Calif., or on *Arenaria fendleri*, a grasslike Caryophyllaceae, in Colo.). Larvae eat leaves, and live in nests of rolled and tied leaves (sometimes in a silk tube under dried cow dung). Larva like that of *H. pahaska* (476), the side of the head light in color in w U.S., dark in SE Canada. Pupa like that of *pahaska*, the proboscis extending very little beyond the legs. Eggs hibernate (and older larvae or pupae in the Arctic).

One flight, mainly L July-E Sep., but L June-E Aug. in s Sask., M July-E Aug. in Nfld. and Lab., M June-E Aug. in w Nev., and mostly June-E July in s Calif.; two flights, mostly M June-July and L Sep.-M Oct. in the Spring Range of s Nev. Biennial in the Arctic, flying in July of odd years in Alaska, of even years at Churchill, Man. Adults sip flower nectar and mud. Males perch all day, generally on hilltops, but ssp. *dodgei* males perch on hilltops or near the host, to await females.

473. Hesperia woodgatei   Fall Skipper

Color Plate 50
Fig. 71

Southwestern, identified by the late-summer flight, large size, dark-brown unh with small rounded spots, and long antennae with tiny clubs. c Tex.-NE Mex. adults are a little smaller, the antennae a little shorter. The valva teeth are farther apart than those of *H. comma* (Fig. 71). The female lamella is similar to that of *comma* (Fig. 71).

Habitat Upper Sonoran to Transition Zone open oak/pine woodland. Ranges to c Mex. Hostplants: not known with certainty, but oviposition on the sedge *Carex planostachys* in Tex., on the grass *Bouteloua uniflora* in Mex.

Eggs pale yellow, turning white.

One flight, M Sep.-E Oct. Males perch all day on hilltops to await females.

474. Hesperia ottoe   Prairie Skipper

Color Plate 53
Fig. 71

Resembles *H. leonardus pawnee* (475) in having a uniformly yellow unh, but males lack a dark patch next to the upf stigma, the stigma has hidden black dust, females have the ups border more blended into the ground color, adults fly June-July, and the genitalia differ (Fig. 71). *H. ottoe* females (along with *leonardus pawnee*, *attalus*, 479, some *metea*, 480, *uncas*, 470, and *dacotae*, 482) may have a transparent white upf spot at the base of fw cell CuA_1. Western populations average paler on the ups, but are variable.

Habitat grazed mixed-grass to tallgrass prairie on the Great Plains, and dry fields and prairies near the Great Lakes. Hostplants (R. Dana) grasses: *Andropogon scoparius*, *gerardii*, *Leptoloma cognatum*, *Bouteloua curtipendula* (the favorites of field larvae), *hirsuta*, *gracilis*, *Panicum* probably *wilcoxianum*, *Sporobolus neglecta*, *Bromus*; sedges (Cyperaceae): oviposition on *Carex geyeri*. Larvae refused the grass *Stipa*.

Eggs creamy-white, laid singly, usually on the host grasses but in Minn. on the disk flowers of *Echinacea angustifolia* (Compositae), on which adults feed also. The young larvae drop off the flowers and crawl to a host, eat the leaves, and live in tied-leaf nests, often in a chamber at the base of the plant. Larva light greenish-brown, without any waxy powder; head dark brown. Fourth-stage larvae (perhaps rarely fifth-stage) hibernate.

One flight, L June-July, June in Kans.-Mo. Males perch all day, mainly on flowers near the larval hostplants (occasionally on bare ground or low plants) on slopes and flats, to await females, and sometimes patrol.

475. Hesperia leonardus   Blazing-Star Skipper

Color Plates 44, 50, 53
Figs. 48, 71

The eastern-woodland ssp. **leonardus** (west to SE Man. and E Kans.) is easily identified by the rust-red unh with rounded cream spots. Ssp. **pawnee** (the Great Plains, east to sw Minn. and sw Man.) is yellowish on the unh with a few vague yellowish spots or no spots; it resembles *H. ottoe* (474) but flies later in the year, males have a dark upf patch outside of the stigma, and females have contrasting ups borders. These two ssp. intergrade completely in Minn. and Wis. (the blend zone is outlined with white on the map). In ssp. **montana** (South Platte River Canyon in the Colo. mountains, threatened by a proposed reservoir), the unh is brownish with small to large cream spots; *montana* is larger, with less-distinct unh spots, than *H. comma* (472). Males of *H. leonardus, pahaska,* and *columbia* (475-477, the "*leonardus* group") are the only *Hesperia* that have yellow dust inside the stigma (to determine the color, run a needle through the stigma from one end to the other, not through the wing, and look at the dust on the needle), a triangular uncus, and small sometimes absent valva teeth (Fig. 71). The female lamella is like that of *H. columbia* (Fig. 71).

Habitat mostly Upper Austral to lower Canadian Zone woodland meadows and clearings (ssp. *leonardus*), prairie (ssp. *pawnee*), and open Transition Zone Ponderosa Pine woodland on crumbling Pikes Peak Granite soil (ssp. *montana*). Hostplants (superscript=first letter of ssp.) grasses: *Panicum virgatum*[1], *Eragrostis alba*[1], *Agrostis*[1], *Danthonia spicata*[1], *Andropogon scoparius*[P], *Bouteloua hirsuta*[P], *gracilis*[m], *curtipendula*[P], *Sporobolus heterolepis*[P], *Stipa*[P], *Poa pratensis*[P], *Tridens*[P].

Eggs greenish-white, turning white, lacking the ventral flange of *H. comma* eggs, laid haphazardly on and near the host. Larvae (Fig. 48) eat leaves, and live in tied-leaf nests. Larva like that of *H. pahaska*, with a cream V-mark on each cheek; head with cream areas on the side only in ssp. *pawnee* and *montana*. Pupa like that of *pahaska*, the proboscis extending 1 mm beyond legs. First-stage larvae hibernate.

One flight, M Aug.-E Sep. northward, mostly L Aug.-M Sep. southward and in Colo., M Sep.-E Oct. in Ark. Adults sip the nectar of flowers, esp. *Liatris punctata* (Blazing Star). Males patrol at flowers all day to seek and court females, and ssp. *pawnee* males also sometimes perch on hilltops in Colo. and Minn. to await females.

476. Hesperia pahaska   Yellow-Dust Skipper

Color Plate 50
Figs. 39, 71

Very similar to *H. viridis* (478), but the male stigma (Fig. 39) has yellow dust, and the unh postmedian band is usually straight at the rear (except in some females, which usually have darker upf borders than *viridis*). The genitalia differ as noted under *viridis* (Fig. 71). The ups is much more orange in SE Calif. (ssp. **martini**). In ssp. **pahaska** (elsewhere in U.S.), the ups is slightly more orange than usual in s Utah, w Colo., and w Tex., and the unh spots are smaller in s Ariz. and w Tex. (the unh spots are very small in w Chihuahua, Mex.). *H. pahaska* is closely related to *H. columbia* (477) because in adults in the Sierra San

Pedro Mártir of Baja Calif. the wing pattern tends toward *columbia*; however, where *pahaska* and *columbia* approach within about 20 km of each other in N Baja Calif., the uncus shape remains distinct.

Habitat Upper Sonoran to lower Canadian Zone desert grassland, chaparral, open woodland, and prairie hills. Hostplants grasses: *Bouteloua gracilis, Erioneuron pulchellum.*

Eggs creamy-white, laid singly on or near the host. Larvae eat leaves, and live in tied-leaf nests. Larva light brown; head dark brown, with two cream vertical stripes on the midline of the forehead above a cream inverted-V-shaped mark, this mark in turn above two cream spots (side by side) above the mouth-parts on the face. Pupa light brown, with tiny pale areas around the dorsal hairs and with brown spots on the abdomen, the proboscis extending 3-4 mm beyond the legs. Larvae hibernate.

One flight, mostly M June-E July northward (L June-July at high altitude and in Sask.); several flights, M Apr.-M Oct., in Ariz.-w Tex. (records mostly M Apr.-M June and M Aug.-M Oct.). Marked males moved an average of about 200 m during their lives, which averaged 4 days in nature (J. Scott). Adults sip flower nectar and mud. Males perch all day on hilltops to await females (*H. viridis* mates in gulch bottoms at the same localities). When a female flies to a hilltop, the male pursues, she lands, he may flutter about her before landing and sometimes after landing, and then they mate. Unreceptive females flap their wings vigorously until the male departs.

Color Plate 50

477. **Hesperia columbia**   Chaparral Skipper

This Calif.-Ore. species is easily identified by the yellowish unh with a silvery straight postmedian band and postbasal dash (not U-shaped) and by the yellow dust in the male stigma. The abdominal structures resemble those of *H. leonardus* (475; see Fig. 71).

Habitat foothill chaparral and open oak woodland. Hostplant grass: *Koeleria cristata* (one oviposition on *Danthonia californica*, but larvae refused it).

Eggs greenish-white, turning white, laid singly on or near the host. Larvae eat leaves, and live in tied-leaf nests. Larva like that of *H. pahaska* (476). Pupa like that of *pahaska*, the proboscis extending about 2 mm beyond the legs.

Two flights, mainly M Apr.-M May and M Sep.-M Oct. Males perch on hilltops all day to await females.

Color Plate 50
Fig. 71

478. **Hesperia viridis**   Black-Dust Skipper

Identified by the unh postmedian band, which has the rear spot in cell CuA_2 bent outward toward the corner. Some *H. pahaska* (476) females also have this spot bent outward, but in *H. viridis* females the upf border is usually blended into the ground color much more. The stigma dust is black (yellow in *pahaska*). The genitalia are distinctive (Fig. 71): the female lamella is smooth without ridges (*pahaska* has four ridges), the uncus is more pointed, and the male valva has two long teeth (the teeth are short in most *pahaska*). Ariz. adults are slightly larger and darker.

Habitat Lower Austral Zone mesquite grassland, and Upper Sonoran to Transition Zone prairie, chaparral, and pine or oak woodland. Hostplants grasses: *Bouteloua gracilis, curtipendula, Erioneuron pilosum, Tridens muticus, Buchloe dactyloides*.

Eggs laid singly on or near the host. Larvae eat leaves, and live in tied-leaf nests. Larva like that of *H. pahaska*, or the head sometimes a little lighter on the side and above the mandible. Pupa like that of *pahaska*, the proboscis extending 2.5 mm beyond the legs.

One flight, mostly July, at high altitude in Colo.; one long flight (and perhaps a partial second) L May-E Aug. (rarely as late as E Sep.) on Colo. plains; several flights, Apr.-M Oct. (mostly Apr.-May and M Aug.-M Oct.), in Tex. Males perch all day in gulches to await females.

Color Plate 53
Fig. 71

479. Hesperia attalus   Dotted Skipper

This SE U.S. species is identified by the greenish-yellow to pale-orangish-yellow to greenish-brown unh with small (sometimes absent) light spots. Less orange on the unh than *H. meskei* (481), and the valva and lamella have different shapes (Fig. 71). *H. sassacus* (483), usually more northern, has different ups borders, unh spots, and abdominal structures. In ssp. **slossonae** (Miss. eastward), the unh is greenish-yellowish-brown with small spots. In ssp. **attalus** (Tex.-Mo.), the unh is greenish-yellow with small or absent spots. *H. ottoe* (474) flies with *attalus* in Kans.-Okla., but *ottoe* is lighter with an almost unmarked yellow unh, and its male uncus is truncated (very pointed in *attalus*). The female lamella differs slightly from that of *ottoe*.

Habitat oak/pine barrens, woodland meadows, and prairie. Hostplants grasses: *Aristida virgata, Leptoloma cognatum, Bouteloua curtipendula* var. *caespitosa*; assoc. with *Panicum virgatum*.

Eggs laid on or near the host.

Two flights, June-E July and Aug.-M Sep. northward, M-L May and L Aug.-M Sep. in Tex.; many flights all year in s Fla. A Mass. record seems to be a stray. Males perch to await females.

Color Plate 49
Fig. 71

480. Hesperia metea   Cobweb Skipper

Easily identified by the eastern range, the spring flight, the blackish-brown unh (sometimes with a reddish-yellow tinge) usually with a white band (sometimes solid black), and the small amount of ups orange. Ssp. **licinius** (Tex.-Ark.) is very dark on the unh with the white band small. Ssp. **metea** elsewhere has a larger white unh band, with white veins next to it in males. The genitalia differ from some other *Hesperia* (Fig. 71).

Habitat Gulf Coast to lower Canadian Zone dry grassy places in woods. Hostplants grasses: *Andropogon scoparius, gerardii, virginicus* var. *abbreviatus*.

Eggs whitish, laid singly on or near the host. Larvae eat leaves, and live in rolled- or tied-leaf nests. Larva grayish-brown, the neck white, the collar black; head black (with orange areas like those of *H. pahaska*, 476), orangish above the mouthparts and behind the eyes. Pupa light brown. Mature larvae hibernate.

One flight, M May-M June northward, Apr. in Ga., M Mar.-M Apr. in Tex. Males perch near the host, apparently all day, to await females. A passing female lands when pursued, the male flies about her briefly, he lands, she may flutter slightly, and then they mate.

481. Hesperia meskei   Gulf Coast Skipper

This species is identified by the orangish-yellow unh with large faint pale (or absent) spots. More orange on the ups and unh (esp. in females and on the hind margin of the unh) than in *H. attalus* (479); males have a dark patch outside the male stigma, and the valva and lamella differ (Fig. 71). Habitat southern open woods and grassy places. Hostplants grasses: *Andropogon scoparius*, *Aristida purpurascens*. Two flights, M-L June and E Sep.-M Oct. northward, L May-M June and M Sep.-M Oct. in Tex.; several flights, at least May-Dec. in s Fla.

482. Hesperia dacotae   Dakota Skipper

This N plains species has yellowish unh spots as in *H. sassacus* (483), but the ups border is mostly suffused with the ground color, the female may have a white fw spot like that of *H. ottoe* (474), and the valva and uncus differ (Fig. 71). Females have a yellowish-gray unh with zero to many spots. *H. dacotae* is smaller and has a less-pointed fw than *ottoe*, and the uncus and female lamella differ. The lamella (Fig. 71) is long, as in *sassacus*, but widest at the end (widest in the middle in *sassacus*).

Habitat northern tallgrass alkaline prairie, generally where *Zygadenus elegans* (Liliaceae) grows. Most N.D.-Man. sites are on shorelines of Ice Age lakes. T. McCabe suggested that hay mowing in Oct. is the best way to preserve the habitat for *H. dacotae* because otherwise shrubs overgrow it (fires originally kept the habitats open, but the remaining sites are too small now to risk burning them). One adult was supposedly caught in 1895 in Chicago, but *dacotae* is unknown east of Iowa now. Hostplants grasses (R. Dana): larvae in nature found on *Andropogon scoparius* (the favorite), *Panicum*, *Poa pratensis*. Larvae eat many grasses and even a sedge (*Carex*) in the lab.

Eggs laid singly on any broad surface, esp. broadleaf plants such as *Astragalus* (Leguminosae), occasionally on grasses such as *Bouteloua curtipendula*, *Andropogon gerardii*, *Stipa*, and *Aristida*. Larvae eat grass leaves, and live in a silk tube among leaves and debris at the base of the plant. Larva light brown, like that of other *Hesperia*, with a black collar; head dark brown, pitted all over (and pitted on lower part, unlike most *Hesperia*). Pupa reddish-brown. Larvae in the fourth stage, and sometimes the third (but not the fifth), hibernate.

One flight, L June-July. Adults sip the nectar of flowers, mainly Compositae, and sometimes *Campanula* (Campanulaceae) and *Oenothera* (Onagraceae); adults refuse *Asclepias*, *Apocynum*, and others that other butterflies visit. Adults usually fly less than 0.5 km during their lifetime. When scared they usually fly about 50 m downwind. Males perch on tall plants or other objects near the larval hostplants, on slopes, etc., to await females. A passing female is pursued until she lands, the male lands behind her, she extends her abdomen, and they mate. Receptive females do not flutter (unreceptive *Hesperia* females flutter strongly).

483. Hesperia sassacus   Indian Skipper

Identified by the eastern range, the brownish-yellow unh (with large but vague yellowish spots usually pointing outwardly along the veins), and the dark contrasting ups borders. The male uncus has a very long point, the valva has small teeth, and the lamella is distinctive (Fig. 71). Habitat upper Transition to

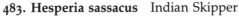

lower Canadian Zone woodland meadows. Hostplants grasses: *Andropogon scoparius, Festuca obtusa, Digitaria sanguinalis* (only in the lab?), *Panicum*, probably *Danthonia spicata*. Eggs (Fig. 45) greenish-white, turning whitish. One flight, June-M July northward, M May-M June southward.

Color Plate 50
Fig. 71

484. Hesperia lindseyi   Lost-Egg Skipper

Occurs only in Calif. and vicinity. The upf borders blend into the orangish ground color, and the unh is yellowish-brown to slightly greenish (with the spots cream to yellowish in males, whitish in females, and extending outward along the veins). On the w side of the Sierra Nevada, the unh spots do not extend onto the veins, and adults resemble *H. comma yosemite* (472), but *lindseyi* flies in L May-E July there, unlike *comma*, and its uncus is pointed (Fig. 71; vs. blunt in *comma*). The female lamella is square in *lindseyi* (Fig. 71), more rectangular in *comma*. The unh spots are yellow in the N Calif. Coast Ranges, cream-colored elsewhere.

Habitat grassy (often not bunchgrass) open chaparral and oak woodland. Hostplants grasses: *Festuca idahoensis, Danthonia californica, Vulpia megalura*.

Eggs whitish, laid singly, mainly on tree lichens at one site, haphazardly at another, often on *Lupinus bicolor* (Leguminosae) at a third. Larvae eat leaves, and live in tied-leaf nests. Larva like that of *H. pahaska* (476); head with the light areas a little darker. Pupa like that of *pahaska*, the proboscis extending 4 mm beyond the legs. Eggs hibernate (the larva fully formed inside).

One flight, M June-M July northward, M May-June southward. Males usually patrol slowly just above the grass all day, and sometimes perch, in grassland (usually near ridgetops) to seek females.

Color Plate 50
Fig. 71

485. Hesperia miriamae   Alpine Skipper

Only in the Alpine Zone (of the Sierra Nevada, Calif., and the White Mts. of Calif.-Nev.); identified by the large white somewhat rectangular unh spots on a grayish background (pale gold if worn) and by the ups orange being somewhat blended with the border. The fw apical spots are large. In *H. nevada* (486) and *H. uncas macswaini* (470), the unh pattern is different. The male valva is serrate at the end, with the outer tooth small, and the female lamella is much broader than in other *Hesperia* (Fig. 71).

Habitat Alpine (rarely straying to Hudsonian) Zone rocky tundra. Hostplants grasses: oviposition on *Festuca brachyphylla*.

Eggs pearly-white, becoming cream speckled with pink.

One flight, L July-M Aug. Adults have a very fast flight. Males perch all day on hilltops and ridgetops to await females.

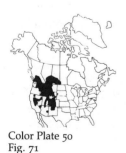

Color Plate 50
Fig. 71

486. Hesperia nevada   Montane Skipper

In this w U.S. mountain species the unh is greenish, the spot in unh cell CuA_2 is more inward than the postmedian band and usually just barely touching the band, and the upf orange is blended into the border. The male uncus has a very long undivided point (Fig. 71). The female lamella helps in identification (Fig. 71). The unh spots are a little larger from B.C. to Calif. and NW Colo. than elsewhere.

Habitat Transition to Hudsonian Zone aspen parkland, sagebrush, grassland. Hostplants grasses: *Stipa occidentalis*, and oviposition on *Koeleria, Sitanion hystrix, Festuca ovina.*

Eggs creamy-white, laid singly on or near the host.

One flight, usually M June-M July (June-E July at low altitude, L June-E Aug. at high). Adults sip flower nectar and mud. Males perch all day on hilltops to await females.

487. Polites draco   Rocky Mountain Skipper

Color Plate 51

The unh postmedian spots are longest in cells M_1 and M_2, as in *P. sabuleti* (488), but *P. draco* is much darker. The unh is brown, slightly greenish, with contrasting cream spots and no light veins. *P. draco* is probably an altitudinal ssp. of *sabuleti*; the abdominal structures and male stigma are the same, intermediates occur on Grand Mesa, Colo. (M. Epstein), and *draco* replaces *sabuleti tecumseh* in the Rockies. Habitat Canadian to Alpine Zone moist meadows and valley bottoms. One flight, M June-July. Males perch all day in low grassy spots and gullies to await females.

488. Polites sabuleti   Saltgrass Skipper

Color Plate 51
Fig. 51

This small species is identified by the unh, which has longer spots in cells M_1 and M_2 (like those of *P. draco*, 487, and *P. peckius*, 489), a yellow U-shaped basal mark, and light veins. The unh spots (yellow in males, cream in females) do not contrast with the yellowish ground color as much as those of *draco*, and the uph has yellow submarginal veins. Ssp. **tecumseh** (high-altitude Sierra Nevada) is darker and smaller (adults in Glenn Co., Calif., and the NW Calif.-SW Ore. Cascades are similar but not as small). Ssp. **ministigma** (San Luis Valley and Arkansas Canyon, Colo.) is yellowish on the ups and lacks the brown patch outside the smaller male stigma. Ssp. **chusca** (SE Calif.-W Ariz.-S Nev.) is yellowish on the ups, and the unh is nearly spotless yellow (without the pattern of all other ssp.). Ssp. **sabuleti** elsewhere is orangish with a complete unh pattern. Ssp. *tecumseh* differs genetically from the low-altitude ssp. *sabuleti* even though spring-form *sabuleti* looks like *tecumseh*; *tecumseh* cannot produce the paler summer form of *sabuleti* (A. Shapiro). Ssp. *tecumseh* requires 3 months from egg to adult in the lab, ssp. *sabuleti* 2 months (in contrast, the high-altitude *Hesperia comma* requires less time at high than at low altitudes).

Habitat Upper Sonoran to Transition Zone moist meadows, urban lawns, and alkali grassland in valley bottoms (ssp. *sabuleti, ministigma*), Lower Sonoran Zone alkali grassland in valley bottoms (ssp. *chusca*), Canadian to Alpine Zone meadows (ssp. *tecumseh*). Hostplants grasses: *Distichlis spicata* var. *stricta* (the main native host for *sabuleti* and *chusca*), *Cynodon dactylon* and *Poa pratensis* (for *sabuleti*), *Eragrostis trichodes* (for *ministigma*), *Agrostis scabra, Festuca idahoensis, brachyphylla* (all three for *tecumseh*).

Eggs pale bluish-green, turning cream, laid singly on the host, nearby dicotyledons, horsetail plants, soil, etc. (and on a sedge, *Carex filifolia*, which larvae refuse). Larvae eat leaves, and live in tied-leaf nests. Larva (Fig. 51) purplish-brown, or green or light gray mottled with brown, with dark dorsal and sometimes lateral lines and a lighter lateral band, the collar black; head black, with two vertical white stripes on the front above a white inverted V on the face, the cheeks white or black. Young larva (first- or second-stage) yellowish-green in ssp. *sabuleti*, purplish-brown in ssp. *tecumseh*. Pupa green, with a dark dorsal line, the abdomen and wing cases yellowish or brown or shaded pink toward the rear, the proboscis about 2 mm longer than the legs. Pupae hibernate.

One flight, mostly M July-M Aug. for ssp. *tecumseh* (mostly Sep. in NW Calif.), L June-July for ssp. *ministigma* in Colo.; mostly several flights, June-E Sep., elsewhere; many flights, M Apr.-Oct., in lowland Calif. and s Nev. Males perch all day in low grassy spots to await females.

489. Polites peckius ("*coras*") Yellow-Patch Skipper

Color Plates 48, 51

The distinctive unh includes a light spot at the base of cell CuA$_2$ and another spot beyond the humeral vein, which are absent in similar *Polites*; the unh is brown around the yellow spots and the margin is yellower-brown.

Habitat mostly Upper Austral to Canadian Zone meadows and prairie. Apparently native in E U.S., the N Rockies, the White Mts., Ariz., and the mountains of Gunnison and Saguache Cos., Colo., but recently invading NE Colo. NE Wash. records are also recent, but *P. peckius* may be native there. Hostplants grasses: *Leersia oryzoides*, undoubtedly *Poa pratensis*; larvae eat grasses in the lab.

Eggs pale greenish-white or cream, later developing irregular reddish mottling, laid singly. Larvae eat leaves, and live in leaf nests. Larva maroon-brown, with a blackish dorsal line and light-brown mottling; head black, with light areas similar to those of *Hesperia pahaska* (476). Pupa reddish-purple with white wing cases and appendages, the proboscis extending nearly to the end of the abdomen. Larvae and pupae hibernate.

One flight, mostly July, northward and at high altitude in the Rockies; two flights, L May-M June and L July-M Sep., elsewhere. Males perch all day in grassy swales to await females.

490. Polites mardon Cascades Skipper

Color Plate 51

Only in sw Wash. (the type locality of Mt. Hood, Ore., was apparently mislabeled, although *P. mardon* probably occurs in Ore.) and extreme NW Calif. The yellow unh spots are like those of *P. mystic* (491), but the front spots (cells Sc+R$_1$ and Rs) are smaller, and the fw is much rounder (the ranges are separate also). The unh spots are smaller than those of *P. peckius* (489). The unh wing veins are not pale (those of *P. sabuleti*, 488, are).

Habitat humid Transition Zone grassy lowlands west of the Cascades (on serpentine in Calif.), and Hudsonian to Alpine Zone grassland. Larvae eat grasses in the lab.

Eggs cream, eventually turning yellowish-orange. Larva light gray, with many brown dots and a black dorsal line, the collar black; head black, with two white dorsal stripes. Pupa ashy-gray, with darker spots, the top of the thorax darker gray, with light-brown areas on the abdomen and wing bases. Pupae hibernate.

One flight, M June-M July. Males rest on rocks and soil (probably perching in grassy areas). Adults mate as late as 5 P.M.

Color Plates 50, 51

491. Polites mystic   Long Dash

Identified by the broad pale unh postmedian band and the pale unh postbasal streak. Somewhat resembles *Ochlodes sylvanoides* (506), but flies earlier in the year, the orange uph postmedian spot in cell CuA_2 is missing, and the pale upf postmedian band is narrower and more blended with the brown border.

Habitat N Upper Austral to Canadian Zone moist meadows and creeksides. Hostplants grasses: *Poa*, *Agropyron repens*[t], *Echinochloa crus-galli*[t], *Phleum pratense*[t]. The sedge *Carex*[t] is questionable.

Eggs greenish-white or pale yellowish-green, laid singly on or near the host. Larvae eat leaves, and live in tied-leaf nests. Larva brownish-green, or dark brown mottled with white, with a dark-brown middorsal line, the collar black; head reddish-brown or blackish. Pupa bluish-black or dark brown with whitish hairs, the proboscis extending to the tip of the abdomen. Fourth-stage larvae hibernate.

One flight, M June-July, in most of the range; apparently two flights, June-E Sep. in s Mich., L May-June and Aug. in coastal N.Y.-N.J., the second flight only partial in N.Y. at least. Males perch all day in low grassy areas to await females.

Color Plate 51

492. Polites sonora   Western Long Dash

Like *P. mystic* (491), but smaller and lives only in western mountains; the unh postmedian band is much narrower and more distinct. The unh varies: brown along the coast from B.C.-c Calif. (ssp. **siris**), brownish-yellow inland (ssp. **sonora**), greenish-brown in the Rockies (ssp. **utahensis**).

Habitat Transition to Hudsonian (mostly Canadian) Zone moist meadows. Hostplant unknown. Larvae eat grasses in the lab.

Eggs greenish-white. Half-grown larva grayish-green; head black.

One flight, mostly L June-M Aug. (M July-M Aug. in Colo.). Adults sip nectar, in Colo. preferring white-flowered thistles at ground level that lack stems (*Cirsium drummondi* var. *acaulescens*). Males perch all day in the low spots of meadows to await females, and court at flowers there.

Color Plate 54
Fig. 71

493. Polites themistocles   Tawny-Edged Skipper

P. themistocles, *P. baracoa* (494), and *P. origenes* (495) have no hw spots (or faint ones). *P. themistocles* is identified by the male stigma, which is in three parts like a tilted J on the right upf (in *origenes* and *baracoa* the stigma is nearly straight), and by the orange upf streak in females. The male valva differs (Fig. 71).

Habitat Gulf Coast to lower Canadian Zone grassy areas and lawns. Hostplants grasses: *Panicum* spp. (including *clandestinum*), *Digitaria filiformis*, *Poa pratensis*.

Eggs greenish-white, laid singly on or near the host. Larvae eat leaves, and live in tied-leaf nests. Larva yellowish, greenish, or purplish-brown, with tiny brown points, a dark sublateral line, and a faint lateral line, the collar black; head black (white near the eyes), with two white vertical stripes above a white inverted V on the face. Pupa dirty-whitish to light mottled-brown (the head dark, the wing cases green), the proboscis extending 0-2 mm beyond the wings. Pupae hibernate.

One flight, M June-July, northward and in the Rockies; several flights, June-Aug., on Colo. plains and in s Mich.; many flights all year in s Fla. Males perch all day in grassy swales and valley bottoms to await females.

494. Polites baracoa   Little Tawny Edge

Color Plate 54
Fig. 71

Like *P. themistocles* (493) and *P. origenes* (495) but smaller (fw length 12 mm in males, about 13 mm in females). The narrow orange streak on the leading edge of the fw of both sexes does not fill the end of the cell (it fills the end in male and female *themistocles* and in male *origenes*), the male unf apical spots are connected to the orange streak on the leading edge (the spots sometimes touch the streak in *themistocles*), the unh usually has a distinct row of postmedian spots (usually weak or absent in *themistocles*), and the male stigma is narrow and straight (angled in *themistocles*). The spine on the end of the valva is at the bottom in *baracoa*, near the top in *themistocles* (Fig. 71).

Habitat subtropical and coastal grassy areas. Ranges south to the Bahamas and Greater Antilles. Larvae eat grasses in the lab.

Eggs cream, later turning yellowish-pink. Larva yellowish-brown, with brownish spots, a dark dorsal line, and a wide dark (light-edged) lateral line; head dull yellow, with two white vertical stripes, and with a white spot above the eyes.

Many flights, Mar.-Nov. (once in Jan. in Fla.).

495. Polites origenes (= *manataaqua*)   Cross-Line Skipper

Color Plate 54
Fig. 71

Resembles *P. themistocles* (493) but slightly larger and darker; the male stigma is straight, females usually (and males often) have faint uph spots, and females nearly lack an orange upf streak. The male valva differs from that of *themistocles* (Fig. 71). Dark males are usual in E U.S. (ssp. **origenes**), rare in the Rockies and vicinity (ssp. **rhena**).

Habitat Gulf Coast to Transition Zone dry meadows (damp meadows eastward), open woodland, and prairie. Hostplants grasses: *Tridens flavus*, *Andropogon scoparius*; larvae eat grasses in the lab.

Eggs greenish-white. Larva mottled brown; head and collar black. Pupa bluish-gray, blacker on the thorax and head. Third- and fourth-stage larvae hibernate.

One flight, L June-M July, northward and in the Rockies; two flights, June-E Sep. in Ill. and N.J., May-Oct. southward. Males perch all day in grassy swales and valley bottoms to await females.

496. Polites vibex   Whirlabout

Color Plates 49, 51

Identified by the peculiar pattern of dark smudged unh dots, somewhat like those of *Hylephila* (465). Males lack the yellow ups marginal veins of *Hylephila*. Males are orangish, but females are dark brown, much darker than *Hylephila* females. In ssp. **vibex** (Conn.-E Tex.), the unh has large dark spots and is yellow in females; in ssp. **praeceps** (s Tex.), the dark spots are smaller, the female unh is grayish, and the ups is lighter.

Habitat Gulf Coast and coastal-plain grassy areas, straying northward.

Ranges south to Argentina and the Greater and Lesser Antilles. Hostplants grasses: *Cynodon dactylon*, *Paspalum setaceum*.

Eggs whitish. Larvae feed mostly at night, and live in a silked-leaf tube. Larva pale green, with a dark middorsal line, the collar black; head black, with two cream vertical stripes, cream spots on each side of the face, and cream on the front. Pupa pale green, the abdomen whitish, the proboscis extending to the end of the abdomen.

Many flights, all year in s Fla. and s Tex., Mar.-Oct. in Miss.; migrates northward, reaching N.J. in late summer (M Aug.-Oct. in N.Y.-N.J.) and rarely Iowa and Ont. Males perch in open fields, etc., to await females.

Color Plate 49

497. Wallengrenia egeremet ("otho")   Brown Broken Dash

The stigma of *Wallengrenia* is split into a long upper and a small lower part, hence the common name. The ups is brown with little orange, long pale spots lie beyond the fw cell, and the unh is brown with vague light postmedian spots extending inward in cells M$_1$ and M$_2$. Females somewhat resemble *Pompeius verna* (499) and *Euphyes vestris* (524; *Polites vibex*, 496, and *Oligoria maculata*, 557, differ on the unh). *P. verna* females have a square fw spot in cell CuA$_1$ (*egeremet* females have an elongated spot in this cell and yellowish scales on the front of the unf). *W. egeremet* females have larger unh spots than *E. vestris* females (which usually lack unh spots), and *vestris* lacks the many spines (it has two spurs) on the middle-leg tibia that *egeremet* and the other spp. have.

Habitat Gulf Coast to Transition Zone moist wooded open areas. Ranges south to the Bahamas and Cuba. Hostplants grasses: *Panicum clandestinum*, *dichotomum*.

Eggs pale green or greenish-white. Larvae eat leaves. Larva (V. Dethier) dark brown, mottled with darker brown and white, with a darker middorsal line; head dark brown to black. Larva (S. Scudder and P. Laurent) pale green, with dark-green mottling, a dark-green middorsal line (bordered by yellowish-green), and indistinct lateral lines; head dark brown, with two pale vertical stripes. Pupa (of *egeremet*?) green, brownish on the head, yellow-green on the abdomen, the proboscis extending nearly to the end of the abdomen. Half-grown larvae hibernate.

One flight, July-E Aug., northward; two flights, M May-M June and Aug.-Sep. (M Sep.-M Oct. in Fla.), southward. Adults fly slowly. Adults sip flower nectar and mud. Males perch on vegetation 1-2 m above ground, esp. in early morning, to await females.

498. Wallengrenia otho   Red Broken Dash

Like *W. egeremet* (497) in stigma shape and wing markings, but the light spots are orangish, and the unh is not brown. In ssp. **curassavica** (s Tex.), the unh is reddish-yellow. In ssp. **otho** elsewhere the unh is rust-red.

Habitat mostly Lower Austral Zone wooded areas and swamps. Ranges south to Argentina and most of the Antilles. Hostplants grasses: *Digitaria sanguinalis*, *Paspalum*, and in Puerto Rico *Oryza sativa*, *Saccharum officinarum*.

Eggs laid singly on or near the host. Larvae eat leaves, and live in tied-leaf nests. Larva green, or mottled with white and reddish-brown, with orange

Color Plate 49

lateral spots and short black hairs; head purplish-brown or black, with two white stripes on the cheeks meeting at the top, or variably marked with white or greenish-yellow. Pupa light green.

Many flights all year in s Fla. and s Tex.; two flights, L May-June and L Aug.-M Sep., in Va. Males perch on forest-edge vegetation near the ground to await females.

Color Plate 49

499. Pompeius verna   Little Glassy Wing

Identified by the blackish-brown ups with distinct whitish fw spots (including a long spot next to the male stigma in cell CuA$_1$) and by the dark-brown unh (often with a faint rusty sheen and a faint blue sheen and sometimes with faint postmedian spots). Females have tiny subapical fw spots, unlike females of *Euphyes vestris* (524), and a darker unh than in *Euphyes bimacula* (522) and *Polites origenes* (495), and they lack the unh pattern of *Lerema accius* (448) and *Wallengrenia egeremet* (497). Females of these species are called "witches" because of their blackish wings.

Habitat Gulf Coast to Transition Zone grassy (often moist) places in wooded areas. Hostplant grass: *Tridens flavus*.

Eggs greenish-white, cream, or white. Larvae eat leaves, and live in nests of rolled or tied leaves. Larva yellowish-green to yellowish-brown, with black dots at the hair bases, a faint dark middorsal stripe, and three faint dark lines on each side; head and collar blackish. Pupa greenish-cream, with dark dots, blackish on the front and rear, the wing veins brown.

One flight, L June-July, northward; two flights, M June-M July and Aug., in Va. and Ill.; several flights, Apr.-Sep., southward. Adults sip flower nectar and (males) mud. Males perch in small sunlit clearings on low plants to await females.

Color Plates 48, 49, 51

500. Atalopedes campestris   Sachem

Males easily identified by the round brown upf spot and very wide stigma. Females have a large transparent upf spot and a yellowish-brown or brown unh with large white to yellow postmedian spots. Females resemble some *Hesperia* females (470-486), but the *Atalopedes* antenna is more hooked, and female *Hesperia* with translucent fw spots generally have an almost unspotted yellow unh or are dark brown on the ups.

Habitat subtropical to Transition Zone grassy areas and lawns. Ranges south to Brazil. Hostplants grasses: *Cynodon dactylon* (sometimes a pasture pest on this grass), *Festuca rubra*, *Stenotaphrum secundatum*, *Digitaria sanguinalis*, *Eleusine indica*.

Eggs greenish-white, laid singly on or near the host. Larvae eat leaves, and live in nests of silked rolled or tied leaves at the base of the grass. Larva dark green, with black dots and a dark-greenish-brown dorsal line; head and collar black. Pupa (similar to 465 in Fig. 52) blackish-brown (lighter on the end of the black-dotted abdomen), the proboscis extending 2 mm beyond the wings.

Many flights all year in s Fla. and s Tex.; a native in lowland Calif. (L Apr.-E Oct.) and se U.S. (Apr.-Nov.), migrating northward as far as Ont. and N.D. (most common northward in late summer). One mass-migration known. Males perch all day in grassy swales and meadows to await females.

Color Plate 54

501. Atrytone arogos   Brown-Rim Skipper

The upf borders are very wide (esp. in females), and the ups veins and unh are yellow. *Atrytone* males lack a stigma.

Habitat Gulf Coast to Transition Zone grassy places and prairie. Apparently absent in most of the middle portion of its range. Hostplants grasses: *Andropogon gerardii*, *scoparius*, possibly *Panicum*.

Eggs pale yellow, developing two reddish rings, laid singly under leaves. Larvae eat leaves, and live in nests of rolled or tied leaves. Larva light green (yellowish in the middle of the thorax), with a dark-green middorsal line, the collar tan; head grayish-white, with orange-brown vertical lines like those of *Problema byssus* (503). Pupa pale yellow, the wing cases and end of the abdomen white, the proboscis extending 3 mm beyond the wing cases. Fourth-stage larvae hibernate.

One flight, July, northward and in Colo.; two flights, M May-E June and M Aug.-E Sep., in Mo. and Ga.; many flights, Mar.-Nov., in Fla. Adults sip flower nectar and mud. Males perch near the host, from about 1:20 to 4 P.M. (usually under cloudy skies), on the bases of slopes and flat areas, to await females.

Color Plate 53

502. Atrytone logan (=*delaware*)   Black-Vein Skipper

Identified by the black ups veins (at least at the margin), the narrow upf borders, and the unspotted yellow unh. Adults are much larger than the small skippers with dark veins (*Thymelicus*, 464, *Pseudocopaeodes*, 468, *Adopaeoides*, 463). Females have wider borders than males, as in male *Problema* (503, 504), but they have darker upf veins and no pale unh spots. Ssp. **lagus** (Great Plains) is lighter with a narrower upf border than ssp. **logan** (eastern woodland). In ssp. **mazai** (s Tex. south to El Salvador), the unh veins are often darker orange.

Habitat subtropical to Transition Zone moist areas with tall grasses. Hostplants grasses: *Andropogon gerardii*, *Erianthus divaricatus*, *Panicum virgatum*.

Eggs laid singly on host leaves. Larvae eat leaves, and live in nests of rolled or tied leaves. Larva bluish-white, with tiny black dots and with a black crescent-shaped band on the rear, the collar black; head white, with a black band around the top and sides and three black vertical streaks on the forehead. Pupa greenish-white, the head and rear black.

One flight, L June-July, northward and in Colo.; several southward; many flights, Feb.-Oct. in Fla., Apr.-Oct. in Tex. Adults sip flower nectar and mud. Males perch all day in grassy swales and gulch bottoms to await females.

Color Plate 53

503. Problema byssus   Golden Skipper

The ups borders are very wide in *Problema*, the males lack a stigma, and some ups veins are black (esp. in females). The unh is yellow in males, brownish-yellow in females (usually with lighter veins), with large faint lighter spots. Male *Problema* look like female *Atrytone logan* (502), but the ups veins are less blackened. Females are much darker than males.

Habitat damp prairie and other grassy areas from the Gulf Coast north to Ill.; the range may be expanding in the north. Hostplants grasses: *Tripsacum dactyloides*, *Andropogon gerardii*.

Eggs whitish, laid singly on the upperside or underside of host leaves. Larvae eat leaves, and live in nests of rolled or tied leaves. Larva dull blue-green, with a yellow dorsal tint; head pale reddish-brown, with many cream vertical lines and streaks. Pupa cream, with tiny brown dots, in a nest of silked-together leaves. Fourth-stage larvae hibernate.

One flight, M June-M July, northward; two flights, June and L Aug.-E Sep., in N Ga.; several flights, Mar.-Oct., in s Fla.

Color Plate 53

504. Problema bulenta   Golden Marsh Skipper

Identified by the extension of the unf black from the corner to vein CuA$_1$, by the uniformly yellow (reddish-tinged) unh without darker veins or dark or pale spots, and by the wide ups borders esp. in females. Habitat Lower Austral Zone freshwater marshes. Adults assoc. with the grass *Zizaniopsis miliacea*. Several flights (recorded in E May, M-L June, L July-Aug.). Adults sip nectar (esp. of *Pontederia* flowers).

Color Plate 53

505. Ochlodes yuma   Giant-Reed Skipper

Bigger than *O. sylvanoides*; the upf border is narrow and blended into the orange, and the unh is spotless yellow in males, tan-yellow in females (sometimes with faint pale spots) in most of the range (ssp. **yuma**) but is grayish-yellow with faint pale spots in N.M. (ssp. **unnamed**). Resembles *Hesperia ottoe* (474) and *H. leonardus pawnee* (475), but the range is west of the Rockies, the male borders and stigma are narrower, and the female generally lacks white spots.

Habitat Lower to Upper Sonoran Zone seeps, springs, riverbanks, sloughs, and canals, near the cornlike host. Hostplant grass: *Phragmites australis* (=*communis*).

Eggs pale greenish-white, laid on or near host leaves. Larvae eat leaves, and live in rolled-leaf nests. Larva pale greenish; head cream, with a narrow brown marginal stripe and a brown vertical median stripe. Pupa brown (dark brown on the head), with two rows of dark-brown dots around each abdomen segment, the proboscis extending about 3 mm beyond wings.

One flight, M July-Aug. in w Colo.-E Utah, M Aug.-E Sep. along the Colorado R.; two flights, June-M July and L Aug.-Sep., in Calif.-s Utah. Adults seldom stray far from the hostplant. A colony may occupy only one hectare of plants, isolated by dozens of kilometers from other colonies. Males perch all day in low spots among the host to await females.

Color Plates 50-52
Fig. 71 (valva)

506. Ochlodes sylvanoides   Western Skipper

This common species is orange on the ups (without white spots) with contrasting toothed brown borders, and the unh is yellowish to brown with large angular yellow or cream spots. The upf has a stigma in males, and a brown patch where the stigma would be in females. In ssp. **santacruza** (Santa Cruz I., Calif., and coastal Santa Cruz, Mendocino, and Humboldt Cos., Calif., intergrading to ssp. *sylvanoides* inland in the Coast Ranges and the other Channel Is.), the unh is chocolate-brown with cream spots. Ssp. **orecoasta** (Ore. coast) has dark ups borders and a brown unh with yellow spots. Ssp. **bonnevilla** (the desert of NE Nev.-s Ida.) is pale, and the unh is orangish-yellow (or even whitish) with faint yellow spots. Ssp. **sylvanoides** (=*pratincola*, the rest of the range) has the unh brownish-orange to orangish-yellow with yellow spots.

Habitat Upper Sonoran to Transition Zone chaparral, sagebrush, and woodland. Hostplants grasses: *Phalaris californica, lemmoni, Elymus cinereus, Agropyron caninum* ssp. *majus, Cynodon dactylon* (larvae were destructive to s Calif. golf courses in 1922).

Eggs cream or greenish-white. Larva pale green, with a darker dorsal line and a pale lateral line, or more yellowish, with seven blackish longitudinal lines; head cream, with black margins and a black vertical forehead stripe. Pupa (similar to 465 in Fig. 52) brownish-cream (the head brownish), the abdomen dotted with brown, covered with a whitish bloom. Mature larvae aestivate about a month before pupating (A. Shapiro). First-stage larvae hibernate.

One flight, mostly L July-Aug. (L Aug.-E Oct. in Calif.); two flights, L June-Oct., in the Central Valley of Calif.; several flights, Apr.-Aug., on Santa Cruz I. Adults sip flower nectar and mud. Males perch all day, in gullies and valley bottoms in Colo., among shrubs often on ridges in Calif., to await females.

507. Ochlodes agricola   California Skipper

Color Plate 53
Fig. 71

Differs from *O. sylvanoides* in being small (male fw length 12-13 mm, female 13-14 mm) and in having fw cells M_3 and CuA_1 with whitish spots instead of the wide orange band of *sylvanoides*, the male stigma wider with a gray streak down the middle, and the unh orange-yellow (bluish-brown in females) with light blurred postmedian and basal spots. The valva (near its end) lacks the keel-like scoop of *sylvanoides* (Fig. 71).

Habitat Upper Sonoran to Transition Zone woodland, streamsides, and chaparral. Larvae eat grasses in the lab.

Eggs gray-green, becoming white.

One flight, L May-June. Males perch all day to await females, mainly in the shade of shrubs at the edges of clearings on hillsides and other places; adults also court at flowers.

508. Ochlodes snowi   Rusty Gully Skipper

Color Plate 49

The unh is rust-red as in *Paratrytone* (515), but *O. snowi* has small yellow unh spots, white fw spots including one in the cell, and a stigma in males.

Habitat upper Transition to Canadian Zone, mostly the upper edge of Ponderosa Pine woodland. Ranges south to Puebla, Mex. Hostplant grass: *Blepharoneuron tricholepis*.

Eggs laid singly on leaves.

One flight, M July-E Aug. in most areas, July in N Colo., Aug.-Sep. in Ariz. Adults sip the nectar of flowers, esp. bluish or purplish legumes. Marked males move an average of 181 m (up to 1,610 m) during their lifetimes, which average a little less than a week in nature (J. Scott). Adults have a very fast flight. Males perch all day in narrow dry gullies to await females, and court there and elsewhere at flowers. A passing female is pursued, and she lands or hovers. If she hovers, the male hovers around her, contacting her occasionally. A receptive female landed without hovering and the male fluttered slightly, he landed, and they mated. Unreceptive females hover, or flutter on a flower, to reject males.

509. Poanes massasoit   Mulberry Marsh Skipper

Easily identified by the rounded dark-brown wings and the characteristic unh pattern. Females have more fw spots than males. The pale unh spots are sometimes absent, esp. in ssp. **chermocki** (s Md.), which usually has only unh postmedian spots; ssp. **massasoit** elsewhere has more unh spots. Habitat mostly N Upper Austral to Transition Zone marshes, bogs, and roadside sloughs. Hostplant sedge (Cyperaceae): *Carex stricta*. Eggs white. Larva dark green. One flight, July-E Aug. Males patrol with a low weak flight to seek females.

510. **Poanes viator**   Broad Marsh Skipper

Easily identified by the large rounded wings, the large orange uph patch, the few upf spots, and the pale unh streak. The fw spots are orange in males, whiter in females. Ssp. **viator** (Great Lakes) has a yellow unh streak and other faint spots. In ssp. **zizaniae** (near the coast and southward) the other spots are just as prominent as the streak or more so.

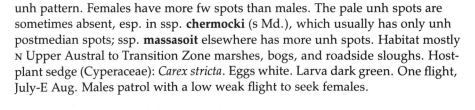

Color Plate 51
Fig. 55 (veins)

Habitat Gulf Coast to lower Canadian Zone marshy areas, even roadside sedge patches. Hostplants sedges (Cyperaceae; ssp. *viator*): *Carex lacustris, rostrata*; grasses (ssp. *zizaniae*): *Zizaniopsis miliacea, Zizania aquatica, Phragmites australis, Panicum*.

Eggs grayish, laid singly under host leaves. Larvae eat leaves, and live between a leaf and a stem without much of a nest, although they reinforce the area with silk before molting. The hibernation site of immatures that eat aquatic grasses is unknown; they may be underwater.

One flight, mostly July, northward; two flights, June-Aug., in Va.; many flights, M Apr.-E Nov., southward. Males patrol all day with a slow and slightly bobbing flight through the vegetation to seek females.

511. **Poanes zabulon**   Southern Dimorphic Skipper

The unh is unmistakable, mostly yellow in males with brown dots and margin, mostly brown in females with faint spots and a bluish margin and often a bluish base. Males lack a stigma. Ssp. **zabulon** (Atlantic west to c Neb., and from E Mex. to Panama) is darker, and females are nearly black with distinct sharp white-to-yellow fw spots. In males of ssp. **taxiles** (westward and NW Mex.), the color is paler, the brown unh spots are longer, and the brown unh marginal spot in cell Sc+R$_1$ lies in front of the one in cell Rs; females have some to much orange on the ups. Ssp. *taxiles* was considered a separate species, but the abdominal structures are the same and the wing pattern is similar; they replace each other geographically, and bear the same relation to each other as the dark eastern ssp. and black females of *P. hobomok* do to the pale western *hobomok wetona*. Also, a ssp. *psaumis* (=*benito*) from Jalisco, Mex., seems intermediate in wing pattern.

ssp. *zabulon*

Color Plates 4 (larva), 5 (pupa), 48, 49, 51

ssp. *taxiles*

Habitat Lower Austral to lower Transition Zone open woods in the east, Upper Sonoran to Transition Zone valley bottoms and high-plains cottonwood groves in the west, often in shady areas. Hostplants grasses: in the east *Tridens* and *Eragrostis*, in Colo. oviposition on the broadleaf grasses *Puccinellia airoides, Poa pratensis, Agropyron repens, smithii, trachycaulum, Dactylis glomerata, Elymus canadensis, Agrostis gigantea*.

Eggs cream, laid singly on the underside of grass leaves. Larvae eat leaves, and live in tied-leaf nests. Larva (ssp. *taxiles*) orangish-tan with a brown middorsal line, fainter subdorsal, supralateral, and sublateral brown lines, and many tiny brown dots, a larger subdorsal brown dot on each segment; prothorax cream; head brownish-red, oranger in front of eyes. Pupa (ssp. *taxiles*) orangish-tan (the head, thorax, and appendages dark bluish-gray, with black crescents on the head) with a brown dot below each of the numerous body hairs, the abdomen with many black transverse dashes and dots, an odd orange patch of bumps near each side of the proboscis on abdomen segments four to six, the proboscis orange on its 5-mm tip beyond the wings, the eyes and cremaster red-brown; inside the larval leaf nest, attached only by the cremaster.

One flight, M June-July, in w U.S.; two flights, L May-E July and M Aug.-M Sep., in the northeast; several flights, Apr.-M Sep., in Ga. Adults sip flower nectar and mud. Males perch all day in valley bottoms and gullies esp. in shaded areas in the west, in forest clearings in E U.S., to await females.

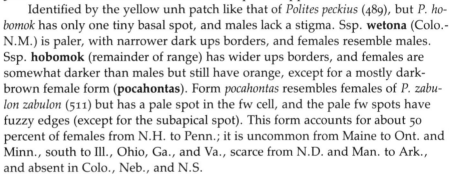

Color Plates 49, 51

512. Poanes hobomok   Northern Dimorphic Skipper

Identified by the yellow unh patch like that of *Polites peckius* (489), but *P. hobomok* has only one tiny basal spot, and males lack a stigma. Ssp. **wetona** (Colo.-N.M.) is paler, with narrower dark ups borders, and females resemble males. Ssp. **hobomok** (remainder of range) has wider ups borders, and females are somewhat darker than males but still have orange, except for a mostly dark-brown female form (**pocahontas**). Form *pocahontas* resembles females of *P. zabulon zabulon* (511) but has a pale spot in the fw cell, and the pale fw spots have fuzzy edges (except for the subapical spot). This form accounts for about 50 percent of females from N.H. to Penn.; it is uncommon from Maine to Ont. and Minn., south to Ill., Ohio, Ga., and Va., scarce from N.D. and Man. to Ark., and absent in Colo., Neb., and N.S.

Habitat mostly Upper Austral to Canadian Zone wooded areas. Hostplants grasses: *Panicum, Poa.*

Eggs pale green, laid singly on or near the host. Larvae eat leaves. Half-grown larva dark green to brown; head and collar dark brown. Pupa reddish, with brown markings.

One flight, mostly June-E July northward and in the Rockies, L Apr.-May in Ga. To await females, males perch all day on vegetation about 2 m above the bottom of gullies and valley bottoms (in clearings on flat land).

Color Plate 53

513. Poanes aaroni   Atlantic Marsh Skipper

Identified by the brown unh with a yellowish streak (and occasionally faint spots), the very narrow stigma (*P. aaroni* and *P. yehl*, 514, are the only *Poanes* spp. that have a stigma), the rounded wings, and the broad brown ups borders. Females have more orange on the ups than females of *P. yehl* and *P. viator* (510), and usually one or two apical fw spots, unlike *yehl*.

Habitat coastal salt marsh, and some inland marshes and lakes. Assoc. with the grass *Spartina alterniflora* var. *glabra*.

Eggs white.

Two flights, L May-June and L Aug.-M Sep., in Va.; several flights, at least L Mar.-E Apr. and Aug.-Oct., in Fla. Adults sip the nectar of flowers, esp. *Pontederia*, as other marsh skippers do.

514. Poanes yehl   Southern Swamp Skipper

Identified by the light reddish-brown unh, which has about five vague post-median spots, by a short pale streak from the end of the unh cell to cell M_1, and by the broad male stigma. The orange fw band of females is generally much wider than in *P. viator* (510) and narrower than in *P. aaroni* (513); the fw of females usually has three apical spots, not two as in *aaroni* and *viator*. The female unh is paler in spring, more cinnamon in late summer. Habitat southeastern woods and swampy woods. Hostplant grass *Arundinaria* (a bamboo). Two flights, L May-M June and L Aug.-Oct. Males perch on sunlit shrubs to await females.

515. Paratrytone melane   Umber Skipper

Identified by the reddish-brown unh with vague yellow spots, the distinct fw spots (reddish in males, whitish in females), and the lack of a male stigma. The ups is blacker with small spots in s Ariz.-w Tex. (ssp. **vitellina**), orangish-brown with vague orange spots in Calif. (ssp. **melane**). Other ssp. range south to Panama.

Habitat urban yards and low-altitude grassy areas in Calif., Upper Sonoran Zone foothills in Ariz.-w Tex. Hostplants grasses: *Deschampsia caespitosa*, *Cynodon dactylon*, *Bromus carinatus*, *Lamarckia aurea*, *Stenotaphrum secundatum*; sedges (Cyperaceae): *Carex spissa*.

Eggs pale greenish. Larvae eat leaves, and live in nests of rolled or tied leaves. Larva dusky yellow-green, with black points, a cream lateral stripe, a blackish dorsal line, and three other dark lines on each side; head yellow-brown. Pupa (similar to 465 in Fig. 52) yellowish with a pink tinge, later becoming grayish-yellow, with many blackish dots on the abdomen, the proboscis extending almost to the end of the abdomen; in nest of tied leaves.

Several flights, Apr.-Oct. (perhaps two flights everywhere, mostly May and Sep.); a stray into s Ariz. from Mex., but native in w Tex. Males perch all day in grassy swales, in gulches, and on lawns to await females.

516. Choranthus haitensis

This species from Hispaniola in the Antilles may have strayed once to N Fla. (Apr.), but probably was mislabeled. Resembles *Atrytone arogos* or *logan* (501, 502) but is small (fw length 14-15 mm), and the male has a narrow upf stigma. Habitat subtropical grassy areas. Hostplant grass: *Saccharum officinarum* in Hispaniola. Published descriptions of the early stages seem to refer to other *Choranthus*. Many flights in the Antilles.

The Cuban *Choranthus radians* (Color Plate 63) was recorded once from Fla., but was undoubtedly mislabeled. It resembles *C. haitensis*, and also has a narrow male stigma, but the unh has pale veins. Hostplant grass: *Saccharum officinarum* in Puerto Rico. Eggs white, changing to pink. Larva grass green, with a dull-green middorsal line; head yellowish, with a black line on each side of the head from the top to the eyes and a black vertical line on the forehead connected to a black W mark on the lower face.

517. Mellana eulogius (= *mexicana*)

The ups has dark veins and broad brown borders almost exactly like those of *Atrytone logan* (502), but *Mellana* is only in s Tex., the upf has a brown streak from the border to the cell, and the unh generally has paler yellow spots. The female has the ups dark brown with several clear upf spots, no uph spots, and no row of yellow fw spots. *Mellana* lack a stigma. Subtropical. Several flights all year in Mex.; a scarce stray to s Tex. (Apr.-Nov.) from Mex.

518. Euphyes pilatka   Coastal Sedge Skipper

This large skipper has wide ups borders. Resembles *Problema bulenta* (504), but the unh is brown (often with faint postmedian spots), and the male has a stigma.

Habitat subtropical and southern marshes near the coast. Hostplant sedge (Cyperaceae): *Cladium jamaicense*.

Larvae eat leaves, and live in rolled-leaf nests. Larva yellowish-green, with tiny dark dots, the collar black; head brownish, the upper part whitish with three black stripes.

Many flights all year in Fla.; apparently two flights, June and Aug.-Sep., northward.

Color Plate 53

519. Euphyes conspicua   Great Lakes Sedge Skipper

Resembles *E. dion* (520) and also has pale uph spots, but the unh lacks paler veins and is rust-brown with four or five vague yellow postmedian spots that are longer at the end of the cell. Some upf spots of females are translucent. Neb. adults are a little larger, and the unf is paler. Habitat mostly N Upper Austral to Transition Zone marshy areas. Hostplant a sedge (Cyperaceae): *Carex stricta*. One flight, July-E Aug. northward, L June-E Aug. southward.

Color Plate 54

520. Euphyes dion   Eastern Sedge Skipper

Identified by the orange uph streak, the orange-brown unh with orange streaks in the cell and in cell CuA$_2$, and the usually paler unh veins. The upf has five to seven orangish spots in females, and a stigma edged by orange in males. In form **alabamae** (=*macguirei*), which is common in N.C., Tenn., and Ark., southward, the orange fw band is narrower. Form *alabamae* was sometimes treated as a separate species because it flies with oranger adults in Va., Mo., etc., but it seems to be just an individual variation (*E. bimacula* has similar variation). C. Bryson found light/dark variation even in Mississippi, and noted that populations are darker on the average where they fly with *E. dukesi* (525) than where they fly with *E. pilatka* (518).

Habitat Gulf Coast to Transition Zone marshy areas, even roadside sedge patches. Hostplants sedges (Cyperaceae): *Scirpus cyperinus, Carex lacustris, hyalinolepis*; assoc. with *C. stricta* var. *brevis* and *Cladium*.

Eggs pale greenish, probably developing a reddish ring and reddish top. Larva bluish-green, with white flecks, yellow between segments, and a dark-green middorsal line; head white, with a black oval spot on the forehead and orange-brown vertical lines. Pupa in a silked-leaf nest. Third-stage larvae hibernate.

One flight, July-E Aug., northward; two flights, May-June and Aug.-Sep., in S.C.; several flights, L Apr.-M Sep., southward. Males perch in marshy areas to await females.

Color Plate 54

521. Euphyes berryi   Florida Sedge Skipper

Resembles *E. dion* (520) in having an orange uph patch and an orange-

Color Plate 54

brown unh with lighter veins, but differs in lacking orange unh streaks. Habitat subtropical to southern coastal-plain marshy sedge areas. Several flights, L Mar.-M Oct. Adults sip the nectar of flowers, esp. *Pontederia*.

522. Euphyes bimacula   Two-Spot Sedge Skipper

Identified by the unmarked brown uph, the orange-brown unh usually with paler veins, and the whitish fringes. Males have a narrow orange upf band next to the stigma, and females have several pale upf spots. Colo. adults are larger.

Habitat Gulf Coast (several valid records) to lower Canadian Zone marshy areas. Hostplant a sedge (Cyperaceae): *Carex trichocarpa*; assoc. with *C. stricta*.

Eggs pale yellowish-green, developing two reddish rings. Larvae eat leaves, and live in nests of rolled or tied leaves. Larva greenish; head cream, with two black vertical bars on the forehead (a brown U-shaped band around and below them) and a brown band over the top and down each side of the head. Half-grown larvae hibernate.

One flight, mostly L June-M July; two flights, M May-E June and L July-M Aug., in s U.S. Adults sip the nectar of flowers such as *Pontederia*. Males perch all day in low spots of sedge marshes to await females.

Color Plate 54

523. Euphyes arpa   Palmetto Skipper

Like *E. bimacula* (522), but the unh is bright unmarked orange, the uph may have a slight orange flush, and the end of the palpi on the head are orange.

Habitat subtropical to coastal open woodland, near palmetto. Hostplant a palm: *Serenoa repens*.

Larvae eat leaves, and live in rolled-leaf nests at the bases of the fanlike leaf segments. Larva pale green, with yellow stripes and with fine streaks of yellow and green, the collar black; head black, with a white border around the sides and top and two white vertical crescents surrounding a black oval on the forehead. Pupa light brown.

Many flights, mostly Mar.-Nov. (Mar.-Dec. on Fla. Keys).

Color Plate 54

524. Euphyes vestris ("*ruricola*")   Sedge Witch (Dun Sedge Skipper)

Identified by the uniformly brown wings and head, and mostly brownish fringes. The male uph has a stigma (rarely with a faint orange tinge around it), and females have several small or faint light fw spots (and rarely faint unh spots). Females of *Wallengrenia*, *Pompeius*, and *Polites* (487-499) have many spines and two spurs on the second long segment (tibia) of the middle legs, whereas those of *vestris* (and all *Euphyes*) have two spurs but no spines.

Habitat Gulf Coast to Canadian Zone moist areas and open woods. Hostplants sedges (Cyperaceae): *Carex heliophila* and *geophila* (both Colo. hillside plants), *lacustris*, *spissa*. The grass *Tridens flavus* is doubtful; larvae eat the sedge *Cyperus esculentus* in the lab, but refuse many grasses.

Eggs pale yellowish-green, developing a reddish ring and a reddish top, laid singly on host leaves. Larvae eat leaves, and live in nests of rolled or tied leaves. Larva pale green, with a whitish overcast, the prothorax white with a thin black collar; head cream, with a black oval on the forehead and two brown vertical bands on each side. Pupa yellow-green, hairy, the abdomen whitish-

Color Plates 47, 49

green, the head tan, the proboscis extending about 2 mm beyond the wings; in nest of tied leaves. Third-stage larvae hibernate.

One flight, mostly July northward and westward, June in s Calif.; two flights, L May-E July and L July-E Sep. in Va.-Mo., May-Sep. in Tex.; many flights, Mar.-Dec., in Fla. Adults sip flower nectar and mud, and feed on dung. Males perch in gullies and swales all day to await females.

525. Euphyes dukesi   Brown Sedge Skipper

Color Plate 49

Easily identified by the dark-brown ups with an orangish uph flush and by the dark-orangish-brown unh with yellow streaks in the discal cell and in cell CuA$_2$. The upf has a stigma in males and several pale spots in females.

Habitat Gulf Coast to Transition Zone marshy areas and wooded swamps, mainly along the coast, in the Mississippi R. system, and around the Great Lakes; these areas have poor drainage and many sedge swamps. Hostplants sedges (Cyperaceae): *Carex lacustris, hyalinolepis, walteriana.*

Eggs laid singly under host leaves. Fourth-stage larvae hibernate.

One flight, mainly July, northward; two flights, June-E Sep., in Va.; about three flights, M May-Oct., southward. Adults sip the nectar of flowers, esp. *Pontederia.* Males seem to patrol to seek females.

526. Asbolis capucinus   Palm Skipper (The Monk)

Color Plate 45

Easily recognized by the large dark-brown wings and the reddish-brown unh. The upf has a stigma in males, a pale patch in females. Habitat subtropical areas near palms. Strays from Cuba established a population in Fla. (first recorded 1947, now widespread and common). Hostplants shrub and tree palms: *Sabal palmetto, Cocos nucifera, Phoenix, Acoelorrhaphe wrightii.* Many flights, all year in s Fla., Mar.-Dec. in c Fla. Adults sip nectar; they may pollinate orchids.

527. Atrytonopsis hianna   Dusted Skipper

ssp. *loammi*

Color Plate 47

ssp. *hianna*

The wings are dark grayish-brown (without orange), the uns margins are gray, the unh has postmedian brown dots or white spots, the uph is unspotted, and the upf cell has a small white spot. The stigma is present on all male *Atrytonopsis,* but in all spp. it is tiny and three-parted as in *Amblyscirtes exoteria* (539). Ssp. **loammi** (Fla., and the coast north to N.C. and west to La., intergrading inland to ssp. *hianna*) has white unh postmedian and basal spots. Ssp. **hianna** elsewhere has few or no white unh spots, esp. westward.

Habitat Gulf Coast to Transition Zone open dry fields, open woodland, and prairie gulches. Ssp. *hianna* seems to be absent from the upper Ohio R. and Missouri R. valley areas. Hostplants grasses: *Andropogon gerardii, scoparius.*

Eggs lemon-yellow, the top turning pinkish-tan. Larvae eat leaves, and live in nests of rolled or tied leaves, higher on the plant than the larvae of *Hesperia metea.* Larva pale pinkish-lavender dorsally (the abdomen pale grayish-white, pale pink at rear); *or* larva pale green to brown, the prothorax gray with a dark-brown or black collar; head deep reddish-purple or dark brown. Pupa brown, the wing cases light brown, the abdomen light orange with a pink overcast; in a nest of leaves. Mature larvae hibernate.

One flight, L May-M June northward, M Apr.-M May (rarely July) south-

Color Plate 47

Color Plate 47

Color Plate 47

Color Plate 47

Color Plate 47

Color Plate 47

ward; many flights, Jan.-Nov., in Fla. Males perch all day in valley-bottom clearings (flats beside the gulch) or near the host to await females.

528. Atrytonopsis deva   Desert Dusted Skipper

Very similar to *A. hianna* (527), with a similar wing fringe, and may be a ssp. of it; *A. deva* is slightly lighter and larger, it occurs only in sw N.M.-Ariz., many males lack androconial scales in the tiny stigma, and the male saccus is slightly thicker. Habitat mostly Upper Sonoran Zone open woodland. Several flights, Apr.-Aug.

529. Atrytonopsis viereki   Four-Corners Dusted Skipper

Like *A. hianna* (527) and *A. deva* (528) but has large white fw spots, including a white bar in the fw cell. The unh is gray. Habitat Upper Sonoran Zone prairie gulches and open woodland. One flight, L May-June in Colo., Apr.-June southward. Males perch all day in gulches to await females.

530. Atrytonopsis lunus   Violet Dusted Skipper

A. lunus has a white bar in the fw cell, and lacks uph spots (as does *A. viereki*, 529), but the unh is dark bluish-brown, and the hw fringe is mostly white except at the corner. Reportedly flies with *viereki* at one site in Grant Co., N.M. Habitat mostly Upper Sonoran Zone open woodland and thorny desert grassland. One flight, L June-E Aug. (one Apr. record in N.M. may be unusual).

531. Atrytonopsis pittacus   White-Bar Dusted Skipper

A. pittacus and the next three species have white spots in the upf cell and on the uph. *A. pittacus* is easily identified by the straight white unh band and by the lack of large white unh postbasal spots. It differs from the other three in having the antennae white (not checkered beneath), the fringes not as checkered, and part of the stigma in cell CuA$_1$ short (only in the lower part of the cell). Habitat mostly Upper Sonoran Zone open woodland and thorny desert grassland. Several flights, L Mar.-July. Males perch all day, usually in gullies, to await females.

532. Atrytonopsis cestus   Baboquivari Dusted Skipper

Like *A. pittacus* (531), but the ups has large white postbasal spots, the unh postmedian band is jagged (formed of large white spots edged outwardly with black), and the fringes are checkered as in the next two species. Habitat mostly Upper Sonoran Zone foothills, in grassy thorn forest and open woodland. Several flights, M Apr.-M May and L Aug. at least. Males perch on rocks on the south-facing sides of deep gullies, from early morning to about noon, to await females.

533. Atrytonopsis python   Yellowspot Dusted Skipper

Like *A. cestus* (532), but the uph lacks a postbasal spot, the unh usually has violet-gray scales, and the unh spots are not as transparent and are sometimes small. The unh postmedian spots are, from the corner, one large, two small, and

two large (in *cestus* they are one small, then four large). Ssp. **margaretae** (N N.M. and perhaps Tex.) has whiter spots. Ssp. **python** elsewhere usually has yellow spots. Habitat Upper Sonoran to lower Transition Zone open woodland. Hostplant grass. Eggs cream, after a day or two developing an orange ring. Larva pinkish to blue-green; head pale brown. Several flights, Apr.-July.

534. Atrytonopsis ovinia   Rounded Dusted Skipper

Similar to the preceding three species, but the uph usually has a small white postbasal spot, the unh is mottled gray with separate rounded white spots (all about the same size), the male fw is more rounded, and *A. ovinia* is larger. Ssp. **zaovinia** is in the U.S.; ssp. *ovinia* is in C. Amer. south to Nicaragua. Habitat mostly Upper Sonoran Zone grassy thorn forest and open woodland. Several flights, L Mar.-Sep. Males perch on rocks on the south-facing sides of gullies, from early morning to about noon, to await females; males feed and rest and do not chase other adults in the afternoon, like male *A. cestus.*

Color Plate 47

535. Amblyscirtes simius   Hilltop Little Skipper

Identified by the pale upf discal-cell spot (rarely absent in dark males), the white uncheckered fringes, the orange in the middle of the unf, and the uniformly gray unh. The ups varies from nearly black (form **nigra**) to quite orange (form **rufa**). The male stigma has just one oval patch in cell CuA$_1$.

Habitat shortgrass and mixed-grass prairie and open pinyon-juniper woodland. Hostplant grass: *Bouteloua gracilis.*

Eggs creamy-white, developing a reddish ring, laid singly under host leaves.

Color Plate 47

One flight, M June-E July northward, L May-June on Colo. plains, July at 2,500 m (8,000 ft) in Colo.; several flights, Apr.-Aug., southward. Marked adults move an average of about 100 m during their life span, which averages 7 days for males in a cool year, and 5 days (males) or 6 days (females) in a hot year (J. Scott). Adults sip the nectar of many flowers, including blue *Penstemon*; they nearly disappear as they crawl among the stamens of yellow cactus flowers sipping nectar. Males perch on top of small prairie plateaus, ridgetops, and hilltops, about 7:40-10:50 A.M., to await females. When a female flies near a perched male on a hilltop, he pursues, she initiates a zigzag dance in which both fly very rapidly back-and-forth or up-and-down (about 15 cm each way) 10-20 times (the male just below her), she then lands, he crawls alongside, and they mate. Some females merely land, and they mate without a dance. *A. simius* may belong in a separate genus because it is the only *Amblyscirtes* species that mates on hilltops, that mates during only a part of the day, and that does not have a very long male aedeagus and saccus.

536. Amblyscirtes oslari   Prairie Little Skipper

Identified by the uniformly rusty-brown ups without pale spots (though faint apical fw spots are rare). The unh is gray and has faint pale postmedian spots, the unf cell is slightly reddish, and the fringes are grayish and slightly checkered. The upper part of the male stigma is very broad, the lower part short and thick. Habitat shortgrass and mixed-grass prairie, plus Upper Sonoran to Transition Zone open woodland and thorn forest. One flight, June-E July north-

Color Plate 47

ward, M May-M June in Colo.; several flights, Apr.-Sep., southward. Males perch all day in gully bottoms and roadside ditches, esp. on sandy spots, to await females.

537. Amblyscirtes cassus   Tawny Little Skipper

Color Plate 47

Identified by the orangish ups spots, including a dipper-shaped orange spot in the fw cell. The unf is quite orange, the unh is mottled gray, and the fringes are checkered. Habitat mostly Transition (sometimes Upper Sonoran) Zone open woodland. One flight, M June-E July; May-Aug. records in N.M. may indicate two flights. Adults sip mud.

538. Amblyscirtes aenus   Bronze Little Skipper

Color Plates 46, 47

Similar to *A. oslari* (536), *A. texanae* (540), *A. cassus* (537), and *A. exoteria* (539) (see them for identification). *A. celia* (543) has sharper fw spots and is blacker, without an orange tint. *A. aenus* is variable, but brown on the ups with a slight orangish tint (adults of only *cassus* and some *A. simius*, 535, are strongly orange). The uph has no spots, the upf may have zero to nine orangish spots (but almost never one in the discal cell), the fringes are checkered tan to cream, the unh is grayish-brown with zero to many vague whitish postmedian spots, and the unf discal cell is usually reddish. The two parts of the male stigma are usually rather small. In ssp. **unnamed** (Ariz.), the unf cell is reddish and the light unh spots are well developed. Ssp. **aenus** has less red and smaller unh spots in N.M.-Colo., and its unh spotting is quite variable from w Tex. to Okla. and SE Colo. (the extreme of this continuous variation, with almost no unh spots, is form **erna**). Form *erna* was considered a species, but normal ssp. *aenus* adults developed from eggs laid by an *erna* female from SE Colo. (J. Scott). Ssp. **linda** (E Okla. eastward) usually has little red in the unf cell, and small pale unh spots.

Habitat Upper Sonoran to Transition Zone open woodland and grassland gulches in the west, woodlands along creeks in the east. Hostplant grass: *Uniola latifolia*.

Eggs whitish. Larvae eat leaves. Larvae and pupae live in nests of rolled or tied leaves. Larva pale bluish-white, with whitish hairs and a faint blue middorsal line, the collar grayish-white; head black, with a white band on each side and the top and two white inverted hooklike marks on the front, these hooks pointed to three white triangles on top of each other on the lower face. Pupa (similar to 465 in Fig. 52) creamy-yellow, the abdomen cream, the proboscis longer than the abdomen. Half-grown larvae hibernate.

One flight, M May-June, in Colo.; two flights, L Apr.-E May and L June-E July in Ark., May-E Aug. in N Tex.; several flights, Apr.-Sep., southward. Adults sip flower nectar and mud. Males perch all day in gully bottoms, esp. in rocky areas (along creeks in E U.S.?), to await females.

539. Amblyscirtes exoteria   Sonoran Little Skipper

Most similar to *A. aenus* (538) but easily identified by the tiny pale fw spot in cell M_1 positioned halfway between the margin and the lowest of the three subapical spots. Adults are large (male fw length 15 mm), the brown ups has an

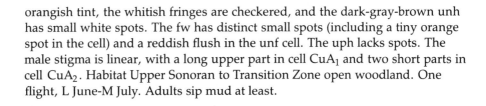

Color Plate 47

orangish tint, the whitish fringes are checkered, and the dark-gray-brown unh has small white spots. The fw has distinct small spots (including a tiny orange spot in the cell) and a reddish flush in the unf cell. The uph lacks spots. The male stigma is linear, with a long upper part in cell CuA$_1$ and two short parts in cell CuA$_2$. Habitat Upper Sonoran to Transition Zone open woodland. One flight, L June-M July. Adults sip mud at least.

Color Plate 46

540. Amblyscirtes texanae   Southwest Little Skipper

Identified by the small yellowish spot in the fw cell (sometimes absent), the large yellowish fw postmedian spots (esp. in cell CuA$_1$), and the three whitish fw subapical spots. The uph is paler in the middle than on the border, the unh is gray with faint pale spots, and the fringe is tan checkered with brown. Habitat Upper Sonoran Zone hilly open woodland and prairie gulches. Several flights, Apr.-Sep. Males perch all day, on rocks or other objects in gullies, to await females.

Color Plate 46

541. Amblyscirtes hegon (=*samoset*)   Greenish Little Skipper (Pepper-and-Salt Skipper)

Identified by the greenish-gray unh with pale postmedian spots, the pale checkered fringes, and the blackish ups with a few postmedian spots (and often a pale spot in the fw cell). *A. celia belli* (543) is similar but has a grayish-black unh. The male stigma has an extra patch on vein CuA$_2$.

Habitat mostly Upper Austral to lower Canadian Zone forest clearings and woods margins. Hostplants grasses: *Uniola latifolia*, *Poa pratensis*, *Sorghastrum nutans*, *secundum*.

Larva pale whitish-green, with dark middorsal and subdorsal lines and a whitish lateral line, the collar black; head dark brown, with two pale vertical crescents on each side of the face and two cream stripes behind them on each side. Pupa pale yellow (tinged with green esp. on the wing cases), the proboscis orange beyond the wing cases. Larvae (first-stage?) hibernate.

One flight, June northward, M Apr.-M May southward.

Color Plate 46

542. Amblyscirtes nereus   Creamy Little Skipper

Identified by the greenish-yellow unh with faint light spots and a blackish hind corner, by the well-developed white upf spots (esp. in cells CuA$_1$ and CuA$_2$, but none in the discal cell), by the white uph spots, and by the whitish slightly checkered fringes. Habitat Upper Sonoran Zone grassy open-woodland areas, often at springs. Several flights, L Mar.-Sep. Adults sip mud and flower nectar.

Color Plate 46

543. Amblyscirtes celia   Creekside Little Skipper

Identified by the blackish-brown ups (without the orangish tint of *A. aenus*, 538), the checkered cream to tan fringes, the small whitish fw postmedian spots, and the vague pale postmedian spots on the grayish-black unh. *A. celia* has more pale unh spots than *A. vialis* (549) or *A. alternata* (548), and the male fw is less pointed than that of *alternata*. *A. celia* is blacker on the ups than *A. hegon* (541) or *aenus*, and the fw spots are more sharply edged than those of *aenus*. In

ssp. *celia*

ssp. *belli*

Color Plate 46

Color Plate 46

ssp. **celia** (s Tex. south at least to s Mex.), the spots are slightly larger, the fw rarely has a tiny cell spot, and the two stigma parts are of average size for the genus or longer. Ssp. **belli** (N Tex. to Kans., east to N.C. and Fla.) is slightly darker, the spot in the unf cell CuA$_1$ is more L-shaped, and both stigma parts are long (as in *A. aesculapius*, 550). Ssp. *belli* is sometimes treated as a separate species because a male and female of ssp. *celia* were caught flying with many *belli* adults at Lancaster near Dallas in L Sep., but the pair were probably both individual variants in the *belli* population or strays from c Tex. Some variation also occurs in the ssp. *belli* population in Ga. (J. Symmes).

Habitat shady thorn forest and canals in s Tex., in woodlands along creeks in E U.S. Hostplants grasses: *Stenotaphrum secundatum*, *Paspalum* for ssp. *celia*, *Uniola latifolia* for ssp. *belli*.

Eggs whitish. Larvae eat leaves, and live in nests of rolled or tied leaves. Larva (Mo.) pale green, with a whitish overcast, a darker-green middorsal line, and a pale-green lateral band, the collar black; head cream-white, with six orange-brown vertical bands meeting at the top, differing from *A. nysa* (547) in having broad cream bands instead of hooks. Pupa pale cream, the thorax pale orange-brown, the abdomen pale yellow with pale-orange rings, the eyes red; in a leaf nest among soil litter. Fourth-stage larvae hibernate.

Several flights, L May-Sep., northward; many flights all year in s Tex. Adults sip flower nectar and mud. Males perch to await females.

544. Amblyscirtes eos   Starry Little Skipper

Identified by the uniformly dark-gray unh with clear-white spots outlined with black, by the solid-black ups with a few white fw postmedian spots, and by the pure-white fringes (checkered with blackish). Habitat southern shortgrass and mixed-grass prairie, plus open juniper-pinyon woodland. Several flights, May-E Sep. in Colo., L Mar.-Oct. southward. Adults seem to have long flights; *A. eos* seems to have invaded SE Colo. recently, where it is now widespread. Males perch all day in gullies and valley bottoms, on flat usually grassy spots on or just beside the gully bottom, to await females.

545. Amblyscirtes unnamed   Atascosa Little Skipper

Most like *A. eos* (544) but identified by the small white spot in the fw cell, the bent postmedian row of uniformly sized white fw spots, the black ups with white (somewhat checkered) fringes, and the grayish-brown unh with distinct white spots like those of *A. eos*, *A. exoteria* (539), and *A. tolteca* (546). *A. eos* lacks a fw-cell spot; *exoteria* and *tolteca* do not have a uniform row of fw spots. Habitat mostly Upper Sonoran Zone desert grassland and open woodland, from the Atascosa Mts. to the Mule Mts. of s Ariz., and Sonora, Mex. One flight, July-Aug. (May?).

546. Amblyscirtes tolteca   Spotted Little Skipper

Identified by the well-developed white spots (including one in the fw cell and another in cell CuA$_2$ of both sexes, and others on the uph of males) and by the clear white unh spots (like those of *A. eos*, 544, but *eos* lacks the fw-cell spot). Males have an unh spot at the base of cell CuA$_2$. The wings are blackish on the ups, the unh is grayish, and the fringes are pale and slightly checkered.

Color Plate 46

The male stigma parts are fairly broad. Ssp. **prenda** is in Ariz. and NW Mex.; ssp. *tolteca* is in the rest of Mex. Habitat Lower to Upper Sonoran Zone open woodland and desert grassland. Ranges south to El Salvador. Several flights, at least May–Sep.

547. Amblyscirtes nysa   Mottled Little Skipper

Color Plate 46

Identified by the peculiar black unh patches (shaped like an N on the right wing) and gray between. The ups is blackish-brown with a few pale fw postmedian spots. The fringes are whitish, checkered with brown. The upper part of the male stigma is long and narrow.

Habitat Lower Austral and Upper Sonoran Zone prairie, open woodland, desert grassland, and city lawns. Ranges to s Mex. Hostplants grasses: *Echinochloa muricata, Setaria glauca, Digitaria sanguinalis, Stenotaphrum secundatum, Paspalum*.

Eggs white, laid on host leaves and stems. Larvae eat leaves. Larvae and pupae live in nests of rolled or tied leaves. Larva pale bluish-green, with a dark-green middorsal stripe, the collar green; head colored as in *A. aenus* (538) except orange-brown, and between the hooks is a whitish line above a whitish triangle (which contains a grayish-white oval). Pupa bright cream, with an orange-brown shading on the head, the proboscis extending about 3 mm beyond the wings. Half-grown to mature larvae hibernate.

Many flights, all year in s Tex., May–Oct. northward. More common in late summer apparently because of migration northward (J. Heitzman). Males perch all day, on or near the bottom of narrow gulches, to await females.

548. Amblyscirtes alternata   Dusky Little Skipper

Color Plate 46

This SE U.S. species is identified by the blackish ups with a few (or zero) tiny white fw postmedian spots, by the whitish checkered fringes, and by the slightly grayish unh mottling. The fw spots are smaller than those of *A. vialis* (549), *A. hegon* (541), and *A. celia belli* (543), and the ups lacks the orange tint of *A. aenus* (538). The male stigma has only one narrow black patch in fw cell CuA_1. Habitat Subtropical to Lower Austral Zone open woods and grassy places. Several flights, at least L Apr.–Aug. northeastward, L Mar.–E Sep. in Tex.; many flights, Feb.–Nov., in Fla.

549. Amblyscirtes vialis   Black Little Skipper

Color Plate 46

Identified by having the unh nearly black at the base but uniformly gray at the margin beyond the faint postmedian spots. The ups is blackish-brown with three white subapical spots (and sometimes two tiny spots behind them); the spot on the front margin is the longest (tiny white streaks lie on the wing edge near this spot).

Habitat Gulf Coast to Canadian Zone mostly wooded areas. Hostplants grasses: *Uniola latifolia, Poa, Agrostis*; larvae eat many grasses in the lab.

Eggs greenish-white, laid singly on the host. Larvae eat leaves, and live in nests of rolled or tied leaves. Larva pale green, yellowish near the rear; head whitish, with reddish-brown vertical stripes. Pupa green, the head slightly reddish, the proboscis reddish beyond the wing cases. Larvae hibernate.

One flight, June–M July northward and at high altitude, L May–June in most places, L Mar.-M May southward; M June-E Sep. records seem to be partial additional flights in the south. Adults sip flower nectar and mud. Males perch all day in narrow shrubby or wooded valley bottoms and in forest glades to await females.

550. Amblyscirtes aesculapius (=*textor*)   Cobweb Little Skipper

Color Plate 49

Easily identified by the brown unh with its distinctive "cobweb" pattern of white lines. Males have smaller spots than females (only females have a spot in the fw cell). Both parts of the male stigma are very long and narrow. Habitat southeastern moist woods. Hostplant grass: *Arundinaria tecta*. Several flights, June-E July and M Aug.-Sep., northward; many flights, at least Feb.-Sep., in Fla.

551. Amblyscirtes reversa   Cane Little Skipper

Color Plate 46

Like *A. carolina* (552), but the unh is reddish-brown with yellow spots and some yellow suffusion (esp. a yellowish streak on the upper part of the unh), and in males the cream spot in the fw cell is smaller than the spot in cell CuA_1. Possibly a form of *carolina*, because *A. reversa* seems to fly with *carolina* in most places and has the same hostplant; this should be studied by raising adults from the eggs of wild females collected where both forms occur. Possibly a separate sp. because the part of the stigma in cell CuA_1 is not much longer than the part in cell CuA_2. Habitat Lower Austral Zone wet woods, near streams or swamps where the host grows. Hostplant grass: *Arundinaria tecta*. Larvae eat leaves, and live in rolled-leaf nests. Several flights, L Mar.-E Sep.

552. Amblyscirtes carolina   Yellow Little Skipper

Color Plate 46

Identified by the yellow unh with many reddish spots, the white uncheckered fringes, and the cream spot in the fw cell (which is usually larger than the spot in cell CuA_1 in males). The fw has many cream spots, including one in cell CuA_2. That part of the male stigma in cell CuA_1 is longer than the part in cell CuA_2, and cuts into the pale spot in cell CuA_1. Habitat Lower Austral Zone wet woods, near swamps or sluggish streams where the bamboo grass *Arundinaria tecta* grows. *A. carolina* may prefer shady areas, *A. reversa* (551) open areas (both spp. near *A. tecta*; R. Webster). Several flights, L Mar.-E Sep.

553. Amblyscirtes phylace   Redhead Little Skipper

Color Plate 47

Easily identified by the unmarked brownish-black wings (bluish-black on the unh), the orange head, and the white fringes (sometimes slightly orange in N.M.). *Euphyes vestris* (524) is similar but lacks spines on the tibia of the middle legs; it has a large male stigma and a browner head and fringes. The stigma is usually an oval blotch over the base of the upf vein CuA_2. Habitat Upper Sonoran to Canadian Zone open woodland and grassy areas. One flight, mostly June in Colo., June-E Aug. in w Tex. Males perch all day, in mostly bare depressions in gulches or at the mouth of tiny gulches, to await females.

554. Amblyscirtes fimbriata   Redrim Little Skipper

Like *A. phylace* (553), but the fringes and the head are both orange, and the male stigma consists of three parts in a line from vein CuA_1 to vein $1A+2A$.

Color Plate 47

Possibly a ssp. of *phylace* because the *phylace* stigma shape and fringe color vary somewhat in Ariz. and N.M. populations, possibly indicating intergradation, and the two species never fly together (K. Roever). Occasional grayish-fringed *A. fimbriata* adults occur in the Chiricahua Mts., Ariz. Habitat Upper Sonoran to Transition Zone pinyon–Ponderosa Pine grassy woodland (1,500-2,500 m, or 5,000-8,000 ft, in the Huachuca Mts.). Ranges south to c Mex. Larvae eat grasses in the lab. Eggs creamy-white. Immature larva grass-green; head black. One flight, M June-M July, in the U.S.; several flights, Mar.-Aug., in Mex.

Color Plate 46

555. Lerodea eufala   Gray Skipper

Identified by the grayish-brown ups (with small translucent fw spots) and by the tan-gray unh (occasionally with faint pale spots). The unf cell seldom has white spots. *Lerodea* males lack a stigma.

Habitat Subtropical to Lower Austral/Lower Sonoran Zone grassy areas and lawns; migrates northward. Ranges south to Argentina and the Greater Antilles. Hostplants grasses: *Cynodon dactylon*, *Echinochloa crusgalli*, *Sorghum halepense*, *vulgare* (and var. *bicolor*), *Setaria verticillata*, *Oryza sativa*, *Saccharum officinarum*, *Zea mays*, *Pennisetum ciliare*.

Eggs pale yellowish-white or greenish-white, laid singly on or near the host (eggs were misplaced on the sedge *Cyperus*, which larvae refused, and on the legume *Medicago sativa*). Larvae eat leaves, and live in nests of rolled or tied leaves. Larva green, with a dark-green middorsal line (edged with yellow) and a yellow lateral stripe above a white line; head whitish (the lower part orange-brown), with an orange-brown vertical stripe. Pupa (similar to 560 in Fig. 52) green, with a dark-green middorsal line and a whitish subdorsal band, the head armed with a long horn.

Many flights, all year in s Tex. and s Fla., Apr.-Oct. in Ga. (perhaps over-wintering on the Gulf Coast); migrates northward by late summer (L July-E Oct. in Va., Sep.-Oct. in Ill. and Mo., Aug.-Oct. and rarely Apr.-July in Calif.), to as far north as Mich. and N.D. Males perch all day in grassy swales and flats to await females.

Color Plate 46

556. Lerodea arabus   Blotchy Gray Skipper

Like *L. eufala*, but the unh has a central dark blotch often edged with white spots. Ssp. **dysaules** (s Tex. south to El Salvador) often has a white spot in the lower part of the fw cell (rarely a spot in the upper part), and the white spot in fw cell M_3 is small. In ssp. **arabus** (Ariz. and w Mex.) the white spot is positioned in the upper part of the fw cell, the spot in cell M_3 is usually larger than that of ssp. *dysaules*, and the unh spots occasionally show through on the uph. The ssp. have been treated as separate spp., but their abdominal structures are identical, and most of the distinguishing features usually cited do not work. The unh has fewer spots around the blotch in the spring in Ariz.

Habitat subtropical thorn forest in Tex., Lower to Upper Sonoran Zone open woodland (mostly in valley bottoms) in Ariz. Hostplant a grass; larvae eat a grass in the lab.

Eggs laid singly on the host.

Several flights, Apr.-Dec. in Ariz., at least June-Nov. in s Tex. (where it reproduces and is apparently native), Jan.-Nov. in Mex. Males perch all day, in gulches and along streams in Ariz., to await females.

Color Plate 47

557. Oligoria maculata   Three-Spot Skipper

Easily identified by the three white round spots on the dark (slightly reddish-brown) unh. The fw also has white spots. *Panoquina panoquinoides* (560) has fainter spots, paler coloration, more-pointed fw, and smaller size.

Habitat Subtropical to s Lower Austral Zone grassy areas. Larvae eat grasses in the lab.

Larva pale green (darker green at the rear); head and collar light brown. Pupa dull green, without a head horn.

Many flights all year in Fla.; two flights M May-M June and M Aug.-M Sep. in Ga., Apr.-May and Aug.-Sep. in Tex.-La.-Miss. Adults rarely migrate north to N.J. (Sep.), N.Y., and Mass.

Color Plate 41

558. Calpodes ethlius   Canna Skipper

Large in size and identified by the linear row of three white hw spots.

Habitat subtropical and Gulf Coast city flower gardens, sometimes in natural habitats. Ranges south to Argentina and throughout the Bahamas and Antilles, a resident on the Galápagos Is. and Bermuda. Hostplants herb Cannaceae: *Canna indica*, *flaccida*, *edulis*, *generalis*, "King Humbert" canna; Marantaceae: *Thalia dealbata*, and in the Antilles *Maranta*. These monocotyledons have showy iris-like flowers. Other records of *Colocasia esculenta*[t] (Araceae), *Phyllanthus* (Euphorbiaceae), and *Apium graveolens* (Umbelliferae) seem to be errors. Most larvae are found on green-leaved *Canna* with red flowers, few on red-leaved or pink-flowered or yellow-flowered plants (E. Bell).

Eggs pale greenish-white, later tinted with reddish, laid singly (or up to seven in a group according to S. Scudder) on host leaves, mainly on the upperside of higher leaves. Larvae eat leaves, mainly after dusk. Larvae and pupae live in rolled-leaf nests. Larva translucent pale grayish-green (the side whiter), with a darker middorsal line and a whitish subdorsal line; head orange to brownish-gray, with a black spot on the face and another black spot around the eyes. Pupa (similar to 560 in Fig. 52) green, with two whitish dorsal lines, the head with a reddish horn, the proboscis extending beyond the abdomen.

Many flights, all year in s Fla. and s Tex., mostly May-Oct. in SE U.S.; migrates northward, esp. in late summer (July-Oct. in Va., Aug.-Sep. in N.J.), as far as Ill. and N.Y. Adults have a very swift flight; several mass flights are known, and past migrants established many island populations. Adults sip the nectar of flowers, including trumpet-shaped ones and *Canna*.

Color Plate 45

559. Panoquina panoquin   Salt-Marsh Skipper

In *Panoquina* species the hw is lobed at the rear, and the fw is long and slightly indented on the outer margin. The middle legs lack spurs on the second long segment (tibia). *P. panoquin* is identified by the pale unh streak and pale unh veins. Females have more fw spots than males.

Habitat coastal salt marsh. Best observed at low tide or from a boat (sometimes found inland). Hostplant possibly the grass *Spartina* or *Distichlis spicata* var. *spicata*.

Eggs pale greenish-white.

Many flights, Feb.-Dec. in Fla., M Apr.-M Sep. in Ga.; several flights, E-M July, L Aug. in N.Y. (perhaps May?).

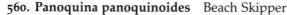

Color Plate 45
Fig. 52

560. Panoquina panoquinoides   Beach Skipper

Like *P. panoquin*, but the unh usually has vague pale postmedian spots, and the unh veins are usually not paler. The pale unh spots are variable. Ssp. **panoquinoides** (Atlantic and Gulf Coast south to Colombia) may have unh spots in cells Rs, M_3, and CuA_1. Ssp. **errans** (Calif.) may have unh spots (usually larger in size) in all cells except cell $1A+2A$ and cell 3A. Some adults of both ssp. lack unh spots. F. Brown proposed that *errans* is a distinct species because the larva and pupa are greener (although his descriptions of the two are reversed). However, the descriptions of many Hesperiinae larvae (and even pupae) vary from brown to green, and the color may depend partly on when and what the larva ate. Young larvae are the same in appearance (C. MacNeill). Other ssp. range south to Peru and Brazil and throughout the Bahamas and Antilles.

Habitat coastal salt marsh and beach grass. Hostplants grasses: in Calif. *Distichlis spicata* var. *spicata*, in the Antilles *Cynodon dactylon*, *Saccharum officinarum*, "Bahama grass," and probably *Sporobolus virginicus*.

Eggs cream or white, laid on the host and on other plants. Larvae eat leaves at night, and live in nests of rolled or tied leaves. Larva (Calif.) green, with four greenish-white dorsal stripes narrowly edged with gray and a yellowish-white lateral stripe; head green. Larva (Jamaica) reddish-brown, with a dark middorsal line and a thin dark lateral line, the prothorax white with a black collar; head black and white. Pupa (Calif.; Fig. 52) translucent green (the thorax and antennae slightly darker), with whitish dorsal lines on the abdomen, the head armed with a brown-tipped horn. Pupa (Jamaica) whitish-green on the head and wing cases, the eyes brownish, the abdomen tan-yellow. Larvae hibernate in Calif.

Many flights, Feb.-Dec. in Fla., at least June-Nov. in Tex., L June-Sep. in Calif. In Colombia, males perch among beach grasses to await females.

Color Plate 45

561. Panoquina ocola   Long-Wing Skipper

P. ocola, *P. sylvicola*, and *P. hecebolus* are larger than the two preceding species and have a more indented fw margin. *P. ocola* is identified by the unmarked brown unh (the unh rarely has a trace of pale spots) and by the lack of a spot in the fw cell (some adults have a pinpoint pale dot above the large fw spot).

Habitat Subtropical to Lower Austral Zone open (usually damp) areas, straying northward. Ranges south to Argentina and the Greater Antilles. Hostplants grasses: *Oryza sativa* in La., *Saccharum officinarum* and *Hymenachne amplexicaulis* in Puerto Rico.

Immatures not described, or confused with those of *P. sylvicola*.

Many flights, all year in s Fla., Apr.-Oct. in Ga.; migrates northward in summer (mostly July-Sep. in Va., reaching Ind. and N.Y. by Sep.-Oct.). T. Walker's malaise traps in N Fla. caught 164 adults moving south in the fall, only one north, and only two in the rest of the year. One mass flight is known in La.

Color Plate 45

562. Panoquina hecebolus

Like *P. ocola*, but the fw has a cell spot, the spot small (1 mm long), rounded, pale, and 1 mm or more from the white spot in cell CuA_1. The spot in cell CuA_1 is smaller and rounder than in *P. sylvicola*. Habitat subtropical open areas and open woodland. Ranges south to Paraguay. Hostplant unknown; adults sometimes fly near *Saccharum officinarum* (sugarcane) in the tropics. Many flights all year in Mex., occasionally common in s Tex. (July-Dec.).

Color Plate 45

563. Panoquina sylvicola   Sugarcane Skipper

Like *P. ocola* and *P. hecebolus*, but the fw cell has a white spot (1-2 mm long) very close to the spot in cell CuA_1. The spot in cell CuA_1 is larger than that of *hecebolus*, is indented outwardly, and extends out along vein CuA_2. The fw cell M_2 contains a small pale spot. The unh, often tinged with blue, usually has small white postmedian spots.

Habitat subtropical open areas and open woodland. Ranges south to Argentina and the Greater and Lesser Antilles. Hostplants grasses in the Antilles: *Saccharum officinarum*, *Oryza sativa*, *Eriochloa polystachya*, *Sorghum halepense*, *Axonopus compressus*, "Pimento grass," bamboo.

Eggs white. Larvae eat leaves. Larva gray-green (blue-green behind the head and yellow between segments), with a dark middorsal stripe, four pale dorsal lines, and a whitish lateral stripe; head green with black eyes. Pupa greenish, with four yellowish dorsal stripes and with a horn on the head, the proboscis a little longer than the wing cases.

Many flights all year in Mex.; migrates northward, occasionally common in s Tex. (Aug.-Dec.), rare in Ariz. and La., and rarely straying from Cuba to s Fla. (July).

Stray only
Color Plate 61

564. Panoquina fusina   White-Barred Skipper

The large size and the white fw spots resemble those of *Calpodes ethlius* (558), but the uph is yellowish-brown in the center without spots, and the unh has a bluish sheen and a vague long whitish postmedian band (the band nearly absent in females). Ssp. **evansi** is in the U.S.; ssp. *fusina* and other ssp. range south to Paraguay.

Habitat subtropical thorn forest. Hostplant probably grass; assoc. with sugarcane in the tropics.

Larva (Brazil) gray-green (gray beneath), with yellowish subdorsal stripes; head gray (the rim black), with a vertical black stripe on the front and a curved black stripe on each cheek.

Many flights in Mex.; an occasional stray into s Tex. (Oct.-Nov.).

Color Plate 45

565. Nyctelius nyctelius

Like *Panoquina* (559-564) on the ups, but the fw has a double white cell spot, the unh has two pale bands (somewhat like those of *Lerema accius*, 448, and *Cymaenes odilia*, 447), the leading edge of the unh has a dark dot, and the head is larger.

Habitat subtropical thorn forest and open areas. Ranges south to Argentina and through most of the Bahamas and Antilles. Hostplants grasses in the Antilles: *Oryza sativa*, *Zea mays*, *Saccharum officinarum*, "coarse grasses."

Eggs greenish-white or cream, laid singly on hostplant leaves. Larvae eat leaves (supposedly at night), and rest in a leaf nest. Larva bluish-gray with gray spots, or bluish-green, the collar black; head dirty-yellow (with a black vertical stripe on the front and a black lateral stripe on each cheek) or brown (with yellow vertical marks). Pupa light yellow, with brown mottling on the head and thorax, the proboscis extending nearly to the end of the abdomen.

Many flights in Mex.; occasionally flies to s Tex. (May-Dec., sometimes common) and rarely migrates to s Fla. (May), s Calif. (Oct.), Ariz. (Sep.), and c Tex.

Color Plate 61

566. Thespieus macareus

Somewhat like *Calpodes ethlius* (558) on the ups, but identified by the distinctive unh. Subtropical. Many flights in Mex., a rare stray into s Tex. (July-Nov.). Ariz. and Fla. records are errors. Ranges south to Venezuela.

Subfamily Pyrginae: Herb, Shrub, and Tree Skippers

The Pyrginae, about 1,150 species, occur throughout the world. Of these, 112 species occur in North America, and a few extend north to tree line.

Adults are mostly brown or gaudy, with antenna clubs usually shaped like boomerangs (rarely merely clubbed but bent a little at the end, Fig. 11). The base of forewing vein M_2 is about equidistant between veins M_1 and M_3 (Fig. 55). In many species the palpi extend forward on the front of the head. Larvae eat many dicotyledons, except for a few species of *Urbanus* that have switched to grasses. The larval head is usually wider on top than in the Hesperiinae, and often has an orange spot near the eyes. Pupae are like those of the Hesperiinae, but there is never a horn or very long proboscis, and the pupa is sometimes stout. Larvae generally hibernate.

A few tropical species seem to be involved in mimicry (see Pyrrhopyginae, below).

Flight habits vary. Most species have a powerful flight, but the wing strokes are fewer and the speed slower than in most Hesperiinae. *Celaenorrhinus* and some other tropical skippers that frequent shady places flap about rather slowly and erratically. *Systasea*, which frequent gullies, have a similar flight. A series of mostly black skippers (*Bolla, Staphylus, Celotes, Pholisora, Hesperopsis*) flutter evenly along in a moderately fast, straight-line flight, sometimes twirling about their larval hostplants. Only a few species migrate. Adults of all species seem to sip flower nectar, but sap-feeding is rare or absent. All adults bask by spreading the wings, but the resting habits vary. Most species close the wings at rest, but many others rest with them flat: species 567-616 generally close the wings while at rest; species 617-678 generally hold them flat, but *Erynnis* may rest with them flat (usually) or closed, and some of the others may also. *Erynnis* and perhaps other species have a peculiar habit of roosting on a twig with the wings wrapped around the twig.

Males generally perch to await females, but some species (such as the small black species noted above) patrol. *Pyrgus* both patrol and perch. Males and females have some unique scent structures for inducing mating (Fig. 39). They lack a stigma, but often have folds on the leading edge of the wing that contain scent scales (costal folds), and often tufts of hairs on the hind legs that fit into pockets behind the thorax during flight. Females sometimes have a patch of scent scales (in some genera occurring in a pouch) on top of abdomen segment 7, and occasionally they have hair pencils on the tip of the abdomen. As in other skippers, when mating pairs are startled, the female flies and totes the male.

567. Phocides pigmalion (=*batabano*)   Mangrove Skipper

Easily identified. The fw bands are absent in Fla. (ssp. **okeechobee**). Ssp. *belus* in Mex. resembles *P. urania*, but the abdomen is brown on top (the ssp.

Color Plate 41

may eventually be found in Tex.). Ssp. *pigmalion* and other ssp. range south to Argentina, the Bahamas, and the Greater Antilles.

Habitat subtropical coastal mangroves. Hostplant shrub Rhizophoraceae: *Rhizophora mangle.*

Eggs laid singly on the hostplant. Larvae eat leaves, and live in silked-leaf nests. Larva dark red to purplish-brown, with yellow or orange rings on each segment; head dark red to brown, with two red or orange eyespots low on the face. Before pupating, the larva becomes covered with white powder. Pupa whitish (greenish on the thorax and appendages), with a yellow stripe on the eye.

Many flights all year in s Fla. Adults sip the nectar of mangrove flowers and others.

568. Phocides urania   Rainbow Skipper

Stray only
Color Plate 62

One of the most beautiful skippers, and easily identified by the blue- or green-striped wings and top of the abdomen. Tropical, supposedly straying into s Tex. and s Ariz., but these old records are doubtful. Ranges south to Costa Rica.

569. Phocides polybius (=*palemon*)   Guava Skipper

Stray only
Color Plate 41

Easily identified in the U.S., although many tropical skippers are similar. Ssp. **lilea** is in the U.S.; ssp. *polybius* and other ssp. range south to Argentina.

Habitat subtropical woodlands, often in cities. Hostplants introduced tree Myrtaceae: *Psidium cattleianum, guajava,* and in Brazil *Eugenia uniflora.*

Eggs pale bluish-green, turning reddish in 1.5 days, laid singly on the upperside of leaves, mainly on young terminal leaves. Larvae eat leaves at night, and live in leaf nests. Half-grown larva red, with yellow rings between the segments; mature larva white, with a brown collar, the thorax enlarged, the head brown with yellow eyespots on the cheeks. Pupa dirty-white or pale green, with a subdorsal row of tiny gray spots and with tiny black dots on the head, thorax, and appendages, the head projecting forward into a double-crested knob between the eyes.

Many flights; regularly moves north from Mex. to s Tex. (Mar.-Oct.).

570. Proteides mercurius

Color Plate 62

Resembles *Epargyreus* (573), but the unh pattern is distinctive.

Habitat subtropics. Ranges south to Argentina and the Greater and Lesser Antilles. Hostplants herb and shrub Leguminosae in Latin Amer.: *Cassia, Derris eliptica* (a liana), *Ecastophyllum, Rhynchosia, Vigna, Muellera moniliformis.*

Larvae eat leaves, and live in leaf nests. Larva dark olive-green or honey-colored, mottled with dark brown, with brown transverse bands, a red subdorsal stripe and a dark middorsal line; head dark reddish-brown, with red eyespots on the cheeks. Pupa dark brown, covered with bluish-white powder. Larvae and pupae on *Muellera* plants may be inundated by tides.

Many flights in Mex.; a rare stray into Tex. (Apr.-Oct.) and from Cuba into Fla. (Apr.-May). Adults sip flower nectar and mud.

571. Epargyreus clarus   Silver-Spotted Skipper

The silver unh spot is unique. By starving larvae, E. Aaron produced adults that had a small silver unh spot like that of *E. zestos* (572).

Color Plates 5 (pupa),
41, 52
Fig. 52

Habitat the Gulf Coast and Upper Sonoran to Transition Zone open woods, canyons, and prairie valleys. Hostplants tree and herb Leguminosae: *Robinia* (the favorite genus) *pseudoacacia, neomexicana, hispida, viscosa, Acacia, Amorpha fruticosa, Amphicarpa bracteata* var. *comosa, Apios americana, Astragalus*[t], *Desmodium marilandicum, nudiflorum, paniculatum, glabellum* or *perplexum, rotundifolium, Gleditsia triacanthos, Glycyrrhiza lepidota, Lathyrus palustris, Lespedeza capitata, Lotus crassifolius, grandiflorus, Phaseolus polystachios, vulgaris, Pueraria lobata, Wisteria sinensis, frutescens.* Females oviposit on *Rhynchosia minima* and *Erythrina herbacea,* but larvae refuse them.

Eggs green, with a bright-red top, laid singly on the upperside of host leaves, rarely on plants in families not eaten by larvae. Larvae eat leaves. Young larvae live in a folded-over flap of a leaf; older larvae live between silked-together leaves. Larva greenish, with black transverse lines, the prothorax black on top and red beneath; the prolegs yellow, the true legs red; head black, with yellow or orange spots in front of the eyes. Pupa (Fig. 52) dark brown, with fine black marks and fine light marks, without the lip on the thoracic spiracle common to most Pyrginae. Pupae hibernate.

One flight, M June-M July, northward and in the Rockies and Sierra; several flights, May-Sep. in s Calif. and Penn., nearly all year in s Fla. Adult *Epargyreus* and many other large Pyrginae such as *Urbanus* have a jerky flight. Adults sip flower nectar and mud. Males perch in gullies (in clearings in woods or suburban yards) from about 7:30 A.M. to 1:15 P.M. to await females; they hang upside down from leaves in the afternoon.

Color Plate 41

572. Epargyreus zestos   Rusty Skipper

Like *E. clarus*, but the unh is red-brown with no silver spot, and the fringes are not checkered. The male abdominal structures are like those of *clarus*. The variability of the silver spot in *Aguna asander* (578) and the reduction of the spot in starved *E. clarus* hint at how *E. zestos* may have evolved. Subtropical. Ranges throughout the Antilles. Hostplant herb Leguminosae: *Galactia spicaformis*. Many flights, Jan.-Nov., in s Fla.

Color Plate 62

573. Epargyreus exadeus

Like *E. clarus*, but the silver unh spot is narrower, and the fw spots are small.

Habitat subtropics. Ranges south to Argentina. Hostplants herb Leguminosae: *Cassia* in Mex., *Phaseolus* and others in Brazil.

Larva olive-green, with white dots, transverse rows of black spots, and a yellow lateral stripe on the abdomen, the thorax tinted with orange, the prothorax red with a black collar; head black with a reddish spot in front of each set of eyes. Pupa light brown, with fine dark-brown lines and spots.

Many flights in Mex.; strays into s Tex. (Oct.) and Ariz. (Mar.).

Color Plates 41, 52
Fig. 71

574. Polygonus leo (=*lividus*)   Violet Skipper

The unh pattern and white fw spots are characteristic. Like *P. manueli*, but the unh has a violet glaze (and lacks a reddish-yellow hind margin), the unf lacks distinct brown spots, the fw spots are dull white, and the basal black unh spot is usually conspicuous. The male valva differs only slightly from that of *manueli* (Fig. 71).

Habitat subtropical wooded areas and desert foothills. Ranges south to Argentina and throughout the Bahamas and Antilles. Hostplants mostly tree Leguminosae: in Fla. *Piscidia piscipula* and *Pongamia pinnata*, in the Antilles *Lonchocarpus sericeus* and *Derris eliptica* (a climber, the source of the insecticide rotenone).

Eggs green, later turning reddish, with the ridges and top white. Larva mottled yellow-green, with a green middorsal line and a yellow subdorsal line (above a row of yellow blotches); head greenish-white (or black or yellow in various localities), with a black margin and two black forehead spots.

Many flights all year in s Fla.; several flights, May-Sep., in the southwest; a rare stray from Mex. into s Tex. (Sep.-Oct.). Adults often rest under leaves, on tree trunks, etc., in the shade.

575. **Polygonus manueli**   Tidal Skipper

Stray only
Color Plate 41
Fig. 71

Like *P. leo* (574), but the unh is powdery-bluish over brown, reddish-yellow scales are on the hind margin of the unh and the lower corner of the unf (around several brown spots), the white fw spots are pearly, the upf is bluish at the base, the uph is paler than the upf, and the black unh basal spot is usually small or absent. The male valva differs slightly (Fig. 71).

Habitat subtropics, probably mostly in tidal mud flats. Ranges south to Argentina and the Lesser Antilles. Hostplant shrub Leguminosae: *Muellera moniliformis* in Brazil.

Larva mottled with green and yellow (translucent like the larva of *P. leo*), with a pale subdorsal stripe; head flattened, glossy pale red (darker behind), with two black eyespots on the forehead. Pupa brown.

Many flights in Mex.; a rare stray into s Tex. (Aug.-Sep.). Supposedly native in s Fla. (Feb.-Nov.), but there are no recent records, and old Fla. records are probably *P. leo* or are mislabeled (*manueli* is absent in the Greater Antilles and Bahamas).

576. **Chioides zilpa**

Color Plate 39

Identified by the long tails and the peculiar white unh patch. Subtropical. Ranges south to Ecuador. Regularly flies from Mex. to s Tex. (Mar.-Nov.) and migrates rarely to Ariz. (May) and Kans.

577. **Chioides catillus**   Silver-Banded Skipper

Color Plate 39

Identified by the long tails and long silver unh band. Ssp. **albofasciatus** is in the U.S.; ssp. *catillus* and other ssp. range south to Argentina and Jamaica.

Habitat subtropical open areas. Hostplants herb Leguminosae: *Tephrosia lindheimeri*, *Phaseolus atropurpureus*, *Rhynchosia minima*, in Brazil *R. senna* and *Mimosa*.

Eggs white, turning yellow after a few days, laid under terminal host leaves. Larvae eat leaves, and live in nests of rolled or tied leaves. Larva olive-green or greenish-yellow, turning pinkish or purplish, with a darker middorsal line and a yellow or red-orange subdorsal line, the prothorax reddish with a black collar; head reddish-brown (scarlet at the margins) or dark brown, with a black mark like an inverted V (or like a bird with its wings spread) on the face. Pupa dark brown, with a bluish-white bloom.

Many flights all year in s Tex. Males may perch to await females.

Color Plate 62

578. Aguna asander

A. asander lacks tails and resembles *Epargyreus clarus* (571), but the silver unh mark is a stripe with a brown dash inside it, this stripe sometimes shrunk to a line or missing, and the fringes are not checkered. Subtropical. Ranges south to Argentina and the Greater Antilles. Hostplant unidentified Leguminosae. A rare stray into s Tex. (Apr.-Nov.) and s Ariz. (Sep.) from Mex. Adults rest under leaves.

Stray only
Color Plate 62

579. Aguna claxon

Identified by the green ups wing bases and body, the hw lobes instead of tails, and the silver unh band. Subtropical. Ranges south to Brazil. A rare stray into s Tex. (Oct.) from Mex.

Color Plate 62

580. Aguna metophis

Identified by the fairly long tails and the long whitish unh band (which blends into the ground color outwardly). The ups is only slightly greenish. Subtropical. Ranges south to Brazil. Hostplant Leguminosae: *Bauhinia mexicana* in Mex. Many flights all year in Mex., a rare stray into s and se Tex. (Aug.-Oct.).

Stray only
Color Plate 62

581. Typhedanus undulatus

The unh is unique, and the hw has long tails.

Habitat subtropics. Ranges south to Argentina. Hostplants (in Latin Amer.) herb and shrub Leguminosae: *Cassia corymbosa, alata, reticulata, occidentalis*.

Eggs grayish-blue, turning gray. Larva greenish-gray, with a darker middorsal line and yellow oblique lateral dashes; head dark brown, with a reddish spot below the yellow eyes. Pupa brown, the head blackish.

Many flights in Mex.; a rare stray into s Tex. (Sep.-Oct.). Males seem to perch to await females.

Stray only
Color Plate 62

582. Polythrix octomaculata

The tails and fw spot pattern distinguish *Polythrix*. Like *P. asine*, but the tail is short in males (long in females), the male lacks a costal fold, the upf cell CuA$_2$ has a brown submarginal spot, and females usually have a large white unh patch. The brown unf postbasal spot is absent or weak.

Habitat subtropics. Ranges south to Argentina and Hispaniola. Hostplants in Latin Amer. tree and shrub Leguminosae: *Pterocarpus indicus, draco, Muellera moniliformis, Toluifera perreirae*.

Larva whitish, with tiny streaks of gray; head flattened, yellow, with a loop of pale red or pale purple across the front. Pupa whitish, with reddish lateral streaks and with angular projections near the front.

Many flights in Mex.; a rare stray into s Tex. (Mar.-Oct.).

Color Plate 62

583. Polythrix asine (= *mexicanus*)

Like *P. octomaculata*, but fw cell CuA$_2$ has two postmedian spots (the upper brown or white, the lower brown) and a postbasal spot, the tails are usually longer, the male has a costal fold, and the male valva has a long sharp spine.

Habitat subtropical woods. Ranges south to Peru. Hostplants tree

Leguminosae (in Mex.): *Ichthyomethia communis* (used by American Indians to poison fish for food), *Amerimnon granadillo*.

Larvae eat leaves, and live in nests of rolled or tied leaves.

Many flights in Mex.; a rare stray into s Tex. (June-Oct.) and s Ariz. (Oct.). Adults land with their wings spread on the underside of leaves.

584. Zestusa dorus   Short-Tailed Arizona Skipper

Easily recognized.

Habitat Upper Sonoran Zone oak woodland. Hostplants tree Fagaceae: *Quercus emoryi, arizonica*.

Eggs laid singly on host leaves, sometimes on buds. Larvae eat leaves, and live in rolled-leaf nests. Larva greenish-yellow, with yellowish dots and yellowish transverse lines, a pale middorsal line beside the heart, and a yellowish subdorsal line; head orange-yellow (orange-brown around the eyes, light brownish-yellow on the lower front). Pupa dark reddish-brown, with a chalky crust. Pupae hibernate.

One flight, May-E June, in Colo.; perhaps two flights, Apr.-July, in Ariz. Adults feed on mud, sap, and spittlebug secretions, rarely on flower nectar. Males perch on trees at the edge of hilltops, at least in the afternoon, to await females.

585. Codatractus arizonensis   Arizona Skipper

Easily identified, but the Mex. species *C. melon* (Color Plate 61) is similar and possibly occurs in s Tex.; *melon* has slightly less white on the unh and a darker-brown uph, the prong on the end of the valva is straight rather than slightly knobbed, and the uncus and gnathos differ (Fig. 71). Habitat Upper Sonoran to Transition Zone desert mountains. Ranges south to Guerrero, Mex. Several flights, Apr.-Oct.

586. Codatractus alcaeus

This tailed species has a unique unh in the U.S., but the Mex. species *C. carlos* (Color Plate 62) is similar and may eventually appear in s Tex.; in *carlos* the yellow fw spot in cell CuA_2 is not partly underneath the yellow spot in cell CuA_1.

Habitat subtropical woodland. Ranges south to Ecuador. Hostplants tree Leguminosae: *Amerimnon granadillo, Ichthyomethia communis*.

Larvae eat leaves, and live in leaf nests.

Many flights in Mex.; a rare stray into s Tex. (Oct. 1973, possibly June) and supposedly into w Tex.

587. Urbanus doryssus   White-Tailed Skipper

Identified by the short white tail, the whitish fw band, and the valva, which has the prong toothed only on the end. Tropical. Ranges south to Argentina. A rare stray from Mex. into s Tex. (Mar.-Nov.).

588. Urbanus esmeraldus

Like *U. proteus* (589), but the brown unh postbasal stripe is broken into

Color Plate 41

Color Plate 41
Fig. 71

Color Plate 62

Stray only
Color Plate 62

Stray only
Color Plate 62

spots, the outer brown spot in unh cell $Sc+R_1$ is smaller than the inner spot or is missing, and the end of the valva has a long club-ended prong that projects upward. Subtropical. Ranges south to Paraguay. Hostplant herb Leguminosae: *Desmodium neomexicanum* in Mex. Eggs laid on young host leaves. Larvae eat leaves. Many flights in Mex.; a rare stray into s Tex. (Aug.).

589. Urbanus proteus Long-Tailed Skipper

Identified by the long tails and by the green body and ups wing bases. In s Tex. it resembles *U. esmeraldus* (588; see its discussion for identification), but the unh details differ and the valva has a short prong.

Color Plates 39, 40

Habitat open areas mainly in the south and Atlantic coastal plain, migrating north. Ranges south to Argentina and throughout the Bahamas and Antilles. Hostplants herb (sometimes tree) Leguminosae: *Clitoria ternatea, mariana, Bauhinia, Amphicarpa bracteata, Desmodium tortuosum, viridiflorum, canescens, neomexicanum* (Mex.), *purpurea, Glycine max*[t], *Phaseolus vulgaris, limensis, polystachios, lathyroides* (Puerto Rico), *Prosopis juliflora* var. *torreyana, Pisum sativum, Wisteria frutescens, Vigna sinensis*. Latin Amer. records on *Canna* (Cannaceae) and *Stigmatophyllon lingulatum* (Malpighiaceae) are doubtful.

Eggs cream or bluish-green, laid in clusters of several (up to 20), mostly under leaves. Larvae eat leaves, and live in nests of rolled or tied leaves. Larvae are sometimes pests on snap beans, but the yield of beans decreases only if a third to a half or more of the leaves are eaten (M. Shepard). Larva yellowish-green or gray, with transverse rows of black and yellow dots, a blackish middorsal line, a lemon-yellow to reddish subdorsal stripe, a pale-green sublateral line, and grayer patches on each side, the rear yellow, the prolegs orange or yellow, the collar black; head reddish-black, with an orange or yellow spot on each side near the eyes. Pupa reddish-brown, covered with a whitish waxy powder.

Many flights all year in Fla. and s Tex. (probably survives the winter only in s Tex., s Fla., and perhaps the Gulf Coast; not native in Calif.). A strong migrant, moving north in spring, reaching the edge of the range (rarely Mich. and Conn.) mainly in late summer, and moving south in numbers in the fall. The N Fla. fall flight goes to the south-southeast from E Sep. to E Nov., peaking about Oct. 1 (many adults caught in malaise traps by T. Walker, A. Riordan); few adults were caught during the rest of the year. The gradual move north (unlike the mass movement of the Monarch Butterfly, *Danaus plexippus*, 89) explains the late dates of captures in the north. Males perch on sunlit vegetation 1-2 m above ground to await females.

590. Urbanus pronus

Stray only
Color Plate 62

The wing bases and body are blue-green, as in *U. proteus* (589), but the uph green stops abruptly at the 3-mm-wide brown border, the male lacks a costal fold, the fw spots in the discal cell and in cell CuA_1 are partly joined, and the tails are short (only about 5-8 mm long). The male valva is similar to that of *proteus*, having a broad end and one rounded projection on top. The only Tex. specimen, a male, was misidentified as a female *U. pronta*; the Mex. *pronta* is like *pronus*, but the male has a costal fold, the fw spots are not joined, and the male valva is pointed with several projections on top. Subtropical. Ranges south to Argentina. A rare stray from Mex. into s Tex. (Oct.).

Color Plates 39, 40
Fig. 45

591. Urbanus dorantes   Brown Tailed Skipper

Identified by the brown body and wings, the checkered fringes, and the long tails.

Habitat subtropical and desert open areas. Ranges south to Argentina and throughout the Bahamas and Antilles. Hostplants herb and tree Leguminosae: *Phaseolus*, *Clitoria*, *Desmodium tortuosum*.

Eggs (Fig. 45) shiny green. Larva pale pinkish-orange to greenish (reddish-brown at the rear), with a dark middorsal line; head blackish. Pupa light brown.

Many flights all year in s Fla. (where it became established in 1969); perhaps a resident in s Tex. (June-Oct. at least) and s Ariz. Migratory, straying north as far as Kans. and N Calif., and present on the Galápagos Is. T. Walker's malaise trap caught three times as many adults flying south as flying north in the fall in N Fla.

s Tex. only
Color Plate 39

592. Urbanus teleus

U. teleus and the next three species (593-595) have long tails, brown wing bases and body, and uncheckered tan fringes. *U. teleus* and *U. tanna* both lack a costal fold and have a long white fw band; *U. simplicius* and *U. procne* have a costal fold and usually lack the band. *U. teleus* usually has only four white fw apical dots, and the valva is much thicker at the base than at the spine.

Habitat subtropical wooded and brushy areas. Ranges south to Argentina. Hostplants grasses: *Panicum maximum*, *Paspalum ciliatifolium*; possibly Leguminosae: *Schrankia* (Brazil). Larvae eat other grasses in the lab.

Eggs laid on the host. Larvae eat leaves, and young but not older larvae make a nest by folding over a grass blade.

Many flights all year in s Tex.

Stray only
Color Plate 62

593. Urbanus tanna

Like *U. teleus* (592), but the fw usually has five white apical dots (including one in cell M$_1$), and the valva is not much thicker at the base than at the spine. Subtropical. Ranges south to Ecuador. A rare stray from Mex. into s Tex. (June).

Color Plate 62

594. Urbanus simplicius

U. simplicius and *U. procne* (595) are totally brown, but they sometimes have white fw apical dots and sometimes a white fw band like that of *U. teleus* (592); their males have a costal fold, which *teleus* and *U. tanna* (593) males lack. *U. simplicius* differs from *procne* in having the brown unh postbasal stripe joined to the brown spot in cell Sc+R$_1$ and a single spine on the valva. Subtropical. Ranges south to Argentina. Hostplants herb Leguminosae: *Phaseolus vulgaris*, in Brazil *Schrankia*; doubtfully the monocotyledon Cannaceae: *Canna*. Many flights in Mex.; a rare stray into s Tex. (Apr.).

595. Urbanus procne

Resembles *U. simplicius* (594) in general appearance and in having a costal fold, but the brown unh postbasal stripe is not connected to (or near) either of the brown spots in cell Sc+R$_1$, and the valva has two spines side by side.

Habitat subtropical open areas. Ranges south to Argentina. Hostplants

Color Plate 39

grasses: *Cynodon dactylon*, *Sorghum halepense*; larvae eat many grasses in the lab, esp. *Panicum maximum*.

Eggs laid on the host. Larvae eat leaves; only young larvae live in nests, which are made by folding the leaf tip over after eating part of the leaf.

Many flights all year in s Tex.; a rare stray northward (Oct. in s Calif.).

596. Astraptes egregius   Green Flasher

Stray only
Color Plate 62

Identified by the narrow yellow unh margin and the male costal fold. *A. fulgerator* and *A. egregius* are the only *Astraptes* that have a male costal fold. The ups wing bases are greenish, and the fw usually has small to large white spots. Subtropical. Ranges south to Brazil. A rare stray from Mex. into s Tex. (Oct.).

597. Astraptes fulgerator   Blue Flasher

Identified by the bluish ups wing bases, the white fw band, and the white fw subapical spots.

Habitat subtropical wooded areas. Ranges south to Argentina. Hostplants Rhamnaceae: *Karwinskia humboldtiana* in Tex. Latin Amer. records possibly refer to other *Astraptes*: *Cassia hoffmanseggi* and *Inga* (both Leguminosae), *Ilex paraguariensis* (Aquifoliaceae), *Vitex mollis* (Verbenaceae).

Color Plate 41

Larva black (the underside maroon), with white hairs and yellow transverse bands, the collar maroon; head blackish, with white hairs, and with reddish-brown marks on the cheeks. Pupa dark brown to black, covered with white powder.

Many flights all year in s Tex. Adults often rest under leaves in the shade. Males may perch to await females.

598. Astraptes alector   Mad Flasher

Stray only
Color Plate 62

Identified by the white unf patch at the corner. The ups wing bases are greenish-blue, the fringe is brown, the unh base is white along the front margin, and the fw has no white spots. Ssp. **hopfferi** (=*gilberti*) is in the U.S. to S. Amer.; ssp. *alector* is in S. Amer. Habitat subtropics. Ranges south to Bolivia. Hostplant shrub or tree Leguminosae: *Bauhinia divaricata*. Many flights all year in Mex.; an occasional stray into s Tex. (Oct.).

599. Astraptes alardus   White Flasher

Stray only
Color Plate 62

Identified by the white hw fringe, the white unh margin, the absence of white fw spots, and the greenish ups wing bases. Subtropical. Ranges south to Argentina, Cuba, and Hispaniola. A rare stray from Mex. into s Tex. (June-Oct.). Adults often rest under leaves.

600. Astraptes anaphus   Yellow Flasher

Stray only
Color Plate 62

Identified by the yellow unh margin, the brown wings and body, and the absence of white spots. Subtropical. Ranges south to Argentina and the Greater and Lesser Antilles. Hostplants Leguminosae: in Mex. the woody vine *Pueraria lobata*, in Brazil a "creeping wild bean." Larva yellow; head brown with prominent "eyespots." Many flights in Mex.; a rare stray into s Tex. (Apr.-Oct.).

Color Plate 41
Fig. 71 (valva)

601. Autochton cellus   Golden-Banded Skipper

Identified by the yellow fw band; *A. pseudocellus* is similar, but it is rare, and found only in s Ariz.

Habitat Lower Austral to s Upper Austral Zone moist valley bottoms in woods in the east, mostly Upper Sonoran Zone foothill canyons in the west. Ranges to s Mex. Hostplants herb Leguminosae: *Amphicarp bracteata* var. *comosa* in the east; *Phaseolus wrightii, grayanus, Clitoria mariana, Vigna* in the west.

Eggs pale yellow, becoming tan, laid on large host leaflets near the base, mostly in clusters of two or three but up to seven in a string. Larvae eat leaves at night, and live in nests of rolled or tied leaves. Larva yellow-green, with tiny yellow dots and a yellow lateral line, the prothorax yellow above and red below, the true legs yellow; head red-brown, with yellow spots on the cheeks. Pupa green, quickly turning dark brown with a green tinge. Pupae hibernate.

One flight, June in Penn., L May-June and a partial second flight L July-M Aug. in Va., M June-Aug. in Ariz.; several flights, Apr.-Sep., in Fla. Males perch in gullies on shrubs, etc., at least in the afternoon (probably all day), to await females.

Color Plate 61
Fig. 71

602. Autochton pseudocellus   Little Golden-Banded Skipper

Like *A. cellus*, but the antenna club has a white ring at the base, the uph lacks yellowish at the front tip (*cellus* has yellowish there), the hw fringe is check-ered to the stubby "tail," and the unh margin lacks blue scales. The male valva differs (Fig. 71). Habitat the oak and pinyon zone in desert mountain foothills. Last found in se Ariz. in 1936, it still occurs in Mex. (south to Puebla). Several flights, at least June-Sep., in Mex.

Color Plate 41

603. Autochton cincta   White-Banded Skipper

The characteristic fw band is narrow and white, and the hw fringe is pure white. Habitat oak/pine woodland of the Chisos Mts., w Tex. Ranges south to El Salvador. Hostplants in Mex. herb Leguminosae: *Desmodium grahamii, angustifo-lium*. Probably several flights, at least L Mar.-E Sep.

Color Plate 42
Fig. 55 (veins)

604. Achalarus lyciades   Hoary Edge

The large yellow fw spots and white unh margin are diagnostic.

Habitat Gulf Coast to Transition Zone woodland. Hostplants herb Legu-minosae: *Amorpha fruticosa*[t], *Desmodium ciliare, paniculatum, glabellum* or *per-plexum, nudiflorum, rotundifolium, canadense, cuspidatum, nuttallii, Lespedeza hirta, Indigofera caroliniana*?[t], *Baptisia, Hedysarum*, "wild bean."

Eggs whitish, laid singly beneath host leaflets. Larva green, with many tiny bumps, a bluish-green middorsal line, and a lateral stripe of yellow-orange dots, the collar dark; head black, with comblike teeth on top. Pupa pale brown (dirty yellow-brown on the abdomen), with black dots. Larvae hibernate.

One flight, M June-July, northward; several flights, Apr.-Sep., southward. Males perch on plants 1-2 m above ground in forest openings to await females.

Color Plate 42

605. Achalarus casica   Desert Hoary Edge

The unh margins are whitish, somewhat like those of *Cogia hippalus* (620), but the white fw spots are small. Habitat mostly Upper Sonoran Zone pinyon-juniper woodland and desert grassland. Ranges south to Guerrero, Mex. Several flights, Apr.-Oct. Adults sip flower nectar and mud.

606. Achalarus albociliatus

Like *A. toxeus* and *A. jalapus*, but males lack the costal fold, the faint pale postmedian spots in fw cells M_3 and CuA_1 overlap, and the male valva differs (Fig. 71). Subtropical. Ranges south to Venezuela. Many flights in Mex.; a rare stray into Ariz. and s Tex.

Color Plate 62
Fig. 71

607. Achalarus toxeus

Resembles *A. jalapus* and *A. albociliatus*. The male has a costal fold like that of *jalapus*, but the hw is not lobed, and the valva differs (Fig. 71).

Habitat subtropical woodland. Ranges south to Panama. Hostplant tree Leguminosae: *Pithecellobium flexicaule*.

Eggs laid singly on host leaves near the trunk. Larvae eat young leaves.

Many flights in Mex.; an occasional stray into s Tex. (all year, common at times). Adults rest on willows along the Rio Grande.

Color Plate 42
Fig. 71

608. Achalarus jalapus

Mostly brown with white fringes, as in *A. toxeus* and *A. albociliatus*; the male has a costal fold (which *albociliatus* lacks), and the hw is lobed (slightly tailed) at the rear (*toxeus* lacks the lobe). The valvae differ in all three species (Fig. 71). Subtropical. Ranges south to Colombia. Many flights in Mex.; a rare stray into s Tex. (July-Oct.).

Stray only
Color Plate 62
Fig. 71

609. Thorybes pylades   Cloudy Wing

Thorybes are medium-sized and gray-brown, with small white fw spots and dark unh bands. *T. pylades* males have a costal fold, unlike all others of the genus (except the s Ariz. *T. drusius*). The white fw spot in cell CuA_1 of both sexes is usually just a small lower spot, never a bar as in *T. bathyllus*; if this spot is large, it is aimed more toward the other postmedian spots. The end of the valva is rounded on the bottom (Fig. 71). In ssp. **albosuffusa** (w Tex.), the unh often has a whitish submargin; ssp. **pylades** (rest of the range) has brown submargins.

Habitat subtropical to lower Hudsonian Zone, mostly in wooded areas. Ranges south to Oaxaca, Mex. Hostplants herb Leguminosae: *Amorpha californica, Astragalus nuttallianus, Desmodium paniculatum, rotundifolium, canadense, glabellum* or *perplexum, nudiflorum*[t], *Lathyrus eucosmus, ochroleucus, Lespedeza intermedia, capitata, hirta, Lotus douglasii, crassifolius, Medicago sativa, Rhynchosia texana, Trifolium pratense, repens, Vicia americana*.

Eggs pale greenish to white, laid singly under host leaves. Larvae eat leaves, and live in nests of rolled or tied leaves. Larva yellowish-orange to dark green, with tiny yellow or orange points, maroon blotches, a brownish or maroon middorsal line, a pale dorsolateral line, and lateral reddish lines, the collar dark; head maroon-black. Pupa dark brown (or slightly greenish-brown), dark between abdomen segments, with tan wing cases. Full-grown larvae hibernate.

One flight, mainly June, in the north, the Rockies, and s Calif.; several flights southward, Apr.-Aug. in w Tex. and N.M., Mar.-Dec. in s Fla., Mar.-Nov.

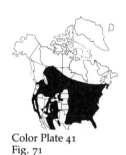

Color Plate 41
Fig. 71

near Dallas. Adults sip flower nectar and mud. Males perch all day among shrubs or small trees, on or near hilltops if available (in gulches in w Tex.), to await females.

610. Thorybes bathyllus   Eastern Cloudy Wing

This E U.S. species is a little smaller than *T. pylades*, and males lack the costal fold. The spot in fw cell CuA_1, a rectangular bar all across the cell, lies next to the spot in cell M_3. The male valva is distinctive (Fig. 71).

Habitat Gulf Coast to Transition Zone woods clearings. Hostplants herb Leguminosae: *Apios americana*[t], *Astragalus engelmannii*, *Centrosema virginianum*, *Desmodium rotundifolium*, *ciliare*, *paniculatum*, *Glycine "reticulata," Lespedeza hirta*, *capitata*, *virginica*[t], *Rhynchosia tomentosa*, *Strophostyles helveola*, *leiosperma*, *Tephrosia ambigua*, *Trifolium pratense*[t].

Color Plate 41
Fig. 71

Eggs pale green, laid singly beneath host leaflets. Larvae eat leaves, and live in nests of rolled or tied leaves. Larva brown (tinged with green), with a darker middorsal line and a paler lateral line; head and collar black. Pupa greenish-brown (with dark-brown marks) or dull brown. Full-grown larvae hibernate.

One flight, June-M July, northward; many flights, Mar.-Oct., in Fla. and Tex. Adults sip flower nectar and mud. Males perch on vegetation 0.5-1.5 m above ground in open areas (esp. hilltops) to await females.

611. Thorybes mexicana   Mountain Cloudy Wing

This western mountain species is smaller than *T. pylades*, the male lacks a costal fold, and the unh has numerous brown striations. The white fw spots vary in size. The male abdominal structures are like those of *T. bathyllus* (Fig. 71). In ssp. **blanca** (White Mts., Calif., and Sweetwater Mts., Nev.), the unh is whitish; ssp. **mexicana** (remainder of the range) has a tan unh.

Habitat mainly Canadian to Hudsonian Zone mountain clearings. Ranges south to Panama. Hostplants herb Leguminosae: *Vicia americana*, *Lathyrus leucanthus*, *Trifolium monanthum*, *longipes*.

Color Plate 41
Fig. 71

Eggs laid singly under host leaves.

One flight, mostly June in Transition Zone foothills, July near timberline. Adults sip flower nectar and mud. Males perch all day on or near the ground on hilltops (or on slight prominences or in swales where there are no hilltops) to await females.

612. Thorybes confusis   Dark Cloudy Wing

In this SE U.S. species the white fw spots are much smaller than in *T. bathyllus*, the male lacks a costal fold (present in *T. pylades*), and the adult size is a bit smaller than that of *pylades*. The palpi are grayish beneath (usually brown in *pylades*). The white spot in fw cell CuA_1, when present, is usually pointed toward the median spots, unlike that of *pylades*. The uncus arms are thick and placed together, and the valva is less divided than that of other *Thorybes* (Fig. 71). Habitat southeastern woodland clearings. Hostplant possibly *Lespedeza* (Leguminosae). Two flights, June-E July and M Aug.-E Sep., northward; many flights, Mar.-Dec., in Fla. and Tex.

Color Plate 41
Fig. 71

Color Plate 41
Fig. 71

613. **Thorybes diversus**   California Cloudy Wing

This Calif.-Ore. species is a little larger than *T. mexicana* and lacks its unh striations. Adults are a little smaller than *T. pylades*, the male lacks a costal fold, and the white fw spot in cell CuA$_1$ is usually long and aimed toward the median spots (unlike that of *pylades*). The valva has a long upcurved spine on the end (Fig. 71).

Habitat Transition Zone tiny coniferous forest clearings. Hostplants herb Leguminosae: *Trifolium wormskjoldii*; assoc. with *Vicia americana*.

Eggs pale bluish-green, quickly turning green, laid singly on the host. Larva dark olive-brown (with a yellowish cast caused by tiny pale dots), a dark-olive middorsal line, and two pale lateral stripes on each side, the prothorax dark reddish-brown; head black.

One flight, M June-M July. Males perch in tiny forest clearings (3 m wide), at least in the afternoon, to await females.

Color Plate 42

614. **Thorybes drusius**   White-Fringed Cloudy Wing

Identified by the white hw fringe and the male costal fold. The male valva is similar to that of *T. diversus*. Habitat Upper Sonoran to Transition Zone oak woodland and desert grassland. Ranges south to Guerrero, Mex. Several flights, at least Apr.-Aug.

Color Plate 41

615. **Thorybes valeriana** (= *mysie*)   Mexican Cloudy Wing

In this s Ariz. species the fw is rounder and the ups is more golden-brown than in other *Thorybes*. The unh has brown crescents on the margin and a pale submarginal band. The male lacks a costal fold. The valva is similar to that of *T. diversus*, but the uncus is not split into two arms. Habitat Upper Sonoran Zone open woodland. Ranges south to Guerrero, Mex. Hostplant unidentified Leguminosae. Larvae hibernate. One flight, M July-M Aug. Adults have a rather weak flight (butterflies with a rounded fw usually fly more weakly than those with a pointed fw). Adults sip mud.

Color Plate 41

616. **Cabares potrillo**

Vaguely resembles *Thorybes* (609-615), but the uns is distinctive, and the two rear white spots on the fw are joined.

Habitat subtropical open areas. Ranges south to Venezuela and the Greater Antilles. Hostplant herb Verbenaceae: *Priva lappulacea*.

Eggs dark green, laid on the host. Larvae eat leaves, and live in leaf nests. Larva light brown (each segment tinted with black on the rear), with orange-brown specks, an orange-brown subdorsal line, and a blackish middorsal line; head black. Pupa light purplish-brown, covered with whitish powder.

Many flights all year in s Tex. Males seem to perch to await females.

Stray only
Color Plate 61

617. **Celaenorrhinus fritzgaertneri**

The white fw spots are joined into a band, and the uph is mottled. Resembles *C. stallingsi*, but the unf lacks a yellow patch, and the fw has a white spot divided by the base of vein CuA$_2$. Subtropical. Ranges south to Costa Rica. A rare stray from Mex. into s Tex. (Feb.-Sep.). Both *Celaenorrhinus* species rest under leaves of shaded plants and in other shady places (small caves, etc.) during the day; they fly near dusk, and sometimes visit flowers at dawn. Both species sip the nectar of papaya and other flowers.

618. Celaenorrhinus stallingsi

Stray only
Color Plate 61

Like *C. fritzgaertneri*, but the lower corner of the unf is pale yellow, and there is no white fw spot divided by the base of vein CuA$_2$. Subtropical. Ranges south to Costa Rica. Sometimes locally common in s Tex. (June-Nov.), perhaps a temporary introduction from Mex.

619. Spathilepia clonius   Falcate Skipper

s Tex. only
Color Plate 41

The truncated fw is unique.

Habitat subtropical wooded areas. Ranges south to Argentina. Hostplants herb Leguminosae in Brazil: *Inga edulis*, *Phaseolus*.

Larva yellow, with brown X-shaped dorsal marks. Pupa light brown, covered with waxy powder.

Many flights, May-Nov., in s Tex. (found regularly and perhaps resident). Males seem to perch to await females, about 3 m above ground on shrubs, etc.

620. Cogia hippalus   White-Edged Skipper

Color Plate 41

The hw fringe is white like that of *Achalarus casica* (605) and *Thorybes drusius* (614), but the fw spots are large, and the unh margin is not as white as the margin of *A. casica*. The antenna shaft is checkered, not brown as in *C. caicus*. Habitat desert grassland and pinyon-juniper woodland. Ranges south to Brazil. Several flights, at least Apr.-Sep., in w Tex. and Ariz., where it is native; rare, perhaps a stray, in s Tex. Adults sip flower nectar and mud.

621. Cogia outis   Texas Acacia Skipper

Like the larger *C. hippalus*, but the white fw spots are smaller, and the fringes are brown or tan. The antenna shaft is checkered. Flies with *hippalus* in Hidalgo and Kinney Cos., Tex.

Color Plate 41

Habitat mostly Lower Austral Zone thorn forest. Hostplants tree Leguminosae: *Acacia texensis*, *angustissima* var. *hirta*.

Eggs laid singly under terminal host leaves. Larvae eat leaves, and live in a nest of leaves silked together. Larvae pupate in a nest of leaves on the ground (as in other *Cogia*) or sometimes in a silk-lined tunnel underground. Full-grown larvae hibernate.

Two flights, Apr.-May and July-Aug., in Mo.-Ark.; many flights, Mar.-Oct., in Tex.

622. Cogia caicus   Arizona White-Edged Skipper

Color Plate 42

The fringe is white like that of the larger *C. hippalus*, but the fw is rounder, the unh bands are more blackish, and the unh margin is whitish with brown striations (without brown marginal spots). The antenna shaft, like that of *C. calchas*, is not checkered. Males of the other *Cogia* spp. have a hair tuft on the uph base, about 3 mm long; it is almost absent in *caicus*. The whitish fw spots vary from large to small. Habitat Upper Sonoran Zone open woodland. Ranges south to Guatemala. Hostplant tree Leguminosae: *Acacia angustissima*. Full-grown larvae hibernate. Many flights, at least Mar.-Aug. Adults sip mud.

623. Cogia calchas   Mimosa Skipper

s Tex. only
Color Plate 41

The fringes are brown like those of *C. outis*, but the upf spots are very small, and the unh is dark brown on the margin and between the grayish-brown median and postmedian bands.

Habitat subtropics, usually near creeks and canals. Ranges south to Argentina. Hostplants herb Leguminosae: in Tex. *Mimosa pigra* var. *berlandieri*, in Latin Amer. *Malicia, Schrankia, Indigofera*.

Eggs laid singly on the host. Larvae eat leaves, and live in nests of rolled or tied leaves. Larva yellowish, with tiny white dots.

Many flights all year in s Tex. Males perch in open grassy areas to await females.

624. Arteurotia tractipennis

Stray only
Color Plate 61

Identified by the dark upf subapical spot, which has three clear dots outside it, and by the white unh median spots. Subtropical. Ranges south to Bolivia. Hostplants herb Euphorbiaceae in Mex.: *Croton reflexifolius, niveus*. Larvae eat leaves, and live in nests of rolled or tied leaves. Many flights, most of the year, in Mex.; a rare stray into s Tex.

625. Nisoniades rubescens   Purplish-Black Skipper

Stray only
Color Plate 63
Fig. 71

Mottled black like *Pellicia costimacula* (627), but the fw has small white subapical spots, and the male valvae differ (Fig. 71). Tropical. Ranges south to Bolivia. Hostplants trailing vine Convolvulaceae in Mex.: *Ipomoea batatas, luteum*. Eggs laid on the upperside of host leaves. A rare stray from Mex. into s Tex. (Oct.-Nov.).

626. Pellicia dimidiata

Stray only
Color Plate 63
Fig. 71

Pellicia lack white fw spots. *P. dimidiata* males have a glandular oval unh patch over the base of vein Rs (in other *Pellicia* this vein is bare and slightly swollen). The wings are not as violet as those of other *Pellicia*, and the valvae lack pointed prongs (Fig. 71). Subtropical. Ranges south to Argentina. A rare stray from Mex. into s Tex. (Oct.). Hostplant Convolvulaceae: *Ipomoea* in Brazil.

627. Pellicia costimacula

Stray only
Color Plate 63
Fig. 71

The wings have a purplish glaze. The uncus tapers evenly, and the valvae are distinctive (Fig. 71). Ssp. **arina** is in the U.S. and C. Amer.; ssp. *costimacula* and other ssp. are in S. Amer. s Tex. records of *Pellicia angra* refer to *costimacula* (*angra* is like *costimacula*, but the uncus resembles a ping-pong paddle when viewed from the top, and the left valva has a spine pointing inward, unlike the valva of other *Pellicia*; Fig. 71). Subtropical: most adults are found on leaves in wooded areas. Ranges south to Paraguay. An occasional stray from Mex. into s Tex. (Mar.-Dec.).

628. Bolla brennus

Stray only
Color Plate 62
Fig. 71

Black like *Staphylus* (630-632), *Bolla* are slightly larger and have a rounder fw. In *B. brennus* the unh has a few scattered orange scales (which *B. clytius* lacks), adults are smaller than *clytius* (fw 14-15 mm), the male lacks white spots (present in *clytius*) although the female has three white dots in a row near the fw tip, and the male valva has an overlapping flange plus a sawtooth truncated end (Fig. 71). Subtropical. Ranges south to Colombia. A rare stray from Mex. into s Tex. (Oct.). Hostplant herb Solanaceae: *Lycopersicon esculentum* in El Salvador.

629. Bolla clytius

Stray only
Color Plate 62
Fig. 71

Like the slightly smaller *B. brennus*, but the unh lacks scattered orange scales, the male and female have three white dots near the upf apex, and the valva is broad and divided at the end (Fig. 71). Subtropical. Ranges south to Honduras. A rare stray from Mex. into s Tex. (June-Nov.).

630. Staphylus hayhurstii   Scalloped Sooty Wing

Color Plate 43
Fig. 71

Like *S. mazans*, but the range is mostly farther north, the fringes are usually checkered brown and tan, making the hw margin look more wavy, and the ups is slightly paler blackish-brown. The male valva has a long spine, and the uncus tip is expanded like an arrowhead (Fig. 71).

Habitat subtropical to Transition Zone wooded areas. Hostplants herb Chenopodiaceae: *Chenopodium album*; Amaranthaceae: *Alternanthera "flavescens."*

Eggs orange-brown with cream ridges, laid singly on the underside of host leaves. Larvae eat leaves, and live in rolled-leaf nests. Larva deep green with a reddish cast, hairy, the collar pale brown; head blackish, deeply cleft vertically. Pupa pale olive-brown (orange-brown on the abdomen), with a whitish bloom. Third-stage larvae hibernate.

Two flights, M May-June and Aug., in Ill.; three flights, M May-E June, July, L Aug.-Sep., in Md.-Va.; many flights, Feb.-Dec., in Fla. Adults rest with the wings spread.

631. Staphylus mazans   Tropical Sooty Wing

Color Plate 43
Fig. 71

Like *S. hayhurstii* (which flies with *S. mazans* in c Tex., apparently without hybridizing), but the fringes are brown, the male valva lacks a spine, and the uncus tip is not expanded (Fig. 71). Habitat subtropical wooded areas. Ranges south to Bolivia. Hostplants herb Chenopodiaceae: *Chenopodium album, ambrosioides*; Amaranthaceae: *Amaranthus retroflexus, Achyranthes aspera* (Mex.). Larvae eat leaves. Many flights all year in s Tex.

632. Staphylus azteca   Aztec Sooty Wing

Color Plate 62
Fig. 71

Like *S. mazans*, but the margins are a little less wavy, the white fw spots are smaller esp. in unf cell CuA_1 (the fw spots are often absent in males, but seldom absent in *mazans*), males are browner black than *mazans* males, and females are slightly more uniformly brown than *mazans* females. The male uncus differs from that of other *Staphylus* in being forked at the tip and not bent downward, and the valva shape differs (Fig. 71). One stray female from Mex. was caught in w Tex. (June), but may be a misidentified *mazans* because identification of *Staph-*

ylus is based largely on males. Habitat subtropical and tropical Mex. south to Brazil. Hostplants in Mex. herb Amaranthaceae: *Celosia nitida, Achyranthes aspera*. Many flights, at least Mar.-Sep., in Mex.

633. Staphylus ceos   Redhead Sooty Wing

Similar to other *Staphylus,* but the head and palpi are orange, the wing margins are not as wavy, and the fringes are not checkered. Similar to *Hesperopsis libya* (677), but the unh lacks white patches. Habitat Subtropical to Upper Sonoran Zone open areas and foothills. Ranges south to Durango, Mex. Many flights, Apr.-Sep. northward, Apr.-Dec. in s Tex. Adults fly faster than *Pholisora catullus* (675). Males patrol all day in gulches and valley bottoms to seek females.

Color Plate 43

634. Gorgythion begga   Variegated Skipper

G. begga has oddly variegated wings, a violet ups sheen, and many dark ups lines. The fw apex is somewhat pointed. Adults vary considerably in the darkness of the ups, in fw shape, and in male valva shape. Tex. records of *G. beggina vox* are misidentified *begga*. Subtropical. Ranges south to Argentina. A very rare stray from Mex. into s Tex. (Mar.-Dec.).

Stray only
Color Plate 63

635. Sostrata bifasciata

Complexly variegated like *Gorgythion* (634). Males are blackish, with blue upf scales and small white fw spots; females are brown, with larger white fw spots. Ssp. **nordica** is in the U.S. south to Costa Rica; ssp. *bifasciata* and other ssp. range south to Argentina. Subtropical. A rare stray from Mex. into s Tex. (Oct., one record).

Stray only
Color Plate 63

636. Carrhenes canescens   Hoary Skipper

Complexly patterned. The wings are tan, some adults paler than others. Other Mex. species are similar. Subtropical. Ranges south to Argentina. Hostplant herb Malvaceae: *Hibiscus* in El Salvador. A rare stray from Mex. into s Tex. (Feb.-Dec.). Adults sip the nectar of flowers, often of lemon trees.

Stray only
Color Plate 61

637. Xenophanes trixus   Glassy-Wing Skipper

Named for the large transparent wing areas. Habitat subtropical open areas. Ranges south to Argentina. Hostplants herb Malvaceae: *Malvaviscus drummondii* in Tex., *Malachra fasciata* in Brazil. Larva whitish-green, mottled; head brown. Pupa mottled brown, with a whitish bloom. Many flights in Mex.; a stray northward, common at times in s Tex. (July-Nov.).

Stray only
Color Plate 43

638. Systasea pulverulenta   Powdered Skipper

The oddly shaped hw is characteristic. Like *S. zampa* (which flies with *S. pulverulenta* in w Tex.), but the white upf central band forms a straight line, the ups is slightly oranger, the hw margin is slightly less wavy, and the prong on the male valva is short (Fig. 71).

Habitat subtropical to Upper Sonoran Zone thorn forest and open areas. Ranges south to Guatemala. Hostplants herb Malvaceae: *Wissadula holosericea,*

Color Plate 43
Fig. 71

amplissima, Abutilon abutiloides, wrightii, incanum, pedunculare, Sphaeralcea angusti-folia, Pseudabutilon lozani.

Eggs laid singly on the host. Larvae eat leaves, and live in nests made by folding over a flap of a leaf after eating the leaf edge. Full-grown larvae hibernate.

Many flights, Feb.-Dec. in s Tex., Apr.-Sep. in w Tex. Males perch in gulches, at least at midday, to await females.

Color Plate 43
Fig. 71

639. Systasea zampa (=evansi)   Arizona Powdered Skipper

Like *S. pulverulenta*, but the white fw band is broken because the spot in cell CuA$_1$ is shifted toward the body, and the prong on the male valva is much longer (the prong is easily seen by brushing away the abdomen-tip scales; Fig. 71). Habitat Lower to Upper Sonoran Zone desert and open woodland. Hostplant unknown, possibly *Hibiscus denudatus* (Malvaceae). Several flights, Apr.-Oct. (sometimes Feb.). Adults sip flower nectar and mud. Males perch in gulches all day to await females.

Color Plates 42, 44

640. Achlyodes mithridates ("thraso")   Sickle-Wing Skipper (Bat Skipper)

The fw is somewhat notched at the tip. Ssp. **tamenund** is in the U.S., ssp. *mithridates* in Jamaica, and other ssp. (including *thraso*) south to Argentina and the Greater and Lesser Antilles.

Habitat subtropical woodland. Hostplants tree Rutaceae: in Tex. *Zanthoxylum fagara*, in Latin Amer. *Z. monophyllum*, *Citrus paradisi*, *sinensis*, *limon*, *aurantifolia*.

Eggs laid singly on the upperside of host leaves. Larvae eat leaves, and live in silked-leaf nests. Larva yellow-green or (Brazil) green or (Jamaica) gray-blue on top and greenish on the sides, all often with a darker-green middorsal line and a broad lateral band of yellow dashes (the band interrupted by a broad transverse dash on each segment consisting of tiny darker spots), the collar yellow; head greenish-brown to tan or brown. Pupa green (the abdomen yellowish-green), with a whitish bloom.

Many flights all year in s Tex. Migratory, straying north rarely to Kans. and Ark. They often rest under or on top of leaves.

Color Plate 61

641. Grais stigmaticus   Hermit

This large species is uniformly mottled brown except for several tiny subapical fw spots. Habitat subtropical wooded areas. Ranges south to Argentina and Jamaica. Occasionally strays from Mex. to s Tex. (June-Dec.) and rarely to Kans. Adults rest under leaves.

Color Plate 42

642. Timochares ruptifasciatus   Brown-Banded Skipper

Identified by the large size, by the mottled wings somewhat like those of *Erynnis* (646-660), by the absence of white spots, and by the orange-brown uns.

Habitat subtropical wooded areas. Ranges south at least to s Mex. and Jamaica. Hostplants shrub and vine Malpighiaceae: *Malpighia glabra*.

Eggs pearly-white, later turning light orange-yellow. Larvae eat leaves, and live in rolled-leaf nests. Larva blue-green (the neck light green), with yellow dots, and with a yellow subdorsal line (which has adjacent orange spots); head mottled white (the cheeks yellow), with a dark-brown line around the margin extending forward on top. Pupa green, the shoulders brown.

Many flights all year in s Tex. Migrates north rarely to Ill. and N.M. Males may perch to await females.

Color Plate 43

643. Chiomara asychis   White-Patch Skipper

The whitish wings are unmistakable. Habitat subtropical woods edges. Ranges south to Argentina, Hispaniola, and the Lesser Antilles. Hostplant shrub Malpighiaceae: in Tex. *Malpighia glabra*, in Mex. *Gaudichaudia pentandra*. Eggs laid singly on host leaves. Larvae eat leaves, and live in leaf nests. Larva and pupa greenish. Many flights all year in s Tex.; migrates rarely to Nev. and Kans.

Color Plate 42

644. Gesta gesta   False Dusky Wing

This species vaguely resembles *Erynnis* (646-660), but the pattern details differ. There are no white spots.

Habitat subtropical open areas. Ranges south to Argentina and the Greater Antilles. Hostplants herb Leguminosae: *Indigofera suffruticosa, lindheimeriana*, in Mex. *Cassia*.

Eggs whitish, later becoming orange-yellow, laid singly on young hostplants. Larvae eat leaves at night, and live in silked-leaf nests. Larva grayish or yellowish-green (whitish at the rear), with a green middorsal stripe, a yellowish lateral band, and an orangish subdorsal band (or yellow subdorsal spots); head white or orange, with many large reddish-brown or black spots. Pupa green, paler at the rear, the eyes turning red before adult emergence, the spiracles behind the eyes large and black. Full-grown larvae hibernate.

Many flights, Apr.-Nov., in s Tex.

645. Ephyriades brunnea   Caribbean Dusky Wing

Easily identified by the fairly large size and the small white fw spots. Males are uniformly brown, but females are paler (often with a violet sheen) and have brown bands. The female scent scales are in a pouch on top of abdomen segment 7 (Fig. 39; *Staphylus, Gorgythion, Chiomara, Gesta, Erynnis*, etc., have these scales only on the surface there).

Habitat subtropical pine-palm scrub in the Fla. Keys. Ranges south to the Bahamas, Cuba, Jamaica, several Lesser Antilles, and possibly Honduras. Hostplants shrub Malpighiaceae: *Malpighia glabra, Byrsonima lucida*.

Eggs laid on hostplant leaves and young shoots. Larvae eat leaves, and live in leaf nests. Larva yellow-green (the neck gray), with yellow transverse bands on the thorax, a dark middorsal line, three whitish subdorsal and lateral stripes on each side, and translucent dorsal stripes. Pupa whitish-green.

Many flights all year.

Color Plate 43
Fig. 39

646. Erynnis icelus   Aspen Dusky Wing

Erynnis have a dark-brown uph and a grizzled and mottled dark-brown upf. *E. icelus* resembles *E. brizo* (647) in lacking translucent white fw spots and in having an upf postmedian row of chainlike spots. *E. icelus* is smaller than *brizo*,

Color Plate 42
Fig. 71

the male hind-leg tibia has a hair plume that fits between the metathorax and abdomen (absent in *brizo*), the upf postmedian spots are more blurred, the palpi are longer, and the valvae differ (Fig. 71). Both *icelus* and *brizo* lack the female abdominal hair pencils that pop out when the abdomen is squeezed (present in other *Erynnis* except *E. martialis*, 648, and *E. pacuvius*, 649).

Habitat Transition to Canadian Zone (plus Upper Austral Zone) open woods, usually near creeks or in moist places. Hostplants tree Salicaceae: *Populus tremuloides, grandidentata, balsamifera, nigra, Salix cordata*; Betulaceae: *Betula populifolia*?; Leguminosae: *Robinia pseudoacacia*.

Eggs laid singly on young host leaves. Larvae eat leaves, and live in nests of rolled or tied leaves. Larva pale green, with white dots, a yellowish tint on top, a dark middorsal line, and a white dorsolateral stripe, the prothorax yellowish; head red-brown. Pupa reddish-brown or yellowish-brown, the mesothorax and abdomen yellowish or tan, the wings greenish-tinted. Full-grown larvae hibernate.

One flight, M May-M June in most areas, L Apr.-June in the southeast, L May-E July in the far north and at high altitude. Adults sip flower nectar and mud. Males perch and occasionally patrol all day in swales to await females.

Color Plates 4 (larva), 42
Fig. 71

647. Erynnis brizo   Banded Oak Dusky Wing

The fw lacks translucent fw spots, as in *E. icelus* (646), but *brizo* is larger, the male hind leg lacks a hair plume, and the male valva differs (Fig. 71). The upf appears more banded (the postmedian chain of spots more uniform) and less dark at the base than in *icelus*. Ssp. **lacustra** (Calif.) is darker on the ups than ssp. **brizo** elsewhere.

Habitat Gulf Coast and Upper Sonoran Zone to lower Canadian Zone oak woodland. Ranges south to Veracruz, Mex. Hostplants tree and shrub Fagaceae: *Quercus gambelii, undulata, turbinella, turbinella × arizonica, ilicifolia, macrocarpa, Castanea dentata*.

Eggs laid singly on young host leaves or leaf buds. Larvae eat leaves, and live in nests of rolled or tied leaves. Larva grayish-green (purplish at the front and rear), with a faint white dorsolateral stripe and a darker middorsal line; head yellowish to dark brown, with an orange spot at the base of the mandible. Pupa green. Full-grown larvae hibernate.

One flight, L Mar.-Apr. in Ariz. and Fla., M Apr.-M May in N.Y. and Calif., mostly May in Colo. Adults sip flower nectar and mud. They roost by folding the wings tentlike downward around a twig. Males perch all day on hilltops (probably in clearings on flat land) to await females. At high density, males also patrol about the hostplant to seek females.

Color Plate 42
Fig. 71

648. Erynnis martialis   Mottled Dusky Wing

Identified by the marginal and submarginal rows of cream unh spots, each edged toward the body by a brown spot (the postmedian spots are brown zigzags). The upf is mottled gray and brown and sometimes tinged with violet. *E. martialis* (and *E. pacuvius*, 649, *E. icelus*, 646, and *E. brizo*, 647) lacks the female abdominal hair pencils found in other *Erynnis*. The male valvae are distinctive (Fig. 71).

Habitat Gulf Coast to Transition Zone, mostly open woodland and chaparral. Hostplants shrub Rhamnaceae: *Ceanothus americanus, ovatus, fendleri*.

Eggs yellow when laid, laid singly on flower pedicels and on other parts of the host. Larvae live in silked-leaf nests. Larva light green (probably having a faint yellow dorsolateral stripe); head black with dark-red markings. Pupa green. Full-grown larvae hibernate (diapause larvae have a whitish translucent cast on the body).

One flight, M May-June in Colo.-Wyo.; two flights elsewhere, M May-M June and M July-M Aug. in the northeast, L Apr.-Aug. in Mo., L Mar.-Apr. and M June-M July on the Gulf Coast (rarely a partial third flight L Aug.-E Sep. in Ga.). Adults sip the nectar of flowers, including *Ceanothus*. Males perch all day on hilltops (and sometimes patrol about the hostplants, even on hillsides) to await females in Colo.; they probably perch in clearings in the east.

649. Erynnis pacuvius Buckthorn Dusky Wing

Color Plate 42
Fig. 71

Geographically variable. Ariz.-Colo. adults have a brown and gray mottled upf. Calif.-B.C. adults resemble *E. propertius* (652), but the upf is less gray. s Ariz.-s N.M. adults resemble *E. juvenalis clitus* (650) and *E. scudderi* (653), but the upf is more mottled gray-brown. Best identified by the male valvae (Fig. 71). Ssp. **pacuvius** (Ariz.-s Utah-N.M.-Colo.) has white fringes (rare N Colo. adults have brown fringes). Ssp. **callidus** elsewhere has brown fringes and is darker (esp. around San Francisco).

Habitat Transition to Canadian Zone open woodland and chaparral. Ranges south to Veracruz, Mex. Hostplants shrub Rhamnaceae: *Ceanothus fendleri, cordulatus, oliganthus*.

Eggs pale green, not changing color.

One flight northward, M May-June at low altitude in Colo. (May-June in N Calif.), June-July at high altitude in Colo. and Calif.; several flights, Apr.-Sep., in Ariz. and lowland s Calif. Adults feed on flowers (including *Ceanothus*) and mud. To seek females, males perch all day on hilltops (and at high density patrol about the hostplants, even on hillsides).

650. Erynnis juvenalis Eastern Oak Dusky Wing

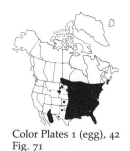

Color Plates 1 (egg), 42
Fig. 71

In this large eastern species the upf is a little more grayish than in *E. horatius* (654), females usually have a white hourglass-shaped unf median spot (seldom a single spot as in *horatius* and *E. tristis*, 655), and both sexes often have a brown unh circle near the apex (like that of *E. telemachus*, 651). Males are readily identified by their valvae (Fig. 71). Ssp. **juvenalis** (most of the range) has brown fringes. Ssp. **clitus** (SE Ariz., south to Chiapas, Mex.) has white fringes, and seldom has the unh circle or the female unf hourglass.

Habitat Gulf Coast to lower Canadian Zone oak woodland. Hostplants tree and shrub Fagaceae: *Quercus ilicifolia, alba, prinus, velutina, rubra, mohriana, macrocarpa, stellata, marilandica, nigra, arizonica, emoryi, gambelii, hypoleucoides*, in N.S. probably *Fagus americana*.

Eggs greenish-white, cream, or pale green, later turning salmon-red, laid singly on host seedlings and young leaves. Larvae eat leaves, and live in nests of rolled or tied leaves. Larvae pale green to bluish-green or dark green, with tiny yellowish-white dots and a yellow dorsolateral stripe; head tan or greenish-brown, with an orange spot on each cheek and two orange spots above this spot on the side (the three orange spots sometimes joined). Pupa tan or reddish-brown, the abdomen tinged with pink above and beneath, the appendages blackish, the center of the wings dark olive-brown. Full-grown larvae hibernate.

One flight, M Apr.-May in NE U.S., June in Sask., M May-June at Ottawa, M Feb.- E Apr. in Fla.; several flights, Apr.-E Sep., in Ariz. Adults sip flower nectar, dung, and mud. Males perch on vegetation 1-4 m above ground in forest margins or clearings to await females.

651. Erynnis telemachus   Gambel-Oak Dusky Wing

This large species has a grayish upf, brown fringes, and almost always a brown circle (the center paler) near the unh apex. Like *E. propertius propertius* (652) and *E. juvenalis juvenalis* (650), but they have different ranges. *E. propertius meridianus* seldom has the unh circle, and is usually less gray on the upf. *E. horatius* (654) is never gray on the upf; its females have a single white unf median spot (not hourglass-shaped as is usual in *telemachus* and *juvenalis*). The valvae of *telemachus* differ from those of most *Erynnis* (Fig. 71).

Habitat Upper Sonoran to Transition Zone oak woodland. Hostplant shrub Fagaceae: *Quercus gambelii.*

Eggs laid singly on new host leaf buds and bark.

One flight, M Apr.-M June southward, M May-M July at high altitude and in the north. Males perch all day in gulches to await females.

Color Plates 40, 42
Fig. 71

652. Erynnis propertius   Western Oak Dusky Wing

Large like *E. telemachus* (651). The upf is grayish, at least in the spring (summer adults of *Erynnis* are less gray on the upf, and summer females have larger white fw spots and slightly lighter wings than spring females). The unh apex usually lacks the brown subapical circle of *telemachus* and *E. juvenalis* (650). Females sometimes have a white hourglass-shaped unf median spot, as in *telemachus*. In ssp. **meridianus** (s Nev.-Tex. south to Mexico City), the upf is a little less gray (esp. in the summer flights) than in ssp. **propertius** (Calif.-B.C.). They have been treated as distinct species, but their male valvae are the same (Fig. 71). Summer ssp. *meridianus* adults resemble *E. horatius* (654), but the valvae differ.

Habitat Upper Sonoran to Canadian Zone open oak woodland. Hostplants tree Fagaceae: in Calif. *Quercus agrifolia* and *garryana*, in Ariz. *Q. arizonica* and *fusiformis.*

Pupa like that of *E. zarucco* (656). Full-grown larvae hibernate.

One flight, M Mar.-May in lowland Calif., June-July in higher Calif. mountains, L Apr.-May in B.C.; about three flights, mostly Apr., M June-M Sep., in Ariz.-Tex. Adults sip flower nectar and mud. Males perch all day to await females, in clearings on the sunny edge of a ridgetop or hilltop (sometimes on banks in valley bottoms) in Calif., on hilltops in Ariz.

ssp. *meridianus*

Color Plate 42
Fig. 71

ssp. *propertius*

653. Erynnis scudderi   Arizona Dusky Wing

The hw fringe is white. The antenna club has a scaleless area of 14-17 segments (the area is 18-21 segments in *E. juvenalis*, 650). Resembles *E. juvenalis cli-*

Color Plate 42
Fig. 71

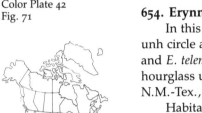

Color Plate 42
Fig. 71

Color Plate 42
Fig. 71

tus so much that males are best identified by their valvae (Fig. 71). The belt of scent scales on top of abdomen segment 7 of females is thick and wider laterally than the plate behind it. Habitat Upper Sonoran to Transition Zone, mostly in mountain woodland although a male was found in the Chihuahua grassland not near trees (J. Scott). Ranges south to Chiapas, Mex. Hostplant unknown, possibly *Quercus*. Two or more flights, at least L May-E July and Aug.

654. Erynnis horatius　Brown Dusky Wing

In this large species the upf is blackish-brown (not gray). There is no brown unh circle and no white hourglass-shaped unf median spot (*E. juvenalis*, 650, and *E. telemachus*, 651, have a gray upf, a brown unh circle, and in females an hourglass unf spot). Resembles summer adults of *E. propertius meridianus* (652) in N.M.-Tex., but the valvae differ (Fig. 71).

Habitat Gulf Coast to Transition Zone oak woodland. Hostplants tree and shrub Fagaceae: *Quercus fusiformis, gambelii, hemisphaerica, laurifolia, marilandica, nigra, phellos, stellata, texana, virginiana, ilicifolia, muehlenbergii, shumardii, rubra, velutina, falcata* var. *pagodaefolia*. J. Heitzman raised larvae on *Wisteria*, so A. Chapman's *Wisteria frutescens* (Leguminosae) record may be valid.

Eggs laid singly on young parts of the host. Larvae eat young leaves, and live in nests of rolled or tied leaves. Larvae hibernate.

Two flights, L Apr.-May and L June-M Aug. in Colo. and NE U.S.; three or four flights elsewhere, as long as M Jan.-M Oct. in Fla. Adults sip flower nectar and mud. Males perch all day on hilltops in Colo. (and probably in clearings in the east) to await females.

655. Erynnis tristis　White-Edged Dusky Wing

Easily identified by the white hw fringes and (in the Ariz.-Tex.-Colombia ssp. **tatius**) by the long white spots on the unh margin (next to the white fringe). In Calif. (ssp. **tristis**), these white spots are faint or absent, but *E. tristis* is one of two Calif. *Erynnis* spp. that have a white fringe (the other is *E. zarucco*, 656, which has a narrow fw). Brown-fringed adults are rare in s N.M. The male valvae are distinctive (Fig. 71).

Habitat mostly Upper Sonoran Zone oak woodland. Hostplants tree Fagaceae: *Quercus agrifolia, lobata, douglasii, suber, wislizenii*.

Eggs pale lemon-yellow, turning deep orange, laid singly on new growth of the host. Larvae eat young leaves, and live in nests of rolled or tied leaves. Larva pale gray-green, with tiny white dots, a dark middorsal line, and a yellowish dorsolateral line; head orange-brown, with three pale orange spots on each side. Pupa olive-gray, with darker wing cases, and with a paler dorsolateral line on the abdomen. Larvae hibernate.

Three or four flights, mostly Mar.-Oct. Adults sip flower nectar and mud. Males perch all day on hilltops in Calif. to await females. O. Shields found that adults fly to hilltops from up to 1 km or more away. He found that 98 percent of the females found on hilltops were virgin, suggesting that they fly there to mate and depart immediately after mating. The male pursues the female and flutters behind and below her (occasionally rising up and making apparent contact), the female lands, the male lands, and they mate. While mating, the female cleans her antennae, which are covered with scales (probably from the male's costal fold). Unreceptive females fly vertically to reject males. *Erynnis* adults produce chemical perfumes that probably allow these confusingly drab butterflies to choose a mate of the right species: all male *Erynnis* have a "costal fold" of yellow scent scales on the fw, and males of some species have hair plumes on the hind legs. All female *Erynnis* have a belt of scent scales on abdomen segment 7, and females of some species have hair pencils on the abdomen. (For similar pheromone structures, see Fig. 39.) *Erynnis* species mate in hilltops, gulches, or swales, which also aids in finding and choosing a mate of the right species.

656. Erynnis zarucco   Streamlined Dusky Wing

Identified by the narrow fw and by the light patch just inside the white upf spots, which contrasts with the dark upf. The male hind leg has a hair plume like that of *E. icelus* (646) and the next four *Erynnis* species (657-660), but *E. zarucco* adults are generally larger (fw length 17-21 mm). The male valvae are distinctive (Fig. 71). Ssp. **funeralis** (Tex. northward and westward, and south to Chile and Argentina) has white fringes. Ssp. **zarucco** (La. northward and eastward, plus Cuba and Hispaniola) has brown fringes, and the fw is less narrow. The ssp. have sometimes been treated as distinct species, but they have similar valvae, migrations, hosts, and early stages. Populations intermediate between the ssp. occur in La. and Fla.; white-fringed adults sometimes occur in w and s Fla.

Habitat Subtropical to Upper Sonoran/Upper Austral Zone open areas. Hostplants herb and tree Leguminosae: for ssp. *zarucco*, *Robinia pseudoacacia*, *Lespedeza hirta*, *Clitoria mariana*, *Centrosema virginianum*, *Wisteria frutescens*, *Daubentonia longifolia*, *Sesbania exaltata*, *grandiflora* (Cuba), *vescicaria*, for ssp. *funeralis*, *Sesbania exaltata*, *drummondii*, *Vicia texana*, *Indigofera leptosepala*, *Lotus scoparius*, *Medicago sativa*, *hispida*, *Olneya tesota*, *Robinia neomexicana*, *Geoffroea decorticans* (Argentina). A Calif. record of *Nemophila membranacea* (Hydrophyllaceae) is doubtful or unusual.

Eggs (Fig. 45) whitish, turning greener, then yellowish, then orange, laid singly, mainly on the underside of host leaves. Larvae eat leaves, and live in nests of rolled or tied leaves. Larva pale yellowish-green (many light hairs produce a light bloom), bluish ventrally, with a dark-green middorsal line, and with a yellow dorsolateral line (which contains a yellow dot on each segment toward the rear of the larva); head black, with three yellow spots on each side of the rim. Pupa green (with yellowish-white clouding on the wing cases), with tiny pale hairs. Larvae hibernate.

Many flights, Mar.-Oct. in most of the range, all year in s Tex. and s Fla.; migratory, ssp. *funeralis* straying rarely north to N Ind., Neb., Ky., and Colo. (strays may have introduced white fringes into Fla. also), and ssp. *zarucco* straying rarely north to Mass., Penn., and Ind. Adults sip flower nectar and mud.

657. Erynnis persius   Hairy Dusky Wing

Small; identified by the numerous white upf hairs on males. The male has a hind-leg hair plume like that of *E. icelus* (646; see Fig. 39), but the fw has translucent spots. The middle appendage of the left valva is boot-shaped, with a rudderlike keel on its inner surface (Fig. 71); it is fingerlike without a keel in the next three species (658-660). During mating, the male bends his left valva in the middle and scrapes it across the female's underside (the reason is not known).

ssp. *funeralis*

Color Plate 43
Figs. 45, 71

ssp. *zarucco*

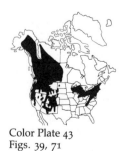

Color Plate 43
Figs. 39, 71

Habitat Transition to Hudsonian Zone open woodland and mountain grass-land (rarely Alpine Zone, and several colonies in c and s Central Valley of Calif.). Hostplants herb Leguminosae: in w N. Amer. *Astragalus flexuosus*, prob-ably *bisulcatus*, *Lotus purshianus*, probably *scoparius*, *Thermopsis pinetorum*, *di-varicarpa*, *Trifolium ciliolatum*, in e N. Amer. *Lupinus argenteus*, *perennis*, *latifolius*, *L.* sp.; in e N. Amer. Salicaceae: *Salix humilis*, *Populus balsamifera*, *tremuloides*, *grandidentata*.

Eggs pale yellowish-green or pale yellow, turning dark red, laid singly on the underside of host leaves. Larvae eat leaves, and live in nests of rolled or tied leaves. Larva pale green, with tiny white dots, a dark-green middorsal line, and a yellowish dorsolateral line; head yellowish to dark reddish-brown, with pale vertical streaks. Pupa dull olive-green (the abdomen pinkish-brown), mottled with pale dots. Full-grown larvae hibernate.

One flight, mostly May-M June in e U.S., mostly June in Canada and w U.S. (June-July at high altitude); two flights, May-Sep., in n Calif.; many flights, Mar.-Sep., in the Central Valley. Adults sip mud and flower nectar. Males perch all day on hilltops in Colo. to await females. In courtship, a passing female is pursued by a male, both hover (the male below the female), she lands, he hovers near her, he lands, and they mate.

Color Plate 43

658. Erynnis lucilius   Columbine Dusky Wing

E. lucilius, *E. afranius* (659), and *E. baptisiae* (660) are very similar (the *lucilius* group); they are small, the male upf lacks white hairs (*E. persius*, 657, has many white hairs), and males have a hair plume on the hind-leg tibia. *E. lucilius* occurs farther east than *afranius*, and usually farther north than *baptisiae*. *E. lucilius* is smaller than *baptisiae* (fw length usually 13-15 mm), the pale upf patch just in-side the white dots is not as prominent as in *baptisiae*, and they have different hostplants. The male valvae are very similar in the three species (see 659 in Fig. 71): the middle appendage of the left valva is fingerlike, without a keel, unlike the valva of *persius*, and the upper appendage of the right valva is narrower.

Habitat Transition to lower Canadian Zone woods edges and gullies. Host-plants herb Ranunculaceae: *Aquilegia canadensis*, *vulgaris*.

Eggs laid singly under host leaves. Larvae eat leaves, and live in nests of rolled or tied leaves. Larva pale green, with a yellowish bloom (the lower sides yellower), a darker middorsal line, and a yellowish dorsolateral line; head black, with three whitish or reddish streaks or spots on each side. Pupa pale green. Mature larvae hibernate.

Two flights, May-E June and M July-M Aug. (perhaps three near Philadel-phia, May, M July-E Aug., E Sep.).

Color Plate 43
Fig. 71 (valvae)

659. Erynnis afranius   Bald Dusky Wing

Like *E. lucilius* (658) and *E. baptisiae* (660) in wing pattern, size (fw length 14-17 mm), and male valvae, but *E. afranius* occurs farther west and has slightly more white upf scales. The male upf is not hairy as in *E. persius* (657).

Habitat Upper Sonoran to Transition Zone open woodland and prairie. Ranges south to Mexico City. Hostplants herb and bush Leguminosae: *Lupinus argenteus*, *Lotus purshianus*, *Astragalus*.

Eggs whitish, later turning to yellowish and probably orange, laid singly under host leaves. Larvae eat leaves, and live in nests of rolled or tied leaves. Larva pale green, with many tiny white points, a dark middorsal line, and a yellow dorsolateral line, the collar black; head black, with tiny white dots, the face orange with a black patch in the center. Pupa green.

Two flights, mostly May and July-E Aug.; several flights, Mar.-Aug., in s Calif. Adults sip flower nectar and mud. Males perch all day in gullies and swales to await females.

Color Plate 43

660. Erynnis baptisiae   Indigo Dusky Wing

Like *E. lucilius* (658) in wing pattern and male valvae shape. *E. baptisiae* flies with *lucilius* only from s Minn. to Penn.-Mass. *E. baptisiae* is a little larger than *lucilius* (fw length usually 16-18 mm) and has a paler upf patch just inside the white dots (like that of *E. zarucco*, 656). *E. baptisiae* is usually smaller than *zarucco*, and its fw is wider.

Habitat Gulf Coast to Transition Zone open woods and brush. Hostplants herb and shrub Leguminosae: *Baptisia tinctoria, leucantha, australis, leucophaea* var. *laevicaulis, Crotalaria sagittalis, Lupinus perennis, Thermopsis villosa, Astragalus canadensis*, introduced *Coronilla varia*, "hop clover." Lab larvae were raised on *Thermopsis mollis* and on *Aquilegia* (Ranunculaceae), the host of *E. lucilius*.

Eggs laid singly on the host. Full-grown larvae hibernate.

Mostly two flights, L Apr.-E June and July-Aug. (sometimes E Sep.). Males perch all day on low shrubs in open areas to await females.

Color Plate 43

661. Pyrgus centaureae   Grizzled Skipper

Identified by the lack of a white spot at the base of upf cell CuA_1. The male has a costal fold. The small ssp. **wyandot** (Mich.-N.Y.-N.C.) is dark on the ups. Ssp. **freija** (Alaska-Que.) has a whitish unh. Ssp. **loki** (B.C.-Colo.) has an olive-brown and blackish unh. Ssp. *centaureae* and other ssp. range from Scandinavia to Siberia.

Habitat Hudsonian to Alpine Zone moist meadows and valley bottoms in the Rockies, in Upper Austral to Canadian Zone clearings and grassy hillsides in forest (even sandy pine barrens) in E U.S., and Canadian Zone to s tundra in Canada and Alaska. Hostplants herb Rosaceae: *Potentilla diversifolia* in Colo., *canadensis* in Va., *Fragaria virginiana* in Mich., *Rubus chamaemorus* in Man. and Europe.

Eggs laid singly on host leaves.

One flight, M Apr.-M May in E U.S., L June-E Aug. in Colo., L July-Aug. in Wyo., M June-July in the Arctic. Ssp. *wyandot* is annual, flying every year, but ssp. *freija* and ssp. *loki* are biennial, flying mostly in odd years in Colo., Wyo., and Lab. and at Churchill, Man. Adults sip the nectar of usually yellow flowers. Males patrol and sometimes perch all day in low spots to seek females.

Color Plate 45

662. Pyrgus ruralis   Two-Banded Checkered Skipper

This small skipper has a white X on the upf and a white uph postbasal dot. Resembles *P. xanthus*, but the range differs, the male has a costal fold, and the unh margin has a large brown triangular spot in cell Rs and smaller brown spots in cells M_3 and CuA_1. Ssp. **lagunae** (San Diego Co., Calif.) is whiter like *P. communis*. Ssp. **ruralis** elsewhere is dark like *P. xanthus* and *P. centaureae*.

Habitat Canadian Zone (sometimes Transition and lower Hudsonian Zone) forest clearings. Hostplants herb Rosaceae: *Potentilla drummondii*, *Horkelia fusca*; assoc. with *H. bolanderi*.

Eggs laid singly on the host.

One flight, mostly May in the Coast Ranges and at low altitude in the mountains, M June-M July at high altitude; ssp. *lagunae* has one flight M Apr.-E June and a complete or partial second flight L June-M July. Males patrol all day (and sometimes perch) near the ground in valley bottoms and swales to seek females.

663. Pyrgus xanthus   Mountain Checkered Skipper

Color Plates 40, 45

Like *P. ruralis*, but the male lacks a costal fold, the white unh spots are larger, and the unh margin has a tan band (wide at the apex, tapering to absent at the rear). The hw fringe has black streaks that extend to the edge of the fringe (the black streaks extend only halfway to the edge in *P. scriptura*), and the uph base has a white dot (which *scriptura* lacks). *P. xanthus* overlaps the range of *ruralis* by only a few kilometers in c Colo. (Jefferson and Gunnison Cos.), which is puzzling. They recently evolved from one species.

Habitat Canadian to lower Hudsonian Zone clearings with grasses and aspen. Hostplants herb Rosaceae: *Potentilla gracilis* var. *pulcherrima*; assoc. with *hippiana* (not *anserina*) and *ambigens*.

Eggs laid singly on host leaves or flowers.

One flight, M May-M June northward, L Apr.-May southward. Adults sip mud, dung, and the nectar of mostly yellow flowers. To seek females, males patrol and sometimes perch near the host, but they usually perch in narrow dry gullies, all day.

664. Pyrgus scriptura   Small Checkered Skipper

Color Plate 45

Very small in size. The black streaks in the hw fringe extend only halfway to the edge of the fringe (the streaks extend to the edge in *P. xanthus* and *P. ruralis*), and the uph base lacks the white dot of *xanthus* and *ruralis*. Males lack a costal fold (which *ruralis* has). The unh marginal spots are very evenly colored, yellowish-tan outwardly. Summer adults are dark with small white spots, but early spring and Nov. adults have larger white spots like those of *xanthus* (form **pseudoxanthus**).

Habitat Upper Sonoran to Transition Zone prairie and open woodland. Hostplants herb Malvaceae: *Sida hederacea*, *Sphaeralcea coccinea*, *ambigua*.

Eggs laid singly on leaves.

Possibly just one flight, July-M Aug., in Mont.-N.D.; three flights, May-Sep., in Colo.; many flights, Mar.-Nov., in lowland Calif. Adults feed on mud, flower nectar, dung, etc. Males patrol and sometimes perch all day in swales and gullies to seek females.

665. Pyrgus communis   Checkered Skipper

Color Plate 45

P. communis, *P. oileus*, and *P. philetas* have white upf submarginal and marginal spots (*Pyrgus* species 661-664 lack them), and males are whiter than females. *P. communis* males lack the hind-leg hair plume that all other *Pyrgus* have. The unh marginal marks (esp. in cells M$_1$ and M$_2$) are rounded (triangular in *oileus* and *philetas*). Ssp. **albescens** (low altitude in s Calif., s Ariz., s N.M., w and s Tex., rare in sw Utah, w Kans., and c Tex.) has one tooth on the male valva. Ssp. **communis** (most of the range, including the higher mountains of s Calif., s Ariz., and N.M.) has two teeth on the male valva. The two ssp. intergrade in many places. Other ssp. range south to Argentina.

Habitat Subtropical to Transition Zone open areas and towns. Hostplants herb Malvaceae: *Althaea rosea, officinalis, Abutilon theophrasti, Anoda, Callirhoe leiocarpa, Hibiscus trionum, Malvastrum rotundifolium, coromandelianum*t*, Modiola caroliniana, Malva moschata, neglecta, rotundifolia, nicaeensis, parviflora, sylvestris, Sidalcea malvaeflora, glaucescens, neomexicana, oregana* ssp. *spicata, Sida filicaulis, lindheimeri, rhombifolia, hederacea, spinosa, Sphaeralcea angustifolia* (and ssp. *cuspidata*), *munroana, lindheimeri, coccinea, ambigua, parvifolia, Iliamna.*

Eggs greenish-white or pale bluish-green, becoming cream just before hatching, laid singly mainly on leaf buds and the upperside of host leaves. Larvae eat leaves, and live in rolled-leaf nests. Larva yellowish-white to brownish, with many tiny white points, a darker middorsal line, and two brownish lines and two thin white lines on each side, the collar black; head black, with short tawny hairs. Pupa light greenish, the abdomen light brown with transverse bands of blackish streaks and dots. Full-grown larvae hibernate.

Several flights, June-M Oct. northward, all year in s Tex. Adults sip flower nectar and mud. Males perch and patrol all day in swales to seek females.

Color Plate 45

666. Pyrgus oileus   Tropical Checkered Skipper

Like *P. communis*, but the male has a hind-leg hair plume, the unh marginal marks are triangles (esp. in cells M_1 and M_2, where a brown triangle is inside a black triangle), males have a whitish suffusion on the ups, and the front edge of the unh has three dark-brown spots.

Habitat subtropical open areas. Ranges south to Argentina and the Greater and Lesser Antilles. Hostplants (in Latin Amer.) herb Malvaceae: *Sida carpinifolia, antillensis, rhombifolia, salviaefolia, Malvastrum.*

Eggs cream, laid singly mainly on the upperside of host leaves. Larvae eat leaves. Larva yellowish-green, with dark-green blotches, tiny white points, and a faint green middorsal line, the neck brown with a brown collar; head black. Pupa greenish (or bright red-brown), the abdomen yellowish-green with a darker middorsal line, with brown spots behind the head.

Many flights all year in s Fla. and s Tex.; migrates rarely north to Ark. and N Tex.

Color Plate 45

667. Pyrgus philetas   Desert Checkered Skipper

Like *P. oileus* (both have a male hind-leg hair plume), but the unh is pale whitish or cream, and most of the marginal marks are triangular. Habitat Subtropical to Upper Sonoran Zone open areas, in the desert at springs and lakes. Ranges south to Guerrero, Mex. Many flights, Feb.-Dec. in Tex., Apr.-Oct. in Ariz. Males patrol and sometimes perch all day in gulches and at springs to seek females.

668. Heliopetes ericetorum   Great Basin White Skipper

Males are mostly white on the ups, but females are mostly black. Identified by the simple unh pattern, by the dark uph marginal crescents, and by the white

Color Plate 45
Fig. 45

unf base. The unh has a long tan indented postbasal stripe, which *H. macaira* lacks.

Habitat mainly Upper Sonoran Zone open woodland and chaparral. Ranges south to Guerrero, Mex. Hostplants herb (sometimes bushy) Malvaceae: *Althaea rosea, Iliamna rivularis, Hibiscus denudatus, Malvastrum rotundifolium, exile, Malacothamnus fasciculatus, orbiculatus, davidsonii, fremontii* ssp. *cercophorum, Malva nicaeensis, Sphaeralcea ambigua, munroana, grossulariaefolia* var. *pedata, angustifolia* ssp. *cuspidata;* Sterculiaceae: *Fremontia.*

Eggs (Fig. 45) pale yellow, turning white, laid singly on young host leaves. Larvae eat leaves, and live in nests of rolled or tied leaves. Larva greenish-yellow (becoming pinkish before pupating), with a green middorsal line, a green line on each side, a yellowish line on each side, and a yellowish lateral band; head black, with short hair. Pupa yellowish-brown (pinkish on the abdomen), with a bluish bloom.

Several flights, L June-Sep. northward, Apr.-Oct. southward (occasionally Dec. in s Calif.). Adults sip flower nectar and mud. Males patrol canyon bottoms to seek females.

669. Heliopetes domicella   Banded White Skipper

Both sexes are blackish on the ups with a broad white band. The unh has a brown postbasal stripe like that of *H. ericetorum* females, but the basal third of the unf is dark (white in *ericetorum* and *H. macaira*). Habitat Subtropical to Upper Sonoran Zone scrub and desert, mostly near water. Ranges south to Argentina. Several flights, mostly Apr.-Oct. (Apr.-Dec. in s Tex.). Adults feed on mud and flowers.

Color Plate 45

670. Heliopetes macaira   Brown-Margined White Skipper

The brown unh marginal patch has an indented inner edge, and there are two brown unh postbasal spots. The black ups markings are a little larger on females than on males.

Habitat subtropical woods and brush. Ranges south to Paraguay. Hostplant herb Malvaceae: *Malvaviscus drummondii.*

Eggs laid on twigs and buds of the host. Larvae eat young leaves, flowers, and fruits. Young larvae hide in crannies on the host without nests, but older larvae may live in a leaf shelter, where they usually pupate.

Many flights all year in s Tex.; one migrant is known from Kans.

Color Plate 45

671. Heliopetes laviana   Tropical White Skipper

The unh has a straight inner edge of the brown postmedian patch, and the brown postbasal spots are almost completely separate from each other. The black ups markings are slightly larger on females than on males.

Habitat subtropical brushy areas. Ranges south to Argentina. Hostplants herb Malvaceae: *Sida filipes, Malvastrum americanum, Abutilon lignosum, hypoleucum, Pseudabutilon lozani.*

Larvae eat leaves, and live in a shelter of folded leaves; young larvae fold over a flap of the leaf at the point where they've eaten.

Many flights all year in s Tex.

Color Plate 45
Fig. 34 (ultraviolet)

Stray only
Color Plate 61

672. **Heliopetes arsalte**   Black-Veined White Skipper

Identified by the black veins on the white unh and by the orange base of the front edge of the unf. Females resemble males. Subtropical. Ranges south to Argentina, rarely straying to Jamaica and Hispaniola. Many flights all year in Mex.; a rare stray into s Tex. (Oct.).

673. **Celotes nessus**   Streaky Skipper

This strange-looking skipper has brown streaks on the wing margins like those of *C. limpia*, but the prong on the male valva is shorter (Fig. 71), the male thorax flap (beneath the abdomen) is brown on top, the female lamella is narrow at the rear (Fig. 71), and *limpia* occurs only in w Tex. In Chihuahua, Mex. (Copper Canyon), two males had the valva prong intermediate to that of *limpia* (J. Scott).

Habitat Subtropical to Upper Sonoran Zone open areas. Ranges south to c Mex. Hostplants herb Malvaceae: *Abutilon incanum, Sida filipes, Wissadula amplissima, holosericea, Sphaeralcea angustifolia* var. *lobata*.

Larvae eat leaves. Larvae hibernate.

Several flights, Mar.-M Sep. northward, Mar.-M Nov. in s Tex. Adults sip flower nectar and mud. Males patrol all day just above the ground in gulches and depressions to seek females.

Color Plate 43
Fig. 71

674. **Celotes limpia**   Chisos Streaky Skipper

The wing pattern is exactly like that of *C. nessus*, although *C. limpia* is slightly larger and occurs only in w Tex. and Mex. The male valva of *limpia* has a long curved prong (Fig. 71; squeezing the abdomen of a fresh male exposes this); *nessus* has a short prong. The ups of the projections from the rear of the male thorax beneath his abdomen are covered with cream linear scales (his hindleg hair plume fits between the bottom of the abdomen and the projection; see similar structures in Fig. 39); these scales are brown in *nessus*. The female lamella is nearly square (Fig. 71); the rear part of the lamella is much narrower in *nessus*.

Habitat Lower to Upper Sonoran Zone open woodland and desert scrub. Hostplants herb Malvaceae: *Abutilon malacum, incanum, Sphaeralcea angustifolia* var. *lobata, Wissadula holosericea*.

Larvae hibernate.

Several flights, Mar.-Sep. Adults sip flower nectar and mud. Males patrol just above the ground in gulches and depressions to seek females.

Color Plate 43
Fig. 71

675. **Pholisora catullus**   Common Sooty Wing (Roadside Rambler)

Identified by the solid-black unh and the rounded wings. The number of white fw spots varies.

Habitat Subtropical to Transition Zone open areas and disturbed ground, but absent in s Fla., the Lower Sonoran Zone desert, and most of the Calif. Coast Ranges and the Cascades. Ranges south to c Mex. Hostplants herb Amaranthaceae: *Amaranthus caudatus, retroflexus, spinosus, hybridus, graecizans, albus, Celosia argentea* var. *cristata*; Chenopodiaceae: *Chenopodium album, ambrosioides, berlandieri, foliosum, paganum, Atriplex rosea*. Other reported hosts such as *Malva, Ambrosia, Monarda*, and *Marrubium* are errors; larvae refuse them.

Color Plate 43
Fig. 45

Eggs (Fig. 45) reddish-tan, laid singly, mainly on the upperside of host leaves. Larvae eat leaves, and live in nests of rolled or tied leaves. Larva light green to yellowish-green, with tiny pale dots (each dot having a short knobbed hair) and with two black plates on top of the prothorax; head black, with short hairs. Pupa greenish-yellow to brown (covered with a grayish-white bloom), hairy except on the wing cases. Full-grown larvae hibernate.

Two flights, L May-E Sep., northward and at higher altitude; many flights, Apr.-Sep. southward, all year in s Tex. Adults sip the nectar of low flowers (usually those 20 cm or less above ground) and mud. They rest and bask with the wings spread nearly horizontal. Males patrol all day just above ground in gulches and depressions to seek females.

Color Plate 43

676. Pholisora mejicanus   Blue Sooty Wing

Like *P. catullus*, but the unh is blue-black with black veins. The number of white fw spots varies.

Habitat Upper Sonoran to Transition Zone open areas, esp. along roadsides, in gulch bottoms, and beside railroad tracks. Adults fly in the same places in the same manner as adults of *P. catullus*. The two species continue to coexist, and larvae of both can be found on the same plant (J. Scott). *P. mejicanus* ranges south to Puebla, Mex. Hostplants herb Amaranthaceae: *Amaranthus retroflexus, graecizans*; Chenopodiaceae: *Chenopodium*.

Eggs reddish-tan, with coarse ribs and bumps, like those of *P. catullus*, laid singly on the upperside of host leaves. Larvae eat leaves, and live in nests of rolled or tied leaves. Larva like that of *catullus*, except the body hairs are twice as long and the hairs lack knobs. Pupa like that of *catullus* but slightly hairier.

Two flights, June-Aug., in Colo.; several flights, May-Sep., southward. Adults sip mud and the nectar of low flowers. Males patrol all day just above the ground in gulches and depressions to seek females.

Color Plate 43

677. Hesperopsis libya   Great Basin Sooty Wing

Hesperopsis have whitish unh patches, and males lack a costal fold (*Pholisora* lack white patches and have a fold). *H. libya* is identified by its uncheckered fringes (checkered in *H. alpheus*) and by the uniformly blackish shade between the white upf spots (*alpheus* has darker patches between the spots). The smaller ssp. **libya** (s Calif.) has many white unh spots. In populations in Inyo Co. and the San Joaquin Valley, Calif., the unh is somewhat suffused with white. The larger ssp. **lena** (c Nev. and Utah to Mont.) has few white unh spots.

Habitat Lower to Upper Sonoran Zone desert washes and alkaline (mostly flat) areas. Hostplant shrub Chenopodiaceae: *Atriplex canescens*; assoc. with *A. confertifolia*.

Eggs dull orange, later turning dirty-white, laid singly on host leaves. Larvae eat leaves, and live in a nest of leaves tied together. Larvae pale blue-green, with many white points beneath the hairs and with three rows of black dots on each side, the collar white; head black, with short orange hair. Pupa light brown, the thorax and wing cases blackish.

One flight, July-E Aug., in N.D.-Mont.; two flights, June-Aug., in Colo. (the early flight darker on the ups); many flights, Mar.-Oct., in s Calif. Males patrol in gulches and around the hostplants, at least in the morning, to seek females.

ssp. *gracielae*

Color Plate 43
Fig. 45

ssp. *texana, alpheus*

678. Hesperopsis alpheus   Saltbush Sooty Wing

Identified by the checkered fringes and rounded wings. In ssp. **gracielae** (along the Colorado River from Yuma, Ariz., to s Nev. and s Utah, and in the Coachella Valley, Calif.), the brown upf postmedian dashes are usually not elongated, the unh has less submarginal white, the ups is darker (esp. in the summer), and the size is slightly less. Ssp. *gracielae* was named as a distinct species, but its male abdominal structures and palpi resemble those of many *alpheus* populations, and ssp. **texana** (from the Rio Grande of s and w Tex.) is also darker, with an unh resembling that of *gracielae*. Ssp. **alpheus** is elsewhere, including the Mojave Desert of Calif. (from Lucerne Valley north, away from *gracielae*). Some *alpheus* from Tucson tend toward *gracielae*.

Habitat Lower to Upper Sonoran Zone washes and alkali flats. Hostplants shrub Chenopodiaceae: *Atriplex lentiformis* (the usual host for ssp. *gracielae*), *argentea* var. *expansa* (one report for *gracielae*), *A. canescens* (the usual host for ssp. *alpheus* and *texana*, and assoc. with ssp. *gracielae* at one site sw of Las Vegas), *Chenopodium* sp. (at Bard, Calif., reported as "near *alpheus*," but refers to *gracielae*).

Eggs (Fig. 45) brownish (the ridges and peaks white), laid on the host. Larvae eat leaves, and live in rolled-leaf nests. Larva dull green, with many white points, without a collar; head blackish, with many short yellowish hairs. Pupa light straw-colored (the abdomen slightly darker), with a whitish bloom, hairy except on the wing cases.

One flight, mostly June, at 2,134 m (7,000 ft) in Colo., Apr.-M May for ssp. *alpheus* in s Nev. and the Mojave Desert of Calif., L Apr.-M June from N Nev. to w Colo.; two flights, M May-M June and July (the latter partial), in SE Colo.; many flights, Apr.-M Oct. for ssp. *gracielae* and for ssp. *texana* in w Tex., Apr.-M Nov. in s Tex. Adults sip flower nectar occasionally. They sometimes fly through brush rather than around it. Males patrol in gulches and around the hostplant all day to seek females.

Subfamily Pyrrhopyginae: Mimic Skippers

The Pyrrhopyginae, about 170 species, live only in the American tropics. One species ranges into the southwestern U.S.

The antenna club in this subfamily is bent back like a putter-type golf club (Fig. 11). The forewing cell is very long, more than two-thirds as long as the leading margin. The subfamily is closely related to the Pyrginae in appearance, and both have the base of vein M_2 on the forewing about as close to M_1 as to M_3 (Fig. 55). Larvae and pupae are like those of the Pyrginae in appearance, and the larvae of both groups eat numerous dicotyledons. W. Evans proposed that the Pyrrhopyginae are related to the Coeliadinae of the African and Australasian tropics, and that these two groups evolved separately when Africa and America split apart in the process of continental drift. In fact, three species of neotropical *Pyrrhopyge* are almost exactly like three species of Coeliadinae from Africa and India in wing pattern, no doubt by coincidence.

Adult Pyrrhopyginae sometimes mimic other tropical American skippers. W. Evans noted that *Pyrrhopyge phidias* looks like *Phocides polybius* (Pyrginae) and *Pyrrhopygopsis socrates* (Hesperiinae); *Jemadia hewitsoni* looks like *Phocides pigma-*

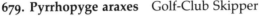

lion (Pyrginae); *Mimoniades yokhara* looks like *Phocides yokhara* (Pyrginae); and *Pseudosarbia phoenicola* looks like *Sarbia xanthippe* (Hesperiinae). Presumably these are cases of mimicry, although it is not known who is mimicking whom or why; the two Hesperiinae probably have grass-eating larvae, and are thus most likely edible to vertebrates. In addition to these cases of apparent mimicry, many Pyrrhopyginae of different genera in the American tropics mimic each other; species that look alike may be in three different genera, and are best identified from the male abdominal structures.

Adults have a strong flight, but do not migrate. They commonly spread the wings while feeding at flowers.

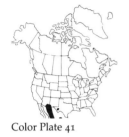

Color Plate 41

679. Pyrrhopyge araxes   Golf-Club Skipper

Identified by the antenna, which is shaped like a putter-type golf club, and by the unique unh pattern.

Habitat Upper Sonoran to Transition Zone oak woodland. Ranges south to Oaxaca, Mex. Hostplant tree Fagaceae: *Quercus arizonica*.

Larvae eat leaves, and live in a nest of a folded-over leaf. Larva red-brown, with narrow yellow transverse stripes and some fairly long white hairs, the collar black; head black, with many long white hairs (the hairs on each cheek orange, and a few hairs on top orange). Pupa brownish-red, the abdomen dull orange (maroon at the joints), covered by white hairs (except on the wing cases), the hairs orange on the top of the head, the pupa covered with flaky white powder.

Several flights, June, Aug.-Nov. (most common in Sep.).

APPENDIXES

REMOTE-ISLAND BUTTERFLIES

Strictly speaking, "North America" includes only the continent of North America south to the Mexican plateau. However, Iceland and Bermuda are included in the book because they involve no new species. Hawaii was also included because it is now part of the United States and has few species that are not on the continent. Butterflies from these areas are listed in the text of Part III and are also listed below (with the number assigned them in text), and ranges in Iceland and Greenland are included on the distribution maps. The species limited to Hawaii are shown on Color Plate 63. Most species listed are introduced and established residents, but some are native (N) and occurred before the Caucasians arrived, and others are temporary strays (*).

ICELAND
Pieris rapae, 76
*Vanessa atalanta**, 184
*Vanessa cardui**, 186
*Vanessa virginiensis**, 187

GREENLAND
Colias hecla (N), 33
*Vanessa cardui**, 186
Boloria titania chariclea
  (N), 240
Boloria polaris (N), 248
Lycaena phlaeas (N), 371
Plebejus glandon (N), 403

BERMUDA
(From L. Ogilvie
  and I. Hughes)
*Papilio cresphontes**, 11
*Colias philodice**, 38
Phoebis sennae, 50
*Eurema lisa**, 63
Pieris rapae, 76
Danaus plexippus, 89
*Danaus gilippus**, 90
*Lethe portlandia**, 94
Precis coenia, 180
Vanessa atalanta, 184
*Vanessa cardui**, 186
*Nymphalis antiopa**, 198
Dione vanillae, 268
*Hylephila phyleus**, 465
*Calpodes ethlius**, 558

HAWAII
Papilio xuthus, 4
Pieris rapae, 76
Danaus plexippus, 89
Vanessa atalanta, 184
Vanessa tameamea (N), 185
Vanessa cardui, 186
Vanessa virginiensis, 187
Dione vanillae, 268
Tmolus echion, 327
Strymon bazochii, 367
Lampides boeticus, 385
Brephidium exilis, 389
Vaga blackburni (N), 394
Erionota thrax, 452
Hylephila phyleus, 465

STUDYING BUTTERFLIES

The study of butterflies can be a very interesting and rewarding hobby. Merely observing butterflies is the simplest way to enjoy them, and many species can be identified without being caught. Butterflies occur everywhere in North America except where there is permanent ice; thus, a pursuit of butterflies can lead to travel. Studying butterflies is less expensive than many other hobbies, and studying them in nature is good exercise. Because caterpillars feed on plants and adults feed on flower nectar, you will learn much about plants, and you may also become interested in geology and climate. In addition, you can make a contribution to science; field observations of behavior are particularly valuable. You may be the first to discover a range extension for a species or a new fact about its natural history. By observing courtships, watching where and when males chase other males and females, and noting whether the male and female were flying or resting before the chase, you can determine the mate-locating behavior of a species. By observing females that seem to flutter slowly, you may watch them lay eggs and discover new hostplants (dig up the plant by the roots and press it in a newspaper; then ask a botanist to identify the plant; if possible, collect the female also to make sure of the identification). Photographing butterflies (particularly immature stages), pickling immatures, and raising butterflies from eggs to adults are also of scientific value, in addition to being intrinsically fascinating. You may publish new distribution records, migrations, hostplants, etc., in the season's summary of the *News of the Lepidopterists' Society* by submitting your records in the fall.

Collecting

Most people who like butterflies collect them at one time or another. Collecting a species one has never found before, or a species in an unusual locality, can be exhilarating. To find butterflies, try a fairly diverse habitat on a warm sunny day (dense forests, for example, have few butterflies). To find a particular species, go within the range of the species, to the proper habitat at the right time of year. To find males, go where mating occurs in the species; but to find females, go where the larval hostplants are. You may have to chase patrolling males, but you can often wait at the mating sites for most perching males. Look, too, at flowers, mud, and sap for feeding butterflies.

You need only two basic items to collect: a net to catch the butterflies, and envelopes to store them in. A net can be purchased, or one can be made out of strong wire, golf-club handles, copper tube, transparent curtain netting, and heavier canvas or cloth (Fig. 68). The wire is bent to fit into grooves and holes drilled into the side of the handle, and a copper tube fits over the wire to hold it onto the handle. The curtain or similar strong netting is sewn into a net bag about two-thirds of a meter long and then onto a canvas or sturdy cloth strip that fits over the wire (the canvas withstands beating the net against plants or rocks).

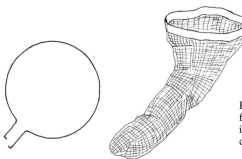

Fig. 68.   An inexpensive collecting net made from a wooden pole (a golf-club handle is ideal), copper tube, heavy wire, canvas or denim, and nylon netting.

When you have caught a butterfly, trap it by rotating the handle to flip the end of the bag over the rim. If you caught the butterfly by dropping the net over it on the ground, trap it in a fold of the net, find the thorax (the legs and wings are attached to the thorax), and kill it by pinching the sides of the thorax with the thumb and finger. Sometimes an adult dies with the wings folded together beneath the body. To fix this, grasp the base of both the left or both the right wings with a pair of forceps, then with a thumbnail or something else move the other set of wings above the body, and place it in the envelope with the wings above the body.

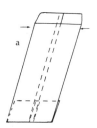

Fig. 69.   Envelopes: *a*, glassine ones that are closed by folding over at the arrows to leave no small openings are best to retard the entry of pests; *b*, paper envelopes can be folded along the lines shown (to stack them before use, the closed end can be taped, and one end can be left open and the next envelope slid into the open end).

Glassine envelopes are best because you can see within. Envelopes that open at one end, which can be folded over to leave no tiny openings (Fig. 69a), are best because dermestid beetles cannot easily get in to eat the butterflies (larvae of dermestids are somewhat hairy with reddish and white rings around the body, up to 7 mm long; adults are blackish with tan spots, round, up to 3 mm long). Flimsy envelopes can cause antenna damage, and gum on the flaps can get on the butterflies when moistened. Paper triangles can be folded from rectangular paper by making a diagonal fold and then closing off the open two sides (Fig. 69b). Store the envelopes in a tight container, so that you can sort and identify the adults in the evening before they dry out. On each envelope, write where and when you caught it, using ink that will not dissolve in water. Write the nearest town, creek, or landmark, the county and state, the date, and, ideally, the altitude and collector. The month should be in letters or Roman numerals to avoid confusion with the day (Aug. 9, 1989, or 9-viii-89). The locality and date are important for scientific reasons and can help in identification. A loose-leaf notebook is useful for recording the locality, date, species caught, and field observations.

Besides these basic items, you may want others. Many people use a killing jar instead of pinching. One sort has a mixture of sawdust and potassium cyanide in the bottom covered by a layer of plaster of Paris. Do not sniff the deadly fumes. Vinegar rejuvenates old cyanide jars. Another sort, the ethyl acetate killing jar, is made with either plaster on the bottom or an absorbent pad on the lid to absorb the fluid, which is applied just before collecting. Killing jars are thought by some to give better specimens, but they are bothersome. Wrap the bottom of the jar with tape for safety, and put crumpled tissue paper in the jar to reduce gumming and sliding of adults.

A rubber-stamp set from a stationery store allows quick stamping of the locality and date on envelopes if you have ten or more from one spot. Forceps are useful for handling specimens (long blunt-tipped forceps will do for most purposes; fine-pointed dissecting forceps and a stereoscopic dissecting microscope are desirable for dissecting genitalia and other fine structures).

Sap-feeding adults can be caught on tree trunks coated with a fermented fruit and beer mash, or caught with a trap. A collecting trap is made of netting and is hung just above rotten fruit on the ground. It is designed like a lobster trap; the butterfly crawls under the trap rim to the fruit, then after feeding it flies upward into a cone made of netting and through a hole in the end of the cone, into the trap made of netting (the trap is larger than the cone, the cone and trap are sewn together at the rim, and the cone must be supported inside the trap by strings or wire). (For most species, the cone may not be necessary.)

You can keep your whole collection in glassine envelopes (ideally in a freezer, so as to kill dermestid beetles), but most people mount several or all of their specimens of each species. To prepare an adult for mounting, "relax" it by placing the envelope containing the butterfly between moist paper towels (wring the water out, since green colors may turn brown if wet; make sure the marking ink is waterproof) in an airtight container for a day. Large butterflies can be quickly relaxed by injecting water into the thorax through the envelope with a syringe.

The butterfly is then pinned onto a mounting board (Fig. 70) constructed from two long wing boards, a long center board, and two end boards to hold the three long boards in place. Thin balsa wood sheets from a craft store are glued onto the wing boards and center board to hold pins (in place of balsa on the

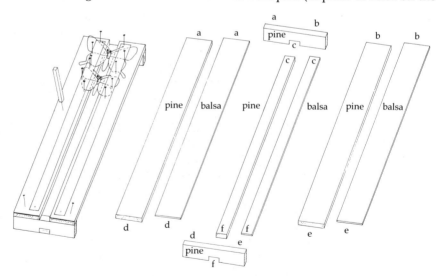

Fig. 70.   *Left,* Mounting board: anchor the tracing-paper strips at the bottom with pins, spread and pin the first adult at the top, release the bottom of the strips, and continue spreading and pinning adults behind the first (see the text). A pin driven into a matchstick helps position the wings. *Right,* Assembly: letters show where to join the pieces. Glue and nail the pine boards together, then glue thin balsa sheets onto the top of the pine. (The balsa sheet for the center is optional; plastic foam can be glued beneath the wing boards instead.)

center, plastic foam can be glued directly to the underside of the wing boards). An insect pin (special pins about 3 cm long bought from dealers: size #3 for most butterflies, and some #2 for the smallest adults) is run vertically through the butterfly thorax until a third of the pin is above the body, and then stuck into the balsa or cork on the center board (or into the foam), so that the body lies between the two wing boards; the positioning of the center board on the end boards determines the position of the body on the pin. Then the wings are brought forward with a pin placed behind a wing vein on the front margin of each wing base (a deheaded insect pin forced backward into a wooden match stick works well), and secured with tracing paper strips and common sewing pins; some people bevel the wing boards inward to account for the sagging of mounted adults in moist climates. The hind margins of the forewings are mounted in a straight line by convention (mainly to display more of the hind-wings; butterflies do not fly with the wings in this position). The antennae are positioned just in front of the forewings (to minimize their vulnerability to breakage), using insect pins placed beside them if necessary. By convention a butterfly is mounted showing the upperside, but with practice you can suc-cessfully mount other specimens with the underside of all wings showing. If you have an adult with the left or right wings damaged, you can mount it sideways with only the good side showing. Other adults are then mounted below the first until the board is full.

Pin the data (the envelope) beside each adult. Make a new small label (15 × 6 mm or as needed) recording the locality, date, and collector, using India ink and a drafting pen. After the butterfly dries, place the label on the same pin with the adult. A storage case can be any box with a pinning bottom glued in (take a pin to a lumberyard to choose an inexpensive bottom, like sound board such as Celotex, or try a craft store), or it can be fancy glass-topped drawers in cabinets that you buy or build. Using mothballs will keep dermestid beetles from eating your butterflies (an outside shed could be used to store your collection where freezing winters will prevent dermestid damage and where you can fumi-gate it freely without breathing the fumes; mice should be excluded). If a fat butterfly gets greasy wings, put it pin and all into unleaded gasoline or acetone for a few days to dissolve the grease.

Little glass bottles and 70-90 percent ethyl or isopropyl alcohol (from a drug-store or supermarket) are very useful for pickling eggs, larvae, and pupae. Pur-ists often kill the larva in near-boiling water first, or place it in KAAD (1 part kerosene, 7-10 parts 95 percent ethyl or isopropyl alcohol, 2 parts glacial acetic acid, 1 part dioxane) for a day, before storing it in alcohol; these techniques are not too important, they supposedly distend the body more so that the structures are more visible. A label marked with India ink giving the locality, date, host-plant, butterfly species, collector, etc., is put in the vial too. The alcohol will preserve the structures, but because some colors may disappear, it is desirable to photograph larvae and pupae in color before killing them. A few people inflate and dry the larva by squeezing the insides out of a hole made in the rear; a complicated apparatus heats the larva while blowing air through it with a tube extended full-length into the rear. Freeze-drying is very useful, either in an airtight box in the freezer with a desiccating chemical for several months, or in a vacuum chamber for several hours or days. Silica gel (bought from a supply house for chemicals) is blue when dry, pink when wet; when a larva is placed in an airtight (taped-shut) container with the dry silica gel for about 5 months in a freezer, it dries completely in its former shape and colors, although some colors, such as green, may later disappear.

Raising and Breeding

Raising butterflies from eggs or larvae is valuable in determining the appearance of the larvae and pupae and in discovering or verifying the habits and larval hostplants. Some people raise butterflies to obtain perfect adult specimens, because many adults can be obtained by raising the eggs of a single wild-caught female and because often the only adults seen in nature are a few worn males. To raise butterflies, search for eggs or larvae in nature or raise them from a wild-caught female. It is very difficult to find the pupae of most species in nature, but eggs and larvae can be easy if you search the right part of the hostplant at the right time. Lycaenidae larvae are often found by noting the ants that tend them.

If you catch a female in nature, it will probably be mated unless it is very young (choose a female with a little wing wear). Put a young sprig of the larval hostplant into wet sand in a quart jar covered with cheesecloth, place the female inside, and position a lamp above it so that the jar is warm but not hot. Better still, put the base of the sprig into a small water-filled vial plugged around the stem with cotton, and place the vial on its side in a clear plastic box, surrounded with many lights. Maintain temperature at about 29-35°C (85-95°F) to avoid cooking the female. Feed her twice a day by soaking some cotton or cloth with a little honey in water (make it watery in consistency but sweet). Place the butterfly's legs on the cotton; the butterfly may unroll its proboscis automatically, but you may have to unroll the proboscis with a pin. Some people make an apparatus using cardboard wing clamps glued to clothespins to hold the butterfly during the 5-10 minutes it is feeding, or you can hold the butterfly's wings by hand. Rinse her legs and proboscis after feeding to prevent the honey from drying onto her. After a week, the female will be tattered, but most of the time she will lay many eggs. Then raise the larvae in containers (for the small larvae, tiny bottles are best to keep the hostplant from drying out and to allow you to find the larva), cleaning the bottles and putting in fresh food every day or two (preferably in plugged water-filled vials). Keeping moisture low will reduce mold. Some diseases may occur, which are minimized by using containers cleaned with hot water and soap, and by dipping the fresh leaves in 5 percent household chlorine bleach, then rinsing in distilled water. Aureomycin or tetracycline (from a veterinarian or physician) mixed with water in a mist sprayer (such as those for cleaning windows) and sprayed on the larval hostplants will prevent bacterial disease. Most people do not use these special techniques, and you should have little problem with disease by just using clean containers and providing low humidity and fresh food. If disease does crop up, isolate each larva, and throw away the sick-looking ones because they probably will not recover and may contaminate the others. (But note that molting larvae are motionless and appear "sick.") Some people have raised butterflies on an "artificial diet" consisting of ground-up hostplant, agar, soy flour, vitamins, minerals, antibiotics, etc., and there are even companies that specialize in making artificial diets for various insects (these techniques are generally used only when raising thousands of insects). When the larvae pupate, remove them from the rearing containers and place them on cotton in a rough cardboard box covered with cheesecloth until the adults emerge, climb the walls, and spread their wings.

Sometimes eggs, larvae, or pupae go into diapause in the laboratory and refuse to develop further. This can be prevented in many cases by shining light on them constantly. Individuals in diapause can be overwintered using large clay planting pots purchased from garden centers (the unglazed kind semipermeable to water); plug the hole in the bottom, place the individuals in small open containers in the pot (cheesecloth prevents their escape from the containers), bury the pot three-fourths of the way into the ground, and cover it with a lid (the saucer for a larger pot). Avoid a sunny hot place where they will cook or dry out, and in a drought water the lid occasionally. This pot will provide natural temperatures and moderate humidity. When the food plant is available in late winter or early spring, bring them indoors and they should develop normally.

"Hand-pairing" of males and females in the lab is a useful technique for raising uncommon or unusual butterflies, or for genetic studies. Position the end of the male abdomen just below the end of the female abdomen (when mating, the male's claspers, or valvae, grasp the female's abdomen beside the plate, or lamella, on the lower end of her abdomen, and the male's uncus fits into a pocket beneath the pillow-shaped structures on the top rear of her abdomen; see Figs. 28, 30). Gently squeeze the abdomens of male and female, and move them slightly around so that the male grasps the female's abdomen just below the tip. Opening the male's claspers with some object (such as a pencil held between the knees) may be necessary. Do this until they remain joined and mate. Hand-pairing works best with large butterflies. Chilling them in the refrigerator briefly makes them easier to handle and gives good results (live adults and other stages can be stored in the refrigerator for days or even weeks, in order to synchronize availability of males and females). Occasionally butterflies will mate in cages placed in the sun. By using these techniques you can hybridize different populations or forms to study inheritance, and raise many adults of uncommon species. First-generation hybrids between two populations or species are called F_1 (short for "filial generation #1"), and second-generation hybrids from brother-sister matings of F_1 individuals are called F_2, etc. Hybrids of F_1 and either of the parent populations are called backcrosses, which determine whether the genes from one of the populations can find their way into the other population (in which case they are the same species, if the hybrids are normal and they can mate in nature). Lab-raised females can be released in front of wild males in nature to obtain hybrids and study courtship.

Marking

To study dispersal, population size, and average life span in nature, each butterfly should be uniquely marked. A small numbered tag can be glued on the forewing of *Danaus* and other large butterflies. F. Urquhart has marked many thousands of Monarchs by making a hole in the cell of the forewing with a hole punch, then folding a printed gummed label over the leading edge of the wing so that the gummed surfaces stick to each other. For large or small species, the number can be written on the wing with a permanent-ink felt-tipped pen, or dots can be placed on the wings to code a number. For instance, a dot on the right forewing tip can represent 1, on the lower corner 2, on the right hindwing tip 4, on the hind angle 7, and the same positions on the left wings can be 10, 20, 40, and 70 (by this scheme, #83 has four dots, in the 70, 10, 2, and 1 positions). With combinations of black dots you can mark 154 butterflies, with red another 154, then 144 more with black dots on the right wings and red dots on the left wings (the first ten numbers cannot be used for these, owing to confusion with the black-dot-only individuals), etc. On small butterflies the lower forewing dot can be moved to the base of the hindwing underside. These pen marks can be made through the material of the collecting net. E. Nielsen used a quick method for studying common migrating *Ascia*; he squirted flower-feeding adults with dye from an oil can. Liquid typewriter correction fluid (toluene-based) can be daubed on the head or spines of larvae to mark them.

For the marking and recapturing process, draw a map of the study area, then record where and when you caught, released, and recaptured each individual. Each should be marked and released immediately where you caught it. Then the places where an individual was marked and recaptured can be plotted to determine how far it flew. (See "Population Size and Population Regulation," in Part I, for the calculation of population size.)

Dissecting Genitalia   To identify some species it may be necessary to examine the hard parts at the end of the abdomen (Fig. 71). Often these parts can be seen merely by brushing the scales away from the tip with a clipped-off fine artist's brush. If the parts cannot be seen, break off the whole abdomen (or the last half) and place it in a warm solution of potassium hydroxide or sodium hydroxide (drain cleaner from a grocery store, about 1 part chemical mixed with 9 parts water; but be careful with these chemicals because they burn the eyes and skin if not washed off); soak until the muscles and soft tissues are dissolved (several hours, or much less if the solution is heated). Then with a stereoscopic microscope and fine tweezers pull the soft parts away from the genitalia to examine them. Rinse them with water and store them with a drop of glycerol in a tiny plastic vial that is pinned through the rubber stopper on the same pin as the adult (if these special tiny vials are unavailable, glue the genitalia to a small card on the same pin as the adult). Do not mount the genitalia on slides, which squash the structures and are often separated from the adult. Acetone-base clear glue is the best glue (it should be thinned with acetone, purchased at a drug store), which is also useful for repairing butterfly wings, legs, antennae, etc. (use a metal probe to dip out the glue, and a moistened fine artist's brush to position the loose part).

Fig. 71 (*facing page*).   Male and female abdominal structures (genitalia) useful for identification. Male structures (see Fig. 28): *v*, valva (inside views); *Lv*, left valva (specified only when left and right valvae differ as shown); *Rv*, right valva; *u*, uncus (dorsal view); *g*, gnathos; *j*, juxta; *s*, saccus; *t*, tegumen. Female structures (see Fig. 30): *l*, lamella (ventral view); *o*, ovipositor.   *18, Papilio glaucus*: A, ssp. *glaucus*; B, ssp. *glaucus*, upper valva prong; C, intermediate from s B.C., upper prong; D, ssp. *rutulus*, upper prong; E, ssp. *glaucus*, flap of lamella; F, ssp. *rutulus*, flap (intermediate flaps occur in SE B.C. also).   *72, Euchloe hyantis*.   *73, E. ausonia*.   *74, E. creusa*.   *120, Erebia dabanensis youngi*.   *121, E. kozhantshikovi lafontainei*.   *122, E. occulta*.   *130, Oeneis bore*.   *131, O. uhleri*.   *133, O. alpina excubitor*.   *134, O. melissa*.   *135, O. polixenes*.   *192, Polygonia gracilis*.   *193, P. progne*.   *200, Euphydryas chalcedona*: A, ssp. *chalcedona*, colon; B, ssp. *anicia* (intermediates occur; see the text for species 200).   *201, E. editha*.   *221, Chlosyne hoffmanni*, with the middle prong short.   *222, C. palla* (similar: *C. gabbii*, 223).   *227, Phyciodes morpheus*, with the uncus divided into two hooks.   *228, P. tharos*, with the hooks thinner and a bit longer.   *229, P. batesii*, with the edge of the uncus more angled in front of the hooks.   *235, P. ptolyca*, dorsal view.   *236, P. frisia*.   *251, Speyeria diana* (similar: uncus of *S. aphrodite, cybele, nokomis, idalia*, 252-255).   *264, S. edwardsii* (similar: uncus of the remaining *Speyeria*).   *282, Calephelis borealis*, ventral view of the male, showing the five-lobed transtilla above the valvae.   *283, C. muticum*.   *284, C. virginiensis*.   *285, C. nilus*.   *286, C. nemesis*.   *287, C. rawsoni*: A, ssp. *rawsoni*; B, ssp. *rawsoni* (similar: female ssp. *freemani*); C, ssp. *freemani*; D, ssp. *arizonensis*.   *288, C. wrighti*.   (*continued on page 515*)

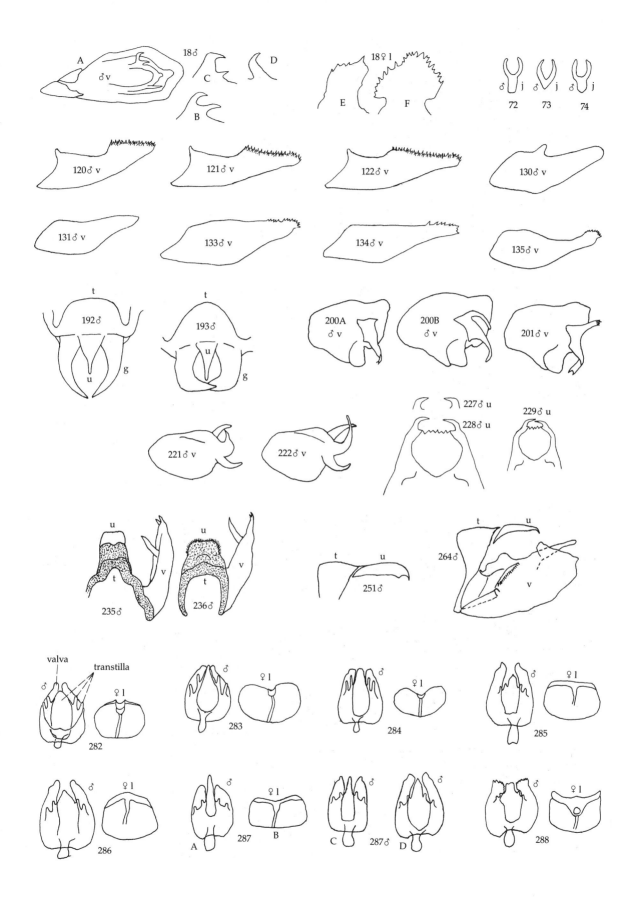

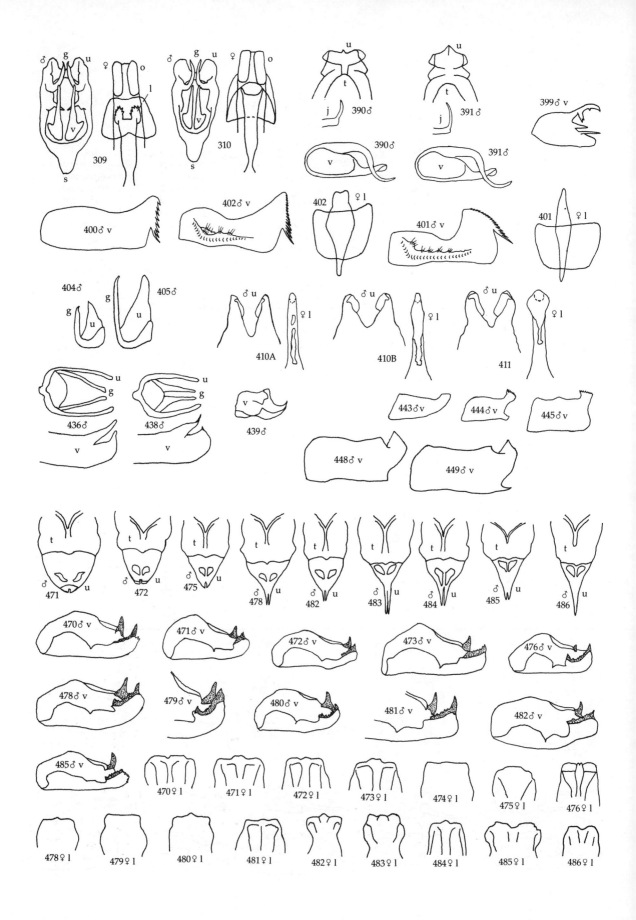

(*Fig. 71, continued*)

309, Satyrium caryaevorus, the male with two spines, the female with two spadelike projections below the mating tube. *310, S. calanus. 390, Everes comyntas. 391, E. amyntula. 399, Euphilotes battoides. 400, E. enoptes. 401, E. rita. 402, E. spaldingi. 404, Plebejus idas,* ventral view, requiring dissection. *405, P. melissa,* same view. *410, P. acmon,* with the female mating tube extending beyond the body and the lamella on it viewed from the top: *A,* ssp. *acmon; B,* ssp. *texanus. 411, P. lupini. 436, Synapte malitiosa,* without a spine. *438, S. syraces,* with a dorsal spine at the tip (similar: genitalia of *S. salenus,* 437). *439, Corticea corticea. 443, Nastra lherminier. 444, N. neamathla. 445, N. julia. 448, Lerema accius. 449, L. ancillaris. 470, Hesperia uncas* (most *Hesperia* after C. D. MacNeill). *471, H. juba. 472, H. comma* (similar: uncus of *H. uncas, woodgatei, ottoe*). *473, H. woodgatei. 474, H. ottoe. 475, H. leonardus* (similar: uncus of *H. columbia* and *pahaska;* lamella of *H. columbia*). *476, H. pahaska* (similar: valvae of *H. columbia, leonardus, sassacus*). *478, H. viridis* (similar: uncus of *H. attalus, metea, meskei;* valva of *H. nevada,* but with the prongs sometimes smaller). *479, H. attalus* (similar: valva of *H. lindseyi*). *480, H. metea. 481, H. meskei. 482, H. dacotae. 483, H. sassacus. 484, H. lindseyi. 485, H. miriamae. 486, H. nevada. 493, Polites themistocles. 494, P. baracoa. 495, P. origenes,* but sometimes without the lowermost of the four teeth on the tip of the valva. *506, Ochlodes sylvanoides:* the stippled part is like a keel with a pocket behind it. *507, O. agricola,* without a keel. *574, Polygonus leo. 575, P. manueli. 585A, Codatractus arizonensis,* ventral view. *[585]B, C. melon* (see the text for species 585). *601, Autochton cellus. 602, A. pseudocellus. 606, Achalarus albociliatus. 607, A. toxeus. 608, A. jalapus. 609, Thorybes pylades* (the uncus is split into two arms in most *Thorybes*). *610, T. bathyllus. 611, T. mexicana. 612, T. confusis. 613, T. diversus.* (*continued on page 516*)

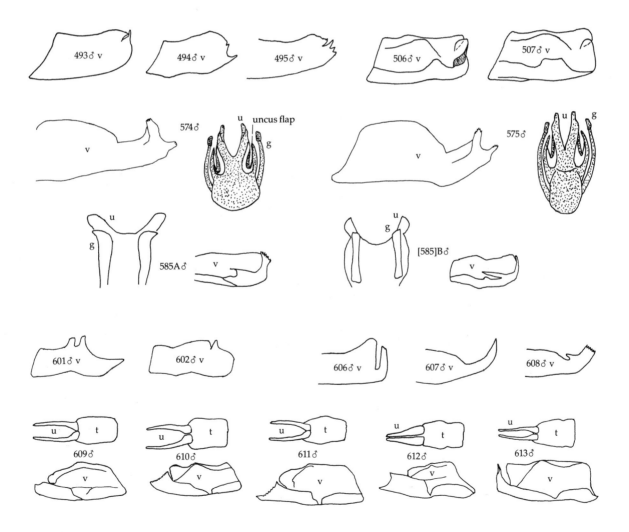

(*Fig. 71, continued*)

625, Nisoniades rubescens. 626, Pellicia dimidiata. 627A, P. costimacula. [627]B, P. angra (see the text for species 627). *628, Bolla brennus. 629, B. clytius. 630, Staphylus hayhurstii. 631, S. mazans. 632, S. azteca. 638, Systasea pulverulenta. 639, S. zampa. 646, Erynnis icelus. 647, E. brizo. 648, E. martialis. 649, E. pacuvius. 650, E. juvenalis: A, ssp. juvenalis; B, ssp. clitus. 651, E. telemachus. 652, E. propertius: A, ssp. propertius; B, ssp. meridianus. 653, E. scudderi,* with two "mouse ears" above the "snout." *654, E. horatius. 655, E. tristis tatius. 656, E. zarucco funeralis* (similar: ssp. *zarucco*). *657, E. persius. 659, E. afranius* (similar: *E. lucilius, 658,* and *baptisiae, 660*). *673, Celotes nessus,* with the lamella in three parts behind the mating tube. *674, C. limpia.*

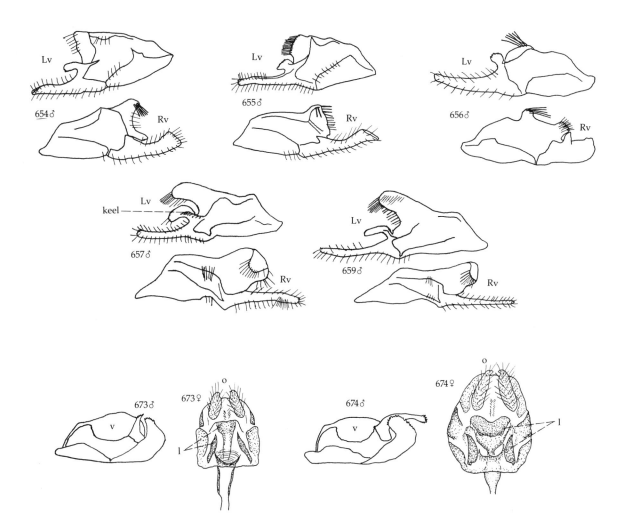

654♂ Lv Rv

655♂ Lv Rv

656♂ Lv Rv

657♂ keel Lv Rv

659♂ Lv Rv

673♂ v

673♀ o l

674♂ v

674♀ o l

REFERENCE MATTER

BIBLIOGRAPHY

Butterfly References   Journal of the Lepidopterists' Society. The society also publishes News of the Lepidopterists' Society, which prints notices from members (without charge) and a
membership list; this list, which includes the addresses and interests of over 2,000
members, enables one member to contact another to exchange information, specimens, etc. A library can provide the current addresses of the two journals.
Journal of Research on the Lepidoptera

A Bibliography of the Catalogues, Lists, Faunal and Other Papers on the Butterflies
of North America Arranged by State and Province. W. Field, C. dos Passos, and
J. Masters. 1974. Smithsonian Contributions to Zoology, No. 157.

Butterflies and Moths of Newfoundland and Labrador. R. Morris. 1980. Agriculture
Canada: Research Branch, Publication 1691.

Butterflies and Skippers of New York State. A. Shapiro. 1974. Search (Cornell University) 4(3).

Butterflies East of the Great Plains. P. Opler and G. Krizek. 1984. Baltimore, Md.:
Johns Hopkins Univ. Press.

Butterflies of California. T. Emmel, J. Emmel, and S. Mattoon. Forthcoming. Stanford,
Calif.: Stanford Univ. Press.

Butterflies of Georgia. L. Harris, Jr. 1972. Norman: Univ. of Oklahoma Press.

The Butterflies of Oregon. E. Dornfeld. 1980. Forest Grove, Ore.: Timber Press.

Butterflies of Saskatchewan. R. Hooper. 1973. Regina: Saskatchewan Museum of
Natural History.

Butterflies of Southern California. T. Emmel and J. Emmel. 1973. Los Angeles County
Museum of Natural History, Science Series, No. 26.

Butterflies of the Delaware Valley. A. Shapiro. 1966. Philadelphia: American Ento-
mological Society.

Butterflies of the Ottawa District. R. Layberry, J. Lafontaine, and P. Hall. 1980. Trail
and Landscape, Vol. 16(1), pp. 3-59.

Butterflies of the Rocky Mountain States. C. Ferris and F. Brown, eds. 1981. Norman:
Univ. of Oklahoma Press.

Butterflies of Virginia. A. Clark and L. Clark. 1951. Smithsonian Miscellaneous Collections, Vol. 116(7).

Catalogue/Checklist of the Butterflies of North America. L. Miller and F. Brown. 1981.
Lepidopterists' Society, Memoir No. 2. Provides the scientific names and the persons who named them, type localities, and library citations for all the species,
subspecies, and synonyms. It includes many minor subspecies and synonyms not
found here in Part III, but the nomenclature for species, genera, and families is
poor in many cases.

Catalogue of American Hesperiidae. W. Evans. 1951–55. Parts I–IV. London: British
Museum of Natural History. Good keys to identify skippers, but the drawings of
male genitalia are crude.

Checklist of Butterflies of Illinois. R. Irwin and J. Downey. 1973. Illinois Natural History
Survey, Biological Notes, No. 81.

Ecology and Distribution of the Butterflies of Southern Central Colorado. J. Scott and G. Scott. 1978. Journal of Research on the Lepidoptera, Vol. 17, pp. 73-128.

Hesperioidea of North America. A. Lindsey, E. Bell, and R. Williams, Jr. 1931. Denison Univ. Bulletin, Vol. 26. Many drawings of skipper male genitalia.

How to Know the Butterflies. P. Ehrlich and A. Ehrlich. 1961. Dubuque, Iowa: Wm. Brown.

Skippers of the Genus *Hesperia* in Western North America. C. MacNeill. 1964. Univ. of California Publications in Entomology, Vol. 35.

Yosemite Butterflies. J. Garth and J. Tilden. 1963. Journal of Research on the Lepidoptera, Vol. 2(1).

Some bibliographies of life histories and hostplants are useful:

Bibliographic Catalogue of the Described Transformations of North American Lepidoptera. H. Edwards. 1889. Bulletin of the U.S. National Museum, No. 35, pp. 7-37.

Bibliography of the Described Life Histories of the Rhopalocera of America North of Mexico, 1889-1937. D. Davenport and V. Dethier. 1937. Entomologica Americana, Vol. 17, pp. 155-94. (Supplement, by V. Dethier, 1946, in Psyche, Vol. 53, pp. 15-20.)

Hibernal Diapause of North American Papilionoidea and Hesperioidea. J. Scott. 1981. Journal of Research on the Lepidoptera, Vol. 18, pp. 171-200.

Index to Life Histories, Early Stages, and Hosts of Macrolepidoptera of the United States and Canada. H. Tietz. 1972. Sarasota, Fla.: Allyn Museum of Entomology. Gives references of papers describing early stages and hostplants but contains many errors; each reference should be checked.

Plant References

Besides providing a useful source for seeing what the plants look like and where they occur, these books contribute to accurate identification. Many other books are also helpful in learning about common plants.

Anderson's Flora of Alaska and Adjacent Parts of Canada. S. Welsh. 1974. Provo, Utah: Brigham Young Univ. Press.

Arizona Flora. T. Kearney and R. Peebles. 1960. Berkeley: Univ. of California Press.

A California Flora. P. Munz and D. Keck. 1959. Berkeley: Univ. of California Press.

Common Weeds of the United States. Agricultural Research Service of the U.S. Department of Agriculture. 1970. New York: Dover.

The Complete Trees of North America: A Field Guide and Natural History. T. Elias. 1980. New York: Van Nostrand/Reinhold.

Flora of Alaska and Neighboring Territories. E. Hultén. 1968. Stanford, Calif.: Stanford Univ. Press.

Flora of Alberta. E. Moss. 1959. Toronto: Univ. of Toronto Press.

Flora of Idaho. R. Davis. 1952. Dubuque, Iowa: Brown.

Flora of Missouri. J. Steyermark. 1963. Ames: Iowa State Univ. Press.

Flora of Southeastern United States. J. Small. 1903. New York: New Era Printing Co., printed by author. Out of date.

Flora of the Prairies and Plains of Central North America. P. Rydberg. 1932. New York: New York Botanic Garden.

Flora of the Rocky Mountains and Adjacent Plains. P. Rydberg. 1917. Lancaster, Pa., and New York: Steinman and Foltz.

A Flora of Tropical Florida. R. Long and O. Lakela. 1971. Miami, Fla.: Univ. of Miami Press.

Gray's Manual of Botany. M. Fernald. 1950. New York: American Book Co.

Hortus Third: A Concise Dictionary of Plants Cultivated in the United States and Canada. L. Bailey and E. Bailey. 1976. New York: Macmillan.

An Illustrated Flora of the Northern United States, Canada, and the British Posses-
    sions. N. Britton and A. Brown. 1913. Lancaster, Pa.: Lancaster Press. Includes
    nice line drawings and the names of plants used in older papers.
An Illustrated Flora of the Pacific States. L. Abrams. 1960. 4 vols. Stanford, Calif.:
    Stanford Univ. Press. Good line drawings.
Manual of Cultivated Plants. L. Bailey. 1949. New York: Macmillan.
Manual of the Grasses of the United States. A. Hitchcock. 1935. Washington, D.C.:
    U.S. Government Printing Office.
Manual of the Vascular Plants of Texas. D. Correll and M. Johnston. 1970. Austin:
    Univ. of Texas Press.
The New Britton and Brown Illustrated Flora. H. Gleason. 1968. 3 vols. New York:
    Hafner.
Range Plant Handbook. U.S. Forest Service. 1937. Washington, D.C.: U.S. Govern-
    ment Printing Office.
Rocky Mountain Flora. W. Weber. 1976. Boulder: Colorado Associated Univ. Press.
Standard Cyclopedia of Horticulture. L. Bailey. 1930. 3 vols. New York: Macmillan.
Trees and Shrubs of Mexico. P. Standley. 1920–26. Contributions to the U.S. National
    Herbarium. Bulletin of the U.S. National Museum, Vol. 23.
Vascular Flora of the Southeastern United States. A. Cronquist. 1980–. Chapel Hill:
    Univ. of North Carolina Press. A continuing series of volumes.
Vascular Plants of Continental Northwest Territories, Canada. A. Porsild and W.
    Cody. 1980. Canada: National Museum of Natural Sciences.
Wildflowers of the United States. H. Rickett, ed. 1974. 6 vols. New York: McGraw-
    Hill. Color photographs of most wild flowers.

HOSTPLANT CATALOGUE

All butterfly larvae, except some Lycaenidae (Miletini), eat plants. Lichens and fungi are eaten by a few Lycaenidae (the tropical tribe Liptenini), and ferns (*Selaginella*) are eaten by some tropical Satyrinae (*Euptychia*). All other butterflies eat advanced seed-bearing plants. The seed-bearing plants are divided into two groups, the gymnosperms and angiosperms. The gymnosperms have the seeds on the surface of a scale, like the scales of pine cones, without a special structure for receiving pollen. They include Cycadaceae (cycads include *Zamia*, eaten by a few Lycaenidae), Pinaceae (conifers, eaten by a few butterflies), and Cupressaceae (cedars and junipers, eaten by a few lycaenids).

Angiosperms, or flowering plants, have the seeds in a closed ovary that has one or more pollen-receiving structures (stigmas) on it. The flowers usually attract insects that pollinate them. The flower typically has small green leaflike sepals at the base, colorful petals, long stamens with pollen at their tips, and one or more stigmas to receive the pollen on a stalk above the ovary. The modifications of the flower parts are used to classify these plants. Flowering plants are divided into two groups, the monocotyledons and dicotyledons, reflecting the number of leaves in sprouting seed.

In the monocotyledons, the leaves usually have parallel veins, the stems are often hollow, the seeds are not split into two parts, and the flowers usually have three of each part (three petals, three sepals, three stamens) or a multiple of three. The monocotyledons eaten by butterflies are Liliaceae, Palmae, Sparganiaceae, Bromeliaceae, Musaceae, Cannaceae, Marantaceae, Gramineae, Juncaceae, and Cyperaceae. Most of these have obvious flowers, but the last three families have tiny inconspicuous flowers because wind pollinates them. Grasses (Gramineae) and sedges (Cyperaceae) are eaten by Satyrinae and Hesperiinae. Grasses have their leaves in two rows on the stem, and cylindrical or flattened and usually hollow stems. Sedges often grow in wet spots, their leaves are in three rows on the stem, and the stems are usually triangular in cross section and solid.

In the dicotyledons, the leaves usually have a network of veins going in all directions, the stems are solid, the seeds are split into two halves, and the flowers usually have five of each part (five petals, five sepals, five stamens). Some families of dicotyledons are important and easily recognized. The Compositae have many tiny flowers clumped into a head, each flower lacking sepals, the outer flowers and sometimes the inner flowers usually having petals. A dandelion has hundreds of flowers in each cluster, and the seeds have hairs to be blown by the wind, for instance. Cruciferae are weedy herbs ("herbs" are plants that die above ground in winter, not shrubs or trees or grasses) that have four petals, four sepals, and six stamens, two stamens shorter than the other four. In the Rosaceae, the sepals are joined into a tube or disk, with the petals and many stamens attached to the rim; they are often shrubs or trees. Leguminosae generally have the leaves split into many leaflets, pea-shaped flowers with a hood, some wings on the side, and a keel, and the seeds are "peas" inside a "bean" pod. The Umbelliferae are herbs with fernlike leaves, and the many tiny flowers are in a flat-topped cluster, from a spray of stalks at the top of a stem. Malvaceae are herbs with fanlike leaves, and the flowers have the stamens all joined into a column around the ovary. Labiatae are herbs that have square stems. Polygonaceae have a translucent sheath around the main stem where each leaf branches off. Scrophulariaceae have the petals joined into a tube having upper and lower lips, usually four stamens (often of different sizes) arising from the tube, and often a fifth stamen lacking pollen. Euphorbiaceae are herbs having milky sap, and their flowers lack petals and are clustered together above colorful leaves that look like petals. Asclepiadaceae are herbs also with milky sap, the flowers have extra petallike lobes above the true petals (like a crown), and the pollen is clustered into bundles that may catch on to butterfly legs. Salicaceae and Betulaceae, usually shrubs or trees, have the flowers clustered into catkins like squirrel tails. Crassulaceae are herbs ("succulents") with thick juicy leaves. Amaranthaceae and Chenopodiaceae are low weeds or shrubs that lack petals or obvious flowers; the Chenopodiaceae generally have gray leaves.

This catalogue lists the plants known to be eaten by the larvae of North American butterflies (the doubtful plants and errors are not listed). Plant genera and plant families are followed by their common names and the species number of each butterfly known to eat them. To find the plant *species*, and the plant family the genus belongs to, consult the species discussions in Part III. The genera of hostplants within each plant family are listed after the common name of each plant family. Common names of hostplants are also listed, followed by their genus or species scientific names, so that you can look up the butterflies that eat them.

References are to
species numbers

GLOSSARY

This glossary treats the important terms used in this book that the reader might not know. The phrasing of the glossary's definitions has been made simple and clear enough that persons who do not know the terms can easily learn them; unless otherwise noted, all definitions implicitly refer to butterflies. The advanced lepidopterist will find most of these terms and many others more technically defined in the glossaries of J. R. de la Torre-Bueno, *A Glossary of Entomology* (Forestburgh, N.Y.: Lubrecht and Cramer, 1973), and Ernst Mayr, *Principles of Systematic Zoology* (New York: McGraw-Hill, 1969).

abdomen. The elongate hind part of the body, behind the thorax (Figs. 7, 18).
aberration. An individual animal not normal in appearance or structure, owing to either environmental or genetic factors. Compare *mutant*.
adult. The final life stage of an insect, capable of reproduction.
aedeagus. The male's mating organ (Fig. 28).
aestivate. To pass all or part of the summer in a dormant (diapausing) state. Compare *hibernate*; see also *diapause*.
allopatric. Not occurring together, as, for example, two or more species whose ranges do not overlap. Compare *sympatric*.
androconia (sing. *androconium*). Scent scales on adults (specifically, those with narrowed brushy tips: Figs. 36-39).
antenna (pl. *antennae*). Either of the two long appendages on the head, which serve to detect odors (Fig. 11).
anterior. Toward the front; toward the tip of the head. Compare *posterior*.
apical. At the tip of; on the wing at its apex (Fig. 54). Compare *basal*.
apiculus. The bent tip of the antenna in skippers (Fig. 11).
arthropod. Any animal with jointed legs, an exoskeleton, and no backbone (a crab or an insect, for example).

backcross. A successful mating between a hybrid and an individual belonging to one of the parent taxa of that hybrid; also, the offspring of such a mating. Compare *interbreed, intergrade, introgression*.
basal. At or toward the base; toward the body or the center of the body; on the wing near its base (Fig. 54). Compare *apical*.
Batesian mimic. An edible species mimicking a poisonous species. Compare *Müllerian mimic*; see also *mimicry*.
biennial. Having a two-year life cycle.
biological species. See *species*.
bursa copulatrix. A sac in the female abdomen wherein the male's spermatophore is stored and, after the sperm are released, digested (Fig. 30).

caterpillar. The larva of any butterfly, and of most moths, having legs and prolegs for crawling (Fig. 1).

cell. In microbiology, a membrane-bounded mass of protoplasm containing a nucleus and other structures; in butterfly study, any area between wing veins (see Fig. 53: each cell is designated according to the vein in front of it—cell CuA_2, for instance, is the area behind vein CuA_2—but the word "cell" used alone refers to the discal cell). See also *vein*.

chaparral. Any dry shrubby thicket (other than sagebrush) in the foothills of the western United States or in ecologically similar regions elsewhere.

chromosome. A structure in the cell's nucleus containing DNA (of which genes consist), held together by special proteins. Compare *DNA, gene*.

chrysalis. See *pupa*.

cline. A gradual change in any species' physical characteristics across some portion of its geographic range; continuous intergradation. Compare *intergrade*.

cocoon. A silk web enclosing a pupa.

collar. A hard transverse plate on the top of the larva just behind the head (Fig. 1).

colony. A local group of individuals geographically separated from other groups belonging to the same species; an isolated population.

compound eye. Either of the two large eyes typical of insects and other arthropods, consisting of many tiny simple eyes (ommatidia) that are crowded together but optically separate (Fig. 8).

convergence. The development of a resemblance between two species or subspecies that are not close genealogical (evolutionary) relatives (includes mimicry).

costal fold. A flap containing scent scales on the leading edge of the forewing in many males and in some females (Figs. 36-39).

coxa (pl. *coxae*). The first segment of the leg, attached to the thorax (Fig. 14).

cremaster. The posterior tip of the pupa, usually having crochets that hook into a silk pad spun by the larva (Fig. 5).

crochets. Tiny hooks, often occurring in species-specific patterns, on the bottoms of the prolegs of larvae and on the cremasters of pupae, providing security against a fall (Fig. 4).

cross (n. or v.). A hybrid (usually a laboratory hybrid); to hybridize.

diapause (n. or v.). A natural (not disease-caused) state of suspended development in any life stage, whether egg, larva, pupa, or adult; to pass through such a state. See also *aestivate, hibernate*.

diaphragm. A muscular sheet extending across the ventral part of the interior of the abdomen, employed in circulation and respiration (Fig. 26). Compare *septum*.

dicotyledon. Any flowering plant whose first sprout from the seed has a pair of leaves (as in maples and potatoes) and whose leaves have branching veins. Compare *monocotyledon*.

dimorphism (adj. *dimorphic*). The occurrence of two different genetic forms in one population (the difference can exist between the two sexes, or within one of them, or within both). Compare *polymorphism*.

discal cell. The area between wing veins that extends from the base to the middle of the wing (Fig. 53).

DNA. Deoxyribonucleic acid, the substance of genes that contains the information needed to make proteins.

dominant. Prevailing over (dominating) a corresponding but different inherited gene in its effect on the appearance, structure, or physiology of a trait when both genes occur in a single organism. Compare *recessive*.

dorsal. Toward the top of the head or body. Compare *ventral*.

egg. The initial life stage of any insect.

electrophoresis. A laboratory procedure in which (for butterflies) ground-up tissue is put into a gel and its proteins are sorted according to their molecular structure and electric charge.

enzyme. A biological catalyst; a protein, produced by an organism itself, that enables the splitting (as in digestion) or fusion of other chemicals.

exoskeleton. The hard case forming the outer surface of the body and appendages of an arthropod.

family. A basic grouping of formal classification (taxonomy): a group of subfamilies, tribes, and genera all of which are related to each other more closely than to any other subfamily, tribe, or genus, designated by a capitalized unitalicized name ending in -idae (for animals) or -aceae (for plants); occasionally a family contains just one genus. Compare *superfamily*.

fauna (pl. *faunas*). All the animal species that occupy the same, or roughly the same, geographic range; also, a subset of all such animals, as, for example, cave fauna or mammalian fauna.

femur. The first long movable segment of the leg, between the trochanter and the tibia (Fig. 14).

flight. A single generation of adults, or the span of time during which they appear (compare *generation*, *partial flight*); also, the act of flying.

form. An optional subordinate grouping of formal classification (taxonomy): a subgroup of a species distinguished in appearance or structure from other, sympatric subgroups, and designated in this book by an uncapitalized italicized name. Compare *dimorphism, polymorphism, subspecies*.

gene. Any of the strings of DNA on a chromosome that make a protein that in turn forms part of the body or acts as an enzyme in the body's chemical factory.

generation. All the individuals of a single life cycle (from egg to larva to pupa to adult) in a single population. Compare *flight, partial flight*.

genus (pl. *genera*). A basic grouping of formal classification (taxonomy): a group of species all of which are related to each other more closely than to any other species, designated by a capitalized italicized name; occasionally a genus contains just one species. Compare *tribe*.

gnathos. A hook (or pair of hooks) on top of the tip of the male abdomen, used in mating (Fig. 28).

hair pencil. A cluster of hairlike scent scales everted during courtship (Figs. 36-39).

herb (adj. *herbaceous*). Any non-grassy annual, biennial, or perennial plant without woody stems or a trunk, generally dying back in winter. Compare *shrub*.

hibernaculum (pl. *hibernacula*). A winter nest (see species 142 and 145).

hibernate. To pass all or part of the winter in a dormant (diapausing) state. Compare *aestivate*; see also *diapause*.

holotype. The single museum specimen that scientists accept as the formal basis for the name of a species or subspecies.

hormone. A chemical produced by one part of the body and circulating in the blood to another part, where it produces an effect (on molting or diapause, for example).

hostplant. Any plant eaten by larvae and on which the eggs are normally laid (often species-specific).

hybrid. The offspring of two animals or plants of different genera, species, subspecies, or forms. Compare *backcross, interbreed, intergrade, introgression*.

inflorescence. The cluster of flowering parts terminating any one main stem of a plant, comprising one to many flowers.

inheritance. The way that the mother's and father's genes are used in the offspring to produce the color pattern, structure, or physiology of a genetic trait. For the usual ways, see also *dominant, quantitatively inherited, recessive, sex-linked*.

interbreed. To mate successfully in nature (typically as between two subspecies or forms), producing healthy fertile offspring. Compare *hybrid, intergrade, introgression*.

intergrade. To interbreed in the geographic area between the ranges of two subspecies, producing individuals or populations intermediate in appearance or structure (if intergradation is gradual, a "cline" is said to occur). Compare *hybrid, introgression*.

introgression. The natural introduction of genes from one species into a second, due to rare successful hybridization between them and requiring a backcross to the second parent species. Compare *interbreed, intergrade*.

juxta. A Y-shaped or V-shaped support beneath the aedeagus (Fig. 28).

labrum. The anterior hardened "lip" of an insect, in front of the mandibles (Figs. 2, 3, 5, 8). See also *mouthparts*.

lamella (pl. *lamellae*). A hard plate sometimes present near the female's mating tube (Fig. 30).

larva (pl. *larvae*). The fleshy, wingless young of advanced insects (butterflies, beetles, bees, etc.) in the life stage between egg and pupa (in butterflies and moths, the larva is commonly called a "caterpillar").

lateral. Toward the side, away from the dorsal or ventral midline of the body.

life zone. A latitudinal or altitudinal range with mostly uniform vegetation, animals, and climate (Fig. 43).

longitudinal. Running from front to back on the body rather than from side to side, as a stripe or structure. Compare *transverse*.

lunule. A crescent-shaped spot on the wing.

mandible. Either of the two toothed jaws of a larva, used for biting and chewing food (Fig. 3). See also *mouthparts*.

marginal. Along the outer margin of the wing (Fig. 54).

mating tube. The channel in the male or female abdomen through which the sperm and spermatophore pass to the bursa copulatrix (Figs. 28, 30).

median. On the middle of the wing (Fig. 54).

mesothorax. The second (middle) segment of the thorax (Figs. 7, 12). Compare *metathorax, prothorax*.

metamorphosis. The process of development through very different life stages, from egg to larva to pupa to adult; also, any change of stage within that process.

metathorax. The third (rear) segment of the thorax (Figs. 7, 12). Compare *mesothorax, prothorax*.

middorsal. Along the midline of the back, or top, of the body.

midventral. Along the midline of the bottom of the body.

migration. The movement of adults (often seasonal) to breed or feed at a place many kilometers away from the area of their birth.

mimic (n. or v.). A species closely resembling a model; to resemble a model closely. See also *Batesian mimic, mimicry, Müllerian mimic*.

mimicry. A process in which one species (the mimic) has come to resemble a second, poisonous species (the model), resulting in a lessened likelihood of the mimic's being eaten by predators that refuse to eat the model. Compare *convergence*.

model. A poisonous species mimicked by another species. See also *mimicry*.

molting. Shedding the larval skin, or exoskeleton (Figs. 7, 23).

monocotyledon. Any flowering plant whose first sprout from the seed has only one leaf (as in grasses and orchids) and whose leaves have parallel veins. Compare *dicotyledon*.

mouthparts. All the appendages of and surrounding the mouth, including the labrum, mandibles, palpi, and proboscis (Figs. 2, 3, 5, 8, 9).

movements. The travel patterns of adults (includes migration if the species migrates).

Müllerian mimic. A poisonous species mimicking another poisonous species. Compare *Batesian mimic*; see also *mimicry*.

mutant. An individual animal genetically different in appearance, structure, or physiology owing to a change (whether accidental or induced by chemicals or radiation) in an old gene in its parent's sperm or egg, and not produced by hybridization, interbreeding, or introgression. Compare *aberration*.

nudum. The scaleless area on the tip of the antenna, where scent detectors are common, occurring especially in skippers (Fig. 11).

ocellus (pl. *ocelli*). Either of the two tiny eyes between the compound eyes on the head of any moth, absent in butterfly adults and larvae (larval eyes are ommatidia, not ocelli).

ommatidium (pl. *ommatidia*). Each facet or individual eye in the adult compound eye (Fig. 8); also, each eye of the larva (Fig. 2).

order. A basic grouping of formal classification (taxonomy): a group of superfamilies or families all of which are related to each other more closely than to any other superfamily or family, designated by an uncapitalized unitalicized name; occasionally an order contains just one family.

osmeterium (pl. *osmeteria*). A reddish, foul-smelling, fork-shaped organ that pops out behind the head in some butterfly larvae, used to startle and deter predators (Fig. 1).

overwinter. See *hibernate*.

oviposit. To lay one or more eggs.

ovipositor. A pair of pillow-shaped structures on the tip of the female abdomen that extrude the egg or eggs (Fig. 30).

palp (pl. *palpi*). A feeding and sensory appendage on the larval head; also (through metamorphosis), the olfactory and cleaning appendage on the front of the adult head (Figs. 2, 3, 8, 9). See also *mouthparts*.

partial flight. A group of adults that have emerged from pupation while most of their generation remains in diapause. See also *flight*.

patrolling. Mate-locating behavior in which the male flies almost constantly in search of females. Compare *perching*.

perching. Mate-locating behavior in which the male waits at a characteristic site and darts out at passing individuals or other flying objects to seek females, generally returning to the same site after unsuccessful flights. Compare *patrolling*.

pheromone. A scent used to attract, seduce, or repel mates; in general, any chemical (not a poison) that stimulates a behavioral response in another individual (Figs. 36-39).

photoperiod. The time between dawn and dusk in any one day.

polarized light. Light vibrating in only one direction (for example, the light filtered through polarizing sunglasses), visible to bees and many butterflies. Compare *ultraviolet*.

polygenic. See *quantitatively inherited*.

polymorphism (adj. *polymorphic*). The occurrence of two or more different genetic forms in one population (the differences can exist between the two sexes, or within one of them, or within both). Compare *dimorphism*.

population. All the individuals of a species that live near each other and have a chance (though some adults may die before others emerge from pupation) of mating with each other. Compare *colony*.

postbasal. On the wing, just beyond its base (Fig. 54).

posterior. Toward the rear; toward the tip of the abdomen. Compare *anterior*.

postmedian. On the wing, just past its middle (Fig. 54).

postnatal seta. Any of a few hairs (setae), present on second-stage and older moth and butterfly larvae, that are absent on first-stage larvae (see also p. 127). Compare *primary seta*, *secondary seta*.

primary seta. Any of a few hairs (setae) present on nearly all moth and butterfly first-stage larvae (Figs. 49, 50). Compare *postnatal seta*, *secondary seta*.

proboscis. The feeding tube of an adult butterfly (Fig. 7). See also *mouthparts*.

process. Any hardened, unjointed protrusion of the exoskeleton (Fig. 6).

proleg. Any of the ten false legs on the posterior segments of a larva (Fig. 4).

prothorax. The first (front) segment of the thorax (Figs. 7, 12). Compare *mesothorax*, *metathorax*.

pupa (pl. *pupae*). The mummylike quiescent stage between larva and adult in most insects, in which the structure of the insect is reorganized (Figs. 5, 6; in butterflies, the pupa is sometimes called a "chrysalis").

pupate. To advance from the larval to the pupal stage.

quantitatively inherited. Affected by many genes, so that all types of intermediate individuals can occur along with the individuals most different in structure or appearance.

race. See *subspecies*.

range. The geographic area occupied by a species or subspecies.

recessive. Suppressed by a corresponding but different inherited gene in its effect on the appearance, structure, or physiology of a trait when both genes occur in a single organism. Compare *dominant*.

resilin. A rubbery protein in the wing base, proboscis, or other bendable sites in the exoskeleton.

saccus. A male mating structure (Fig. 28).

sclerite. Any hardened plate constituting part of the exoskeleton.

scolus (pl. *scoli*). Any branching spine or seta-bearing cone on a larva (Fig. 1).

scudders. Butterflies of the superfamily Papilionoidea, distinguished from skippers (see also p. 160).

secondary seta. Any of numerous extra hairs (setae) that develop as a larva grows from the first stage to maturity. Compare *postnatal seta*, *primary seta*.

septum. A muscular sheet extending across the interior of the base of the abdomen (Figs. 24, 26). Compare *diaphragm*.

seta (pl. *setae*). Any tiny socketed projection from the exoskeleton (except the highly flattened ones, which are called "scales"), commonly hairlike in appearance.

sex-linked. Determined by a gene on a sex chromosome, so that males and females may differ in structure or appearance; also, located on a sex chromosome, as a gene.

shrub. Any non-grassy perennial plant with a number of woody stems (as distinct from a tree). Compare *herb*.

skippers. Butterflies of the superfamily Hesperioidea, distinguished from scudders (see also p. 160).

species (pl. *species*). A basic grouping of formal classification (taxonomy): a group of organisms, usually scattered as a number of populations, constituting all the individuals that could if brought together in nature mate readily and produce healthy fertile offspring, designated by an uncapitalized italicized name (actually the genus name and the species name together designate the species). Compare *genus, hybrid, subspecies*.

spermatophore. The sperm sac transferred to the female during mating (Fig. 30). See also *bursa copulatrix*.

sphragis. A hard deposit left on the female abdomen by males of some species just after mating, which prevents the female from remating (Fig. 62; Pl. 9).

spinneret. The silk-dispensing lobe beneath the larval head (Fig. 3).

spiracle. Any of a series of breathing holes along the sides of the body (Figs. 24, 25).

spur. Either of the two (or, in some skippers, any of the four) long spinelike projections on the tibia (Fig. 14: spines are smaller; see species 524).

stigma. Any conspicuous patch of scent scales, usually occurring on the wing if present (but often absent).

stink club. A process on the tip of the abdomen of most female Heliconiini, bearing scent scales (Fig. 37).

subdorsal. Just below the top of the head or body, between the middorsal and lateral areas (closer to the middorsal).

subfamily. An optional intermediate grouping of formal classification (taxonomy): a group of tribes or genera all of which are related to each other more closely than to any other tribe or genus, designated by a capitalized unitalicized name ending in -inae (for animals) or -oideae (for plants); occasionally a subfamily contains just one genus. Compare *family*.

sublateral. Just below the side of the head or body, between the lateral area and the legs (closer to the lateral area).

submarginal. On the wing, just inside its marginal zone (Fig. 54).

submedian. On the wing, just before its middle (Fig. 54).

subspecies (pl. *subspecies*). An optional subordinate grouping of formal classification (taxonomy): a subgroup of a species that occupies a distinct geographic range and in which most individuals differ in appearance or structure from those belonging to other subgroups of the same species living elsewhere, designated by an uncapitalized italicized name (usually given along with the genus and species names). Compare *form, species*.

sulcus (pl. *sulci*). An internal strengthening ridge of the exoskeleton, visible under a light microscope as a dark line beneath the exoskeleton (Figs. 2, 19; often misnamed "suture").

superfamily. An optional intermediate grouping of formal classification (taxonomy): a group of families all of which are related to each other more closely than to any other family, designated by a capitalized unitalicized name ending in -oidea (for animals) or -ideae (for plants); occasionally a superfamily contains just one family. Compare *order*.

supralateral. Just above the side of the head or body, between the lateral and subdorsal areas (closer to the lateral).

sympatric. Occurring together, as, for example, two or more species whose ranges overlap (such species are said to be sympatric in the area where they occur together). Compare *allopatric*.

taiga. The vast cold coniferous forest at high latitude or high altitude. Compare *tundra*.

tarsus (pl. *tarsi*). The tip, or concluding segment, of the leg (Figs. 1, 14).

taxon (pl. *taxa*). Any group, of any size, that has a scientific name; also, the name assigned to such a group.

tegula (pl. *tegulae*). Either of the two dorsal flaps between the prothorax and the forewing (Figs. 13, 59).

tegumen. A hardened dorsal plate on the male genitalia (Fig. 28).

thorax. The middle section of the body, to which the legs and wings are attached (Figs. 1, 7).

tibia (pl. *tibiae*). The second long movable segment of the leg, between the femur and the tarsus (Fig. 14).

transverse. Running from side to side on the body rather than from front to back, as a stripe or structure. Compare *longitudinal*.

tribe. An optional intermediate grouping of formal classification (taxonomy): a group of genera all of which are related to each other more closely than to any other genus, designated by a capitalized unitalicized name ending in -ini (for animals) or -ieae (for plants); occasionally a tribe contains just one genus. Compare *subfamily*.

trochanter. The second segment of the leg, between the coxa and the femur (Fig. 14).

tubercle. Any hairless projection on a larva or pupa (Fig. 1).

tundra. The grassy treeless zone at high latitude or high altitude. Compare *taiga*.

tympanum (pl. *tympana*). A hearing organ on the exoskeleton or wing, consisting of a thin membrane with air behind it (Fig. 64; see also p. 40).

type. See *holotype*.

ultraviolet. A range of light with a wavelength shorter than violet, visible to butterflies but not to humans. Compare *polarized light*.

uncus. A projection or pair of projections (commonly hook-shaped) on top of the tip of the male abdomen, used during mating (Fig. 28).

valva (pl. *valvae*). Either of the two viselike ventral appendages on the tip of the male abdomen that grip the female during mating (Fig. 28).

vein. Any of the tubular struts of the wings (Figs. 53, 55; blood veins, such as those of vertebrates, do not occur in butterflies).

ventral. Toward the bottom of the head or body. Compare *dorsal*.

wing vein. See *vein*.

zone. See *life zone*.

INDEX

The hostplant catalogue (pp. 524-42) indexes all hostplants; the index below lists everything else, including subjects and butterflies. For North American species, subspecies, and forms, the butterfly's name is followed by parentheses that contain the genus the name belongs in, and the number assigned to its species (sp.) in this book; after the parentheses are listed the numbers of the pages and plates (pl.) on which that butterfly is mentioned or shown. Genera, tribes, subfamilies, families, and superfamilies also have the included North American species' numbers in parentheses. If you wish to look up a butterfly and know the names of both the genus and the species (or subspecies, or form) for it, look under the name of the species (or subspecies, or form) rather than the name of the genus; look under the name of the genus only if you want the page numbers for the entire genus. Much information that is of a sort standard for most of the species accounts in Part III has not been indexed here; see pages 157-59 for the usual information to expect in the accounts in Part III. The word "improper" appears in parentheses in this index after any name that either is a synonym, or else is a valid name properly belonging to another species.

Library of Congress Cataloging in Publication Data

Scott, James A., 1946-
  The butterflies of North America.

  Bibliography: p.
  Includes index.
    1. Butterflies—North America.   2. Butterflies—
North America—Identification.   3. Insects—Identification.
4. Insects—North America—Identification.   I. Title.
QL548.S38   1986   595.78'9097   82-60737
ISBN 0-8047-1205-0 (cloth)
ISBN 0-8047-2013-4 (pbk.)

This book is printed on acid-free paper